A NEW HISTORY OF IRELAND

UNDER THE AUSPICES OF THE ROYAL IRISH ACADEMY
PLANNED AND ESTABLISHED BY THE LATE T. W. MOODY

VI
IRELAND UNDER THE UNION, II
1870–1921

A NEW HISTORY OF IRELAND

UNDER THE AUSPICES OF THE ROYAL IRISH ACADEMY
PLANNED AND ESTABLISHED BY THE LATE T. W. MOODY

*Already published

A NEW HISTORY OF

IRELAND

VI

IRELAND UNDER THE UNION, II
1870–1921

EDITED BY

W. E. VAUGHAN

CLARENDON PRESS · OXFORD
1996

Oxford University Press, Walton Street, Oxford OX2 6DP

Oxford New York
Athens Auckland Bangkok Bombay
Calcutta Cape Town Dar es Salaam Delhi
Florence Hong Kong Istanbul Karachi
Kuala Lumpur Madras Madrid Melbourne
Mexico City Nairobi Paris Singapore
Taipei Tokyo Toronto
and associated companies in
Berlin Ibadan

Oxford is a trade mark of Oxford University Press

Published in the United States
by Oxford University Press Inc., New York

British Library Cataloguing in Publication Data
Data available

Library of Congress Cataloging-in-Publication Data
(Revised for vol. 6)
A new history of Ireland.
Includes bibliographies and indexes.
Contents: —v.2. Medieval Ireland, 1169–1534.—
v.3. Early modern Ireland, 1534–1691.—v.4. Eighteenth-century Ireland, 1691–1800.—v.5.
Ireland under the union. Pt 1. 1801–70.—v.6. Ireland under the union. Pt II. 1870–1921—v.8.
A chronology of Irish history to 1976.—v.9. Maps, genealogies, lists.—[etc.]
1. Ireland—History—Collected works. I. Moody,
T. W. (Theodore William), 1907–84. II. Martin,
F. X. (Francis Xavier), 1922–   . III. Byrne, F. J. (Francis John),
1934–   . IV. Vaughan, W. E. (William Edward), 1944–   .
V. Cosgrove, Art, 1940–   . VI. Hill, J. R. (Jacqueline Rhoda), 1948–
DA912.N48   941.5   76-376168
ISBN 0–19–821751–X

Typeset by Pure Tech India Ltd., Pondicherry
Printed in Great Britain on acid free paper by
Bookcraft Ltd., Midsomer Norton, Nr Bath, Avon

PREFACE

THIS volume, together with volume V (1801–70), completes the coverage of the period of the parliamentary union of Ireland and Britain. As mentioned in the preface to its predecessor, the present volume includes chapters on the Irish economy from 1850 to 1921 and on university education from 1793 to 1908, as well as a bibliography for the whole period of the union.

Once again we are grateful to the late Dr John A. Mulcahy, of New York, and the directors of the American Irish Foundation, for the generous financial help that enabled us to carry out much-needed research in the early stages of work on the *New history*, particularly in what was then the virtually untouched field of art history. We also thank David Hall, bookseller of Enniskillen, County Fermanagh, and the Augustinian Order in Ireland, for supplying our office with a typewriter and a word processor at a time when the Royal Irish Academy was unable to replace our worn-out equipment.

We acknowledge the generous help we received from the National Library of Ireland and the libraries of Trinity College, Dublin, and of the Royal Irish Academy, and from other Academy projects, in particular the cordial cooperation of the Irish Historic Towns Atlas and the Dictionary of Irish Biography. In compiling the illustrations we were greatly assisted by the research of John McHugh and the photography of Brendan Dempsey; we are also grateful for the assistance of Belfast City Council, the Ulster Museum, the director and staff of the National Gallery of Ireland, Keith Jeffery, Gordon Herries Davies, Jeanne Sheehy (who suggested the jacket illustration), and E. J. McParland, our adviser on jacket design; and for the work of Janet McKee, Helen Litton, and Daniel Gallen in proof-reading. We also take this opportunity of recording our debt to our typist, Peggy Morgan, who retired from full-time employment in July 1991 but continued regular work for the *New history* to December 1994, completing over twenty-four years of invaluable service.

The major part of the primary narrative in this volume was written by the late F. S. L. Lyons, several years before his death in 1983. It is a mark of the quality of his work that we found little amendment necessary, except for annotations indicating recent work on the topics that he covered. For the work of annotation we are indebted to Deirdre Lindsay, and to the advice and assistance of R. F. Foster and Eunan O'Halpin. We also record with sorrow the deaths of Vivian Mercier (3 November 1989) and Aloys Fleischmann (21 July 1992). Both had made unique contributions to their fields of study, and we are grateful that their work appears in this volume.

F. X. MARTIN
F. J. BYRNE
W. E. VAUGHAN
ART COSGROVE
J. R. HILL
DÁIBHÍ Ó CRÓINÍN

Royal Irish Academy
12 April 1995

CONTENTS

IV THE AFTERMATH OF PARNELL, 1891–1903   by F. S. L. Lyons

XIII LITERATURE IN ENGLISH, 1891–1921   by Vivian Mercier

XIV IRISH LANGUAGE AND LITERATURE, 1845–1921
by Brian Ó Cuív

XVI VISUAL ARTS AND SOCIETY, 1900–21   by Cyril Barrett and Jeanne Sheehy

XX ADMINISTRATION AND THE PUBLIC SERVICES, 1870–1921
by R. B. McDowell

XXIII THE IRISH IN AUSTRALIA AND NEW ZEALAND, 1870–1990
by Patrick O'Farrell

XXIV THE REMAKING OF IRISH-AMERICA, 1845–80
by David Noel Doyle

CONTRIBUTORS

Donald Harman Akenson	B.A. (Yale), M.Ed., Ph.D. (Harvard); F.R.S. (Can.); professor of history, Queen's University, Kingston, Ontario
Cyril Barrett	M.A., Ph.D. (Lond.); fellow of Campion Hall, Oxford; emeritus professor of philosophy, University of Warwick
Charles John Benson	M.A., Dip. in Lib. Stud. (Q.U.B.); keeper of early printed books, Library of Trinity College, Dublin
Richard Vincent Comerford	M.A. (N.U.I.), Ph.D. (Dubl.); professor of modern history, St Patrick's College, Maynooth
Lewis Perry Curtis, jr	B.A. (Yale), D.Phil. (Oxon.); professor in history and in modern culture and media, Brown University, Rhode Island
David Noel Doyle	M.A. (Marquette), Ph.D. (Iowa); college lecturer in modern history, University College, Dublin
David Patrick Brian Fitzpatrick	B.A. (Melb.), Ph.D. (Cantab.); fellow, and associate professor in modern history, Trinity College, Dublin
Aloys Fleischmann	M.A., D.Mus. (N.U.I.); emeritus professor of music, University College, Cork (died 21 July 1992)
Henry Derwent Gribbon	B.Comm.Sc., Ph.D. (Q.U.B.); honorary research fellow in economic and social history, Queen's University, Belfast
Francis Stewart Leland Lyons	F.R. Hist. Soc.; F.B.A.; M.R.I.A.; F.R.S.L.; professor of history, Trinity College, Dublin (died 21 Sept. 1983)
Robert Brendan McDowell	M.A., Ph.D., Litt.D. (Dubl.); M.R.I.A.; fellow emeritus, Trinity College, Dublin
Vivian Herbert Samuel Mercier	B.A., Ph.D. (Dubl.); emeritus professor of English and comparative literature, University of California at Santa Barbara (died 3 Nov. 1989)

Helen Frances Mulvey

B.A. (Brown), M.A. (Columbia), Ph.D. (Harvard); emeritus professor of history, Connecticut College, New London, Connecticut

Brian Ó Cuív

M.A., D.Litt. (N.U.I.); M.R.I.A.; emeritus senior professor, School of Celtic Studies, Dublin Institute of Advanced Studies

Patrick James O'Farrell

M.A. (N.Z.), Ph.D. (A.N.U.); F.A.H.A.; professor of history, University of New South Wales

Susan Mary Parkes

M.A., M.Litt., P.G.C.E. (Cantab.); senior lecturer in education, Trinity College, Dublin

Jeanne Iseult Sheehy

B.A. (Hons) (N.U.I.), M. Litt. (Dubl.); principal lecturer in history of art, Brookes University, Oxford

William Edward Vaughan

M.A., Ph.D. (Dubl.); senior lecturer in modern history, Trinity College, Dublin

The maps have been drawn by Matthew Stout, under the direction of Mary Davies, B.A., cartographical adviser to this history, from material supplied by contributors. The index is the work of Helen Litton, M.A.

MAPS

FIGURES

ILLUSTRATIONS

at end of volume

7 Margaret Anne Cusack (Mary Francis Clare) (1832–99), the 'Nun of Kenmare', prolific writer, organiser, and land league sympathiser, from the frontispiece of her autobiography (London, 1889); for her controversial role in connection with the apparitions at Knock, see Donnelly, 'Marian shrine of Knock', pp 89–95

8 'Waiting for the landlord!', cartoon by Charles Keene in *Punch*, lxxv (July–Dec. 1878), p. 27; the impatient ribbonman, saying 'Bedad, they ought to be here be this toime! Sure, Tirince, I hope the ould gintleman hasn't mit wid an accidint!!!', became an enduring stereotype of agrarian disturbance, though it was later affirmed in G. K. Chesterton's *The flying inn* (1914) that the man was English

9 'The right pig by the ear', cartoon by Linley Sambourne in *Punch*, lxxxv (July–Dec. 1883), p. 267: the 5th Baron Rossmore is removed from the magistracy (the constable on the left, with Rossmore's commission in his belt, is Earl Spencer, lord lieutenant of Ireland) after endangering the peace at a confrontation between Orangemen and nationalists during the 'invasion of Ulster' in the autumn of 1883

10 Rev. James Healy (1824–94), parish priest of Bray, Co. Wicklow, renowned for wit and sociability; 'I was at the Castle in Lord Zetland's time [1889–92], when Fr Healy had just returned from a fortnight's visit to Monte Carlo, where he had been the guest (of all people in the world!) of Lord Randolph Churchill. "May I ask how you explained your absence to your flock, Fr Healy?" asked Lady Zetland. "I merely told them that I had been for a fortnight retreat to Carlow; I thought it superfluous prefixing the Monte," answered the priest' (Lord Frederic Hamilton, *The days before yesterday* (London, 1920), pp 83–4)

11 Cartoon by Percy French (1854–1920) from *The Jarvey* (1890), an example of French's work as a black-and-white artist, the growing use of the modern 'safety' bicycle, and the limerick verse-form, the popularity of which would reach epidemic proportions in 1907

12 'Parnell and Young Ireland', cartoon by Harry Furniss (1854–1925), in *Black and White*, ii, no. 33 (19 Sept. 1891), with his account of the incident: '. . . soon music, shouting, and cheering seemed to surround the hotel. I went down, and there saw, standing in a brake and haranguing a surging mass of people, the familiar figure of Charles Stewart Parnell. He descended from the waggon . . . and literally fought his way into the hotel, while his admirers, who had invaded the hall, clung to his coat-tails till they were summarily ejected by the hotel servants. I am thankful to say this is all I saw of political life in Ireland' (Harry Furniss, *Flying visits* (Bristol and London, 1892), pp 38–9); Furniss, born in Wexford, saw – as illustrator of H. W. Lucy's 'Essence of parliament' column in *Punch* – a great deal of Irish politicians at Westminster

13 'A dramatic incident at Mr Parnell's funeral in Dublin', by W. S. Stacey (*Black and White*, ii, no. 37 (17 Oct. 1891), p. 518), showing members of the crowd at Westland Row station breaking up for mementoes the packing case in which Parnell's coffin had been brought to Dublin

14 The dining room, Carton House, Maynooth, Co. Kildare, *c*.1890 (Imperial 2284, Lawrence Collection, N.L.I.)

15 The Grand Lodge room, Freemasons' Hall, Dublin, typifying the decor of Victorian lodge rooms

16 Mr MacSimius: 'Well, Oi don't profess to be a particularly cultivated man meself; but at laste me progenitors were all educated in the hoigher branches!'; cartoon by Bernard Partridge in *Punch*, cxiii (July–Dec. 1897), p. 10

17 'Last of the vi-kings and first of the tea-kings', cartoon by Leonard Raven Hill in *Punch*, cxxv (July–Dec. 1903), p. 129; Sir Thomas Johnstone Lipton (1850–1931), born in

Glasgow of famine refugees from Co. Monaghan, made his fortune as a grocer (dealing largely in Irish produce), dispensed munificent charity, and maintained a steam-yacht, *Erin*, and a succession of sailing-yachts named *Shamrock* with which he competed for the America's cup

18a Edward VII inspecting a guard of honour of the R.I.C. at Leopardstown racecourse, Co. Dublin, July 1907 (*Illustrated London News*, cxxxi, no. 3561 (20 July 1907), p. 94)

18b 'The royal visit to Ireland: their majesties at the viceregal lodge, Dublin' (*Illustrated London News*, cxxxix, no. 3769 (15 July 1911), p. 114); those shown in the photograph as published include (in addition to the duke of Connaught, the lord lieutenant and Lady Aberdeen, and the O'Conor Don) Robert MacGregor Bowen-Colthurst, vice-chamberlain to the lord lieutenant, who was killed in action in 1915 and whose elder brother John ordered the shooting of Francis Sheehy Skeffington and others in 1916

19 Rev. James Cullen (1841–1921) in the centre of members of the Society of St Vincent de Paul attached to the Pioneer Total Abstinence League of the Sacred Heart; Fr Cullen founded the League in June 1889 (Lambert McKenna, *Life and work of Rev. James Aloysius Cullen, S.J.* (London, 1924))

20 'Irish Tichbornites reading the verdict: 14 years penal servitude' by W. H. Hill Marshall, 1874; based on 'The Ryans and the Dwyers, calumniated men' by Erskine Nicol, 1858 (see *History Ireland*, i, no. 1 (spring 1993), cover and p. 6); Marshall's title refers to the widespread interest in the court cases arising from Arthur Orton's claim to be heir to the Tichborne estate in Hampshire (1871–2) and his subsequent trial for perjury (1873–4), in which his counsel was Edward Vaughan Hyde Kenealy (1819–80), Corkman, T.C.D. graduate, and (in his own judgement) twelfth and last messiah

21 'The marriage of Princess Aoife of Leinster with Richard de Clare, earl of Pembroke (Strongbow)' by Daniel Maclise (detail) (National Gallery of Ireland)

22 'The Aran fisherman's drowned child' by F. W. Burton (National Gallery of Ireland)

23 'The banks of the river Seine, near Paris' by Nathaniel Hone the younger (National Gallery of Ireland)

24 'Towards the night and winter' by Frank O'Meara (Hugh Lane Municipal Gallery of Modern Art)

25 'The Four Courts, Dublin' by Walter Osborne (National Gallery of Ireland)

26 'The fish market' by Walter Osborne (Hugh Lane Municipal Gallery of Modern Art)

27 'The fine art academy, Antwerp' by Dermod O'Brien (Ulster Museum)

28 'Field of corn, Pont Aven' by Roderic O'Conor (Ulster Museum)

29 'In the west of Ireland' by Paul Henry (National Gallery of Ireland)

30 'The rogue' by Jack B. Yeats (Hugh Lane Municipal Gallery of Modern Art)

31 'John O'Leary' by John B. Yeats (National Gallery of Ireland)

32 'Roger Casement' by Sarah Purser (National Gallery of Ireland)

33 The buildings of the Dublin industrial exhibition, 1853, Sir John Benson architect (photo by J. & S. Harsch, Dublin)

34 St Fin Barre's cathedral, Cork, William Burges architect (Irish Architectural Archive, 33/84x16)

35 St Patrick's church, Jordanstown, Co. Antrim, under construction, W. H. Lynn architect (Irish Architectural Archive, 54/29x2)

36 St Patrick's College, Maynooth, Co. Kildare; design drawings by A. W. N. Pugin, 1846 (Irish Architectural Archive, 29/18 129)

Ireland (London, 1979), p. 51). The car was fully restored in 1985 by Denis Dowdall of Irish Motor Distributors; its representation on an Irish postage stamp in 1989 was based on the original of this photograph, which hangs in Hunter's Hotel, Rathnew, Co. Wicklow

55 James (Jimmy) Tyrrell (1866–1921) of Ballyfoyle, Co. Kilkenny, as Irish countryman and British colonial official: (a) with his parents James and Anastasia (sitting), both native speakers of Irish, and his brother Paddy (standing, right); (b) as assistant superintendent of police, Singapore, *c.*1900. Tyrrell, son of a small farmer, was a farm labourer before joining the R.I.C.; he later joined the D.M.P., then the Straits Settlement police, serving in Malacca and Singapore until retiring in 1908 to Ballyfoyle, where he had married Mary Brennan while on leave in 1903

56 'A negligible quantity', cartoon by Bernard Partridge in *Punch*, cxxx (Jan.–June 1906), p. 57; Redmond, after the general election, finds himself unable to hold the balance between Campbell-Bannerman and Balfour

57 'Desperate remedies', cartoon by Linley Sambourne in *Punch*, cxxxiii (July–Dec. 1907), p. 443, representing Birrell's 'softly, softly' approach to cattle-driving:

'There was an old man who said "How
Shall I stop the pursuit of that cow?
I will sit on this stile
And continue to smile."
(But it gave no relief to the cow)'

58 ' "We want to remain with you": Edward Carson 1914: an Orange man' by Cecil Cutler

59 ' "A" Company, 2nd Royal Inniskilling Fusiliers' (1911); though the 2nd battalion was at Dover on the outbreak of war, mobilisation for active service took two weeks; the battalion left for France on 21 Aug. 1914 and went into action on the extreme left of the British line at Le Cateau on 26 Aug. (Sir Frank Fox, *The Royal Inniskilling Fusiliers in the world war* (London, 1928), p. 39).

60 First page of the recruiting booklet *Ireland's cause* [1915], with parallel texts in Irish and English

61 'Major-general Sir Oliver Nugent', by William Conor (Belfast City Council); Nugent (1860–1926), commanding 36th (Ulster) Division, issued before battle on the Somme a special order of the day, expressing confidence 'that the honour of the British army and the honour of Ulster are in safe keeping' and calling on his men to show 'resolution, self-reliance, discipline, and the spirit which knows no surrender and no defeat' (Fox, *Royal Inniskilling Fusiliers*, p. 66)

62 Two Irish chaplains of the third battle of Ypres: (a) Rev. William Doyle (1873–1917), chaplain to 16th (Irish) Division, killed at Frezenberg; his colonel, brigadier, and divisional general recommended him for the V. C. (Alfred O'Rahilly, *Father William Doyle, S. J.: a spiritual study* (3rd ed., London, 1925)); (b) Rev. G. A. Studdert Kennedy (1883–1929), T.C.D. classics graduate (1904), poet, and Christian socialist, who won the M.C. at Messines (frontispiece of William Purcell, *Woodbine Willie: an anglican incident . . .* (London, 1962))

63 'H.M.S. *Vindictive*' by K. D. Shoesmith; *Vindictive* was laid down in 1916 at Harland & Wolff, Belfast, as an 'improved Birmingham class' cruiser, and completed in Oct. 1918 as an aircraft-carrier of 9,750 tons

64 Memorial at Thiepval to the 36th (Ulster) Division, designed by the architects J. A. Bowden and A. L. Abbott as a copy of 'Helen's tower' (erected in memory of Helen Selina,

mother of the 1st marquis of Dufferin and Ava) at Clandeboye, Co. Down, where the division trained before going to France; the idea of using this design for the memorial appears to have come from Sir James Craig
65 Missionaries about to leave for Africa; Cork, 1920 (*Cork Examiner*)

The originals of these illustrations were made available through the courtesy of the following, and are published by their permission: the National Museum of Ireland, plate 1; the Board of Trinity College, Dublin, plates 2, 3, 4, 5, 6, 7, 8, 9, 12, 13, 16, 17, 18a, 18b, 19, 37, 40, 47, 48, 49, 56, 57, 62a, 62b; the director of the National Archives of Ireland, plate 10; the National Library of Ireland, plates 11, 14; the Grand Lodge of A. F. & A. Masons of Ireland, plate 15; the late R. F. V. Heuston, plate 20; the National Gallery of Ireland, plates 21, 22, 23, 25, 29, 31, 32, 41; the Hugh Lane Municipal Gallery of Modern Art, plates 24, 26, 30, 39; the Ulster Museum, plates 27, 28, 43, 44; Professor Cyril Barrett, plate 33; the Irish Architectural Archive, plates 34, 35, 36, 38; An Post, plate 42; the Museum of Decorative Arts, Prague, plate 45; Mrs Mary Boydell, plate 46; the late Vivian Mercier, plates 50, 51, 52, 53; Mrs Maureen Gelletlie, plate 54; Dr Éamonn Ó hÓgáin, plates 55a, 55b; Mr Raymond Duff, plate 58; Dr W. E. Vaughan, plate 59; Professor Brian Ó Cuív, plate 60; Belfast City Council, plate 61; Dr H. D. Gribbon, plate 63; Dr Stephen Royle, plate 64; the *Cork Examiner*, plate 65; the *Irish Times*, jacket illustration.

ABBREVIATIONS AND CONVENTIONS

Abbreviations and conventions used in this volume are listed below. They consist of (a) the relevant items from the list in *Irish Historical Studies*, supplement I (Jan. 1968) and (b) abbreviations, on the same model, not included in the *Irish Historical Studies* list. Where an article is cited more than once in a chapter, an abbreviated form is used after the first full reference. Occasionally, however, the full reference is repeated for the convenience of the reader. A similar convention is used for titles of parliamentary papers.

A.H.R.	*American Historical Review* (New York, 1895–)
Akenson, *Ir. education experiment*	D. H. Akenson, *The Irish education experiment: the national system of education in the nineteenth century* (London and Toronto, 1970)
An Cosantóir	*An Cosantóir: a military review* (Dublin, 1940–)
Anal. Hib.	*Analecta Hibernica, including the reports of the Irish Manuscripts Commission* (Dublin, 1930–)
Annual Reg., 1758 [etc.]	*The Annual Register, . . . 1758* [etc.] (London, [1759]–)
Archiv. Hib.	*Archivium Hibernicum: or Irish historical records* (Catholic Record Society of Ireland, Maynooth, 1912–)
Arklow Hist. Soc. Jn.	*Arklow Historical Society Journal* (Arklow, 1982–)
Ashby, *Universities*	Eric Ashby, *Universities, British, Indian, and African* (London, 1966)
B.L., Add. MSS	British Library, Additional MSS
Béaloideas	*Béaloideas: the journal of the Folklore of Ireland Society* (Dublin, 1927–)
Belfast Natur. Hist. Soc. Proc.	Proceedings and Reports of the Belfast Natural History and Philosophical Society (Belfast, 1873–)
Bessborough comm. rep.	*Report of her majesty's commissioners of inquiry into the working of the Landlord and Tenant (Ireland) Act, 1870, and the acts amending the same* [earl of Bessborough, chairman] [C 2779], H.C. 1881, xviii
Bew, *Conflict & conciliation*	Paul Bew, *Conflict and conciliation in Ireland, 1890–1910: Parnellites and radical agrarians* (Oxford, 1987)
Bibliog. Soc. Ire. Pub.	*Bibliographical Society of Ireland* [*Publications*] (1918–58, 6 vols)
Black, *Econ. thought & Ir. question*	R. D. C. Black, *Economic thought and the Irish question, 1817–1870* (Cambridge, 1960)
Bodkin, *Lane*	Thomas Bodkin, *Hugh Lane and his pictures* ([Dublin], 1932)
Booth, *Life & labour*	Charles Booth (ed.), *Life and labour of the people in London* (4th ed., 17 vols in 3 series, 1902–3)
Boyce, *Englishmen and Irish troubles*	D. G. Boyce, *Englishmen and Irish troubles: British public opinion and the making of British policy, 1918–22* (Cambridge, Mass., and London, 1972)

Boyce, *Nationalism in Ire.*	D. G. Boyce, *Nationalism in Ireland* (Baltimore and London, 1982; revised ed., 1991)
Boyce, *Revolution in Ire.*	D. G. Boyce (ed.), *The revolution in Ireland, 1879–1923* (Basingstoke, 1988)
Breifne	*Breifne: journal of Cumann Seanchais Bhreifne (Breifne Historical Society)* (Cavan, 1958–)
Brit. Acad. Proc.	*Proceedings of the British Academy* (London, 1903–)
Butler Soc. Jn.	*Journal of the Butler Society* ([Kilkenny], 1968–)
C.S.B.	Crime Special Branch (papers in N.A.I.)
C.S.O., R.P.	Chief Secretary's Office, Registered Papers (papers in N.A.I.)
Cal. S. P. Ire., 1509–73 [etc.]	*Calendar of the state papers relating to Ireland, 1509–1573* [etc.] (24 vols, London, 1860–1911)
Capuchin Annual	*Capuchin Annual* (40 issues, Dublin, 1934–77)
Carty, *Bibliog. Ir. hist., 1912–21*	James Carty, *Bibliography of Irish history, 1912–21* (N.L.I., Dublin, 1936)
Cath. Hist. Rev.	*Catholic Historical Review* (Washington, D.C., 1915–)
Celtica	*Celtica* (Dublin, 1946–)
Census Ire., 1841 [etc.]	[The sources denoted by these titles are the reports and other material relating to the censuses of Ireland taken by the British government in the years indicated; corresponding abbreviations are used for the censuses in Great Britain]
Childers comm.	*First report of the royal commissioners appointed to inquire into the financial relations of Great Britain and Ireland; with evidence and appendices* [C 7220], H.C. 1895, xxxvi
Clogher Rec.	*Clogher Record* ([Monaghan], 1953–)
Collect. Hib.	*Collectanea Hibernica: sources for Irish history* (Dublin, 1958–)
Comerford, *Fenians in context*	R. V. Comerford, *The fenians in context: Irish politics and society, 1848–82* (Dublin and Atlantic Highlands, N.J., 1985)
Connell, *Population*	K. H. Connell, *The population of Ireland, 1750–1845* (Oxford, 1950)
Corish, *Ir. catholicism*	Patrick J. Corish (ed.), *A history of Irish catholicism* (16 fascs, Dublin and Melbourne, 1967–72)
Cork Hist. Soc. Jn.	*Journal of the Cork Historical and Archaeological Society* (Cork, 1892–)
Cosgrove & McCartney, *Studies in Ir. hist.*	Art Cosgrove and Donal McCartney (ed.), *Studies in Irish history presented to R. Dudley Edwards* (Dublin, 1979)
Coyne, *Ireland: industrial and agricultural*	W. P. Coyne (ed.), *Ireland: industrial and agricultural* (2nd (expanded) ed., Dublin, 1902)
Curriculum of the secondary school	Department of Education [Ireland], *Report of the council of education: the curriculum of the secondary school* (Dublin, 1962)
Curtis, *Coercion & conciliation*	L. P. Curtis, *Coercion and conciliation in Ireland, 1880–92* (Princeton, N.J., and London, 1963)

Cymmrod. Soc. Trans.	*Transactions of the Honourable Society of Cymmrodorion* (London, 1892–)
D.M.P.	Dublin Metropolitan Police
Dáil Éireann proc. 1919–21	*Dáil Éireann, miontuarisc an chead dala, 1919–1921: minutes of proceedings of the first parliament of the republic of Ireland, 1919–1921, official record* (Dublin, [1921?])
Dáil Éireann rep. 1921–2	*Dáil Éireann, tuairisg oifigiúil (official report)* [1921–2] (Dublin, [1922?])
Davitt, *Fall of feudalism*	Michael Davitt, *The fall of feudalism in Ireland: or the story of the Land League revolution* (London and New York, 1904)
Decies	*Old Waterford Society: Decies* ([Waterford], 1976–)
Denvir, *Irish in Britain*	John Denvir, *The Irish in Britain* (London, 1894)
Denvir, *Life story of an old rebel*	John Denvir, *The life story of an old rebel* (Dublin, 1910)
Dept. Agric. Jn.	*Éire, Department of Agriculture, Journal* (Dublin, 1938–)*
Devonshire comm.	*Royal commission on labour: assistant commissioners' reports on the agricultural labourer, vol. iv, Ireland* [C 6894], H.C. 1893–4, xxxvii, 1–483
Devoy's post bag	*Devoy's post bag, 1871–1928*, ed. William O'Brien and Desmond Ryan (2 vols, Dublin, 1948, 1953)
Donnelly, *Land & people of Cork*	J. S. Donnelly, jr, *The land and people of nineteenth-century Cork: the rural economy and the land question* (London, 1975)
Dublin Hist. Rec.	*Dublin Historical Record* (Dublin, 1938–)
Dublin Mag.	*Dublin Magazine* (Dublin, 1923–58)
Dudley comm.	*First report of the royal commission appointed to inquire into and report upon the operation of the laws dealing with congestion in Ireland: evidence and documents* [Cd 3266–7], H.C. 1906, xxxii
Duiche Néill	*Duiche Néill: journal of the O Neill Country Historical Society* (Benburb, 1986–)
Econ. Hist. Rev.	*Economic History Review* (London, 1927–)
Econ. & Soc. Rev.	*The Economic and Social Review* (Dublin, 1969–)
ed.	edited by, edition, editor(s)
Edwards, *Pearse*	Ruth Dudley Edwards, *Patrick Pearse: the triumph of failure* (London, 1977)
Éigse	*Éigse: a journal of Irish studies* (Dublin, 1939–)
Éire-Ireland	*Éire-Ireland: a journal of Irish studies* (Irish American Cultural Institute, St Paul, Minn., 1965–)
Études Irlandaises	*Études Irlandaises* (Lille, 1972–)
F. J.	*The Freeman's Journal* (Dublin, 1763–1924)
First taxation comm.	*Report from the select committee on the taxation of Ireland . . .*, H.C. 1864 (513), xv
Fitzpatrick, *Ir. emigration, 1801–1921*	David Fitzpatrick, *Irish emigration, 1801–1921* (Dundalk, 1990)

* For the antecedents of *Dept. Agric. Jn.*, see *I.H.S.*, supplement I (Jan. 1968), p. 94.

Fitzpatrick, *Politics & Ir. life*	David Fitzpatrick, *Politics and Irish life, 1913–1921: provincial experience of war and revolution* (Dublin, 1977)
Fleischmann, *Mus. in Ire.*	Aloys Fleischmann (ed.), *Music in Ireland* (Cork, 1952)
Foster, *Churchill*	R. F. Foster, *Lord Randolph Churchill: a political life* (Oxford, 1981)
Foster, *Parnell*	R. F. Foster, *Charles Stewart Parnell: the man and his family* (Hassocks (Sussex), 1976)
Gailey, *Ire. & death of kindness*	Andrew Gailey, *Ireland and the death of kindness: the experience of constructive unionism, 1890–1905* (Cork, 1987)
Galway Arch. Soc. Jn.	*Journal of the Galway Archaeological and Historical Society* (Galway, 1900–)
Garvin, *Evolution of Ir. nationalist politics*	Tom Garvin, *The evolution of Irish nationalist politics* (Dublin, 1981)
Goldstrom & Clarkson, *Ir. population*	J. M. Goldstrom and L. A. Clarkson (ed.), *Irish population, economy, and society: essays in honour of the late K. H. Connell* (Oxford, 1981)
Gregory, *Lane*	Augusta Gregory, *Hugh Lane's life and achievement, with some account of the Dublin galleries* (London, 1921)
Gwynn, *Redmond*	Stephen Gwynn, *The life of John Redmond* (London, 1932)
H.C.	house of commons papers
Hall, *Bank of Ire.*	F. G. Hall, *History of the Bank of Ireland* (Dublin, 1949)
Hansard 3, i [etc.]	*Hansard's parliamentary debates*, third series, 1830–91 (vols i–ccclvi, London, 1831–91)
Hansard 4, i [etc.]	*The parliamentary debates (authorised edition)*, fourth series, 1892–1908 (vols i–cxcix, London, 1892–[1909])
Hansard 5 (*commons*), i [etc.]	*The parliamentary debates (official report)* fifth series, *house of commons*, 1909– (vols i– , London, [1909]–)
Hansard N.I. (*senate*), i [etc.]	*The parliamentary debates (official report)*, first series, volume i: *first session of the first parliament of Northern Ireland, 12 George V, the senate, 1921* [etc.] (vols i–lvi, Belfast, 1921–72)
Hermathena	*Hermathena: a series of papers . . . by members of Trinity College, Dublin* (Dublin, 1874–)
Hist. Studies	*Historical studies: papers read before the Irish Conference of Historians* (vols i–vii, London, 1958–69; viii, Dublin, 1971; ix, Belfast, 1974; x, Indreabhan (Co. na Gaillimhe), 1976; xi, Belfast, 1978; xii, London, 1978; xiii–xv, Belfast, 1981–5; xvi, Cork, 1987; xvii, Dublin, 1991; xviii, Derry, 1993; in progress)
Historical Studies	*Historical Studies, Australia and New Zealand* (Melbourne, 1940– ; from 1967, title *Historical Studies*)
History	*History: the quarterly journal of the Historical Association* (London, 1916–)
Hist. Jn.	*The Historical Journal* (Cambridge, 1958–)

Hoppen, *Elections, politics and society*	K. T. Hoppen, *Elections, politics, and society in Ireland, 1832–85* (Oxford, 1984)
I.B.L.	*The Irish Book Lover* (32 vols, Dublin, 1909–57)
I.E.R.	*Irish Ecclesiastical Record* (171 vols, Dublin, 1864–1968)
I.H.S.	*Irish Historical Studies: the joint journal of the Irish Historical Society and the Ulster Society for Irish Historical Studies* (Dublin, 1938–)
I.R.B.	Irish Republican Brotherhood
I.T.	*The Irish Times* (Dublin, 1859–)
Intelligence notes, *1913–16*	Chief Secretary's Office, Dublin Castle, Intelligence notes, *1913–16, preserved in the State Paper Office*, ed. Breandán Mac Giolla Choille (Dublin, 1966)
Ir. Baptist Hist. Soc. Jn.	*Irish Baptist Historical Society Journal* (Belfast, 1969–)
Ir. Bookman	*Irish Bookman* (Dublin, 1946–)
Ir. Builder	*The Irish Builder and Engineer* (Dublin, 1867–) [formerly *The Dublin Builder* (8 vols, 1859–66)]
Ir. Econ. & Soc. Hist.	*Irish Economic and Social History: the journal of the Economic and Social History Society of Ireland* ([Dublin and Belfast], 1974–)
Ir. Educational Studies	*Irish Educational Studies* (Dublin, 1981–)
Ir. Folk Song Soc. Jn.	*Journal of the Irish Folk Song Society* (29 vols, London, 1904–39)
Ir. Geneal.	*The Irish Genealogist: official organ of the Irish Genealogical Research Society* (London, 1937–)
Ir. Geography	*Irish Geography (Bulletin of the Geographical Society of Ireland)* (Dublin, 1944–)
Ir. Georgian Soc. Bull.	*Quarterly Bulletin of the Irish Georgian Society* (Dublin, 1966–)
Ir. Jn. Med. Sc.	*Irish Journal of Medical Science* (Dublin, 1922–)
Ir. Jurist	*The Irish Jurist: new series* (Dublin, 1966–)
Ir. Political Studies	*Irish Political Studies* (Galway, 1986–)
Ir. Railway Rec. Soc. Jn.	*Journal of the Irish Railway Record Society* ([Dublin], 1947–)
Ir. Sword	*The Irish Sword: the journal of the Military History Society of Ireland* (Dublin, [1949]–)
Ir. Theol. Quart.	*Irish Theological Quarterly* (17 vols, Dublin, 1906–22; Maynooth, 1951–)
Ir. Univ. Rev.	*Irish University Review: a journal of Irish studies* (Dublin, 1970–)
Irishman	*The Irishman: a weekly journal of Irish national politics and literature* (Belfast, 1858–9; Dublin, 1859–84)
Jackson, *Ulster party*	Alvin Jackson, *The Ulster party: Irish unionists in the house of commons, 1884–1911* (Oxford, 1989)
Jn. Brit. Studies	*Journal of British Studies* (Hartford, Conn., 1961–)
Jn. Ecc. Hist.	*Journal of Ecclesiastical History* (London, 1950–)
Jn. Econ. Hist.	*Journal of Economic History* (New York, 1941–)
Jn. Hist. Ideas	*Journal of the History of Ideas* (Lancaster, Pa., 1940–)

Jn. Mod. Hist.	*Journal of Modern History* (Chicago, 1929–)
Jn. Relig. Hist.	*Journal of Religious History* (Sydney, 1960–)
Kerr, *Peel, priests, &* *politics*	Donal A. Kerr, *Peel, priests, and politics: Sir Robert Peel's* *administration and the Roman Catholic church in Ireland,* *1841–46* (Oxford, 1982)
Kerry Arch. Soc. Jn.	*Journal of the Kerry Archaeological and Historical Society* ([Tralee], 1968–)
Laffan, *Partition of Ire.*	Michael Laffan, *The partition of Ireland, 1911–1925* (Dundalk, 1983)
Lee, *Ir. histor., 1970–79*	J. J. Lee (ed.), *Irish historiography, 1970–79* (Cork, 1981)
Lee, *Ire. 1912–85*	J. J. Lee, *Ireland 1912–1985: politics and society* (Cambridge, 1989)
Lee, *Modernisation of Ir.* *society*	J. J. Lee, *The modernisation of Irish society 1848–1918* (Dublin, 1973; 2nd ed. 1989)
Louth Arch. Soc. Jn.	*Journal of the County Louth Archaeological Society* (Dundalk, 1904–)
Lowe, 'Irish in Lancashire'	W. J. Lowe, 'The Irish in Lancashire, 1846–71: a social history' (Ph.D. thesis, University of Dublin, 1975)
Lyons, *Dillon*	F. S. L. Lyons, *John Dillon* (London, 1968)
Lyons, *Ir. parl. party*	F. S. L. Lyons, *The Irish parliamentary party, 1890–1910* (London, 1951; reprint, Westport, Conn., 1975)
Lyons, *Ire. since famine*	F. S. L. Lyons, *Ireland since the famine* (London, 1971)
Lyons, *Parnell*	F. S. L. Lyons, *Charles Stewart Parnell* (London, 1977)
Lyons & Hawkins, *Ire.* *under the union*	F. S. L. Lyons and R. A. J. Hawkins (ed.), *Ireland under* *the union: varieties of tension. Essays in honour of T. W.* *Moody* (Oxford, 1980)
McClelland, *English* *Roman Catholics*	V. A. McClelland, *English Roman Catholics and higher* *education, 1830–1903* (Oxford, 1973)
MacDonagh, *Pattern of* *govt growth*	Oliver MacDonagh, *A pattern of government growth,* *1800–60: the passenger acts and their enforcement* (London, 1961)
McDowell, *Ir.* *administration*	R. B. McDowell, *The Irish administration, 1801–1914* (London, 1964)
McDowell & Webb, *Trinity College*	R. B. McDowell and D. A. Webb, *Trinity College, Dublin,* *1592–1952* (Cambridge, 1982)
McElligott, 'Intermediate education'	T. J. McElligott, 'Intermediate education and the work of the commissioners, 1870–1922' (M. Litt. thesis, University of Dublin, 1969)
McNeill, *Ulster's stand for* *union*	Ronald McNeill, *Ulster's stand for union* (London, 1922)
Macardle, *Ir. republic*	Dorothy Macardle, *The Irish republic: a documented chronicle* *of the Anglo–Irish conflict . . .* (London, 1937; later eds)
Maguire comm.	*Report from the select committee on Tenure and Improvement of* *Land (Ireland) Act . . .* , H.C. 1865 (402), xi, 341
Mansergh, *Unresolved* *question*	Nicholas Mansergh, *The unresolved question: the Anglo–* *Irish settlement and its undoing, 1912–72* (New Haven, Conn., and London, 1991)

Martin, 'Eoin MacNeill on the 1916 rising'
F. X. Martin (ed.), 'Eoin MacNeill on the 1916 rising' in *I.H.S.*, xii, no. 47 (Mar. 1961), pp 226–71

Mitchell, *Labour in Ir. politics*
Arthur Mitchell, *Labour in Irish politics, 1890–1930: the Irish labour movement in an age of revolution* (Dublin and New York, 1974)

Mitchell & Deane, *Brit. hist. statistics*
B. R. Mitchell and Phyllis Deane, *Abstract of British historical statistics* (Cambridge, 1962)

Mitchell & Ó Snodaigh, *Ir. pol. docs 1869–1916*
Arthur Mitchell and Pádraig Ó Snodaigh, *Irish political documents 1869–1916* (Blackrock, 1989)

Mitchell & Ó Snodaigh, *Ir. pol. docs 1916–49*
Arthur Mitchell and Pádraig Ó Snodaigh, *Irish political documents 1916–1949* (Blackrock, 1985)

Moody, *Davitt*
T. W. Moody, *Davitt and Irish revolution, 1847–82* (Oxford, 1981)

Moody, *Ir. histor., 1936–70*
T. W. Moody (ed.), *Irish historiography, 1936–70* (Dublin, 1971)

Moody & Beckett, *Queen's, Belfast*
T. W. Moody and J. C. Beckett, *Queen's, Belfast, 1845–1949: the history of a university* (2 vols, London, 1959)

Morrissey, *National university*
Thomas J. Morrissey, *Towards a national university: William Delany, S. J., 1835–1924* (Dublin, 1983)

Moss & Hume, *Shipbuilders to the world*
Michael Moss and John R. Hume, *Shipbuilders to the world: 125 years of Harland and Wolff, Belfast, 1861–1986* (Belfast and Wolfeboro, 1986)

N.A.I.
National Archives of Ireland

N.I. Legal Quart.
Northern Ireland Legal Quarterly: [the journal of the incorporated Law Society of Northern Ireland] (Belfast, 1936–)

N.L.I.
National Library of Ireland

N.U.I.
National University of Ireland

N. Munster Antiq. Jn.
North Munster Antiquarian Journal (Limerick, 1936–)

Nation
The Nation (Dublin, 1842–91; absorbed in *The Irish Catholic*, 1891–6; continued as *The Nation*, 1896–7; as *The Weekly Nation*, 1897–1900)

Nineteenth Century
The Nineteenth Century (148 vols, London, 1877–1950; title *The Nineteenth Century and After* from 1900; continued as *The Twentieth Century*, 1951–)

Norman, *Cath. ch. & Ire.*
E. R. Norman, *The catholic church and Ireland in the age of rebellion, 1859–1873* (London and Ithaca, N.Y., 1965)

O'Brien, 'Dear, dirty Dublin'
J. V. O'Brien, *'Dear, dirty Dublin': a city in distress, 1899–1916* (London and Berkeley, Calif., 1982)

O'Brien, *Parnell and his party*
Conor Cruise O'Brien, *Parnell and his party, 1880–90* (Oxford, 1957; corrected impression, 1964)

O'Brien & Travers, *Ir. emigrant experience*
John O'Brien and Pauric Travers (ed.), *The Irish emigrant experience in Australia* (Dublin, 1991)

Ó Broin, *Revolutionary underground*
Leon Ó Broin, *Revolutionary underground: the story of the I.R.B., 1858–1924* (Dublin, 1976)

O'Day, *Parnell and first home rule episode*
Alan O'Day, *Parnell and the first home rule episode, 1884–87* (Dublin, 1986)

O'Farrell, *Catholic church*	Patrick O'Farrell, *The catholic church and community: an Australian history* (revised ed., Sydney, 1992)
O'Farrell, *Documents*	Patrick O'Farrell and Deirdre O'Farrell, *Documents in Australian catholic history* (2 vols, London, 1969)
O'Farrell, *Ir. in Australia*	Patrick O'Farrell, *The Irish in Australia* (Sydney, 1987)
O'Farrell, *Vanished kingdoms*	Patrick O'Farrell, *Vanished kingdoms: the Irish in Australia and New Zealand: a personal excursion* (Sydney, 1990)
Ó Gráda, *Ire. before & after famine*	Cormac Ó Gráda, *Ireland before and after the famine: explorations in economic history, 1800–1925* (Manchester, 1988)
O'Halpin, *Decline of the union*	Eunan O'Halpin, *The decline of the union: British government in Ireland 1892–1920* (Dublin and Syracuse, N.Y., 1987)
Old Kilkenny Rev.	*Old Kilkenny Review* (Kilkenny, 1948–)
P.R.O.	Public Record Office of England
P.R.O.N.I.	Public Record Office of Northern Ireland
Past & Present	*Past and Present: a journal of historical studies* (London, 1952– ; subtitle *A journal of scientific history*, 1952–8)
Pearse, *Educational writings*, ed. Ó Buachalla	*The educational writings of P. H. Pearse: a significant Irish educationalist*, ed. Séamas Ó Buachalla (Dublin and Cork, 1980)
Pearse, *Plays, stories, poems*	P. H. Pearse, *Plays, stories, poems* (Dublin, 1917)
Pearse, *Political writings*	P. H. Pearse, *Political writings and speeches* (Dublin, 1922)
Q.U.B.	Queen's University, Belfast
R. Hist. Soc. Trans.	*Transactions of the Royal Historical Society* (London, 1872–)
R.I.A. cat. Ir. MSS	T. F. O'Rahilly and others, *Catalogue of Irish manuscripts in the Royal Irish Academy* (fascs 1–27 and indexes, Dublin, 1926–58; fasc. 28, Dublin, 1970)
R.I.A. Proc.	*Proceedings of the Royal Irish Academy* (Dublin, 1836–)
R.I.C.	Royal Irish Constabulary
R.M.	resident magistrate
R.S.A.I. Jn.	*Journal of the Royal Society of Antiquaries of Ireland* (Dublin, 1892–)
Reportorium Novum	*Reportorium Novum: Dublin Diocesan Historical Record* (Dublin, 1955–)
Rev. Pol.	*Review of Politics* (Notre Dame, Ind., 1950–)
Richmond comm. evidence	*Minutes of evidence taken before her majesty's commissioners on agriculture* [C 2778–I], H.C. 1881, xv
Ríocht na Midhe	*Ríocht na Midhe: records of the Meath Archaeological and Historical Society* (Drogheda, [1955]–)
Saothar	*Saothar: journal of the Irish Labour History Society* (Dublin, 1975–)
Seanchas Ardmhacha	*Seanchas Ardmhacha: journal of the Armagh Diocesan Historical Society* ([Armagh], 1954–)
Spenser, *View*	Edmund Spenser, *A view of the state of Ireland . . . in 1596* [edition cited]

Stat. Soc. Ire. Jn.	Journal of the Statistical and Social Inquiry Society of Ireland (Dublin, 1861–)
Stewart, Ulster crisis	A. T. Q. Stewart, The Ulster crisis (London, 1967; repr. Aldershot, 1993)
Strickland, Dict. Ir. artists	Walter G. Strickland, A dictionary of Irish artists (2 vols, Dublin and London, 1913; repr. Blackrock, 1989)
Studia Hib.	Studia Hibernica (Dublin, 1961–)
Studies	Studies: an Irish quarterly review (Dublin, 1912–)
T.C.D.	(Library of) Trinity College, Dublin
Thornley, Isaac Butt	David Thornley, Isaac Butt and home rule (London, 1964)
Townshend, British campaign	Charles Townshend, The British campaign in Ireland 1919–1921: the development of political and military policies (Oxford, 1975)
Townshend, Political violence	Charles Townshend, Political violence in Ireland: government and resistance since 1848 (Oxford, 1983)
U.C.D.	University College, Dublin
Ulster Folklife	Ulster Folklife (Belfast, 1955–)
University Rev.	University Review: official organ of the Graduates Association of the National University of Ireland (5 vols, Dublin, 1954–69)
Vaughan & Fitzpatrick, Ir. hist. statistics	W. E. Vaughan and A. J. Fitzpatrick, Irish historical statistics: population, 1821–1971 (Dublin, 1978)
Walker, Ulster politics	B. M. Walker, Ulster politics: the formative years, 1868–86 (Belfast, 1989)
Ward, Unmanageable revolutionaries	Margaret Ward, Unmanageable revolutionaries: women and Irish nationalism (London, 1983)
Yeats, Autobiographies	W. B. Yeats, Autobiographies (London, 1926)
Yeats, Plays	The variorum edition of the plays of W. B. Yeats, ed. Russell K. Alspach (London, 1966)
Yeats, Poems	The variorum edition of the poems of W. B. Yeats, ed. Peter Allt and Russell K. Alspach (London, 1989)

INTRODUCTION

Ireland, 1870–1921

R. V. COMERFORD

CONSIDERING the wealth both of the developments that it encompasses and of the source material that it has deposited, the half-century covered by this volume might be judged the richest available to historians of Ireland.[1] Documentation abounds at home and abroad. The British sources for Irish history in this period are particularly profuse because for much of the time Irish affairs were at or near the centre of high politics in Britain. Even without that added British or imperial dimension, Irish life in many of its aspects—and not only the political—can be seen as going through an epoch of exceptional interest between 1870 and 1921. The wealth of political incident and development, much of it of epic proportions, merging ultimately with armed conflict, was matched by long drawn out agrarian upheaval, assorted crusades and popular mobilisations, a many sided campaign for cultural revival, and a literary movement that has made a lasting impression on the world stage.

At least by comparison with the fifty years that followed, this period has the sense of being replete with possibilities for Ireland. This is true even of politico-constitutional developments, so often seen in hindsight as following the dictates of some ineluctable paradigm. In 1870 Norway, Poland, Bohemia, and Catalonia, like Ireland, were countries with a history of political and cultural distinctiveness currently subordinate to a greater power. By 1920 Norway had become an independent kingdom; Poland was an independent country with disputed frontiers and a minorities problem; Bohemia was the dominant region in a multi-ethnic, democratic republic; Catalonia was still subordinate to a greater whole. Neither the full independence that won such an impressive endorsement from a majority of Irish constituencies at the general election of 1918 nor the eventual partition settlement of the years 1920–21 was the working out of a design of nature: they were two of numerous potential developments. So, too, in social, cultural, associational, and intellectual life Ireland might be said to have been refashioned in the period between 1870 and 1920, but, again, not in accordance with the demands of a predetermining national genius or any other precise

[1] This introduction is indebted to many published works; see the extensive bibliography below, pp 764–879.

prescription, but mostly by haphazard and distinctive participation in the movements of the age, British, European, Atlantic, and world-wide.

Though much was in flux, not everything was. The aspect of Irish society least open to possibilities of change and development in 1870 may have been religion: the time of fluidity and unpredictability in the ecclesiastical contours of the country had been much earlier in the century. By 1870 the reinvigorated catholic church, commanding the allegiance of almost 80 per cent of the population, had settled into heavy Gothic moulds. For generations to come its combined strength of both spirit and structure would make it the most formidable institution in the land. Power provokes its own counteractions, and many of the most interesting developments of the period, especially around the turn of the century, embody reactions, internal and external, to this power. Irish protestantism in its various forms was also a beneficiary of fairly recent waves of revival. The disestablishment of the Church of Ireland, effective from 1 January 1871, while it involved a loss of legal status and ancient wealth, provided for the creation of new structures, which soon became a source of increased strength and confidence.

In Ireland, as was also the case in other societies to a greater extent than is often allowed, much of the population defined its sense of political belonging in terms of religion. There were significant exceptions, but most catholics felt themselves to belong to a nation that was specifically catholic, and when they acted politically did so as members of such a nation, even if some of their leaders rationalised the situation in terms of an all-embracing Irish nationality. By the same token most—though certainly not all—protestants of every denomination felt quite definitely that they did not belong to the same political community as the catholics. The political developments of the period under review, especially the democratisation of politics, led to a hardening of these certainties.

The role of religion was enhanced by the part that all the churches played in promoting the all-pervading ethos of the age best summed up in the word 'respectability': 'Victorianism' conveys the correct connotation but suggests limitations of place and time that are not appropriate. The standing of individuals and communities in the eyes of the world and ultimately in their own estimation depended on conspicuous adherence to a strict code of manners and morals (originating with the bourgeoisie and spreading through all classes) that was inseparable from specific forms of social accomplishment and material attainment. Because it was part of the daily life of so many ordinary people who might never cast a vote or attend a political meeting, the striving for respectability in all its forms undoubtedly absorbed more Irish time and energy than all the famous politics and conspiracy of the era. The consequent individual and social discipline was readily identified by the churches with the Christian moral and spiritual order and promoted accordingly. Cleanliness was self-evidently next to godliness.

As promoters and invigilators of order, uniformity, and respectability, priests and elders had most effective collaborators in the personnel of the Royal Irish Constabulary. By 1870 this centrally controlled force covered the entire country, apart from Dublin, which had its own metropolitan police force. An armed body, available for upholding the constitutional order when required, the R.I.C. was expected to provide the authorities in Dublin Castle with reliable information on the state of the country. From the early 1880s this function was formalised into a system of regular reporting from each county. Involvement in the agrarian troubles of the 1880s brought much popular opprobrium, and the force became in 1919–21 the target of revolutionary nationalist attack, which undermined its character and drew it into an ugly and, for it, fatal armed conflict. However, the great bulk of constabulary resources and energies over a period of more than eighty years went into an enterprise that was political only in a general sense and was primarily social. As the enforcers of a myriad of laws intended to create an orderly society—laws covering everything from illicit distillation of spirits to shopkeepers' weights and measures and the licensing of dogs—the constabulary constituted one of the prime agencies for the modernisation of the country. In this they had at least the implicit support of almost everyone else concerned with 'peace, progress, and prosperity'. There were always those who had reservations on political grounds, but by and large the R.I.C. man was a respected figure, and one of the pillars of respectability in Irish towns and parishes in the early twentieth century.

Despite the strongly antidenominational tendencies of parliament and government, even publicly funded social institutions in Ireland came to be more thoroughly segregated along religious lines. Among voluntary institutions this was still more pronounced. In schools, colleges, hospitals, reformatories, and on the sports field, Irish people by the early twentieth century could expect to be dealing almost exclusively with those of their own denomination.

If the churches were entrenched along securely fixed lines, that did not preclude a great fluctuating contest between their members for individual places and collective influence in civil life. The very clear advantages enjoyed by protestants in this regard before 1870 did not dissipate with disestablishment. It took the gradual effects of expanding educational opportunities for the lower middle classes, local government reform, and active government policy, to bring about significant change in the relative balance of advantage. Many of the political and cultural developments of the period derive much of their impetus from interconfessional rivalry for places, high and low. In Belfast the contest was conducted in the context of large-scale factory employment with ultimately explosive political consequences.

Elsewhere in the country manufacturing industry prospered only in small pockets after 1870, and apart from the glories of shipbuilding, engineering, and linen manufacture in the north-east there is little enough that sparkles on the pages of Irish economic history in this period. In fact, the economy was next only to religion as a source of continuity. Over most of the country this period witnessed what amounted to the institutionalisation of a demographic system that had prevailed since the great famine and was to prove remarkably enduring. This required the emigration of a large proportion of every age cohort in order that those remaining behind might sustain or improve their standard of living without necessarily achieving a compensatory increase in total wealth. Identification of this as a regional phenomenon within the wider United Kingdom and thus as a corollary of political subordination would be more plausible for the period under review if we did not know that it was subsequently to endure for generations in an independent Irish state.

Official figures indicate that some 2.5 million people emigrated from Ireland between 1870 and 1920, representing roughly 50 per cent of the population of the country in the latter year. Migration was preponderantly to the English-speaking world, as it had been for generations, and the consequent links with the United States of America were particularly important. Kin in America, particularly if they were willing and able to make financial remittances, constituted a substantial presence in scores of thousands of Irish families. Throughout this period there was at all times a significant Irish-American public opinion ready in its response to news from Ireland but ultimately concerned with American rather than Irish politics, and a small and usually fragmented group of dedicated American-based conspirators, typified by John Devoy, watching every opportunity to give practical assistance to revolutionary efforts in Ireland. While Devoy and his friends could intervene, sometimes decisively, in Irish affairs, they were powerless to initiate large movements. These came about typically in response to events at home or as part and parcel of some of the wider movements of the age.

A case in point is the land war, in the initial stages of which Devoy played some part.[1] However, it was the local impact of an international agricultural crisis that made the struggle possible. After the phase of greatest intensity, from 1879 to 1882, the war against Irish landlords continued episodically for another twenty years as the Irish version of the war against privilege, which in one guise or another had been a leading theme in European history for more than a century. When Michael Davitt entitled his book of 1904 on the land war *The fall of feudalism in Ireland*, he was making an equation that was technically quite incorrect, but with a rhetorical thrust that was impeccable. Irish landlords might have considered themselves unlucky that unlike their counterparts at various times over much of continental Europe they did not have a privileged church beside them on the ramparts to draw some of the fire.[2] And their position was greatly weakened by the fact that in Britain also landlordism was on the defensive, both economically and politically. On the other hand they were fortunate in the British connection in that no Westminster government of the period, given the balance of interests in British political life, could be seen to countenance open expropriation, not even in Ireland. The balance of Irish politics, which could not be ignored either, was much different, favouring the interests of tenant farmers in particular.

---

[1] For the interaction between emigration and the land war, see below, p. 630.
[2] Above, v, 225.

By a series of measures spread over a period of more than a quarter century the law was changed, initially to limit the rights of landlords to set rents and evict tenants, and ultimately to induce them to sell the farms outright to their tenants, at prices that seemed generous before the inflationary hurricane of the first world war period. These transactions were conducted under the supervision of a body having its origins in the land act of 1881,[1] the Irish land commission, which was for nearly a century one of the central institutions in Irish life. In 1921 there were still estates that had not been vested in the farmers, but the focus of land agitation for some years had been on the question of distribution rather than ownership. In assessing the decline of the Irish landlord it is important to bear in mind that in Britain, where there was no comparable legislative intervention, social and economic change alone had a similarly devastating effect on many of the landed aristocracy.

The Irish land war transcended the interests of tenant farmers because it assumed the character of a nationalist movement. One of the most effective weapons used by the opponents of the landlords was to brand them as aliens whose property claims were in conflict with the rights of the national community. This device could be used selectively and was not extended to Parnell, the political master of the campaign, who was himself a landlord. Parnell, who even before the land crisis had displayed a formidable genius for leadership, used the pulling power of the land question to create a movement that became the most impressive political embodiment of Irish nationalism since the days of O'Connell. Just as O'Connell had extended the frontiers of popular democracy, Parnell and his party were pioneers in the democratisation of parliamentary politics in the United Kingdom.

The high point of Parnell's achievement came in 1886 when, backed by the eighty-six M.P.s of his nationalist party, he succeeded in winning the support of Gladstone's liberals for Irish home rule. Parnell's party was seriously split at the time of his death in 1891 and though it was reunited in 1900 under John Redmond further fission was to follow. But, whole or fragmented, it had the character of a great political establishment, the government-in-waiting of a home rule Ireland. The first phase of this destiny was accomplished when in 1898 the country was granted a fully elective system of local government, after which nationalist party supporters won control of the great majority of county councils and other local bodies, and so of a great web of patronage in jobs and contracts, which was to grow over the years. The stereotypical local Irish party stalwart was a small-town merchant and creditmonger (referred to disparagingly as a 'gombeen man') with a finger in every local pie, and with a rate-collector and a priest in the family. The type, and his supporting society and culture, nauseated intellectuals from William Butler Yeats to Peadar O'Donnell, but the reality was more complex and was apparently acceptable enough to most of those affected by it.

---

[1] 44 & 45 Vict., c. 49 (22 Aug. 1881); for the land commission, see sects 41–56.

The Irish party was now the secular counterpart of the catholic church in Ireland, and between the two there was an implicit understanding. The feeling of living under this joint establishment of their own choosing seems to have been enough to content a great many Irish people around the turn of the century, including the farmers as they prepared to become the new lords of the soil. It also seemed as if the *status quo* quite suited many of the Irish party M.P.s at Westminster as they grew accustomed to membership of the most exclusive club on earth.

The writ of the catholic–nationalist establishment did not run throughout the island. The land war had defined a political community by exclusion of the gentry, and they were put out of politics definitively over much of the country by subsequent local government legislation. Outside, too, was a large (though diminishing) segment of the administrative class and much of the commercial and professional élite of Dublin and other cities and towns. It was only in the north-east and in the constituencies of Dublin University and Dublin South County that dissenters from the majority had sufficient numerical strength to put their own into parliament. The unionist party represented the constitutional aspirations (or non-aspirations) and the manufacturing interests of the areas of protestant majority but also the aspirations and interests of a variety of groups with a near country-wide spread. Its operators at parliamentary and local level had little to learn from their nationalist counterparts.

A significant number of the Irish party M.P.s had been members at some stage of their careers of the Irish Republican Brotherhood but had left it behind for the parliamentary politics that were more in tune with the temper of the country and the age. Nevertheless, the organisation endured as the standard-bearer of the alternative, if discredited, nationalist policy of armed insurrection. In the period 1879–82 much of its membership and its energy were drawn into the Parnellite movement and in subsequent decades its main function was as a meeting place, and one with a wide assortment of *habitués*: devotees of the separatist ideal, adventurers, conspirators, and intelligent men of the lower middle class who felt their genius being rebuked by state, party, and especially church in the form of smug, authoritarian priests wanting to dictate to every committee and to preside over every parochial initiative. The organisation exerted little influence over what these people actually did and the most talented of those who joined seem to have moved on fairly quickly to seek elsewhere a focus for their dreams and ambitions. That situation was not greatly altered even when a more energetic leadership began to emerge from about 1907.

The years before and after the turn of the century were marked by intellectual, cultural, and associational ferment, much of it implicitly critical of the *status quo*: not merely the British connection, but also the catholic–nationalist establishment. Like any large, entrenched party the nationalists served their supporters in ways that reeked of corruption and chicanery to the nostrils of young idealists. The maliciousness of the infighting between, at various stages, Parnellites, anti-Parnellites, Healyites, Dillonites, and O'Brienites was thoroughly disedifying. Besides, there were those who were not content to enjoy an indefinite wait for home rule; and there were those who were coming to realise that home rule might not after all change very much and that simply having a parliament in Dublin would not of itself guarantee achievement of any of the thoroughgoing nationalist's dreams of a distinctive, prosperous, and creative society. There were also those who feared the combination of forces likely to rule in a self-governing Ireland and who hoped to establish counterbalances to church and party in advance of the dreaded day. The consequent crusades, programmes, publications, and organisations lacked any mutual coherence and simply bounced off one another, mostly within the narrow confines of lower-middle-class urban society. The Church of Ireland clergyman James Owen Hannay, himself both observer and participant, summed up the situation in the title of a didactic novel published in 1904 under the nom de plume 'George Birmingham': *The seething pot*. What would eventually come to the top or sink to the bottom, nobody could tell.

Even among the catholic clergy a note of unease was sounded. The centenary of Maynooth College in 1895 was marked by an amount of triumphalism but also by the inauguration of the Maynooth Union, intended as a forum for the discussion of problems raised by the contemporary age. There were at least two strands to this implicit criticism of the *status quo*: one, represented by Gerald O'Donovan, saw the church as in need of escape from the grip of Irish-party gombeenism; another, represented by Canon P. A. Sheehan, worried about the complacency of catholic nationalist Ireland in the face of the menacing infidelity of the age, as Sheehan himself had witnessed it at first hand while on mission in England. In the event the self-questioning trend did not flourish very widely and the majority of the catholic clergy, understandably, continued to act as custodians of a smoothly running and impregnable system. By comparison with their counterparts elsewhere in Europe they displayed little initiative in the promotion of Catholic Action or other associational activity among the laity, being instead generally content—although there were notable exceptions to this—with a monitorial role at parochial level in movements generated by others.

Possibly the most influential individual in the midst of the ferment was Arthur Griffith. A printer by trade and an ardent nationalist, he took up ideas about national self-sufficiency that had been commonplace among nationalists elsewhere in Europe and applied them to the Irish situation with a thoroughness not previously attempted. He articulated a vision of nationality in which mere political independence appeared as a bauble if not matched by a more profound self-sufficiency. Griffith perceived that if the majority of Irish people really did desire home rule as ardently as their voting patterns seemed to suggest, they could institute *de facto* self-government without having to wait for an act of the Westminster parliament. In this spirit he took up and developed the concept of abstentionism, calling for the election of M.P.s committed to remaining in Ireland and forming a national assembly. A number of clubs influenced by him combined in 1907 and soon took the name Sinn Féin. Ironically, in view of the connotations that that name was later to assume, Griffith could entertain quite flexible views on the question of Irish constitutional arrangements, as he displayed when he advocated a resolution of the Anglo–Irish relationship along the lines of the Austro–Hungarian dual monarchy, as he understood it.

Well before Griffith began his crusade, campaigns for cultural nationalism had been launched, even though it was not until the turn of the century that they, too, made a significant impact. The Gaelic Athletic Association (founded 1884) was ultimately successful to the point that over most of the country the leading field game of the twentieth century has been one of those that it codified—Gaelic football or hurling. This major contribution to the distinctiveness of Irish cultural life was outmatched in scope, if not in eventual achievement, by the project for the revival of Irish as the spoken language of the population at large set forth by the Gaelic League (founded 1893). The census of 1891 had shown that less than 15 per cent of the population claimed a knowledge of the language, which during the century had been abandoned on a large scale in favour of the evidently more useful and more fashionable English. Like Griffith, Douglas Hyde, first president of the Gaelic League, had had revealed to him the superficiality of mere political independence. What the country needed, he declared, was to be 'de-anglicised' in every aspect of its life.

In the early years of the new century the league acquired widespread membership and support. Like the Gaelic Athletic Association it became a very significant social movement. This was an era of remarkable development of associational life in many parts of Europe, with open and legal club and societal organisation spreading down the social scale, and outwards, as never before. Not least in Ireland, the increasing availability of the bicycle had a significant impact on social life. The social dimension of the Gaelic League—which progressed from language classes to drama, singing, Irish dancing, and other occasions of socialisation—upset some of the restrictive conventions of Irish rural and small town life, just as its formal objective amounted to an implicit criticism of the existing order as represented by church and party. Both institutions responded by giving the league their blessing, patronising it, occasionally exploiting its energy, and generally making sure that it did not get too far out of control. By 1910 or thereabouts deference to Irish—but not necessarily the language itself—was on the lips of almost every nationalist politician and catholic cleric. After 1921 the rulers of the Irish Free State automatically assumed that the pursuit of the revival policy was one of their duties. Not that the appeal of the Irish revival movement was exclusively catholic-nationalist. Hyde himself was of protestant gentry background and a significant, if small, number of others like him were attracted to the Gaelic League by the prospect of creating an alternative to the politico-religious realities that loomed about them. Seldom have hopes been more comprehensively dashed.

Horace Plunkett was another protestant of landed background who endeavoured to change the face of Ireland for the better and at the same time render the country less menacing to his own class and creed. If he failed in the latter objective, he had some success with the former. Plunkett's great project was agricultural cooperation. He saw that ownership of the land would not of itself increase the prosperity of Irish farmers. Elsewhere in Europe, and in the U.S.A., farmers had responded to the new era heralded by the agricultural slump of the late 1870s with more efficient and customer-orientated modes of production, including cooperative dairy enterprises. Meanwhile agrarian life in Ireland was distracted from business by the land war and Irish produce was failing to keep pace with competition from other countries in terms of quality and marketing. Plunkett's efforts to propagate the cooperative creamery in Ireland were so successful that it soon became an integral feature of rural society, especially in south Leinster and Munster.

The groups of planners and dreamers to be found in Dublin in the late 1890s included a tiny Irish Socialist Republican Party under the direction of the Edinburgh-born James Connolly, who hoped to transcend preexisting divisions by means of the doctrine of non-sectarian labour. Outside the north-east, industrial society was so sparse that there was little by way of a potential rank and file for a socialist movement. Nevertheless, in the course of the next twenty years, as general trade unionism was taking hold extensively elsewhere in Europe, Ireland followed suit. The reality of trade union achievement in Ireland, as well as its limitations, was demonstrated by the episode of the 1913 lock-out in Dublin. In the following five years the Irish Transport & General Workers' Union, founded by James Larkin in 1908, achieved remarkable enrolment figures throughout the country, so remarkable that many of them may have represented very perfunctory attachment indeed. It nevertheless remains true that labour organisation was a much more significant factor in Irish public life in the period 1914–21 than is usually recognised or than might appear from the reminiscences of some participants in the independence movement.

Formal education, whether viewed as cause or sign, is inseparable from the social, cultural, and political transformations of the age. Already by 1870 the national education system, after nearly forty years in existence, was providing at primary level a service that went very near to meeting demand. The less well-off undoubtedly demanded less than others, if only because their families could afford to allow them less time in school, but, by and large, ambitious parents had access to standardised, publicly funded instruction in the three Rs for their offspring. The system worked all the more smoothly after 1870 because that was approximately the point at which the state came to accept definitively that the churches would manage the schools along denominational lines. Rising demand for more advanced schooling led to the creation of the intermediate education board under an act of 1878 and the subsequent widespread, if not overgenerous, funding of secondary schools, again with maximum scope allowed to religious interests.

Soon there was an increasing demand for university education, especially from catholics, for it was they who benefited most from the expansion at secondary level. In the closing years of the century University College, run by the Jesuits on Stephen's Green, was providing for scores of students, many of them exceptionally talented and ambitious. Their degrees were awarded by the royal university, an examining institution chartered in 1880. A definitive answer to the long-standing Irish university question was not achieved until 1908: the Irish universities act of that year managed to reconcile various warring interests, including the conflict between denominational Irish realities and the antidenominational outlook of the British liberal party, and the tensions between indigenous religious and educational interests. The act might have presaged elaborately contrived reconciliation on larger political issues, but that was not to be: the architect of the 1908 act, Augustine Birrell, would leave office as a failure following Easter week 1916.

Rising educational levels went hand in hand with an expanding civil service. Numbers grew significantly in existing government bodies and there was a series of new bodies to be served, including the Irish land commission, the intermediate education board, the local government board, the congested districts board, the department of agriculture and technical instruction. Besides, many Irish people won positions in the British and imperial civil services. Recruitment by competitive examination had a democratising effect and resulted in much improved representation of catholics.

Within all denominations the extension of formal education improved the position of many women of the middle and lower middle classes and boosted the numbers of them leaving an individual mark on the historical record. On the catholic side the progress of schooling for girls meant the flourishing of the convent both as provider of much of the education and as destination of many of the educated. Touching as it did on so many aspects of life—religious, economic, educational, cultural, and aesthetic, and the ethos of disciplined cleanliness and godliness—the convent was one of the nodal institutions of Irish catholic society. Educated and independent women made a vital contribution to the ferment that was early twentieth-century Dublin, notably through Inghinidhe na hÉireann (Daughters of Ireland), launched in 1900 under the direction of Maud Gonne. This organisation was responsible for radical initiatives, especially in the area of nationalist propaganda and culture.

The widespread participation of women in the work of the Gaelic League is further, if less spectacular, evidence of a new-found public role. Indeed, one of the strengths of the league was precisely that it tapped the resources of women. Nevertheless, its implications for the place of women in society can be seen as ambiguous: the question has been asked, whether they were welcomed as equals or as supporters.

Needless to say the predominant assumptions of the time assigned a subordinate role to women in general, although all the evidence suggests that collectively women were moved as much as men by the political sagas of the age. In a number of crises, groups of women (in particular relatives of male leaders) were ready to channel their enthusiasm into what were intended to be ancillary or even stop-gap organisations. Probably the earliest instance of this was the prisoners' relatives support fund, conducted mainly by sisters and wives of prominent fenians arrested in 1865–6. A somewhat better remembered case is that of the Ladies' Land League of 1881–2, which assumed a life of its own and made a notable mark in the land war. The Ulster Women's Unionist Council (1911) and the nationalist Cumann na mBan (1913) exemplify a further stage of female mobilisation.

The Irish contribution to the classic women's rights movement of the age, the demand for suffrage, brought many impressive figures on stage, intermittently, over half a century, beginning with Isabella Tod of Belfast and Anna Haslam of Dublin. The latter was founder in 1876 of the Dublin Women's Suffrage Association, the best-known of its type in Ireland. The fortunes of it and its associates waxed and waned over the decades until a more militant phase was ushered in with the formation of the Irish Women's Franchise League by Hanna Sheehy Skeffington and Margaret Cousins in 1908. The years leading up to the first world war witnessed a lively suffrage campaign, especially in Dublin. Irish women gained the vote for local elections in 1898 and for parliamentary elections in 1918, but subject to a lower age limit of 30 (as was provided for in the United Kingdom generally). The constitution of the Irish Free State in 1922 accorded the same voting rights to women as to men. It is also worth noting that the first woman to win election to the house of commons was Constance de Markievicz in the Dublin constituency of St Patrick's in 1918 (albeit on an abstentionist platform).

Expansion in the numbers receiving higher education helped to make possible a burgeoning of literary activity. The call for a national literature had been raised on a number of occasions during the nineteenth century. Fr Matthew Russell, S.J., launched the *Irish Monthly* in 1873 with moderately expressed but very definite ambitions in that direction. Most prominent among the writers published by him in the decade that followed was a group of women including Rosa Mulholland, Katharine Tynan, and Rose Kavanagh. He also carried an early piece by Yeats, who was soon formulating his own grand designs for a national literature. While Russell was primarily interested in promoting writing by Irish authors, Yeats was more concerned with dictating the style and tone of an ideal Irish literature. Without Yeats there would still have been a great quantity of new and diverse Irish writing in the thirty years or so after 1890 now generally recognised as a golden age of Irish literature, but its impact would have been immeasurably different. He contributed immensely to the promotion of the Celtic movement in literature and so to the wider revivalism, which also inspired the Gaelic League and whose beginnings were in evidence at least from the 1870s. But there was no Celtic exemplar for the national theatre that he helped to found: Yeats, as is usual with revivalists, utilised the riches of the past as props in a thoroughly contemporary enterprise, improvising at will.

Like Hyde with the language, Plunkett with the cooperatives, and Connolly with socialism, Yeats hoped to transform Irish society; in his case the medium was to be celticising aesthetic culture. The term 'renaissance' is freely used of the epoch in Irish letters over which he presided, and it certainly reflects the scope of the ambitions of literary and Irish language enthusiasts of the period: there were those who thought in terms of reproducing the miracle of classical Greece. There certainly was world-class achievement: in December 1921 James Joyce's *Ulysses* was within two months of publication; Sean O'Casey's 'The shadow of a gunman', the first of his celebrated dramas, was within eighteen months of its première; and Yeats was within two years of receiving the Nobel prize for literature. However, the cultural lives of those who seemed to believe, in Yeats's words, that 'man was born to pray and save' were scarcely touched. Charles Kickham's *Knocknagow, or the homes of Tipperary* (1873) was their idea of literature.

While Irish language sources were explored by poets and playwrights for myths and folklore they also yielded material for the writing of scholarly history. Eoin MacNeill, one of the founders of the Gaelic League, became a pioneering figure in the study of early Irish society. His major work *Phases of Irish history* appeared in 1919. The influential Edmund Curtis used Irish-language sources in writing his *History of medieval Ireland* (1923). James Connolly, author of *Labour in Irish history* (1910), felt that he had sufficient information to speculate analytically on the social structures of Gaelic Ireland. The most successful exploiter of Gaelic history in the service of contemporary attitudes was Alice Stopford Green. In *The making of Ireland and its undoing* (1908) and *Nationality* (1911) she promoted a quite well informed but partisan and passionate view of the Irish past, replete with unquestioned assumptions about its contemporary significance, which appealed to all Irish nationalists but especially to the young enthusiasts in the Gaelic League, Sinn Féin, and the literary movement.

If the study of early Irish history gained momentum in the early twentieth century, the single most influential Irish historian of the years between 1870 and 1921 was an authority on the eighteenth century, W. E. H. Lecky. The substantial Irish segment of his eight-volume *A history of England in the eighteenth century* (1878–90) was reissued in 1892 as *A history of Ireland in the eighteenth century*. This masterpiece of history-writing supported the catholic–nationalist outlook in a liberal kind of way, so much so that commentators then and since have been surprised at Lecky's opposition to home rule. And Lecky was not the only liberal scholar-gentleman historian at work in Ireland at the time: Richard Bagwell's multi-volume masterpieces *Ireland under the Tudors* and *Ireland under the Stuarts* first appeared in 1885 and 1909 respectively. Publication of G. H. Orpen's four-volume *Ireland under the Normans* began in 1911 and concluded in 1920. A young barrister, George O'Brien, created a landmark with his three-volume *Economic history of Ireland* (1918–21). Besides, the period was marked by the appearance of a large quantity of works in ecclesiastical and local history, varying greatly in their standards of scholarship but with many of them having enduring value. Some of them have subsequently acquired particular importance because they incorporate archival material lost when the public record office of Ireland was destroyed in 1922 in the course of civil hostilities.

When in 1868–70 Gladstone proffered and delivered disestablishment and land law reform he was consciously deferring to Irish democratic demands. As he saw the matter, Ireland ought to be governed in accordance with majority 'Irish ideas' and Britain ought not to stand in the way. Implicitly, at least, this came to be accepted by British politicians on all sides, as in the transformation of the land law and and the generally conciliatory policies of the decades after 1881. The main area in which this consensus did not apply was that of constitutional arrangements. Gladstone broached home rule in 1886 as another issue between Britain and Ireland, but his opponents succeeded in turning it into a party political one. In fact it became ostensibly the question that defined the difference between parties, a perilous development for any important issue. Instead of being a matter between Britain and Ireland, home rule became a matter between the liberals and their Irish nationalist allies on the one hand, and the tories and their Irish unionist allies on the other. This meant that the way to the enactment of home rule was blocked until the power of veto of the tory-dominated house of lords was broken in 1911.

Irish opposition to home rule had two bases of strength: the landlords and the collectivity of Irish protestants. As democratic trends weakened the former throughout Ireland, they gave strength to the latter in the area where protestants were a majority, in the north-east. The three home rule bills—1886, 1893, and 1912—were the occasions of increasingly thorough popular mobilisations in the name of unionism, centred on Belfast. Encompassing as it did an industrial proletariat and manufacturing and commercial proprietors, in addition to the full range of agrarian classes, unionism in the north-east drew its strength from a wider social spectrum than the numerically superior nationalist movement did in the country at large.

The dependence of the liberal government of the day on Irish nationalist support meant that the home rule bill of 1912 seemed destined to become law by 1914. Faced with the prospect of rule by a Dublin parliament certain to have a catholic majority, the unionists declared their determination to resist, by force if need be. Hence the fateful move to form and arm a mass military organisation, the Ulster Volunteer Force, a move that was facilitated by the partisan character of the home rule question in British politics. The unsurprising consequence was the formation and arming of the Irish Volunteers in support of the nationalist cause. Preventing the arming of mobilised political opinions had been vital to the maintenance of peace in Ireland throughout the nineteenth century. In particular Irish nationalism had been by the standards of the age—and despite the efforts of some Young Irelanders and fenians—a particularly unmilitarised creed. In the space of twelve months armed mobilisation came about and as a consequence the ability of the government to determine the future of Ireland was radically diminished. And those on both sides in Ireland whose power had been simultaneously enhanced had little capacity for compromise.

The outbreak of the first world war in August 1914 provided a plausible excuse for putting home rule on ice and deferring the moment of truth. Both sides saw an opportunity to use the interval before the anticipated 'victory by Christmas' to manoeuvre for the strengthening of their influence over the government and its future Irish policy. With this in mind the unionist leader, Edward Carson, and the leader of the Irish nationalist party, John Redmond, encouraged their followers to enlist in the British army. The allies' defence of Belgium permitted Irish nationalists to see participation in the war effort as part of a crusade for the rights of small nations, although this rationalisation is not of itself adequate to explain the subsequent rush to enlist. But with the duration and enormity of the war exceeding all expectations it was to destabilise the political élites of country after country, not sparing the Irish nationalist party.

The initiative in forming the Irish Volunteers had come from a group of cultural and conspiratorial nationalists. In the well practised fashion of his party Redmond had subsequently taken the organisation under his own control. When he advocated enlistment in the imperial war effort the original founders withdrew, taking a small segment of the rank and file with them to form an independent organisation, dedicated to bearing arms in Ireland alone, which continued to be called the Irish Volunteers. British involvement in a major war altered the balance of the pragmatic argument against nationalist insurrection and gave hitherto unprecedented credibility to the Irish Republican Brotherhood's position. If the brotherhood had not existed somebody would surely have invented it following the outbreak of the war. A small band of cultural revivalists and I.R.B. activists answering to nobody but themselves, but operating under the aegis of the brotherhood, sought help from Germany and planned a rising to involve the Irish Volunteers, the leaders of which were not party to the plans. Significant parts of the arrangements came unstuck, but the rising went ahead, mainly in Dublin, on Easter Monday 1916, under the leadership of Patrick Pearse, and lasted almost a week before it was suppressed.

While the leaders of the rising, and others, forfeited their lives, the principal political victim was the Irish party. In two decades it had generated precious little energy of its own but had drawn on that of others, particularly the generation of cultural revivalists and activists among whom the rising was conceived. These now, under the name of Sinn Féin, came forward as a party on their own account and found that over much of nationalist Ireland they faced no serious local opposition. In the space of a year or so Sinn Féin refurbished the symbolic paraphernalia of Irish nationalism—new martyrs, new heroes, new flag, new anthems. The further extension of the suffrage in 1918 could not but have aided the prospects of such a dynamic new party. Its victory at the general election in December was followed by the convening of Dáil Éireann and the declaration of an independent Irish republic.

If Sinn Féin were the major beneficiaries of the rising of 1916, the unionists too turned it to advantage. The insurrection seriously weakened Redmond's already faltering hand in the contest for influence over government policy and strengthened Carson accordingly. After Easter 1916 the chances that the protestant- dominated north would be coerced into accepting rule from Dublin went from very slight to nonexistent. On the other hand the events of 1916–18 made the granting of home rule in some form inescapable. The British government's resolution of the dilemma was presented in the government of Ireland act of 1920, providing for partition and for two home rule parliaments—subordinate to Westminster—in Dublin and Belfast. A council of Ireland was provided for as a forum for future cooperation.

Meanwhile the government appointed by Dáil Éireann was endeavouring to make a reality of its declared independence, and with some success over much of the country. The ability of crown forces to uphold the authority of the British government was seriously restricted by a campaign of guerrilla warfare conducted by members of the Irish volunteers, now increasingly being referred to as the Irish Republican Army. A truce agreed in July 1921 was followed by negotiations that produced the Anglo–Irish treaty of 6 December, under which the southern state went well beyond home rule to acquire the status of self-governing dominion and the title of the Irish Free State. Provision for a boundary commission to redraw the frontier between the two new Irish states was a palliative to sweeten the bitter pill of partition.

In the period 1920–23 many thousands of Irish people, protestant as well as catholic, were forced by fear or intimidation to leave their homes or their employment. Terrible though this was, it did not compare in extent or intensity with the horrors of displacement experienced following the collapse of imperial authority or the outbreak of civil conflict elsewhere in Europe at various times throughout the century. It remained to be seen how successfully the two new political entities would cope with the island's unresolved intercommunal tensions. Similar problems faced numerous new regimes in the Europe of the 1920s.

The war had not only produced political upheaval but had also loosened many social and economic bonds. Some were never fully restored again. In Ireland, north and south, the distancing from Britain provided by new political institutions facilitated a fuller return to antebellum order than was possible in 'pagan' England. The Sinn Féin élite, like most of their immediate predecessors among the cultural and political enthusiasts, were dedicated to the perfection of Irish respectability. The relatively smooth accession of Sinn Féin to national leadership was made possible by the sending of clear signals of reassurance to the church, employers, farmers, and shopkeepers. Indeed Sinn Féin did much to smother some Irish aftershocks of the Bolshevik revolution. In both Northern Ireland and the Irish Free State constitutional change seemed to offer the prospect of obviating drastic social change and of salvaging some of what people valued from the social order that had evolved between the great famine and the great war.

CHAPTER I

Isaac Butt and the home rule party, 1870–77

R. V. COMERFORD

THE political exuberance that had marked the late 1860s in Ireland declined in the spring of 1870. The publication of Gladstone's long-awaited land bill in February had a quietening effect, not because it satisfied tenant expectations but because it ended the uncertainty that had seriously disturbed the equanimity of tenant and landlord alike since Gladstone's rise to power in 1868 promising 'justice for Ireland'.[1]

The question of the fenian prisoners had been another, but a less potent, source of tension. Fenian sympathisers insisted—and others had come to accept—that the reconciliation desired by Gladstone would not be complete without an amnesty for the prisoners, and this became the object of an impressive public agitation. The belief that this had been the great issue in Irish political life in 1869—indeed one of the great focal points of popular protest in mid-Victorian Ireland—owes much to a pamphlet published in March 1870, *Ireland's appeal for amnesty: a letter to W. E. Gladstone*, by Isaac Butt. In summing up and embellishing the campaign of the Amnesty Association, including its series of mass meetings in the previous autumn, Butt was signalling that as far as he was concerned—and he implied that his was the moving spirit—that phase of activity was over and done with. Butt was planning to move on to greater things.

The cessation of mass campaigning for amnesty allowed the prime minister to display his deeply felt desire to be accommodating. It was too soon for an amnesty, too soon at least for Gladstone's cabinet colleagues and Dublin Castle officials to contemplate that concession. But another aspect of the problem could be tackled. Concern for the prisoners and anger against the government were being constantly nurtured by reports of the alleged ill-treatment of incarcerated fenians, most notably Jeremiah O'Donovan Rossa. He, like most of the fenians convicted in Irish courts in 1865, 1866, and 1867, was imprisoned in England; the others had been transported to Western Australia in 1868. On 17 March 1870 Gladstone informed George Henry Moore, the Irish M.P. (Kilkenny County)

[1] Above, v, 441–50.

most openly and consistently critical of the government on the prisoner issue, that a commission of inquiry would examine the allegations of ill-treatment in English jails. This served to defuse further criticism, and the effect was enhanced when the membership of the commission, chaired by the earl of Devon, was made public weeks later. Included were Dr R. D. Lyons of Dublin, who had been expressing concern about the prisoners; Dr E. H. Greenhow, a Londoner with radical connections; and Stephen de Vere, a County Limerick landlord who was universally held in high regard. The report of the commission was published in 1871; it was a model of fairness, balance, and conciliatory wording.[1] However, the Devon commission had made its principal contribution to conciliation by providing all concerned with the occasion to drop heated public airing of the prisoner question. The relative silence of the Amnesty Association while the commission was sitting helped Gladstone to persuade ministers and officials in November 1870 that the time had arrived for a fenian amnesty. Those benefiting were primarily prisoners convicted in Ireland between 1865 and 1867, and they included such prominent personalities as John O'Leary, Thomas Clarke Luby, Jeremiah O'Donovan Rossa, John Devoy, and Denis Dowling Mulcahy. After delays caused by legal technicalities these and others were released in January 1871, but on the condition of exile from the United Kingdom for the period of their prison sentences.

The conciliatory advance announcement of the Devon commission on 17 March 1870 had been balanced by the publication of a coercive measure, the Peace Preservation (Ireland) Bill. Its provisions amounted in the main to continuation in a milder form of measures reenacted continuously for decades past (and due to expire at the end of the next session of parliament) that were applied by the proclamation of disturbed districts. The willingness to renew the legislation was more important than its terms and the effect was less to frighten the disaffected than to reassure those, including Dublin Castle officials, who worried about the maintenance of order, and about the liberal government's preparedness to make special legislative arrangements for the peace and government of Ireland. A novel feature of the measure was a series of provisions allowing for the suppression of treasonable newspapers.[2] This smacked of something more than empty gestures. The *Irishman*, a Dublin-based weekly under the proprietorship of Richard Pigott, was the unofficial organ of the élite group that had reorganised the Irish Republican Brotherhood under a new controlling authority, the supreme council, in the late 1860s.[3] The paper had been outspoken in its denunciations of the government over the fenian prisoners, and of the catholic church over the papal condemnation of fenianism *ipso nomine*, delivered in January 1870.[4] That condem-

---

[1] *Report of the commissioners appointed to inquire into the treatment of treason-felony convicts in English prisons, together with appendix and minutes of evidence* [C 319], H.C. 1871, xxxii, 1–60; [C 319–I], H.C. 1871, xxxii, 61–602.

[2] Peace Preservation (Ireland) Act, 33 Vict., c. 9 (4 Apr. 1870), sects 30–32.

[3] Above, v, 444–6.

[4] E. R. Norman, *The catholic church and Ireland in the age of rebellion, 1859–1873* (London, 1965), pp 129–33; P. J. Corish, 'Political problems, 1860–78' in Corish, *Ir. catholicism*, v, fasc. 3, pp 41–3.

nation reflected the perception by both civil and ecclesiastical authority of the strength of the fenians. But the strength was more apparent than real, and was a product of the general sense of uncertainty that had already begun to drain away by the end of 1870.

The last great wave of a three-year cycle of political excitement was caused by the outbreak of the Franco-Prussian war in July 1870. Irish catholics identified with France and held many enthusiastic pro-French demonstrations throughout the country. Large sums of money were collected to aid the French war effort and, later, to send medical aid. In response there was an amount of popular protestant mobilisation in support of the king of Prussia.[1]

While the country in general settled back into a more normal state in 1871, pockets of disturbance remained. Cork city witnessed a confused series of labour disputes. Much greater government and press attention was devoted to persistent agrarian violence in County Westmeath. Exaggerated assessments of what was essentially petty criminal activity, extending to an occasional murder, led to the enactment in June 1871 of the so-called 'Westmeath act', which permitted the suspension of habeas corpus in proclaimed districts.[2]

LIKE catholic Ireland, nonconformist Wales had achieved a new level of self-expression and identity within Gladstone's liberal coalition at the general election of December 1868. Exactly fifty years later, after an epoch of very considerable development along distinctive lines within the United Kingdom, each of these national majorities again plumped for a panacea: in one case the socialism of the British labour party, in the other the separatism of Sinn Féin. Neither one outcome nor the other was the inevitable consequence of the national recognition achieved in 1868. None the less, the notion that the 'justice for Ireland' promised by Gladstone should take the form of self-government was indeed given expression in the late 1860s. The fenians, in so far as they were concerned with ideology, stood for separation, but they had just proved that they were incapable of achieving it. A handful of the survivors and heirs of O'Connell and Young Ireland—such as W. J. O'Neill Daunt, John Martin, A. M. Sullivan, P. J. Smyth, and Dean Richard O'Brien—dreamt of a new repeal movement of some kind, but they failed to launch anything. In any case most heirs of the 1840s movements were now adherents of Gladstone. It was an old tory opponent of O'Connell, Isaac Butt, who began agitation for Irish self-government in 1870.

Butt's proposals envisaged not the dismantling of the United Kingdom but its federalisation, with England, Scotland, and Ireland having local parliaments subordinate to Westminster.[3] He envisaged the Irish parliament having a house

---

[1] Above, v, 726–7.

[2] Protection of Life and Property in Certain Parts of Ireland Act, 34 & 35 Vict., c. 25 (16 June 1871); see A. C. Murray, 'Agrarian violence and nationalism in nineteenth-century Ireland: the myth of Ribbonism' in *Ir. Econ. & Soc. Hist.*, xiii (1986), pp 56–73.

[3] Isaac Butt, *Home government for Ireland: Irish federalism, its meaning, its objects and its hopes* (Dublin, 1870).

of lords with powers of veto. This offered the prospect that protestant landowners could prevent any further legislative assaults on their interests or sensibilities, assaults of the kind represented by the Irish church act of 1869 and the land act of 1870. Since the spring of 1869 protestant annoyance had produced expressions of serious disenchantment with the union,[1] and Butt had reason to hope that protestants of substance would rally to his campaign for what quickly became known as 'home rule'. Such people formed the largest group at the private meeting in Bilton's Hotel, Dublin, at which Butt's Home Government Association took shape on 19 May 1870. Included were protestant landowners, proprietors of conservative newspapers, and fellows of Trinity College. However, this promise of substantial protestant support was not to be realised. There might be much disillusionment with the union and much passive goodwill towards Butt's project, but in the cold light of day few could accept that a self-governing Ireland might be made safe for protestant ascendancy. In any case, Butt for all his political insight and intellectual acumen seems to have had little awareness of the popular element in Irish protestantism burgeoning in the north-east. The Dublin-centred tory élite with which he was dealing could not speak for the presbyterian farmers, or for the Belfast proletarians who had rioted so spectacularly in July 1864. And even among those of rank and wealth, active advocates of home rule were few and soon became fewer.

If it was difficult for many protestants to believe that home rule would serve their interests, it must have been even more difficult for landlords in general to see it serving theirs. Few notions commended wider (albeit not frequently spoken) assent in post-famine Ireland than the assumption that self-government would involve change in the land system to the detriment of landlord interests. Gladstone's land act of 1870, the cause of so much landlord ire, had amounted to an acknowledgement that the balance of Irish opinion demanded a different land law in Ireland from that in England. Butt, as everyone knew, had close contacts with organised tenants. No doubt this enabled him to offer silent or at least implied assurances to his landlord cooperators concerning the possibility of compromise on the land question in an Irish parliament. Only a small number can have been convinced.

While discussions preliminary to the formation of the Home Government Association were still under way, home rule was put to the electoral test. Major Laurence Knox, proprietor of the *Irish Times*, stood on the platform of home government in a by-election in Mallow on 10 May 1870. He had been unsuccessful in the same constituency a few months earlier as a tory. This time he lost again, and by the same margin as previously. On 16 May 1870 a by-election in County Longford—a constituency controlled for over thirty years by an alliance of whig landowners and priests—was contested by the tory E. R. King-Harman

---

[1] David Thornley, *Isaac Butt and home rule* (London 1964), pp 86–7; L. J. McCaffrey, 'Isaac Butt and the home rule movement: a study in conservative nationalism' in *Review of Politics*, xxii, no. 1 (Jan. 1960), pp 72–95.

under the flag of home rule. He lost, but with an encouraging 43 per cent of the votes cast. He was unsuccessful in a Dublin city by-election in August 1870. He again had 43 per cent of the vote, but this time the figure was no source of encouragement. The tory vote in the constituency was around 50 per cent, and as he had only a liberal opponent against him King-Harman might have been expected to achieve that figure at least.

By the autumn of 1870 A. M. Sullivan, P. J. Smyth, O'Neill Daunt, John Martin, and Dean O'Brien had overcome their qualms about abandoning the principle of repeal of the union and were supporting Butt's programme. Early in 1871 Martin contested a by-election in County Meath. This was a constituency where the tenant interest was particularly strong and particularly actively supported by the priests. And here the home rulers profited from tenant disillusionment with Gladstone as Butt's strategy calculated they would. The Gladstonian who was Martin's only opponent, the Hon. George J. Plunkett, initially enjoyed clerical acquiescence in his candidature, but when opposition materialised the priests did not rise to meet it. Their apathy reflected that of the farmers and allowed Martin to win a clear-cut victory on 17 January.

The result marked the beginning of the end of Gladstone's first phase of collaboration with majority Irish opinion. At this point home rule inherited the remnants of the independent opposition tendency within the catholic body politic, which had been forced to bow before liberalism in 1868. People such as Archbishop MacHale of Tuam and the former Callan curates Thomas O'Shea and Martin Keeffe, who had been waging factional warfare against the liberals for two decades, now eagerly declared for home rule. Those politicians who had invoked the name of Gladstone to secure catholic votes in 1868 now decided that 'home rule' was the new open sesame to the constituencies. When a by-election campaign opened in Galway county in February 1871 three candidates of liberal type and antecedents presented themselves, all invoking home rule, however circumspectly. One of them, Mitchell Henry, was eventually returned unopposed. What happened in Galway was bad news for Gladstone. However, it was also bad news for Butt, or at least for the kind of movement he had launched less than a year previously. For in addition to invoking home rule Henry had also committed himself to support 'denominational education' (a code for the recognition and endowment by the state of a catholic university) and the restoration of the pope to the position of temporal power that he had recently lost at the hands of the Italian kingdom.[1] In other words, 'home rule' was the key to electoral success, but only if it was accompanied by invocation of catholic concerns. In a comparatively short time home rule came to be synonymous with the assertion of popular catholic sentiment.

A by-election in Westmeath in June 1871 put matters to the test once more. This time P. J. Smyth presented himself as a home rule candidate. A prominent catholic liberal, J. A. Dease, was eager to run in the Gladstonian interest but

---

[1] Thornley, *Isaac Butt*, p. 117.

withdrew when the bishop and priests threw their influence behind Smyth. But in addition to home rule Smyth had denominational education as one of the planks in his platform. The internal inconsistencies of the movement were highlighted more spectacularly in a very different kind of constituency, County Monaghan, where a by-election took place in July 1871. A chapter of confusions led to the belated drafting of Butt himself as a candidate, only for him to trail home at the polls behind the tory John Leslie, who was defending a family seat.[1] In September 1871 a by-election in Limerick city gave Butt the opportunity to try again. He was successful, but only after he had disarmed the opposition of priests, intending to run a pro-Gladstone candidate, by a ringing declaration for denominational education. By the late autumn of 1871 home rule had acquired the support of the catholic–liberal *Cork Examiner* and *Freeman's Journal* and had lost the support of the protestant–conservative *Irish Times*.[2]

A factor of considerable significance in the electoral successes of home rule was its possession of a cadre of activists. Most of them were members of the I.R.B. They were referred to as fenians, the party of action, or the 'advanced' men, and they sometimes referred to themselves as the 'nationalists'. These intimations of principle notwithstanding, the group in question is best understood in terms not of ideology but of function. They had been given a modernising education, inculcating personal ambition, by a society that still expected deference to wealth, order, and the professions in all areas of life including politics. There may have been a disproportionately large gap in mid-Victorian Ireland between the output of the primary education system and the availability of employment within the country itself. That is not to suggest, however, that jobs or mere monetary success would have pacified the advanced men. They sought significance, influence, and acceptance. In certain protestant cultures religion provided appropriate outlets for such people, Welsh congregationalism being an outstanding example of this. In France they embraced radicalism, and in catholic Ireland republican separatism. Significant numbers of them were in evidence in Ireland in the late 1850s and early 1860s before the greater part (but by no means all of them) became drawn into James Stephens's fenian organisation. By 1870 they had been fully initiated into the excitements of electioneering, contradicting the policies and defying the directives of the I.R.B. supreme council, to which they were supposedly subject, by their participation in parliamentary by-elections. They displayed, in the County Tipperary by-elections of November 1869 and January 1870, and in supporting John Martin as an independent nationalist in the Longford by-election of February 1870, that they could constitute a dynamic election machine at short notice. That was a potentially momentous innovation, given that in so many counties the only effective existing machine was that of the priests. The principal authors of the innovation included Charles G. Doran, James F. X. O'Brien, John 'Amnesty' Nolan, James O'Connor, John O'Connor Power, Richard Pigott, and Peter E. Gill.

[1] Ibid., pp 119–20.   [2] Ibid., pp 122–5.

From 1868 G. H. Moore had been in close contact with fenian activists, obviously hoping to use their energy and talents in the new national movement that he and others were thinking about. Moore died suddenly on 19 April 1870. Butt had been in contact with the advanced party through the Amnesty Association. Before the launching of the Home Government Association he had a meeting with two members of the supreme council of the I.R.B. Each side could help the other in various ways. There were many examples from the 1860s of how extremists could inflict injury on a public nationalist movement, if only by the disruption of meetings.[1] By means of friendly overtures Butt could hope to ward off that danger. Better still, he might hope for actual assistance. Discreet dealings with fenian types were not likely to stick in the throats of Butt's tory friends in the Home Government Association; whenever independent oppositionists or the advanced party posed an electoral challenge to the liberals over the previous decade and a half, tory encouragement was usually forthcoming and on a few occasions there had been substantial amounts of tory money.[2] The enemy's enemy is a friend. Discretion entered into the business, but not squeamishness.

The principal internal problem of the I.R.B. in the early 1870s was how to reconcile its functional, socio-political *raison d'être* with its theoretical *raison d'être* which was a burden and was being raised to the level of dogma by influential individuals such as Charles J. Kickham, who insisted that the fenian oath obliged them to wait patiently for the day of the pitched battle against England, eschewing in the meantime all contact with the contamination that was public agitation and parliamentary politics.[3] Butt's movement provided the best possible pretext for activism. It was anti-liberal and, though not separatist, could be said to be heading in the right direction. The fenian cadres were of considerable assistance in the early years of the home rule movement and never more so than in Butt's successful by-election campaign in Limerick in September 1871. Even where it was not called into action the election machine of the advanced men may have influenced events. Unless a candidate was particularly committed to Gladstone's government, what was the point of his incurring the trouble and expense (and risk of losing) involved in fighting against an enthusiastic electoral machine, when all of this inconvenience could be avoided by the simple invocation of home rule? One could subsequently vote as one thought best in parliament. If a candidate invoking home rule was at the same time prepared to declare for denominational education, that satisfied most of the priests. Even when the clerical election machine was at its most effective, some priests had no liking for the work. Many more of them would have reservations about a campaign where they could be depicted as taking on 'the people', and might well lose on top of that.

[1] Above, v, 431–2.
[2] For an example from 1865 see James O'Shea, *Priests, politics, and society in post-famine Ireland: a study of County Tipperary, 1850–91* (Dublin, 1983), p. 158.
[3] R. V. Comerford, *Charles J. Kickham: a study in Irish nationalism and literature* (Dublin, 1979), pp 179–81.

The excavations of nineteenth-century Irish political culture conducted by K. T. Hoppen demonstrate the insufficiency of national issues on their own for explaining much of the electoral behaviour of the period.[1] The home rule by-election victories of 1871 turn out on close inspection to be ambiguous. They owed much to the fenian-related cadres, but not because of any widespread public conversion to the principles of either the I.R.B. or the Home Government Association. The machine was influential simply because it existed, a source of unaccustomed energy and a product of Irish political precociousness, at a time when electoral politics generally were still conducted on the presumption of deference to property and the social order. But the principal political effect had been to make home rule into another tune in the already extensive repertoire of the typical parliamentary hopeful, seeking to charm an Irish catholic constituency. Any one tune could be taken for them all. On the hustings in Limerick Butt himself had declared simultaneously for home rule and denominational education. It is doubtful if many of the voters cared tuppence about the university question, but they recognised an Irish catholic catch-cry when they heard it. 'Home rule' was well on the way to becoming another such catch-cry. As far as Westminster politics was concerned this was all evidence that enthusiasm for Gladstone had declined significantly; but it did not mean anything as definite and clear-cut as a deliberate repudiation of the liberal alliance by Irish catholic opinion.

The place achieved by home rule in the politics of the catholic counties was illustrated by two by-elections in February 1872. A vacancy occurred in Kerry when Viscount Castlerosse, who had been returned as a liberal M.P. for the county without challenge since 1852, succeeded his father as earl of Kenmare. A young protestant landlord, Rowland Ponsonby Blennerhassett, presented himself as a home rule candidate and thereby faced the liberal interest in the county with the prospect of the first contested election in over thirty years. Where a less politicised churchman might have let things pass, Bishop David Moriarty of Kerry resolved to make a stand for liberalism and the alliance with Gladstone. He was supported by the archbishop of Dublin, Cardinal Cullen. They shared an intense dislike both of the tory element in the Home Government Association and of the fenian-related activists, whom they saw as harbingers of revolution and godlessness. Both ecclesiastics hoped that Gladstone would produce university legislation acceptable to the church, although their emphases may have been different, with Cullen interested only in concessions to the church while Moriarty was also interested in seeing Gladstone get credit for such concessions. The bishop of Kerry encouraged J. A. Dease to carry the liberal banner against home rule. However, division soon emerged among his priests, with numbers of them supporting each candidate. There was also landlord influence and money on each side. However, an invasion of enthusiastic campaigners from outside combined

---

[1] K. T. Hoppen, *Elections, politics, and society in Ireland, 1833–85* (Oxford, 1984).

with indigenous enthusiasm for home rule to swing the contest in favour of Blennerhassett, who garnered 62 per cent of the votes cast.[1]

Galway county had almost as little experience as Kerry of contested elections. A vacancy arose in February 1872 following the appointment of W. H. Gregory, liberal M.P. for the county since 1857, as governor of Ceylon. Captain J. P. Nolan, one of those who had given way to Mitchell Henry in 1871, was quickly agreed upon as the candidate in the majority (that is to say popular and clerical) interest. He was a proponent of home rule, but in other respects was a liberal candidate of a well-established type. Instead of enjoying the unopposed return that he might have expected, Nolan had to face a challenge at the polls from a tory, William Le Poer Trench. In a contest that was embittered by sectarian controversy, Nolan easily carried the day with the support of the united priesthood of the county and of the home rule activists, the two cadres in this case pulling together. Mark Ryan, then a young local adherent of the advanced party and subsequently a noted I.R.B. man, recalled in his later years that in the 1872 election he had marshalled carloads of cudgel-bearing supporters of Captain Nolan.[2]

There is a tendency to think of the priests of mid-Victorian Ireland as past masters of the art of getting out the vote. In fact a contested election was a rare event in the career of most priests. Clerical electoral influence generally took the form of influencing or determining the selection of an acceptable and unbeatable candidate who could then be expected to have an unopposed return. The necessity to go to the polls, when it arose, constituted a crisis in which the temptation was to abandon caution and decency for the sake of victory. That was what some of the priests of County Galway did in February 1872, with the result that Trench, defeated heavily at the polls, was able to lodge a successful petition against Nolan on the grounds of improper clerical influence, and was given the seat. The judge who tried the petition was William Keogh, a catholic who had himself experienced the wrath of some politically minded priests when member of parliament for Athlone in the 1850s. Keogh's judgment in the Galway case, delivered on 27 May 1872, included a generalised and unrestrained denunciation of the manners and influence of the catholic priesthood. A wave of public protest ensued, as newspapers and politicians sensitive to catholic sensibilities rushed to denounce Keogh. Protestants, including many who would have wished that he had not stirred matters up in the first place, felt impelled to come to his defence. The sectarian polarisation of Irish life revealed by this episode was no new revelation to anybody, but as with all such waves of renewed emotion it added to the cumulative effect. For home rule the result was an intensified identification with Irish catholic causes. Butt found himself obliged to support publicly the campaign against Keogh, even as far as the floor of the house of commons.[3]

[1] Thornley, *Isaac Butt*, pp 126–30.
[2] Mark Ryan, *Fenian memories* (Dublin, 1945), p. 42.
[3] Thornley, *Isaac Butt*, p. 131.

Interconfessional tension was high in Western Europe generally in the early 1870s, in the wake of the definition of papal infallibility by the Vatican council in 1870. (Cardinal Cullen played a prominent part in the work of the council.) The occupation of Rome by Italian forces in September 1870 brought to a high point the widespread tension that existed between the catholic church and the modern state. In Germany Bismarck was shortly to embark on his *Kulturkampf* against the institutions of catholicism. Questions were raised about the force of canon law and episcopal authority in Ireland by the controversial case of Father Robert O'Keeffe, who was suspended from office as parish priest of Callan, County Kilkenny, in November 1871 for having brought an ecclesiastical dispute before the civil courts.[1] The subsequent series of court cases and debates in parliament stoked both the anti-clerical dread of ultramontanism and the catholic sense of enduring discrimination.

In this charged atmosphere Gladstone worked to produce legislative proposals for the future of the Irish universities. His university bill was published in February 1873 and amounted to a far-reaching, imaginative, and complex plan.[2] It would have left the country with one comprehensive national university embracing every university institution in the country—including the Catholic University. What Gladstone could not propose, because of the opposition of his nonconformist supporters, was endowment of any denominational institution, in particular the Catholic University. None the less Cardinal Manning of Westminster urged the Irish bishops to accept the proposed measures. The process whereby they moved to a rejection was complicated, but it had much to do with Irish politics, just as it was to have repercussions for Westminster politics. It was a case where the main body of the bishops could unite only on a negative line, and even at that there were two, including Moriarty of Kerry, who wished to stand by the liberal alliance. The majority was variously motivated. Cullen, like Moriarty, had no desire to bring down Gladstone, and he might have been glad enough to put up with the prime minister's proposals as a *fait accompli*. But he could not bring himself positively to endorse compromise, especially with the sounds of *Kulturkampf* ringing in the air. Archbishop MacHale of Tuam revelled in this opportunity to denounce the liberals, and by implication all those, especially Cullen, who had ever advocated trust in them. He had published his own denunciation of the bill before the meeting of the bishops on 25 February 1873, at which a collective condemnation was agreed.[3] MacHale was now behind home rule as he had been behind independent opposition in the 1850s. With home rule achieving a popularity that independent opposition had not enjoyed outside of a few months in 1852, liberals sitting for Irish catholic constituencies had more than educational principles in their minds when they came to vote on the second reading of Gladstone's university bill. Episcopal urgings would not of themselves have mattered very much but for the certainty that anyone standing by Gladstone would be challenged by clerically supported

<hr/>

[1] Norman, *Cath. ch. & Ire.*, pp 431–6.   [2] Below, pp 557–8.
[3] Norman, *Cath. ch. & Ire.*, pp 449–51.

home rulers at the next election. The great majority decided, in concert, to vote against, and the bill was lost by a narrow margin on 12 March 1873. Gladstone's authority was severely dented; with the tories refusing to form a minority government he retained office, but as head of an administration that had lost its capacity for initiative.

The defection of the Irish liberals in March 1873 signified the end of the phase of alliance between Irish catholics and the British liberal party that had enjoyed such a triumph in 1868 on a wave of euphoria about the governing of Ireland in accordance with 'Irish ideas', that is to say, in accordance with majority Irish demands. The arrangement held up admirably in the disestablishment of the church; it lost some of its gloss on account of the fenian prisoner question; and it showed signs of strain with the land act of 1870, which gave some useful security to the yearly tenants but did not change the facts of economic and legal life in favour of the Irish farmer.[1] Gladstone in 1868 had offered in effect home rule without constitutional structures. The transition from that to the explicit home rule so popular with Irish catholics by 1873 was not very great. Whatever he may have been hoping for, what Butt actually achieved was not a realignment of Irish parties but a tilt of the balance of advantage inside one party, namely that consisting of the catholics and those protestant politicians reliant on catholic constituencies. There had been no ideological upheaval. Butt and home rule now constituted the prime focus within the catholic–liberal party where previously it had been Gladstone and 'justice for Ireland'. Most of the catholic bishops, the priests, the enfranchised farmers, and unenfranchised popular opinion had pushed and pulled one another into the new alignment. A significant part had been played in the process by the cadres of advanced activists; they, and small contingents of former tories (including Butt himself) and ageing Young Irelanders were the only additional elements acquired over and above what had been there in 1868. There were also losses: the segment of northern presbyterians that inclined towards voting liberal, and a small number of catholic notables having close affiliations with Gladstone, did not adopt home rule.

Except for those who had connections with the government (which usually implied prospects of preferment) candidates seeking popular and clerical support in by-elections from early 1872 onwards had flown the home rule flag. After the defeat of the universities bill in March 1873 and the obvious ending of the alliance with Gladstone, sitting M.P.s returned as Gladstonians in 1868 made preparations to present themselves as home rulers at the next general election. Their accession to the home rule ranks was facilitated by the holding of a home rule conference in Dublin from 18 to 21 November 1873. Here the former Gladstonians were seen to have a say in the shaping of the home rule movement. The Home Government Association was replaced by the Irish Home Rule League; Butt's federalist policy was adopted; the conduct of a home rule party in parliament was debated.[2]

[1] Above, v, 449–50, 464–7, 746–55. [2] Thornley, *Isaac Butt*, pp 159–72.

The home rule conference ultimately yields very little evidence about the state of Irish thought on the constitutional question. But it provides much evidence of the precocious attachment of some Irishmen to advanced modes of political organisation and activity. The kind of countrywide mass mobilisation achieved by O'Connell's campaigns in the 1820s and 1840s had been without precedent anywhere, except perhaps in the United States of America. In subsequent decades the possibility of a revival was constantly on the minds of nationalist ideologues. In particular A. M. Sullivan, proprietor of the *Nation* from 1855, canvassed the idea in and out of season. He was one of those who saw the new beginning of November 1873 as a necessary development for the home rule movement, which should create an organisation that would 'strike its roots deep in the population of every barony and parish'.[1] The Home Government Association had been an association of gentlemen; the Home Rule League was a similar—if expanded— entity at its inception, with a subscription of one pound, but the home rule conference had also agreed that steps should be taken 'to enrol the great mass of the people in the league'.[2] Making provision for this was an obvious task for the rules committee of sixteen, established by the conference and charged with reporting in a matter of weeks.

Notwithstanding its democratic aspect, the repeal association of the 1840s— which Sullivan and others now hoped to reconstitute in the form of the Irish Home Rule League—was controlled internally on the basis of rank and order, with lawyers, priests, shopkeepers, and strong farmers being awarded roles commensurate with their social status. The advanced men of the 1870s were seeking political influence that was not linked with, or dependent on, their social antecedents. Although Butt had little sympathy with the advance of democracy, he was astute in his dealings with them. The November conference had been preceded by contacts and some understanding was achieved. Charles S. Doran and John O'Connor Power, two prominent I.R.B. men, proposed and seconded a resolution calling on future home rule M.P.s to be guided, in any 'emergency' that might arise, by a national conference representative of 'the opinions and feelings of the Irish nation' and recommending that after each parliamentary session M.P.s 'should render to their constituents an account of their steward-ship'.[3] The resolution was adopted unanimously, which is not to say that everyone took it seriously, but does prove the extent to which it was felt necessary to humour quite advanced notions of parliamentary democracy. A significant proportion of the pressure for democratisation came from home rule supporters in Britain, where young activists—the equivalent of the advanced cadres in Ireland—had succeeded in fomenting among the Irish exiles more popular enthusiasm than was evident at home. Vigorous local Irish home rule clubs in the midlands and the north had come together in August 1873 to form the Home Rule Confederation of Great Britain.

[1] Ibid., p. 158.   [2] Ibid., p. 169.   [3] Ibid., p. 165.

The development of the Home Rule League was greatly influenced by the occurrence of a general election—that of February 1874—so shortly after its inauguration. There was no time for testing the credentials of candidates presenting themselves as home rulers, so that those inclined to invoke the cause merely for the sake of convenience and advantage had full scope. Of the 103 Irish seats, 60 went to self-proclaimed supporters of home rule, 33 to the tories, and 10 to liberals. In all, 18 of the 60 home rulers had sat as liberals in the previous parliament, and a further 12 or so were of typical liberal stamp. It can safely be said that a clear majority of the home rule M.P.s would have stood as Gladstonians if that was what the political need of the hour dictated.

The 1874 election, which gave England two working-class M.P.s for the first time, had a notable effect on the social composition of the Irish representation in the house of commons. Only seven of the twenty-four home rule M.P.s who were new to parliament were landowners or sons of landowners.[1] The degentrification of the Irish representation had begun; it had done so under cover of a slogan originally intended to reassure landlords about their place in Irish political life. Some of the principal facilitators of the change had sworn allegiance to an organisation, the I.R.B., which professedly shunned all dealings with parliamentary politics. Rhetoric and ideology, as is so often the case, were very imperfect guides to what was really happening.

The introduction in 1872 of the secret ballot for parliamentary elections must be seen as both symptom and cause of changing assumptions about electoral democracy, assumptions that were reflected in actual behaviour. At the 1868 elections sixty-nine Irish members were returned unopposed; in 1874 only seventeen were so fortunate. Of course, to be unopposed at the polls could be the reward for success in a bitter intra-party contest; or it could be the result of deference to wealth and status. In either case the choice was likely to be highly restrictive in social terms. The ballot certainly contributed to the more widespread consultation of the electors in 1874, but its impact on how they voted is not easy to assess. In so far as they trusted the secrecy of the ballot box, tenants could now defy the wishes of their landlords without fear of reprisal, but deference to aristocracy was in any case undergoing significant diminution in both British and Irish society. Voters were still under pressure, but the balance had swung in favour of the influence wielded by party machines playing on communal loyalties.

In the north, where home rulers, priests, and fenians were least influential, the swing against landlord dominance in 1874 was at least as spectacular as elsewhere, with tenant right activists and presbyterian ministers to the fore. In 1868 two tories were returned unopposed in each of seven of the nine Ulster counties (the exceptions being Cavan and Monaghan), whereas in 1874 liberals challenged the tories in five of these seven. The challengers took both seats in Londonderry and one in Down, and came close to victory in both Antrim and Donegal. The three

[1] Ibid., p. 207.

new county liberal M.P.s were all middle-class. The success of the liberals in Ulster (they also won three borough seats) was made possible by cooperation between presbyterian and catholic voters.[1]

Whatever its long-term socio-political significance, the 1874 election lacked the sense of a great issue being at stake that was so evident in 1852 and 1868. True, most candidates (outside of the north) seeking popular catholic support felt obliged to declare for home rule, but feeling was not stirred by the issue as deeply as it had been by the ecclesiastical titles act or the disestablishment question. M.P.s who had invoked it might well be forgiven for thinking that it need not concern them very much once they had returned to Westminster. Such attitudes were hardly changed very much by the conference of home rule M.P.s held in Dublin on 3 March 1874. It was agreed that in the house of commons they ought to form 'a separate and distinct party',[2] but this meant different things to different people. The same ambiguities had bedevilled the attempt to create an independent Irish party following the 1852 election.[3] That party held the balance of power in the commons and so its weakness was quickly exposed and exploited. In 1874 the tories under Disraeli had a secure majority, so that there was no parliamentary pressure on those home rulers with liberal leanings to break ranks and help form a government, as had happened with the independent oppositionists in 1852–3. On the other hand the parliamentary statistics meant that the home rulers could put no voting pressure on the government, and so faced years of frustration. Unlike the independent party of the 1850s, the home rulers possessed in Butt an obvious leader. However, he had limited notions of what was possible or even desirable in the way of maintaining an independent party. At the conference in November 1873 he had resolutely and successfully resisted a proposal that home rule M.P.s vote *en bloc* by majority decision on all matters concerning Ireland. Butt made it clear that he saw subordination of the individual member to any collective control as an attack on the true nature of parliamentary representation. He would demand nothing of those elected as home rulers except that they support home rule.[4] Even that proved too much for some of them.

Butt opened his parliamentary campaign for home rule by proposing on 20 March 1874 an amendment to the queen's speech in which he requested an examination of Irish political dissatisfaction. It was no surprise that the amendment was defeated; but what was surprising was the failure of up to a dozen of the home rule M.P.s to appear for the vote. Some months later Butt obtained parliamentary time for a debate on home rule and brought forward a motion calling for a committee of the whole house to examine parliamentary relations between 'England and Ireland'.[5] In the debate, running from 30 June to 2 July 1874, Butt was impressive while his supporting cast was disappointing and

---

[1] B. M. Walker, *Ulster politics: the formative years, 1868–86* (Belfast, 1989), pp 91–116.
[2] Thornley, *Isaac Butt*, p. 123.   [3] Above, v, 402–6.
[4] Thornley, *Isaac Butt*, pp 165–8.   [5] Ibid., pp 230–34, 279–84.

disorganised. Six home rule M.P.s failed to vote for the motion: four of them had paired and two were absent without explanation. There was a similar display of indiscipline, and again a handful of absentees from the voting lobby, when two years later Butt proposed a motion for the appointment of a select committee to inquire into the demand for the restoration of an Irish parliament.

WHATEVER inconsistencies, incongruities, and failures it exhibited, the home rule movement of 1874 was a considerable achievement for Butt, and keeping the land question in the background was perhaps the most impressive part of this achievement. But he could not maintain his stream of reassuring sounds for the landlords if his followers were shouting for tenants' rights. Even more critically, the land was a touchy subject with the fenians and their fellow travellers. Many of the advanced activists had had their initiation into politics in 1869 as amnesty campaigners who viewed the contemporaneous tenant right campaign as a serious rival and resented it accordingly. Just like the chartists and other English radicals most of them resented the existing system of landed proprietorship and they assumed that it would be changed in any new order they might succeed in bringing about. The farmers also wanted major change in agrarian arrangements, but only on the basis of the extension of the rights and advantages of existing landholders. 'Tenant right', which since the early 1850s had signified the interests and objectives of the farmers, had few attractions for landless radicals, a point of which farmers were keenly conscious.[1]

To avoid giving offence to landlords and activists Butt as home rule leader had to sing dumb about tenant right. At the same time he was relying on tenant farmers for most of his votes. The facts of Irish economic life, together with the Representation of the People (Ireland) Act of 1850, gave farmers a preponderant share of the votes in most county constituencies.[2] From the mid-1860s Butt had been identified with tenant right and he had worked in 1869 and 1870 to establish himself in the confidence of the tenants. In the spring of 1870 he had adopted the strategy of advising the farmers to cease agitation for tenant right and to place their trust instead in home rule, declaring that only an Irish parliament would meet their demands. When farmers voted for home rule at the general election of 1874 (as at the by-elections of the preceding few years) they believed that they were also voting for tenant right, whether the subject was explicitly mentioned or not. In the northern counties, tenant right agitation was the principal driving force behind the liberal candidates.

To point out one of the ambiguities on which Butt had built his movement is not to condemn him as a mere manipulator. Just as his original home rule plans

---

[1] See R. V. Comerford, *The fenians in context: Irish politics and society, 1848–82* (Dublin, 1985) pp 115–16.

[2] Hoppen, *Elections, politics, and society*, pp 17–29.

were an honest and creative attempt to find a balance between the advantages of the union and those of self-government, so he was concerned to find an answer to the conflict of interests between landlords and tenants within Ireland. He was genuinely anxious to ameliorate what he could see as a source of economic debilitation and a potential cause of social disruption. His capacity for seeing both sides of a question and endeavouring to reconcile them marks out Butt as one of the most remarkable Irish public men of the century. In the case of the land the framework of his proposal for a solution—set out in his pamphlet *Land tenure in Ireland: a plea for the Celtic race* (Dublin, 1866)—was that tenants be given the security of sixty-year leases, the interests of the landlords to be protected by regular independent review of rents.

Butt did not encourage tenant agitation in the 1870s but he never completely lost contact with what agitation there was. By the middle of the decade a few dozen farmers' clubs and tenants' associations existed in some shape or other, dispersed irregularly around the country.[1] While the 1870 land act had given a measure of very welcome security to many tenants—to the annoyance of landlords—it created new grievances, among other reasons because its benefits did not extend to long-term leaseholders, and the cumulative effect was an exacerbation of landlord–tenant tensions. The prosecution of their cause in parliament gave the farmers little satisfaction. In May 1874 Butt introduced a land bill designed to remedy some of the weaknesses of the 1870 act in the area of compensation for eviction, but it came to nothing. By the end of 1874 plans were being laid for a conference that eventually convened in Dublin on 20 February 1875. Although Butt and fifteen other home rule M.P.s were present, the farmers themselves kept a firm grip on the proceedings. When they omitted Butt from a committee set up to draft a new land bill they were expressing dissatisfaction with the home rule leader's attitudes. The proposals for legislation produced by the committee went further than Butt was prepared to follow—especially in not allowing for periodic revision of rents—with the result that the 1875 session of parliament passed without the expected bill being introduced. Butt introduced a land bill of his own devising in March 1876. As well as again proposing the closing of loopholes in the 1870 act it provided for a mechanism that would give yearly tenants secure leases, but with safeguards for the landlords' interests. The bill was defeated at the second reading on 29 June 1876.[2] When the representatives of organised farmers met in conference in Dublin in October 1876 they were in dissatisfied mood. Their frustration owed much to the small extent of their organisation. Tenant farmers constituted the most extensive and powerful constituency in the country, but their political energy was dormant. Any threat to their interests would evoke a powerful reaction. But with prices and seasons good until 1876, the great majority of them did not feel moved to agitation.

[1] See Samuel Clark, *Social origins of the Irish land war* (Princeton, N.J., 1979), pp 219–20; Hoppen, *Elections, politics, and society*, pp 468–9; Walker, *Ulster politics*, p. 91.
[2] Thornley, *Isaac Butt*, pp 259–60, 261.

THE home rule movement, too, suffered from the lack of any widespread enthusiasm even among those who were very willing to vote for its parliamentary candidates. The decision of the conference of November 1873 to open up membership of the Home Rule League to the populace had little effect: there was little demand, but that does not explain fully why the attempt was not made. Butt had no liking for popular mobilisation. His suggested way of involving the masses—as adopted in January 1874—was to open a 'national roll' of all home rule sympathisers with an enrolment charge of one shilling. This allowed the league to remain as a monolithic élite body, as distinct from the articulated popular movement with local branches, reading rooms, and intensive socialisation that A. M. Sullivan and others had in mind. In the event, interest in the national roll proved to be slight.[1] One consequence was a failure to raise any substantial financial wind. Unlike the repeal campaign of the 1840s, the home rule movement of the 1870s did not benefit from any worthwhile popular subscriptions, nor indeed from any substantial wave of middle-class donations. Butt might have been a more effective party leader if, like O'Connell, he could have abandoned his work at the bar to devote himself to politics. In the absence of party funds that might have permitted this, an effort was made—on Butt's initiative—to raise a sum of money specifically for the support of the leader. A few thousand pounds were collected. However, much of whatever special support Butt received seems to have come by way of loans from a handful of men of substance. Unfortunately, Butt had apparently insoluble financial problems and any money he received went into a bottomless pit, leaving him still obliged to work for more at the bar.

Butt's party never succeeded in having an impressive series of public demonstrations. The most serious attempt took place in the autumn of 1874 and included gatherings intended to promote the cause in Ulster, as well as a number of constituency meetings that were presumably held in the spirit of the conference resolution of November 1873 concerning answerability to the electorate.[2] The seconder of that resolution had been John O'Connor Power, one of the most active and vocal of the fenian activists, and representative of an important Connacht–Lancashire subgroup within the movement. A native of Ballinasloe, he was coming in November 1873 to the end of a few years of study at St Jarlath's College, Tuam, where he had betaken himself after a youth spent as house painter and I.R.B. organiser in Lancashire.[3] At the 1874 general election O'Connor Power had presented himself as a potential candidate in County Mayo with the support of a team of fenian organisers, but he withdrew when confronted by two candidates of more traditional stamp who like himself were declaring for home rule, but unlike him had the support of the priests. As it happened, the Mayo election was subsequently invalidated on a technicality, and in the resulting rerun O'Connor Power and his supporters pressed home their challenge. Men came

---

[1] Ibid., pp 241–2.   [2] Ibid., pp 243–5.
[3] T. W. Moody, *Davitt and Irish revolution, 1847–82* (Oxford, 1981), pp 45–8.

from all over Connacht and money was drawn from the north of England to sustain the ensuing contest with clerical and landlord power. The outcome was close run, with O'Connor Power coming second, and so taking the second seat and becoming the first man of no property to represent Mayo in parliament.

A similar personage was Frank Hugh O'Donnell, a 26-year-old journalist endowed with great talent but few material resources, who was returned for Galway city in an 1874 by-election, again with the support of a clique of young activists. However, he was subsequently unseated on petition and did not establish himself as an M.P. until returned for Dungarvan in a by-election in January 1877. The link between the fraternity of the activists and the advent to politics as home rulers of previously unlikely social types is well illustrated in the case of Joseph Biggar, an unpolished Belfast provision merchant of presbyterian background who was elected for Cavan county at the 1874 general election. He subsequently took the I.R.B. oath and became a member of the supreme council. For good measure he converted to catholicism in 1875.

The fenian cadres were a great source of support for home rule but they could also cause embarrassment, as was illustrated when John Mitchel, the veteran Young Irelander, stood for parliament in 1874 and 1875. Mitchel's outspoken advocacy of extreme nationalist attitudes and policies had resulted in his transportation to Van Diemen's Land as a convicted felon in 1848. He had escaped to America in 1853, and through his writings and his political postures he had maintained his position as the prime personification of extreme nationalism. At the time of the 1874 general election advanced nationalists in Cork and Tipperary hit upon the idea of nominating Mitchel as a candidate, and by telegraph he signalled his consent. Those proposing his candidature disagreed with the majority of their fellow fenian activists, who were supporting home rulers. Mitchel was identified with outspoken rejection of Westminster and of parliamentary politics. It was axiomatic that if elected to the commons he would not take his seat. His candidature was calculated to injure the home rule party by embarrassing those advanced nationalists participating in its election campaign. The embarrassment was not great in 1874 as the Mitchelite campaigns began too late to make a serious impact. However, Mitchel was so encouraged as to visit Ireland later in the year and before he returned to America arrangements were made for him to contest any suitable by-election that might arise. The opportunity came with a vacancy in County Tipperary early in 1875. At once a vigorous campaign was put in motion and Mitchel himself set out from New York. Before he reached Queenstown he had been returned unopposed on 16 February. However inconvenient they may have found it, all claimants to nationalist credentials had felt obliged to declare for Mitchel, the living legend, including home rule M.P.s such as John Martin (his brother-in-law) and O'Connor Power, who also felt obliged to disown Mitchel's policies. With the activists' election machine united and all set for a contest, the home rule leadership and the Tipperary priests accepted the humiliation involved in giving Mitchel a walk-over

rather than risk the greater humiliation—and the bitterness—that might follow
from challenging him in the name of the home rule on which he was accustomed
to pour so much scorn.[1]

Mitchel was soon declared ineligible for parliament as an undischarged felon.
Even some of his keenest supporters advocated leaving the matter to rest there,
but Mitchel announced that he would stand as often as he was rejected by
parliament. It was now more difficult than ever for any home ruler or priest to
think of opposing him. No such inhibitions affected tory supporters, and a tory
candidate—the first the county had seen since 1852—was nominated to challenge
him. About 60 per cent of the electorate stayed away on polling day, 11 March
1875; of those who did vote, a very comfortable majority voted for Mitchel. The
runner-up was eventually given the seat by the house of commons, but in the
meantime Mitchel had died on 20 March, thereby ending a life devoted to making
trouble for England, but which in its final weeks had created most embarrassing
trouble for home rule.

A cold caught at Mitchel's funeral has been blamed for the death a few weeks
later, on 29 March 1875, of John Martin. The resulting vacancy in Meath was
filled by a young County Wicklow landowner of protestant stock, Charles Stewart
Parnell. For forty years and more, counties such as Meath where the landlords
had lost collective control of politics had been sending to parliament, generally as
liberals or whigs, landed gentlemen—usually protestants—who were prepared to
identify with popular catholic interests or causes. This customarily involved
achieving a tacit or open understanding with the priests, and a willingness to meet
the expenses of the election from private resources. The 1874 general election had
seen the beginnings of the democratisation of the representation, but social
standing and the ability to pay expenses still mattered, even if they had to be
accompanied by new measures of political flexibility. If anything distinguished the
newly elected member for Meath from the many others of his type it was probably
the hard-necked determination that he had shown in his pursuit of a seat. Little
time needs to be spent asking what views he had on public affairs. From the
opening of his parliamentary quest early in 1874 Parnell had made the mandatory
obeisances to home rule, denominational education, and tenant right. But he went
beyond these intimations of availability to seek out the wielders of popular
electoral influence with a brazen directness that could be the product of either
naïveté or genius. He had his local parish priest write to fellow priests in
relevant counties setting out his qualities; he attended the tenant right conference
of February 1875 and made himself known to the farmer activists; in a number
of ways he introduced himself to the nationalists, not least by making a
contribution to the fund covering the expenses of Mitchel's election and then
advertising the fact in a letter to the *Freeman's Journal* (in which he also carefully
recorded his disapproval of Mitchel's policies). Prevented by a technicality from

---

[1] R. V. Comerford, *Charles J. Kickham: a study in Irish nationalism and literature* (Dublin, 1979),
pp 126–7.

contesting his native county in February 1874, he challenged a tory unsuccessfully in a County Dublin by-election in March 1874, and staked his claim in Tipperary in March 1875 (when Mitchel's death opened up the possibility of another by-election there) before his successful intervention in Meath.[1]

O'Connor Power, Biggar, O'Donnell, and Parnell came in the period 1874–7 to make up an aggressive advanced group within the home rule representation in parliament that stood in obvious juxtaposition to the moderate and politically cautious Butt. In Ireland they received some encouragement from nationalist newspapers, but there was no formal rank-and-file mobilisation in support of them. It was otherwise across the Irish Sea, where among the exiles the Home Rule Confederation of Great Britain was a vibrant popular organisation that increasingly looked to the activist M.P.s. Parnell, Biggar, and O'Donnell were elected to honorary offices in the confederation at a convention it held in Dublin in August 1876. Although Butt was appointed president at the same time it was very obvious that he was out of sympathy with recent trends within the organisation, and especially with the desire to extend its grass-roots system to Ireland, which had been the original purpose behind the holding of the convention in Dublin.[2]

The participation of its activists in electoral and parliamentary politics had profound implications for the I.R.B. The decade had opened with the brother-hood probably more numerous and better armed than in the mid-1860s, when it had promised to be a power in the land. But 1867 had shown that the promise was illusory, and the influx of new members in 1868–70 did nothing to change that. The years 1870–71 witnessed not only the enthusiastic involvement of the I.R.B. cadres in public affairs but a slump in the numbers of the rank-and-file fenians. Subsequently the I.R.B. was an affair of many chiefs with relatively few followers. The former were seriously divided among themselves in their assump-tions about what membership of the brotherhood implied. Most acted as if they saw themselves in a fellowship of activists with a broadly anti-establishment and nationalist outlook. But in the early 1870s, just at the time that the vibrant English republicanism of the 1860s was petering out to nothing, the republican doctrine of the I.R.B. was being tacitly abandoned by many of its supposed adherents. The fenian fellowship also began to display something of a masonic-style mutual self-help character. This it always possessed to some degree, as was illustrated by supreme council advice to its followers in January 1870 that 'common sense would also point out to us the advisability of giving the preference to our friends in all our dealings'.[3] The impression was added to in the early 1870s with the emergence to prominence in nationalist ranks of a handful of businessmen. Joseph

---

[1] See R. F. Foster, *Charles Stewart Parnell: the man and his family* (Hassocks (Sussex), 1976), pp 131–46.

[2] Thornley, *Isaac Butt*, pp 291–6.

[3] 'Address of the I.R.B. supreme council to the people of Ireland, January 1870', quoted in T. W. Moody and Leon Ó Broin (ed.), 'The I. R. B. supreme council, 1868–78' in *I.H.S.*, xix, no. 75 (Mar. 1975), p. 310.

Ronayne is a case in point: an engineer by trade, he had made a fortune in California before returning to Ireland to become proprietor of the Cork–Macroom railway line. A less wealthy example was Matt Harris, who along with his other interests was a building contractor in Ballinasloe. Patrick Egan was manager of a milling company with headquarters in Dublin and branches in the north midlands and Connacht. Employees of Egan played a notable part in O'Connor Power's successful election campaign in Mayo in 1874.

The supreme council made an attempt in 1873 to come to terms with changing circumstances, and one of the consequences was a new constitution for the I.R.B. This, in one of its sections, effectively subordinated the brotherhood to the politics of the ballot box by a stipulation that 'war against England' should await 'the decision of the Irish nation as expressed by a majority of the Irish people' and by decreeing that in the meantime the I.R.B. should 'lend its support to every movement calculated to advance the cause of Irish independence consistently with the preservation of its own integrity'.[1] Other sections of the document, by contrast, reasserted the objective of an Irish republic to be achieved by force of arms. The indications are that only a minority took these reiterations of old orthodoxy fully seriously. The policy difference between activist participants in public politics and intransigent opponents of this trend gave rise to controversy and was in its turn—and more importantly—used as a proxy in struggles based on factional and personality conflicts.[2]

In advance of the home rule convention of November 1873 the potentially disruptive opposition of the intransigents had been neutralised through negotiations, which were largely an internal I.R.B. affair.[3] Butt made, or allowed to be made on his behalf, a promise to the effect that if a further three years of political effort failed to achieve home rule, he would admit defeat and place the cause, in some unspecified way, in the hands of the intransigents. Within twelve months two individuals—Biggar and O'Connor Power—were simultaneously members of the supreme council and members of parliament. They had thus sworn fealty both to the Irish republic and to Queen Victoria, an ambivalence that was deplored by intransigents such as Kickham, who had become president of the supreme council by 1874.

Intransigents and activists might have continued indefinitely in mutual toleration but for intervention from across the Atlantic. In June 1875 the supreme council ratified a 'compact of agreement' with Clan na Gael (or the United Brotherhood), which by this time had become the most efficient of the Irish-American organisations dedicated to the promotion of revolution in Ireland. This distinction it had achieved under the direction of Dr William Carroll, a Donegal-born presbyterian, and John Devoy, one of the fenians released into American exile in January 1871. The compact provided for a Clan na Gael

---

[1] 'Amended constitution of the I.R.B. and of the supreme council, 17 March 1873', quoted ibid., p. 314; see also Mitchell & Ó Snodaigh, *Ir. pol. docs 1869–1916*, p. 22.
[2] Comerford, *Fenians in context*, pp 203–5.
[3] Above, pp 11–12.

subvention for the supreme council, but at the price of giving Devoy *de facto* influence over the council's affairs. Soon he was prodding the intransigents into a decisive move against the activists. His most likely motive was the establishment of discipline within the supreme council and its following, so that it would be a more effective instrument of his own designs. Inextricably linked with this consideration were personal animosities, some that already existed within the supreme council and others that affected Devoy himself.

Following pressure from Devoy and a complicated round of manœuvrings, the supreme council decided on 10 August 1876, by a majority of one, that all cooperation of I.R.B. members with the home rule movement should cease within six months. Devoy ensured that the resolve of the majority did not flag and on 5 March 1877 four activists were called on to resign from the supreme council. Patrick Egan and John Barry did so; the two others, Biggar and O'Connor Power, were subsequently expelled. One consequence was to show that the link between the I.R.B. and the activist politics of the 1870s was largely incidental: it had provided the activists with a congenial ambience, but they did not have any absolute need for the I.R.B. Their fellowship was wider than the I.R.B. and in the last analysis independent of it. The coup within the supreme council did have the effect of rendering that body apparently more amenable to Devoy's influence, at least for a time. In the summer of 1877 the supreme council adopted a plan for a joint 'revolutionary directory' of the I.R.B. and Clan na Gael, advocated by Devoy and Carroll and certain, if implemented, to give the Irish-Americans a means of controlling the I.R.B.

The standing of Devoy and Clan na Gael had been enhanced in 1876 by the brilliantly conceived and executed rescue of six fenian convicts, spirited out of captivity in Western Australia on board the *Catalpa*. The effectiveness of Clan na Gael in America was amply demonstrated in the story of the 'skirmishing fund' launched in September 1875 by Jeremiah O'Donovan Rossa and Patrick Ford, editor of the New York *Irish World*. Their declared purpose was to finance the use of the recently perfected weapon of dynamite against British cities as an alternative to the hitherto unsuccessful 'conventional' strategies of Irish revolutionists. The considerable financial success of their appeal posed a challenge to the position of Clan na Gael. The Clan's answer was to take over the 'skirmishing fund'; following some adroit application of pressure, Devoy, Carroll, and a number of other Clan members had become trustees of the fund by March 1877. O'Donovan Rossa remained on as secretary but eventually he was ousted from that office and his fund was renamed the National Fund.

Since the early 1870s Clan na Gael had similarly outmanœuvred and outshone the Fenian Brotherhood, its principal rival for Irish revolutionary support in America. The conclusion of the compact of agreement between Clan na Gael and the supreme council in 1876 was a severe shock to the Fenian Brotherhood.[1] In

---

[1] For earlier divisions in American fenianism, see above, v, 436–8, 444–6.

a desperate attempt to restore the balance now so seriously tipped against it, the brotherhood made overtures to James Stephens, who from his chosen place of exile in Paris claimed to be still the rightful fenian chief. He had retained a faithful, if attenuated, following in Ireland of men who claimed that they, and not the adherents of the supreme council, were the rightful Irish Republican Brotherhood. The Fenian Brotherhood now effectively began to recognise Stephens's claims, a development that gave a temporary fillip to his organisation and may have helped it to draw away several hundred supporters from the supreme council by early 1877. But the Fenian Brotherhood itself remained in the doldrums. Its fortunes were symbolised by the death in poverty on 6 February 1877 of John O'Mahony, who had been its head centre until a few weeks previously.

IT is difficult to assess the degree of seriousness with which anyone regarded the call for home rule in 1874, more particularly after the general election had placed Disraeli and the tories in power with a comfortable majority. What cannot be doubted, however, is that there was popular expectation that the home rulers would work in parliament to secure benefits and ameliorations for 'Ireland'. In popular perception home rule and Gladstone's 'justice for Ireland' may both have meant the same thing, namely, the government of Ireland in accordance with the wishes of the catholic majority. Success in winning benefits and concessions would have maintained the morale of the party, and the lack of success was not caused by want of effort, at least on Butt's part. His attempts in the area of tenant right have already been mentioned. In addition, between 1874 and 1877 Butt and colleagues, acting in accordance with party plans, introduced Irish bills on a wide range of issues going from grand jury reform to fisheries and from university education to borough franchise. The only measure that they succeeded in having carried was the Municipal Privileges (Ireland) Act, 1876.[1] This was short on substance, but it ministered to urban civic pride, an otherwise poorly promoted commodity in modern Ireland. One of its provisions allowed the various city councils to institute rolls of freemen. In both Dublin and Cork the name of Isaac Butt stands where it was placed in 1876 at the head of a select list of freemen.

Some of the unsuccessful bills and parliamentary motions of the home rulers were voted down after debate in the commons. Many others were lost without even the satisfaction of full debate, simply through running out of time. This fate became increasingly common for Irish bills from 1875, following the reintroduction—with that explicit intention—of a procedural rule terminating debate after 12.30 a.m. on any non-money bill that was not passing unchallenged. As the parliamentary schedule forced most private members' business into the late night and the small hours of the morning, the home rulers' bills could now effectively be killed by the proposing of amendments.

---

[1] 39 & 40 Vict., c. 76 (15 Aug. 1876).

In addition to promoting their own private members' bills the home rule M.P.s—or many of them—felt obliged to take a stand on the government's Irish legislation, and particularly on coercive measures. In July 1874, as the end of the session approached, parliament was asked to take the expiring laws continuance act covering *inter alia* Ireland's exceptional, and rarely used, coercive legislation. Butt fought the second reading and formally opposed the motion to go into committee. Biggar and others carried opposition even further before giving way to the irresistible force of numbers.[1] In 1875 the familiar package of Irish coercive legislation was reformulated in a new measure with a five-year life, the Peace Preservation (Ireland) Act.[2] Butt and his party opposed it vigorously, taking up more than a week of house of commons time on the committee stage.

Not all of the Disraeli government's Irish legislation was coercive, although in the three sessions from 1874 to 1876 major items were scarce. Two measures enacted in 1877 drastically reorganised control of the prison system and the structures of the superior courts.[3] The Dublin Science and Art Museum Act,[4] passed on the same day, was a major step in the long-drawn-out development of the national library and a national museum.

Inability to make a mark with legislation for Ireland seriously demoralised the home rule party. Butt's instinct was to accept such disappointments and adhere to conventions of parliamentary debate and procedure on the firmly held assumption that there was no alternative to reasoned argument and no other acceptable means of achieving political ends. The great majority of home rule M.P.s were at one with Butt on this. Like their liberal and tory fellow M.P.s, the generality of home rulers in parliament felt themselves bound by gentlemanly mid-Victorian norms of procedure and behaviour and their notions of party discipline scarcely extended beyond that. But what was there to constrain members who were not susceptible to the pressures of gentlemanly convention? The activist supporters of home rule, including the handful of them in parliament, were—almost by definition—in rebellion against the prevailing norms of deference. So, a member like Biggar could refuse either to abide by the conventions of parliament or to be constrained by party discipline that was analogous to that of a gentleman's club.

As early as July 1874 Butt had felt obliged to rebuke Biggar in the commons for carrying opposition to the expiring laws continuance bill beyond that invisible point at which a true parliamentarian and gentleman would have known instinctively to stop.[5] Biggar was to transgress repeatedly in the years ahead, and he was joined or emulated in this by O'Connor Power and a small minority of the party. By 1876 this policy of opposition exceeding the accepted norm, generally referred

---

[1] Thornley, *Isaac Butt*, pp 235–6.

[2] 38 Vict., c. 4 (28 May 1875).

[3] General Prisons (Ireland) Act, 40 & 41 Vict., c. 49 (14 Aug. 1877); Supreme Court of Judicature (Ireland) Act, 40 & 41 Vict., c. 57 (14 Aug. 1877).

[4] 40 & 41 Vict., c. ccxxxiv (14 Aug. 1877); above, v, 395.

[5] Thornley, *Isaac Butt*, p. 236.

to as 'obstruction', had caught the imagination of the activists, being presented to them as a novel and effective form of retaliation against a government unresponsive to Irish demands. By this time Parnell had become one of the principal advocates and practitioners of obstruction. The disdain for convention, and the capacity to recognise and tap the well-springs of power, that had marked his search for a parliamentary seat, enabled him once in parliament to adopt obstruction and turn his back on the values and perceived interests of his class. In the parliamentary session of 1877 Parnell made himself the most notorious of the obstructionists and the clear leader of the group by pursuing the policy with a degree of thoroughness and brazenness that not even Biggar had previously attained. In February Parnell and Biggar put down notices of opposition to all the major English and Scottish bills tabled for the session, thus turning the 12.30 a.m. rule back against the government. Subsequently, with the particular assistance of O'Connor Power and Frank Hugh O'Donnell, they talked out various bills and delayed the progress of others by means of motions for adjournment and amendment. The climax came with the committee stage of the South Africa bill in July. It eventually passed, after a sitting lasting almost twenty-one hours, when the small band of obstructives were no longer physically capable of delaying progress by means of the amendments, interminable speeches, and repeated divisions with which they filled the time from 5.15 p.m. on 31 July to 2.10 p.m. on 1 August.

The 1877 campaign split the home rule party in parliament irrevocably: by April Butt and Parnell were exchanging rebukes in the press.[1] There was no question of Parnell ousting Butt from the leadership, because the great majority, even if disillusioned with Butt, could not bring themselves to embrace obstruction. The triumph of Parnell's methods would be tantamount to the end of the political world as they knew it. However, Parnell had brought obstruction into favour with a significant section of public opinion and of the press in Ireland, and he had established himself as the leader of the activists, in and out of parliament. When the Home Rule Confederation of Great Britain met in annual convention on 27 and 28 August 1877, it dropped Butt from the presidency and appointed Parnell in his place.[2]

[1] Ibid., pp 300–27.
[2] F. S. L. Lyons, *Charles Stewart Parnell* (London, 1977), p. 67.

CHAPTER II

The land war and the politics of distress, 1877–82

R. V. COMERFORD

GLADSTONE disembarked at Kingstown on 17 October 1877 for an Irish visit that lasted nearly four weeks. At 67 he was busily reestablishing himself as the leader of the liberal party and he saw in Ireland sufficient potential to bring him to the country for the first time in his life. Ireland had contributed handsomely to his 1868 general election triumph and he now looked for a renewal of that year's alliance between whigs, liberals, and Irish voters. The recent attachment of many of the latter to the home rule slogan was a nuisance in Gladstone's eyes, but by no means an insurmountable problem. Local government reform of some kind he saw as the answer. Most home rule M.P.s were only too obviously ready to be taken off the hook and given the opportunity to reenter the liberal fold. And the vast majority of their supporters seemed to have no very serious and definite objectives and could be expected to rally for another round of Gladstone's concessions. The power struggle within the home rule parliamentary group might be an inconvenience but Gladstone could assume that once it was resolved the leadership would respond sensibly to his overtures.

In order to re-form his old Irish constituency Gladstone needed in the first instance to mend his relations with the catholic church. Erstwhile catholic admirers had been shocked in 1874 by the vehemence with which he (just then out of office) had attacked the claim of papal infallibility asserted by the first Vatican council in 1870.[1] The gratitude towards the author of disestablishment that had been diluted already between 1870 and 1873 was replaced with suspicion and resentment in the minds of many bishops and priests. A visit to Maynooth College and interviews with a number of priests elsewhere passed off amicably enough. But when Gladstone called on Cullen, the cardinal did not conceal his resentment: 'You know, Mr Gladstone, we could have given you a warmer reception if it had not been for certain pamphlets which we in Ireland did not like very well.'[2]

[1] W. E. Gladstone, *The Vatican decrees in their bearing on civil allegiance* (London, 1874).
[2] H. C. G. Matthew (ed.), *The Gladstone diaries* (9 vols, Oxford, 1968–86), ix, 258–67, covers the Irish visit.

Alert tories were determined to thwart Gladstone's Irish prospects. The lord lieutenant, the duke of Marlborough, entertained Gladstone to lunch on 20 October 1877 and kept a jealous watch on the visitor's other activities in Ireland. Since their arrival in January 1877 the duke, the duchess, and their son Lord Randolph Churchill, M.P. for Woodstock, had been engaged in a lively courtship of public opinion up and down the country. The Irish press was flattered, especially by the duchess. Irish manufactures and Irish tourism were patronised. Popular sentiment was indulged on the public order and agrarian questions. Speaking in his English constituency in September 1877 Lord Randolph had gone so far as to decry England's years of 'tyranny', 'crime', 'oppression', and 'general misgovernment' in Ireland.[1]

Education was the key question, not because it was a highly popular political issue in itself, but because it meant so much to the catholic clergy. Gladstone had disappointed them on this in 1873, but that did not preclude the possibility that he might make a new offer that, as happened in 1868, would swing the clerical machine into action on his behalf at the next election. This the tories very effectively preempted. Marlborough and Churchill demonstrated a warm readiness to make concessions to catholic demands both at the university level—where Gladstone had failed in 1873—and at the secondary level—where Gladstone had not even made an attempt.[2] Butt gave his encouragement. He favoured concessions to denominational education, and his home rule movement stood to benefit from anything that hindered a liberal resurgence in Ireland. Perhaps even more important to him was the hope that by being associated with a government concession he would have something to present as evidence of the effectiveness of conventional as opposed to obstructionist tactics. The Intermediate Education (Ireland) Act, 1878, and the University Education (Ireland) Act, 1879,[3] fell far short of catholic clerical hopes and of the lord lieutenant's ambitions, but through them the tories made provision for state support for denominational education, if only on a limited basis and by the back door. As far as the subsequent general election was concerned Gladstone's clothes had been stolen.

Fenian amnesty was yet another political plank dislodged from Gladstone's platform. Though it created very little public excitement in the middle years of the decade the fate of those still in prison for fenian activities had strong emotive potential and was regularly aired by home rule M.P.s with fenian connections. Before coming to Ireland Gladstone had publicly declared himself in favour of release. Michael Davitt, sentenced in 1870 to fifteen years' penal servitude for arms trafficking on behalf of the I.R.B. in the north of England, was set free from Dartmoor on a ticket of leave on 19 December 1877. Early in January 1878 three of the 'military fenians'—members of her majesty's forces in Ireland convicted by

[1] R. F. Foster, *Lord Randolph Churchill: a political life* (Oxford, 1981), p. 43.
[2] Below, pp 524–5, 557–60, 579.
[3] 41 & 42 Vict., c. 66 (16 Aug. 1878), and 42 & 43 Vict., c. 65 (15 Aug. 1879); see below, pp 524, 561.

court martial in 1866–7—were released again on ticket of leave. When one of these—Colour-sergeant C. H. McCarthy—a few days later collapsed and died at a Dublin reception in his honour, the amnesty question was thereby given a new impetus. The remaining prisoners were released in ones and twos over the next thirteen months.

GLADSTONE's impressions of Ireland as he found it in the late autumn of 1877 were highly positive. He discerned prosperity and improvement on all sides. Chance had timed his long-postponed visit for the Indian summer of post-famine prosperity. The great houses at which he stayed—Carton, Kilruddery, Coolattin, Powerscourt, and Abbeyleix—would soon have their ease disturbed and their prosperity threatened by agricultural recession and agrarian and political unrest. Following a cold and wet summer the 1877 harvest was disappointing, but the Irish agricultural economy was sufficiently resilient to absorb the effects of one poor year. Nobody could know that this was but the first of several, and that as the decade came to a close serious reduction in yields would be aggravated by plunging prices for crops and cattle. The outcome was not only agrarian unrest but a political movement that was to overturn Gladstone's and everyone else's assumptions about Irish politics. The activists prominent as obstructionists inside parliament and their allies outside took advantage of the agrarian crisis to create a popular political movement that brought them from the periphery to the centre of Irish affairs. This development not only secured dominance for the activist group but involved an internal power struggle in which the main prize went to Parnell; Michael Davitt was the clear runner-up.

A native of Mayo who had grown up in a working-class Lancashire environment, Davitt was the quintessential fenian activist at the time of his arrest in 1870—a young man whose talent, energy, and hard-won education stood little chance of recognition, owing to his origins and his want of wealth and connections. While in prison he became the object of attention for a number of reasons: he had personal links with the activist élite inside and outside parliament, being especially well acquainted with John O'Connor Power, M.P.; he had succeeded in smuggling out accounts of his prison life that provided substance for charges of ill-treatment;[1] and he attracted sympathy because of his ardent personality and because of the cruel industrial accident that had left him without his right arm from the age of 11. On his release he quickly rejoined the north of England fenian fellowship. A decade earlier that had involved running guns; when Davitt returned to the scene the dominant preoccupation was promotion of the Home Rule Confederation of Great Britain and of a vibrant public social movement, which indeed had always been an aspect of fenianism in England. Davitt still accepted the fenian premise that armed Irishmen should be available to strike for

---

[1] The less exacting regime informally introduced from late 1868 onwards for the main body of fenians in English prisons was not extended to convicted members of the British army or to those, including Davitt, convicted for fenian activities in England.

Irish independence, but he was not amenable to the purist approach to the question that had been raised to the level of dogma within the supreme council of the I.R.B. by its president, Kickham. Although he quickly became north of England representative on the supreme council, Davitt argued publicly for cooperation with parliamentarians. Like so many of his associates inside and outside parliament he was primarily interested in having an enterprise to conduct. He was sufficiently astute, pragmatic, and ambitious to discard physical force when he came to see its irrelevance to the kind of enterprise he could actually sustain.

The supreme council that Davitt joined in 1878 was largely a dependency of Clan na Gael and John Devoy. William Carroll of Philadelphia, Devoy's chief collaborator in the Clan at this time, subjected the I.R.B. to a thorough visitation in the first half of 1878. He saw to changes in the supreme council and the revitalisation of the rank-and-file organisation.[1] The latter was now concentrated in north Connacht and south Ulster. The weakness of the I.R.B. in its strongholds of a decade earlier—Leinster and Munster—could be partially explained by the existence there of a small rival organisation owing allegiance to Stephens, now living in poverty in Paris but still claiming to be the only rightful fenian chief. But the attractions of fenian conspiracy of any kind had largely faded for the young townsmen of the south and the east, whereas in Mayo, Sligo, Leitrim, Roscommon, Cavan, and Monaghan, the I.R.B. retained much of its appeal for numbers of hard-pressed smallholders. These were attracted to the brotherhood because it promised them the opportunity to mobilise in support of their perceived economic interests. The poor harvest of 1877, and especially the partial failure of the potato crop, was a serious blow to those on marginal holdings and certainly helped Carroll's work of revitalisation in Connacht and south Ulster in 1878. He was also helped by the rumours of Anglo-Russian war, rife since 1876, which enabled him to re-create the illusion of imminent action such as had served the I.R.B. so well on earlier occasions.[2] But undoubtedly Carroll's principal asset was a plentiful supply of Clan na Gael funds. Money and the determination of Devoy, ably assisted by Carroll, had given Clan na Gael an apparently firm grip of the I.R.B.

Devoy intended using the I.R.B. to foment an Irish revolution, hoping that international war and 'England's difficulty' were at hand. He overestimated the resources at his disposal but not to the extent of imagining that the I.R.B. could do very much on its own. He hoped to mastermind and dominate a wider movement, including home rule M.P.s who would agitate in parliament for Irish independence and then withdraw from Westminster at an appropriate point and give their support to a campaign combining resort to arms and the overthrow of the landholding system. The process would be aided very considerably if Ireland were denuded of troops by a war in the near east. The M.P. most obviously suited

[1] Comerford, *Fenians in context*, pp 207–8.   [2] Above, v, 417–21, 436–7.

to cooperate in such a strategy was John O'Connor Power, but Devoy (and he was not alone in this) had developed an intense personal antipathy for the member for Mayo from at least as early as 1876. Devoy was behind O'Connor Power's expulsion from the supreme council, arguing that his membership of parliament amounted to unacceptable compromise with constitutional politics. Yet Devoy himself was more than willing to do business with parliamentarians who might serve his purpose, and he soon believed he had found one in Parnell. J. J. O'Kelly, a New-York-based journalist and Clan na Gael activist, called on Parnell and Biggar in August 1877 and subsequently recommended the member for Meath in the warmest terms to Devoy. Carroll on his transatlantic mission met Parnell in Dublin in January 1878 and again in London in March, this time in the company of Frank Hugh O'Donnell, M.P., W. H. O'Sullivan, M.P., J. J. O'Kelly, John O'Leary, and John O'Connor (the newly appointed secretary of the supreme council of the I.R.B.). For Parnell's part these meetings appear to have been exercises in that masterly keeping of silence that did so much to advance his career. He created the impression of being prepared for anything, but had committed himself to nothing. By contrast, O'Donnell, another obstructionist with leadership ambitions, presented Carroll with a written statement of policy and viewpoints. For his pains he was made the butt of private ridicule by Carroll and Devoy.

Devoy had further reassurance about Parnell from Davitt when he arrived in America in August 1878. While Davitt remained in the New York area for some weeks, he and Devoy explored together the possibilities for radical Irish nationalism. Then on 24 October 1878, while Davitt was touring in the mid-west, Devoy moved dramatically to initiate, as he hoped, the new phase of Irish agitation in which he himself would pull the strings. The occasion for this move was the announcement in the New York *Herald* of 24 October that Parnell had been reelected president of the Home Rule Confederation of Great Britain at its annual convention held in Dublin a few days earlier. It was scarcely an astounding development but Devoy seized on it with the eagerness of someone who had been anxiously awaiting a pretext. His anxiety was surely based on the fear that, if he did not act, someone else—O'Connor Power, or Matt Harris, or Davitt—would take an initiative. Besides, Devoy had sufficient acquaintance with fenianism over two decades to know that the revitalisation recently achieved under Clan na Gael auspices was likely to be a short-lived phenomenon unless something was done to maintain morale. One of the factors in that revitalisation had been the prospect of an Anglo–Russian war over Bulgaria, and that had disappeared after the Berlin congress of the European powers in June–July 1878. Whatever his precise motivation, Devoy hurriedly contacted a handful of Irish Americans—some in New York, others elsewhere in the U.S.A., by telegram—for consultations of the kind that implicate those consulted without giving them any opportunity to influence what they are consulted about. Before the day was out he had dispatched this telegram to Dublin in his own name and in the names of Carroll and three others:

Show following to Kickham, and if approved present to Charles Parnell and friends: Nationalists here will support you on following conditions: (1) abandonment of federal demand [and] substitution [of] general declaration in favour of self-government; (2) vigorous agitation of land question on basis of peasant proprietary, while accepting conditions tending to abolish arbitrary eviction; (3) exclusion of all sectarian issues from platform; (4) [Irish] members to vote together on all imperial and home questions, adopt aggressive policy, and energetically resist all coercive legislation; (5) advocacy of all struggling nationalities in British empire and elsewhere.[1]

The recipient of this telegram was James O'Connor, one of the founders of the supreme council,[2] and elder brother of that body's newly appointed secretary, John. Devoy addressed his telegram to James O'Connor's place of work, the office of Richard Pigott's *Irishman*, of which weekly he was sub-editor. Kickham, the president of the supreme council, had fallen on hard times and was living at O'Connor's family home in Blackrock, County Dublin. Devoy sent his message by way of the supreme council leadership, expecting to hustle that body into acceptance of his scheme. The suggestion of a power of veto contained in the words 'if approved' was no more than a verbal courtesy. Far from waiting on any verdict from Dublin Devoy had the text of his telegram carried in the New York *Herald* of 25 October. He followed this up two days later with an elaborately contrived article in the same paper highlighting the support of a selection of prominent American fenians for 'the new Irish departure'. Devoy had moved without any formal approval from Clan na Gael—that body, like the I.R.B., was presented with a *fait accompli*—and he seems to have expected more serious opposition from his American colleagues than from the supreme council. Davitt, hearing about Devoy's initiative while still on tour, was taken aback, but on returning to New York he was prevailed upon to swallow his reservations and to side with Devoy against an emerging coalition of critics.

The 'new departure' telegram was poorly received in Dublin. The office of the *Irishman* was a particularly inhospitable destination, since it was well known that Devoy and Carroll had the ambition of putting Pigott out of business and breaking his influence with the I.R.B. Making soundings with a view to establishing a new fenian-controlled newspaper had been one of the principal items on Carroll's agenda during his Irish tour. Apart altogether from whatever influence may have been exerted on him by Pigott or O'Connor, Kickham was unlikely to find the new departure attractive. He had no liking for Parnell and was not impressed by the capers of the obstructionists. Devoy and Davitt and others cited obstructionism as an excuse for supporting Parnell. Kickham held that ideally Irish nationalists should not go to Westminster at all, but that if they did they should behave like gentlemen and not bring their country's good name into disrepute by breaking the rules of the club. In other words, as an observer of the bitter struggle for leadership of the home rule party Kickham gave his

---

[1] Moody, *Davitt*, p. 250.   [2] See above, v, 445–6.

sympathy to Butt and not to the obstructionists. He had no desire to give any support to Parnell, much less to offer him the leadership of a nationalist front.

Of course Devoy did not expect Kickham to like the new departure; what he did expect was that the president of the supreme council would feel obliged to go along with the coup, realising that financially and organisationally the rank and file of the I.R.B. depended on Clan na Gael. But Kickham refused to be coerced by such considerations: his fenianism had long since become a purely mental posture and was indifferent to the existence or absence of rank-and-file followers, as distinct from a handful of close associates. Since he felt no need for an organised rank and file, Kickham could not be blackmailed by fear of losing it.

In the attack that they now prepared to launch against the new departure Kickham, O'Leary, and others had to hand the weapon of principled fenian intransigence, which Devoy himself had used barely two years before to help expel O'Connor Power and the others from the supreme council.[1] Soon Devoy and Davitt were being denounced publicly and privately for heresy and deviation by Kickham, Pigott, O'Leary, Stephens, and others, on the grounds that the new departure would involve participation by fenians in supposedly untouchable parliamentary politics and would contaminate the purity of the physical force ideal. For most of these critics the doctrine of intransigence was a justification for doing nothing, whereas in the written and spoken defence of the new departure made by Devoy and Davitt it is impossible not to discern a burning desire to precipitate an Irish revolution. Their attempts to define that revolution were not without coherence but left unspoken its one essential feature—that they should control it.

At a meeting of the executive of Clan na Gael, held in New York on 24 November, the new departure was approved and there was agreement that Devoy and Davitt should proceed across the Atlantic to carry it through. Davitt attended the New York meeting as an I.R.B. representative under the provisions of the 1877 agreement to set up a revolutionary directory. On the same basis Devoy was enabled to attend a meeting of the supreme council held in Paris from 19 to 26 January 1879. Here Devoy and Davitt endeavoured unsuccessfully to win approval for their initiative. This outcome was a setback but not a defeat, for Devoy had more influence with the main body of the I.R.B. than anyone else had, a fact recognised by the supreme council when it agreed in Paris to allow him to embark on a tour of inspection of the organisation in Britain and Ireland. In subsequent months he was able to treat with Parnell as the effective commander of the fenian forces on both sides of the Atlantic. Parnell crossed the channel to meet Devoy at Boulogne in early March 1879 and they had further discussions in Dublin, with Davitt present, in April and June 1879. They were facing the challenge of what the new departure was to amount to in practice. At least, Devoy and Davitt were facing a challenge. Parnell had not committed himself, and if the

[1] See above, p. 22.

initiative petered out he would have lost nothing. For the two fenians there was no turning back, or so they felt. But how to start a revolution? The engine was provided by a local group in County Mayo.

On a visit to his native county in February 1879 Davitt discovered that plans were afoot for a mass meeting at Irishtown to voice the demands of hard-pressed local tenant farmers. Two bad years had left many unable to pay their rents and in consequent danger of losing their farms. Public protest was intended to put pressure on landlords to reduce rents and to desist from evictions. The organisational impetus came principally from James Daly, proprietor of the Castlebar-based *Connaught Telegraph*, who had been endeavouring for years to foment tenant right agitation in Mayo. The county had acquired since the late 1860s an impressive cadre of lay political activists of whom Daly was only the most prominent. Not surprisingly most of them—but not Daly—were fenians. Equally unsurprisingly they were all eager to participate—without any reference to I.R.B. authority—in the emerging movement. As the rank and file fenians of Mayo and adjacent counties would so obviously rally to any agrarian campaign, Davitt and Devoy were left with little choice. Even if they wanted to have nothing to do with the land question they would now have to adopt it or else risk losing the I.R.B. in the west.

Davitt joined in the preparation of the Irishtown meeting, leaving detailed arrangements to be settled locally but ensuring for himself some influence over the list of speakers and the resolutions to be adopted. He apparently obtained guidance on the complex world of Mayo connections from two Dublin-based I.R.B. men, Patrick Egan and Thomas Brennan, who had obtained a knowledge of the county while engaged there in a commercial capacity. It is unlikely that Davitt ever understood the exact local circumstances that gave rise to the proposal for the Irishtown gathering. When the demonstration took place on 20 April 1879 with, perhaps, 7,000 participants, Brennan was on the platform having brought from Dublin two resolutions framed by Davitt. These reflected Davitt's anxiety to assimilate the meeting to the new departure. The first incorporated a demand for self-government; the second was a ringing denunciation of landlordism as an institution. The only other resolution to be adopted was framed locally and emphasised immediate concerns in calling for a reduction of unfairly high rents.

Persuading Parnell to identify with the Mayo campaign was Davitt's next preoccupation. On 1 June the M.P. confirmed to Davitt and Devoy that he would address a meeting arranged for Westport one week later. As at Irishtown the affair was essentially a local County Mayo endeavour, with Daly in the chair, but the primacy of honour was accorded to Parnell. The leadership of this new movement was now his for the taking. The radical John O'Connor Power, M.P. for Mayo and long-time advocate of 'the land for the people', was thus displaced from a position he might very reasonably have expected to occupy. Deference is an insidious habit: as Mayo farmers and fenians, and Devoy and Davitt, were about to defy the landlords, they were emboldened by the self-assurance of someone who was himself a landlord and who spoke with the accent of command. They had chosen well; indeed, as it was to prove, too well for the sake of their own objectives and ambitions.

Clerical opposition to the agrarian campaign in Mayo was highlighted by a letter in the *Freeman's Journal* of 7 June from Archbishop MacHale of Tuam, warning against attendance at the Westport meeting. It has been suggested that the real author was the ageing prelate's secretary, but in any case the sentiments were exactly those evinced by the majority of the clergy five years earlier when the new fenian activists of Mayo defied bishops and priests to campaign for the election of O'Connor Power. By and large the same people were active in the new agrarian movement and at least some of the clergy were still profoundly distrustful of them. The intent of the new movement, as conveyed by its platform rhetoric, was another cause of clerical concern. Landlords were being menaced by gesture and word into reducing rents. The tenants were being given the impression that they need not pay rent other than at a 'reasonable' level, and perhaps not at all under current conditions, and that in any case they could defy eviction, the landlords' ultimate sanction. The flouting of legal and moral convention contained in this was a worry for the more conservative minded even among those most eager for the advancement of the tenant cause. The spectre of 'communism' was raised, a codeword for a perceived threat to the basis of private property.

Even if the policy of the agitators were morally acceptable, would it be expedient? With the summer of 1879 unfolding as one of the worst on record, the third bad harvest in a row was inevitable, so that the need for rent abatements and other concessions on the part of landlords was escalating. Already rent reductions had been granted by some landlords, usually in response to respectful petitions drawn up under priestly guidance. Such non-confrontational pressures, combined with the obvious inability of so many tenants to pay at previous levels, might have been expected to yield results on a wide front, and to constitute a more fruitful line of approach than the belligerent stance promoted at the Mayo demonstrations. However, belligerency was particularly attractive to those who could not afford to pay rent at any level. The many thousands in the west, especially in Mayo, who depended on the proceeds of migratory labour to maintain them on small, impoverished holdings were in a particularly serious plight in 1879 with recession in British agriculture wiping out their accustomed seasonal employment just as disease and weather were destroying their potato crop. The most powerful attraction of the agrarian campaign was the prospect of forestalling eviction: 'You must show the landlords that you intend to keep a firm grip of your homesteads and lands', Parnell had declared at Westport. Anti-landlord sentiment was endemic in the wider Irish society, and the economic conditions of 1879 made tensions and readjustments in landlord–tenant relations unavoidable. But collective confrontation leading to virtual civil war was scarcely inevitable. That was the course embarked upon thanks to a mainly non-farming activist élite who found in Mayo in the spring and summer of 1879 a tenantry sufficiently distressed to abandon conventional and cautious courses. When Canon Ulick Burke together with other local priests appeared on the platform at an agrarian meeting in Claremorris, County Mayo, on 13 July 1879, this was acknowledgement by the older established popular leadership that the new movement had taken hold. That was given a formal structure on 16 August 1879 in the shape of the National Land League of Mayo, in the institution of which Davitt played a central part.

In subsequent weeks and months the campaign of mass meetings spread to other counties in the west and began to cross the Shannon. At this stage the reactions of the many preexisting local and county tenant farmers' associations became important. Difficult times had prompted increased activity by a number of them from the middle of 1878 onwards and had brought some new ones into existence.[1] One part of the challenge Davitt set himself was to capture these and harness their potential. Predictable enough was the support of the Ballinasloe Tenants' Defence Association, a body that had itself held many demonstrations since its foundation in 1876. Its founder was Matt Harris, businessman and fenian, and now a close ally of Davitt. The other tenant associations generally represented the interests of large farmers and had a decidedly more cautious outlook. What they did have in common with the Mayo and Ballinasloe movements was a membership sensitive to economic crisis and a politically ambitious leadership. Andrew J. Kettle, founder of the County Dublin Tenants' Defence Association, was also the dominant figure in the umbrella Central Tenants' Defence Association. When he agreed to cooperate with Davitt the way was made smooth for the emergence of the Irish National Land League. The involvement of Kettle was of great importance in persuading Parnell to commit himself to such a venture. For Davitt a nation-wide agrarian campaign under Parnell's presidency and with himself and his fenian friends strategically placed was by autumn 1879 the shape of the Irish revolution. However, Parnell and Kettle would participate only in an organisation within the law.

The Irish National Land League was founded on 21 October 1879 at a meeting summoned by Parnell and with Kettle in the chair. Its stated aims were to secure the reduction of rack rents and 'to facilitate the obtaining of the ownership of the soil by the occupiers'.[2] On the surface these objectives were amenable to a thoroughly law-abiding and constitutional interpretation, and the impression of moderation was underlined by the inclusion of a wide range of mostly well known and respectable persons including fourteen priests and a few gentlemen farmers, on a committee that the league gave itself. On the other hand the new organisation had a seven-man executive not clearly answerable to anyone and dominated by radical activists, including Davitt.[3] Such people could read into the stated

---

[1] Samuel Clark, *Social origins of the Irish land war* (Princeton, N.J., 1979), pp 220, 247–8.
[2] *F.J.*, 22 Oct. 1879, quoted in Moody, *Davitt*, p. 335.
[3] The league had no constitution; for its organisation, see Moody, *Davitt*, pp 342–3.

objectives of the league a very radical social interpretation; or they could hope to use the policies of the league to spark radical political developments.

The *Freeman's Journal*, the leading organ of Irish catholic and moderate nationalist opinion, was at this time engaging its readers' attention with a series of articles highly critical of the land system. The principal author was a talented professional journalist, William O'Brien, who visited some of the most deprived agricultural districts in the country and reported on a depressing situation in the darkest colours. O'Brien drove home relentlessly the message that landlordism was to blame, without seriously considering other possible contributors, such as natural disadvantages of soil and climate, overpopulation, rural usury, and fluctuating markets. Despite their obvious willingness to agitate the land question both O'Brien and the *Freeman's Journal* were slow to rally to the land league.[1]

The land league did not immediately ignite the entire country. In the weeks and months following its launching, meetings and the formation of branches were again concentrated in Connacht. True, Parnell was rapturously received at meetings elsewhere in Ireland and at various venues in England, but the rising young hero had been receiving adulation of this kind for quite some time before the land league's existence. The government inadvertently gave the league a much needed publicity boost in November and December 1879 by arresting Davitt, Brennan, and two others and (unsuccessfully) pressing charges against them arising out of platform speeches. But active measures were needed to spread the movement and by early 1880 a band of peripatetic organisers had been engaged. Membership of a league branch required an annual subscription—one shilling at a minimum—and branches were encouraged to make contributions to the central body, but the land league, unlike O'Connell's repeal association, was not financially self-sustaining. Outside money was required. On 21 December 1879 Parnell set sail for 'the land of Columbia, land of dollars'.[2]

By December 1879 there was no denying that the coming winter threatened to bring misery on a large scale to the poorest of those left by a third bad year without adequate supplies of food or fuel, and without money or credit to buy them. There was a wide consensus that a large increase in the availability of employment on public works for the 'working agricultural classes' was essential. The government agreed, but refused to become directly involved, recommending instead that local authorities and landlords should avail themselves fully of the loans obtainable from the board of works for improvement projects. By legislation[3] and special provision the amount available was substantially increased and

[1] Sally Warwick-Haller, *William O'Brien and the Irish land war* (Dublin, 1990), pp 27–42.
[2] Translation from Irish-language verse in *Irishman*, 27 Mar. 1880.
[3] Relief of Distress (Ireland) Act, 43 Vict., c. 4 (15 Mar. 1880); Relief of Distress (Ireland) (Amendment) Act, 43 & 44 Vict., c. 14 (2 Aug. 1880).

within six or seven months loan applications had been made for projects costed at over £1,500,000. An even more timely and practical government measure was an act of 1 March 1880 authorising the poor law boards of guardians to provide smallholders in distressed districts with supplies of seed potatoes and seed oats, repayment to be made in two instalments as convenient.[1] As a direct consequence destitute smallholders were enabled to make an investment worth more than £600,000 in the harvest of 1880.

However, the crisis winter of 1879–80 was more noteworthy for private than for public relief ventures. Charitable individuals, both ecclesiastical and lay, were already at work before it was announced in mid-December that the duchess of Marlborough was seeking contributions to a fund under her own auspices for the relief of distress. With Lord Randolph Churchill as secretary devoting his considerable talent and energy to the project, large sums were forthcoming from England and elsewhere. By early summer about £120,000 had been dispensed by the Marlborough fund on food, fuel, clothing, seeds, and some relief works. Genuine though the duchess's humanitarian intentions undoubtedly were—not to mention the motivation of those who subscribed a total of £135,000 to her fund—there was also a political dimension to the charity. The fund was the culmination of that campaign for 'hearts and minds' that was the hallmark of the Marlborough viceroyalty.

The political implications of the Marlborough fund induced added urgency in the promotion of the Mansion House fund established under the presidency of the lord mayor of Dublin, Edmund Dwyer Gray, M.P., on 2 January 1880. Having succeeded his father, Sir John, as proprietor of the *Freeman's Journal*, Gray was a major figure in Irish public life. The Mansion House fund drew on the sensibilities of all those who as catholics, catholic nationalists, or liberals were unwilling to give the duchess a free run for the title of chief benefactor of Ireland. The needy were the ultimate beneficiaries as emulation supplemented philanthropy to push the Mansion House fund to a figure in excess of £180,000.

Parnell began his American tour just as enthusiasm for Irish famine relief was erupting at home and abroad. He at once became the focus of an outpouring of humanitarian sympathy for his country, which, allied with his own charisma (and the fact that his maternal grandfather Charles Stewart was famous as the commander in 1815 of U.S.S. *Constitution*, 'Old Ironsides', an icon of U.S. naval history), secured for him a warm and open welcome not just from the Irish-American masses but from the great and powerful also. He addressed the house of representatives and was received by the president, Rutherford B. Hayes. Generous subscriptions were forthcoming for Irish relief everywhere he went. This was not what Parnell had come for, but he was sufficiently adroit to make the most of the unexpected by setting himself up as relief fund patron. Soon he was engaged in recriminatory transatlantic exchanges with the managers of the

[1] Seed Supply (Ireland) Act, 43 Vict. c. 1 (1 Mar. 1880).

Dublin-based funds. Davitt in Ireland and Devoy and Carroll of Clan na Gael, who had expected Parnell's tour to raise money not for relief but for the land league, were tantalised. Displaying true revolutionary impatience with palliatives Davitt wrote to Devoy on 6 February 1880 complaining that their work of twelve months was now in danger of being undone by 'meal and money'.[1] Parnell did indeed seek 'the sinews of war' but the time was not opportune. He alienated James Gordon Bennett, owner of the New York *Herald*, by requesting money for the land league. Bennett created his own Irish relief fund, launching it with a personal subscription of 100,000 dollars. Completing the political cycle, William Shaw, M.P. (since the death of Butt in May 1879, leader of the moderate faction of the home rulers and chairman of the party), was chosen to preside over the committee that saw to the distribution of the Bennett charity. Some of this arrived at Queenstown in kind on board a ship provided by the U.S. government.

The Royal Navy brought relief supplies to remote points on the west coast and to a number of islands. Elsewhere what impressed was the effectiveness of the country's communications and retail systems in translating public and private money into food on the table during the late winter, spring, and early summer of 1880, a period of hardship that ended with the arrival of a good potato crop in June–July. Independently of the great subscription funds, numerous individual donations were made from home and abroad to local committees and to individual clergymen. One contemporary estimate put the total of private gifts at about £830,000.[2] This was greatly exceeded by the increase in family remittances from America. The poor law system as the last line of defence came under pressure but was able to take the strain. There were deaths in 1880 from diseases related to malnutrition but the general picture is one of successful aversion of threatened calamity through practical and sensible effort on many fronts.

The land league found itself unexpectedly acting as a relief agency. Of the £70,000 collected by Parnell on his American tour more than 80 per cent was contributed for charity, as distinct from the purposes of the league. However, even relief money could be allocated in such a way as to promote the cause, and in any event the league closed its relief account on 25 August 1880 so that thenceforth all its expenditure was for political ends.[3] By then the philanthropic wave had subsided and as Irish-Americans discerned a political crisis rather than a threatened famine in Ireland, money flowed to the league without humanitarian strings attached. Much of it came by way of Patrick Ford of the *Irish World* who had helped O'Donovan Rossa to assemble the 'skirmishing' fund a few years earlier.

Ford controlled a section of the Irish National Land League of the United States, a body for which Parnell made hurried provision as he was about to

---

[1] *Devoy's post bag*, i, 483.
[2] *The Irish crisis of 1879–80: proceedings of the Dublin Mansion House relief committee* (Dublin, 1881), p. 73.
[3] Moody, *Davitt*, p. 416.

embark for Ireland in March 1880. Parnell's departure from America was hurried because a general election was pending, the imminent dissolution of parliament having been announced on 8 March. Gladstone, now presented with the opportunity of turning the electoral tables on Disraeli, made no serious attempt to harness the forces behind home rule in Ireland, although many of his party's radical candidates in Britain were playing for the Irish votes in their constituencies. When the prime minister vilified home rule in his election address, one result was to inhibit his opponent from making overtures to what both leaders recognised as the liberals' natural constituency in Ireland. It was thanks largely to tory spoiling tactics over a number of years that 'the people's William' was unable to promote in Ireland anything equivalent to the Midlothian campaign of 1879 and 1880 with which he whipped up liberal support in Scotland in preparation for the election. But in the event of a hung parliament not even Disraeli's wiles were likely to prevent Gladstone from securing the support of the bulk of home rule M.P.s. The fundamentally liberal affiliation of the majority of those under the home rule banner in the outgoing parliament had been highlighted when they elected William Shaw as chairman. It was still possible to see Parnell and the other obstructionists as no more than an irritant.

Parnell used the election to augment his faction within the party, a tactic that he had already tested successfully at a by-election in Ennis in July 1879. He had in his favour the enthusiasm and devotion that his name and his enigmatic presence already evoked in a section of the populace. He had come to be identified with the obstructionist policy, and that had the advantage of being exciting (especially as written up by sympathetic journalists) at a time when the mainstream of the party had nothing new to offer. Parnell had the support of a cadre of activists, of whom Davitt was the most prominent. Finally, he had identified himself with the cause of the tenantry.

Parnell was not over-particular about the credentials of candidates if they were willing to join his train. He exerted his influence to secure the return of a number of individuals who had little to recommend them in party terms except that they were prepared to meet their own election expenses—or at least to find the money privately. Such were the O'Gorman Mahon and Captain William O'Shea, both returned for County Clare, and J. C. McCoan, one of the new M.P.s for Parnell's native county, Wicklow. But returned also—perhaps somewhat to Parnell's surprise—were some ardent young men of advanced views. J. J. O'Kelly was elected for Roscommon, ousting the O'Conor Don, a catholic landlord and home ruler; Thomas Sexton, a railway clerk turned leader-writer, was elected for County Sligo, ousting Captain E. R. King-Harman, a protestant landlord and home ruler. Of similar stamp were T. P. O'Connor and Arthur O'Connor, returned for County Galway and Queen's County respectively. No more angry or action-hungry young man was ever returned to parliament than John Dillon, son of the late John Blake Dillon, and an outspoken supporter of obstructionism, now elected for County Tipperary.

The second member for Queen's County, Richard Lalor, exemplifies another kind of 1880 Parnellite. He was a gentleman farmer with long-standing claims on local loyalties, who took advantage of the split within the home rule party from 1877 onwards to undermine the position of the two liberal-type landlord home rulers returned for the county in 1874. In Kildare James Leahy fired previously frustrated local interests with the Parnellite magic to secure his return at the expense of the outgoing liberal, the Rt Hon. W. H. F. Cogan. In County Westmeath the same ingredients produced the election of two outsiders, H. J. Gill and T. D. Sullivan (editor of the *Nation*).

The land question was an important issue in many Irish constituencies in 1880, and it helped Parnell. But there was nothing in the results to suggest a vote of confidence by enfranchised farmers in the land league, except perhaps west of the Shannon. In Counties Donegal, Monaghan, Armagh, and Tyrone a total of six landlord tories lost their seats before a wave of tenant self-assertion and demand that spread right across Ulster and owed nothing whatever to Parnell or his land league. In County Carlow a successful assault on two tory seats held unchallenged for nearly a quarter of a century was headed by Edmund Dwyer Gray, proprietor of the *Freeman's Journal*, a noted exponent of tenant right views who was as yet deeply suspicious of the land league. Meanwhile in agricultural County Cork the land leaguer Andrew J. Kettle failed in his bid against two home rulers of the other stamp, William Shaw (the party leader) and Lt-col. David La Touche Colthurst.

Home rulers won sixty-three seats in the 1880 election. Of these the Parnellite group constituted twenty-seven at most. The news from Britain rendered the Irish results to all appearances insignificant, for the liberals had captured sufficient seats in England, Scotland, and Wales to give them a clear majority at Westminster. When the home rule M.P.s met in Dublin on 17 May 1880 to elect a chairman for the ensuing parliamentary session, more than twenty were missing, partly no doubt because the outcome did not appear to matter very much. However, Parnell's supporters were there in strength and by a majority of five votes he defeated Shaw. In the given parliamentary situation Parnell now had, if not power, then advantage, but without that responsibility that is typically the greatest constraint on a political leader—the responsibility of maintaining party unity.

The general election of 1880 was a turning-point in the story of the Irish land agitation, not because Parnell was given a mandate by the Irish electorate—he was not—but because it returned Gladstone to power. Ireland had returned only fifteen liberals *ipso nomine*, but the liberal leader was widely seen as a friend of Ireland, that is to say, as being prepared to make concessions to majority Irish opinion. That perception was reinforced when in the queen's speech at the opening of parliament on 10 May it was indicated that the Peace Preservation (Ireland) Act, 1875,[1] embodying and continuing a variety of long-standing

---

[1] 38 Vict., c. 4 (28 May 1875).

repressive measures due for renewal on 1 June 1880, would be allowed to lapse. Added to this, an admission that the land question was the government's highest Irish priority—although any legislation would have to await the next session—completed the sense of expectation. Against this background O'Connor Power introduced a private member's bill proposing to extend to tenants evicted for failure to pay rent the same rights to compensation for disturbance that Gladstone's land act of 1870 accorded to those dispossessed for any other reason. In the spirit of conciliation the government a few weeks later adopted the essentials of O'Connor Power's bill in its own compensation for disturbance bill. The establishment on 29 July of a commission chaired by the earl of Bessborough to inquire into the working of the 1870 land act was a sure earnest of larger legislation later. Ireland, it appeared, was about to be pacified by another round of Gladstonian concession. Then on 3 August the lords struck down the compensation bill and in so doing shattered the government's authority in rural Ireland.

The stalwarts of the land league executive, Davitt, Egan, Kettle, and Brennan, had reacted to the introduction of O'Connor Power's bill with bitter denunciations, which did not spare Parnell himself. Either O'Connor Power's proposal or the government's substitute measure would have drastically reduced the incidence of eviction, at least in the short term, and so would have deflated the land agitation and robbed the league of its prospects. That outcome would have pleased O'Connor Power, who had been cold-shouldered by the league; and it might have pleased Parnell also. The defeat of the bill was a major fillip for agitation not simply because disappointed tenants were angry but because the government itself was seen to have conceded that a grievance existed. Why should a tenant meekly obey the law in the matter of rents and evictions when the house of commons had implicitly accepted the injustice of the law by voting to change it?

In rejecting the government's bill the lords were taking part in a much wider discourse on the land question, with little thought for particular circumstances in Ireland. The 1870s had marked a high point of that questioning of the basis of landlordism that was a recurrent theme in Victorian Britain. On 10 February 1880 Davitt had been warmly received at a London conference of trade union and land reform groups, held under radical patronage. In the Scottish highlands an agrarian agitation had been in progress since 1876. The post-1873 depression in the United States of America had given rise to vigorous criticism of land monopolies and of the very principles of landlordism. Indeed, for a time the land league was to receive very substantial support from American reformers such as Henry George and James Redpath, and from militant American trade unionists, precisely because it was seen as part of a wider struggle.[1]

At the beginning of Gladstone's first administration the prospect of imminent land legislation had given rise to a period of considerable agrarian unrest. The

---

[1] Thomas N. Brown, *Irish-American nationalism, 1870–90* (Philadelphia, 1966), pp 101–15.

same effect was created in 1880 but in a form greatly exacerbated by the hardships of the three preceding years and by the existence of the land league. The return of good weather and a reasonable harvest in 1880 removed the danger of starvation but brought other problems to a head as landlords who had held off before this prepared to recover arrears of rent. Only in the summer and autumn of 1880 did the land league finally shed its predominantly western orientation and acquire extensive support elsewhere in the country. It became a country-wide movement with an impact that was to be great in the midlands, the south, and south Ulster, as well as Connacht, but less so in the north-east and the south-east.

In spreading the land league in the second half of 1880 the organisers did not neglect Ulster. The warmth of the northerners' welcome was variable. The league was soon firmly established in catholic areas. The reaction of the protestant farmers was more complex. They had themselves been engaged in a long-term tug of war with their landlords that had become increasingly politicised, to the point where in the recent general election tenant right liberals had enjoyed spectacular successes. The Ulster tenants were now waiting expectantly for the legislative triumph of their campaign and were keeping pressure on their landlords and on Westminster. Under the circumstances the campaign of the land league was a welcome additional pressure on the government. The coincidence of purpose disarmed the opposition of many and even induced some to participate, to the extent of forming a few land league branches and providing audiences for a few meetings. However, just as Davitt and his friends were 'nationalising' farmers in the south, the Orange order set about reminding land- and money-minded protestant farmers that they, too, had higher responsibilities. Davitt might adopt a special rhetoric for northern purposes, eschewing references to invader races and alien institutions, and including jibes at King James II, but it cut very little ice. The order had little enough difficulty making the point that the league was a nationalist movement, and when the protestant tenants in 1881 achieved their tenant right objectives they had no further incentive to indulge the league.

Outside Ulster the league organisers did spectacularly well in taking advantage of the opportunity that presented itself with the defeat of the government's compensation bill. However, the land league in itself marked little advance in organisational terms on the repeal association of the 1840s. What structures there were at local level rested mainly on the pattern of catholic parishes. This gave the priest a key role if he wished to take it, which he might do either because he was a keen league supporter, or because, though not being one, he wished to keep some upstart off the parochial pedestal. The received impression that all or nearly all of the priests did participate in the land league is incorrect. While O'Connell had been lord and master of the repeal association, Parnell, the nominal president of the land league, had little choice in September 1880 but to add his weight to a campaign that would have been waged with or without him by the real controllers of the league. In so far as O'Connell had activists to link national and local levels they were mainly from the professions, especially law. It was professionals in another sense who fulfilled that function in the land league—the travelling organisers who, like Davitt himself, were prepared to live both for and from politics. The money that supported them and with which they in turn energised the movement came principally from the U.S.A.

The league brought to local prominence many whose political ambitions and talents had previously lain dormant. They were usually not themselves farmers. Indeed, the most prominent branches were to be found in substantial towns such as Tralee, Ballinasloe, or Carrick-on-Suir, where individual farmers carried little weight but where farming fortunes were of vital economic importance. Merchants and shopkeepers in town and village were major beneficiaries of post-famine agricultural prosperity. Because they sold on credit to so many of their customers, big and small, a reduction in agricultural incomes threatened them not only with a decline in business but with a disruption of the cash flow that they needed in order to satisfy a higher order of moneylenders, usually the commercial banks. Landlords, big and small, operated under similar fiscal constraints. By autumn 1879 tenants, farmers, shopkeepers, and bankers had become aware that there was no longer enough money in the rural economy to keep them all in the manner to which they had grown accustomed. Moralising deprecation of 'predatory' land-lordism has too often distracted attention from the fact that, faced with a diminution of their common resources, individual landlords, shopkeepers, and farmers simply reacted, as individuals almost invariably will in such circumstances, by endeavouring to extract as much as ever for themselves, not because they were vicious but because they needed it to maintain the lifestyle on which their socio-economic standing and their self-esteem depended. Not unnaturally, farmers and shopkeepers responded readily to the idea that agricultural rents lacked the moral legitimacy of other debts and might be delayed, reduced, or withheld to facilitate the meeting of other commitments. It was the landlords' bad luck that this viewpoint commanded widespread sympathy in and out of Ireland, even among people who proclaimed the sanctity of all other forms of property. In economic terms—though of course there was much more to it than economics— the land war was an attempt to force a change in the allocation of seriously reduced agricultural income, to the benefit of tenants and merchants and the detriment of landed proprietors.

There was no uniformity from place to place either in the demands on landlords or in the form of agitation patronised by the league. On many estates there was no agitation as landlords granted abatements or other concessions that took account of the difficult times; Parnell's estate at Avondale was an example of this. In the absence of such consensus, anti-landlord tactics would vary according to time and place. So, in one parish the advice would be to pay no rent or only what the tenant 'believed he could afford' (usually the same thing); elsewhere tenants would refuse to pay more than the valuation put on their farms for purposes of local taxation by Griffith's survey of a generation earlier; somewhere else the demand would be for an abatement of 20 or 25 per cent. When eviction threatened, the serving of processes might be resisted actively with the help of neighbours; or the landlord might be challenged in the courts; or there might be passive resistance up to the last moment before physical ejectment, and the rent paid at that point; or, rent not having been paid, eviction might be allowed to take its course. An evicted tenant might attempt to resume possession; or he might be reinstated—illegally and possibly against his inclinations—by the local leaguers; or he might camp near the property with a view to deterring any potential successor tenant and so keeping the way clear for his own eventual restoration by the landlord. Some of these modes of operation entailed loss for the tenant, and the essence of the land league's function was to provide recompense. In its most spectacular form this involved the building of houses for evicted persons. The costs of compensation might be partially met from local resources but most typically they came from headquarters in Dublin. American money channelled through the central office in Dublin made a sustained land war possible by indemnifying agitators against their losses in the fray.

The open-air meeting with marching bands and platform oratory was one of the land league's principal modes of operation. By means of it popular interest was engaged and the establishment of new branches in important centres was promulgated. There could also be a more specific target, as when gatherings were held near a particular property to bring public opinion to bear on an individual case of eviction, 'land-grabbing', or refusal to reduce rents.

In conducting their varied local campaigns the leaguers refurbished an old weapon of social conflict, formerly used by the chartists and others, the systematic ostracisation of uncooperative individuals. The operation of this against Captain Boycott of Lough Mask House, County Mayo, in the autumn of 1880 attracted so much attention that his name has been given to the practice. He had offended in his capacity as land agent; and while many landlords and agents were boycotted, the victims were more typically at a lower social level, and included those who paid rents contrary to local policy and especially the 'land-grabbers'. From the very beginning of the campaign in Mayo in early 1879 the greatest emphasis had been laid on dissuading anyone from taking a farm from which another had been evicted, in the belief that landlords would thus be deprived of any incentive to evict.

Whatever the justice or morality of the boycott in itself, its infliction was frequently determined on the basis of personal vendettas and preexisting antagonisms. Weekly meetings of the parish land league presided over by the parish priest could be tyrannical against individuals. When, as happened in many localities, land league 'courts' were instituted and began to deliberate in public-house back rooms, tyranny was inescapable. And it was not unknown for a shopkeeper to engineer the blacklisting of a competitor in trade, or for a vociferous delator of land-grabbers to be himself transacting business clandestinely with his landlord.

The 'moral' force of the boycott gave way quite easily in the circumstances to physical violence and its essential accompaniment, the threatening letter. The violence could range from the burning of ricks of hay to the maiming of animals, to bodily assault, and even murder. The mean number of agrarian murders a year from 1852 to 1878 was five. For the years 1879 to 1882 it rose to seventeen. The rise in the reported incidence of lesser agrarian crime was much more spectacular, reaching a peak in the last quarter of 1880 at more than twenty-five times the level in the same period of 1878, and not returning to pre-1879 levels until 1883.

Apart from individuals acting alone, three possible sources of violence can be identified without making any pretence that they are separable from one another. It seems likely that within or on the edges of many local land league branches some of the members got together to plan physical intimidation in support of whatever campaign was being waged against local landlordism. Secondly, the exciting times facilitated the coming together of small bands of young men with a taste for nightly prowling and conspiracy. These were endemic in rural society. When they became ramified or assumed a durable profile, as some of them did in certain parts of the country during the land war, such groups came to resemble (and probably were) the continuation of some of the multifarious older forms of nocturnal rural conspiracy including the followers of 'Captain Moonlight'. They might act against the targets of the league or simply in accordance with their own anarchic instincts. Despite the land league's public disowning of violence it seems possible that some of these groups received support from league funds and with the knowledge, in particular, of Patrick Egan. Thirdly, and least important, were the possible activities of rank-and-file I.R.B. members who went over to the land league, as apparently almost all of them in rural areas did. They were certainly armed to some extent, and at least as late as February 1880 Davitt was endeavouring to procure arms for them, or so it appears from his correspondence with Devoy. I.R.B. men undoubtedly contributed to the other two types of land league 'physical force' but there is little evidence that they acted as a separate force. In so far as there are indications of I.R.B. members acting together as such during the land war, what is in question is harassment by supporters of the supreme council directed against some of their fellows who had gone over to the agrarian campaign.

The evidence of widespread acquisition of arms during the land war is no proof of a popular thrust towards political revolution. The desire to possess a gun was a recurrent nineteenth-century fad and one not by any means confined to Ireland. When the peace preservation act lapsed in June 1880 there was no further legal constraint on the possession of arms until March 1881. When Davitt was arrested in February he had a revolver in his possession; at his request the police passed this on to Thomas Brennan whom they knew to be a fenian of the deepest dye.[1]

---

[1] Moody, *Davitt*, p. 464. On the possession of arms in nineteenth-century Britain and Europe, see above, v, 763–4.

Hit by the first shock of the league at its full strength, the landlords as a group reeled somewhat in the last quarter of 1880. From early 1881 they began a recovery, thanks to more determined government support in the exercise of their legal rights, and to the creation of organised private support in the shape of the Orange Emergency Committee and the Property Defence Association, both founded in December 1880. Soon 'emergency men' (mostly northerners) were available on call to work for boycotted landlords, to occupy evicted holdings in the landlord's interest, and to place bids at the auction of goods or cattle distrained for rent.

Gladstone's new chief secretary for Ireland, W. E. Forster, who had come to office full of conciliatory intentions, had decided by late October 1880 that a renewal of coercive legislation was necessary, but the cabinet postponed action until January. An elaborate case, beginning on 28 December, in which Parnell and thirteen others were put on trial for conspiracy, ended with the jury failing to agree on a verdict, and underlined the inadequacy of the ordinary law for dealing with the agitation. On 3 February 1881 Davitt, whose release in 1877 had been granted on a ticket of leave, was arrested and returned to jail in England. For weeks after its opening on 6 January the new session of parliament was dominated by the obstructive resistance of Parnell and his followers to the government's proposals for coercive legislation. The protection of person and property act finally became law on 2 March and was supplemented by the peace preservation act of 21 March.[1] The former, which in effect suspended habeas corpus in proclaimed districts, empowered the Irish government to detain without trial persons suspected of agrarian or treasonable offences; the latter, despite its comprehensive title, was concerned with the importation, sale, and possession of arms, and was similarly applied only in proclaimed districts.

The land war placed a mighty burden on the Irish administration and its agents. Numerous public meetings had to be observed or, at a later stage, prevented; landlords' agents had to be given support in the face of physical and moral resistance to their attempts to serve writs, auction distrained livestock, or effect evictions; persons whose lives were under threat for resisting the demands of the league had to be protected; and a multitude of incidents had to be anticipated, investigated, or reported. By autumn 1880 the constabulary was heavily dependent on military support. Large contingents of accompanying soldiers served to bolster the authority of necessarily smaller numbers of policemen facing defiant or hostile crowds. When called upon to protect sheriffs, bailiffs, and process servers in the course of their work—as happened so frequently in the period 1880–82—the police needed military backing to make up sufficiently intimidating numbers. The possibility that soldiers might be required to act in a specifically military role prompted the setting up of a number of flying columns, but the

---

[1] 44 & 45 Vict., cc 4, 5 (2, 21 Mar. 1881).

armed rebellion feared by alarmists (and hoped for by some of the originators of the league) did not come to pass.

On 7 April 1881 Gladstone introduced a major Irish land bill that became law on 22 August.[1] It tackled the problem of fair rents by instituting a quasi-judicial commission, with regional subcommissions, to which individual tenants or landlords could appeal for adjudication. Rents fixed in this way would remain unchanged for fifteen years. A tenant paying his rent could not be evicted. In addition the tenant could sell his interest in the holding on the open market. Thus were conceded the 'three Fs' sought by tenant righters since the 1840s. As in the 1870 land act there was provision for loans to facilitate the outright purchase of their farms by tenants—the terms were actually improved—but there was no new incentive for landlords to sell. The 1881 act was one of the most momentous pieces of legislation in the history of modern Ireland, granting as it did to the tenants a form of coownership of their holdings. The Irish land commission that emerged from its provisions for rent fixing was in time to assume a pivotal role in the socio-political life of the country.[2]

The declared objective of the land league was the achievement of peasant proprietorship and thus the end of the landlord system, and this objective was constantly reiterated by platform speakers. But emphasis could vary enormously, with Parnell implying handsome compensation for the landlords, while Davitt's rhetoric about the evils of landlordism gave a very different impression. Peasant proprietorship was the league's stated objective precisely because it was amenable to an extremist interpretation. In 1879 Devoy and Davitt and his activist henchmen had seen it as a token of the wider revolution that they believed they were launching. While others clung to it because of these ulterior militant-nationalist overtones, Davitt had come to see the elimination of landlordism as an end in itself, an ideological imperative. But the anti-landlord feeling tapped by the land league in the country was neither extremist nor ideological. The land league appealed to the farmers by and large because, whatever was said on platforms, it was seen as offering the promise of security and tangible financial benefit within a continuing landlord–tenant relationship.

Such people saw the 1881 land act as a very substantial gain. When it became clear within a few months that the rents being fixed under the new act were in general substantially lower than previous rents the majority of Irish farmers lost interest in any further agitation. A condition for approaching the commission was the settlement of outstanding rent. Up to 20 per cent of farmers—that is, over 100,000, usually the smaller and poorer ones such as those among whom the agitation had first begun—were too deeply in arrears to clear their debts and enter the new order. They provided potent material for the indefinite perpetuation of the agitation, which was precisely what the activists of the land league hoped to achieve. Parnell adroitly balanced between the now satisfied majority and the

[1] Land Law (Ireland) Act, 44 & 45 Vict., c. 49 (22 Aug. 1881).   [2] Below, pp 583–6.

advocates of continued agitation. He contributed constructively to the passage of the land bill through the commons, yet abstained in the final vote. At two land league conferences on the measure, in April and September, he maintained an ambivalent stance and effectively thwarted the efforts of the radical group—weakened as it was by the enforced absence of Davitt—to have the measure rejected out of hand. But the government finally concluded that Parnell either would not or could not wind down the agitation and on 13 October he was arrested under the protection act and confined in Kilmainham jail. The many leaguers already detained there included Brennan and Kettle. They were soon joined by Dillon, J. J. O'Kelly, Sexton, and O'Brien. The latter, previously the leading journalist with the *Freeman's Journal*, was editor of a newspaper, *United Ireland*, owned by Parnell and others, which had begun publication in August. In Kilmainham O'Brien composed, and Parnell, Dillon, Kettle, Brennan, and Sexton signed, a manifesto calling on farmers to pay no more rent until the government came to its senses. This was the kind of extreme move that Parnell had always hitherto avoided. Like the proposal to withdraw from parliament that had been made at crucial stages by Davitt, Dillon, and others, the rent strike was seen by some as the prelude to that total conflict with British power in Ireland that the new departure had been intended to initiate. But if the farmers ever possessed the stomach for that they no longer did in October 1881. Bishops and priests, the *Freeman's Journal*, and the *Nation* repudiated the manifesto. Picking his moment well, Forster proclaimed the land league as an illegal organisation on 20 October. With all its principal figures locked up or out of the country the central body simply folded. However, centralised support and encouragement soon returned in the form of the Ladies' Land League.

Two of Parnell's sisters, Fanny and Anna, who normally lived at their mother's home in Bordentown, New Jersey, became active in the American wing of the land league under the influence of a Clan-na-Gael-type extremist understanding of the movement's purpose. Fanny founded the Ladies' Land League in New York and late in 1880 Anna went to Ireland to establish it on home soil. Davitt had cleared the way, overcoming the misgivings of the land league leaders, not least those of Anna's brother.[1] She soon had enlisted a solid corps of activists, many but by no means all of them relatives of male leaders. The driving force came from Anna herself. From October 1881 the Ladies' Land League not only had the field to itself but was able to draw on the land league's substantial funds. Will-power and money enabled Anna to maintain a formidable campaign in the face of a rising tide of evidence that many of the rank and file had little inclination to soldier on. By early 1882 the Ladies' Land League had been proscribed and a number of its local activists had been imprisoned.

Much though the activities of the ladies' league inconvenienced the government, the most serious threat to civil order in late 1881 and early 1882 came from

---

[1] Moody, *Davitt*, pp 456–7.

a high level of localised violence over most of which, it seems, nobody except the perpetrators had any control. The arrears problem and the incarceration of the leaders were continuing provocations, but in any event the violence triggered by the land war was likely to need some time to subside. The detention without trial of over 800 local activists, of various kinds, in 1881 and early 1882, ultimately had a calming effect but in some places it may have initially made matters worse. Such was the pressure on the R.I.C. in early 1882 that several hundred soldiers were assigned to take over the protection of individuals under threat and other work of a police nature.[1] The belief, or hope, that a freed Parnell might have the power to control 'Captain Moonlight' enhanced his political capital in the eyes of the government.

HIS incarceration had a profound effect on Parnell's political career. To his already great popularity there was added the aura of martyrdom that prison confers on patriots. But his months of not uncomfortable confinement led him to a more moderate political path. In April 1882 he conveyed by intermediaries to Gladstone that he was eager to make his peace with the government. The proposal had obvious attractions for Gladstone and they came to a mutual understanding whereby Parnell and his chief lieutenants would be released and the government would introduce a substantial measure of relief for small tenants in arrears, thereby enabling Parnell to use his influence to end the disorder in the countryside and to cooperate 'cordially' with the liberal party.[2] This so-called 'Kilmainham treaty' was repudiated by Forster, who resigned the chief secretaryship on 2 May. Parnell, Dillon, and O'Kelly were released on the same day and Davitt on 6 May. That evening there came the shocking news of the assassination in Dublin's Phoenix Park of the newly appointed chief secretary, Lord Frederick Cavendish, and the permanent under-secretary, Thomas Henry Burke.

To the present-day reader the most surprising feature of the affair may be the fact that such eminent personages should have felt safe walking through the city from the castle to their residences in the park without protection during troubled times. The conventional immunity of the great was violated by a group named the Irish National Invincibles. Although five of their number were eventually hanged for the Phoenix Park murders, the workings of the society were never fully uncovered. Most of those implicated were part of a pinched Dublin lower-middle-class and artisan milieu, and as a group they had multifarious connections with various forms of nationalism and fenianism. They were drawn together about the autumn of 1881 in a new conspiracy explicitly committed to political assassination. Political passion and a liking for conspiracy would not of themselves have brought these people together into a new, select grouping. That required in addition outside initiative and money. What little is known about the initiators is

---

[1] Richard Hawkins, 'An army on police work, 1881–2; Ross of Bladensburg's memorandum' in *Ir. Sword*, xi (1973–4), pp 75–117.
[2] Lyons, *Parnell*, pp 196–202.

suggestive of links with the upper but non-parliamentary echelons of the land league; and the league had very substantial funds, which since February 1881 had been located in Paris under the supervision of Patrick Egan. There is also the possibility of direct Irish-American involvement.

Writing to Devoy on 16 December 1880 Davitt had mentioned the possibility of something being done 'by way of retaliation in England' if the expected government moves against the land agitation should prove draconian, but he did so in a way that suggests he was trying to put Devoy off the idea.[1] In a public address delivered in New York some weeks later Devoy spoke of taking the lives of British ministers and reducing London to ashes. By February 1881 a Clan na Gael agent, William Mackey Lomasney, had crossed the Atlantic to plan a bombing campaign in Britain. He had a meeting with Parnell in Paris and reported back enthusiastically to Devoy about the parliamentarian's advanced attitudes. But it is doubtful if Parnell knew of Lomasney's precise mission, and in any event Lomasney did not carry out any bombing on this occasion. However, agents of O'Donovan Rossa, an outspoken opponent of the new departure, perpetrated a series of bomb attacks on public buildings in Lancashire and London in the first half of 1881, and Lomasney and his associates would return to the attack a few years later. Some of those implicated in the assassination of Cavendish and Burke may have believed that they were pursuing a line of which Parnell or other league leaders approved. In the case of Parnell, at least, they were grievously mistaken. He not only suffered acute political embarrassment but was thrown off stride more visibly than at any other time in his public career.

The assassinations impelled Parnell all the more quickly along the route of moderation to which the months in prison and the understanding with Gladstone had already committed him. They also forced Gladstone to introduce a new and drastic coercion measure before giving parliamentary time to any other Irish measures. The 'crimes act'—the Prevention of Crime (Ireland) Act[2]—became law on 12 July, providing the Irish government with a comprehensive armoury of most of the powers that had been used against crime and agitation during the nineteenth century, and including provision for the trial of certain cases by a commission of three judges in place of a jury. The Arrears of Rent (Ireland) Act[3] followed on 18 August. Confining itself to holdings of less than £30 by Griffith's valuation this provided that tenants with the kind of substantial arrears that so many had accumulated owing to the bad years and the campaigns against rent would now be liable for only one year's total, while the government would pay half the balance and the landlords would suffer the loss of the remainder. Over 120,000 tenants availed themselves of this scheme. With this great source of popular grievance diminished, Parnell felt free to remove the agents of agitation. By the end of August he had seen to the dissolution of the Ladies' Land League. In October he took control of the land league fund out of the hands of Egan.

---

[1] *Devoy's post bag*, ii, 24.   [2] 45 & 46 Vict., c. 45 (12 July 1882).
[3] 45 & 46 Vict., c. 47 (18 Aug. 1882).

Like so many other Irish crises, the land war of 1879–82 ended with an exodus to America. Egan went, and so did Brennan. Putting a brave face on his disillusionment Dillon followed in early 1883, though he was to return in a few years. The most eminent of these thwarted revolutionists, Davitt, had gone earlier (and also returned). In prison from February 1881 to May 1882 he had had time to work out the philosophy of his policies. Thanks to the inspiration of Henry George's *Poverty and progress*, he arrived at the eminently logical conclusion that 'the land for the people' was a sham if it did not mean nationalisation or state control of land.[1] The contrast was startling between that programme and the compromise, moderation, and self-seeking that he found to be rampant when he emerged from prison, as the comfortable majority of farmers quietly settled for the benefits of the 1881 act, with Parnell's tacit encouragement. He travelled to America in June 1882, hoping to win support that would give him leverage at home, but while his nationalisation policy was strongly endorsed by some Irish-Americans it provoked so much hostility from others that Davitt realised he had lost. Eventually Davitt would come to celebrate what had taken place, but it was not the agrarian revolution he had set his heart on so recently; much less was it the radical nationalist revolution that he and Devoy thought they were launching in 1878 and recruiting Parnell to in 1879. The opportunistic parliamentarian now held all the trumps.

More significant than the westward movement of the revolutionaries was the departure of so many of the intended beneficiaries of the revolution. This agricultural recession took its toll, as surely as had the unpoliticised recession of the early 1860s. The emigration rate rose from 7.7 per thousand of population in 1878 to 8.8 in 1879 and doubled in 1880 to 17.6. The figures remained high in 1881 and 1882 and jumped in 1883 to 21.6 per thousand, the highest since 1854. In the five years following the Westport meeting at least 25,000 people emigrated from Mayo, the equivalent of 10 per cent of the population.[2] Few of those who left Mayo or any other county were holders of middling to large farms; and very few were landlords.

For some of those who remained there were apparent benefits, such as reduced rents and security of tenure, but at a perhaps unnecessary price for Irish society at large. The social and economic configuration of post-famine Ireland was such that the landlord interest stood little chance in the long run against the tenants. It must be remembered that the northern Irish tory landlords advocated the 1881 land bill in the lords, and thus secured its passage, not because they were seriously menaced by the land league (which they were not) but because they could not downface the demands of their own tenantry (presbyterian, protestant, and catholic) as expressed in the ballot box and through other organs of public opinion. The fact that over so much of the country the agrarian readjustment of

---

[1] Moody, *Davitt*, p. 519.

[2] W. E. Vaughan and A. J. Fitzpatrick, *Irish historical statistics: population, 1821–1971* (Dublin, 1978), pp 262, 337–8.

the early 1880s was accompanied by a poisoning of social relations, agitation, violence, and disturbances sufficiently severe to earn, however hyperbolically, the description of 'war', reflected to some extent a different quality of landlord–tenant relations, but it did not mean that war had been inevitable. As ever, war had its costs, long-term and short-term, for the entire country, and these have to be balanced against the gains of the tenant farmers under the legislation of 1881.[1]

The land war did much to define and strengthen the sense of national identity that, at least from O'Connell's time, was part of the world-view of the mass of Irish catholics. And it brought to high prominence a leader and a leadership élite who—if only in order to retain their prominence—were likely to look for new wars to fight.

[1] Essential books on the land war not already cited in the footnotes to this chapter include J. S. Donnelly, *The land and the people of nineteenth-century Cork: the rural economy and the land question* (London, 1975); J. J. Lee, *The modernisation of Irish society, 1848–1918* (Dublin, 1973); Barbara Solow, *The land question and the Irish economy, 1870–1903* (London, 1971); W. E. Vaughan, *Landlords and tenants in Ireland, 1848–1904* (Dublin, 1984); Paul Bew, *Land and the national question in Ireland, 1858–82* (Dublin, 1979); see also Andrew W. Orridge, 'Who supported the land war? An aggregate-data analysis of Irish agrarian discontent, 1879–1882' in *Economic & Social Review*, xii (1980–81), pp 203–33.

CHAPTER III

The Parnell era, 1883–91

R. V. COMERFORD

PARNELL and his parliamentary associates used the prominence they had won in the land war years to fashion, during the period 1882–5, a new kind of Irish political party.[1] The formal structure was provided by the Irish National League as established at a conference in Dublin on 17 October 1882. This soon absorbed the Home Rule League of 1873, which had been virtually non-existent outside of its ineffectual Dublin central body, and this in any case had been taken over by obstructionists before 1880. Thus deprived of their formal organisation, the non-Parnellite home rule M.P.s made no effective effort to create a new focal institution. By-elections from 1881 onwards highlighted their vulnerability in the constituencies as avowal of support for Parnell came to be synonymous with being a home ruler. The new leader did not raise a finger to maintain the unity of the old home rule party in parliament, and the thirty or so home rulers of 1880 who for reasons of policy or personality could not bring themselves to follow in Parnell's train were sloughed off. Among them were not only the former leader, William Shaw—who did not contest the 1885 general election—but also two of the most ambitious and able—along with Parnell himself—of the obstructionists of the 1870s: John O'Connor Power, who joined the liberals and stood unsuccessfully for an English constituency at the next election in 1885; and Frank Hugh O'Donnell, who was not a candidate.

The extent of the popularity on which Parnell could rely for the business of party-building was strikingly demonstrated by the success of a collection raised in 1883 in aid of his personal finances. After it became public knowledge early in the year that debts totalling £18,000 were forcing him to dispose of his properties in County Wicklow, various well-wishers canvassed the idea of a testimonial. Soon a committee was formed and subscriptions eventually materialised from home and abroad. Before the end of 1883 Parnell was presented with a cheque for £37,000.

Financial considerations formed one of the principal obstacles to the emergence of a disciplined political party. Men who could afford to pay their own election

---

[1] O'Brien, *Parnell and his party* (1964).

expenses and to keep themselves at Westminster—in practice the usual requirements in candidates of every political colour—were likely to give much rein to
individualistic inclination and to view the party whip with a certain nonchalance.
By amassing a substantial parliamentary fund from which election expenses and
members' salaries could be paid, Parnell and his henchmen were enabled to make
provision for the return to parliament at the 1885 elections of a phalanx of M.P.s
for whom loyalty to the party was a *sine qua non*. The submission of the individual
to the collective—in practice of course to the leader and his surrounding
oligarchy—was copper-fastened by a signed pledge demanded of all candidates
before they could receive the party's nomination. This included an undertaking
to resign forthwith if formally convicted by a majority of colleagues of failing to
'sit, act, and vote' with the party.[1]

Most home rule candidates in elections down to and including that of 1880 were
adopted by *ad hoc* gatherings of local notables, frequently including a strong
contingent of priests. In preparation for the contest of November–December
1885, Parnellites formalised this practice. For each of the thirty-two counties a
convention was summoned consisting of four representatives of every local branch
of the national league and as many of the county's catholic clergy as wished to
attend. Parnell and his close collaborators were not interested in associational
structures as such, and the purpose of the formal conventions was to give the
central authority influence over the nominations. Every convention was chaired
by an M.P., who came with clear instructions from Dublin as to who should be
nominated. Largely because the Dublin directorate had chosen with an eye to
local and ecclesiastical sensibilities, it had its way in most cases.

The success of the convention system was evidence of extensive cooperation
between the Parnellites and the catholic church. From the very beginning of his
career Parnell had been eager to avail himself of the assistance of the priests at
constituency level, and he always declared himself in favour of denominational
education. Thomas Nulty, bishop of Meath (1866–98), and Thomas Croke,
archbishop of Cashel (1875–1902), were early supporters of his. There were still
churchmen who distrusted him because of the political company he kept, but
from 1882 onwards he went out of his way to prove himself trustworthy. Even
the founding of the national league was taken as a good earnest, providing as it
did for local branches with abstract and safe political ends to take the place of the
inflammable agrarian movement. Complications were caused by papal interven-
tions—indirectly encouraged by the government—that culminated in a Vatican
circular, 'De Parnellio', to the Irish bishops in May 1883 deploring clerical
support for the Parnell testimonial. This made so little impact on Irish realities
that in October 1884 the bishops in conference entrusted to 'the Irish parliamentary party' the promotion of their educational demands at Westminster. Alignment of church and party was further advanced in 1885 when Cardinal McCabe,

---

[1] Ibid., pp 133–43.

archbishop of Dublin since 1878, was succeeded by William J. Walsh. Unlike his predecessor, Walsh was enthusiastic for the emerging national mobilisation. He was also determined to put his mark on developments, and he claimed that it was his insistence that secured all the nominations at the conventions for Dublin city and county, Kildare county, and Wicklow county for catholics.[1]

The building of the Parnellite electoral machine was watched with special interest because of the likelihood that it would convert the popularity of the leader into a solid phalanx of loyal followers in the next parliament. Electoral reform enhanced the expectation. The representation of the people act of 1884,[2] giving the vote to male heads of households without requiring a property qualification, increased the Irish electorate from a little under a quarter-million to a little under three-quarters of a million. Democratisation was taken a stage further in June 1885 with the passing of the redistribution of seats act,[3] which allocated seats roughly in relation to population. However, the Irish redistribution was kept separate from that in Britain, so that the country retained its 103 seats and continued to be over-represented in the house of commons.

The most problematic of the new voters were the agricultural labourers. In general they had rallied behind the land league, but in many instances their antagonism to the farmers had been but barely prevented from disrupting the anti-landlord front. Parnell had frequently shown sensitivity to their concerns, and the promotion of their welfare was among the stated objectives of the national league. The challenge was to keep the labourers happy without showing so much concern for them as to alienate the farmers, who had a highly developed sense of proprietorial right when it came to their dealings with those below them in the economic order. Parnell's advocacy of the Labourers (Ireland) Act, 1883[4]—enabling local authorities to provide decent housing for the families of rural workers—was part of his low-key and successful endeavour to assure the labourers that his political enterprise had something in it for them.

The Parnellite organisation was effective, but as an exercise in popular politics it had limitations. It was designed to facilitate the transmission from the top downwards of directives largely concerned with achieving coordination of electoral strategy. While in theory the local branches could have served as political clubs sustaining the lively discourse of aspiring democracy—and no doubt a few of them did—in general they amounted to little more than a formalisation of the political aspect of the authority-orientated catholic parish (and so were much the same thing as most land league branches). There lies a difference between the league and the contemporary mobilisation of working-class and middle-class

---

[1] Emmet Larkin, *The catholic church and the creation of the modern Irish state, 1878–86* (Dublin, 1975), p. 341.

[2] 48 Vict., c. 3 (6 Dec. 1884).

[3] 48 & 49 Vict., c. 23 (25 June 1885).

[4] 46 & 47 Vict., c. 60 (25 Aug. 1883); on the labourer question see Donnelly, *Land & people of Cork*, pp 237–41, and James O'Shea, *Priest, politics and society in post-famine Ireland: a study of County Tipperary, 1850–1891* (Dublin, 1983), pp 119–35.

radical opinion in Britain. And whereas Gladstone was regarded as the embodiment of their ideals by only a section of his party, the image of Parnell the leader suffused the entire Irish movement. The image and the organisation were cultivated not only by Parnell himself but by the efforts of a knot of a dozen or so M.P.s, many of whom disliked the leader but accepted him for the indispensability of his charisma.

Like his radical counterparts in Britain, Parnell had a following that was fired by various and contradictory social and economic grievances, which, particularly the land question, occasionally threatened to divert or disrupt his movement. The advantage of being the leader of a nationalist movement was that Parnell could when necessary call for the deferral of all else pending the achievement of self-government. And the meaning of home rule was itself conveniently vague. A wide variety of constructions could be put on the demand in the constitution of the national league for 'the restitution to the Irish people of the right to manage their own affairs in a parliament elected by the people of Ireland'.[1]

Ironically, one consequence of the great success of the Parnellite party was that it became involved as no Irish group had been for half a century with the higher echelons of Westminster politicians. Popular myth might visualise Parnell as battling the ancient enemy to vindicate Irish nationhood, but the reality was more complex. The two great British parties were not only in competition with one another but each was in turn a coalition of contending cliques and potential leaders. The Parnellites they saw as yet another interest to be weighed in the endless calculations for the acquisition and retention of majorities in parliament. British politicians might have their various principles and concerns and prejudices concerning Ireland or the unity of the empire but at the end of the day their actions were governed by the imperative of winning votes—at Westminster or in the constituencies.[2] Parnell entered confidently into this tangle. He was all the more confident—and all the more deeply drawn in—because of the Irish vote in Britain, greatly increased by the extension of the franchise. The Irish National League of Great Britain was a vibrant organisation and, formal objectives apart, it had more in common with its British contemporaries than with its Irish equivalent.[3]

IN the rich—and richly documented—discourse of the high politics of the 1880s, exchanges and negotiations between the principal actors followed a bewildering variety of channels. Parnell brought a distinctive line to this elaborate signalling system by the use of Captain William O'Shea, M.P., and Mrs Katharine O'Shea as intermediaries. The captain was an Irishman of upper-middle-class catholic

---

[1] Lyons, *Parnell*, p. 236.
[2] A survey of this length cannot deal with the myriad complexities and nuances; see Curtis, *Coercion & conciliation*; A. B. Cooke and J. R. Vincent, *The governing passion* (Hassocks (Sussex), 1974); Foster, *Churchill*; Alan O'Day, *Parnell and the first home rule episode, 1884–87* (Dublin, 1986).
[3] Below, pp 679–84.

background who had not found any means of generating income to match his pretensions. Mrs O'Shea came from an English clergy family with aristocratic connections, and might have hoped to make a better match. By the time of his election to parliament for County Clare in 1880 O'Shea was residing in London in bachelor accommodation paid for by his wife's wealthy aunt, while Katharine and their children lived at Eltham in Kent. On a visit to London in July 1880 as hostess for one of her husband's social evenings Katharine met Parnell. They quickly formed a deep attachment and he became a regular visitor to Eltham. Their first child was born in 1882. The full extent of Captain O'Shea's complaisance is unclear, but he saw the possibility of achieving status at Westminster by acting as intermediary between Parnell and the government. He played an important part in the manœuvres that preceded the Kilmainham 'treaty' of May 1882. Quite independently of her husband's diplomacy Mrs O'Shea became a kind of agent for Parnell, meeting Gladstone on his behalf on three occasions and writing many letters to the prime minister and other important personages.[1] Doors were open to her, as the niece of a former lord chancellor, at which even Parnell might hesitate to knock.

To ascribe Parnell's involvement with Katharine O'Shea to simple infatuation is probably to underrate her place in his career. There was assuredly a meeting of minds and a matching of personalities. And it would be hard to credit that this forceful woman was merely a passive conveyor of messages. We can take it that at least from 1882 onwards Parnell's political actions were informed by the influence and ambitions of Katharine O'Shea. She had put her feckless husband into parliament in 1880; what might she not hope to do with Parnell? It seems probable that, like Captain O'Shea, Parnell was financially dependent on Katharine, or rather on the monies she received from her aunt, Mrs Benjamin Wood. The £37,000 testimonial of 1883 did not lift Parnell out of debt and in subsequent years he continued to lose huge amounts on mining and quarrying enterprises in County Wicklow.[2] With £4,000 a year and a house convenient to London Katharine was a source of security at many levels.

In the autumn of 1884, Captain O'Shea, presumably acting with Parnell's consent, opened an important exchange with Joseph Chamberlain, a key member of Gladstone's cabinet and acknowledged leader of the radical wing of the liberal party. They were soon engaged in the formulation of proposals for a sweeping reform of local government in Ireland, and early in 1885 there emerged an ambitious scheme under which new, democratically elected, local councils would send representatives to a central board that would direct a wide range of matters including poor law, public works, and education.[3] Chamberlain, additionally, intended that the board should have legislative powers, and he made clear that he

---

[1] Lyons, *Parnell*, pp 224–5.
[2] Foster, *Parnell*, pp 190–96; Lyons, *Parnell*, p. 458.
[3] C. H. D. Howard, 'Joseph Chamberlain, Parnell and the Irish "central board" scheme, 1884–5' in *I.H.S.*, viii, no. 32 (Sept. 1953), pp 324–61.

saw it as the definitive answer to the demand for home rule. It was against the background of these negotiations that Parnell on 21 January 1885 made his celebrated assertion that 'no man has the right to fix the boundary to the march of a nation'.[1]

At one level this was powerful platform oratory; at another it was a reminder to Chamberlain, O'Shea, and others (a warning repeated in private correspondence) that Parnell was not prepared to accept the proposed board as a final offer. The game was but beginning and he could hope to do much better by playing it through. Others were indeed eager to accept Chamberlain's proposal, including Archbishop Croke, who informed Cardinal Manning of Westminster of the enthusiasm of the Irish bishops for the project. An intensive round of negotiations involving Manning, Chamberlain, O'Shea, and Parnell resulted in Chamberlain obtaining assurances that if the government adopted a revised scheme of his—with the legislative element now watered down so that it looked less like a substitute for an Irish parliament—Parnell would be favourably disposed and would hold off obstruction of a measure to renew the crimes act for one year. The lord lieutenant, Earl Spencer, however, who fundamentally disliked exceptional coercive measures and hoped to supersede them by a general reform of criminal law for the United Kingdom, was nevertheless not satisfied with a mere one-year renewal, and while he proposed local government reform (along with other ameliorative measures) he was opposed to Chamberlain's more far-reaching scheme. On 9 May a deeply divided cabinet turned down the central board scheme. Shortly afterwards Chamberlain and another radical minister, Sir Charles Dilke, tendered their resignations, though not ostensibly on the local government issue.[2]

From the tory side, too, came various displays of friendly interest. In the early 1880s, while directing a disruptive clique within the tory ranks in the commons (the 'fourth party'), Randolph Churchill had established a rapport of sorts with some of the Parnellites, who were being disruptive for different if not totally dissimilar reasons. Speaking in the house in October 1882 he had referred in flattering terms to Parnell and more than hinted at the potential of a tory–Irish alliance.[3] His Irish experience gave him an advantage and he used it when it suited his purposes. By the second half of 1884 his trouble-making in the wings had won him a place in the party hierarchy, where he was unlikely to forget Ireland, or any other question with potential.

From early 1885 some level of cooperation between Parnellites and tories was evident in the commons; and on 17 February Parnell actually conferred with the opposition chief whip, and subsequently rumours of an understanding abounded. By the middle of May Parnell was conferring with Churchill. On 15 May Gladstone informed the commons that legislation to continue coercive powers in

[1] Lyons, *Parnell*, p. 260; Mitchell & Ó Snodaigh, *Ir. pol. docs 1869–1916*, p. 62.
[2] Lyons, *Parnell*, p. 273; O'Day, *Parnell and first home rule episode*, pp 24–6.
[3] Foster, *Churchill*, pp 58–97.

Ireland was on the way. Five days later Churchill publicly announced that the tories saw no need to renew coercion, and although he subsequently back-pedalled that was scarcely noticed. It was against this background that Irish members turned out in force on 9 June to support a tory amendment to the budget on which a weary government, with many of its own M.P.s suspiciously absent, was defeated. When two weeks later a minority tory government under the marquis of Salisbury took office in the knowledge that the technicalities of the new franchise made the holding of a general election impracticable before the end of the year, politics had entered a period of exceptional uncertainty.

The choice of the earl of Carnarvon as lord lieutenant of Ireland was the act of a prime minister bent on avoiding trouble with the Parnellites. Carnarvon had very advanced ideas on the desirability of Irish self-government, and he had been taken through the question in detail by Sir Charles Gavan Duffy, the Young Irelander, now back from the antipodes after his second career as a lawyer and prime minister in Victoria. The new lord lieutenant soon confirmed the abandonment of coercion and otherwise set about displaying his good will. When the Munster Bank suspended payments in the middle of July 1885 he promised to provide government money in a bid to avert a collapse that would cause serious hardship for many small depositors. Like the minority tory regimes of 1858–9 and 1866–8,[1] but even more markedly so, the first Salisbury government displayed a great eagerness to legislate generously for Irish interests. By the middle of August there was a new and very significant land act,[2] a new act to improve the housing of agricultural labourers,[3] and an act affecting educational endowments, which could only result in their redistribution in a manner favouring catholic secondary schools.[4] Behind the scenes even more startling novelties were unfolded. Carnarvon had a meeting with the vice-chairman of the Irish party, Justin McCarthy, M.P., and in the course of an amicable discussion of Irish policy let it be known that he was personally in favour of home rule. When the lord lieutenant met Parnell in great privacy on 1 August the main topic of discussion was apparently the outline of a home rule scheme.

The Parnellites were not only taking advantage of a pliable government to wring concessions for their supporters while opportunity offered; they were also creating the possibility of cooperation with a tory government after the election. Concurrently there were unmistakable gestures of hostility towards the recently departed liberal government, which had fought the land war and imprisoned the leaders. A proposal by Chamberlain and Dilke to go on a fact-finding visit to Ireland was brutally denounced in *United Ireland*; what killed it was the unhelpful attitude of Irish bishops and of Cardinal Manning, a reminder of how much more promising

---

[1] Above, v, 416–17, 439–42.
[2] Purchase of Land (Ireland) Act, 1885, 48 & 49 Vict., c. 73 (14 Aug. 1885); below, p. 69.
[3] Labourers (Ireland) Act, 1885, 48 & 49 Vict., c. 77 (14 Aug. 1885).
[4] Educational Endowments (Ireland) Act, 48 & 49 Vict., c. 78 (14 Aug. 1885); see also below, p. 579.

tories were as opposed to radicals for those concerned about denominational education. Animus against Earl Spencer's recently departed regime at Dublin Castle lay behind Parnell's decision to put down a motion in the commons for the reopening of capital cases of recent years, including the Maamtrasna affair. One of three men executed for this grisly murder of five members of a Connemara family, in August 1882, was widely believed to have been innocent. The consequent humanitarian concern was used to bludgeon Spencer, but the motivation was political. Asking one administration to reopen its predecessor's business was a violation of unwritten laws and precedents, but that did not deter Parnell. Neither did it deter Churchill, even though he now held cabinet office as secretary of state for India. Other tories were appalled and saw in it all a grim reminder of the hazards of a Parnellite alliance.

The alliance, informal as it was in 1885, was heavily laden with anomalies, not least of which centred on the fact that any concessions to home rule would be anathema to a great many tories. When Herbert Gladstone, son of the liberal leader, urged the tories, in a speech on 14 July, to think about giving Parnell a parliament on College Green, he was attempting to sow discord between the two. The elder Gladstone pursued the same objective more diplomatically. Enquiries directed by way of Mrs O'Shea, as to where Parnell now stood on the 'central board' scheme, brought a response (some days after the tête-à-tête with Carnarvon), which in effect asserted that the stakes were now much higher than six months earlier. When he came to publish his election manifesto in mid-September Gladstone was at his most elusive, juxtaposing a reference to the 'desires of Ireland, constitutionally ascertained' with an expression of qualified approval for 'every grant to portions of the country [i.e. the United Kingdom] of enlarged powers for the management of their own affairs'.[1] But this was the epitome of straight talking when compared with Salisbury's treatment of the Irish question a few weeks later.[2] The fact that the prime minister, who personally had a deep antipathy to any notion of meddling with Ireland's constitutional position, felt it necessary to raise the possibility of such a development—as he did—is an indication of the urgency of the question. In responding to it the party leaders were hamstrung by the exigencies of the British constituencies. In a few score of these the votes of Irish labourers could be decisive. But in these and in many other constituencies there was potential for a powerful backlash against a party identifying with Irish or catholic interests.

Both British parties were allowing the Irish party to envisage the possibility of a substantial constitutional development in the next parliament. The great advantage possessed by the tories was that any measure they might put through the commons was likely to be accepted by the lords. A liberal concession on the constitution was likely to be annihilated in the upper house, unless perhaps Gladstone had received a mandate for it at the polls. For this reason (and others)

---

[1] O'Day, *Parnell and first home rule episode*, p. 91; Lyons, *Parnell*, p. 295.
[2] Lyons, *Parnell*, p. 298.

Parnell pressed Gladstone very hard in the run-up to the 1885 election to give a more unequivocal undertaking. In late October he forwarded privately to Gladstone a draft home rule constitution, an extraordinarily forward move for him. Some days later the liberal leader declared in an election speech that if the vast majority of Irish M.P.s in the new parliament were to demand 'large local powers of self-government' then the question would have to be dealt with as a matter of priority.[1] Parnell immediately and publicly acknowledged the significance of these words but he still insisted that Gladstone should formulate specific proposals before the election. His insistence was in vain.

Two days before polling, when all hope of further movement by Gladstone was gone, Parnell issued a manifesto calling on the Irish in Britain to vote against liberals and radicals.[2] A number of unanswered questions surround this dramatic development. The number of seats captured by the tories with the help of Irish votes has been variously estimated but was probably between twenty and forty. What is not clear is the extent to which Parnell controlled these Irish votes. Cardinal Manning had already indicated that on the basis of educational policy catholics ought to vote tory, and Parnell might have simply exposed the limits of his own influence if he had gone against the cardinal. And in so far as he had discretion there is no telling whether Parnell saw himself as assisting the tories because he thought them to be his most likely benefactors in the new parliament or as endeavouring to cut down the likely liberal majority so that he might hold the balance and be enabled to bargain with Gladstone.[3]

In Ireland the general election was a triumph for Parnell and his machine. Dublin county had been represented exclusively by tories since 1841 and Parnell himself had been soundly defeated there in a by-election in 1874. An increase of almost fivefold in the electorate brought also a dramatic change in its political complexion, with the result that the nationalist candidates were easy winners in each of the two constituencies into which the county was now divided. Up and down the country the same story was repeated, if not always so dramatically: the catholic vote, swelled by the franchise act, rallied to Parnellite nationalism. In only two constituencies was the official home rule candidate challenged by another nationalist: the more serious of these challengers was the colourful and experienced Philip Callan in North Louth, the only home rule M.P. of 1880 to stand against the new party. In a straight contest with the unspectacular Joseph Nolan he won 35 per cent of the vote. Tories—or in a few cases liberals—contested seats throughout the south in the hope of attracting dissident nationalist votes, but all were overwhelmed (though they did have the satisfaction of putting the Parnellites to the expense of a contest). Excluding Trinity College's two seats, the Parnellites carried all before them in twenty-seven counties, including the two seats in Fermanagh; in addition they captured seats in Tyrone (three out of four), Londonderry (one out of three, counting the city), Armagh (one out of three),

---

[1] Ibid., pp 300–01.   [2] Below, p. 674.
[3] O'Day, *Parnell and first home rule episode*, pp 120–21.

and Down (two, including Newry, out of five). Only in Antrim were they unrepresented. Eighty-five of Ireland's 103 M.P.s belonged to the nationalist party, which also had one member—T. P. O'Connor—elected for a Liverpool constituency.

The United Kingdom results as a whole put the liberals exactly eighty-six seats ahead of the tories. This left Parnell holding the balance of power indeed, but not as effectively as he would have wished. He had little to offer the tories: at best he could keep them in office as a demoralised caretaker administration. Carnarvon still advocated the tackling of the Irish constitutional situation but he was shot down so decisively by the cabinet that he quickly resigned. Churchill swung from an urge to leave office as quickly as possible to exploring various stratagems for holding on to power: these ranged from killing home rule with kindly educational or agrarian initiatives to throwing the Irish party M.P.s in jail on a charge of high treason.[1]

An arrangement securing the support of the Irish party would offer the liberals a serious opportunity of retaking and holding office. Even before all the returns were in, Parnell announced himself as expecting the opposition to meet the home rule demand. However, his private approaches to Gladstone failed to elicit any definite undertaking, much less any firm proposals. Behind the veil the liberal leader was moving ponderously towards a home rule policy. Interpretation of his motives tends to dichotomise between moral duty founded on intellectual conviction about Irish nationality, and political manœuvre designed to bring a confused parliamentary situation under his control. However, one explanation does not exclude the other, for Gladstone was adept at infusing what was politically expedient with his gigantic sense of moral obligation. When he took up home rule in December 1885 or early 1886 he ignited a sense of personal mission to put Ireland to rights, and he simultaneously placed himself at the centre of his political universe.

The first public intimation of these momentous developments came in a newspaper interview given by Herbert Gladstone as published on 17 December and subsequently dubbed the 'Hawarden kite', with reference to the elder Gladstone's residence near Chester. The implication—perhaps mistaken—was that the son had been sent to test the wind when he told journalists that his father was about to declare for home rule. The likelihood is that the liberal leader had not intended a public unveiling until later: the precipitate revelation had the effect of killing an attempt he was making to interest the tories in an all-party approach to the Irish question.

After the convening of the new parliament on 21 January 1886 the Irish party took the earliest convenient opportunity to join the liberals in defeating the government, which thereupon resigned. Gladstone became prime minister for the third time on 1 February and in constituting his government he gave the

---

[1] Foster, *Churchill*, pp 240–45.

Parnellites a sure earnest of his intentions by appointing John Morley, a radical advocate of home rule, as chief secretary for Ireland. For nearly two months more the prime minister applied his gargantuan powers to the framing of legislation on Irish land and home rule, taking no more than a few close advisers into his confidence. Not until 13 March did he reveal the shape of his plans to the cabinet as a whole. Then, and at subsequent cabinet meetings, much rancour was in evidence, with Gladstone resisting pressure for modifications. The resignations of Chamberlain and G. O. Trevelyan on 26 March raised the likelihood that a sufficiently large section of the party would reject the proposed measures to cause their defeat and the downfall of the government. Even if Gladstone realised at this point that he had miscalculated, he had no choice but to press on.

Gladstone had Parnell's draft for a home rule constitution[1] to hand when framing his own scheme, but the Irish party was not consulted. On 5 April, just three days before introducing his government of Ireland bill in the commons, Gladstone finally agreed to see Parnell but he was in his most pedagogical mood and had no inclination to take advice. Reporting back to a small group of his most prominent M.P.s Parnell guarded his own position by emitting expressions of disappointment, but he must have been quite pleased with what was on offer.

All pronouncements about constitutional change in Ireland emanating from British sources—and most of those from Irish sources also—had carried weighty stipulations about the preservation of the union and the supremacy of the imperial parliament. The home rule bill[2] sought to provide for an 'Irish legislative body' with wide domestic powers but with no function in a series of 'imperial' matters ranging from the making of peace and war to control of military forces, coinage, and customs and excise. Gladstone was especially eager to have what he saw as the great Irish social evil—the land problem—made the responsibility of the Irish legislature. But he wished to ensure that mere superiority of numbers would not enable its opponents to overwhelm the propertied interest. To counterbalance precipitate democracy he had an ingenious scheme. The unicameral Irish legislature would have within it two orders. The first would consist of twenty-eight representative peers and seventy-five others meeting high property qualifications (a minimum of £4,000 or an annual income of £200) elected by voters meeting a £25 qualification. The second order was to consist of 204 members elected in accordance with the current United Kingdom franchise. Normally both orders would sit and vote as a single chamber, but either could demand a separate vote on any particular issue, and exercise a veto. In the case of the first order the veto would have a three-year limit.

The land measure[3] prepared by Gladstone alongside the home rule bill would have facilitated the sale of tenanted land to the occupiers on statutory terms, and can be seen as another device intended to ease the fears of landlords unwilling to

[1] Above, p. 61.
[2] Reproduced in O'Day, *Parnell and first home rule episode*, appendix II, pp 234–51.
[3] Ibid., appendix III, pp 252–73.

trust their future welfare to the proposed new political regime in Dublin. However, a more subtle interpretation sees the land bill as a concession to the tenant interest, and one that Gladstone may have envisaged not as an accompaniment to the home rule bill but as a possible alternative legislative gesture to the Irish party in the parliamentary session of 1886. In any event, both bills were introduced in the commons in April 1886. Both were lost, the land bill through effective abandonment, the home rule bill in a memorable defeat.[1]

For all its safeguards the government of Ireland bill proposed embarkation on a startling and unpredictable course. Nothing exemplified this better than the provision for an end to Irish representation at Westminster. For some British politicians, including Gladstone presumably, this was one of the great attractions of the scheme; but while the prospect of a return to 'normal' two-party politics might be appealing it was easy for those so inclined to see the removal to Dublin as a prelude to total separation, a token of menace to Britain and of diminution of the empire.

Just as Gladstone would not have taken his initiative if it had not promised to suit his party purposes, so it was now opposed by many not on its merits or demerits but out of political calculations and antipathies. The tories with few exceptions combined sentiment and opportunism in opposing home rule. Within a matter of weeks it was clear that the prime minister could not hope to hold his own party together on the subject, as whigs led by Lord Hartington, and a significant number of radicals following Chamberlain, raised insurmountable objections or demanded impossible concessions. In the early hours of 8 June the government of Ireland bill was lost on the second reading by thirty votes, with more than ninety liberals voting against.

The general election of July 1886 precipitated by Gladstone's defeat on home rule consolidated the position of the nationalist party. Sixty-five Parnellites were returned unopposed; losses in South Tyrone and South Londonderry were balanced by gains in West Belfast and (following a petition) in Derry. Counting T. P. O'Connor's Liverpool seat the total was again eighty-six. All the evidence suggests that defeat in the commons, far from demoralising the party's following, only served to install Parnell all the more securely as the patriotic champion. The financial terms of the home rule bill were widely criticised as being disadvantageous to Ireland, but outside of a numerically insignificant minority it did not matter that the measure of self-government offered by Gladstone and declared by Parnell in parliament and elsewhere to be acceptable as a final settlement fell so far short of sovereignty or the ideals of national self-determination. 'Home rule' for most of its followers remained as it had been from the beginning an assertion of a sense of identity and an expression of discontent over grievances but possessing little or no doctrinal content.

---

[1] See John Vincent, 'Gladstone and Ireland' in *Proceedings of the British Academy*, lxiii (1977), pp 225–9.

The home rule initiative secured Gladstone's leadership of the liberals but at the cost of diminishing the party. From the 335 seats won by liberals at the end of 1885, the general election of 1886 reduced Gladstone's following to 191 seats, while 75 were taken by those who had parted company with him—henceforth known as liberal unionists. Profiting from liberal divisions, the tories increased their representation to 300 and Salisbury became prime minister for a second time. Parnell, who in 1885 had instructed the Irish in Britain to vote against the liberals, spent much of July 1886 working up support for liberal candidates in British constituencies. An ironical consequence of the political success of the home rulers was that they became more than ever before part of the Westminster system. And the English statesman who had endeavoured to remove the Irish representatives from the imperial parliament became once again, as he had been in the late 1860s, a popular hero in Ireland.

THE euphoria of home rule predictably encompassed Irish-America. Following the home precedent the American Land League gave way in April 1883 to the Irish National League of America. With Clan na Gael pulling the strings the presidency of the new body went to Alexander Sullivan of Chicago, who had replaced John Devoy as the most influential individual in the Clan. The league was launched with great ambitions and some of its founders envisaged it becoming the central and dominant representative of Irish-American political opinion and action.[1] Following the well established laws of Irish-American associational life the Irish National League of America lived a torpid existence until high action became visible in Ireland in 1885-6.

The league and other American sympathisers provided the Parnellite movement in Ireland with funding. Money was vital to the success of the Irish nationalist party as it had been for the conduct of the land war. Without a ready supply of money for the customary and statutory expenses of electioneering Parnell could not have carried the series of by-elections from 1880 onwards that demoralised all opposition, and without ready cash for train fares and hotel expenses the crucial convention system of 1885 could not have been operated. It was the availability of money for stipends and expenses that made possible the forging of an unprecedentedly disciplined parliamentary party out of the M.P.s of 1885 and 1886.[2] While direct income from the U.S.A. was low in the early years of the national league, Parnell had at his back the residue of the land league funds, which were preponderantly of American origin. In 1885 and 1886 money flowed in very substantial amounts from the Irish National League of America and other transatlantic sources. From 1886 to 1890 the Irish party disbursed over £116,000, including approximately £48,000 in salaries to M.P.s, over £28,000 in election expenses, and about £13,000 for a sophisticated propaganda project in Britain, the Irish Press Agency.[3] To the extent that like most political movements money was

---

[1] Thomas N. Brown, *Irish-American nationalism 1870–1890* (Philadelphia, 1966), pp 155–68.
[2] O'Brien, *Parnell and his party*, pp 133–6.   [3] Ibid., p. 267.

sine qua non for its success, the Irish parliamentary party, like the fenians and the land league, is scarcely conceivable without the burning interest of so many Irish-Americans in the homeland.

Once Gladstone brought home rule into the realm of practical politics Irish-America assumed another kind of importance: here was an example of what could be expected from the 'Celtic race' when given its head. Accordingly, advocates of home rule cited the progress, prosperity, and sobriety of the Irish in America. Opponents depicted them as feckless troublemakers, corrupt Tammany Hall operators, and violent fanatics. The campaign of bombing in British cities, initiated under O'Donovan Rossa's direction in 1881, was intensified in the period 1883–5 with the participation of emissaries of Alexander Sullivan's wing of Clan na Gael. On 14 January 1885 explosions rocked Westminster Hall, the Tower of London, and the house of commons chamber. It is impossible to say to what extent anger about the bombings may have affected British public attitudes to home rule. In any event a consensus that further explosions would be detrimental to Parnell's progress was one factor that discouraged a resumption, although one further campaign was attempted in 1887. Parnell sent a high-powered delegation to the convention of the Irish National League of America meeting in Chicago on 18 August 1886 for the purpose of ensuring that disappointment with the defeat of home rule in parliament and in the British constituencies would not lead to the adoption of extremist attitudes. Moderation prevailed. For all the veneration given his name and leadership in America, especially from 1886 to 1890, it is noteworthy that Parnell never returned there after his hasty departure in March 1880. An important part of his genius lay in knowing what *not* to do. Unsurpassed adulation awaited him, but also perhaps factional jealousies and loss of mystique.

ALTHOUGH about a dozen of the Irish party M.P.s of 1885 and 1886, including Parnell himself, were protestants, the thrust for home rule was perceived, not least by the mass of voters, as essentially an assertion of catholic power. Polarisation of voting along religious lines was a concomitant of the consolidation of Parnell's party and of the further democratisation of the electoral system. The process was most evident in Ulster. There liberals had done well in 1880, drawing on the support of presbyterian and catholic tenants. At a by-election in Tyrone in September 1881 there was remarkable cross-confessional support for the victorious Gladstonian liberal candidate. Less than two years later a by-election in Monaghan (where two liberals had been returned in 1880) provided evidence of a significant change when a home rule candidate, T. M. Healy, took the seat with almost all the catholic vote (and a small number of votes from presbyterian farmers impressed by his contribution to the 1881 land act). The subsequent promotion of national league organisation throughout Ulster took on the character of an invasion in many protestant eyes and prompted the beginnings of a counter-mobilisation that moved the Orange order towards the centre of political life. By 1885 the catholics were incorporated into the home rule machine, and while many protestant farmers remained with the liberals, protestants of every other class were looking to the tories as the defenders of the constitution. To complete the ruin of the liberals, Parnell's followers, in a number of constituencies without home rule candidates, voted for the tories, who won all the non-home-rule seats.

The intimation in late December of Gladstone's option for home rule sparked off a lively mobilisation in Ulster. By 1 February the newly formed Ulster Loyalist Anti-Repeal Union, with the cooperation of the Orange order, had launched a series of demonstrations. The most celebrated was that of 22 February in Belfast, addressed by Lord Randolph Churchill. Taken with other pronouncements before and after, his Belfast speech was reminiscent of the Parnellite style: it was sufficiently emotive to win an ecstatic response; he toyed with illegality in envisaging the struggle becoming extraconstitutional; at the same time the language did not mean all that the audience might take it to mean and was sufficiently vague to permit of subsequent back-tracking. Nevertheless, Churchill's Ulster foray (together with the motto 'Ulster will fight and Ulster will be right', which he coined some months later) signified the emergence of opposition to home rule as the touchstone of tory orthodoxy for the years ahead.

Tory encouragement reinforced the unionists' objections to home rule: that their religious and civil liberties would be menaced by a catholic-dominated Dublin government not only out of sectarian animosity but through Tammany-Hall-style corruption; and that the industrial economy of the north-east would be wrecked by any breach of the union. In the outline proposals for an Irish constitution submitted to Gladstone in October 1885 Parnell envisaged 'special arrangements for securing to the protestant minority a representation proportionate to their number' in an Irish legislative assembly.[1] Of course the problem as the protestants saw it was that even such an apparently generous guarantee would still condemn them to subordination. In any case landowners and gentry were the only Irish protestants who were of serious political importance in Parnell's eyes, and this was even more true of Gladstone. The home rule bill had complex provisions for protecting the political power of the landed minority but nothing similar for the religious minority. The proposed Irish legislature was indeed to be prohibited from making any law 'respecting the establishment or endowment of religion or prohibiting the free exercise thereof or imposing any disability or conferring any privilege on account of religious belief' but that, even with guarantees about denominational education and corporate bodies, did very little to placate protestants. The publication of the bill drove Ulster liberals, with few exceptions, into alliance with the tories and the Orangemen, a development formalised in the shape of the Ulster Liberal Unionist Association, founded in June. A remnant had just formed the interesting, but numerically insignificant, Irish Protestant Home Rule Association.

---

[1] O'Day, *Parnell and first home rule episode*, appendix 1, p. 232.

The idea of making special provision for Ulster or part of Ulster—possibly by an assembly and local administration quite independent of Dublin's—had already been well aired in 1885, and very soon all the inherent problems had been exposed. There would still be a minority problem on each side of any dividing line. The confessional minority question was one that Gladstone wished to sweep under the carpet. And protestants were hopeful that recognition of their difficulty would result in the total defeat of home rule rather than some special provision for the north-east. In Orange circles there were proposals for a refusal to pay taxes to a Dublin administration, and vague talk of massive armed resistance. Temporary deliverance came with the defeat of the home rule bill and the return of a tory government at Westminster. In Ulster the 1886 election witnessed a further consolidation of protestant voters behind the unionist cause, while catholics were even more solidly united behind the nationalists.

Just as the home rule mobilisation created a nationalist party at Westminster, so too did it produce by way of response an Irish unionist party when in 1886 the Irish tory members began to meet and act as a separate group, devoted above all else to keeping the wider tory party up to the mark on home rule.[1] This perfected the incorporation of Irish preoccupations into the parliamentary system. Drawing its strength from the north-east, from some Irish holders of Scottish and English seats, and from the two members returned by the graduates of Trinity College, Dublin, it was as distinguished in its own way as the nationalist party. While the latter group was remarkable for the number of journalists it contained, the unionist party bristled with lawyers. It was symptomatic of the changes in Irish politics over a short period of years that the first leader of the unionist party, Colonel E. J. Saunderson, M.P. for Armagh North from 1885, had been returned unopposed as liberal M.P. for his native—and predominantly catholic—County Cavan in 1865 and 1868.

The summer of 1886 brought a stark reminder—in the form of Belfast riots—of the depths of the popular feelings that underlay the polarisation at the polling booths. The trouble began in early June and continued spasmodically until August. In a particularly violent five-day period in the latter month eight persons were reported killed and more than 120 injured. Most of the violence occurred in clashes between protestants and the Royal Irish Constabulary, with catholic groups less frequently involved. The rioting was allegedly sparked off when a catholic worker at Harland & Wolff's shipyard taunted a protestant with the threat that home rule would mean no more jobs for protestants. The threat may or may not have been made: what matters is that it had verisimilitude. A political conflict that was understood in such terms by the rank and file was unlikely to be resolved as readily as Gladstone and Parnell and Churchill and other practitioners of high politics might assume.

[1] Alvin Jackson, *The Ulster party: Irish unionists in the house of commons, 1884–1911* (Oxford, 1989), pp 44–52.

BEHIND the high political spectacle of 1885 and 1886 the land question was once again coming to a crisis. Poor seasons, falling prices, and weak markets in 1884 and following years served to underline the fact that the 1881 act had not removed the basic problem. Even among those with rents fixed judicially—usually at a much lower level than previously—there were many for whom the latest decline in prices rendered payment extremely difficult if not impossible; and the judicial rents were fixed for fifteen years. More seriously, in the popular mind the legitimacy of agricultural rents had been undermined, so that at the first setback even those who could well afford to pay had no qualms about defaulting on any available pretext. The conciliatory gestures of the tory administration in 1885, including the abandonment of special legislation when the crimes act of 1882 expired, could only reinforce the confidence of the tenants in the correctness of their instincts. Thoughtful tories had been saying at least since 1882 that the answer to the land problem lay in adequate provisions for the voluntary sale of holdings to the occupiers. The land purchase act of 1885[1]—drafted by Lord Ashbourne (lord chancellor 1885–6, 1886–92)—provided government loans to the purchasing tenant covering the whole of the purchase price and at a rate of interest sufficiently low for the annual repayment to be less than the late rent.

The course was thus set for a task that would take decades to accomplish. But it was no instant panacea and by the autumn of 1885 not a few branches of the national league, especially in the south-west, were taking up where the land league had left off three or four years earlier, by inaugurating the 'second phase' of the land war.[2] From such areas came reports of combinations against 'unjust' rents, backed up by league courts and boycotting. With the encouragement of some leading nationalist M.P.s many rent strikes occurred towards the end of 1885 but as no financial assistance or other encouragement was forthcoming from the national league headquarters—though it had been expected—these local efforts collapsed fairly quickly. The politicians were deterred from too close an identification with agitation while they were playing for high stakes at Westminster, and this constraint remained until after the general election of 1886.

The second Salisbury government, on coming to office in July 1886, gave early evidence of constructive, if unformed, intentions by appointing a commission to investigate the working of the land acts of 1881 and 1885.[3] With a view to securing some interim amelioration Parnell moved the tenants relief bill in September 1886, proposing that judicial rents be open to immediate review and that the courts be given power to disallow eviction if a sum of half the arrears and half the current rent had been paid. Its rejection by the government was a relief to landlords, who read it as a 50 per cent cut in their rents. But the defeat of this potentially moderating influence was welcome also to those lieutenants of Parnell

---

[1] Above, p. 59.
[2] Donnelly, *Land & people of Cork*, pp 308–76.
[3] The Cowper commission; see *Report of the royal commission on the Land Law (Ireland) Act, 1881 and the Purchase of Land (Ireland) Act, 1885* [C 4969], H.C. 1887, xxvi.

who relished the prospect of a new round of agrarian agitation. As parliament went into recess the circumstances of autumn 1880 were uncannily duplicated: immediate relief had been refused, but there was an implicit promise of later concessions, whose generosity was likely to be a direct reflection of the intensity of agitation in the interim. But this time Parnell was determined to be cautious. He agreed to the setting up of a national league fund to assist evicted tenants but he displayed no inclination to give a lead, and it was Dillon who set the headlines for a new round of politician-directed and centrally coordinated agitation, in a form subsequently disowned by the party leader.

Dillon enunciated on 17 October 1886 a scheme adumbrated earlier by Tim Healy, subsequently filled out and finally set down by another M.P., Timothy Harrington, and published as a 'plan of campaign'. Tenants were given clear directions and succinct legal advice as to how they could combine to force rent reductions. All the tenants on an estate should agree on what was a fair rent and collectively tender that amount to the landlord or agent. In the event of rejection the reduced rent should be handed over to a trustee to constitute a fighting fund. If evicted, tenants would be supported from the fund while it lasted and subsequently, if necessary, by the national league. The promise was that this course would 'reduce to reason any landlord in Ireland'.[1]

The plan of campaign was promoted vigorously by Dillon, William O'Brien, and a dozen or so M.P.s besides, at public meetings up and down the country. Travelling organisers and some priests also played vital roles. It has been calculated that over a period of three years the plan was adopted on just over 200 Irish estates ranging in size from less than 100 acres to more than 100,000.[2] Some landlords settled almost at once; others carried through evictions and then settled; yet others evicted their recalcitrant tenants and held out with the aid of the Land Corporation of Ireland and other organs of landlord solidarity; in a number of cases new tenants were brought in, usually from Ulster.

The estates where the plan was enforced were not necessarily those where the landlords were most grasping or the tenants hardest pressed. The organisers were waging war against an institution rather than seeking justice for individuals. This class struggle was invested with the rhetoric of a national and holy war, and the weapons used included the boycott and intimidation as well as the rent strike and public demonstrations. The crusader premise served again, as in the earlier phase of the land war, to justify departures from normal standards that would otherwise be denounced as such. Thus the archbishops of Dublin and Cashel both gave approval to the plan. Other bishops viewed the matter very differently. Faced with conflicting advice from Ireland the Vatican dispatched Archbishop Persico to the country on an extensive fact-finding mission in 1887. In the light of his findings, and prompted by British representations, the Congregation of the Holy Office issued a solemn condemnation of the plan of campaign, and of boycotting, in

[1] Laurence M. Geary, *The plan of campaign, 1886–1891* (Cork, 1986), p. 145.
[2] Ibid., pp 151–78.

April 1888. The Irish M.P.s responded with an assertion of their independence of Rome in political matters. The assembled bishops reiterated their loyalty and obedience to the holy see but fudged the implications in order to avoid exposing their disagreements. If nobody was seen to give way before the papal rescript and if some priests appeared to dismiss it truculently, that is not to say that it had no effect on the subsequent attitudes of bishops, priests, and laity.

Whatever its moral ambivalences, the plan of campaign, like the land war of 1879–82, did draw on the well-springs of popular nationalist feeling and the energy of a vibrant socio-economic interest. For tenants on the vast majority of estates not taking part, it was a vicarious war from which they could hope to benefit as their own landlords pondered the risks of refusing abatements. Turning the goodwill of non-participants into financial aid was the primary objective of the Tenants' Defence Association set up by the Irish party on 24 October 1889 with Parnell's consent but without his active assistance; but the formal objective of the new organisation was defensive and it appealed both to supporters of the plan of campaign and those who wished to see the campaign wound up without loss of face. A series of county conventions and chapel-gate collections amassed £61,000. The total collected in Ireland in support of the plan from 1886 to 1890 was almost £130,000[1] (not including more than £40,000 deposited by participating tenants), a sum that compared very favourably with indigenous subscriptions to various other Irish causes from O'Connell's time onwards.

Sir Michael Hicks Beach (chief secretary, July 1886–March 1887) was very wary of committing the forces of the crown to the support of evicting sheriffs, so much so that in January Chief Baron Christopher Palles publicly upbraided the authorities for failure to fulfil their legal obligations in this regard. Hicks Beach's successor was Arthur James Balfour, the 38-year-old nephew of the prime minister, and one of the few British statesmen whose reputation was to be made in Ireland. Balfour, too, did what he could to make unreasonable landlords see sense but he was prepared to enforce the law of the land relentlessly. Evictions began at once on plan of campaign estates and in the early summer public opinion in Britain and in Ireland was excited by mass evictions such as those at Bodyke in Clare and Luggacurran in Queen's County. This was the great era of the transportable battering-ram and of the set-piece eviction scene, producing images that have been frequently superimposed on earlier times.

Balfour's hand was greatly strengthened by the Criminal Law and Procedure (Ireland) Act passed in July 1887.[2] This permitted the private questioning under oath by a resident magistrate of an individual believed to have information relevant to crimes. A series of offences associated with agrarian agitation were made amenable to summary jurisdiction and so could be determined—subject to a maximum sentence of six months imprisonment—at petty sessions where resident magistrates and justices of the peace sat without juries. As a further

---

[1] Ibid., p. 141.   [2] 50 & 51 Vict., c. 50 (19 July 1887).

measure against the intimidation that made it so difficult for juries to convict in political or agrarian cases, the attorney general was empowered to move cases from one county to another. The enforcement of the new act gave rise to many confrontations including one particularly serious incident at Mitchelstown, County Cork, on 9 September 1887 during a protest meeting held outside the court to which O'Brien and John Mandeville, a local gentleman farmer, had been summoned on a charge of incitement to resist eviction. The crowd impeded the repeated efforts of a force of constabulary to approach the platform escorting a police note-taker, a figure customarily tolerated at such gatherings. Driven back inside their barracks by a hail of stones and sticks, the panic-stricken constables opened fire on the crowd, killing two and injuring dozens, one of whom subsequently died of his injuries. The consequent outcry on both sides of the Irish Sea did not deflect the authorities—numerous activists including a few dozen M.P.s were jailed on summary convictions over the next few years—but the 'Mitchelstown massacre' undoubtedly taught both sides a lesson about the limits beyond which the conflict could not be allowed to pass. Some of the loudest protests against the tyranny of 'Bloody Balfour' came from the Irish party's liberal allies, who a few short years before were themselves pursuing coercion in Ireland. Their new emphasis was calculated especially to embarrass the liberal unionists, on whose support the government to some extent depended, and especially Chamberlain.

Balfour fought against the plan of campaign both in his official capacity and privately.[1] It was at his insistence that a syndicate of wealthy landowners was formed to sustain the Ponsonby estate near Youghal. Chagrin at the success of this resistance brought the wrath of plan supporters down on the spokesman of the syndicate, A. H. Smith-Barry, and the attempt to get even with him led the promoters of the plan into the disastrous venture of 'New Tipperary'. Smith-Barry was the landlord of much of Tipperary town, and, under the influence of a local curate, David Humphreys, and others, the shopkeepers were persuaded to leave their premises rather than pay ground rent, and to set up business in new—and inferior—facilities nearby. The cost of supporting this venture was a most serious drain on the available funds, and when most outstanding instances of the plan collapsed in 1891 no surrender was more abject than that of New Tipperary.

IF the coercion act of 1887 was an embarrassment to the liberal unionists, they had some compensation in the influence they exerted over the terms of the accompanying land act.[2] As enacted (and to the great disgust of many government supporters) this had many resemblances to Parnell's failed bill of the previous year. Judicial rents fixed in the period 1881–6 could be reviewed at once, and all

[1] Catherine Shannon, *Arthur J. Balfour and Ireland, 1874–1922* (Washington, D.C., 1988), pp 36–44.
[2] Land Law (Ireland) Act, 1887, 50 & 51 Vict., c. 33 (23 Aug. 1887).

future judicial rents could be reviewed after three years. Leaseholders were admitted for the first time to the benefits of the 1881 act. And where a tenant could not pay his rent and could show a county court judge that this was through no fault on his part, the court could give him an extended time to pay his arrears and forbid an eviction. This came too late to prevent the plan of campaign from gathering a head of steam, but it undoubtedly had the eventual effect of moderating the practical grievances and hardships in which agrarian agitation was grounded, and it contributed handsomely to the falling off of the second phase of the land war in the closing years of the decade.

By about 1890 the main (if largely unarticulated) question about the agrarian problem was: under what terms would the landlords' interest be bought out by the occupiers? If the proprietorial stake were to be whittled down in law to its level in nationalist propaganda and popular estimation, the farmers would have their land for next to nothing. Hence the small interest of tenants outside Ulster in taking up the Ashbourne act: they hoped, in a home rule Ireland, to get the land more cheaply, and perhaps—as the platform orators hinted—for nothing. Tory politicians, like most landlords, accepted the inevitability of peasant proprietorship, but they were determined that the vendors should be paid a price reflecting their current nominal income from the property—the rent. The 1885 act was supplemented in 1888 by further legislation, which in essence provided more money for land purchase.[1] By 1891, after many years of preparation, Balfour had ready another purchase scheme under which the burden on the treasury was eased by paying landowners in government bonds.[2]

Of course, turning tenants into owners on any terms whatsoever would do nothing to solve the problem posed by holdings too small and unproductive to support their occupiers. Parnell was keenly aware of this problem and in 1884, along with Captain O'Shea, he had ventured some money in a private (and unsuccessful) scheme to provide for migration of smallholders to more economic farms.[3] The land act of 1891 created a congested districts board empowered, among other things, to purchase land and create viable holdings in the poorest districts on the western littoral from Donegal to Cork. The board offered advice on modern farming methods and promoted small local industry. It also took charge of relief projects of a kind that Balfour had initiated in 1890 to counteract the effects of a serious potato failure in that year.[4] New roads, harbours, piers, and a series of light railway lines were the result. Many thousands had been given temporary employment and a communications infrastructure had been created which was a monument to goodwill and hope, if not to realism. The 'saving of the west' was on its way.

The interest of so many liberal M.P.s and propagandists in the agrarian campaign (one English M.P. was actually jailed in Ireland under Balfour's

---

[1] 51 & 52 Vict., c. 49 (24 Dec. 1888).
[2] Purchase of Land (Ireland) Act, 1891, 54 & 55 Vict., c. 48 (5 Aug. 1891).
[3] Lyons, *Parnell*, p. 263.   [4] Below, pp 86, 283-7, 587-9.

coercion regime), taken together with Parnell's pointed distancing of himself from the same movement, serves to highlight the progress of the 'union of hearts' between the liberals and Parnellites. The Irish party leader now assumed, in liberal eyes, the appearance of a respectable and trustworthy statesman, and himself took to describing Gladstone in most laudatory terms. The liberal leader followed up his embracing of home rule by adopting a strain of historicist Irish nationalist rhetoric such as the unerudite Parnell could never match.[1]

The old polarity of parliament was reasserting itself and as surely as the liberal unionists were settling into an alliance with the tories (a combination now usually called unionist), even more obviously were liberals and Irish nationalists sheltering together contentedly under the one umbrella of home rule. The coalition would be committed to its own dissolution if it meant to carry through home rule on the exact terms of the 1886 bill with its provision for the ending of Irish representation in the imperial parliament, but, as Gladstone began to consider the details with his senior colleagues and with Parnell in 1888 and 1889, exclusion began to look less and less like practical politics. The existence of a Dublin parliament, whatever its exact shape, need not imply the complete banishment of the Irish nationalist M.P.s from the metropolis, which for so many of them was home.[2] The 'agrarian' M.P.s might be more persistently troublesome in Ireland than even the most advanced of their British radical colleagues could be in the constituencies, but at Westminster the conformity to custom and precedent after 1886 was most striking. Before the end of the decade the Parnellites were being chided for poor attendance and inattention to parliamentary business—the very failings that they had once denounced so purposefully in their home rule opponents.

By cultivating the connection with the liberals and keeping them up to the mark on home rule Parnell made himself appear as the almost certain arbiter of Ireland's destiny after the next general election. At the same time he was drawn all the more directly into the white heat of British party conflict, while government partisans sought to find in his past the Achilles heel of the opposition alliance. That Parnell had condoned illegality during the land war and that his collaborators had included people on both sides of the Atlantic associated with fenianism were matters of public knowledge. A series of articles in *The Times* under the heading 'Parnellism and crime', running from March to December 1887, sought to establish that his complicity was even deeper and darker than appeared. The newspaper's evidence included a purported letter from Parnell—reproduced in facsimile in the issue of 18 April 1887—conveying that his condemnation of the Phoenix Park murders had been a mere pretence. More material of the same kind was produced in court by counsel for *The Times* when Frank Hugh O'Donnell brought a libel action arising out of references to himself in the controversial

---

[1] James Loughlin, *Gladstone, home rule and the Ulster question, 1882–93* (Dublin, 1987), pp 172–96.
[2] Alan O'Day, *The English face of Irish nationalism: Parnellite involvement in British politics, 1880–86* (Dublin, 1977), pp 23–4.

articles. The letters were forgeries naïvely bought by *The Times* from Richard Pigott, the indigent former owner of the *Irishman*, who bore a deep grudge against everyone connected with the new departure of the late 1870s. Parnell requested a select committee to investigate the letters. Instead the government put through parliament an act[1] establishing a special commission of three judges to investigate the charges of *The Times* in their totality, including those relating not only to Parnell but to his closest political associates. By departing in this way from the conventions of judicial procedure the government was using state power for party purposes, a point that was underlined by the appearance of the attorney general as counsel for *The Times*. The chief secretary, Balfour, who played a central part in this strategy, was a good match for Parnell: both were unhampered by any sense of unwritten constitutional principles, or moral conventions, or political ethics, governing the operation of political life. Sensitivity to the 'taint of illegality' was for devotees of the bourgeois liberal world-view, not for aristocrats.

The special commission sat 128 times between October 1888 and November 1889. Its highlights included the appearance of Thomas Miller Beach as witness for *The Times*: for twenty-five years, under the name of Henri Le Caron, he had lived as a British agent at the heart of fenian and Clan na Gael activity in the U.S.A. In 1881 he had been sent to Europe as a Clan envoy and in this revolutionary guise had conferred with Parnell in the very palace of Westminster. However, not even Beach could establish a sufficiently tangible link between Parnell and serious crime, and in the great mass of evidence put before it the special commission found nothing to damn the Irish party leader. The turning-point of the tribunal's history was the uncovering through cross-examination that Pigott had forged the controversial letters. The effect of the special commission was to enhance Parnell's stature on both sides of the Irish Sea and to exorcise the ghost of past illegalities. But another spectre soon hove into view.

Just as his revulsion from the plan of campaign tended to keep Parnell out of Ireland during the years of the liberal alliance, so his private 'union of hearts' with Katharine O'Shea gave him a positive incentive to remain in England. Following the death of their first child in 1882, a daughter was born to them in 1883 and another in 1884, Captain O'Shea's honour being preserved by the fiction that he was the father. O'Shea refused to take the Irish party pledge before the 1885 general election, presumably because it would bar him from the political advancement that he hoped for from the liberals. Having failed to win a seat in England as a liberal he turned to Parnell to secure his return at the Galway city by-election of February 1886. In one of his most brazen political manœuvres the leader prevailed upon the party to drop a local candidate and accept in his place an outsider who refused to take the party pledge. Four months later, when O'Shea walked out of parliament rather than vote on the home rule bill, it was clear that both his political and his personal relations with Parnell had deteriorated badly.

---

[1] 51 & 52 Vict., c. 35 (13 Aug. 1888).

The expectation that his wife would inherit a large fortune from her aged aunt kept O'Shea from drastic measures, of which the most obvious was a divorce petition. When 'Aunt Ben' died in May 1889 leaving her entire fortune of £140,000 to Katharine but in such a way as to exclude her husband from benefiting from it, Parnell found himself enmeshed in a legal tangle more challenging than any political problem. The cast of the unfolding drama included O'Shea, Katharine, her disappointed siblings, and a chorus of lawyers who would insist on pushing matters at least to the point at which they received their fees. O'Shea made a tentative move on 24 December 1889 by filing a petition for divorce in which Parnell was named as co-respondent. It appears likely that he expected an offer from Katharine's side—the sum of £20,000 was subsequently mentioned in this connection—in order to secure the dropping of his case. Parnell also apparently expected matters to follow this course: his followers would then be confirmed in the belief that the divorce petition had been yet another ploy of his political opponents. But, with the disputed inheritance frozen, money to buy off O'Shea was not forthcoming, and the trial of his petition went ahead in November 1890. Parnell and Mrs O'Shea had not prepared any defence, with the result that there was no challenge in the court to the opposing counsel's detailed, biased, and unflattering account of their liaison. The court's ruling in favour of O'Shea freed Katharine to marry Parnell—which she did in June 1891 when the decree was made absolute—but it created insurmountable political problems.

Parnell's lieutenants and his episcopal supporters had swallowed so many camels over a decade or more that they were slow to accept that this time they would have to disown him. Davitt, no longer a lieutenant since 1882, was the first to recognise, and to say, that Parnell would have to go. Perhaps the Irish catholic collectivity could have tolerated in its protestant hero flagrant departures from the code that it enforced so strictly on its own members; but there was no possibility that Gladstone's nonconformist following could suffer a continued alliance with a politician subjected to moral disgrace in the high court as Parnell had been. On 25 November 1890 (the date determined well in advance for what had since 1880 become an annual formality) the Irish party unanimously reelected Parnell as chairman, some members naïvely believing that this would be the prelude to a dignified voluntary resignation. Gladstone responded by expressing publicly (as he had already endeavoured to convey privately) that Parnell's continued leadership would make his own position untenable. In other words, the maintenance of the 'union of hearts' and of the liberal commitment to home rule demanded the retirement of Parnell, at least temporarily.

Parnell's answer to this sentence of political death was a combination of the self-centredness, ruthlessness, and brilliance that had made him a great charismatic leader in the first instance. Vain were the hopes that he would put the cause—the liberal alliance, or party unity, or home rule—before his own ambition. On 28 November 1890 he issued 'to the people of Ireland' a manifesto of breathtaking audacity. Without any reference to the divorce proceedings that were the cause of the current trouble, he accused the liberals of endeavouring to undermine the independence of the Irish party. Belying the policy that he had pursued assiduously for so many years, and jettisoning the 'union of hearts', he denounced what he alleged were the limitations of liberal plans for home rule, and in so doing broke the confidentiality of discussions he had held with Gladstone at Hawarden in December 1889. He was to be repeatedly reminded in the days and weeks ahead that at the time he had publicly expressed his extreme satisfaction with the Hawarden negotiations. But consistency mattered little in his calculations. Since he no longer had a future with the liberals he was reverting to the policy of independence and on this basis he intended to consolidate his leadership of the party, throwing off those who refused to follow, as he had previously discarded so many of the home rule M.P.s of 1880. It remained to be seen how many would resist—and how effectively—the alternative of being discarded or being led into the wilderness.

The issue of Parnell's continued leadership was debated by the Irish party in Committee Room 15 of the house of commons from 1 to 6 December 1890. Parnell used his position as chairman to thwart any decisive motion of his opponents, who were clearly in a majority. A Parnellite motion to remove the business in hand to an Irish venue was defeated by forty-four votes to twenty-nine. The one ray of hope to light up the gloomy proceedings was the endeavour to obtain undertakings from Gladstone about the contents of his home rule plans, upon receipt of which undertakings Parnell might stand down. But the hope was misleading: Gladstone found it impossible to offer anything, and in any case there was nothing cast-iron about the intimation of Parnell's willingness to retire. Despairing of any definite outcome to the deliberations, the anti-Parnellites, forty-five in all, withdrew on 6 December leaving Parnell with twenty-eight followers. Both sides would recruit from the absentees and the eventual breakdown was probably fifty-four to thirty-two.

The verdict of Irish voters on the contending factions would be crucial, and an early sampling of this was forthcoming in the Kilkenny North by-election of 22 December. In the final weeks dozens of M.P.s descended on the constituency, Parnell giving vigorous leadership on his side. The dominant figure on the other side was not one of the M.P.s but Davitt. He more than anyone had been responsible in 1879–80 for setting Parnell's career on a heightened trajectory; his forceful intervention in December 1890 helped to ground his old leader. Even more decisive was the contribution of the priests directed by Abraham Brownrigg (bishop of Ossory 1884–1928) and urged on by Thomas Croke (archbishop of Cashel 1875–1902), one of the most politicised of prelates.

The bishops had strengthened the resolve of the anti-Parnellites just before and during the debates in Committee Room 15, but, Archbishop Walsh setting the tone, they did so with notable circumspection. They held back because they preferred to have the parliamentarians strike the first blow, and because, like so many others, they hoped that Parnell would end the nightmare by providing some honour-saving reinterpretation of the divorce court revelations. Failing that, the bishops could scarcely be seen as less censorious than the English nonconformists, but not until 3 December did their standing committee issue a statement declaring that Parnell was unfit, on both moral and political grounds, for the leadership. Once battle was joined between the rival factions, political necessity and, as they saw it, the interest of religion demanded that the bishops should spare no effort in the anti-Parnellite cause. Not all priests followed the episcopal lead but most of them in Kilkenny North did, and the defeat of the Parnellite candidate that they helped to secure by extraordinary effort was of vital significance.[1] The chief was not invincible.

Six M.P.s, including Dillon and O'Brien, being in the U.S.A. to raise funds for the plan of campaign, participated in the events surrounding the split only indirectly—through the newspapers and transatlantic telegrams. As a group they leaned heavily to the anti-Parnellite side. However, distance gave them a detached status and some of them became the focus of a desperate attempt to repair the split. Basing himself in Boulogne (because a prison sentence awaited him on his return to British jurisdiction) O'Brien conducted a series of negotiations between late December and early February, Parnell crossing the Channel to meet him on a number of occasions. A scheme was devised whereby Parnell and Justin McCarthy (the leader of the anti-Parnellites) would resign simultaneously. Dillon would head a reunited party and lead it into the coming general election and a new parliament, which—it was expected—would have a majority in favour of home rule. In various ways Parnell was guaranteed great influence in the party and his eventual return to the leadership was not precluded. One of his demands was the obtaining from the liberals of guarantees about some features of the next home rule bill, including Irish control of the constabulary. These guarantees would be seen as concessions wrung from Gladstone by Parnell as the price of his standing down. The liberals did offer guarantees of the kind sought, but Parnell declared them to be inadequate and so ended the hopes of a negotiated solution.[2] It is doubtful if he could ever have brought himself to submit to terms from his lieutenants. He would no longer have been Parnell.

Through the spring, summer, and autumn of 1891 the struggle was waged in Ireland. Parnell travelled the country indefatigably, weekend after weekend, addressing his supporters and preparing for the general election at which he hoped once again to work his magic. He had installed a reliable supporter as editor of *United Ireland*, and the *Freeman's Journal* was on his side until September. The anti-Parnellites issued their own daily, the *National Press*, from March onwards. Bitter verbal abuse became the currency of rival newspapers and platforms. Most wounding were the many ribald references to the revelations of the divorce court. On both sides the abuse could pass from verbal to physical: Parnell received an

---

[1] The Parnellite candidate received 1,362 votes against his opponent's 2,527; at a further by-election ten months later the anti-Parnellite candidate was returned unopposed.
[2] Lyons, *Parnell*, pp 549–75.

eye injury when a white substance, apparently lime, was thrown at him in Castlecomer, while in Cork Parnellite groundlings roughed up T.M. Healy, the most outspoken and wounding of the chief's opponents. However, the intensity of the conflict should not detract from the fact that it was conducted within limits that testified to a reasonably sophisticated political culture. This was already suggested by the ability of the party majority to decide on the deposition of its charismatic leader in the face of complex political difficulties. In the struggle that followed there was no organised resort to physical force; lines of communication across the divide were maintained; and within a decade party unity was to be restored. All of this suggests a very favourable comparison with the performance of the successor nationalist élite, the Sinn Féin party of 1918, when it faced its time of testing in 1921–3.

Even if Parnell's refusal to accept the majority decision of his parliamentary party colleagues was inspired by a primal egotism, his appeal to the country was nothing if not sophisticated. Then and later his supporters could see themselves as upholders of an ideal and defiers of self-serving politicians and oppressing churchmen. However, any defence of Parnell has to face the fact that in refusing to surrender his post he defied the cardinal principle of representative democracy, namely that when the votes go against them leaders give way, no matter how mistaken or misguided they may believe the voters to be. Although it might be said that in this, his final contest, Parnell drew the support of many for whom the psychic thrills of nationalism outweighed its practical applications, there is no simple guide to the alignment of forces. In reality there was principle and opportunism on both sides, playing on the complex of interests, loyalties, and connections, collective and local, that went to make up the world of Irish nationalist politics. Those fenians who still resented the disruption of their own world by the land war and the rise of the parliamentary party now rallied to Parnell as to the opponent of party. O'Leary, Stephens, and—from a very particular perspective—Devoy all declared for Parnell, who encouraged such support by ambiguous pronouncements about the alternative to constitutional home rule. Observing the first stirrings of modern trade union organisation in Ireland, Parnell was prepared to take advantage of it; he addressed a conference of labourers in Dublin on 14 March 1891. And speaking in Belfast in May he adopted the friendliest of lines towards the Ulster protestants, a group that he had previously ignored or dismissed.[1]

By-elections for North Sligo in April 1891, and for Carlow in July, were both won by anti-Parnellites, but, taken together, they suggested that Parnell still had much to fight for in the general election, especially as everyone knew that Dublin—both city and county—was a stronghold of his supporters. But he did not live to see the general election. The physical and mental strain of his incessant campaign played havoc with a physique already affected by kidney disease,

---

[1] Paul Bew, *C. S. Parnell* (Dublin, 1980), pp 128–30.

rheumatism, and possibly heart disease. Following a few days' acute illness he died at Brighton on 6 October 1891 in his wife's presence. He was 45.

Charles Stewart Parnell was gifted beyond most men with political qualities of a particular kind. We do not know how well he would have exercised executive authority, but that he possessed an instinctive, unsurpassed capacity for the exercise of political leadership is patent. In the Ireland of the 1870s and 1880s he found conditions that offered this capacity very full scope. From 1886 the task became more difficult but ultimately it was his luck rather than his instincts that betrayed him. He presided over a time of great changes in Irish public life and he helped to shape these changes, but he can hardly be seen as the author of change, and some of it he would have preferred to stop dead in its tracks. For instance, he scarcely wished for the social and political overthrow of the gentry that the land war helped to precipitate.

A major source of change in Parnell's time was the upheaval in agricultural and industrial prices and in consumer demand on the British food market—and in western Europe generally—that began in the 1870s. Innovations in processing and manufacturing were coupled with the new or greatly increased availability of supplies from North America, Argentina, Australia, and New Zealand. Farmers in Denmark, Sweden, Normandy, and the Netherlands responded by becoming more competitive in terms of quality, reliability of supply, and diversity, and generally making advances in dairying, bacon production, and horticulture. Did the political developments of which Parnell was the figurehead blind Irish farmers to the necessity of economic initiative and instil in them the delusion that the solution to their problems lay in acquiring—at the expense of the landlords—a greater share of the declining proceeds of static production? Parnell did indeed have high hopes for the economic progress of a self-governing Ireland but he did nothing to inspire Irish farmers to find out how two blades of grass might be made to grow where one grew before. If a particular mental attitude is vital for economic initiative, so too is capital. The land war boosted the capital of middle-sized and large farmers but perhaps at the cost of diminishing the sum total of the capital value of Irish land. There is no guarantee that much of this would have gone into new agricultural enterprise in any event, but after 1879 the possibility did not even exist.

Parnell's charismatic political leadership undoubtedly gave a boost to the collective self-confidence of his catholic nationalist followers, which had been slowly rebuilding since the famine, and to which in his person and name he gave enduring expression. He had less success in directing the country towards any of the more substantial bases of self-respect, such as economic enterprise, intellectual achievement, or cultural enrichment. That is to say that his genius, and his bequest to the country, were confined to the arena in which—thanks in no small measure to Parnell himself—nineteenth-century Ireland excelled, namely party political mobilisation.

CHAPTER IV

The aftermath of Parnell, 1891–1903

F. S. L. LYONS

IT is strange how the pendulum of historical fashion can swing from one extreme to another even within the space of a single generation. It was formerly commonplace for historians to regard the two decades following the death of Parnell as a political vacuum that remained untenanted until the reunion of the Irish parliamentary party in 1900, and the return of the liberals to power six years later, allowed the struggle for home rule to be taken up again almost as if nothing had changed in the interval. The post-Parnellite record of the parliamentary party, however, cannot be dismissed as an embarrassing appendix to a volume already closed. To do so would be to overlook the constitutional movement's dominant position in the life of the country at least up to 1914 and, no less serious, it would also be to underestimate the extent to which continuity was subsequently preserved between a party that had experience but no power and a dáil that had power but no experience. Equally, however, it is plain that it will not suffice to view the home rule crisis of 1912–14 as a simple continuation of those of 1886 and 1893. It will not suffice because the Ireland of 1912–14 was not the Ireland either of 1886 or 1893. Too many things had happened in the intervening years for comparison to be more than superficially valid.

This narrative will attempt to review—and hold a reasonable balance between—the various developments that competed for attention in the aftermath of Parnell, but the task presents formidable problems of selection and arrangement. Almost any scheme will appear arbitrary and open to objection, but it may serve the interests of clarity to suggest that while the whole period from 1891 to 1914 may indeed be regarded as a unity, within that unity a watershed occurs between about 1903 and 1907. To put the same point in another way, it will be argued here that, between 1891 and the middle of the first decade of the twentieth century, events in Ireland moved not only sedately but in a variety of directions that at first sight seem, if not random, at least to have little obvious connection with each other. After the watershed (which itself will have to be examined in its place) many different paths begin perceptibly to converge. The pace quickens and the complexity deepens almost year by year. Before long we become conscious of an impending crisis far larger and more dangerous than any in the memory of those then about to be drawn into the vortex.

If we turn now to the earlier of these two periods, the first and most obvious fact to be recorded is the impotence of the parliamentary party. Whatever hopes might have been secretly cherished that the Parnellite and anti-Parnellite factions might join hands over the leader's grave were shattered almost before his coffin was lowered into that grave. He was buried in Glasnevin on Sunday 11 October 1891. On 10 October *United Ireland*, still the mouthpiece of his adherents, printed a hysterical editorial in which it not only repeated the old charge that Parnell had been 'sacrificed by Irishmen on the altar of English liberalism', but added for good measure that he had been 'murdered . . . as certainly as if the gang of conspirators had surrounded him and hacked him to pieces'.[1] It was hardly surprising that when the funeral procession moved through the city the following day his opponents were conspicuous by their absence; indeed, the temper of the Parnellite crowd was such that if they had appeared they would quite literally have been taking their lives in their hands.

However, as Parnell himself had found to his cost, Dublin was not Ireland; and the events of the next few months, culminating in the general election of 1892, indicated clearly enough that in the country at large the Parnellite cause enjoyed only limited support. John Redmond, the new leader of the Parnellite party, was defeated when he contested his chief's seat in Cork city; and although he won Waterford city shortly afterwards, this was partly due to family influence, and even that did not save him from having a very rough passage. What this meant in national terms was demonstrated in the general election itself, when the Parnellite group was reduced to nine members compared with the solid seventy-one seats (seventy-two if T. P. O'Connor's Liverpool constituency be included) retained by their opponents.[2] The Parnellites did not disappear, as might perhaps have been predicted. On the contrary, they continued to maintain their own organisation, the Irish National League; their own newspaper, the *Irish Daily Independent*; and their own separate existence in the house of commons, where, indeed, their strength actually went up to eleven after the general election of 1895. But despite this brave show of independence, nothing could conceal the fact that they had failed to carry the country with them, or that, apart from Redmond's prestige as a parliamentary orator and the respect still accorded to one or two individuals such as Timothy Harrington or Patrick O'Brien, they had little to contribute to the mainstream of Irish political life.

But was there any longer such a thing as a mainstream? Increasingly, it came to seem as if there was not and as if all the enthusiasm and passion engendered by Parnell in his prime must now waste themselves in the arid desert of internecine strife. It cannot, however, be too often stressed that the most deadly

---

[1] *United Ireland*, 10 Oct. 1891.

[2] Cf. above, pp 64–5. In 1892 the nationalists lost Dublin County South, Fermanagh North, and Londonderry City to unionists, and Belfast West and Dublin (St Stephen's Green) to liberal unionists.

and damaging aspect of this strife was not the open, honourable, and perfectly comprehensible war between Parnellite and anti-Parnellite. It was rather the semi-secret, half-veiled vendetta between two sections within the anti-Parnellite party itself that did more than anything else to discredit the parliamentarians in the eyes of the public and to turn people's minds towards other and less squalid forms of nationalist activity. The roots of the quarrel went back to the original split in the party. It will be recalled that in the absence of John Dillon and William O'Brien the main burden of conducting the campaign against Parnell had fallen not on the gentle and ineffective chairman of the anti-Parnellites, Justin McCarthy, but on T. M. Healy, whose love–hate relationship with his leader had already—at the Galway election of 1886—involved the party in its one serious internal crisis before 1890.[1] In fighting his duel to the death with Parnell— both on public platforms and in the newspaper, the *National Press*, which he ran almost single-handed—Healy had gone to savage extremes of vilification. But this savagery, while it no doubt sickened and alienated many moderates and helped to destroy all hope of reconciliation, struck others as no more than appropriate to the occasion. It was observable that among these others were numbers of the catholic clergy whose bishops, after an initial period of pru-dent reserve, had thrown their full weight against Parnell in the last phase of his career.

Even at the time it had seemed to Dillon and O'Brien, watching helplessly from Galway gaol, that Healy was consciously constructing a clerical party, which would serve him as a power base for the future when Parnell was dead and done with.[2] Whether or not their apprehensions were well founded (and the evidence suggests that they were), when they reemerged into public life they found to their distaste that the struggle into which they were reluctantly drawn seemed to concern itself less with principle than with the debris left behind after the fall of Parnell. The immediate point of conflict was over the question of whether or not the *National Press* should be amalgamated with the *Freeman's Journal*. The latter was a late convert from Parnellism, but it was a genuinely national newspaper and far more eminent than the *National Press*. Eventually Healy was forced to allow his paper to be amalgamated, but the ill-tempered negotiations dragged on so long that at one point it appeared likely that the party's performance at Westminster during the crucial home rule debate in the summer of 1893 would be jeopardised by the withdrawal of one key member, Thomas Sexton, who, as chairman of the *Freeman's Journal*, was deeply involved in the controversy. This particular disaster was averted, but the archbishop of Dublin, William Walsh, spoke for many nationalists when he asked pointedly how anyone 'could now regard them as a

[1] Above, p. 75.
[2] For the role of the catholic clergy in the 1892 election, see C. J. Woods, 'The general election of 1892: the catholic clergy and the defeat of the Parnellites' in F. S. L. Lyons and R. A. J. Hawkins (ed.), *Ireland under the union: varieties of tension. Essays in honour of T. W. Moody* (Oxford, 1980), pp 289–319. For the later and wider role of the church in politics, see David W. Miller, *Church, state, and nation in Ireland, 1898–1921* (Dublin, 1973).

body in whose hands any public interest would be safe . . . So far as I am concerned, the party has committed political suicide.'[1]

This was an exaggeration, though during the next few years it was often to seem the only possible verdict open to reasonable men. The bickering over the newspaper war spilled over into related, and equally bitter, disputes over membership of the committee that supposedly governed the party and over the choice of candidates for vacant parliamentary seats. The details of these unedifying squabbles need not concern us. They seemed to reach a climax after the general election of 1895, when the divisions within the anti-Parnellite ranks were openly and ruthlessly advertised by both groups. Nevertheless, although that election was marked by disgraceful scenes, it did produce a slight but significant shift in the balance of power. As a result of this it proved possible in August 1895 to expel Healy and his more vociferous supporters both from the national organisation, the Irish National Federation, and from the committee of the parliamentary party. When in the following year Dillon took over from McCarthy as chairman of the majority section, his firm, if sometimes dictatorial, style of leadership did something to restore morale. Even so the irrepressible Healy remained for some time further a thorn in the side of his former colleagues. Before long he had formed his own organisation, the People's Rights Association, and it was not until the major drive for unity succeeded at the turn of the century, in circumstances soon to be described, that he was finally isolated and rendered politically impotent.

In the broad perspective of history the quarrel between Dillonites and Healyites may seem a triviality over which it is unnecessary to linger. Yet it ought not to be dismissed out of hand, for in three distinct ways it affected the future of the home rule movement. The first and most obvious of these was that it brought that movement into discredit at precisely the moment when constitutional nationalism needed all the support it could get. The downfall of Parnell might be justified if it could be seen to have preserved intact a unified and powerful party. When what in fact emerged from the split were three divided and powerless parties, the movement of opinion away from the parliamentarians was both immediate and profound.

In another sense, however—and this was the second significance of the controversy—the disgusted onlookers who were sickened by the methods used by both sides were misled by their aversion to the means into failing to realise how important were the ends involved. In reality two vital and interrelated issues were in dispute. On the one hand, Dillon's fight against Healy could be seen as an endeavour, in the end successful, to prevent Irish politics from being dominated by a 'clerical' party, with all the sinister implications for home rule that that was likely to have. And on the other hand, the fight could be seen as a conflict between localism and centralism. What Healy seemed to be saying, and what his short-

[1] Walsh to Dillon, 11 June 1893, quoted in F. S. L. Lyons, *John Dillon* (London, 1968), p. 150.

lived People's Rights Association was dedicated to proving, was that the individual politician ought to be directly responsible for his words and actions to his own constituency. What Dillon was asserting was—to adopt the phraseology of a resolution he carried successfully at an eve-of-session meeting of the party in January 1897—that 'unity and discipline' were central to the continued existence of a properly functioning parliamentary party. The party must be a tightly controlled instrument, as it had been in Parnell's day, or it would be nothing. In Parnell's day, admittedly, control had been exercised by a dictator, and the establishment of a governing committee immediately after the split had begun had been a laudable attempt to democratise the leadership. Laudable, but ineffective; and it was no surprise to anyone when Dillon, after he had settled into the saddle, allowed the committee system to expire. This is not to say that his own personal rule did not encounter criticism. On the contrary, it encountered such acute criticism that he was constantly on the verge of resignation. But this should not obscure the fact that by the time he was ready to vacate the chair he had maintained intact among the anti-Parnellites the essentials of the old-style Parnellite party. Though shaken by their experiences and reduced to all sorts of humiliating shifts to keep their organisation afloat, they still remained a party composed of individuals who, so far from being mere delegates from their constituencies, were pledged to 'sit, act, and vote together'.

The full consequences of this victory—for it was nothing less—belonged to the future, and the benefit would be reaped by other hands than Dillon's. Meanwhile, however, it was he who had to reckon with the third, and on the face of it the most damaging, consequence of the party's continuing disunity. This was of course the fact that it was in no condition to apply the same sort of pressure at Westminster as Parnell had applied in his prime. Thus, although the general election of 1892 had resulted in the return of the liberals to power—but dependent for that power on the Irish nationalist vote in the house of commons—and although Gladstone duly fulfilled his pledge to introduce a second home rule bill in the summer of 1893, even this ritual gesture was made only after fierce internal argument within the liberal party. Everyone knew, in fact, that it could only be a ritual gesture and that a home rule bill that got through the commons (as this one did) solely on the strength of the Irish vote would be mercilessly destroyed by the house of lords.

When this duly happened, and when in March 1894 Gladstone at last retired, the Irish factions were soon made to realise that they faced a new and bleak situation. Gladstone's successor, Lord Rosebery, lost no time in making it brutally plain that before home rule could be conceded 'England, as the predominant member of the partnership of the three kingdoms, will have to be convinced of its justice and equity'.[1] This was no more than the truth, but to blurt it out in this fashion was hardly tactful. Not surprisingly, unionists were filled with

---

[1] *Hansard 4*, xxii, 32 (12 Mar. 1894).

jubilation and nationalists were correspondingly dismayed. But among the latter there was a significant differentiation. Whereas the followers of Redmond and Healy treated Rosebery's remark as virtually ending the liberal alliance, Dillon, as the spokesman for the main anti-Parnellite section, did not allow his deep resentment of Rosebery's outburst to deflect him from his settled policy of maintaining the closest possible contact with Gladstone's heirs. Indeed, no other course was open to him. Parnell had been sacrificed because the choice for Ireland had seemed to narrow down to a choice between the man and the demand for home rule; and since, after 1886, it seemed as if only the liberals were prepared to meet the demand, to break with them *after* jettisoning Parnell would have been nothing less than suicide. In time to come, this stoical acceptance of unpleasant realities was to pay dividends after a fashion, but nothing could disguise the result that in 1894 and for a dozen years thereafter the liberal alliance was so anaemic as to be almost invisible. To be fair, however, the blame for this was by no means wholly to be laid at the door of any of the Irish parliamentary factions. The liberals themselves were in scarcely better case after Gladstone's retirement than their Irish allies after Parnell's death. Rent by personal rivalries and unable to agree on a coherent programme once the cohesive influence of home rule had been withdrawn, they drifted miserably into the general election of 1895 where they went down to substantial, predictable, and deserved defeat. For the next ten years power was to rest firmly in unionist hands.

For Ireland this new turn of fortune's wheel was to have enduring consequences that could scarcely have been anticipated at the time. Between 1886 and 1892, the tory government had been associated with 'resolute government', and the idea that a peaceful social revolution might stem from such a regime would have been dismissed as laughable. Yet precisely this was what was now about to happen. It had in fact already begun to happen in the closing years of Salisbury's second administration, for it was in 1891, when most people's minds were on other things, that the chief secretary, Arthur Balfour, succeeded in carrying a land act of major importance.[1] To contemporaries the most striking feature of this act was that it provided a larger sum for state-aided land purchase—£33 million—than any previous act, but in practice the process of buying was made so complicated that tenants were easily discouraged, while landlords were alienated by the device of paying them not in cash but in land stock, whose value was only too vulnerable to market fluctuations. The outcome was, therefore, that although a further act was passed in 1896[2] in an attempt to retrieve the situation, the amount actually advanced under the scheme was only £13.5 million, while the number of tenants utilising it to buy their farms, though not inconsiderable (47,000), was much less than had been expected.[3]

In the long run, however, the real significance of the 1891 act was that it broke genuinely new ground in quite a different direction. This was the attempt,

[1] 54 & 55 Vict., c. 48 (5 Aug. 1891).   [2] 59 & 60 Vict., c. 47 (14 Aug. 1896).
[3] Below, pp 274–5.

through the establishment of the congested districts board, to relieve poverty in the remoter parts of the south and west of Ireland. The board consisted of the chief secretary himself, two land commissioners, and five experts appointed by the government. Its objects were to develop local industries by subsidies and technical instruction; to amalgamate uneconomic holdings by promoting land purchase; to assist migration from impoverished areas to the newly amalgamated holdings; and to improve the quality of agriculture in the congested districts themselves. A congested district was defined as one in which the total rateable value divided by the number of inhabitants amounted to less than 30s. (£1.50) per person. In 1891 this definition covered an area of slightly more than 3.5 million acres (1.4 million hectares) and a population of about half a million, spread over parts of the counties of Donegal, Leitrim, Sligo, Roscommon, Mayo, Galway, Kerry, and Cork. In the course of time this area was extended until by 1910 it was twice what it had been in 1891, while the income available to the board had grown from the initial grant of £41,000 to over half a million pounds. No doubt the board made mistakes, but these were minimised by the practice that it early established of detailed investigation of local conditions (right down to poor law union level and beyond) and of intelligent application of resources not merely to land purchase and agricultural education, but also to the encouragement of cottage industries, the stimulation of fishing, and the building of roads, bridges, and harbours.[1] To these benevolent and, on the whole, beneficent labours should be added the incentive given by Balfour between 1889 and 1891 to the building of light railways.[2] Devised originally as a means of providing employment, especially during the recrudescence of famine conditions in 1890, these played an important role in opening up the far west and bringing the people into contact with the remainder of the country.

All this was to the good, but, like most governmental initiatives at this time, Balfour's reforming policy suffered from the fact that it, like the tenants whom it was designed to placate, was primarily concerned with the tenure and transfer of land rather than its cultivation. Consequently, while two decades of almost incessant legislation had certainly done much to clarify the relations between tenants and landlords, they had done little or nothing to improve the quality of agriculture. The congested districts board indeed pointed in that direction, but its sphere of operation was by definition limited. Ultimately this function too would come within the purview of the government, but, as so often happens in such cases, the running was made in the first instance by a private individual. This was Sir Horace Plunkett. Born in 1854, the third son of the sixteenth Baron Dunsany, he had lived the life of a rancher for ten years in Wyoming but had returned to Ireland in 1889 to manage the family's estates and also to oversee its

[1] For a more critical assessment of the achievements of the congested districts board, see Eunan O'Halpin, *The decline of the union: British government in Ireland, 1892–1920* (Dublin and Syracuse, N.Y., 1987), pp 12–14; see also below, pp 283–7, 587–9.
[2] Under 52 & 53 Vict., c. 66 (30 Aug. 1889).

business interests in England. Unmarried, energetic, of a turn of mind at once practical and visionary, Plunkett saw in the Irish countryside the challenge he needed to absorb his surplus energies. For him the remedy for agricultural backwardness was luminously self-evident—it was cooperation. But cooperation itself was only a means to the greater end of diverting the average Irishman's attention from home rule agitation to economic self-help. Plunkett was a unionist in politics, of a somewhat eccentric kind (he was in fact to end as a supporter of dominion status),[1] and it was often to be argued against him that his much vaunted social reforms were in reality a subtle means of preserving the political *status quo*. This was less than just. Plunkett certainly was an outspoken critic of his fellow countrymen—the fact that the critic seemed so invincibly assured of his own rightness did nothing to make his criticisms more palatable—but he directed his derogatory remarks with a fine impartiality alike at tenant and landlord, priest and minister, businessman and politician. Those who thought of him as a gigantic red herring missed altogether the central fact about him, which was that he was as much concerned with national regeneration as any of those who gave that concept the kind of political interpretation to which Plunkett himself always remained unalterably opposed.

Although his considered ideas did not reach a wide public until the appearance in 1904 of his outspoken and controversial book *Ireland in the new century*, Plunkett had by that time begun to make a considerable impact both on Irish agriculture and on Dublin Castle. His earliest tentative step towards agricultural cooperation—more specifically, the creation of cooperative dairies, or 'creameries'—was taken as early as 1889 when with immense difficulty he founded his first society at Doneraile. Despite the opposition of conservative farmers and suspicious parish priests, he acquired allies—the Jesuit, Father Tom Finlay; Lord Monteagle; a young land-agent, R. A. Anderson; and the poet A E (George William Russell)—with whose help he began to spread his gospel. By 1894 there were over thirty cooperative societies in existence, and Plunkett felt strong enough to launch a permanent body, the Irish Agricultural Organisation Society. Within ten years of its establishment there were 876 cooperative societies, with an annual turnover of some £3 million.

Inevitably, Plunkett was drawn on from this essentially private initiative into a public career. In 1891 Arthur Balfour appointed him one of the founding members of the congested districts board and in 1892 he entered politics by winning the South Dublin seat as a unionist in the general election of that year. Three years later, with home rule to all appearances dead and buried, he suggested that Irishmen of diverse political persuasions should combine to press on the government the need to create a special department of agriculture and also to stimulate 'technical' or vocational education. Not all politicians accepted his

---

[1] For Plunkett's development up to openly describing himself as a home ruler in 1911, see for example Trevor West, *Horace Plunkett: cooperation and politics, an Irish biography* (Gerrards Cross and Washington, D.C., 1986), pp 109–19.

invitation—the Ulster unionists and the followers of Dillon both remained aloof and critical—but Plunkett received enough support to enable him to hold a series of conferences during the parliamentary recess of 1895. When the report of this group—known as the recess committee—was published in 1896, it was at once obvious that Plunkett had secured substantial backing for his ideas.

Not too much should be made of the revolutionary character of this all-party cooperation. It was for the very limited and specific purpose of extracting money from the treasury, and did not extend beyond that. Indeed, an incident the very next year suggested that unanimity even in the agreeable pastime of despoiling the government could not be counted on indefinitely. During the home rule debate of 1893 Gladstone had promised a commission to inquire into the financial relations between Britain and Ireland. In 1896 this body—the Childers commission—reported (with various minority reservations) to the effect that Ireland had been overtaxed since the union.[1] The report understandably caused a sensation in Ireland and out of the clamour there emerged in 1897 the All-Ireland committee, which was even more widely representative of the political spectrum than the recess committee had been. But when a conference was summoned to consider what action should be taken, Dillon's suggestion that all Irish parties unite to press the government for early redress was unpalatable to the Irish unionists, and since no formula could be found, the government was able to shelve the commission's report with impunity. Such were the springs of cooperation and their limitations.

Fortunately, conditions were propitious for Plunkett's movement. The return of the unionists to power in 1895 signalled a resumption of the policy of 'killing home rule with kindness'[2] and though we shall presently have to question some of the premises on which that policy was constructed there can be no denying that its immediate effect was to maintain the flow of beneficial legislation for Ireland. Thus one of the first constructive steps taken by the new chief secretary—Arthur Balfour's brother Gerald—was to pass the land act of 1896,[3] which increased the amount of money available for purchase under the 1891 act and also reduced the complications surrounding the process of land purchase. Two years later he successfully carried through a reform that had eluded his predecessor but was arguably one of the most important measures to have been carried by a British government during the entire nineteenth century. This gave

[1] See also above, v, 784–94; below, pp 327–31.

[2] For a consideration of the origins and significance of Gerald Balfour's phrase and of how it has tended to obscure the complex motives behind unionist policies in this period, with particular reference to the reform of Irish local government, see Andrew Gailey, 'Unionist rhetoric and Irish local government reform, 1895–9' in *I.H.S.*, xxiv, no. 93 (May 1984), pp 52–68. Gailey examines the same subject in ch. 1 of his *Ireland and the death of kindness: the experience of constructive unionism, 1890–1905* (Cork, 1987), which also includes (pp 35–50) a discussion of tory land policy in this period. Gailey has argued that there was 'a discrepancy between intention and outcome' in the 'constructive unionism' of both Balfour brothers. See also Gailey, 'Failure and the making of the new Ireland' in D. G. Boyce (ed.), *The revolution in Ireland, 1879–1923* (London, 1988), pp 61–5, 67–70.

[3] 59 & 60 Vict., c. 47 (14 Aug. 1896).

Ireland a system of elected local government on the lines adopted in Britain in 1888, with county councils and urban and rural district councils. Elected on a wide franchise (which included women), the new councils took over the admin- istrative and financial functions of the old grand juries (though not their legal functions) and were eligible for treasury grants as well as being empowered to levy their own rates. Inevitably the councils over most of the country were strongly nationalist in character, and in time this was to be a political factor of considerable importance. But their real significance was more profound. On the one hand they provided a potentially invaluable forum for training in self-government; on the other, they marked a decisive shift away from the traditional leadership of the landlords and towards the dominance of a new bourgeoisie of shopkeepers, publicans, and farmers.[1]

In 1898 a countryside where tenants had become owners still seemed a distant enough prospect, but enough had already happened to maintain the impetus of Plunkett's recess committee. Almost immediately, in 1899, their persistence was rewarded by the creation of the department of agriculture and technical instruc- tion and by the installation of Plunkett himself as its first vice-president. In effect Plunkett became a minister though he was still responsible to the chief secretary. The new department took under its wing not merely the areas of activity indicated in its title, but also fisheries, the collection of agricultural statistics, the prevention of plant and animal disease, the supervision of the national museum and the national library, and (from 1905 on) the geological survey of Ireland. It was equipped, perhaps over-equipped, with semi-representative bodies, but although these did undoubtedly do something to bring the department into direct touch with the rural population to which it was presumed to be ministering, the organisation soon began to suffer from bureaucratic elephantiasis, which in turn led to complaints of delay, rigidity, and conservatism. Nevertheless, within the limits that it set itself, it did make commendable efforts to improve the quality of certain aspects of agriculture, though the necessity to work within a strict budget prevented it, even if it had been so disposed, from achieving anything like an agricultural revolution. Perhaps, if Plunkett had remained in charge of it for a long period, he might have been able to weld the two parts of his vision—private cooperation and public assistance—into a coherent whole. But this was not to be.[2] He lost his seat in parliament in 1900, and although he was able to continue as vice-president so long as a unionist government remained in office, the return of

[1] For a more critical evaluation of the effects of the local government reform, see Joseph Lee, *The modernisation of Irish society, 1848–1918* (Dublin, 1973; 2nd ed. 1989), pp 127–8; while admitting the administrative benefits accruing from Balfour's legislation (61 & 62 Vict., c. 37 (12 Aug. 1898)), O'Halpin argues (*Decline of the union*, p. 16) that the reforms were the 'fortuitous outcomes of the chief secretary's efforts to safeguard the essentials of his policy, rather than . . . an essential part of that policy'. See also below, pp 590–94

[2] See O'Halpin, *Decline of the union*, pp 18–21, for an account of the clashes between the department of agriculture and technical instruction and the congested districts board, and for difficulties that arose from Plunkett's personality and style of management; and below, pp 282–7, 588–94.

the liberals to power in 1906 signalled his doom. In 1907 he was manœuvred into retirement—mainly, it must be said, as a result of nationalist pressure—and was succeeded by T. W. Russell, an Ulsterman (and liberal unionist M.P. for Tyrone South) with a possibly inflated reputation for defending the interests of the tenant farmers. Evidently he did not rate agricultural cooperation very high among those interests, for one of his first actions was to cut off the department's grant to the Irish Agricultural Organisation Society. For the next few years—until a fresh grant was made available in 1913 from the newly established development fund—Plunkett's own money was virtually all that kept his dream alive; and although the cooperative movement seemed in good health on the eve of the first world war—in 1914 it had over a thousand societies, with a turnover of more than £3.5 million—its impact on rural conservatism had been less than his sanguine expectations had originally led him to hope for.

A similar charge might be directed against the department of agriculture, and in both cases the explanation is the same. These efforts to guide farmers towards more efficient methods of production and marketing always had a faintly *ad hoc* air about them, because they were devised in a situation that was itself in a state of permanent flux. Neither the cooperative movement nor the department asked the key question about Irish agriculture—what was the right kind of development to make it truly competitive in the modern world?—because, despite Plunkett's own desire to guide the debate into more constructive channels, most men, and virtually all farmers, were still obsessed by questions of tenure rather than of technique. Until 'the land for the people' became a reality rather than an aspiration, no one had much time for discussion about how the land itself should actually be used. But a final irony remained. Because 'the land for the people' was automatically assumed to involve the creation of a multitude of small family farms worked by their owners, the political crusade to bring about this end was dedicated, whether the fact was realised or not, to buttressing precisely that rural conservatism that Plunkett had been seeking to demolish.

We shall understand this paradox better if we realise that at the very moment the department of agriculture and technical instruction was coming into being, the west of Ireland—and soon parts of the south as well—was in the grip of yet another land agitation. Like the land war it began in Mayo, and like the plan of campaign it looked to William O'Brien for leadership, but as it developed it turned out to be significantly different from those earlier upheavals. O'Brien had withdrawn from politics in the mid-1890s and had, somewhat ostentatiously, dissociated himself from the squabbles of the various parliamentary factions, though his close personal friendship with Dillon ensured that his lines of communication with the anti-Parnellite majority remained open. He had settled near Westport where he was at once struck by the contrast between the small farmers eking out a meagre living from their small plots of stony land and the more prosperous graziers on the neighbouring grass farms, or 'ranches'. To O'Brien the remedy was obvious—it was to buy out the ranches and redistribute the land among the population. The chances of legislation along these lines being conceded without pressure were minimal, so O'Brien decided to apply the pressure. In January 1898 he formed a new organisation, the United Irish League, with both economic and political ends in view. The economic objective was to break up the ranches, but this was essentially a western problem and, as the league spread to other parts of the country, its programme broadened out to include the time-honoured demand for the conversion of tenants into owners, by compulsion if necessary.

The political objective was much less advertised, though it seems to have been in O'Brien's mind from the outset. Beginning his labours in the very year— 1898—in which the centenary of the United Irishmen was being celebrated, O'Brien, like most people who thought about the matter at all, longed for the reestablishment of unity among nationalists. But, as his movement took root, he thought of reconciliation in terms not of a simple merger of parliamentary parties, but rather of using the United Irish League as an umbrella under which all other sectional interests would eventually shelter.[1] For nearly two years he sought to urge his view on anyone who would listen, but most particularly on his old ally Dillon. The ensuing argument subjected their friendship to the first of the cumulative strains that were in due course to rupture it beyond repair. O'Brien was totally unable to understand why his old comrade should still choose to immerse himself in political intrigues, which, as Dillon himself repeatedly admitted, were deeply repugnant to him. Dillon, for his part, was equally unable to bring home to O'Brien the importance of maintaining intact the essentials of the party as it had been in the great days of Parnell, and he failed utterly to convey to O'Brien—a man often impervious to logic and never more so than when in the grip of a new enthusiasm—that no purely popular movement could be an adequate substitute for a trained and disciplined parliamentary group poised to exploit to the full its potential as a third force at Westminster.

The drift of events, however, favoured O'Brien. On the one hand, the parliamentarians remained so bitterly divided that the 1798 centenary celebrations were little better than a farce; worse still, the continuing split served to paralyse the energies of the different factions at the very moment when the outbreak of the second Boer war reawakened intense anti-British feeling in Ireland, feeling that the party leaders should have been able to canalise or, at least, adequately to represent in the house of commons. On the other hand, the United Irish League, having once succeeded in provoking the government into coercive counter-measures, never looked back. Whereas in the midsummer of 1899 it had no more than an estimated 33,000 members, two years later there were close on 100,000 members organised in nearly a thousand branches. Although the league was

---

[1] Paul Bew has offered an examination of the strategy and tactics of the United Irish League (including O'Brien's attempt to use the League as a grass-roots pressure group for ending the split among nationalists) in his *Conflict and conciliation in Ireland, 1890–1910: Parnellites and radical agrarians* (Oxford, 1987), pp 35–69.

essentially non-violent in its methods, its employment of the boycott sometimes spilled over into intimidation, and by 1902 large areas of the country had been 'proclaimed' under the 1887 crimes act because of the illegal activities of O'Brien's followers. In reality the government's efforts to repress the league were less stringent than those of, say, Arthur Balfour at the time of the plan of campaign, and there is reason to believe that George Wyndham, the chief secretary, who had succeeded Gerald Balfour in October 1900, was much less interested in repressing agitation than in redressing the grievances that caused it.[1] But the very fact that coercion was being applied led predictably to increased support for the league, and there can be no doubt that by the end of 1899 O'Brien held the key to the situation.

It is against this background that the cautious manœuvres of the parliamentarians towards some kind of reconciliation have to be judged. Dillon, though still convinced of the absolute necessity of a strong parliamentary representation at Westminster, had been planning for some time to resign the chairmanship of his own group in 1899 and there was a possibility that this might open the way to an amicable conference at least with Redmond's Parnellites if not with Healy and his group of dissidents. Since all three groups were suffering severely from the refusal of a thoroughly disillusioned public to subscribe to their funds, financial stringency was an additional—and perhaps the most important—incentive towards reunification. The prospects of peace were improved by the fact that both Dillon and O'Brien had been able to maintain contact over the years with one of the most respected of the Parnellite M.P.s, Timothy Harrington, and Dillon apparently hoped that Harrington would eventually emerge as the chairman of a reunited party. Since, however, there were strong indications that Redmond and Healy were also drawing closer together, it became more than ever necessary for Dillon to assure himself of O'Brien's continued support. Increasingly, therefore, his letters and speeches in the latter part of 1899 leaned in the direction of the United Irish League. It is almost certain that for Dillon this was a tactical manœuvre rather than a real change of heart, but it reflected the advice given to him at the time by the friends whose opinion he valued most (they included Davitt, T. P. O'Connor, and the distinguished Irish-Canadian Edward Blake, who was at this period an influential member of the party), that he would be in grave danger of being isolated by a Redmond–Healy pact unless he held fast to O'Brien. In the end, though only after much intrigue, the warring factions came together at a conference in January and February 1900, at which the fundamental decision to reunite under a Parnellite chairman was finally taken. The choice of chairman was not made until 6 February. That it turned out to be Redmond was the result of an unexpected intervention by O'Brien and Davitt.

[1] See Gailey, *Ire. & death of kindness*, pp 162–72, for an account of Wyndham's background, personal characteristics, political ideas, and attitude towards Ireland, derived in part (Gailey argues) from his attraction to the romanticised Ireland of the literary revival, and in part from his desire as an imperialist to reverse economic, social, and moral decay through industrialisation.

Believing, perhaps wrongly, that Harrington was lukewarm in his support of the United Irish League, they sent a last-minute letter to Dillon urging him to support Redmond's nomination even though it was known also to have Healy's backing. The bleak presumption was that if Dillonites and Healyites could agree on Redmond as chairman they could fight each other afterwards for the monopoly in manipulating him.

This was exactly what happened. But what could rapidly have become a very ugly situation was unexpectedly obviated by Healy's shortsightedness in falling into the very trap that Dillon had just avoided. An essential part of the agreement reached at the reunion conference had been that a national convention of the United Irish League should be summoned to set the seal on the grand process of reconciliation. All the parliamentarians were in varying degrees nervous about what might happen at the convention, for O'Brien made no secret of his intention to use it as the means of subordinating the party to the league. But Healy alone came out strongly against it, and in doing so not only incurred the wrath of O'Brien but wrecked his entente with Redmond, who had not taken long to see where the centre of power really lay. And when Healy further compounded his heresy by running his own candidates against those of the league at the general election in October 1900, his isolation was complete. When the new parliament assembled, he himself supplied the best commentary on what had happened when he observed that 'the right honourable gentleman [George Wyndham] stated that the United Irish League has deposited a united Irish party in this house. As a matter of fact it has deposited two parties, of which I am one'.[1] His colleagues promptly took him at his word and in December he was formally expelled from the parliamentary party.

There was a certain irony in this dénouement since, in a sense, Healy was suffering not just because of his insubordination but because he was, in the short term at any rate, too acute a political prophet. He disliked the league, as Dillon did at bottom, because it represented a serious threat to the freedom of action of members of parliament; though of course he differed from Dillon as to the extent to which that freedom should be constrained by an interior discipline imposed by the parliamentary party itself. With the league in full flood in the summer of 1900, such ideas were not merely dangerous but visionary. The national convention solemnly established the elaborate and hierarchical organisation after which O'Brien had always hankered, and if words on the printed page meant anything they meant that the league had become the dominant political force in the country, equipped as it was with machinery for the selection of parliamentary candidates in the constituencies and, through its projected annual conventions, with the means of reviewing the parliamentary party's record at the end of each session. The reality, however, was rather different. The league did indeed become a genuinely national organisation, but it did not long remain independent of the

---

[1] *Hansard 4*, lxxxix, 964 (22 Feb. 1901).

parliamentary party. Since its president was Redmond, its secretary was Joseph Devlin (perhaps the ablest recruit to join the party after the reunion), and its executive committee contained a strong representation of influential M.P.s, it was obvious that the parliamentarians were bent on reasserting the same kind of control over the grass-roots organisation that Parnell had done over the league's predecessor, the Irish National League. While O'Brien remained at the centre of things this process—which, in retrospect, seems almost inevitable—was held in suspension, but, as we shall see presently, he came to differ so completely from his colleagues on a fundamental matter of principle that within a few years of the reunion he was as bitterly estranged from them as was Healy, with whom, by a final irony, he then began to construct the nucleus of a fresh independent party.

In 1900 such a consummation would have seemed inconceivable. On the contrary, the power of the league and its continuing success as an agrarian organisation placed it and its creator in a very strong position not only *vis-à-vis* the politicians, but also *vis-à-vis* the government. It has already been suggested that the chief secretary, George Wyndham, preferred reform to coercion, and a curious sequence of events was now to give him the opening he had long been seeking. In 1902 he made his first attempt to introduce a comprehensive measure of land purchase, but his bill was defective in various ways and had to be withdrawn. Then, on 3 September of that year there appeared a letter in the newspapers from a Galway landlord, Captain John Shawe-Taylor. The letter contained a simple invitation to certain named representatives of the landlords and the tenants to meet in conference and attempt to reach a final settlement of the land question. Most landlords were intensely suspicious of this initiative, and those originally invited by Shawe-Taylor refused to act. Others, however, were prepared to put his eccentric proposal to the test, and on 20 December 1902 eight negotiators sat down together in Dublin. The chairman was the earl of Dunraven, whose fellow landlord representatives were the earl of Mayo, Colonel Hutcheson-Poë, and Colonel Nugent Everard. The tenants were represented by Redmond, O'Brien, Harrington, and Russell.

After only two weeks deliberation the land conference produced a report, which, though brief, was in its way a historic document. It dealt with a number of issues, but its essence was contained in the recommendation that the government should at once launch a massive scheme of land purchase. Compulsory powers were not to be sought, but the landlords were to be guaranteed a fair price through state aid to purchasers, who would repay their loans by annuities extending, it was suggested, over a period of sixty-eight and a half years. In more general terms, the conference laid down what it considered to be the three necessary guidelines that must be followed if there was to be any hope of success: the new owners must not be burdened with excessive repayments; the landlords should receive a special inducement to sell; and, if the community as a whole was to derive the full benefit from the operation, 'it is of the greatest importance that income derived from the sale of property in Ireland should continue to be expended in Ireland'.[1]

The report, when published, understandably made a great sensation. True, it had critics—some of them, like Davitt and Thomas Sexton, extremely formidable—who maintained from the start that the tenor of the proposals was altogether too favourable to the landlords, but it was easy to overlook such warnings when Wyndham introduced in 1903 a new land bill that quite obviously owed a great deal to the report of the land conference. In brief, what he proposed was that landlords should be encouraged to sell entire estates, not just individual holdings, and that such sales should take place provided three-quarters of the tenants on any given estate were in favour. The prices to be paid would range from 18 ½ years purchase up to 24 ½ years purchase on 'first-term rents' (rents fixed by the land courts under the act of 1881), or from 21 ½ to 27 ⅔ years purchase on the lower 'second-term rents' fixed in and after 1896. The money for purchase was to be advanced to the tenants by the state and repaid by annuities at the rate of 3 ¼ per cent over 68 ½ years. The incentive to the landlords called for by the conference report was to be a 12 per cent bonus on each sale, to be paid out of the Irish revenue. There were, of course, some features of Wyndham's scheme that nationalists disliked—they thought the price too high, the bonus repugnant, and the regulations governing rent reductions too complex—but on balance this was such an advance over all previous offers that it was difficult to condemn it out of hand. It was in fact accepted by the party and the league subject to certain amendments and without prejudice to the subsequent introduction of the principle of compulsion. In the event, and largely as a result of secret negotiations between Redmond and Wyndham through a third party, the measure ran smoothly along its parliamentary course and became law before the year was out. Its immediate effect was to give an immense impetus to the transfer of land. Even though its financial provisions were soon shown to be defective, and even though compulsion was not resorted to until an amending act was passed in 1909 (and then only minimally), the tenants seized eagerly the opportunity now presented to them.[2] The principle of compulsory sale was in fact first embodied in legislation designed to resettle tenants who had been evicted during one or other of the various phases of the land war, but this—the evicted tenants act of 1907—was by its very nature of strictly limited application.[3] When in March 1920 the estates commissioners calculated the effect of the 1903 and 1909 acts together, they found that £83 million had been advanced for purchase (another million had been lodged by purchasers in cash payments) and that sales totalling a further £24 million were pending. Between 1903 and 1920 nearly 9 million acres (3.6 million

---

[1] The report is reprinted in William O'Brien, *An olive branch in Ireland and its history* (London, 1910), pp 475–9; the words quoted appear on p. 478; see also Mitchell & Ó Snodaigh, *Ir. pol. docs. 1869–1916*, pp 112–15.

[2] 3 Edw. VII, c. 37 (14 Aug. 1903); 9 Edw. VII, c. 42 (3 Dec. 1909).

[3] 7 Edw. VII, c. 56 (28 Aug. 1907).

hectares) had changed hands and 2 million more (810,000 hectares) were in process of being sold. Even this did not completely exhaust the problem, and after 1922 both the Northern Ireland and Irish Free State governments had to wind up the business, but this should not be allowed to detract from Wyndham's achievement. His act was, and was seen by contemporaries to be, the vital breakthrough from which all subsequent developments followed.

This in itself would be sufficient to justify the importance that historians have always attached to the Wyndham act. But it was significant also on two other grounds. First, it represented the climax of what may be called 'constructive unionism', that blend of private enterprise and government intervention from which so many of the reforms of the previous fifteen years had flowed. Indeed, the Wyndham act went beyond the previous achievements of constructive unionism in that it was a concession not handed down *de haut en bas*, but actually worked out in collaboration with leading nationalists. It seemed, in short, as if Plunkett's mantle had not only fallen on Lord Dunraven, but had been transformed in the process into a coat of many colours to the fashioning of which all shades of political opinion had contributed. But, and this was the second and more profound significance of the act, it was a climax that was also a termination. Some of those who had taken part in the land conference had hoped that this coming together of ancient enemies would be the prelude to a new era of reconciliation in which other problems—for example, the establishment of a university acceptable to catholics[1]—and even the ultimate question of the future government of Ireland would be solved by agreement reached through other, and possibly more far-reaching, conferences.

This hope was blasted almost before it had been formulated. Moreover, it was blasted on both sides of the fence. The first to suffer was O'Brien, who, with characteristic over-optimism, had seen the settlement of the land question as merely the opening gambit in the evolution of a policy to which he gave the name 'conference plus business'. By this he meant quite simply that further instalments of negotiation devoted to strictly practical ends would not only yield positive benefits for the country but would in time so diminish old antagonisms that large issues could be discussed without rancour. The history of his subsequent career is largely the history of his bitter awakening from this dream and of his progressive alienation from his former colleagues. The ink was hardly dry on the royal signature to the Wyndham act before the trouble began. Initially, it took the form of an all-out attack on the terms of the settlement, the more formidable because it brought into play such an array of talent—Davitt, Dillon, Sexton, and the *Freeman's Journal*—that Redmond, whose finely developed instinct for survival was one of his most remarkable qualities as a party leader, had little option but to swing into line with the critics even though he had been one of the principal architects of the act. In fairness to these critics it should be said that, to

[1] Below, pp 539–70.

the extent that they concentrated their fire on the financial clauses, they were to be more than justified in the event: within a very few years the government got into serious difficulties over the system of buying out the landlords, and the complicated and not wholly successful land act of 1909 had to be passed as a matter of urgency in an attempt to put this right.

It was observable, however, that the main weight of criticism was directed not so much towards land purchase finance *in toto* as against the excessive benefits the landlords were alleged to be reaping from their sales, and particularly against the cash bonus they received on each transaction. Whether the benefits were or were not excessive is an arguable case on which it is impossible to generalise—circumstances obviously differed from estate to estate—but that they were widely believed to be excessive was in itself an important contemporary fact. It was important because it could be exploited to undermine the whole concept of conference plus business. If negotiating with landlords could be equated with being outsmarted by landlords, then public opinion could the more easily be mobilised against fresh landlord initiatives such as the letter proposing another conference—this time on the university question—that Captain Shawe-Taylor sent to the press in September 1903, but which, largely because of the developing anti-landlord prejudice, fell on stony ground.

But, it may be asked, why this wariness, why this nationalist reluctance to come to close quarters with the ascendancy class? Was it really due to a kind of collective inferiority complex, which assumed almost as a matter of course that the majority would be cheated of its rights by the minority? The answer must be that while this certainly contributed to shaping the nationalist attitude it was only the symptom of a deeper malaise. Nationalists feared landlords bearing gifts because they could not be certain that home rule might not, in deadly earnest, be killed by kindness. The point was put with brutal clarity by Dillon in a speech at Swinford in October 1903, which O'Brien was soon to describe as marking the final parting of the ways between them:

Some people believe . . . that all the obstacles in the path of Irish freedom are now levelled . . . that all that remains for us to do is to clasp hands in affectionate friendship with Lord Dunraven . . . and co., and advance more or less under their inspiration along the smooth and easy and short road to that goal of Irish freedom for which we have so long and so arduously struggled. I wish I could share that view . . . but I do not believe it . . . And I say, beware of doctrines of conciliation which may drive out of our ranks those young men who, although they may . . . be mistaken in [their belief in] the possibility of force, are the salt of any movement they come into, because they are ready for sacrifice.[1]

The immediate consequence of this mounting criticism of the policy of conciliation (of which criticism the Swinford speech still stands as the classic statement) was the abrupt resignation of O'Brien from the parliamentary party. It is true that his health had been undermined by his exertions in creating the

[1] *F.J.*, 21 Oct. 1903, quoted in Lyons, *Dillon*, pp 239–40.

United Irish League, and his temporary retirement from public life was in part quite genuinely due to illness. But it was much more due to the realisation that, although the country appeared to be accepting the fruits of the Wyndham act quite happily, it was not prepared to draw the same conclusions from the land conference as O'Brien himself was. Outgeneralled and outgunned, he not only withdrew from the party but by his very absence in effect handed over his own creation, the United Irish League, to those who had defeated him in this crucial battle.[1] Nor was the permanence of this defeat in any way affected by the fact that in 1907 he was received back into the fold, for the reconciliation then effected was never more than fragile and was speedily shattered, with appropriate irony, by fresh disagreements over the land act of 1909. O'Brien at once resigned again and this time he went for good. He did not leave politics altogether—later we shall glimpse him again at the head of a new movement and of a group of independent M.P.s[2]—but his final breach with the party made it absolutely certain that the concept of conference plus business would have no backers among those who spoke for 'official' nationalism.

The argument as to whether home rule was or was not in danger of being killed with kindness had implications far beyond the fate of a single politician, however prominent. We shall have to consider some of those implications when we examine the 'minority' revolution of 1916, but this is probably the place at which to make the point that there may actually have been more substance to the anxieties of Dillon and Davitt and the rest than they themselves realised. This was not because reforming landlords posed a potent threat—on the contrary, as we shall see shortly, they had troubles of their own no less serious than O'Brien's. It was rather because the country itself was undergoing steady and undramatic, but nevertheless profound, social and economic change. Some of this, as already suggested, derived from conscious acts of policy by both individuals and governments. It is obvious, for example, that the progressive amelioration of the land question, the creation of the congested districts board and the department of agriculture and technical instruction, the building of railways, roads, and harbours, the improvement of rural housing by the various labourers' acts from the 1880s onward,[3] all worked towards a more prosperous society.

But this prosperity, which began to be widely evident from about the mid-1890s and continued at a high level up to 1914, reflected a general improvement in the economic environment. This in turn was due to a rise in prices that was of particular advantage to Ireland, where the market was limited and where exports therefore played a crucial role. Not every industry benefited from this

[1] For an examination of the challenge posed to the Irish party by the passage of the Wyndham act (i.e. to develop a new strategy for Irish nationalism) and the far-reaching consequences of the rejection of O'Brien's conciliation policy, see Philip Bull, 'Land and politics, 1879–1903' in Boyce, *Revolution in Ire.*, pp 30–46.

[2] Below, pp 126–7.

[3] 45 & 46 Vict., c. 60 (18 Aug. 1882); 46 & 47 Vict., c. 60 (25 Aug. 1883); 48 & 49 Vict., c. 77 (14 Aug. 1885); 6 Edw. VII, c. 37 (4 Aug. 1906).

buoyancy and some of the most prestigious were already showing symptoms of decay, but it is fair to say that, compared with the lean years of the late 1870s and the 1880s, most of the main staples on which Ireland depended for her modest wealth were enjoying, relatively speaking, a period of boom. This was true of the all-important cattle industry (though less true of dairying, which did not sufficiently adapt to the competition from Denmark and New Zealand), of brewing and distilling, of milling and baking, and of most of the key manufactures of the industrial north. Of these, linen remained important, but had in fact reached the limits of its expansion mainly because it was facing increasing competition from cotton, to which was later to be added a variety of synthetic fabrics. Thus, while linen exports continued to grow, they grew more slowly than before and grew at all only because they were capturing a larger share of a declining market. Moreover, in other respects the state of the industry was far from satisfactory. It depended excessively on the labour of women (and indeed of 'young persons' also), conditions of work were hard, wages were low, and net output per worker inferior to that of other textile workers. Much the same criticisms could be levelled at that other Ulster textile industry that came to full flower in the second half of the nineteenth century, the shirt-making of Derry; for although that city doubled its population between 1851 and 1901, its economic future was highly precarious since it had virtually no alternative source of wealth. In this respect Belfast, of course, was in a vastly stronger position. Even if linen was suspect, the manufacture of textile machinery and also of rope were both expanding rapidly, while in the shipping industry the town (city from 1889) had one of the wonders of modern industrialisation. Dominated by two firms— Harland & Wolff, founded in the 1850s, and Workman & Clark, dating from 1879—it specialised at this time in the building of passenger liners, and produced a staggering total of over 250,000 tons of shipping in 1914 alone. Nor was this all. Belfast was also a large-scale exporter of tobacco, of whiskey, and of aerated waters. From this single city derived about a third of the net industrial output of the whole of Ireland and possibly two-thirds of its total industrial exports.

Another way of putting this is to say that outside Belfast, and to a lesser extent Dublin, industry was thinly spread and, on the whole, of modest proportions wherever it occurred. Even so, there is considerable evidence of prosperity not only in the countryside, but in the towns. As farmers grew more prosperous, and as the wages even of labourers increased, so too did the amount of cash available for the purchase of consumer goods. Improved transport, the use of the bicycle, and the coming of the mail-order catalogue, all helped to develop the potential market for the retail trade. Retailers responded eagerly to the challenge and the result was seen both in a greater range of commodities and in a striking improvement of diet. The picture, of course, was not without its dark corners. There was considerable unemployment in the towns and underemployment in the countryside; housing, though generally better than it had been, was still inadequate, and particularly appalling in the slums of Dublin; disease and drunkenness abounded, while the death-rate in Dublin and Belfast (especially the former), though declining, was still ominously high; and, as we shall see presently, out of these lower depths a desperate, or despairing, labour movement was soon to arise. Nevertheless, it cannot be too often emphasised that as Ireland entered the twentieth century she exhibited many of the features of high rather than low development: a large foreign trade; major export industries, some of them extremely sophisticated; an elaborate network of banking, commerce, and transport; a rising income from the proceeds of foreign investment.

Not all of this was immediately visible to contemporaries, though some of it was. What seems to have been least visible was the degree to which the new prosperity depended on factors outside the control of Irishmen. It depended primarily on the continuing buoyancy of prices in the outside world and on the continuing capacity of Irish exports to profit from this buoyancy. To a very large extent, though by no means exclusively, 'the outside world' meant Britain, which just before the war took about four-fifths of Irish exports and supplied two-thirds of Irish imports. This was one economic fact of which contemporaries were well aware, though neither unionists nor nationalists seem thoroughly to have grasped its implications. Nationalists, in the decade or so before 1914, were much preoccupied with the demand for tariff autonomy as an essential element of home rule, this being regarded as the indispensable preliminary to an Irish industrial revolution. We shall see shortly that this was an integral part of Arthur Griffith's Sinn Féin policy, and it was also pursued by others who had no time for Sinn Féin, like the journalist D. P. Moran in his influential weekly the *Leader*, or those whose concern was more purely economic, like the businessmen who founded the Cork Industrial Development Association in 1903 and extended this two years later into an Irish Industrial Development Association.

Unionists viewed the question of economic relations with Britain even more simplistically, if that were possible. Access to raw materials and markets being vital to the export industries of the north-east, it was to be expected that the attachment of Belfast manufacturers to the British connection would have a strong commercial content, and that the modest Irish hinterland should seem to them to have little to offer in comparison with the United Kingdom free trade area of which they insisted on remaining members. But for the landed gentry who supplied the leadership of Irish as distinct from Ulster unionism, the British connection, to which they were just as passionately attached as the northern industrialists, had on balance involved economic loss rather than gain. Their rents had risen little if at all over the past half-century, they had been obliged by successive governments to yield concession after concession to their tenants, and in the end they were thankful to be allowed to wind up their estates in the more or less beneficent shade of the Wyndham act. But neither they, nor the northern industrialists, nor nationalist advocates of protection, understood what, with hindsight, seems so obvious to us: that the argument about whether or not to retain the union was, in economic terms, almost irrelevant. Whatever political solution might in the future be applied to the Irish question, the immutable facts of geography, climate, and history would ensure in the foreseeable future that for Ireland the British market would be indispensable, and that for Britain the Irish market would be too valuable to relinquish.[1]

Unionists and nationalists alike would no doubt have replied that the debate about the union was not wholly, or even principally, economic, and that what was at stake was far wider, in fact nothing less than the distribution and ultimate control of power. The time was approaching when the nationalists would state their view of the case, but the emergence of the concept of conference plus business prompted the unionists to give their own answer without further delay. The earl of Dunraven had been as impressed as O'Brien by the success of the land conference and, like him, wished to repeat that success in other spheres. Accordingly, in 1904 he and a group of fellow landlords established the Irish Reform Association with the object of promoting what they called the devolution of certain local government functions to financial and legislative councils in Ireland. In framing their proposals Dunraven and his friends had enlisted the help of Sir Antony MacDonnell, who had been persuaded to give up a brilliant career in India to become under-secretary for Ireland. Partly because of this sacrifice, and partly because he was a forceful personality, MacDonnell believed that he would have a greater say in matters of Irish policy than was usually permitted to civil servants—even to under-secretaries. Indeed, MacDonnell seems to have obtained assurances to this effect from Wyndham himself, on his appointment as under-secretary.[2] The fact that Irish policy was in his mind bound up with progress towards home rule in itself suggests that in appointing him the unionist government was taking a serious risk. Nevertheless, in this particular matter MacDonnell behaved with admirable discretion, telling the lord lieutenant of his connection with Dunraven's scheme and writing to the same effect to his immediate superior, George Wyndham. Unhappily, Wyndham not only failed to grasp the message his under-secretary was conveying to him but also succeeded in first forgetting and then mislaying the letter. When the devolution proposals were published, therefore, he had no hesitation in condemning them publicly. This, however, did not prevent Irish unionists, with certain Ulster M.P.s in the lead, from launching a scathing attack on devolution as a form of creeping home rule. The bitterness of this attack was accentuated because they suspected MacDonnell's complicity and therefore placed little confidence in Wyndham's repudiation of the scheme. The under-secretary naturally defended himself by explaining the precautions he had taken to keep his minister informed. Inevitably, the hurricane then changed course towards Wyndham, and in 1905 he was forced to resign—a disaster from which his career never recovered.[3]

---

[1] For economic development see also below, pp 260–342.

[2] O'Halpin, *Decline of the union*, pp 33–4.

[3] For the background to the 1904 crisis, including a discussion of MacDonnell's impact on the making, as well as the administration, of Irish policy, and his difficult relationship with hard-line Irish

The devolution proposals fell a long way short of home rule, and the Irish Reform Association itself never at any stage ceased to regard itself as impeccably unionist. Yet even the faintest indication of a willingness to experiment in limited self-government had created a major crisis. This in itself was highly revealing of the nature of unionist psychology. But even more revealing were two consequences that flowed from the crisis. One was the creation of the Ulster Unionist Council (originating in a conference of M.P.s on 2 December 1904, though the name was not adopted until March 1905), with the object of linking the main organs of unionism in the north in a common organisation 'with a view to consistent and continuous political action',[1] which, being interpreted, meant simply the uncompromising defence of the union. The other consequence of the crisis was that it brought to a close the brief but fascinating episode that we have called constructive unionism. Even at its height this had never attracted the attention of more than a tiny minority of protestants, and with the ending of the experiment Irish unionists retreated, as if in response to an irresistible impulse, into a dour, rigid, and unimaginative defence of the British connection. Not for many years would they again seek accommodation with nationalists, and then it would be too late.

It will be obvious that in pursuing thus far the history of the Wyndham act and of the devolution crisis we have moved very close to the watershed mentioned at the beginning of this chapter. And it is indeed true that the virtual solution of the land question, the collapse of conference plus business, the retirement of O'Brien into the political wilderness, the ruin of Wyndham and the discrediting of Dunraven, the creation of the Ulster Unionist Council, and the hardening of unionist, and especially northern, opinion—all these developments point towards the ending of one phase and the beginning of another. But before we explore further the way in which this transition came about, it is necessary first to examine four other factors in the situation, which themselves contributed to the overwhelming impression of change of pace and direction conveyed by the events of these crucial and crowded years.

The first of the four factors in point of time was the foundation and growth of the Gaelic League.[2] The reawakening of popular interest in a distinctively Irish culture had actually begun while Parnell was still in his prime—the creation of the Gaelic Athletic Association after all dates from 1884.[3] But the really powerful

---

unionists, see O'Halpin, *Decline of the union*, pp 32–43, and Jackson, *Ulster party*, pp 244–53. Jackson also sets out the contradictory accounts by contemporaries of what passed between Dunraven, MacDonnell, Wyndham, and Dudley in Sept. 1904 before the publication of the Reform Association's scheme, and analyses the extent and nature of Wyndham's involvement in the discussions (pp 253–60). A full narrative of the episode is in O'Halpin, op. cit., pp 44–50, and Gailey, *Ire. & death of kindness*, pp 255–91.

[1] Agenda of meeting of 2 Dec. 1904, quoted in Patrick Buckland, *Irish unionism, 1885–1923: a documentary history* (Belfast, 1973), p. 204, and Mitchell & Ó Snodaigh, *Ir. pol. docs 1869–1916*, p. 118.

[2] Below, pp 403–12.

[3] Above, p. l.

thrust towards an 'Irish', as distinct from an English or even an Anglo-Irish, Ireland belongs to the period after his death when nationalist energies were seeking new outlets and new modes of expression. It was in 1893 that three pioneers together launched the Gaelic League. One, Father Eugene O'Growney, was professor of Irish at Maynooth. A second, Eoin MacNeill, was an Antrim catholic (born in 1867) who came south to work in the civil service but who was in time to become not only one of the foremost exponents of early Irish history, but also a leading figure in the politics of the next thirty years. The third member of the group, the first president of the league, and closely identified with its ideals all his life, was Douglas Hyde. Born the son of a Church of Ireland rector in Sligo in 1863, Hyde grew up in the neighbouring county of Roscommon, where he learned Irish and absorbed Irish stories and song from the country people around him. He went next to Trinity and almost as a matter of course entered the Anglo-Irish protestant circle where the young W. B. Yeats was then beginning to make a name. These writers collaborated in producing *Poems and ballads of Young Ireland* in 1888 and followed this by founding the Irish Literary Society in London in 1891 and the National Literary Society in Dublin in 1892. At this time the whole emphasis of Hyde's thought was on liberating Irish culture from English influence, hence the title of his early and influential lecture to the National Literary Society (given in November 1892), 'The necessity for de-anglicising the Irish people'.[1] Although it was in fact MacNeill who suggested the establishment of the league, it was Hyde who was its principal propagandist. A gentle, simple man and a poet of great delicacy and feeling in both English and Irish, his conception of the league was non-political (despite the admiration for the physical force tradition in his early writings) and, of course, non-sectarian. Its functions, as he and the other founders insisted, were quite simple—to preserve and extend the daily use of the Irish language, and to create favourable conditions for the study and publication of existing Gaelic literature, as well as for the creation of new works in Irish. Up to a point the league certainly fulfilled the hopes of its progenitors. It was never, indeed, more than a very small pressure group and its numbers, even after twenty years of growth, remained small. In 1908, after it had been fifteen years in existence, it had only 599 branches; but though these were to be found in all parts of the country, many were no more than little groups of enthusiasts who were often regarded as distinctly, though amiably, eccentric. But this was not really the point. The chief significance of the league lay not in the quantity of its recruits but in their quality. It was very much a young people's organisation and it attracted into its ranks some of the most gifted and dedicated of the post-Parnellite generation. This undoubtedly gave the kind of stimulus to the language that Hyde had been seeking, but it also produced other results that he had not envisaged, and which, when he had fully grasped their tendency, led him to resign the

[1] For some acerbic comments on Hyde's concept of 'de-anglicisation', see Lee, *Modernisation of Ir. society*, pp 137–41.

presidency in the vastly different and doom-laden atmosphere of 1915. These results can be summed up in a single phrase—the league, despite its origins and within a very short time of its foundation, became in essence a partisan body. This expressed itself in two main ways. First, the more politically conscious of its members found that the study of the Irish language and the Irish past made them more rather than less political, with the consequence that, when opportunities arose for action more direct and far-reaching than anything the parliamentarians could offer, it was very frequently the Gaelic enthusiasts who were in the van. The league, it is scarcely too much to say, was the nursery for the revolutionary generation of 1916.

Yet to describe it simply in those terms is to underestimate the complexity of its influence. For the second and unforeseen way in which its partisan character emerged was that, despite the affection in which Hyde was held, and despite the fact that protestants were welcomed into its ranks, the Gaelic League did in practice become very closely identified in people's minds with catholicism. This was partly because priests often took a prominent part in organising local branches, but partly also because its emphasis, which was necessarily on the cultural past of Ireland, was naturally seen to be an emphasis on a golden age before English and Anglo-Irish influences, both by definition protestant, had together driven 'the hidden Ireland' underground. Some modern scholars are now highly critical of the whole concept of a hidden Ireland,[1] and golden ages are not part of the historian's stock in trade; but what is important here is the contemporary assessment of the Gaelic League. The true significance of this tendency was only to be seen when the question of home rule came once more to the fore in 1912, and when the Ulster protestant resistance to an Irish Ireland began to reveal its full strength. When that happened the image that the league projected of an Ireland that should be both Gaelic and catholic came into direct and baneful conflict with the unionists' insistence that they would have no part in a state that claimed to be exclusively, or even mainly, both of those things. It is a conflict that has yet to be resolved.

Whatever the ultimate ingredients of the national identity might be, the Gaelic League was certainly a major instrument in the search for that identity. But its early concern with culture and its avowed abstinence from politics meant that it would not be the only instrument. And before the 1890s were over, a more mundane movement had begun tentatively to take shape. In origin it was no more than a journalistic crusade, and it was in fact the creation of a journalist of genius, Arthur Griffith. In 1899, Griffith, who was then 28 years old, returned from South Africa to launch a paper, which, with memories of the 1798 centenary celebrations still fresh, he called *United Irishman*. By inclination Griffith was a separatist. He was apparently a member of the I.R.B. for a period of his youth, and in the very first issue of his paper (4 March 1899) he claimed that his

---

[1] See L. M. Cullen, 'The hidden Ireland: reassessment of a concept' in *Studia Hib.*, ix (1969), pp 7–47; and above, iv, 129–30.

nationalism was the nationalism of '98, '48, and '67—that is, militantly republican and in the tradition of Tone and of the fenians.

But if he was a separatist, Griffith was also a pragmatist. Physical force in the circumstances of 1899 was a chimera. What was needed, he thought, was not romantic gestures but prosaic organisation, not rhetoric but self-help. About the turn of the century he began to devise the outlines of a programme to give Irishmen an objective to aim at, which, though theoretically extreme, was not so far out of reach as to be hopelessly discouraging. He intended his own contribution to be primarily didactive, and aimed his newspaper at the various clubs and literary societies based on Dublin, Belfast, and a few other towns. But they hungered for some common ground or forum in which to meet and discuss the new Ireland of their dreams. To meet this hunger Griffith reluctantly agreed to the formation of a loose-knit organisation called 'Cumann na nGaedheal', which would encourage its members to support Irish industries, to study the language, literature, and history of Ireland, to play Irish games, and in general, like Hyde's Gaelic Leaguers, to resist the anglicisation of the country.

With rather more enthusiasm than he showed for the routine of organisation, Griffith began to work out in greater detail the intellectual basis of his programme. In defining his ideas he was much influenced by his (mistaken) notion of the so-called independent parliament that he believed Grattan had gained for Ireland between 1782 and 1800. More eccentrically, he was also deeply impressed by the Austro–Hungarian *Ausgleich* of 1867 and by the writings of the German economist Friedrich List. From the latter he learned the gospel of protectionism and the absolute necessity (as he conceived it) of a newly independent state being able to develop its own infant industries behind its own tariff barriers. The lesson he derived from central Europe seemed more obscure but rapidly became absolutely central to his political thinking. In his reading of Austrian history (like his reading of Irish history, it was defective, but that did not deter him) he had observed that in their successful attempt to resurrect their own assembly the Hungarian deputies to the imperial diet had in 1861 withdrawn from Vienna, a form of non-cooperation that, in Griffith's view, had helped them ultimately to gain their essential point. Thus on 26 October 1902, for the benefit of a Cumann na nGaedheal convention, he proposed a resolution calling on the Irish members of parliament to put the 'Hungarian policy' into effect and while absenting themselves from Westminster 'remain at home to help in promoting Ireland's interests and to aid in guarding its national rights'.[1]

At the time this seemed no more than idle talk. Certainly no one, not even Griffith, could have foreseen the vital role the Hungarian policy was to play in Anglo–Irish relations only seventeen years later. And it is important to be clear that although he was encouraged by the initial reception of his ideas to elaborate them still further, and even to provide a more permanent organisation to

---

[1] *United Irishman*, 1 Nov. 1902.

propagate them, the doctrines of 1902 were a portent for the future rather than a present reality. But they were soon to become a reality, and Griffith's direct intervention in politics was, as we shall see, to be an important element in the shaping of the watershed between 1903 and 1907.

The third of the influences that began to manifest themselves between the death of Parnell and the watershed was in one important respect like the two that have just been mentioned, though in other respects, no less important, it could hardly have been more different. This was the movement that had been foreshadowed when Yeats and Hyde were founding their literary societies in 1891 and 1892, but only blossomed when Yeats, Lady Gregory, Edward Martyn, and George Moore combined in and after 1898 to found the Irish Literary Theatre, out of which, in a few years' time, the celebrated Abbey Theatre was to develop.[1] The intention of these writers, and of others whom they gathered round them, was to create a modern literature that should, initially at least, be in English, but should look for its inspiration to Irish sources, whether the sagas as Standish O'Grady had revealed them in his 'bardic' *History of Ireland* published in 1878–80,[2] or in the speech and traditions of the Irish countryside as first Lady Gregory and Hyde, and then J. M. Synge, collected them.

Many influences went to the making of this literary renaissance. With some of them—for example, occultism and theosophy, which attracted both Yeats and AE—we need not here concern ourselves. What does concern us, however, is that this movement was not merely Anglo-Irish in essence and largely protestant in ethos, but that it was created by a very small group of people, all of whom knew each other very well and most of whom were closely connected with the west of Ireland. They were not politically minded people—Yeats's involvement with the I.R.B. was quite exceptional and even this, which was temporary, partly reflected his hero-worship of the old fenian John O'Leary, and partly his love-lorn attachment to Maud Gonne—and although controversy was to be the element in which their movement lived and throve, there is a sense in which, no less than Plunkett or Dunraven, they stood for the reconciliation not merely of different interests but of different cultures.

This did not, however, mean that reconciliation involved any loss of artistic independence. On the contrary, all of them preached and practised an almost fanatical creed of creative freedom, for, although their intention was to use Irish themes and Irish material, the best of them never lost sight of a wider European civilisation to which they felt an instinctive allegiance. It soon became obvious that, between the freedom they claimed and the propaganda for an Irish Ireland, which the revivalists held to be the supreme task of that generation, no bridge could possibly be built. And in fact one of their very first ventures, Yeats's play 'The Countess Cathleen', which the theatre produced in 1899, demonstrated at once how great the gulf was between the two cultures. In that play Yeats had

---

[1] Below, pp 119–21, 362–3.   [2] Above, v, 517–18.

imagined two devils coming to a famine-stricken Ireland to tempt the peasants to sell their souls for gold. The Countess Cathleen interposes and in the last resort agrees to sell her own soul to save them. The very notion of such a traffic was deeply repugnant to catholic morality, and the stormy scenes at the first-night performance set off a controversy that was to break out again and again in the years to come. Yeats himself was by no means always intent on going against the grain of his audiences, and in 1902 he was to produce a patriotic play, 'Cathleen Ni Houlihan', of such intensity that years later he was to wonder

> Did that play of mine send out
> Certain men the English shot?[1]

Nevertheless, the early furore over 'The Countess Cathleen' was significant because it revealed the sensitivity and the essentially puritan character of the Irish-Ireland movement. And when in 1903 the theatre produced 'In the shadow of the glen', the first of two plays by John Synge that looked at peasant Ireland with an unwinking gaze, the storms that then burst on his head and Yeats's were so central to what the journalist D. P. Moran called 'the battle of two civilisations' that they too came to form an essential element of the watershed.

Before turning to discuss that watershed in more detail, one further phenomenon of the 1890s needs to be mentioned, especially since it also contributed to the excitement and complexity of the period 1903–7. At the time, admittedly, this could hardly have been anticipated, for its origins were modest in the extreme. We are speaking of the first faint beginnings of the Irish labour movement. Although trade unionism in one form or another had been in evidence in the eighteenth century, since then there had always been two serious obstacles to the growth of labour as either an economic or a political force. The political obstacle, which was to continue into the twentieth century, was that the great question of the retention or repeal of the act of union comprehended, or dwarfed, all other questions, which were regarded as relevant only in the degree to which they contributed to the main debate.[2] And of course, from the viewpoint of organised labour, the fact that the protestant working man in Belfast took a different view of the union with Britain from that taken by his catholic counterpart, either in Belfast or in Dublin, was a further indication that labour matters would continue to seem only marginally relevant. The economic reason for the failure of labour to organise was very simple. Outside north-east Ulster there was not enough heavy industry, or industry heavily concentrated, for the workers readily to combine in powerful unions. Moreover, among the workers themselves there were important distinctions of status between the skilled minority and the much larger mass of unskilled and unemployed or underemployed carters, porters, and general labourers who supplied the bulk of the work-force in most Irish towns. From this difference two consequences resulted. One was that when Irishmen joined trade unions they tended on the whole to join 'amalgamated' unions, which frequently

---

[1] Below, p. 358.   [2] For Parnell's brief *rapprochement* with trade unionism, see above, p. 79.

had their headquarters in Britain and had little time to spare for Irish problems. The second consequence was that although an Irish trade union congress did finally emerge—partly in reaction against this neglect on the part of the British-based unions—it only came into being as late as 1894. Even then the link with the British unions remained strong. By 1910 some 70,000 workers were represented in the Irish trade union congress; most of these came from about fifty unions, of which roughly half had their headquarters in Britain.

It was hardly surprising that the tone of the congress should have been exceedingly undoctrinaire, not to say conservative. A careful attention to wage negotiation and working conditions seemed the be-all and end-all of the Irish labour movement at the end of the nineteenth century. Yet even here the first stirrings of a radical approach could be detected, albeit with difficulty. In 1896 there arrived in Dublin a 28-year-old organiser for the Dublin Socialist Society. His name was James Connolly and he had been born in Edinburgh of Irish parents. There he was early imbued with the two doctrines—socialism and nationalism—that it was to be his life's work to seek to reconcile. Within a few weeks of his arrival he founded the Irish Socialist Republican party, but the name was always more grandiose than the reality and Connolly found it so hard to support his young family that in 1903 he was obliged to emigrate to the United States. With his departure the infant party languished and there seemed no future for it in the circumstances then prevailing in Ireland.

The true significance of the Irish Socialist Republican party is to be found not in its influence on the course of events—this was virtually negligible—but in the programme with which Connolly provided it and in the explanation that he himself gave of that programme. The programme itself, as defined in the party's inaugural manifesto, looked forward to the creation of an Irish socialist republic 'based upon the public ownership by the Irish people of the land and instruments of production, distribution, and exchange'. But as Connolly himself realised, 'the struggle for Irish freedom has two aspects; it is national and it is social.'[1] The question he had to grapple with was whether these two aspects could be dealt with simultaneously or whether one should take precedence of the other, and if so which. In the end, as was perhaps inevitable in the circumstances in which he was placed, he came down, or seemed to come down, in favour of the primacy of political action when he wrote that 'the conquest by the social democracy of political power in parliament, and on all public bodies in Ireland, is the readiest and most effective means whereby the revolutionary forces may be organised and disciplined' for the achievement of a socialist republic.[2]

Later we shall see along what strange paths and towards what an agonising choice this doctrine would lead him. When he left Ireland in 1903 the whole question seemed utterly remote, a theoretical argument with no basis in reality. What was real and evident was the condition of the urban, and especially the

---

[1] Quoted in C. Desmond Greaves, *The life and times of James Connolly* (London, 1961), pp 60–61.
[2] Ibid., p. 62.

unskilled, workers crowded into the slums of Belfast and Dublin. When the labour movement woke into new life it would do so not in response to any sophisticated arguments about socialism but under the impulsion given to it by James Larkin, an agitator and orator of genius. In 1903 his arrival in Ireland was still four years away. But when he landed in Belfast in 1907 he too would make his contribution, highly individual but still essential, to the stresses and confusion of the watershed.

CHAPTER V

The watershed, 1903–7

F. S. L. LYONS

THE full significance and complexity of the watershed in Irish history, which the previous chapter repeatedly defined as falling between 1903 and 1907, can best be grasped if, before attempting to view it as a whole, we simply enumerate the series of apparently random events that took place at the second of those two dates. From what happened in that single year, 1907, may be derived most of the clues to the crisis that was to develop so swiftly between then and 1914. The list includes the introduction and withdrawal of the Irish council bill; the resignation from the Irish parliamentary party of C. J. Dolan and his decision to contest his old seat as a Sinn Féin candidate; the formation of the Joint Committee of Unionist Associations; the promulgation by the pope of the *Ne temere* decree; the death of the old fenian John O'Leary; the return of a younger fenian, Thomas Clarke; the arrival of James Larkin in Belfast and the consequent outbreak of strikes and lock-outs in that city; finally, the Abbey Theatre riots at the first production of 'The playboy of the western world'.

To contemporaries, few of these occurrences can have seemed to have had much contact with each other, but taken together they suggest to the historian a heightened temper, a sharper tone in Irish life, which foreshadows the onset of a period altogether different in character from what had gone before. The chief fascination of this concatenation of events is that it exhibits the same kind of change operating simultaneously at several different levels. It will be the purpose of this chapter to examine the levels individually before drawing the argument together and attempting a general evaluation of an episode that hitherto has been strangely neglected.

The most obvious point at which to begin is the point that also seemed most obvious at the time—the fact that the general election at the end of 1905 had produced in the new year of 1906 a major political upheaval. Since the effect of that upheaval was to end the almost uninterrupted tory domination of the previous twenty years and to substitute for it a liberal government, which, after its landslide victory at the polls, now had a majority over all other parties in the house of commons, the Irish reaction to the news might have been expected to be joyful and enthusiastic. So no doubt it was, at least among the politically unsophisticated, whose simple pleasure in the result was enhanced by the spectacle of John Redmond leading back to Westminster a party of eighty-one members (eighty-two, including T. P. O'Connor's Liverpool seat), which at least seemed to have recovered the solidity and discipline of the Parnellite heyday.

Yet very little thought would have suggested that rejoicing was premature. Certainly Redmond and his advisers, especially Dillon, had no illusions about the difficulty of the task with which they were now about to be confronted. A liberal government was doubtless an improvement on a tory government, but a liberal government that, by virtue of its huge majority, could float serenely out of reach of Irish pressure, was a phenomenon that could inspire only a very qualified rapture. Nor, unfortunately, was it simply a question of electoral statistics. Much also depended on how far this new government regarded itself as the inheritor of Gladstone's policies as well as of his prestige. From about the beginning of 1905, when it was becoming obvious to everyone that the tory government could not last much longer, the Irish leaders had sought to elicit from the liberals what they would do about home rule. The results of this exploration were not encouraging. The liberals, indeed, were so immersed in the byzantine complexity of their own internal quarrels—the disunity that had broken out after Gladstone's retirement had been intensified by a fundamental split over the question of whether to oppose or to support the Boer war—that it was difficult to determine how they stood on anything, or even who was competent to speak for them. Broadly speaking, however, it was possible to discern three different liberal attitudes towards Ireland. The first was the simple acceptance of Gladstonian home rule as a sacred trust to be fulfilled when the party returned to power. The custodians of this trust, who tended to be even more Gladstonian than Gladstone himself, included such influential figures as Earl Spencer, John Morley, and, most important, Sir Henry Campbell-Bannerman; since the last of these was in fact the leader round whom the party rallied at the general election, it was obviously gratifying to find that his heart was still in the right place. But Sir Henry was a Scotsman whose heart was habitually ruled by his head, and he could not be unaware either that many members of his party had come to regard home rule as an albatross around the neck of liberalism, or that the electorate was much more intent on domestic reform than on the redress of Irish grievances.

At the opposite pole from the Gladstonian old guard stood Gladstone's successor, Lord Rosebery. Rosebery had not been a success either as prime minister or as leader of the party, but he still enjoyed considerable prestige, and his occasional sallies into the political fray were regarded by liberals who differed from him with more trepidation than perhaps they warranted. Rosebery had in fact moved even further away from home rule than the position he had taken up in his discouraging speech of 1894,[1] and in October 1905 he warned his colleagues publicly that the policy 'of placing home rule in the position of a reliquary, and only exhibiting it at great moments of public stress, as Roman Catholics are accustomed to exhibit relics of a saint, is not one which will earn sympathy or

[1] Above, p. 85.

success in this country'.[1] Irish nationalists, it was clear, could expect little comfort from him.

There remained a third attitude. It was one that had been outlined as far back as 1901 by H. H. Asquith, unquestionably one of the ablest of the rising young men in the party. While declaring himself in favour of the supremacy of the imperial parliament, he had also suggested 'as liberal a devolution of local powers and local responsibilities as statesmanship can from time to time devise'. But it was Asquith's friend, Sir Edward Grey, who expressed this doctrine in a formula more acceptable to Irish ears: 'Things must advance towards home rule, but I think it must be step by step.'[2] As the downfall of the tory government drew nearer during 1905, there was no sign that this doctrine was likely to secure the general allegiance of all liberals. On the contrary, when Asquith made it clear that in his view the liberals should not advance towards home rule in the lifetime of the coming parliament, this provoked a strong protest from Morley, which indicated that Gladstonians were as divided from Asquithians as both were from Roseberyites.

In the end it was the common sense of Campbell-Bannerman that pulled the party together on the vexing Irish issue. On the eve of the election he not only accepted the 'step by step' policy as the one on which liberals were likely to disagree least, but also continued to reassure his nationalist allies that the lesser did not necessarily preclude the greater. The formula by which he expressed this—and to which he committed himself publicly in a speech at Stirling on 23 November 1905—was that, while no one should expect home rule to be granted overnight, the Irish would be well advised to accept an instalment of reform, which, however, 'must be consistent with and lead up to the larger policy'.[3]

With this the nationalist leaders had perforce to be content, but their patience was soon to be exposed to a cruel test. This was not altogether due to the reluctance of their liberal allies to face up to Irish realities. It was partly the consequence of what appears to have been a deliberate strategy by the tory party to use its control of the house of lords to veto, or in some cases to subject to sweeping amendment, legislation that had passed through the house of commons by large liberal majorities. The time was fast approaching when this 'wrecking' policy would involve not merely the tory party but the constitution itself in grave dangers, but in the short term it certainly succeeded in reducing the liberal programme to a shambles. An immediate consequence of this was that no advance was made at all during 1906 towards the implementation of the 'step by step' policy. But when in 1907 the government did unveil its plans, these were deeply disappointing to Redmond and his colleagues. It was proposed to introduce a measure, the Irish council bill, which was in effect a new version of the devolution

---

[1] R. R. James, *Rosebery* (London, 1963), p. 453.
[2] H. W. McCready, 'Home rule and the liberal party, 1899–1906' in *I.H.S.*, xiii, no. 52 (Sept. 1963), p. 325.
[3] Stephen Gwynn, *The life of John Redmond* (London, 1932), p. 116.

scheme that had ended Wyndham's career, and, like that ill-fated notion, the new one bore the heavy imprint of MacDonnell's powerful personality. The projected council, partly nominated but mainly elected, was to be given control over eight departments of the Irish administration (including education, local government, and agriculture and technical instruction). The moneys necessary to service these departments were to be transferred to the council, but the lord lieutenant was to retain wide powers of veto, and ultimate authority was of course to reside, as before, with the British government and the imperial parliament. Redmond and Dillon worked hard, and not unsuccessfully, to amend the proposals so as to make the council more effective and more representative, but nothing could conceal the fact that, even when so improved, it would fall very far short of anything resembling a home rule parliament. Since that was the standard by which the measure was bound to be gauged, it was not surprising that opposition to the Irish council bill should have been both widespread and intense.[1] The predictable result was that when in May 1907 a national convention of the United Irish League met to consider the bill, Redmond, whose own view of it had been steadily hardening, anticipated the feeling of the meeting by denouncing it as totally unacceptable. The bill was then promptly withdrawn by the liberal government and the policy of 'step by step' lay, or seemed to lie, in ruins.

It would be too much to say of this fiasco that it ended the honeymoon period of the post-1905 liberal–nationalist alliance, since there had scarcely been any question of a liaison let alone a marriage; but it certainly did nothing to improve relations between the two parties, and not even the fact that the liberals did manage to squeeze into the session of 1907 an act that at last provided for the reinstatement of the evicted tenants (by now not so much the wounded soldiers as the Chelsea pensioners of the land war)[2] succeeded in effecting any real reconciliation. Yet it is arguable that for the Irish party the most damaging injuries inflicted by the crisis over the council bill were internal, not external. Friction with the liberals was disagreeable, but it was no more than an incident in politics, which would soon be forgotten—would have to be forgotten, indeed, for the brutal fact remained that it was only from the liberals that the nationalists could obtain home rule. Friction within the party was, however, a very different matter. This took two distinct forms. One was the emergence of a group of Young Turks—that is to say of nationalists of the rising generation who, while giving their loyalty to the parliamentary party, did not regard that loyalty as unconditional. They were mostly centred on Dublin, where their platform was the Young Ireland branch of the United Irish League, and they included a handful of intellectuals—T. M. Kettle, Francis Cruise O'Brien, Francis Sheehy-Skeffington,

---

[1] See Bew, *Conflict & conciliation*, pp 130–33, for the argument that Redmond's initial reaction to Birrell's proposals was ambivalent, and that his own and his colleagues' initial silence on the bill allowed other public commentators to set the tone in condemning its limitations, thus putting pressure on the party's convention to reject the proposals out of hand.

[2] Above, p. 96, n. 3.

Thomas Dillon—who would eventually move in diverse directions but who in 1907 wished both to purify and reinvigorate the party. By purifying it they meant primarily freeing it from the machine politics of which the United Irish League had become the symbol and the agent, and also purging it of a sectarian influence, which they believed was inescapable from the fact that Joseph Devlin combined the post of general secretary of the league with that of grand master of the Ancient Order of Hibernians. In practice, those in the Young Ireland branch were too few, and perhaps too inexperienced, to make much direct impact on decisions of party policy, but the fact that in 1907 they became so active and so articulate was a warning light, which the party should not have ignored. That it did ignore it was a symptom of a growing aloofness from the grass roots, for which eventually a heavy price was to be paid.

The second indication of a deep-seated malaise was the tendency of a few members of the party to look over their shoulders at Sinn Féin. Griffith's organisation was still not very large and the appeal of his doctrines did not extend beyond a very limited circle, but in the years immediately before the council bill dispute he had apparently begun to make some headway. The visit of Edward VII to Dublin in 1903 had provided a basis for protest, and to organise this protest a so-called National Council had been formed under the chairmanship of the dramatist and patron of the arts Edward Martyn.[1] The council itself led a rather shadowy existence, but it remained in being after the king's departure and under its auspices a convention was held in November 1905. At this convention Griffith was prevailed on to outline a detailed policy for the future. It was in fact the policy of political and economic self-reliance that he had been preaching since the turn of the century, but on this occasion it acquired the name by which it was to become famous—Sinn Féin ('ourselves'). Griffith's speech to the convention was much concerned with the economic objectives by which he set such store, but he also seized the occasion to call once again for abstention from Westminster. The Irish parliamentary party, he suggested, should come home to Ireland and there, together with delegates from local bodies, they should set up a Council of Three Hundred and assume the powers of a *de facto* parliament.

It all seemed highly visionary, but the vision was beginning to be provided with the rudiments of a practical organisation. During 1905, through the agency of two energetic young Ulstermen, Bulmer Hobson and Denis McCullough, there began to appear, mainly in the north, a few scattered bodies known as Dungannon Clubs.[2] But although the clubs were in no sense secret societies, and although they were ostensibly commemorating the very constitution that Griffith wanted to reanimate, there was rather more to them than that. Hobson and McCullough were both members of the I.R.B., and the real object of their enterprise was to educate the rising generation in the separatist doctrine. It was therefore more

[1] Below, pp 363, 490–91.
[2] An allusion to the Volunteer conventions that had contributed to political reform in 1782–3 (above, iv, 230, 270).

significant than appeared on the surface when in April 1907 the Dungannon Clubs and Cumann na nGaedheal came together to form the Sinn Féin League, which the following September merged with the National Council to become one body known from September 1908 by the generic name of Sinn Féin. It was still more significant that the political aim of the new body should have been defined simply as 'the reestablishment of the independence of Ireland'.[1] If this meant what it said, it committed Sinn Féin to total separation from Britain. But, though Griffith proclaimed himself a separatist as heretofore, he made it quite clear that in his opinion the Irish people were not separatists and that the constitution of 1782 offered the best base on which to unite them. For the young men of the Dungannon Clubs, independence of course did mean separation, though for the immediate future the vagueness of Griffith's formula suited them well enough. With the wisdom of hindsight we can see how this initial failure clearly to define the movement's objective held within it the seeds of future confusion and division. At the time, however, this does not seem to have crossed anyone's mind, and 'the constitution of 1782' still seemed a more than adequate rallying cry to enthusiastic nationalists.

Not the least interesting consequence of the council bill crisis was that it revealed that even a few parliamentarians were to be numbered among these enthusiasts. Within a month of the bill having been withdrawn (3 June 1907), a small group had proposed a resolution at a party meeting demanding a temporary secession from parliament and a reunion with O'Brien and Healy. The resolution in fact lapsed after a debate had shown how little support there was for it, but two of the group, James O'Mara and C. J. Dolan, resigned their seats in parliament and a third, Sir Thomas Esmonde, resigned his post as senior whip. Dolan then caused a major sensation by deciding to stand again in his constituency, North Leitrim, as a Sinn Féin candidate. After a long-drawn-out campaign he was eventually (on 21 February 1908) defeated by a substantial majority, but nothing could alter the fact that Sinn Féin had taken a halting step on to the stage of national politics. It is true that what followed was mainly anticlimax. Griffith and his followers had neither the men, the money, nor the support to fight other by-elections as they occurred. Some of the movement's meagre funds were wasted in the latter part of 1909 in a vain attempt to convert Griffith's weekly paper into a daily, and political impotence was soon added to financial stringency when the parliamentary situation changed dramatically to the Irish party's advantage in 1909 and 1910. All the same, the North Leitrim election and the ripple of insubordination within the party had alike indicated that there were limits to the frustration and disappointment that constitutional nationalists would accept. And here, even more than in the admittedly less serious instance of the Young Ireland branch of the United Irish League, the parliamentary leaders would have done well to recognise that their hold on public opinion was strictly conditional.

[1] P. S. O'Hegarty, *A history of Ireland under the union, 1801 to 1922* (London, 1952), p. 651.

At least it could be said that these eddies and flurries were on the surface of politics. But two of the symbolic events of 1907 suggest that deeper, subterranean tides were also beginning to flow. These events were the death of John O'Leary and the return from America of Thomas Clarke. O'Leary had been allowed to return from political exile in 1885 and for the next twenty years had exerted a strong influence over a small circle of associates (of whom Yeats was one of the most devoted), while himself abstaining from direct political action. O'Leary stood as a monument to an antique style of nationalism. He had little interest in the Irish language, and although he had belonged to a republican movement he was pragmatically ready to approve a constitutional monarchy. Above all, he was an austere patriot who believed that 'a man ought not to cry in public for his country'[1] and who had accordingly accepted years of imprisonment and exile with a stoic resignation. The man who returned at the very moment that O'Leary's passing left a void among separatists was of a different kind. He too had committed himself to fenianism in his youth and he too had paid a heavy price—even heavier than O'Leary's—in terms of loss of liberty. Born in 1857, Thomas James Clarke had become involved in the dynamite campaign in England in the early 1880s.[2] For this he was sentenced to penal servitude for life in 1883. Released after fifteen years, he went to America where he worked closely with Devoy. On his return Clarke set up a business in a small tobacconist and newsagent shop in North Great Britain Street, but this was little more than a front for his political activities. Almost immediately he was coopted on to the supreme council of the I.R.B. and threw himself at once into conspiratorial politics, the only politics he knew. Where O'Leary was large-minded, amateur, aristocratic in his approach to life, Clarke was much closer to the ground, more secretive, more professional, and ultimately far more ruthless. That he should have returned to the fray just as interest in the I.R.B. was beginning to revive among the separatists was, in 1907, no more than a portent, but it was a portent that pointed towards a harsher and more dynamic approach to the manufacturing of a minority revolution. This, of course, was still in the future, and presently we shall look more closely at how Clarke and his associates surmounted the formidable obstacles in their path; but from 1907 onwards his very presence in Ireland was an indication that the process of polarisation between moderate and extreme nationalism was about to resume.

It was a process that, in these watershed years, extended far beyond the rivalries of one breed of nationalist with another. Unionists were scarcely less affected. We have seen already that the immediate effect of the devolution crisis of 1904–5 had been to cause a hardening of Ulster unionist opinion, epitomised by the hounding of Wyndham out of office and the creation of the Ulster Unionist Council to work for the defence of the union. Yet, at the very moment this was happening Ulster

---

[1] ' "There are things a man must not do to save a nation", he had once told me, and when I asked him what things, had said "To cry in public" ' (W. B. Yeats, *Autobiographies* (London, 1926), p. 263).
[2] Above, pp 50, 66.

unionism was itself in turmoil, arising from the foundation in June 1903 of the Independent Loyal Orange Institution (commonly known as the Independent Orange Order). This was the creation of a shipyard worker, Thomas Sloan (he was also a temperance enthusiast and evangelical preacher), who for a short period became the spokesman for a section of the Belfast protestant working class, irked by the continued domination of unionism by landowners and big business. In July 1902 Sloan heckled and criticised the leader of the Ulster unionist parliamentary group, Colonel E. J. Saunderson. Expelled from the Orange Order for this insubordination, Sloan, who had won a by-election in Belfast South in August 1902, retaliated by forming the Independent Orange Order, into which he breathed his own brand of aggressive protestantism and his own concern for the condition of the workers. Some degree of intellectual respectability was conferred on this rogue elephant by the adhesion of an able journalist, Robert Lindsay Crawford, who gave up his post as editor of the Dublin-based *Irish Protestant* to come north and produce a liberal paper in Belfast. In 1905, just before he moved from Dublin, Lindsay Crawford wrote for the Independent Orange Order the Magheramorne manifesto, which appealed for religious toleration and came out in favour not only of a reorganisation of Irish government, but also of social betterment for the working people of the province.[1] Under this banner Sloan and his colleagues campaigned in the general election of 1906, in the course of which Sloan himself retained Belfast South, another independent unionist took Antrim North, and T. W. Russell, also standing as an independent unionist (though primarily on a platform of compulsory land purchase), was returned for his old constituency, Tyrone South. It seems moreover that the victory by a narrow margin in Belfast West of the nationalist Joseph Devlin was almost certainly due to disarray among the unionist voters, confused by the appearance on the scene of another independent unionist, Alexander Carlisle. He only secured 153 votes, but since Devlin won by only 16 votes in a poll of 8,413 it is likely that Carlisle's intervention was decisive.

Almost at once, however, the process of polarisation began. Sloan had shown signs of backsliding towards orthodox unionism even while the election was in progress, and when in May 1908 Lindsay Crawford was deprived of his editorship and expelled from the Independent Orange Order for advocating home rule and attacking sweated-labour conditions in the linen industry, Sloan quickly reverted to his sectarian base, although this was not enough to save him from losing his seat at the next election in January 1910. What seems to have been happening from 1907 was that Ulster unionism was closing its ranks in face of the liberal majority in the house of commons and the renewed nationalist pressure for home rule. Nor was it only Ulster unionism that reacted to that threat in that way. The

---

[1] The manifesto saw the order's members as standing 'once more on the banks of the Boyne, not as victors . . . but to . . . hold out the right hand of fellowship to those who, while worshipping at other shrines, are yet our countrymen' (John Boyle, 'The Belfast Protestant Association and the Independent Orange Order, 1901–10' in *I.H.S.*, xiii, no. 50 (Sept. 1962), p. 134).

southern unionists likewise began, not merely to look to their own defences, but to work for a closer understanding with their Ulster brethren and with the British tories. The latter aim was facilitated by Colonel Saunderson's death in 1906 and by the succession to the leadership of Walter Long, an English squire who had a deep, romantic attachment to Ireland and to the union.[1] Since closer cooperation between unionists of north and south was almost simultaneously achieved by the creation on 19 December 1907 of the Joint Committee of Unionist Associations, which was designed to harmonise the work of the Irish Unionist Alliance and the Ulster Unionist Council, it was evident that the opponents of home rule were poised to begin their counter-offensive the moment it should prove necessary.

In the long run the battle would have to be fought out in the sphere of politics, for that was where the overriding issue—the control and distribution of power—could alone be decided; but the ultimate bitterness of that battle cannot be properly understood unless it is constantly borne in mind that it subsumed other conflicts that coloured the central struggle for power with sectarian, cultural, and even class rivalries. On these rivalries certain events of 1907 shed a lurid, if premonitory, light. One of them was the promulgation by the papacy at the end of the year of the *Ne temere* decree.[2] This dealt with mixed marriages—always a delicate problem in Ireland—in such a fashion as to make it incumbent on a catholic marrying a protestant to ensure that the children of the marriage would be brought up as catholics. The decree did not come into operation until Easter Sunday 1908, and it was several years after that before its full implications could be grasped; but this does not affect the significance of the papal initiative, which was to widen the existing gulf between catholics and protestants in Ireland at the very moment when the renewal of the agitation for home rule presupposed, or appeared to presuppose, that both communities could be successfully reconciled in a self-governing Ireland.

Protestant doubts about such a halcyon future can only have been intensified by a further symbolic event in 1907—the prolonged and vehement riots that greeted the first production of J. M. Synge's 'The playboy of the western world' at the Abbey Theatre in January. Superficially, the riots were occasioned partly by the language Synge put into the mouths of the peasants—Dublin grundyism was outraged especially by the reference to girls in their 'shifts'—and partly by the story, which elevates the peasant boy Christy Mahon into a local hero when it is believed he has killed his father, and deflates him into an anti-hero when it turns out that he is incompetent even at parricide. It was in vain for Synge to insist that both the language and the incident came out of his intimate personal

---

[1] Jackson has, however, argued (*Ulster party*, pp 286–98 and ch. 7, *passim*) that from 1905 to 1911 Irish unionism was undergoing a period of flux, with unionists (particularly in Ulster) experiencing an increasing sense of isolation from their British counterparts and an increasingly frosty and mistrustful relationship with the tory leadership in Britain; and that Long's impact on this situation was more apparent than real.

[2] See I. M. Ellis, *Vision and reality: a survey of twentieth-century Irish inter-church relations* (Belfast, 1992), pp 5–7.

knowledge of the west of Ireland. To his critics, he was and remained a foul-mouthed slanderer of his country. This, however, was not a new quarrel. We have seen already that Yeats had collided with the conventional pieties with his very first play for the new theatre, and Synge himself had provoked a controversy very similar to that of 1907 with the first production in 1903 of 'In the shadow of the glen', in which he had depicted the loneliness and frustration of a young wife married to an old man in a remote Wicklow cottage, and had resolved her crisis by having her elope with a 'travelling man'.[1]

The storm that burst in 1903, like its successor of 1907, was symptomatic of a deep cultural division in Irish society. To nationalists in general, and to Gaelic enthusiasts in particular, literature and the theatre presented themselves primarily as instruments of propaganda to be used for the creation, or re-creation, of an indigenous Irish culture. The essential ingredients of this culture were that it should be Gaelic, that it should be catholic, and that it should hold up to nature a mirror in which Irish life, especially rural Irish life, should be reflected in an image of flawless purity. One can readily understand the psychological mechanism that made it imperative to compensate in this way for centuries of inferiority, but it was perhaps inevitable, given the prevailing tone of Irish catholicism, that purity should involve puritanism.

For the creators of the Irish theatre purity and puritanism were equally irrelevant. They were intent on developing, in English, a literature that, while certainly derived from their Irish experience, would be a part of the wider European civilisation to which they were highly conscious of belonging. For them, therefore, the freedom of the artist to express himself without regard to the demands of propaganda, and without pandering to religious, cultural, or political susceptibilities, was a principle on which there could be absolutely no compromise. It was this principle that Yeats defended with great courage and tenacity in 1903 and 1907 and, in the sense that the Abbey Theatre continued to exist and to put on controversial plays, he can be said to have gained his point. Indeed, only two years later he and Lady Gregory once more demonstrated their independence of censorship from quite a different quarter, by performing Bernard Shaw's 'The shewing up of Blanco Posnet' after it had been banned in England, and in the teeth of determined efforts by Dublin Castle to prevent them.

Yet despite these successes, and although both Yeats and Lady Gregory were to survive to fight similar battles on behalf of Sean O'Casey in the vastly different circumstances of the 1920s, the furore of 1907, when added to that of 1903, suggests that the long-term battle they were fighting was an uneven one, which they would probably lose. Anglo-Irish and protestant as most of the group were, they found themselves isolated in Irish life. On the one hand, they could look for little support from the ascendancy class, which as a whole preferred the hunting field to the theatre, and which certainly looked askance at a theatre that seemed

[1] Above, p. 108; below, pp 366–8, 372–5.

to deal mainly with legendary Irish gods and earthy Irish peasants. On the other hand, the uncompromising demand for artistic freedom, allied to the fact that several of these writers openly expressed their preference for cosmopolitanism as opposed to nationalism in art, meant that whatever bridges they had hoped to build between the two cultures were never likely to span the chasm that separated Gaelic idealism from Anglo-Irish liberalism.[1] In fact, of course, as we can now see in retrospect, the whole cultural movement of which the Abbey Theatre was the supreme embodiment was founded on an illusion—the illusion that politics was no longer of primary importance and that what mattered was to reconcile different traditions by providing them with a common fund of artistic achievement. But politics had not ceased to be of primary importance, and the Abbey controversies were in reality significant of far deeper conflicts in Irish society than the creators of the literary revival had allowed themselves to realise. Characteristically, it was James Joyce rather than Yeats who judged the cultural climate most accurately. Brought up in the world of catholic nationalism that Yeats could never really penetrate, Joyce remained embedded in that world even while repudiating it and repudiated by it. For him, Dublin had already come to seem 'the centre of paralysis',[2] and at this very time he was completing in Trieste the stories, *Dubliners*, that were to convey that paralysis as nothing else in literature has ever succeeded in doing, unless it be his own subsequent writings. Less self-confident (despite appearances) than the Anglo-Irish and certainly lacking their reserves of material support, he was groping his way towards his famous conclusion that the only way to 'fly by' the nets of nationality, language, and religion that Ireland spread in the path of the artist was to resort to 'silence, exile, and cunning'.[3] In 1907 this would have seemed to the Anglo-Irish much too extreme a response, but the time was coming when for many of them also it would seem the only one.

By comparison with the theatre imbroglio, which naturally focused the attention of the intelligentsia and thus ensured it the widest possible publicity, the final event of 1907 that we have still to note made a mainly local impact, even though it contained within itself the seeds of something potentially far more wide-ranging in its consequences than the quarrel between Yeats and Synge and their critics. This was the outbreak of severe labour trouble in Belfast, following the arrival there of a new organiser, sent by the British-based National Union of Dock Labourers to stimulate the dockers into self-protection. This was James Larkin. Born in Liverpool of Irish parents in 1876, he had, like James Connolly, endured a poverty-stricken childhood in which the need to earn a living had effectively barred him from formal education. Built on the large scale, he had

[1] D. G. Boyce has offered a somewhat different analysis of the complex motivations, both artistic and political, of the leading protestant figures of the cultural revival in his ' "One last burial": culture, counter-revolution, and revolution in Ireland, 1886–1916' in Boyce, *Revolution in Ire.*, pp 115–36.
[2] Joyce to Grant Richards, 5 May 1906 (*Letters of James Joyce*, ii, ed. Richard Ellmann (London, 1966), p. 134).
[3] James Joyce, *Portrait of the artist as a young man* (Everyman ed., London, 1991), p. 251.

trained himself to become an extremely effective open-air orator, and his obvious sympathy for the poor combined with his hatred of exploitation and bureaucratic indifference to make him a flamboyant, explosive force in the labour movement. Within a few months of his arrival in Belfast the city was torn apart by strikes and lock-outs that affected not merely the dock workers, but also the carters and coalmen, and even a section of the police. More remarkable still, he succeeded briefly—with some help from Joseph Devlin and also from the Independent Orange Order—in persuading catholic and protestant working men to present a common front to their employers. It has to be admitted, however, that in this, as in so many other of the episodes we have been considering, 1907 was a portent rather than a climax. Larkin did manage to win wage increases for the carters and coalmen, but he failed to obtain acceptance for a closed-shop policy in the future, and the dockers, who were supposed to be his special responsibility, had eventually to go back to work on the employers' terms. Moreover, the non-sectarianism of his organisation was short-lived, and before long the Belfast workers were to be found once more firmly entrenched in their traditional antagonisms. Yet if Larkin largely failed in Belfast, his mission there was only the beginning of his crusade. He moved to Dublin in 1908 and there at once began that frenetic campaign of agitation that in five years time was to add a new dimension to Irish politics.

If class warfare was a new dimension, the watershed we have been considering may be said in general to have thrown the old landscape of Irish politics into sharper, clearer relief. In whatever direction we turn between 1903 and 1907, we seem to be faced with a heightening of tension and an increasing rigidity of attitudes. This was so even within the comparatively placid ranks of the parliamentarians; it was so among the revolutionaries of the I.R.B. and also within that broad spectrum of nationalist opinion to which contemporaries had already given the name of Irish-Ireland; it was so no less among the unionists, north and south; and, though perhaps to a less obvious degree, among the writers and artists of the Anglo-Irish ascendancy. The true significance of this heightened tension and rigidity was by no means clear at the time it was happening; on the contrary, it would only become clear when extraneous events—the breaking of the political pack-ice from 1910 onwards—served to reawaken men to the still persisting fissures in Irish society.

CHAPTER VI

The developing crisis, 1907–14

F. S. L. LYONS

IF in retrospect we can see that the watershed of 1903–7 was a watershed precisely because the events of those years were creating a situation that was deeply inimical to the solution of Ireland's problems by a process of benevolent legislation, the immediate sequel seemed to point rather in the opposite direction. True, in 1908 and 1909 a constructive political initiative by the government seemed as remote as ever, but the chief secretary, Augustine Birrell (1907–16), did register a degree of success in the field of social reform. Birrell had become chief secretary in somewhat unpromising circumstances. His own labours at the board of education had been nullified by the action of the house of lords in rejecting an important education bill in 1906, and he had subsequently been transferred to the Irish office. There, he inherited the legacy of frustration and annoyance that his ineffectual predecessor, James Bryce (1905–7), had created among the Irish parliamentary leaders. Birrell's first attempt to make his mark as a more dynamic minister—the Irish council bill—could scarcely have been a more dismal début,[1] but he had reserves of tenacity and resilience that only gradually became apparent. He was in fact to hold office for nine years—far longer than the normal stint for chief secretaries—and it was not until the Easter rising utterly discredited his regime that he finally left Ireland. Long before that, however, his style of government had been a matter of controversy.[2] Like many chief secretaries, he spent considerably more time in London than in Dublin, but this, though disliked, was probably less objectionable to his 'subjects' than the fact that he approached their affairs with what seemed to some of them an uncalled-for levity. Birrell was indeed a witty man who compensated for the burdens of his official position by finding a good deal to laugh at in the humours and absurdities that he had no difficulty in detecting in Irish life. For this, and for his famous indiscretion in admitting that he took his evidence of public opinion as much from the programmes of the Abbey Theatre as from the reports of the R.I.C., he was

---

[1] For Birrell's attitude towards the council bill proposals, see O'Halpin, *Decline of the union*, pp 76–8, 81.

[2] Patricia Jalland has offered an examination of the attitudes of near-contemporary writers and more recent historians to the achievements, as well as the failings, of Birrell, highlighting some of the factors that have contributed to the somewhat obscure picture often painted of him (Jalland, 'A liberal chief secretary and the Irish question: Augustine Birrell, 1907–1914' in *Hist. Jn.*, xix, no. 2 (1976), pp 421–6).

later to be condemned and ridiculed. It remains arguable, however, that to govern
Ireland on a light rein rather than to bear down heavily in the traditional manner
may have been a more appropriate response to what Birrell himself was sensitive
enough to diagnose as a delicate and potentially explosive situation.[1]

His principal monument is probably the legislation that he succeeded in
carrying in 1908: the Irish universities act, which was intended to remove, and
which, despite certain defects, did remove from the political arena the long-
standing grievances of Irish catholics in regard to higher education.[2] Cutting
through the tangle of argument and the mountain of evidence assembled by recent
commissions of inquiry into the whole question, Birrell's act avoided the rock on
which so many earlier reforming efforts had foundered—what to do with Trinity
College—and instead created two new universities out of the other existing
institutions. One was the Queen's University of Belfast, which was the old queen's
college given independent status. The other was a federal structure, the National
University of Ireland, composed of the two former queen's colleges of Cork and
Galway, together with the university college in Dublin that had evolved out of
Newman's foundation in the middle of the nineteenth century. Both the new
universities were empowered to award their own degrees, and so the royal
university, which had acted as an examining body since 1882, was now abolished.
Though both the Queen's University and the National University were deliberately designed to be interdenominational, this intention was in the long run to be
more completely fulfilled in Belfast than elsewhere. The National University,
though not precisely what catholics had been seeking over the years, did to a very
large degree become their university, just as Trinity remained to all intents and
purposes the protestant university.[3]

The Irish universities act by no means exhausted the liberal impulse towards
reform. On the contrary, between 1906 and 1909 legislation reached the statute
book that provided improved housing for the working classes in town and
country, afforded protection to town tenants, increased payments to national
school teachers and grants for school-building, renewed the grant in aid of the
study of the Irish language, and applied to Ireland the provisions of the British
old age pensions act of 1908.[4] To this list should be added the decision to allow

---

[1] See, for example, an account of the relationship that Birrell built up with the Irish party, which
led Dillon to comment in 1913 that Birrell's administration was the most successful since the union,
and in 1914 that Birrell was 'one of the best of Irish secretaries' (Jalland, art. cit., pp 428–9). Jalland
ascribes the degree of cooperation given by Redmond and his colleagues to Asquith, from 1911 on, to
their confidence in and respect for Birrell, rather than any trust they put in the prime minister. She
has also offered a useful analysis of the difficulties of Birrell's task in the aftermath of the introduction
of the third home rule bill, and of his weakness in coping with the problems that confronted him after
1912 (ibid., pp 441–51). O'Halpin's assessment (*Decline of the union*, pp 91–6) is more critical of the
nature of the Irish government under Birrell and his under-secretary (1908–14), Sir James Dougherty.

[2] 8 Edw. VII, c. 38 (1 Aug. 1908); and see below, pp 566–7.

[3] See Lee for the limitations of the legislation, particularly in the financial provisions made for the
colleges of the new national university (*Modernisation of Ir. society*, pp 128–9).

[4] 8 Edw. VII, c. 40 (1 Aug. 1908); the act provided for a pension of 1s.–5s. a week to be paid to
any person over the age of 70 who had been a British subject resident in the United Kingdom for

the arms act of 1881 to expire at the end of 1906, and two further concessions already mentioned—the evicted tenants act of 1907 and the land act of 1909.[1] Ironically enough, the latter, which was intended to redress some of the financial grievances arising out of the Wyndham act, had to be paid for by a price that was all too familiar in the political economy of Ireland—that is to say, a renewed split among the constitutional nationalists. Once again it was O'Brien who was at the centre of controversy. Towards the end of 1907, in an effort to offset the Irish council bill fiasco and the subsequent challenge from Sinn Féin, Redmond had entered into negotiations with O'Brien with a view to reestablishing unity. The main point at issue was whether the pledge to be taken by all parliamentary candidates was still regarded as binding those who took it to 'sit, act, and vote' with the party in parliament only, or whether O'Brien's own version of 1900—imposing obedience to the party line outside as well as inside the house of commons—was now acceptable to the party as a whole. Redmond was quite ready to agree to this wider interpretation of the pledge, but refused to concede O'Brien's demand for a national convention of the United Irish League to be summoned to ratify the reconciliation. O'Brien, whose political judgement seems from this time onwards to have become increasingly erratic, thereupon set on foot a curious intrigue whereby, with the help of Captain Shawe-Taylor, Lord Dunraven, and Sinn Féin, he hoped to form a new comprehensive party dedicated to his old nostrum of conference plus business. Not altogether surprisingly, his plan came to nothing; and, since it simultaneously became clear that feeling in the Irish party and in the league was strongly in favour of unity without delay on the basis of his negotiations with Redmond, O'Brien hurriedly changed course and in January 1908 agreed to come back into the fold. With him appeared a group of other M.P.s, including the irrepressible Healy, who for sometimes divergent reasons had found themselves at odds with the party in the recent past.

So far so good. Unhappily, however, no sooner had O'Brien and Healy rejoined the party than the old question of land purchase finance, which had been the immediate cause of O'Brien's previous resignation, reared its head again. When in April 1908 the party discussed how best to improve the financial aspects of the Wyndham act, O'Brien promptly proposed a second dose of his old panacea, a land conference between representatives of the landlords and tenants. His motion was heavily defeated—a party intent on bringing the liberal government to the brink of home rule was in no mood to coquet with Irish landlords—and from that moment, it seems, O'Brien recognised that the gulf between him and the party leaders was still as wide as it had ever been. Characteristically, he responded to this by attempting to sway a national convention of the United Irish League into accepting his doctrine—or dogma as it might more properly be called—of conference plus business. The meeting was held in Dublin in February 1909, and

twenty years, and whose means did not exceed £31. 10s. a year; paupers, convicts, lunatics, and the chronically idle were excluded, however.

[1] Details of Birrell's land policy can be found in Jalland, art. cit., pp 431-4.

O'Brien suffered the traumatic experience of being refused a hearing by the organisation he had himself created. He blamed this rowdyism on Devlin's followers from the Board of Erin wing of the Ancient Order of Hibernians but, although there may indeed have been an element of organised heckling, it was noticeable that Dillon also was much interrupted during a debate on the Irish language at the same convention. Whether this malice was specific, or reflected a general frustration at the grass roots, O'Brien did not pause to inquire. Loudly proclaiming his contempt for the 'baton convention', he withdrew to his stronghold in Cork and there, just over a year later, founded yet another organisation, the All-for-Ireland League, intended to be the vehicle for his policy of conciliation towards those who, he hoped, would cooperate with him. The parliamentary leaders at once responded by placing the new league under an interdict; but although this presaged a fresh split, the full implications remained hidden for a further year, since O'Brien's health collapsed and, having resigned his parliamentary seat, he disappeared once more from the scene.

This was not the last the country was to hear of him by any means, but when he did eventually reemerge in 1910 it was to confront a vastly changed situation. The catalyst, as is well known, was Lloyd George's celebrated budget of 1909. Faced with the need to find more money for the new old-age pensions and the beginnings of social insurance, and also for additional naval expenditure, the chancellor of the exchequer proposed to increase income tax, to levy a supertax, to introduce a range of land taxes, and to increase death duties and the duties on liquor licences, spirits, and tobacco. The budget was intensely controversial in Britain, and although the liberal majority in the house of commons was large enough to enable the government to press on with their proposals, it very soon became evident that the tories were prepared to go to the limits of the constitution, or even beyond them, by using the house of lords to veto the budget.

For the Irish parliamentary party this was a situation full of hope, but also full of danger. If a major quarrel developed between the two houses—and such a quarrel had been impending ever since 1906—it might, if pushed to a conclusion, result in a limitation of the lords' veto and, as it had been obvious for many years that this was an indispensable preliminary to the achievement of home rule, Redmond and his colleagues were bound to try to give new life and meaning to the liberal alliance. On the other hand, the budget was not only as controversial in Ireland as in Britain, but, because it bore most heavily on the liquor interest on which the party depended for much of its support, the nationalist leaders had virtually no option but to criticise Lloyd George's proposals at the same time as they urged the liberal government to stand firm against the house of lords. They tried to reconcile these two aims throughout the wearing and anxious session of 1909, seeking to extract concessions on those parts of the budget that related most directly to Ireland, while at the same time making their general support conditional on an effective limitation of the veto power of the upper house. They failed to make much headway on the budget, and it was not until the lords finally braced themselves to reject it, on 30 November 1909, that the situation was dramatically changed in their favour. Parliament was at once dissolved and the country plunged into what was probably the most critical election since 1832. From an Irish viewpoint the supreme advantage of this development was that it removed at one stroke the incubus of the large liberal majority that for the past four years had made the government almost impervious to Irish pressure. Now, that pressure could again be applied with maximum effect, and the first indication of this was a public statement in December by Asquith (who had succeeded Campbell-Bannerman as prime minister in April 1908) at an eve-of-election meeting in the Albert Hall, London, that the problem of Ireland could only be solved 'by a policy which, while explicitly safeguarding the supremacy and indefectible authority of the imperial parliament, will set up in Ireland a system of full self-government in regard to purely Irish affairs.'[1]

This statement was later to be extensively exploited by nationalists to counter the unionist claim that home rule had not been an issue at the election, and it is probably fair to say that although 'lords versus people' occupied the stage to the exclusion of almost anything else, perceptive observers (and these included some unionist politicians) recognised that part of the seriousness of the veto question was that it was inextricably bound up with the Irish question. In Ireland itself, admittedly, this proved a difficult point to bring home to the electorate, and although Redmond came out of the election in a seemingly strong position he was vulnerable on two counts. One was that he was not at the head of a united party. True, his following numbered seventy-one, but there were also eleven independents. Eight of these were later supporters of O'Brien's All-for-Ireland League, and, since they included both Healy and the redoubtable O'Brien himself, it was clear that nationalist critics of nationalists would be formidably represented in the new house of commons, though Redmond could take comfort from the fact that they were not formidably represented in the country at large, since six of the independents sat for seats in Cork city and county, where O'Brien's personal ascendancy had always been very strong.

The other sense in which Redmond was vulnerable was that the support he had won in the constituencies was strictly conditional. He must turn the constitutional crisis to immediate account or he would very soon face trouble at home. Fortunately for him, the effect of the election was to place him in a position of leverage undreamt of since Parnell's day and potentially even more powerful than that achieved by Parnell himself in 1886. When the dust had settled it appeared that the liberals had won 275 seats as against the 273 won by the unionists and that the balance of power rested in the hands of the Irish members and of the bloc of forty labour members, whose presence in parliament was itself one of the most revolutionary consequences of a revolutionary election.

At first sight, admittedly, it did not seem as if the revolutionary election was going to produce a revolutionary situation. The instinct of moderate politicians

[1] Gwynn, *Redmond*, p. 169.

on both sides was not to push the argument to extremes, and this tendency was much accentuated when the death of Edward VII in May 1910 brought to the throne an inexperienced successor in the person of George V. For six months, from June to November, liberal and tory representatives were locked in conference in an attempt to find an agreed solution to the problem confronting them. Indeed, for some leading politicians, notably Lloyd George, an 'agreed solution' meant agreement not only on the question of the house of lords, but on a whole range of contemporary questions of which he, like many others, was inclined to regard tariff reform as the most fundamental, though Ireland—to be dealt with on federal lines—also came within his purview. The logical outcome of such a manœuvre would presumably have been a coalition government of the kind Lloyd George was eventually to lead in wartime; but although the idea was not unattractive to some of the younger tories, it collapsed, as did the constitutional conference itself, in the face of Arthur Balfour's unwavering hostility to any settlement either of the house of lords issue or of the Irish question on terms that he thought might imperil the integrity of the empire or the unity of the tory party.

With the failure of the conference and of these other more subterranean manœuvres, the contestants were once more left face to face. But so grave was the situation that the government did not feel able to move towards its final sanction—to ask the king to create sufficient liberal peers to swamp the unionist majority in the upper house—without holding a second general election within the year, in December 1910. This time the result was even more extraordinary than in February. Liberals had 271 seats, tories and liberal unionists 273, labour went up to 42, and Irish nationalists (including T. P. O'Connor) to 84, of whom 74 were Redmondites. This meant, of course, that Irish pressure could now be applied with even greater intensity, and in the end, though only after the threat of a mass creation of liberal peers, the house of lords capitulated and accepted the limitation of its powers embodied in the parliament act of 1911.[1] The effect of this was to reduce the veto of the upper house to a power to delay for two years. Any bill passing through the house of commons in three successive sessions would thus automatically become law. With Redmond still holding the balance of power at Westminster, it was obvious that the way had now been prepared for a third attempt to pass a home rule bill.

In Ireland this had been obvious to unionists for some time and, as we saw earlier, there had been a marked tendency among them to close their ranks and obliterate internal disputes the moment the return of the liberals to power had signalled the probable reappearance of the spectre of home rule. It is important to be clear, however (in view of the emphasis that was later to be laid on the theory that two nations existed in Ireland), that, in this preliminary stage of unionist preparation to resist home rule, argument was directed not

[1] 1 & 2 Geo. V, c. 13 (18 Aug. 1911).

towards demonstrating the existence of separate communities in the country but rather towards insisting on the oneness of Ireland with the rest of the United Kingdom.

That it was this line that was so persistently followed at the outset reflects the prominence, if not preeminence, of the southern unionists in the counsels of Irish unionism as a whole at this time. Attention has been drawn[1] to the fact that Irish unionism was by no means monolithic, either in its protestantism, its social organisation, or its politics, and this essential disunity of unionism would soon again be even more starkly demonstrated. But in 1911 it was not obvious, at least on the surface. The reason is that despite the evident weaknesses of their situation—they were thin on the ground and widely scattered geographically—the southern unionists enjoyed a degree of influence within the tory party altogether out of proportion to their numbers. Not only were their principal leaders, the marquess of Lansdowne and Viscount (later Earl) Midleton, also leaders of British toryism, but southern unionists contributed eighty-six to the total of peers in the house of lords who had Irish interests, while no fewer than eighteen southern unionist M.P.s had British seats in the house of commons. When to this is added a considerable amount of intermarriage between British and Irish families and the further fact that it was by no means uncommon for individuals to hold property in both countries, it is clear that the ties between this small yet influential minority and the British governing class were very close. The Ulster unionists, on the other hand, were much more *sui generis*. They had a stronger local base, which contributed to their sense of independence, but it is not unreasonable to suppose that this in itself may have been heightened by the fact that some of them differed from their southern brethren in being presbyterian and either middle-class or working-class.[2] It was scarcely accidental that there were only eighteen Ulster unionist peers in the house of lords, or that Ulster unionists should supply only two M.P.s to British constituencies. These figures do not in themselves signify a great deal, but they help to explain not only a fundamental distinction between northern and southern unionists, but also why the alliance that was so soon to develop between British tories and Ulster unionists turned out in the end to be a marriage of interests rather than a union of hearts.

This, however, only gradually became apparent. In 1910 and 1911, while the crisis over the lords' veto was coming to its climax, changes in leadership seemed to emphasise unity rather than difference. Thus in 1910 Sir Edward Carson took over from Long as leader of the Irish unionists, and in 1911 Andrew Bonar Law replaced Balfour at the head of the tory party. Since both Carson and

---

[1] Above, pp 117–19.
[2] Alvin Jackson (*Ulster party*, pp 307–10) has given detailed attention to this aspect of the development of Ulster unionism, describing the emergence of middle-class leaders from commercial and legal backgrounds, who were not only less deferential to local landlords but closely tied to their local constituencies. This development, he argues, both influenced and was in turn reinforced by the founding of the Ulster Unionist Council, whose standing committee 'encouraged a more gritty and a more populist articulation of faith' and also encouraged local reorganisation (ibid., p. 311).

Bonar Law had been prominent in tory politics for years past, it seemed reasonable to assume that the partnership between them would be both formidable and—from a unionist viewpoint—fruitful. To a certain extent, but to a certain extent only, this turned out to be true. That it was not wholly true is to be explained partly perhaps by important differences of temperament and responsibility, but also by scarcely less important differences of origin. Carson was a southerner, educated at Trinity College and rising through his own superlative abilities to the highest position at the bar and to early political advancement. Bonar Law, born in Canada and entering politics in Britain only after he had made a fortune in the Canadian iron industry, was much less articulate and forceful than Carson. But he was of Ulster extraction, and had a certain dour tenacity characteristic of the province. Behind these obvious divergences of background and personality lay something more fundamental. It is important to be clear that Carson was a quintessential southern unionist who had first risen into prominence as crown prosecutor at the time of the plan of campaign. He had seen agrarian agitation at first hand and had not liked what he saw. He knew how vulnerable unionists were outside the north-east corner of the island, and for him therefore the essence of the matter was that the connection with Britain must never be broken, for this was the sole guarantee of their security that would be acceptable to the people whom he represented. To this doctrine Bonar Law would no doubt have given an intellectual assent, but it was consistent neither with his nature nor with his position to push it to the uttermost. He could indeed use extreme language and adopt very intransigent stances, but with his Ulster predilections and his responsibilities as tory leader to influence him, he was bound to take a more elastic view than Carson of what was possible and what was not.[1]

But that was for the future. In 1911 everything seemed to point towards a consolidated and powerful resistance to home rule. The motives that guided unionists in the critical years that now lay ahead of them were essentially the same as those that had guided them in the earlier crises of 1886 and 1893, though their perceptions had no doubt been sharpened by the devolution crisis of 1904–5, which had brought home to them a new awareness of the necessity for cultivating self-reliance. These motives remained as mixed as they had been when home rule first swam into their ken in the days of Isaac Butt. They feared it as the thin end of an entering wedge. They did not accept that self-government meant only local self-government, and dreaded that it would lead on to total separation. They were convinced that home rule would mean Rome rule and were ready to point to catholic clerical control of education over most of the country, to the undoubted intervention of bishops and priests in nationalist politics, and to the attitude of the church towards protestants as most recently evinced by the promulgation of

[1] For an alternative analysis of the unionism of Carson and Bonar Law, and for an account of Law's ascent to the tory leadership, views on Ulster, and concept of his role as leader of the opposition, see Nicholas Mansergh, *The unresolved question: the Anglo–Irish settlement and its undoing, 1912–72* (New Haven, Conn., and London, 1991), pp 45–9.

the *Ne temere* decree.[1] They disliked the economic panaceas of Griffith and his friends, believing that the commercial ties between Britain and Ireland must remain close if the smaller island was to retain the late and precarious prosperity it had just achieved.[2] Finally—and, though impossible to quantify, this must have weighed heavily with many of the ascendancy class, eroded though their position had been during the forty-odd years since Gladstone's first land act—they would scarcely have been human if they had not seen in the approach of home rule both the passing of their long supremacy and also the probable elimination of those opportunities for younger sons in the service of the empire that they had seized so avidly for generations.

These were considerations that most unionists could share, though the emphasis would naturally shift depending on whether they were viewed from the 'big house', from Dublin, or from Belfast. But precisely because it was in and around Belfast that unionists were most numerous and most highly organised, it was there that Carson made the first of his intensely dramatic public appearances. On 23 September 1911 in the grounds of Craigavon—the house of the Ulster unionist M.P. James Craig, who was to become his right-hand man and eventual successor—Carson warned his audience to prepare themselves 'with such measures as will carry on for ourselves the government of those districts of which we have control. We must be prepared . . . the morning home rule passes, ourselves to become responsible for the government of the protestant province of Ulster.' And in fact, before he had left Belfast, the Ulster Unionist Council had appointed a small group to frame a constitution for the Ulster provisional government of which he had spoken.[3]

All this was by way of premonitory rumbling, for the actual introduction of a home rule bill was still several months away. When it was finally introduced by Asquith on 11 April 1912 it did not on the face of it seem a very extreme measure. It was proposed to give Ireland a separate parliament with jurisdiction over her

[1] Lee (*Ire. 1912–85*, p. 11) gives an account of the McCann case in Belfast (1910), which seemed to unionists a proof of the insidious implications for protestants of the *Ne temere* decree.

[2] Lee has argued (ibid., p. 8) that at this period unionists made few references to the Sinn Féin movement and its policy, as Sinn Féin was still a 'fringe nationalist faction'. While some unionist spokesmen referred to tariffs as a threat, it was not until later that the protectionist issue became important in the economic arguments. The leading unionist economic spokesman, J. Milne Barbour, was in 1913, Lee argues, at least as concerned that 'the rural interest might outweigh the manufacturing interest' in a home rule Ireland as he was about the prospect of protectionism, and conceded that Ulster unionist opposition was 'very largely religious'.

[3] Ronald McNeill, *Ulster's stand for union* (London, 1922), p. 51. Jackson has argued that while the Craigavon demonstration and the plans for a provisional government *were* timed to follow the promulgation of the parliament act, the framework for such a government had long been present in the standing committee of the Ulster unionist council, and that the significant overlap in personnel between this committee and the 'commission of five', appointed in September 1911 to prepare for provisional government, is an indication of this. In addition, he claims that moves towards militancy among extreme unionists also predate the passing of the act, and that this historic legislation was significant less as a motivation for militants than as a means by which they could bring their measures of resistance into the open, and it seemed to be the point at which Carson gave his sanction to militancy (*Ulster party*, pp 313–19).

own internal affairs, but to withhold from that parliament not only large issues of policy (peace and war; defence; relations with the crown; even, initially, control of the police), but also effective control over revenues, which, including customs and excise, were to be reserved to Westminster.[1] Partly because of this, and partly because it was assumed that a self-governing Ireland would make a contribution in return for the 'imperial services' she shared, it was intended that forty-two Irish members should still continue to be elected to the British house of commons. As with the attempts in the bills of 1886 and 1893 to solve the technical problems connected with the grant of home rule, the Achilles' heel was once again finance. What was suggested could hardly be permanently acceptable to the nationalists, and if it was not permanently acceptable then where would they be prepared to stop? Carson had no doubts whatever. There could not be, he said, any permanent resting-place between complete union and total separation because legislative autonomy could only be coupled with financial independence, and Redmond himself had already admitted that financial independence was what nationalists would eventually claim. Moreover, and if this were not a cogent enough reason to regard the third home rule bill as essentially provisional in character, it appeared—on the surface at any rate—that there was no intention to make any special provision for Ulster.

This was to some extent an illusion. We know now that in February 1912—two months before the bill had been introduced—the cabinet had decided, and had so informed Redmond, that if it became necessary to make concessions to Ulster the government must be free to do what it thought best.[2] The form such concessions might take was left entirely vague, but an inkling of their possible character appeared as early as 11 June 1912 when a liberal member, T. G. Agar-Robartes, proposed that four counties—Antrim, Armagh, Down, and Londonderry—should be excluded from the jurisdiction of the projected home rule parliament. Carson and the Ulster unionists voted for the amendment, but this was not so paradoxical as it seemed. It was in fact a tactical manœuvre.[3] At that stage, and indeed for long afterwards, it was widely believed—they believed it themselves—that they

---

[1] See Patricia Jalland, 'Irish home rule finance: a neglected dimension of the Irish question, 1910–14' in *I.H.S.*, xxiii, no. 91 (May 1983), pp 233–53, for an examination of the findings of the committee set up under Sir H. W. Primrose in January 1911 to investigate the financial relationship between Britain and Ireland and to recommend a fiscal scheme for the home rule bill. Jalland traces the development of the bill's financial clauses, which were largely the creation of Herbert Samuel and gave the British exchequer much more control over Irish financial affairs than the Primrose committee had recommended.

[2] The cabinet's decision is quoted in Roy Jenkins, *Asquith* (London, 1964), pp 276–7.

[3] Richard Murphy has argued, however, that the Agar-Robartes proposal brought divisions among unionists to the surface for the first time, and that there was deep opposition from Long and others to supporting the proposed amendment, even on tactical grounds; moreover, its defeat on 18 June served only to reinforce the view that southern unionists should not be sacrificed. See Murphy, 'Faction in the conservative party and the home rule crisis, 1912–1914' in *History*, lxxi, no. 232 (1986), pp 222–34; cf. also Patrick Buckland, *Irish unionism: one–the Anglo-Irish and the new Ireland, 1885–1922* (Dublin and New York, 1972), p. 18, and *Irish unionism: two–Ulster unionism and the origins of Northern Ireland, 1886–1922* (Dublin and New York, 1973), pp 46–7.

had only to take a significant part of Ulster out of the scheme for the whole edifice
to collapse.

In the event the motion was defeated and the home rule bill began to move
slowly forward on the three-year cycle at the end of which, if constitutional
procedures were to be allowed to operate without interruption, it would become
law.[1] But would the constitutional procedures be allowed to operate without
interruption? And was there any general consensus that these procedures were in
fact constitutional? The two questions were inextricably interlinked, and the tory
party was beginning to give disturbing answers to each of them. On 27 July 1912,
at a great demonstration at Blenheim Palace, Bonar Law made a deliberate and
far-reaching onslaught on the government. It was, he said, a revolutionary
committee 'which has seized by fraud upon despotic power', and for that very
reason tories would be justified in going beyond the ordinary restraints of the
constitution to resist it, for, even if home rule were passed through the house of
commons, 'there are things stronger than parliamentary majorities'. As for the
Ulster protestants, if any attempt were made to deprive them of their 'birthright'
as the result of what he called 'a corrupt parliamentary bargain', then 'I can
imagine no length of resistance to which Ulster will go . . . in which they will not
be supported by the overwhelming majority of the British people'.[2]

This tone was so ominous and so novel in modern British history as to require
explanation. There are three things that need to be said about it. One is that by
the summer of 1912 the old conventions and certainties of parliamentary politics
seemed in a state of dissolution. If this was not, as one historian has described it,
'the strange death of liberal England',[3] it was at any rate a paroxysm from which
it was doubtful if the patient would recover. The passions roused by the house of
lords crisis, the growing militancy of the suffragettes, the worsening relations
between labour and capital, and the prospect—even the reality—of massive
industrial stoppages influenced by the syndicalist yearning for a general strike—all
these things created a hectic and superheated atmosphere in which it was very
easy to take up extreme positions on the Irish question, which, after all, had so
often provoked violence and passion even in much quieter times.[4]

But there were in addition two more specific reasons why the tory leader spoke
as he did. One was that he, like many of his followers, felt that because the liberals
were dependent on the Irish vote if they were to stay in power, and because in
their early years of office those same liberals had shown themselves at best

[1] For the attitudes of British liberals to the Ulster opposition to home rule, and the possibility of
offering concessions to the unionists, see Michael Laffan, *The partition of Ireland, 1911–1925* (Dundalk,
1983), pp 25–7.

[2] *Times*, 29 July 1912; Robert Blake, *The unknown prime minister* (London, 1955), p. 130, gives a
slightly different wording.

[3] The title of George Dangerfield's book (New York, 1935; London, 1936; reprint, New York,
1961).

[4] Jackson (*Ulster party*, p. 117) argues moreover that Bonar Law's comments should have been seen
in the context of traditional tory rhetoric on Ireland, and that he was merely repeating the substance
of older commitments by leading tories.

lukewarm in their support for home rule, their decision to introduce a bill in 1912 represented a surrender to nationalist blackmail—a feeling that was undoubtedly heightened by the success of the Irish party's fund-raising efforts to secure Irish-American support for their cause during the critical year of 1910. A liberal government that could survive only by the favour of an Irish vote that was itself sustained by American dollars was, in Bonar Law's view, the very essence of that 'corrupt parliamentary bargain' he had denounced at Blenheim.

A second argument reinforced this view. It was quite simply that since the British people had not been asked to vote on home rule *per se* (the two elections of 1910 having been fought on the house of lords issue) the government had no mandate to bring in its bill and force it through. As we saw earlier, it was in fact incorrect to say that home rule had not been an issue at either of those elections, since Asquith had unequivocally committed himself to it at his Albert Hall speech on 10 December 1909,[1] and it had been perfectly plain during the constitutional conference of 1910 that the stumbling-block to agreement between the two parties on the veto had been that the elimination of the permanent veto of the house of lords would infallibly clear the way for home rule. If, against this, it was still maintained that the ordinary voter had not been consulted and that the existing majority for it in the commons was invalid because it was merely an Irish majority, the nationalists were entitled to reply that if the act of union meant anything then it meant that an Irish vote was as valid as a Welsh, a Scottish, or an English vote and that a liberal government dependent on an Irish vote was just as legitimate as a liberal or a tory government dependent on any other regional or sectional support.

Behind these often technical and abstract altercations there loomed something much more fundamental—the question of whether a British government responding to the pressure of a parliamentary party that represented the majority of the people of Ireland could in justice impose on a minority of those same people a form of self-government to which they were deeply opposed. And behind this again was the even more profound question whether there really was any such entity as 'the people of Ireland'; whether, in short, Ireland consisted of one nation, two nations, or no distinguishable nation or nations at all. This question was not new. On the contrary, its historic roots went back 300 years, and it had assumed an urgent contemporary relevance from the moment home rule became a possibility in the 1880s. But hitherto the changes and chances of British politics, and the existence of the lords' veto, had enabled liberals, unionists, and nationalists alike to avoid facing up to the ultimate reality of what was to be done with Ulster.

Now, that reality could no longer be avoided, and very rapidly it began to take on a most menacing shape. While in Britain Bonar Law exerted the substantial pressure at his disposal in an endeavour to persuade George V to refuse the royal assent to the home rule bill (an endeavour that failed in the face of the king's

---

[1] Above, p. 127.

determination not to involve the monarchy in party strife if he could possibly avoid it),[1] in Ulster the unionists bent every nerve to demonstrate their solidarity and their intransigence, both symbolised in the signing of the Solemn League and Covenant on 28 September 1912, an undertaking to resist home rule. Since this act of dedication was followed on 31 January 1913 by the formation of the Ulster Volunteer Force, 100,000 men who were to be trained and eventually armed, it was becoming increasingly clear that the situation was in imminent danger of passing out of the control of politicians.

To avert this danger the pressures for some kind of compromise became intense. Intermittently, during 1913 and at the beginning of 1914, the leaders of the two main British parties came together to explore the possibility of separate treatment for a number of predominantly protestant Ulster counties.[2] Although the hope of agreement was very faint it was sufficient for Asquith to begin to exert pressures of his own on Redmond. The latter predictably responded that he could not consent to 'the mutilation of the Irish nation' and assured the prime minister that 'the magnitude of the peril of the Ulster situation is considerably exaggerated'.[3] Looked at in retrospect, this seems a breathtaking oversimplification, and it is tempting to assume that in making it Redmond was bluffing, which in his situation was virtually obligatory. After all, if he was committed to maintaining that Ireland was one nation, he could only do so by dismissing the Ulster resistance to home rule as itself a form of bluff. It is more likely, however, that he genuinely believed what he said. And if this seems strange, not only in the light of the bitter hindsight we have ourselves acquired, but also of the information available to him at the time, we have to remember two countervailing influences. One was that Irish unity was not simply an unquestioned element in the mystique of nationalism (though it certainly was that), but that it had been an administrative and political reality from the time when the conquest of Ulster had been finally completed; it was easy, when contemplating that long perspective, to forget the periodic manifestations of Ulster restiveness and, worse still, to overlook the differences of race, religion, and social and economic organisation that had been the perennial obstacles to genuine assimilation. But if Ireland was not an obvious entity, then neither was Ulster itself, and this was the second fact in the situation that was bound to impress itself on Redmond. Given that almost half of the population of the province were catholic in religion and nationalist in politics, and that in Devlin they had a representative in the inmost circle of the party leadership, it was impossible, or then seemed impossible, for Redmond to waver in his insistence on the essential unity of Ireland.

[1] However, see Laffan, *Partition of Ire.*, p. 34, for reference to a letter from George V to Asquith in Sept. 1913, in which the king echoed demands by tories for a general election on the question of home rule.

[2] Mansergh (*Unresolved question*, pp 61–7) has attributed much significance to these meetings between Bonar Law and Asquith, from Oct. to Dec. 1913, in determining the course of liberal policy on Ulster; see also Murphy, 'Faction in the conservative party', pp 224–30, for these negotiations.

[3] *F.J.*, 13 Oct. 1913, and Redmond memo. 24 Nov. 1913, quoted in Lyons, *Dillon*, pp 333, 341.

Yet while Redmond appeared to stand firm the ground was beginning to quake under his feet. During 1913 one of the most dedicated of Ulster unionists, Major Fred Crawford, had organised the import into the north of several thousand rifles, a number of machine-guns, and a large quantity of ammunition, but when on 4 December the government prohibited the import of arms and ammunition into Ireland Crawford received the backing of the Ulster Unionist Council for a more audacious exploit. This was to purchase further weapons and ammunition in Germany, transport them secretly to Ulster, and distribute them all over the province when a suitable occasion arose. This perceptible movement towards the brink of war was matched by developments in the south towards the end of 1913, which, from the viewpoint of both Asquith and Redmond, were no less ominous. Ironically, these southern developments were themselves in part the outcome of northern initiatives. For although, as we saw earlier, the return of Clarke to Dublin in 1907 had presaged a revival within the republican movement, the actual impetus towards modernisation stemmed initially from Ulster. It came in fact from the Dungannon Clubs founded from 1905, which, despite their affiliation with Sinn Féin, stood, as we have seen, for the full separatist ideal. This was the ideal to which the originators of the clubs, Bulmer Hobson and Denis McCullough, were pledged as members of the I.R.B., and it was to this ideal that in 1906 they introduced their most promising recruit, Sean MacDermott, who two years later also became a full-time organiser for Sinn Féin. While Hobson moved with MacDermott to Dublin—where in 1910 the former established the militantly republican newspaper *Irish Freedom*—McCullough remained in the north, becoming in 1908 the Ulster representative on the supreme council of the I.R.B. With this infusion of new blood and the gradual exclusion of veterans who had lost their revolutionary edge, it was inevitable that 'the movement', as it was revitalised, should become more attractive to a generation that the Gaelic League had already taught to think of Ireland in terms of an autonomous cultural nationality. To move from this to the idea of autonomous political nationality was a short enough step, and one that was to be made by many individuals during the coming years.

Nothing, however, could disguise the fact that the I.R.B., even though revitalised, was small (about 2,000 in 1912), poor, and lacking in any means of making a significant impact on the current situation. This last deficiency was now about to be abruptly changed. Southern nationalists had watched as closely as anybody else while northern unionists had begun to organise and to drill, and the thought had certainly crossed Bulmer Hobson's mind by the summer of 1913 that it would be well for the south to equip itself in the same kind of way. He did in fact arrange for secret drilling by the I.R.B., but he needed an open movement on a much larger scale. The impetus towards this larger movement was supplied, quite suddenly and dramatically, by the appearance on 1 November 1913, in the Gaelic League newspaper *An Claidheamh Soluis*, of an article entitled 'The north began'. It was written by the much respected professor of early Irish history at

University College, Dublin, Eoin MacNeill, and it derived particular significance from the fact that he was known to be a political moderate for whom the conventional home rule platform was still at that time amply sufficient. Apparently influenced to some extent by reports of a local initiative in the autumn of 1913 to create a Midland Volunteer Force based on Athlone,[1] MacNeill was affected to an even greater extent by what was happening in the north. He saw the emergence of the Ulster Volunteers less as a threat to home rule than as a demonstration of an Ulster version of home rule—that is, of the determination of Ulstermen to present an organised resistance to what they conceived as an attempt by the British parliament to impose on them a settlement that they refused to accept. Both the determination and the organisation could be imitated by nationalists, and it was MacNeill's purpose to drive that fact home to his readers.

It is doubtful, however, if he quite expected the sort of reaction he actually got. He had been asked to write his article by the managing director of the paper, Michael Joseph Rahilly, or 'the O'Rahilly', as he had taken to calling himself. A few days after 'The north began' had appeared, the O'Rahilly, prompted by Hobson, asked MacNeill if he would be prepared to follow up his words with actions. MacNeill agreed to the extent of attending a meeting at Wynn's Hotel in Dublin that had been called to discuss what practical steps might be taken to translate his vision into a reality. Of the ten men present at that meeting, four were members of the I.R.B., and their presence indicated that the republicans had already begun to see here the nucleus of the front organisation they were seeking. More meetings were held and the outcome was the formation of a committee to launch a volunteer force. Of the thirty members forming this committee, the I.R.B. accounted for twelve, and their proportion of the membership was subsequently even higher. It was decided to hold a mass meeting to promote the force, and for this occasion—it was held in Dublin on 25 November 1913—Mac-Neill repeated in the form of a manifesto the ideas he had first put forward in his article. The effect of tory policy in Ulster, he asserted, had been to make violence the determining factor in the relations between Britain and Ireland. To acquiesce tamely in this trend would be for nationalists to surrender their rights as men and as citizens. 'In a crisis of this kind the duty of safeguarding our own rights is our duty first and foremost. They have rights who dare maintain them.' This could only be done effectively by creating a 'citizen army' or corps of Irish Volunteers. 'The duties', he insisted, 'will be defensive and protective, and they will not contemplate either aggression or domination.'[2] The meeting was an overwhelming success. Between three and four thousand recruits enrolled on the spot and within about six months the Irish Volunteers numbered 75,000.

[1] These reports were in effect a hoax; see F. X. Martin, 'MacNeill and the foundation of the Irish Volunteers' in F. X. Martin and F. J. Byrne (ed.), *The scholar revolutionary: Eoin MacNeill 1867–1945 and the making of the new Ireland* (Shannon, 1973), pp 123–9.
[2] Quoted in Bulmer Hobson, *A short history of the Irish Volunteers* (Dublin, 1918), pp 21–3, and F. X. Martin (ed.), *The Irish Volunteers 1913–1915: recollections and documents* (Dublin, 1963), pp 99–100.

MacNeill's reference to a 'citizen army' was not as novel as it may have seemed to most of those who attended the meeting, for it is further evidence—if such were needed—of the increasing complexity of the Irish situation that both the description and the actuality of a 'citizen army' had been annexed by others only a few days before the Irish Volunteers were launched. These others were the leaders of militant labour, and they consisted in effect of the irrepressible Larkin and of Connolly, who had returned from America in 1910. When Larkin moved south after his Belfast battles of 1907 he immediately became absorbed in other similar battles in Dublin, Wexford, and Cork. These involved him not only in clashes with the employers, but with his own English-based Dockers' Union, which was by no means enthusiastic at having to support the numerous strikes called by its impulsive but dynamic organiser. Because of friction with the union's general secretary, Larkin was suspended at the end of 1908. He immediately responded by forming the Irish Transport & General Workers' Union, into which he gradually attracted most of the dockers and carters in the principal ports of the country. Although to some extent influenced by the syndicalist ideas that were then in vogue among more militant trade unionists, and apparently conceiving of the I.T.G.W.U. as roughly analogous to the 'one big union' beloved of American syndicalists, Larkin was in no sense a doctrinaire, and most of such intellectualising about the role of labour in Ireland as was done in these years was done by Connolly, who, as of old, combined the hard grind of union organisation with a remarkable output of forthright socialistic journalism. But neither Larkin nor Connolly had to be doctrinaire to grasp the meaning of the new 'industrial unionism' that was convulsing the labour movement in Britain—that it was the business of trade unionists to extend their movement downwards to include the hitherto unorganised masses and also to use their influence so as to imbue these masses with militant class-consciousness.

If Belfast seemed a likely field for the development of industrial unionism—though even there the advance of militant agitation was hampered by the high proportion of women in industry and by the continuance of sectarian and political differences within the working class—Dublin presented a very different aspect. Under-industrialised, depending on distribution rather than manufacture, its large labouring population wretchedly housed, poorly paid, and chronically unemployed or underemployed, it had an unenviable record for disease and mortality, drunkenness, and prostitution.[1] Into these lower depths Larkin, who was a man of deep compassion as well as of reckless ardour, flung himself with a concentrated fury that set the city in almost continual commotion between 1908 and 1913. During that time, despite some severe setbacks, he registered sufficient successes to alarm some of the more powerful and more conservative employers. In the summer of 1913 one of the most influential among them, William Martin Murphy, who controlled the Dublin tramways, a large store, an hotel, and various

---

[1] Above, pp 121–2; below, pp 171–2, 336–7.

other businesses in addition to the *Independent* newspaper, decided to forestall Larkin's intention of unionising the tramway workers by refusing to recognise the I.T.G.W.U. Larkin responded by calling the men out on strike, and a chain reaction of strikes and lock-outs rapidly spread through Murphy's commercial empire and thence into a wide range of other industries. By the end of September 25,000 men were off work and they and their families faced a bleak winter, only partially alleviated by large grants of money and food from the British Trades Union Congress. This, however, dwindled almost to nothing by the new year, after Larkin had alienated the T.U.C. by the violence and crudity with which, in his desperation, he had pressed his syndicalist views on that organisation, which, in labour terms, was still deeply conservative.

The outcome was predictable. In the early months of 1914 the men drifted back to work, and although Larkin's union was not totally destroyed many of those who did return to their jobs were only readmitted on condition that they would not belong to the I.T.G.W.U., that they would not engage in sympathetic strikes, and that they would not refuse to work with non-unionists. Larkin himself left shortly afterwards for America where he was to remain for the next nine years. Yet, though the collapse of his movement and his own departure testified to the extent of his defeat, the great Dublin labour war of 1913 left behind it three legacies. The first and most intangible was that it had made manifest in the most brutal and dramatic way the fact of class war in a society that was habitually preoccupied with sectarian and political differences. These differences still remained the dominant obsession of most people, but among the more militant trade unionists the lesson of 1913 was not that workers' solidarity had been proved to be impossible, rather that next time there must be greater discipline and tighter organisation if the union were to stand its ground. Connected with this stoical resolve to do better in the future was the second legacy of the crisis: the fact that the leadership passed from Larkin to Connolly. With Connolly's move from Belfast to Dublin towards the end of 1914, and with the launching of his new paper, the *Workers' Republic*, on 29 May 1915, a new tone and a new intransigence began to be infused into the labour movement, with consequences that we shall presently have to examine.

The final outcome of 1913 was more directly physical. During the dispute a former army officer, Captain J. R. White, had suggested that the locked-out men should be formed into a small force and given some elementary military training. The purpose was partly to counter the demoralising effects of idleness and partly to provide self-protection against police brutality. The tiny force never numbered more than a few hundred, and when the dispute was over it practically lapsed. It was revived, however, through the initiative of a self-taught genius, Sean O'Casey, or Ó Cathasaigh as he signed himself at that time. O'Casey had yet to begin his career as a writer, but, as a general labourer and an admirer of Larkin, he knew the Dublin slums from the inside and was as determined as Larkin or Connolly that the workers should organise in their own defence. Accordingly, in March

1914 the Citizen Army was reconstituted with membership composed primarily of trade union members but also including anyone who accepted the broadly socialist programme that O'Casey drew up for it. He himself left it shortly afterwards, mainly because of personal differences with one of its most exotic members, the Countess Markievicz; but the Citizen Army remained in being as a witness, not merely to the continuing militancy of one section of the labour movement, but to the growing tendency for authority in Ireland to pass out of the hands of government and into those of private groups prepared in the last resort to use violence in pursuit of their own ends.

Such a development was of course a recipe for anarchy. Two further episodes in that dangerous spring of 1914 pointed in the same direction, and did so all the more dramatically because, on the political front, it had seemed for a moment as if there might be a break in the deadlock. During the winter of 1913–14 Redmond and his colleagues had been brought with the utmost reluctance to agree to the government's proposal that individual Ulster counties might be allowed to opt out of the home rule settlement for a period of three, subsequently increased to six, years after which they would automatically come under the jurisdiction of the Dublin parliament. For Redmond to have conceded even this was a dangerous manœuvre, which made logical nonsense of his 'one nation' theory, but it seems probable that he felt it necessary to offer a show of reasonableness in the face of what he knew about the divisions in the cabinet and the anxieties of the king. Moreover, it is reasonably certain that he expected the concession to be rejected by Carson, in which case he would have gained credit for his moderation without having had to abandon the substance of his position. Nor did Carson disappoint him. When Asquith put the proposal for county option and temporary exclusion to the house of commons on 9 March 1914 the Ulster leader contemptuously refused what he called 'sentence of death with a stay of execution for six years'.[1] A few days later he ostentatiously left the house of commons to put himself, as he said, at the head of his people, and there was widespread speculation that he had gone to Belfast to proclaim the provisional government for which the Ulster Unionist Council had laid its contingency plans the previous autumn.

In fact, what came out of Ireland was not a declaration of Ulster independence but something that, from the government's point of view, was scarcely less ominous. For some time past the government had been bracing itself to take the necessary military and naval precautions against the danger of just such a declaration, but, equally for some time past, disquieting rumours had been circulating to the effect that the army could not be relied on to coerce Ulster if coercion there needed to be. This was not altogether surprising. Not only were many officers themselves from the Anglo-Irish ascendancy class, and strongly unionist in their sympathies, but in the inmost circles of the tory party, to which at least one high-ranking soldier (the Anglo-Irishman Major-general Henry

[1] *Hansard 5 (commons)*, lix, 934 (9 Mar. 1914).

Wilson, director of military operations at the war office) had access, a scheme was on foot to have the annual army bill rejected by the house of lords and thus to deprive the government of the means of keeping the army in being as a regular force.[1] This desperate expedient was in fact ruled out by Bonar Law; but, while the issue was still in doubt, news arrived that a group of army officers stationed at the Curragh camp had proffered their resignations rather than face the prospect of being ordered north, as they expected, to coerce Ulster. Their action seems to have arisen partly from the natural stress of their situation and partly from a simple misunderstanding of orders,[2] but it took on a more serious character when one of the generals stationed in Ireland, Sir Hubert Gough (like Wilson, of Anglo-Irish stock), went post-haste to London and with Wilson's assistance extracted from the secretary of state for war, Colonel J. E. B. Seely, a promise that the government had no intention of using the army 'to crush political opposition to the policy or principles of the home rule bill'.[3] Asquith had no option but to act swiftly. Seely and two senior generals were obliged to resign, and the prime minister, who temporarily took over the war office himself, repudiated Seely's pledge. This indeed he was bound to do, but, although the incident went no further than this, it revealed, as by a vivid flash of lightning, that in this delicate area the loyalty of the army could no longer be taken for granted.

No sooner had this dire fact been demonstrated than the situation in Ireland deteriorated still further. On the night of 24–5 April 1914 Major Crawford, who had completed his arms purchases in Germany with the aid of a defence fund subscribed to by British as well as Irish unionists, succeeded in landing them at three harbours in Ulster (Bangor, Larne, and Donaghadee) whence they were distributed over the province within twenty-four hours. It was a formidable display both of efficiency and of militancy, and, with the memory of the Curragh incident still fresh in his mind, it was not surprising that Asquith's instinct to search for a compromise should once again have reasserted itself. He and his colleagues would have preferred to reach such a compromise on the basis of a separate, if temporary, deal for Ulster, but when on 23 June a proposal was brought forward in the house of lords to offer county option for six years, this was immediately amended to indefinite exclusion for all nine counties. Clearly nothing was to be hoped for from that quarter, and in despair the government invoked the authority of the king to summon representatives of the contesting

---

[1] Gregory Phillips has claimed that the scheme was first espoused in June 1912, by Lord Willoughby de Broke, but was made public by him only in 1914, and although he received some initial support from Lord Milner and others, the tory leadership was firmly opposed to the idea (Phillips, 'Lord Willoughby de Broke and the politics of radical toryism, 1909–1914' in *Jn. Brit. Studies*, xx, no. 1 (fall 1980), pp 205–24.

[2] However, on the political content of military attitudes see Charles Townshend, *Political violence in Ireland: government and resistance since 1848* (Oxford, 1983), pp 268–74.

[3] Memo to Gough, 23 Mar. 1914 (Ian F. W. Beckett (ed.), *The army and the Curragh incident, 1914* (London, 1986), p. 218).

parties to a conference at Buckingham Palace. The liberals were represented by Asquith and Lloyd George, the nationalists by Redmond and Dillon, the tories by Bonar Law and Lord Lansdowne, and the Ulster unionists by Carson and James Craig. Between 21 and 24 July, during days when the threat of a European war came steadily nearer, the conference blankly contemplated the convoluted borders of the Ulster counties and ended with an all too predictable failure to agree on any scheme of exclusion that would be fair to both catholic and protestant.[1]

But while the negotiators manœuvred, events in Ireland continued to gather momentum. On 26 July the Irish Volunteers unloaded a cargo of arms and ammunition in broad daylight at Howth on the north side of Dublin Bay, and under the very noses of police and troops continued to distribute them to their members. Behind this startling variation on an Ulster theme there lay a curious history. The trio who had been mainly responsible for the foundation of the Irish Volunteers in November 1913—MacNeill, Hobson, and the O'Rahilly—had lost little time in setting up machinery for raising money to be used in the purchase of arms and for organising the transport of the arms to Ireland. Most of the money was raised with the help of Irish nationalist sympathisers living in London. These included the historian Alice Stopford Green and also Sir Roger Casement. Casement had just retired from a distinguished career in the British consular service, but he had been for some years an enthusiastic supporter of nationalist and Irish-Ireland causes and within a few months of his retirement he had become a member of the provisional committee that had been set up to act as the governing body of the Volunteers. But while he was largely instrumental in raising the money for buying the arms, the arrangements for the actual transaction were made by a journalist, Darrell Figgis, and a celebrated amateur yachtsman, Erskine Childers. English by birth and education, Childers had an Irish mother and this may have helped to incline him towards home rule from about 1908 onwards, though he had served in the British army against the Boers and retained a deep and abiding interest in both military and naval matters. As a yachtsman he was familiar with the German coast, which had provided him with material for his famous spy story *The riddle of the sands*, and it was decided that he, together with a group of friends—mostly Anglo-Irish and English gentry—should transport the cargo in two yachts, the *Asgard* and the *Kelpie*. Against all rational calculation the plan succeeded to perfection. A portion of the arms was transferred to another yacht off the Welsh coast and landed subsequently at Kilcoole in County Wicklow, while the main part was unshipped at Howth in the circumstances already described.

[1] Murphy has argued that there was considerable opposition among tories to the Buckingham Palace conference, many still preferring the prospect of a general election on the issue, and that Bonar Law was going through the motions of negotiating; furthermore, Murphy claims, the outbreak of war saved Law from the possibility of a split in his party ('Faction in the conservative party', pp 231–3). Mansergh concludes merely that the conference was 'designed to serve a time-honoured purpose of conferences and committees—that of delaying the day of decision. So much it achieved—and no more' (*Unresolved question*, pp 74–5).

But the Howth episode did not end as the Ulster gun-running had ended. Although the troops had to march back to Dublin almost empty-handed, they clashed with the crowd that followed them, and eventually, in the centre of the city, at Bachelor's Walk, they turned, fired, and used their bayonets. This was almost certainly the result of a misunderstanding of orders, natural enough in the confusion of the moment, but the consequences were tragic. Three people were killed and thirty-eight wounded, and this event, coming as it did immediately on the heels of the breakdown of the Buckingham Palace conference, seemed for a moment as if it might be the prelude to the violent explosion that the news from Ireland had been leading most people to expect for so long.

That this did not happen was due to two reasons—one local and obscure, the other international and obvious. The local and obscure reason was that the Irish Volunteers themselves were in the grip of a crisis. The scheme to import arms had been a closely guarded secret and in Dublin was known only to MacNeill, Hobson, and the O'Rahilly. But while it was maturing, these three, and the Volunteer movement in general, had come under pressure from two quite different directions. So far as it was a public movement it was naturally of concern to the parliamentary leaders, and in May and June 1914, of course in ignorance of the arms plot, Redmond manœuvred to bring the Volunteers under his control. This he did by winning the acceptance of the provisional committee that twenty-five members nominated by the Irish parliamentary party should be added to the committee. His strength in the country at that critical moment was such that it would probably have been fatal to the Volunteer organisation to resist him. Yet—and here was the second source of pressure—the republican element in the movement, as ignorant as Redmond of the fact that arms were on the sea, argued bitterly that he should be resisted in the interest of preserving the Volunteers as an independent force. They were outvoted, and they never forgave Hobson, who strongly influenced the final decision. He swayed the decision towards acceptance of Redmond's dictation partly because he believed that it would be a relatively easy matter to hoodwink the Redmondite nominees should that prove to be necessary, but even more because he wanted the weapons to be delivered to a united Volunteer movement. In this he succeeded, but he was made to pay a price for his success. Before long he resigned from the supreme council and ceased to be editor of *Irish Freedom*; he was never again to be in the inner councils of either the Volunteers or the I.R.B.

If the Volunteers remained passive, despite the affray at Bachelor's Walk, because of their internal differences, they may have done so still more because their attention and that of other people had been abruptly transferred to the international stage where the great powers of Europe were taking their last faltering but apparently inevitable steps into war. It was the belated realisation that Britain too was about to be engulfed in the crisis that deflected the rival parties in Ireland from their collision course, which, up to the last days of July, seemed as if it must lead to actual conflict. The shadow of war did not make either nationalists or unionists any more conciliatory towards each other, but it did convince the government, and eventually the opposition as well, that it was imperative that the Irish imbroglio should be shelved as quickly as possible. There remained, however, a delicate question. As the parliamentary session neared its end the time was fast approaching when the home rule bill, now completing its third circuit, would need only the royal assent to become law. Should this assent be given or should it not? Redmond demanded vehemently that it should. Carson objected as vehemently that it should not. In the end, Asquith evaded his dilemma by a characteristic manœuvre. He agreed to place the government of Ireland act on the statute book, but did so subject to two conditions. One was that it was not to come into operation while the war lasted. The other was that before it did come into operation parliament must have the opportunity to make provision for Ulster by special amending legislation. Given these conditions it is a little difficult to understand the widespread rejoicing among nationalists when the royal assent was finally pronounced on 18 September.[1] Perhaps it was simply a psychological release of long-pent-up emotion and frustration. Perhaps, also, it reflected an instinctive feeling that what had been given could never be retracted and that whether the war was short or long—most people assumed it would be short—Ireland at last had self-government within her grasp. It was, of course, an illusion. The Irish problem had been refrigerated, not liquidated. Nothing had been solved and all was still to play for.

---

[1] 4 & 5 Geo. V, c. 90 (18 Sept. 1914), suspended by 4 & 5 Geo. V, c. 88.

CHAPTER VII

Ireland in 1914

L. P. CURTIS, JR

IRELAND in 1914 was a country still seeking a national identity, while deeply divided by issues inherited from a past that always seemed to impinge on the present. The country resounded with the speeches of men who thought that they could solve complex social, economic, cultural, and religious problems with purely political remedies. Years of agitation against the act of union, above and below ground, seemed only to have widened the divisions of opinion about the meaning and the consequences of home rule. The apparent readiness of so many protestants in the north, not all of them Orangemen, to fight against home rule caused the politics of bluff and bluster to give way to preparation for the mobilising of armed volunteers and the onset of civil war. To the members of Asquith's cabinet, already buffeted by militant workers and feminists and increasingly anxious about the prospects of war on the Continent, the Irish question appeared to have lost none of its power to embitter British political life.

To turn to people rather than issues, the population of the country in mid-1914 stood at 4,381,398, of whom roughly 74 per cent were Roman Catholics.[1] Although many protestants in Britain regarded Ireland as a priest-ridden country, the actual ratio of pastoral clergy (exclusive of monks, nuns, and other servants of the church) to worshippers belied this stereotype. As the following table reveals, the catholic church had a far less favourable ratio of priests to parishioners than did the protestant denominations.

The most notable feature of the Irish population on the eve of the first world war was its continuing decline. A combination of excess mortality during the famine years (when so many thousands starved to death or died from diseases arising out of malnutrition), heavy emigration, late marriage, and a relatively low birth-rate had reduced the population to almost half of what it had been in 1845.[2]

---

[1] *Statistical abstract for the United Kingdom . . . 1900 to 1914*, p. 381 [Cd 8128], H.C. 1914–16, lxxvi, 855. The percentage of Roman Catholics is based on the census of 1911.

[2] Joel Mokyr discusses the controversial issue of famine-related mortality in *Why Ireland starved: a quantitative and analytical history of the Irish economy, 1800–1850* (London, 1983), pp 261–9, wherein he estimates excess mortality from 1846 to 1851 at between roughly 1.1 and 1.5 millions—depending on whether averted births are counted. Further demographic analysis of the famine and post-famine periods may be found in Mary E. Daly, *The famine in Ireland* (Dundalk, 1986), Cormac Ó Gráda, *Ireland before and after the famine* (Manchester, 1988), and James S. Donnelly, jr, 'Excess mortality and emigration', above, v, 350–56.

Religious denominations in Ireland, 1911

denomination	persons	% of population	pastoral clergy	ratio of clergy to worshipper
Roman Catholic	3,242,670	73.9	3,924	1 : 826
Church of Ireland	576,611	13.1	1,575	1 : 366
Presbyterian	440,525	10.0	667	1 : 660
Methodist	62,382	1.4	244	1 : 256
Other	65,652	1.5	171	1 : 384
Information refused	2,379	0.1		
	4,390,219	100.0	6,581	1 : 667

Source: *Census Ire., 1911: general report*, p. xviii [Cd 6663], H.C. 1912–13, cxviii, 18.

Although overseas emigration tapered off after the early 1850s, fluctuating in a series of smaller peaks and troughs, Ireland's emigration rate far exceeded that of every other European country up to the outbreak of war in August 1914.[1]

With the numerical balance between the sexes almost even in 1911 (49.9 per cent male and 50.1 per cent female) the Irish population could lay claim to the lowest birth and marriage rates in the British Isles, while the death rate was somewhat higher than that in Great Britain, as the following table indicates.

A striking feature of Irish society was the propensity of unmarried men and women to leave both country and town in order to seek gainful employment and fuller lives abroad. Most of these emigrants had every intention of settling where members of their families and friends had preceded them. This meant in the main

Birth, death, and marriage rates in Great Britain and Ireland in 1914
(per 1,000 population)

country	births	deaths	marriages
England and Wales	23.8	14.0	15.9
Scotland	26.1	15.5	14.8
Ireland	22.6	16.3	10.8
U.K. average	23.9	14.4	15.3

Source: *Statistical abstract for the United Kingdom . . . 1900 to 1914*, p. 382 [Cd 8128], H.C. 1914–16, lxxvi, 856.

[1] See the graph of Irish emigration from U.K. ports in David Fitzpatrick, *Irish emigration, 1801–1921* (Dundalk, 1990), p. 4. Two indispensable studies of Irish emigration, emigrant communities, and demographic trends are Robert E. Kennedy, jr, *The Irish: emigration, marriage, and fertility* (Berkeley, Calif., 1973) and Kerby A. Miller, *Emigrants and exiles: Ireland and the Irish exodus to North America* (Oxford, 1985), esp. pp 280–426. For some comparative figures of net population loss through emigration in Europe during this period, see below, pp 607–8.

America, the destination of choice for over 80 per cent of all Irish emigrants who sailed from Irish and British ports between 1876 and 1914.[1] When they had saved enough money, many of these recent arrivals would send for their nearest kith and kin, whose decision to leave also hinged on the marked disparities between economic opportunities at home and overseas. Lured by the prospect of better wages, travel, and urban adventure overseas, and depressed by the meagre wages, the menial status, the loneliness, and the friction with their employers, many male labourers decided to leave. At the same time many of their sisters had grown weary of the endless round of household and farm chores and yearned for a glimpse of city lights. If these poor young women managed to find a husband, the security they might receive rarely compensated them for all the responsibilities of child-rearing and catering to the needs (or demands) of a hard-drinking spouse.[2]

The sum of these push–pull factors proved strong enough to sever the ties that bound many young people to family, friends, and the local branch of the Gaelic League or Gaelic Athletic Association. So they left their villages, townlands, and counties for New York, Boston, or Philadelphia with little idea of the grim conditions that awaited them in tenements and factories. In the half-century following the famine (1851–1901) over 3,840,000 men, women, and children left Ireland, depleting the country further of energy, talent, and enterprise.[3]

As in previous years, the great majority of emigrants in 1914 came from rural districts and were both young and unmarried. The counties with the highest emigration rates were Mayo (10.1 per 1,000), Longford (8.9), Galway (8.6), Kerry (8.4), Leitrim (8.3), Clare (7.3), Cavan (7.2), Sligo (6.9), Louth (6.3), and Roscommon (6.3). With regard to age structures, 86.6 per cent of all emigrants in 1914 were between 15 and 35, even though this cohort constituted only 22.7

[1] For the breakdown of emigrant destinations, see below, p. 641. Besides the mainstream exodus to America, significant numbers of Irish men and women also headed for Canada, Australia, and South Africa.

[2] For an example of this bleak outlook, see Mary (Sissy) Fogarty's recollection in Mary Carbery, *The farm by Lough Gur* (Dublin, 1973), p. 47. Glimpses of the hard lives led by ordinary labourers in the post-famine era may be found in Marilyn Silverman and P. H. Gulliver, *In the valley of the Nore: a social history of Thomastown, County Kilkenny, 1840–1983* (Dublin, 1986), pp 105–12. According to David Fitzpatrick, 'the cyclical peaks in emigration corresponded closely with business "booms" in the New World, which themselves coincided broadly with recessions in the British Isles' (*Ir. emigration, 1801–1921*, p. 29).

[3] The role of gender in emigration patterns requires more critical attention. But younger historians have tried to address this issue in the wake of the pioneering work of Kennedy, *The Irish: emigration, marriage, and fertility*, esp. chs IV–VI. See *inter alia*, Ó Gráda, *Ire. before & after famine*, esp. pp 153–69; and David Fitzpatrick, 'The modernisation of the Irish female' in Patrick O'Flanagan, Paul Ferguson, and Kevin Whelan (ed.), *Rural Ireland: modernisation and change, 1600–1900* (Cork, 1987); and David Fitzpatrick, 'Review article: Women, gender, and the writing of Irish history' in *I.H.S.*, xxvii, no. 107 (May 1991), pp 267–73. Between 1904 and 1913 the average annual number of emigrants dropped slightly to 31,732. In 1914 this figure fell sharply to 20,314, equivalent to a rate of 4.6 emigrants per 1,000 population. For emigration by counties and provinces from 1851 to 1920, see Vaughan & Fitzpatrick, *Ir. hist. statistics*, pp 269–353.

per cent of the population in 1911. Only 7.4 per cent of all emigrants were 15 or under, while 6 per cent were over 35.[1]

As for celibacy and marriage rates, the overwhelming majority of emigrants were single. Only 7.7 per cent of the men and 10.7 per cent of the women had been married or widowed. Of the 8,954 men and women in the 20–25 cohort, only 136 (45 and 91 respectively) were married. With a mere 5.2 per cent of the emigrants in 1914 expressing a wish to settle in Great Britain, it becomes clear just how strong a pull North America exerted on those who wished to escape from the realities of rural life.

With regard to occupations, 7,480 of the 10,867 male emigrants (72.8 per cent) in 1914 were classified as agricultural labourers, while 6,932 of the 9,716 female emigrants (77.2 per cent) were grouped under the heading of 'servants', which covered a variety of lowly valued forms of work. The 'middle-class' category contained 462 females, including clerks, typists, governesses, schoolmistresses, shopkeepers, and their assistants as well as 1,665 men (15.3 per cent of all male emigrants) whose occupations ranged from clerks to accountants, schoolmasters, shop assistants, and farmers.[2]

As Ó Gráda and Fitzpatrick have made clear, this haemorrhaging of the population affected every aspect of Irish society—from the tangible to the intangible. The near equality of male and female departures and their relative youth were bound to alter marriage and celibacy rates. The magnitude of this exodus, moreover, may have moved some farmers towards a partible rather than impartible inheritance. In other words, the custom of leaving the farm and livestock to one child—a favoured son or, less likely, a daughter—probably increased during the post-famine era, as the 'joint' family system gradually gave way to the 'stem' system. While the drain of people from rural areas lessened the competition for land, the practice of not dividing the farm among several children must have aggravated already fierce sibling rivalries. Impartible inheritance meant that the ageing father or mother could always hold the succession over the heads of the children and threaten to disinherit anyone who misbehaved.[3]

Since the famine, Ireland had experienced not only a marked shift from tillage to pasturage but also an increase in the number of strong farmers and graziers, who worked holdings of 30 acres and above. Skilled at managing livestock and driving hard bargains, they constituted a prosperous rural middle class that would make even larger profits out of any wartime food shortages. Some 48 per cent of all holdings in 1910 fell into the 5 to 29 acre range, exclusive of gardens and allotments. The men and women who worked these 290,769 medium-size farms

[1] These figures reflect the general trend of the decade 1901–10, when 59.2 per cent of all emigrants fell into the 15–25 cohort and 24.1 per cent into the 25–35 cohort, with 7.8 per cent above 35 (*Emigration statistics of Ireland for the year 1914*, pp 3–8 [Cd 7883], H.C. 1914–16, lxxx, 321–6).

[2] Ibid., pp 7–14 (MS 325–32).

[3] Ó Gráda deals with some of the tensions and conflicts arising out of the inheritance problem, arguing on the basis of probate evidence that most parents tried to treat their children as fairly as possible (*Ire. before & after famine*, pp 153–61).

belonged to a rural *petit bourgeoisie* that was vulnerable not only to the vagaries of the market and weather but to the clutches of the gombeen men or moneylenders. For these smaller farmers, whether or not they had acquired title to their holdings under the land purchase acts, life was a long struggle to keep indebtedness within bounds and to meet interest payments on time.

One of the more subtle and significant changes in Irish social organisation before 1914, too often obscured by the land question and the home rule issue, was the gradual encroachment by urban culture on the countryside. This was an irregular and intermittent process that brought the country people in all but the most remote or inaccessible parts of Ireland into closer contact with urban values and town-dwellers. The diffusion of urban products through the rural districts did not, of course, change the outlook of country people in a fortnight or even a single generation. In remote parts of the west, such as the Blasket and Aran Islands, patterns of life changed slowly if at all, and the threat, not to say reality, of distress through crop failure hung heavy over the rocky soil. But the active intervention of the congested districts board in the fishing industry and land purchase operations, the advent of the telegraph, and a nascent tourist industry exposed islanders to the values of the modern market-place.[1]

One symptom of this transformation was the steady decline in the number of Irish-speakers, especially after the 1840s, as Brian Ó Cuív makes clear below. Although they should be treated with caution, the census figures reveal a sharp fall in Irish-speaking monoglots—from 38,192 in 1891 to 16,873 in 1911, even though the efforts of Gaelic Leaguers helped to triple the number of Irish-speakers in Leinster over the same period.[2] Those who were bilingual amounted to 582,446 or 13.3 per cent of the population.[3] Some of the counties with the highest proportion of Irish-speakers (bilingual and otherwise)—Galway (54.1 per cent), Mayo (46.1 per cent), Kerry (38 per cent), Clare (35.2 per cent), Donegal (35.2 per cent), and Cork (23.8 per cent)—were also areas of high emigration. The language revival inspired by Douglas Hyde and his fellow Gaelic Leaguers did, however, make substantial gains in Dublin and the surrounding counties.[4]

If the more obvious differences between town and country life still persisted in 1914, this did not mean that there was no blurring of rural and urban elements. In practice, the distinction made by the Irish census commissioners between civic and rural districts, which was based on a population of 2,000, may have had some justification for certain administrative purposes. But generally in Ireland, it made

---

[1] See Brian Harvey, 'Changing fortunes on the Aran islands in the 1890s' in *I.H.S.*, xxvii, no. 107 (May 1991), pp 237–49. In his reminiscences, *The islandman* (Oxford, 1978), Thomas Ó Crohan alludes to the emergence of a more monetary economy. See, for example, his reference to lobster-catching off the Blaskets (pp 153–6).

[2] According to the census, there were only 13,677 Irish-speakers in Leinster in 1891, compared with 40,225 in 1911; see table below, pp 431–2.

[3] *Census Ire., 1911: general report*, p. 291 (MS 357).

[4] Between 1891 and 1911, the percentage of people speaking Irish rose from 0.7 to 3.4 in the county borough of Dublin, from 0.9 to 3.9 in Kildare, from 0.5 to 3.4 in King's County, and from 0.5 to 3.5 in Westmeath (ibid.).

little sense to relegate all areas with less than 2,000 people to the category of 'rural'.

According to the criteria used by the census commissioners the civic or urban sector of the Irish population had grown from 17.0 per cent in 1851 to 33.5 per cent in 1911. In the same period the civic part of the English and Welsh population had increased from 50.2 per cent to 78.1 per cent.[1] Changes in the distribution of the Irish population may seem small alongside those in England, but statistical appearances can be deceiving. If one adopts another definition of 'town', a different picture becomes discernible. In Ireland there were many small towns that had, despite their smallness, most of the attributes of urbanism: regular markets, churches, schools, petty sessions, constabulary barracks, and post offices. The differences between towns and villages were often subjective in character, based in part on whether or not the local shopkeeper sold shoelaces or boots, ropes or nets, spades or ploughs. Those who lived in villages or small towns regarded themselves as set off, rather than cut off, from the surrounding countryside. One has only to consider the contrast in size, character, and facilities between Quin (with a population in 1911 of 164) and Ennistymon (1,204) in County Clare or between Collon (195) and Ardee (1,773) in County Louth to realise the problematic nature of the census commissioners' figure of 2,000 inhabitants as the definition of a 'civic district'. It would make more sense to apply a separate label, 'semi-urban', to those settlements ranging in size from 120 to 1,000 inhabitants, and, in addition, to lower the criterion of what is urban to incorporate all towns with a population of 1,000–2,000. Lowering the urban boundary in this way would include such towns as Cappoquin and Tramore, County Waterford; Dingle and Cahirciveen, County Kerry; Killybegs and Buncrana, County Donegal; Rathkeale, County Limerick; Moate, County Westmeath; Portstewart, County Londonderry; Millstreet and Passage West, County Cork; and Tullow, County Carlow. The application of these new criteria to the census data results in the following pattern of distribution. The expanded urban category now makes up some 36 per cent of the population (1,580,095), and when it is added to the 6.1 per cent of the semi-urban category, the total population living in non-rural areas becomes 42.1 per cent (1,848,445). This revised estimate suggests that the country was considerably more urbanised than the census commissioners' definition implied.

A curious feature of the urban category was the paucity of cities above the 20,000 mark. Not counting Dublin's burgeoning suburbs of Pembroke, Rathmines, and Rathgar, there were only three towns or cities in the 20,000–50,000 class: Limerick (47,247), Londonderry (40,780), and Waterford (27,464). Only Cork (102,435) occupied the huge gulf between Limerick and Belfast (386,947). This urban imbalance accounted for the unchallenged ascendancy of Belfast in the

---

[1] *Census Ire., 1911: general report*, p. xx (MS 20). See also *Census of England and Wales, 1911*, pp xv–xx [Cd 6258], H.C. 1912–13, cxi, 15–20. The 1851 figure for urban population includes inmates of public institutions.

Population distribution in Ireland in urban, semi-urban,
and rural areas, 1911

class	number of units	estimated population	% of total population
I urban			
1,000–1,999	73	109,500	2.5
2,000–19,999	101	467,487	10.65
20,000 and up	8	1,003,108	22.85
sub-total	182	1,580,095	36.0
II semi-urban			
120–499	510	158,100	3.6
500–999	147	110,250	2.5
sub-total	657	268,350	6.1
III rural		2,541,774	57.0
total	839	4,390,219	100.0

Source: *Thom's official directory ... 1914* (Dublin, 1914), pp 1373–4*b*. The compilers of this list of Irish 'towns' exceeding 120 inhabitants derived their data from the Irish census of 1911.

north, Dublin (398,235) in the east, and Cork in the south-west. Urbanisation in Ireland had assumed an uneven pattern, with small settlements of several hundred persons and country towns of several thousand persons being much more characteristic of the interior than the major provincial cities that loomed so large in the midlands of England.[1]

However important the distinctions between urban, semi-urban, and rural areas in Ireland, they should not be exaggerated. There were no high walls or impassable barriers between town and country. In countless ways city, town, village, and countryside all depended on one another for both material and human replenishment. On market days the farmers and graziers invaded the towns, jamming the streets and squares with their livestock, their vegetables, and their families. The shops and pubs teemed with people and throbbed with such timeless activities as gossiping, bargaining, and drinking.

WHAT Irish men and women did, how they occupied their lives and tried to make a living, matters even more than where they lived. Even though agriculture still overshadowed all other occupations in 1914, the large number of Irishmen who worked as farmers, agricultural labourers, farm servants, herdsmen, and dairy

---

[1] A suggestive discussion of urbanisation and the relationship of urban, semi-urban, and rural districts (in the context of late eighteenth-century France) may be found in Charles Tilly, *The Vendée* (New York, 1967), pp 1–57. Although based on rather subjective field studies in the 1930s, the observations of Conrad Arensberg and Solon Kimball in their *Family and community in Ireland* (Cambridge, Mass., 1940; reprint, Gloucester, Mass., 1961) shed some light on the interaction of town and country a generation earlier. See especially pp 282–308, and also Conrad Arensberg, *The Irish countryman* (Cambridge, Mass., 1937; reprint, Gloucester, Mass., 1959), pp 146–80.

hands should not be allowed to conceal certain shifts away from the traditional pattern of work and wage-earning.

In 1911, 43 per cent of all occupied Irish males were involved in agriculture—including the management of livestock. In 1851, by comparison, using a slightly different number basis, roughly 53 per cent of all Irish families had been engaged in agriculture. The following table, comparing occupations in 1901 and 1911, provides some clues about the distribution of the Irish labour force before the first world war. The classification used must be treated with care, however, given the relegation of 58.6 per cent of the population to the category of 'indefinite and non-productive'. Almost one-half of these so-called unoccupied persons (49.8 per cent) consisted of children under 15 years of age, while the remainder ranged from gentlemen and ladies of rank and independent means to housewives, retired businessmen, and inmates of almshouses as well as lunatic asylums. The five other classes used by the census commissioners contained a rich, not to say confusing, variety of occupations, divided into orders and sub-orders. The three orders within Class I, for example, consisted of persons in local and national government, the army and navy as well as pensioners, and members of 'the liberal and learned professions'.[1]

Occupations in Ireland 1901 and 1911

class	numbers		% of labour force	
	1901	1911	1901	1911
I professional	131,035	141,134	6.6	7.7
II domestic	219,418	170,749	11.1	9.3
III commercial	97,889	111,143	4.9	6.1
IV agricultural	876,062	780,867	44.6	43.0
V industrial	639,413	613,397	32.5	33.7
VI indefinite and non-productive	2,494,958	2,572,929	[55.9]	[58.6]
total labour force or all workers with specified occupations	1,963,817	1,817,290	[44.1]	[41.4]

The figures in square brackets give the classes as percentages of the total population.

Source: *Census Ire.*, *1901, general report*, pp 115–16 [Cd 1190], H.C. 1902, cxxix, 159–60; *Census Ire.*, *1911, general report*, pp xxvii–xxx, 7–8, 104–5 (MS 27–30, 73–4, 170–71).

[1] *Census of England and Wales, 1911*, x. *Occupations and industries, pt I*, pp 2–5 [Cd 7018], H.C. 1913, lxxviii, 474–7. It is worth noting, in passing, that in England and Wales only 7.6 per cent of the labour force fell into the agricultural category; whereas the percentage of those involved in government and the professions in 1911 came close to that in Ireland.

Among the more noteworthy changes in the Irish labour force since the early 1850s was the steep decline of farmworkers—from a ratio of 229 to every 100 farmers in 1851 to one of 131 : 100 in 1911.[1] By contrast the number of metalworkers increased after the 1850s, especially those employed in foundries and factories as well as engineering and shipbuilding firms. The growth of a national school system and the slow expansion of higher education swelled the ranks of those in the teaching profession: by 1911, schoolmasters and schoolmistresses, lecturers, and professors numbered 22,204. In both law and medicine, those traditionally exclusive professions, the numbers fell. In 1911 there were 2,246 barristers and solicitors, compared with 3,268 in 1851. Physicians and surgeons had fallen slightly from 2,439 to 2,259 in the same period.[2] The growth of white-collar workers was one of the most impressive occupational changes since the great famine, as the number of civil engineers and surveyors (1,692 in 1911), and male commercial clerks (19,723 in 1911) attested. Female commercial clerks, including typists and general office workers, doubled their numbers between 1901 and 1911, rising from 3,437 to 7,849, while bankers and bank clerks increased from 2,675 in 1901 to 3,033 in 1911. These gains seemed to indicate that the pursuit of wealth through banking, finance, insurance, and property sales was attracting more wage-earners as well as entrepreneurs.

There was at least one new entry in the Irish census of 1911—the sub-order of 'motor car driver and chauffeur', which contained 1,349 males. The presence of this masculine occupation not only signalled the arrival of a new form of leisure activity for the rich but made possible more frequent and rapid trips around the country by government officials, royalty, and, of course, British tourists. Among the earliest car owners in Ireland were Sir Horace Plunkett, Sir William Goff, and the viceroy, Lord Dudley. When that keen motoring enthusiast King Edward VII visited Ireland in 1903, he toured western Connacht by car. Despite many bumps and stray livestock on the roads Ireland became known as 'a paradise for motorists' owing to the tolerant attitude of the police towards speeding. As a result rich drivers came over from England in big and fast vehicles 'to gratify their lust for speed' while enjoying the awesome landscapes of the west. The Edwardian era was also the heyday of the élite owner-mechanic, who had to learn how to cope with breakdowns given the scarcity of garages outside cities. Aided and abetted by the Royal Irish Automobile Club, founded in 1901, the era of automotive transport was well and truly, if not safely, under way.[3]

[1] David Fitzpatrick discusses the ambiguities of such categories as farmer and labourer and analyses population trends in the agricultural sector in an important article with a rather misleading title, 'The disappearance of the Irish agricultural labourer, 1841–1912' in *Ir. Econ. & Soc. Hist.*, vii (1980), pp 66–92.

[2] The basic figures for this comparison may be found in *Census Ire., 1851: general report*, pp xxiii–ix, 634–6 [2134], H.C. 1856, xxxi, 33–9, 774–6, and *Census Ire., 1911: general report*, pp xxvii–xxviii (MS 27–8). For a discussion of the significant shifts in occupations since the famine years, see below, pp 333–5.

[3] *Census Ire., 1911: general report*, p. xxviii (MS 28). For some amusing anecdotes about touring the Irish countryside in a motor car with the king, the chief secretary, and other officials in the pre-war

Although the census often obscured the variety of women's work, some of the occupational data afford fleeting insights into the nature of the female labour force. Few working-class women in town or country managed to avoid the exhausting daily round of unpaid domestic chores and child care as well as low-paid work outside the household. Most of those who tried to escape this fate by emigrating overseas found little relief from such burdens in their new domiciles. The women who stayed behind constituted 84.9 per cent of all persons in domestic service in 1911 and 66.8 per cent of the work-force in the textile and dressmaking trades.[1]

If middle-class women were entering the public sphere in the first decade of the twentieth century in greater numbers than ever before, they still faced many doors that were either closed or only slightly ajar. Only 26.6 per cent of those classified as 'professional' in 1911 were women. But this represented a slight increase (up from 24.9 per cent) since 1901. In the higher professions women had scant access to positions of power. Of the 4,848 persons engaged in legal services in 1911, only 60 were women. (This was an improvement on the figure of 38 in 1901.) While the number of female medical workers had risen from 2,093 in 1901 to 6,679 in 1911, most of these were low-paid nurses of working-class origins.[2] In sum, even educated and reasonably affluent women found it hard to enter, let alone ascend to positions of rank in, institutions other than convents, elementary schools, and the professions of nursing and midwifery. Just as in Britain, entry into universities came slowly and often at the price of male resentment. In 1914 the 300 or so women enrolled in Irish colleges and universities were outnumbered by a margin of ten to one. And yet the sheer fact of their presence there held out the promise of better jobs and greater autonomy for generations of daughters not yet born.[3]

The pursuit of profit or higher salaries did provide some Irishmen with avenues of upward social mobility, although the Knights of Columbanus and the Ancient Order of Hibernians might not have agreed that there were no religious obstacles in the way of those who sought careers open to talent. Religious barriers alone did not prevent many catholics from advancing. In Dublin, Cork, Limerick, and

period, see Sir Henry Robinson, *Memories: wise and otherwise* (London, 1924), pp 180–82, and *Further memories of Irish life* (London, 1924), pp 160–78.

[1] The number of female domestic servants fell from 169,769 in 1901 to 128,457 in 1911 (*Census Ire., 1901: general report*, table 19, pp 115–16 (MS 159–60); *Census Ire., 1911: general report*, table 19, pp 7–8 (MS 73–4)). A fuller discussion of women and work may be found in Maria Luddy and Cliona Murphy (ed.), *Women surviving: studies in Irish women's history in the 19th and 20th centuries* (Dublin, 1990).

[2] *Census Ire., 1901: general report*, table 19, pp 115–16 (MS 159–60); *Census Ire., 1911: general report*, table 19, pp 7–8 (MS 73–4). Maria Luddy alludes to nursing in 'An agenda for women's history in Ireland, part II: 1800–1900' in *I.H.S.*, xxviii, no. 109 (May 1992), pp 31–2. In 1911 women occupied 63.4 per cent of 22,204 teaching positions. And they almost equalled the number of men in the clerical worker category: 9,175 and 9,840 respectively.

[3] On women's education, see Mary Cullen, *Girls don't do honours: Irish women in education in the 19th and 20th centuries* (Dublin, 1987).

other large towns many of the most prosperous bankers, merchants, lawyers, and doctors were catholics who had used their talents and connections to good effect. Although the legal and medical professions enabled qualified catholics to climb out of a lower-middle-class ambience, there were many signs that protestants, in proportion to their numbers in the country, were still over-represented in the upper echelons of the professions, the civil service, commerce, banking, and industry.

In a country where catholics formed almost 74 per cent of the population, their distribution in different occupations was uneven. In the professions catholics were under-represented, accounting for only 48.7 per cent of physicians and surgeons, 44.5 per cent of barristers and solicitors, 37 per cent of architects, and 36.2 per cent of civil engineers, although they were better represented among male teachers (73 per cent), among officers and clerks in the civil service (59 per cent), and among journalists (60 per cent). Only in the teaching profession did their share approach their proportion of the population. (In the more humble reaches of official life, however, they were well represented, accounting for 81.6 per cent of civil service messengers, 78 per cent of policemen, and 68.8 per cent of army pensioners, who were a better guide to Irish representation in the British army than the troops actually stationed in Ireland.) In the skilled manual occupations their position varied. They were strong among coopers (86.3 per cent), brewers (85.5 per cent), masons (85.4 per cent), blacksmiths (77.4 per cent) engine drivers and stokers (76.9 per cent), tailors (74.9 per cent), and shoemakers (74.6 per cent), where they were over-represented: they were under-represented, however, among builders (71.9 per cent), carpenters (68.8 per cent), painters and glaziers (63.7 per cent), bricklayers (61.3 per cent), printers (57.8 per cent), and motor car drivers (54.7 per cent). Among retailers and service occupations their positions also varied; they were over-represented among publicans and hotel-keepers (88.7 per cent), fishmongers (83 per cent), general shopkeepers (82.1 per cent), butchers (80.7 per cent), and bakers (77.5 per cent); they were under-represented among grocers (62.7 per cent), commercial clerks (49.7 per cent), commercial travellers (42.1 per cent), auctioneers (39.5 per cent), chemists (37.2 per cent), and bank clerks (35.7 per cent). In agricultural occupations they were consistently over-represented, accounting for 81.7 per cent of farmers, 84.9 per cent of agricultural labourers, and 86.8 per cent of farm servants. Although catholics did not monopolise the lowliest occupations they were usually over-represented, accounting for 81.1 per cent of general labourers, 78.1 per cent of male domestic servants, 82 per cent of female domestic servants, and 92.4 per cent of chimney sweeps. Among scavengers and crossing sweepers, however, which were not exactly the most exalted members of the labour aristocracy, they were under-represented, accounting for only 71 per cent; they were just slightly over-represented among rag gatherers (76.7 per cent).

The relationship between religious denomination, status, and occupation was a complicated one in Belfast where catholics made up 24 per cent of the population.

Catholics were under-represented in the professions, occupying much less than the 24 per cent that they should have had if their numbers in the population had generated a proportionate share of positions. They were worst off in accountancy where they were 6.4 per cent and in the medical profession where they were 8.6 per cent of those enumerated in the 1911 census; they were best off in teaching where they accounted for 36.7 per cent and among journalists where they accounted for 24 per cent. Between the sparseness of accountancy and the proportionate propriety of journalism there were gradations: 10.3 per cent of civil engineers were catholics, as were 13.7 per cent of architects and 16.9 per cent of lawyers. In skilled manual trades the pattern was mixed: catholics were 30.3 per cent of engine drivers and stokers, 30 per cent of woodturners and box-makers, 22.4 per cent of bricklayers, 20.2 per cent of builders, 20 per cent of painters and glaziers, but they were only 15.4 per cent of printers, 15 per cent of motor car drivers, 13.4 per cent of fitters and turners, and 12.6 per cent of carpenters. In retailing and similar services, however, they were well represented: they were 81.3 per cent of publicans and hotel-keepers, 77.5 per cent of wine and spirit merchants, 64.8 per cent of fishmongers, 46.4 per cent of general shopkeepers, 40.4 per cent of butchers, 31.5 per cent of shoemakers and dealers, and 27.9 per cent of carters and carriers, although they were only 18.7 per cent of bakers, 16.5 per cent of commercial travellers, 14.8 per cent of photographers, and 7.6 per cent of bank clerks. In the two great staples of Belfast, linen and shipbuilding, catholics were relatively well represented in one and poorly represented in the other; in linen they were over-represented among spinners (33.8 per cent) and under-represented among weavers (17.2 per cent); in shipbuilding, however, they accounted for only 7.8 per cent of the 5,497 males who described themselves as shipbuilders and only 6.7 per cent of 1,312 who described themselves as ship-wrights or ship carpenters. At the bottom of the occupational hierarchy, among the general labourers, catholics were over-represented, accounting for 33.1 per cent.

Occupations reflected to some extent patterns of external trade, and Ireland's increasing reliance on imports of both raw and finished goods did not prevent the country from achieving a slight trade surplus in 1913. Although the outbreak of war in August 1914 reversed the trend, Irish exports had managed to keep slightly ahead of imports from Great Britain and overseas since 1900.[1] Among the leading items imported in 1913 (listed in descending order of value), were hosiery and drapery, cotton goods (exclusive of raw cotton and yarn), maize or Indian corn, wheat, coal, wheat flour, flax, bacon, sugar, steel, machinery, and linen goods. Textiles of all kinds accounted for almost 26 per cent of imported goods. As for exports, linen goods and yarn led the way with an estimated value of £15,845,604. These were followed (again in descending order of value), by cattle (fat and store), butter, bacon, shipping, eggs, cotton goods, porter or beer, spirits, and horses.

[1] In 1913 the total estimated value of all commodities imported into Ireland amounted to £73,673,149, and the total estimated value of Irish exports came to £73,886,411; see also below, pp 298–309.

Finished and raw textiles, mostly linens, amounted to 31.9 per cent of the value of exports; followed by livestock (including cattle, horses, and swine), which accounted for 26.3 per cent. Taken together, the linen and shipbuilding industries, concentrated in the north-east, produced almost one-quarter of all Irish exports.[1]

Judged by pre-famine demographic patterns, one of the occupations that seemed to have lost some of its appeal over the years was that of married parent. Few observers of Irish society since the 1850s have failed to remark on the high celibacy rate, especially for men. In 1911 there were 850,437 unmarried males and 751,738 unmarried females in Ireland aged 15 and upwards. Only 38.5 per cent of all males over 15 were married, while 6 per cent had been widowed, compared with 38.6 per cent and 13.1 per cent respectively for all women over 15. Of all men and women in the 25–34 cohort, only 37.2 per cent were married, compared with 9 per cent of those aged between 20 and 24, and 59.5 per cent for those between 35 and 44.[2]

In a society marked by an austere sexual code, the implications of repression ought not to be ignored. The prevalence of so many taboos against extra-marital sex must have given rise to profound emotional conflict and guilt. The sanctions visited by society and the church on those who indulged in illicit affairs or who bore children out of wedlock may well have precipitated decisions to migrate or emigrate.[3] Even if there was no clear-cut relationship between celibacy rates and emigration, the circumstantial evidence would suggest that sexual frustrations played some part in spurring young people to leave home long before they could afford to marry and raise a family. The European war soon shut off this escape route on which so many restless and underemployed people had long depended.

Irish rural society gave the appearance of more tranquillity than unrest in 1914. Both the land agitation and the land act of 1881 had greatly pruned the power of the landlords, who could no longer expect much deference from their remaining tenants. Under the fair rent provisions of that measure and later amendments, the rental of some 528,457 holdings had been reduced in aggregate by 20.7 per cent for the first statutory term, 19.4 per cent for the second, and 9.5 per cent for the third, and the cumulative effect of this was to reduce the total rental by 16 or 17 per cent.[4] Only landowners fortunate enough to own valuable urban property, untenanted grazing land, or stocks and bonds were able to absorb the loss of agricultural rental without plunging into bankruptcy.[5]

[1] *Thom's official directory . . . 1916*, pp 776*a*–*b*.

[2] Vaughan & Fitzpatrick, *Ir. hist. statistics*, p. 90.

[3] For a provocative discussion of this sensitive subject, see K. H. Connell, *Irish peasant society* (Oxford, 1968), pp 51–86, 113–61. According to the report of the registrar-general for Ireland, only 3 per cent of all births in Ireland in 1914 were illegitimate. The provincial breakdown for that year was: Ulster, 4.0 per cent; Leinster, 3.2 per cent; Munster, 2.4 per cent; Connacht, 0.7 per cent (*[Fifty-first] annual report of the registrar general . . . 1914*, pp xi, 2 [Cd 7991], H.C. 1914–16, ix, 699, 753).

[4] *Thom's official directory . . . 1916*, p. 776*d*.

[5] An example of one who took this plunge was Frederick Oliver Trench, 3rd Baron Ashtown, who owned some 37,257 acres in eight counties, valued at £26,936 around 1880, which made him nominally one of the richest landlords in the country. In order to borrow £45,000 from the Church of Ireland

After fair rents came land purchase, or the sale of holdings to the tenant occupiers. By the spring of 1915 £86,130,530 had been advanced under the various land purchase acts passed since 1881 in order to enable tenants to buy their farms.[1] Between 1870 and 1917 roughly 309,000 tenants took advantage of the opportunity to convert themselves into owner occupiers.[2] This transformation in landlord–tenant relations was, indeed, momentous, and could never have been consummated without a huge treasury subsidy, which bridged the gap between what owners and occupiers regarded as an acceptable price. Hoping to tempt landlords to sell, Wyndham included a cash bonus of 12 per cent on the purchase price, which many hard-pressed vendors found irresistible. By injecting over £66 million into the land market, this measure, which the liberal government supplemented in 1909, raised great expectations among buyers and sellers alike. But accusations by John Dillon and more radical members of the United Irish League that the estates commissioners were charging exorbitant prices for farmland were matched by landlord fears that the estates commissioners were biased in favour of the tenantry.[3] Besides these political charges, there were long delays in the land commission, owing in part to the amount of legal and clerical work required to process all the applications for sale. Financial problems also took their toll as the treasury reacted with traditional parsimony when the chief secretary and his advisers asked for more infusions of capital in order to narrow the gap between vendor and buyer. Given all these impediments it is remarkable that some 9 million acres were bought or sold under these two acts between 1903 and 1920, with another 2 million acres in sales pending.[4] Not only the under-financing of the Wyndham act but the increase in anti-grazing outrages caused grave concern among officials responsible for administering land purchase.[5]

in 1907 he took out six life insurance policies with a face value of £61,000. But two years later a London moneylender hauled him into court for failing to repay a loan. The bailiffs soon seized Woodlawn House along with his cattle and held them for several weeks. New creditors helped only to postpone the day of reckoning in May 1912, when he entered into bankruptcy. After more litigation, Ashtown's trustees authorised a loan of £130,000 from another insurance company, which annulled the bankruptcy order (*Minute book of the legal committee*, vol. 11, 1901, pp 138, 150, and *Minutes of finance committee*, vol. 15, 1904, p. 493, and vol. 17, p. 99, Archive of the Representative Church Body, Church of Ireland, Church House, Rathmines; 'Epitome of abstract of title', Ashtown estate, Box 6801, pp 25, 32–3, Irish Land Commission).

[1] *Thom's official directory . . . 1916*, pp 778–9.

[2] A full statement of the working of the land purchase acts may be found in a special memorandum prepared by the subcommittee on land purchase in the *Report of the proceedings of the Irish convention*, pp 86–107 [Cd 9019], H.C. 1918, x, 782–803.

[3] Paul Bew discusses the partisan nature of these charges about the pricing of land under the zone system adopted by Wyndham and MacDonnell in his *Conflict & conciliation*, pp 99–102.

[4] F. S. L. Lyons, *Ireland since the famine* (London, 1971), p. 214. The slumping value of land stock after 1906 did not help matters. For the deep concern of officials in Dublin Castle and the Irish Office about the parlous state of land purchase finances, see W. R. Davies to James Bryce, 25 Oct. 1907 and 8 Feb. 1908 (Bryce Papers, U.B. 22, Bodleian Library); W. F. Bailey to Bryce, 22 Sept. 1908 (ibid., U.B. 46/F19); George Wyndham's memorandum on Irish land purchase, 29 Oct. 1907 (Lansdowne papers, Bowood).

[5] As Frederick Wrench wrote to Arthur Balfour, 'If things are allowed to go on as at present, there will be a general surrender on the part of the graziers and the mob will have prevailed—as no

While some proprietors tested the market with sporadic sales of tenanted land, others decided to hold on for a few more years, hoping that prices would recover. In the meantime the impatience of tenants turned into anger, and some resorted to harassing tactics, hoping to force their landlords into selling.[1] The amount of land sold before 1915 varied considerably across the country, with landowners in the north-east showing more reluctance to take advantage of the Wyndham act than those in the south and west. In County Clare, where rents remained relatively high, landlords did not relish the prospect of losing some 34 per cent of their existing rent, compared with 28 per cent for the country as a whole. The financial gap between vendors and buyers in this county meant that sales 'lagged well behind the general trend' before the outbreak of war.[2]

Although most vending landlords planned to stay on and farm their untenanted land, some insolvent owners put everything up for sale, including their houses and demesnes, and moved to England or abroad. A few combative proprietors objected to the whole policy of land purchase and accused the Balfour brothers and Wyndham of throwing them to the nationalist wolves.[3]

If some landlords withdrew more into the privacy of their demesnes and clubs after selling thousands of acres, they also continued to take part in such public outings as hunting and shooting, quarter sessions, and rural district council meetings. In the meantime their former tenants faced the familiar difficulties of extracting profit from farms despite the vagaries of weather and prices. At least they had the compensation of pride of ownership, security of tenure, freedom

respectable people who can avoid doing so will continue to live in the west, which will be a calamity' (Wrench to Balfour, 3 July 1907; Balfour papers, B.L. Add. MS 49816, ff 182–3).

[1] Tenants were not the only ones who had to wait years to complete purchase transactions. In general, landlords who sold early fared better than those who waited. Apart from the long delays after 1907, the liberal land purchase act of 1909 whittled down the amount of the bonus due on the purchase price. Henry Lyle Mulholland, 2nd Baron Dunleath, filed his originating application for the sale of some property in Oct. 1908. But the transaction was not completed until 16 Mar. 1923, by which time several family members, who stood to gain portions of the purchase money, had died. See the originating application and final schedule of incumbrances, Dunleath Estate, E.C. 7792, P.R.O.N.I.

[2] See David Fitzpatrick, *Politics and Irish life, 1913–1921* (Dublin, 1977), p. 48. According to Fitzpatrick's calculations, the landlords of Clare by 1915 had parted with only 57 per cent of all the land that would eventually be sold under the various purchase acts, compared with an average of some 72 per cent for the whole country.

[3] Among these disgruntled landlords was Lord Ashtown of Woodlawn House, Co. Galway, who owned and managed a large cattle ranch in eastern Galway along with estates in seven other counties. He accused the architects of land purchase of political cowardice because they hoped to quell the land agitation by means of a measure that actually increased the intimidation of landlords and graziers. Ashtown blamed the Wyndham act for driving out landlords who were not only loyal unionists but large employers of labour, thereby inflicting 'irreparable injury' on the country. Too many protestant gentry, he complained, had sold their estates under pressure and left Connacht: 'It is simply lamentable to see their empty demesnes, with their houses falling down.' Calling himself a 'fighting unionist', who refused to sell his property 'at the dictation of the United Irish League', Ashtown vowed to continue defending the lost cause of southern unionism. He bitterly resented the way the state was facilitating the transfer of property from men whose forebears had fought to preserve English rule to 'men who have always been rebels' (Ashtown to A. Bonar Law, 21 Apr. 1912; Bonar Law MS 26/2/37, House of Lords Record Office).

from land agents, and the savings arising out of a land annuity that was lower than the former rent and spread out over 68 ½ years.

Initially, the publicity given to land purchase by its promoters tended to disguise the fact that some of the best grazing land in the country, located in a broad belt running from Meath and Westmeath westwards through King's, Leitrim, Roscommon, and into eastern Mayo, Sligo, and Galway counties, was owned by graziers or cattle ranchers who were determined not to sell. The concentration of so much lush pasturage in so few hands provoked Laurence Ginnell, M.P. for Westmeath North, and David Sheehy, M.P. for Meath, and other leaders of the United Irish League to launch a campaign in October 1906 against cattle ranchers, demanding that their lands be distributed among small-holders.[1] Although the land war had receded into the collective memory and folklore of most people, there were still vivid reminders of the old struggle between landlords and tenants. While most evicted tenants had been reinstated under the act of 1907, memories of traumatic ejectments and long years of separation from the homestead lingered on, moving some to exclaim privately that all land agents (and most landlords) deserved to be shot.[2]

The desire of many farmers to buy their holdings at low prices aggravated relations with landlords who refused to sell or held out for higher prices. Wyndham and his friends failed to realise that land purchase would open a Pandora's box of frustrations and resentments, even if the amount of money available to finance these transactions made it less necessary for Irish tenant right advocates to approach British ministers 'with the head of a landlord in one hand, and the tail of a cow in the other'.[3] Disputes over rent and arrears, land tenure, turbary, and other matters continued to provoke bad feelings, while the cattle drives and anti-rent combinations sponsored by the United Irish League provoked officials to proclaim certain districts as disturbed, and reopened some of the wounds of the land war. Agrarian outrages did, however, diminish after 1910, apart from a dozen estates in Connacht, where relations between landlords and tenants remained adversarial.[4]

---

[1] Bew, *Conflict & conciliation*, p. 139.

[2] In 1906, some 4,950 tenants had applied for reinstatement. Almost one-quarter of their holdings were still in landlords' hands. The evicted tenants act of 1907 (above, p. 96) empowered the estates commissioners to buy land—by compulsion if necessary—to be distributed among the 'wounded soldiers of the land war'. As a result, at least 3,500 evicted tenants or their representatives were settled on 26,000 acres acquired for this purpose under the act. Dublin Castle continued to keep an eye on rural evictions and noted 734 evicted farms as 'unlet' in 1914—most of them either in landlords' hands (375) or derelict (356) (Breandan Mac Giolla Choille (ed.), *Intelligence notes, 1913–16* (Dublin, 1966), p. 252; see also Lyons, *Dillon*, p. 298). An example of the animus many tenants bore towards their (former) masters may be found in Carbery, *The farm by Lough Gur*, pp 28–9.

[3] An expression used by Horace Plunkett in the house of commons and quoted by R. Barry O'Brien in *Dublin Castle and the Irish people* (London, 1912), p. 258.

[4] From 1907 to 1912 the annual totals of indictable agrarian offences stayed above 300. In 1913, the figure fell to 190 and then rose in 1914 to 235 (*Intelligence notes, 1913–16*, p. 246). By 1910, county inspectors all over the country were reporting generally peaceful conditions, except for certain chronically disturbed districts in the west. See the note written by Sir James B. Dougherty,

Most indictable agrarian offences in 1914 involved threatening letters and other forms of intimidation. While serious boycotting had declined, the revival of cattle drives in parts of Meath and Galway caused a flurry of police activity.[1] The efforts of the United Irish League to break up the large grazing farms in Meath, which were used for the final fattening of cattle on their way to market in Dublin, met with scant success. Neither graziers nor gentry were prepared to surrender their valuable lands, least of all under the pressure of such agrarian outrages as cattle driving, broken fences, and nails or spikes strewn in fields. In some cases threatening letters forced landowners to request police patrols or full-time protection.[2]

One continuing source of anxiety to both officials and the farming community was the flourishing state of the moneylending business. Although the evidence is sketchy as well as contradictory, owing in part to the secrecy with which private loan transactions were carried out, there can be little doubt that many farmers were caught in a net of credit, high interest rates, and judgments for debt. Whether the creditors were called moneylenders, shopkeepers, usurers, or gombeen men made little difference to those clients who were led down the debtor's path to bankruptcy. What kept the moneylenders in business was a combination of deceptive advertising in the local press and the expanding credit needs of farmers, many of whom were compelled to borrow money at exorbitant interest rates. In some districts the gombeen men took advantage of the peasant proprietor's newly acquired collateral in land by allowing him more credit than he could handle and then foreclosing after the interest payments fell into arrear.[3]

In spite of these dangers many people preferred to deal with the local moneylender, rather than avail themselves of the lower interest rates at the local bank. The joint-stock banks were not always equipped to deal with the special needs of farmers, and the fifty-one loan fund societies (which had survived from the original 300 societies in 1842) were precarious ventures with little capital at their disposal. Some enterprising farmers took Horace Plunkett's advice and joined the Irish Agricultural Organisation Society, borrowing small sums from local cooperative credit societies. But these cooperatives struggled against many odds. In 1914 no more than 176 of the original 310 credit societies were operational—of which only sixty-one held deposits in excess of £100.[4] Frugal

---

under-secretary for Ireland, on the cover of the monthly confidential report sent by the county inspector of the east riding of Galway to the inspector general, R.I.C., 16 Feb. 1910 (P.R.O., C.O. 904/80, p. 2). In 1916 Dublin Castle received reports of 51 cattle drives around the country, more than half of which took place in Connacht (*Intelligence notes, 1913–16*, p. 254).

[1] *Intelligence notes, 1913–16*, pp 123, 144, 186.

[2] On 30 June 1914, 49 persons were under 'constant protection' by police and 250 others were protected by police patrols (ibid., p. 120).

[3] For details of these moneylending activities, see *Report of the departmental committee on agricultural credit in Ireland*, pp 51–61 [Cd 7675], H.C. 1914, xiii, 69–79, and below, p. 325.

[4] *Report . . . on agricultural credit*, pp 2, 121, 166–7 (MS 20, 139, 184–5); and above, pp 87–91.

farmers with money to spare might lodge their capital in the post office savings bank, which had the double attraction of government security and privacy. Needless to say, the diversion of some £13 millions to these savings banks deprived the cooperative movement of an important source of capital.

On the whole the sales of so much land to occupiers under the land purchase acts withdrew the sting from landlordism, even though many tenants complained about exorbitant prices and delays in completing the sale. Contrary to nationalist hopes the Wyndham act did not purge the countryside of the resident landlords, however. Leaving aside the businessmen or *arrivistes*, who had bought property under the encumbered estates acts and were mostly absentees, the older landlord class clung to their ancestral houses and birthplaces. Local people knew full well who the 'old quality' were and how they differed from newer owners who had made their money in trade.

When the war broke out, many of the younger men from the big houses rushed to enlist (or rejoin their regiments), keen to prove both their patriotism and manhood. No doubt they looked forward to a short campaign and an early return to their hunting and house-partying after vanquishing the king's enemies. If the Anglo-Irish gentry provided many an officer in the British Expeditionary Force, the ranks of the army contained thousands of catholic Irishmen, many of whom were nationalist volunteers, who answered Redmond's call in September to join the fight against the Germans who had crushed catholic Belgium.[1] Needless to say, countless Irish soldiers signed up for the pay and the pension that would come their way on discharge. But by October 1914 the casualty lists in the newspapers made it painfully clear that some scions of the big house as well as many tenants or workers on their estates were never going to return.[2]

However reduced in acreage and shorn of political power—at least outside north-east Ulster—most of the old resident gentry still commanded respect and influence around their estates and in nearby market towns, where shopkeepers competed for their custom. Here and there groups of loyal tenants continued to memorialise such traditional milestones as the coming-of-age or marriage of the heir apparent of the big house. Occasionally, rural district councils would congratulate a local aristocrat for some honour received, or express regret when a 'good' landlord or aristocratic 'big spender' decided to pull up stakes and leave the country.[3] Not only did the resident gentry and plutocracy inspire endless gossip, but they also remained the largest single employers of labour—indoors and outdoors—in many parts of the country. Their patronage and goodwill still mattered. If landlordism no longer cast a chilling shadow across the land, there were enough residual fears and resentments lingering in the minds

---

[1] Below, p. 190.

[2] For glimpses of the repercussions of the great war in a small community, see Silverman & Gulliver, *In the valley of the Nore*, pp 162–9.

[3] For two such instances, involving the earl of Carrick and Baron Southampton, see ibid., pp 168, 177.

of Irishmen reared on tales of rack-rents and evictions to cause trouble in the future.[1]

The position of owners of middling estates with gross rentals of between £1,000 and £5,000 and encumbrances was not always enviable. On many of these estates the claims of needy relatives and various other charges on the property ate deeply into the owner's income, forcing the trustees of a settled estate to adopt stringent economies or to raise new capital through mortgages, sometimes secured by a cluster of life insurance policies. Once the estates commissioners had approved the sale of land, vendors might receive less than half of the purchase money advanced, because every creditor who could prove a claim on the lands sold received the principal sum due plus interest before the residue went to the vendor.[2] The crumbling demesne walls, the shabby carriage, the unweeded gardens, the empty stables, or the water-stained ceilings that characterised so many big houses after 1900 were not just symbols of gentility but proof of chronic financial distress.

The extensive transfer of ownership of tenanted land under the land purchase acts did not remove that vital distinction in rural society between 'them' and 'us'. Even the humblest labourer knew the difference between the strong farmer, the businessman speculator in land, and the genuine 'quality'. Country people tended to regard the 'ould gintry' with more than ambivalence. Around the families of resident proprietors there flourished a dense undergrowth of lore and legend about their behaviour in good times and bad. If relations between landowner and tenants were mostly amicable, especially after the rent nexus had been abolished, landlords and tenants (or ex-tenants) had other deeper loyalties of a political and religious nature that could prove irreconcilable. The minority status of protestants of all classes in the south and west made their political position increasingly vulnerable in so far as they opposed home rule. And they had good reason to worry about their future as the number of southern unionist M.P.s dwindled to only three in 1906.[3] If they wished to survive in the midst of a catholic nationalist majority, protestant unionists had to avoid antagonising the parish priest, as well as local Redmondite leaders, United Irish Leaguers, Sinn Féiners, and radical republicans. Alternatively, they could embrace home rule, as did some of the more liberal veterans of the devolution imbroglio of 1904–5, along with a few sons and daughters of landlords who had fought both the land league and Parnellism.[4]

---

[1] See for example Dan Breen's early memories of landlord oppression in County Tipperary in *My fight for Irish freedom* (Tralee, 1964), pp 11–13, 100.

[2] For a sample of the mortgages and other debts carried by landowners at the time of sale under the Wyndham act, as evidenced by the final schedules of incumbrances in the land commission, see L. P. Curtis, jr, 'Incumbered wealth: landed indebtedness in post-famine Ireland' in *A.H.R.*, lxxxv, no. 2 (Apr. 1980), esp. pp 349–55.

[3] The two unionists returned for Dublin University in this year were Sir Edward Carson and J. H. M. Campbell, Q.C., along with Walter H. Long, M.P. for Dublin County South.

[4] Among the former were Lords Dunraven and Monteagle, Sir Nugent Everard, and Sir William Hutcheson Poë. Among the latter were Walter MacMorrough Kavanagh, the 2nd Baron Ashbourne, the 6th earl of Carrick, and, of course, Countess Markievicz (Constance Gore-Booth).

Far more numerous than the remnants of the old ascendancy and the middle-class protestants living in towns and cities were the tenant farmers and new owner-occupiers, whose lives had changed little since the 1890s. This class still had to endure the caprices of climate and harvest, as well as fluctuations in the price of their produce. Land purchase may have lifted the spirits of the new owners, but it did not noticeably improve the quality of Irish agriculture. Horace Plunkett was not the only informed observer to express concern over the poor quality of agricultural products, especially dairy goods and seeds.[1] The cooperative creameries sponsored by the Irish Agricultural Organisation Society after 1894 were designed to modernise the Irish dairy industry in order to make it competitive with its Danish and British rivals. With the help of such able deputies as R. A. Anderson and A E (George Russell), the indefatigable Plunkett embarked on his long crusade to spread the faith in cooperation and promote the regeneration of rural Ireland.[2]

The decline of tillage as a whole in Ireland did not quite match that of wheat, the acreage of which decreased by 81.7 per cent between 1867 and 1910, as compared with a decrease of 46.3 per cent in the acreage of wheat in Great Britain during the same period.[3] While the amount of arable land was slowly shrinking, yields per acre of cereal crops showed a significant increase between the 1890s and the decade 1905–14.[4] Measured in starch tons, the total output of crops was slightly higher in 1909–13 than in 1873–7.[5]

Increases in livestock signified the movement away from labour-intensive tillage. After several sharp fluctuations in the period 1850–73, the number of cattle in the country had remained fairly constant until 1889, when it began to rise steadily, attaining a record high in 1921. In 1914 the number of sheep was still declining from the peak of 4,396,000 reached in 1892. The quinquennial average of pigs stayed roughly the same between the late 1850s and the years 1912–16. But one category of livestock increased dramatically after the famine—namely,

---

[1] See, for example, the leading article in the *Irish Homestead* (24 Apr. 1915) by A E condemning the flagrant adulteration of seeds, especially in the west. Tests of seed samples between 1910 and 1915 revealed that the percentage of worthless seeds ranged between 54 and 69 per cent.

[2] Plunkett's mission to enhance both the efficiency of the Irish dairy industry and the quality of rural life is treated in R. A. Anderson, *With Horace Plunkett in Ireland* (London, 1935); Margaret Digby, *Horace Plunkett* (Oxford, 1949), pp 51–7, 63–6, 94–5, 101–2; and Trevor West, *Horace Plunkett: cooperation and politics, an Irish biography* (Gerrards Cross, Bucks., 1986), pp 20–25.

[3] See Mitchell & Deane, *Brit. hist. statistics*, pp 78–9; 'Statistical survey of Irish agriculture' in W. P. Coyne (ed.), *Ireland: industrial and agricultural* (Dublin, 1902), pp 304–14. Total tillage in Ireland fell by 45.7 per cent (from 4,344,330 to 2,358,140 acres) between 1861 and 1910. See also Raymond D. Crotty, *Irish agricultural production* (Cork, 1966), appendix, table II, p. 353.

[4] Besides the impressive gains for wheat, barley, and oats, the yield per acre of potatoes, turnips and swedes, and mangolds also showed an increase between these two periods (Mitchell & Deane, *Brit. hist. statistics*, table 8, pp 92–3).

[5] In 1860, 28.3 per cent of all cultivated land (pasturage and tillage combined) was given over to crops, exclusive of meadow and clover. But by 1914, this figure had fallen to 13.5 per cent. At the same time pasturage or grass composed 72.1 per cent of cultivated land (*Agricultural statistics of Ireland . . . for the year 1907*, p. 2 [Cd 4352], H.C. 1908, cxxi, 832; and *Thom's official directory . . . 1916*, pp 782–93).

poultry. While the number of sheep doubled between 1851 and 1910, poultry rose threefold in the same period, indicating not only a higher consumption of eggs and fowl in rural households but the growing reliance of farmers' wives on this cash crop for their spending money.[1]

In general the swing from 'corn to horn' was more pronounced on medium-sized and small farms than on large farms, which had already reached a closer balance between pasturage and tillage. Smaller holdings tended to have the highest number of livestock in proportion to land, exclusive of dry cattle over two years old. On smaller farms, where mixed agriculture predominated, more workers were needed for crop cultivation. Much of the work was carried out by family members, who accounted for 89 per cent of all labourers on farms of 1–15 acres. On farms of more than 200 acres, by contrast, family members made up only 24 per cent of the work-force.[2] In 1912, only 26 per cent of all 862,000 males and females engaged in agriculture were classified as wage-earners. In other words, 74 per cent of all agricultural workers consisted of farmers and their families or relatives, who were located on home farms. In all, 15 per cent of all labourers were more or less permanent wage-earners, and another 11 per cent were temporary or short-term hired hands. Family labour was more in evidence on small farms of 1–15 acres, as compared with the 24 per cent figure for workers on farms of 200 acres and above. The contrast between farms of 15–30 acres, which employed an average of 110 workers per 1,000 acres of cultivated land, and farms of over 200 acres, which employed an average of twenty-two workers, mostly hired labour, reveals the difference between the extent of pasturing activities on large and small farms.[3] The other major difference involved productivity. On farms of 50 acres and under, labour-intensive methods produced higher crop yields per acre than was the case on larger farms where workers had a higher average output per man.[4] The actual relationship of farm size to output may be judged from the following table, which points up the disparities of agricultural activity according to size of farm.

These figures reveal nothing about the quality of life on farms in different parts of the country, and they are silent about the subordinate position of women in rural society. In rural areas the myriad responsibilities of mother, cook, and housekeeper were supplemented by equally onerous duties in the yard and field. At harvest time country women worked alongside their men and then returned at intervals to the kitchen to prepare the meals. In 1912, one out of every four

[1] In 1851, there were 7,470,694 poultry in Ireland, compared with 24,339,015 in 1910. In this population, chickens greatly outnumbered ducks, geese, and turkeys. See Crotty, *Ir. agricultural production*, p. 91, and table III, p. 354. In the poor law union of Thomastown, Co. Kilkenny, the number of poultry shot up from 33,088 in 1850 to 124,052 in 1914 (Silverman and Gulliver, *In the valley of the Nore*, p. 104).

[2] On farms of 15–30 acres, the average number of workers was 110 per 1,000 acres of cultivated land, compared with an average of 22 workers (mostly hired labour) for farms over 200 acres (Department of Industry and Commerce (Saorstat Éireann), *Agricultural statistics, 1847–1926: report and tables* (Dublin, 1928, 1930), pp l–lii).

[3] Ibid., pp l–lii.   [4] Ibid., p. li.

Acreage of crops and livestock per 100 persons engaged in agriculture in Ireland, 1 June 1912

	size of holding (acres)						
	1–15	15–30	30–50	50–100	100–200	over 200	all holdings
area ploughed	123	168	208	258	302	268	196
hay	116	187	247	319	409	476	236
milch cows	88	126	160	200	211	155	141
cattle (under 2 years)	112	178	235	309	380	426	223
cattle (2 years and over)	15	35	60	112	252	648	105
total: all cattle	215	338	455	621	842	1,229	470
sheep	122	209	299	452	838	1,827	402
pigs	98	129	146	157	137	77	128
poultry	2,286	2,234	2,146	2,060	1,880	1,398	2,221

Source: Department of Industry and Commerce (Saorstat Éireann), *Agricultural statistics, 1847–1926: report and tables* (Dublin, 1928, 1930), p. li.

workers on farms of less than 200 acres was a female, and roughly 86 per cent of all women in agriculture belonged to families working their home farm.[1]

In the view of that impassioned socialist and feminist, James Connolly, the women of Ireland were the slaves of the male slaves in capitalist society; and he inveighed against their continuing exploitation: 'The daughters of the Irish peasantry have been the cheapest slaves in existence—slaves to their own family who were in turn slaves to all the social parasites of a landlord and gombeen-ridden community.'[2] Because the feminist revolt in Great Britain coincided with the participation of militant women in the Irish labour movement, Connolly had hopes that the Irish people would soon combine the goal of sexual equality with 'civic conscience' for the betterment of all.[3] But this dream was not fulfilled, and Irish women had to wait many years for even tokens of the emancipation envisaged by Connolly.

Up to 1918 Irish women remained outside the parliamentary arena despite a decade of militant protests against their exclusion in both Ireland and Great Britain.[4] Instead of participating in national politics, women activists had to settle for the modest role of poor law guardian, until 1911, when they became eligible for election to the county as well as the rural and urban district councils created in 1898. By 1914, dissension within the women's suffrage movement had reached a breaking-point over the question of whether or not home rule should take

[1] Ibid., p. liii.   [2] James Connolly, *The reconquest of Ireland* (Dublin, 1934), p. 292.
[3] Ibid., p. 290.
[4] For an informative study of the militant phase of the suffragette movement, which resulted in acts of arson and vandalism in north-east Ulster as well as England, see Andrew W. Rosen, *Rise up women! the militant campaign of the Women's Social and Political Union, 1903–1914* (London and Boston, Mass., 1974).

precedence over the franchise. Many feminists wanted to achieve the best of both worlds: votes for women and full equality with men in an independent Ireland. But this promised land lay far ahead; and it was not attained without some acrimonious quarrels over priorities. Since the 1860s both the agitation against the contagious diseases acts and the campaign for women's suffrage had served as recruiting and training grounds for women who were eager to enter the public sphere. Prominent among these were the daughters of middle-class Dubliners, both protestant and catholic, who resented their isolation from national politics and had no wish to spend their lives within a private sphere of stultifying respectability. Although they had taken part in protest meetings and anti-eviction activities during the land war, many country women accepted their subordinate role in matters political and social. And it took two daughters of one big house—Avondale—to run the Ladies' Land League with an authority and verve that proved threatening to male land leaguers in 1881–2.[1]

In 1900 a group of women activists, some of them radicalised by the Boer war, launched a new association that fused feminism with nationalism and socialism in a dynamic manner. Calling themselves 'Inghinidhe na hÉireann' (Daughters of Erin), Maud Gonne, Jenny Wyse Power, Annie Egan, and their followers also published a newspaper, *Bean na hÉireann* (Woman of Ireland), which shared Sinn Féin's commitment not only to independence but to the promotion of Irish culture and manufactures. Seeking to foster solidarity and improve security, the founders made admission contingent on Irish ancestry and the sponsorship of at least two members. Combining hard work with a flair for publicity, the Inghinidhe organised picnics and school meals for poor children, opposed recruiting for the British army, and protested against royal visits to Dublin. As membership grew, so, too, did the national network—until 1911, when disagreements and shortage of funds forced *Bean na hÉireann* to cease publication and moved some members to join more radical groups.[2]

In the meantime the cause of women's suffrage was attracting many daughters of the middle class. Four years after its founding in 1908, the Irish Women's Franchise League boasted a thousand members, who found inspiration in the activities of the Women's Social and Political Union in Britain. To coordinate the various suffrage associations in Dublin and elsewhere a more moderate body, the Irish Women's Suffrage Federation, soon came into being.[3] The vitality of the Irish suffrage movement seems to have nettled John Redmond, however. Having set his sights

---

[1] For details of the Ladies' Land League and the leadership qualities of Anna and Fanny Parnell in particular, see T. W. Moody, 'Anna Parnell and the Land League' in *Hermathena*, cxvii (summer 1974), pp 5–17; Jane McL. Cote, *Fanny and Anna Parnell: Ireland's patriot sisters* (Dublin, 1991); and Janet K. TeBrake, 'Irish peasant women in revolt: the land league years' in *I.H.S.*, xxviii, no. 109 (May 1992), pp 63–80.

[2] For further details of Inghinidhe na hÉireann, see Margaret Ward, *Unmanageable revolutionaries: women and Irish nationalism* (London, 1983), pp 50–87.

[3] Founded by Louie Bennett and Helen Chenevix in 1911, the federation worked hard to achieve the semblance of a feminist popular front. Other Dublin-based feminist associations in 1914 were the Irish Woman's Suffrage and Local Government Association, launched (or renamed) in 1901 by the

firmly on home rule, he had no wish to divert his party's attention towards female suffrage—thereby dashing feminist hopes of support from the parliamentary party.

While the third home rule bill was being debated in the house of commons, dissension over goals and tactics widened the divisions among Irish feminists, some of whom adopted the rallying cry of the *Irish Citizen*, founded by Francis Sheehy-Skeffington and James Cousins in May 1912—'Suffrage first—before all else'. Others devoted their energies to achieving home rule or equal rights for working-class women. To the declaration that 'there can be no free nation without free women' the champions of home rule replied: 'neither can there be free women in an enslaved nation.'[1]

The founding of Cumann na mBan ('the women's association') on 5 April 1914 marked another new departure in the history of Irish feminism and nationalism. Led by Agnes O'Farrelly, a graduate of U.C.D. and keen Gaelic Leaguer, along with several other fervently republican women, this association encouraged members to serve as the fundraisers, helpmates, and auxiliaries of the male Volunteers in the coming struggle. Pledged 'to assist in arming and equipping a body of Irishmen for the defence of Ireland', the women of Cumann na mBan raised funds and took lessons in first aid and military tactics in preparation for the eventual call to arms.[2] Not surprisingly, the I.W.F.L. criticised Cumann na mBan for assigning women the 'slavish' role of minions to the men in the Volunteer movement, while diverting valuable resources from the cause of female emancipation. As Cumann na mBan drew more young women away from the suffragette cause, the tensions between these rival goals added to the acrimony of Irish politics in this momentous year.

By way of contrast a small but powerful cohort of Irishmen, predominantly protestant and upper-middle-class, made a good living in the Irish civil service.[3]

---

seasoned quaker activist Mrs Anna M. Haslam (with offices located at 125 Leinster Road, Rathmines) and the Irish Women's Reform League (29 South Anne Street). A northern affiliate of the federation was the Belfast Women's Suffrage Society. For further details, see Rosemary Cullen Owens, *Smashing times: a history of the Irish women's suffrage movement, 1889–1922* (Dublin, 1984), pp 42–5; and Cliona Murphy, *The women's suffrage movement and Irish society in the early twentieth century* (Hemel Hempstead, 1989).

[1] Quoted in Owens, *Smashing times*, p. 108. See also Margaret Ward, 'Suffrage first above all else! An account of the Irish suffrage movement, 1876–1922' in *Feminist Review*, x (1982), pp 21–36. After Cousins resigned as co-editor of the *Irish Citizen* in Mar. 1913, Sheehy-Skeffington's wife Hanna contributed even more articles and ideas to the paper. See Leah Levenson and Jerry H. Natterstad, *Hanna Sheehy-Skeffington: Irish feminist* (Syracuse, 1986), pp 35–6. For the story of Irish women workers organising their own militant union, see Mary Jones, *Those obstreperous lassies: a history of the Irish Women Workers Union* (Dublin, 1988).

[2] For the origins and early activities of Cumann na mBan, see Margaret MacCurtain, 'Women, the vote and revolution' in Margaret MacCurtain and Donncha Ó Corráin (ed.), *Women in Irish society* (Dublin, 1978), pp 52–5, and Ward, *Unmanageable revolutionaries*, pp 92–118. Besides 'organising and training the women of Ireland to take their places by the side of those who are working and fighting for a free Ireland', Cumann na mBan also raised money for 'the Defence of Ireland Fund' (Owens, *Smashing times*, p. 108).

[3] The denominational difference between the salaries paid to the 650 professionally trained officers was considerable: in one department the protestant officials earned on average £358 a year, the

The cost of governing the country was no trivial matter, least of all to those 'young watch-puppies of the treasury' whose bristles, as Sir Henry Robinson of the Irish local government board once observed, 'would stand up like the fretful porcupine when schemes from Irish departments came before them'.[1] The expense of the Irish administration, including all the special social and economic measures that were supposed to appease Irish voters, must have persuaded some British taxpayers to support the third home rule bill if only to relieve themselves of the extra burden of the Irish administration.

The discrepancy between the *per capita* cost of governing Britain and Ireland also caused dismay in Whitehall and Westminster. In 1892–3, for example, according to one critic of the system, civil government charges were 11s. 5d. per head in Great Britain and 19s. 7d. per head in Ireland.[2] During the Edwardian era public expenditure in Ireland threatened to absorb every penny of hard-won Irish revenue. In addition to the normal tendency of bureaucracy to expand—in Ireland as elsewhere—various laws were enacted that swelled the ranks of officialdom. The local government act of 1898 virtually trebled the size of the local government board by 1914; and the Irish land acts multiplied the number of inspectors, assistant commissioners, surveyors, and accountants in order to deal with the huge volume of business at the land commission.[3] Few Irishmen showed much gratitude for all this costly treatment, unless, of course, there was a government job in the offing.

One significant occupation for Irishmen in good health and with a taste for law and order was police work. By the early twentieth century, the Royal Irish Constabulary had acquired the dubious distinction of being both 'a standing army and the most expensive police force in the world'.[4] In 1914 there was one constable or policeman (including the Dublin Metropolitan Police) to every 377 people in Ireland, whereas the ratio in England and Wales was 1 to 664 and in Scotland 1 to 802. The total bill for the Irish police establishment in 1914 came to the princely or imperial sum of £1,582,849. The ratio of police to population

catholics £202. By 1900, catholics occupied the majority of rank-and-file positions in the bureaucracy, while protestants still dominated the top positions, even though their former monopoly was being eroded. In 1911 the thirty-nine departments of Irish government employed 27,222 persons, of whom 2,248 earned more than £160 a year. According to the latest historian of Dublin Castle, 39 per cent of appointments to the 1,611 principal positions in the Irish administration were made by nomination, 48 per cent were made after a special qualifying examination, and 13 per cent were made on the basis of an open competitive examination (Lawrence W. McBride, *The greening of Dublin Castle: the transformation of bureaucratic and judicial personnel in Ireland, 1892–1922* (Washington, D.C., 1991), pp 10–37).

[1] Sir Henry Robinson, *Memories: wise and otherwise* (London, 1924), p. 94.

[2] A. E. Murray, *A history of the commercial and financial relations between England and Ireland . . .* (London, 1907), pp 388–9.

[3] McDowell, *Ir. administration*, pp 29–35, 189–90, 218–23; and below, pp 571–95.

[4] To support this opinion, Alice Murray cited the calculations of Thomas Lough, M.P., who estimated the cost of the Irish constabulary in 1895 as 6s. 7d. per head compared with 2s. 3d. per head in Scotland. In addition, he calculated the ratio of policemen to citizenry as 1 : 257 in Ireland and 1 : 1,000 in Scotland (*England's wealth, Ireland's poverty* (London, 1895), p. 81).

varied widely in Ireland. Counties Antrim, Down, and Londonderry had the lowest proportion with 13 police per 10,000 persons. County Galway had the highest ratio with 48 per 10,000, followed by Clare (45), by Westmeath (35), and then by Belfast (32), and Dublin (27).[1]

The special training and weapons carried by the R.I.C. were hardly justified by the rate of ordinary crime in Ireland, which was only slightly higher in a few categories than that in England and Scotland. In 1914 some 8,504 indictable offences were recorded, while 163,041 persons were tried for non-indictable offences. The number of indictable offences in 1914 was thus 1.94 per 1,000 persons, as against an average in England and Wales of 1.81 per 1,000 persons for the years 1900–13.[2]

In terms of geographical or regional distribution the major cities had the highest crime rates, with the Dublin metropolitan area coming first, followed by Belfast, Derry, Waterford, Limerick, and Cork. These urban areas were followed in descending order by Counties Kildare, Tipperary (South Riding), and the King's County. In other words, the six most urbanised areas, which contained 22.5 per cent of the population in 1911, accounted for 34 per cent of all criminal offences. In general, the regions with the lowest crime rates had the lowest population densities: Counties Leitrim, Donegal, and Mayo.[3] Of the 19,353 males and females convicted and sent to Irish prisons in 1914, 20.8 per cent were declared to be 'absolutely illiterate', compared with an illiteracy rate of 9.7 per cent for the population at large. The female prisoners in that year were significantly less educated than the males. Only 57.7 per cent of the females could read and write well, compared with 72.1 per cent of the males.[4]

In view of the ordinary crime rate in Ireland, the only excuse for maintaining such an extensive police force had to be a political one. The principal function of the R.I.C. was not just to prevent crime and catch offenders but to serve as the eyes and ears of Dublin Castle. Among the myriad duties of these men were counting people, animals, and agricultural produce, observing weather conditions and harvests, reporting outbreaks of agrarian outrage and animal disease, maintaining surveillance of nationalist societies (both secret and those above ground), enforcing the game laws and licensing acts, and keeping the peace with a minimal use of force.[5] Needless to say, the physical stature as well as the distinctive

---

[1] *Judicial statistics, Ireland, 1914. Part I: criminal statistics*, pp xxiii–xxiv [Cd 8077], H.C. 1914–16, lxxxii, 473–4. For further details see McDowell, *Ir. administration*, pp 136–45.

[2] *Judicial statistics, Ireland, 1914*, p. ix (MS 459), and *Judicial statistics, England and Wales, 1913. Part I: criminal statistics*, p. 18 [Cd 7767], H.C. 1914–16, lxxxii, 18.

[3] *Judicial statistics, Ireland, 1914*, p. xv (MS 465).

[4] Ibid., p. xix (MS 469).

[5] For an informed account of the role played by the Royal Irish Constabulary in Ireland as well as within an imperial context, see Richard Hawkins, 'The "Irish model" and the empire: a case for reassessment' in David M. Anderson and David Killingray (ed.), *Policing the empire: government, authority, and control, 1830–1940* (Manchester, 1991), pp 18–32, esp. p. 27. Considering all these duties and activities, it might be argued that taxpayers were getting their money's worth—especially in view of the low wages paid to these servants of the crown.

dark-green uniforms and weaponry of the constabulary inspired awe or respect among those being policed. Had there been no rebellions, tithe wars, land wars, intimidation, and boycotting in Irish history, it is unlikely that the treasury would have condoned so costly a police establishment. The activities of the political intelligence unit within the R.I.C., known as the 'special crimes branch', which functioned under the supervision of the inspector general and reported directly to the under-secretary, probably kept a number of county and district inspectors a good deal busier than the political suspects whom they were supposed to observe.

The persistence of poverty should not be allowed to conceal the distinct, if selective, rise in the Irish standard of living. Outside the hard-core pockets of poverty in Dublin[1] and Belfast and the congested districts of western Munster and Connacht, there was ample evidence of improvement in the household amenities, dietary habits, and dress of the people.

As the newer suburbs of Ballsbridge, Foxrock, Rathmines, Rathgar, and Kingstown began to sprout sturdy little villas for sturdy little businessmen, as tramlines and trains began to reach out more regularly into these suburbs, and as motor cars fought their way through traffic jams of horse-drawn carriages in the city, the signs of modernity, as distinct from progress, became unmistakable. The Dublin of 1914 was a metropolitan mixture of grimy tenements, Georgian elegance, Victorian commercialism, and red-brick bastions of respectability, both Redmondite and unionist. The city, in short, was a congeries of designs and districts as well as moods and experiences.

The growing affluence of suburban Dublin contrasted sharply with the pockets of hard-core poverty in the Coombe and tenements north of the Liffey. Judged by the criterion of mortality rates, Dublin was one of the unhealthiest cities in the British Isles, even though Ireland as a whole had a lower infant mortality rate (87 per 1,000 live births) than England and Wales (105), Scotland (111), and most of the continental countries except for Norway (68) and Sweden (73).[2] Unsanitary, overcrowded, and rickety tenements abounded in such wards as the North city, the Rotunda, the Mountjoy, the Merchant's Quay, the Inn's Quay, and Wood Quay. According to a government report, 25,822 families, consisting of 87,305 persons, were then living in 5,322 tenement houses. Some 78 per cent of

---

[1] See *Report of the departmental committee appointed . . . to inquire into the housing conditions of the working classes in the city of Dublin* [Cd 7273], H.C. 1914, xix, 61–106; and below, pp 335–8.

[2] According to Joseph V. O'Brien, Dublin stood 'first among major towns and cities of Britain and Ireland' in terms of mortality and compared unfavourably with many cities in Europe and the eastern seaboard of America. In 1866 the city's death rate of 33.1 per 1,000 surpassed that of Glasgow (29.3), Manchester (31.9), and Leeds (32.5), while falling far below Liverpool (41.8). Despite some sanitary improvements in the intervening decades, Dublin's death rate did not drop below 26.6 before 1900 and continued to reach appalling heights in the poorest courts and back streets in the early 1900s. See *'Dear dirty Dublin': a city in distress, 1899–1916* (Berkeley, Calif., 1982), pp 21–2. Working-class children bore the heaviest burden of death: from 1875 to 1900 the average rate for Dublin-born infants in their first year was 171 per 1,000. In 1898 the figure stood at 196. If infant mortality remained high in most British cities, Dublin's record in this respect was lamentable.

the tenants in these buildings were crowded into single-room dwellings, which were breeding grounds of tuberculosis as well as alcoholism and petty crime.[1]

The scarcity of heavy industry in the metropolis made it all the more difficult for tenement dwellers to find regular work. Most adult males had to settle for irregular and low-paid work as stevedores, porters, coal-shovellers, carters, and street-sellers or pedlars. And when no one hired their services, they had to beg or steal to provide their families' basic needs. The stark contrasts between the living standards of Dublin's rich and poor stirred James Larkin and James Connolly to make Dublin's proletariat aware of their potential strength as well as dignity by means of the mass trade union and the sympathetic strike.[2] Quick to notice that some of the most overcrowded and decaying tenements were owned by prominent aldermen, a few of whom received tax rebates on this urban property, Connolly denounced these middle-class profiteers and held out hope to the depressed slum-dwellers of a new social order designed to fulfil the needs and aspirations of the working class.[3]

In the early months of 1914, the supporters of Larkin and Connolly, who had gone out on strike or been locked out by the owners, were still nursing memories of the batons wielded by the D.M.P. in the previous autumn. Having seen the hand of red socialism in the activities of the Transport & General Workers' Union, the employers were bent on teaching the workers a lesson they were not likely to forget. The demoralising effects of weeks without work and the indifference of British trade unionists to the sufferings of their Dublin brothers eventually forced most of the strikers to submit to the employers' terms. Apart from the bitter taste of defeat at the hands of William Martin Murphy and his fellow employers, Connolly learned much from this encounter with the propertied élite of Dublin. While Larkin pursued schemes that took him to America in 1914, Connolly decided to reorganise the Irish Citizen Army into a self-defence force.

[1] See the map of the city of Dublin (and the vivid photographs) in *Report of the departmental committee appointed . . . to inquire into the housing conditions of the working classes in the city of Dublin,* pp 2–3 [Cd 7273], H.C. 1914, xix, 66–7; the photographs are on MS pp 95–106, and the map between pp 344 and 345 (MS 456–7). In 1891, 37 per cent of all Dublin families lived in fourth-class (the poorest) accommodations compared with 49.9 per cent in 1851 (O'Brien, *'Dear, dirty Dublin',* p. 24). To take another criterion of bad housing conditions—namely, the number of persons per 1,000 population living in one-room tenements—Dublin had the dubious distinction of 229, compared with 132 in Glasgow, 59 in London, 56 in Edinburgh, 23 in Liverpool, 7 in Manchester, 4 in Birmingham, and only 3 in Belfast.

[2] The story of Dublin's labour strife in 1913–14 may be pieced together from Emmet Larkin, *James Larkin* (Cambridge, Mass., 1965), pp 85–184; Peter Berresford Ellis, *A history of the Irish working class* (London, 1972), pp 184–210; Arthur Mitchell, *Labour in Irish politics, 1890–1930* (New York, 1974), pp 25–63; and O'Brien, *'Dear, dirty Dublin',* pp 212–40. Although somewhat dated, there is still good value in J. Dunsmore Clarkson, *Labour and nationalism in Ireland* (New York, 1925). For a vivid fictional account of Dublin in these years, see James Plunkett, *Strumpet city* (London, 1969).

[3] Connolly, *Reconquest of Ireland,* pp 337–8. For a list of the seventeen members of the Dublin corporation who owned or had an interest in tenement housing, and mention of those five members who had applied for tax rebates on that housing, see *Appendix to the report of the departmental committee appointed . . . to inquire into the housing conditions of the working classes in the city of Dublin: minutes of evidence with appendices,* pp 286–91, 344 [Cd 7317], H.C. 1914, xix, 396–401, 456.

Under the command of Captain Jack White, who had the good sense to call himself a 'misfit', and with the help of a young working-class playwright, Sean O'Casey, the Irish Citizen Army embodied the aspirations of both ardent trade unionists and revolutionary socialists. Given the intensity of political conflict and economic hardship it was not surprising that this proletarian private army should attract the flamboyant daughter of a Sligo landlord, Constance de Markievicz (née Gore-Booth), and should be drilled by the son of a distinguished general and Ulster unionist, Sir George White, V.C.[1]

Dublin in 1914 presented a striking contrast between the poverty of its slums and the richness of its intellect. Admittedly some of the brilliant lustre of the literary revival had faded with age and emigration. But there were still enough gifted writers and talkers left to make Dublin a centre of literary and theatrical creativity. Even though Synge had died too young and both George Moore and James Joyce had left for different destinations, the Abbey Theatre retained much vitality despite the skirmishes with what Yeats called the forces of philistinism. In Plunkett House, Sir Horace and George Russell (A E) made certain that the Irish Agricultural Organisation Society would deal with issues loftier than egg prices and bacteria counts in milk, cream, and butter. Douglas Hyde, the 'catholic protestant' of Moore's protestant-catholic imagination, had left his Connemara-made dug-out to enjoy the fame and popularity that were denied to Moore.[2] Susan Mitchell's satirical verses continued to deflate Orange politicians and pompous authors.[3] In south-west Cork Edith Somerville and Martin Ross, with their best work behind them, were beginning to explore those psychic phenomena so fashionable at that time.[4] If Lady Gregory and Edward Martyn seemed to have passed their prime in 1914, there were new talents waiting to be discovered and to find patronage as well as hospitality at Coole, among them James Stephens and Sean O'Casey. As for Yeats, whose formidable muse was not always appreciated by middle-class catholic Dublin, the quest for ultimate truth was drawing him ever deeper into spiritualism and psychic research. The poems he published early in 1914 under the title *Responsibilities* were filled with such antithetical themes as life and death, fantasy and reality, love thwarted and fulfilled, and shades of the past superimposed on the present. This collection contained the famous lament on the occasion of John O'Leary's death, 'September 1913', with its haunting refrain:

> Romantic Ireland's dead and gone
> It's with O'Leary in the grave.

[1] Lyons, *Ire. since famine*, pp 283–4; Jacqueline van Voris, *Constance de Markievicz: in the cause of Ireland* (Amherst, Mass., 1967), pp 97–131. See also Captain J. R. White, *Misfit: an autobiography* (London, 1930).

[2] George Moore, *'Hail and farewell!' Vale* (London, 1920), pp 251–3.

[3] See her pointed verses in *Aids to the immortality of certain persons in Ireland* (Dublin and London, 1908, 1913).

[4] Maurice Collis, *Somerville and Ross, a biography* (London, 1968), pp 164–5.

Most of these poems were woven out of legends, fables, and 'old mythologies', revealing glimpses of a man 'close on forty-nine', yearning for the nourishment of love, wishing for an end to the years of 'barren passion'. In the more topical poems, Yeats vented his anger on those myopic Irishmen who had reviled Parnell after the O'Shea scandal, condemned Synge's *Playboy of the western world*, and scorned Hugh Lane's plan for an opulent gallery in Dublin to house his fine collection of modern art.[1] These verses formed a poetic prelude to the autobiographical reflections he published in 1915—*Reveries over childhood and youth*.

Ireland in 1914 retained many of the features of a traditional society still steeped, outside the north-east, in the ways of agriculture and barter. But it was a country sufficiently complex to defy attempts to reduce it to a series of melodramatic contrasts between rich and poor, castle and cabin, or landlords and peasants. For all the outward signs of poverty in town and country, there were many indications of improvement in the material condition of the working classes. The conversion of tenants into peasant proprietors, who were paying the state less than the judicial rent in the form of land annuities, contributed to a slight rise in their living standards. And if the remaining agricultural labourers still worked long days for low wages, and had to eat a stirabout of Indian meal instead of potatoes in the summer, at least they could exchange their old well-worn frieze and corduroy suits (made in Ireland) for the durable shoddy produced in Yorkshire.[2] Another indicator of improvement was the amount of money kept in savings banks. The absence of reliable information about the extent of indebtedness obscures net savings, but gross savings had increased noticeably since the 1890s. In June 1914, the post office savings banks reported an all-time high of £13,303,000 in deposits—a figure almost three times the amount lodged in 1894. During the same period the number of savings accounts in both post office savings banks and trustee savings banks rose from 307,380 in 1894 to 713,356 in 1914.[3] The growth of a relatively prosperous urban and rural middle class was reflected, too, in the record sum of £61,955,000 on deposit in joint-stock banks on 30 June 1914.[4]

As so often in the past the relative tranquillity of the countryside contrasted with the frantic quality of political life in Dublin and Belfast. With the waning of the

---

[1] W. B. Yeats, *Later poems* (New York, 1924), pp 171–234; Richard Ellman, *Yeats: the man and the masks* (London, 1961), pp 196–213. The contrast between the paternalistic values of Yeats and Lady Gregory and the bourgeois materialism of Dublin's middle classes is brought out by Vivian Mercier (below, pp 358–9, 375–6).

[2] *Royal Irish Constabulary and Dublin Metropolitan Police: appendix to the report of the committee of inquiry, 1914: containing minutes of evidence with appendices* [Cd 7637], H.C. 1914–16, xxxii, 359–752.

[3] *Banking, railway, and shipping statistics, Ireland, June 1914*, pp 9–15 [Cd 7675], H.C. 1914–16, lxxx, 245–53, and *Banking and railway statistics, Ireland (December 1914)*, pp 8–20 [Cd 7884], H.C. 1914–16, lxxx, 278–92.

[4] Ibid., pp 6–8 [Cd 7675] (MS 242–4), and pp 6–7 [Cd 7884] (MS 276–7), and *Thom's official directory . . . 1916*, pp 818–20. For further details about the expansion and the assets of this class, see below, pp 334–5.

anti-grazier campaign most farmers were content to focus their minds on the weather, crop yields, livestock, prices, local gossip, and the politics of 'the parish pump'. For some the debate over the third home rule bill seemed almost as remote as the war clouds looming over Europe, although local Redmondite and Sinn Féin leaders were not about to let them forget the dangers of political apathy. Moderates on both sides of the great divide found themselves caught between extreme republicans and unionists, who talked much the same language of physical force, while taking steps to arm and drill in preparation for a showdown. As Conor Cruise O'Brien has written, 'The confusion of the time was rich and explosive. And it was the man of action rather than the man of prudence who flourished in it.'[1]

The main features of Irish political life in 1914 were so closely locked together that even to separate them for purposes of identification creates distortion. They belonged to an organic whole, connected at countless points by overlapping ideas, tactics, and symbols. First and foremost, the tension between the ideologies of constitutional agitation and physical force methods came close to the bursting-point in the course of this year. Second, the polarisation of the protestant north and catholic south gathered momentum as the day of reckoning, when the home rule bill received royal assent, approached. And, third, the prospect of partition became ever more likely as Carson and Craig mobilised Ulster unionists into a formidable political army backed by Bonar Law and most tory M.P.s.[2]

First, the disenchantment of republicans and other separatists with the home rule bill, which continued the political tie to Westminster, undermined the cause of constitutionalism in the country. By the same token, the leaders of northern unionism, aware that they could not block the government's plan to include Ulster in their home rule scheme by constitutional methods, had decided to bypass the parliamentary process altogether by founding and arming the Ulster Volunteer Force. In their bid to wreck the third home rule bill Carson and Craig kept their tory allies at Westminster, especially Bonar Law, informed of their intentions. If they did not relish the prospect of fighting British soldiers, they were prepared to go to prison for their convictions.[3] The launching of the Ulster Volunteer

---

[1] Conor Cruise O'Brien (ed.), *The shaping of modern Ireland* (London, 1960), p. 22.

[2] For a comprehensive treatment of Irish unionism north and south during this time of crisis, see Patrick Buckland, *Irish unionism: one—the Anglo-Irish and the new Ireland, 1885–1922* (Dublin and New York, 1972), esp. pp 15–35, and id., *Irish unionism: two—Ulster unionism and the origins of Northern Ireland* (Dublin and New York, 1973), esp. pp 1–91 (Buckland discusses the problem of partition on pp 92–126). See also Patricia Jalland, *The liberals and Ireland: the Ulster question in British politics to 1914* (London, 1980); George Dangerfield, *The damnable question* (London, 1977); David Miller, *Queen's rebels* (Dublin, 1978); Michael Laffan, *The partition of Ireland, 1911–1925* (Dundalk, 1987); Nicholas Mansergh, *The unresolved question: the Anglo-Irish settlement and its undoing, 1912–72* (New Haven, Conn., and London, 1991), pp 43–78; and Alvin Jackson, *The Ulster party: Irish unionists in the house of commons, 1884–1911* (Oxford, 1989), pp 284–321.

[3] Carson allegedly told Major Fred Crawford, the indispensable gun-runner, who transported 20,000 new rifles along with ammunition from an island near Kiel to Larne: 'Crawford, I'll see you through this business, even if I should have to go to prison for it' (Frederick H. Crawford, *Guns for Ulster* (Belfast, 1947), p. 20).

Force had grave repercussions in Ireland and at Westminster. Deeply impressed by this move towards military force, the leaders of separatist nationalism in Dublin immediately began to lay plans for a counter-force—the Irish Volunteers, who came into being in November 1913. Shortly thereafter arrangements were made for a secret shipment of arms from Hamburg in the hope of achieving a rough parity with their rivals in the north.

Estimates of the strength of the volunteers north and south varied substantially, and the leaders in both camps were quite content to allow any exaggerations in number to go unchallenged. According to police estimates, the Irish Volunteers numbered 182,000 in September 1914.[1] To the north, the U.V.F. comprised around 85,000 men, who were far better armed and trained than their rivals.[2] Even if some of the drilling was amateurish and many of the weapons, especially in the south, were old shotguns, the government could not dismiss these volunteer forces as mere bluff or bluster. By the summer the chances of solving the Irish question peacefully seemed more than remote.[3]

Secondly, the polarising effects of the home rule bill assumed different forms in the north and south. In general Ulster unionists could boast of a united front, ready to resist any invasion of their self-declared territory or their rights. In the spring of 1914 rumours spread that the government was planning to attack the U.V.F. with a combined naval and military expedition. Unionist commanders put their companies in a state of readiness, as the war of nerves between Belfast and Westminster reached a new intensity. However apprehensive they might be, those who had signed the Solemn League and Covenant did not seem to flinch at the prospect of fighting soldiers of the king to whom they were ostensibly loyal. The misnamed 'mutiny at the Curragh' in March involved the decision of over fifty British and Anglo-Irish cavalry officers to resign rather than obey orders that would force them into a military confrontation with the U.V.F. Needless to say, this highly publicised act raised suspicions, not exactly ill-founded, that Ulster unionism enjoyed the support of many officers in the British army.[4]

If there were some cracks in the apparent unity of Ulster unionism, these were superficial when compared with the divisions and sources of friction within Irish nationalism. Quite apart from the shadowy or secret presence of the Irish

[1] *Intelligence notes, 1913–16*, pp 104–12. For the origins of the volunteer movement—north and south—see above, pp 134–7.

[2] *Intelligence notes, 1913–16*, pp 100–02. For the Ulster Volunteer Force, see A. T. Q. Stewart, *The Ulster crisis* (London, 1967).

[3] Winston Churchill, then first lord of the admiralty, wanted to call what he regarded as Ulster's bluff. In a bellicose mood he told an audience at Bradford that there were 'worse things than bloodshed even on an extended scale' (Stewart, *Ulster crisis*, p. 142). By mid-1914, the U.V.F. possessed roughly 37,000 modern rifles and carbines along with six new Maxim machine-guns and countless shotguns and revolvers. An R.I.C. report in Jan. 1915 estimated the number of rifles at 53,341. The U.V.F. in Belfast alone probably had more weapons than all the Irish Volunteers in the south. For the weaponry of the U.V.F., see Stewart, *Ulster crisis*, pp 244–9, and *Intelligence notes, 1913–16*, p. 178.

[4] For the Curragh incident, see A. P. Ryan, *Mutiny at the Curragh* (London, 1956); Sir James Fergusson, *The Curragh incident* (London, 1964); Stewart, *Ulster crisis*, pp 168–75; and above, pp 140–41.

Republican Brotherhood, Redmond's party found it harder after 1906 to satisfy voters who ranged across a spectrum of social class and cultural interests—including big and little businessmen, members of the professions, strong and small farmers, office-workers, domestic servants, West Britons, and Irish-language enthusiasts. By 1913 Redmondism was losing supporters to Sinn Féin and the Irish labour movement; and feminists were reluctant to help a party that showed so little interest in giving them the vote. At the same time the party's critics were too divided over ideology, tactics, and personality to constitute an effective alternative to the parliamentary party. But the longer the fate of home rule hung in the balance, the greater was the appeal of physical force to ardent nationalists who were afraid of political deals or compromises at Westminster. Those who stood to profit most from Ulster's defiance of the constitution were the separatists and republicans, who could now justify their extremism on the grounds that the Orangemen had more respect for the gun than the law. Faced with mounting criticism of the third home rule bill, Redmond agreed to support the Irish Volunteers. But he had to move with care lest he alienate those who abhorred even the threat of violence. On 3 August Redmond lost what little remained of his credit among the militants, when he announced that Ireland would support the British war effort against the Central Powers. This pledge of political allegiance to the United Kingdom in its time of crisis and his proposal that the Volunteers of north and south defend Ireland from invasion was interpreted by the republicans as aiding and abetting the enemy of Irish freedom.[1] Since the parliamentary party supported Redmond's position on the war, the inner circle of the I.R.B. concluded that only a military strike against Dublin Castle's forces, at a time when the government was preoccupied with a war in Europe, would awaken the Irish people from their semi-lethargy and force them to choose sides.

Thirdly, Ulster's role in forcing the pace of Irish political life during this period can hardly be overstated. It was Ulster unionism, backed by Bonar Law, Walter Long, and other leading British tories, that brought the country close to civil war by putting so many weapons in the hands of political partisans. And even though Carson and Craig had resigned themselves by 1914 to the loss of the three southern provinces to home rule, they were prepared to fight the government in order to save Ulster from this fate.[2] Surrounded by so many historic and symbolic reminders of a protestant nation that had withstood what was perceived as a state of siege by a catholic majority ever since the seventeenth century, Orangemen and unionists alike adopted the posture of 'no surrender' with a resolve that British liberals were reluctant to test.

In their attempts to justify the exclusion of an entire province from the home rule bill, Ulster unionists often indulged in a form of cultural appropriation,

---

[1] For the position and policies of Irish nationalists at this time, see Lyons, *Ire. since famine*, pp 313–57, and his *Dillon*, pp 312–68. See also below, pp 190–91.

[2] For details of the political manœuvrings leading up to partition between 1911 and 1914, see Laffan, *Partition of Ire.*, pp 19–48.

speaking of the nine counties as though there were no catholics and home rulers
living there. Bonar Law, the conservative party leader who took such pride in his
Ulster ancestry, described the province's population as 'homogeneous' in a letter
to a catholic aristocrat.[1] This denial of the catholic presence was, of course, an
essential part of Ulster unionist ideology. The opposite tendency, which belittled
unionism as a sectarian movement strong only in two north-eastern counties, was
an essential part of nationalist ideology. Both parties distorted the facts of Ulster's
religious demography; protestants were indeed a majority in the province, but
they were only a slight majority, accounting for 56.33 per cent of the population
in 1911; in three counties (Cavan, Donegal, and Monaghan), they were a small
minority, comprising between one-fifth and a quarter of the population; they were
also a minority, albeit a substantial one, in Fermanagh, Derry county borough,
and Tyrone, accounting for roughly 45 per cent of the population (their position
in these areas resembled that of the catholics in the province as a whole). In
the remaining four counties they were a majority in Armagh and Londonderry
and only in Antrim and Down were they overwhelmingly strong.[2] If Ulster
was not unionist, neither was unionism a mere appendage of the latter two
counties; for one thing the two counties included Belfast and had a combined
population of 750,000, which made them a rather large appendage; secondly,
protestants physically dominated most of the area that would later become
Northern Ireland.

The leaders of Ulster unionism belonged to a protestant plutocracy composed of big businessmen and landed magnates, who shared a number of
financial as well as social and political interests. Indeed the wealth of this élite
caused some resentment among protestant workers, one of whom, the evangelical shipyard worker Tom Sloan, launched the Independent Orange Institution
in 1903 to promote working-class interests as well as the protestant faith.
This short-lived experiment in Orange populism represented an attempt by
Sloan and, later, his ally Robert Lindsay Crawford, a talented liberal journalist,
to temper northern unionism with concern for the poor, along with a modest
proposal for democratic self-government.[3] By 1914, however, the ranks of
the Orange order had closed over the threat to impose a Dublin government
on the province. The pressure of polarisation had made it difficult for moderates of any kind to gain much of an audience, let alone financial support, in the
north.

Many northern landowners relished their role as officers in the U.V.F. Drawing
on their experience in the British army, they taught their loyal (and loyalist)
tenants close-order drill and infantry tactics, and turned over parts of their

[1] In a letter to Lady Ninian Crichton Stuart, as quoted in Robert Blake, *The unknown prime minister*
(London, 1955), p. 126.
[2] *Census Ire., 1911, iii: Province of Ulster; summary tables,* pp vii, 37 [Cd 6051–x], H.C. 1912–13,
cxvi, 1335, 1375.
[3] John Boyle, 'The Belfast Protestant Association and the Independent Orange Order' in *I.H.S.,*
xiii, no. 50 (Sept. 1962), pp 117–52; above, pp 117–18.

demesne for rifle practice and manœuvres.[1] While Carson and Craig were plotting to keep Ulster out of an all-Ireland scheme of home rule, Redmond was losing his hold on radical nationalists, who criticised him for accepting such a modest measure of home rule. Neither his cautious moderation nor the king's efforts to work out a compromise, however, could overcome the deep differences between north and south. Asquith, the master of wait and see, saw no point in tripartite talks until all other expedients had been exhausted. After the house of commons had approved the home rule bill for the third time on 25 May 1914, he tried to buy some time and peace with an amending bill that contained a stay of execution by allowing each county to opt out for six years. But the unionist majority in the lords pounced on this proposal and amended the bill so as to ensure the indefinite exclusion of all nine counties. Worried about the possibility of violent conflict, Asquith won the king's consent to a conference of the various party leaders at Buckingham Palace on 21 July. Besides Asquith and Lloyd George, this meeting was attended by Carson, Craig, Bonar Law, Lord Lansdowne, Redmond, and Dillon. But the talks broke down over failure to agree on which areas in the north should be excluded from the measure.[2] Once again the policy or mentality of 'no surrender' had won the day.

Two days after the collapse of those talks, some 1,500 Mauser rifles were landed at Howth and distributed to waiting Irish Volunteers. Alerted to this activity, the police and a detachment of the King's Own Scottish Borderers tried to seize some of the contraband weapons. Several hours later a crowd of Dublin citizens began to harass the soldiers on their way home. Some troops then opened fire on their assailants in Bachelor's Walk, killing three and wounding thirty-eight.[3] This 'massacre' not only outraged nationalists but revealed the government's double standard, which allowed unionists in the north to run guns with impunity while volunteers in the south were attacked by the forces of the crown for daring to imitate the U.V.F. The moral of this tale was not lost on the I.R.B.: what the situation required was many more rifles and bullets to protect the people against British soldiers and Orange Volunteers.

When the home rule act finally received the royal assent on 18 September, the opposition benches in parliament were almost empty. The streets of Belfast were unnaturally quiet, and even nationalist celebrations in the south were restrained. The contest had been long and exhausting, and now there was a sense of hollowness about the victory. No sooner had the measure been passed than its provisions were suspended by an amending act for the duration of the war. If any Redmondites were moved to celebrate the end of their long journey, they were

---

[1] An epitome of aristocratic Ulster unionism was Charles, 5th earl of Leitrim, who commanded a U.V.F. regiment in Donegal and arranged to run guns from Germany on board his steam yacht, the *Ganiamore* (Stewart, *Ulster crisis*, pp 93, 95–6; Crawford, *Guns for Ulster*, pp 19–20).

[2] Details of the Buckingham Palace conference may be found in Blake, *The unknown prime minister*, pp 210–30; Roy Jenkins, *Asquith* (London, 1965); and Lyons, *Dillon*, p. 353. See also Laffan, *Partition of Ire.*, pp 43–6.

[3] Above, pp 142–3.

not to know that August 1914 marked not only an ending but the beginning of several new departures in Ireland that would eventually lead to insurrection and their own political extinction.

Just as the culture of political extremism in 1914 fostered the growth of revolutionary ideology, so, too, the outbreak of war among the civilised nations of Europe promoted the view that violence was a legitimate, indeed necessary, means of attaining political ends. By defying the authority of parliament, and by backing up that defiance with the threat of arms, the unionist coalition had created a model of resistance that was bound to be emulated by militants in the south. At the heart of this hardening of attitudes was the revitalised I.R.B., some of whose leaders—Clarke, Hobson, MacDermott, McCullough, and McCartan—had been raised in the harsher sectarian climate of the north. Unlike many of their predecessors, these men were puritanical in temperament, determined to forsake the comforts of family life and to avoid when necessary the pleasures of the pub for the sake of the revolution. The I.R.B. was, of course, more than a group of Belfast republicans translated to Dublin. Among the prominent southern members in 1914 were the O'Rahilly, P. S. O'Hegarty, Seán T. O'Kelly, and, later, Patrick Pearse.[1]

During 1914 the supreme council of the I.R.B. worked to infiltrate nationalist organisations in preparation for the day when they could thrust the moderates aside and proclaim the republic in the name of 'the people'. The I.R.B. had played a vital part in launching the Irish Volunteers and took care to secure a working majority on the provisional committee. At long last its security arrangements were tight enough to prevent the special crimes branch in Dublin castle from learning how deeply the brotherhood had penetrated not only the Volunteers but also the Gaelic League and the Gaelic Athletic Association. The outbreak of the European war spurred the I.R.B. leaders to press forward with their plan for a rising, which was agreed on at a meeting held on 5 September at the Gaelic League headquarters in Rutland (later Parnell) Square. Among those present were Pearse, Ceannt, MacDermott, Clarke, Griffith, and O'Kelly. Four days later, the I.R.B. leaders held another council of war and resolved to take advantage of the European conflict 'to rise in insurrection against England'.[2] These meetings did more than pave the way for the rising. They also symbolised the increasing appeal of physical force to some who had heretofore placed their faith in Redmondism. Even Hyde, the scholarly godfather of the Irish language revival, who had

[1] Considering the relative lack of documentation, the literature about the Irish Republican Brotherhood is extensive. See especially Maureen Wall, 'The background of the rising . . .' in Kevin Nowlan (ed.), *The making of 1916* (Dublin, 1969), pp 157–97, and Leon Ó Broin, *Revolutionary underground: the story of the I.R.B., 1858–1924* (Dublin, 1976). In addition to the contributions of Professors Martin and Nowlan in F. X. Martin (ed.), *Leaders and men of the Easter rising: Dublin, 1916* (London, 1967), pp 95–108 and 109–21, respectively, see F. X. Martin's useful historiographical article '1916—myth, fact, and mystery' in *Studia Hib.*, vii (1967), pp 7–124; also his 'The 1916 rising—a coup d'état or a "bloody protest"?', ibid., viii (1968), pp 106–37.

[2] Wall, 'The background of the rising', p. 166, and Kevin B. Nowlan, 'Tom Clarke, MacDermott, and the I.R.B.' in Martin, *Leaders and men of the Easter rising*, pp 115–16.

struggled so hard to keep the Gaelic League above partisan politics, succumbed to the allure of arms. In March 1914 he went well beyond the home rule convictions of his youth by telling an assembly of Volunteers that 'our duty is to be prepared to take the field as one man against any enemy tyrant or oppressor'. And in July he exhorted volunteer recruits to make the hills resound with the thunder of their rifles. If he stopped well short of encouraging volunteers to shoot British soldiers and R.I.C. constables, his rhetoric came close at times to that of Pearse, Hobson, and other guardians of the phoenix flame.[1]

In some respects 1914 marked the culminating point of conflicts that had long been stirring between the two dominant cultures of the country—Irish or Gaelic and English. But this binary division distorts the reality because it ignores the vital, if divided, culture known as Anglo-Irish. And it also obscures the political controversies swirling around such questions as whether Irish writers should use the English language and just how Gaelic the new Irish Ireland should be. According to Lyons, 'the chief work of the generation between the death of Parnell and the Easter rising had been to lay bare as never before the socio-cultural roots of difference in Irish society'. This task was crucially important because any and all 'political solutions in the future' depended on the resolution of those differences.[2] Leaving aside the vital subcultures of Ulster and minorities elsewhere, the principal cultural battles in this era were fought over the challenge posed by 'Irish-Ireland' to 'Anglo-Ireland'. But the latter was divided between the champions of English culture, epitomised by J. P. Mahaffy, the provost of Trinity College, Dublin, on the one hand, and the Young Ireland tradition that revered literature 'racy of the soil', on the other. Whatever the latter phrase might mean to Dublin journalists and their readers, the purists of Irish-Ireland regarded the English language along with Anglo-Saxon laws, values, and institutions as corrupting. In their view, so long as Irish politicians played political games according to English rules, so long would Ireland remain unfree. Prominent among the new apostles of Gaelic truth and beauty was D. P. Moran, founder and editor of that bristling paper, the *Leader*, wherein the true Gael was the uncorrupted, Irish-speaking peasant, who shared all the virtues attributed to the kings, warriors, saints, and bards of ancient Ireland. Appealing to the ethnic and cultural consciousness of their readers, Moran and his friend W. P. Ryan warned against the baneful influence of *raiméis* and held up 'shoneens' or West Britons to ridicule. They also drew a clear distinction between genuine nationality—the approved goal of a gaelicised politics—and the sordid compromises of Redmondite politics.[3] In pamphlets and newspapers, Ryan and Moran hammered away at

---

[1] For the evolution of Hyde's position on nationalism, see Janet E. and Gareth W. Dunleavy, *Douglas Hyde: a maker of modern Ireland* (Berkeley, Calif., 1991), pp 320–28. The radical implications of Hyde's plea in 1893 for the 'de-anglicisation' of Ireland had, of course, made a deep impression on republicans and cultural separatists. Cf. also some of his earlier writings: below, p. 400.

[2] F. S. L. Lyons, *Culture and anarchy in Ireland, 1890–1939* (Oxford, 1979), p. 83.

[3] D. P. Moran, 'The battle of two civilisations', reprinted in his *The philosophy of Irish Ireland* (Dublin, 1905), pp 94–114. For insights into cultural conflicts in this era, see Brian Inglis, 'Moran of

the passivity and indifference of their fellow Irishmen, hoping to lead the way towards the promised land of purity and plenty for every son and daughter of the Gael.

The new cultural nationalism contained more than predictions about the moral and material improvement that would come after separation from England. There were elements of fantasy or wishful thinking about the unity of the Irish race; there was nostalgia for the imagined paradise of pre-Norman Ireland; and there was resentment over centuries of English misrule, culminating in the great famine. Irish-Irelanders drank deep from the well spring of Irish myth and folklore; and they listened devoutly to tales of perfidious Sassenachs and wicked landlords. Despite conflicts of personality and politics, Sinn Féin, the Gaelic League, the Gaelic Athletic Association, and the Dungannon Clubs shared a commitment to solving the Irish question on Irish rather than English terms. Like the extremists of the north, they conceived of themselves as crusaders fighting a holy cause. To many advocates of Gaelic renewal or revival, catholicism and nationalism were as intimately bound together as were protestantism and unionism in Ulster.[1] Impelled by a hunger for fame and driven by fantasies of dying for Ireland in the manner of Tone, Emmet, and other martyrs, Pearse was no narrow-minded advocate for physical force. The romantic nationalism of this young schoolteacher and lawyer contained much respect for Davis, O'Connell, and Parnell. And yet Pearse insisted that Irishmen must take up the rifle and the sword, if they were ever to regain their lost manhood. In speech and writing after 1912 he praised the virility and courage of the Fianna, the legendary warriors of Gaelic antiquity. 'A citizen without arms', he reminded his audience, 'is like a priest without religion, like a woman without chastity, like a man without manhood.'[2] What he called the 'murder machine' was the educational system that the English had imposed on Ireland. This machine did not just kill its victims but castrated them, turning Irishmen into 'very eunuchs, with the indifference and cruelty of eunuchs'.[3]

To the age-old allure of physical force, Pearse and his admirers added the ingredient of blood sacrifice, derived in part from the paradigm of Christ's crucifixion and resurrection and also from a belief in the ability of rebellion to cleanse or cauterise the wounds of the past. These votaries of political violence

the *Leader* and Ryan of the *Irish Peasant'* in Conor Cruise O'Brien (ed.), *The shaping of modern Ireland* (London, 1960), pp 108–23; F. S. L. Lyons, 'The battle of two civilisations' in *Ire. since famine*, pp 219–42, and *Culture and anarchy in Ireland*, pp 57–83; D. G. Boyce, 'The battle of three civilisations' in *Nationalism in Ireland* (London, 1991), pp 228–58; and Tom Garvin, *Nationalist revolutionaries in Ireland, 1858–1928* (Oxford, 1987), esp. pp 57–138.

[1] Patrick O'Farrell pursues this important theme in *Ireland's English question* (London, 1971), pp 223–40, 279–92.

[2] Pearse, *Political writings*, p. 196. For other allusions to the theme of virility and weaponry in the national struggle, see ibid., pp 75, 86, 97, and 183–8. Ruth Dudley Edwards provides a shrewd assessment of Pearse's *mélange* of romantic and religious ideas in *Patrick Pearse: the triumph of failure* (London, 1977), esp. pp 152–97.

[3] Pearse, op. cit., p. 9. The cult of the blood sacrifice and the messianic streak in the new nationalism are discussed below, pp 192–6, 377–8.

had persuaded themselves that only a resort to arms would convince Englishmen that Irish nationalism, in particular the republican movement, should be taken seriously and not be dismissed as the whim of feckless Paddies or mercurial Celts.

Arthur Griffith was a brilliant journalist with a gift for excoriating criticism of opponents. Like Pearse he venerated Young Ireland and believed in cultural as well as political separatism. But he was much more ambivalent about physical force, appreciating its value in theory but shying away from its practice unless all the alternatives had been tried and found wanting. Raised in the orthodox physical force tradition and a member of the I.R.B., he preferred wielding a sharp pen rather than a sword. An ideologue with a vivid historical imagination, he blended the best of the constitutional and the physical force traditions, as he saw them, into a Gaelic context and then mixed in the tactics of passive resistance. What emerged as Sinn Féin's programme was thus cobbled out of disparate elements, which proved more revolutionary in the long run than anything the I.R.B. had to offer. The eclectic Griffith spread the gospel of pride in race and culture by promoting not only Irish but Hungarian solutions to Irish questions.[1]

Political extremism also included radicals who dreamed of reconstructing Irish society. Chief among these was Connolly, who by the end of 1914 had become the leader of the Irish labour movement. Connolly invested much time and energy in organising labour and recruiting for the Irish Citizen Army, hoping that this force would protect defenceless workers against the batons of the Dublin Metropolitan Police and serve as the vanguard of revolutionary social change. Avoiding some of the rigidities of orthodox Marxism, he fought against the exploitation of Irish workers by merchants, moneylenders, stockbrokers, solicitors, and aldermen. Polemical excess notwithstanding, Connolly's writings afford many insights into Irish society and the condition of working men and women in the early twentieth century.[2]

For some Irishmen, at least, 1914 was a year of painstaking investigation of conditions in the country rather than a time of political confrontation. In January, the lord lieutenant's commission completed its hearings on the recent disturbances in Dublin arising out of the bitter labour disputes of the previous year.[3] No sooner had the local government board committee finished examining witnesses on the housing of the working classes in Dublin,[4] than another committee of inquiry was busy looking into the rates of pay, allowances, functions, and expenses

[1] For illuminations of Griffith's complex personality and political ideas, see Richard Davis, *Arthur Griffith and non-violent Sinn Féin* (Dublin, 1974), as well as Lyons, *Ire. since famine*, pp 244–55; and Boyce, *Nationalism in Ire.*, pp 295–300.

[2] In addition to Connolly's own writings, especially *Labour and Irish history* (Dublin, 1914), see C. Desmond Greaves, *The life and times of James Connolly* (London, 1961); Owen Dudley Edwards (ed.), *The mind of an activist: James Connolly* (Dublin, 1971); and Mitchell, *Labour in Ir. politics*, pp 25–63.

[3] *Report of the Dublin disturbances commission* [Cd 7269], H.C. 1914, viii, 513–22; *Evidence and appendices* [Cd 7272], H.C. 1914, xviii, 533–990.

[4] *Report of the departmental committee appointed . . . to inquire into the housing conditions of the working classes in the city of Dublin* [Cd 7273], H.C. 1914, xiv, 61–106; *Evidence and appendices* [Cd 7317], H.C. 1914, xix, 107–506.

of the R.I.C. and D.M.P.[1] In October the department of agriculture and technical instruction investigated the Irish pig-breeding industry;[2] and in the same year the departmental committee on agricultural credit finally completed its report on the state of the rural economy.[3] The government also set up a royal commission on the massacre at Bachelor's Walk. After hearing much testimony, the three commissioners found the assistant commissioner of the D.M.P., William Harrell, whom Birrell had suspended from duty on 27 July, at fault for having used the police and the military to confiscate the rifles landed at Howth, and also for having tried to disperse a procession that was not a riotous assembly.[4] Harrell's resignation could no more undo the damage of the 'massacre' than it could bolster the sagging morale of the police and other officials in Dublin Castle who were alarmed at the growth of extremist activities.

The outbreak of war in Europe was not altogether unwelcome to many Irishmen. Besides providing fuller employment and causing a boom in agriculture, the war forced Asquith's government to suspend the home rule act; it depleted the ranks of the U.V.F. more than it did those of the Irish and National Volunteers; it lessened the chances of a clash between the Volunteers of north and south; and it enabled republicans and feminists to revive and improve on the anti-recruiting campaign they had launched during the Boer war. The I.R.B. now had a golden opportunity to exploit Britain's involvement in a major war and to link the Irish-Ireland movement with the cause of neutrality or even of sympathy for Germany. The war also divided many nationalist households, often along generational lines, between the supporters of Redmond's imperial or patriotic position and those who opposed sending young Irishmen to serve as cannon fodder in the army of the hereditary enemy.

In the wartime atmosphere rumours were rife about negotiations between Irish extremists and German agents. Officials in Dublin Castle responsible for law enforcement made fewer efforts after August 1914 to draw distinctions between fervent nationalism and treason. The special crimes branch of the R.I.C. kept busy shadowing and reporting on the activities of republican or separatist suspects. In November the government imposed restrictions on the import and sale of firearms; and early in December four Dublin newspapers were suppressed under the defence of the realm act.[5] Intelligence officers in the Castle were already hard at work compiling the names and particulars of those who spoke

---

[1] *Royal Irish Constabulary and Dublin Metropolitan Police: report of the committee of inquiry, 1914* [Cd 7421], H.C. 1914, xliv, 247–84; *Appendix, containing minutes of evidence . . .* [Cd 7637], H.C. 1914–16, xxxii, 359–752.

[2] *Report of the departmental committee on the Irish pig-breeding industry* [Cd 7890], H.C. 1914–16, vi, 855–78; *Evidence, appendices, and index* [Cd 8004], H.C. 1914–16, vi, 879–1024.

[3] *Report of the departmental committee on agricultural credit in Ireland* [Cd 7375], H.C. 1914, xiii, 1–430; *Evidence, appendices, and index* [Cd 7376], H.C. 1914, xiii, 431–1116.

[4] *Royal commission on the circumstances connected with the landing of arms at Howth on July 26th 1914: report of commission* [Cd 7631], H.C. 1914–16, xxiv, 805–20; *Evidence* [Cd 7649], H.C. 1914–16, xxiv, 821–900. For the Howth incident, see above, pp 142–3, 179.

[5] *Intelligence notes, 1913–16*, pp 116–18.

out against recruiting, including twenty-four catholic priests in various parts of the country.[1]

If one looks beyond the immediate issues of Irish politics, it is possible to discern, however faintly, the pressure of social and economic forces on political affiliation. Although many qualifications are needed, there were signs that occupation, income, status, or the ways in which people defined themselves in social groups had something to do with the decision to join a particular party or group. In the protestant enclaves of Ulster, by contrast, the urgency of the home rule issue and the prevalence of a sectarian tradition tended to minimise the number of options open to loyalists. The home rule crisis of 1912–14 had effectively closed unionist ranks in the north-east.

In 1914 the Redmondite party still dominated more than three-quarters of the constituencies in the country.[2] In social terms the gap had been widening between the middle-class leaders of the party and the rank-and-file M.P.s, many of whom sprang from more modest or obscure backgrounds.[3] Redmondism drew its strength from catholic merchants and shopkeepers, newspaper and hotel proprietors, lawyers and doctors, minor civil servants, clerks, publicans, journalists, and commercial agents. Their allies and social analogues in the countryside were strong farmers, cattle-dealers, and graziers. In country towns the staunchest Redmondites tended to be the publican, the auctioneer, and the gombeen man—assuming that they were not one and the same person. These men made a formidable alliance, especially when they were reinforced by the parish priest.

This partnership of small but ambitious entrepreneurs in town and country, men well versed in the value of land, livestock, and dowries, had supplied much of the thrust of the land war during the 1880s.[4] Aware of the need for low rents, especially in times of distress or crop failure, in order to sustain consumer demand, these men were not just content to make a decent profit. Ultimately they wanted to supplant the old landed élite as the dominant or hegemonic class. After the founding of the Irish Agricultural Organisation Society in 1894, some of these townsmen had tried to undermine the cooperative stores and credit societies promoted by Horace Plunkett and his supporters. Local shopkeepers and moneylenders were bound to resent a movement that tried to help small farmers

---

[1] Ibid., p. 119.

[2] In the general election of Dec. 1910, the Irish parliamentary party won 84 seats or 80.6 per cent of Irish constituencies. Unopposed candidates in this election numbered 53. The average vote for nationalist candidates who were opposed amounted to 81.9 per cent (David Butler and Jennie Freeman, *British political facts, 1900–1960* (London, 1964), p. 122). The extent of uncontested elections makes it well-nigh impossible to calculate the popular support enjoyed by the Redmondite party. For a breakdown of the results by constituency, see Brian M. Walker (ed.), *Parliamentary election results in Ireland, 1801–1922* (Dublin, 1978), pp 325–82.

[3] Lyons, *Ir. parl. party*, pp 163–76, 180–81.

[4] For a pioneering exploration of this theme during the era of the land war, see Sam Clark, 'The social composition of the Land League' in *I.H.S.*, xvii, no. 68 (Sept. 1971), pp 447–69; and also 'The political mobilisation of Irish farmers' in *Canadian Review of Sociology and Anthropology*, 12 (4: part 2) (1975), pp 483–99.

by selling fertilisers and other goods at almost wholesale prices, and by offering loans to 'coop' members at interest rates of only 5 to 6.25 per cent. As the courageous Patrick Gallagher of West Donegal could attest, one did not challenge the local shopocracy with impunity. The latter had too much at stake to allow the cooperative stores to take away their customers; and in some cases they resorted to underhand means in order to drive the 'coops' out of town. After visiting Paddy the Cope's store in Dungloe in 1903 on behalf of the I.A.O.S., George Russell (AE) recalled years later the heavy odds Gallagher faced in his fight:

[The gombeen men] were the bosses of the Rosses. The farmers were tied customers of theirs. Seventy-five per cent of the farmers were born in debt and were never out of it. It was not the policy of the bosses that they should be out of debt . . . . The landlord owned the land. The gombeen men owned the people, and the profits the gombeen men got out of the men was greater by far than the profit the landowner got out of his for the holding.[1]

In Dublin, Connolly and Larkin confronted much the same kind of adversary, albeit on a bigger scale, in the form of rich businessmen like William Martin Murphy, who owned people and property all over town. According to Connolly, the gombeen men were 'leeches' who joined forces with middlemen in the country towns and 'sucked the life blood of the agricultural population around them'.[2]

While the G.A.A. contained a preponderance of urban and rural labourers, Sinn Féin had more appeal to middle-class journalists, teachers in schools and universities, shopkeepers, clerks, and solicitors. In this respect such gentry rebels as Edward Martyn, Roger Casement, Mary Spring Rice, and Constance Gore-Booth (Countess Markievicz) were the rare exceptions that proved the existence of a middle- and working-class majority among more extreme nationalists. Some impression, however faint, of the mixture of occupations and ages among the advocates of physical force may be gained by looking at the 171 persons, mostly Irish Volunteers, who were tried by general court martial in 1916 for 'complicity' in the Easter rebellion. Analysis of these prisoners according to the criteria of occupation, geographical origin, and age reveals a few significant patterns.[3]

Of the 162 prisoners with specified occupations, 31 (19.1 per cent) may be categorised as 'professional people'—with teachers and journalists heading the list. Farmers accounted for the second largest category with 27 (16.7 per cent), of whom 22 came from County Galway. There were 20 labourers (12.3 per cent), most of whom (70 per cent) lived in Dublin and environs. Sixteen of these defendants (9.9 per cent) owned or worked in retail stores. (Most of these shopkeepers and shop assistants came from Dublin.) There were also 17 skilled

[1] *Selection from the contributions to the Irish Homestead by G. W. Russell (A E)*, ed. Henry Summerfield, ii (Gerrard's Cross, 1978), pp 566–7.
[2] Connolly, *Reconquest of Ire.*, p. 316.
[3] The sample contained in 'The list of persons "tried by field general court martial for complicity in the Irish revolt", 1916' is not confined to those who fought in Dublin but includes Volunteers from Counties Cork, Galway, Kildare, Meath, and Waterford, who were arrested during Easter week. The Countess Markievicz had the distinction of being the only female in this group (*Intelligence notes, 1913–16*, appendix i, pp 255–70).

workers (10.5 per cent), who ranged from masons and carpenters to painters, followed by 16 clerks and secretaries, 12 teachers, 6 journalists, 6 printers, 5 university students, 2 weavers, 2 railway fitters, 3 insurance agents, and an assortment of artisans.

In terms of age, there was a distinct gap between farmers and labourers, whose average age was 25.7 and 25.5 years respectively, and professional persons, who averaged ten years older (35.9 years). In view of the preponderance of teachers and journalists among the leaders of the rising, it becomes clear that the decision to rebel was not just a function of impetuous working-class youth. However inadequate this sample, we may conclude that these so-called rebels represented a cross-section of middle- and working-class society.[1]

Granting the imprecisions of status categories, there remains a strong connection between Redmondism and middle-class respectability.[2] What underlay that respectability was first of all property: not great estates but a decent house in town, a modest income from shop or pub, rental from urban property or a prosperous farm, and a little income, too, from the interest on loans as well as savings accounts in the bank. As the tax collectors knew, it was often difficult to gauge the real worth of these middle-class families because so many of their dealings and assets were shrouded in secrecy. Secondly, the drive towards respectability owed much to the insecurities attendant on the recent emergence of this class from rural and urban obscurity. But the country's future belonged to these shopkeepers, hotel and newspaper proprietors, lawyers, doctors, and teachers, not to mention politically active priests, all of whom had contributed in one way or another to subverting the old ascendancy.

Ireland in 1914, then, hovered on the brink of new departures, whose destinations were obscured by the clouds of war on the Continent, the old rhetoric of home rule, and the dust of Volunteer drilling at home. There was, however, one visionary who had some inkling of what lay ahead. In a letter to a friend, AE wrote:

You asked . . . why was I scared about Ireland. I can hardly tell you because I can hardly explain it to myself. I have a conviction deep inside me that we are going to have one more heart-searching trial, baring our lives to the very spirit, and that within the next few years. May be much sooner. The dragons of the past have not died and were only sleeping and recent events have stirred them.[3]

---

[1] The sample of the prisoners on trial in May 1916 excludes the 12 prisoners who were found guilty of taking part in a mêlée at Tullamore, King's County, on 20 Mar. Of the 171 names listed as tried by court martial, 161 were assigned occupations. But Countess Markievicz was not given an occupation (or a first name), and her age was incorrectly stated as 43, instead of 48. In this survey I have counted her as an 'author' and political organiser (in the manner of her friend Connolly) (*Intelligence notes, 1913–16*, pp 263, 267). Tom Garvin discusses the nature of 'separatist nationalism' in *Nationalist revolutionaries in Ireland, 1858–1928*, esp. pp 107–38.

[2] Above, p. xliv.

[3] A E to Charles Weekes, 14 Oct. 1914 (Alan Denson (ed.), *Letters from A E* (London, 1961), p. 99).

Presumably, those dragons breathed the fire of past insurrections and represented the kind of violence that would create more martyrs to the cause of Irish
freedom. 'Romantic Ireland' had not died with John O'Leary after all, as Yeats
tried to persuade his readers, but lived on with Pearse, Plunkett, MacDonagh,
and other young men who were determined to confront the forces of British
imperialism with rifles not words. Given the scale of state-authorised slaughter
taking place in Europe, their decision to shed blood seems more understandable.

And yet, appearances to the contrary, not all Irish men and women lived by
politics alone. They had much on their minds besides the historic struggle for
independence, as any reading of the novels, plays, newspapers, and government
reports published that year is bound to reveal. In many a household north and
south the issue of home rule took second place to family quarrels, neighbourly
feuds, money deals, marriage contracts, expectations of inheritance, and harvest
prospects. The country fairly bustled with intellectual and artistic as well as
economic and sporting activity. Besides national and parish-pump politics there
were race meetings, market fairs, Gaelic and English games, and Irish dance and
musical competitions. And all the while workers in cottages, workshops, and
factories were producing commodities for domestic or foreign markets. While
politicians wrestled with the momentous problems of nationality, schoolchildren
and Gaelic Leaguers struggled with the intricacies of the Irish language, farmers
worried about the weather, interest rates, and agricultural prices, and priests tried
to cope with lapses of faith and morals among parishioners. The political crises
in that fateful year should not obscure the ways in which ordinary people went
about their daily rounds of work and play and found fulfilment or passing pleasure
in pursuit of goals less sublime than national independence and less demanding
than the search for their 'true' cultural identity.[1]

---

[1] Readers interested in the condition of Ireland and the activities of the Irish people in 1913–14
should consult, in addition to Francis Hackett, *Ireland: a study in nationalism* (New York, 1918), the
series of articles sponsored by *The Times* of London in 1913 and revised for publication as *The Ireland
of today* (Boston, Mass., 1915). A chronology of events in 1914 may be found below, viii, 386–9, and
also in Carty, *Bibliog. Ir. hist. 1912–21*, pp xxviii–xxx. See also the *Annual Reg., 1914*, which deemed
the publication of Mrs O'Shea's *Charles Stewart Parnell: his love-story and political life* 'perhaps the
greatest biographical sensation of the year' (p. 39).

CHAPTER VIII

The revolution in train, 1914–16

F. S. L. LYONS

IT was suggested above[1] that the outbreak of the first world war did not so much liquidate the Irish question as refrigerate it. Even this statement, however, though true within limits, is an oversimplification. The war certainly refrigerated the Irish question at the official or public level, but the question itself, precisely because it remained unliquidated, continued to evolve, stimulated rather than stifled by the new circumstances that the war introduced.

At the official and public level the tone for the wartime relations between the two countries had apparently been set by John Redmond's celebrated intervention in a debate in the house of commons on 3 August 1914, when in a highly emotional speech he pledged Ireland's support for the allies in the coming conflict and urged the government to leave the defence of Irish shores to the Irish and Ulster Volunteers. The speech may not have been quite so spontaneous as was thought at the time (Redmond had been urged by Margot Asquith, the prime minister's wife, to say something on these lines), but it seems clear that it was made without consultation with his senior colleagues and it is quite certain that it very soon turned into a major political liability. This, however, was not evident all at once. The almost hysterical enthusiasm with which the call to arms was greeted in Britain had its counterpart in Ireland also, and in the early weeks and months of the war thousands enlisted.[2] It is important, in view of the emphasis that is so often laid on Irish revulsion from the war, to stress this initial reaction, which was not indeed seriously checked until the Somme offensive in the summer

---

[1] p. 144.

[2] David Fitzpatrick has argued that 'the war-fever which swept middle-aged England in August 1914, and the consequent communal and family pressure on young men to join up, scarcely affected Ireland outside Ulster' and that reaction in nationalist Ireland was 'cool' and 'businesslike'. Furthermore, he argues that despite the efforts of leading home rulers to encourage recruitment, the rates of recruitment varied considerably from region to region and, while the loyalty of the press to the Irish party did not waver under the stress of the recruiting campaign, the enthusiasm feeding that loyalty gradually diminished (Fitzpatrick, *Politics & Ir. life*, pp 109–11). Joseph Lee also argues that the early decline of recruiting figures is evidence that Irish enthusiasm for the war was not widespread (Lee, *Ire. 1912–85*, pp 23–4), while Eunan O'Halpin has claimed that 1915 saw an increase in war-weariness, particularly with the heavy Irish casualties at Gallipoli, and that thenceforth apprehension grew regarding the increasing possibility of conscription in Ireland (O'Halpin, *Decline of the union*, p. 111). See also Philip Orr, *The road to the Somme* (Belfast, 1987), pp 54–84, for an account of the complexity of local responses to the recruitment drive in Ulster.

of 1916. As a result of it over 50,000 men enlisted in Ireland in the first six months of war,[1] and it was possible in the autumn of 1914 to give the title 'Irish' to no less than three divisions in the first of Kitchener's new armies, though only the third of these divisions—the 36th or Ulster—could be said to have been thoroughly homogeneous, being composed, as it mainly was, of Carson's Ulster Volunteers.

Yet, massive though the Irish response was, it quickly fell foul of official rigidity and distrust. Partly perhaps this may have been no more than the usual bureaucratic reaction of the military authorities to any new situation, but partly also it reflected the deep-seated hostility of Kitchener, whom Asquith, in a moment of inspired folly, had brought into the cabinet as a non-political secretary for war. Kitchener had been born in Ireland, had moved all his life in the atmosphere of the officer caste, and was inflexibly opposed to any suggestions—for example, of separate badges, flags, and bands—that would harness the emotions of traditional nationalism to the needs of the British war machine. Although Craig's proposal that the Ulster Volunteers should form the nucleus of the 36th Division was, after some negotiation, conceded by the military authorities, a similar proposal for the creation of a territorial force incorporating the National Volunteers was refused.[2] This obduracy persisted, with dire consequences, even after Redmond had shifted his position in a very remarkable fashion. When Redmond made his speech in August he intended that the Volunteers whom he was offering to the government should not be asked either to take an oath of allegiance to the crown or to serve outside Ireland. Within a very few weeks, however, it had become obvious that the immediately decisive battles were going to be fought in Flanders and northern France. It may have been this fact that caused Redmond to change his mind; it may have been a desire to compete with Carson who was eager for the Ulstermen to fight overseas; it may have been a sudden surge of gratitude for the fact that home rule was at last on the statute-book; it may even have been a desire to force a showdown with the militant section of the Volunteers—but, whatever the explanation, in a speech at Woodenbridge on 20 September he urged the Volunteers not just to fight for Ireland but to go 'wherever the firing line extends'.[3]

This speech, as casual as it seemed, and as unpremeditated as it actually may have been, at once produced a predictable crisis within the Volunteer movement. The organisation split into two sections, the larger of which (about 170,000 men) stayed with Redmond to form the National Volunteers and contribute a steady

[1] This figure covers recruitment in Ireland to all armed services, and does not allow for those Irish who enlisted in Britain; see Patrick Callan, 'Recruiting for the British army in Ireland during the first world war' in *Ir. Sword*, xvii (1987–90), p. 42; and Terence Denman, *Ireland's unknown soldiers: the 16th (Irish) Division in the Great War, 1914–1918* (Blackrock, 1992), pp 15–16, 31, 36–7, 131–41.
[2] Laffan, *Partition of Ire.*, p. 50; Patrick Buckland, *James Craig* (Dublin, 1980), pp 35–6; Orr, op. cit., pp 37–54.
[3] Gwynn, *Redmond*, pp 391–2; cf. Mitchell & Ó Snodaigh, *Ir. pol. docs 1869–1916*, pp 176–7, quoting *F.J.*, 21 Sept. 1914.

stream of recruits to the British army, while the minority, consisting of about
11,000 of the more extreme members, broke away to form their own force, which,
however, retained the name 'Irish Volunteers'.[1] On the face of it this clarification
of the situation may have seemed advantageous to Redmond: at last he was rid of
his critics and had, or so it seemed, isolated them by a manœuvre that left them
so depleted as to be an insignificant factor in his future calculations. Yet in reality
nothing could have been further from the truth, for thereafter the initiative rested
with the dissident minority and not with the Redmondite majority. While
Redmond continued to struggle with the inanities of the war office, and while he
and Dillon held elaborate discussions with the under-secretary for Ireland, Sir
Matthew Nathan, about how the transfer of power should take place when home
rule came into operation, a revolutionary conspiracy began to take shape to which
the whole concept of home rule was simply irrelevant.

It was, if the expression may be allowed, a strictly orthodox conspiracy. Based
on the classical assumption that England's difficulty was Ireland's opportunity, it
bore in its inception many of the marks of traditional fenianism. Thus it was
traditional that part at least of the impetus should have come from America, where
Clan na Gael, the organisation still dominated by John Devoy, informed the
German ambassador of their intention to foment a rising in Ireland and to seek
German assistance. And it was equally traditional that the supreme council of the
I.R.B., being informed of this intention, should themselves have decided within
a month of the outbreak of the war to plan for an insurrection, which, they were
determined, should take place whether German aid was forthcoming or not.[2]

What was decidedly less traditional was the profound secrecy that soon
enveloped these preparations. Apart from an initial flurry of consultation with
'advanced nationalists' who were not then members of the I.R.B., such as Griffith
and Connolly, and which led to nothing but the creation of a short-lived and
ineffectual Irish Neutrality League,[3] the leading figures in the conspiracy were
content to work entirely behind the scenes. The split in the Volunteer movement,
so far from weakening their position, actually strengthened it. When the minority

[1] Historians have differed in their estimates of the numbers of Volunteers on each side after the
split of Sept. 1914. W. F. Mandle has given a useful summary of the government's estimates of the
numerical strength of the 'Sinn Féin' Volunteers, as MacNeill's followers were misleadingly known in
Dublin Castle (Mandle, *The G.A.A. and Irish nationalist politics 1884–1924* (London and Dublin, 1987),
pp 170–71). Leon Ó Broin has given the division as 11,000 Irish Volunteers, 184,000 National
Volunteers (Ó Broin, *Revolutionary underground*, p. 155). Both Charles Townshend and Michael
Tierney have followed Bulmer Hobson, who gave the numbers as 2,000–3,000 and 150,000; Tierney,
however, cites Colonel Moore's claim that not more than 10,000 men remained with MacNeill, but
he qualifies this with the comment that this figure was probably not reached until after a year had
passed (Townshend, *Political violence*, p. 279; Tierney, *Eoin MacNeill: scholar and man of action
1867–1945*, ed. F. X. Martin (Oxford, 1980), p. 154).

[2] For a fuller account of the timing of the I.R.B. decision, the nature of the decisions taken at this
point, and the influence of Devoy and Clan na Gael on the I.R.B. organisation in Ireland, see Ó Broin,
op. cit., pp 156–60.

[3] For an account of the meeting with 'advanced nationalists' in Sept. 1914 in the Gaelic League's
headquarters in Parnell Square, see ibid., pp 158–9.

group of Irish Volunteers was reconstituted in October 1914, the old provisional committee was replaced by a general council, consisting of one representative from each of the thirty-two counties and one from each of the nine chief cities and towns; in addition there was to be a president and eight other members elected by an annual convention of the Volunteers from candidates resident within ten miles of Dublin. These nine members were to form a central executive, and it was obvious from the outset that this was where the real power would be. One of the first acts of the executive was to create a headquarters staff in order to put the Volunteers on a military footing. Eoin MacNeill, though a decidedly unmilitary person, was chief of staff, Bulmer Hobson was quartermaster, and the O'Rahilly was director of arms. Thus far, it seemed as if the reorganisation had done no more than confirm the founding fathers in office; but their authority was balanced, and before long transcended, by the holders of three other offices. These were Patrick Pearse, director of military organisation; Thomas MacDonagh, director of training; and Joseph Plunkett, director of military operations. All three were either then, or soon afterwards, members of the I.R.B.; and since, unknown to MacNeill, the I.R.B. also had a controlling majority on the general council of the Volunteers, it is clear that the process of infiltration was already far advanced.

Pearse, MacDonagh, and Plunkett shared some striking characteristics that gave their insurrection a colouring that was to have a profound influence on succeeding generations. They were all poets, they were all Gaelic enthusiasts, they were all romantic revolutionaries cast in the same fanatical mould. While not themselves trained to arms—Plunkett was a consumptive who would probably in any event have died young, MacDonagh was a dramatist and university don, and Pearse was a highly original educationist—these three young men belonged to a European generation, which even before 1914 had begun to react against the 'great ennui' of nineteenth-century bourgeois capitalism by a deliberate cult of violence and destruction. It was a generation that looked, with a strange mixture of innocence and ruthlessness, towards what they imagined to be the purging and cleansing effects of war as an essential preliminary to the creation of a new and more just and beautiful world.[1]

Naturally, the manifestations of this blood-lust, for that is what it was, differed according to local circumstances. In Ireland, so long isolated and insulated from continental influences, it was perhaps inevitable that the contemporary mood

[1] Seán Farrell has offered a provoking analysis of the psychological and emotional conflicts that, he claims, Pearse displayed in his character and behaviour, as well as in his writings. Farrell argues that this experience formed part of a wider ideological 'revolt against modernity' evident throughout Europe at this time, and exemplified most vividly by the writings, actions, and ultimately the deaths of the English poet Rupert Brooke, the French poet Charles Péguy, and Pearse himself (Farrell, 'Patrick Pearse and the European revolt against reason' in *Journal of the History of Ideas*, l (1989), pp 525–43). This analysis has been challenged by Brian P. Murphy, who argues that Pearse's motivation as an insurgent was less irrational than has been suggested, and offers an analysis of Pearse's conversion from home ruler to revolutionary (Murphy, *Patrick Pearse and the lost republican ideal* (Dublin, 1991), pp 41–5). The starting-point for any study of Pearse remains Ruth Dudley Edwards, *Patrick Pearse: the triumph of failure* (London, 1977).

should express itself partly through a nostalgic view of the revolutionary past and partly through the prism of the Gaelic revival. Of both these tendencies Pearse was the supreme embodiment. Born in 1879 (the same year as MacDonagh and nine years earlier than Plunkett), the son of an English father and an Irish mother, Pearse grew up in a middle-class catholic environment. Educated by the Christian Brothers, and a B.A. of the Royal University, he had early been deflected from the law into education. In 1908 he founded his famous school, St Enda's, at Rathmines, moving it two years later to Rathfarnham. Financially a precarious venture, the school broke with most of the usual pedagogical conventions, and with its absence of stern discipline and rigid timetables bore witness equally to its founder's hatred for the official education system ('the murder machine', as he called it)[1] and to his passionate wish to inspire rather than to instruct his pupils.

Since he had himself as a young man become deeply involved with the Gaelic renaissance, it was inevitable that he should have made his school a nursery for the teaching of the Irish language and of Irish history and literature. But with this ardent cultural revivalism went something much more fundamental. To Pearse, more perhaps than to anyone else in his generation, the ancient culture was important because it could be made the vehicle of a modern nationalism. Or rather, the cultural values of the remoter past could in his view be combined with the revolutionary doctrines of the more recent past to create not just a republic separated from England, by force if need be, but also a nation that had become a nation by the deliberate act of recovering and re-creating its submerged civilisation.

As exemplars of the old Ireland and the new, Pearse chose Cú Chulainn and Tone. Cú Chulainn, the legendary figure who in the Irish sagas was described as fighting to the death in defence of Ulster, might have seemed a fitter hero for a northern unionist than for a southern nationalist, but he played a central role in Pearse's fantasies because he could be identified as the pagan version of Christ crucified, the man willing to sacrifice all for his people. It was the measure of Cú Chulainn's psychological importance to Pearse that at the entrance to St Enda's, where every boy must see it, he had inscribed the famous saying attributed to the hero: 'I care not though I were to live but one day and one night, if only my fame and my deeds live after me.'[2]

From Tone, Pearse drew a very different kind of inspiration, the kind that he himself defined in the title of the pamphlet *The separatist idea*, written in February 1916. The lesson Pearse learnt from Tone may have been in part the political ecumenism that lay at the root of the society of United Irishmen (at least in its earliest days), but no one can read his pamphlet without feeling that it was the

---

[1] The title of one of Pearse's major pamphlets, published in 1916 and reprinted in Pearse, *Political writings*, pp 1–50, and in *The educational writings of P.H. Pearse: a significant Irish educationalist*, ed. Séamas Ó Buachalla (Dublin and Cork, 1980), pp 371–85.

[2] The wording here is as in Pearse, *Educational writings*, ed. Ó Buachalla, p. 324; a slightly different wording appears in Edwards, *Pearse*, p. 117.

smaller part. No doubt he derived his assumption that 'the Irish nation is one nation' from Tone's determination 'to substitute the common name of Irishman in place of the denominations of protestant, catholic, and dissenter', but it is abundantly clear that what interested him much more was Tone's declaration of his objective—'to break the connection with England . . . and to assert the independence of my country'. It was this, the pursuit of sovereign independence, that drew Pearse towards Tone and led him to end his pamphlet with a piece of characteristic hyperbole:

That God spoke to Ireland through Tone and through those who, after Tone, have taken up his testimony, that Tone's teaching and theirs is true and great, and that no other teaching as to Ireland has any truth or worthiness at all, is a thing upon which I stake all my mortal and all my immortal hopes.[1]

To the extent that Tone had shown himself prepared to fight and die for his objective he was no doubt entitled to a place beside Cú Chulainn in Pearse's private pantheon, and it was significant that as Pearse's own thoughts turned increasingly towards political action it was on the separatist ideal rather than on the gospel of reconciliation that he preferred to dwell.[2]

It seems in fact to have been only about 1913 that Pearse turned decisively in this direction. Up to that time such reputation as he had rested on his school and on his work for the Gaelic League, and as late as 1912 he had spoken upon a home rule platform when it had seemed that Redmond's policy might after all be crowned with success. Within a year, however, Pearse had accepted an invitation to speak at the annual commemoration of Tone and chose to use the occasion to urge his hearers to prepare themselves to fight for Ireland in their day as Tone had done in his. The invitation itself was an indication that the I.R.B. regarded him as worth cultivating, and, though it was not until about the end of 1913 that he was sworn into the organisation, the events of that year, and especially the foundation of both the Ulster Volunteers and the National Volunteers, so worked on his imagination as to swing him more and more into the orbit of the physical-force movement. In November 1913 he had proclaimed that he thought the Orangeman with a rifle much less ridiculous than the nationalist without one. And a month later he asked if the reason why Ireland was not free was because she had not deserved to be free.

Men who have ceased to be men cannot claim the rights of men; and men who have suffered themselves to be deprived of their manhood have suffered the greatest of all indignities . . . For in suffering ourselves to be disarmed . . . we in effect abnegate our manhood.[3]

---

[1] Pearse, *Political writings*, pp 269–70, 293.
[2] See Edwards, *Pearse*, pp 152–322, for the development of Pearse's interest in political questions, for the course of the conspiracy, and for his role in the events of Easter 1916.
[3] 'From a hermitage' in Pearse, *Political writings*, pp 185, 194–5.

Gaelic culture and republican separatism were an explosive mixture, but they did not exhaust Pearse's thinking on the subject of revolution. Brought up in an atmosphere of deeply felt faith, he did not hesitate to adapt this faith to the needs of his nationalism. Not only could he compare national freedom to a 'divine religion', because it bore 'the marks of unity, of sanctity, of catholicity, of apostolic succession',[1] he could envisage his own role in that religion of national freedom as one that combined the function of messiah and of blood sacrifice. Thus the hero in his play 'The singer', returning from exile to lead his people's resistance to the Gall, is prepared to go forward alone even if no one follows him. And he speaks for Pearse himself when he says: 'One man can free a people, as one Man redeemed the world. I will take no pike, I will go into the battle with bare hands. I will stand up before the Gall as Christ hung naked before men on the tree.'[2]

Were this no more than a personal fantasy, a form of religious delusion suffered by one obscure individual, it would not occupy our attention for more than a passing moment. But it becomes important when we remember two additional facts about it. One is that it was shared by MacDonagh and Plunkett, and that while all three may have been dreamers, they were dreamers who occupied high office in the Irish Volunteers and were also at the centre of the I.R.B. They were, in short, in a position to give weight and substance to their dreams. The second is that for these romantic revolutionaries the concept of the blood sacrifice was not envisaged as the prelude to a military triumph, but rather as an inspiration, which, because it would dignify failure by its idealism, would change the political climate of the country and inspire those who came after them to pursue the separatist goal to the end. Once again it is Pearse who provides us with the most explicit statements of this doctrine, though it is to be found also in such poems as MacDonagh's 'Wishes for my son' and Plunkett's 'The little black rose shall be red at last'. Pearse signalled his conversion to militancy in the essay 'The coming revolution', published in November 1913, opening with a deliberate onslaught on the Gaelic League, with which he himself had been so intimately associated for so long and which he now dismissed as 'a spent force'. 'We never meant', he said, 'to be Gaelic Leaguers and nothing more than Gaelic Leaguers'; their intention was rather to go forward 'to accomplish the revolution'. And so, whenever the inoffensive and non-political Douglas Hyde had produced his dove of peace at meetings, 'I have always been careful to produce my sword; and to tantalise him by saying that the Gaelic League has brought into Ireland "not peace, but a sword".'[3]

The logical extension of this, and one very understandable in the excitement and confusion of 1913, was that he should recommend to his fellow Irishmen that they must accustom themselves to arms. 'A thing that stands demonstrable is that nationhood is not achieved otherwise than in arms.' They might, he conceded,

[1] 'Ghosts', ibid., p. 226.   [2] Pearse, *Plays, stories, poems*, p. 44.
[3] Pearse, *Political writings*, pp 91, 92, 95–6.

with what in the light of events may seem a chilling casualness, shoot the wrong people at first, 'but bloodshed is a cleansing and a sanctifying thing, and the nation which regards it as the final horror has lost its manhood'.[1] With the coming of the war, when the nations of Europe set about losing their manhood in the literal sense through the slaughter of each other's armies, Pearse's obsession with blood grew shriller and more intense. At the end of 1915, after a year of carnage on the western front, he could write like this: 'The last sixteen months have been the most glorious in the history of Europe.' And again: 'It is good for the world that such things should be done. The old heart of the earth needed to be warmed with the red wine of the battlefields. Such august homage was never before offered to God as this, the homage of millions of lives given gladly for love of country.' War, he conceded, was a terrible thing, but it was not an evil thing:

It is the things that make war necessary that are evil. The tyrannies that wars break, the lying formulae that wars overthrow, the hypocrisies that wars strip naked, are evil. Many people in Ireland dread war because they do not know it. Ireland has not known the exhilaration of war for over a hundred years. Yet who will say that she has known the blessings of peace? When war comes to Ireland, she must welcome it as she would the angel of God. And she will.[2]

Hysterical though the language of these passages must have seemed to many of those who read them, Pearse himself took them, and meant others to take them, with the most deadly seriousness. And because of Pearse's own crucial role in the drama that was now about to unfold, the historian has no option but to take them seriously as well.[3] It was not necessary to Pearse's purpose that they should reach or convince the multitude, it was enough that the few should come under his spell. For what he had in mind was not so much a mass movement as a revolutionary conspiracy. Indeed, he went one better, for what he actually achieved was a conspiracy within a conspiracy.

We have seen already that the Volunteer movement had been heavily infiltrated by the I.R.B., but it is important to be clear that within the I.R.B. itself there was gradually developing an inner directing group to which not even all the members of the supreme council belonged. The crucial issue during 1915 and the early months of 1916 was the control of the Irish Volunteers. Outwardly this was still vested in MacNeill, assisted by Hobson and the O'Rahilly. But MacNeill's conception of the force—which, after some fluctuation following the split with Redmond, had reached a strength of about 16,000 by the spring of 1916—remained, as it had always been, essentially defensive. He wanted to use the Volunteers as a powerful lever after the war, not to dissipate them in what he

---

[1] Ibid., pp 97, 99.   [2] Ibid., pp 216–17.

[3] Lee has argued that in the light of the publication of new material in *The letters of P. H. Pearse*, ed. Séamas Ó Buachalla (Dublin, 1980), it seems that the emphasis given by historians to the literary works of Pearse has resulted in a distorted picture of his motivations and the aims of the conspiracy as a whole (J. J. Lee, 'In search of Patrick Pearse' in Máirín Ní Dhonnchadha and Theo Dorgan (ed.), *Revising the rising* (Derry, 1991), pp 122–38).

would have regarded as a hopeless rebellion during the war.[1] To this waiting policy, however, there were two important exceptions. If the country as a whole were threatened with conscription, or if any attempt were made to disarm the Volunteers, then in MacNeill's view a *casus belli* would undoubtedly exist. To meet either of these contingencies—and each was perfectly possible—it was necessary not only to keep the Volunteers in being but to train them and to devise an appropriate strategy for a conflict that might come at any moment. It was not surprising, either that during 1915 there should have been unofficial discussions among some of the more militant Volunteer officers about a possible plan of campaign, or that these should have broadened out to embrace the possibility of the Volunteers being committed to the offensive rather than being obliged to wait until they were attacked, by which time it might be too late for them to organise in their own defence. But casual and informal discussion of such life-and-death matters as these was too dangerous to be allowed to continue unchecked.

Consequently, in May 1915[2] the executive of the supreme council of the I.R.B. took a vital decision, probably at the instigation of Thomas Clarke. This was to set up a military committee, or military council as it came to be called, consisting initially of Pearse, Plunkett, and a young activist named Éamonn Ceannt (Kent) who had been sworn into the I.R.B. by Seán MacDermott. At that time none of the three was on the supreme council, but in September 1915 they were strengthened by the addition of Clarke and MacDermott. The council was further reinforced when Connolly joined it in January 1916 and when MacDonagh was coopted in April. These seven men were to be the signatories of the proclamation of independence, but more immediately they were the real progenitors of the rising. It seems to have been about the end of 1915 when they first decided that the date for the rising should be Easter 1916, but so closely did they keep this secret that even when in January 1916 the supreme council of the I.R.B. took a general decision that there should indeed be a rising as soon as possible, the date that the military council had already agreed on was not disclosed to them. In addition, the leading spirits on the military council—Clarke and MacDermott— not only pursued their own independent policy of recruiting into the I.R.B., but also devised their own private chain of command.[3] If the object of this deviousness was secrecy, then it must be said that it was largely achieved, for no rebellion in modern Irish history was so free of informers as the 1916 rising; but for this

[1] F. X. Martin, (ed.), 'Eoin MacNeill on the 1916 rising' in *I.H.S.*, xii, no. 47 (Mar. 1961), pp 228–9.

[2] Lee has stated that the military committee had been set up by the I.R.B. supreme council in Sept. 1914, but only began to plan insurrection in May 1915, with plans initially for a rising in Sept. 1915; and that it was at this period that MacDermott and Clarke recruited Pearse into this military council, which would also include MacDonagh, Plunkett, and Ceannt (Lee, *Ire. 1912–85*, p. 24).

[3] F. X. Martin and Leon Ó Broin agree that the chief protagonist in the 'conspiracy within the conspiracy' was MacDermott: Martin has credited him with developing and refining plans for the insurrection, while Ó Broin states that MacDermott 'was effectively the executive' of the I.R.B. (Martin, 'Easter 1916: an inside report on Ulster' in *Clogher Rec.*, xii, no. 2 (1986), pp 198–9; Ó Broin, *Revolutionary underground*, pp 165–6).

secrecy a heavy price had to be paid in terms of local confusion and paralysis when the moment for action arrived.

A further reason for secrecy, of course, was to try to win the advantage of surprise. For this, however, it was necessary to prevent unauthorised outbreaks, which, by altering the authorities, might lead to a general move to suppress the Volunteers. From the conspiratorial point of view the greatest menace to the plans of the military council was the alarming disposition being shown by Connolly to take independent action with his tiny Citizen Army of some 200 men. Connolly had been passing through a period of deep disappointment and frustration. His initial hope had been that the war might usher in the collapse of capitalism and the triumph of international socialism, but when each of these consummations obstinately failed to occur he was driven to reexamine his own attitude to the local Irish situation. He remained, of course, fully committed to his ideal of a people's, or workers', republic, based on the public ownership of the means of production, distribution, and exchange. Yet the very environment in which he had to live and work presented him with an excruciating dilemma. So far as there were revolutionary forces at work in Ireland they were nationalist rather than socialist, obsessed with the winning of political independence and little concerned with social justice.[1] Of the leading figures among the conspirators of the I.R.B., only Pearse appeared to share some of Connolly's views about the redistribution of wealth, and even Pearse adopted a disconcertingly casual attitude towards programmes of nationalisation.

There is nothing divine or sacrosanct in any of these arrangements; they are matters of purely human concern, matters for discussion and adjustment . . . matters in which the nation as a whole can revise or reverse its decision whenever it seems good in the common interests to do so.[2]

In the short term, however, the issue was not whether they could agree on a post-insurrection utopia, but whether Connolly could be persuaded to throw in his lot with the conspirators. Excluded as he was from that circle during the whole of 1915, he came very easily to believe that no action was in prospect at all. From that it was an easy step to decide that it was up to him to take an independent initiative, and by October 1915 he was writing ominously that where there was no 'forward movement' the Citizen Army reserved 'the right to step out of the alignment and advance by itself if needs be'.[3] Since he was at that moment

---

[1] Michael Gallagher ('Socialism and the nationalist tradition in Ireland, 1798–1918' in *Éire-Ireland*, xii, no. 2 (1977), pp 63–102) has discussed some of the statements made by the leading extreme nationalists on the labour movement and questions of social reform. Ronald Munck ('At the very doorstep: Irish labour and the national question' in *Éire-Ireland*, xviii, no. 2 (1983), pp 36–51) argues that labour rose in 1913 before the nationalist movement was ready, and that by the 1916 rising the working class had been weakened and demoralised.

[2] Pearse, *Political writings*, p. 340.

[3] James Connolly, 'For the Citizen Army' in *Workers' Republic*, 30 Oct. 1915, reprinted in *Labour and Easter week: a selection from the writings of James Connolly*, ed. Desmond Ryan (Dublin, 1949), p. 93.

carrying out battle exercises under the very noses of the authorities, there was an obvious risk that his autonomous gestures might provoke the government into a policy of general repression and thus imperil the whole enterprise. About the middle of January 1916, therefore, MacNeill saw Connolly (Pearse was present) and urged him to be cautious. Connolly—ignorant, like MacNeill, of what was already in train—continued obstinately to press for an immediate insurrection even though MacNeill warned him not to suppose that by leading the Citizen Army on to the streets he would pull the Volunteers after him into the vortex. There then occurred a curious incident. After the interview, Pearse assured MacNeill that he could handle Connolly, and a few days later came to tell him that he had succeeded. During the interval, in circumstances that are never likely to be completely explained, since Connolly chose to say little about them, the labour leader disappeared from view and was absent from 19 to 22 January without either his family or his colleagues having the slightest idea where he was. He was in fact in close and constant discussion with members of the military council, who had realised in the nick of time that if they were to win his cooperation they could only do so by admitting him to their secret. This they did, and from that time forward he was one with them, being sworn into the I.R.B. and at once becoming a member of the military council. He was the only member of that body, incidentally, who had any claim to professional military experience; though even this was minimal, consisting as it did of a brief spell in the ranks in early youth, which had ended with his being posted as a deserter. What he lacked in recent experience, however, he more than made up by his powers of leadership, which rapidly secured for him a weight and authority within the conspiracy far greater than the tiny army he contributed to the insurgent forces might have entitled him to expect.

But if the conversion of Connolly was kept secret from MacNeill, there were other things that were less easy to conceal. As the I.R.B. strengthened its hold on the Volunteers, and as the recruiting activities of Clarke and MacDermott pursued their own highly individual course, scattered indications began to reach headquarters that orders were being issued to certain units that had not been authorised by MacNeill as chief of staff. Not being an assertive man, at least in any military sense, he did not bestir himself to regain direct control of the Volunteers, and relied instead on the false assurances with which he was plied by Pearse, Plunkett, and MacDonagh, who were at that very moment manipulating the Volunteers for their own ends. Nevertheless rumours of an impending rising continued to proliferate to such an extent that he could no longer ignore them. Consequently he wrote a letter to Pearse, intending it to be read to the executive of the Volunteers; and, not content with this, he embodied his own views in a memorandum couched in similar terms. From this memorandum (dating, it would seem, from mid-February 1916), which has since been published,[1] but of

[1] Martin, 'Eoin MacNeill on the 1916 rising', pp 226–71.

course was unknown to most people at the time, it is clear that MacNeill was
utterly opposed to the reckless launching of an insurrection on what he called *a
priori* grounds: that Ireland must strike while the war was on, that her history was
a record of lost opportunities, and that the advantage of surprise must not be
sacrificed. An essential criterion—moral as well as military—was a 'reasonably
calculated' prospect of success. To overrule actualities by dogmas would, he said,
be a proof of mental incapacity. 'To act on them would be madness, to act on
them without otherwise justifying the action would be criminal.'[1]

He showed that he was aware that there was another justification then in
circulation when he turned to consider the argument—to which Connolly was
scarcely less susceptible than the romantic revolutionaries—that some action was
necessary, that some lives must be sacrificed, in order to produce such a revulsion
of feeling among the public as to give a rebellion the impetus needed for success.
It is interesting evidence of how seductive this argument was, even to men of
mature intelligence, that MacNeill could not bring himself to condemn it out of
hand. If it were true that the destruction of Irish nationality was actually at hand,
and if it were felt that 'at least the vital principle of nationality would be saved'
by Irishmen laying down their lives, then for him that would be a comprehensible
and an honourable sacrifice.[2] But at that moment he did not believe that any such
apocalyptic situation threatened, and he exhorted his comrades to confine
themselves to the realities of military planning. Their main concern, he insisted,
must be to build up their forces, to avoid provocation, and above all to hold on
to their weapons. He himself, he said, would fight to the death against any attempt
to deprive him, or any of the Volunteers, of the arms that were their ultimate
guarantee. Yet in advancing this counter-argument he was, no doubt in all
innocence, leaving his flank dangerously exposed. If a governmental seizure of
arms really was to be the *casus belli*, then those who wished to bring on an
irrevocable rebellion had only to manufacture an incident, or even the rumour of
an incident, for the Volunteers to be committed apparently in defence of
MacNeill's principle, in reality for motives of which it was intended he should
remain entirely ignorant.

Not that even romantic revolutionaries could evade the practicalities of their
situation indefinitely. However strong Pearse's death wish may have been, it is
doubtful whether he could have led many of the Volunteers into action if they
had not felt some glimmering of hope that against all the odds they might snatch
victory for their cause. But for such victory to come even remotely within the
realm of possibility, the insurgents must have help from outside. In the
circumstances, as Devoy in America had realised from the moment war broke out,
this could only come from Germany.[3] This was also the view of Casement, who
happened to be in the United States when hostilities began. He at once offered
to travel to Germany to do what he could to obtain assistance, and was duly

[1] Ibid., p. 235.   [2] Ibid., p. 236.   [3] Above, p. 191.

dispatched with Irish-American backing, though only after Devoy had reluctantly stifled his inmost conviction that Casement was not the man for the job. Perhaps it was a job that no man could have performed adequately. Certainly Casement's inadequacies all too rapidly became apparent. Apart from some personal episodes that cast doubt on his judgement and general suitability, he was intermittently ill, and he did not carry enough weight to impress the Germans, who were anyway prone to regard Ireland as a remote and improbable sideshow in which it would be folly to make a major investment of men and materials at a critical moment in the war.

True, at the end of 1914 Casement did elicit from the Germans a declaration—or 'treaty' as he grandly but erroneously called it—that gave him *carte blanche* to form an Irish brigade from among prisoners of war, held out promises of arms and ammunition (to be provided after a German naval victory), and graciously signified an intention to recognise and support an independent Irish government after the Irish had achieved it.[1] The declaration was in fact hardly worth the paper it was written on. Casement, who had virtually signed his own death warrant by going to Germany, should he ever be subsequently captured, encountered only humiliation in his attempt to form an Irish brigade, and he grew steadily more despondent about the possibility of any insurrection taking place at all. In the end, as we shall see, he was to suffer the cruel irony of being arrested and hanged after he had returned to Ireland to halt rather than to promote the rising.

But that was still in the future. Given Casement's ineffectiveness, other plans had to be made to secure German help, which, if only on the most modest scale, would make the whole difference between the viability and the non-viability of the conspiracy. The key figure in these transactions was Devoy, who not only engineered a mission by Joseph Plunkett to Berlin in the spring of 1915 to arrange for a shipment of arms, but was also responsible for coordinating the German movements with the timetable worked out by the military council. In wartime, and in the face of British naval power, this was a hazardous operation, a tenuous thread on which to hang the fortunes of the entire enterprise. Early in February 1916 the military council told Devoy that the rising was to take place on Easter Sunday, 23 April 1916. However, in his dispatch to Germany he changed this to 'Easter Saturday' and suggested that the arms should be landed 'between Good Friday and Easter Sunday'.[2] The Germans for their part replied that they would land 20,000 rifles and ten machine-guns between 20 and 23 April. Not surprisingly, this drew from Devoy a demand for greater precision, and in the end it was agreed to aim for Easter Sunday as the most suitable date. Requests for German troops and submarines were firmly refused, and when the arms were at last released they were loaded on to a single steamer, the *Aud*, which, though it had in Captain Karl Spindler an audacious commander, lacked the all-essential

[1] Mitchell & Ó Snodaigh, *Ir. pol. docs. 1869–1916*, pp 180–82.
[2] *Devoy's post bag, 1871–1928*, ed. William O'Brien and Desmond Ryan (2 vols, Dublin, 1948, 1953), ii, 487.

wireless that it needed if it was to be able to keep in touch with a rapidly changing situation.

It was in fact a situation that was changing rapidly for the worse. Not merely had the British navy broken the German code used for messages between Berlin and Washington, but a raid by the American authorities on a German agency in New York on 18 April disclosed the transcript of a cipher message from Dublin that had just been wirelessed to Germany, a message so important that it was immediately passed to British intelligence. It consisted of an urgent request from the military council narrowing the time at which the arms should reach the Kerry coast to the night of Easter Sunday. The reasoning was sound enough: if the arms arrived too early, it would jeopardise the chances of surprise; but having to make sure they arrived on time obviously made Captain Spindler's task far more difficult.[1] Or rather it would have done so if the message had ever reached him. Since, however, he had sailed on his mission long before the message arrived, and was incommunicado while he was at sea, he kept to the original timetable and reckoned he had done well to arrive, as he did, on Thursday 20 April. That he found no one awaiting him was no doubt due primarily to the confusion about dates, but it is a legitimate criticism of the military council that they assumed until too late that their instruction pinpointing the time of arrival to the night of Sunday 23 April had got through successfully. A more intelligent appreciation of the situation would surely have suggested that the margin of error was too great, and that contingency plans ought to have been laid to cover all the dates that had been discussed.

Up to a point, it is fair to say, they were unlucky. The Germans did inform Devoy that they could not reach the *Aud* with news of the altered date, and Devoy did his best to get this crucial information to Dublin. His message miscarried, and it was not until Friday, 21 April, that Plunkett sent his agents down from Dublin to make the final arrangements to receive the arms that they fondly expected would not arrive for another forty-eight hours. In reality, of course, they had already been cruising up and down the coast in the *Aud* since the night of 20 April and were in imminent danger of seizure. It was remarkable, indeed, that Spindler's luck should have held as long as it did, for the British navy, alerted by the intercepted German code messages, had been searching the area intensively. Eventually on the morning of Friday 21 April the *Aud* was intercepted by British warships, and all that was left to Spindler to do he did. On being ordered into Queenstown harbour on the morning of 22 April, he abandoned his ship and sent her and her cargo to the bottom. With that dénouement, it is scarcely too much to say, all hope of a successful uprising, at least of one on an extended scale, was irretrievably doomed. But it was typical of the air of tragicomedy that hung over these proceedings like a pall that the remaining scene enacted on the Kerry coast

[1] See Townshend, *Political violence*, p. 298, for some comments on the shortcomings of the plans regarding the timing of the *Aud*'s arrival; for example, the lack of any strategy for the distribution of the German arms.

should have been in some ways the most genuinely pathetic. In Germany Casement had pleaded to be conveyed home to Ireland, and the Germans had eventually agreed to risk a submarine to transport him and two companions, Robert Monteith and Daniel Bailey, to the same spot on the coast that had been selected for the *Aud*'s rendezvous. Punctually on 21 April Casement and his companions were put ashore. Half-drowned in the process, they were picked up by the police and identified, and Casement was sent to London for the trial that, a few months later, was to result in his conviction for treason and his execution by hanging.

These disastrous events on the Kerry coast effectively destroyed the basis for a national rising. The original plan for such a rising—drawn up by Pearse, Ceannt, Plunkett, and Connolly, and kept extremely secret—had envisaged simultaneous action in Dublin and in the provinces. In the capital, a number of strategic buildings were to be seized and held for long enough, it was hoped, to allow operations to get under way elsewhere. The chief of these were envisaged as taking place in the south and west, where it would be the task of the Volunteers to land, protect, and distribute the arms that the Germans were to transport to Fenit in Tralee Bay. At the same time the Galway brigade was to be mobilised to hold what was rather grandly described as 'the line of the Shannon', and a corridor to the west was to be kept open in case it should be necessary for the Dublin garrison to retreat in that direction. There was to be no large-scale manœuvre in the north, but the Volunteers from Belfast, Derry, and Tyrone were expected to rendezvous at Belcoo, County Fermanagh,[1] and then make their way towards that magnetic 'line of the Shannon'. A further touch of fantasy was added to this extraordinary scheme by the facts that when it was concocted the Volunteers had no heavy guns—indeed, not even a machine-gun—and that only one man in five had a rifle. When the weapons on the *Aud* went to the bottom, the Volunteers in most parts of the country were in effect paralysed. In Munster and Leinster this had particularly serious consequences, for it meant that the guerrilla role assigned to the Volunteers in those parts of Ireland could not be undertaken. Since the prime objective here had been to prevent British reinforcements from moving on Dublin, the fact that it could not now be done meant that any rising in the city would have to face the full force of the British counterstroke with virtually no hope of help from elsewhere. Or, to put the matter another way, the military justification for going on with an unsupported Dublin insurrection had ceased to exist.

This, however, only gradually became clear at headquarters as the news from Kerry began to filter in. For those who were bent on a blood sacrifice at any cost, the news was largely irrelevant; but on the nominal head of the force, MacNeill, it was bound to have a decisive effect. His position during April had not been

---

[1] According to a letter written by Patrick McCartan to Joseph McGarrity of Clan na Gael during Easter week 1916, the northern insurgents were to have assembled at Belcoo (Martin, 'Inside report on Ulster', p. 194).

enviable. Fresh rumours had reached him at the beginning of the month about an impending outbreak, and on 5 April he secured the agreement of the headquarters staff that no orders other than those dealing with routine matters would be issued to the Volunteers without his countersignature. But two weeks later (19 April) there was published the 'Castle document', which purported to be a government order for the suppression of the Volunteers, the arrest of various suspects, and the occupation of certain key points that were regarded as centres of conspiracy (grotesquely, it included the catholic archbishop of Dublin's Drumcondra residence in the list, but compounded the error by calling it 'Ara Coeli', the name of the official residence of the archbishop of Armagh). The government at once denounced the document as a forgery and, though to this day some of the facts are still in dispute, the available evidence has inclined historians to think that a forgery was what it was.[1] Certainly, one can see that from the point of view of those who wished to precipitate a rising, the 'Castle document' was a powerful psychological lever. MacNeill had always said that he would regard a threat to suppress the Volunteers as a legitimate *casus belli*; and now that he was presented with what, in the first spasm of alarm, he regarded as conclusive proof that this was what was being contemplated (though later he came to view the document as false), his reaction was prompt. Having been shown the document ahead of publication, he conferred rapidly with his staff and then sent out a general order to all Volunteers to be prepared to resist suppression.

This was on Wednesday 19 April. Late on Thursday night Hobson, who shared MacNeill's defensive conception of the Volunteers, learned by chance that orders were either being issued, or had been issued, to the various commands to be ready for an insurrection three days later, on Easter Sunday. Going at once with his informants to MacNeill's house at Woodtown Park, Rathfarnham, he roused the chief of staff from sleep with this grave news. Deeply angered, MacNeill went straightaway to St Enda's to confront Pearse and demand an explanation. It was then that he learned for the first time of the extent to which he had been deceived by his comrades, and heard from Pearse's own lips the brutal truth that the Volunteers were really in the hands of another organisation, the I.R.B., and that they had tolerated him only to make use of him.

MacNeill's reaction was to countermand the mobilisation orders already issued by Pearse. But before he could do this, he was subjected to further pressure from the extremists. On the Friday morning Pearse, MacDonagh, and MacDermott came to urge him not to throw the country into confusion by countermanding the mobilisation, adding the clinching argument that German arms were at that moment on their way. This revelation, which was entirely new to MacNeill, persuaded him to let the plan for Sunday stand, and he himself went so far as to add a further circular of his own warning the Volunteers that government action to suppress them was inevitable and might begin at any moment. All the same,

---

[1] See Desmond Ryan, *The rising* (Dublin, 1949), pp 64–75; Martin, 'Eoin MacNeill on the 1916 rising', pp 247–8, 257–8. In the published version the 'Ara Coeli' error did not appear.

to make sure that he had no second thoughts, the I.R.B. kidnapped Hobson, who would have had the responsibility for sending out any further orders MacNeill might have wished to issue, and kept him prisoner while the crisis lasted.

The irony of all this was of course that MacNeill only learnt of the approaching shipment of German arms on the morning of Friday 21 April, at about the time the *Aud* was being intercepted and after Casement had already been picked up. That afternoon, at a meeting with Connolly in the latter's headquarters in Liberty Hall, Pearse apparently heard the first indications that things had gone wrong in Kerry, though this did not in the least affect his resolve, or Connolly's, to proceed with the Dublin rising as planned. But clearly it might very well have the opposite effect on MacNeill once he came to hear of it. On the Saturday morning he, like everyone else, read in the paper of the arrest of a mysterious stranger in Kerry, but although he did not and could not know that this was Casement the news was enough to induce in him a mood of fatalism. The authorities would now be on the alert and more likely than ever to move against the Volunteers, who would resist suppression and thus precipitate the crisis. MacNeill later recorded that the news had helped to persuade him that the situation was beyond recall—this being so, he felt bound to join in an insurrection for which he saw no possible hope of success. 'I consented because I held that we were entitled to protect ourselves in the most effective way and to the utmost in our power.'[1]

This fatalistic mood did not last for long. That night he received more specific information about what had happened in Kerry—that the *Aud* was sunk and that it was Casement who had been arrested. At the same time he received evidence that convinced him that the 'Castle document' had been a forgery. If this was so, and if the German arms had been irretrievably lost, then it might just be true that the government had not made up its mind to strike, that his own warning to the Volunteers had been premature, and that, in the absence of arms, it might still be possible to call off the rising scheduled for Sunday. Before doing so, however, he had one further brief but angry interview with Pearse, in the course of which the latter, according to the later recollection of an eye-witness, excitedly turned on MacNeill: 'We have used your name and influence for what they were worth', he said, 'but we have done with you now. It is no use trying to stop us: our plans are all made and will be carried out.' MacNeill retorted that he was chief of staff and would forbid the mobilisation. Pearse replied that the men would not obey him. In which case, rejoined MacNeill, the responsibility would lie at Pearse's door.[2]

Little time was left for calling off the rising, but MacNeill dealt with the problem partly by sending out special messengers to various parts of the country countermanding the rising, and partly by inserting in the *Sunday Independent* of 23 April an order forbidding all Volunteer movements for that day. Effectively this, following hard upon the débâcle at Kerry, prevented any nation-wide insurrection and undoubtedly saved a great deal of blood from being shed in what

[1] Martin, 'Eoin MacNeill on the 1916 rising', p. 249.   [2] Ibid., p. 266.

could only in the circumstances have been a hopeless cause. But those to whom the shedding of blood had become a redemptive act, and thus an end in itself, were unmoved by this latest turn of fortune's wheel. On the Sunday morning the conspirators met at Liberty Hall to discuss what they should do. Clarke was for marching out at once, but this was held to be impracticable and the insurrection was postponed for twenty-four hours to enable as many as possible of the Dublin units to be assembled and prepared for action. In the meantime, and in order to prevent any further intervention by the chief of staff, Pearse sent word to MacNeill informing him that the Sunday parade had been cancelled according to his instructions. Needless to say he did not tell him what had been arranged instead for Monday. But this was to be Pearse's last act of deception. Now he had only to step from history into myth, to act out his dream, and in so doing to transform both dream and myth into a political reality with which all who came after him would have to reckon.

CHAPTER IX

The rising and after

F. S. L. LYONS

IN view of the frenetic comings and goings described in the previous chapter, it may seem strange that the authorities, whose intervention MacNeill so constantly expected, failed to move against the conspirators until it was too late. We shall see presently that they were indeed contemplating action, and that they were forestalled only by a matter of hours, but behind the mystery of their passivity up to the very eve of the rising there lies a deeper mystery—why it was that they should have allowed the situation in Ireland to deteriorate, not just for days or weeks before the outbreak, but for months and even years.

There seem to be two main explanations. One is bound up with the undoubted fact that the war had brought to Ireland an unprecedented prosperity. No doubt the boom was reflected in higher prices, and for the poor, especially in the large towns and cities, life, which was always hard, grew harder still. But up and down the country, in industry and in agriculture, all the signs were that prosperity was both more solid and more widely diffused than at any time in living memory. The intelligence reports from the police that arrived regularly on the chief secretary's desk spoke with extraordinary unanimity of the good times the farmers were enjoying, and it seems clear, from subsequent calculations made by the economist C. H. Oldham,[1] that linen, woollen goods, and shipbuilding also benefited substantially from the increased demand that the war itself had stimulated. And even for those who had nothing to sell but their labour, there was a greater prospect of well-paid employment than before, not just in Ireland but in the munitions and other industries in Britain, which were desperately short of manpower. Moreover, the fact that by 1916 there were perhaps 150,000 Irishmen serving in the forces created an additional cash flow into the country in the form of separation allowances and other remittances. All of this suggests that MacNeill, when setting out the arguments for and against a rebellion in his memorandum of February 1916, was right to warn his officers against assuming that others shared their discontent with English rule. The only possible basis for a successful revolution, he said, was deep and widespread popular discontent. 'We

[1] C. M. Oldham, 'Changes in Irish exports' in *Stat. Soc. Ire. Jn.*, xiii, pt 97 (Oct. 1919), pp 629-37.

have only to look around us in the streets to realise that no such condition exists in Ireland.'[1]

This seems, on the whole, to have been the opinion of the government also, and herein lies the second explanation for its apparent inactivity. But although this inactivity was a product of deliberate policy rather than of drift, the policy itself was the product of an all too familiar dilemma. It was not to be expected that a country that had been seething with discontent right up to July 1914 should relapse overnight into perfect quiescence; and although it is true that the first shock and excitement of the war obliterated most of the more obvious signs of disaffection, as the causes of disaffection remained untouched so too did the malaise itself. Before long, indeed, it was to be reinforced by a predictable movement of opinion away from enthusiasm for the war and towards a very real revulsion. This was partly because of the hardships, the separations, and the casualties it caused; partly because, so far from being brief, it seemed to stretch drearily into an illimitable future; but most of all because, as the strain on manpower intensified, the possibility of conscription drew closer. And if it seems a strange paradox that Irishmen were able to combine affluence with alienation, one can only reply that in wartime the seeming paradox is not really a paradox at all, since the affluence and the alienation are generally experienced by different sections of the population.

So, at any rate, it turned out in Ireland. While, as we have seen, the affluence was widely diffused, the alienation was confined to those whose business in life it was to be irreconcilable to British rule. At first their numbers were very few, and police reports during 1915 of anti-recruiting activities by Sinn Féin indicated that these did not receive much popular support. The same appeared to be true of the more extremist newspapers. Most of these were closed down by the government on the outbreak of war, but though they had a tendency to reappear under other names their circulation remained small. Nevertheless, they—and those who produced them—presented the government with a difficult problem, which was complicated by the fact that it was a problem shared by the Irish parliamentary party. The party's views on how to deal with extremists and their journalistic excesses were conveyed by Dillon to the under-secretary, Sir Matthew Nathan, on numerous occasions. The burden of Dillon's refrain was always the same. If the government bore down heavily on the militants, the only effect would be to drive them underground where they would become less accessible and therefore more dangerous. It would be even worse if the authorities were to go further and try to suppress the Volunteers, for this would probably provoke a major outbreak that would enlist popular feeling behind the Volunteer leaders—a development, as nobody knew better than Dillon, likely to be as prejudicial to the parliamentarians as to the government.

[1] Martin, 'Eoin MacNeill on the 1916 rising', p. 240. By February 1916 some 94,000 men had enlisted in Ireland, but it should be noted that not all of these would have been accepted; see Callan, 'Recruiting for the British army', pp 42, 56 (above, p. 190, n. 1).

Thus, although he was privately much disturbed by what seemed to him to be an increasing swing towards militancy, Dillon counselled caution and restraint. Since this advice coincided with Birrell's own inclinations, the under-secretary was restricted to a policy of compromise.[1] From time to time, particularly abusive newspapers were suppressed and agitators were banished from the scene of their activities, a few of the more intransigent even being sent out of the country altogether. But no action was taken against the Volunteers, and recruiting for that force (and also, secretly, for the I.R.B.) went steadily ahead without any effective interruption. From the government's point of view this was not a healthy situation, and in Nathan's opinion—as also in Dillon's—it was a situation that was apparently deteriorating rather rapidly in the closing months of 1915. If this was so, then the prime cause is probably to be sought in the menace of conscription, which then seemed to be coming perceptibly closer. The question of compulsory service had first been raised in the cabinet in June 1915, and in January 1916 the government followed this up by securing parliamentary sanction for the conscription of bachelors. Redmond had managed to secure the exemption of Ireland from this measure, but no one could be sure how long this exemption might last, and the general uneasiness was in no sense removed. Indeed, among those who had any political awareness at all, it can only have been increased by the realisation that the government that was moving towards compulsion was, from May 1915 onwards, a coalition of liberals and unionists. For the leaders of the Irish parliamentary party the formation of the coalition represented a double blow. On the one hand it led to the inclusion of Carson in the cabinet, where obviously he could exert enormous pressure on Irish policy. And on the other hand it confronted Redmond and Dillon with an acute dilemma. To balance Carson's inclusion, Asquith and Birrell urged one or other of the nationalist leaders to enter the coalition as well. This, however, they could not do without compromising the principle of independent opposition that was vital to the party's existence. In the end, they had the worst of both worlds. Obliged to acquiesce in Carson's inclusion, they stayed outside themselves and thus preserved their independence at the expense of their influence.

Meanwhile on the streets of Dublin the Volunteers and the Citizen Army continued to parade openly, the Citizen Army indeed carrying its audacity to the length of staging a mock attack on Dublin castle. These activities were not apparently regarded by the Irish government as being particularly menacing, though the military took a rather more serious view. They had good reason for doing so. On 22 March 1916 Sir John French, at that time in command of home forces, had been told by the director of intelligence in Britain that the latter had

---

[1] The lack of effective action by Birrell's administration has been fully considered in O'Halpin, *Decline of the union*, pp 108–11. O'Halpin identifies four main factors: political reasons; conflicts between civil and military jurisdiction, with ambiguity as to what constituted sedition; limitations in the Castle's intelligence system (including the lack of effective communication between British external intelligence and the Dublin administration); and the personal style of Birrell.

received information 'from an absolutely reliable source' that a rising was being planned, and that German assistance for it was expected.[1] According to this information the rebellion would begin on Saturday, 22 April, by which time arms from Germany would have been landed at Limerick. It seems probable that the details about dates and places—which were not wholly accurate, but near enough to constitute impressive evidence—were derived from the navy's success in breaking the code used for the transmission of German messages to and from the United States. At any rate, they were thought important enough to be passed on to Major-general L. B. Friend, the general officer commanding in chief the forces in Ireland; and although he was inclined to dismiss it, he did make some provisional arrangements for reinforcement in case of need.

One of the oddest features of these exchanges is that it is not known for certain whether the report from intelligence ever got as far as the civil authorities—Birrell, his under-secretary Nathan, or the lord lieutenant, Lord Wimborne. It seems that there was no direct communication between the admiralty and the Irish government, and if the details intercepted by the navy got through to Dublin Castle at all they presumably did so through the somewhat tepid agency of General Friend. If they did get through they made remarkably little impression. On 10 April Nathan bestirred himself to answer French's query as to whether 'the government was satisfied that there was no likelihood of a rising'. What he had to say was certainly revealing. 'Though the Irish Volunteer element has been active of late, especially in Dublin,' he wrote, 'I do not believe that its leaders mean insurrection or that the Volunteers have sufficient arms if the leaders do mean it.'[2]

But evidence to the contrary continued to accumulate. On 17 April Nathan was handed a letter that General Friend had received from the officer commanding the defences of the port of Queenstown. It mentioned that a landing of arms somewhere on the south-west coast was imminent and that a rising would take place on 22 April. Nathan showed the letter to the head of the Royal Irish Constabulary, Sir Neville Chamberlain; and, although they were both inclined to dismiss it as a rumour, Chamberlain put his men on the watch in the southern and south-western counties while the Dublin Metropolitan Police were similarly alerted in the capital. The events of that fateful Saturday, 22 April, seemed to confirm them in their scepticism. With the *Aud* sunk and Casement captured, all prospect of an outbreak seemed at an end. Nathan, who, like nearly everyone else at this time, had totally misunderstood Casement's essentially negative role, now felt secure enough to write to Birrell in London that he could 'see no indications of a "rising" '.[3] On the other hand, if the danger seemed to be over, information derived from one of Casement's companions (Bailey) revealed that it had been a real and not an imagined danger. This in itself, as the lord lieutenant urged on Nathan on the morning of Sunday, 23 April, provided ample grounds for moving

---

[1] Leon Ó Broin, *Dublin Castle and the 1916 rising* (London, 1966), p. 135.
[2] Ibid., pp 72–3.   [3] Ibid., pp 81–2.

against the leaders of the Volunteers, the more so as word had just come in that a quantity of gelignite had been taken from a quarry to Connolly's headquarters at Liberty Hall. Nathan would not move, however, without the chief secretary's permission, which he immediately sought by telegram, but which would nevertheless take some time to reach Dublin. Later that day there was another conference at the viceregal lodge, and Wimborne again pressed for instant action. He failed to get it, partly because of Nathan's reluctance to do anything until he heard from Birrell, and partly also because the military authorities demanded more time for their preparations.[1] There was general agreement that a move should be made against Liberty Hall, regarded, with some justice, as the nerve-centre of the conspiracy, but the majority opinion was that the next day, Easter Monday, would be inappropriate since it was a public holiday and there would be too many Volunteers at leisure—hence the decision to postpone the attack for at least a further twenty-four hours and to allow army leave to continue as planned.

The consequences of that decision were momentous. While citizens and officers disported themselves at Fairyhouse races outside Dublin, the Volunteers and the Citizen Army moved towards their appointed objectives in the city. Their leaders committed them to the insurrection in the virtually certain knowledge that it was doomed to failure. The orders and counterorders of the weekend had produced confusion and paralysis in most parts of the country.[2] This, together with the absence of arms and ammunition, meant that although there were a few local actions of some consequence—in Wexford, Galway, and Meath—the rising was effectively confined to Dublin. There, too, uncertainty and divided allegiance had ensured that the actual striking force assembled on the morning of Easter Monday would be of the most meagre proportions. In fact, even if all those are included who joined after the fighting had started, it does not seem that the combined total of the Volunteers and the Citizen Army amounted to more than about 1,600, of which the latter supplied just over 200. All that could be done with such numbers was to occupy certain key buildings and hope to hold them long enough either to enable outbreaks to occur elsewhere in Ireland, or to secure sufficient recognition from Germany as to guarantee representation at the peace conference at which, so the conspirators fondly believed, a defeated Britain would sooner or later have

[1] For two diverging views of Nathan's abilities and shortcomings, see O'Halpin, *Decline of the union*, pp 105–6, and—a more detailed analysis of Nathan's military and administrative career—Anthony Haydon, 'Sir Matthew Nathan—Ireland and before' in *Studia Hib.*, xv (1975), pp 162–76.

[2] F. X. Martin has pointed to the personal reputation of, and high regard for, MacNeill among Irish Volunteers in the provinces as a key factor in their failure to mobilise in large numbers outside Dublin during Easter week. See, for example, the comments by Patrick McCartan recorded in Martin, 'Inside report on Ulster', pp 202, 204. In 'The decline and fall of the I.R.B.' in *Éire-Ireland*, x, no. 1 (1975), pp 15–16, Joseph M. Curran argues that the conspirators had destroyed any hope of a nation-wide insurrection by keeping MacNeill, and most of the I.R.B. supreme council and local Volunteer leadership, in the dark. Townshend has, however, pointed out that the conspiracy had aimed, rather vaguely, for an uprising throughout the country without providing the machinery to mobilise and coordinate it (*Political violence*, pp 299–302).

to sue for terms. It is doubtful, however, if military considerations were uppermost in the minds of Pearse and his fellow revolutionaries. Obsessed as they had been for so long with the concept of the blood sacrifice, it seems certain that they went into battle not only courting death, but in the belief, as Pearse had expressed it the previous year at the funeral of O'Donovan Rossa, that 'from the graves of patriot men and women spring living nations'.[1]

Because the whole undertaking was so desperate, and because, as we have seen, the authorities had underrated the urgency of the situation, the opening moves of the insurgents went far more smoothly than might have been expected. Their military headquarters and their seat of government were both to be housed in the General Post Office half-way up Sackville Street (O'Connell Street), while other garrisons occupied the Four Courts, the South Dublin Union, the Mendicity Institution, Jacob's biscuit factory, Boland's mills, and St Stephen's Green. The first shot was fired by the Citizen Army when it opened its assault on the castle at noon. The unarmed policeman on duty outside was shot dead and, if they had pressed home their attack, the insurgents could have had both the castle itself and Sir Matthew Nathan (who was inside) for the asking.[2] They did not do so, however, perhaps because they did not really believe that the centre of British power in Ireland could be so vulnerable, but also, it may be, because the occupation of such a large and widely dispersed conglomeration of buildings would have overstretched their resources. Elsewhere the initial occupation went more or less as planned, though it was not long before the futility of occupying St Stephen's Green (where valuable time was lost digging useless trenches) dawned on the Citizen Army officer in charge, Michael Mallin, and his second in command, Constance Markievicz. But although they withdrew in good order to the College of Surgeons on the west side of the Green, even this was inadequate because it was overlooked by the taller Shelbourne Hotel, which was promptly occupied by the troops. The consequence was that the contingent in the College of Surgeons was pinned down and in effect taken out of the battle during almost the whole of the six days the rising lasted.

The same was true of Jacob's biscuit factory and to a lesser extent of Boland's mills, though in the latter case—where Eamon de Valera commanded—the necessity of patrolling the railway line and some of the neighbouring road approaches to the city imposed on the Volunteers in this sector a more active and exacting role than was possible for others who were simply cooped up in isolated buildings. On the other hand, it was in some of these buildings—notably the Mendicity Institution, the South Dublin Union, the City Hall, and the Four

---

[1] Pearse, *Political writings*, pp 136–7. Joseph Lee has challenged the traditional emphasis on the blood sacrifice idea as an element in the plans for an insurrection, arguing that this aspect of motivation among the leadership came fully into play only after the failure of the *Aud*'s mission, and has been overemphasised in the wake of the execution of the leaders (*Ire. 1912–85*, pp 25–7).

[2] An account of this incident and an interesting narrative of Nathan's activities immediately before and during the rising can be found in Leon Ó Broin, *Protestant nationalists in revolutionary Ireland* (Dublin and Totowa, N. J., 1985), pp 69–106.

Courts—that the fiercest fighting occurred. It was, however, fighting that could have only one end, as British reinforcements poured into the city and as artillery was systematically used to dislodge the insurgents from one strongpoint after another. Had the rebel strategy been more flexible, and had the leaders been prepared to experiment with street fighting based on the exploitation of local knowledge, the final result might not have been very different, but the struggle would probably have gone on longer and the British casualties would certainly have been heavier. Such at least is the conclusion suggested by the one episode where approximately this kind of warfare was attempted. That was at Mount Street, where on 26 April a dozen Volunteers prevented for a whole day the entry of British reinforcements from Kingstown and inflicted on the Sherwood Foresters almost half the losses incurred by the military during the entire week.

This, however, was unique. Elsewhere the strategy of fixed positions prevailed, and nowhere was the position so fixed, or the strategy so futile, as at the General Post Office. It was admittedly a substantial building, and it was not until late on Friday night that it was so thoroughly set alight that Pearse and his followers were forced to evacuate it; but as a headquarters it suffered from the overwhelming defect of being too remote from the other centres of resistance, which had therefore to conduct their own battles without much guidance from the centre. It is necessary to insist, however, that the role of the G.P.O. was symbolic and political rather than practical and military. Indeed, it had largely served its symbolical and political function within a few minutes of being occupied, when Pearse stepped outside to read the proclamation of the republic on behalf of the provisional government. Of the seven members of the provisional government who signed the proclamation—Pearse, Clarke, Connolly, MacDermott, MacDonagh, Plunkett, and Ceannt—all but Ceannt and MacDonagh were in the G.P.O., a concentration of the leadership that may have been necessitated by the decision to place the civil authority alongside the military one, but which may also have weakened the effectiveness of the insurgents at other points in the city.

The primary purpose of the proclamation was of course to bring into being the Irish republic that had been the goal of militant nationalism ever since Tone. That the framers of the document—Pearse, probably assisted by MacDonagh—were intensely conscious of the connection with the past was shown in the preamble, where the revolt was described as taking place 'in the name of God and of the dead generations from which she [Ireland] receives her old tradition of nationhood'. Moreover, the fact that it was explicitly stated that the rising had been organised not merely by the open action of the Volunteers and the Citizen Army but through the 'secret revolutionary organisation, the Irish Republican Brotherhood', emphasised that the 'old tradition of nationhood' was assumed to be republican.[1] This was not an assumption with which most Irishmen at that time

[1] Curran has pointed to the fact that although a few key men in the I.R.B. planned and led the insurrection, some I.R.B. members opposed it and most took no part in either the preparations or the fighting. But, he argues, the tribute to the I.R.B. in the proclamation 'enveloped the organisation in

would have agreed, and it was not in fact an assumption to which the leaders themselves were committed so uncompromisingly as appeared on the surface. Evidence has come to light that suggests that while the proclamation of the republic was the affirmation of an ideal, both Pearse and Plunkett, and apparently MacDonagh as well, were prepared to discuss among themselves the more prosaic possibility of accepting a German prince, in the short term at least, as king of an independent Ireland. This was, no doubt, only idle speculation, and could never be more than that unless Germany won the war, but the direct reference that was made in the proclamation to 'gallant allies in Europe' showed very clearly that the provisional government was quite ready to incur the penalty of treason, which this traffic inevitably attracted, if it would serve to secure for an independent Ireland recognition of her belligerent status and therefore the right to present her case at the peace conference that must eventually end the war.

In a very different vein were the passages in the proclamation asserting 'the right of the people of Ireland to the ownership of Ireland' and declaring a resolve 'to pursue the happiness and prosperity of the whole nation and of all its parts, cherishing all the children of the nation equally, and oblivious of the differences carefully fostered by an alien government, which have divided a minority from the majority in the past'.[1] In these phrases it is not unreasonable to see the influence of Connolly (though also, to an extent, that of Pearse), but their very vagueness suggests that the social programme of the new republic had been tacitly shelved until the republic itself should have fought its way into existence. Even so, the promise of a new and better life that these generalities held out was not to be forgotten in the future; nor was the ensuing gap between the dream and the reality to go unremarked or uncriticised.

Events after Pearse's somewhat melodramatic ceremony outside the G.P.O. followed a predictable course. Given that the rebels were committed to their strategy of fixed positions, and given also their numerical weakness, it was only a matter of time before the British superiority in manpower and in weapons asserted itself overwhelmingly. When the rising broke out, there were about 6,000 effective British soldiers in Ireland as well as a considerable number of war wounded.[2] In addition, the armed Royal Irish Constabulary accounted for a further 9,500 men and the unarmed Dublin Metropolitan Police for slightly more than another

---

the mystique of the rising and the enthusiasm of many members remained undimmed' ('Decline and fall of the I.R.B.', p. 16). For the text of the proclamation, see Mitchell & Ó Snodaigh, *Ir. pol. docs. 1916–49*, pp 17–18, based on National Museum of Ireland EW 2L.

[1] Mitchell & Ó Snodaigh, *Ir. pol. docs 1916–49*, p. 17.
[2] See G. A. Hayes-McCoy, 'A military history of the 1916 rising' in K. B. Nowlan (ed.), *The making of 1916* (Dublin, 1969), p. 315, for details of military strength in Ireland at the outbreak of the rising: Hayes-McCoy estimates that under 2,500 soldiers were available in Dublin on 24 Apr. 1916, and in Ireland a total of 3,000 cavalry, 17,000 infantry, and 1,000 artillery, all of them draft-finding units and third-line troops.

thousand, though the latter were withdrawn from duty very early in the proceedings. It seems probable therefore that the insurgents were outnumbered by between two and three to one before they had even started; within forty-eight hours the odds had lengthened to twenty to one, and right to the end of the week troops continued to pour into the city. But the decisive factor was probably the ruthless use of artillery. Connolly, perhaps in an effort to reassure his inexperienced men, had forecast that a capitalist-imperialist government would never turn its guns on the property of the bourgeoisie. If he really did believe this he could not have been more wrong. Field guns were employed as early as the afternoon of Tuesday 25 April to sweep barricades off the streets. On the following morning the fishery patrol vessel *Helga* used her gun to help blow the empty Liberty Hall to pieces, and thereafter artillery was used at each stage of the operations. The resultant damage—from high explosive, but still more from fire—reached massive proportions. Sackville Street was almost entirely burnt out, as were the streets around the G.P.O., and many other parts of the city were severely damaged. The rebuilding grants and compensation payments of nearly £2 million, which were paid when it was all over, almost certainly fell far short of the actual cost of the destruction the city had experienced.

It was perhaps inevitable in the confusion and stress of the fighting that the civilian population should have suffered severely. Initially attracted to the scene of the fighting by sheer curiosity, a section of the population—mostly the tenement-dwellers who lived closest to Sackville Street—were quick to sense the breakdown of law and order and to indulge in indiscriminate but highly dangerous looting. Numbers of them were killed in this way: some perished as their homes came into the line of fire, and yet others died in circumstances that suggested, even where positive proof was lacking, that officers and men of certain British units, their nerves stretched beyond bearing, yielded to the temptation to carry out their own grim and unauthorised reprisals. The most famous incident, where guilt was positively established, was the murder of Francis Sheehy-Skeffington and two journalists, Patrick Mackintyre and Thomas Dickson. Sheehy-Skeffington was a well known and well loved figure in Dublin. An argumentative but good-hearted man, he was a supporter of all kinds of minority causes and quite fearless in his pursuit of whatever seemed to him right. As a pacifist he abhorred the rising, but as a citizen he felt it his duty to help the wounded and to do what he could to put a stop to the orgy of looting. Returning home on the evening of Tuesday 25 April he was arrested at Portobello Bridge. That night he was taken as a hostage to accompany a raiding party and witnessed the officer in charge—an Irishman, Captain J. C. Bowen-Colthurst—shooting dead an unarmed youth. The next morning, on the orders of that officer, he and the two journalists were themselves shot, without any semblance of a trial or opportunity to vindicate themselves. Their bodies were buried in quicklime, and the officer himself led a raid on Sheehy-Skeffington's home, apparently in an effort to secure incriminating evidence that might in some way retrospectively palliate his crime.[1] In this, of course, he totally failed because there was no evidence; but it was only after several days, during which he had shown marked signs of derangement and committed other atrocities, that he was removed from his post. In due course he was tried and found guilty of murder while insane; imprisoned for a time in Broadmoor, he was later released and allowed to go to Canada, where he died in 1965.[2]

The Sheehy-Skeffington case became famous overnight, partly because the victim was a person of consequence, and partly because Dillon raised the matter in the house of commons. It was more difficult for humbler victims to obtain justice, and the outcome of one episode, almost as well known as the murder of Sheehy-Skeffington, suggested to a public predisposed to imagine the worst that the widespread rumours of dark deeds in every part of the city were only too well founded. North King Street had been utilised by the rebels as part of the outworks of the Four Courts, and in order to clear it the troops had to work through it house by house. The unhappy civilians were caught between two fires, but the persistent story was that men of the 2/6th South Staffordshire regiment had taken deliberate reprisals against them. In fact it was alleged that fifteen people had been done to death and, after two bodies had been recovered from a shallow grave in one of the houses, an official inquiry was held. No culprits were identified, but the circumstantial evidence was never satisfactorily refuted and Dubliners remained obstinately convinced that some sort of massacre had occurred and was being hushed up by the authorities.

It was only gradually, of course, that such details became public knowledge. At the time, the fears and anxieties of most citizens were concentrated on the destruction of Dublin. No doubt it seemed as if it would go on for ever, but in reality it lasted effectively for only six days, though even this was sufficient to disrupt business and communications and to cause serious hardship, especially to the very poor. By Friday night the end was very near. The G.P.O. was burning fiercely and Pearse had to order its evacuation, taking with him Connolly, who had been severely wounded earlier in the week. Leaving by the Henry Street exit, they turned into Moore Street with the intention of breaking through the military cordon and making their way towards the Four Courts where the garrison still held out. But Moore Street was dominated by a military barricade, and the O'Rahilly demonstrated the impossibility of forcing it by leading a forlorn charge in which he was killed.[3] The rest of the evacuating party scattered into the houses

---

[1] For the activities of Francis and Hanna Sheehy-Skeffington in the weeks preceding the insurrection, their movements in the early part of Easter week, and Francis Sheehy-Skeffington's death, see Leah Levenson, *With wooden sword* (Boston, Mass., and Dublin, 1983), pp 210–34.

[2] For the aftermath of these shootings, Bowen-Colthurst's court martial, and Hanna Sheehy-Skeffington's campaign for a public inquiry, see ibid., pp 235–7.

[3] See Aodogan O'Rahilly, *Winding the clock: O'Rahilly and the 1916 rising* (Dublin, 1991), pp 219–25.

further down the street, and it was from there, on Saturday, 29 April, that Pearse and Connolly authorised the capitulation. Their surrender was repeated at the various strongpoints until the whole process was completed during 30 April. In the six days of fighting 450 people had been killed, 2,614 were wounded, and 9 were missing—the vast majority of these casualties, in the nature of the case, occurring inside Dublin itself. Military casualties were 17 officers killed and 46 wounded; 99 other ranks killed, 322 wounded, and 9 missing. The R.I.C. lost 13 killed and 22 wounded, the D.M.P. 3 killed and 7 wounded. The official figures make no distinction between insurgents and civilians, but give a combined total of 318 killed and 2,217 wounded.

The most obvious and immediate effect of the rising was to put the city at the mercy of the military authorities. Martial law had been proclaimed in Dublin on Easter Monday and extended to the rest of the country on the following day. In practice this meant that dictatorial powers rested in the hands of the commanding officer. At the outset this had been Brigadier-general W. H. M. Lowe, but on Friday he was superseded by Major-general Sir John Maxwell,[1] on whom devolved the responsibility for deciding the fate of the insurgents. His first reaction to the collapse of the rising was an interesting foretaste of the way in which a potentially strong British position was to be progressively destroyed during the next two years by a combination of simple ignorance and political ineptitude. Starting from the totally incorrect premise that because Sinn Féin had been the most prominent of the militantly nationalist organisations up to 1916, therefore the rising must be the handiwork of Sinn Féin, he began by ordering a general round-up of 'suspects'—a term that was interpreted in a manner so bizarre as to have been ludicrous, had not the consequences been so disastrous—not merely in Dublin but all over the country. In a very short time 3,430 men and 79 women were swept into the net.[2] Of these, 1,424 men and 73 women were released after interrogation, but a total of 170 men and one woman (the Countess Markievicz) were tried by court martial for direct complicity in the rebellion; all but one man were convicted. The remaining prisoners, 1,836 men and 5 women, were sent to Britain for internment, but of these 1,272 were discharged after further investigation and most of the others were released at Christmas.

It is necessary both to preserve a sense of proportion about these arrests and at the same time to emphasise the seriousness of what was being done. A sense of proportion suggests that this reaction was not really an excessive one on the part of a government that was in the middle of a great struggle for survival, and at a

[1] Lowe continued as commander of forces in the Dublin area under Maxwell, who held general authority for the exercise of martial law throughout Ireland.

[2] The extent to which the women of Cumann na mBan had involved themselves in the rising is described in Margaret Ward, *Unmanageable revolutionaries* (Dublin, 1983), pp 107–18; the effect of this participation on the Irish feminist movement is examined in Beth McKillen, 'Irish feminism and nationalist separatism, 1914–1923' in *Éire-Ireland*, xvii (1982), no. 3, pp 61–7; no. 4, pp 72–7. See also above, pp 168, 186.

moment of crisis in that struggle found itself attacked in the rear, and its soldiers distracted from graver tasks, by what appeared to be the conspiracy of a minority that openly boasted that it had been trafficking with the enemy. Yet there was a fundamental inconsistency here to which the official mind remained oblivious until it was too late. If the rising really was the work of a minority—and in this at least British intelligence was not at fault—then the path of wisdom would have been to confine arrest, detention, and, if need be, death, to those who had figured, or figured prominently, in the actual events of Easter week. But to define the minority in such a way as to broaden the definition into a catch-all for as nearly as possible everyone who had incurred official suspicion in the past two years was a crass psychological blunder. It was so because it was based on a total misconception of the mood that the rising had engendered in Ireland. Dubliners may indeed have been fascinated at the outset by the spectacle of a handful of their fellow citizens—some of them well known to be dreamers rather than soldiers—taking on the full might of the British empire; but as their city became an inferno of fire and smoke and destruction, hostility towards those who had recklessly precipitated this ordeal became so intense that when, after the surrender, the leaders were marched away to captivity, they passed through crowds from whom, it is scarcely too much to say, they, and not the troops who guarded them, needed protection.[1]

The initial unpopularity of the rising should have been regarded by the government as a priceless asset. This indeed it would have been, had it not been squandered in part by the internment policy which, by herding innocent men and women into camps alongside dedicated revolutionaries, exposed the former to a process of indoctrination of which the full consequences were only to be seen in the years that lay ahead.[2] But in part, and still more, the asset of public hostility to the rising was squandered by the policy adopted towards its admitted leaders. Here again, and once more taking the wartime situation into account, it could be argued that the price exacted—fourteen shot in Dublin and one in Cork, and Casement hanged in London—was not disproportionately high. And in this connection it should be remembered that the total initially sentenced to death was ninety, of whom seventy-five (including de Valera and the Countess Markievicz) had their sentences commuted to various terms of penal servitude. But what deprives this argument of all validity was the way in which the price had to be paid. Not only were the leaders tried by secret courts martial, not only were they executed at dawn with only the briefest warning to priests and relatives, but the executions themselves were spun out over ten days (from 3 to 12 May), a period

---

[1] This widely held view—that public reaction in Dublin to the insurgents was initially hostile, then gradually became sympathetic in the wake of the arrests and executions—has been reexamined in some detail in Lee, *Ire. 1912–85*, pp 28–36. Lee's arguments suggest a much more complex and varied response from the press and other commentators, both in Dublin and in the provinces. See also O'Rahilly, *Winding the clock*, for some contemporary comments on reaction in Dublin (e.g. letter from Nell Humphreys to her sister, appendix 6, p. 236).

[2] See Sean O'Mahony, *Frongoch* (Dublin, 1987), pp 17–28, 58–65.

that was amply sufficient to allow time for feelings of compassion for the victims and anger against the authorities to replace the original public condemnation of the rising.[1] Moreover, as the list of men shot—usually in batches of three or four—grew from day to day, it could be seen that it included the names of some who hardly seemed to merit such punishment. The role of Pearse's brother Willie, for example, had been entirely subordinate, and the only conceivable reason for shooting him was the simple fact that he was Pearse's brother. And if there were understandable grounds for executing the signatories of the proclamation—after all, they had not only been the chief conspirators, but also included the leading devotees of the cult of the blood sacrifice—it was somewhat gratuitous to kill Connolly while he was too weak to stand up to be shot, and it was perhaps extending the definition of treason unwisely far to execute such subordinate commanders as Michael Mallin, Edward Daly, Con Colbert, or Seán Heuston for carrying out what they had conceived to be their military duty.

Had military law, courts martial, and executions been the only official reaction to the rising, Irish resentment might have been impossible to contain without the risk of further violence. This at any rate was the opinion of Dillon, who had been virtually blockaded in his house in Dublin (in North Great George's Street only a few hundred yards from the G.P.O.) throughout the days of fighting. This gave him a perspective on the rising different from that of Redmond, who was in London and naturally sensitive to the currents of British indignation that eddied round him. Both men recognised instinctively that the rising was almost as serious in its implications for the future of the Irish parliamentary party as it was for the relations between the two countries, but they differed significantly in their reactions to it. Whereas Redmond immediately expressed in the house of commons his feelings of 'detestation and horror'[2] and ascribed the outbreak to German machinations, Dillon, though equally severe in his strictures, saw at once that unless the British reaction were exceedingly restrained—more restrained even than it was reasonable to expect—the effect on Irish sentiment might well be devastating. As soon as he could leave his house with impunity he did what he could to exert pressure on Sir John Maxwell, and as early as 30 April he urged Redmond to bring home to the British government the necessity for caution. 'The wisest course', he wrote, 'is to execute *no one* for the present . . . If there were shootings of prisoners on a large scale the effect on public opinion might be disastrous in the extreme.'[3]

Two days later the shootings began, and although Redmond did his best to obey Dillon's frequent and increasingly excited admonitions to persuade Asquith that the executions must cease forthwith, they continued remorselessly; indeed, the fact that some of them occurred after Asquith had given the required assurances

---

[1] O'Halpin has, however, pointed out that the pattern of executions was dictated by legal and procedural factors (*Decline of the union*, p. 120).

[2] *Hansard 5 (commons)*, lxxxi, 2512 (27 Apr. 1916).   [3] Lyons, *Dillon*, p. 373.

suggested to the Irish leaders the alarming conclusion that the prime minister had lost control of the situation. So tormented was Dillon by this mysterious, and to him intolerable, state of affairs that he left Dublin, his family, and his efforts to restrain the military authorities, in order to intervene in a commons debate on the rising with the express purpose of attempting to secure parliamentary support for a cessation of the executions. The speech that he made on 11 May was one of the most famous in his career, and it had consequences far beyond the immediate occasion. Speaking to a deeply hostile house, and himself much overwrought by his experiences, he gave members the first direct account most of them had heard of what life had been like in beleaguered Dublin. The house was stunned into silence when he spoke of the Sheehy-Skeffington case, but it erupted into fury when he proclaimed that, while he deplored the rising, he could not conceal his admiration for the rebels. Fury turned to bafflement when he prophesied that to continue the policy of executions would not only let loose 'rivers of blood' in Ireland, but would also destroy the whole work of reconciliation carried out by his party since the days of Parnell.[1]

Before many years had passed both these prophecies were to be fulfilled with a sombre exactitude, but at the time Dillon was much censured in political circles for making a 'fenian' speech at a time when it behoved Irishmen to ride out the storm in prudent silence. Yet in reality his policy, of combining condemnation of the rising with criticism of the military rule that had followed it, probably offered the best hope of survival for the constitutional movement. If the repressive regime were to continue in Ireland, and if it were to excite an all too predictable resentment (Dillon had already detected signs of this), then the parliamentary party must canalise this resentment in order to control it. Failure to do this would lead inevitably to rejection by the people and to the rise of a more intransigent nationalism, which in its turn, as Dillon bleakly foresaw, would precipitate a fresh revolutionary outbreak.

For a brief moment in the aftermath of 1916 it seemed that this fate would be avoided.[2] The day after Dillon's speech in the commons the prime minister left for Ireland where he spent a week exploring the situation. What he saw and heard convinced him that an attempt must be made to achieve a political settlement even while the war was still in progress. He entrusted the task to Lloyd George who, with his habitual energy and skill, appeared at first to make remarkable progress. Starting from the assumption that some kind of partition was inevitable, he made

[1] Ibid., pp 380–82.

[2] D. G. Boyce has argued that reaction to news of the rising in the British press, delayed as it was by a combination of government censorship and damaged communications, was 'surprisingly moderate in tone'; that although the insurgents were universally condemned, there was no denunciation of Irish nationalists as a whole, except in the extreme right-wing press. The rising was seen as an insult and blow to Ireland as much as to Britain. Even the *Daily Telegraph* admitted that it was 'unreasonable to make capital against home rule by this criminal insurrection of Sinn Féiners'. Boyce contends that the ground was thus well prepared for Asquith's visit (Boyce, 'British opinion, Ireland, and the war, 1916–1918' in *Hist. Jn.*, xvii (1974), pp 578–9).

it his primary aim to secure the support of both nationalists and unionists for his proposals. These envisaged that the government of Ireland act of 1914 should be brought into operation for twenty-six counties as soon as possible, and that the six north-eastern counties of Antrim, Armagh, Down, Fermanagh, Londonderry, and Tyrone should be excluded. The excluded counties would be administered by a secretary of state responsible for the area. Lloyd George also proposed that Irish representation in the imperial parliament would remain unchanged (103 members); but that this would probably have been only a temporary expedient is suggested by the final clause of his 'Headings of a settlement',[1] which laid it down that the legislation embodying his scheme was to remain in force during the war and for twelve months thereafter; it was only to be further extended if at the end of that time parliament had failed to make permanent provision for the government of Ireland and needed more time to do so. Linked with this was the notion that when, as expected, an imperial conference was held at the end of the war, the conference should be empowered to address itself to the task of framing an enduring solution to the problem.

The crux of the scheme was obviously the exclusion of the six north-eastern counties, and it may well seem extraordinary that in the space of a few weeks Lloyd George should have won the assent of the opposing Irish factions to something that had brought them to the verge of civil war in 1914. The sad and simple answer is that he achieved this spectacular result by a piece of political illusionism. Having first called the contending parties to meet him round the conference table, he thereafter negotiated with them separately. In this way he was able to allow Redmond to understand that the exclusion of the Ulster counties would only be temporary, while to Carson he gave a written promise that it would be permanent.

Even so, and despite these precarious acrobatics, he had the greatest difficulty in obtaining the consent he wanted. Redmond had of course to reckon with the bitter criticism of his fellow nationalists, and especially with the alarm of northern catholics, deeply apprehensive at being cut off from their co-religionists in the south; it was only after a passionate plea by the leading northern catholic in the party, Devlin, and his own threat to resign if he were not supported, that Redmond was able to carry the day. Carson had a similarly rough passage and only persuaded the Ulster Unionist Council to agree after long and stormy argument.[2] That they did agree was perhaps a symptom of the changing times. With the formation of a coalition government, Ulster unionism was no longer an instrument that the tory party needed to use to lever itself back to power, and it was a prudent tactic for the Ulstermen not to presume too much on the memory of the pre-war alliance. Moreover, though this only began to emerge during the first half of July when the crisis reached its climax, Ulster unionism was no longer

---

[1] Lyons, *Dillon*, pp 485–6.

[2] McNeill, *Ulster's stand for union*, pp 246–9; and see Patrick Buckland (ed.), *Irish unionism, 1885–1923* (Belfast, 1973), pp 404–5.

in the position of strength it had been in when the Ulster Volunteers stood ready to back an independent Ulster government. Now those self-same Volunteers were falling in their thousands in the Somme offensive, and Ulster was at one stroke plunged into mourning and bereft of its protecting shield. It was a strange irony that put the rising and the Somme in such close juxtaposition. The first strengthened the determination of the Ulstermen never to be ruled from Dublin, whereas the second weakened their ability to ensure that this should be so. From their standpoint, therefore, exclusion from home rule, combined with continuing government from Whitehall, offered a guarantee of which prudence, if not affection, counselled acceptance.

The real losers from Lloyd George's ingenious scheme were of course the small minority of protestants in the south, the 'southern unionists' or 'loyalists', to use terminology that became increasingly common at this time. Not unnaturally, their opposition was vehement and intense. More important, it was successful and a demonstration, never again to be repeated, of the influence they could bring to bear in high places. Once the terms became known to them, their organisation devoted a tremendous effort of propaganda to convincing ministers, members of parliament, and the British press that they must not be abandoned. They were of course greatly helped both by the fact that inside the government they had sympathetic champions—Lord Lansdowne and Walter Long—and by Lloyd George's failure to keep the cabinet fully informed about either the course or the scope of his negotiations. The end result was that not only were the proposals strongly resisted, and partially blocked, by Lansdowne and Long in the private sessions of the cabinet, where they were denounced as a surrender to force that would only breed more violence, but, after Redmond had been pressed into agreeing to additional safeguards for British military and naval interests in Ireland, Lansdowne stated publicly in the house of lords that, if the scheme were to go through, the partition of the country would be 'permanent and enduring', adding—in language that seems to have been intended to be deliberately offensive to nationalists—that Britain would be sure to make her own defence arrangements in Ireland with which a Dublin government would be unable to interfere.[1] After some further vain and irritable exchanges with the government, Redmond withdrew from the negotiations, which thereupon lapsed. Probably they had never stood much chance of success, but their failure, though hailed with relief by many on either side, was ominously significant for the future.[2] If Irishmen could not

---

[1] *Hansard 5 (lords)*, lii, 645–52 (11 July 1916).
[2] Some further details of the 1916 negotiations can be found in J. D. Fair, *British inter-party conferences, 1867–1921* (Oxford, 1980), pp 122–34. Nicholas Mansergh agrees with the emphasis given here to the role played by the thorny issue of partition in the breakdown of the negotiations (*Unresolved question*, pp 92–100). Boyce has argued that Redmond was, however, receptive to Lloyd George's attempts to gloss over the issue of partition because of his anxiety for a quick settlement, and eventually withdrew from the negotiations not so much because he suddenly discovered that he had been deceived, but because British and southern Irish unionists had forced the issue and obliged him

come to terms with one another in the shadow of the two greatest tragedies of their generation, what likelihood was there that they would agree when they had had time to rebuild their old defences and refurbish their ancient enmities?

to take a stand that he would otherwise have avoided (Boyce, 'British opinion . . . 1916–18', pp 580–81). Fair has concluded that ultimately it was the Asquith government, widely blamed for its inept handling of the negotiations, who were the real losers in the fiasco of the Lloyd George initiative (Fair, op. cit., p. 139).

CHAPTER X

The new nationalism, 1916–18

F. S. L. LYONS

ALTHOUGH hindsight suggests that the Irish parliamentary party was the chief sufferer from the events of 1916, this was by no means clear at the time. True, the failure of the home rule negotiations—even, in the eyes of some of his critics, Redmond's very eagerness to participate in those negotiations—had struck a serious blow at the party's prestige and greatly reduced the morale of its supporters, but up to about the end of 1916 there was no reason to suppose that those supporters were not a substantial majority over most of the country. For if the party had been thrown into disarray by the aftermath of the rising, so too had its militant rivals. Casualties among the leadership of the I.R.B. had been very heavy, and although a move had begun within a few days of the executions to resuscitate the organisation, this was bound to take time and the activists were obliged to shelter behind apparently innocuous front organisations such as the Irish National Aid Association and the Irish Volunteers' Dependants Fund.[1] These, while openly devoted to helping the families of those who had died or been wounded, or were in exile, also provided a focus for the fierce anti-British sentiment that was one of the chief legacies of the executions. Sinn Féin was in similar, or worse, straits. The fact that the government attached the Sinn Féin label to the rising may ultimately have worked to the advantage of Griffith and his friends, but in the short term it earned them the opprobrium of many of the Volunteers who had no love for what they regarded as Griffith's pacifist and monarchist views. This was not quite fair, for while Griffith had been excluded from the inner councils of the conspiracy, he had offered his services to the provisional government when hostilities began, only to be told that he would be more useful later on in his accustomed role as propagandist.[2] This had not prevented him from being arrested in the general round-up of nationalist suspects after the collapse of the rising, but although he was released later that year and immediately resumed publication of his newspaper *Nationality*, his personal

---

[1] For the importance of nationalist women (most of whom remained at liberty throughout this period) in carrying out the work of these front organisations, and in particular for the role played by the Cumann na mBan, see Ward, *Unmanageable revolutionaries*, pp 119–27.

[2] There is some disagreement as to whether Griffith, on hearing of the insurrection, actually went in person to the G.P.O. to offer his services, or sent a message there to that effect; accounts agree, however, that his offer was declined (Calton Younger, *Arthur Griffith* (Dublin, 1981), pp 54–5).

following was small and it was by no means certain that Sinn Féin, or at least his version of it, would succeed in maintaining itself, let alone expand into a great national movement.

Yet, despite all the evidence of shock and confusion that the rising left in its train, the fact remained that in the latter part of 1916 public opinion was changing swiftly and profoundly. A good part of the reason for this, as we have already seen, was the executions and the widespread deportations, but the deep and permanent alienation of Irish opinion was completed by the almost uncanny mishandling of the situation by the British government. During that dismal summer of 1916, stroke after stroke seemed to emphasise that Ireland's fate was a matter almost of indifference to her rulers. In a sense it was, of course, for the energies and anxieties of the cabinet were centred primarily on the critical military situation created by the massive failure of the Somme offensive, but even at those points where official policy impinged on nationalist sentiment the effects were rasping and unsettling. The continuance of martial law (Maxwell was only withdrawn in November, even though a new chief secretary, H. E. Duke, had been appointed long before that),[1] the failure of the home rule negotiations and the peculiarly brutal way in which Redmond had been publicly humiliated, the trial and hanging of Sir Roger Casement in the face of strong American and Irish protest, the publication of the report of the inquiry into the Sheehy-Skeffington case—all these things combined to produce a mood of savage resentment. This expressed itself most dramatically in a rapidly developing cult of the dead leaders, a cult that found expression in the frequent commemorative masses then being held in the Dublin churches, and that easily passed into the singing of patriotic songs and the formation of vast processions, highly charged with emotion.

When therefore the interned men came back at Christmas from the jails and the camps, many of them more militant than when they went in,[2] they found a

---

[1] The divergence in policy, between the conciliation expressed by Asquith and the continued repression used by Maxwell, has been explained by O'Halpin as partly due to neglect by the prime minister, who did not restrain the general until the second week in May. There was an additional problem for Asquith in trying to find replacement civil administrators; after the diversion created by Lloyd George's negotiations, it was not until 31 July that H. E. Duke was appointed chief secretary, and 18 Aug. that Wimborne was reappointed lord lieutenant. O'Halpin also points to evidence that after the early days of the rising Maxwell eschewed the use of martial law on the grounds that the military regulations allowed by the defence of the realm act were sufficient, and that it was for the Dublin Castle authorities to govern the country rather than the military. The public perception, however, seems to have made no distinction between the use of D.O.R.A. and martial law; and although as late as July 1916 Asquith praised Maxwell's policy as merciful, the general's continuance in his post became a liability, and three months later he was removed from Ireland and denounced for those same actions (O'Halpin, *Decline of the union*, pp 120–22, 135).

[2] The question whether to release the remaining Irish prisoners was a difficult one for the Irish administration in the latter part of 1916. The problem of finding a system to sort out the small fry from serious troublemakers, particularly given the refusal of the prisoners themselves to cooperate with the inquiries of the authorities, proved insoluble; with the result that it was decided to release all the remaining prisoners before Christmas 1916 (O'Halpin, *Decline of the union*, p. 126). Tom Garvin has argued that the mixing together of revolutionary élites and potential élites in Frongoch and elsewhere had the effect of minimising the differences between various ideological tendencies, encouraging

situation that was already greatly changed. Exactly how that situation would develop in the immediate future no one could then have predicted. All that could safely have been said was that a groundswell of discontent and frustration had begun to make itself felt in the country, and that the repressive regime which had been the almost automatic reaction of the authorities had already revealed its bankruptcy.

The first inkling that a new kind of nationalism was beginning to emerge came with the North Roscommon by-election on 3 February 1917. The seat, which had been virtually the private property of the parliamentary party for many years, was contested by George Noble, Count Plunkett, the father of the executed Joseph Plunkett. Count Plunkett, as his subsequent conduct amply demonstrated, was anything but a professional politician. He stood on this occasion as an independent but, under pressure from Sinn Féin, agreed, after he had won the election with heterogeneous support from extreme nationalists of various persuasions, that he would not take his seat at Westminster. Since this had always been the central political tenet of Sinn Féin, it was thus possible to claim that the North Roscommon by-election marked the first breach by the new nationalism of the defences of the old nationalism.

We shall see presently that although this claim was partly true, it was certainly not the whole truth. First, however, it is necessary to consider the effect of the North Roscommon defeat on the Irish parliamentary party. On its leader the effect was nothing less than catastrophic. Indeed, Redmond actually drew up a memorandum, which he would have published if he had not been restrained by the protests of his senior colleagues, warning the country against the new trend evidenced by the election, but admitting that it would not be in the least surprising if, after so many years, the voters had grown tired of the men who had represented them for so long. He then continued:

Let the Irish people replace us, by all means, by other and, I hope, better men, if they so choose. But in the name of all they hold most sacred, do not let them be led astray by any passion of resentment or will-o'-the-wisp of policy into courses which must end in immediate defeat of their hopes for the present and permanent disaster to their country.[1]

What he intended, of course, was to attack the Sinn Féin doctrine of withdrawal from Westminster, and behind it the republican doctrine of total separation from Britain; but what came through most strongly in the document was his own fatalistic despair. This was an extreme reaction to what was, after all, only a single electoral setback, but the very fact that it was so extreme was ominously significant, and though his colleagues managed to suppress this outburst, they

solidarity, and providing the opportunity for the formation of friendships and contacts, which (he claims) resulted in a 'remarkably cohesive' revolutionary group by 1917 (Tom Garvin, *The evolution of Irish nationalist politics* (Dublin, 1981), p. 115). For an extensive analysis of the make-up of this 'revolutionary élite', see Tom Garvin, *Nationalist revolutionaries in Ireland, 1858–1928* (Oxford, 1987), pp 48–56.

[1] Lyons, *Dillon*, 411.

could not but realise—as Dillon especially was to realise with increasing clarity in the months to come—that their chairman was a beaten man.

Redmond's pessimism had this much justification: that there now began a sequence of events that almost seemed to indicate—Dillon, again, was convinced of it—that it was an essential part of the government's policy to weaken or destroy the parliamentarians so as to provoke a head-on collision between authority and the forces of extremism. There is in fact no convincing evidence that Lloyd George, who had become prime minister on the fall of Asquith in December 1916, cherished any such Machiavellian scheme. It is far more likely that, immersed as he was in the problems of the war, he dealt with Ireland on an *ad hoc* basis. If it was necessary to make gestures to keep the country quiet, or, more important, to placate American opinion, then he would make whatever minimal concessions he thought sufficient to secure his aims, but a coherent and consistent Irish policy was not something that, at this crucial stage, he had either the time, the energy, or the inclination to construct.

In practice, therefore, and in the absence of any grand design, the Irish government was left to its own devices. Propped up by the military and increasingly dependent on them, Dublin Castle fell back on its traditional response to trouble, which was to strike at what it conceived to be the roots of disaffection. Soon after the North Roscommon by-election on 3 February, and presumably in answer to the growing vociferousness of extreme nationalists, the authorities began once more to rearrest some of the suspects who had been set free earlier.[1] With seismographic sensitivity, three new by-election results registered three new successes for Sinn Féin in May, July, and August 1917. These traumatic events are exemplified by what happened in East Clare in July. The seat had fallen vacant because of the death in battle of Redmond's brother Willie on 7 June at Wytschaete Ridge—a personal tragedy that still further weakened the leader's power to grapple with the crisis confronting him—and the election soon assumed a symbolic importance, partly because of the Redmondite association with East Clare, but still more because Eamon de Valera, fresh from prison, was chosen to contest it for Sinn Féin. In fact, he campaigned mainly on his 1916 record and took his stand on the Easter Monday proclamation. It is true that his republicanism was not entirely unqualified. 'We want an Irish republic', he said, 'because if Ireland had her freedom, it is, I believe, the most likely form of government. But if the Irish people wanted to have another form of government, so long as it was an Irish government, I would not put in a word against it.'[2] This was a characteristically flexible position, to which he was to revert many times in

---

[1] According to O'Halpin, the arrest of these thirty-one prominent separatists (ten of whom were subsequently deported without charge) in the aftermath of the North Roscommon by-election was carried out at the behest of the G.O.C.-in-C., General Mahon, because of British intelligence reports that new shipments of arms were being sought from Germany. O'Halpin further contends that misleading intelligence reports from London pressed Duke into taking repressive measures, contrary to the conciliatory policy that he originally intended (*Decline of the union*, pp 126, 137–8).

[2] Quoted in Macardle, *Ir. republic*, p. 233.

the years ahead, but it is not surprising that in the heat of the contest what mattered most to the electors was that here among them was the senior surviving commandant of the rising, and that in voting for him they were voting not just against the parliamentary party but against the whole British connection. The party indeed was so unequal to the fight that it did not even choose the candidate who had the temerity to oppose him. The result was entirely predictable, but the size of de Valera's majority (he won by 5,010 votes to 2,035) suggested that East Clare marked a significant milestone on the road along which the constitutional movement was reeling to destruction.

Yet, although the tide seemed to be running irresistibly for Sinn Féin, this became apparent only very gradually. True, several factors were now working in its favour. First, the entry of the United States into the war on 6 April 1917 gave new hope to militant nationalists, not merely because their traditional links with the Irish-Americans would now acquire additional significance, but because in the first flush of enthusiasm it was possible to believe that the high-flown declarations about the rights of small nations in which President Wilson had already indulged might have a specifically Irish application. In the second place, the emergence of de Valera as a charismatic national leader at this juncture suggested that a consolidation of the forces of militant nationalism was taking place, and if this was true (it was not, in fact, until October that it was shown to be true), then it was a further encouragement to the claims of Sinn Féin to be heard at the peace conference that, presumably, would decide the fate of all those small nations whose hopes President Wilson had so rashly raised. Finally, and partly as a result of the American involvement in the war, members of the extreme party in Ireland were powerfully, if negatively, helped by Lloyd George's decision to interrupt the regime of coercion by a new constructive initiative. Initially, he renewed, on 16 May 1917, his old offer to Redmond of immediate home rule for the twenty-six counties. When this was flatly rejected he took up a suggestion that Redmond himself had privately made to a leading liberal, Lord Crewe,[1] that a conference or convention of Irishmen should be brought together in the hope that they might themselves work out their own salvation. Even at the time it seemed a desperate expedient, and it is doubtful if Lloyd George valued it any higher than as a breathing-space that would allow him to get on with the war unimpeded by Ireland. That Redmond himself should have clutched at it so eagerly was a measure of his political bankruptcy, and it was in fact to be the last tragic chapter in the history of his efforts to bring order out of chaos.

[1] The idea for the convention had originated early in 1917 among the proponents of federalism in the cabinet's secretariat (for example, Lord Amery, one of Lloyd George's aides, suggested the idea to the prime minister in Feb.) and Redmond's initial reaction, voiced in his commons speech of 7 Mar., was negative. It was not until 16 May that Redmond raised the idea with Crewe, who immediately relayed his opinion to Lloyd George and persuaded the prime minister that the suggestion was feasible. The decision to implement it was announced to the house on 21 May (J. D. Fair, *British inter-party conferences, 1867–1921* (Oxford, 1980), pp 199–201).

The Irish Convention first met on 25 July 1917 and continued to labour hard, if with a gathering sense of unreality, until the following spring, but it never recovered from two fatal defects. One was that it was ignored by Sinn Féin and by organised labour.[1] The other was that the Ulster unionists revealed themselves to be still as adamantly opposed to any form of home rule as they had ever been, and in the process succeeded in alienating not only Redmond and his colleagues, but also those southern unionists who, under the guidance of Lord Midleton, were inching their way towards an acceptance of some limited form of Irish self-government. One consequence of this was to throw the leader of the parliamentary party and the southern unionists into a precarious alliance; but even that development, which in 1914 would have been heralded as a major triumph, turned out badly for the unfortunate Redmond. So eager was he to preserve this new-found friendship that he went very far towards accepting Midleton's proviso that if there was to be an Irish parliament then it ought not to be entrusted with the power to levy its own customs duties. Such docility availed him nothing—on the contrary, it only separated him from his own party, and his last speech to the convention was a melancholy swan-song to a distinguished but frustrated career. On 6 March 1918 he died, having failed to recover from an operation for gallstones that was not expected to be serious. His place was taken on 12 March by Dillon, who had refused to serve on the convention and had long chafed under what seemed to him the tired, defensive leadership of his chairman. Had Dillon been chairman in 1916 it is possible, though unlikely, that he would have been able to arrest the subsequent disastrous decline in the party's popularity and morale, but the situation he inherited in the spring of 1918 was desperate beyond any reasonable hope of redemption.

There were two main reasons for this—one arising directly from the course of the war, the other connected with the transformation of Sinn Féin. Although both were to contribute to the final eclipse of constitutional nationalism, the exigencies created by the war might not have been quite so disastrous to the party had not Sinn Féin been in a position to exploit them with spectacular success. But that position was only finally achieved during the latter part of 1917. As we saw earlier, Count Plunkett's election for North Roscommon, though it seemed a great triumph for militant nationalism, was in reality only a first faltering step along a road of which no one quite knew either the length or the direction. The count, whose head was quickly turned by his success, imagined himself to be the very personification of a new-style Sinn Féin. He was, of course, nothing of the kind. Indeed, at the moment his victory was being proclaimed at the polls it would have

[1] After the two main labour organisations in the south (the trades councils of the cities of Dublin and Cork) refused to participate in the convention, the Irish administration sent an agent to Belfast to make contact with organised labour in the north. He secured the assent of several labour activists to attend the convention as representatives of labour organisations; details of these men and the groups they represented can be found in R. B. McDowell, *The Irish convention, 1917–18* (London and Toronto, 1970), pp 85–6. This remains the standard work on the convention's proceedings, but for more recent analyses see Fair, op. cit., ch. 10, and Mansergh, *Unresolved question*, pp 103–7.

been a brave man who would have dared to define either what Sinn Féin was or who best embodied it. The original Sinn Féiners who had not been 'out' in 1916—and these included Griffith—were still looked at very much askance by the survivors of the I.R.B. and also by many Volunteers. Moreover, apart from Count Plunkett and his friends, they had to reckon with a splinter group, the Irish Nation League, formed by northern nationalists in the wake of their disillusionment with the parliamentary party over the acceptance of a form of partition in 1916.[1] The new league did not succeed in spreading far outside Ulster, but it had intervened, alongside Sinn Féin, in the North Roscommon election, and this early experience of cooperation had suggested the possibility of some more permanent alliance. To Count Plunkett, however, alliance seemed to mean fusion, or rather the absorption of the existing movements into a new all-embracing organisation to be called the Liberty League. Such, at any rate, was the plan he announced at a convention that he summoned in April 1917. Not unnaturally he met with spirited opposition, especially from Griffith's followers who were beginning to be conscious of once more making an impact on public opinion, mainly through the medium of Griffith's incomparable journalism: then, as always, much better than that of any of his competitors. The outcome was a nominal defeat for Plunkett in that the various existing groups were to be allowed to retain their separate identities. Lip-service, however, was paid to his ideas on unity by the creation of a new body, later called the Mansion House Committee, which contained both Plunkett and Griffith and an equal number of their respective supporters, together with a representative of the Irish Nation League and William O'Brien of the labour movement.

Notwithstanding this reverse, Plunkett persisted in forming his Liberty League, and soon his followers and Griffith's were at loggerheads up and down the country. The spring and early summer of 1917 witnessed the peak of this competition, which was mainly at the constituency level and often the result of local enterprise rather than central direction. As a result the number of Sinn Féin clubs rose quite spectacularly from 166 with a membership of about 11,000 in April 1917 to 1,200 clubs and a membership of a quarter of a million by October. The chief beneficiary of this expansion was Griffith—his organisation was superior, his writings were more widely read, and he retained the monopoly of the name Sinn Féin—but long before then it had become apparent that he would have to share with others whatever power this expansion might bring him. More specifically, he would have to share it with the men who came back from internment and, later, from prison. It would appear, indeed, that the missionary work that was done at the grass roots in the first half of 1917 was done by released internees, 'the men of Frongoch' (and of Reading). When in June the important prisoners were released from Lewes (they included not only de Valera but also Cathal Brugha, who had survived multiple wounds during the rising and came

---

[1] Above, p. 221.

back from prison at least as much an *enragé* as when he went in) they came back to a situation that had recently and suddenly simplified itself. The running fight between Sinn Féin and the Liberty League was abandoned, and in late May or early June the two sets of clubs amalgamated under the common name of Sinn Féin.

It still remained, however, to determine what the long-term aims, as distinct from the tactical weapons, of Sinn Féin should be. Most people could agree without too much difficulty that to contest each by-election as it occurred on a programme of abstention from Westminster was the tactic that would be most likely to pay dividends, but there was considerable debate as to whether the constitution of the Ireland of the future should be monarchical or republican. The argument was complicated by the reentry of the I.R.B., albeit in a somewhat ambiguous fashion, into Irish politics. It was ambiguous because some of those who had been members of the I.R.B. at the time of the rising had in the interval come to the conclusion that, since circumstances had changed so radically, a secret conspiratorial movement was no longer either necessary or desirable. This attitude was important because it was shared by leaders as prominent as Cathal Brugha and de Valera, though in the latter's case, it is proper to add, the argument of expediency appears to have been reinforced by scruples of conscience.

There were, however, others who felt quite differently. For them the I.R.B. was as necessary as it had ever been, not merely to instil a new fighting spirit into the slowly reviving Volunteer movement, but also to act as the guardian of the republican ideal. But if the I.R.B. again became important, it is no exaggeration to say that it did so less because of its message than because it had thrown up a leader who in the space of the next five years was to establish a remarkable personal ascendancy over his fellow countrymen. This was Michael Collins. Collins in 1917 was still only 27 years of age and, though he had joined the I.R.B. as far back as 1909, only began to attract attention when he served with some distinction as Joseph Plunkett's aide-de-camp in the G.P.O. Arrested after the rising, he was imprisoned at Frongoch detention camp and at once set about re-creating a branch of the I.R.B. from among the internees.[1] After his release at the end of 1916 he became prominent in the work of the Irish National Aid Association, assisted in the reorganisation of the Volunteer movement, and became a member of the supreme council of the I.R.B. Given his energy, ruthlessness, and undoubted powers of leadership, nothing was more certain than that he would make a major impact on events and would do so primarily as a representative and exponent of the physical force tradition. It was ominously symbolic, therefore, that his first public appearance after his return to Ireland— and the occasion that first directed attention to him as one of the heirs of 1916—should have been in circumstances that strangely recalled Pearse's oration over the grave of O'Donovan Rossa. During the summer of 1917, the government

---

[1] A useful account of the organisation of the internees at Frongoch into military units, and of their recruitment into the I.R.B., is to be found in O'Mahony, *Frongoch*, pp 58–66.

reverted to one of its periodic spasms of coercion, 'proclaiming' meetings, prohibiting the wearing of uniforms or the carrying of arms, and arresting some of its more outspoken critics.[1] Among these was Thomas Ashe who, when sent to Mountjoy jail in Dublin, resorted, as did others, to a hunger-strike. He was subjected to forcible feeding and, apparently as a result of this, died on 25 September 1917. The I.R.B., under the fairly transparent disguise of the Wolfe Tone Memorial Committee, resolved to use his funeral as the opportunity for a major political demonstration. In defiance of the official ban the Volunteers marched, armed and in full uniform, to the graveside and there, after the firing of the ritual three volleys, Collins made the brief speech that more than anything else illustrated the change of style that had come over the movement in the eighteen months since the rising. There was no flamboyance, no rhetoric, no reference to the blood sacrifice, or even to the republic—merely two sentences: 'Nothing additional remains to be said. The volley which we have just heard is the only speech which it is proper to make above the grave of a dead fenian.'[2]

Although the situation continued to be confused until the meeting of the crucial *árd-fheis* of Sinn Féin on 25–6 October 1917, it is clear in retrospect that it had been transformed in the summer of 1917 in three important respects. First, the summoning of the Irish convention had in effect paralysed the parliamentary party at the moment when it most needed to be aggressive and articulate. While the convention remained in being, the party was precluded from defining its position on the future of Ireland and was thus obliged to leave the initiative in the eager hands of more extreme nationalists. Secondly, those extreme nationalists who had been so much at loggerheads with each other were at last showing signs of consolidating under the banner of Sinn Féin, which remained, as hitherto, loyal to Griffith. Finally, the release of the prisoners had begun to result in the emergence of new leaders, of whom de Valera on the political wing, and Collins on the military wing, were already assuming a degree of prominence that marked them out from their fellows.

These three developments, although in one sense they represented clarification, posed certain key questions. What would be the relation of Sinn Féin to the extremer nationalism that was so rapidly striking new roots in the country? Within that extremer nationalism, what would be the role of the I.R.B.? And in the face of this rising competition, what future remained for the constitutionalists of the Irish parliamentary party? None of these questions could be quickly or easily answered, and it would be many months before an answer to the last two could even be attempted. But the *árd-fheis* of October 1917 at least settled—or appeared to settle—the relationship between Sinn Féin and the republicans. It was not an

---

[1] O'Halpin has identified an abrupt change of policy on the part of Duke at this period towards a much tougher line, which marks the beginning of a drift in government policy towards Ireland (*Decline of the union*, pp 140–43).

[2] Piaras Béaslaí, *Michael Collins and the making of a new Ireland* (2 vols, Dublin, 1926), i, 166; according to Béaslaí, Collins first spoke a few words in Irish, which were not recorded. Cf. Mitchell & Ó Snodaigh, *Ir. pol. docs 1916–49*, p. 31, citing *Ir. Independent*, 1 Oct. 1917.

easy matter to achieve accord, and the convention itself was preceded by strenuous negotiation at a committee charged with preparing a constitution for whatever joint body might emerge from the confrontation between the two groups. At one time, indeed, it seemed as if the committee might break up without reaching agreement and it was only at the eleventh hour that de Valera produced the formula that finally gained general assent. It was as follows:

Sinn Féin aims at securing the international recognition of Ireland as an independent Irish republic.
Having achieved that status the Irish people may by referendum freely choose their own form of government.[1]

For both sides this represented a compromise, though it is perhaps not unfair to say that Griffith made the greater sacrifice. Nor was his contribution limited to giving ground on the point of principle. When the árd-fheis met, it was attended by over a thousand delegates, and if he had wished to force a division over the question of the presidency of the reorganised Sinn Féin movement he, as the founder and president in office, would have been certain of a very large vote, possibly a majority. In fact, he (and also the third candidate, Count Plunkett) conceded the presidency to de Valera, an act of magnanimity that did much to set the tone for the unexpected harmony of the proceedings. The definition of the movement's aims that de Valera had devised was accepted with remarkably little dissension. This was probably because a compromise was so exactly what most people present passionately desired at that moment. No one—or at least only the tiniest minority—was thinking then of another insurrection, and although of course the assembly included its quota of dyed-in-the-wool republicans, for most delegates the whole concept of a republic was so vague that it probably amounted to little more than a synonym for independence. Nevertheless, there was an ambiguity about the formula that was to exact a terrible penalty in the not too distant future. The movement, however loosely, had declared its commitment to the republican ideal and in doing so had demonstrated its loyalty to the men of 1916. But if that loyalty were in due course to lead to further fighting in the cause of the republic, then it needed little imagination to see that the second clause of the formula, proclaiming the freedom of the Irish people to choose their own form of government, might ring more than a little hollow.

This, however, was still hidden in the mists of time. The immediate impression of a growing consolidation of the nationalist forces was strengthened by the fact that the day after the Sinn Féin árd-fheis de Valera became president of the Volunteers, thus achieving a notable concentration of power in his own hands. Yet even here a question remained unanswered. How far were the Volunteers really the masters of their own fate, or how far were they about to repeat their earlier experience of being penetrated by the I.R.B.? Since their chief of staff was Cathal Brugha, and since Brugha was now firmly opposed to the traditional role

[1] Macardle, *Ir. republic*, p. 242; Mitchell & Ó Snodaigh, *Ir. pol. docs 1916–49*, p. 35.

of the I.R.B. as a conspiratorial agency, it seemed as if the autonomy of the
Volunteers had been safely preserved. But in fact this was largely an illusion.
History had already begun ominously to repeat itself. Among the high command, Collins was director of organisation, Diarmuid Lynch was director of
communications, and Sean McGarry was general secretary. These appeared to be
innocuous enough appointments, but they were all vital to the efficient functioning of the Volunteers and each of them was held by an officer high in the councils
of the I.R.B.

Yet, despite the consolidation that had been achieved by the autumn of 1917,
the career of the revitalised and transformed Sinn Féin was by no means one of
uninterrupted progress. The winter and spring that followed witnessed three
by-election victories in succession for the Irish parliamentary party (Armagh
South, Waterford, and Tyrone East), and though these could, with some justice,
be explained away in each case as the outcome of exceptionally favourable
conditions for the party, the other feature of that dark season was distinctly more
ominous. It was a time when war weariness was rising and morale was falling—not
surprisingly, it was also a time when in various parts of the country there appeared
unmistakable symptoms of social unrest, expressed in terms of raids on private
houses to secure arms and attacks on graziers with the object of breaking up their
ranches and converting them into tillage farms for small farmers and labourers.
Carried out as they were without instructions from Volunteer headquarters—indeed, in the face of very precise instructions to the contrary—these activities
suggested that discipline among the militants was fragile and that unless some
external pressure reimposed discipline the movement might quite easily degenerate into a series of unrelated and impotent fragments.

The external pressure was punctually applied, and applied, as so often before,
by the British government. When in March 1918 the German offensive on the
western front once more brought the war to a state of crisis, the need for
additional manpower became overwhelming. In such circumstances it was almost
inevitable that ministers should at last brace themselves to grasp the nettle of
conscription for Ireland. For several weeks the cabinet hung on the horns of a
familiar dilemma. If it did not conscript young men in Ireland at a time when it
was conscripting the middle-aged and even the elderly in Britain, then it would
face a storm of criticism at home, accompanied perhaps by serious divisions inside
the coalition.[1] But if it did adopt conscription to find the 150,000 Irishmen it
needed, then it would face such resistance that additional troops would have to
be sent to Ireland to obtain recruits who, when drafted so unceremoniously,
would quite likely be so disaffected as to be virtually useless. Lloyd George's

---

[1] That these were the factors that influenced Lloyd George's decision to introduce conscription for
Ireland is beyond dispute. But see A. J. Ward, 'Lloyd George and the 1918 conscription crisis' in *Hist.
Jn.*, xvii (1974), pp 107–29, for details of cabinet discussions and for the argument that the prime
minister's decision was not so much forced on him by cabinet opinion as based on mistaken
assumptions regarding parliamentary and public opinion.

reaction was characteristic in its mixture of ingenuity and ruthlessness. He was quite prepared to risk bloodshed to get the recruits he wanted, but he believed—and there is no reason to doubt his sincerity—that conscription should be linked with home rule. Up to the beginning of April he seems to have been clinging (against all the odds) to the hope that the Irish convention, which met for the last time on 5 April and published its report a week later, would produce an agreed solution on which he could then act.[1] But even without that unlikely miracle, he was still prepared to offer home rule—including, of course, separate treatment for Ulster—as a legislative initiative to be introduced before conscription began to take effect. In practice, however, little attention was paid to this part of the bargain and the furious debate that ensued was centred mainly on the military service bill that he introduced in the house of commons on 9 April.

The result was a foregone conclusion, though the ultimate consequences could scarcely have been anticipated. The measure itself passed through the house of commons inside a week, despite the protests of the Irish members.[2] What then happened was truly remarkable. Dillon, who had succeeded Redmond as leader of the parliamentary party only the previous month, led his colleagues out of the house, thus putting into practice with startling exactitude one of the central tenets of Sinn Féin. Back in Ireland, the party joined in an anti-conscription conference on 18 April at the Mansion House, Dublin, which was attended by representatives of virtually the whole spectrum of Irish nationalism, including as it did not only Dillon, but also Devlin, de Valera, Griffith, Healy, William O'Brien of the All-for-Ireland League, and the other William O'Brien, the labour leader. The conference rapidly agreed on a pledge, drafted by de Valera, which bound those who took it to resist conscription 'by the most effective means at their disposal'.[3] This was, it is true, significantly different from the terminology used by the standing committee of the Irish bishops, who publicly proclaimed that the Irish people had a right to resist conscription 'by every means that are consonant with the laws of God'.[4] Not surprisingly, in the fever of the moment the qualification introduced by the last part of the clause went largely unnoticed. What was noticed, or assumed, was that bishops and laity were united on this issue, and the pledge was accordingly taken by many thousands of people outside the chapel doors on Sunday, 21 April. It was backed by action of a more prosaic kind. The trade unionists were as opposed to compulsory military service as the clergy or the politicians, and on 23 April they organised a one-day general strike, which, outside unionist areas of the north, was universally observed. Since, at the same time, 'committees of defence' were being organised at the parish level, and a National Defence Fund was being launched by the Mansion House Committee,

[1] Above, p. 229.   [2] 8 Geo. V, c. 5 (18 Apr. 1918).
[3] *Speeches and statements by Éamon de Valera, 1917–73*, ed. Maurice Moynihan (Dublin and New York, 1980), p. 13; Mitchell & Ó Snodaigh, *Ir. pol. docs 1916–49*, p. 42.
[4] Mitchell & Ó Snodaigh, op. cit., pp 42–3; for a dissentient opinion see Walter McDonald, *Some ethical questions of peace and war with special reference to Ireland* (London, 1919).

it was evident that a formidable resistance to the imposition of military service was already building up.

This unanimity was undeniably impressive, but it was also highly precarious. There had been no real meeting of minds between Sinn Féin and the parliamentary party, only an *ad hoc* alliance in the face of a common peril. And even that *ad hoc* alliance survived for barely a fortnight before it was blown apart by yet another by-election, this time in East Cavan. What gave East Cavan its particular significance was partly that Griffith decided to contest the seat himself, and partly the fact that the election was fought in circumstances peculiarly favourable to the Sinn Féin cause. Griffith's candidature virtually ensured that the fight would be especially bitter, since he had long been a virulent critic of the parliamentary party. Even with the conscription crisis still looming over the country, he made no concessions to what he plainly regarded as a fictitious or unnatural unity. Before there could be real unity, he declared, the party 'would have to accept the Sinn Féin programme of absolute independence for Ireland, abstention from the British parliament, and that the peace conference was the place where freedom was to be won'. Since Dillon predictably denounced this programme as 'a policy of lunatics', it was clear that the common ground that these two irreconcilable factions had appeared to find at the Mansion House was little better than a mirage.[1]

Yet the decisive stroke was delivered, almost with the inevitability of Greek tragedy, by the British government. Impressed, however reluctantly, by the strength and seeming universality of the anti-conscription movement in all of Ireland save the north-east corner, the cabinet deemed it expedient to take certain precautions. Early in May Field-marshal Lord French replaced Lord Wimborne as lord lieutenant. He went to Dublin with wide powers to suppress disorder, and had in fact told the cabinet before his departure that he proposed to issue a proclamation and arrest anyone against whom evidence of 'intriguing' could be produced. The cabinet approved the terms of this proclamation on 15 May and on 18 May it was published in Ireland. On the night of 17 May virtually the whole of the Sinn Féin leadership (with the vital exceptions of Collins and Brugha) were seized, though it is possible that they awaited seizure, well knowing the effect this would have on public opinion. The proclamation itself, however, was sufficiently explosive to create unaided all the impact that was needed, for the main burden of its message was that fresh coercive action was necessary because the government had become aware that Sinn Féin had been engaged in a treasonable conspiracy with the Germans.

On the face of it, and in the conditions then prevailing in Ireland, the very notion of a 'German plot' was so absurd that to most people then, and to most historians since, it was explicable only as a manœuvre to justify arrests that were in reality intended to paralyse the Irish resistance to conscription. In view of the

[1] Lyons, *Dillon*, pp 438–9.

evidence we now have of the cabinet discussions and the briefing of Lord French, this still seems the most probable explanation, but it is proper to record that even though nothing was uncovered that could remotely be described as an 'official' Sinn Féin liaison with the Germans, there had undoubtedly been contacts with them of one kind or another. Devoy in America, for example, had repaired his lines of communication with Germany only a few weeks after the collapse of the rising, and from that time forward there had been persistent rumours that arms shipments were either on their way or had failed to arrive, and that U-boats were frequent visitors to remote points off the west coast of Ireland. But apart from all this somewhat nebulous speculation there was one identifiable incident when a survivor from Casement's Irish brigade, James Dowling, was actually arrested in Galway after having landed from a submarine. It is probable that his mission was exploratory and that the Germans themselves had sent him to see whether any prospect for a rising actually existed. He is said to have carried a code message for Collins, but if the latter ever replied to it, which is doubtful, the advice he would have given would surely have been negative.

The by-product of the 'German plot' was that Griffith from his prison cell became a far more formidable contender for East Cavan than when he had been a free man. 'Put him in to get him out' was the slogan, and put him in the electors did, with a majority of over 1,200 votes in a total poll of 6,376. But this victory itself was only a symbol of something far more profound and dangerous. The East Cavan election gave outward expression to what Dillon, with his usual perception, called the people's 'desperate hatred of L.G. and the government'.[1] This hatred, compounded of an immediate dread of conscription and a frustration derived from many months of uncertainty, was intensified by the comprehensive banning early in July of the Volunteers, the Gaelic League, and any organisation that could be labelled as Sinn Féin in its sympathies. The effect of this was not to destroy Sinn Féin, merely to drive it underground and so to make it more dangerous.

Indeed, the very effectiveness of revolutionary nationalism in the struggle that now lay only a short distance ahead owed much to the experience that was, as it were, thrust on the movement by the government's efforts to suppress it. Since not all the leaders had been swept into the internment net, those who survived were able, provided they avoided detection and arrest, not merely to keep Sinn Féin and the Volunteers intact, but actually to expand their following in the country. From these months of more or less secret activity dates the emergence of a group of men who were to play a major part in the transition from passive to active resistance. Foremost among them was Collins, who, together with his I.R.B. responsibilities, combined in his person the Volunteer posts of adjutant-general and director of organisation. In these capacities he developed what in the future was to be almost his own personal instrument of power—an intelligence service that continued to penetrate not only key government departments but

[1] Ibid., p. 441.

even the police themselves. The training, discipline, and recruitment of the Volunteers, on the other hand, was largely the work of Brugha (chief of staff), his deputy Richard Mulcahy, and Rory O'Connor (director of engineering). Propaganda was the responsibility of an able journalist, Piaras Béaslaí, and his editorship of the Volunteer journal, *An tÓglach*, the first number of which appeared on 15 August 1918, must be accounted a major factor not only in whipping up opposition to conscription, but in giving the widespread anti-British sentiment of the time a coloration of almost hysterical violence that augured ill for the future. Finally, and no less important, the work of political indoctrination was indefatigably carried forward by one of Collins's closest friends, the Dublin tailor Harry Boland, who was largely responsible for the immensely significant fact that during 1918 the membership of Sinn Féin clubs in the country grew from 66,270 to 112,020.

The growth of Sinn Féin as a political force was an immensely significant fact because, although all this furious activity was ostensibly directed against conscription, that particular threat had lost nearly all its terrors by the summer of 1918 when it had become virtually certain that the triumph of the allies could not be much longer delayed. In order to understand the epochal importance of the semi-underground movement that was developing such momentum in the last months of the war, we have to remember that, as the ceasefire approached, parties and organisations of every political persuasion began to look forward to the general election that was to follow the ending of the war, in the knowledge that this would be the crucial test of how far the country had changed its allegiance in the thirty months that had elapsed since the Easter rising.

The result surpassed all expectations. Although the leader of the parliamentary party, Dillon, was full of fight, his party went into battle in a deeply defeatist mood and he himself anticipated a serious reverse, though scarcely the virtual annihilation that took place. Sinn Féin fought on a four-point programme that proposed, first, withdrawal from Westminster; secondly, 'making use of any and every means available to render impotent the power of England to hold Ireland in subjection by military force or otherwise';[1] thirdly, the establishment of a constituent assembly in Ireland; and finally, an appeal to the peace conference to endorse Irish independence. The manifesto in which these points appeared was heavily censored, many of the Sinn Féin candidates were still in jail, and the electoral machinery of the organisation was much hampered by interference from the authorities. Yet despite these drawbacks—and compensating for them by what its victims described, with some justification, as unabashed intimidation or, alternatively, impersonation—Sinn Féin won a shattering victory. On the eve of the election (polling took place on 14 December) Dillon's party had held sixty-eight seats, William O'Brien's following and a few other independents ten, the unionists eighteen, and Sinn Féin seven. After the election (the result was

---

[1] Mitchell & Ó Snodaigh, *Ir. pol. docs 1916–49*, p. 48.

declared on 28 December; redistribution had increased the total of Irish seats from
103 to 105), the unionists had increased to twenty-six; the O'Brienites and
independents had disappeared; the parliamentary party's total had sunk almost
unbelievably to six seats of which four were border constituencies in which, by
agreement, there was no Sinn Féin challenge; and the remainder, seventy-three
in all (held, actually, by sixty-nine candidates as there were several cases of double
election), had been captured by Sinn Féin. It is true that on closer inspection this
was not quite the landslide it seemed at first glance. Over a third of the electorate
did not vote, and of those who did vote just under 48 per cent voted for Sinn
Féin (though, to balance this, it needs to be recorded that in twenty-three seats
Sinn Féin candidates were returned unopposed). But perhaps the most significant
feature of the election was that for very many voters this was their first chance to
go to the polls—indeed, the Irish electorate actually rose from about 740,000 in
1910 to just under 2 million in 1918. Much of the increase naturally occurred in
the boroughs, and it seems highly probable that this worked to the advantage of
Sinn Féin. Such, at any rate, is a reasonable inference to be drawn from the fact
that if the predominantly unionist six counties of the north-east be excluded, then
the Sinn Féin proportion of the vote rises from 47.7 per cent to almost 65 per
cent. In this connection, it is relevant to mention that in certain constituencies
the candidates of the parliamentary party actually increased their votes as
compared with the previous general election in 1910. That this availed them
nothing was primarily due to the great increase in the size of the electorate, of
which a large proportion presumably voted for Sinn Féin,[1] but also, to a certain
extent, to the fact that organised labour, after much hesitation, decided not to
stand as a separate party so as to leave the main issue—self-determination—free
of other complications. Electoral statistics are usually capable of more than one
interpretation and December 1918 is no exception. However, reservations about
the size and distribution of the Sinn Féin vote pale into insignificance beside the
effect of the election in terms of the transfer of power. Sinn Féin was able, as
never before, to claim a mandate for its programme on the basis of massive
support in the constituencies. But what it would do with that mandate, or how
the mandate would even be defined, remained to be seen.

[1] The assumption that the newly enfranchised electors voted mainly for Sinn Féin has been
questioned in David Fitzpatrick, 'The geography of Irish nationalism, 1910–1921' in Past & Present,
no. 80 (1978), pp 113–44; and see Garvin, Evolution of Ir. nationalist politics, pp 118–22.

CHAPTER XI

The war of independence, 1919–21

F. S. L. LYONS

WHEN in January 1919 the newly elected Sinn Féin members refused to take their seats at Westminster and instead assembled in Dublin, they were of course carrying out to the letter the doctrine of abstention as Griffith had formulated it nearly twenty years earlier.[1] This much was plain even at the time. What was harder to determine was whether the body that assembled in Dublin was merely acting out some kind of pseudo-historical charade, or whether it really meant business. Certainly, it did not seem very impressive when it met as Dáil Éireann for the first time on 21 January. Invitations had gone out to the members elected for all constituencies, but, as was to be expected, these were ignored by the unionists and by the survivors of the parliamentary party. Since no fewer than thirty-four of the newly elected Sinn Féin members were still in prison, and eight others absent for various reasons, the number of members present at this first meeting was only twenty-seven, all of them representatives of Sinn Féin.

No time was lost in adopting a provisional constitution that was redolent of the newly fashionable doctrine of popular sovereignty. There was to be an executive government, consisting of a prime minister (*príomh-aire*) chosen by the dáil, and ministers of finance, home affairs, foreign affairs, and defence, nominated by the prime minister but subject to ratification by the dáil, which also had full powers of legislation and absolute control of finance. At this same constituent session, which lasted only about two hours, the dáil solemnly approved three documents of major importance. The first was a declaration of independence, which the dáil ratified as establishing the republic that had been proclaimed in 1916. The second was a 'message to the free nations of the world', which demanded that Ireland should have the right to confront Britain at the peace conference 'in order that the civilised world, having judged between English wrong and Irish right, may guarantee to Ireland its permanent support for the maintenance of her national independence'.[2] Delegates to the peace conference were actually appointed, and later danced attendance for a considerable period in the corridors of Versailles. This, however, was a fantasy world that had little or no connection with reality. The great powers had more urgent preoccupations, and the combination of

---

[1] Above, p. 106.   [2] *Dáil Éireann proc. 1919–21*, p. 20 (21 Jan. 1919).

American indifference and British veto proved conclusive. Nothing came, or ever looked like coming, out of the appeal to the free nations.[1]

Much the same has to be said of the third document that the dáil approved. This was the Democratic Programme—an attempt to translate into specific terms the rather vague social ideas of Pearse without going so far as to engage in any commitment to the more precise Marxism of Connolly, whose name, significantly, was not mentioned in the document. That this was so, and that the degree of socialistic commitment was so slight as to be almost non-existent, reflected the Democratic Programme's curious genesis. In its original form—drafted mainly, it would appear, by the labour leader Thomas Johnson—it had been more explicitly socialist, but discussions of the draft between representatives of Sinn Féin and labour had disclosed so much disagreement—partly on ideological grounds, but partly also because extreme nationalists, and especially Collins and the I.R.B., feared any deflection of effort away from the goal of political independence—that Seán T. O'Kelly was deputed, only a few hours before the meeting of the dáil, to produce a modified version. Even this version, however, did declare that the nation's sovereignty extended to all its material wealth and resources and asserted that 'all right to private property must be subordinated to the public right and welfare'. Various proposals were included in the document for exploiting these resources for the common good, but the phrases that attracted most attention and, in retrospect, most ironic criticism, were those that pledged the government of the republic 'to make provision for the physical, mental, and spiritual wellbeing of the children', and 'to secure that no child shall suffer hunger or cold from lack of food, clothing, or shelter, but that all shall be provided with the means and facilities requisite for their proper education and training as citizens of a free and Gaelic Ireland'.[2] In reality, the fears of Collins and his friends that this promised social revolution might get out of hand were quite unfounded. So far from getting out of hand, the social revolution never even got off the ground. For his part, de Valera announced the postponement of much of the Democratic Programme on 12 April, asserting that 'he had never made any promise to Labour, because, while the enemy was within their gates, the immediate question was to get possession of their country'.[3] The pressures of the struggle for independence were too intense, the aftermath of that struggle was too divisive, the labour movement was too weak, the social structure of the country too rigidly conservative, for the Democratic Programme to be more than a pious gesture,

[1] Efforts by the dáil to obtain international recognition by establishing a network of envoys, to promote its interests in the major European cities, were also largely unsuccessful. This early initiative was, however, important in forming the nucleus of a diplomatic corps after 1921. For details of these early envoys, see Dermot Keogh, *Ireland and Europe, 1919–1989* (Cork and Dublin, 1990), pp 7–10); early relations with the Vatican are further explored in id., *The Vatican, the bishops and Irish politics, 1919–1939* (Cambridge, 1986).

[2] *Dáil Éireann proc. 1919–21*, pp 22–3 (21 Jan. 1919).

[3] For a discussion of the varying fortunes of the labour movement at this period, see David Fitzpatrick, *Politics and Irish life, 1913–1921* (Dublin, 1979), pp 254–67; the words quoted above appear on p. 263.

which the post-revolutionary generation felt no impulsion to transform into any kind of recognisable reality.

One final point needs to be made about this first session of Dáil Éireann before considering the events that were to give the assembly much greater authority and relevance. It has sometimes been remarked that because so many of the major figures were absent on this occasion, the dáil behaved irresponsibly and committed itself to positions, notably with regard to the republic, that it would later find embarrassingly difficult to maintain. There is some truth in this, but it would be unwise to press the accusation too far. For although it was certainly significant that the chairman, Cathal Brugha, was a diehard republican, this was hardly true of the membership as a whole. On the contrary, it would not be unfair to say that for many members, and certainly for those who had elected them, the republic to which so much attention was devoted on 21 January was an aspiration or ideal, rather than an immediately realisable objective. All present were certainly committed to independence as the goal to the achievement of which they were dedicated, but precisely what form that independence would take was still for some—though not for all—as open a question as when de Valera had produced his exquisitely ambiguous formula at the *árd-fheis* of 1917.[1]

Meanwhile, between 22 January and 1 April, when the dáil reassembled, the situation was radically changed, first by a series of prison escapes so blatant as to lead an impartial observer to suspect a degree of official connivance, and next by the government's decision to release all the remaining prisoners in March. The consequence was that the second session of the dáil, which was attended by fifty-two members, was much more representative than the first and was also better placed to institute constructive policies. De Valera was elected prime minister or 'president' and, the constitution having been amended to permit of a larger executive, he submitted the names of eight ministers (apart from himself) to the dáil for ratification. These were Griffith (home affairs and deputy-president), Collins (finance), Brugha (defence), Count Plunkett (foreign affairs), Countess Markievicz (labour), W. T. Cosgrave (local government), and Eoin MacNeill (industries). In addition provision was made for non-ministerial directors of agriculture (to which Robert Barton was appointed) and of propaganda—a post held successively by Laurence Ginnell (a convert from the parliamentary party), Desmond FitzGerald (after Ginnell was imprisoned in May 1919), and Erskine Childers (during FitzGerald's imprisonment in early 1921).

Particular importance attached to these nominations in view of the fact that de Valera had set his mind, almost from the moment of his escape from Lincoln jail, on visiting America in order to raise funds and secure support for the cause. Even though it can scarcely have been envisaged at the time that he would be away for as long as turned out to be the case—he did not return until Christmas 1920—the fact of his absence threw a heavy responsibility on his cabinet colleagues. This

[1] Above, p. 233.

was intensified when on 12 September 1919 the government finally made up its mind to take the dáil seriously enough to suppress it. Thereafter the assembly had to meet in secret, and inevitably the occasions when it could meet grew fewer and fewer. Thus, whereas there were six sessions comprising fourteen actual meetings in 1919, there were three sessions in 1920 and three in 1921, which together produced a total of only seven actual meetings. The result was that a great deal came to depend on the initiative of individual ministers, and the sometimes grandiose policies of the dáil flourished or dwindled according to the capacity of those who were responsible for carrying them out. The most remarkable successes were, however, registered in four of the most important areas—finance, agriculture, local government, and the courts. In the first of these, Collins's exuberant energy turned an unlikely gamble into a resounding achievement. Faced with the task of raising a 'national loan' he produced in a remarkably short space of time the sum of close on £358,000. Barton's work in agriculture was less dramatic, but possibly more permanent. Having set up a land bank to advance loans to farmers so as to keep the process of land purchase in operation, he followed this with the establishment of a land commission to administer a scheme of land acquisition and distribution in the west of Ireland; this, which was very much in the tradition of the congested districts board, laid the foundation for the more extensive reforms that were carried through after 1921.

Perhaps the most spectacular results were obtained, however, by the minister for local government, W. T. Cosgrave, and his forceful assistant, a rising politician named Kevin O'Higgins, whose formidable reputation owed its first beginnings to his work in this department. Their aim was to persuade the county and borough councils to transfer allegiance from the official administration—which still, of course, purported to function as if nothing had happened— to Sinn Féin. They were considerably assisted by the fact that the local election results of January and June 1920 reflected the national swing (outside the north-east) that had first been registered by the general election in 1918. The outcome was that at every level of administration—from the county council and corporation at one end of the scale to rural district councils and poor law boards at the other—Sinn Féin secured a dominant majority. When, therefore, the dáil recommended in the summer of 1920 that the councils should break off their connections with the local government board and come under the authority of the dáil ministry, the vast majority outside north-east Ulster agreed to do so.

Side by side with this massive erosion of Dublin Castle government went the creation of the so-called Sinn Féin courts. Intended at first to arbitrate in difficult cases, and especially to deal with disputes involving land, they proliferated and developed to such an extent that during 1920 the dáil found it necessary to arrange for a systematic hierarchy of courts, which at once began to function up and down the country to such good effect that the legal profession itself gave it *de facto* recognition in the sense of turning a blind eye whenever barristers and solicitors appeared before these courts. Despite their prohibition by the government, several hundred of them were functioning at various levels by the summer of 1921.[1]

It is clear that the experiments here briefly described had a collective importance far beyond that of the exertions of individual dáil ministries. What was gradually taking shape, especially during the critical year of 1920, was a determined effort to supplant the official administration in as many areas of government as possible, and in doing so to make good the claim of Dáil Éireann to be a true national parliament with fully functioning departments directly responsible to it. Sooner or later the British government would have to meet this challenge to its authority. It was, moreover, not merely a challenge directed towards taking over the machinery and trappings of power, it was also a deliberate bid to wrest from the authorities their control over law and order. It had been ominously significant that, on the very day the dáil had first met, two policemen of the Royal Irish Constabulary were shot dead at Soloheadbeg by a group of Tipperary Volunteers led by Seumas Robinson, Dan Breen, and Sean Treacy, all three of whom were destined to become notable guerrilla commanders in the struggle that was coming steadily closer. The Soloheadbeg incident and others like it that occurred during 1919 were not, it is true, intended to be the first shots in a general war of independence, though that is what they turned out to be. Indeed, the government itself, both then and for long afterwards, refused to attach the name of war to the wave of attacks on police barracks that developed. On political grounds, it was no doubt undesirable to enter into a state of war with a republic that officially did not exist. Nevertheless, as the attacks mounted and the already sagging morale of the police deteriorated still further it soon became necessary to reinforce them, and in doing so to treat the Irish 'troubles' as a war *de facto* if not *de jure*.

The first serious indication of a change in official attitudes[2] was the recruitment at the beginning of 1920 of the body of men who rapidly became notorious as the Black and Tans. The name, deriving from a famous hunt in the south of Ireland, was attached to them because a supply shortage obliged them at first to wear a mixture of khaki with the rifle-green clothing and black equipment of the R.I.C.

---

[1] While the success of the dáil departments in overseeing the transfer of local allegiance to unofficial civil and judicial authorities is generally acknowledged, see Fitzpatrick, *Politics & Ir. life*, pp 174–97, for a consideration of the extent to which dáil policy consisted primarily of 'propagandist gestures' and in maintaining the semblance of central control over local initiatives. Fitzpatrick argues that the change of allegiance was due to the initiatives taken by local Sinn Féin clubs rather than to any directive from Dublin, and that local government functioned successfully in proportion to the ingenuity and persistence of local Sinn Féin leaders. With reference in particular to County Clare, he also examines the merits of the Sinn Féin courts in their administration of justice, the weakness of central control over local factional influences, and the inability of the courts to dispense punitive justice effectively because of the continued presence of the civilian and military forces of the official administration.

[2] A discussion of the personal frictions and disagreements about the formulation and execution of policy among officials within the Irish administration, and also of the lack of attention to, and clear direction of, Irish policy by the British cabinet at this time, can be found in O'Halpin, *Decline of the union*, pp 185–207.

The Black and Tans were not soldiers, though they included many ex-soldiers in their ranks. They were police and, in the beginning at least, were recruited by the same rules as ordinary members of the R.I.C. Their numbers are difficult to gauge, since contemporary estimates do not usually distinguish between the regular police and their supplementary recruits. Originally, the latter were merely intended to fill the vacancies—about 1,500—that existed in the R.I.C. at the beginning of 1920, but as the situation grew worse their numbers rapidly increased. It has been estimated that between 1 January 1920 and the end of August 1922, when the R.I.C. was formally disbanded, about 12,000 men were enrolled, of whom about 7,000 seem actually to have been taken into the service.[1] It would have been surprising if in the unsettled conditions of the post-war world the force had not attracted a considerable number of ruthless and reckless young men to whom neither property nor life were particularly sacred. Whatever predisposition towards brutality they may have had was certainly likely to have been strengthened by their experiences in Ireland. Constantly under threat of attack by rifle or bomb, subject to frequent and damaging ambushes, often unable to identify their enemies, their nerves at full stretch day and night, it is not surprising that the hallmarks of their behaviour were drunkenness and indiscriminate violence. Hating the population among whom they found themselves, they attracted only hatred in return, and thus began a vicious cycle of violence to which there seemed no logical end.

These reinforcements, which brought the R.I.C. from about 10,000 in mid-1920 to over 14,000 a year later, did not constitute the whole of the British forces in Ireland, nor even the whole of the R.I.C. itself. In the summer of 1920 a second, smaller body—consisting for the most part of ex-officers—was recruited as the auxiliary division of the R.I.C. Popularly known, and detested, as 'the Auxies', they amounted to about 770 in late October 1920 and were nearly double that number by July 1921. Contemporary views about them were less unanimous than about the 'Tans', but they seem to have been just as uninhibited in action as the latter; and their commander, Brigadier-general F. P. Crozier, though himself scarcely the most reliable of officers, provided his own comment when he resigned his post rather than go on leading 'a drunken and insubordinate body of men'.[2] When to these somewhat unusual policemen is added a military establishment that brought the combined security forces up to at least 40,000, it will be clear that a great expenditure of effort and of manpower was centred on Ireland in the years when the struggle was at its most intense.

Against these numbers the forces available to the dáil were not only fewer, but also generally less well armed and equipped. The full strength of the Volunteers

---

[1] Cf. Charles Townshend, *The British campaign in Ireland, 1919–1921: the development of political and military policies* (Oxford, 1975), pp 209–12.

[2] In *Ireland since the famine* (London, 1971), F. S. L. Lyons cited Crozier's *Impressions and recollections* (London, 1930); but both drunkenness and indiscipline figure more largely in Crozier's *Ireland for ever* (London, 1932; reprint, Bath, 1971).

may have been about 15,000, but this total was never fully deployed at any one time, since the tactic was to use only small bodies of men unless in quite exceptional circumstances. The active elements perhaps amounted to as little as 5,000, and Collins, whose expert opinion is not lightly to be disregarded, reckoned the regular 'working' force to be perhaps only 3,000. Small as this force was, it presented the dáil with a difficult problem of control, which, indeed, was not really solved while the fighting lasted and was to persist even into the post-revolutionary period. It has to be remembered not only that from their earliest days the Irish Volunteers had been an autonomous force, but also that after 1916 (as before it) they had been deeply infiltrated by the I.R.B., whose own constitution laid down that the supreme council of the I.R.B. was the sole government of the republic 'until Ireland secures absolute national independence and a permanent republican government is established'.[1] From the point of view of those who were seeking to make Dáil Éireann the sole government of the republic—some of whom were in any event antagonistic to the I.R.B. as a secret conspiratorial agency—it was axiomatic that the Volunteers ought to be brought under civilian control as quickly as possible.

Accordingly, on 20 August 1919 Brugha, as minister of defence, persuaded the dáil to require of each of its members and officials, and also of the Volunteers, that they take an oath of allegiance to the state, swearing that they would 'support and defend the Irish Republic and the government of the Irish Republic, which is Dáil Éireann, against all enemies, foreign and domestic . . .'.[2] The Volunteers took this oath as individuals, but their organisation never formally ratified the change in status that the oath implied, and which was exemplified by the gradual dropping of the title 'Volunteers' and the substitution of that of 'Irish Republican Army' or, more familiarly, 'I.R.A.' Since those members of the force who were also members of the I.R.B. had already taken an oath to the latter organisation, there was obviously cause here for confusion if not for suspicion. It was unfortunately complicated by personal frictions between Collins and his friends—who were indispensable in their military and political roles, but none the less remained I.R.B. men to the core—and ministers such as Brugha or, later, Austin Stack, whose suspicion of the I.R.B. seems to have been paralleled by a certain jealousy of the prestige that soon surrounded the name and exploits of Collins.

These disagreements rankled and were presently to have important political repercussions, but it does not seem that they interfered seriously, or even directly, with the conduct of the war. The war itself, indeed, was such a sporadic and fragmented affair that it often appeared to owe more to the initiative of local

---

[1] Quoted in H. B. C. Pollard, *The secret societies of Ireland: their rise and progress* (London, 1922), p. 299, where the constitution (revised after the 1916 rising) is mistakenly dated 1914 (Leon Ó Broin, *Revolutionary underground: the story of the Irish Republican Brotherhood, 1858–1924* (Dublin, 1976), p. 176).

[2] *Dáil Éireann proc. 1919–21*, p. 151 (20 Aug. 1919).

commanders than to any central direction.[1] During 1919 it scarcely deserved the name 'war' at all. At that time the prime targets were the police, for the obvious reasons that on them depended the rule of law and that from them could be extracted the arms and ammunition that the insurgents so urgently needed. Even so their casualties were not unduly heavy at the outset. Eighteen R.I.C. men were killed between 1 May and the end of 1919, but during the winter of 1919–20 the operations of the I.R.A. underwent a significant change. In December there was an attempt to assassinate Lord French, which only narrowly failed, and about the same time Collins unleashed his special agents—the 'squad' as they were called—for the purpose of shooting down the G-men, the detectives of the Dublin Metropolitan Police, whose expert knowledge of the I.R.A. made them a special hazard.

The pattern of assassination and counter-assassination, once embarked on, has an ugly tendency to repeat itself almost indefinitely. As the year 1920 progressed, such incidents multiplied and each side could claim both to have suffered and to have inflicted atrocities, of which the killing of Tomás Mac Curtáin, lord mayor of Cork and commandant of the Cork No. 1 Brigade of the I.R.A.—widely assumed to have been carried out by the police—and that of an elderly magistrate, Alan Bell, in broad daylight in the Dublin streets—known to have been carried out by the I.R.A. because of his investigation of Sinn Féin funds—are only two of the more notorious incidents.

The strengthening of the R.I.C., to which reference has already been made, was an obvious reaction by the government to this worsening situation, but it was not the only one. Lloyd George still nursed the fragile hope that he could successfully combine coercion with a constitutional settlement. To that end he introduced in 1920 yet another variation on the theme of home rule. It was significantly different from all its predecessors in that it actually embodied the principle of partition instead of reserving this, as hitherto, for special amending legislation.[2] It was proposed to set up two parliaments in Ireland, one for the six counties in the north-east and one for the rest of the country. The powers to be entrusted to these legislatures were not extensive, and responsibility, not merely for imperial matters, but also for financial control, remained with the parliament at Westminster in which it was envisaged that Irishmen would still be represented, though in reduced numbers. In the hope that partition might not be the be-all and end-all of the Irish question, the bill also contained provision for setting up a council of

---

[1] For a useful analysis of the question of G.H.Q.'s direction and control of the Volunteer campaign, see Townshend, *Political violence*, pp 332–40, particularly his comments on the limitations of I.R.B. influence, on the importance of 'the process of military professionalisation', and on the three distinct phases that he identifies in the 1919–21 war: a long period of low-level operations in 1919, driving in the outposts of the R.I.C.; attacks on larger police posts in the first half of 1920; and, after the restoration of order act in Aug. 1920, the formation of full-time I.R.A. fighting units.

[2] The process by which the decision on partition was reached by the cabinet's 'Irish situation committee' (appointed in Oct. 1919 and chaired by Sir Walter Long) is given in detail in Mansergh, *Unresolved question*, pp 116–40.

Ireland, consisting of representatives of the two local parliaments. The council was to be entrusted with certain modest powers and, in an ideal world, was to have been the bridge over which the two parts of the island would in time advance towards reunification.[1]

The world, alas, remained obstinately less than ideal. Although the measure passed into law as the government of Ireland act by the end of 1920,[2] it was entirely ignored by Sinn Féin except for the purpose of staging the elections to the second dáil in the summer of 1921. The new act was accepted by the Ulster unionists without affection, but as the best guarantee they were likely to get of the continuing connection with Britain, which, as always, was the rock on which they stood. They acquiesced in an 'Ulster' of six counties rather than the historic nine, because that was the maximum in which a permanent protestant and unionist majority could be assured, though even in the six counties it was certain that there would be a substantial and fractious catholic-nationalist minority. Just how far the government of Ireland act was from being an ideal solution was demonstrated by serious disturbances in the north while the legislation was on its way through parliament. The tense and difficult balance between the communities was violently upset by I.R.A. attacks on the police and on protestant workmen, and these in turn provoked protestant reprisals that led to the killing of over sixty people and the wounding of some 200 others. Many catholic families were driven from their homes and, since the Ulster Volunteers were simultaneously being reorganised in response to Sir Edward Carson's promise to use them to defend the province against Sinn Féin, it was plain that the drift towards civil war, which had only been arrested by the all-embracing European crisis in 1914, had now again begun to be resumed, this time in even more unpromising circumstances.[3]

---

[1] There has been some difference of opinion on the primary motivation behind the 'council of Ireland' provision of the 1920 act. Richard Murphy has argued that, while the inclusion of the clause was a sign of British hopes for eventual reunification, the concession to the Ulster unionist lobby of a six-county boundary, rather than the nine-county option originally recommended by Long's committee, made the prospect of reunification less likely. He further contends that, after a deliberately long delay in finalising the text of the bill, the 'council of Ireland' clause had become in Sept. 1920 'a harmless sop to nationalist sentiment', and was conceded only in the certain knowledge that it would never be used (Murphy, 'Walter Long and the making of the government of Ireland act' in *I.H.S.*, xxv, no. 97 (May 1986), pp 86–94. Mansergh (*Unresolved question*, pp 129–31) points to evidence that one of the principal aims of British government policy was to produce a good effect in the dominions as well as the U.S.A., and that this object could not be achieved by anything short of a measure paving the way for a single parliament. He argues further that provisions for facilitating reunification were ultimately subordinated to the practical consideration of meeting Ulster unionist wishes on the question of the area to be within their jurisdiction. Ronan Fanning has argued that the act of 1920 was fashioned with Britain's 'tactical position before the world' (according to a comment of Lord Birkenhead) in mind, and that the 'Ulstercentricity' of the government of Ireland act reveals it to be 'not so much a sincere attempt to settle the Irish question as a sincere attempt to settle the Ulster question' (see his 'Anglo–Irish relations: partition and the British dimension in historical perspective' in *Irish Studies in International Affairs*, ii, no. 1 (1985), pp 1–20).

[2] 10 & 11 Geo. V, c. 67 (23 Dec. 1920).

[3] See Jonathan Bardon, *A history of Ulster* (Belfast, 1992), pp 466–74.

That the Ulster problem was not seen in its true dimensions by either London or Dublin seems obvious in retrospect. To contemporaries it was not obvious because the larger problem of Anglo–Irish relations, of which it was but a part, dominated the thoughts and energies of soldiers and politicians alike. In its essentials it was a deceptively simple problem—to defeat the I.R.A. and to destroy the alternative government that Dáil Éireann had set up. In order to do this it was felt necessary to intensify the ordinary methods of coercion. We have already seen that the year 1920 marked the introduction of the Black and Tans and the Auxiliaries. It was a year that witnessed also an almost blanket suppression of organisations suspected of helping or giving allegiance to Sinn Féin, numerous arrests of individuals suspected of political 'crimes', and a vigorous attempt to stamp out revolutionary propaganda. Yet though these measures caused great hardship and furious resentment, they did not succeed in their purpose. For this there were two main reasons. One was that the I.R.A. found itself in the ideal guerrilla situation where over much of Ireland it was assured of support, whether active or passive, whether willing or fearful, from the civilian population. This alone would have made it difficult if not impossible for the troops and the police to pin down and exterminate their enemies. But here the second reason for the comparative ineffectiveness of the measures came into play. By an all-out assault and the employment of uninhibited methods of frightfulness, from which innocent bystanders were likely to suffer as much as the actual combatants, the forces of the crown could no doubt have brought their superior resources to bear and won a kind of victory. But apart from the obvious political fact that to make a desert and call it peace was in no sense a solution, the British government had to face the realisation that the Irish struggle was a struggle in the mind as well as on the ground. And that struggle in the mind was being won, or so it seemed, by Sinn Féin. Despite enormous difficulties, their propaganda continued to reach the outside world—often through no more substantial medium than the cyclostyled pages of the *Irish Bulletin*—and this powerfully reinforced the opinion already being formed independently by many journalists, M.P.s, churchmen, and public figures, that the war in Ireland was brutal and degrading and one that could not possibly bring honour to those engaged in it. The mobilisation of public opinion in Britain against coercion was necessarily a slow business and no overnight pressure to end hostilities could reasonably be expected, but in the long run British revulsion from the struggle was to play an important part in the restoration of peace.[1]

In the short run, however, the war not only continued, but continued with increased momentum. In the latter part of 1920 the restoration of order in Ireland act[2] gave the general officer commanding-in-chief in Ireland, General Sir Nevil Macready, very wide powers to arrest and imprison without trial anyone suspected of Sinn Féin connections, to try prisoners by court martial, and to

[1] For pressure on British opinion, see below, pp 684–5.
[2] 10 & 11 Geo. V, c. 31 (9 Aug. 1920).

institute military inquiries, rather than coroners' inquests, into violent deaths. In addition, the military were, if not actually encouraged, permitted to employ reprisals against terrorism. There was much academic debate at the time about the difference between 'official' and 'unofficial' reprisals, but there seems little doubt that both in fact occurred and no doubt at all that reprisals of any kind immediately provoked counter-reprisals from the I.R.A.

It was inevitable in such circumstances that the savagery of the fighting would be intensified, and in the closing months of 1920 it seemed to reach a climax of horror with each side dealing terrible blows to the other. This was the period of the burning of Balbriggan by the Black and Tans (20 September), and of Cork by the Black and Tans and the Auxiliaries (11–12 December, after the latter had suffered heavy casualties in ambush at Kilmichael on 28 November); of 'Bloody Sunday' (21 November), when Collins's men killed a dozen men believed to be British intelligence agents, breaking into their rooms and shooting some of them in front of their wives; of the Croke Park 'massacre' on the afternoon of that same Sunday, when the Black and Tans opened fire on a football crowd, as a result of which twelve people died and sixty were wounded; of the deaths—also on that fatal day—of two of Collins's lieutenants, Peadar Clancy and Dick McKee, who had helped to plan the attack on the British intelligence officers and who were themselves 'shot while attempting to escape'.

This list scarcely begins to exhaust the catalogue of atrocities, and it would be possible to compile another list for the first six months of 1921 of which the deaths of harmless citizens would be the principal items.[1] It would be possible; but it would obscure an all-important fact, which was that during those same six months the first faltering and difficult steps were taken along the road to a cease-fire. That this should have coincided with the return of de Valera to the scene was no accident. His long mission to the United States had had many vicissitudes but, though he failed in some of his objectives—he did not secure the government's recognition of the republic, and his effort to commit the two main parties to the Irish cause at their presidential nominating conventions in 1920 only served to embroil him to no purpose in domestic American, or Irish-American, politics—he did win much popular sympathy and he did raise in a bond-drive for his 'victory fund' the vast sum of $5 million, of which $4 million was actually spent in Ireland, where it provided the resources without which the war of independence would have been impossible. By the end of 1920, however, it was imperative that he should return to Ireland, for in November Griffith had been arrested, and although Collins was able to act as his deputy, Collins's own multitudinous preoccupations, combined with the fact that his liberty, if not his life, was constantly at risk, made de Valera's presence all the more essential. He himself, as he told the dáil after he got back to Ireland, was deeply concerned at

---

[1] See for instance Robert Kee, *The green flag: a history of Irish nationalism* (London, 1972), p. 699; the outrage returns tabulated in Townshend, *British campaign*, p. 214, give an inevitably incomplete tally of civilian casualties.

the stage that the war had reached and anxious to ease the burden of the people if any way could be found to do so without an unworthy compromise.[1]

In fact, even before he left America there had been tentative moves towards a truce, some of them by well intentioned but bungling amateurs, others through agents whose importance suggested that even while Lloyd George was proclaiming that he 'had murder by the throat', he was seeking a basis for opening negotiations.[2] But such a basis was extremely difficult to find. On the British side, although, as we have seen, there was considerable revulsion against the war in many different quarters, there was also a deep detestation of the I.R.A. and its methods. Moreover, inside the coalition government, where since the 1918 election tories were dominant, the general consensus was that no settlement could be made that either coerced Ulster unionists into accepting rule from Dublin, or set up in Ireland a regime that might constitute a standing danger to the security and integrity of the empire. It seemed almost impossible that these conditions could be reconciled with the Irish demand for total separation and republican status. Indeed, it was as difficult to see how the contending parties could contrive to sit down at the same table, let alone agree on a settlement, since the British started from the position that the Irish must first surrender their arms while the Irish were absolutely adamant that they had not the slightest intention of doing so.

Nevertheless, both sides were afflicted with war-weariness and both were aware that if the government of Ireland act were not to come into full operation at its appointed date in mid-1921, the penalty for the twenty-six counties would be the imposition of crown colony government; and although the British cabinet naturally shrank from the greatly increased military effort that this would involve, the records of the time show quite clearly that contingency plans had been laid to produce that effort if it were needed.[3] Since, however, it would involve the deployment of perhaps 100,000 men, it was essential to explore every avenue of conciliation before proceeding to extremes,[4] and Lloyd George enlisted the services of a variety of helpers ranging from General Smuts to George V. It is often said, indeed, that the king's speech at the opening of the Northern Ireland parliament (22 June 1921) did more than anything else to break the ice. In this speech, which bore the influence of Smuts,[5] the king appealed to all Irishmen 'to pause, to stretch out the hand of forbearance and conciliation, to forgive and to

---

[1] Dáil Éireann proc. 1919–21, pp 240–41 (25 Jan. 1921).

[2] Mansergh, however, argues (Unresolved question, pp 154–61) that until May 1921, at the earliest, Lloyd George was firmly opposed to negotiating with the leadership of Sinn Féin. The quoted words were reported in The Times, 10 Nov. 1920.

[3] Under section 73 of the act, the 'appointed day' was to be 'the first Tuesday in the eighth month after the month in which this act is passed, or such other day not more than seven months earlier or later, as may be fixed by order of his majesty in council . . .'.

[4] For a useful discussion of the military considerations that influenced attitudes on each side towards a truce, see Townshend, British campaign, pp 183–96.

[5] Smuts had contributed to earlier drafts, but the text delivered was by Lloyd George's speech-writer, Edward Grigg (R. F. Foster, Modern Ireland, 1600–1972 (London, 1988), p. 504 n.).

forget, and to join in making for the land which they love a new era of peace, contentment, and goodwill'.[1]

However effective this may have been in predisposing British opinion in favour of a settlement, it is unlikely that a speech from the king, on the occasion when for the first time the partition of Ireland received institutional expression, would have appealed very much to the republicans of the south. In purely political terms their hands appeared to have been strengthened by the election of May 1921 when the machinery of the government of Ireland act was utilised to elect the second dáil. This body, which was somewhat larger than its predecessor, seemed no less uncompromising.[2] At the election, with a unanimity that was not calculated to set at rest suspicions of intimidation, all the constituencies—except Dublin University whose four independents were in effect unionists—returned Sinn Féin candidates unopposed. Yet there were two good reasons why even intransigent republicans should think twice before they rejected all possibility of a truce. One was that when Lloyd George followed up the king's speech with an offer to hold a tripartite conference between the British government and representatives of Northern and Southern Ireland, he dropped his previous conditions about the necessity for the I.R.A. to surrender their arms and abandoned also his prohibition on certain Irishmen attending the conference table. The second was that the I.R.A. itself was hard pressed and faced critical shortages of both men and weapons. It is true that this situation varied from brigade to brigade, and some local commanders were later to go on record to say that they could have continued the struggle much longer, but against this must be weighed the reported statement of Collins, who is said to have remarked to the chief secretary afterwards that the Irish resistance could not have continued another three weeks.[3] General Smuts appears to have played a significant role in persuading Sinn Féin leaders to accept Lloyd George's offer to talks when, at de Valera's invitation and with Lloyd George's consent, he travelled to Dublin on 5 July to discuss the issue.[4]

Lloyd George's offer was therefore taken seriously, though de Valera did not actually go to London until he had established that the conference would be between Lloyd George and himself (the Northern Ireland prime minister, Sir James Craig, being excluded),[5] and that a truce would be established before he left Dublin. In fact the cease-fire began to operate at noon on 11 July 1921, and the following day de Valera, accompanied by several of his ministers, arrived in London. He found that Lloyd George was prepared to offer him something

---

[1] *Hansard N.I. (senate)*, i, 11 (22 June 1921).
[2] Under the government of Ireland act the house of commons of Southern Ireland had 128 seats; John Mahoney, a Sinn Féin member for Fermanagh and Tyrone, also sat in the second dáil.
[3] See Townshend, *British campaign*, pp 192–3.
[4] Mansergh, *Unresolved question*, p. 193; John Bowman, *De Valera and the Ulster question 1917–1973* (Oxford, 1982), pp 49–50.
[5] Craig nevertheless also travelled to London for talks with Lloyd George, and although no tripartite meeting took place several unsuccessful attempts were made to bring the two leaders towards an accommodation on the issue of unity (Bowman, op. cit., pp 50–56).

approximating to dominion status. This, which seems to have been in the prime minister's mind at least since the previous April,[1] was, however, to be accompanied by certain significant qualifications—limits were to be set on the size of the Irish army, voluntary recruiting for the British forces in Ireland was to continue, air and naval facilities were to be granted to Britain, Ireland was to pay a contribution to the British war debt, and the final settlement 'must allow for full recognition of the existing powers and privileges of the parliament of Northern Ireland, which cannot be abrogated except by their own consent'.[2] Not surprisingly, de Valera's impulse was to reject these terms, which still fell far short of the republican demand, without even bringing them back to the dáil. But Lloyd George warned him that the alternative would be war, so the Irish leader agreed to have them discussed by his cabinet and by the second dáil.

As was to be expected, they were turned down by both bodies. Indeed, the second dáil seemed bent on underlining rather than modifying its republican bias. De Valera's own title was altered from 'president of Dáil Éireann' to 'president of the Irish Republic'. All deputies took an oath of allegiance to 'the Irish Republic and the government of the Irish Republic, which is Dáil Éireann'.[3] And finally, within de Valera's reconstituted cabinet, although Griffith (foreign affairs), Cosgrave (local government), and perhaps Barton (economic affairs) might have been classed as political moderates, they were balanced, if not indeed outweighed, by the inclusion of a group of prominent republicans—Stack (home affairs), Brugha (defence), and Collins (finance). De Valera himself would presumably have been classed by his colleagues among the more rigid republicans, but this would have been a gross oversimplification of his position and a gross underestimate of his capacity for political evolution. In the long and tortuous correspondence that was the immediate sequel to the apparent breakdown of the negotiations, it was noticeable that he made very little overt reference to the republic *per se*, but that he was prepared to consider ways and means whereby an independent Ireland might be 'associated with' the empire. And at the opening of the new dáil shortly afterwards he reminded deputies that the setting up of the first dáil had been a vote for freedom and independence rather than for a particular form of government, because 'we are not republican doctrinaires'.[4] It is true that this was not a great deal to build on, but it was enough to encourage Lloyd George to persist, and at last, by the end of September, he had found an apparently acceptable formula. De Valera was invited to send delegates to London on 11

---

[1] Mansergh argues that 'down to May 1921 dominion home rule, as it was generally termed, or dominion status was not on offer' and remained until that date 'an outcome expressly and repeatedly' ruled out of consideration by the prime minister and leading members of the coalition cabinet (*Unresolved question*, pp 145–8, 150–53, 157–61, in particular, for an examination of Lloyd George's views regarding the basis for a settlement). Townshend also takes the view that before mid-May 1921 Lloyd George was very reluctant to put dominion status on offer (*British campaign*, p. 181).

[2] Macardle, *Ir. republic*, p. 502.

[3] *Dáil Éireann rep. 1921–2*, p. 77 (26 Aug. 1921); for the oath, see above, p. 246, n. 2.

[4] *Dáil Éireann rep. 1921–2*, p. 9 (16 Aug. 1921).

October 1921 'with a view to ascertaining how the association of Ireland with the community of nations known as the British empire may best be reconciled with Irish national aspirations'.[1]

This was vague enough to allow negotiations to begin in earnest, but it was far from reassuring to the republican element in the Irish cabinet, and it was ominous that the two most extreme devotees of the republic, Stack and Brugha, refused to serve on the delegation that was to go to London. Even more significant was the fact that de Valera himself did not go either. Of the various explanations that have been advanced for this crucial decision, the most plausible are that by staying at home he could best ensure that the final vote on whatever settlement was achieved would be taken in Dublin; that he would be better placed to continue to press his doctrine of association—or 'external association', to give it the name it was soon publicly to acquire—on his more extreme republican colleagues; and above all, perhaps, that as 'head of state' he was himself the symbol of the republic and that this symbol should be kept out of the arena and thus uncompromised.

If, however, his intention was to reserve to the cabinet in Dublin the ultimate responsibility for peace or war, then there was a grave ambiguity about the instructions issued to the delegates. Their credentials (which were approved by dáil and cabinet, but for obvious reasons not formally accepted by the British government) described them as 'envoys plenipotentiary', charged 'to negotiate and conclude' a treaty or treaties with the representatives of the crown,[2] but at the same time the actual instructions issued to the delegates made it very clear that they were to submit to Dublin the complete text of any draft treaty and to await a reply before signing it.

It was reasonable to suppose that in actual fact the delegates would refer back to their colleagues, but they were a formidable group in their own right and it was no less reasonable to anticipate that they would be quite ready to use their initiative where necessary. They were led by Griffith and included Collins (who went with a foreboding of tragedy), Barton, Eamon Duggan, and George Gavan Duffy, with, as principal secretary, Erskine Childers, now a fanatical republican who had come a long way from the home rule summer of 1914. Facing the Irish delegates was a very powerful British team headed by Lloyd George himself and including Winston Churchill, Austen Chamberlain, Lord Birkenhead (lord chancellor), Sir Laming Worthington-Evans, Sir Hamar Greenwood (chief secretary), and Sir Gordon Hewart (attorney-general). It was particularly noteworthy that the tory element in the coalition government was heavily represented. This would make it more difficult for Lloyd George to carry his points in committee, but it meant also that if he did carry them his chances of controlling the tory back-benchers on whose vote the coalition largely depended would be correspondingly improved.

---

[1] Mitchell & Ó Snodaigh, *Ir. pol. docs 1916–49*, p. 115.   [2] Ibid., p. 116.

The negotiations, which began on 11 October and continued until 6 December with scarcely a break, were concerned with three main issues: the British demand for military and naval facilities; the constitutional status of the Irish state; and the question of partition versus the 'essential unity' of Ireland. Although the first of these had far-reaching implications for Irish foreign policy—and more specifically for Irish neutrality in a British war—it was not seriously contested by the Irish delegates, who recognised that British anxiety about defence was legitimate and were prepared to allay that anxiety, at any rate in the early stages of independence.

The other two questions turned out to be, as indeed they always had been, closely interwoven. The dáil cabinet had decided beforehand to press for the unity of Ireland, and that if the delegates had to break off negotiations they should break on Ulster. But in British eyes the Ulster question, though undeniably important, was only part of the larger issue of the future relationship between the new dominion and the commonwealth. For them the crux of this matter was whether or not the Irish were prepared to accept an oath of allegiance to the crown, which would stamp them unmistakably as being inside the empire. Griffith, following his instructions, put forward instead de Valera's concept of external association, suggesting that, while Ireland could not permit any intervention by the crown in her internal affairs, she might recognise the king as head of the association of commonwealth states. In making this suggestion the Irish were ten years ahead of their time, for a doctrine that was to form the basis of the statute of Westminster in 1931[1] was much too strange and suspicious in 1921 to find any favour in British eyes.

On the other hand, Lloyd George did hold out some promise of a fruitful exchange of concessions. If, he hinted, the Irish could satisfy him on the constitutional question in such a way as to enable him to muzzle his own diehards, he might be able to help them to secure the essential unity of Ireland. This was so momentous a suggestion that Griffith, after a private interview with Lloyd George, drafted a letter explaining just how far he would be prepared to go if assured that Lloyd George really meant what he said about Ulster. This letter was shown to his colleagues and, as amended by them, it seemed innocuous enough. In it Griffith agreed, provided he was satisfied on other points, to recommend to the dáil cabinet that Ireland should agree to recognise the crown as head of the association of free states of the commonwealth and that she should join in 'free partnership' (on terms subsequently to be defined) with the commonwealth. Shortly afterwards, however, he and the rest of the delegation were persuaded to alter this to 'free partnership with the other states associated within the British commonwealth', which was decidedly and seriously more than he had meant to convey in the first place.[2]

It now remained to be seen what, if anything, Lloyd George could make of Ulster. He saw Craig twice early in November and made absolutely no impression

---

[1] 22 Geo. V, c. 4 [U.K.] (11 Dec. 1931).   [2] Macardle, *Ir. republic*, pp 575–6.

on him. This was scarcely surprising. Apart from the fact that Ulster unionists were as instinctively hostile to rule by a Dublin parliament as they had ever been, their intransigence had been still further hardened by the running fight they were carrying on with the I.R.A., in spite of the truce, and by the boycott of northern products that the south had instituted in retaliation for the anti-catholic pogrom of 1920. But if Craig could not be reasoned with, might he not be coerced? The precedents were the reverse of encouraging, but Lloyd George, with his usual ingenuity, hit on a possible way of exerting pressure on Northern Ireland, which seems to have been proposed originally by Craig himself in December 1919, during discussions with the British cabinet on the possible boundary for the jurisdiction of the proposed parliament of Northern Ireland.[1] The suggestion was that if Northern Ireland refused to enter an all-Ireland settlement she should be obliged to submit to a boundary commission, which, it was implied, might transfer such substantial areas of the six counties to the south as to make total reintegration the only feasible solution. To this suggestion the Irish delegation responded cautiously that it was entirely Lloyd George's affair, but that if he found it useful as a means of exerting pressure on Northern Ireland they would not stand in his way. Yet in making even that reply they were taking a grave risk. Hitherto Lloyd George had been threatening resignation if baulked by Ulster. Now he was being allowed to step back from the brink and embark on another initiative, which might or might not work to the envoys' advantage.

In fact it worked only to Lloyd George's advantage. On 13 November Griffith was visited by Thomas Jones, a Welsh member of the cabinet secretariat and a personal confidant of Lloyd George's, with whom he could converse in Welsh as in a code impenetrable to outsiders. Jones extracted from Griffith his agreement to a written record of a conversation he had had with Lloyd George the previous day. During that conversation the prime minister had explained that Northern Ireland would be offered an all-Ireland parliament with the right to opt out of it in twelve months, but that if the right were exercised a boundary commission would be set up. Lloyd George, who had still to carry this policy through the tory party conference, which was due to be held at Liverpool on 17 November, had pleaded with Griffith not to make the task of his tory colleagues at this conference impossible by repudiating the policy. Griffith consented to this and reported the fact to de Valera at home. But when Jones visited him on 13 November and got him to agree to the written record of the conversation, that record contained the phrase that the boundary commission should revise the frontier of Northern Ireland 'so as to make the boundary conform as closely as possible to the wishes of the population'.[2] This document seemed to Griffith a matter of no great significance, but it was presently to be used against him with enormous effect at the most crucial moment in the negotiations.

[1] Patrick Buckland, *James Craig* (Dublin, 1980), p. 44; Mansergh, *Unresolved question*, p. 130.
[2] Frank Pakenham, *Peace by ordeal* (London, 1935), p. 218.

Meanwhile, however, it began to seem as if the break might not come on Ulster at all, for while the Liverpool conference was being persuaded to accept the prime minister's policy that Northern Ireland must either accept inclusion in an all-Ireland parliament or submit to a frontier revision, Lloyd George ran into fresh difficulties with the Irish delegation. In presenting them with a progress report on 16 November he evoked from them a counter-document six days later, which not only ignored the boundary commission and still insisted on the 'essential unity' of Ireland, but also contained virtually nothing to reassure either Lloyd George or his colleagues that the Irish would accept an oath of allegiance that would place them unequivocally inside the empire.[1] So wide was the gulf that still separated the two sides that on 22 and 23 November Lloyd George came within an ace of breaking off the negotiations. Indeed, had it not been for the strenuous efforts of Jones to keep the lines open for further discussion, the talks might have ended there and then. They did not do so, however. On the contrary, after Griffith's stand on the constitutional question had been fortified by a visit to Dublin, it was the British who broke the ice by a considerable concession, undertaking to draft a more innocuous form of the oath of allegiance and also inviting the Irish to invent whatever phrase they wished to ensure that the crown would in practice intrude no more in their internal affairs than it did in those of Canada or any other dominion.

But the time for negotiating was drawing rapidly to a close. Lloyd George had promised Craig that he would send him the final decision not later than 6 December, and although this deadline could conceivably have been extended, to prolong the conference would be to prolong a situation that had never ceased to be dangerous. As the critical moment approached the Irish delegation returned once more to Dublin where the dáil cabinet sat for most of Saturday, 3 December, in tense and apparently bitter debate. The case for accepting the terms so far hammered out was that dominion status, even with certain strings attached, was still the best offer that could be obtained in the circumstances, that the safeguards against crown interference were perfectly adequate, and that if the crown were not accepted in some way then the hold over Ulster afforded by the boundary commission would be lost. Against this it could be argued that the 'essential unity' of Ireland had already been compromised, that the British could be pushed further on the constitutional question, and that the republic itself seemed as far out of reach as ever. In the end, after Griffith had made it clear that he would not take the responsibility of breaking on the issue of the crown, and after de Valera had redrafted the oath to bring it nearer his concept of external association, the delegates were given their instructions only a few minutes before they were due to travel back to London. They were instructions that reflected the confusion now reigning within the Irish cabinet. They stated that the delegates were to press for the amendment of the oath and 'to face the consequences assuming that

[1] Ibid., pp 232–3.

England will declare war'; that Griffith was to tell Lloyd George that no agreement could be signed—'to state that it was now a matter for the dáil' and to show Ulster as the difficulty; finally, that if the delegation should think it necessary, they were empowered to meet Craig.[1]

Such divided counsels left them very much at Lloyd George's mercy, and they found him in the next three days at his most brilliant and his most ruthless. Sensing the uncertainty and confusion among his opponents, he worked on them individually, concentrating on Griffith and Collins. Griffith, as we have seen, had already come to the conclusion that the terms offered were so favourable that they should be accepted. Collins, though much more closely identified with the republic and therefore faced with a more agonising dilemma, inclined towards acceptance partly because of the inexpediency of renewing the war and also because Lloyd George appears to have convinced him that the boundary commission would be an efficient instrument in restoring the 'essential unity' of Ireland. Desperately, the delegates tried to reopen the question of Ulster, but when Griffith was confronted with the document he had approved on 13 November his resistance collapsed, and it was clear that he at least would stand by the boundary commission solution. As to the oath, on the other hand, the British did make a considerable concession, revising their formula to read

I . . . do solemnly swear true faith and allegiance to the constitution of the Irish Free State as by law established, and that I will be faithful to H.M. King George V, his heirs and successors by law, in virtue of the common citizenship of Ireland with Great Britain and her adherence to and membership of the group of nations forming the British common-wealth of nations.[2]

At the last moment, and with characteristically superb timing, Lloyd George also threw into the scales the much sought after tariff autonomy for the Irish parliament. Given these concessions, and assuming that the Irish accepted both the boundary commission and the general definition of dominion status, would they, Lloyd George demanded, be prepared to sign the treaty embodying these terms? And with a dramatic gesture, he held out to them two letters, one of which had to go to Craig that night (5 December). Would the letter announce a settlement or would it tell of the resumption of the struggle? 'If I send this letter it is war, and war within three days. Which letter am I to send?'[3]

Late that evening the Irish delegation withdrew to consider what was in effect an ultimatum. After hours of agonised discussion the objections of Barton and Gavan Duffy to signing were finally overcome, and in the early hours of 6 December 1921 Griffith, Collins, and Barton signed the articles of agreement for a treaty, the others adding their signatures later. They signed in the end without consulting de Valera and their other colleagues at home. To telephone would have seemed the obvious thing, but de Valera was in Limerick at the crucial moment

---

[1] Ibid., pp 261–2.   [2] Mitchell & Ó Snodaigh, *Ir. pol. docs., 1916–49*, p. 117.
[3] Wording as in Pakenham, *Peace by ordeal*, p. 298; cf. Macardle, *Ir. republic*, p. 608.

and not readily accessible. To return to Dublin without signing would no doubt have led to another acrimonious and probably barren debate within the cabinet. This might still have been the right thing to do, but it would have involved a fearful responsibility—the responsibility of deciding that Lloyd George was bluffing and that when he threatened imminent war he did not mean what he said. Moreover, the terms that these exhausted men had won were such that, it could be argued, they had a moral duty to sign and to throw on their fellow countrymen the ultimate decision as to whether the future for their country should be one of peace as a dominion or of war as a republic.

CHAPTER XII

Economic and social history, 1850–1921

H. D. GRIBBON

THE Irish, it is said, tend to refer to events long past as though they had taken place only recently, and of nothing is this more true than of the famine of 1845–9. In any company anywhere in Ireland mention of 'the famine' will not provoke query, everyone will know what is being discussed, no one will regard the reference as incongruous or archaic. Folk memory, which thus recalls the famine as an event, also regards it as a watershed—certain events took place either before or after the famine—and it is so treated in most history textbooks, where it neatly bisects the nineteenth century. But for economic history this impression of discontinuity is belied by the facts. Forces at work outside Ireland—growing population and increasing industrialisation in Great Britain, the development of overseas interests by most western European states, the gathering economic strength of the Americas—were all evident before 1845 and exerted determinant pressures after 1850. From this point of view the famine was an irrelevance. On the other hand the external pressures were applied to a country that had passed through a traumatic experience. Before the famine it was assumed that things would go on much as they had always done; that, bad as conditions might be, the land would always somehow be able to sustain the people; that leaving Ireland was the ultimate misfortune. After the famine these traditional attitudes had undergone a fundamental change. The economic history of the period 1850–1921 may therefore be treated neither as a completely new departure nor simply as a continuation of earlier trends. The picture is rather of an accelerated deterioration of the ideas and institutions of the past combined with a slow and experimental development of those that came to replace them.[1]

IRELAND in 1850 was rather in the position of a patient who has survived the crisis of a serious illness—it is probable that he will live but evident that recovery will be a long and slow business. The haemorrhage associated with the illness, having taken probably over a million emigrants out of the country since 1846,

[1] For the effects of the famine and developments in mid-Victorian Ireland, see above, v, 332–95.

continued for some years before reducing to a smaller but still steady flow—an indication that the predisposing cause of the malady had yet to be dealt with. Meantime the physicians seemed all too ready to assume that further treatment could be left to nature. As quickly as possible therefore expenditure by the board of works was scaled down[1] and outdoor relief for the unemployed virtually eliminated.[2] It was hoped too that the encumbered estates act, by introducing into the ranks of the landowning class fresh proprietors with capital and energy to replace those whose estates had been worst affected by the famine, would promote the aim that Irish property should bear the cost of Irish poverty. Trevelyan, assistant secretary at the treasury, wrote to Larcom in Dublin in 1850:

The famine, the poor law, and the encumbered estates commission have given a new stimulus to the principle of individual exertion as contrasted with the old habit of depending upon the government . . . and considering this and the other circumstances mentioned we may reasonably expect that the system of advances from the consolidated fund of Great Britain and Ireland to Ireland *exclusively* should cease . . .[3]

The premature reduction in assistance from United Kingdom funds was naturally unpopular, even more so the requirement that Ireland should reimburse the exchequer for monies spent on relief during the height of the famine. As one contemporary put it, 'What I complain of is the subsequent conduct of the English government. I complain of your taxing the Irish proprietors and occupiers with charges . . . for the repayment of sums which we did not borrow, which you expended for us, and which after all rather relieved *your* minds than *our* distress.'[4]

In general, the outlook at the beginning of 1850 was bleak, the people exhausted and apathetic, and those with means to do so still leaving the country in considerable numbers. A director of the Provincial Bank of Ireland wrote: 'The state of Ireland this year as compared with the relative period last year is not, I am sorry to say, improved. I do not think as a whole it can be said to have retrograded, but there are no general symptoms of amendment.'[5] Nevertheless, there were signs that if too much hope could not be placed as yet in improvement, the worst was probably over. The harvest of 1849 had been good and, though mostly sold for ready money at the earliest possible date, there remained a marginal surplus over immediate requirements.[6] In the north a good demand for linen stimulated the further mechanisation of the spinning section of the industry,[7] and encouraged an extension of the acreage sown to flax. Banking statistics showed small but significant increases in the balances held by joint-stock

[1] R. D. C. Black, *Economic thought and the Irish question, 1817–1870* (Cambridge, 1960), p. 124.
[2] *Third annual report of the commissioners for administering the laws for relief of the poor in Ireland*, pp 4–6 [1243], H.C. 1850, xxvii, 462–4.
[3] Larcom papers, N.L.I., MS 7746, f. 42. Thomas Larcom, deputy chairman of the board of works in Ireland, was appointed under-secretary at the beginning of 1853 and held the post until his retirement in 1868; for a portrait, see above, v, plate 31(*b*).
[4] N. W. Senior, *Journals, conversations and essays relating to Ireland* (2 vols, London, 1868), ii, 4.
[5] Larcom papers, N.L.I., MS 7600, f.3 .   [6] Ibid.
[7] *Belfast News Letter*, 18 Jan. 1850.

and trustee saving banks. To see how the forces making for recovery steadily gained the upper hand during the next few years it will be necessary to look in turn at the main sections of the economy—agriculture, industry, and finance—and then to consider how improvements in these fields affected social conditions generally.

Compared with the years immediately before 1845 some features of the period 1850–70 showed little change, others were profoundly affected by events inside Ireland, and still others by developments in Great Britain and beyond. The landholding system falls into the first category, for although over 7,000 purchasers bought land under the encumbered estates acts of 1848 and 1849, the legal powers of both old and new landlords, to whatever extent they were exercised in practice, continued undiminished. Indeed the new proprietors were said to have been less inhibited than their predecessors in forcing up rents, though equally negligent of their responsibilities.[1] Some were speculators attracted by the very low prices at which the land could be bought, their main object being to obtain from their expenditure the maximum return with the least practicable delay. Institutional purchasers, typically assurance societies who had lent money to now insolvent landowners, were conspicuously unwilling to invest further in their reluctantly acquired estates.[2] A few were tenants who bought at prices beyond their means because they feared the replacement of a negligent landlord by an extortionate one. But it would be wrong to attach to all landlord purchasers under the encumbered estates acts the opprobrium earned by a few: 'It is much easier to prove that it was practically universally *believed* that small landowners who purchased in the landed estates courts raised rents than to estimate the extent to which they actually did so.'[3] On the other hand, if the acts harmed tenants less than contemporaries believed, they certainly did Irish agriculture little good. It had been hoped that the legislation would encourage purchasers from Great Britain to invest capital in the acquisition and development of Irish estates; in fact few purchasers came from Great Britain,[4] little fresh capital was invested in farming, standards were not improved, and tenants were, generally, no better off than before. But there were changes arising from other causes.

The greatest change, of course, resulted from a major and continuing decrease in rural population. Initially, in the areas that had been worst affected, the competition for land ceased, farms fell vacant, and of the tenants who remained

---

[1] 11 & 12 Vict., c. 48 (14 Aug. 1848); 12 & 13 Vict., c. 77 (28 July 1849); *Report from the select committee on Tenure and Improvement of Land (Ireland) Act*, p. 2, H.C. 1865 (402), xi, 354; *Report from the select committee on general valuation, etc. (Ireland)*, p. 177, H.C. 1868–9 (362), ix, 189; *Reports from poor law inspectors in Ireland as to the existing relations between landlord and tenant*, p. 14 [C 31], H.C. 1870, xiv, 50; *Report from the select committee on Irish land act, 1870*, p. xii, H.C. 1878 (249), xv, 12.

[2] P. G. Lane, 'The management of estates by financial corporations in Ireland after the famine' in *Studia Hib.*, xiv (1974), pp 67–89.

[3] Barbara L. Solow, *The land question and the Irish economy, 1870–1903* (Cambridge, Mass., 1971), pp 72–3.

[4] It was estimated that of some £26 million spent, less than 12 per cent came from non-Irish sources (R. W. McDonnell, 'Statistics of Irish prosperity' in *Stat. Soc. Ire. Jn.*, iii, pt xxii (Dec. 1862), p. 274).

many were unable to pay their rents. Landlords, or their agents, took advantage of the holdings made vacant by eviction or emigration to consolidate their land into fewer and larger units. A great many very small holdings remained, particularly in Connacht, but calculations based on census and land commission returns show that between 1845 and 1851 there was a decrease of 213,000 in the number between 1 and 15 acres, and an increase of 14,000 of those above 15 acres.[1] Subdivision, frowned on even before the famine, became (save for the western seaboard) virtually a thing of the past.

Agricultural labourers, whose perquisites included the right to use a plot of ground for growing potatoes, had suffered at least as much as the occupiers of land, and with this class may be included cottiers and casual labourers, whose margin above starvation level, normally slight, disappeared with the smallest adversity. Here rather than among farmers of any substance the famine had produced its most severe effects. The loss of all these people, and their families, due to disease, starvation, and emigration, resulted in a shortage of labour on the land and a consequent rise in wage levels from 1854—on the farms, at the handlooms, and in small rural industries.[2] As significant, at least, for agricultural labourers was the fact that they now began to receive a higher proportion of their wages in cash, and to obtain more regular employment.[3]

The decreasing number and increasing average size of holdings, the decreasing numbers and increasing wages of agricultural labourers, accompanied more fundamental changes in the pattern of Irish farming, for at the same time began a long-term shift in balance between tillage and pasture, between the growing of crops and the raising of livestock.[4] Prompted at home by post-famine conditions, the shift was given impetus by the free trade in grain made possible by the 1846 repeal of the corn laws[5] and subsequently by the influence in world markets of expanding American grain production. Irish agricultural census figures show a fluctuating acreage of wheat in the years between 1850 and 1857 but thereafter a steady fall. The acreage under meadow and clover began its climb rather before

[1] P. M. A. Bourke, 'The agricultural statistics of the 1841 census of Ireland: a critical review' in *Econ. Hist. Rev.*, 2nd ser., xviii (1965), pp 376–91 (reprinted in id., *'The visitation of God'?: the potato and the great Irish famine*, ed. Jacqueline Hill and Cormac Ó Gráda (Dublin, 1993), pp 74–89).

[2] *Seventh annual report of the commissioners for administering the laws for relief of the poor in Ireland*, p. 9 [1785], H.C. 1854, xxix, 545.

[3] *Eighth annual report of the commissioners for administering the laws for the relief of the poor in Ireland*, pp 11–15 [1945], H.C. 1854–5, xxiv, 533–7; *Ninth annual report . . .*, pp 10, 45 [2105], H.C. 1856, xxviii, 424, 459.

[4] Thomas Kennedy, 'Fifty years of Irish agriculture' in *Stat. Soc. Ire. Jn.*, x, pt lxxix (Aug. 1899), pp 398–404; John O'Donovan, *The economic history of livestock in Ireland* (Cork, 1940), pp 205–6; Redcliffe N. Salaman, *The history and social influence of the potato* (Cambridge, 1949), p. 318; Hans Staehle, 'Statistical notes on the economic history of Irish agriculture, 1847–1913' in *Stat. Soc. Ire. Jn.*, xviii (1947–52), p. 444; Raymond D. Crotty, *Irish agricultural production: its volume and character* (Cork, 1966), ch. III; see also review by J. J. Lee in *Agricultural History Review*, xvii (1969), pp 64–76; J. P. Huttman, 'The impact of land reform on agricultural production in Ireland' in *Agricultural History*, xlvi (1972), p. 354.

[5] 9 & 10 Vict., c. 22 (26 June 1846); Crotty, op. cit., p. 71.

1850 and continued to move upwards throughout the period under review, and indeed beyond the end of the century. The change in balance between grass and tillage was, however, even more pronounced than these figures suggest because over a million acres of waste land were reclaimed between 1850 and 1870, most of it suited primarily for permanent pasture or rough grazing.[1]

Associated with the movement from tillage to grass was the restocking of farms with cattle and sheep, and a rapid growth in numbers of pigs and poultry. Total cattle on farms increased from 1,393,000 in 1850 to 3,800,000 in 1870, sheep from 1,876,000 to 4,337,000, and pigs from 927,000 to 1,461,000. There was as yet little progress in breeding and rearing or in the preparation of agricultural produce for sale, but an expanding market in Great Britain, whose industrial population demanded continually more food than she herself could supply, provided an outlet for a wide range of cattle and carcass meat, sheep and mutton, bacon, butter, and eggs.

The rate of change in the farming pattern was influenced by a number of factors, the most important in the 1850s and 1860s being the relative selling prices of different types of agricultural produce, good and bad seasons, conditions of land tenure, technical change, and the availability of capital. It must be noted, however, that regional differences were considerable; agriculture became more backward as one moved westward, and in Connemara and Donegal subdivision of holdings and reliance on the potato persisted until the 1890s.

The price pattern is most clearly illustrated in figure 1, using index numbers with base 100 at 1840,[2] averaged over five-year periods. The following table shows

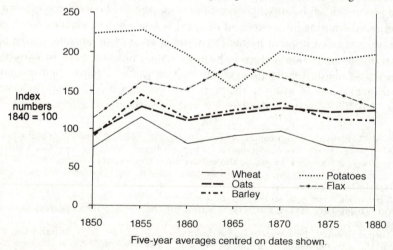

Five-year averages centred on dates shown.

Figure 1   CROP PRICES, 1850–80, by H. D. Gribbon

---

[1] T. W. Grimshaw, 'Notes on the statistics of waste lands in Ireland' in *Stat. Soc. Ire. Jn.*, vii, pt lxii, (July 1884), p. 523.

[2] Thomas Barrington, 'A review of Irish agricultural prices' in *Stat. Soc. Ire. Jn.*, xv, pt ci (Oct. 1927), pp 251–3.

Prices per cwt of agricultural produce, 1840–45, 1853,
1865, 1870

	1840–45		1853		1865		1870	
	s.	d.	s.	d.	s.	d.	s.	d.
wheat	12	3	15	3	12	4	10	4
oats	6	8½	7	7	7	6	7	11½
barley	7	4½	9	3½	7	10½	8	1½
flax	53	0	57	0	106	0	60	0
potatoes	2	2	4	10	3	3	4	0
butter	81	0	83	6	119	0	120	0
beef	46	3	53	0	65	3	71	3
mutton	49	0	59	6	74	8	75	10
pork	39	0	47	6	56	6	56	0

typical prices per hundredweight in actual values, with a column to illustrate pre-famine levels.[1]

Allowance should be made for the effect of the American civil war on the 1865 price of flax, but otherwise the very modest increase for oats, associated with use for animal feed, and the decrease (comparing 1870 with 1853) in the prices of other cereals contrasts markedly with the substantial increases in the prices of animal products. There was clearly an inducement for farmers to concentrate on the livestock side of the industry, and their response to price trends is illustrated by the total value of crops and livestock on farms (averaged for five-year periods) arrived at by multiplying output and numbers respectively by estimated average prices. With the exception of flax and hay, crop acreages had fallen by something like one-third, while the increase in livestock values reflected both rising prices and increased numbers in all categories.[2]

Crop and livestock values, 1851–5,
1866–70

	crops	livestock
1851–5	£58,000,000	£39,000,000
1866–70	£45,000,000	£60,000,000

Good harvests seem to have been a feature of the 1870s, but yields of oats and potatoes fell in 1859 and this marked the beginning of a series of poor harvests that lasted until 1864–5. Caused by adverse weather conditions, the 1859–64 depression was most severely felt by livestock producers who had to contend with

[1] Prices quoted are medians calculated from *Purdon's Almanac* as cited in *Report of the royal commission on the Land Law Ireland Act, 1881, and the Purchase of Land (Ireland) Act, 1885. ii. Minutes of evidence and appendices*, pp 89–92 [C 4969-I], H.C. 1887, xxvi, 121–4. Flax prices for 1840–45 and 1853 are drawn from the *Belfast News Letter*.

[2] T. W. Grimshaw, presidential address in *Stat. Soc. Ire. Jn.*, x, pt lxx (July 1890), pp 441–2.

shortage of fodder, animal disease, and the forced selling of unfinished stock at panic prices.[1] Depletion of capital and accumulation of rent arrears followed inevitably even for those normally secure.[2] Something was recovered during the rest of the decade, when harvests, with the exception of 1869, were reasonably good. Livestock numbers recovered, but it is evident that some of the prosperity reported, for instance, by the poor law commissioners in 1865 represented recovery rather than advance.[3] Those who detected a reluctance by occupiers to invest in their holdings[4] may have been looking for fencing and houses while available money was going towards increasing livestock numbers. Also, of course, farmers were meeting rising costs and wages[5] on one hand and increasing rents on the other as competition for land for the expansion of livestock farming became more intense. When leases fell in they were replaced by yearly tenancies.[6] At the same time farms in the lowest acreage groups became steadily less viable.[7] This is not to say that agriculture saw no accumulation of capital. On the contrary, dealers and cattle traders in 1870 had sufficient funds to contemplate the purchase and operation of their own transport across the Irish Sea;[8] the rising totals of bank deposits in rural areas were indicative of much larger sums held in cash by small farmers who were still wary of bankers;[9] technically, there was an increasing use both of artificial fertilisers and agricultural machinery;[10] while not only proprietors and leaseholders, but some yearly tenants, were reported as spending money, a few proprietors considerable sums, on long-term improvements.[11]

[1] Senior, *Journals*, ii, 196; J. S. Donnelly, jr, 'The Irish agricultural depression of 1859–64' in *Ir. Econ. & Soc. Hist.*, iii (1976), pp 33–54.

[2] W. N. Hancock, *Report on the supposed progressive decline of Irish prosperity* (Dublin, 1863), p. 63; *Report from the select committee on the taxation of Ireland*, p. 177, H.C. 1864 (513), xv, 211 (hereafter cited as *First taxation comm.*).

[3] *Annual report of the commissioners for administering the laws for the relief of the poor in Ireland, etc.*, pp 30–46 [3507], H.C. 1865, xxii, 376–92.

[4] *Report from the select committee on Tenure and Improvement of Land (Ireland) Act*, pp 3, 23, 124, H.C. 1865 (402), xi, 355, 375, 476 (hereafter cited as *Maguire comm.*).

[5] A. L. Bowley, 'The statistics of wages in the United Kingdom during the last hundred years: part III; agricultural wages—Ireland' in *Journal of the Royal Statistical Society*, lxii (1899), pp 395–404.

[6] *Maguire comm.*, p. 2 (MS 354).

[7] *First taxation comm.*, pp 199, 211 (MS 233, 245).

[8] *F.J.*, 25 Jan. 1871.

[9] *Report of the departmental committee on agricultural credit in Ireland*, pp 21, 39 [Cd 7375], H.C. 1914, xiii, 37, 57.

[10] The *Irish Times* (30 June 1860) carried advertisements for haymaking machines, threshing machines, patent corn-drilling, grass-mowing, corn-reaping, and potato-digging machines. From 1865 the agricultural statistics began to include farm machinery, at which date a well equipped farm in Co. Kilkenny offered for sale one two-horse mowing machine, a one-horse patent reaper, a two-horse grubber, a one-horse hoe, and one clod crusher, besides ploughs, harrows, a chaff cutter, hay rake, etc. (*Kilkenny Journal*, 7 Jan. 1865).

[11] *Reports from poor law inspectors in Ireland as to the existing relations between landlord and tenant*, pp 19, 23, 40, 153 [C 31], H.C. 1870, xiv, 55, 59, 76, 189. It was commonly reported that, unless protected by tenant right or an understanding with their landlord, most yearly tenants were reluctant to risk money on capital improvements.

THE period 1870–81 was marked at the beginning by the passage of the Landlord and Tenant (Ireland) Act, 1870, and at the end by the price slump of 1879–82; neither interrupted the steady transition from tillage to livestock. During this period, however, Irish agriculture came increasingly under pressures from outside, and the consequences of, and responses to, these pressures deserve comment.

With the end of the American civil war the cotton famine disappeared and the linen trade no longer demanded flax at any price; the fall in value of scutched fibre was reflected in a reduction in the acreage sown to flax in the years immediately after 1870. Again, the high price of wool consequent on the cotton famine had affected the numbers of sheep in Ireland, which reached their peak for the century in 1868 but by 1870 were falling away. As the American economy gathered strength and the prairies were opened up for the growing of cereals and the raising of cattle, these and their products began to flow across the Atlantic in increasing quantity, competing in the British market with Irish produce. Prices were not affected immediately because the Franco-Prussian war of 1870–71 interfered with the normal European trade in foodstuffs, and livestock prices reached their highest level in 1874–5; thereafter, however, they began to sag. Prices of Irish bacon and butter began to fall from about 1876–7 while that of wheat declined towards pre-war levels soon after 1872.[1]

American participation was evident not only in the British but also in the Irish market where it had been noted as early as 1863 that 'as American corn has been followed by American bacon, so American bacon is followed by American butter'.[2]

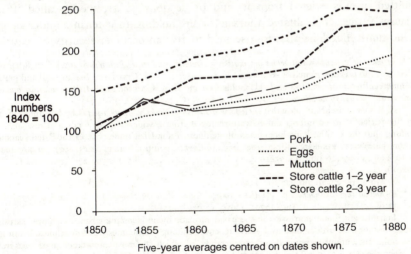

Five-year averages centred on dates shown.

Figure 2 LIVESTOCK PRICES, 1850–80, by H. D. Gribbon

[1] The proportion of home-grown wheat sold in the United Kingdom market declined from 60.9 per cent in 1870 to 27 per cent in 1880 (*Ministry of reconstruction: report of the agricultural policy sub-committee of the reconstruction committee*, p. 9 [Cd 9079], H.C. 1918, v, 109).

[2] Larcom papers, N.L.I., MS 7606, f. 4.

Thus imported maize meal tended to replace local oatmeal as a supplement to the potato diet still standard in western areas,[1] and cheap American bacon began to replace Irish bacon in poorer homes, leaving the latter to be shipped to Great Britain. The position with butter was rather different, for it was European, not American, butter that ousted the Irish product from the London market where, between 1850 and 1875, supplies of imported butter and cheese trebled.[2]

Other influences from outside included the reduction in demand for migrant Irish harvest labour, brought about by the increasing use of machinery on cereal farms in Great Britain.[3] One effect was to narrow the areas from which such people came to those parts of the western seaboard, later to be designated 'congested districts', where seasonal labour in Great Britain was a regular and traditional feature of the economy. Elsewhere, in the more fertile districts, occupiers of smallholdings who might have sought casual work in difficult years tended more and more to emigrate or to seek employment as 'herds' or regular workers on the larger livestock farms.[4]

Even had external conditions been more favourable it is open to doubt whether the Landlord and Tenant (Ireland) Act, 1870,[5] could have produced the results hoped from it. The act dealt with three main topics. It gave legal sanction to the Ulster custom or tenant right,[6] but without defining it, and sought to extend its principles to those parts of Ireland where they did not currently apply: it prescribed compensation for the value of improvements (up to a maximum of £250) that a tenant had made to his holding, but only at the point where he quitted or was evicted from it, and by sections 32–41, the so-called 'Bright clauses',[7] the act facilitated the sale of his holding to a tenant, under defined conditions. The Ulster custom seemed to give an occupier security of tenure so

---

[1] *Minutes of evidence taken before her majesty's commissioners on agriculture*, p. 102 [C 2778–1], H.C. 1881, xv, 130 (hereafter cited as *Richmond comm. evidence*); E. M. Crawford, 'Indian meal and pellagra in nineteenth-century Ireland' in J. M. Goldstrom and L. A. Clarkson (ed.), *Irish population, economy, and society; essays in honour of the late K. H. Connell* (Oxford, 1981), pp 113–33.

[2] C. S. Orwin and E. H. Whetham, *History of British agriculture, 1846–1914* (London, 1964), p. 145. In the period 1846–60 import duties were removed from a wide range of foods and raw materials coming into the United Kingdom: items of significance for Irish trade with Great Britain included bacon, beef, pork, woollens, hides, hams, linen, sausages, poultry, butter, cheese, eggs, and leather (9 & 10 Vict., c. 23 (26 June 1846); 16 & 17 Vict., c. 54 (4 Aug. 1853); 23 & 24 Vict., c. 22 (15 May 1860)).

[3] Orwin & Whetham, op. cit., pp 110–14, 256.

[4] *Richmond comm. evidence*, p. 371 (MS 399).

[5] 33 & 34 Vict., c. 46 (1 Aug. 1870); above, v, 464–7, 751–8.

[6] Tenant right found expression in the payment made by an incoming tenant to his predecessor in occupation of land usually held as a yearly tenancy, although sometimes this was applicable also to a leasehold. Its amount recognised several elements, of which the most important was the difference between the actual rent and the theoretical rack-rent of the holding. Other elements were the value of the improvements made by the outgoing tenant and, where there was danger of contention, assurance of peaceable possession. Tenant right existed most commonly in Ulster, but it was to be found in some of its elements, with different emphasis at different times, in most parts of Ireland. A Co. Down farmer defined it in 1880 as 'the free sale by the tenant of his interest and improvements to any person to whom the landlord cannot show reasonable objection' (*Richmond comm. evidence*, p. 409 (MS 437)).

[7] So called because they were added to the bill at the instigation of John Bright, M.P.

long as his rent was paid. The unfortunate consequences of such security, however, were the readiness with which traders were now prepared to extend credit to the smaller farmers, and the recklessness with which, in the good years to 1875, the latter availed themselves of it. In consequence, 'the indebtedness of the small farmer is one of the worst features of the present [1881] depression'.[1] The presumed security of tenure, moreover, proved illusory: 'there is no protection against arbitrary eviction; such evictions are merely made more costly for the landlord.'[2] Indeed, they need not always have been more costly, for there was nothing in the act or in practice to prevent landlords raising the rents of yearly tenants and driving them into debt so that on eviction they were not entitled to compensation for disturbance.[3] A tenant holding a lease for thirty-one years or more, granted after 1 August 1870, was automatically debarred from claiming compensation for disturbance or for certain improvements. In granting such a lease landlords customarily required the tenant to abrogate his remaining entitlements under the act. A large farmer whose holding was valued at not less than £50 could contract out of the provisions of the act and thus forgo any claim he might later have; hence every effort was made to create such tenants, and to force them by the threat of eviction or rent increases to sign covenants excluding themselves from the benefits of the act.[4] If the law on compensation for disturbance was complex and open to abuse or evasion, that on compensation for tenants' improvements, when tested in court, proved even more so. Under the Ulster custom the money that an incoming tenant paid to his predecessor was agreed between them and took into account the improved, or dilapidated, state of the holding. The law could not make allowance for the variety of circumstances in which improvements had been made, or their effectiveness, particularly where there was any difference between landlord and tenant as to who had made them and when. In general, the improvement provisions of the act depended for their value on the fairness and honesty of the people concerned; they could not change a bad landlord into a good one, and were double-edged because even conscientious landlords became afraid of assisting in, or sanctioning, them, fearing to incur obligations for compensation at a later date.[5] But compensation for improvements, arising as it did on the termination of a tenancy, was the lesser of a tenant's concerns. As the Bessborough commission put it,

In nearly all cases of dispute between tenant and landlord, what the aggrieved tenant wants is, not to be compensated for the loss of his farm, but to be continued in its occupancy at a fair rent. This, as the law now stands, he cannot have; and in order to raise the question before the court, he is forced to begin by a surrender of the only thing for which he really

---

[1] *Richmond comm. evidence*, pp 89, 93, 118 (MS 117, 121, 146).

[2] Louis Paul-Dubois, *Contemporary Ireland* (Dublin, 1911), p. 248.

[3] John E. Pomfret, *The struggle for land in Ireland, 1800–1923* (Princeton, N.J. 1930), p. 95; David L. Armstrong, *An economic history of Northern Ireland, 1850–1900* (Oxford, 1989), p. 37.

[4] James S. Donnelly, jr. *The land and people of nineteenth-century Cork* (London, 1975), pp 205–9; above, v, 753.

[5] *Richmond comm. evidence*, pp 902, 910 (MS 930, 938).

cares . . . In a word, once a tenant comes into court, all the law can give him is compensation in money. The very fact of his making a claim at all presupposes that he is to leave the land.[1]

Even the Bright clauses, intended to assist tenants to purchase their holdings, met with a mixed reception. Useful in a few instances, they meant in others that land was bought too dear and involved too heavy repayments, purchasers being left with insufficient capital to farm properly their newly acquired holdings.[2] Much the same criticisms applied to the purchase of land under the Irish Church Act, 1869.[3]

Evidence is ambiguous about rent levels. Undoubtedly rents were rising but on livestock farms this was not unreasonable; there were cases of rents being doubled between 1850 and 1879, with no more than the usual complaints; there were cases of rents not being increased at all; most rents, however, were increased only moderately. In Ulster the value of tenant right rose steeply and there was said to be intense competition for land. The numbers of evictions between 1865 and 1878 also declined markedly from the level of 1861–4.[4] In the years 1876–8 emigration fell to the lowest level since the famine and was not to be so low again until almost the end of the century.[5] The evidence is therefore that, while good crop yields and high livestock prices brought prosperity to the larger farmers, even the smaller occupiers were comfortable.[6] Over the whole decade there was a slow but continuing increase in average farm size; there was a growing interest in the technical aspects of the industry fostered by the Royal Dublin Society and by an increasing number of local farming societies; an impressive cattle export trade was built up and maintained; the use of fertilisers and machinery on farms developed steadily if slowly. But on the whole there was nothing like the technical advance, the specialisation, the capital investment, and the improvement in conditions of tenure that would have enabled the economy to withstand the effects of the prolonged depression that, preceded by a poor harvest in 1878, began in 1879–82.

Several features combined to produce this phenomenon, which was felt throughout western Europe, the most important being overseas competition and a succession of bad seasons. Ireland suffered severely, being more backward and less prepared than most other parts of the United Kingdom, and the people worst affected included the large body of tenant farmers who had insufficient capital to weather the storm, some of whom were already in debt before it started.

---

[1] *Bessborough comm. rep.*, p. 7 (MS 11).

[2] *Richmond comm. evidence*, p. 975 (MS 1003).

[3] 32 & 33 Vict., c. 42 (26 July 1869); Hugh Shearman, 'State-aided land purchase under the disestablishment act of 1869' in *I.H.S.*, iv, no. 13 (Mar. 1944), pp 58–80.

[4] *Return, 'by provinces and counties . . . of cases of evictions which have come to the knowledge of the constabulary in each of the years from 1849 to 1880 . . .'*, p. 3, H.C. 1881 (185), lxxvii, 727.

[5] W. E. Vaughan and A. J. Fitzpatrick, *Irish historical statistics: population, 1821–1971* (Dublin, 1978), pp 261–2.

[6] *Thirty-fifth annual report of the commissioners of the loan fund board of Ireland*, p. 4 [C 753], H.C. 1873, xxi, 272; *Report from the select committee on Irish Land Act, 1870*, p. xxx, H.C. 1878 (249), xv, 30.

There had been a poor potato crop in 1878. Then in 1879 excessive summer rainfall, combined with low temperatures,[1] resulted in a deficient grain harvest and a blighted potato crop that yielded an average of only 1.3 tons per acre against a normal 4 tons. The supply of turf saved in 1879 was unusually small;[2] cattle prices fell, the market being over-supplied by involuntary sellers; Irish butter, fetching at home only 6d. to 7d. per pound, could hardly be disposed of on the London market; there was a lack in Great Britain of seasonal employment even for the currently reduced numbers of Irish agricultural labourers. Conditions at the beginning of 1880, particularly in the west, must have seemed all too reminiscent of the late 1840s. This time, however, remedial measures were more readily available. For one thing there was more workhouse accommodation; for another, outdoor relief was quickly afforded—to 225,000 applicants in 1880 compared with 86,000 in 1879. Emigrant ships were able to take 95,500 passengers in 1880 (compared with the previous annual average of 43,000), in better conditions and with better prospects of safe arrival than those of thirty years earlier; and this time the emigrants did not carry disease with them. At home, private and official relief funds were quickly made available (government grants in the period 1880–82 amounted to £99,000 and loans, of which substantial repayments were ultimately remitted, to £2,070,000); arrangements were made to supply on credit seed potatoes and seed oats to those unable to pay cash for them;[3] finally the prevailing distress accelerated the introduction of the Land Law (Ireland) Act, 1881, with its provisions for the fixing of judicial rents, which put an end to the time-honoured system of increasing rents slowly and erratically in times of prosperity, according to the temper or circumstances of particular landlords, while reducing them even more slowly and uncertainly in face of general adversity.

The slump of 1879–82 ushered in for Irish agriculture a period of depression that lasted until about 1896. There then followed a few years of uncertainty, until, around the turn of the century, a sustained upward movement began.

THE features that deserve particular attention during the period 1881–1914 include: changes in agricultural prices and production; the effects of land legislation; the condition of agricultural labourers; technical developments, such as the more extensive use of machinery, improvements in animal husbandry, and changes in the marketing of agricultural produce; the creation in 1899 of the department of agriculture and technical instruction; and, dealing specifically with the western coastal areas, the work of the congested districts board.

---

[1] Solow, *The land question and the Irish economy, 1870–1903*, p. 122: 'it is almost impossible for the imagination to devise a worse combination of weather conditions than befell the Irish in 1879.'

[2] *Royal commission on agriculture. Preliminary report of the assistant commissioners for Ireland*, p. 1 [C 2951], H.C. 1881, xvi, 841.

[3] Seed Supply (Ireland) Act, 1880, 43 Vict., c. 1 (1 Mar. 1880).

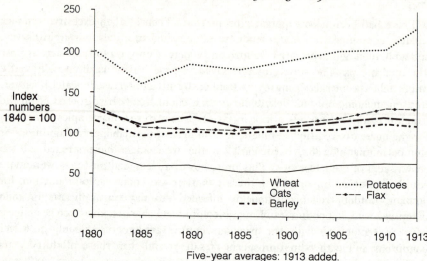

Five-year averages: 1913 added.

Figure 3   CROP PRICES, 1880–1913, by H.D. Gribbon

The course of agricultural prices is best illustrated by figures 3 and 4, using index numbers, with base 100 at 1840,[1] averaged over five-year periods. The response to these prices in terms of acreage of crops and numbers of livestock produced on farms will be clear from agricultural census figures. In general, tillage crops continued to decline, hay and pasture to increase. Cattle numbers moved upwards fairly steadily throughout the period as did numbers of poultry. There was little long-term change in pigs, but sheep numbers, after moving from the low levels of 1879–82 to a plateau around 1892, began to fall.

Too much emphasis should not be placed on the diminishing acreage of food crops because the reduction in area sown was offset by long-term improvements in crop yields; total food produced, in starch tons, probably increased rather than decreased between 1881 and 1914.[2] Prices too should be treated with caution because, with the exception of wheat and flax, and to a lesser extent barley, a high proportion of all crops grown was retained on the farm. Thus less and less produce from the land was reaching the consumer direct from the plough, more and more after conversion into livestock and livestock products.

On the livestock side of the industry it is significant that, whereas cattle numbers increased by 20 per cent between 1875–9 and 1910–14, exports rose by 33 per cent. Some of the difference may have been due to reduced home demand, although population fall was probably outbalanced by increasing urban consumption on the eastern side of the country, but the greater part reflects the fact that store cattle formed an increasing proportion of those exported. Fat cattle were not normally marketed under 2½ to 3 years old whereas store cattle could be sold at

[1] Source as above, p. 264, n. 2.

[2] Department of Industry and Commerce (Saorstat Éireann), *Agricultural statistics, 1847–1926* (Dublin, 1928, 1930), pp xxxi, xxxvii.

1½ to 2 years; by selling a greater proportion of young stock Irish farmers were able to achieve greater output from the same total area of crops and pasture and a largely stable breeding herd. In proof of this, fat cattle accounted for nearly half the total numbers exported in 1875 but for only one-third after 1900. Not that exports of fat animals declined; on the contrary they increased steadily between 1875–9 and 1890–94 and, despite downward fluctuations between 1895 and 1904, reached record high levels during 1910–14. The rearer of young stock found that his animals were wanted by both local and cross-channel graziers; there was competition among dealers for a wide variety of stock; while improved rail and steamship facilities helped to reduce transport delays and costs. Moreover the emphasis on young store cattle meant that it was worth while to improve the grazing on marginal upland pastures formerly devoted mainly to sheep. Unlike fattening, which was the business of large midland graziers, the rearing of young stock was practicable for the occupiers of the smaller poorer holdings, which comprised so high a proportion of the rest of Ireland. The changes outlined thus had widespread repercussions.

The increase in poultry numbers also indicated a growing participation in the money economy by the smallest landholders. There was a rise of 5.5 million birds between 1880 and 1906 with a further rise of 2.5 million between 1907 and 1914. The consequent increase in egg production was to some extent a continuation of

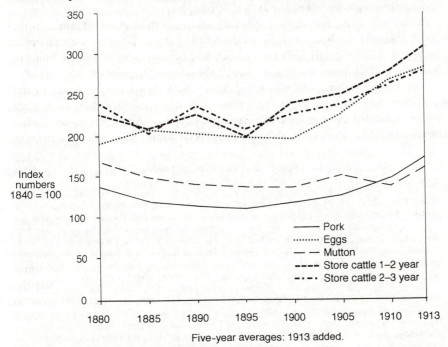

Figure 4 LIVESTOCK PRICES, 1880–1913, by H. D. Gribbon

the trend observable from before the mid-century, suggesting some amelioration of living conditions at home, but progressively reflecting a growing export business in which even the remote holdings on the western coast were able to take part. By 1914 exports of eggs were worth over £3 million a year.

As discussed elsewhere, several acts of parliament led to the gradual transition into owner-occupiers of something approaching 500,000 tenant farmers, a process that by 1920 had made substantial progress. There had been a few tenant purchasers under the encumbered estates acts, a further 6,057 under the Irish church act, 877 under the Landlord and Tenant (Ireland) Act, 1870, and 731 under the Land Law (Ireland) Act, 1881.[1] Under specifically land purchase legislation there were, up to 31 March 1920, 25,367 purchasers under the 1885 act, 46,834 under the acts of 1891 and 1896, and 278,748 under the Wyndham act of 1903 and the Birrell act of 1909. By 1919 358,614, that is over three-fifths of all holdings, either had been or were in course of being bought out.[2] In all, some 72 per cent of occupiers of land in Ireland had become or were in the process of becoming owners, most of them by means of annuity payments that fell below judicial rent levels. Since insecurity of tenure, rack-renting, and landlord negligence were traditionally blamed for the plight of tenant farmers it is relevant to inquire whether change of status from tenant to owner-occupier produced any practical effect in the use or management of land. As with other apparently simple questions the answer is complex.

In the first place, not all landlords had neglected their responsibilities. In the period 1840–81, Irish landlords were thought to have invested on their estates at least £3.5 million, partly their own money and partly money borrowed from the board of works.[3] At the latter date, despite the alleged deterrent effect of the 1870 act, a number of them were still acting jointly with their tenants in carrying out improvements, such as supplying timber and slates for farm buildings while tenants provided stone and did the actual construction. After 1881 falling rentals meant that, even where they wished, landlords could no longer afford to invest in

---

[1] 11 & 12 Vict., c. 48 (14 Aug. 1848); 12 & 13 Vict., c. 77 (28 July 1849); 32 & 33 Vict., c. 42 (26 July 1869); 33 & 34 Vict., c. 46 (1 Aug. 1870); 44 & 45 Vict., c. 49 (22 Aug. 1881).

[2] 48 & 49 Vict., c. 73 (14 Aug. 1885); 54 & 55 Vict., c. 48 (5 Aug. 1891); 59 & 60 Vict., c. 47 (14 Aug. 1896); 3 Edw. VII, c. 37 (14 Aug. 1903); 9 Edw. VII, c. 42 (3 Dec. 1909). The statistical difference between numbers of holdings bought out and of owner-occupiers created arises from the fact that in making one farm occupiers of land commonly put together two or more holdings, perhaps combining a home farm with a piece of upland grazing used as an 'out-farm'. Or, a farmer marrying a widow with land would normally operate both holdings as a single enterprise. Thus, as land purchase proceeded, the number of tenancies extinguished always exceeded the number of owner-occupied units created; see W. P. Coyne (ed.), *Ireland: industrial and agricultural* (2nd (expanded) ed., Dublin, 1902), pp 315–16.

[3] *Report of her majesty's commissioners of inquiry into the working of the Landlord and Tenant (Ireland) Act, 1870 . . . Minutes of evidence, part II*, p. 1290 [C 2779–II], H.C. 1881, xix, 540. The fourth earl of Fitzwilliam, who succeeded to the family properties in 1857, spent over £300,000 up to 1879 in improving his 90,000 acres in Wicklow (E. D. Steele, *Irish land and British politics, 1865–70* (Cambridge, 1974), p. 21; Lindsay Proudfoot, 'The management of a great estate: patronage, income, and expenditure on the duke of Devonshire's Irish property, *c.* 1816 to 1891' in *Ir. Econ. & Soc. Hist.*, xiii (1986), pp 32–55).

tenants' farms, while yearly tenants were deterred from doing so because they hoped run-down holdings would qualify for enhanced rent reductions. Leaseholders on the other hand, who did not come within the jurisdiction of the land courts until 1887, continued to improve their farms. In any case, it was difficult for a good farmer deliberately to neglect his land, or for a poor farmer to be transformed overnight: 'Land purchase will not turn the present small inefficient farmer into a good one', as an experienced land agent said in 1886.[1] Thus in terms of improvements to land it was not to be expected that ownership would bring about any spectacular change.

That this proved to be the case is evident, for example, from the absence of any regular upward trend in farmers' applications for board of works loans. To some extent of course reluctance to borrow money was a good thing; as W. F. Bailey, one of the land commissioners, said in 1903, 'A noteworthy proof of the improved financial circumstances of the tenant purchasers is the great care and evident hesitation with which they accept a loan. They are more cautious than of old in availing themselves of their credit.'[2] Nevertheless, improvements were made to farms, buildings, and equipment; independent of loan sources, farmers did invest capital in the holdings they now owned, but the timing of these activities, after 1895 and more noticeably after 1900, makes it difficult to say whether the response was due to the spur of ownership or the prevailing improved agricultural conditions. A committee that considered the question in 1903 expressed the view: 'that the holdings of tenant purchasers have largely improved in all parts of Ireland as regards cultivation, treatment, and general improvement is unquestionable.'[3] The committee thought that while the improvements noted were not necessarily the outcome of land purchase, tenants as well as owners being better off, certain important, including psychological, benefits must be attributed to the occupiers' change of status.

There were of course disadvantages. Whereas in bad times a landlord might grant rent remissions, the estates commissioners expected regular payment of the full annuity. Major drainage works were possible with cooperation from perhaps three or four landlords but virtually impossible where a multiplicity of owner-occupiers had to cooperate.[4] Professional land-agents, notably Scots, employed by improving landlords had usually been helpful rather than oppressive and their advice was missed by the new tenant purchasers, who now also became liable for poor rates and income tax. Tenant purchase helped to crystallise existing land divisions and to make rationalisation of occupation patterns more difficult than ever. Nor did land become cheaper since a tenant purchaser selling his interest

---

[1] *Report of the royal commission on the Land Law Ireland Act, 1881, and the Purchase of Land (Ireland) Act, 1885. Vol. II: Minutes of evidence and appendices*, p. 134 [C 4969-I], H.C. 1887, xxvi, 166.

[2] *Report . . . of an inquiry into the present condition of tenant purchasers under the land purchase acts*, p. 10, H.C. 1903 (92), lvii, 344.

[3] Ibid., p. 5 (MS 339).

[4] *Report of the departmental committee on agricultural credit in Ireland*, pp 278-9 [Cd 7375], H.C. 1914, xiii, 296-7.

was at least as likely as a landlord granting a tenancy to exact its full scarcity value.[1]

More significant than these general considerations, however, were the circumstances of individual holdings. Where the initial deposit was so high that the new owner had insufficient working capital, or the holding was too small, or the land too poor, no amount of work by the most assiduous occupier could mend matters and the owner of such a holding was worse off than a tenant in that he was unable to move elsewhere. Once the landlord–tenant relationship envisaged by the 1881 act had been achieved, therefore, a change to owner-occupation involved in principle a fairly even balance between benefits and disadvantage. The former could be outweighed more easily than the latter by the circumstances of a particular holding or the general conditions of the agricultural industry.

The number of agricultural labourers continued to diminish and wages continued to increase during the period 1881–1914, while the steady change in emphasis from tillage to livestock farming meant that of those employed a smaller proportion was required for seasonal and a larger proportion for regular work. Moreover, real wages during the period tended to rise faster than money wages so that regularly employed skilled men, such as herds, ploughmen, and shepherds, could be as well off as occupiers of small holdings.[2] On the other hand, hours were long—6 a.m. to 7 p.m. in summer was not unusual, Saturday half-holidays were unknown, and cottage accommodation usually appalling. Rural housing had often been the subject of adverse criticism and in 1867 was referred to as 'very wretched' and 'the disgrace of Ireland'.[3] By 1893 typical cottages were still referred to as 'utterly wretched cabins unfit for habitation'[4] and 'frequently deplorable'.[5] These largely pre-famine conditions were relieved here and there where landlords built cottages for their workers or where tenant farmers with long leases invoked the act of 1860, but while this made some contribution towards the housing of permanent men who could pay a modest rent or whose perquisites included a free house, it did nothing for day labourers whose low earnings would not stretch to the economic rent of cottages costing the usual £50–£150. Even for permanent men the attitudes of employers differed. One farmer in Mayo who had built several houses for his workers liked to have their families on his farm

---

[1] *Royal commission on the income tax. Sixth instalment of the minutes of evidence*, pp 1024–7 [Cmd 288–6], H.C. 1919, xxiii, pt 2, pp 298–301.

[2] *Royal commission on labour: the agricultural labourer. Vol. IV: Ireland, pt II. Reports by Mr W. P. O'Brien . . .*, pp 19–20 [C 6894–XIX], H.C. 1893–4, xxxvii, pt 1, pp 149–50.

[3] E. D. Mapother, M.D., 'On labourers' dwellings' in *Journal of the Royal Dublin Society*, v (1870), p. 35; *Report from the select committee of the house of lords on the Tenure (Ireland) Bill [H.L.], together with the . . . minutes of evidence . . .*, p. 261, H.C. 1867 (518), xiv, 701.

[4] *Royal commission on labour: the agricultural labourer, Ireland, pt 1. Reports by Mr R. McCrea . . .*, p. 10 [C 6894–XVIII], H.C. 1893–4, xxxvii, pt 1, 10.

[5] Ibid., pt 4, *Reports by Mr Arthur Wilson Fox*, p. 32 [C 6894–XXI], H.C. 1893–4, xxxvii, pt 1, 372. Fox adds 'After having had a large experience of cottage bedrooms in Norfolk and Suffolk . . . I can unhesitatingly say that the bedrooms in the older cottages in England are far worse ventilated than any of the rooms in an Irish cottage, notwithstanding the presence of cattle and pigs' (ibid., p. 34 (MS 374)).

'because they are always at my command when I want them',[1] but tenants who had achieved security and reduced rents under the 1881 act were conspicuously reluctant to provide accommodation for their workers, even when required by the land courts to do so.

Beginning in 1883, therefore, a series of acts was passed that enabled local authorities to borrow money from public funds on the security of the rates and to erect cottages specifically for agricultural labourers. Initial progress was slow, and initiative shown by poor law guardians so uneven that by 1892 the building of only seventy-eight cottages had been sanctioned in Ulster and eighty-seven in Connacht, while 4,464 had been sanctioned in Leinster and 7,242 in Munster.[2] The disparities may be explained by the fact that on the smallholdings of Connacht few labourers were employed and unions did not welcome any additional calls on the rates. In the north it was said that farmers did not want cottages to be built by local authorities because labourers would thereby become more independent;[3] in fact handloom weavers' cottages were still habitable and available in most parts.[4] By March 1906, 20,634 cottages had been provided, less than half the number estimated to be required.[5] Under the Labourers (Ireland) Act, 1906, however, defects in existing legislation were remedied and additional funds provided, largely by the labourers' cottages fund set up under the act, so that the rate of building more than doubled, producing a total of 43,702 cottages by 31 March 1914 and 47,966 by 31 March 1920.[6] The recommended maximum expenditure on a cottage and plot was £170, made up of £130 for building and £40 for the land, including in both cases legal and incidental costs.[7] The average rent of 'union' cottages, 1s. per week, required considerable subvention from local rates and government grants but was still an amount of consequence to a labourer earning 12s. per week. The provision of a half-acre plot with each cottage was, however, intended to facilitate the growing of potatoes at least and the keeping of a few poultry or pigs.

Between 1871 and 1911 the number of agricultural labourers fell by more than half but the acreage under tillage crops and hay by only one-seventh.[8] With livestock production expanding, the number of permanently employed men can

---

[1] Sources as for p. 276, n. 3.

[2] *Royal commission on labour: the agricultural labourer. Vol. IV: Ireland, pt 1. Reports by Mr R. McCrea*, p. 10 (MS 10). For legislation, see above, p. 99, n. 3.

[3] Ibid. For the diminished number of labourers through emigration, see below, pp 613–15.

[4] *Report from the select committee on land acts (Ireland); together with the ... minutes of evidence ...*, p. 431, H.C. 1894 (310), xii, 491.

[5] Elizabeth R. Hooker, *Readjustments of agricultural tenure in Ireland* (Chapel Hill, N.C., 1938), p. 183.

[6] 6 Edw. VII, c. 37 (4 Aug. 1906); *Annual report of the local government board for Ireland, for the year ended 31 Mar. 1914*, p. 168 [Cd 7561], H.C. 1914, xxxix, 824; *Annual report ... for the year ended 31 Mar. 1920*, p. lxxvi [Cmd 1423], H.C. 1921, xiv, 858.

[7] *Annual report of the local government board for Ireland for the year ended 31 Mar. 1908*, p. 268 [Cd 4243], H.C. 1908, xxxi, 338.

[8] *Agricultural statistics, Ireland 1912. Report and tables relating to Irish agricultural labourers*, p. 9 [Cd 6928], H.C. 1913, lxxvi, 477.

have decreased little, if at all, so that the reduction must have been concentrated among casual or day labourers. The gross underemployment of these men, their low earnings, and the uneconomic use of human resources in Irish agriculture could hardly be better illustrated. The drastic reduction in numbers and increase in output per man, made possible by better farming and increased use of machinery, were essential prerequisites for, and indications of, economic progress. Undoubtedly numbers fell faster than was convenient for farmer-employers, many of whom complained. Their difficulties were partially overcome by migrant labour; for example, men came from Cavan and Monaghan into the Ardee district during harvest and young men and women from Kerry and West Cork travelled to the dairying district around Limerick in spring and summer. Mutual help or 'neighbouring' was another solution for smaller-scale operations. So far as permanent men were concerned no great reduction in numbers was possible until the horse was replaced as the major motive power on the farm, and this had to await more than another decade.

FOLLOWING the lessons of the famine and the reappearance of blight in 1859, disease resistant strains of potatoes were developed and came into general use during the 1870s, but spraying with Bordeaux mixture was not tried until 1885 and was not universally adopted until 1910. Commercial interests ensured that the cultivation of flax received more than average attention, and between 1848 and 1857 the Royal Dublin Society was given annual government grants of £1,000 to pay the expenses of instructors, whose attention was directed particularly to the south and west, but their efforts met with little more success than those of their eighteenth-century predecessors. In the north, government grants to the Joint Flax Committee between 1864 and 1871, and the work of the Flax Supply Association, encouraged the improvement of flax-scutching machinery and the introduction of fresh strains. Despite these efforts the price of Irish scutched flax fell fairly steadily after 1866 and was consistently below that of imported Belgian flax, which gradually replaced it.

Despite an increasing livestock population, the growing of root crops—turnips, mangolds, fodder beet—made little headway. Indeed, turnips were grown partly at least for human food as an alternative to the vulnerable potato, and acreage decreased after 1895. Perhaps the most marked difference between knowledge and ignorance, between progress and stagnation, arose in cultivating Ireland's premier crop—grass. Progressive farmers introduced new types, the government tried to ensure the sale of good quality seed, and some pastures were laid down on well drained and prepared ground; but much of the area taken out of tillage in the post-famine years was simply 'allowed to cover itself naturally' with a poor weedy scrub.[1] Here as so frequently elsewhere progress was painfully slow. In 1865 agriculture in Ireland was said to be backward both absolutely and in comparison

---

[1] *Richmond comm. evidence*, pp 102–3 [C 2778–I], 1881, xv, 130–31.

with Great Britain, France, and Belgium.[1] In 1876 it was pointed out that the current prosperity owed little if anything to improved farming.[2] Horace Plunkett in 1896 said that 'ours is by common consent one of the simplest and most barbarous systems of agriculture in western Europe, both as regards to want of variety in the crops and the scantiness of the produce'.[3] But Plunkett's view was coloured by his desire to promote the panacea of agricultural cooperation, whereas recent appraisals of Irish post-famine agriculture paint a more cheerful picture. Total factor productivity growth turns out to have been a good deal higher than that recently calculated for Britain at a similar period, and also higher than that calculated for the United States for 1840–1900.

It was not that the Irish cultivator lacked energy or patience. The spade was more ubiquitous than the plough in many districts long after the famine and so continued on smallholdings and hilly areas into the twentieth century; only a people of timeless industry could have built farms on the rocky western seaboard by cutting and carrying seaweed from the shore to remote mountain holdings whose stone dykes round each tiny field represented generations of clearance work with bare hands or the simplest of tools. When he went to Great Britain the Irish harvest labourer or navvy was conspicuous for his endurance and hard work, but at home much of his energy was misapplied, underemployed, and made ineffective by the conditions under which he worked.

Fortunately the mild Irish climate allowed cattle, other than milk cows, to be wintered in the open, while stall fattening was the exception rather than the rule; but milk yields were low and beef animals slow in maturing. Landlords, large farmers, and graziers were therefore particularly interested in improvements in the breeding of cattle, so that in 1864 the improved quality of cattle and sheep on the larger farms was singled out by one observer as a bright feature in an otherwise depressing agricultural scene.[4] A few progressive farmers found during the depressed conditions of 1879–90 that it paid to house-feed beef cattle for sale in winter and spring instead of in the usual autumn glut period. Later, in 1898, a Scottish importer of store cattle referred to an immense improvement in animals coming from Ireland.[5] The improvement was due not only to the better breeding and management on large farms but also to the better transport facilities that enabled animals to be carried by rail and steamship with less damage and loss of condition

[1] *Report from the select committee on Tenure and Improvement of Land (Ireland) Act; . . . minutes of evidence*, pp 1, 44, 119, 193, H.C. 1865 (402), xi, 353, 396, 471, 545.

[2] James Macauley, *The truth about Ireland: tours of observation in 1872 and 1875 etc.* (London, 1876), pp 253, 261.

[3] *Report of the recess committee on the establishment of a department of agriculture and industries for Ireland* (Dublin, 1896), p. 11; Cormac Ó Gráda, *Ireland before and after the famine* (Manchester, 1988), p. 130.

[4] *Report from the select committee on taxation of Ireland*, p. 173, H.C. 1864 (513), xv, 207.

[5] J. Gillespie, 'The cattle industry in Scotland' in *Transactions of the Highland and Agricultural Society of Scotland*, 5th ser., x (1898), p. 236.

than formerly,[1] and to the operation from 1866 onwards of the diseases of animals acts.

The mild damp climate favouring cattle was less suitable for sheep, which were affected by disease, notably liver fluke, throughout the period and, possibly because of their relatively low unit-value, received from breeders less attention than cattle. Their wool was suitable for only a limited range of fabrics and they were reared primarily for meat. With few exceptions, pigs were kept in small numbers, chiefly on the smaller holdings and fed on surplus potatoes when available, but otherwise on scraps. Their owners had neither the knowledge nor the resources for breeding improvements. After 1887 belated support came from the government and the Royal Dublin Society,[2] but this was largely offset by an increased incidence of swine fever between 1880 and 1895. Apart from some improvements in feeding, therefore, any advance before the end of the century was mainly in the curing side of the industry.

Improvements in the handling of agricultural produce were probably as significant as changes in production towards the end of the nineteenth and beginning of the twentieth centuries. The use of ice in bacon curing after 1860 and refrigeration from about 1887 meant that bacon could be cured all the year round, enhancing its keeping quality and leading to more efficiently run factories. It also made possible a milder type of cure, enabling Irish bacon on the London market to face increasing Danish competition. The introduction of line slaughter, after the Chicago pattern, around 1900 represented unusually progressive thinking. These changes were of importance in the main curing centres of the south, Dublin, Limerick, and Waterford; less so in Belfast and Derry, which handled the typical Ulster farm-killed pig, although the former built up a reputation, particularly in the Scottish market, for 'Belfast hams'. Together the northern and southern districts contributed to an industry whose exports were valued at £2.5 million in 1904, increasing steadily to £4.4 million in 1913.

Facing similar competition the butter industry proved less flexible. In the main producing areas of Munster butter was made on a multitude of farms of all sizes and in widely varying conditions while the Cork market through which much of it passed was hampered by anachronistic regulations. Little improvement took place before the last quarter of the century when, gradually, mild-cured butter began to replace the over-salted type no longer required on the British market; the bulky and frequently dirty firkins in which it was sold began to be replaced after 1879 by lighter more convenient packaging; the reactionary Cork market

---

[1] The deterioration in Irish cattle during transit, reflected in their lower market price in Britain compared with animals from England and Scotland, added an incentive to the switch from fat cattle to stores (*Report . . . relative to the trade in and the movement of animals intended for exportation from Ireland to Great Britain . . . for the year 1877* [C 2104], H.C. 1878, xxv, 537–78; John O'Donovan, *The economic history of livestock in Ireland* (Cork, 1940), p. 230).

[2] Until 1902 it was claimed that most of the funds allocated to the R.D.S. for stock improvement went to horse-breeding (J. P. Huttmann, 'The impact of land reform on agricultural production in Ireland' in *Agricultural History*, xlvi (1972), p. 363).

committee was reformed in 1884; by 1885 the efforts of the Munster Dairy School in training farmers' daughters in dairying had begun to affect the quality of local butter;[1] and in the late 1880s weekly fresh-butter markets and blending factories were established in many places in the south of Ireland, leading to both an improved product and useful competition with the traditional firkin butter centres. All these things combined to reinstate Irish butter in the British market from which it was in danger of being ousted by continental, particularly Danish, competition. One problem was that Irish butter production and marketing were concentrated in the six spring and summer months whereas Danish butter appeared on the British market uniformly throughout the year.[2] Winter dairying was more expensive but on the other hand markets lost in the autumn had to be regained each summer. It was not so much that Irish butter had declined in quality as that the appearance of a superior, more regular product had emphasised its defects. Finally, the mechanical cream separator, available from 1879, began to be adopted and by 1889 creameries were in operation in Limerick, Tipperary, and Cork. With trained staff and up-to-date equipment, creameries contributed largely to the £4 million gross output of the industry in 1907.

The poultry industry owed its rapid expansion at the end of the century to refrigeration and to developments in packaging and transport, though as late as 1906 breakages among Irish eggs on arrival with British wholesalers were conspicuously higher than among imports from Denmark. Nevertheless by 1913 the value of exports from Ireland had reached £4 million.

Production and marketing were both affected by the development after 1889 of agricultural cooperation. The start was slow. Plunkett wrote: 'My own diary records attendance at fifty meetings before a single society had resulted therefrom.'[3] However, thirty societies, all cooperative creameries, had been established by 1893 and by 1903 there were over 800 societies—300 dairy societies, 140 agricultural societies, nearly 200 agricultural banks, 50 home industry societies, 40 poultry societies, and 40 others with miscellaneous objects.[4] The 80,000 members were nearly all occupiers farming on a very small scale, with tenant-purchasers forming an increasing proportion of the total. By buying seeds, fertilisers, and feeding stuffs in bulk, by providing a marketing organisation, by operating creameries and bacon factories, by small-scale lending from Raiffeissen-type banks, the cooperatives used their strength effectively in the prevailing favourable market conditions. By instruction and encouragement they helped to improve their members' standards of farming. Up to 1914, when there were around 1,000 societies, the movement seemed destined to play an increasingly

---

[1] For an account of the origin and functions of the Munster Dairy School or 'Munster Institute', see *Departmental committee on the Irish butter industry [vol. ii]*, pp 463–76 [Cd 5093], H.C. 1910, viii, 475–8, and Coyne, *Ireland: industrial and agricultural*, pp 137–45.

[2] *Report of the departmental committee on the Irish butter industry*, p. 21 [Cd 5092], H.C. 1910, vii, 861.

[3] Horace Plunkett, *Ireland in the new century* (London, 1905), p. 190.

[4] Ibid., p. 192; above, pp 87–90.

important part in Irish agriculture. Its subsequent failure to do so must be attributed more to political than to economic causes.

THE background to the setting up in 1899 of the department of agriculture and technical instruction for Ireland will be found elsewhere;[1] it is sufficient to comment here on the new department's influence on agricultural development in the opening years of the present century. For a number of reasons the breadth of the department's responsibilities was extraordinarily wide. Agriculture, fisheries, veterinary work, agricultural statistics, agricultural education, these were within its legitimate sphere. But it was saddled also with technical education in the widest sense: supervision of certain colleges and institutions, including the national library; the collection and compilation of banking, railway, and shipping statistics; the administration of government grants for science and art; and, in 1905, the carrying out of the geological survey of Ireland. The multiplicity of duties, however, does not seem to have interfered with the department's major agricultural interest, in which progress was steady rather than spectacular.

In the first place, the department had the duty of enforcing the diseases of animals acts, involving veterinary inspection of animals entering and leaving the country, and the slaughter of those with anthrax, swine fever, or foot-and-mouth disease.[2] These preventive measures were long-term in their effects. Other duties required by legislation, under for example the fertilisers and feeding stuffs act,[3] were more immediately beneficial. So too were schemes aimed at the improvement of livestock by selective breeding, the encouragement of butter production, and the handling of milk and dairy products. Throughout, the department avoided doing things that farmers could do for themselves or interfering with prices and normal trade competition. Even its loans were directed towards those farmers whose means were limited: 'In order to encourage farmers of small means to provide themselves, either with a registered stallion or a premium bull, a sum of money was allotted by the department . . . for the purpose of granting loans for the purchase of approved sires.'[4] 'These loans [for hay barns] are not intended for occupiers who can afford, or may reasonably be expected to pay, cash for the required barn . . . '[5] It was not simply that funds were insufficient for grant or subsidy schemes but that the whole philosophy of the day was opposed to any such idea.

Much more in conformity with the spirit of the times, the department directed particular efforts towards experiment and instruction. Experiments on manuring, disease-resistant strains of potatoes, calf-rearing, flax growing and handling, and

---

[1] Above, pp 90–91, and below, pp 588–9.

[2] 57 & 58 Vict., c. 57 (25 Aug. 1894); 59 & 60 Vict., c. 15 (20 July 1896).

[3] 56 & 57 Vict., c. 56 (22 Sept. 1893).

[4] *Department of agriculture and technical instruction for Ireland: first annual general report*, p. 30 [Cd 838], H.C. 1902, xx, 546.

[5] *Report of the departmental committee on agricultural credit in Ireland*, p. 288 [Cd 7375], 1914, xiii, 306.

many others were accompanied by the propagation of modern ideas and methods by instruction leaflets, itinerant instructors, and exhibitions. In the field of more formal education it provided instruction at its Glasnevin farm (the Albert College, 'institute', or 'department') for students in the agricultural faculty, established in 1900, of the Royal College of Science; also at Glasnevin its own instructors were trained. The Munster Dairy School trained women and girls in dairying and poultry keeping; several agricultural stations were opened where short courses were given to farmers' sons and daughters. The total effect of such work or indeed the total effect of the department's agricultural activity is impossible to quantify. To some extent the department replaced the advisory activity of the few enlightened landlords who had regarded themselves as having duties toward their tenants; to some extent it continued and supported the agricultural work of the Royal Dublin Society; to some extent it applied to the whole country the ideas and activities of the congested districts board. If the conservative nature of the industry made new ideas uncertain of welcome, if bureaucracy came in practice to temper zeal, if more time than had been anticipated had to be spent in laying foundations, the first decade or so of the department's work saw important steps taken from the passive attitude of the nineteenth to the more active tempo of twentieth-century agriculture.[1]

THE congested districts board was established in 1891 to deal with the pre-famine conditions still persisting in many northern and western coastal areas.[2] A 'congested' district was one where more than 20 per cent of the population of a county lived in electoral divisions of which the average rateable value was less than £1. 10s. per head.[3] This, translated into geographical terms, produced the pattern shown below (volume ix, map 85). Within the areas indicated the land was exceptionally poor and quite unable to sustain the population settled on it. Farming of its tiny holdings had to be supplemented by fishing, migrant harvest labour, kelp burning, and minor domestic industry. Emigrant remittances and, after 1909, old age pensions made a significant contribution, but when all sources of income had been taken into account the area remained conspicuously impoverished, badly farmed, deficient in communications, and with a population regularly drained of its most active members. As one report put it, 'There are two classes in the congested districts mainly, namely, the poor and the destitute. There are some shopkeepers and officials . . . but their numbers are very small, and there are hardly any resident gentry . . . Nearly all the inhabitants are on one dead level of poverty.'[4] The manner of life of the people was described thus:

[1] Coyne, *Ireland: industrial and agricultural*, pp 271–94.
[2] 54 & 55 Vict., c. 48 (5 Aug. 1891), pt II.
[3] The average valuation per acre of holdings in the congested districts was 3s. 6d. compared with 12s. 1d. in the rest of Ireland.
[4] *Royal commission on local taxation: minutes of evidence, vol. V: Ireland*, p. 126 [Cd 383], H.C. 1900, xxxvi, 744.

In the poorer districts the food consists largely of potatoes from harvest time until the spring, and of flour and Indian meal during the 'hungry' months, supplemented by bread and tea. Oatmeal seems to be little used; milk is scarce, and the diet is entirely vegetable, with the exception of salt fish at times, which is generally used more as a relish than as an ordinary article of food, or a little fat bacon used as 'kitchen'. Some beer and whiskey and a comparatively large amount of tobacco are used, whilst in many districts the consumption of tea seems excessive. Most of these articles may, however, be regarded as stimulants for a badly fed population rather than as ordinary luxuries.[1]

A more picturesque account from George Wyndham's pen when he visited the area in 1901 includes

They manure with [seaweed] the starved soil that has given potatoes for 50 years . . . [they] carry pieces of [granite] to make walls round enclosures the size of a room . . . Some wild colts and lean cattle roam like goats over the intricate waste . . . The women toil over the slippery rocks laden with creels of seaweed. The men lean and loaf and look with soft idle blue eyes at the sea. The place is a beautiful, stagnant desolation.[2]

Despite such conditions, including the worst possible housing, the health of the population was remarkably good and the excess of births over deaths considerably above that in the rest of rural Ireland.

The board had two major tasks: to reform the landholding pattern, which was dominated by rundale and intermixed plots, and to raise the total income of the area. Chronologically the latter was tackled first, land reform having to await the passage of legislation, particularly the acts of 1903 and 1909, of which the second gave the board compulsory purchasing powers.[3] The tasks were of course linked, for agricultural advance was impossible on holdings where even 'a field of one acre may belong to a dozen persons, each of whom owns his particular plot . . . '[4] Even a list of the board's activities would be lengthy but, as they are fully detailed in its annual reports, a few only need be mentioned here. These are grouped under fisheries, agriculture, rural industry, and communications.

Aids to the fishing industry included the bringing to Ireland of Scottish instructors in curing and fishing; the building of curing stations; marine works, such as piers, harbours, and navigation marks; loans to fishermen for the purchase of boats and gear; the carrying on of barrel-making and boat-building. At one stage the board operated its own steam drifters. The value of fish landed on the congested districts coast in 1891 was estimated at £51,000, and in 1913 at £167,000. Total board expenditure on fisheries from 1891 to 1917 was £484,000, of which £298,000 was recovered, mainly from sales, leaving a net expenditure of £186,000. Loans to fishermen for boats and gear amounted to a further £232,000.[5]

[1] *Royal commission on congestion in Ireland: final report*, p. 6 [Cd 4097], H.C. 1908, xlii, 746.
[2] I am indebted for this delightful though possibly superfluous reference to L. P. Curtis, *Coercion and conciliation in Ireland* (Princeton, N.J., 1963), p. 356.
[3] 3 Edw. VII, c. 37 (14 Aug. 1903); 9 Edw. VII, c. 42 (3 Dec. 1909).
[4] Coyne, *Ireland: industrial and agricultural*, p. 262.
[5] W. L. Micks, *An account . . . of the congested districts board for Ireland from 1891 to 1923* (Dublin, 1925), p. 57.

The limited tillage of the congested districts provided an uncertain livelihood for the people and their livestock, and depended on a very primitive system; but there was little scope for innovation. The board's assistance was therefore directed toward improvements within the existing pattern. Instructors were appointed to teach better farming methods; schemes were initiated to improve the breeding of livestock and poultry; assistance was given towards sheep-dipping, fencing, potato-spraying, and the purchase of agricultural implements. When in 1903 this side of the board's work was transferred to the department of agriculture and technical instruction, over £140,000 had been spent on agricultural work and a further £14,000 had been advanced in loans for agricultural purposes. £49,000 was spent under 'parish committee schemes' to encourage improvements, mainly to dwelling houses and farm buildings. The energy and idealism with which the board approached the agricultural side of its work may be illustrated by Micks's reference to the bee-keeping instructor who 'combined the enthusiasm of a missionary with the sagacity and endurance of a commercial traveller. He . . . travelled on his push bicycle over all the congested districts from Donegal to Kerry and West Cork.'[1] No doubt the board's agricultural activities were amateurish, and they were of necessity financially modest, but in the prevailing conditions of the congested districts, they were practical, reasonably effective, and consistent with the policy of helping the people to help themselves.

Wool was one of the few industrial raw materials available in the board's area and fortunately a demand existed in Great Britain for tweeds and homespun fabrics. Accordingly the board was able by the use of instructors and the supply of equipment to aid the domestic woollen manufacture. Loans and grants were made to a woollen mill at Foxford and a machine-knitting factory at Ballaghader-reen (both backed by the Sisters of Charity), while in west Donegal four small carpet factories were set up with the board's encouragement, each employing 150–200 workers. Hand- and machine-knitting were promoted and numerous schools set up to train women and girls in lace and crochet work. Small-scale as these efforts may have been, they were, up to 1914 at least, remarkably successful, and in households where total cash income might be as low as 14s. a month every small addition meant a significant improvement in living standards. Of particular value in this as in other aspects of the board's work was the support it received from convent schools and the local clergy.

The improvement in communications served several purposes, providing employment, opening up the area to tourists, and affording facilities for the speedier marketing of perishable goods such as fish and eggs. The board had insufficient funds to assist in the construction of light railways in its area, though it encouraged and benefited from them. Instead it spent some £418,000 up to 1919 on the building of causeways, roads, and bridges. It also granted subsidies to certain steamship services including those from Galway to the Aran Islands,

---

[1] Ibid., p. 32.

from Derry to ports in County Donegal, from Sligo to Belmullet, and from Bantry railway pier to Castletownberehaven; it operated its own steamer, generally on the business of the board but sometimes to carry cargo in default of other services.

Land purchase, on a scale not envisaged when it was set up, completely altered the balance of the board's work. Holdings in the congested districts were generally too small to make tenant purchase economic. The board, therefore, bought complete estates, rearranged, consolidated, and, where possible, enlarged holdings, built roads, carried out fencing and drainage, and repaired or occasionally built dwelling houses before selling the improved holdings to the tenants under land purchase annuity terms. Begun on an experimental basis in 1893, and after legislation had sufficiently widened the board's powers,[1] the work resulted, in the course of ten years, in the purchase for £536,168 of forty-six estates containing 169,829 acres, £179,054 being spent on improvements before resale to 6,211 tenants. The Wyndham act of 1903 increased the powers of the board to make purchases and its annual income by £20,000; the Birrell act of 1909 increased the area of its operations by over 4 million acres. Under the former, the board purchased for £1,685,189 a total of 158 estates containing 227,723 acres with 9,516 tenants. Under the Birrell act most purchases were made between 1910 and 1914—some 733 estates containing 1,768,000 acres and costing about £7 million. Resale to tenants had not been completed at the time of the board's dissolution in 1923 but by that date over 2 million acres had been purchased under its auspices at a cost of £9 million; and on the holdings created, improvements worth £2,249,477 had been made.[2]

The board's annual income was originally £41,250, which was interest at 2.75 per cent on a grant of £1.5 million, known as the church surplus grant because it was charged on the Irish church temporalities fund. At its foundation the board also became responsible for the Irish reproductive loan fund, amounting to about £66,000 in cash, securities, and outstanding loans, and for part of the sea and coast fisheries fund, amounting to about £18,000.[3] The last two funds had their origins in public subscriptions collected—mainly in London—in 1822 to relieve current distress on the Irish western seaboard, and their residues had been transferred to the board of works in 1874 and 1884 respectively, for issue as loans in those counties for which the congested districts board subsequently became responsible.[4] Additional income was provided in 1899 by a parliamentary grant of £25,000, but since £8,000 of this was required for administrative expenses, previously voted separately, the board gained a net £17,000 only.[5] From 1903 there was a further allocation of £20,000 a year from the Ireland development

---

[1] 56 & 57 Vict., c. 35 (24 Aug. 1893); 47 & 58 Vict., c. 50 (25 Aug. 1894).

[2] Curtis, *Coercion & conciliation*, p. 361.

[3] 54 & 55 Vict., c. 48 (5 Aug. 1891), pt II.

[4] 37 & 38 Vict., c. 86 (7 Aug. 1874); 47 & 48 Vict., c. 21 (3 July 1884).

[5] 62 & 63 Vict., c. 18 (1 Aug. 1899); *Royal commission on congestion in Ireland: final report*, p. 10 [Cd 4097], H.C. 1908, xlii, 750.

grant[1] and finally in 1909 an annual parliamentary provision of £144,750.[2] This brought the board's total grant income to £231,000. The money handled each year, however, was considerably greater, amounting in 1919/20 to £866,448, of which the major items outside parliamentary income were £348,618 from rents of tenanted land and revenue from untenanted land. On the expenditure side, the major items were £147,460 spent on estate improvements and £170,405 paid to the Irish land commissioners, mainly in interest on money used to purchase estates. Fisheries expenditure, in grants and loans, totalled £53,698, with sales and loan repayments of £70,332.[3]

Set up with the widest terms of reference, the congested districts board was able generally to adopt an empirical approach to its problems, and almost uniformly met with cooperation, if not from the treasury at least from the people it sought to help. It is worth remarking that none of its resources was directed towards promoting emigration, the most obvious remedy for many of the area's ills.

THE Irish fishing industry enjoyed a number of advantages—immediate access to rich fishing grounds, a deeply indented coast with natural harbours, and a fishing tradition spanning several centuries—yet in 1850 it was in a most unsatisfactory condition. The immediate cause was the extreme poverty accompanying and following the famine, which had led to boats being sold or left unrepaired, equipment neglected, and Atlantic coast fishing villages decimated; as emigration continued the number of boats and men engaged in fishing diminished steadily. In 1850, for instance, 14,800 boats and 63,000 men and boys were shown by coastguards' returns to be employed; by 1880 the numbers had shrunk to 6,500 boats and 24,500 men and boys.[4] Contemporary observers recognised and lamented the facts but seemed unable to suggest remedies.

There were several difficulties. With an industry whose equipment was in the hands of individual fishermen or small groups, capital to purchase new boats and gear, even in good times, was not readily available. Again, a high proportion of crews fished only part time, and most boats were suitable for inshore fishing only. Meantime the provision of piers and harbours where fish could be landed, of curing and packing facilities, and of transport to take the fish to distant markets, were outside the direct control of the industry.

From the point of view of government interest, fishing seems to have been the Cinderella of the Irish industries. The support given to it in 1819 was reduced in 1824 and eliminated in 1830; as part of famine relief works seven fish-curing houses were built in 1847–8, only to be closed shortly after 1850 when they were

---

[1] 3 Edw. VII, c. 37 (14 Aug. 1903), sect. 38; the Ireland development grant was created by 3 Edw. VII, c. 23 (11 Aug. 1903).

[2] 9 Edw. VII, c. 42 (3 Dec. 1909), sect. 49.

[3] *Twenty-eighth report of the congested districts board for Ireland* [1 Apr. 1919–31 Mar. 1920], pp 5, 13 [Cmd 1409], H.C. 1921, xiv, 617, 625.

[4] *Nineteenth report from the board of public works, Ireland*, p. 161 [1414], H.C. 1851, xxv, 233.

beginning to be efficient;[1] the fishery inspectors appointed in 1869 were not given control of any funds that could be loaned or granted for fishery purposes,[2] and their numbers compared unfavourably with those in Scotland. But a description of their garret apartment in Dublin castle as 'a cock-loft more resembling the *sanctorum* [*sic*] of an astrologer than the office where the onerous public duties of the fisheries of Ireland are conducted' seems rather unkind.[3] However, partly as famine relief and later under a series of fishery acts the board of works made loans to local authorities for the construction and repair of piers; loans that, between 1848 and 1887, totalled over £375,000.[4] Then in 1874 the fishery inspectors were given power to recommend loans to fishermen from the Irish Reproductive Loan Fund.[5] Between 1874 and 1880 £31,079.10s. from this source was advanced to 1,737 applicants.[6] Clearly the average loan was insufficient to build deep-sea fishing boats costing around £800; but the assistance helped inshore fishermen and arrested the decline in total numbers of boats and crews employed. Apart from public funds there were private charities (Lady Burdett Coutts was said to have £10,000 out on loan, free of interest, to Baltimore fishermen in 1885),[7] and normal capital investment exceeded the charitable funds. Also, railway extensions to some of the fishing ports were beginning.[8] By 1880 therefore the decline had been halted and the future had begun to look healthier than for some years.

Bad as it was, however, the extent of the decline between 1850 and 1880 should not be exaggerated. The east and south-east coast fisheries whose produce could be landed directly in Britain never experienced decline to the same extent as those on the Atlantic coast,[9] and if the number of boats declined, the proportion of larger types able to stay at sea and to fish the more distant grounds, equipped with better gear and manned by full-time crews, started to increase. With better transport to take fish to the British market, returns from catches landed became gradually more remunerative. When, therefore, contemporary observers stressed the inadequacy of landing facilities and deplored the numerical decline in boats and crews they were referring mainly to the Atlantic coast; elsewhere the

---

[1] *Report from the select committee on industries (Ireland); . . . minutes of evidence*, p. 42, H.C. 1884–5 (288), ix, 60.

[2] 32 & 33 Vict., c. 92 (9 Aug. 1869).

[3] John Hoare, 'The resources of the sea fisheries of Ireland' in *Journal of the Royal Dublin Society*, v (1870), p. 8.

[4] 9 & 10 Vict., c. 3 (5 Mar. 1846); 10 & 11 Vict., c. 75 (22 July 1847); 16 & 17 Vict., c. 136 (20 Aug. 1853); 19 & 20 Vict., c. 37 (30 June 1856); 29 & 30 Vict., c. 45 (28 June 1866); 43 & 44 Vict., c. 4 (15 Mar. 1880); 46 & 47 Vict., c. 26 (2 Aug. 1883); *Second report of the royal commission on Irish public works: appendix*, pp 707–11 [C 5264–1], H.C. 1888, xlviii, 951–5.

[5] 37 & 38 Vict., c. 86 (7 Aug. 1874).

[6] *Second report of the royal commission on Irish public works: appendix*, pp 768–9 [C 5264–1], H.C. 1888, xlviii, 1012–13.

[7] *Report from the select committee on industries (Ireland): . . . minutes of evidence*, p. 36, H.C. 1884–5 (288), ix, 54.

[8] *Nineteenth report from the board of public works, Ireland*, pp 67, 161 [1414], H.C. 1851, xxv, 70, 233.

[9] This is the general tenor of successive reports of the commissioners of Irish fisheries.

post-famine depression was neither so deep nor so lasting as some reports suggested. Indeed the considerable sales of Scottish herring indicated that despite population decrease there was still a market for fish to be exploited within Ireland.[1]

The remainder of the nineteenth century was characterised by improvement rather than growth. Rising population in Great Britain, combined with better refrigeration and specialised transport, created a growing market for fish which should have meant expansion for the Irish industry. Unfortunately the whole pattern of supply to the British market was changing; an increasing proportion of fish was coming from Iceland and the far northern seas, and whereas only five steam trawlers were registered at Irish ports in 1899 there were in England and Wales over 1,100.[2]

In local waters the Irish Sea was being fished by boats from Fleetwood, the Isle of Man, and the Welsh and Scottish ports, while on the Atlantic shelf well-equipped French boats competed with the Irish. Setting distant grounds apart, therefore, the Irish industry was faced with at best a limited supply of fish and these mainly seasonal—herring and mackerel. Around the Irish coast, however, there was still room for improvement. Greater quantities of fish could be landed and better prices obtained given proper handling facilities; rail transport was lacking at many fishing ports. There was no reason why boats should not be built locally instead of being bought from the Isle of Man; nets and gear could be made as well in Ireland as in Great Britain. In 1887 there were said to be herring curing facilities only at Dublin, Dungarvan, and Castletown; on the west coast more boats above 25 to 30 tons were needed to fish beyond the Aran Islands.

A difficulty was that even the established fishing ports on the south and east coasts bore little resemblance to Grimsby, Lowestoft, or Aberdeen with their concentration of ancillary services and capital, while the industry in the north and west of Ireland depended on many small harbours and ill-equipped landing places. Considerable encouragement by government was therefore necessary if the industry was to be maintained and modernised, let alone expanded. Railway extension was a case in point. Connections were completed to Bantry, Skibbereen, Dingle, Baltimore, Ardglass, Killybegs, Valentia, Kenmare, Achill, Clifden, and Burtonport among others in the period 1881–1903, generally under the Balfour act (1889), of which it was said that the government bore £1,554,000 of the £1,850,000 expenditure under the act.[3]

Work on fishery piers and harbours was also financed in the main from public funds, for example the £250,000 granted under the Sea Fisheries (Ireland) Act,

---

[1] John de Courcy Ireland, *Ireland's sea fisheries: a history* (Dublin, 1981), p. 68.

[2] *Report of the inspectors of Irish fisheries . . . for 1899*, p. 5 [Cd 222], H.C. 1900, xii, 315; *Sea fisheries (England and Wales): fourteenth annual report of the inspectors*, p. 8 [Cd 326], H.C. 1900, xii, 122.

[3] 52 & 53 Vict., c. 66 (30 Aug. 1889); Patrick Flanagan, *Transport in Ireland, 1880–1910* (Dublin, 1969), p. 172.

1883, and the £100,000 under the Marine Works Act, 1902.[1] Additional money came from the department of agriculture and technical instruction, the Ireland development fund, the congested districts board, and the county councils. But the £3,000 a year available to Howth, for instance, was considered to be misapplied, and elsewhere financial restrictions meant that piers were not extended far enough into deep water to ensure berthing at all states of the tide.[2] Annual figures do not exist but the total spent in the period 1880 to 1914 cannot have been far short of £1,000,000.

It is difficult to be sure of the size and significance of the Irish fishing industry. The census of production for 1907 shows the value of fish landed as £341,000 and the number of persons regularly employed as 8,027 and occasionally employed as 16,405. The annual official figures for numbers of boats and men engaged and for quantities and values of fish landed have, however, substantial shortcomings. They do not attempt to record fish landed in Great Britain by Irish boats nor the proportion of time spent fishing by part-time crews—some 15,000 to 18,000 men, representing more than three-quarters of the total. Nevertheless some facts of significance can be noted; for instance that, despite fluctuations during the period, the average number of boats fishing full-time fell by only 12.5 per cent between 1880–85 and 1905–10 while the number of boats fishing part-time marginally increased. Significant and consistent falls in both boats and crews occur only after 1905. The report for 1913 points out that the fall in total number of boats was offset by an increase in the number of high-powered motor vessels fishing full-time.[3] The 1914 picture is distorted by the enlistment or calling up of men in the Royal Naval Reserve. The quantities of fish landed in Ireland, recorded from 1887, showed rather less change than did numbers of boats and crews. The value did not fall below £300,000 and only once exceeded £400,000. Representative figures in the period 1883–94 show salmon earning more than herring, mackerel, and cod combined in nine English markets, despite relatively minor assistance from public funds. In 1912, 1913, and 1914 just over one-quarter of salmon arriving in Billingsgate market came from Ireland.

On the whole the period 1850–1914 shows no consistent trend, much less any indication of long-term expansion. Figures are inadequate to judge the return on capital invested or to compare the economics of operating different types of boats, but a comment in 1912 indicates that the wages of fishermen compared unfavourably with those in other occupations.[4] Nor does the type of organisation seem to have mattered—while most boat owners were independent there were fishery companies operating from Galway, certainly between 1857 and 1885, but with little more success than anyone else. Overseas markets for Irish fish were

[1] 46 & 47 Vict., c. 26 (2 Aug. 1883); 2 Edw. VII, c. 24 (8 Aug. 1902).
[2] *F. J.*, 1 Nov. 1886; *Second report of the royal commission on Irish public works*, pp 7–9 [C 5264], 1888, xlviii, 151–3.
[3] *Report on the sea and inland fisheries of Ireland for 1913*, p. v [Cd 7751], H.C. 1914–16, xxii, 279.
[4] *Report on the sea and inland fisheries of Ireland for 1912*, p. v [Cd 7146], H.C. 1914, xxxi, 5.

repeatedly promising and as regularly disappointing. It is hard to escape the conclusion that the quite considerable efforts by various private and public bodies and the money spent on piers, harbours, curing stations, and railways were not so much wasted as misdirected. According to W. L. Micks, in 1907, 'no new trading or commercial fishery development has been attempted in recent years, although many of the present methods of capture of fish and transmission to market, even outside congested districts, will soon be more interesting to persons of antiquarian tastes than to modern fish merchants'.[1] The real problem seems to have been the limited Irish market for locally caught fish and the cost of sending to Great Britain a surplus consisting mainly of the cheaper types.[2] The Irish market suffered both from the decreasing demand of a declining population and from the fact that fish was held in very low esteem as an item of diet as compared with most other countries in western Europe, notably the Scandinavian countries and Germany. Even when consumed as a matter of obligation, there was no guarantee that it would come from local sources. William Andrews, fisheries committee chairman, said in 1865 that 'during last Lent . . . 850 tons of ling, also Newfoundland codfish were imported into Ireland, and 80,000 barrels of Scotch herrings . . . as well as a large quantity of Norway herrings'. He went on: 'In the last twenty years, every town in Ireland during Lent has been supplied by imported fish.'[3] The extension of light railways to the Irish fishing ports did something to help, but transport by rail involved boxes, ice, and handling at junctions and termini, while, compared with salmon, the prices of cod, mackerel, and herrings could not stand the addition of even modest transport charges (and those of Irish railways were under constant criticism). The major centres of population on the east coast, where alone population was expanding, could be supplied from the Irish Sea, but even here the distribution system was often primitive. In the 1901 census 1,612 people returned themselves as 'fishmongers', but in the southern provinces 62 per cent of these were female, suggesting a preponderance of itinerant vendors. In the north also vendors were usually itinerant but generally male.

The picture was transformed between 1914 and 1919 when, with the British trawling fleet diverted to minesweeping and other wartime duties, the English market was anxious for all that the Irish boats could land, at much enhanced prices. Under these conditions, loans were eagerly sought and readily granted for motor vessels and new gear on both the Irish Sea and Atlantic coasts. The indebtedness incurred had not been cleared, however, when the British trawling

---

[1] *Committee of inquiry into the provisions of the Agriculture and Technical Instruction (Ireland) Act, 1899 . . . Minority report*, p. 143 [Cd 3575], H.C. 1907, xvii, 1117.

[2] In times of glut cured herring and mackerel were also sent to the Continent and to the United States where they found a ready sale. But profit margins were too low and too uncertain to make a regular trade worth while.

[3] *Report from the select committee on the taxation of Ireland*, pp 61, 67, H.C. 1865 (330), xii, 103, 109.

fleet resumed fishing in 1920; and by 1921, compared with other Irish industries, fishing had resumed its position as a poor relation.[1]

INDUSTRIAL development during the period 1850–80 followed a simple pattern—the contraction of industries dependent on the home market and the expansion of those with a major export trade. The distinction was not new, for the conspicuous poverty of the mass of the Irish people had long held effective demand for consumer goods at a very low level. After the famine the continuous reduction in population caused further contraction of the home market, which was open also to increasing competition from British mass-produced goods.

The decline in population of the country as a whole concealed an important variation between city and town, between east and west. Whereas, in general, population declined by 21 per cent from 6,552,000 in 1851 to 5,175,000 in 1881, the decrease in cities and towns with over 10,000 inhabitants was considerably less and there were in fact increases in Dublin and Belfast (and their suburbs), Kingstown, Derry, and Newry. Thus the decrease in rural population was above the national average, in some counties exceeding 33 per cent: Tipperary lost 39 per cent and Kilkenny 37 per cent. Some villages disappeared completely, many small towns survived in an attenuated form, and everywhere the tempo of small-scale industrial activity slowed down.

In the towns and villages local breweries and distilleries fell idle; corn mills closed (affected by falling cereal acreage as well as by reduced demand); the smaller numbers of spade mills, and flax scutch mills in the north (after 1867), reflected increasing farm size and a general decline in tillage. Flour mills at the ports, as well as the few inland ones remaining, felt the effects of increased importation of American flour. Even bleach greens, despite the healthy condition of the linen industry, were affected by the tendency for bleaching to be concentrated into fewer and bigger units; in the process many small rural concerns closed. Exceptions to the general pattern were paper manufacture, which for the moment was able to hold its own, and the woollen industry.[2]

Of the industries that expanded the most obvious examples were linen, shipbuilding, and engineering in the north, brewing and distilling in the south. Factories for spinning flax yarn and weaving linen cloth increased from 69 in 1850 to 129 in 1878, their employees from 21,000 to 56,000. The corresponding increase in numbers of power looms from 58 to over 19,000 in weaving premises was accompanied by the wholesale displacement of handloom weavers in country districts. To some extent this was offset in County Londonderry by the cottage shirt-making industry,[3] in parts of Down by the sewed muslin trade,[4] and in the

[1]　J. D. Rush, 'Our sea fisheries' in *Manannán*, i, no. 5 (July, 1946), pp 12–15.

[2]　Above, p. 285.

[3]　Coyne, *Ireland: industrial and agricultural*, p. 417.

[4]　*Children's employment commission (1862): second report . . . with minutes of evidence*, p. 210 [3414], H.C. 1864, xxii, 290.

Lurgan–Portadown area of Armagh by handkerchief manufacture,[1] but elsewhere in Ulster the depressing effects on the rural economy were marked. The traditional combination of small-scale farming and handloom weaving characteristic of the province for almost 200 years disappeared. Henceforward industry and agriculture pursued separate paths, and, particularly when machinery became more highly developed, women and girls from the surrounding districts began to travel for work into town factories rather than to find it at home. The movement of course was gradual and by 1875 three-quarters of the 16,000 to 20,000 employees in the Derry-based shirt manufacture were still outworkers.[2] Handloom weaving in the Ballymena area, using yarn put out by 'manufacturers', was still on a sufficient scale in 1880 to merit the holding of a weekly linen market.[3]

From an employer's point of view the putting-out system combined minimum overheads with maximum flexibility in the use of labour. Where, as in Ireland, there were many unemployed women and girls in rural areas, the system had the further advantages of low wages and absence of workers' organisation. Even when work was centralised in factory premises the fact that so many firms in the finishing and making-up trades were employed by English and Scottish business houses on materials sent to them meant, in effect, that the putting-out system was extended to the manufacturing side of the business and that the relationship between Irish firms and their cross-Channel principals was much the same as that between outworkers and their Irish employers. Thus, shirts were made in Derry for wholesalers in Glasgow, Manchester, and London,[4] the sewed muslin trade was largely in the hands of Scottish agents,[5] and as early as 1851 cotton was being printed in the Belfast district for Manchester firms.[6] In consequence, trade depressions had an immediate effect on the livelihood of both employers and workers, the earnings of the latter being particularly subject to fluctuation. Workers on manufacturing premises, however, had the advantage that, to cover overheads, production was often maintained even when outworkers were on short time or idle. Unpopular as work in city mills may have been, therefore, and despite long hours and regimented conditions, their comparative regularity of employment undoubtedly stimulated the influx of the rural population into the linen manufacturing centres of the north.

Despite short recessions in 1854–5 and 1857–8, the linen industry expanded rapidly until 1861. The American civil war (1861–5) at first caused a sharp fall in sales, but the ensuing dislocation of the cotton trade led to several years of exceptional prosperity lasting until 1867. After a recession in 1868–9, progress,

[1]   Ibid., p. 222 (MS 302).
[2]   *Report from the commissioners appointed to inquire into the working of the factory and workshops acts, with a view to their consolidation and amendment*, p. 823 [C 1443–I], H.C. 1876, xxx, 825.
[3]   *Belfast News Letter*, 1 Jan., 13 Jan. 1880.
[4]   *Report from the commissioners appointed to inquire into the working of the factory and workshops acts, with a view to their consolidation and amendment*, p. 823 [C 1443–I], H.C. 1876, xxx, 825.
[5]   David Bremner, *The industries of Scotland* (Edinburgh, 1869), p. 307.
[6]   *Northern Whig*, 15 Feb. 1851.

though at a slower rate, was resumed until 1875 when there was a levelling-off
that lasted until beyond the end of the decade.

Much has been made of the growth of shipbuilding in Belfast during the second
half of the nineteenth century; in fact it was simply part of a larger pattern. A
world-wide increase in trade and in the movement of goods and people and in the
development of iron steamships led inevitably to increased shipbuilding, particularly in Europe and the United States. The tonnage of ships built and first
registered in the United Kingdom rose from 134,000 in 1850 to 404,000 in 1880,[1]
and it was only natural that Ireland, with her many harbours and her dependence
on seaborne trade, should have been affected. The feature of shipbuilding
deserving of comment is not that it increased but that the increase was largely
confined to Belfast.

Many ports in Ireland had facilities for building vessels for the coasting
trade—Cork, Derry, Dublin, Drogheda, Larne, and Waterford—but only Belfast
developed an industry based on the construction of large ocean-going ships.[2] The
reason is to be sought in a peculiar combination of circumstances—the making of
an island in the harbour (later Queen's Island) when the channel of the Lagan was
straightened in 1841–6; the Belfast harbour commissioners' provision there in
1847 of a nucleus of trained engineering workers; the appointment in 1854 of
Edward James Harland as a manager of Robert Hickson's small shipbuilding
concern occupying the site; that firm's subsequent personnel and financial
problems; the partnership between Harland and G. W. Wolff in the acquisition
and subsequent running of the shipyard; and the proximity of Harland & Wolff's
shipyard to the busy port of Liverpool.[3] Thus, of the increase in Irish shipbuilding from 1,092 tons in 1850 to 13,842 in 1880 (from 0.8 per cent to 3.4 per cent
of the U.K. total), the greater part must be attributed to the Belfast firm. Their
connection with the White Star Line (later amalgamated with Cunard) is well
known and their early work for John Bibby & Sons, Liverpool; their successful
use of iron in the construction of ships' hulls marked a significant technical
advance. Employees of Harland & Wolff increased from 120 in 1855 to 2,400 in
1870,[4] and the fact that these were exclusively men meant that shipbuilding and
linen manufacture (with its predominantly female work-force) complemented one
another and added to the stability of working conditions in Belfast. The
construction of Harland & Wolff's engine and boiler shops in 1880 ensured the
continued development of both the local shipbuilding and engineering trades.

Engineering also experienced improved conditions during the third quarter of
the nineteenth century. More widely based than shipbuilding, it included in 1856

---

[1] B. R. Mitchell and Phyllis Deane, *Abstract of British historical statistics* (Cambridge, 1962), p. 221.
[2] E. H. Wadge (ed.), *The Irish industrial magazine* (Dublin, 1866), p. 229, refers, however, to the
launching at Waterford in 1865 of a large ship for the Atlantic trade.
[3] Michael Moss and John R. Hume, *Shipbuilders to the world: 125 years of Harland and Wolff*,
Belfast, 1861–1986 (Belfast and Wolfeboro, 1986), pp 7–35.
[4] Denis Rebbeck, 'The history of iron shipbuilding in the Queen's Island up to 1870' (Ph.D. thesis,
Q.U.B., 1950).

thirty-five foundries in Dublin, fifteen in Belfast, and one or two in most provincial centres.[1] However, the industry's products were mainly for local use rather than for export—agricultural and textile machinery, equipment for flax and corn mills, steam engines, railway rolling stock, and the many appurtenances of developing urban life such as lamp posts, railings, and water cisterns. Some textile machinery was exported from Belfast,[2] but the major developments in this field, as in marine engineering, took place after 1880. During the earlier period an increase in the number of foundries and engineering workshops throughout the country must be attributed to the use of power driven in place of manually operated machinery in some processes, such as weaving, to the development of public transport, and to a generally increased sophistication of urban life, rather than to the service of an expanding industrial economy.

Production of both beer and spirits increased steadily after the famine. Illicit distillation apart, the average annual output of Irish whiskey rose from 8,293,000 gallons during 1851–5 to 11,138,000 gallons during 1876–80. Output of beer rose from an estimated 752,000 barrels to 2,069,000 barrels during the same period.[3] Exports of whiskey to Great Britain more than doubled,[4] while exports of beer, at more than 40 per cent of production,[5] also increased considerably—trends that were not unexpected in the light of Britain's steadily increasing population. More interesting was the general tendency in Ireland for the consumption of spirits to decline while that of beer was rising.[6] In part the former must reflect upward changes in excise duties but the pattern is consistent with depopulation in the rural areas, where mainly spirits were drunk, and improved living standards (and in some cases increased population) in the towns, where the demand was principally for beer; contemporary temperance campaigns, whose promoters saw beer as less harmful than spirits, may also have contributed.[7] A feature of the period was the concentration of production in fewer and bigger units, with growing emphasis on Cork and Dublin.

Cotton, an industry whose products were predominantly for local use, experienced a continuous reduction in spinning machinery (from 150,000 spindles in 1857 to 79,000 in 1878) accompanied by an increase in power looms, presumably using imported cotton yarn, from 1,600 in 1857 to 3,400 in 1871, falling to 2,700

---

[1] Slater's *Directory of Ireland*, 1856.

[2] W. E. Coe, *The engineering industry of the north of Ireland* (Newton Abbot, 1969), pp 51, 52, 55.

[3] *First report of her majesty's commissioners appointed to inquire into the financial relations between Great Britain and Ireland*, p. 456 [C 7720], H.C. 1895, xxxvi, 464.

[4] Ibid., p. 418 (MS 426).

[5] Calculated from Guinness's proportion of export to home sales (Patrick Lynch and John Vaizey), *Guinness's brewery in the Irish economy, 1759–1876* (Cambridge, 1966), pp 199–200.

[6] *Report of the commissioners of inland revenue on the duties under their management for the years 1856 to 1869 inclusive, vol. II*, pp 9, 20 [C 82–I], H.C. 1870, xx, 387, 398; *Twenty-eighth report of the commissioners of her majesty's inland revenue . . .*, pp 146, 155 [C 4474], H.C. 1884–5, xxii, 188, 197.

[7] Elizabeth Malcolm, *'Ireland sober, Ireland free': drink and temperance in nineteenth-century Ireland* (Dublin, 1986), pp 275, 323–4.

in 1878.[1] Employment in factories, at between 3,000 and 4,000 during most of the period, absorbed only a very small proportion of the working population but, unlike the linen industry, cotton was well represented outside Ulster, particularly in Waterford where Malcolmsons of Portlaw had the largest cotton factory in Ireland, and exceptionally had built up an export trade.[2] This last was not typical and clearly cotton, whether for home use or export, could not long survive the competition of cheaper, better, and more varied goods increasingly available from Great Britain.

As distinct from cotton, the woollen industry presented the unusual feature that in terms of equipment and labour employed in factories it multiplied about four times between 1850 and 1880.[3] Essentially small-scale rural concerns, many of them driven by water power, these factories employed a total of less than 2,000 people in 1878; but factory returns do not include small carding mills, tuck mills, or the diminishing number of outworkers, who were members of families producing homespun tweeds and frieze. Despite its small scale, however, the industry's products were of good quality and in 1864 attracted praise from an English woollen manufacturer who commented on some he had seen: 'The goods were well mixed, well made, well finished—above all they were thoroughly sound, and I have never yet seen Yorkshire goods to surpass them, except in the finer qualities of fancy trouserings . . .'[4] The same observer mentioned the poor quality of the machinery used in Ireland, referring to its obsolescence in the light of English technical advance, but the scale of enterprise, the amount of capital available, and the extent of the market for Irish goods meant that in practice some degree of obsolescence was inevitable. Nevertheless, the Irish woollen industry continued to expand throughout the second half of the century, its multiplicity of small concerns[5] being entirely appropriate to its early stage of industrial development.

The paper industry too presented the anomaly that it expanded although its products were almost entirely for local use. So far as inland revenue statistics can be relied on in the face of massive evasion of duty, production was rising between 1850 and 1861 (when duties were removed).[6] An increase in demand was to be expected because paper is an urban requirement and its extended use an invariable accompaniment of a rising standard of living. Thus the market for paper in Ireland's major cities was steadily expanding, but while Irish manufacturers got some of the increased business, mainly for commercial paper (including newsprint), much of it was imported from Great Britain.[7]

[1] *Factory returns*, p. 16, H.C. 1857 (7 Sess. I), xiv, 188; p. 71, H.C. 1871 (440), lxii, 179; p. 4, H.C. 1878–9 (324), lxv, 204.

[2] Anthony Marmion, *The ancient and modern history of the maritime ports of Ireland* (London, 1855), p. 558.

[3] *Factory returns*, p. 10, H.C. 1850 (745), xlii, 464; p. 9, H.C. 1878–9 (324), lxv, 209.

[4] Letter to *The Times*, 3 Oct. 1864.

[5] E. H. Wadge (ed.), *The Irish industrial magazine* (Dublin, 1866), p. 229.

[6] *Report of the commissioners of inland revenue on the duties under their management for the years 1856 to 1869 inclusive; vol. II*, p. 26 [C 82–I], H.C. 1870, xx, 404.

[7] *Report from the select committee on industries (Ireland); . . . minutes of evidence*, p. 113, H.C. 1884–5 (288), ix, 131.

Other industries with a purely local demand for their products were boot and shoe manufacture and furniture making. The former suffered from the effects of cheaper machine-made products from England.[1] In connection with the latter Edward Senior said in 1864: 'If you buy any furniture in Dublin, the man tells you that it was all made in England.'[2] His explanation was that trade union activity had ruined the craft trade, an explanation in which there may have been some substance, for skilled tradesmen's wages in Ireland were admittedly high, but it is equally likely that local craftsmen, who had been dispersed after the disappearance of the quality trade after 1800, were no longer available to make the type of furniture Senior sought; the current demand for the citizens' houses being built around an expanding Dublin was for cheaper articles, both imported and locally produced.

The proportion of the Irish working population engaged in mining remained constant at around 0.4 per cent during the period 1851–81, but with a declining total population this meant an actual reduction in the labour force of around 6,000. There is little reflection of this in the returns showing the quantities of coal, iron, copper, and lead produced—which probably means that if less labour was used it was used more efficiently, and indeed the figures suggest that the less economic mines were steadily closed in favour of those with better yielding ores or more easily workable seams. Coal-mining produced an average of around 130,000 tons a year;[3] production of iron ore was negligible until large-scale working of the County Antrim beds began in 1862,[4] but from that date it rose to an annual average of 155,000 tons in 1877–80, the ore being shipped to Scotland and Barrow-in-Furness for smelting.[5] Copper-mining showed a marked decline from a peak of 18,000 tons of ore raised from ten mines in 1860 to 2,000 tons from five mines in 1879–80. In the period 1856–64 pure copper to the value of about £156,000 a year was being produced from Irish ore. The decline of the industry (like that in Britain) was due to the discovery and working of much richer ores elsewhere, particularly in Spain and South America.[6] Irish lead-mining also declined, due to price competition. From a peak of eleven mines working in 1859 the number had shrunk to two in 1879–80 as smaller, less productive units were closed. However, production was still being maintained in 1879–80 from Wicklow, the major mining area, at an annual average of about 1,500 tons. Silver extracted from lead ore reached a maximum of 16,800 ounces in 1865 but thereafter declined rapidly.

---

[1] Ibid., p. 33 (MS 51).

[2] *Report from the select committee on taxation of Ireland; . . . minutes of evidence*, p. 214, H.C. 1864 (513), xv, 248.

[3] Figures here and subsequently are from annual reports of inspectors of mines.

[4] This was in fact a resumption of small-scale eighteenth-century working (P.R.O.N.I., 572/11–4, 5, 10, 16: correspondence between George Black, Belfast (agent for Lord Macartney) and Robert Walsh, Antrim, 1789–90).

[5] *Report from the select committee on industries (Ireland); . . . minutes of evidence*, pp 75–6, H.C. 1884–5 (288), ix, 93–4.

[6] Ibid., p. 18 (MS 36).

The general picture for copper, lead sulphur, and zinc (the last two being of some importance in the 1860s) is one of contraction in the face of increasing price competition, since apart from short spurts during the Crimean war and the American civil war the wholesale price indices for minerals fell almost continuously during the period.[1] The effect in Ireland was not only to hasten the closure of low-yielding mines but to discourage further prospecting. The latter was also discouraged by the generally exaggerated ideas of landlords, owners of the mineral rights in their lands, of the monetary value of such rights. In the case of coal, iron ore, and rock salt, mining continued to be at least marginally profitable until the end of the century; although, even from these, gross profits were visibly shrinking.[2]

THE progress of Irish industry between 1880 and 1914 and particularly in the period 1880–96 must be seen in the context of expanding industrial output by the major European countries and the United States of America. It was a time of intense competition, of national rivalry, of growing influence by cartels and industrial empires; a time when, by comparison with Germany and the United States, Great Britain seemed to be falling behind. For Ireland, selling the products of her industry meant competing in a world market where success required an industry to be either very large or highly specialised or to be favoured with some particular cost or technical advantage. In effect Irish industry on the necessary scale was confined to Belfast and Dublin and to firms engaged in linen manufacture, shipbuilding, certain types of engineering, brewing, and distilling. Specialisation allowed the continuation or development of the woollen industry, ropeworks, tobacco manufacture, shirt-making, the biscuit trade, and lacemaking. Local circumstances permitted the survival on a small scale for the home market of a few others, like bookbinding or the manufacture of chemical fertilisers and cement. Net industrial output, however, was by value only about half that of agriculture and was a fraction of the industrial output of the United Kingdom—in distilling about one-quarter, in shipbuilding less than one-fifth, in brewing less than one-tenth. Only in linen did Ireland occupy a significant place, with some 46 per cent of total United Kingdom production, and this mainly because of a decline in Great Britain. While, therefore, there was growth in all the industries mentioned, greater towards the end of the period than at the beginning, the rate of increase was slower than in Britain, and considerably slower than in other major industrial countries. Based on *per capita* consumption of coal, Ireland was (as one would expect) below Britain and Germany, also France, the Netherlands, Denmark, and Sweden, but above Italy, Spain, and Russia.[3] In other words,

---

[1] Mitchell & Deane, *Brit hist. statistics*, p. 474.

[2] *Report of the commissioners of inland revenue . . . for the years 1856 to 1869 inclusive*, II, p. 199 [C 82–I], H.C. 1870, xx, 577.

[3] By interpolating Irish figures for coal imports, after 1905, into fig. 16 in Rondo Cameron, 'A new view of European industrialisation' in *Econ. Hist. Rev.*, 2nd ser., xxxviii, no. 1 (Feb. 1985), pp 1–23. The result is compatible with table 13, aimed at on a different basis in Paul Bairoch, 'International

despite increases in production Ireland's industrial output declined in relation to most of the rest of Europe. More significant, Ireland did not produce basics for heavy industry but rather consumer goods and services of a kind that were most easily sold when times were good but for which demand fell rapidly in times of recession.

Just as the early shipbuilding industry owed much to the engineering genius of Edward Harland, so the later expansion of Harland & Wolff depended on the salesmanship of W. J. Pirrie. It was principally his concept of transatlantic liners as floating luxury hotels, combined with his interest in the White Star and other shipping lines, that boosted the output of his firm from an average of 62,000 tons during 1890–95 to 82,000 tons during 1903–8.[1] At the same time advances by another Belfast firm, Workman & Clark (established in 1879), together with the output of one or two smaller shipyards elsewhere in Ireland, raised total tonnage of merchant ships built from under 14,000 tons in 1880 to an average of 180,000 tons during the period 1910–14. Workman & Clark specialised in cargo liners, frozen meat carriers, and insulated fruit carriers and their output during 1903–8 averaged 54,000 tons. Employment in Belfast shipyards was said to have been 15,000 in 1907 but the significance of the figure is qualified by the amount of work subcontracted to ancillary firms whose employees may or may not be included in the total.

The Irish linen industry emerged surprisingly well from the depression of the 1880s and early 1890s compared with most other European producers. Probably the spinning section was worst affected, with seventeen mills containing 175,000 spindles dismantled, yarn imports increasing, and prices of Irish flax driven downwards. However, both home usage and exports of yarn increased after 1895. Installation began after 1904 of additional spindles capable of spinning finer yarn, and a boom period extended from early 1905 to the end of 1907. In 1913 and 1914 spinning capacity was at an all time peak of over 950,000 spindles.[2] The depression in the weaving section had been less marked, though changes in the type of goods that the market required caused difficulties of adjustment for some factories. Unexpectedly, quite a few handlooms survived the depression and, though numbers were falling, handloom wages were estimated to total £220,000 in 1893;[3] by 1912 there was still work for handlooms in the Lurgan area though handloom weaving had largely disappeared from its stronghold around Ballymena. The number of power looms increased fairly steadily after 1885 and reached 37,000 in 1912. In both spinning and weaving, wages increased by about 20 per cent between 1886 and 1903[4] with further increases to 1914, but the industry

industrialisation levels from 1750 to 1980' in *Journal of European Economic History*, xi, no. 2 (spring 1982), pp 269–333.

[1] C. H. Oldham, 'The history of Belfast shipbuilding' in *Stat. Soc. Ire. Jn.*, xii, pt xci, (Dec. 1911), pp 417–34, and Moss & Hume, *Shipbuilders to the world*, pp 513–18.

[2] *Forty-seventh annual report of the Flax Supply Association* (Belfast, 1915), p. 12.

[3] Edward J. Riordan, *Modern Irish trade and industry* (London, 1921), p. 116.

[4] D. L. Armstrong, 'Social and economic conditions in the Belfast linen industry, 1850–1900' in *I.H.S.*, vii, no. 28 (Sept. 1951), p. 264.

remained conspicuous for low wages and long hours, particularly among out-workers.[1] Three-quarters of the linen manufactured in Ireland in 1910 was said to have been exported, with the United States taking about half the total, followed by Australia, Canada, Cuba, Argentina, India, Brazil, Germany, Egypt, and Japan. The fact that so high a proportion of Irish linen was exported to so many different markets meant that trade was subject to unexpected setbacks, for instance, from suspension of payments by several Australian banks in 1893 and the financial crisis in the United States in 1908. The existence of many small family firms with limited capital also involved risks of widespread failure in any prolonged crisis.

The engineering industry's major dependence on shipbuilding and textiles gave it a firm base and, between 1880 and 1914, a moderate prosperity. But it confined manufacture for export to the industrial area of Ulster. Particularly in shipbuilding there were interesting developments with the establishment of engine works by Harland & Wolff in 1880, MacIlwaine & McColl in 1886, and Workman & Clark in 1891, the last becoming pioneers in marine turbine engines.[2] All three firms built engines not only for ships launched on the Lagan but for many others as well. So far as the making of textile machinery was concerned, as distinct from its installation or repair, there was a similar concentration into the hands of a small number of Belfast firms who exported flax-spinning and preparing machinery to a wide market in Europe, the United States, and Japan. Too late perhaps they recognised the long-term implications for their local customers.[3] During the same period other Belfast firms began to develop an export business in tea-drying, ventilating, and heating equipment.

Machinery repair and installation with their associated skills were of course more diversified and widespread than manufacture. Census returns showed 14,571 blacksmiths in 1881, 11,712 in 1911 scattered throughout the counties of Ireland; small foundries continued to serve the needs of most towns; there were railway workshops at Dundalk and Inchicore; the making of agricultural machinery was developed by several firms in County Wexford; millwrights and engineers were available to serve the needs of rural flour mills, distilleries, and woollen mills. Machinery came, however, in increasing quantity and sophistication from Birmingham, Wolverhampton, Cleveland, and Essen. Failure to develop engineering in the southern part of the country was doubtless due to the limited extent of the local market and the increasing complexity of the industry's products. Even the making of bicycles, for which there was a good demand, never extended beyond a few small workshops in Dublin, Belfast, and Wexford, while most relatively

[1] *Committee of inquiry into the conditions of employment in the linen and other making-up trades in the north of Ireland: report and evidence*, p. vii [Cd 6509], H.C. 1912–13, xxxiv, p. 371; Marilyn Cohen, 'Working conditions and experiences of work in the linen industry: Tullylish, County Down' in *Ulster Folklife*, xxx (1984), pp 1–21.

[2] Coe, *The engineering industry of the north of Ireland*, p. 83.

[3] See correspondence of Fairbairn Lawson Combe Barbour Ltd in P.R.O.N.I., D. 769.

simple vehicles such as the Dublin tramcars were in 1885 being imported from England.[1]

In brewing, the last two decades of the nineteenth and the opening years of the twentieth centuries were marked both by steady increase and the concentration of the industry in Dublin, which produced about three-quarters of the 2.9 to 3.5 million barrels brewed annually between 1899 and 1914. At the same time exports were absorbing a bigger proportion of output, rising between 1905 and 1913 more than twice as fast as production and earning in the latter year an estimated £2,274,000. The fall in the number of licensed brewers from 56 in 1880 to 28 in 1914 and 24 in 1920 is less significant than the fact that by the turn of the century the single firm of Guinness accounted for more than two-thirds of total Irish output and was already the largest brewery in Europe.[2]

Expansion of distilling was less marked and more erratic. From an 1879 peak of around 12 million gallons, production fell to just over 9 million gallons in 1882 and rose to an average 13.5 million gallons during the years 1910–14. Simultaneously there was a shift in emphasis from pot-still to patent-still production with the latter predominant in the Belfast area. The number of distilleries at work varied little between 1880 and the opening years of the twentieth century, but then fell from 28 in 1906 to 22 in 1914, though it rose to 23 in 1919. Two general features of the period deserve comment—the consistent fall in home consumption, from just over 5 million gallons in the 1880s to around 2.75 million in 1914, and the increasing exportation of spirits from Ireland to an ever widening market. Unlike brewing, distilling was not dominated by any single firm, but it was highly capitalised, with considerable quantities of spirits always in bond, and its products subject to unpredictable changes in excise duties at home and abroad. There was thus in the cities a tendency towards amalgamation rather than closure and towards the taking over or elimination of the smallest country firms. Using largely home-produced raw materials and employing a work-force of approaching 10,000 people, the brewing and distilling industries accounted by value for between 5 per cent and 8 per cent of total Irish exports in the period under review.

Contemporaries saw the woollen industry as a success story, which indeed it was, with the added satisfaction that a long-standing reproach was at last being removed. 'The woollen manufacture is the principal industry that is going on in the country', said an observer in 1886;[3] another referred to it as 'the most successful of the existing nascent industries of the country'.[4] Mills were small but numerous; forty made returns in 1884 under the factory acts; the quality, finish, and durability of their goods was acknowledged to be satisfactory. Sir Robert

[1] *Report from the select committee on industries (Ireland) . . . minutes of evidence*, p. 118, H.C. 1884–5 (288), ix, 136.

[2] Above, v, pp 146, 380.

[3] *Report of the royal commission on the Land Law Ireland Act, 1881, and the Purchase of Land (Ireland) Act, 1885, vol. II. Minutes of evidence . . .*, p. 102 [C 4969-I], H.C. 1887, xxvi, 134.

[4] *Report from the select committee on industries (Ireland); . . . minutes of evidence*, p. 21, H.C. 1884–5 (288), ix, 39.

Kane's sour comment that they were 'toys of those [aristocratic] gentlemen rather than . . . serious developments of industry',[1] was scarcely justified in view of growing exports, principally to England, Scotland, and America but including some specialised items such as, for instance, frieze for Canadian police uniforms. The goods produced were not cheap; specialisation and economic use of manpower were rare but output included no cotton or shoddy yarn and sales were mostly to a high-class market. The fact was that changes in taste had made popular in London and other fashion centres the tweeds and homespuns that for generations the Irish peasant had made for his own use. Initiative and small capital were available, fortunately, to organise finishing and marketing in such a dispersed and still largely domestic industry; something was owed too to the public spirit of people such as Mrs Ernest Hart, who helped to organise the Donegal industry.[2] In 1890 there were 3,443 workers in woollen factories alone, and from the evidence of census returns there must have been at least another 3,000 domestic and ancillary workers. The smaller number of people who recorded themselves in 1911 as occupied in the woollen and worsted trades were doubtless mainly factory workers. Exports of woollen goods alone passed the £500,000 mark in 1909 and, together with woollen yarn, carpets, and felt, were estimated at almost £1 million in 1914.[3]

Other Irish industries that made progress during this period included biscuit and tobacco manufacture, shirt-making, and the domestic production of lace and crochet. Each had a substantial export component and, with the exception of shirt-making, all were in some sense luxury goods. A brief account of each follows.

The post-famine increase in Irish tobacco consumption was of little industrial importance, while the conversion of imported leaf into plug or twist required only simple manual equipment. Every port had one or more workshops equipped for the purpose;[4] in 1850 Belfast had about fourteen.[5] At that date 14,460 dealers and 159 manufacturers held licences to trade in tobacco;[6] however, the very small scale of business must have made regulation difficult and the true numbers may well have been higher. But if absolute numbers are uncertain the trend after 1850 was unmistakable—a steady increase in the number of dealers, as retail outlets became

---

[1] Ibid., p. 144 (MS 162).

[2] Mrs Hart, whose husband was president of the British Medical Association, visited west Donegal in 1883 and subsequently promoted a knitting and tweed-making cottage industry around Gweedore, Ardara, and Glenties. She arranged for the goods produced to be exhibited in London, and for fine Donegal tweeds to be sold through prominent retail stores (ibid., pp 161–9 (MS 179–87)).

[3] *Report on the trade in imports and exports at Irish ports during the year ended 31 Dec. 1909*, pp 106–7 [Cd 5354], H.C. 1910, lxxxv, 168–9; . . . *year ended 31 Dec. 1915*, p. 20 [Cd 8498], H.C. 1917–18, xxix, 574.

[4] B. W. E. Alford, *W. D. & H. O. Wills and the development of the U.K. tobacco industry, 1786–1965* (London, 1973), p. 8.

[5] D. J. Owen, *History of Belfast* (Belfast, 1921), p. 313.

[6] *Report of the commissioners of inland revenue . . . for the years 1856 to 1869 inclusive . . .*, vol. II, p. 107 [C 82-1], H.C. 1870, xx, 483.

Tobacconists and manufacturers of tobacco and
snuff, 1871–1911

	1871	1881	1891	1901	1911
male	1,374	904	779	747	815
female	96	345	536	1,020	1,316
total	1,470	1,249	1,315	1,767	2,131

more numerous, and a steady decrease in the number of manufacturers to 32 by 1875 and 25 by 1900.[1] A parallel though opposite trend appears in the quantities of tobacco that paid duty on importation into Ireland, an annual average of 4.6 million lb in 1850–54 becoming 9.1 million in 1890–94 and 13.2 million in 1910–14[2] (on the basis that unmanufactured tobacco reexported from Britain had been held in bond and paid excise duty on importation into Ireland). Census figures for occupations are interesting. The number of tobacconists and manufacturers of tobacco and snuff is recorded in the table above.[3] The number of tobacconists, that is retailers specialising in tobacco products, was negligible outside the largest cities; snuff manufacture was no more than an adjunct to the main process; so that the figures quoted must refer almost entirely to the production of pipe tobacco and cigarettes. If this is so then the reducing number of males reflects the steady elimination of small ill-equipped businesses (in line with the reduction in the number of licensed manufacturers) by a few growing firms using female labour to operate more advanced power-driven equipment, particularly, after 1900, cigarette-making machinery.

It has been estimated that by 1900 some 20 per cent of U.K. retail tobacco sales was in the form of cigarettes, a proportion that doubled by 1910 and increased to 54 per cent by 1920.[4] In Ireland, pipe tobacco gave way to cigarettes more slowly and still accounted for 60 per cent of sales in the early 1920s.[5] Nevertheless the main Irish manufacturers installed cigarette-making machinery soon after the turn of the century,[6] influenced no doubt by the increasing popularity of cigarettes imported from Great Britain—of which Thomas Gallagher at least had first-hand experience because cigarettes were being made in his London factory as early as 1895.[7] In 1911 he built a new factory in York Street, Belfast, specifically for cigarette manufacture and was popularly reputed to be the largest tobacco

[1] Annual reports of commissioners of inland revenue.

[2] *Customs tariffs of the United Kingdom from 1800 to 1897*, pp 197–8 [C 8706], H.C. 1898, lxxxv, 201–2; *Report on the trade in imports and exports at Irish ports during the year ended 31 Dec. 1914*, p. xvi [Cd 8208], H.C. 1916, 548.

[3] *Census Ire.* [C 1377], H.C. 1877, lxxxi, 1; [C 3365], H.C. 1882, lxxvi, 385; [C 6780], H.C. 1892, xc, 1; [Cd 1190], H.C. 1902, cxxix, 1; [Cd 6663], H.C. 1912–13, cxviii, 1. These MS page numbers denote the first pages of the documents, not the pages giving the data shown in the table.

[4] J. B. Jefferys, *Retail trading* (Cambridge, 1954), p. 271.

[5] Alford, *W. D. & H. O. Wills*, p. 387.

[6] Gallaghers in 1902; P. J. Carroll & Co. in 1905.

[7] Information from Mr W. H. Hall, local historian and ex-employee of Gallagher Ltd.

manufacturer in the British Isles if not in the world.[1] Even before that, in 1907, Belfast accounted for 5.3 million lb of Ireland's exports of 5.7 million lb of manufactured tobacco.[2] Unfortunately the 1907 census of production does not distinguish Irish tobacco manufacture from that of Great Britain but it was clearly a capital-intensive industry in which a high proportion of women workers kept average wages low. On the other hand the high level of exports of manufactured tobacco in 1919 (8.4 million lb),[3] continuing the pre-war trend, suggested an industry with little to fear from the future.

Apart from Limerick and a few places along the Munster coast, Irish lace and embroidery manufacture in the closing decades of the nineteenth century and the opening decades of the twentieth was carried on mainly in those parts of Ulster where the domestic linen industry had disappeared without being replaced by mechanical production—east Down, south Armagh, Cavan, Monaghan, west Donegal, and the border of Fermanagh and Tyrone. Unlike domestic spinning, however, the necessary skills were difficult to acquire and the finished material could not find an adequate market in the areas in which it was produced. Sponsors were therefore necessary to organise production and sale and these ranged from the Royal Dublin Society, the congested districts board,[4] the department of agriculture and technical instruction, and the Irish Agricultural Organisation Society, together with some thirty convents and as many private individuals. In most cases the latter were either businessmen, principals or agents of retailing concerns, or wives of major landowners. For most of these sponsors commercial gain was only a secondary motivation and large profit margins were not sought. Wages were low, though by no means out of line with those paid for example to linen outworkers. Judging from the prizes won by Irish lace and embroidery at national and international exhibitions, the work produced was of good quality and found a ready sale in Dublin, London, and North America (notably in Chicago and Toronto). But despite these favourable circumstances the industry grew very slowly. Census returns show an average of 4,500 women and girls employed in lacemaking and embroidery in the years 1871–91, rising to 5,900 in 1901 and 7,800 in 1911. By the last date, however, numbers were thought to be declining from a peak reached between 1905 and 1909, though it must be said that in an industry with so many part-time workers census figures for employment are particularly difficult to interpret. Similarly the value of output can only be guessed. The managing director of the Irish Lace Depot in Dublin said in 1907: 'the annual value of the lace manufactured in Ireland cannot be less than £100,000.' But it is not clear whether he included or excluded crochet and embroidery in this figure, which Elizabeth Boyle considers too low, nor how much

---

[1] Owen, *Belfast*, p. 50.
[2] L. M. Cullen, *An economic history of Ireland since 1660* (London, 1972), p. 161.
[3] *Report on the trade in imports and exports at Irish ports during the year ended 31 Dec. 1919*, p. 21 [Cmd 1105], H.C. 1921, xxxi, 423.
[4] Above, pp 283–7.

he knew of lace that did not pass through the depot. Fashion changes, competition from machine-made lace, the introduction of new fabrics, and the marginal importance of lace during the years 1914–19 made the prospects for the industry after that date far from optimistic.[1]

The replacement of hand-spun yarn in the linen industry created a large pool of skilled but unemployed female labour, particularly in counties such as Donegal (where production had been predominantly yarn rather than cloth) and Londonderry (where, unlike Antrim and Down, spinning mills did not proliferate). As early as 1831, therefore, an entrepreneur from Derry had some shirts made locally and established a connection with a Glasgow firm interested in buying them.[2] From that small beginning an industry developed in the 1840s based on city workshops where material (linen and cotton) was cut out and distributed to female workers to be sewn up into shirts in their own homes. Regular steamship services to Glasgow and later to Liverpool brought in cotton cloth and took out the finished garments. At this stage all operations in both workshop and home were carried out by hand.[3] The business flourished and by 1845, apart from workshops engaged in cutting out and packaging, an estimated 500 females were employed in their own homes.[4] The cross-channel demand was such that the original pioneer became agent for twenty-two firms while others from London, Manchester, and Glasgow set up their own factories in Derry to take advantage of the seemingly endless supply of skilled female labour available at wages well below those paid in England and Scotland.[5] The industry extended in the 1850s to Strabane and Coleraine, with three shirt-making agencies in the former and two independent concerns in the latter.[6] Further afield, between 1849 and 1855, shirt-making appeared in Belfast, Dublin, Cork, and Limerick, though on a smaller scale than in Derry and generally in premises where it was subsidiary to some other manufacturing process or business.[7]

The sewing machine was first applied to Derry shirt-making on an experimental basis in 1856, and as improved models appeared they were installed in increasing numbers. With an elastic market this led to boom times for the city; existing firms expanded and new ones were established, some of considerable size. In 1862 Tillie & Henderson could accommodate 1,000 workers in their factory and employed six times that number outside. M'Intyre & Hogg had 700 on the premises and

[1] Coyne, *Ireland: industrial and agricultural*, pp 420–42; Elizabeth Boyle, *The Irish flowerers* (Belfast, 1971), *passim*; *Report from the select committee on home work; . . . minutes of evidence*, p. 47, H.C. 1908 (246), viii, 97; *Committee of inquiry into the conditions of employment in the linen and other making-up trades in the north of Ireland; report and evidence*, pp v–viii [Cd 6509], H.C. 1912–13, xxxiv, 369–72.

[2] Geraldine McCarter, *Derry's shirt tale* (Derry, 1991).

[3] E. H. Slade, 'A history of the Londonderry shirt industry' (M.A. thesis, Q.U.B., 1937).

[4] *Derry Journal*, 24 June 1845.

[5] J. A. Grew, 'The Derry shirtmaking industry 1831–1913' (M.Phil. thesis, Ulster, 1987), p. 31. For wages, see n. 18.

[6] *Ibid.*, pp 42–3.

[7] *Children's employment commission (1862): second report . . . with appendix*, pp lxvii, 51–62, 65–7 [3414], H.C. 1864, xxii, 67, 131–42, 145–7.

employed outworkers within a forty-mile radius; R. Sinclair & Co. had between 500 and 900 workers in their factory and four or five times as many outside.[1] Steam power was applied to factory sewing machines from 1859 and to machinery for cutting out shirts from 1864. In 1871 there were sixteen shirt factories in the county, employing, by 1875, between 4,000 and 5,000 factory hands and 12,000 to 15,000 outworkers.[2] Agencies were spread as far afield as Ballymena and Sligo (both connected to Derry by rail) and branch factories were set up in Omagh and Magherafelt.[3]

The period of expansion halted in 1879, with factories working short time and numbers of outworkers reduced. But favourable conditions returned in 1882 and from then until the end of the century, taking one year with another, the industry experienced a fairly steady trade. Competition was increasing, however, and tariffs applied in the American and colonial markets created pressure to reduce costs.[4] This was achieved, partly by adopting machinery for making collars, cuffs, and buttonholes, and partly by setting up laundries and box-making premises so that shirts could be exported in a finished state instead of in bundles requiring further handling in Great Britain. This increased mechanisation led to the establishment of branch factories, where the various machines could be installed, in at least nine towns and villages in the counties of Donegal, Londonderry, and Tyrone.[5] At the same time the number of home workers was reduced. By 1901 there were estimated to be 80,000 workers engaged in shirt-making in Derry and its hinterland, including 18,000 in the city with the remainder distributed between branch factories and their own homes.[6]

The early twentieth century saw some decline in the first few difficult years, some improvement in 1905, a struggle for existence in 1908, and a return to boom times in 1910–13. The switch to khaki in 1914–18 meant a steady trade but some uncertainty in the supply of raw materials, particularly in 1915. With increasing coal and transport costs the operation of branch factories became uneconomic, while low-wage outworkers were not so readily available. Peacetime conditions therefore found a more concentrated industry able to resume prewar levels of output fairly quickly but with continued dependence on British entrepreneurs and world markets and with the prospect of political uncertainty at home.

Access to shirt-making statistics is not difficult but they need some interpretation. For instance, the concentration of the industry in County Londonderry is

[1] Ibid.

[2] 'Return of the number of manufacturing establishments in which the hours of work are regulated by any act of parliament . . .', p. 201, H.C. 1871 (440), lxii, 309; Report of the commissioners appointed to inquire into the working of the factory and workshops acts, with a view to their consolidation and amendment, p. 823 [C 1443–I], H.C. 1876, xxx, 825. See also above, pp 292–3.

[3] Grew, 'Derry shirtmaking industry', p. 139.

[4] To combat the Australian tariff Welch, Margetson, & Co. opened a factory in Melbourne with a nucleus of trained staff from Derry (Sarah Levitt, 'Cheap mass-produced men's clothing in the nineteenth and twentieth centuries' in Textile History, xxii, no. 2 (1991), p. 188).

[5] Grew, 'Derry shirtmaking industry', pp 173, 179, 181.

[6] Coyne, Ireland: industrial and agricultural, p. 418.

Shirt makers and seamstresses, 1901

	Leinster	Munster	Ulster	Connacht	total
males	16	7	720	2	745
females	5,499	4,714	42,440	3,543	56,196
total	5,515	4,721	43,160	3,545	56,941

illustrated by (*a*) the 1,485 sewing machines in that county's factories in 1871, which was over 73 per cent of the total for Ulster and over 71 per cent of the total for Ireland,[1] and (*b*) the 1901 census figures for 'shirt makers and seamstresses'.[2] The number of men employed, though small, had been growing since 1871 and must reflect increased mechanisation with its need for maintenance of machinery and motive power. But absolute numbers of females are not to be relied on, partly because seamstresses were also employed in occupations other than shirt-making, and partly because not all outworkers would have regarded their sewing activities as a full-time or even a main occupation. Coyne's figure of 80,000, though an estimate and probably including laundry workers, may be nearer the mark, taking into account family members who assisted from time to time.

Exports of 'cotton goods' from ports other than Belfast, Dublin, and Cork, and noted as 'almost all from Londonderry' were as follows:[3]

year	1905	1907	1909	1911	1913	1915	1917	1919
exports (cwt)	50,300	51,999	55,985	64,772	67,909	59,709	62,619	69,843

Some shirts made in Derry were doubtless exported through Belfast, but they cannot be distinguished in that port's figures, which reflect mainly traffic in cotton sent from Britain for printing in County Antrim printworks.[4]

In 1863 sewing machine workers in Derry were being paid 5s. to 7s. a week, workers at home 3d. to 4d. a day. The latter was not considered exceptionally low and was much the same as, or even a little better than, could have been earned at the spinning wheel thirty or more years earlier. A major employer, however, spoke of girls in his factory as being from 11 years of age and upwards, and some of those working at home would have been of similar age, so that doubtless the averages discussed at that date must have been influenced considerably by rates for juveniles. By 1886 the very young workers had disappeared, in the factories at least, with learners starting at 14 or 15 years of age and average wages for

---

[1] '*Return of the number of manufacturing establishments in which the hours of work are regulated by any act of parliament . . .*', pp 201, 206, H.C. 1871 (440), lxii, 309, 314.

[2] *Census Ire, 1901: general report*, pp 122, 129 [Cd 1190], H.C. 1902, cxxix, 166, 173.

[3] *Reports on the trade in imports and exports at Irish ports* [for the years given]: [Cd 3631], H.C. 1907, lxxxi, 21; [Cd 4429], H.C. 1908, xciv, 191; [Cd 5354], H.C. 1910, lxxxv, 23; [Cd 6397], H.C. 1912–13, lxxxviii, 39; [Cd 7639], H.C. 1914–16, lxiv, 1; [Cd 8498], H.C. 1917–18, xxix, 533; [Cmd 338], H.C. 1919, xlv, 1; [Cmd 1105], H.C. 1921, xxxi, 377.

[4] *Vice-regal commission on Irish railways . . .: appendix to the final report, vol. VII*, p. 15 [Cd 5248], H.C. 1910, xxxvii, 191.

trained workers 5s. to 12s. a week: outworkers using treadle machines at home could make up to 8s. The factory wages compared with payment for similar work in Manchester, at 6s. to 18s. a week. By 1906, when the U.K. average, excluding London, was 13s. 4d. for power machinists, shirt factories in Belfast were paying 12s. 3d. and in Derry 10s. 5d. a week. A board of trade inspector referred in 1907 to the fact that earnings of Irish workers were very much lower than those in England, adding the interesting comment: 'It is quite impossible for Londoners really and truly to compete with the Irish workers and, of course, the best class of shirt is made in Ireland.'[1] In 1912 when it was estimated that one-third of the work-force was employed in the factories and two-thirds as outworkers, the former were able to earn about 14s. a week, the latter 9s. Rates in Derry had reached 14s. to 16s. a week in 1914, when, with the introduction of trade boards, the disparity between Irish and British rates, though not necessarily earnings, tended to disappear. In general then, until wartime inflation and minimum wage legislation affected them, wages in Derry factories and their branches were at least 2s. a week below those paid in Great Britain. On the other hand conditions in the Derry factories were good, comparing favourably with those elsewhere. Factory inspectors reported the usual hours as 8 a.m. to 6 p.m., with an hour and a half for a midday meal, enabling those who lived locally to go home; there was little overtime working. One employer, with a large proportion of married women among his workers, found that by delaying the starting time to 9 a.m. production increased.[2]

Census of production figures show that in 1907 Ireland contributed 23 per cent of the gross value of United Kingdom output of shirts, cuffs, and collars,[3] by far the greatest proportion of which must have been from the north-west.

It is difficult to account for the sudden rise, though possibly resurgence would be a better term, of the biscuit trade. With origins in the ships' provision business carried on principally in Belfast, Cork, Derry, Dublin, and Waterford, and given a boost by the post-1847 emigrant traffic, the trade was facilitated in the latter part of the nineteenth century by the importation of American flour through the same ports. The prosperity attending the early years of the twentieth century is

---

[1] *Report from the select committee on home work*, p. 38, H.C. 1907 (290), vi, 55.
[2] *Reports from the inspectors of factories for the half year ending 31 Oct. 1862*, p. 120 [3076], H.C. 1863, xviii, 437 (this report says that outworkers could earn up to 1s. a day, which conflicts with other evidence); *Children's employment commission (1862): second report . . .*, pp lxvii–lxxi, 57–62 [3414], H.C. 1864, xxii, 67–71, 137–42; *Report of the commissioners appointed to inquire into . . . the factory and workshops acts . . .*, p. 823 [C 1443–I], H.C. 1876, xxx, 825; *Report of the royal commission on the Land Law Ireland Act, 1881, and the Purchase of Land (Ireland) Act, 1885, ii. Minutes of evidence . . .*, p. 183 [C 4969–1], H.C. 1887, xxxvi, 215; *Report of the royal commission on labour; the employment of women*, p. 325 [C 6894–XXIII], H.C. 1893–4, xxxvii, pt 1, p. 545; *Report of an inquiry by the board of trade into the earnings and hours of labour of workpeople of the United Kingdom, ii; clothing trade in 1906*, pp 70–72 [Cd 4844], H.C. 1909, lxxx, 325; *Report from the select committee on home work*, pp 186–97, H.C. 1908 (246), viii, 236–47; *Report of the departmental committee on the insurance of outworkers (Ireland): minutes of evidence*, pp 59, 84 [Cd 7658], 1914–16, xxxi, 637; Dorothea Barton, 'The course of women's wages' in *Journal of the Royal Statistical Society*, lxxxii (1919), pp 530, 537.
[3] *Final report of the first census of production of the United Kingdom (1907)*, p. 425 [Cd 6320], H.C. 1912–13, cix, 433.

associated both with the rise of the major Dublin firm of Jacobs, established in Waterford in 1851, and the improved living standards in most United Kingdom cities and towns. Exports in 1914 exceeded £530,000.[1]

Industries that managed to survive, even in an attenuated form, included boot- and shoemaking and paper manufacture. Mass production in England spelled the decline of the former, which in 1884 was providing from local resources only one-eighth to one-quarter of Irish requirements. In 1907 imports were valued at £1,728,000 against an estimated value of goods made and work done in Ireland of £264,000.[2] Part of the trouble was that Irish handmade boots and shoes were too good, too long lasting, and were undersold by machine-made footwear of reputedly inferior quality. The remedy of reducing prices while maintaining quality was impracticable and the alternative was unacceptable. 'No Irish manu- facturer, as far as I am aware, has yet attempted the experiment of putting out a still worse boot than his cross-channel opponent.'[3] In the event machinery was applied to the industry, beginning in Cork in 1892 and providing a firm if small basis for later expansion.

It would be tedious to present even a thumbnail sketch of other industries mentioned—paper manufacture, rope-making, the production of agricultural machinery—let alone several others existing here and there on a smaller scale. This has in any case been done by Riordan.[4] The general pattern is fairly clear. In a mainly agricultural economy Irish industry developed along a few specialised lines, with some firms growing to European if not world stature on the basis of their export trade. Lack of raw materials, shortage of skilled manpower, and proximity to a mass-producing neighbour inhibited development of others. Expansion where it existed was insufficient to absorb the quantity of industrially unskilled labour being displaced from agriculture, but an escape route existed to relatively better paid employment in Great Britain and elsewhere. On the whole, the industrial scene in the latter part of the nineteenth century and early years of the twentieth century was not discouraging. People could look back to times that had been very much worse; there was a general air of optimism in the north; commerce, if not manufacturing industry, was expanding in the south; both earnings and real wages were rising. The fact that outside Ireland things were moving a great deal faster did not for the moment seem important.

ON average, each year between 1850 and 1880 saw an additional sixty miles of track added to Irish railways (515 miles of line open in 1850, 2,370 miles

---

[1] *Report on the trade in imports and exports at Irish ports during the year ended 31 Dec. 1915*, p. 14 [Cd 8498], H.C. 1917–18, xxix, 568.

[2] *Report on the trade in imports and exports at Irish ports during the year ended 31 Dec. 1909*, p. 83 (MS 145); *Final report of the first census of production of the United Kingdom (1907)*, p. 419 [Cd 6320], H.C. 1912–13, cix, 427.

[3] James Winstanley to Thomas Sexton, M.P., 13 June 1885 (*Report from the select committee on industries (Ireland); ... minutes of evidence*, p. 740, H.C. 1884–5 (288), ix, 758).

[4] Riordan, *Modern Irish trade and industry*.

in 1880).[1] In an economy characterised by industrial lethargy, and with an agricultural system undergoing a metamorphosis as slow as it was painful, the vigour of railway expansion was conspicuous. Labourers with money to spend, remote districts visited by engineers and surveyors, towns brought within hours of Dublin rather than days, new stations and equipment to be seen—these must have conveyed a sense of change and an air of progress long absent from the Irish scene. The railways did facilitate emigrant traffic (and migrant harvest labour), they did bring British goods to the village shop to compete with local products, but they also contributed in no small measure to the advancement in the quality of living that made conditions in rural Ireland gradually more tolerable.

In terms of finance there was both major expansion and an influx of capital from Irish sources. Paid up and loan capital of £14 million in 1856[2] had risen to £34 million (£25 million paid up and £9 million loan capital) by 1880,[3] while the extent of Irish participation in total railway financing showed a marked improvement over the period.[4] In 1850, for instance, Irish investors held only 36 per cent of the capital in the Great Southern & Western Railway of Ireland but by 1862 this had risen to almost 77 per cent.[5] Local support was encouraged by dividend rates rather better than those available in Great Britain[6] and came in at the point where Irish railways were considered to have passed the speculative stage—confirmation of a tendency, noted in connection with banking and insurance, that Irish capital, of which there was not in fact any real shortage, followed rather than preceded English capital and government support.[7]

Unlike railways in Great Britain, those in Ireland received considerable help by way of loans from official sources. Between 1850 and 1871 the public works loan commissioners added a further £3 million to the £1 million already advanced for railway construction.[8] Then, between 1871 and 1882, the board of works, within whose ambit they now came, provided another £936,000.[9] The amounts were not, of course, cumulative because earlier loans were usually repaid before the later ones were issued; nevertheless the extent of government involvement in Irish railway construction was substantial. Railway loans were regarded as a form of

---

[1] T. W. Grimshaw, 'A statistical survey of Ireland from 1840 to 1888' in *Stat. Soc. Ire. Jn.*, ix, pt lxviii (Nov. 1888), pp 321–61.

[2] G. W. Hemans, 'On the railway system in Ireland' in *Proceedings of the Institution of Civil Engineers*, xviii (1858–9), p. 34. Paid up share capital alone, at 31 Dec. 1857, was £12,623,000 (*Total share capital of every railway and canal company on 31 Dec. 1857*, p. 10, H.C. 1857–8 (385), li, 510).

[3] *Railway returns . . . for the year 1880*, p. xviii [C 2996], H.C. 1881, lxxx, 670.

[4] Joseph Lee, 'The provision of capital for early Irish railways, 1830–53' in *I.H.S.*, xvi, no. 61 (Mar. 1968), pp 47–50.

[5] W. N. Hancock, *Report on the supposed progressive decline of Irish prosperity* (Dublin, 1863), p. 55.

[6] Hemans, 'On the railway system in Ireland', p. 34.

[7] Joseph Lee, 'Capital in the Irish economy' in L. M. Cullen (ed.), *The formation of the Irish economy* (Cork, 1969), p. 54.

[8] *A return 'of all monies lent to railway companies in Ireland'*, pp 2, 3, H.C. 1850 (159), li, 552, 553.

[9] *Report of the committee appointed to inquire into the board of works, Ireland*, p. xix [C 2060], H.C. 1878, xxiii, 19; *Return 'showing the amounts of the several loans advanced to railways in Ireland through the board of public works, . . .'*, p. 1, H.C. 1883 (15), lxi, 471.

public works, like fishery harbours, land reclamation, or drainage, intended to help the general development of the economy rather than the success of particular railway companies.[1]

A feature of Irish railway construction was its comparatively low cost, £15,000 per mile, compared with £39,000 per mile in England. The reason is to be sought in lower labour costs, much less double tracking, and ease of construction in Ireland. Few viaducts were required and not many tunnels of significance.[2] On the other hand railway operations seemed to assume that low wages would continue indefinitely, and Irish lines had a multiplicity of level-crossing gates (where in England cuttings transversed by bridges would have been used), signal boxes at minor junctions, and stations manned on a scale that would have been justified if traffic had been three or four times what it was. This did not seem important, assuming that industrial development bringing additional traffic would follow the creation of a railway system, on the false analogy that 'it was not traffic that made communications, but communications that made traffic'.[3] The accuracy of the assumption became of more consequence when it was found that industry remained obstinately on the east coast and substantial goods traffic failed to develop, as illustrated by the figures of revenue per mile of line open by 1864: England £3,229, Scotland £1,789, Ireland £882.[4]

There was much criticism of the way in which the railways were run—lack of coordination between the various companies, exorbitant and illogical freight charges, and excessive overheads. There was also considerable pressure for amalgamation and government control,[5] but while the former was achieved in the normal course of development (thirty-five companies in 1867; nineteen companies in 1874),[6] the latter had to wait until 1916.

Roads in Ireland had generally been adequate for the traffic they carried. There was no shortage of stone or suitable labour, indeed there had probably been too much unselective road-making as part of famine relief work and, apart from the activity in remote areas by the congested districts board, little needed to be done during the remainder of the nineteenth century. Better surfaces were required when motor passenger services began in 1904, with tourist charabancs making an appearance between 1905 and 1910. The expansion of total motor traffic may be gauged by the number of licences issued to motor spirit dealers—increasing from 712 in 1910 to 1,473 in 1914.[7] The bicycle, ultimately ubiquitous in Ireland, was at first too expensive to have an important economic effect. British manufacturers,

[1] Black, *Econ. thought & Ir. question*, pp 189–202.
[2] Hemans, 'On the railway system in Ireland', pp 34, 36.
[3] Coyne, *Ireland: industrial and agricultural*, p. 83, quoting Sir Arthur Cotton on canals (1883).
[4] *Memorial to the chancellor of the exchequer . . . on the subject of railway reform*, p. 4, H.C. 1866 (265), lxiii, 272.
[5] J. C. Conroy, *A history of railways in Ireland* (London, 1928), pp 55–70.
[6] *Royal commission on railways: report of the commissioners*, p. xciii [3844], H.C. 1867, xxxviii, pt 1, p. 93; Conroy, op. cit., p. 66.
[7] From inland revenue annual reports.

producing 'safety' bicycles from the 1880s, aimed at a middle-class market with high-quality, high-priced machines, and it was not until 1897, partly to meet American competition and partly to offset a slump at home, that prices began to fall. In this year Rudge-Whitworth reduced the price of their standard model from £20 to 12 guineas, in 1898 to 10 guineas, and in 1908 to £5.15s. Most other firms followed suit, though slowly. Average export prices at British ports fell from £6.15s. in 1905 to £4.2s. in 1914.[1] Although, in January 1901, the *Freeman's Journal* carried half a column of bicycle advertisements, including a Champion Roadster at £10.10s., these prices were well beyond the reach of the average Dublin wage-earner, the majority of whom in the years before the first world war had less than £1 a week. But they might have been afforded by craftsmen in the north earning 36s. to £2 a week.[2] Even so, in a 1911 illustration showing a home-going crowd of Belfast shipyard workers there is not a bicycle in sight,[3] a very different picture from that of the inter-war years when pedestrians had to contend with hundreds of them. Similarly, a picture of Sackville Street in 1902 shows tramcars, many horse-drawn vehicles, and pedestrians, but no cyclists.[4] Cullen refers to the bicycle becoming 'commonplace' between the end of the century and 1915,[5] but this was in the context of rural areas and receives support from a photograph taken near Rostrevor in the early 1900s which includes a well dressed man accompanied by two very well dressed children, and his bicycle.[6] It seems that in Ireland the bicycle remained a status symbol, or even a necessity, as in the R.I.C., until during, or perhaps even after, the first world war.[7]

Tramway services, begun in both Belfast and Dublin in 1872, were gradually electrified, the former after 1904, the latter after 1896. Cork's system, also begun in 1872, was electrified after 1898. The rural Giants' Causeway line, the first of its kind in the British Isles, used hydroelectric power from 1883. An important consequence of the city electric tramway systems was that they enabled skilled men and white-collar workers to move to the suburbs, creating the familiar concentric pattern of an inner zone in which transport, industry, and the houses of unskilled workers were interspersed, surrounded by an outer zone containing the houses of skilled and white-collar workers, with this in turn surrounded by the houses of managers and administrators.

Railway expansion after the 1880s was partly commercial and partly subsidised; the former consisted principally of links joining city termini, standard-gauge

---

[1] A. R. Harrison, 'The competitiveness of the British cycle industry, 1890–1914' in *Econ. Hist. Rev.*, 2nd ser., xxii, no. 2 (Aug. 1989), pp 287–303.

[2] F. S. L. Lyons, *Ireland since the famine* (London, 1971), p. 56.

[3] Jonathan Bardon, *Belfast: an illustrated history* (Belfast, 1982), p. 173.

[4] Patrick Flanagan, *Transport in Ireland, 1880–1910* (Dublin, 1969), p. 79.

[5] L. M. Cullen, *An economic history of Ireland since 1660* (London, 1972), p. 156.

[6] Flanagan, *Transport in Ire.*, p. 59.

[7] 'A bicycle becomes a necessary part of a man's equipment now, and every young man is supposed to have a bicycle' (*Royal Irish Constabulary and Dublin Metropolitan Police: appendix to the report of the committee of inquiry*, p. 30 [Cd 7637], H.C. 1914–16, xxxii, 394); the R.I.C., however, did not initially issue bicycles, but paid its members an allowance for using their own machines on official business.

feeder lines, and new construction in support of cross-channel traffic; the latter consisted of lines built in remote rural areas with the assistance of grants and guarantees under the tramway act of 1883 or the light railway acts of 1889 and 1896.[1] Under these acts and subsequent legislation 309 miles of railway were built at a cost of £1,850,000, of which the government paid £1,554,000. Lines open to traffic increased from 2,465 miles in 1882 to 3,215 miles in 1902 and 3,410 miles in 1913. While on the one hand the process of amalgamation among existing companies continued, there was a steady addition of small companies operating the newly constructed light railways. Not without reason was there constant complaint about excessive numbers of directors, managers, and office staff. Inefficiency, abuse of monopoly powers, and lack of bulk goods traffic were mainly responsible for the complaints about high railway charges that figured largely in the evidence of witnesses before various committees and commissions.

It was easier, however, to point to particular rates or fares that seemed excessive than to make valid comparisons with charges in Great Britain or Europe. For instance in 1899 average charges per ton for the carriage of general merchandise were: England 4s. 11d., Scotland 5s. 0d., Ireland 6s. 6d.; for mineral traffic 1s.6d., 1s.4d. and 2s.7d., respectively.[2] But such figures give no indication of the average size of consignments, which were certainly bigger in Great Britain than in Ireland. Similarly, average passenger fares per mile in 1889, without distinguishing average lengths of journeys, are shown in the following table.[3]

Average passenger fares per mile, 1889

	1st class d.	2nd class d.	3rd class d.
England	2	1.25	1
Ireland	2.125	1.625	1

But whereas in 1899 an average of 64,000 passengers travelled over each mile of line in England and Wales, the corresponding number in Ireland was just over 9,000. For goods traffic the figures were 23,000 tons and 1,700 tons respectively. The basic facts of Irish railway economics were that, despite government assistance, despite low construction costs and capital charges, despite the absence of passenger duty, and despite weekly railway wages averaging some 3s. to 6s. below those in Great Britain, the volume of traffic was barely sufficient to sustain a free enterprise system. Critics who pointed to a plethora of directors or to

[1]   46 & 47 Vict., c. 43 (25 Aug. 1883); 52 & 53 Vict., c. 66 (30 Aug. 1889); 59 & 60 Vict., c. 34 (14 Aug. 1896); and see *Royal commission on congestion in Ireland: final report*, p. 97 [Cd 4097], H.C. 1908, xlii, 695.
[2]   Calculated from *Statistical abstract for the United Kingdom . . . from 1890 to 1904*, p. 238 [Cd 2622], H.C. 1905, xciv, 244. See Coyne, *Ireland: industrial and agricultural*, p. 80, for similar figures for 1880, 1890, and 1900.
[3]   J. T. Pim, 'A review of the economic and social condition of Ireland' in *Stat. Soc. Ire. Jn.*, x, pt lxxix (Aug. 1899), p. 496; see also *Hansard 4*, lxvi, 1295–1347 (17 Feb. 1899).

'unfair' through rates charged by cross-Channel railway companies were of course correct but the real difficulties lay much deeper. Interestingly enough, even the witnesses to the 1910 viceregal commission (like their predecessors at earlier inquiries) who were most vocal about high fares and charges were almost uniformly in favour of the further extension of the Irish system into even more remote districts. By 1910, however, the last of the standard-gauge lines was already under construction (Castleblayney, Keady, and Armagh) and the last of the light railways (Strabane–Letterkenny) nearing completion.

The years immediately preceding 1914 have been referred to as 'golden years' for the Irish railways, and in terms of passengers and goods carried and of revenue earned on the main lines the expression is appropriate enough, but the light railways recently constructed with government assistance (almost £2 million by 1907) were in a different position. Few of them ever paid their way and most imposed heavy burdens on the ratepayers of the guaranteeing districts. But they did open up remote areas that could not have been served on a commercial basis, they facilitated the fishing industry in particular, provided important employment in their construction and operation, and inspired an affection in their users proportionate rather to their social than to their economic advantages.

Canals no longer attracted passenger traffic after 1850, but up to the end of the century they did share in the increase in the movement of goods within Ireland, a total of 1,052,000 tons being moved by water in 1898 compared with 865,000 tons in 1888.[1] This traffic was confined of course to certain major waterways such as the Royal, Grand, Lagan, and Newry canals, but even here the canal companies had the problem that railway competition kept tolls at a minimum while maintenance costs were rising. Thus a £34,000 increase in revenue between 1888 and 1898 produced an increase in profits of only £12,000 (with the railway-owned Royal showing a profit decrease of £1,600). After the turn of the century, when road was added to rail competition, the position of the canals became steadily less tenable.

The increase in shipping using Irish ports and the rising values of imports and exports must be regarded as some indication of improved prosperity. Totals for ships entered and cleared in 1870 were 8,123,000 tons and in 1890 10,362,000 tons. The total estimated value of imports and exports combined rose from £108 million in 1905 to £148 million in 1913. At the same time cross-Channel passenger services increased in number and frequency. All this meant increased capital expenditure by harbour boards and commissioners and a significant expansion in employment of wharf and dock labour.

IRISH retail prices between 1850 and 1920 were largely determined in Great Britain. This was because the greatest part of Ireland's agricultural produce found

---

[1] *Royal commission on canals and waterways: final report . . . Ireland*, pp 16–17 [Cd 5626], H.C. 1911, xiii, 46–7. In 1836 on the canals completed by that date the total was probably about 550,000 tons.

Bread prices and U.K. wheat production, 1860–1910

	average price of 4 lb. loaf		percentage of U.K. wheat
	Dublin	London	home grown
	d.	d.	%
1860	6.0	8.75	64.1
1870	6.75	8.0	60.9
1880	7.5	7.5	27.0
1890	6.0	6.0	23.1
1900	5.25	5.23	22.8
1910	6.0	5.9	20.3

a market there, and export prices of cattle and sheep, bacon and butter, became the ruling wholesale prices in Ireland. At the same time Britain provided almost all of Ireland's coal, iron, and manufactured goods. There were exceptions, because Ireland exported very little of her wheat, oats, and potatoes and produced part of her own cotton, woollen goods, and footwear. Excise duties on the one hand and the American market on the other were the major influences on the prices of whiskey, beer, and linen. So far as food is concerned a comparison of bread and potato prices is interesting. A reducing wheat acreage should have meant a steadily rising price for bread but instead, due to the availability of cheap American flour, prices tended to fall, except for 1865–8, and were lowest when Irish production was at a minimum in 1901–5. The table above compares Irish (generally Dublin) prices with those in London.[1] It illustrates what trade and agricultural statistics would lead one to expect, namely that falling wheat acreage and increasing use of imported grain or flour occurred some ten to fifteen years earlier in Ireland than in Great Britain; also that when total U.K. imports exceeded 50 per cent of consumption, British and Irish bread prices tended to coincide. It is accepted that inland prices would have varied by a small margin from prices at the ports, but quite clearly bread prices in Ireland (although subject to fluctuations, for instance during the years 1867–8 and 1871–4)[2] fell fairly steadily during the whole period 1850–1914, and in so far as bread formed a substantial part of diet must have done something to reduce living costs.

The Irish potato crop fell from 875,000 acres in 1850 to 583,000 in 1920. With a population that fell by 2.5 million during the same period it might have been expected that prices would remain reasonably steady; but in fact, as Barrington explains, 'no other crop has varied so much in market price from year to year as the potato'.[3] The explanation lies largely in the weather, at least in so far as the

[1] *Report on wholesale and retail prices in the United Kingdom in 1902*, p. 231, H.C. 1903 (321), lxviii, 287; Mitchell & Deane, *Brit. hist. statistics*, p. 498; *Ministry of reconstruction: report of the agricultural sub-committee of the reconstruction committee*, p. 9 [Cd 9079], H.C. 1918, v, 109.

[2] Mary E. Daly, *Dublin, the deposed capital . . . 1860–1912* (Cork, 1984), p. 74.

[3] Thomas Barrington, 'A review of Irish agricultural prices' in *Stat. Soc. Ire. Jn.*, xv, pt ci (Oct. 1927), p. 262.

weather affected crop yields, which varied from 6.4 tons an acre in 1853 and 1855 to 1.6 tons in 1861 and 2.6 tons in 1872.[1] The low yields in these last two years were due to blight, which appeared also in 1852, 1859, 1860–64, 1872, 1890, and 1894.[2] This meant that while the average Dublin price in 1865 or 1886 was in the range of 2s. 4d. to 3s. 2d. a cwt (3½d. to 4¾d. a stone) the price reached 6d. to 9d. a stone on the west coast during the blight year 1891.[3] As in previous times of severe shortage, relief measures had to be organised by the government, and wheat meal, Indian corn, and oatmeal brought into the area. The people themselves seemed at last to have realised that reliance on the potato for three-quarters or more of their basic diet was no longer practicable. Elsewhere in Ireland the predominance of the potato had weakened steadily since the famine; now, with improved transport and a widening variety of other foods available, this tendency spread among the small farms of the congested districts too. A curious result noted by Barrington was that by 1913 increasing acreages of potatoes (comparing that year with 1850–78) were in evidence among almost all the countries of Europe, except Ireland.[4] Despite all this the potato remained and remains a major article of diet in most homes 'because it is liked, not because it is necessary'.[5]

The prices of meat—beef, mutton, and pork—moved upward in unison from 1850 until the end of the 1870s, then, after a brief though appreciable fall, there began a slow downward movement until the opening decade of the new century. The rise is illustrated by the figures given in the following table, with comparative prices given for Indian meal, oatmeal, and tea.[6] Bacon prices were above those for pork (1860, 7½d. to 10d.; 1870, 9d. to 11d.), but from at least 1850 imported American bacon was available at 20 to 25 per cent below Irish prices. It is clear that for the lower levels of society meat of any kind had become a barely attainable luxury. But for the Belfast millworker or Dublin stevedore the falling prices of

---

[1] *Agricultural statistics (Ireland)*, annually.
[2] Donnelly, *Land & people of Cork*, pp 146, 148, 150, 252–3.
[3] T. P. O'Neill, 'Food crises in the 1880s' in E. M. Crawford (ed.), *Famine: the Irish experience* (Edinburgh, 1989), p. 185.
[4] Barrington, 'Review of agricultural prices', p. 263:

	Area under potatoes ('000 acres)	
	*	1913
Denmark (1871)	106	173
Belgium (1855)	371	395
Norway (1865)	79	101
Holland (av. 1850–5)	237	421
Sweden (1865)	316	376
Germany (1878)	6,815	8,431
France (1850)	2,303	3,825

* Year shown in brackets.

[5] Redcliffe N. Salaman, *The history and social influence of the potato* (Cambridge, 1949), p. 331.
[6] Daly, *Dublin*, p. 74.

Prices of foodstuffs, 1850–79

	beef lb	mutton lb	pork lb	Indian meal cwt	oatmeal cwt	tea lb
1850	4d.	4½d.	3½d.	7s. 0d.	10s. 0d.	5s. 0d.
1860	6½d.	7½d.	5d.	8s. 3d.	13s. 2d.	4s. 0d
1870	7d.	7½d.	6d.	6s. 10d.	12s. 0d.	3s. 6d.
1879	7½d.	8½d.	8d.	6s. 8d.	11s. 6d	2s. 8d.

the staples, bread, butter (rejected on quality by the British market), and tea were becoming easier. Outside the cities, the falling price of Indian meal was significant and there was always the possibility of a turnip or rabbit or skimmed milk; in the north, oatmeal and buttermilk were seasonally available. Meat did not of course enter into official calculations of the cost of living for in 1864–5 'the provisions which enter most largely into their [the labouring population's] consumption are good, cheap, and abundant. Bread, oatmeal, flour, Indian meal, and potatoes as well as tea and sugar are all to be had at much lower prices than formerly'.[1] Even so it is difficult to see how the guardians at Midleton in 1867 were able to keep the workhouse paupers' bodies and souls tenuously together for 1s. 8d. a week.[2]

Since the products of most of Ireland's minor industries were sold within Ireland their prices were determined by local circumstances and local demand. This usually meant that they were of excellent handmade quality but rather dearer than mass-produced articles from Great Britain, from which they were to some extent protected by transport costs. As transport costs fell, however, within and between the British Isles, and as wholesaling and retailing facilities developed within Ireland, competition became a greater threat. During the 1850s and 1860s British prices tended to rise[3] and competition was held in check, but in 1874 with the collapse of a world-wide industrial boom British manufactures flooded the Irish market and prices fell.[4] The fall, or at any rate the downward price pressure, continued until around 1898. Falling prices, though advantageous to consumers, were disastrous to small non-exporting manufacturers, many of whom collapsed. The only ground for consumers' complaints was the inferior quality of some of the articles imported (such as footwear and the cheaper cottons). There were some minor complaints about the regular increases in excise duty on beer and spirits, though this did not seem to affect the number of retail outlets.[5] For most people in Ireland the years from 1894 to the end of the century were as comfortable a period as they could remember. Unemployment was falling, living costs stable, and wages beginning ro rise.

[1] *Annual report of the commissioners for administering the laws for relief of the poor in Ireland*, p. 32 [3507], H.C. 1865, xxii, 378.
[2] *Cork Examiner*, 16 Sept. 1867.
[3] Mitchell & Deane, *Brit. hist. statistics*, p. 472.
[4] L. M. Cullen, *An economic history of Ireland since 1660* (London, 1972), p. 146.
[5] Numbers of licensed retailers of spirits, beer, etc., from customs and excise reports.

The second Boer war pushed up both wholesale and retail prices. In Ireland food was little affected but clothing, footwear, and household goods became dearer. With little fall between 1901 and 1905 retail prices in Belfast, Derry, Dublin, Cork, and Limerick were comparable at the latter date with those in Great Britain—a little cheaper than in the London area, a little dearer than in the west and north (though not so dear as in Scotland).[1] House rents in Ireland, even in cities undergoing expansion, were, however, conspicuously lower than elsewhere in the United Kingdom.[2] Then came a steep rise in prices generally. Between 1905 and 1912 average increases in retail prices of food and coal were calculated as 9 per cent in Dublin, 13 per cent in Belfast, 15 per cent in Limerick, 16 per cent in Cork, and 18 per cent in Derry; increases that, with the exception of Dublin, were steeper than those in Great Britain.[3] By 1914, save for rents and services it was cheaper to live in London than in most places in Ireland—but rents were of major importance in working-class households and services in those of the higher income groups, so that overall there was little cause for concern.

An area of retail prices seldom noted is worth some consideration. In 1842 W. M. Thackeray stayed at the Shelbourne Hotel for 6s. 8d. a day, which included three substantial meals.[4] In 1860 Dublin eating houses in respectable areas of the city advertised in the *Freeman's Journal* breakfast at 6d. to 1s. 3d., lunch at 5d. to 8d., dinner at 10d. to 1s. 2d., and accommodation at 1s. a night.[5] In 1897 the Clarence Hotel on Wellington Quay offered a five-course dinner from 2s.[6] By 1900 prices had advanced a little, for the XL Café in Grafton Street was charging for hot dinners 10d., 1s. 2d., and 1s. 6d.,[7] while Wynn's Hotel had first-class bedrooms available at 2s. 6d. a night.[8] There was little further rise before 1914, when the Clarence Hotel was charging for accommodation (bed and breakfast) 3s. to 4s. 6d. a night.[9] All of these very reasonable charges were based, not only on the cost of food and manufactured goods (sheets, furniture, furnishings), already discussed, but on the very low wages of domestic labour.

ON the subject of wages, an agricultural labourer who got 6d. to 8d. a day before the famine would earn 1s. to 1s. 4d. a day at work in 1855 and might get 1s. 6d. to 2s. a day at certain busy seasons.[10] In the 1860s there was a levelling off and

---

[1] *Sixteenth abstract of labour statistics*, pp 152–8 [Cd 7131], H.C. 1914, lxxx, 476–82.

[2] Ibid., pp 147–9 (MS 471–3).

[3] Ibid., pp 152–3 (MS 476–7).

[4] W. M. Thackeray, *The Irish sketch book of 1842* (London, 1879), p. 263.

[5] *F. J.*, 8 Sept. 1860.

[6] *Daily Nation*, 16 June 1897. In late 1993 a four-course dinner at the Clarence Hotel cost £12.50, including value-added tax.

[7] *F.J.*, 14 Dec. 1900.

[8] Ibid., 16 Jan. 1901.

[9] Ibid., 6 Jan. 1914. The corresponding rates at the Clarence Hotel for 1994 were £37–£50 (low season) and £44–£54 (high season), including value-added tax. For this and the additional information in n. 6 above, the editors are indebted to the management of the Clarence Hotel, Dublin.

[10] *Eighth annual report of the commissioners for administering the laws for the relief of the poor in Ireland*, pp 11–15 [1945], H.C. 1854–5, xxiv, 533–7.

by 1865 an average wage would have been 1s. 2d. a day or 5s. to 9s. a week.[1] By 1870 wages were moving upwards again and by 1880 they had reached 9s. to 12s. a week.[2] Real wages were less satisfactory in the light of increasing retail prices, though it seems unlikely that at any point they actually fell. On the whole, and despite rising money wages, the increase in what an agricultural labourer (or any other unskilled man) could buy with his earnings was relatively slow.

In other respects the average agricultural labourer's position improved markedly. There was less casual and more full-time work. As farms became bigger few of those above 50 acres would have been without at least one permanent man, employed in tending livestock, repairing fences, earthing up potatoes, clearing ditches, making hay, or any of the multiplicity of jobs found about a mixed farm. The many skills that a good agricultural labourer needed were every bit as exacting as those of the town industrial worker, and his hours considerably longer. On this basis the best men were doubtless underpaid; the employer who in 1880 was paying 12s. a week, with a free house, a garden, and potato ground, was ahead of his neighbours.[3]

Unskilled labour in Ireland, whether agricultural or otherwise, was poorly paid because it was worth so little, and the margin between the wages of unskilled labourers in Ireland and Great Britain was of the order of 4s. to 5s. per week,[4] which was significant in relation to an Irish wage invariably under 15s., and altered little during the period under review. Moving up the ladder, however, to semi-skilled and skilled workers the margin diminished and for some specialist skills the Irish worker was paid a little above his British counterpart. For instance, in Liverpool bookbinders earned 4s. 2d. an hour in 1859 against 4s.–5s. an hour in Dublin; lithographers earned 4s. 2d. an hour in 1860 compared with 3s. 4d. to 6s. 6d. an hour in Belfast.[5] Such figures confirm the complaints of Irish employers that it was difficult to retain skilled men, because wages offered had to approximate to British levels.

Wages in the semi-skilled trades tended to reflect labourers' rather than skilled rates;[6] for example, riveters in Belfast shipyards, who were skilled men, earned 3s. 6d. to 4s. 2d. for a ten-hour day in 1866, 4s. 2d. in 1871, and 28s. for a fifty-four-hour week in 1877. There was a considerable differential between these and, for example, the wages paid to men at bleach fields near the town of 2s. 6d. in 1867/8, 3s. in 1871, and 21s. for a sixty-hour week in 1877. Semi-skilled rates for women spinners in the Belfast mills were lower again at 1s. 4½d. for a ten-hour day in 1866, 1s. 1d. to 1s. 4d. in 1871, and 8s. for a fifty-six-hour week

[1] *Chronicle*, 19 Aug. 1865; *Report from the select committee on Tenure and Improvement of Land (Ireland) Act*, p. 212, H.C. 1865 (402), xi, 564.

[2] R. M. Barrington, 'The prices of some agricultural produce and the cost of farm labour for the past fifty years' in *Stat. Soc. Ire. Jn.*, ix, pt lxv (Feb. 1887), pp 137–53.

[3] *Richmond comm. evidence*, p. 371 [C 2778–I], H.C. 1881, xv, 399.

[4] *Returns of wages published between 1830 and 1886* [C 5172], H.C. 1887, lxxxix, 273–714.

[5] Ibid., pp 304, 312, 314 (MS 580, 588, 590).

[6] Coe, *The engineering industry of the north of Ireland*, p. 178.

in 1877.[1] Daily rates do not of course necessarily indicate earnings, which were affected by short-time or overtime working. As compared with wages for skilled workers, Dublin wages in the semi-skilled category seem to have been a little lower than those prevailing in the north. That skilled workers were better able than unskilled to maintain a relatively favourable wage position was due at least in part to their earlier trade union organisation.

Wage levels and wage movements in Ireland after 1880 have certain features that deserve consideration. Of these, the steady rise in agricultural labourers' wages is best attested.[2] The weekly rates of cash wages for ordinary labourers rose between 1880 and 1913 by some 30 per cent; for farm servants the rise was of the order of 25 per cent but these men and women were lodged and fed by their employers and there is reason to believe that standards of accommodation and subsistence were better at the end of the period than at the beginning. Skilled men, such as shepherds, ploughmen, and herds, had such a varied range of perquisites that comparison is particularly difficult, but increases in the range 25 to 30 per cent would probably be representative. The earnings of the last two classes were regular whereas ordinary labourers found less work in winter than in summer and one can think therefore of a general rise in earnings of something above 25 per cent. Average figures, however, are a convenient abstraction. In practice there were in each group quite wide variations between different parts of the country. In 1885 it was said that agricultural labourers normally earning 9s. to 12s. weekly could earn 12s. to 15s. in the vicinity of towns or near places where public works were in progress; in 1893 summer wages in Skibbereen were higher by 3s. near the coast because mackerel fishing was available as an alternative; in 1903 the range was from 8s. 9d. a week in Mayo to 13s. a week in Down. Irregularity of employment as much as difference in wage rates is reflected in the 1893 estimate of £20 being the annual average earnings of labourers near Ballyshannon, compared with £30 to £35 near Downpatrick or Limavady. Agricultural wages in Ireland advanced during the period rather faster than in England or Scotland, but from a much lower base. Thus there was still in 1903 a differential of 5s. to 9s. per week between average wage rates in Ireland and those in Britain, a differential that could be doubled in terms of earnings by intensive harvest labour. By 1914 the average wages of ordinary agricultural labourers in Ireland had risen to 11s. to 13s. weekly, and in England to 17s. to 20s., leaving the differential relatively unaffected.

[1] *Return of wages published between 1830 and 1886*, pp 75, 88, 221 (MS 351, 364, 497).

[2] There are many sources for agricultural wages during the period. The most useful include: *Royal commission on labour: the agricultural labourer* [C 6694–XVII to XXI], H.C. 1893–4, xxvii, pt 1; *Abstracts of labour statistics of the United Kingdom from 1894*; A. L. Bowley, 'The statistics of wages in the United Kingdom during the last hundred years. Part III. Agricultural wages: Ireland' in *Journal of the Royal Statistical Society*, lxii (1899); *Agricultural statistics (Ireland)*: reports and tables relating to agricultural labourers. From 1901; *Second report by Mr Wilson Fox on the wages, earnings, and conditions of employment of agricultural labourers in the United Kingdom* [Cd 2376], H.C. 1905, xcvii, 335–616; *Report of an inquiry by the board of trade into the earnings and hours of labour of workpeople in the United Kingdom: V. Agriculture in 1907* [Cd 5460], H.C. 1910, lxxxiv, 451–534.

An agricultural labourer who came to Dublin in 1880 and found unskilled employment would have received between 12*s*. and 14*s*. a week.[1] In 1885 he would have been paid 9*s*. to 14*s*. in a small country town, a little higher in most cities, and 15*s*. to 20*s*. in Belfast, although the highest rate must have been exceptional.[2] By 1910 he might have averaged 16*s*. a week in Dublin,[3] a shilling or two more in Belfast. But he would have found that accommodation in the cities was dearer than in the country, that he no longer had access to ground for growing potatoes or vegetables, and that the irregularity of agricultural labour (which was in any case diminishing) was replaced by an industrial and commercial irregularity of a less predictable kind. Had he chosen Belfast, of course, his wife might have found employment in the textile industry and his older children as 'half-timers' in a spinning mill. The possibility of going to England and Scotland would have occurred to him, but with unskilled labour no longer required for railway construction, with unemployment rising in the years 1875–95, and with evidence of considerable poverty among earlier immigrants from Ireland, the prospects were not encouraging. Hence there remained in Ireland, particularly in Dublin, a sufficient pool of unskilled labour to keep wages down to subsistence level, which meant in 1914, for the considerable number of carters, porters, and messengers in the city, something less than 18*s*. a week.[4]

The wages of skilled and semi-skilled workers contrast with those just discussed. In 1892 skilled men in Dublin were getting 33*s*. weekly, which was considered equal to the English average outside London.[5] In 1895 over a wide range of trades Belfast and Dublin rates compared with those in many British cities. But this was a time of quickening economic activity and at the beginning of the twentieth century, in a period of slackening demand, Irish workers seem to have lost ground. At any rate Irish city wages in 1906 were generally below those of British workers in all but the most remote areas.[6] By 1910 some of the lost ground had been regained and in the favoured shipbuilding and engineering trades Belfast fitters at 37*s*. a week were said to be among the highest paid in the British Isles.[7] This was not typical, but bears out the view that the wages of skilled workers in Ireland were pulled upward by the rates prevailing in Great Britain rather than pushed downward by the poor wages paid locally to the unskilled.

[1] *F.J.*, 13 Jan. 1881.

[2] *Report from the select committee on industries (Ireland); . . . minutes of evidence*, p. 631, H.C. 1884–5 (288), ix, 649.

[3] Emmet Larkin, *James Larkin: Irish labour leader, 1876–1947* (London, 1965; reprint, 1977), p. 46.

[4] *Report of the departmental committee . . . to inquire into the housing conditions of the working classes in the city of Dublin*, p. 8 [Cd 7273], H.C. 1914, xix, 72.

[5] *Royal commission on labour: minutes of evidence . . . group 'C', ii*, pp 209–10 [C 6795–VI], H.C. 1892, xxxvi, pt II, pp 657–8.

[6] *Report of an inquiry by the board of trade into the earnings and hours of labour of workpeople of the United Kingdom. VI: metal, engineering, and shipbuilding trades in 1906* [Cd 5814], H.C. 1911, lxxxviii, 1–252.

[7] *Standard time rates of wages in the United Kingdom at 1 Oct. 1910*, p. 54 [Cd 5459], H.C. 1910, lxxxiv, 894.

Average figures, however, conceal internal wage differentials within the United Kingdom and fail to reflect the lower incidence of overtime working in Ireland. As to regional differences, carpenters in 1900 were paid only 26s. 8d. a week in Armagh and 32s. in Limerick, but 37s. 1d. in Dublin, and 38s. 3d. in Belfast.[1] In 1914 iron moulders in Cork got 34s., in Dublin 38s., and in Belfast 42s. to 44s.[2] The lack of mobility of skilled labour within Ireland, which these figures suggest, was at least as conspicuous in Great Britain.

On an even lower level than those of unskilled men were the wages paid to women, who found employment mainly in textile factories, garment-making, domestic service, or cottage industry. Not only were wages low but, except where regulated by legislation, hours of work were excessive. A few instances must suffice. Average weekly wages for spinners in the Belfast linen mills were estimated in 1875 at 7s. 9d., in 1884 at 7s. 6d., in 1886 at 8s. 5d., in 1906 at 10s. 5d., and in 1914 at 15s.[3] The better Dublin householders, paying their resident domestic servants £10 to £12 a year in 1901, were indignant at an English agency seeking to recruit them at better wages, but can hardly have been surprised that many of them went.[4] Perhaps the most glaring cases of exploitation occurred among domestic workers in the linen and making-up trades, where an investigation in 1912 showed that the majority of firms were paying for work at rates equivalent to less than 3d. an hour and a considerable number at less than 1d. an hour.[5] By these standards shirt-making at 14s. to 16s. a week was a prestige occupation. Not surprisingly emigrants from Ireland in the 1890s contained a majority of women.

It is difficult to present a simple account of finance in the Irish economy because the main elements in the picture seldom move together. In terms of available capital there were clear indications in the second half of the nineteenth century of steady, almost uninterrupted accumulation. Overlaying this were fluctuations in trade, in agricultural conditions, in government taxation, and expenditure. At longer range were changes in British monetary policy and in world gold supplies.

On the first there is adequate evidence. In Irish joint-stock banks, trustee savings banks, and, after 1862, in post office savings banks, deposits rose from £9,500,000 in 1850 to £33,400,000 in 1880.[6] Contemporary observers noted the

[1] A. L. Bowley, 'The statistics of wages in the United Kingdom . . . Part VII' in *Journal of the Royal Statistical Society*, lxiii (1900), pp 492–3.

[2] *Seventeenth abstract of labour statistics of the United Kingdom*, p. 48 [Cd 7733], H.C. 1914–16, lxi, 364.

[3] D. L. Armstrong, 'Social and economic conditions in the Belfast linen industry, 1850–1900' in *I.H.S.*, vii, no. 28 (Sept. 1951), p. 264; Riordan, *Modern Irish trade and industry*, p. 109.

[4] *F.J.*, 23 Jan. 1901.

[5] *Committee of inquiry into the conditions of employment in the linen and other making-up trades of the north of Ireland: report and evidence*, pp vii–ix [Cd 6509], H.C. 1912–13, xxxiv, 371–3.

[6] T. W. Grimshaw, 'A statistical survey of Ireland, from 1840 to 1888' in *Stat. Soc. Ire. Jn.*, ix, pt lxviii (Dec. 1888), pp 321–61. Grimshaw's figures are misleading in detail, if not in direction, because the total of bank deposits and current accounts was falling between 1877 and 1887; see Philip

fact but were unable to explain it. Some thought the money represented accumulation by farmers who, unwilling to put profits back into their holdings for fear of rent increases, chose instead to hold it in liquid form; others attributed at least the savings bank deposits to increasing prosperity among the artisan class. Possibly both contributed, but to the extent that, as confidence grew, the new facilities replaced the traditional one of simple concealment, the increase in savings bank deposits cannot be taken completely at its face value. The average size of deposits in trustee savings banks in 1880 was under £40.[1] The increased deposits in joint-stock banks doubtless included profits from family firms, which were liable to be abstracted for land purchase or private use instead of being ploughed back,[2] and, while accumulating, would have been placed on deposit. They would have been joined by the customary large dowries being held for daughters of the more substantial farmers. Commentators have pointed out that what was missing in Ireland was not so much capital as risk capital, and this was true. It was also true that some of the capital on deposit with joint-stock banks was not regarded by the owners as available for investment because it was earmarked for other purposes. Nevertheless banks could have used it as a base for extending credit to industry. It remains to be explained why, in the light of the resources available to them, lending by banks was on so limited a scale and played so little part in stimulating the economy.

Generally speaking, Irish banks regarded themselves primarily as custodians of their clients' money, as providing facilities for its transfer, and as acting in support of commercial transactions: by discounting bills, for example. They regarded their lending function either as incidental—where an account was allowed to be overdrawn for a short period—or as a means of earning what was needed to cover their expenses and pay their shareholders modest but assured dividends. It was only with reluctance, and because so few other outlets were available, that they lent money for, for example, railway construction.[3] They frequently came under fire for investing in government funds moneys that their critics thought should have been made available to business,[4] but there was some excuse for this in the 1850s in the light of recent experience of land values on the one hand and with legislation on the other that inhibited acceptance of land or houses or factories as security. The latter situation was not remedied for the Bank of Ireland until 1860.[5]

Ollerenshaw, *Banking in nineteenth-century Ireland* (Manchester, 1987), pp 115–16; David K. Sheppard, *The growth and role of U.K. financial institutions, 1880–1962* (London, 1971), pp 120–21.

[1] *Report of the departmental committee on agricultural credit in Ireland*, p. 39 [Cd 7375], H.C. 1914, xiii, 57.

[2] Joseph Lee, 'Capital in the Irish economy' in L. M. Cullen (ed.), *The formation of the Irish economy* (Cork, 1969), p. 55.

[3] F. G. Hall, *History of the Bank of Ireland* (Dublin, 1949), p. 223.

[4] *Report from the select committee on industries (Ireland) . . . minutes of evidence*, p. 792, H.C. 1884–5 (288), ix, 810; W. N. Hancock, 'Complaints against bankers in Ireland' in *Stat. Soc. Ire. Jn.*, vi, pt xlix (Feb. 1876), pp 523–38.

[5] 23 & 24 Vict., c. 31 (3 July 1860), removed the inhibitions in 21 & 22 Geo. III [Ir.], c. 26 (4 May 1782), sect. 7.

Even after 1860 there was the problem that a tenant farmer could not offer land as security, while industry more often needed money to keep going than to expand. Exceptions were the major shipbuilding and brewing concerns, which had access to the share market, or the linen firms of the north, often represented on the boards of local banks, who had few serious complaints. However, banking services did become more extensive and, as the century advanced, a network of branches and agencies began to offer to farmers and traders in provincial towns the services previously available only in the cities. The total number of branches and agencies open was 174 in 1850, 180 in 1860, 304 in 1870, and 479 in 1880.[1] All the major banks took part in the expansion.

If their conservative lending policies attracted criticism, Irish banks had at least the benefit that they passed largely unscathed through a succession of financial crises that affected their counterparts in Great Britain. The collapse of the Tipperary bank in 1856 was the result not of exterior pressures but of local mismanagement and fraud.[2] It was the last Irish bank failure. The crisis of 1857, during which banks in England, Scotland, and America suspended payment, affected particularly the trade of Belfast,[3] but was of short duration and, as the Northern Bank noted, 'through this severe ordeal the joint stock banks of Ireland have passed most creditably, proving . . . the soundness of their management and the strength of their resources'.[4] The collapse of Overend, Gurney, & Co. in 1866 with liabilities exceeding £10,000,000 affected Irish investors but again the banks survived unscathed.[5] Similarly, the collapse of the City of Glasgow bank in 1878, while it dislocated the extensive business carried on between Scotland and the north of Ireland, did not affect the Irish banks.[6] Agricultural distress, however, compounded by the defalcation of the managing director, led the Munster Bank to suspend payments in July 1885 and to go into liquidation. Its remaining assets were taken over later in the year by the newly formed Munster & Leinster Bank, which proved a more soundly run successor.[7]

Because few agricultural borrowers had any title to land, the banks required as an alternative sureties who had to attend personally on the granting of a loan and at subsequent renewals—a tedious and expensive process for the borrower.[8] Also, loans liable to recall at short notice were not suited to an industry whose money was tied up irrevocably in stock and crops for considerable periods. Farmers,

---

[1] *Report of the departmental committee on agricultural credit in Ireland*, p. 18 [Cd 7375], H.C. 1914, xiii, 34.

[2] Hall, *Bank of Ire.*, pp 224–31.

[3] *Report from the select committee on the bank acts*, p. 342, H.C. 1857–8 (381), v, 420.

[4] *Northern Banking Co. Ltd., Belfast. Centenary volume 1824–1924* (Belfast, 1925), p. 131.

[5] Hall, *Bank of Ire.*, p. 246.

[6] Ibid., p. 264.

[7] Donnelly, *Land & people of Cork*, pp 308–13; *Ann. Reg., 1885*, pp 43–4; Coyne, *Ireland: industrial and agricultural*, p. 125.

[8] *Report of the departmental committee on agricultural credit in Ireland*, p. 13 [Cd 7375], H.C. 1914, xiii, 29.

however, had available other sources of credit—cattle dealers, butter merchants,[1] and general agricultural suppliers; indeed there is evidence that between 1870 and 1880 farmers sometimes found loans too easy to obtain.[2]

Finally, there was the loan fund board, whose constituent societies made available sums up to £10 to very small borrowers among 'the industrious agricultural poor'. From 198,000 loans issued and £900,000 in circulation in 1860 the board's activities fell to 89,000 loans issued and £428,000 in circulation in 1880, and the fall continued.[3] This was less an indication that farmers' credit needs were diminishing than that in the 1880s money was required for more urgent purposes than capital investment. But banks, traders, and the loan fund board were equally averse to meeting, for example, rent arrears. Relief of distress loans might be sought from the commissioners of public works—who issued 2,607 loans in 1879/80 compared with the normal annual 200 to 300—but otherwise recourse was to a much longer established system. The rural gombeen man and the back-street moneylender are easier to condemn in social than to assess in economic terms. Living closer to less reticent clients than institutional lenders to their more respectable borrowers, their place in folk memory is assured. They charged exorbitantly for services nobody else was willing to provide but it would have to be demonstrated that they were less disposed than bigger lenders to distinguish between the unfortunate and the improvident. There may have been some tendency to exaggerate their rapacity. A modern assessment suggests that they charged around 15 per cent for their services and that interest rates below 10 or above 20 per cent were exceptional. This was in the early 1890s, however, when other lending agencies had been established; twenty years earlier, they were in a much stronger position, but even for that time it has never been suggested that they were in the same league as their counterparts in rural Burma or Laos, whose charges even at the present day can exceed 100 per cent.[4]

With the establishment in 1885 of the Munster and Leinster Bank,[5] the complement of Irish joint-stock banks was complete, but the opening of new branches, particularly in provincial towns, continued, the total reaching 863 by 1913. Deposits also continued to rise, totalling £74.5 million in 1914 and £166 million in 1919. The allocation of resources between cash, advances to customers, and investment in government securities is interesting. For instance, between 1897 and 1911 investment increased from £18 million to £24 million and was

---

[1] *Richmond comm. evidence*, p. 108 [Cd 2778–I], H.C. 1881, xv, 136. Butter merchants of Cork were believed to have lent almost £500,000 to farmers in the neighbourhood.

[2] Ibid., p. 93 (MS 121); *Bessborough comm. evidence*, p. 220 (MS 438).

[3] *Report of the departmental committee on agricultural credit in Ireland*, p. 109 [Cd 7375], H.C. 1914, xiii, 127. There were 133 societies in 1850 falling to 78 in 1873, mainly in Ulster, and the average loan was under £5 (*Report from the select committee on loan fund societies (Ireland)*, H.C. 1854–5 (259), vii, 321–94; *Thirty-fifth annual report of the commissioners of the loan fund board of Ireland* [C 753], H.C. 1873, xxi, 269–88).

[4] Liam Kennedy, 'A sceptical view of the reincarnation of the Irish gombeenman' in *Economic & Social Review*, viii, no. 3 (1977), p. 217.

[5] Above, p. 324.

about 5 per cent higher than for Scottish and 15 per cent higher than for English banks. At the same time the totals of bills discounted and advances to customers were also higher by about 8 per cent and 10 per cent respectively.[1] Sample figures for the earlier years 1883, 1891, and 1896 show that in relation to deposits, Irish banks' lending was much the same as that of London banks and consistently higher than that of Scottish banks.[2] Again, while it is true that Irish banks' profits were generally higher in relation to resources than those of British banks, the proportion represented by bank premises was conspicuously lower.[3] In other words, whatever may have been the earlier position, Irish bankers after the 1880s were at least as ready lenders as their colleagues elsewhere—though perhaps more apt to hedge their bets. Their policies are consistent with, and further confirm, the view that investment in Ireland required to be attracted by a rather higher proportionate rate of profit than elsewhere in the United Kingdom. In this connection it is of some interest that in Ireland discount rates on bills of exchange were 1–3 per cent higher than in England, and the practice of the Bank of Ireland, at least, was to charge rather more on Irish than on English bills. In other respects banking policies were closely tied to English practice, with overdraft rates, which were more important for general lending purposes, keeping in close touch with movements in the Bank of England's bank rate.[4]

Bank lending, however, was essentially short-term; capital for buildings, plant, and machinery had to be sought elsewhere. Inquiry as to its source and extent presents considerable problems. In the first place, apart from banks and railway companies, few pre-1900 Irish manufacturing firms had recourse to the stock market. Some breweries and distilleries, some flax-spinning mills, and one or two builders had, but this was not so with weaving, making-up, or engineering concerns. New firms tended to be financed by the private capital put up by partners, established firms by the ploughing back of profits. On the whole, Irish industries were labour- rather than capital-intensive, but capital employed in industry, building, and public services was growing fast after 1880, as evidenced from a number of sources. For example, imports of machinery, iron castings, boilers, and building materials, notably glass and slates, increased markedly in the decade 1890–1900, levelled off for a few years, and then rose to a peak around 1910; the amount of paid-up capital in joint-stock companies registered in Ireland increased steadily between 1885 and 1914 from around £13 million to £50 million;[5] expenditure by local authorities on roads and bridges, water supply, sewage works, paving, and lighting more than doubled between 1880 and 1914.

[1] D. D. Fraser, 'Some modern phases of British banking, 1896–1911' in *Journal of the Institute of Bankers*, xxxiv, pt 2 (Feb. 1913), p. 98.

[2] James Dick, 'Banking statistics of the United Kingdom in 1896' in *Journal of the Institute of Bankers*, xviii, pt 4 (Apr. 1897), p. 196.

[3] 'Notes and comments' in *Journal of the Institute of Bankers in Ireland*, xiii (1911), p. 13.

[4] Hall, *Bank of Ire.*, appendix D, pp 331–90.

[5] *Companies: twenty-third general annual report by the board of trade*, p. 121, H.C. 1914 (348), lxxix, 129.

The expenditure on roads and bridges alone increased from £702,176 in 1879/80 to £1,192,137 in 1912/13.[1] The pattern, it seems, was not greatly different from that in Great Britain, where capital formation increased slowly after 1886, rapidly from 1895, and then slackened in the first decade of the new century. Ireland, of course, did not have the highly capitalised mining and heavy engineering industries of Great Britain. Apart from the few major export-orientated concerns, Irish manufacturing firms were generally small-scale, and Irish railways and public services much less highly developed. Returns on investment were therefore satisfactory because of the lower levels of capital employed, and despite lower net output per worker (estimated in 1907 as England and Wales £104, Scotland £98, Ireland £78)[2] Ireland was not infrequently attractive to investors from, for example, Liverpool and Glasgow.

THE subject of taxation attracted a great deal of attention after 1850 (as indeed it had since the union).[3] Unfortunately, interest was concentrated on three main questions, or rather, on three aspects of the same question—whether the taxation of Ireland was excessive, whether it was in conformity with the financial provisions of the act of union, and whether Ireland bore a disproportionate share of the United Kingdom burden. Much less attention was given to the influence of particular taxes on the economy or to the general effects of government expenditure. In 1864 the position was examined by a select committee of the house of commons[4] and in 1895 by a royal commission.[5] In connection with several other official inquiries the question of taxation was constantly mentioned.

The main facts were not in dispute. Income tax and succession duty had been extended to Ireland in 1853, and rates of duty on spirits increased threefold between 1853 and 1860.[6] The effect was to raise by about £2.5 million the annual amount contributed by Irish property and Irish consumption to the imperial exchequer, an increase of about 40 per cent.[7] More difficult to assess was the amount of government expenditure in Ireland. In some departments figures could not be provided to distinguish one part of the kingdom from another; for other items the distinction was arbitrary—should the cost of keeping soldiers in Ireland, for instance, be regarded as expenditure in Ireland?[8] Critics put the amounts contributed to imperial funds, over and above the amount of expenditure in

---

[1] *Returns of local taxation in Ireland for the year 1879*, p. 12 [C 2738], H.C. 1880, lxii, 217; *1912–13*, p. xii [Cd 7289], H.C. 1914, lxix, 5.

[2] *Final report of the first census of production of the United Kingdom (1907)*, p. 19 [Cd 6320], H.C. 1912–13, cix, 27.

[3] Above, v, 784–92.

[4] *Report from the select committee on taxation of Ireland*, H.C. 1864 (513), xv; H.C. 1865 (330), xii, 1–282.

[5] *Royal commission on the financial relations between Great Britain and Ireland: first report, evidence and appendices* [C 7720], [C 7720–I], H.C. 1895, xxxvi; *final report* [C 8262], H.C. 1896, xxxiii, 59–554.

[6] Ibid., *final report*, p. 157 (MS 219).

[7] Ibid., p. 9 (MS 71).

[8] Ibid., p. 124 (MS 186).

Percentage of revenue collected in Ireland attributable to indirect, non-tax, and direct tax sources

	1859	1860	1869	1870	1879	1880
customs and excise	82	84	83.5	85	85	86
stamp duties	7	6.5	7.5	7	8	7.5
income tax	11	9.5	9	8	7	6.5
total revenue	£6,738,000		£6,773,000		£6,988,000	
	(£7,700,000)		(£7,426,000)		(£7,281,000)	

The figures in parentheses show the 'true' revenue of Ireland, calculated by the treasury, taking into account amounts of duty charged in Great Britain on goods consumed in Ireland and amounts charged in Ireland on goods consumed in Great Britain.

Source: Calculated from data in appendix III of *Royal commission on the financial relations between Great Britain and Ireland; minutes of evidence* (hereafter cited as *Childers comm. evidence*), pp 392–414 [C 7720–1], H.C. 1895, xxxvi, 400–22.

Ireland, as £5,396,000 in 1859–60, £4,488,000 in 1869–70, £3,226,000 in 1878–80, and £2,677,000 in 1889–90.[1]

Of particular interest was the way in which Irish revenue was raised. Indirect taxation accounted for much the largest proportion of the total. Clearly, the figures mean that revenue was levied on wants rather than means, confirming complaints throughout the period that it was the poor of Ireland who bore the heaviest part of the tax burden because it was they who consumed the greatest proportion of the most heavily taxed articles—spirits, tea, and tobacco. As Edward Senior put it: 'I do not believe that Ireland is a poor country because she is over-taxed; but I think she is over-taxed because she is poor.'[2] But prima facie the actual amounts convey very little. That they were increasing could mean that rates of duty were increasing,[3] that consumption was rising because of improved living standards, or that measures to suppress illicit distillation and smuggling were becoming more successful.[4] High spirit duties, it was frequently alleged, caused the closure of distilleries; but they also meant that production was forced to concentrate in larger and more efficient units, and that the brewing industry received an artificial boost.

In connection with direct taxation, it is to be noted that while net receipts fell (1859/60, £718,000; 1869/70, £613,000; 1879/80, £471,000) both gross and net amounts assessed for tax rose. The fall in yield (with basic rates relatively

[1] Thomas Kennedy, *A history of the Irish protest against over-taxation* (Dublin, 1897), p. 6.
[2] *Report from the select committee on taxation of Ireland*, p. 221, H.C. 1864 (513), xv, 255.
[3] After the duty on spirits reached the United Kingdom level of 10s. a gallon in 1861 the disparate effects of changes in rates of duty appear to have been small (*Childers comm. evidence* [interim report], appendix XII, p. 480 (MS 488)).
[4] Smuggling of tobacco was not large but was widespread. Reports by commissioners of inland revenue regularly mention seizures at Dublin, Passage West, Derry, and Inishowen, also in the Channel Islands, of cargoes intended for Ireland. But there was much more activity around the British coast, in 1880 for instance. It looks as though preventive measures were more effective in England than in Ireland; it is rather harder to believe the Irish were more law-abiding.

unchanged in the years selected) seems to have been due to rising rebates on taxation of low income. Landed property in Ireland was taxed on the basis of its valuation rather than as in Great Britain on the rental that it realised,[1] a system that operated to the advantage of landlords when rents were rising and to their disadvantage when they were falling,[2] which they did not begin to do until after 1880. Certainly it did nothing to encourage the reduction or remission of rents in difficult years.

More important than direct taxation was the incidence of local rates, which amounted to £3.3 million in 1850, £2.9 million in 1860, £3.9 million in 1870, and £4.5 million in 1880.[3] These amounts, despite their size, were paid with relatively little protest, perhaps because expenditure of the money was largely under the control of those who paid it. The fact that immediate payment was made by the property-owning class (though recouped where possible through rents) did tend, however, to reduce the disparity in the proportion of total public expenditure borne by the different sections of the community.

On the expenditure side, ignoring uncertainties of definition, official figures showed expenditure from United Kingdom funds in Ireland as £2,304,000 in 1859-60, £2,938,000 in 1869-70, and £4,055,000 in 1879-80.[4] Both these and the figures already quoted agree in showing an increasing proportion of Irish revenue spent in Ireland and a decreasing proportion spent elsewhere.

The influence of public finance on the Irish economy during the second half of the nineteenth century needs much more study than it has so far received before conclusions can be drawn whether lower scales or a different incidence of taxation would have been more appropriate to Irish conditions than the system in fact adopted. That Ireland should initially have been required to pay out of later income moneys spent on famine relief was obviously unsound, but the removal of this requirement in 1853 coincided with the extension of the income tax to Ireland, with the result that Irish taxation rose by some £2 million a year.[5] This was naturally unpopular, but in an economy without large-scale industry and with an in-built propensity to save, the effects of government taxation and expenditure may well have been beneficial in stimulating a sluggish circulation. To the extent that money raised by indirect taxation was invested in public buildings and transport or made available as loans for harbours, land improvement, or drainage (for which private funds were not forthcoming), the long-term effects must also have been useful—however they appeared to contemporaries.

[1] *Childers comm. evidence*, evidence of J. G. Barton, particularly p. 231 (MS 239).
[2] Ibid., question 5800, p. 235 (MS 243).
[3] Thomas Lough, *England's wealth, Ireland's poverty* (London, 1896), p. 205; T. W. Grimshaw, 'A statistical survey of Ireland from 1840 to 1888' in *Stat. Soc. Ire. Jn.*, ix, pt lxviii (Dec. 1888), pp 354-5. Local rates consisted of grand jury cess, poor rates paid to boards of guardians, town rates, the Dublin police tax, and the Belfast water commissioners' taxes.
[4] *Childers comm. evidence*, p. 404 (MS 412).
[5] Above, p. 327.

As to the suggestion that local funds otherwise available for investment were syphoned off by excessive taxation, an inquiry in 1893–4 found that Ireland was indeed overtaxed, providing one-eleventh of the tax revenue of the United Kingdom although her 'taxable capacity' was estimated to be below one-twentieth. The excess taxation, estimated at £2.75 million a year, had increased to £3.5 million a year by 1908, and was thought to be around £3 million in 1910–11. It has to be said that these figures cannot be precise, as there was no consensus among contemporaries on what Ireland 'ought' to contribute to the United Kingdom common financial pool. Subsequent dispassionate analysis shows that Ireland was not in fact overtaxed,[1] but at the time observers saw things differently. The argument in 1908 ran as follows:

Since 1894 the population of Ireland has fallen by more than 200,000. . . . There has been an enormous increase in the wealth of Great Britain but no corresponding increase in that of Ireland. Judged by the yield of the income tax, the taxable capacity of Ireland was about 1/22 that of Great Britain: judged by the same test in 1908 it is less than 1/30. If we take 1/24 as representing the present relative incomes of Ireland and Great Britain . . . Ireland ought to have contributed last year 4 per cent (or 1/25) of the total revenue of the United Kingdom. As a matter of fact she contributed 6.29 per cent, or more than 1/16. On the basis of these figures she ought to have contributed in 1907–8 a total revenue of £6,120,000. As a matter of fact she paid £9,621,000; in other words she was over-taxed to the amount of £3,501,000.[2]

Taxation per head of the population, 1819–20, 1849–50, 1859–60, 1893–4

	on commodities		other taxes		total	
	Great Britain	Ireland	Great Britain	Ireland	Great Britain	Ireland
	s. d.	s. d.	s. d.	s. d.	s. d.	s. d.
1819–20	48 7	11 0	21 8	3 5	70 3	14 5
1849–50	30 3	12 2	17 5	1 9	47 8	13 11
1859–60	31 7	20 7	18 5	4 9	50 0	25 4
1893–4	24 1	22 0	20 9	6 10	44 10	28 10

Weight was added to the argument by figures published in 1911[3] as shown in the above table. Any disquiet felt about Ireland's contribution to imperial funds must have been offset by the steady change in her receipts from such funds, as indicated in the treasury calculations shown in the following table.[4] In other words, from being a financial asset to the United Kingdom,

[1] Above, v, 784–94.
[2] Editor's note in Louis Paul-Dubois, *Contemporary Ireland* (first published as *L'Irlande contemporaine* (Paris, 1907); ed. T. M. Kettle, Dublin, 1908), pp 525–6.
[3] 'The finance of Irish government' in *Journal of the Institute of Bankers in Ireland*, xiii (1911), p. 158.
[4] C. H. Oldham, 'The public finances of Ireland' in *Journal of the Institute of Bankers in Ireland*, xiii (1911), p. 286.

Revenue and expenditure in Ireland

financial year	Irish 'true' revenue £'000	expenditure in Ireland £'000	balance £'000
1859/60	7,700	2,304	−5,396
1869/70	7,426	2,938	−4,488
1879/80	7,281	4,055	−3,226
1889/90	7,735	5,058	−2,677
1899/1900	8,664	6,980	−1,684
1909/10	8,355	10,712	+2,357

Ireland had become a liability, and the balance in Ireland's favour was to continue. It was not that Ireland was becoming poorer or contributing less to the common pool but that she was drawing more from it.[1] Many items on the expenditure side showed increases over time—education, the cost of running the post office, law and order, police—but the biggest single addition and the most important socially and financially arose from the granting of old age pensions in 1909, giving Ireland an annual average of £2.5 million from the imperial exchequer in the years 1910–14.[2] It was not only the granting of pensions that was significant but the fact that the proportion of the Irish population qualifying for them was more than double the United Kingdom average. Repercussions in social terms (in 1912 old age pensions in Mayo exceeded earnings brought back by migrant labourers)[3] as well as in government thinking about the economic, as distinct from the political, side of the problem were bound to be far-reaching. As a government-appointed committee reported in 1913,

For these reasons we are emphatically of the opinion . . . that, quite apart from any question of a change in the political relations between Great Britain and Ireland, some radical change in the financial relations is imperatively required in the interest of both countries alike, of Great Britain no less than of Ireland.[4]

SOCIAL changes in Ireland between 1850 and 1914 were at least as marked as those in agriculture and industry. At the top of the pyramid the landed gentry had seemed in the 1860s to be in an unassailable position, yet land legislation first

[1] See figures in appendix for net assessments to tax under Schedules D and E, 1880–1916, below, p. 355.
[2] *Seventeenth abstract of labour statistics of the United Kingdom*, pp 184–6 [Cd 7733], H.C. 1914–16, lxi, 500–02.
[3] *Departmental committee on food production in Ireland; minutes of evidence . . .* , p. 5 [Cd 8158], H.C. 1914–16, v, 837.
[4] *Report by the committee on Irish finance*, p. 7 [Cd 6153], H.C. 1912–13, xxxiv, 13. The view that the 'excess expenditure' in Ireland was partly the result of administrative extravagance comes from at least two sources: Windham Thomas Wyndham-Quin, Lord Dunraven, *The finances of Ireland before the union and after* (London, 1912); and Antony MacDonnell (the former under-secretary, later Lord MacDonnell of Swinford), 'The finance of Irish government' in *Nineteenth Century*, ccccxix (Jan. 1912), p. 1. See also Patricia Jalland, 'Irish home-rule finance: a neglected dimension of the Irish question, 1910–14' in *I.H.S.*, xxiii, no. 91 (May 1983), pp 233–53.

regulated their relationship with their tenants, then drastically reduced their rental income, and ultimately eliminated them as rentiers. As their estates were exchanged for capital (over one-half by 1914, around two-thirds by 1921) they were steadily relieved of the responsibility and embarrassment, not to say danger, of landowning in Ireland. Some removed to Great Britain; others remained to make a considerable personal contribution to society as justices of the peace, presidents of farming societies, or chairmen of boards of guardians; they served on the governing bodies of church and educational establishments, and their wives and daughters graced the more prestigious charitable committees. More relevant in a British than an Irish context, they continued to supply recruits to the upper echelons of the armed forces and, up to 1921, representative peers to the house of lords. Meantime, in Ireland, the big house and walled demesne provided useful employment, examples of good husbandry, and the background to a justly famed horse-breeding industry. It is impossible to generalise about income but there is evidence that, if conspicuous expenditure was no longer the norm, few of the landed gentry who remained in Ireland found any need to curtail the social activities that continued to be reported in the appropriate society journals.

At a lower level alterations in the pattern of wholesaling and retailing (apart from the effects of inventions and innovations) meant that a wider range of goods was available to the ordinary consumer. Capital investment in housing, schools, and hospitals and in the development of community services—water supply, sewage, lighting, and transport—led to a general improvement in the quality of living. On the whole, most people in Ireland were better off in 1880 than in 1850 and there was further, though perhaps slower, improvement by 1914. Published statistics attest to better housing and health, a lower incidence of pauperism, and increasing literacy.[1] But there were wide variations regionally and between different social classes. In the congested districts of the western seaboard, improvements were minimal compared with those in the east coast towns. Similarly, while farm labourers and large farmers were better off at the end of the period than at the beginning, the position of the smallest farmers had probably deteriorated. Totals and averages must therefore be treated with caution.

One indicator of growing prosperity was the steady increase in shipping using Irish ports. From an annual average of 5,400,000 tons in 1851–5, tonnage increased to an average of 11,580,000 in 1876–80 and to 16,020,000 tons in 1914, suggesting a considerable increase in the volume of goods being moved.[2] Interestingly, the increase was not confined to the major ports, Dublin, Belfast, and Cork, but extended to the smaller ones as well.[3] Increased rail traffic indicated

---

[1] The proportion of the population over 5 years of age able to read and write rose from 33 per cent in 1851 to 87.6 per cent in 1911.

[2] *Childers comm. evidence* [report], p. 458 (MS 466); *[Sixty-eighth] statistical abstract of the United Kingdom, . . . 1908 to 1922*, pp 234–7 [Cmd 2207], H.C. 1924, xxiv, 242–5.

[3] J. T. Pim, 'A review of the economic and social condition of Ireland' in *Stat. Soc. Ire. Jn.*, x, pt lxxix (Aug. 1899), pp 492–5.

not only the extension of the railway system but its greater use.[1] In the same
general category one could cite the increased activity of the post office—64 million
letters delivered in 1870, 79 million in 1880, and 113 million in 1894.[2] A change
in format of Irish national newspapers to suit a wider reading public was
accompanied by the development of a thriving local press.

In terms of the work that people did, the slow upward drift of agricultural and
certain other wage rates, the influence of improving emigration facilities, and the
contraction of domestic manufacture are illustrated by changes of another kind,
as shown in the following table.[3] Ignoring marginal uncertainties in classification,

*Occupations of the people of Ireland, by
percentages, 1851–81*

	1851	1861	1871	1881
agriculture	48.4	42.9	40.7	41.1
fishing	.4	.3	.4	.5
mining	.4	.4	.3	.4
building	2.0	2.4	2.2	2.4
manufacture	22.8	20.7	19.5	16.0
transport	1.4	1.8	2.1	2.2
dealing	3.6	4.1	4.6	4.8
industrial service	2.3	7.5	7.5	6.7
public and professional service	2.2	3.7	4.3	5.0
domestic service	9.4	13.3	15.2	18.0
others	7.1	2.9	3.2	2.9

the pattern is clear enough—a reduction both absolutely and proportionately in
numbers employed in agriculture and manufacture. For present purposes it is not
important that general labourers may sometimes have been put in one category
rather than the other, or that there were possibly changes of category as
hemstitching, embroidery, or shirt-making moved from home to factory or vice
versa; what is important is the alteration in quality of employment, which the
figures conceal rather than illustrate. The elimination of many small agricultural
holdings and the increased average size of those remaining has already been
discussed, so too the decline of small-scale rural industry; not evident is the major
reduction in home industries, particularly handloom weaving. Factory returns

[1] Mitchell & Deane, *Brit. hist. statistics*, p. 228.
[2] *Childers comm. final report*, p. 206 [C 8262], H.C. 1896, xxxiii, 268.
[3] From census reports; but see Charles Booth, 'Occupations of the people of the United Kingdom,
1801–81' in *Journal of the Royal Statistical Society*, xlix (1886), p. 314, and *Financial relations report*,
appendix x, pp 478–9 [C 7720–1], H.C. 1895, xxxvi, 486–7. Census reports of 1891, 1901, and 1911
show a continuation of the same trends but detailed comparison is impossible because of differences
in the definition of certain occupations.

show the other side of the picture—the increasing work-force in textile mills and in shipyards and engineering workshops.

More detailed tables show that the reduction in numbers employed as metalworkers is almost balanced by increases under 'machinery and tools', 'shipbuilding', and 'railways', and outweighed by the increase in 'unspecified manufacture', which included general engineers, firemen, and mechanics. The increases under domestic service reflect the increasing number of women returned as 'domestic indoor servant' or 'charwoman'. With little scope here for confusion in the definitions it seems reasonable to infer increased employment of these very low wage categories by a rising middle class.[1] Figures for 'army (at home)', representing as they do members of regiments stationed in Ireland, fail to disclose the interesting fact that the British army relied quite heavily on Irish recruits, who in the 1860s were about 20 per cent of total intake; even from a falling population the peacetime proportion seldom fell below a fairly steady 10 per cent. Of equal significance, regular soldiers born in Ireland were over 30 per cent of army strength in the 1870s before falling to around 20 per cent in the 1880s, with a reduction thereafter to between 9 and 12 per cent as second-generation emigrants joining in Britain were classified as born in England or Scotland.[2] No doubt the incidence of recruitment in Ireland reflected the scarcity of male employment, but it also perpetuated the tradition in many garrison towns of 'marrying into the regiment' with sons following their fathers.

Contemporary observers expressed concern at the increase in numbers under 'dealing' and 'other employment', which were regarded as non-productive, contrasted with the reduction in the number of primary producers, and concluded that the economy was in a parlous state.[3] Conditions were admittedly difficult, with industrial production overwhelmed by the output of a powerful neighbour, but objectively the figures also reflect a necessary stage in economic progress—increasing efficiency in primary production and increasing elaboration in marketing and distribution. The introduction into many Irish towns and villages of railway staff, bank clerks, and local government officials, people with permanent and reasonably paid jobs, meant increased social diversity; a growing number of retail shops gave an air of progress, even modest affluence, to the streets, while the settling of doctors, solicitors, and other professional men indicated the presence of a growing middle class. Dentists from Dublin and Belfast made regular visits as far afield as Galway and Strabane well before the turn of the century.[4]

[1] A similar though proportionately smaller increase occurs in Great Britain, but from a rising population.
[2] From recruitment returns and general annual reports on the British army, e.g. H.C. 1864 (346), xxxv, 473; H.C. 1872 (315), xxxvii, 427; H.C. 1872 (171), xxxvii, 433; H.C. 1878–9 (15), xliii, 513; [C 6196], H.C. 1890, xliii, 1; [Cd 1496], H.C. 1903, xxxviii, 769; [Cd 3798], H.C. 1908, xi, 1; [Cd 7252], H.C. 1914, lii, 267. See also above, v, 793.
[3] Charles Booth, 'Occupations of the people of the United Kingdom, 1801–81' in *Journal of the Royal Statistical Society*, xlix (1886), pp 338–46.
[4] *F.J.*, 30 Oct. 1886; *Belfast News Letter*, 18 Sept. 1893.

It is perhaps the expansion and influence of the middle classes that emerges as the most significant social trend of the period and for the future. The position of the landed gentry has already been noted; at the lowest levels peasant proprietors of the poorer holdings, landless labourers, unskilled or semi-skilled industrial workers, and the unemployed found life as precarious as ever, with emigration offering the most hopeful future for those who could afford to go. The classes that prospered during the period covered a very broad spectrum—strong farmers, industrialists, managers, shopkeepers, bankers, professional men, administrators, wholesalers, and the upper levels of skilled artisans. Most numerous in Dublin, Belfast, and Cork, they appeared also in other cities and towns where banks opened branches, where specialised shops replaced the general store, where solicitors set up practice, or the government appointed senior officials. It was these people who built villas on the outskirts of towns, who lived in suburbs such as Rathgar or Knock, or in the fringeing respectable artisan terraces. The urban dwellers among them exchanged the horse-drawn carriage for the suburban train or the new motor car; their younger members made social use of the pneumatic-tyred bicycle. Census figures showed the number of central and local government officials rising from 29,600 in 1891 to 35,000 in 1911, professional people from 53,500 to 65,300, and those in commercial occupations from 29,200 to 48,200. Literate and articulate, these were the people who pushed up the circulation of newspapers, the number of university entrants, the importation of small luxuries; who attended theatres and the new suburban churches; and who conveyed the impression that, despite the political agitation of the times, life in Ireland was far from intolerable.

There were, of course, critics of 'enhanced salaries or additional government appointments';[1] the Irish courts system, costing £369,000 in 1907/8, was compared unfavourably with the Scottish system at £203,000;[2] similarly it was pointed out that there were only 5,435 police in Scotland against 11,144 in Ireland with a smaller population.[3] In Dublin the splendour of the viceregal court was in marked contrast to the living conditions of the capital's low paid and unemployed.[4]

Middle-class people either bought or had houses built for them; those who could not afford to buy but had to rent houses found a variety of conditions. Legislation in the period 1850–79,[5] intended to encourage house building by private enterprise, had been relatively ineffective, but better progress was made

[1] A. P. MacDonnell, 'The finance of Irish government' in *Nineteenth Century*, ccxix (Jan. 1912), p. 12.

[2] *Hansard 4*, clxxxvi (26 Mar. 1908), 1641–2.

[3] Louis Paul-Dubois, *Contemporary Ireland* (Dublin, 1908), p. 523. The Irish figure had increased by 1914 to 12,000 R.I.C. and 1,200 Dublin Metropolitan Police.

[4] J. V. O'Brien, *'Dear, dirty Dublin': a city in distress 1899–1916* (London, 1982), pp 126–58.

[5] 13 & 14 Vict., c. 31 (15 July 1850), sect. 8; 19 & 20 Vict., c. 65 (21 July 1856); 23 & 24 Vict., c. 19 (15 May 1860); 29 & 30 Vict., cc 40, 44 (28 June 1866); 33 & 34 Vict., c. 46 (1 Aug. 1870), sect. 10; 35 & 36 Vict., c. 32 (18 July 1872), sect. 1; 44 & 45 Vict., c. 49 (22 Aug. 1881), sects 18, 19; 45 & 46 Vict., c. 60 (18 Aug. 1882).

with the Housing of the Working Classes (Ireland) Acts, 1890 to 1896[1] under which local government loans were sanctioned to towns such as Armagh, Bantry, Enniscorthy, and Waterford. On the whole, however, the provisions of these acts were most used where they were least needed, in, for instance, Rathmines, Rathgar, or Killiney in the hinterland of Dublin city.[2] Particularly in villages the situation remained unsatisfactory.

I have met a very large number of unfit houses in different parts of Ireland, but with the exception of two dwellings in the Skibbereen union I have never been confronted with houses so wretched and unsanitary as some I met in the village of Ballylongford and Tarbert. Any attempt to describe the wretchedness of the so-called house occupied by Michael Carmody and his family in the street of Ballylongford would be futile.[3]

More generous loans with extended periods of repayment under an act of 1908[4] produced better results.

In the north, building was more often from private resources than by municipal authorities. In 1893 it was noted that good cottages had been provided by factory proprietors for their workers in Ballymena and Limavady;[5] in Belfast some linen manufacturing firms were still building houses for their workers on the eve of the first world war.[6] Elsewhere, in Coleraine, Derry, and Lurgan construction by local builders seems to have flourished. Most striking, however, was the difference between Belfast and Dublin. In the former before 1914 about 99 per cent of house building was thought to have been by private enterprise; indeed, despite the rapid growth in population, there was considerable over-building in the early years of the twentieth century.[7] The houses so built were of good quality and let at reasonable rents, although the position was probably exaggerated by a writer in 1891 who said:

The artisans' dwellings in Belfast are . . . self-contained houses of good size, . . . constructed in a style which renders them exceptionally comfortable and thoroughly sanitary. In many a busy and prosperous manufacturing town of Great Britain the abodes of the hard-working factory hands and mechanics will not bear comparison with these neat and cleanly industrial dwellings of Belfast.[8]

---

[1] 53 & 54 Vict., c. 70 (18 Aug. 1890), 56 & 57 Vict., c. 33 (24 Aug. 1893); 57 & 58 Vict., c. 55 (25 Aug. 1894); 59 & 60 Vict., c. 11 (2 July 1896).
[2] This is obvious from examination of *Supplement to the twenty-ninth annual report of the local government board for Ireland, 1900–1901* [Cd 1260], H.C. 1902, xxxvii, 429–756.
[3] *A return . . . of reports of inspectors of the local government board*, p. 5, H.C. 1906 (135), c. 25.
[4] 8 Edw. VII, c. 61 (21 Dec. 1908).
[5] *Royal commission on labour: the agricultural labourer, Ireland. A. Summary report by Mr. R. McCrea*, p. 9 [C 6894], H.C. 1893–4, xxxvii, pt 1, p. 9.
[6] From Belfast city hall records of streets adopted 1861–1917.
[7] *Belfast News Letter*, 1 Jan. 1903.
[8] Historical Publishing Company, *Industries of Ireland, part 1; Belfast and the towns of the north* (London, 1891; facsimile reprint in *Industries of the north one hundred years ago*, with introduction by W.H. Crawford, Belfast, 1986), p. 132.

Health and sanitary regulations following the Public Health (Ireland) Act, 1878,[1] had done much to improve the poorest property but there were still black spots. The 1911 census showed 447 families living in single-room accommodation, 3,305 families living in two-roomed apartments, and mortality rates well above the average for the major industrial towns in Great Britain.

Dublin on the other hand had even higher mortality rates; its central area included some of the worst slums in the United Kingdom, and the building of working-class housing by private interests was negligible. An inquiry in 1914 found that only about half a dozen employing firms had provided housing and that some 45 per cent of the working population lived in very bad tenements, most of them in filthy condition.[2] Even where houses were provided by the corporation or by bodies such as the Artisans Dwellings Co., the rents were usually beyond the means of those for whom they were intended.[3] (The position in Cork was similar to that in Dublin, the Improved Dwellings Co. and the corporation having between 1870 and 1900 built a small number of houses on cleared slum sites, but the weekly rents at 3s. to 3s. 6d. attracted mainly white-collar and artisan tenants.)[4] A certain amount of blame for the deplorable record of slum tenements was attributable to non-enforcement of health regulations, but a major reason for Dublin's housing difficulty and for the contrast with Belfast lay in the fact that Belfast's building was mainly on the expanding periphery where land was relatively cheap, whereas the cost of acquiring and clearing slum property in Dublin was very high. 'It is quite clear that if legislation stepped in and prevented the robbery of public bodies by exorbitant awards for valueless property, one obstacle to more extensive operations would be removed.'[5] The regular wages of skilled and semi-skilled men made it possible for houses to be built in Belfast and let profitably at rents ranging from 2s. 6d. to 5s. a week and for owners of house property to obtain between 7 and 16 per cent on their capital.[6] In Dublin not only were building costs higher than in Belfast but the preponderance of lowly paid, irregularly employed, unskilled labourers among the prospective tenants meant that rents of 5s. 3d. to 7s. were wildly beyond the reach of those accustomed to paying as little as 10d. per week (1875) for a single tenement room.[7] Slum clearance usually meant in practice increased rents for, and even more overcrowding in, the tenements that remained. Comparative rent levels of working-class houses in Ireland in 1907 were calculated as: Dublin 100,

---

[1] 41 & 42 Vict., c. 52 (8 Aug. 1878).

[2] *Report of the departmental committee appointed . . . to inquire into the housing conditions of the working classes in the city of Dublin*, pp 3, 5 [Cd 7273], H.C. 1914, xix, 67, 69, and above, pp 171–2.

[3] O'Brien, 'Dear, dirty Dublin', pp 126–58.

[4] Maura Murphy, 'The working class of nineteenth-century Cork' in *Cork. Hist. Soc. Jn.*, lxxxv (1980), p. 30.

[5] Charles Dawson, 'The housing of the people, with special reference to Dublin' in *Stat. Soc. Ire. Jn.*, xi, pt lxxxi (Aug. 1901), p. 48.

[6] From newspaper advertisements of sales of profit rents, which show that the poorer the property the higher the nominal profit.

[7] O'Brien, 'Dear, dirty Dublin', p. 33.

Limerick 67, Cork 66, Belfast 61, Derry 54, Waterford 53.[1] Even so, in 1913 only one of the companies building such houses in Dublin was able to pay a commercial dividend.[2]

NOT surprisingly, the differences in wage levels between skilled and unskilled workers throughout Ireland, combined with the appalling living conditions of the lowest paid in Dublin, are reflected in differing levels of trade union activity.[3] With production usually based on small units, the earliest and simplest form of organisation was the friendly society type of craft union, of which a great many existed in Dublin in the 1850s and 1860s, their preoccupations being largely with apprenticeship, mutual help, and inter-union demarcation. The British unions that shortly began to establish branches in Ireland, and to affiliate with some of the local unions, were at first of the same élitist type but drew members from the industrial north as well as from such towns as Cork, Dundalk, Limerick, and Waterford. Attempts before 1907 to form unions of unskilled workers[4] or agricultural labourers[5] met with only limited success. Meantime, members of the skilled unions enjoyed wage rates not dissimilar from those in Great Britain, and in their occasional disputes with employers had access to cross-channel resources. On the whole therefore the position was probably reflected correctly in the view, expressed for instance in 1892, that the relations between employers and skilled workers in a wide range of trades in Dublin and Belfast were 'good' and 'very amicable'.[6]

In the linen industry with its large number of female and domestic workers organisation was particularly difficult; in 1892 the Irish Linen Lappers Trade Union was virtually the only union in the trade and the only one represented before the royal commission of that year. A typical craft union, with 450 members and a six-year apprenticeship, there was little cause for complaint over wages of 15s. to 30s. for a 48-hour week.[7] The Irish Congress of Trade Unions established in 1894, although bedevilled by nationalist and personality issues, adopted a more militant stance and gradually shed the aura of respectability that had prevented participation by, and the showing of concern for, the semi-skilled. For the lowest paid, however, the pattern was better reflected by the 1907 strike by Belfast's

[1] *Report of an inquiry by the board of trade into working class rents . . .*, p. xxii [Cd 3864], H.C. 1908, cvii, 342.

[2] F. H. A. Aalen, 'Approaches to the working-class housing problem in late Victorian Dublin' in R. J. Bender (ed.), *New researches on the social geography of Ireland* (Mannheim, 1984), pp 161–90.

[3] Particularly useful for trade union activity are Lyons, *Ireland since the famine*, pp 267–84, and Dermot Keogh, *The rise of the Irish working class* (Belfast, 1982); see also above, p. 172, n. 2, and below, p. 376.

[4] Andrew Boyd, *The rise of the Irish trade unions* (Tralee, 1971), p. 48.

[5] Pamela L. R. Horn, 'The National Agricultural Labourers' Union in Ireland, 1873–9' in *I.H.S.*, xvii, no. 67 (Mar. 1971), pp 340–52.

[6] *Royal commission on labour*, ii. Group 'C', p. 214 [C 6795–VI], H.C. 1892, xxxvi, pt II, p. 662; iii. Group 'A', pp 82, 442 [C 6894–VII], H.C. 1893–4, xxxii, 96, 456.

[7] Ibid., *vol. ii: group 'C'*, p. 72 (MS 520).

carters, dockers, and coal labourers, which ended in defeat,[1] the long struggle of Dublin's carters and dock workers in 1908, which met with little better success, and the formation of the Irish Transport & General Workers Union in December of that year. More widespread industrial unrest occurred in 1911 and 1913, the latter leading to serious riots in Dublin and resulting in a severe defeat for organised labour. It is true that a good deal could be laid at the door of competing sectarian rivalry in the north and to the inconstancy of British unions' support in the south, but the basic economic reason was the lack of employment for the total supply of unskilled labour available, a problem for which succeeding decades found palliatives but not solutions.

Finally, there were changes in social life due to economic developments outside Ireland. Indices for the United Kingdom show that the depression of the 1880s and early 1890s was accompanied by a fall or at best a stagnation of money wages, but retail prices were falling due to changes on the supply side, and in consequence real wages, which between 1875 and 1879 had fallen by between 8 and 9 per cent, began to move upward again.[2] The fall in retail prices was due to mass production methods applied to consumer goods, to improved wholesaling and distribution methods, to free trade, and to the development of railway networks into the interior of newly settled regions abroad and to improved steamship services. Money wages rose between 1896 and 1903 producing at first an accelerated rise in real wages, which reached a peak around 1900 but then fell off as retail prices moved ahead. The tendency between 1900 and 1914 was generally downward save for a minor plateau in 1907–9 caused by the inelasticity of money wages at a time of downward pressure on retail prices. The position in Ireland was much the same as in the rest of the United Kingdom. In the linen industry it was estimated that 'in terms of bread, real wages rose by . . . 50 per cent between 1875 and 1906. In terms of potatoes . . . by . . . 100 per cent'.[3]

It would thus appear that the Irish linen workers shared in the rise which took place in the standard of living in the United Kingdom during the half century [1850–1900]. It was not only that food became cheaper; as the century advanced the workers were able to clothe themselves better, as is strikingly illustrated by the fact that by the end of the century it was rare for adults to work in bare feet.[4]

Again, the contemporary view in 1893 was that the cost of food and clothing had declined during the preceding few years and that some workmen at least had cheaper living conditions than their counterparts in Great Britain. With rising retail prices, however, Ireland did less well, and in the period 1905–12 only Dublin showed increases for food and coal below the United Kingdom's average;

---

[1] John Gray, *City in revolt: James Larkin and the Belfast dock strike of 1907* (Belfast, 1985).

[2] Mitchell & Deane, *Brit. hist. statistics*, ch. XII.

[3] D. L. Armstrong, 'Social and economic conditions in the Belfast linen industry, 1850–1900' in *I.H.S.*, vi, no. 28 (Sept. 1951), p. 267.

[4] Ibid., p. 268.

Belfast was exactly on the average, Cork, Derry, and Limerick above it.[1] The year 1908 was perhaps the worst of the series. With rural distress due to a wet summer and a poor potato crop in 1907, increased outdoor relief became necessary in the spring, the linen trade had a difficult year, while average unemployment rates rose sharply and did not decline until well into 1909.[2] The few years immediately before 1914 were for most people years of seeking to hold on to earlier gains in real wages and improved living standards rather than of making any further progress.

Other developments outside Ireland, technical advances such as the invention of the internal combustion engine, also had an effect on social conditions, and the holiday habits of the growing English middle classes led to a small but significant tourist industry. The latter part of the nineteenth century and the early years of the twentieth saw the building of the big railway hotels, the construction of seaside golf courses, and steamer services on the Erne and Shannon systems. Paid holidays for workpeople with their quite different needs were still on the horizon, although the railways did provide cheap fares for attendance at important football matches.[3]

Gas lighting had long been available in many Irish towns, the 45,000 consumers of 1885 rising to 185,000 by 1914 and 190,000 by 1919.[4] The 1890s saw the beginning of municipal electricity supplies,[5] which soon provided power as well as light and made possible the siting of new small-scale industry outside traditional centres. Belfast's tiny motor-car manufacture was started in 1904 in Cuba Street, virtually a back street;[6] not that motor cars contributed greatly to the predominantly horse-drawn traffic on Irish roads, although the 2,688 cars registered in 1912 grew rapidly to 4,435 by 1914, almost all being imported.[7] The picture of the telephone services is more confused. In 1895 the National Telephone Co., licensed by the post office, had networks in Belfast, Cork, Derry, Dublin, and Limerick with a total of 3,300 subscribers. By 1898 their lines had reached Armagh, Portadown, and Waterford together with a score of other towns, mainly on the east coast, and they were seeking to extend into other areas.[8] The

[1] *Sixteenth abstract of labour statistics of the United Kingdom*, pp 152–3 [Cd 7131], H.C. 1914, lxxx, 476–7.

[2] *Annual report of the local government board for Ireland for the year ended 31 March 1908*, p. xiii [Cd 4243], H.C. 1908, xxxi, 31; *Annual reports of the poor law commissioners*; *Belfast News Letter*, 1 Jan. 1909.

[3] See for instance the advertisement by the Dublin, Wicklow, & Wexford Railway in *F. J.*, 30 Oct. 1886.

[4] From annual *Returns relating to . . . gas undertakings in the United Kingdom*: e.g. H.C. 1884–5 (124) and (238), lxxi, 613, 649; H.C. 1914 (137), lxxxi, 377; H.C. 1914 (138), lxxix, 481; [Cmd 1021], H.C. 1920, xlix–l, 113; [Cmd 1210], H.C. 1920, xxxvi, 57.

[5] In 1895 there were public supplies in Belfast, Bray, Carlow, Derry, Dublin, Galway, Killarney, and Larne.

[6] John Moore, *Motor makers in Ireland* (Belfast, 1982), p. 7.

[7] *Sixth report of the commissioners of his majesty's customs and excise, (for the year ended 31 March 1915)*, p. 71 [Cd 7621], H.C. 1914–16, xiii, 231.

[8] *Report from the select committee on the telephone service, together with . . . minutes of evidence . . .*, p. 325, H.C. 1895 (350), xiii, 355; *Report from the select committee on telephones*, pp 529, 550, H.C. 1898 (383), xii, 569, 590.

post office, however, already operated a comprehensive telegraph system throughout the country and it was decided, following an inquiry in 1905, that when the company's licence expired in 1911 the post office would take over the whole concern with a view to securing a better service. An act of 1911[1] provided the necessary funds, and the take-over was completed towards the end of 1912.

These were among the more obvious, visible, changes in social living and affected mainly town-dwellers, who by 1911 constituted just over 33 per cent of total population. Rural society was affected by changes less obvious but in the long run more fundamental.

The concept of a pre-famine rural society subsisting on potatoes and multiplying through improvident marriage and continuous subdivision of holdings has received major qualification.[2] Substantial farmers never did behave in the manner suggested, nor indeed did some of the smaller men. Post-famine, with a reducing population and an emphasis on livestock as distinct from tillage farming, there was a tendency at all levels to increase rather than to reduce the size of holdings; subdivision became anathema. Owner-occupation accentuated the feeling that land must at least be kept intact and so handed down to the next generation. This meant of course that if only one son could inherit, and if inheritance had to await the demise or incapacity of a father, that son's marriage must be postponed until living accommodation became available or was a reasonable expectation. For the rest of the family the alternatives were migration, including emigration, or continued residence on the farm as unmarried, and generally unpaid, helpers. Occasionally land was farmed by brothers in partnership, sometimes it descended to a daughter or widow whose marriage or remarriage prospects were related to stock rather than family rearing considerations. The pattern is well known—high rates of celibacy, late marriage, and an ageing generation of small landholders whose conservative attitude to change or innovation was ill-suited to a competitive world. For those who remained unmarried the catholic church, already placing a premium on celibacy, offered spiritual rather than material consolation. In consequence Ireland became a major source of men and women dedicated to teaching, nursing, and missionary and pastoral work not only in Ireland but throughout the world. In the north, where the so-called protestant ethic of hard work for its own sake was reinforced by climatic and soil conditions less favourable than Leinster or Munster, to be 'careful' was an admired attitude, but it was not a progressive one. Again, although careers in industry were open to some, there was a need for employment outside Ireland, which a surprising number found in the British colonial service, in India, and the dominions.[3]

---

[1] 1 & 2 Geo. V., c. 26 (18 Aug. 1911).

[2] J. J. Lee, 'Marriage and population in pre-famine Ireland' in *Econ. Hist. Rev.*, 2nd ser., xxi, no. 2 (Aug. 1968), p. 284; L. M. Cullen, *An economic history of Ireland since 1660* (London, 1972), pp 116–18; and above, v, 108–32.

[3] This, mainly from observation, receives support, for upper- and middle-class families at least, in W. T. Pike (ed.), 'Contemporary biographies' in *Belfast and the province of Ulster in the 20th century* (Brighton, 1909).

Marriage patterns in Ulster, despite greater industrialisation, were not significantly different from those in the southern provinces. If in the west, in contrast to
Ulster or the midlands, a more spontaneous spirit prevailed, it was paid for by an
even slower amelioration of living conditions.

In the period 1850–1914, therefore, Ireland saw extensive changes in agriculture,
industry, and society. In agriculture these were much the same as in Great Britain
where rural depopulation, falling rents after 1875, and, in many districts, poor
living conditions for agricultural workers were equally marked.[1] There were not of
course the same facilities for land purchase, nor the same need for them. Cheap
grain from the new world and the need to feed her growing cities exerted the same
pressure on British farming as on Irish farming to expand on dairy and poultry
products. In England rather than in Ireland there was significant growth in market
gardening. In industry, the changes were of the same kind in Ireland as in the rest
of the United Kingdom but, with a few exceptions, on an infinitely smaller scale.
Ulster industrialists were innovative and ingenious but the talents of some had to
find fulfilment elsewhere.[2] In the prevailing conditions Irish industry was inevitably
overmanned, net output per worker in 1907 at £78 comparing with £104 in
England and £98 in Scotland.[3] Most social changes—falling population, late
marriage, and urban stagnation—were in a direction opposite to these in the rest
of western Europe. In education, in science, and in the arts Ireland suffered
alternatively from sectarian rivalry and treasury parsimony.[3] Only in general and
mental health does there seem to have been a sustained effort to make good past
neglect and deal at least with the outcome of a deficient diet and poor living
conditions.[5] A solution for the underlying causes was much harder to find, as
indicated by the continued high incidence of tuberculosis, which accounted for an
official 14 per cent of all deaths in 1909[6] but was probably much higher.

THE opening months of 1914 contained little in the economic sphere that was
unusual, nothing that was spectacular; nor were there indications that the future

[1] H. Rider Haggard, *Rural England* (2 vols, London, 1906), i, 128, 417; ii, 153, 449. In 1901 the
author made an Arthur Young-type tour through the English counties and produced an informative
non-fictional account of agricultural conditions.
[2] W. E. Coe, *The engineering industry of the north of Ireland* (Newton Abbot, 1969), pp 120–21, 200.
Men whose reputations were made principally outside Ireland include John Boyd Dunlop (1840–1921),
Harry Ferguson (1884–1960), and Lord Kelvin (1824–1907).
[3] *Final report of the first census of production of the United Kingdom (1907)*, p. 19 [Cd 6320], H.C.
1912–13, cix, 27.
[4] Lyons, *Ire. since famine*, pp 72–86; R. A. Jarrell, 'The department of science and art and control
of Irish science, 1853–1905' in *I.H.S.*, xxx, no. 92 (Nov. 1983), pp 330–47.
[5] Annual reports of the poor law commissioners show a steady increase in expenditure on medical
relief from £54,000 in 1852 to £206,000 in 1914. On Dublin health see Mary Daly, *Dublin, the deposed
capital . . . 1860–1912* (Cork, 1984), pp 4, 90, 255–70; Mark Finnane, *Insanity and the insane in
post-famine Ireland* (London, 1981).
[6] The figure in the decade 1901–10 was 15.2 per cent as calculated from *Supplement to the
forty-seventh report of the registrar general . . . in Ireland . . . for the years 1901–1910*, p. xxxi [Cd 7121],
H.C. 1914, xv, 31.

contained any particular difficulties or expectations. The chancellor of the exchequer (David Lloyd George) in his budget speech on 4 May was at something of a loss, saying 'I have never found greater difficulty in forming a judgement as to what is likely to happen to the trade and industry of the country and of the world during the coming year . . .'.[1] In Ireland the June agricultural census showed crop acreages and livestock numbers at about the average of the preceding five years, with the exception of cattle, which continued their steady slow increase, and poultry numbers, which were up by about 4 per cent on 1913. By the autumn it was clear that crop yields were going to be above rather than below average, though by small margins. The main industries of the country, little disturbed by the political events of the previous year, enjoyed a reasonable prosperity. In linen there was some accumulation of stocks due to a slackness in the American market but the naval building programme promised increased activity in the shipyards. The brewing, distilling, and biscuit industries continued the steady progress of the preceding few years, but 1914 was a bad year for pigs and bacon due to the high incidence of swine fever. Butter exports in 1914 were at a peak of 42,780 tons.

Apart from the calling up of reservists and some flurry in the business of buying horses for the army, the first effect of the outbreak of war was the autumn budget of November which doubled income tax for the remainder of the year and added 15s. 3d. (later 16s. 3d.) a barrel to the duty on beer and 3d. a lb to that on tea. In the north, war office orders for heavy cloth and canvas for equipment and tents, and for iron stoves for huts and hospitals, began to affect weaving factories and foundries. In the engineering trade the calling up or volunteering of skilled men soon began to reveal just how poorly off Ireland was for this type of labour. Of the crops harvested and sold in 1914 wheat, oats, and flax fetched their highest prices since the 1880s and there were upward movements in the prices of all livestock and livestock products, particularly fat cattle, which advanced between 5s. and 10s. a cwt. There were very heavy shipments of the latter, mainly to replenish depleted stocks in Great Britain rather than to meet any shortfall in meat supplies. By Christmas, and despite a rise of 10 per cent in the cost of living since August, few people in Ireland felt much effect from the war; those who were adversely affected (some workers in the woollen and cotton industries, temporarily on short time) were outnumbered by others earning more, the workhouse population was reduced, fewer harvest labourers were away from home, and in the city shops the new treasury £1 and 10s. notes added variety to the season's usual spending.

Meagre as were the symptoms in these first few months they nevertheless set for the remainder of the war a pattern of changes, wholly predictable in nature, whose interest for the historian lies principally in their extent and duration. The response of agriculture to steeply rising prices will be noted from the census returns, which show a 55 per cent increase in cereal acreage between 1914 and

---

[1] *Hansard 5 (commons)*, lxii, 58 (4 May 1914).

1918, wheat increasing from 37,000 to 157,000 acres. Flax too was conspicuous, rising from 49,000 to 143,000 acres. Even then, with supplies from Belgium cut off and Baltic flax practically disappearing in 1917, the supply was far below the needs of the linen industry. There was an increase of about 50 per cent in the acreage of oats but considerably smaller increases in barley and potatoes, while hay remained little above the pre-war average. On the livestock side numbers of grazing animals changed very little, while pigs tended to decline due to a shortage of imported feedingstuffs. The relatively static numbers of cattle did not, however, indicate a lack of response to higher prices; rather it meant that cattle were being kept longer on the grass and sold in more finished condition. This is clear from export figures, which show that in the period 1900–13 fat cattle formed 37 per cent and stores 63 per cent of those shipped; during the years 1914–19, the figures were 52 per cent and 48 per cent respectively. That farmers tried to increase the numbers of animals reared is shown by the drop in calf exports from an annual average of 50,000 (1904–13) to 24,000 (1914–18). On the other hand the export of milch cows, which started rather below the pre-war average, rose in 1916–17 to 53,000 per year, threatening to deplete the breeding stock, and had to be prohibited by legislation. There were of course production difficulties—shortages of imported fertilisers and feeding stuffs, restrictions on the use of building materials, fencing wire, and the like—but, with the drying up of emigration, labour was seldom a problem; agricultural machinery was given special manufacturing priority and, apart from 1916, weather conditions were not unfavourable. On the other hand, the congested districts board found their land improvement work hampered by the treasury's cutting back of loan funds. Compulsory tillage, introduced in 1917, and price controls on most agricultural produce, imposed at varying dates and with varying degrees of success, placed emphasis on food production rather than good husbandry. In fact, the expansion of tillage in Ireland took place with less difficulty than in England and Wales because, with a higher proportion of grassland available, a smaller percentage of rotation grazing had to be sacrificed and little if any permanent pasture was touched. Nevertheless cereal and flax yields tended to decline after 1915 and with some relief conditions reverted after 1919 to the more balanced traditional pattern. By 1920, and despite a continuing rise in agricultural prices, the acreage of all crops except barley and flax had fallen, numbers of breeding animals had begun to increase, and exports of pig products began to return to pre-war levels. Permanent change was to be seen in the continuing production of cheese, which though small in quantity had developed considerably during the war, and in the maintained high export levels of eggs and poultry.

The spectacular feature of farming in 1914–18 was, of course, the steep rise in agricultural prices, which are illustrated in the following table. With prices like these it is hardly surprising that farmers referred to the war years as a boom time. They were, however, accompanied by higher costs for materials, transport, and wages, and by rising land prices and rents. By 1920 the wages of ordinary farm labourers had reached 30s. to 32s. 6d. a week and those of ploughmen and

Annual average prices of agricultural produce, 1913–20

	wheat cwt		oats cwt		barley cwt		potatoes cwt		flax stone		butter cwt		eggs 120		cattle 1–2 year			cattle 2–3 year			cattle over 3 year			sheep lambs		sheep hoggets	
	s.	d.	s.	d.	s.	d.	s.	d.	s.	d.	s.	d.	s.	d.	£	s.	d.	£	s.	d.	£	s.	d.	s.	d.	s.	d.
1913	7	5½	6	0	7	4½	3	9¾	7	2¼	103	0	9	5¼	8	14	6	11	12	3	13	4	6	28	6	36	9
1914	8	8¾	7	1¼	7	3½	3	4½	9	3¼	108	6	9	11	8	16	9	11	17	3	13	4	3	30	0	37	3
1916	14	1	11	3	14	7	5	5	23	2	161	3	15	4	12	16	3	17	14	6	21	6	6	43	3	53	9
1918	17	0	16	5	17	2	5	6¾	30	10	236	6	35	7	16	5	3	23	11	0	29	19	0	55	0	78	0
1920	21	6	17	3	22	5	10	2	39	5	320	6	31	2	18	6	3	27	19	3	35	2	9	76	9	109	6

Source: *Agricultural prices (Ireland) . . . Return 'showing . . . annual average prices . . . from 1881'*, p. 2, H.C. 1921 (181), xli, 94.

cattlemen 33s. 6d. to 36s. od.[1] A cottage that could have been built in 1914 for £180 cost £450 in 1920.[2] Nor did the pace of cost increases show any sign of slowing down; railway goods rates were increased in September 1920 by no less than 120 per cent and the board of trade's wholesale price index (1900 = 100) moved from 297 to 367 between 1919 and 1920.[3] The stage then was set for real problems in the agricultural industry, with food supplies from primary producing countries and a recovering Europe coming back into world markets, but with taxation, costs, and wages showing a marked tendency to maintain at least their wartime levels. The collapse came in 1921, which marked an agricultural as well as a political watershed.

On the industrial side a notable contribution to the war effort was made by shipbuilding. Harland & Wolff quickly became specialists in ship conversions— passenger liners into troop transports and hospital ships, cargo liners into dummy battleships—work which began as early as November 1914. The building of naval vessels began in 1915 with a series of monitors, that is, ships of 6,180 tons armed with 12-inch and 14-inch guns for coastal bombardment. Also in 1915 the keel was laid down of a battlecruiser, launched and completed in 1916. This was followed in 1917 by six destroyers and finally in 1918 by another cruiser adapted to carry aircraft.[4] Meantime Workman Clark & Co. completed three patrol boats and two sloops (2,300 tons) in 1916, two more patrol boats, ten boom defence vessels, and a hospital ship in 1917, and a further six boom defence vessels in 1918. But conversions and naval building were only part of the work of the Belfast shipyards, for both firms were involved in the building of at least a score of tankers and supply ships for the fleet auxiliary, besides many conventional cargo carriers to replace those lost to U-boats. In addition there was an unending queue of naval and commercial craft requiring refitting and repair. On the repair side a contribution was also made by shipyards in Dublin, Derry, and Cork. By the end of the war Harland & Wolff were employing some 25,000 men in Belfast, Workman & Clark a further 10,000, and the smaller yards perhaps 2,000. A somewhat novel development was the construction in Belfast of aircraft for the Royal Flying Corps. Of these, 100 had been delivered by February 1918 and work was still in hand by the end of the war, with Aldergrove being used for test flying.[5]

In the linen industry, the immediate demand in 1914 was for such things as tents, kitbags, and lorry covers, made of the heaviest material,[6] but the major

---

[1] *Standard time rates of wages and hours of labour in the United Kingdom at 31 December 1920*, p. 203 [Cmd 1253], H.C. 1921, xl, 921.

[2] *Annual report of the local government board for Ireland for the year ended 31 March 1920*, p. lxxvi [Cmd 1432], H.C. 1921, xiv, 858.

[3] Mitchell & Deane, *Brit. hist. statistics*, pp 476–7.

[4] Below, plate of H.M.S. *Vindictive*.

[5] Michael Moss and John Hume, *Shipbuilders to the world: 125 years of Harland & Wolff, Belfast, 1861–1986* (Belfast, 1986), pp 175–207, 520–24; Workman Clark Ltd, *Shipbuilding at Belfast, 1880–1933* (London, 1934), appendix (not numbered) shows list of ships completed; Riordan, *Modern Irish trade and industry*, pp 196–214.

[6] Riordan, op. cit., p. 198; *Belfast News Letter*, 1 Jan. 1915.

requirement, beginning in 1916, was for rather lighter aeroplane linen. The ministry of munitions alone placed contracts worth £11 million with Irish firms, chiefly in the Belfast area.[1] Production of this strong, closely woven fabric meant that damask looms had to be put aside, but not entirely, since exports to the United States were still necessary to help pay for war materials purchased there. The German occupation of Belgium and northern France cut off a major source of Ireland's supply of flax and yarn, which had to be replaced by increased imports from Russia up to 1917, and then in the final year of the war Ireland's own flax crop was pushed up to 143,000 acres, compared with a pre-war average of 53,000 acres. A Flax Control Board was instituted in October 1917 and for three years commandeered the whole crop at advertised prices. After the war the board continued in existence in conditions for which it was quite unsuited, particularly when the short-lived boom of 1919 was replaced by falling demand in 1920. Its abolition in that year was greeted by the trade with relief.[2]

Several other industries were directly affected by the war. Government contracts for shirt manufacture in Ireland amounted to nearly £4 million; the woollen industry was fully engaged on war work, for which alone imported raw material was allocated; and engineering too came under government control, working at maximum capacity.[3] Distilleries, however, found their output of spirits severely curtailed and when the use of barley was prohibited in 1916 pot stills were put out of business; distillers using patent stills, however, contributed to the war effort by producing nearly pure alcohol for use in the making of cordite. Brewing output was similarly restricted with production in 1919 running at about one-third of its pre-war level. Of raw materials there was expansion in the production of bauxite and iron ore in Antrim, barytes in Cork, but, despite its high price, a negligible increase in the Irish output of coal.

Ireland's record on the production of munitions *per se* was not impressive, due mainly to lack of interest if not actual obstruction by the war office. Small shell factories employing a total of 2,148 people were established eventually at Dublin, Waterford, Cork, and Galway, but (with the exception of Dublin) did not reach production stage until October 1917. Munitions production in the north was in the hands of private firms but they seem to have had as little success in attracting work as those elsewhere (although a few were fully employed making fans and heaters and parts for submarines). By September 1919 the total value of shells and components actually delivered was, by private firms in the Belfast area, £939,900, by private firms in the Dublin area, £1,672,726, and, by national factories in the Dublin area, £662,458, totalling altogether £3,275,084. This can be compared with the value of aeroplane linen (£11,380,468) or with the total expenditure of the ministry of munitions up to 31 March 1918 of over £1,101

---

[1] Riordan, op. cit., p. 114; *Belfast News Letter*, 1 Jan. 1916, 1917.
[2] Riordan, op. cit., p. 119; *Belfast News Letter*, 1 Jan. 1918; *Flax Supply Association annual report, 1920*, p. 10.
[3] Riordan, op. cit., pp 123, 128.

million. In supplies and clothing Ireland provided goods and materials worth £24,595,000 out of the total army requirement of £943,442,000.[1]

The total effect of increased agricultural and industrial employment, of an estimated 130,000 to 150,000 men who by 1916 had joined the British army, of the considerable numbers of men and women who went to Great Britain to work in munition factories and hospitals, plus the employment provided in Ireland in the servicing of army camps and naval bases, coupled with steadily rising wages in all sectors, was to transform the traditional pattern of unemployment and underemployment. One outcome appears in the annual reports of poor law guardians, which show steady falls not only in the number of people on outdoor relief but also in the number of sick and aged in workhouses, suggesting that at the lowest stratum of society it was becoming possible to care for more of these people at home. The fact that old age pensions did not increase from 5s. weekly to 10s. until 1919 and even then failed to keep pace with living costs certainly suggests that some other cause for the trend must be sought. Another consequence, although the evidence is slight, was the tendency of firms to become less labour- and more capital-intensive, by, for example, spending more money on larger-scale labour-saving equipment. The Ford Motor Co. must have considered that the time was ripe for their highly mechanised system when they set up in Cork in 1919.

The effect of the end of wartime conditions was at least as marked in industry as in agriculture. By 1920 there was a considerable backlog of house building and a need to rebuild stocks of raw materials, to replace worn-out machinery, and to catch up on postponed public works. Trouble came in later years when production from these high-cost resources had to be sold on falling markets, and debt incurred during this time of inflation had to be serviced with money which was restored to its parity with gold from April 1925.

One major effect of wartime conditions on the total Irish economy appears from examination of her changed trading position.[2] The detailed figures are shown in the following table, and despite possible deficiencies in the data[3] it is evident that Ireland moved during this period into a strong creditor position. It is true, though not immediately relevant, that value figures reflect rising prices rather than volume of trade, which was in fact falling, but it is noteworthy that, with the exception of 1915 and 1916, the percentage increases were greater for exports than for imports. Exports exceeded imports by 4 per cent in 1914 and by 11 per cent in 1919.

To the inflow of cash from trade must be added income from increasing investments outside the country, from money brought or sent home by workers in Britain, from army pay and pensions, and from government payments for services (transport, fodder, victualling) at camps and bases. Totals are impossible to estimate

---

[1] Ibid., pp 201–14, 307.

[2] *Report on the trade in imports and exports at Irish ports during the year ended 31 Dec, 1919*, p. vi [Cmd 1105], H.C. 1921, xxxi, 383.

[3] Returns of exports and imports were on a voluntary basis until the end of 1918 and published value figures are only estimates.

Imports and exports, 1914–19

	1914	1915	1916	1917	1918	1919
	(£ million)					
Imports (from all sources)						
farm produce, food, and drink	27.1	33.4	39.0	41.4	34.4	55.3
raw materials	11.1	14.0	17.8	21.3	21.7	24.4
manufactured goods	35.9	39.8	47.7	56.4	69.9	79.0
total	74.1	87.2	104.5	119.1	126.0	158.7
Exports (to all destinations)						
farm produce, food, and drink	41.6	48.5	62.6	71.8	78.2	93.7
raw materials	4.3	3.9	4.6	5.3	5.4	6.8
manufactured goods	31.4	32.0	40.0	56.7	69.3	75.5
total	77.3	84.4	107.2	133.8	152.9	176.0
excess of exports over imports	3.2	− 2.8	2.7	14.7	26.9	17.3

but the period 1914–20 saw balances in joint-stock banks increased by £132 million, deposits in trustee and post office savings banks by £2.2 million, paid-up capital of joint-stock companies registered in Ireland by £19.8 million, and holdings of government stocks, the interest on which was paid through the Bank of Ireland, by £64.8 million.[1] Further money, probably in excess of £100 million, went into local loans and shares of companies registered outside Ireland. The major amounts must have represented institutional funds, company reserves, and money from traditional investors, with some smaller savings of wage earners. In general a pattern appears, particularly among traders, the lower middle classes, and skilled tradesmen, of spending rather than saving and of the acquisition of minor luxuries relatively unknown before 1914. Other groups of wage-earners benefited less, finding little margin between higher wages and the rising cost of living, particularly as unskilled wages in Ireland lagged considerably behind those in Great Britain although living costs increased very much in step in the two countries. It seems therefore that the economic benefits of wartime prosperity were unevenly distributed. Those who could cushion future adversity by investment outside the country did so; skilled workers tended to raise their living standards with comparatively little saving; firms in general found the rising costs of 1920 and 1921 eating into reserves that would otherwise have been adequate; while workers at the lowest end of the scale found that it required considerable tenacity to maintain their limited gains[2] under post-war conditions. It was a feature of post-war activity by organised labour that shorter working hours became a more practicable and more widely achieved objective than higher wage rates.

---

[1] [Sixty-eighth] statistical abstract of the United Kingdom . . . from 1908 to 1922, pp 280, 283, 285 [Cmd 2207], H.C. 1924, xxiv, 288, 291, 293.
[2] Because so many wartime wage awards were on the basis of flat-rate war bonuses, unskilled workers tended to improve their position relative to skilled men.

A few individual features of the economy require further mention. Irish railways were seen to have reached by 1914 a position of unstable equilibrium: some parts of the system were bound by their nature to be uneconomic, while the whole was subsidised by a level of wages well below the British average. At the same time fares and charges provoked a recurrent outcry from traders who compared them unfavourably with those in the rest of the British Isles and Europe. There were few changes in the first two years of the war but by December 1916 a threatened strike forced government action and the whole system was taken into government control from 1 January 1917. From that time a series of wage rises was granted, which by 1919 totalled 33s. a week, effectively doubling pre-war rates and more than trebling the wage bill (from just over £1.5 million in 1913 to almost £6 million by 1920). These additional costs were partly passed on to railway users, partly borne by government traffic. Both declined steeply after 1919 and in August 1920 it was found necessary to advance passenger fares by 33.33 per cent while goods traffic, which was always less profitable than passenger traffic on Irish railways, was forced to bear a 120 per cent rise in September. Government control of the railway system ended in August 1921, coinciding with wage rises to railway staff that brought porters to between 43s. and 60s. for a 48-hour week, guards to 65s., and engine drivers to 90s. Fairly obviously the costs to users at a time when road competition was increasing and agricultural (and later, industrial) prices were falling posed considerable difficulties for the future of the system.

Despite difficulties, the sea fishing industry prospered during the war—after an initial drop in 1915 catches increased up to 1919, fetching considerably increased prices—but when the more distant grounds became open again the relative advantage of Irish inshore fishing disappeared. There were wartime increases in certain minor activities also, such as tanning and paper manufacture, due mainly to the need to supplement reduced supplies from Great Britain. On the other hand, industries such as cotton and tobacco manufacture, dependent on raw materials from overseas, were adversely though not permanently affected. By 1920–21, on economic considerations alone, it seemed that the scene was set for a continuation of the pattern of slow change and growth that had characterised industry in the opening years of the century. Linen had not lost its overseas markets; there was a demand for ships to replace wartime losses; brewing and distilling returned fairly quickly to pre-war levels of production; the engineering industry was, temporarily at least, without continental rivals.

In the social sphere there were two small but significant changes. Women had been employed in the civil service as early as 1901; in 1914 about sixty were working in Irish offices.[1] During the war they were appointed to banks to replace men who had joined up, but they continued to be employed after the war. The number of women assistant teachers increased both absolutely and in proportion

---

[1] McDowell, *Ir. administration*, p. 35.

to men during the same period, while in commercial offices throughout most of Ireland lady typists and secretaries soon came to be regarded as normal rather than unusual members of staff. At the universities too, while still a very small minority, an increasing number of women achieved academic qualifications. As in the rest of the western world, therefore, Irish women began to play their role in academic, business, and professional activity. The Public Health (Medical Treatment of Children) (Ireland) Act, 1919,[1] made provision for regular inspection of, and attention to, children attending elementary schools; in the same year the scope of the compulsory national insurance scheme, which since 1911 had provided sickness benefit to the employed through approved societies, was widened to cover almost all workers; and the year 1920 saw the introduction of unemployment insurance.[2] All these, together with steadily increasing expenditure by local authorities on dispensaries and hospitals,[3] indicated acceptance of the principle, in Ireland as in Great Britain, that even outside the poor law there existed aspects of welfare that could no longer be left for individual provision.

It is unfortunate that many statistics for the period 1914–18 are unavailable and those for 1920–21 sketchy. To that extent some of the patterns traced and conclusions reached in this section must be regarded as tentative, yet the overall impression remains that if, in the famine, Ireland suffered a national tragedy from which recovery was slow and difficult, in 1914–18 she shared a common experience with most of Europe and America from which she emerged, economically at least, ready to play her part in the reconstruction that was to follow.

Few of the problems that beset Ireland in the period 1850–1921 were new, none was unique. An older generation of economists used to draw comparisons with India; more modern studies have looked at Denmark, Scotland, and France. Equally valid would be comparison with Italy, which had a predominantly catholic population, a relatively prosperous industrial north, a depressed peasantry practising a primitive agriculture in the south, and a steady drain through emigration. The basic and perennial problem of most west European societies in the second half of the nineteenth century was how to find employment for people surplus to the requirements of agriculture, as more and cheaper food became available from overseas and while agriculture itself needed less labour per unit output. Great Britain was more fortunate than most in that her early industrialisation provided both employment for displaced agricultural labour and, with her increasing urban population, an expanding market for food and raw materials. To have kept even a part of her emigrants at home, Ireland would have had to embark on a massive programme of industrial development that was quite outside the bounds of possibility. Apart from the lack of mineral resources there were other factors that discouraged even quite modest attempts. In the first place, the native genius, if

---

[1] 9 & 10 Geo. V, c. 16 (29 May 1919).

[2] 1 & 2 Geo. V, c. 55 (16 Dec. 1911); 10 & 11 Geo. V, c. 30 (9 Aug. 1920).

[3] Expenditure increased from £242,000 in 1907/8 to £457,000 in 1918/19. *[Sixty-eighth] statistical abstract of the United Kingdom . . . from 1908 to 1922*, pp 56–7 [Cmd 2207], H.C. 1924, xxiv, 64–5.

one can talk of such a thing, was in other directions. The north was industrialised overwhelmingly by entrepreneurs either from Britain or of British origin, and even in the south, among the few industrialists who were active, it is almost impossible to recollect Irish names (Guinness being a conspicuous exception); it was not that there was any lack of capital in Irish hands, but it tended to be used in commerce rather than industry.[1] Secondly, the catholic church, aware of conditions in many British industrial cities, was opposed or at best apathetic towards producing similar conditions in Ireland.[2] Thirdly, and most importantly, a programme of industrial development just could not pay, as is clear from a glance at labour costs, the lack of a developed infrastructure, and the poor technical facilities that existed everywhere other than in the major exporting industries.

What was surplus in Ireland was not labour, but unskilled labour. Skilled men, with wages approximating to British levels, had a long history of intractability allied to a scarcity part natural, largely contrived. Thus it was pointed out in 1885, for instance, that Dublin tramcars were all imported from England,[3] but this was not simply a case of failure to encourage native enterprise but rather of prudence because it would have cost more, even if skilled labour had been available, to have them made locally. Again, the Irish infrastructure was rudimentary and her railways used mainly for passenger traffic.[4] In 1865 it was noted that the streets of Dublin were being paved with setts obtained from Penmaenmawr in north Wales whereas material quite as good was said to be available within forty miles in County Carlow.[5] But stone from Penmaenmawr was loaded direct from the quarry into coastal shipping, which delivered it to the centre of Dublin; from Carlow it had to be taken from the quarry by horse-drawn wagons, then transferred to rail, and on arrival in Dublin had to be handled again before delivery to its destination. No doubt north Wales was further away than Carlow, possibly the local material was equally good, but transport costs clearly favoured the former. Ireland imported around 4 million tons of coal annually and herself mined between 90,000 and 145,000 tons. Could she have produced more and saved on imports? Geologically perhaps a little, but Irish coal cost on average 2s. a ton, or around 30 per cent, more *at the pit head* than British.[6] These examples must suffice, but clearly, without government subvention, there were many areas where it would have been unrealistic to expect private investment. Indeed, a

---

[1] Maureen Wall, 'The rise of a catholic middle class in eighteenth-century Ireland' in *I.H.S.*, xi, no. 42 (Sept. 1958), pp 91–115.

[2] Liam Kennedy, 'The early response of the Irish catholic clergy to the cooperative movement' in *I.H.S.*, xxi, no. 81 (Mar. 1978), pp 56–8.

[3] *Report from the select committee on industries (Ireland) . . . minutes of evidence*, p. 118, H.C. 1884–5 (288), ix, 136; above, pp 300–01.

[4] *Royal commission on railways: appendices to evidence*, p. 31 [3844–II], H.C. 1867, xxxviii, pt ii, p. 37.

[5] *Royal commission on railways: evidence and papers relating to railways in Ireland*, p. 105 [3607], H.C. 1866, lxiii, 355.

[6] 'Report on wholesale and retail prices in the United Kingdom in 1902', p. 7, H.C. 1903 (321), lxviii, 63.

wealth of experience suggests that risk-taking in Ireland required rather better prospects of success than elsewhere and, whatever his proclivities at the race-course, in business the Irish investor seems to have preferred certainty to speculation.

A further facet to be considered is the effect of British administration in Ireland. Was the system wasteful, its efforts misdirected, the hand of the treasury unduly restrictive? Certainly it was expensive. 'But of government officials assessed for income tax, there are in Scotland 963, in Ireland 4,539. Their salaries are in Scotland £311,694; in Ireland, £1,412,520.'[1] There was, too, a reluctance to concede special treatment to Ireland.[2] Robert Lowe, vice-president of the privy council in London, writing to the treasury in 1863 about the museum of Irish industry, said: 'My lords are unwilling to admit that there are any circumstances in the condition of Ireland so exceptional to the rest of the kingdom as to justify a breach of the well established principle of non-interference by government in private enterprise.'[3] Yet despite such views the British government time and again provided money through the board of works for relief of distress, for railway construction, for the clearance of rent arrears, for drainage and land improvement, on the basis of loans whose repayment was often remitted. Above all, the land purchase acts provided very considerable sums (by 1922 £119 million) to enable Irish tenants to buy out their holdings. In the event, the repayment annuities were paid with negligible default, but at the time and in the light of landlord experience of trying to collect rents in difficult years, the original advances represented a remarkable act of faith. On the civil service there were conflicting views. One observer referred to 'loose congeries of independent departments',[4] another in 1912 wrote that 'no such chaotic jumble of administrative agencies exists in any country of the world as Ireland presents at the present time'.[5] On the other hand Lord Spencer, who should have been in a position to know, wrote: 'I worked so long with the Irish officials that I think better of them than many people, and think them undeservedly the best abused people I know.'[6] Perhaps it depended on the level at which one looked. There must have been an attitude of professional detachment in the administrations of the Dublin Reconstruction (Emergency Provisions) Act, 1916, under which loans to rebuild or restore houses damaged or

---

[1] Louis Paul-Dubois, *Contemporary Ireland* (Dublin, 1908), p. 526; these figures show, at any rate, that Scottish officials were on average paid more than Irish officials.

[2] Emphasis is on 'reluctance'. Prevailing *laissez-faire* principles were breached on many occasions, but only after urgent need was clearly confirmed and a remedy devised and argued over. This often meant, in an overworked modern phrase, 'too little and too late', so that those providing the remedy got little thanks for it.

[3] Cited by R.A. Jarrell, 'The department of science and art and control of Irish science, 1853–1905' in *I.H.S.*, xxiii, no. 92 (Nov. 1983), p. 337.

[4] Cited in Curtis, *Coercion & conciliation*, p. 337.

[5] A. P. McDonnell, 'The finance of Irish government' in *Nineteenth Century*, cccxix (Jan. 1912), p. 13.

[6] Cited in Peter Gordon (ed.), *The red earl: the papers of the fifth Earl Spencer, 1835–1910*, i: *1835–1885* (Northampton, 1981), p. 180.

destroyed during the rising were being approved, even if on a small scale, right up to 1920.[1] As for the clerk who, in the middle of a world conflict and with Ireland moving towards insurrection, could record in 1915: '£12.10s.0d. received through the commissioners of public works from the Dingle harbour commissioners on account of the balance due by them for the hire of the dredger *Sisyphus*',[2] what can one feel but admiration? Interdepartmental confusion and financial pedantry apart, Ireland owed much to the dedicated work of men such as Thomas Drummond, J. F. Burgoyne, Richard Griffith, and W. T. Mulvany,[3] who exemplified the best traditions of the service.

Finally, Ireland's problems were exacerbated in a direction already mentioned but not perhaps sufficiently stressed. She lost continuously by emigration, by army recruitment, and in other ways people who were in the prime of life. But in addition the Irish incidence of tuberculosis was the worst in Europe.[4] Deaths from the disease were most prevalent within the age group 15–55 but there was a particular concentration between the ages 25 and 35.[5] Nor were deaths the only consequence of this debilitating condition that sapped the energies of so many who should have been among the most active members of society. The registrar general's figures reviewing the period 1871–1910 showed almost no improvement,[6] while Lady Aberdeen in 1908 thought that in contrast to other countries the incidence of tuberculosis in Ireland was still increasing.[7] Significantly, the province least affected was Connacht where, as distinct from the more varied but less healthy food of Belfast and Dublin (where there was the highest incidence), there remained a large measure of reliance on the potato, bearing out Connell's view of the nutritional adequacy of the traditional diet.[8] If to all this one adds the tragic loss of many thousands of vigorous and active men during the first world war, a new dimension appears, not to the economic problems faced by the new regimes of 1921 but to the human resources available to cope with them.

---

[1] 6 & 7 Geo. V, c. 66 (22 Dec. 1916); *Annual report of the local government board for Ireland for the year ending 31 March 1915*, p. 1 [Cd 7936], H.C. 1914–16, xiii, 275.

[2] *Report of the lord lieutenant of all his proceedings under the 'Ireland Development Grant Act, 1903' for the financial year ending on the 31 March 1915*, p. 1 [Cd 7936], H.C. 1914–16, xiii, 275.

[3] John O'Loan, 'Origin and development of arterial drainage in Ireland and the pioneers' in *Department of Agriculture Journal*, lix (1962), pp 46–73; John Ryan, 'William Thomas Mulvany' in *Studies*, xii (1923), pp 378–90; G. L. Herries Davies and R. C. Mollan (ed.), *Sir Richard Griffith, 1784–1878* (Dublin, 1980).

[4] *Encyclopædia Britannica* (11th ed.), 'Tuberculosis', p. 355.

[5] *Supplement to the forty-seventh report of the registrar general . . . in Ireland*, p. xxxiii [Cd 7121], H.C. 1914, xv, 33.

[6] Ibid., p. xxxi (MS 31).

[7] *Royal commission on the poor laws and relief of distress. Appendix, X. Minutes of evidence*, p. 30 [Cd 5070], H.C. 1910, 1, 224.

[8] Connell, *Population*, pp 121–62.

1 REPORTS OF COMMISSIONERS OF INLAND REVENUE: NET ASSESSMENTS TO TAX UNDER SCHEDULES D AND E

year ending 31 March	Schedule D				Schedule E			
	Great Britain		Ireland		Great Britain		Ireland	
	£,000	%	£,000	%	£,000	%	£,000	%
1881	207,212	96.12	8,366	3.88	24,485	94.22	1,502	5.78
1886	243,333	96.60	8,559	3.40	27,964	94.50	1,627	5.50
1891	272,559	96.93	8,626	3.07	32,660	95.15	1,665	4.85
1896	276,778	96.89	8,887	3.11	33,544	95.26	1,669	4.74
1897	289,494	97.30	8,036	2.70	34,946	95.37	1,697	4.63
1901	358,901	97.42	9,490	2.58	45,126	95.93	1,914	4.07
1906	357,254	97.82	7,980	2.18	48,885	96.16	1,950	3.84
1912	414,557	97.37	11,204[a]	2.63	60,366	96.01	2,507	3.99
1916	509,438	97.80	11,455	2.20	77,341	96.34	2,937	3.66

[a]Increase due to inclusion (for the first time in 1906/7) of a large amount of interest on the purchase of estates under the land purchase acts. The interest referred to was collected from the tenants by the land commission and paid out to the vendors of the estates, less tax.

Sources: [C 2967], H.C. 1881, xxix, 181; [C 4816], H.C. 1886, xx, 279; [C 6537], H.C. 1890–91, xxvi, 307; [C 8226], H.C. 1896, xxv, 329; [C 8548], H.C. 1897, xxiv, 353; [Cd 764], H.C. 1901, xviii, 427; [Cd 3110], H.C. 1906, xxvi, 419; [Cd 6344], H.C. 1912–13, xxix, 549; [Cd 8425], H.C. 1916, xi, 101.

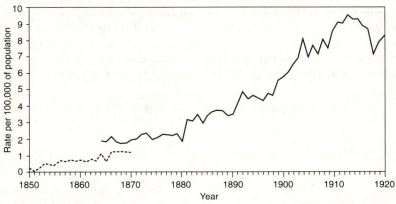

Figure 5 DEATH RATE FROM DIABETES MELLITUS IN IRELAND, 1850–1920, by Margaret Crawford

This figure is based on a more extensive graph, covering the period 1833–1983, which was published in *Ulster Medical Journal*, lvi, no. 2 (1987). This present version is used with the permission of the editors of *Ulster Medical Journal*. The broken line denotes figures from census returns, and the solid line figures from the returns of the registrar general.

2 HOUSING, 1851–1911

years	rural districts only				rural and civic districts			
	first class	second class	third class	fourth class	first class	second class	third class	fourth class
1851	22	243	501	131	50	319	542	136
1861	26	273	451	86	55	361	490	89
1871	28	275	329	38 [110]¹	60	381	363	39 [118]¹
1881	33	301	352	39	67	422	384	41
1891	37	327	286	20	71	467	313	21
1901	39	350	229	9	75	521	252	10
1911	43	392	171	5	84	583	189	5

Sources: *Census Ire., 1851–1911.* All figures are in thousands.

'Houses were classified in four divisions—first, according to extent, as shown by the number of rooms; second, according to quality, as shown by the number of windows in front; and third, according to solidity and durability, as shown by the material of the walls and roof. If numbers be adopted to express the position of every house in a scale of each of these elements, and if the numbers thus obtained for every house be added together, a new series of numbers will be produced, giving the position of each house in a scale compounded of all the elements, i.e., its actual state. . . . In the lowest of the four classes are comprised houses built of mud or perishable material, having only one room and window; in the third a better description of house, varying from one to four rooms and windows; in the second, what might be considered a good farm house, having from five to nine rooms and windows; and in the first class all houses of a better description than the preceding' (*Census Ire., 1901, general report,* p. 11 [Cd 1190], H.C. 1902, cxxix, 29).

Civic districts were all towns containing 2,000 inhabitants and upwards; rural districts were everything else (Vaughan & Fitzpatrick, *Ir. hist. statistics.,* p. xiii).

¹ Third- and fourth-class houses, built of brick or stone, in 1871.

CHAPTER XIII

Literature in English, 1891–1921

VIVIAN MERCIER

THE relationship of Irish literature to Irish politics in the thirty years under review in this chapter offers both paradox and symmetry. The paradox lies in the fact that the Anglo-Irish literary revival, which saw itself at first as an alternative to, or even a denial of, politics, helped to foster a new separatist political tradition. The symmetry will be found in the fact that although the writers' disillusionment with politics gave way temporarily to a celebration of revolution—'A terrible beauty is born'—the setting-up of the Irish Free State soon led to a new disillusionment. In Nicholas Mansergh's words, 'Irishmen felt as Italians had felt after 1870, that an heroic age was over, that prose had succeeded to poetry.'[1]

F. S. L. Lyons has stressed the importance of the Gaelic League as 'the nursery for the revolutionary generation of 1916'.[2] But Thomas MacDonagh at least among the 1916 leaders shared in the literary revival, having a play performed at the Abbey Theatre and assessing the Irishness of Anglo-Irish literature in his *Literature in Ireland* (1916). He, Pearse, and Plunkett, for all their nationalist passion, were no more willing than Yeats that poetry should be made to serve propagandist ends. Among the work they wished to preserve there are only a handful of overtly patriotic poems such as Pearse's 'The *dord féinne*' and Plunkett's '1867'. A few others veil patriotic feeling in symbolism: Pearse's 'The fool' and 'The rebel'; MacDonagh's 'Of Ireland'; Plunkett's 'The little black rose shall be red at last':

> Praise God if this my blood fulfils the doom
> When you, dark rose, shall redden into bloom.[3]

The bulk of their poetry consists of personal lyrics and religious or philosophic meditations.

Yeats had prophesied 'an intellectual movement at the first lull in politics';[4] after the death of Parnell he began to fulfil his own prophecy by helping to found the Irish Literary Society in London in 1891 and the National Literary Society

---

[1] Nicholas Mansergh, *Ireland in the age of reform and revolution* (London, 1940), p. 230.
[2] Above, p. 105.
[3] *The 1916 poets*, ed. Desmond Ryan (Westport, Conn., 1963), p. 201.
[4] *Autobiographies* (London, 1955), p. 199.

in Dublin in 1892. Like the Gaelic League, these organisations insisted on their freedom from politics. The rules of the National Literary Society as printed in 1897 ended thus: 'N.B. The society is non-political.'[1] Yet one cannot help noticing the recurrence of the words 'Irish' or 'national' or both—e.g. Irish National Theatre Society—in the titles of the various revival organisations. It was bound to be hard to keep cultural nationalism separate from political nationalism. What Yeats and his co-workers had become disillusioned with was a certain kind of bourgeois democratic politics, which they rejected not in the name of socialism or communism but because they hankered after a feudal harmony between gentry and peasantry that may never have been more than a convention of pastoral poetry or a myth fostered by conservative ideologists. Their vision of a two-class rural society ignored the existence of the hated bourgeoisie, whom nineteenth-century poets and painters had identified as the enemies of art. Yeats was to write long afterwards, in 'The Municipal Gallery revisited':

> John Synge, I and Augusta Gregory thought
> All that we did, all that we said or sang
> Must come from contact with the soil, from that
> Contact everything Antaeus-like grew strong.
> We three alone in modern times had brought
> Everything down to that sole test again,
> Dream of the noble and the beggar-man.[2]

'Contact with the soil' makes a point that is partly contradicted by 'the noble and the beggar-man'. The peasant, especially if he had participated in the land war, was a little too close to the middle-class anti-Parnellite nationalist for comfort. There is a cult of the tramp or travelling man or tinker, seen as a rebel against society, not only in the plays of Synge but in a number of plays by Yeats and in Lady Gregory's one-act 'The travelling man', where the title character is revealed to be Jesus Christ. If we look closely at 'Cathleen Ni Houlihan' we see not only that Ireland appears as an old beggar-woman but that Michael, in order to serve her, rejects all the symbols of a settled existence: money, new clothes, a farm, a wife. In a late poem, 'The man and the echo', Yeats wondered

> Did that play of mine send out
> Certain men the English shot?

He was obviously referring to 'Cathleen Ni Houlihan', but indeed any Abbey play that rejected bourgeois values might be seen as encouraging revolution.[3]

---

[1] Quoted in Una Ellis-Fermor, *The Irish dramatic movement* (2nd ed., London, 1954), p. 218.

[2] *The variorum edition of the poems of W. B. Yeats*, ed. Peter Allt and Russell K. Alspach (London, 1989) (hereafter cited as Yeats, *Poems*), p. 603.

[3] The rules of the Irish National Theatre Society, as incorporated in the patent of the Abbey Theatre, did not forbid politics altogether: 'No play shall be accepted or rejected on political grounds, and the literary, dramatic, and acting merits of the play shall primarily be considered . . . ', but there must be no 'degradation of national ideals' in the work.

It is very curious to read contemporary Dublin criticism of the first performances of 'The king's threshold' in 1903. Seanchan, the hero of Yeats's tragedy, fasts
to death against King Guaire rather than give up a jot of his privileges as a poet.
(The plot comes from the medieval Irish story 'Tromdámh Guaire'.) The
reviewers thought it basically improbable that any man would continue his fast to
death, no matter how great the injustice he had suffered. Yet within twenty years
more than one Irishman was to die on hunger strike against imprisonment by the
British—the best remembered being Terence MacSwiney, republican lord mayor
of Cork, whose fast lasted for seventy-four days. An essayist and poet, MacSwiney
was the author of a play, 'The revolutionist', performed at the Abbey in 1921,
after his death. Many examples of hunger strikes (including those against native
governments) since that time could also be cited. If Yeats's play did not contribute
directly to the adoption of the hunger strike tactic, it at least contributed to the
atmosphere of messianic self-sacrifice that pervaded the ranks of the extreme
nationalists before and after 1916. The late Herbert Howarth wrote an ingenious
book, *The Irish writers, 1880–1940: Irish literature under Parnell's star* (1958), about
six of the leading revival writers—George Moore, Lady Gregory, Yeats, AE,
Synge, and Joyce—which suggests that they all regarded Parnell as a crucified
messiah; that each regarded himself or herself as a potential messiah; and that each
wanted to write a 'sacred' book. Howarth failed to mention that Pearse had
written more often on the theme of one man dying for the people than any of his
six authors. It can hardly be denied that the literary movement influenced the
unconscious minds of the young revolutionists as well as their conscious minds.
At the same time it is conceivable that writers like Joyce, Synge, and Yeats, who
never consciously thought that an armed rising was possible, drew unconscious
sustenance from the revolutionary mood of some of their contemporaries. The
'heightened temper of Irish life'[1] that Lyons points to about 1907 was, after all,
a literary phenomenon as well as a political one. 'The playboy' provoked an
explosive response because it was an explosive play. Joyce completed *Dubliners* in
1907, but the book was considered so subversive in various ways that it did not
reach the public for another seven years. Where plays are powerful enough to
provoke riots, it is at least conceivable that riots will evoke plays. Is it pure
coincidence that just after 1916 Yeats and Joyce decisively broke the traditional
moulds that their writing had so skilfully exploited up to then?

THERE is a tendency to imagine the Anglo-Irish literary revival emerging full
grown from the head of Yeats, as Pallas Athene sprang from the head of Zeus.
The intellectual history of Dublin has yet to be written, so that we fail to realise
how vigorous the official culture of the capital in fact was. Maurice Craig's *Dublin,
1660–1860* (1952), the nearest thing to such a history, ends too soon for our
purpose. Possessing two universities and such old established cultural institutions

---

[1] Above, p. 111.

as the Royal Irish Academy and the Royal Dublin Society, Dublin could rival any provincial city in the British Isles, Edinburgh included, in its literary culture. The anthology *Echoes from Kottabos* (1906) shows how skilful Trinity men could be in pastiches of Tennyson, Browning, Swinburne, and even Whitman. No doubt the revival writers congratulated themselves from time to time on having less awe-inspiring models to emulate—Mangan, Ferguson, Allingham—as well as on the comparative novelty of native Irish subjects. The unofficial culture of the city was a lively enough affair too: 1885, for instance, saw the founding of two organisations as different from each other as the Dublin Hermetic Society (later the Dublin Theosophical Society) and the Contemporary Club, where intelligent people from many walks of life met to discuss ideas. There were political clubs like the Young Ireland Society, and of course the various student societies. The National Literary Society, at its founding in 1892, was unique only in its special emphasis on literature.

When we look at the organisations that hived off from this parent society, we get a sense of what its founders really felt their priorities were. The stated priorities were very different. According to the 1897 *Rules* of the society, it 'was formed in June 1892, with the object of promoting the study of Irish literature, music and art (1) by means of the circulation of Irish literature; (2) by lectures and discussions; (3) by concerts of Irish music; and (4) by the establishment of lending libraries throughout the country'.[1] One might expect that the first step would have been to found a literary magazine, but nothing of the kind seems to have been thought of: this suggests that Irish periodical literature was in a reasonably healthy state.[2] The first significantly productive step taken was to set up a subcommittee, out of which the Gaelic League emerged as a separate entity in 1893. On this occasion, the movement showed a correct sense of its priorities. To achieve 'the circulation of Irish literature', it was considered urgent that the society should publish an inexpensive series of Irish books. Yeats has told[3] how his plans to make the New Irish Library preponderantly literary in content were frustrated by Sir Charles Gavan Duffy, who insisted that its first volume should be Thomas Davis's *The patriot parliament of 1689*. Yeats's prophecy of doom for the series was quickly fulfilled. After this failure, the next genuine priority was to create an Irish theatre: the Irish Literary Theatre officially began as yet another subcommittee of the parent society, appointed on 16 January 1899.

The failure to found a magazine may have arisen partly from the feeling that a purely literary magazine could not survive in Ireland. All the reasonably successful journals that published literature in 1892 or later served other ends as well: political, religious, scholarly, or even agricultural, as in the case of the *Irish Homestead*. The *Dublin University Review* (1885–7) was perhaps the most self-consciously literary periodical yet published in Dublin, and it had been short-lived.

[1] Quoted in Ellis-Fermor, *Ir. dramatic movement*, p. 218.
[2] See Barbara Hayley and Enda McKay, *300 years of Irish periodicals* (Dublin, 1987).
[3] *Autobiographies*, pp 224–8.

The *Irish Monthly* (1875–1954), a Jesuit periodical, flourished, however, and published poetry by Yeats and others. A later Jesuit periodical, the *New Ireland Review* (1894–1911), published Hyde, Yeats, Synge, and translations into Irish of short stories by George Moore; it had succeeded the *Lyceum* (1888–94) and was itself succeeded by the quarterly *Studies* (1912–). Under various names a theosophical periodical, of which A E was for a time editor, appeared in Dublin continuously from 1892 to 1904.

Among political journals the Parnellite daily *United Ireland* (1881–93) was always willing to shelter literary controversy and published several poems by Yeats. Arthur Griffith's weekly *United Irishman* (1899–1906) and its successor *Sinn Féin* (1906–14) regretted the absence of nationalist fervour in the revival writers, but often published them nevertheless. Entire plays appeared as supplements to the former, while James Stephens published all his earliest writings in the latter. Standish O'Grady's extraordinary one-man weekly, the *All Ireland Review* (1900–06), dealt mainly with politics but published some of its editor's literary work too, as well as poems, plays, and prose by other writers. The *Irish Homestead* (1895–1923), the weekly organ of the Irish Agricultural Organisation Society, being edited by A E, welcomed poetry and even printed short stories, usually rather naïve, but including Joyce's first three published works ('The sisters', 'Eveline', and 'After the race') in that genre. It also published an annual literary supplement, *A Celtic Christmas*. The *Irish Homestead* was later incorporated into the *Irish Statesman* (1919–20, 1923–30), whose literary aims were higher.

Periodicals combining literature with scholarship included *Kottabos* (1869–81, 1888–95), which contained a section of translations into classical Greek and Latin as well as the poetry in English already mentioned; and the *Gaelic Journal* (1882–1909), the longest-lived Irish periodical for Celtic studies before the twentieth century. The *Irish Book Lover* (1909–37) also deserves mention for its literary content.

The literary revival was destined never to have a distinguished periodical exclusively identified with it. *Beltaine* (1899–1900), *Samhain* (1901–8), and the *Arrow* (1906–9) were occasional publications of the theatre movement; *Dana* (1904–5), edited by John Eglinton, soon came to an undeserved end; *The Shanachie* (1906–7) was exclusively literary, but, lacking both a point of view and rigorous standards, was deservedly short-lived. Most ambitious was the *Irish Review* (1911–14), describing itself as 'a monthly magazine of Irish literature, art, and science', whose contributing editors included Padraic Colum, James Stephens, Joseph Plunkett, and Thomas MacDonagh; it also published work by Pearse and Francis Ledwidge as well as by many others who survived 1916. It ceased publication in November 1914 after the seizure of a large number of copies by the London police.

Although Dublin in the 1890s had a fairly large printing and publishing industry for a city of its size, most of the books published were either educational or religious. Sealy, Bryers, & Walker were the Dublin publishers of the New Irish

Library; Gill & Son included several books by Hyde in an otherwise undistinguished list. Eventually, however, Joseph Maunsel Hone financed a new Dublin publishing company, Maunsel & Co. (later Maunsel & Roberts), that published a number of works by revival writers, including many Abbey plays and the first collected edition of Synge. Yeats's sister Elizabeth established the Cuala Press in 1903 to print fine limited editions, mainly of works by her brother, on a hand press. There were other Irish publishing efforts of limited scope, but the majority of works by revival writers were published in London—T. Fisher Unwin and, later, Macmillan being the most active English firms in this respect.

Impressive as was the publishing output of Maunsel's in its heyday, the only permanent institution established by the Anglo-Irish revival is the Abbey Theatre. Although Yeats and Lady Gregory may have begun to plan for a theatre in 1896 and their plans were certainly well under way by November 1897,[1] they were to need the help of many people before a permanent theatre with an acting company and a repertory of plays came into being. Nevertheless, in 1921 we find them in sole charge of that theatre. The three annual series of performances staged by the Irish Literary Theatre during the years 1899–1902 had the great disadvantage of being dependent on English actors recruited specially for each series. A permanent company of Irish players to perform Irish plays was obviously needed; the nucleus of this company was found in an amateur group, the Irish National Dramatic Society, headed by the brothers William G. and Frank Fay, which in its turn had resulted from the merging of two nationalist clubs, one of which had been staging patriotic *tableaux vivants*. The atmosphere was exactly that of Joyce's story 'A mother', yet when the group was offered plays of literary merit, AE's 'Deirdre' and Yeats's 'Cathleen Ni Houlihan', they performed them with simple but adequate technique and deep feeling. The amateur, unofficial culture of Dublin was continuing to show vitality.

In 1902 the Irish Literary Theatre combined with the Fays' group to become the Irish National Theatre Society. Then in 1904 an English admirer of Yeats, Miss A. E. F. Horniman, acquired and renovated the buildings that became the Abbey Theatre, which opened on 27 December; a limited company, the National Theatre Society, was established to run it in 1905. Yeats, Lady Gregory, and Synge became directors of this company, thus ensuring their permanent control of the theatre; some of the actors were nominally shareholders, but they came to feel that they were regarded as mere employees of the directors. Most of the original acting company, including the Fays themselves, left during the first four years of the Abbey, but not before they had trained successors and established the Abbey tradition of acting and speaking. Mostly Dubliners from the lower middle class, the actors and actresses worked out a style of ensemble playing without stars through democratic give and take. Before the advent of Yeats in 1902, they chose their plays democratically too, but in the Abbey Theatre the directors decided the

[1]Yeats to Lady Gregory, 1 Nov. 1897 (*Letters of W. B. Yeats*, ed. Allan Wade (London, 1954), pp 288–9).

programme. The actors were often unhappy about the plays chosen, tending to apply political or social rather than aesthetic criteria. These tensions resulted in the loss of many fine performers but saved the theatre from any danger of bureaucratic stagnation.

Yeats and Lady Gregory had earlier parted company with two authors, Edward Martyn and his cousin George Moore, who had been important in the Irish Literary Theatre, of which Martyn was the principal financial guarantor.[1] Martyn wrote one fine play in the manner of Ibsen, 'The heather field' (1899), in part an allegory of attempts to modernise Ireland and their defeat by stubborn native tradition. Moore's 'The bending of the bough' (1900), a sort of Irish 'Pillars of society', also had affinities with Ibsen. Yeats, on the other hand, detested Ibsen's social drama and aimed at a less sophisticated, more poetic type of play. In any case, there were temperamental as well as aesthetic differences between him and Moore. Helped by Joseph Plunkett and Thomas MacDonagh, Martyn founded the Irish Theatre in 1914 for the production of non-peasant drama by Irishmen, of plays in the Irish language, and of English translations of European drama. Performances were staged at the Hardwicke Hall; MacDonagh, Eimar O'Duffy, and H. B. O'Hanlon were among the Irish dramatists who shared the stage with Chekhov, Strindberg, and of course Martyn himself. Dublin at the time simply was not big enough for two theatres, however small, that regularly performed Irish or other non-commercial plays. The majority of Dublin playgoers clearly preferred West End successes at the Gaiety Theatre or melodramas at the Queen's; otherwise these two theatres, each considerably larger than the Abbey, could not have stayed open. The Abbey Theatre was prevented by the terms of its patent, granted on 4 August 1904 to Lady Gregory, from performing modern plays originally written in English unless their authors were of Irish birth or they dealt with Irish subjects. It is surprising that, operating under these conditions and in competition with the wealth of London, the Abbey could obtain enough playwrights and performers of talent to keep its doors open. National feeling was one of the motives prompting both authors and actors, especially as most Abbey plays were of a kind unacceptable to the commercial theatre of the time. If Yeats and Lady Gregory had not seen the need for a purely Irish theatre, some of the greatest plays of the twentieth century might never have been written.

In Thomas Flanagan's chapter on 'Literature in English, 1801–91', Emily Lawless and Canon Sheehan were seen to embody two divisive tendencies, which between them might have destroyed Anglo-Irish literature.[2] Lawless resented the element of class war—too apt to degenerate into sectarian conflict—that she found implicit in nationalist politics. Sheehan, on the other hand, defined Ireland 'almost entirely in terms of its catholicism' and summoned his catholic Ireland 'to a

[1] For Martyn's patronage of the visual arts, see below, pp 490–91.
[2] Above, v, 510–14.

"mission" that is nothing less than warfare against modernity'.[1] Yet instead of splitting into two camps, protestant and catholic, Anglo-Irish literature entered its golden age (roughly 1899–1939) during which members of both communities joined in a united, if not always harmonious, outpouring of creativity. In another section of the present chapter[2] the writers' diversity of background is examined in some detail.

There are two main reasons why the Lawless–Sheehan split did not continue: first, the attempt to separate politics from literature already discussed; secondly, the strong tendency among protestant writers to adopt Sheehan's position by celebrating the Irish countryman. Yeats, Synge, Lady Gregory, and Hyde were all as opposed to modernity as Sheehan was, defining it as materialism, uniformity, and the breaking of tradition. They saw in the life of the Irish-speaking small farmers and fishermen of the western seaboard the perfect antithesis to modern, industrialised, urbanised man. Because these men of the west were in fact catholics, though Synge and Yeats liked to stress the survival among them of pagan beliefs, the literature of the revival became decidedly catholic in tone, no matter what the origins of its authors.

The Anglo-Irish revival can most reasonably be thought of as continuous with the Gaelic revival, for Yeats and his followers were trying to revive and reinterpret in English the whole culture of Gaelic Ireland.[3] Most immediately attractive to Yeats, an essentially romantic poet, were the pre-Christian myths and legends. William Morris—and probably also Richard Wagner, though Yeats was no musician—had revealed to him the artistic possibilities of a mythology that was unfamiliar and therefore, unlike the classical one, unhackneyed. Furthermore, as an occultist, Yeats believed that all myth and folklore contained ancient and unchanging wisdom. This view is most explicitly stated in his *The Celtic twilight* (1893), a book whose title cast an unfair aura of dimness over both Gaelic literature and the revival itself. Also, as an Irish nationalist and a lover of the Irish landscape, especially that of Sligo, he found in the mythology not only the names of many places that he loved but explanations of why these places bore their names (what was called *dindsenchas* in Old Irish). Other Irish poets whom Yeats admired, notably Ferguson, had already ·begun to use this mythology, while Standish James O'Grady had drawn attention to the great imaginative power of the Ulster cycle of tales, especially those that told of the exploits of Cú Chulainn.

Thomas Flanagan has already done sufficient justice to O'Grady.[4] We need to remind ourselves, however, that O'Grady knew no Irish, unlike his older kinsman, Standish Hayes O'Grady, whose translations in *Silva Gadelica* (1892) and elsewhere may attract a present-day reader more than the younger man's Carlylean flourishes. Also, when Standish James O'Grady's first volume appeared in 1878, there was already a good deal of Gaelic literature available in published translations—mainly English, but also German and French— and more came into

[1] Ibid., pp 512–13.   [2] Below, pp 369–72.
[3] Below, pp 385–430.   [4] Above, v, 515–20.

print every year thereafter, though often only in learned journals. The most important translators of Irish birth, besides the senior O'Grady, were John O'Donovan, Eugene O'Curry, John O'Daly, George Sigerson, P. W. Joyce, and Whitley Stokes; the last named had a knowledge of Old and Middle Irish not available to his predecessors, who were completely at home only in modern and classical modern Irish. Later, a German, Kuno Meyer, was the first to make felicitous English translations of Old Irish poetry in his *Selections from ancient Irish poetry* (1911).[1]

The first major works of the revival based on Gaelic mythology came from the Finn cycle: Yeats's *The wanderings of Oisin* (1889), Alice Milligan's 'The last feast of the Fianna' (1900), and the Yeats–Moore 'Diarmuid and Grania' (1901). (Lady Gregory's fine 'Grania' was never performed at the Abbey.) Then attention turned to the Ulster cycle, beginning with A E's 'Deirdre' (1902). In 1904 Yeats staged 'On Baile's strand', the first of his five plays based on the legends of Cú Chulainn, the last being completed just before his death thirty-five years later. Yeats also wrote a 'Deirdre' (1907) and Synge a 'Deirdre of the sorrows' (1909).[2]

Thanks to O'Grady and Yeats, with the help of a number of more popular retellings by Eleanor Hull, Lady Gregory, T. W. Rolleston, O'Grady himself, and others, Cú Chulainn was restored to the Irish people. It used to be said that, except for the story of Deirdre, the Ulster cycle had been replaced in the folk mind by that of Finn; this was not strictly true, but the fact remains that Cú Chulainn was seriously neglected by the later oral tradition. The choice of a statue of Cú Chulainn to commemorate the Easter rising of 1916 inevitably had a literary, perhaps even a highbrow, basis, but of course it has added to the standing of the Ulster hero in the popular mind. Conversely, Cú Chulainn contributed to the mythic aura surrounding the rising: his youth (in spite of the ages of Clarke, Connolly, and MacBride) reinforces the popular idea that the rising was the work of young men. (F. S. L. Lyons reminds us that to Pearse Cú Chulainn seemed 'the pagan version of Christ crucified'.)[3]

Appropriating Cú Chulainn thus as the symbol of one particular group of Irishmen has of course diminished his value as a unifying symbol, and one particularly attractive to Ulstermen. Nevertheless, by focusing attention on an Irish way of life that predated Christianity, let alone religious, ethnic, or cultural divisions, the revival did encourage a sense, however illusory, of the unity of Ireland. The revival's interest in folklore, too, pointed back to a timeless past when modern divisions did not exist. Furthermore, the literature in modern Irish is so archaic in spirit that it is possible to read a great deal of it without being reminded of religious differences at all. Unless they had read certain translations

---

[1] For a full account of the Celtic scholarship that made this aspect of the revival possible, see the first chapter of J. F. Kenney, *The sources for the early history of Ireland* (New York, 1929).

[2] It should be borne in mind, however, that even before the 1890s long poems about Deirdre had been written by Robert Dwyer Joyce, Ferguson, and Aubrey de Vere.

[3] Above, p. 193.

in Hyde's *The religious songs of Connacht* (1906), people who knew no Irish might remain quite unaware of the presence of sectarianism in its literature. Similarly, the more bitterly anti-English political poems were hidden by a plethora of sentimental Jacobite songs and visions of suffering Ireland that now seem charmingly innocuous.

Love and respect for a tradition beget love and respect for the carriers of that tradition. Earlier Anglo-Irish literature had tended to patronise the Irish country-man, portraying him as full of good qualities, no doubt, especially loyalty to 'the master', but ever prone to shocking or absurd behaviour. Was he really witty or was he merely perpetrating 'Irish bulls'? Even Kickham patronises him, some-times by stopping the narrative to praise him. It would be hard to find a literary work before Synge's 'Riders to the sea' that is totally free of patronising and presents Irish country people as genuinely tragic figures. Once Synge had done this, writers from a catholic background did it too: Seumas O'Kelly in 'The shuiler's child', Padraic Colum in 'Thomas Muskerry', and T. C. Murray in a number of plays.

Anglo-Irish literature thus ceased to be colonial. In the words of Daniel Corkery:

This colonial literature was written to explain the quaintness of the humankind of this land, especially the native humankind, to another humankind that was not quaint, that was standard, normal . . . The same note is found everywhere in Kipling's Indian books.[1]

Technically, what marks the break with colonial literature is the suppression of a mediating character. This character may be a colonist who has lived many years in Ireland, like Major Sinclair Yeates, R.M., in Somerville and Ross's *Irish R.M.* books, or a native of Ireland, like Charles O'Malley and others of Lever's first-person heroes, or someone brought up in England who is in Ireland for the first time, like the hero of Maria Edgeworth's *The absentee*. Shaw's 'John Bull's other island' contains both Larry Doyle, a native, and Broadbent, the greenhorn. But whether he be native, old China hand, or greenhorn, the mediating character's function is to act as a colonist explaining the colonised people to those in the mother country. He is a *raisonneur*, a spokesman for the author, and very useful as such. In Synge's peasant plays we find no such character: this may be one reason why 'The playboy of the western world' provoked such a hostile response in its first audiences. Even a very sophisticated playgoer of the time, being accustomed to Ibsen's use of the *raisonneur*, might find himself baffled: what attitude ought he to adopt to Christy's apparent murder of his father, or to the Mayo people who seem to approve of it? If there were a single urban middle-class character in the play, it might be possible to identify with him, but Synge leaves his presumably middle-class audience disorientated. Much writing about the working class everywhere is colonial too; O'Casey's tenement plays, however, lack a *raisonneur* and are in consequence still the least patronising plays of their kind

[1] Daniel Corkery, *Synge and Anglo-Irish literature* (Cork, 1931), pp 7–8.

in the world. Many Abbey peasant plays do in fact still contain a *raisonneur*, but he is no longer a colonist; instead he (or she) is a priest or an older man or woman of standing in the rural community.

More immediately striking than the absence of the mediating character is another significant technical innovation: the attempt that ran its course within our period, to create an 'Irish-English' literary language out of Irish folk speech. It began almost accidentally in the process of literal translation from Irish: anticipation can be found in the *Transactions of the Gaelic Society of Dublin* (1808), and elsewhere, but Hyde revealed the full potential of such Irish-English by the literal translation of his own Irish prose commentary in *Love songs of Connacht* (1893), as well as his almost literal translations of the songs themselves. He had already translated Irish folktales literally in, for example, *Beside the fire* (1890), and Ferguson and others had sometimes given colloquial versions of Gaelic songs: what was wholly new was the idea that a modern scholar could express himself in the English of the country people without loss of dignity. Lady Gregory took the hint in her *Cuchulain of Muirthemne* (1902) first of all, retelling the Ulster cycle in a language approximating to the dialect of the village of Kiltartan near Coole Park. A whole series of similar volumes by her followed—retelling myths, folktales, history—many with the word 'Kiltartan' in the title. The most startling of these was *The Kiltartan Molière* (1910), in which three plays of the classic French dramatist were rendered into the dialect.

This dialect was naturally most appropriate to peasant plays. Lady Gregory not only used it in many of her own, but helped Yeats with the dialogue in 'Cathleen Ni Houlihan' and 'The pot of broth', to both of which he signed his name, and in the revised edition of his *Stories of Red Hanrahan* (1904). Synge, however, did not restrict himself to the reproduction of a particular Irish-English dialect: such dialects contain much Gaelic syntax, as P. L. Henry has demonstrated,[1] but Synge often translated literally from the Irish of the Aran Islands as well. He was so well pleased with the literary qualities of this language that he wrote original poetry in it, translated poems by Petrarch, Villon, Leopardi, and others into it, and at his death in 1909 was within sight of completing a play, 'Deirdre of the sorrows', that would be a tragedy in the fullest sense of the word, noble in its thought and including characters of the highest rank, yet couched in the language of the poorest countrymen. George Fitzmaurice was another playwright who devised a unique language from folk materials. Eventually, these various styles became too easily parodied—as in the 'Scylla and Charybdis' and 'Cyclops' episodes of *Ulysses*—and fell into disrepute. This ultimately unsuccessful linguistic experiment finds an imperfect parallel in the successful choice of *cainnt na ndaoine* (the speech of the people, folk speech) as the norm for the revived Irish language.[2]

---

[1] See P. L. Henry, *An Anglo-Irish dialect of North Roscommon* (Dublin, N.D.), *passim.*
[2] Below, pp 420, 428–9.

All that we have said up to now about the choice of subject-matter and technique by the revival writers can be summed up in one sentence: they were writing, to the best of their ability, for an Irish audience. Lyons has pointed to various ways in which the founders of the revival, all protestants, failed to attune themselves to the catholics in their audience: there were discrepancies in their views on politics, religion, and morality.[1] Partly, though, the discrepancies were those that often separate any artist from his society. In one of his Wicklow essays Synge specifically compares the tramp with the artist, saying that the same gifts that produce the artist's alienation from his middle-class family go to the making of a tramp in a poor, uneducated family: both are unfit to make a living in any orthodox way. The characters in Synge's comedies divide into two groups, one belonging to an anti-society of tramps, beggars, tinkers, or perhaps actual criminals (in the case of the playboy and his father), while the other represents settled society. Synge's sympathies are with the anti-society, what William Empson has called 'mock pastoral' heroes.[2] Yeats, too, seeks to enlist our sympathy for a number of mock pastoral figures in his plays, as well as for Crazy Jane and similar personae in his poems. He records that an audience of farmers once sat through a performance of his little comedy 'The pot of broth' without laughing.[3] He thought the reason was that they had never seen a play before: it did not occur to him that they might have found the theme of the comedy offensive in that it shows a tramp outwitting a decent enough farmer and his rather stingy wife.

Such problems will always occur when members of one class consciously attempt to create literature for members of another. What the Irish theatre movement achieved with astonishing rapidity—and the literary revival as a whole with less speed and certainty—was what Yeats described in 1919, only twenty years after the Irish Literary Theatre's first performances, as 'the making articulate of all the dumb classes each with its own knowledge of the world, its own dignity . . .'.[4] Once the Abbey Theatre had provided a stage, and once playwrights like Synge, Yeats, and Lady Gregory had provided models, dramatists who had grown up in circumstances quite different from theirs were able to express the ideals and attitudes of their own regions and classes. In the open letter to Lady Gregory just quoted, Yeats admitted that their theatre had become something very different from what he and she had intended. Instead of myth, tragedy, and poetry, it had grown more and more concerned with reality, comedy, and prose. Yet if the revival writers had not taken the essential first step of addressing an Irish audience, that audience might have taken much longer to learn how to express itself to itself.

---

[1] Above, pp 120–21.

[2] William Empson, *Some versions of pastoral* (London, 1935), pp 195–250.

[3] *The variorum edition of the plays of W. B. Yeats*, ed. Russell K. Alspach (London, 1966) (hereafter cited as Yeats, *Plays*), p. 254.

[4] W. B. Yeats, 'A people's theatre: a letter to Lady Gregory' in *Explorations* (London, 1962), pp 244–59, especially p. 249.

To what extent were the makers of Anglo-Irish literature 'Anglo-Irish' in the narrow sense—members of the peerage or landed gentry and of English protestant ancestry? If we look back to the beginnings of this literature in the nineteenth century, not allowing ourselves to be dazzled by the prestige of its founder, Maria Edgeworth, we recognise that several very significant novelists—Carleton, Griffin, the Banim brothers, Kickham—were catholics. Carleton was by origin an Irish-speaking peasant, while the other novelists came from farming and shop-keeping families. Mangan and Thomas Moore, perhaps the two most important poets, were also of middle-class catholic origin, as was J. J. Callanan. George Darley, Davis, Ferguson, Lover, Lever, Le Fanu, and Mitchel were all from professional or commercial middle-class protestant stock; Maturin was a Church of Ireland clergyman, and Lady Morgan the daughter of an actor who was a native speaker of Irish.[1] In fact apart from Maria Edgeworth and the de Veres, father and son (both catholics), no serious creative writer whose work was complete by 1891 could be described as a member of the gentry.

During 1891–1921, some leading Irish writers did indeed come from the landed classes, including an authentic peer, Lord Dunsany, though we rarely find an Irish scene or character in his work. In certain cases, it might be more correct to speak of the ex-landed classes: George Moore makes no bones about the need to earn money that turned him from painting to writing after the land war cut off his rents; Maurice Collis's biography of Somerville and Ross[2] shows their dependence on their royalties for mere living expenses as well as the upkeep of Drishane House and the West Carbery Hunt. Lady Gregory had no need of royalties to maintain Coole Park; her work for Irish literature no doubt appealed to her as a new manifestation of *noblesse oblige*: at the beginning of the Irish Literary Theatre she coaxed a number of monetary contributions from the Anglo-Irish nobility and gentry on this principle. Indeed, to the extent that the revival was truly Anglo-Irish, it can be seen as an attempt, whether conscious or unconscious, to substitute cultural leadership for the political and economic leadership that was slipping from the gentry's grasp.

Two of the literary gentry, George Moore and his wealthy cousin Edward Martyn, were in fact catholics, but the most gifted writers of all—Shaw, Wilde, Yeats, Joyce, Synge—came from the middle classes and were all protestants except Joyce, whose impoverished family had originally been among the better-off members of the catholic middle class. Almost all those protestant writers who threw in their lot with Ireland were sons or grandsons of Church of Ireland clergymen, at a time when that church as a whole was strongly evangelical. Is it too far fetched to suggest that their families' evangelical tradition found a new outlet in serious cultivation of literature and the other arts? After all, it has become almost a truism of English literary history that the Bloomsbury group were mostly descended from members of the Clapham sect. The evangelical

---

[1] Above, iv, 394, 597.　　[2] Maurice Collis, *Somerville and Ross: a biography* (London, 1968).

movement in the established church in Ireland prompted the founding of many charitable and missionary institutions: its concern for the souls and bodies of the Irish poor led to charges, well or ill founded, of proselytism. While the Erastianism prevalent in the eighteenth-century Church of Ireland may have been congenial to the Synges who became bishops then, the relative who visited the Aran Islands, forty-three years before J. M. Synge, went there in search of converts. In any case, Synge's maternal grandfather and his brother Edward were clergymen; both this brother and his mother were strongly evangelical and puritanical. Yeats's paternal grandfather and great-grandfather were also clergymen; his great-uncle Matthew Yeats and the latter's large family he describes as 'very religious in the evangelical way'.[1]

The list can be continued among the lesser writers: Hyde was the product of four generations of clergy on his father's side and originally intended to continue the tradition; Standish James O'Grady's father was considered 'a bit wild' for taking orders—surely under the influence of strong convictions—contrary to the tradition of his family; Lennox Robinson's father gave up stockbroking in middle age to become a Church of Ireland curate; George Fitzmaurice was the son of a clergyman who had married a catholic. Although Lady Gregory had no clergy in her immediate ancestry, the Persse family were known for their piety, which she herself shared to the end.

Wilde and Shaw, not usually included among the revival writers, came from the same clerical and evangelical background. Two of Wilde's father's brothers were Church of Ireland clergymen, as was a grandfather of Lady Wilde. Shaw's paternal grandfather, Bernard, was a leading evangelical layman, married to a clergyman's daughter. One of G.B.S.'s paternal uncles was also a clergyman, but it is ultimately more significant that his wealthy uncle Henry was a leading evangelical layman who contributed generously to the building of Christ Church in Leeson Park, Dublin.[2]

When realism asserts itself in contrast to the myth and fantasy of much writing of the early days of the revival, its practitioners are often northern protestants: 'St John Ervine' (John Greer Ervine) and 'Rutherford Mayne' (Samuel Waddell) from Belfast; Forrest Reid, also from Belfast, who mingled realism with the occult; Shan F. Bullock, son of a Fermanagh farmer; 'Lynn Doyle' (Leslie A. Montgomery), combining a bank manager's shrewdness with abundant humour. On the other hand, 'A E' (George W. Russell), in spite of his Lurgan methodist origin, was attracted by theosophy and Celtic myth, as was his presbyterian friend 'John Eglinton' (W. K. Magee), son of a minister and best known as a trenchant critic. Another writer much influenced by theosophy was James Stephens, a Dublin protestant who had known stark poverty: he is mostly remembered for

[1] Yeats, *Autobiographies*, p. 20.
[2] For a fuller discussion of evangelical origins, see Vivian Mercier, 'Victorian evangelicalism and the Anglo-Irish literary revival' in Peter Connolly (ed.), *Literature and the changing Ireland* (Gerrards Cross and Totowa, N.J., 1982), pp 59–101.

works of fantasy and retellings of Irish myths, but he has moments of savage realism in both prose and verse.

The catholic playwrights, novelists, and short-story writers of these years, who come from middle-class and lower-middle-class backgrounds, are in general more given to realism than their southern protestant counterparts: at the very beginning of the theatre movement, Padraic Colum's 'Broken soil' (1903) and, especially, 'The land' (1905) established a genre of plays about peasant life that were less flamboyant and more concerned with economic and social factors than Synge's. W. F. Boyle's alleged comedies are often harshly realistic. Colum knew country and small-town life in County Longford; other realists who had contact with a life very unlike that of Dublin were T. C. Murray from Macroom, Seumas O'Kelly from Loughrea, and Daniel Corkery from Cork city. We must also include a Donegal catholic, Patrick MacGill, author of crude but powerful books about Irish migrant labourers in Scotland. But the supreme realist, at least in his earlier work, was a Dubliner, James Joyce.

To be a member, especially a not too prosperous member, of the catholic community surely helped to make writers aware of discrimination and hardship not only in their own lives but in the lives of less fortunate members of their church. Similarly, northern protestant writers belonged to a community that included a large proportion of tenant farmers, farm labourers, and members of the urban working class. Realism of a socially conscious type therefore came naturally to writers from these groups, whereas a southern protestant author (with the exception of Sean O'Casey) would find it hard to gain a really intimate knowledge of the life of his poorer co-religionists, who were decidedly outnumbered by middle-class protestants. The title of St John Ervine's play 'Mixed marriage' (1911) distracts us from its true originality: it is indeed about a protestant–catholic marriage, but it also happens to be the first Abbey play about urban working-class characters, seen of course through the author's middle-class eyes.

Generalisations break down when we turn from the playwrights and novelists to the lesser poets, all of whom were overshadowed by Yeats. Beside A E and Stephens, already mentioned, we may set 'Seumas O'Sullivan' (James S. Starkey), son of a Dublin Wesleyan pharmacist. Of the catholic poets who gave their lives in 1916, Plunkett had a father who was independently wealthy, thanks to *his* father's success in building and letting houses; Count Plunkett was an art historian and director of the National Museum (1907–16). MacDonagh, both of whose parents were national schoolteachers in Cloughjordan, County Tipperary, was a lecturer at University College, Dublin. Pearse, son of an English monumental sculptor, was the headmaster of his own boys' school, St Enda's. Among other poets, Padraic Colum was the son of a one-time master of the Longford workhouse, Patrick Colum, who deserted his family. Joseph Campbell was a Belfast catholic, son of a road contractor. Two catholic poets with a rural background were Katherine Tynan, daughter of a well-to-do County Dublin farmer, and Francis Ledwidge, son of a County Meath labourer, who was killed in France in 1917 while serving as a lance-corporal in the 1st Battalion, Royal Inniskilling Fusiliers. The one thing common to all the poets on this representative list is that none of them could possibly be described as in the narrow sense Anglo-Irish.

THE point at which literature and society impinged most sharply on one another was necessarily the theatre, where the literary movement confronted its audience in the too, too solid flesh. An organisation that called itself successively the Irish Literary Theatre, the Irish National Theatre Society, and, from 1911, the National Theatre Society obviously claimed to speak for the Irish nation: if it did not, why include the words 'Irish' and 'national'? When large segments of the Irish nation were offended, or thought they were offended, by this or that play, they felt they had a right to protest against what was being done in their name. Yeats and Lady Gregory could easily have chosen a neutral title (as the Dublin Gate Theatre did later), but they too were in fact inspired by a nationalist feeling. Unlike many of their fellow nationalists, however, they felt that the dignity of Ireland and her right to independence could not be demonstrated by the production of bad art. Yeats's didactic articles in *Samhain* and *The Arrow* continually stress the need for playwrights to express something personal to themselves, not the sentiments, however pious or patriotic, that they have read in the newspapers.[1]

The outcry against 'The Countess Cathleen' in 1899 may have begun in the personal spite of Frank Hugh O'Donnell, but it evoked a bigger response than he had perhaps expected. After the 1798 commemoration Dublin, especially the University College students, was in a protesting mood. There must in any case have been uneasiness about the predominantly protestant and Dublin Castle sponsorship of the Literary Theatre.[2] Yeats's play did contain scenes likely to offend catholic audiences; that the blasphemies were supposedly uttered and the acts of sacrilege supposedly committed by demons or under the influence of demons did not necessarily make them palatable. Police were in the auditorium, but they did not have to make any arrests, as no attempt was made to stop the performance, though there were jeers and hisses in plenty.

There were no disturbances at the first performance of Synge's 'In the shadow of the glen' (1903), but its presentation of an unfaithful Irish wife was regarded by many as a national insult, although Synge found most of his plot in a Gaelic folk-tale. Not only did the daily press, especially the *Irish Independent*, denounce it, but Arthur Griffith's *United Irishman*, at first approving, became indignant. Griffith and his fellow nationalists would have liked all Abbey plays to be as patriotic as Yeats's 'Cathleen Ni Houlihan'; they held the view that 'he that is not

---

[1] W. B. Yeats, *Explorations* (London, 1962), pp 73–243.
[2] The list of sponsors is given in Lady Gregory's *Our Irish theatre* (London and New York, 1914), pp 15–16; in the edition by T. R. Henn and Colin Smythe (Gerrards Cross, 1972), see p. 23.

with me is against me'. When Lady Gregory was applying to the Irish privy council for a patent for the Abbey Theatre, reference was made to a play ('In the shadow of the glen') 'which was an attack on marriage'.[1] The growing hostility against the theatre movement became an organised disturbance on the second night of 'The playboy of the western world' (28 January 1907) and continued all week. The police were called in again and made a number of arrests this time, because there was enough noise to prevent the hearing of the play and attempts were even made to drive the actors off the stage. I have suggested earlier that the absence of a spokesman for the author made the play bewildering even to the sophisticated.[2] The profanity and supposed impropriety of Synge's version of country speech offended some: Lady Gregory's classic telegram to Yeats said 'Audience [at the first night] broke up in disorder at the word shift.'[3] But the chief objection, undoubtedly, was to the whole picture of the Irish countryman: such an ignoble savage, without respect for any of the ten commandments, would never be fit for any form of self-government. The point has been made by AE and others that the original production of the play was brutal in its realism; later productions made it seem more of a fantasy. That there was something of a ghetto mentality behind the protest became explicit during the Abbey's first American tour in 1911–12: 'The playboy' aroused hostility in the Irish communities of Boston, Chicago, and Philadelphia, the cast being arrested in the last named city for taking part in an immoral performance.

Andrew E. Malone felt that the strongest objections to 'The playboy' were political, offering as proof the protests of the first-night audience against Conal O'Riordan's 'The piper' (1908). This is a play about 1798, in which the chief character, Black Mike, 'has some very unpalatable things to say about the Irish character. The play is a rather obvious satire upon Irish political tactics of the then recent past . . .'[4] Thomas MacDonagh's play about a future Irish revolution, 'When the dawn is come', was also performed at the Abbey in 1908. In 1909 Yeats and Lady Gregory, having previously taken a stand on behalf of art against both the ultra-devout and the ultra-nationalist, were able to prove their impartiality by defending art against the imposition of censorship by Dublin Castle. Against the expressed wish of the lord lieutenant they went to court, obtained a ruling that the lord chamberlain's writ did not run in Dublin, and performed Shaw's 'The shewing-up of Blanco Posnet', which had been censored for blasphemy.[5] Thereafter, Sinn Féin and the other nationalist organisations felt better disposed to the Abbey. More by accident than by design, the theatre remained open on the night of King Edward VII's death in 1910. This may have pleased the nationalists, but

[1] Ibid., pp 41 (1914), 35 (1972).

[2] Above, p. 366.

[3] Gregory, *Our Irish theatre*, pp 112 (1914), 67 (1972); for a survey of the reaction to the play, see Robert Hogan and James Kilroy, *The Abbey Theatre: the years of Synge, 1905–1909* (Dublin, 1978), pp 123–62.

[4] A. E. Malone, *The Irish drama* (London, 1929), p. 104.

[5] Above, p. 120.

it so incensed Miss Horniman that she severed her connection with the Abbey; however, she sold her interest to Yeats and Lady Gregory for the nominal sum of £1,000. Until 1922, when they coopted Lennox Robinson, they remained in sole control of the theatre as the only directors of the limited company. Until 1926, when rioting broke out against 'The plough and the stars', they were also in control of their recalcitrant audience.

Actually, in spite of their increased control of the theatre, Yeats and Lady Gregory seem in about 1910 to have temporarily lost their sure sense of direction. 'The death of Synge in 1909 had marked the end of an extraordinary decade. During it, Synge himself had written at least three masterpieces, 'The playboy', 'The well of the saints', and 'Riders to the sea'. Yeats had written almost all the heroic plays and folk plays that he was to produce in conventional forms; his next peak of dramatic energy would manifest itself in experimental 'Noh' plays, also known as 'plays for dancers'. Lady Gregory had written the most effective of her brief folk comedies and tragedies, collected in *Seven short plays* (1909), as well as most of her more ambitious plays on Irish mythological and historical subjects, collected in two volumes as *Irish folk-history plays* (1912).

Curiously enough, although Padraic Colum was not yet 30, all his major work for the Irish theatre was finished by 1910. His 'The land' (1905) is rightly considered prophetic of the direction that Irish drama was to take after 1910. Its concern with social problems suggests that the example of Ibsen had won over Irish drama, in spite of Yeats. In this play, the more vigorous children of two peasant families find Irish rural life too constricting and emigrate to America, leaving only the weaklings to inherit the farms for which their fathers struggled so long. The country speech given by Colum to his characters lacks the strong rhythm and poetry of Synge, more resembling that of Lady Gregory. Colum is writing about country and small-town life from inside rather than outside. The same can be said of T. C. Murray and Seumas O'Kelly, though Murray usually keeps within a single household, as in his tragedy of rivalry between brothers, 'Birthright' (1910), whereas O'Kelly shows the individual in relation to society, as in his play on corruption in local politics, 'The bribe' (1913). Realism rather than poetry or fantasy became the hallmark of the Abbey after 1910. George Fitzmaurice, who had begun as a realist with 'The country dressmaker' (1907), his charming study of a country girl who expects life to be like a romantic novel, became a writer of brilliant fantasy, but after 'The magic glasses' (1913) the Abbey ignored this development in his work, while finding room for the rather conventional imagination of Lord Dunsany.

The danger of making generalisations about literary movements is shown by the comment of Augustine Birrell, explaining why the Easter rising took him by surprise: 'the Abbey Theatre made merciless fun of mad political enterprises, and lashed with savage satire some historical aspects of the Irish revolutionary.'[1] He

---

[1] *The royal commission on the rebellion in Ireland: minutes of evidence . . .* , p. 21 [Cd 8311], H.C. 1916, xi, 205.

was thinking primarily, no doubt, of Conal O'Riordan and Lennox Robinson. The
latter, a man who shrank instinctively from violence, wrote a whole series of plays
about the futility of revolution: 'Patriots' (1912); 'The dreamers' (1915), about
Robert Emmet; 'The lost leader' (1918), based on the popular belief that Parnell
was not dead and would intervene in Irish politics again in his own good time.
These two playwrights cannot be said to stand for the whole movement, especially
when one thinks not only of 'Cathleen Ni Houlihan' but of Lady Gregory's 'The
rising of the moon' and especially 'The gaol gate', in which the mother rejoices
so fiercely that her son has died rather than betray his comrades.

Plays now forgotten, because they never reached print, explored previously
undramatised areas of the social scene: for instance, W. F. Casey's 'The suburban
groove' (1908), and R. J. Ray's 'The gombeen man' (1913). As already mentioned,
St John Irvine in 1911 was the first to put the Belfast working class on the stage.[1]
In 1917 there appeared the first Abbey play about Dublin slum-dwellers, 'Blight'
by 'Alpha and Omega' (Oliver St John Gogarty). Daniel Corkery wrote a
disappointing play on a related subject, 'The labour leader' (1919). The year 1921
saw the production of George Shiels's first two plays of lower-middle-class
small-town life, 'Bedmates' and 'Insurance money', but 'the making articulate of
all the dumb classes' would not be complete until 1923, when a Dublin working
man who had lived in the slums became an Abbey dramatist with 'The shadow
of a gunman'.

In the years 1912–16 poetry and politics came closer together in Ireland than they
had since the seventeenth century. Poets died for their country in 1916 as none
had died since Pierce Ferriter in 1653; a great poet, Yeats, commented on history
in the making in a way unparalleled since Dáibhidh Ó Bruadair composed poems
on the Williamite war in 1689–91.[2] For a moment in 1912–13, it seemed that the
poets had made common cause with the workers against the bourgeoisie. The old
feudal ideal was restated in an urban setting. In a note to his volume *Responsibilities* (1914) Yeats wrote of the shortcomings of religious and political Ireland,
concluding as follows:

Against all this we have but a few educated men and the remnants of an old traditional
culture among the poor. Both were stronger forty years ago, before the rise of our new
middle class which made its first public display during the nine years of the Parnellite split,
showing how base at moments of excitement are minds without culture.[3]

In writing this note, Yeats primarily referred to the efforts made in 1912–13 to
persuade the Dublin corporation to build a new municipal gallery worthy of the
fine collection of nineteenth- and twentieth-century paintings, mainly French,
that Lady Gregory's nephew Hugh Lane had offered to the city.[4] In December
1912 he published in the *Irish Times* the poem entitled 'To a wealthy man who
promised a second subscription to the Dublin Municipal Gallery if it were proved

---

[1] Above, p. 371.   [2] Above, iii, 542–5.   [3] Yeats, *Poems*, p. 819.   [4] Below, pp 480–85.

the people wanted pictures'. Its burden is that the people are not competent to decide and that one should, like the Italian nobility of the renaissance, give

> What the exultant heart calls good
> That some new day may breed the best
> Because you gave, not what they would,
> But the right twigs for an eagle's nest![1]

On 8 September of the next year, in the same paper, Yeats published one of his most famous poems, 'September 1913'. It reproaches those to whom it is addressed—whether the whole Irish people or only some of them is not made clear—for believing that their only duties are 'to pray and save'—save money, that is—and laments again and again that 'Romantic Ireland's dead and gone | It's with O'Leary in the grave.' The reference is of course to John O'Leary (d. 1907), the old fenian who had been Yeats's mentor in nationalism. Although the poem and the note to *Responsibilities* contain no explicit reference to the Irish Transport & General Workers' Union strike or to the lockout that was to reach its peak that very month, most readers at the time must have read into the poem a rebuke to the Dublin employers. The praise of Lord Edward Fitzgerald, Robert Emmet, Wolfe Tone, and the 'Wild Geese'—who seem to have died or gone into exile only to bring about the unromantic Ireland of 1913—looks forward unconsciously to the Easter rising. The chief inspiration for the poem, however, must have been the final rejection of the plans for the new gallery. 'To a shade', dated 29 September 1913, addresses Parnell and likens Sir Hugh Lane's rejection to his; it ends with a bitter warning to Parnell's ghost: 'Away, away! You are safer in the tomb.'[2]

It fell to another poet, A E, to make explicit the connection between the rejection of the Lane pictures and the lock-out. In his 'Open letter to the employers', published in Dublin newspapers on 7 October 1913, he was primarily concerned to denounce their 'collective and conscious action as a class in the present labour dispute', but he also taunted them with being 'an uncultivated class' because of 'recent utterances of some of you upon art'. Furthermore, he went on,

You are bad citizens, for we rarely, if ever, hear of the wealthy among you endowing your city with . . . munificent gifts . . ., and Irishmen not of your city who offer to supply the wants left by your lack of generosity are met with derision and abuse.[3]

A E also let loose his eloquence in a powerful speech at the Albert Hall on 1 November 1913, in which he said of the strikers; 'these men are the true heroes of Ireland today, they are the descendants of Oscar, Cú Chulainn, the heroes of our ancient stories.'[4]

---

[1] Yeats, *Poems*, p. 288.   [2] Ibid., p. 293.

[3] *Letters from A E*, ed. Alan Denson (London, 1961), p. 86.

[4] Richard M. Kain and James H. O'Brien, *George Russell (A.E.)* (Lewisburg and London, 1976), p. 36; and see A E, *The Dublin strike* (London, 1913).

In that same month of November 1913 another poet, Pearse, wrote an article in *An Claidheamh Soluis* entitled 'The coming revolution'. He called the Gaelic League 'a spent force' but prophesied that 'the vital work to be done in the new Ireland will be done . . . by men and movements that have sprung from the Gaelic League'. What that work was likely to be can be seen from the highly rhetorical conclusion to the article:

A thing that stands demonstrable is that nationhood is not achieved otherwise than in arms . . . We must accustom ourselves to the thought of arms, to the sight of arms, to the use of arms. We may make mistakes in the beginning and shoot the wrong people; but bloodshed is a cleansing and a sanctifying thing, and the nation which regards it as the final horror has lost its manhood. There are many things more horrible than bloodshed; and slavery is one of them.[1]

Some of these words are spoken by the orator off stage in the second act of O'Casey's 'The plough and the stars', where their frightening implications cannot be ignored; but Pearse intended that some or all of the blood shed would be his own. In 1913 a play that he had written in Irish for the boys of his own school, St Enda's, was performed at the Abbey. 'An rí' (The king) shows a king who is unable to defeat the invader; a boy of humble origin, Giolla, is elected king in his place. Giolla dies in battle, but the invader is driven out. The messianic parallel is brought out more strongly in 'The singer', a play that Pearse wrote in English in 1915. The singer, MacDara, deliberately sacrifices himself at the hands of the invaders, saying: 'One man can free a people as one Man redeemed the world.'[2]

After Pearse and his comrades had made their sacrifice, Yeats honoured them in three fine poems, but his reactions were not as public or as prompt as they had been in 1912–13. 'Easter 1916', dated 25 September 1916, was 'published' in London as a pamphlet the same year, but 'Sixteen dead men' and 'The rose tree' had to wait until 1920 for publication. The title of 'Easter 1916' was clearly designed to stress that it was an answer to 'September 1913'. Where previously Yeats had felt certain that romantic Ireland was dead and that he 'but lived where motley is worn', just as Joyce had felt when he made Stephen Dedalus treat Davin's earnest preparations for a new rising as play acting, now all is '. . . changed, changed utterly: a terrible beauty is born'. It does not matter that the sacrifice of Pearse and the others may have been 'needless death after all'; we must be content 'to murmur name upon name' in celebration of their transfiguring deed. As so often before, it seemed that the chief political use of Irish poetry was to keep alive the memory of the dead. (By no coincidence, Pearse and Yeats had both participated in the commemoration of Thomas Davis in 1914.)[3]

---

[1] Pearse, *Political writings*, pp 91, 97–9.
[2] Patrick Pearse, *Plays, stories, poems* (Dublin, 1924), p. 44.
[3] W. B. Yeats, *Tribute to Thomas Davis*, ed. Denis Gwynn (Cork, 1947); and see Yeats, *Poems*, pp 391–6.

Other attitudes of course were possible: Yeats himself stressed the theme of national regeneration through the leaders' sacrifice in 'The rose tree', coming very close to the actual views of Pearse. Indignation was also natural: in 'Sixteen dead men' Yeats suggested that compromise—'give and take'—had become impossible after the executions. On the whole, there was surprisingly little indignation in the response of the poets: Ledwidge simply grieved; Stephens expressed hope for the future; A E, like Yeats, saw the dead transfigured:

> Their dream had left me numb and cold,
> But yet my spirit rose in pride,
> Refashioning in burnished gold
> The images of those who died . . .[1]

Stephens also wrote *The insurrection in Dublin* (1916), a valuable eye-witness account in prose. Maurice Dalton's 'Sable and gold', the first Abbey play on the Easter rising, was performed in 1918. In 1919 Yeats published a Noh play set in the days immediately following Easter week 1916, 'The dreaming of the bones'. Diarmuid and Dervorgilla, the unhappy pair traditionally regarded as responsible for the Anglo-Norman invasion, cannot rest in peace until 'somebody of their race' has forgiven them. A young man 'on the run' after fighting in Dublin is momentarily tempted to do so, but 'never, never shall Diarmuid and Dervorgilla be forgiven'.[2] The myth-makers and the men of action, in so far as they were not already the same people, had made common cause. Literature and politics, for a short time at least, travelled parallel courses.

IN an earlier chapter, Thomas Flanagan has dealt with some novelists—Sheehan, Lawless, Somerville and Ross—who prolonged nineteenth-century trends into the twentieth century.[3] Inevitably, the revival had less impact on prose fiction than on drama and poetry. Because the novel had been realistic from its beginnings, it could not easily accommodate, for example, a concern with Celtic myth and legend. Virtually the only writer to graft myth and folklore on to what might loosely be called a novel was Stephens. When he ignored decorum, mingling policemen, philosophers, leprechauns, and gods both classical and Celtic, he produced that inimitable fantasy *The crock of gold* (1912). *The demi-gods* (1914), which mixed tinkers with angels who were Celtic heroes in disguise, was more coherent and no less amusing. But when he attempted to retell the saga literature in the idiom of the modern novel, he reduced Deirdre to a 1920s 'flapper'. *The charwoman's daughter* (1912), Stephens's one novel about the Dublin slums, where he lived until the age of 6—before spending ten years in an industrial school—is pastoral comedy rather than realism. Only a few poems and

---

[1] See Edna C. FitzHenry (ed.), *Nineteen-sixteen: an anthology* (Dublin, 1935), for the response of these and many other poets.

[2] Yeats, *Plays*, pp 773, 775; the allusion is to Diarmait Mac Murchada, king of Leinster (d. 1171), and Derbforgaill, wife of Tigernán Ua Ruairc, king of Bréifne (d. 1172).

[3] Above, v, 510–15.

an occasional short story such as 'Hunger' look directly at the Irish society of his time.

Though George Moore served his apprenticeship to the realistic novel, producing a masterpiece of the genre, *Esther Waters* (1894), which is set in England, the literary revival in the long run decisively altered the direction of his career. His first piece of fiction set in Ireland, *A drama in muslin* (1886), realistically satirised Dublin Castle society as a marriage market for young ladies. After he had moved to Ireland in 1900, initially to help Yeats and Martyn with the Irish Literary Theatre, he proceeded to write the realistic short stories of Irish rural life published in *The untilled field* (1903), 'in the hope of furnishing the young Irish of the future with models'.[1] Several of these stories were translated into Irish and issued—with others not included in the English edition—as *An t-úr ghort* (1902). There is said to have been a plan at one time for Moore to destroy his English originals; the Irish versions by Tadhg Ó Donnchadha and Pádraig Ó Súilleabháin would then be retranslated literally into the Irish-English idiom of Hyde or Lady Gregory! One of the recurring themes in these stories, for example, 'Some parishioners' and 'Julia Cahill's curse', is that the parish priests' suppression of crossroads dancing, courting by the roadside, and love matches has made life in rural Ireland so depressing that the young flee to America. The protagonist in 'Home sickness' returns from America to Ireland on a nostalgic impulse; he almost settles down there with a local girl, but the priest's ban on dancing and drinking sends him back to New York. In 'A letter to Rome', a more sympathetic priest suggests the ending of clerical celibacy, so that surplus women may get good husbands and raise children to replace the emigrants. Moore went on to write *The lake* (1905), a novel in which a country priest realises he is in love with a girl whom he has driven from his parish; he eventually loses his vocation and goes off to England, making it appear that he has drowned himself in the lake that provides the setting and central symbol of the novel.

Moore's portrayal of a priest in *The lake* ought to be contrasted with an interesting autobiographical novel by Jeremiah O'Donovan, an ex-priest who wrote under the pseudonym of 'Gerald O'Donovan'.[2] The title character of *Father Ralph* (1913) is coaxed into taking orders by a devout mother. Maynooth College strikes Ralph as a forcing house for careerists. Both it and the diocesan seminary, especially the latter, contain many small farmers' sons seeking a short cut into the middle classes. Ralph finds the life of a country curate, including its chaste flirtations with pious spinsters, almost unbearable. He becomes a convert to the movement within the church known as modernism, an anticipation of the more recent *aggiornamento*; knowing that his narrow, ignorant bishop will silence him if he speaks his mind, Ralph leaves both the church and Ireland. O'Donovan does not show much gift for character-drawing here, though he later wrote five other

---

[1] George Moore, preface to *The untilled field* (revised ed., London, 1936), p. ix.
[2] *The lake* is said to have been inspired by O'Donovan's career; see article on O'Donovan by Peter Costello in Robert Hogan (ed.), *Dictionary of Irish literature* (Dublin, 1980), p. 509.

novels; he might have been better advised to tell his story quite frankly as autobiography, but he does give us an insight into the catholic church in Ireland quite different from Moore's on the one hand or Canon Sheehan's on the other.

After he had left Dublin, Moore wrote a mocking account of his ten-year experience with the revival in the three volumes known collectively as *Hail and farewell* (1911–14). His egotism and envy of Yeats mar the book, but Edward Martyn emerges as a great comic character in the tradition of Don Quixote. Joyce probably took from Moore the idea of using real people under their own names as characters in *Ulysses*. After his brush with the revival, Moore wrote very little fiction about contemporary life—except, of course, in his autobiographies—turning instead to the New Testament, Greek myth, and medieval history for his themes. With the help of Kuno Meyer he wrote a number of comic and romantic stories based on legends of Irish saints and heroes in *A story-teller's holiday* (1918) and *Ulick and Soracha* (1926).

It is hard to assess the effect of the revival on Seumas O'Kelly: if it had never existed, he would surely still have felt the same respect and affection for the country people of Counties Galway and Kildare. He was an active nationalist, dying of a heart attack in 1918, aged at most 43, while editing the Sinn Féin weekly *Nationality* in place of the imprisoned Griffith. *Hillsiders* (1921) and *The golden barque* (1919) are two groups of six linked stories each, which had originally appeared serially in the *Irish Weekly Independent*. Though written for an unsophisticated audience, they have style and psychological depth; the first series deals with a Galway village, the second with the crew of a canal boat. *The lady of Deerpark* (1917) is a powerful novel about the destruction of a well bred woman by her marriage to a brutal ex-peasant who has made money. *Wet clay* (1922), published posthumously, was written earlier than *The lady of Deerpark*; it is a weak novel about the miseries of a small farmer's life. 'The weaver's grave',[1] a long short story that is O'Kelly's masterpiece, tenderly reworks the theme of Synge's 'In the shadow of the glen': the weaver has lived so long that only two other old men are likely to know where his family lie buried; as they quarrel about where the grave should be dug, the weaver's young widow and fourth wife falls in love with one of the twin gravediggers.

Shan F. Bullock, the son of a strong farmer in County Fermanagh, earned his living as a civil servant in London, but wrote all his life about the country people living on the shores of Upper Lough Erne. He can be sentimental or humorous, but his best vein is one of sober realism, as in the short story 'The emigrant' from *Ring o' rushes* (1896): a young Fermanagh girl is going back to America because the man she loves is a drunkard and will never make a home for her. Bullock's last novel, *Loughsiders* (1924), is usually considered to be his best: Richard Jebb, a dour northern farmer, tries to marry a girl much younger than himself; when she rejects him, he bides his time until her father dies; then, having manœuvred

---

[1] First published in *The golden barque and The weaver's grave* (Dublin, 1919).

her and her brothers into leaving home, he marries her widowed mother and adds another farm to his possessions. Bullock also wrote one of the very few Irish novels about boarding-school life, *The cubs* (1906).

Another novelist who wrote directly from experience was Patrick MacGill. From a poor Donegal family, he worked as a farm labourer in County Tyrone, then joined the migrant labourers who worked in the Scottish potato fields, and later worked as a navvy in Scotland. *Children of the dead end* (1914), describing the hardships of a labourer's life, is more a series of autobiographical sketches than a novel. *The rat pit* (1915) tells of a Donegal girl who goes to work in Scotland, is seduced there, becomes a streetwalker in Glasgow, and dies of tuberculosis. Benedict Kiely sums up MacGill's work thus:

The bulk of his work was waste: shapeless novels that attained to a great popularity and are now deservedly forgotten. But for his comic novel *Lanty Hanlon* [1922], for his eye-witness sketches of war in *The great push* and *The red horizon* [1916], for his observation of the exiled Irish living in conditions that are surpassed only by the nineteenth-century coffin ships, this crude unshapen novelist—a sort of Donegal Gorki—is worth remembering.[1]

Forrest Reid, who began his long career as a novelist in 1904, serves to remind us that novels were being written by and about the urban middle classes as well as the gentry and the rural poor. Except that he was the author of the first book on Yeats by an Irishman, he may be thought of as unaffected by the revival. *Pirates of the spring* (1919), a story of adolescent schoolboys in the suburbs of Belfast, is a good example of his work. His psychological insight and his moral sense, which has little or nothing to do with revealed religion, link him with his friend E. M. Forster, who much admired his work. 'In life, no doubt as in everything else, it is very hard to be fine, to be rare; but if one does not make an effort, has no ideals, then one simply lapses into vulgarity, ceases to count.'[2] Put baldly like this by one of Reid's characters, his morality sounds dangerously like snobbery, but his feeling for psychological nuances is often rare and fine. Even as a psychologist, however, he can hardly be said to rival Joyce, while his awareness of the details of an urban scene appears minimal beside that of Dublin's circumnavigator.

THE greatest Irish literary event of 1921 was the completion of James Joyce's *Ulysses*, to be published in Paris the following year. Its final page bears the notation 'Trieste–Zürich–Paris, 1914–1921'. Although written in this multiple exile, it deals with events, real and imagined, occurring in Dublin on 16–17 June 1904. Joyce had left Ireland in October of that year, returning three times in later years for a matter of a few weeks in all, but his letters show that he was aware of

---

[1] Benedict Kiely, *Modern Irish fiction* (Dublin, 1950), p. 125.
[2] Forrest Reid, *Pirates of the spring* (Dublin, 1919), p. 322. For a more thorough analysis of Reid's work in a social context, see John Wilson Foster, *Forces and themes in Ulster fiction* (Dublin, 1974), pp 139–48, 197–211. Note pp 207–8, on Reid's youthful gesture towards realism.

much that had happened there since his departure. Nevertheless *Ulysses* not only preserves an astonishing amount of the physical appearance of Dublin in 1904 but also records a mood that must have some validity for the historian, if only because Joyce himself clearly experienced it at the time. It seems as though nothing in the Ireland of *Ulysses* will ever change. Molly Bloom remarks of the architect of the Irish Free State: '. . . he [her husband] says that little man he showed me without the neck is very intelligent the coming man Griffith is he well he doesnt look it thats all I can say . . .'[1] Joyce apparently could not stop thinking of Dublin as 'the centre of paralysis', the description he had used in writing to Grant Richards about *Dubliners*.[2]

Yet the value of Joyce's earlier work—in effect everything but *Finnegans wake*—to the historian is always twofold: on the one hand he documents the paralysis; on the other, however satirically, he documents the movements, political and cultural, that aimed at ending that paralysis. If it were not for *Ulysses* and, to a lesser extent, *A portrait of the artist as a young man*, it would be easy for everyone but the social historian to forget that Dublin so recently contained a well defined brothel quarter; even the names of most of the streets concerned have since been changed, as Joyce students discover when they try to follow the 'Circe' episode on a modern map. The glimpse we get of paid political canvassers in 'Ivy day in the committee room' is invaluable to the historian, though hardly reassuring to a fervent apostle of democracy. Countless other instances of paralysis could be cited, but we are also shown, in *A portrait of the artist as a young man*, the young patriot Davin, with his drilling, his Gaelic games, his Irish classes, and his uncomplicated love for his country; Joyce's touching glimpse of him is given added poignancy if we know that George Clancy, the model for Davin, was murdered while serving as the republican mayor of Limerick in 1921.

Similarly, although Joyce was sceptical of the literary revival and attacked it for parochialism in 'The day of the rabblement', we can hardly fail to be impressed with the cultural level of the conversation in the National Library during the 'Scylla and Charybdis' episode. A E and John Eglinton were not the brightest stars of the revival, but their wide reading, poetic feeling, and keen intelligence prove a match for those of the precocious Stephen. Even though they are parodied and ridiculed—Shakespeare is described by Buck Mulligan as 'the chap that writes like Synge'[3]—the greater figures of the period—Yeats, Synge, Moore, Lady Gregory—are kept constantly before our minds in the episode.

Up to the completion of *Ulysses*, indeed, Joyce's work seems almost a deliberate antithesis to the revival. Apart from his choice of the classical myths of Daedalus and Ulysses, he categorically rejects Celtic mythology and the Gaelic tradition in

[1] James Joyce, *Ulysses* (London, 1960; Penguin Twentieth-Century Classics, Harmondsworth, 1992), p. 886.
[2] Joyce to Grant Richards, 5 May 1906 (*Letters of James Joyce*, ii, ed. Richard Ellmann (London, 1966), p. 134).
[3] Joyce, *Ulysses*, p. 254.

the 'Cyclops' episode, both in his parodies of translations from the Irish and in his realistic presentation of that cantankerous Gaelic revivalist, 'the Citizen' (based on Michael Cusack, a founder of the G.A.A.). Instead of idealising the Irish countryman, he pitilessly exposes his Dubliners of the lower and lower-middle classes. In sending *Dubliners* to Grant Richards, he wrote of 'the special odour of corruption which, I hope, floats over my stories'.[1] In truth, almost every story contains at least one blighted character: spongers, lechers, drunkards, cowards, petty tyrants, the suicide of 'A painful case', or the pervert of 'An encounter'. Nor is the eloquence and poetry of the revival to be found in *Dubliners*, which Joyce fairly claimed to have written in a style of 'scrupulous meanness'.[2] As for *A portrait*, although it contains passages of great beauty and poignancy, its burden is that Irish religion, Irish politics, and even Irish family life are shams. Stephen says: 'I will not serve that in which I no longer believe, whether it call itself my home, my fatherland, or my church.'[3] The one thing Joyce had in common with the revival was his detestation of the bourgeois mentality; instead, however, of turning away from it in disgust to contemplate pleasanter prospects, he 'chooses to bend upon these present things' and documents middle-class urban life without pity—or so at first it seems. Joyce's bitterness understandably sprang from his own experience: thanks to his father's shiftlessness and alcoholism, he had seen his own family tumble from solid bourgeois comfort to virtual pauperism. The miracle is that he found pearls on the dunghill, beginning with Gabriel and Gretta Conroy in 'The dead', and culminating in his version of a flawed but 'truly good' man, Leopold Bloom, a twice baptised (protestant and catholic), uncircumcised Jewish Dubliner.

We all know something of the difficulty Joyce had in getting *Ulysses* accepted anywhere in the English-speaking world. It would be natural to assume that the book was banned in the Irish Free State under the Censorship of Publications Act, 1929,[4] but in fact it never was: even the customs prohibition order against it was withdrawn in 1932. Nothing of Joyce's was ever openly banned in Ireland except, inexplicably, the posthumous *Stephen hero* (1944), a portion of the original draft of *A portrait of the artist as a young man*. 'The day of the rabblement', which appeared in *Two essays* (1901), was refused publication by the Jesuit censor of the University College, Dublin, student magazine; it was then published in a pamphlet along with 'A forgotten aspect of the university question', a feminist essay by Francis Sheehy Skeffington that had been similarly rejected. Maunsel & Co. actually had an edition of *Dubliners* in print and ready for publication in 1912 when the printer, John Falconer, who depended for most of his work on religious and educational publishers, insisted on destroying it. This experience probably strengthened Joyce in his determination to continue his self-imposed exile. One

---

[1] Richard Ellman, *James Joyce* (revised ed., Oxford, 1982), p. 210.
[2] Ibid.
[3] James Joyce, *A portrait of the artist as a young man* (Everyman ed., London, 1991), p. 251.
[4] 1929/21 [I.F.S.] (16 July 1929).

should never forget, though, that his refusal (until 1931) to legalise his union with Nora Barnacle would have created social and perhaps legal difficulties had the Joyce family returned permanently to Ireland. His awareness of this fact can be seen in his only play, 'Exiles'.

After the publication of *Ulysses*, Joyce soon embarked on his last major work, *Finnegans wake*, long known as *Work in progress*. Here he finally paid homage to the revival, at least to the extent of making important structural use of Irish myth from the Finn cycle. Many of the rhythms of this great comic poem are also strongly Irish, so much so that a critic has written of Joyce's 'Synge-song'. Meanwhile, as Joyce characteristically swam against the stream, back to the sources of the revival, Irish fiction, both in the short story and the novel, was moving towards the scrupulous realism evident in his early work.

CHAPTER XIV

Irish language and literature, 1845–1921

BRIAN Ó CUÍV

WRITING early in the seventeenth century about the hostile attitude to the Irish people and their language shown by a contemporary, Richard Stanihurst, the priest-historian Séathrún Céitinn (Geoffrey Keating) said 'It is not possible to banish a language without banishing the people whose language it is.'[1] Four and a half centuries had elapsed since Henry II had been acknowledged as lord of Ireland and over eighty years since Henry VIII had been acknowledged as king, but Irish was still the language of most of the native Irish and of many of the descendants of settlers whom Céitinn termed *sean-Ghaill* (old foreigners)—a class to which he himself belonged. Three centuries later Irish had ceased to be the everyday language of all but a small proportion of the people of the island although the population still consisted mainly of descendants of those about whom Céitinn had written. Nevertheless at the close of the period covered by this chapter the status of being 'the national language' was accorded to Irish under a native government representing the people of the greater part of Ireland. An attempt is made in this chapter to explain how this anomalous situation came about.

Some indication has already been given[2] of the linguisto-demographic situation about the middle of the nineteenth century. Accordingly it seems appropriate to deal at this point with later stages of the decline as shown in reports of the censuses of population carried out between 1851 and 1911. It would be unwise to accept the census figures as completely accurate. Questions about language were included for the first time in the enumeration of 1851, and it is probable that in that year the numbers of Irish-speakers were underestimated.[3] It was claimed for the 1881 census that it was more accurate than that of 1871.[4] The 1891 census

---

[1] *Foras feasa ar Éirinn* (4 vols, London, 1902–14), i (Ir. Texts Soc., vol. iv), pp 36–7.
[2] Above, iv, 384–7.
[3] Ibid., p. 384.
[4] *Census Ire., 1881*, pt II, *general report* [C 3365], H.C. 1882, lxxvi, 385; also see Garret FitzGerald, 'Estimates for baronies of minimum level of Irish-speaking amongst successive decennial cohorts: 1771–1781 to 1861–1871' in *R.I.A Proc.*, lxxxiv, sect. C (1984), at pp 117–18.

provides a useful basis for comparison with that of 1851, for it reflects the situation before the revival movement[1] began to distort the figures seriously. The 1911 figures must be assessed against the background of nearly twenty years of exhortation to people to learn Irish and to speak it. Unfortunately there are no figures for 1921, as there was no census in that year because of the disturbed state of the country.

It is clear from the 1851 census figures that by that time English had become the everyday language of the vast majority of the people of Ireland. Out of every 1,000 persons in the country 767 could not speak Irish whereas only 49 could not speak English. The total number of Irish-speakers was 1,524,286 or 23.3 per cent of the population, of whom 319,602 (4.9 per cent of the population) were Irish-speaking monoglots.[2] Of those aged under 10, only 11.4 per cent of boys and 10.5 per cent of girls could speak Irish. The percentages for all age-groups for the provinces were Leinster 3.5, Ulster 6.8, Munster 43.9, and Connacht 50.8. Nine counties of the east and north-east had each less than 1 per cent recorded as being able to speak Irish. On the other hand, in the three Leinster counties of Kilkenny, Louth, and Meath, with roughly 21,000, 19,000, and 9,000 Irish-speakers respectively, Irish was certainly an everyday language in some areas; and in most of the counties of Munster and Connacht[3] and in Donegal there were large areas where the number of Irish-speakers exceeded 50 per cent of the population.[4] Irish was still in general use in many towns throughout the country, although of course the towns were more anglicised than the surrounding districts; it was still necessary for many urban shopkeepers in dealing with their customers and continued to be so for several decades. The town of Galway was remarkable in having 61.4 per cent of its inhabitants Irish-speaking and 14.8 per cent of the Irish-speakers knowing only Irish. Also noteworthy is the fact that the three Munster cities had each a substantial number of Irish-speakers: Cork with 10,381 (12.1 per cent of the population), Limerick with 4,204 (7.9 per cent) and Waterford with 4,103 (16.2 per cent).

From 1851 onwards the decline in the use of Irish continued steadily, with successive enumerations revealing an acceleration in the decline in the numbers of those who spoke Irish only and in the numbers of those in the younger age-groups who could speak Irish. By 1891 the total Irish-speaking population had dropped to 680,245 (compared with 1,524,286 in 1851) or 14.5 per cent of the population, and there were only 38,121 Irish-speaking monoglots. Out of

---

[1] Below, pp 399–410.

[2] The importance of the existence of a substantial proportion of monoglots for the survival of any spoken language is generally recognised by linguistic scholars.

[3] Leitrim was an exception.

[4] Apart from some urban areas the smallest territorial unit used for enumerating Irish speakers in the census reports down to 1891 was the barony. In the whole of Ireland there were sixty-one baronies in 1851 in which the number of Irish-speakers exceeded 50 per cent of the population. The barony showing the greatest proportion of Irish-speakers was Aran (Co. Galway) where 92.4 per cent of the population were recorded as Irish-speaking and 60 per cent could not speak English.

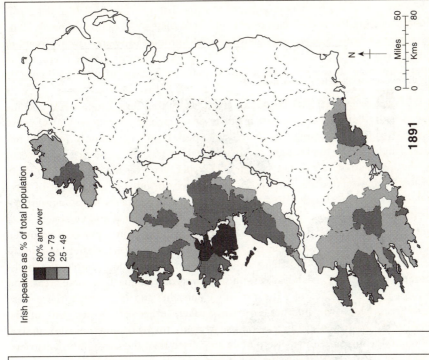

Irish speakers as % of total population

80% and over

50 - 79

25 - 49

1851

Miles
Kms

Map 1   IRISH-SPEAKERS, 1851, BY BARONIES, by Brian Ó Cuív

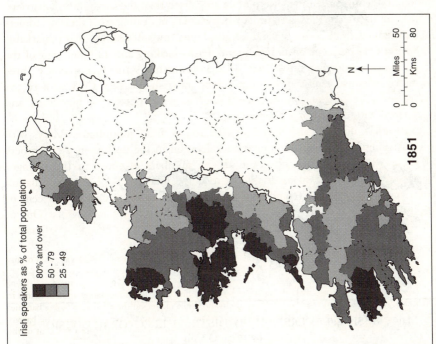

Irish speakers as % of total population

80% and over

50 - 79

25 - 49

1891

N

Miles
Kms

Map 2   IRISH-SPEAKERS, 1891, BY BARONIES, by Brian Ó Cuív

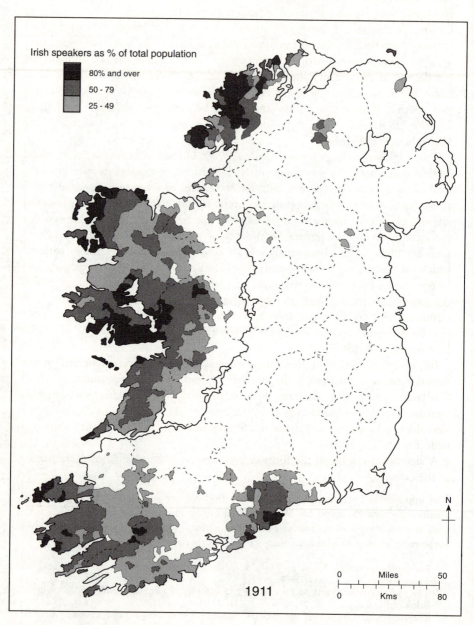

Irish speakers as % of total population

80% and over

50 - 79

25 - 49

1911

Miles
0　　　　　　　　　　　50

Kms
0　　　　　　　　　　　80

Map 3　IRISH-SPEAKERS, 1911, BY DISTRICT ELECTORAL DIVISIONS,
by Brian Ó Cuív

every 1,000 persons in Ireland 855 could not speak Irish whereas only 8 could not speak English. All counties showed a decrease in the total number of Irish-speakers,[1] some having dropped as much as 75 per cent since 1851, including Cavan, Fermanagh, Kilkenny, Limerick, Louth, and Meath. Donegal alone showed an increase in the percentage of the population that was Irish-speaking— 33.4 per cent compared with 28.7 per cent in 1851. Thus at the beginning of the last decade of the century the Irish-speaking areas were mainly to be found in Clare, Cork, Donegal, Galway, Kerry, Mayo, and Waterford; to a lesser extent in Limerick, Roscommon, Sligo, and Tipperary; and as small pockets of Irish-speakers in Armagh, Cavan, Londonderry, Kilkenny, Leitrim, Louth, Meath, Monaghan, and Tyrone.

Two factors significant for the future survival of Irish as a community language may be noted here: the percentage of Irish-speaking monoglots in relation to the total number of Irish-speakers, and the percentage of Irish-speakers aged under 10 in relation to the total population under 10. In the country as a whole the relevant figures for 1891 are 5.6 per cent for the first group, and 3.1 per cent for the second.[2] While the figures for most areas are much lower, those for certain areas are higher, and some remarkably so. This fact is demonstrated in table 2,[3] which lists, according to each county, the baronies that in 1891 showed more than 40 per cent of the people as Irish-speaking, and gives both the relevant figure and the percentage of the total number who were monoglot Irish-speakers. It is significant that on the whole Irish as a community language has survived in the twentieth century in those areas that showed a high proportion of monoglot Irish-speakers in 1891.

By 1901 the effects of the Gaelic revival movement were reflected in the census returns, for although the number of Irish-speakers continued to fall in Gaeltacht[4] areas, that is areas with substantial Irish-speaking communities, increases were recorded elsewhere in the country. These trends continued in the next decade, as can be seen from the figures for 1891, 1901, and 1911 shown in table 1.

A significant change in the form of presentation is noted in the general report of the census of 1911:

The information regarding district electoral divisions appears for the first time in the census reports of 1911, and has been tabulated in response to representations made to us that, in connection with the teaching of Irish in national schools, it was necessary to arrive at the particulars of smaller areas than those formerly dealt with.[5]

[1] For figures see table 1, below, pp 431–2. More detailed analysis will be found in Ó Cuív, *Irish dialects and Irish-speaking districts* (Dublin, 1951).

[2] This may be compared with 28.8 per cent, which is the figure for the age-group 50 and under 70.

[3] Below, pp 433–4.

[4] The term 'Gaeltacht' (earlier spelling 'Gaedhealtacht') is used in a broad sense here, but has acquired a technical administrative connotation since 1921, designating areas that are accorded special treatment under various government departments and agencies.

[5] *Census Ire., 1911, general report*, p. lvii [Cd 6663], H.C. 1912–13, cxviii, 57.

The change was mainly due to the introduction of the 'bilingual programme',[1] which for the most part was carried out in schools where Irish was the native language of a large number of the pupils. Thus the statistics contained in the 1911 report give a much clearer view of the areas where Irish was still the normal community language, as well as other areas where it continued to be spoken, but to a more limited extent.

Analysis of the figures shows that 80 per cent or over of the population were recorded as Irish-speaking in 101 district electoral divisions (D.E.D.s), between 50 per cent and 79 per cent in 317 D.E.D.s, and between 25 per cent and 49 per cent in 426 D.E.D.s.[2] These D.E.D.s covered much of the seven coastal counties of Waterford, Cork, Kerry, Clare, Galway, Mayo, and Donegal, with a few areas in Limerick, Tipperary, Leitrim, Roscommon, Sligo, Antrim, Cavan, Monaghan, Tyrone, Louth, and Kildare.[3]

The total number of Irish-speakers in the country was given as 582,446, or 13.3 per cent of the population, but there were only 16,873 Irish-speaking monoglots, that is 2.9 per cent of the Irish-speaking population, and the total number of Irish-speakers in the areas covered by the highest category referred to above,[4] that

---

[1] Below, pp 405–6.

[2] The 'commission of inquiry into the preservation of the Gaeltacht', appointed in 1925, applied the term 'Irish-speaking district' to any district where 80 per cent or more of the population was Irish-speaking and 'partly Irish-speaking district' to any district where not less than 25 per cent and not more than 79 per cent of the population was Irish speaking; and it applied the term 'Gaeltacht' to those districts combined (*Report of Coimisiún na Gaeltachta, 1925*, sects 18, 19, 23). The term 'Fíor-ghaeltacht' came to be applied to the first category.

[3] I have included Maynooth D.E.D. in Co. Kildare which showed 26.1 per cent Irish speaking, but this figure is misleading, being due to the location there of St Patrick's College.

[4] These are areas that under the terms devised by the Gaeltacht commission would be classed as 'Fíor-ghaeltacht'. Attention must be called to a disparity between the figure of 93,684 cited here and the figure of 149,677 cited in vol. viii ('Irish language with special tables for the Gaeltacht areas') of *Census Ire., 1926* as the 'actual numbers of Irish-speakers in 1911' in those districts of Saorstát Éireann (the 26 counties of the Irish Free State) that it classified as 'Irish-speaking areas' (Fíor-ghaeltacht). That the '80 per cent or over' criterion was not applied strictly is manifest from table 4 of the census report, where the figures for Irish-speakers as a percentage of total population in the so-called Fíor-ghaeltacht were given as 79 per cent in 1911 and 77.3 per cent in 1926. The basis for this obvious statistical contradiction is the decision of those charged with carrying out the census of 1926 and compiling the report to identify the Fíor-ghaeltacht (Irish-speaking areas) and Breac-ghaeltacht (partly Irish-speaking areas) as 'these areas . . . as defined in the report of the Gaeltacht commission, 1925' (op. cit., p. vi). Reference is made to this matter in vol. x (general report), p. 130, where we read: 'The delimitation of areas by the Gaeltacht commission . . . has been adopted in this report. The unit of delimitation was the district electoral division.' This must be read in conjunction with the report of the Gaeltacht commission, from which it emerges that the figure of 149,677 cited both there (sect. 25) and in vols viii and ix of *Census Ire., 1926* does not relate to the 101 D.E.D.s referred to above, but to a very different area. In determining the delimitation of the districts forming the Gaeltacht the commission adopted the D.E.D. as the 'unit of area employed in building up these districts', but also took 'the circumstances of the immediate locality . . . into consideration in determining the boundary lines of the Gaeltacht areas', with the result that 'these boundary lines are not always coterminous with the boundaries of the district electoral divisions' (sect. 24). The report goes on: 'It is not feasible, nor necessary, to define a unit of area for purposes of differentiation. Some district electoral divisions, in which the percentage of Irish-speakers is less than 80, have been included in the "Irish-speaking districts".'

is 80 per cent and over, was only 93,684. We can conclude that while the majority of those recorded as Irish-speaking still belonged to Gaeltacht areas, there was a significant number for whom Irish was an acquired second language. Although statistical information is lacking for the decade 1911–21, there is little doubt that the regional trends of decline and growth seen in the two decades 1891–1911 continued between 1911 and 1921.

IN considering the causes of the decline of Irish between the famine and the end of the union it is necessary to look at the decline against a very varied background. This includes the attitude of the government to the use of the Irish language in various areas of public life, the altered status of the catholic church after 1829, the economic condition of the majority of the people, and the demographic changes that followed the great famine of the 1840s.

Government policy was linked to the continuing belief that a difference of language contributed to a spirit of separateness and disaffection—a belief that had been expressed in the seventeenth century in Spenser's phrase 'The speech being Irish, the heart must needs be Irish'.[1] The fact that the existence of Irish was taken into account when plans were drawn up for the 1851 census of population, and that questions about Irish continued to feature in all subsequent censuses, did not imply that Irish would be given due recognition for use in government business or in education. English was the sole official language of government officials, of local authorities, and of the courts.[2] Of course Irish was used in various circumstances by government employees, such as members of the constabulary, who of necessity used it in their duties in districts that were mainly Irish-speaking. But in general little heed was paid to the disadvantages suffered by those whose normal language was Irish and who at most had only a very limited

---

[1] Spenser, *View*, ed. Renwick (1970), pp 67–8; see above, iii, 513; v, 536–7. The attitude referred to here is reflected in the period under review in, for example, the suspicion with which members of the Gaelic League were treated by the authorities, and especially the police, in the early decades of the twentieth century; see below, pp 413, 417. For other aspects of government action see below, pp 395–6, 399–400, 405–9, 411, 415.

[2] A contributor to *Irishman*, 13 Aug. 1859 (pp 74–5), wrote of Irish-speaking witnesses being insulted and refused expenses by judges. In 1897 a witness was committed for contempt of court at Dungarvan petty sessions for insisting on giving evidence in the Irish language. A protest by Dungarvan town commissioners led to an assurance being given by the lord chancellor that 'he fully recognises the obligation upon all magistrates of securing to Irish-speaking witnesses the utmost facility for expressing themselves fully and clearly when giving evidence in a court of justice, and trusts that magistrates will satisfy themselves before requiring any such witness to give evidence in English that he is as fully capable of giving evidence in that language as in his own.' See *Report of the executive committee of the Gaelic League, 1897*, p. 7.

EDITOR'S NOTE: In *Rex* v. *Burke* (1858), it was decided in the Irish court for crown cases reserved that a witness electing to give evidence in Irish was not to be harassed on the grounds that there was some evidence that the witness spoke and understood English; in cross-examination of a witness, linguistic competency was to be regarded as a collateral issue (8 Cox's Criminal Cases 44). The treatment of the Irish language and of Irish-speakers at the hands of the common law legal system in Ireland is being researched by Benedict Ó Floinn. We are indebted for this reference and information to Professor W. N. Osborough of the school of law, University College, Dublin.

command of English. The disregard for Irish was manifested in a variety of ways. For instance, Irish-speakers were often denied justice in the courts because of their inability to understand evidence given against them, and anglicised forms of names, both personal and place names, were used for official purposes instead of Gaelic forms, with the result that within a few generations one of the most distinctive marks of Irish identity was blurred.[1]

Increasingly in the course of the nineteenth century St Patrick's College, Maynooth, was a training ground for priests destined to a considerable extent to minister to their flocks through the medium of English. There seems to be no evidence that the Irish hierarchy ever planned collectively to ensure that the clergy would be competent in both Irish and English.[2] There were of course exceptions among the bishops,[3] just as there were many priests who were fluent Irish-speakers and used Irish in carrying out their religious duties, but the trend nationally and locally was to use English in church affairs—in public prayers, sermons, instructions, notices, inscriptions, church documents, and so on—except in circumstances where Latin would be the normal language.

It is true that shortly after St Patrick's College was founded a chair of Irish was established and this was held from 1802 to 1820 by Paul O'Brien. In 1828 James Tully was appointed and held the chair for forty-eight years, that is, until 1876. These years could have been vital for the development of a policy favourable to the use of Irish in the church, but Tully seems to have achieved nothing of note for the language during his career. An tAthair Peadar Ua Laoghaire (Canon Peter O'Leary), who entered Maynooth in 1861, tells in his autobiography of the dismissive attitude to Irish that he encountered among his fellow students and of the consequent waning of his own interest in the language.[4] Elsewhere he recalled Tully, whom he referred to as 'an sean duine bocht a bhídh sa chathaoir sin le m' línn féin' (the unfortunate old fellow who occupied that chair in my time) and commented that his being professor was sufficient to bring about the demise of the language.[5] In striking contrast to Tully was Ulick J. Bourke of Tuam who, while studying in Maynooth during Tully's time as professor, compiled a grammar of Irish 'to supply a want under which my fellow students in Maynooth College have laboured in the study of their mother tongue'.[6] Bourke went on to become president of St Jarlath's College, Tuam, and continued to be a staunch advocate of the use of Irish. The chair of Irish in Maynooth remained vacant from

---

[1] Use of an Irish name-form could lead to prosecution in the courts; see below, pp 410–11.

[2] A positive policy to use the Irish language to the greatest possible extent might have been expected as a reaction to the activities of the Bible societies (for which see above, iv, 376–8) but this did not come about.

[3] Among them was John MacHale (archbishop of Tuam 1834–81). Peadar Ua Laoghaire tells in his autobiography how MacHale made him aware of the neglect of Irish literature that he (Ua Laoghaire) had shown in a prize-winning essay in English that he wrote while a student in Maynooth (*Mo sgéal féin* (Dublin, 1915), ch. XIII).

[4] Ibid.

[5] Pádraig Ó Fiannachta, *Léann na Cléire* (Maigh Nuad, 1986), p. 177.

[6] *The college Irish grammar* (Dublin, 1856), p. 1.

1876 to 1892 when Eugene O'Growney, an ardent supporter of the language, was appointed. His appointment marked the beginning of a new phase during which Irish in university education became a subject of controversy in the college.[1]

The catholic church's attitude to Irish is reflected in the small number of devotional works in that language printed in the second half of the nineteenth century. These included a few 'catechisms' of doctrine and reprints of earlier works.[2] The only substantial new work was a translation by John MacHale of part of the Old Testament.[3] It may be noted, by way of contrast, that on the protestant side a collection of sermons, translated from English, was published in 1847,[4] a revised version of the complete New Testament in Munster Irish was published in 1858,[5] and a new edition of the Book of Common Prayer, in Irish and English, was published in 1861.[6]

It must also be noted that the activities of the Bible societies, which reached their peak in the first half of the nineteenth century, continued to a limited extent in the second half, and that there were Irish-speaking clergymen in a number of places.[7] One such was Séamas Goodman, a native of west Kerry. He studied in Trinity College, Dublin, from about 1848 to 1852, after which he became curate, then incumbent, in Skibbereen (County Cork) and subsequently (1879–96) professor of Irish in Trinity College. There is ample evidence of his genuine interest in the Irish language and also in Irish music.[8]

BEHIND the statistical information set out in the first part of this chapter is the fact that the majority of the Irish-speaking population was to be found in rural areas and belonged to the poorer sections of the community. Migration from these

---

[1] See below, pp 407–8.

[2] An edition of *An Teagasg Críosduidhe*, a dual language (Irish and English) catechism of Christian doctrine first published in Paris in 1742, was published 'for the royal catholic college of St Patrick, Maynooth' in 1848. Ulick J. Bourke's *Sermons in Irish-Gaelic* (Dublin, 1877) was a re-edition of James Gallagher's *Sixteen Irish sermons* (Dublin, 1736), and *Searcleanmhain Chríosd* (Dublin, 1886) was a reprint of the translation of Thomas à Kempis's *De imitatione Christi* by Domhnall Ó Súilleabháin, first published in Dublin in 1822.

[3] John MacHale, *An Irish translation of the Holy Bible*, i: *Genesis to Joshua* (Tuam, 1861). MacHale also translated non-religious works, including some of Moore's *Melodies* and the 'Iliad'.

[4] Séamus Ó Súilliobháin, *Seanmoirighe Gairid agus Abharáin Diaga do leanbhuighe* (Dublin, 1847).

[5] Ríobeárd Ó Catháin, *Tiomna Nuadh ár dTighearna agus ár Slánuightheóra Íosa Críosd* (Dublin, 1858).

[6] For this, and for another edition published in 1856, see H. R. McAdoo, 'The Irish translations of the Book of Common Prayer' in *Éigse*, ii (1940–41), pp 250–7.

[7] Proselytising activity by protestants, which was particularly marked during the famine period and in the following years, led to the introduction of the word *súpar* (from English 'souper'), which was applied to protestant ministers and others who distributed free soup to needy catholics and at the same time encouraged them to abandon the catholic faith; see Desmond Bowen, *The protestant crusade in Ireland, 1800–70: a study of protestant–catholic relations between the act of union and disestablishment* (Dublin and Montreal, 1978). Proselytisers were particularly active in Achill (Co. Mayo) and even had their own printing press and published several religious works in Irish; see Raymond Gillespie and Gerard Moran (ed.), *'A various country': essays in Mayo history, 1500–1900* (Westport, Co. Mayo, 1987), p. 124.

[8] See *Béaloideas*, xiii (1943), pp 286–91; xxii (1953), pp 112–14; *Kerry Arch. Soc. Jn.*, vi (1973), pp 152–65.

areas existed in the eighteenth century and the first part of the nineteenth century, but the pace of migration, and of emigration from the country as a whole, accelerated after the famine. Thus the twin features of high mortality in the famine years and of continuing emigration thereafter reduced the rural population. But along with this reduction came a reduction in the proportion of the population whose normal language was Irish. Economic and social pressures played a major part in the changing linguistic situation. Long before the famine the upper strata of the catholic population—landed gentry, merchants, and professional men—had abandoned Irish for English in their efforts to gain acceptance on terms of equality with protestants. In the course of the nineteenth century more and more Irish-speaking catholics in rural Ireland and in the country towns followed suit. The 'utility' argument for learning and speaking English, voiced by O'Connell before the famine,[1] had more force than ever when opportunities for rural employment diminished. For emigrants heading for Britain, America, or Australia the advantage of being able to speak English was obvious. Likewise, English was a necessity for those with ambitions to avail themselves of opportunities of employment in Ireland, such as in the police forces, or as national teachers, or in various branches of business or administration. Hence it became a common practice for Irish-speaking parents to speak such English as they had to their children while using Irish with one another. Thus in many homes the vernacular changed from Irish to English in one or two generations. This drastic course taken by parents might have been avoided if there had been at that time an effective advocacy of bilingualism—what Peadar Ua Laoghaire so aptly described as 'dhá arm aigne' (two tools of the intellect).[2]

Whereas the various Bible societies had recognised the benefit of teaching Irish, and Thaddeus Connellan of the London Hibernian Society had favoured a policy of bilingualism, Irish was allowed no place in the system of national education that was established in 1831.[3] A policy of bilingualism for those areas in which Irish was the common language was recommended by Thomas Davis in 1843[4] but his views were regarded as idle dreaming even by most of his friends in the Young Ireland group. Twenty-five years after the beginning of the national schools, the advantages of bilingualism were recognised and pointed out by one of the national education board's chief inspectors, P. J. (later Sir Patrick) Keenan.[5] In 1856 he wrote:

The children of parents who at present speak Irish only, will, through the course of education pursued in the national schools and the experience of home, speak English and

---

[1] Above, iv, 381.

[2] Ua Laoghaire was born in 1839, so his formative years were just before and after the famine. From his childhood he was given the facility of knowing both Irish and English. He was taught English reading and writing at home by his mother, but he also attended two national schools before going to study in lay catholic 'Latin' schools. See *Mo sgéal féin*, chs V and VII (especially pp 51–3).

[3] Cf. above, iv, 376–8; v, 536–7.

[4] In the article 'Our national language' in *Nation*, 30 Dec. 1843.

[5] Below, p. 524.

Irish when they grow up; but *their* children will in nine cases out of every ten speak English only. In this way the Irish language will gradually fall into disuse, and be, perhaps, forgotten. Many good men would rejoice at this; but they seem to me to forget that the people might know both Irish and English, and they also forget that by continuing to speak Irish and *learning English through its medium*, the latter language would be enriched by the imagery and vigour of the mother tongue, and the process of learning would be a mental exercise of so varied and powerful a character, that its disciplinal effect upon the mind would be equal, in itself, and by itself, to a whole course of education of the ordinary kind. The shrewdest people in the world are those who are bilingual: borderers have always been remarkable in this respect . . . The real policy of the educationist would, in my opinion, be to teach Irish grammatically and soundly to the Irish-speaking people, and then to teach them English through the medium of their native language.[1]

Keenan's recognition of what would have been sound educational practice in mid-nineteenth-century Ireland did not blind him to the reality of the situation: that people felt the need to be able to speak English. Writing in 1857 of the passion of the Donegal islanders for education he stated that it

may be traced to one predominant desire—the desire to speak English. They see, whenever a stranger visits their islands, that prosperity has its peculiar tongue as well as its fine coat; they see that whilst the traffickers who occasionally approach them to deal in fish, or in kelp, or in food, display the yellow gold, they count it out in English; and if they ever cross over to the mainland for the 'law', as they call any legal process, they see that the solemn words of judgement have to come second-hand to them through the offices of an interpreter. Again, English is spoken by the landlord, by the stray official who visits them, by the sailors of the ships that lie occasionally in their roadsteads, and by the schoolmaster himself; and whilst they may love the cadences, and mellowness, and homeliness of the language which their fathers gave them, they yet see that obscurity and poverty distinguish their lot from the English-speaking people; and accordingly, no matter what the sacrifice to their feelings, they long for the acquisition of the 'new tongue', with all its prizes and social privileges. The keystone of fortune is the power of speaking English, and to possess this power there is a burning longing in their breasts that never varies, never moderates. It is the utilitarian, not the abstract, idea of education which influences them, for they know nothing of the pleasures of literature, or of the beauties and wonders of science. The knowledge which they thirst for in the school is, therefore, confined to a speaking use of the English language.[2]

Modern scholars differ in their assessment of the attitude of the commissioners towards the Irish language, but in the light of Keenan's comments, which they themselves published, it can hardly be true that they were unaware in 1857 of the fact that Irish was the vernacular of a sizeable proportion of the rural population.[3] Not many years later a commentator, writing about Irish, said that 'the so-called

---

[1] *Twenty-second report of the commissioners on national education in Ireland*, ii, 75 [2142-11], H.C. 1856, xxvii, pt 2, p. 81.
[2] *Twenty-third report of the commissioners on national education in Ireland*, i, 143-4 [2304], H.C. 1857-8, xx (no MS pagination).
[3] For such a view see above, v, 537.

board of national education, which should have been a channel for its [the Irish language's] cultivation side by side with English (the one aiding the other), has been deliberately made an instrument to stamp it out withal'.[1]

In spite of Keenan's observations and advocacy more than twenty years passed before permission was given in 1878 for a limited use of Irish in national schools. In the same year a system of support from public funds for intermediate education was set up,[2] and Irish was included in its programme as an optional subject under the title 'Celtic language and literature'. It must be remembered that secondary education had been available to only a small proportion of the population and that, in the lay and ecclesiastical intermediate schools providing it, Irish was not generally a subject.[3] The new developments were milestones in the history of Irish in education, and it is appropriate at this point to consider how they came about.

The official admission of Irish into the schools came after more than thirty years of activity relating to Irish in various quarters during which awareness of the decline in the use of the language in everyday life was paralleled by a growing realisation of the importance of Irish as a key to the country's historical, literary, and linguistic heritage. Interest in Ireland's manuscript remains on the part of the ascendancy was not new,[4] but it was given an impetus through the activities of the Royal Irish Academy, and especially through the work initiated under the authority of the ordnance survey office.[5] Since membership of the academy was very limited, it is not surprising that a number of learned societies came into being to cater for this growing interest. The work of men such as George Petrie, Eugene O'Curry, and John O'Donovan resulted in the publication of editions of Irish texts from manuscripts under such auspices as the Irish Archaeological and Celtic Society (which published twenty-two volumes in the period 1841–80), the Celtic Society (six volumes, 1847–55), and the Ossianic Society (six volumes, 1854–61). These societies were all non-sectarian and were supported by many belonging to the upper levels of society as well as by both protestants and catholics.

Financial support for antiquarian Irish studies was given by the government on a number of occasions. Thus in 1843 it contributed £600 for the purchase by the Royal Irish Academy of a valuable collection of Irish manuscripts that had been built up over the preceding years by the Dublin firm of Hodges, Smith, & Co.; in 1852 it established the brehon law commission to make provision for the editing and publication of early Irish law texts; and from 1865 on it granted funds to the Royal Irish Academy for the support of Irish studies. The subsequent publication

---

[1] *Irishman*, 13 Oct. 1866, p. 250.

[2] 41 & 42 Vict., c. 66 (16 Aug. 1878); below, pp 524–5.

[3] There were some exceptions. For instance Irish was taught in the catholic diocesan college of St Jarlath in Tuam. Also there is mention in *Nation*, 7 Sept. 1844 (p. 762, col. 3) of Irish being taught in a school in Galway endowed by James Hardiman. And of course Irish was taught in St Columba's College in Stackallen, Co. Meath, which was established 'to supply the Church of Ireland with a body of clergy, able to convey the gospel to their countrymen in their own language'; see above, iv, 377.

[4] See, for example, above, iii, 530; iv, 392–402; also Nessa Ní Shéaghdha, 'Collectors of Irish manuscripts: motives and methods' in *Celtica*, xvii (1985), pp 1–28.

[5] Above, iv, 418–19.

by the stationery office of the *Ancient laws of Ireland* (6 vols, 1865–1901), and the inclusion in the Rolls Series of editions of Irish historical texts, including *Chronicon Scottorum* (1866), *Cogadh Gaedhel re Gallaibh* (1867), *Annals of Loch Cé* (1871), and *Annals of Ulster* (1887–1901), provided substantial volumes to take their place beside John O'Donovan's pioneering work *Annals of the Kingdom of Ireland*, published in seven volumes in 1848–51 by Hodges, Smith, & Co. Special mention must be made of the *Bibliography of Irish philology and of printed Irish literature*, published under the authority of the stationery office in 1913. This indispensable research tool, which demonstrates the extent of Irish scholarship in the preceding years, was compiled by Richard Irvine Best in the National Library of Ireland, established in 1877, one year before the developments in educational policy that have been referred to above.

Irish found a permanent place in the university system with the establishment in 1838 of a chair of Irish in Trinity College, Dublin. Not long after this came the establishment of the queen's colleges, all of which had chairs of Celtic languages. John O'Donovan was appointed professor in Belfast but had few students. In Cork the first professor was Owen Connellan, one-time proselytiser and, according to himself, Irish historiographer to George IV and William IV. He had published a few works on Irish grammar, and according to a record in the minutes of the council of the Royal Irish Academy he had been employed in 1831 to make a copy of the fourteenth-century Book of Ballymote for William IV.[1] In Galway the first professor was Cornelius Mahony, succeeded in 1856 by John O'Beirne Crowe who produced some editions of medieval Irish texts during the following twenty years. The most notable feature about the subject 'Celtic' in the queen's colleges was the almost complete lack of students. Indeed the dearth of students was such that a royal commission reported in 1858: 'We cannot recommend that the chairs of the Celtic languages should be retained.'[2] Quite different was the situation in the catholic university in Dublin, where Cardinal Newman had determined that Irish studies would have a place of high honour, and Eugene O'Curry's lectures[3] fully justified the decision whereby Irish literature and antiquities were provided for under a chair of Irish history and archaeology.

Outside Ireland the Celtic languages, and Irish in particular, had attracted the interest of scholars in the eighteenth and nineteenth centuries, but in 1853 came an event that ushered in a new era for Irish studies and ensured that henceforth Irish would be of academic importance in continental Europe, in Britain, and eventually in America. This was the publication of Johann Kasper Zeuss's *Grammatica Celtica*, which laid a sound basis for all future study of Old and Middle Irish. The second half of the nineteenth century saw the burgeoning of

[1] This is one of two Irish manuscripts in Windsor castle library.
[2] *Report of the commissioners appointed to inquire into the progress and condition of the queen's colleges* . . ., pp 21–2 [2413], H.C. 1857–8, xxi, 81–2.
[3] His great learning is reflected in the lectures and related material published in *Lectures on the manuscript materials of ancient Irish history* (Dublin, 1861) and *On the manners and customs of the ancient Irish* (London, 1873).

interest in Celtic studies and the emergence into prominence of scholars such as Alexander Bugge, Henry d'Arbois de Jubainville, Georges Dottin, Joseph Loth, Kuno Meyer, Holger Pedersen, John Strachan, Rudolf Thurneysen, Ernst Windisch, and Heinrich Zimmer, all of whom contributed to the new prestige that attached to the study of Irish. The scholarly activity outside Ireland was matched by the labours of successive generations of Irish scholars: O'Donovan and O'Curry, together with others such as George Petrie and James H. Todd, from the 1830s to the 1860s, and, in the later years of the century, Robert Atkinson, William Hennessy, Standish Hayes O'Grady, and Whitley Stokes were followed by the generation of Douglas Hyde, John MacNeill, and Osborn Bergin, all of whom combined academic scholarship with activity in the revival movement.

While solid foundations for the higher academic study of Irish were being laid from the 1830s on, the call that Davis had made in the *Nation* for the retention and cultivation of Irish as a vernacular evoked no major response in any quarter although there were a few positive reactions.[1] The great famine, with its consequent deaths and emigration, was a major factor in the declining use of Irish, and from time to time there were signs in the columns of the *Nation* and elsewhere that some Irishmen were aware of this decline and appreciated what the loss of the language might mean in relation to nationhood. Among the politicians of his day William Smith O'Brien deserves mention for his role as Irish scholar and scribe and as an advocate of teaching Irish in schools.[2] Also deserving of mention is Richard D'Alton of Tipperary, a prosperous businessman who recognised the threat to Irish and decided to set about a revival in its use. To encourage people to learn it he founded in 1862 a short-lived journal, *An Fíor-Éireannach*, which began publication in Tipperary. He saw the need for organised effort and in his journal he wrote about establishing societies for the promotion of Irish as a spoken language in cities, towns, and villages. However, his efforts failed for lack of support.[3]

At yet another level interest in later Irish literature was being kept alive by such men as Edward Walsh and John O'Daly. In their joint work *Reliques of Irish Jacobite poetry* (1844), in Walsh's *Irish popular songs* (1847), and in O'Daly's *The poets and poetry of Munster* (1849) many readers got their first knowledge of eighteenth-century poetry in Irish. Walsh, born in 1805, was sympathetic to the Young Ireland movement and was dismissed from his post as teacher in the prison

---

[1] For Davis and the Irish language see above, iv, 382. One such reaction is seen in *Nation*, 17 May 1845, p. 513, which carried an advertisement of the opening in Liverpool of a school in which Irish would be taught in evening classes.

[2] For examples of his activity in relation to Irish manuscripts see *R.I.A. cat. Ir. MSS*, general index. He appears as an advocate of bilingualism in *Irishman*, 21 Aug. 1858, p. 83. Four years later Irish was introduced to schools in Co. Clare on his advice (*Irishman*, 22 Aug. 1863, p. 118).

[3] D'Alton collected several Irish manuscripts and also transcribed a number of items. Eleven of his manuscripts were presented to the Royal Irish Academy by his son W. F. D'Alton in 1941 and 1943. The academy was also the beneficiary of sizeable bequests made in memory of Richard D'Alton by his son, and by his daughter Mrs Alice Kennedy.

school on Spike Island in Cork because he had a clandestine meeting with John Mitchel who was being transported to Bermuda.[1] Walsh died in 1850, but O'Daly, born in 1800, lived on until 1878 and thus bridged the gap between the Young Irelanders and the later political and revolutionary movements that saw a shift in attitudes to Irish. In his capacity as author, publisher, and bookseller over a period of nearly forty years O'Daly had many contacts with scholars and quietly passed on his interest to others, including the young Hyde.[2]

Interest in the language was also sustained to some extent in this period by the inclusion of items in Irish in newspapers and journals. Thus between 1866, when it first appeared, and 1882 the *Shamrock* published a number of Irish songs, some with music, and also a series of 'Lessons in Irish' (1872–5). Other periodicals that carried Irish-language contributions at that time were *Young Ireland* and the *United Irishman*.[3] In the later years of the century, and especially after the foundation of the Gaelic League, Irish contributions became a regular feature in a number of newspapers and periodicals and attracted a fair degree of interest.[4]

The combination of forces and interests outlined in the preceding paragraphs led to the foundation in 1876 of the Society for the Preservation of the Irish Language, with Archbishop MacHale as its patron, Lord Francis N. Conyngham as its president, and Isaac Butt and the O'Conor Don among its vice-presidents in its first year, these being joined later by Marshal MacMahon, president of the French republic. Among the objects of the society was 'to procure that the Irish language shall be taught in the schools of Ireland, especially in the Irish-speaking districts'.[5] In pursuit of this aim the society addressed a memorial to the commissioners of national education urging that Irish be placed on the results programme for national schools. There were 1,300 signatories including members of the catholic hierarchy, the Church of Ireland bishop of Ossory and other dignitaries of that church, the lord mayor of Dublin, forty M.P.s, and many others prominent in various walks of life. Within three months of the date of the memorial (17 June 1878) it was announced that Irish would be placed on the same footing as Greek, Latin, and French as regards results fees. Although this was only a minor concession it represented a beginning in the process of establishing an official place for Irish in the educational system. This success was soon followed by another when, largely through the urging of the O'Conor Don in

---

[1] See John Mitchel, *Jail journal* (Dublin, 1913; reprint, 1982), ch. 1.

[2] See 'Congantóirí Sheáin Uí Dhálaigh' in *Éigse*, i–iv (1939–44); Dubhglas de híde, *Mise agus an Connradh* (Baile Átha Cliath, 1937), pp 15–19; also Dominic Daly, *The young Douglas Hyde* (Dublin, 1974).

[3] In this connection see P. S. O'Hegarty, 'Notes on the Irish language columns of "The Shamrock"' in *Irish Book Lover*, xxix (June 1945), pp 104–8.

[4] As a result of the growth of interest in the language among emigrants to the United States of America such journals as *An Gaodhal* (New York) and *The Irish Echo* (Boston) published items in Irish. It may also be noted at this point that Irish emigrants began to show an interest in the preservation of Irish manuscripts: see below, p. 414.

[5] *Society for the Preservation of the Irish Language, list of the council, officers, etc., 1878–9* (Dublin, 1879), p. 17.

parliament, Irish was introduced into secondary schools when the Irish intermediate education board was set up in 1878. Two years later Irish was placed on the curriculum for the royal university.[1]

These achievements of the society were followed in 1880 by the formation of a breakaway body called the Gaelic Union whose aim was to promote more vigorously the retention of Irish in the Irish-speaking districts and to encourage English-speakers to learn the language. To this end its founders established the *Gaelic Journal*, a monthly periodical 'exclusively devoted to the interests of the Irish language'.[2] In its first issue it contained an article that had appeared in *The Times* on 4 October 1882, which derided the idea of Irish being cultivated as a 'national instrument'. In the light of subsequent events a sentence in this article is of particular interest: 'In deprecating the artificial cultivation of Irish as the national language, we are actuated by no dread or jealousy of its power to raise up fresh obstacles to political amalgamation.'[3] In fact the Irish language was destined to become a major factor in Irish politics and in resistance to British rule during the next forty years.

One of the contributors of original items in Irish to the first issue of the *Gaelic Journal* was Hyde, who had already contributed some Irish poems to the *Irishman* and was then a student in Trinity College, Dublin. He was to play a central role in matters relating to the Irish language and education during the next sixty years or so, culminating in his inauguration in 1938 as the first president of Ireland under the constitution of 1937. Despite the fact that his parents were English-speaking protestants of planter stock, Hyde had imbibed a love for the Irish language during his childhood in Roscommon, together with a sympathy with catholic fellow Irishmen that influenced his views on contemporary affairs. One of his earliest compositions was a patriotic song in Irish in which landlords were cursed for their treatment of their tenants.[4] In a poem composed a little later in honour of O'Donovan Rossa, he advised each of his fellow countrymen to buy a rifle and a revolver, telling them that no bank would pay them so much interest as such an investment would, for all that they might desire would come to them in a free Ireland, but in order to attain a free Ireland they would have to abandon talk and return to 'the old fashion'.

In the years before Hyde came to Dublin the writings on Irish literature and history by O'Donovan, O'Curry, O'Grady, Stokes, and others had opened up new cultural vistas, thus adding to the inspiration that was drawn from the writers of the Young Ireland movement. In Dublin Hyde found himself associating with two groups. The first, represented by the Society for the Preservation of the Irish

---

[1] For a summary of the achievements in education claimed by the Society for the Preservation of the Irish Language, see its report for 1910, p. 39.

[2] *Gaelic Journal*, i (1882), p. 17.

[3] Ibid., p. 30.

[4] *Irishman*, 29 Nov. 1879, p. 343. For a comment on this and others of these early compositions (including that for Rossa, quoted below) see pp xiv–xv of my introduction to Douglas Hyde, *A literary history of Ireland* (new ed., London, 1967).

Language and the Gaelic Union, was interested in the language, and Hyde not merely gave it his full support but also applied himself to the task of learning about earlier Irish literature. The second group consisted of littérateurs writing in English on Irish or Celtic themes. It may have been through John O'Leary, who had settled in Ireland in 1885 and was giving support to various nationalist and Irish cultural movements, that Hyde became so closely identified with the latter group, among whom were Yeats, Rolleston, and Katherine Tynan. He was held in high esteem by them and his connection with them was important for his future as a writer on Irish literary themes and a proponent of the revival of the Irish language.

Hyde had published a few traditional songs in Irish as far back as 1881. During the next seven or eight years he wrote down songs and prayers, stories and other items in many places in Connacht, and in 1889 came the first of many books in which this material was published, *Leabhar Sgeulaigheachta*, a collection of short folk-tales taken down from speakers in Roscommon, Leitrim, Galway, and Donegal. What makes this book particularly significant is that it contains a note 'On the reasons for keeping alive the Irish language', in which he condemned the attitudes towards Irish of the Anglo-Irish gentry, the authorities who appointed English-speaking magistrates and local officials to serve 'among a people to whom they could not make themselves intelligible', and 'the board of education, who do not recognise the language of those baronies where no English is spoken'.[1] In using such phrases as 'our living language' and 'our long slavery as a nation' Hyde identified himself with Irish-speaking Ireland. He now reinforced his words with an appeal:

I do not think there is much to add to what I have said here, except to observe that it is a national duty—I had almost said a moral one—for all those who speak Irish to speak it to their children also, and to take care that the growing generation shall know it as well as themselves: and in general, that it is the duty of all Irish-speakers to use their own language amongst themselves, and on all possible occasions, except where it *will not run*. For, if we allow one of the finest and richest languages in Europe, which, fifty years ago, was spoken by nearly four millions of Irishmen, to die out without a struggle, it will be an everlasting disgrace and a blighting stigma upon our nationality.[2]

In his next book, *Beside the fire*, Hyde was outspoken in his condemnation of 'the influential leaders of the race' from whom, he thought, a lead might have been expected:

The inaction of the parliamentarians, though perhaps dimly intelligible, appears, to me at least, both short-sighted and contradictory, for they are attempting to create a nationality with one hand and with the other destroying, or allowing to be destroyed, the very thing that would best differentiate and define their nationality. It is a making of bricks without straw. But the non-parliamentarian nationalists, in Ireland at least, appear to be thoroughly in harmony with them on this point.[3]

[1] Douglas Hyde, *Leabhar Sgeulaigheachta* (Dublin, 1889), pp 215–18.
[2] Ibid., p. 219.   [3] Douglas Hyde, *Beside the fire* (London, 1890), p. xlv n.

It is clear from a further comment that in referring to 'non-parliamentarian nationalists' he had O'Leary in mind. The fact that he was willing to criticise publicly a close friend shows how strongly he must have felt on the subject.

The academic year 1890–91 was spent by Hyde in Canada as visiting professor in the University of New Brunswick in Fredericton. By the time he returned Parnell's ten years of superb leadership of the Irish parliamentary party had come to an end and in political matters Ireland was entering the dark period that William O'Brien subsequently described as 'years of hellish strife'.[1] In the meantime Eugene O'Growney, a young priest from a district in County Meath where Irish was still spoken by some of the older generation, was organising the teaching of the language in Maynooth, and as a result of his frequent contributions to the *Gaelic Journal* his advice about learning Irish was being sought by people who were becoming conscious of the importance of Irish as a living language. Among these was John MacNeill, a young law clerk working in Dublin, who was a native of the Glens of Antrim. In an article published in 1891,[2] in which he appealed to the clergy to take up the cause of Irish, he spoke about the forces that in the past had prevented the fusion of the Irish people with the British, citing, among these, difference of language and physical resistance. Looking to the future he wrote 'Physical hostility is not to be dreamt of', and he made it clear that he saw language as the one possible differentiating force. He concluded his article by exhorting the 'young men of Ireland' to 'strike a good blow for Irish' by speaking it. Those who did not know Irish should, if possible, learn it, and he added: 'If we cannot learn Irish, we can at least stand up for it.' The years ahead were to prove how much easier it is to stand up for Irish than to learn it or to speak it consistently. They were also to prove that physical hostility towards British rule would not only be dreamed of but would become a reality and that MacNeill himself would play a central role in this unforeseen course of events.

Soon another voice was raised in support of Irish. As if to show the injustice of Hyde's condemnation of the parliamentarians for their supposed attitude to Irish, William O'Brien addressed the Cork National Society in 1892 and made a convincing case for the restoration of Irish.[3] Not the least interesting point in his address was the statement that he had put six months spent in jail in Galway to good use in learning to speak Irish. History was to repeat itself in this respect many times during the next fifty years and more.

Hyde returned to the attack in November 1892 in a presidential address to the National Literary Society in Dublin where he spoke of 'the necessity for de-anglicising the Irish nation'.[4] It is perhaps worth noting that he included games

---

[1] William O'Brien, *The Parnell of real life* (London, 1926), p. 206.

[2] 'Why and how the Irish language is to be preserved' in *I.E.R.*, xii (1891), pp 1099–1108.

[3] William O'Brien, *The influence of the Irish language on Irish national literature and character* (Cork, 1892).

[4] Douglas Hyde, 'The necessity for de-anglicising Ireland' in Charles Gavan Duffy, George Sigerson, and Douglas Hyde, *The revival of Irish literature* (London, 1894), pp 117–61.

and music in his remarks against what he called 'West-Britonism', and he even urged people to wear Irish clothes. His appeal for de-anglicisation, as he himself recalled years later,[1] evoked no great response among his audience. Undaunted, he delivered another address in Cork in the same strain. Then came the fateful meeting on 31 July 1893 at which a new organisation called Connradh na Gaedhilge, or the Gaelic League, was founded. Hyde provided the inspiration, but it was MacNeill who took the initiative and who did much of the work in the early years. One thing on which the founders were agreed was that the organisation, whose proclaimed object was 'to keep the Irish language spoken in Ireland', should be non-political and non-denominational. This was one of its sources of strength, for it enabled it to draw support from all quarters, and it continued to do so for twenty years during which there emerged a new Ireland, no longer satisfied with the measured concessions of British legislators but determined to have as of right a degree of independence consistent with its separate and ancient nationhood and willing to take up arms to attain it. There were other forces, concerned with cultural, social, economic, industrial, and political affairs, that contributed to the new spirit of independence, but the Gaelic League provided a forum where those of divergent views, interests, and loyalties could associate.

It is significant that the Gaelic League put down its roots so well in the years following the Parnell split. In the nation-wide despondency following the political débâcle, the language movement offered an outlet for the energies of those with nationalist inclinations. It already had an attraction for scholars and for the literary persons working through the medium of English, and in due course people in the Irish-speaking areas—who were fundamental to it—became aware of it. So it was that the call issued by Hyde and MacNeill and their colleagues from a room in 9 Lower Sackville Street in Dublin in 1893 was heard and acted upon, not only in Dublin, but throughout the country. It has been said that 'the weakness of the league from the beginning was that it was essentially a townsmen's organisation, centralised in Dublin, and never took real root in the Irish-speaking or semi-Irish-speaking districts'.[2] While it is true that the primary aim of preserving Irish as the everyday language of the Gaeltacht areas was not achieved, it is an undoubted fact that through its activities the league was instrumental in spreading a new consciousness of national distinctiveness throughout the country, and this was reflected in the number of people, adults as well as children, learning the language; and as a result of this the number of people registered as Irish-speaking in the censuses of population of 1901 and 1911.[3] After fifteen years of growth only thirty-four of the 599 league branches in existence were in Dublin and there was no county in Ireland without a branch. Moreover, branches in Britain provided

---

[1] De hÍde, *Mise agus an Connradh*, pp 33-4. On the adoption of Irish clothing, see below, p. 471.

[2] Thomas F. O'Rahilly, *Irish dialects past and present* (Dublin, 1932), p. 14.

[3] See above, pp 389-91, and appendix, table 1, pp 431-2.

centres for Irish activities,[1] and allied organisations in America, through their members, maintained a link with bodies sympathetic towards Irish political nationalism.

The earliest lists of members of the league show that bishops, priests, protestant clergymen, M.P.s, lawyers, journalists, teachers, students, civil servants, post office workers, soldiers, policemen, tradesmen, and labourers had joined. Although it was non-political its widespread organisation was to prove important in the spread of new ideas. Its branches were primarily concerned with fostering the Irish language by means of classes and allied activities. But through them many young men and women became aware of something far removed from the material attitude to life so common around them. Even if they did not pursue their linguistic studies very seriously they were liable to be receptive to other ideas that would not be looked on favourably by the British authorities. Moreover, during the first fifteen years of its existence the league pursued a policy of agitation that drew attention to it and established it as a powerful national force. The fact that the president of the league was a protestant intellectual and a graduate of the University of Dublin gave the movement a standing that was invaluable. Hyde's friendship with Yeats, Sigerson, Rolleston, George Moore, and others of the Anglo-Irish group carried their support. Members of the parliamentary party saw merit in the league's objectives and some of them were whole-hearted in their support. Once it became clear that an Irish Ireland was the league's aim and that its leaders really meant business, support came from other quarters, such as the Sinn Féin leader, Arthur Griffith, writing in the *United Irishman*, W. P. Ryan in the *Irish Peasant*, D. P. Moran in the *Leader*, and George Russell (A E) in the *Irish Homestead*. At an early stage Gaelic organisers were put on the road to foster interest in Irish in the Gaeltacht and elsewhere, and these did pioneer work. The contacts established by them in the language campaign were to prove useful later on in political and military organisation, but in the early years there was little, if any, thought of such developments.

Since the schools seemed to be the strongest single force militating against Irish, the league set out specially to tackle the problem caused by them, and for fifteen years it was constantly fighting on the educational front. The concern of the league was well founded, for Davis's dictum 'educate that you may be free' began to have added meaning with the spread of education. Among those who learned Irish in schools in Dublin in those years were Patrick Pearse (Pádraic MacPiarais) and Seán T. Ó Ceallaigh. Fate was to bring them together in the league, in the Irish Volunteers, and in the G.P.O. in Dublin in 1916.

---

[1] An Oxford University branch, which was established in 1904, had among its members Edmund Curtis (later Lecky professor of history in Trinity College, Dublin), T. A. Spring-Rice (whose sister took part in the gun-running to Howth in 1914), and Claude Chavasse (whose father was Anglican bishop of Liverpool). The branch seems to have ceased to function in 1916, in which year Chavasse, who was then its president, was arrested and imprisoned for speaking only Irish to a police constable in Ballingeary, Co. Cork. See Diarmaid Ó Briain, *Traolach Mac Suibhne* (Baile Átha Cliath, 1979), pp 73–4.

Ó Ceallaigh, inheritor of a fenian tradition, started as an unwilling student of Irish but came to find in the language a motive force with a considerable potential for political ends. So it came about that as early as 1902—long before either MacNeill or Pearse was involved in political activity—Ó Ceallaigh was a member of the Irish Republican Brotherhood and, as such, was ordered to use his position in the Gaelic League to infiltrate its central organising committee with I.R.B. members.[1] In his subsequent career as a Sinn Féin member of Dublin corporation he played an important part in the various moves to bring the Irish language into public life. Ó Ceallaigh, then, was involved at a young age both in political—and potentially revolutionary—activity and in the language movement.

Pearse, on the other hand, had been a dreamer, but his dreams at first were not of an Ireland freed by force of arms but rather of an Ireland with an intellectual mission. Addressing the New Ireland Literary Society in 1897 he said:

I believe that the ends which, as a nation, we have hitherto striven to attain are ignes fatui which are fated to elude us forever.

Others have been struck before now by the fact that hundreds of noble men and true have fought and bled for the emancipation of the Gaelic race, and yet have all failed. . . . May it not be that the ends they struggled for were ends never intended for the Gael? . . . The Gael is not like other men; the spade, and the loom, and the sword are not for him. But a destiny more glorious than that of Rome, more glorious than that of Britain awaits him: to become the saviour of idealism in modern intellectual and social life, the regenerator and rejuvenator of the literature of the world, the instructor of the nations, the preacher of the gospel of nature worship, hero worship, God worship—such, Mr Chairman, is the destiny of the Gael.[2]

Here we have an immature Pearse addressing a literary society, but it is perhaps significant that already the idea of hero worship was in his mind, for he was to become the greatest exponent of the cult of Cú Chulainn, which for him was in no way incompatible with the full practice of Christianity and which was to be one of the strands in the weaving of the new nationalism.[3] The following eighteen years, during which the promise of home rule was often repeated but never fulfilled, were to see a change in the spirit of many of the Irish people. In that time, too, there was a metamorphosis in Pearse himself. For him these years were to be years of labour for the Irish language, for education, and finally for Irish freedom, during which his dreams for Ireland changed and he came to see himself playing a central role in yet another sacrifice 'for the emancipation of the Gaelic race'. All that lay before him in 1897 when the league was so concerned with Irish in the schools.

The Gaelic League was unrelenting in its agitation to bring Irish into the forefront of the educational scene. Thus in the year 1900–01 it issued over 100,000 copies of eighteen pamphlets dealing mainly with education in primary

[1] Seán T. Ó Ceallaigh, Seán T. (Baile Átha Cliath, 1963), p. 50.
[2] P. H. Pearse, Three lectures on Gaelic topics (Dublin, 1898), pp 47–9.
[3] Above, pp 193, 365.

and secondary schools and the universities. Before 1900 Irish in the national schools was an extra subject for which the teacher received results fees from the national commissioners, but which had to be taught outside normal school hours.[1] Between 1900 and 1906 it became an optional ordinary subject for such senior pupils as wished to learn it, provided that the teacher was able and willing to teach it and that the inspector found that the other school subjects continued to be taught satisfactorily. From 1905 bilingual schools were encouraged in Irish-speaking districts, and 'a very liberal scale of fees for instruction in Irish in bilingual schools' had been granted by 1907.[2] Figures given in the house of commons in March 1906 showed that Irish was then being taught as an ordinary subject in 566 schools and as an extra subject in first-year courses in 1,062 schools, and that there was no county in Ireland where Irish was not being taught in some school.

An obvious difficulty in the promotion of Irish in the schools arose from the lack of trained teachers. The classes organised by various branches of the Gaelic League had a limited measure of success. However, in 1904 came the first of a number of Irish summer colleges established by private initiative mainly to provide adults with advanced and elementary instruction in the speaking, reading, and writing of Irish, and these assisted in giving the necessary training in Irish to teachers wishing to carry out the schools programmes. The first college, established in Ballingeary (County Cork), was followed by others in Cloughaneely (County Donegal), Toormakeady (County Mayo), and elsewhere, and by 1906 the national board had arranged that these colleges should be granted a £5 fee for each teacher who, having studied there for at least four weeks, was considered qualified to receive a bilingual certificate. When Irish was added to the programme in the teachers training colleges the way was open for a further expansion in the teaching of Irish in national schools. It is clear from the parliamentary debates on the home rule bill in 1912 that unionists were well aware of the influence of the Gaelic League and of the possibility of compulsion in the matter of Irish. In 1913 the *árd-fheis* of the league adopted a series of recommendations on education proposed by MacNeill and Ó Ceallaigh, including one that said that Irish should be taught to all pupils in every national school in Ireland, and another proposing that no student be admitted to a national teachers training college unless he had a good knowledge of Irish. At the same meeting a resolution was adopted condemning John Dillon for a statement he had made in the house of commons implying that if a policy of compulsion with regard to Irish were proposed in an Irish parliament it would meet with such opposition from many nationalist members that the unionist minority would be changed to a majority on the question. The resolution put forward by the league standing committee was very strongly worded: 'That we regard as a grave national danger Mr Dillon's pronouncement on the Irish education question . . . and that in the event of any

---

[1] Above, p. 396; below, pp 535–6.
[2] *The seventy-third report of the commissioners of national education in Ireland, school year 1906–7*, p. 11 [Cd 3699], H.C. 1907, xxii, 1085.

such policy being embodied in any future educational system in this country, we pledge ourselves to meet it with the most strenuous and uncompromising opposition.'[1] It appeared that as far as the league was concerned there would be no compromise—universal compulsory Irish was to be the rule. It is not certain what, in fact, would have been the attitude of the parliamentary party to the Irish language in an all-Ireland parliament. The 1918 general election and the government of Ireland act of 1920 ensured that the matter would never be put to the test. In the meantime support for Irish in the national schools continued to grow so that by 1919–20 it was being taught as an extra subject in 1,525 schools and the bilingual programme was being operated in 232 schools.

For the first twenty years after the establishment of the intermediate examination board Irish made slow progress at secondary level. In 1890 only 18 out of 230 boys who sat for the senior grade examination (that is, 7.8 per cent) took Irish. By 1900 the proportion had increased slightly to 25 out of 309 (8.1 per cent). But in 1910 the situation was very different for by then the figures were 295 out of 550 (53.6 per cent), and by 1919 805 out of 1,116 (72.1 per cent). This remarkable change was mainly due to the Gaelic League. The league's struggle in this area had come to a head in 1899 with the royal commission on intermediate education,[2] which considered the position of Irish in the secondary school system. Strong opposition to the teaching of Irish came from the provost of Trinity College and some of its professors but this was countered successfully by the league, which mobilised an array of scholarly experts from Ireland, Britain, and continental Europe who testified to the academic advantages to be derived from the study of Irish. Here Hyde proved to be a tower of strength, and it is greatly to his credit that when the battle over Irish brought the league into conflict with the authorities of Trinity College he did not stand aside. Indeed, although he regretted the need for doing so, he gave Provost George Salmon and Professors John Pentland Mahaffy and Robert Atkinson more than they bargained for, and in so doing he established the claims of Irish scholarship and research to recognition in Ireland. In fact he may have contributed indirectly to the revolutionary movement, for his successful campaign was followed by the foundation of the School of Irish Learning in Dublin, and one of its most generous supporters was Alice Stopford Green, who later became an equally strong supporter of Ireland's claims to political freedom. She was a friend of Casement and MacNeill, and when the Irish Volunteers were founded she gave considerable help in obtaining guns. After the rising she was one of the few who stood by Casement during his trial and, indeed, she bore a substantial part of the expenses of his defence.

The Gaelic League won its greatest battle on the education front when it brought to a successful conclusion in 1910 its campaign to have Irish made a compulsory subject for matriculation in the newly founded National University

<hr>

[1] *Connradh na Gaedhilge, Árd-Fheis 1913*, Clár na hOibre, p. 8.   [2] Below, pp 525–6.

of Ireland.[1] Yet with that campaign came the first serious differences among nationalists over a policy adopted by the league. Although compulsory Irish for matriculation was supported by many of the catholic clergy, it was opposed by the majority of the bishops, with whom the leaders of the parliamentary party, Redmond and Dillon, aligned themselves. During the campaign a manifesto, signed by Hyde and MacNeill and other members of the central committee, was issued on behalf of the league. It concluded:

If the Irish public stand by the declarations they have made, they cannot be defeated. The fears and apprehensions of the more timid will soon be dispelled. The Irish nation will achieve the most decisive victory it has ever achieved for nationality. The power of education is the greatest power possible to men. Hitherto it has been employed against Irish nationality. Henceforth it must be employed in the service of nationality.[2]

Among those who criticised the opponents of Irish as a requirement for matriculation was Michael O'Hickey, who had succeeded Eugene O'Growney as professor of Irish in Maynooth in 1896 and was fostering an interest in the language there.[3] His outspoken comments on the role played in the opposition to compulsory Irish by some members of the senate of the university,[4] including prominent ecclesiastics, as well as the support given to him publicly by students in Maynooth, outraged Daniel Mannix, president of the college, and led to O'Hickey's dismissal from his chair.[5] The day was won for Irish when the general council of county councils decided to agree to a university scholarship scheme only if Irish were made compulsory for matriculation. This was indeed a measure of the impact that the league had made on a representative body of Irishmen.

While campaigning on the educational front the league did not hesitate to use its influence whenever it saw an opportunity for some advantage for the language. Thus as early as 1896 it called on candidates in the parliamentary election for Kerry East to have speeches delivered in Irish at their meetings. In the following year it had some success in seeking rights for Irish-speakers when giving evidence in Irish in the courts of law. In the same year the very active Lee branch in Cork reported that a circular issued by it 'was the means of bringing a battering-ram of resolutions at the doors of the queen's college, Cork, urging the establishment of a Celtic lectureship, which is now as a fact established'.[6] The man appointed

---

[1] Below, p. 568.

[2] *Connradh na Gaedhilge, Árd-Fheis, 1909*, pp 5–6. See also MacNeill's pamphlet *Irish in the National University of Ireland* (Dublin, 1908).

[3] He was a prime mover in establishing in the college the Columban League, whose aim was the promotion of the study and use of Irish among students and priests. Early members included Paul Walsh and Lawrence Murray, both of whom became noted Irish scholars and historians. The league began publishing a journal, *Irisleabhar Muighe Nuadhad*, in 1907. It also published four volumes of sermons between 1906 and 1911.

[4] See Michael O'Hickey, *An Irish university, or else* (Dublin and Waterford, 1909).

[5] See Pádraig Ó Fiannachta, *Léann na Cléire* (Maigh Nuad, 1986), pp 140–99.

[6] *Report of the executive committee of the Gaelic League, 1897*, p. 16.

to the post was Osborn Bergin, a young protestant who had graduated in classics in Cork but had taken up the study of Irish some years earlier and had become a prominent member of the Gaelic League. He was later to be a member of the Celtic faculty in University College, Dublin, along with Hyde and MacNeill.

By 1900 the league had made Irish such an important issue that a full debate on it took place in the house of commons, with a large number of Irish members speaking in support of the language.[1] At the same time the league succeeded in getting support among the county councils and in Dublin corporation. With its strength growing it took up fresh issues. In 1901 it began a campaign to have St Patrick's day observed as a general holiday and this was achieved in the small space of two years.[2] By that time the national parade, organised by the league for St Patrick's day, had become an important event. In 1902 an industrial committee was formed by the league for the promotion of Irish industries, and some league branches even succeeded in having Irish made compulsory for employment under Dublin corporation, and within a few years the cause of Irish was reinforced by the election to that body of a number of members of Griffith's Sinn Féin party who were also ardent workers in the league. The league kept up the pressure on many fronts. In 1905 it organised a campaign to force the post office to accept mail addressed in Irish only. In its determination to win its point it sent 200 supporters in a body to the G.P.O. in Dublin to hand in parcels addressed in Irish. Because of the unwillingness of the post office officials to accept the mail, business was disrupted for a considerable time. None of those who took part in the 'battle of the G.P.O.' in 1905 foresaw that the G.P.O was to become the symbol of a resurgent Ireland.

The league's tactics in 1905 annoyed those who regarded Ireland as an English-speaking province of Britain, just as Parnell's policy of obstruction had infuriated his parliamentary opponents in the 1870s and 1880s. The London *Daily Mail* commented caustically:

It has been said that the root of the Irish problem lies in the fact of a dull people (the English) trying to govern a singularly witty people. No one will surely be so bold as to suggest that the latest agitation, by which Irishmen are induced to fill the postboxes with letters addressed in the uncouth characters of a barbarous language, has its origins in a sense of humour.[3]

---

[1] *Hansard 4*, lxxxvi, 674–766 (20 July 1900). In the course of the debate the chief secretary for Ireland, Gerald Balfour, was guilty of misleading the house when, in justification of government policy towards the use of Irish in the schools, he stated: 'According to the census of 1891 the total number of Irish-speaking persons in Ireland was only 31,121.' In fact, as already stated (above, p. 386), the census report gave 680,245 as the total number of Irish-speakers with 38,121 as the number of Irish-speaking monoglots. Balfour, however, gave a less misleading statement later in the debate (*Hansard 4*, lxxxvi, 706).

[2] 3 Edw. VII, c. 1 (27 Mar. 1903).

[3] Quoted by Casement in 'On the prosecution of Irish', for which see H.O. Mackey, *The crime against Europe* (Dublin, 1958), p. 96.

And the *Morning Post* disparagingly likened Irish to 'kitchen Kaffir'.[1] One immediate effect of the comments in the English press is told by Casement, who had returned to Ireland in the previous year and had got caught up in the language movement:

I bethought me that a people's language was a living thing, and that it was a shameful thing for an Irishman to stand by and see the soul of his country being dragged out through its lips. I accordingly gave up my club in London, and devoted the amount of the annual subscription thus saved to a training college in Munster where Irish teachers are perfected in a fuller knowledge of, and more scientific methods of imparting, 'kitchen Kaffir'.[2]

It was the college in Ballingeary[3] that was helped by Casement's generosity at that time, and among those who went to improve their Irish there in the following years were young men who in the fullness of time took their place in the ranks of the revolutionaries: men such as Terence MacSwiney,[4] who, as lord mayor of Cork, died on hunger strike in Brixton prison in 1920, and Richard Mulcahy, later chief of staff of the I.R.A. during the war of independence and one of the founders of the Irish Free State in 1922.

In 1906 Casement left Ireland for South America where he spent five years in the broader service of humanity; yet his interest in Irish and his belief in the usefulness of summer schools in the Gaeltacht were undiminished. On his return to Ireland in 1912 he became patron of the Irish summer school on Tawin Island (County Galway), which had as its headmaster that summer, as in 1911, a young mathematics teacher named Eamon de Valera who had begun to learn Irish while he was studying for a degree in science and who, ever since, had been committed to the cause of the language.

A major event in the struggle for home rule was the rally in O'Connell Street in Dublin on 31 March 1912, attended by M.P.s and local councillors and by members of a wide spectrum of organisations and institutions. Among those on one of the four platforms were Hyde, MacNeill, and Bergin as members of the Celtic faculty in University College, Dublin. Alongside them was Pearse, who had devoted himself fully to the cause of Irish since his 1897 address to the New Ireland Literary Society.[5]

Although he had qualified as a barrister as well as gaining a B.A. degree, Pearse's only professional appearance in court seems to have been in 1905 when he unsuccessfully argued before three judges in Dublin in an appeal against the imposition of a fine on Niall Mac Giolla Brighde of Creeslough in Donegal who was adjudged to have broken the law by having his name written on his cart in

---

[1] Ibid., p. 98.   [2] Ibid., p. 101.   [3] Above, p. 406.

[4] MacSwiney's commitment to Irish is reflected in his last letter from Brixton to his colleagues in Cork corporation in which he appealed to them to elect no future lord mayor without proficiency in Irish, and also to use Irish habitually in the conduct of official business. See Diarmaid Ó Briain, *Traolach Mac Suibhne* (Baile Átha Cliath, 1979), p. 139.

[5] Above, p. 405.

the Irish form and in Irish letters only.[1] Having been introduced to Irish in the Irish Christian Brothers school in Westland Row in Dublin, Pearse had pursued his studies in the Gaelic League and in Gaeltacht areas of Connacht with such success that he became a teacher of Irish, an Irish author, editor of the Gaelic League periodical *An Claidheamh Soluis* in 1903, and paid secretary of the league's publication committee in 1906. His enthusiasm for Irish and his unorthodox ideas on education led him to found the school St Enda's in 1908, but during the course of the next five years he began to show an interest in politics. Thus it was that he was among the few chosen to speak on the 'academic' platform at the 1912 meeting. His speech was in Irish and it contained a note of warning:

If we are let down this time there are people in Ireland, and I am one of them, who will advise Irishmen never again to enter into discussions with the English, but to answer them with force and the sword. Let the English understand that if we are betrayed again, there will be bloody war throughout Ireland.[2]

But it was to MacNeill that it fell to issue a call to arms. Twenty eventful years had passed since he had taken the initiative that had led to the founding of the Gaelic League. The reaction of the Ulster unionists to the progress of the home rule bill was to establish the Ulster Volunteers and to threaten armed revolt against the British government. On 1 November 1913 MacNeill published in *An Claidheamh Soluis* a reasoned case for action on the part of the nationalists in response to the founding of the Ulster Volunteers, and this was followed by a meeting in the Rotunda in Dublin at which the Irish Volunteers were launched under the presidency of MacNeill. It surprised no one that members of the league were to the fore in answering MacNeill's call, nor did it cause any surprise that supporters of the league followed MacNeill in refusing to answer Redmond's call to the Volunteers to join the British forces when war came in 1914.[3]

In fact there was in the league a number of influential members who were also members of the Irish Republican Brotherhood, and behind the scenes they were contemplating military action. Some of them considered that the time had come when the league should identify itself with the aim of political freedom, and towards this end Seán MacDermott, supported by Tom Clarke and others, suggested privately that the league's constitution should be amended, and steps were taken to bring the matter up for discussion at the annual conference that was to be held in Dundalk in July 1915, despite the likelihood of the resignation of Hyde from the presidency and a split in the league if a proposal for such an amendment were carried.[4] In the past Hyde had steered the league on a safe

---

[1] See *Dírbheathaisnéis Néill Mhic Ghiolla Bhríghde* (Baile Átha Cliath, [1938], pp 97–103; Ruth Dudley Edwards, *Patrick Pearse: the triumph of failure* (London, 1979), pp 79–81). In a later case it was decided that use of the Irish form constituted an offence, even if it appeared in roman letters.

[2] Translated from Irish original, for which see *Scríbhinní Phádraig Mhic Phiarais* (Baile Átha Cliath, 1919), pp 267–8.

[3] A bilingual booklet for recruitment to the British army was issued early in the war.

[4] Ó Ceallaigh, *Seán T.*, pp 153–5.

course, skilfully avoiding contentious political matters while being uncompromising on those things that, according to his evaluation, were fundamental to the organisation. Now, however, in the explosive situation caused by the founding of the Ulster Volunteers, the fiasco over the home rule bill, Ireland's involvement by Britain in the European war, and the Irish party's attitude to this, the political issue became preeminent and the conference eventually adopted a resolution whereby rule 2 of the league was altered to read: 'Connradh na Gaedhilge shall be strictly non-political and non-sectarian, and shall devote itself to realising the ideal of a free Gaelic-speaking Ireland.'[1]

This was the parting of the ways for Hyde and MacNeill. Hyde, convinced that a grave disservice was being done to the league, left the presidency that he had held for twenty-two years. The conference, hoping that he would reconsider his action, elected no one to replace him, but when he proved adamant MacNeill was elected to the position.

Three years earlier Pearse had said of the league that it was a spent force:

There is need for a new 'league' in Ireland today. The power of the old leagues is broken and their force is spent. Nothing is lasting. Each generation has its own achievement. The Land League was the achievement of the second last generation. The Gaelic League is the achievement of the generation coming to an end.[2]

Pearse was not altogether correct in his judgement. What happened was that he and others associated with him adopted new priorities in their plans for Ireland and found themselves in a coalition of revolutionary forces in which the Irish Republican Brotherhood, as heirs to the fenian tradition of the 1860s, represented militant separatism, and Connolly's Citizen Army represented militant socialism. The events of 1916 were the prelude to the eclipse of the Irish parliamentary party and the emergence of a state in whose constitution the Irish language would be given a primary position. From the early years of the century Arthur Griffith's Sinn Féin party had been trying unsuccessfully to challenge the power of the parliamentary party. The British government, by labelling the 1916 rising as the 'Sinn Féin rebellion', put his party on a new plane, and in the events of 1917 to 1921 Connolly's heirs in the Irish labour party found themselves playing a minor role. In the aftermath of the rising the ranks of Sinn Féin were swelled by 'politicians by accident'—men who, as Pearse had put it, had 'been to school to the Gaelic League'. They included MacNeill and de Valera, who was the sole surviving commandant of the rising. MacNeill had considered the rising ill advised; had done his best at the last minute to try to prevent it; and did not take part in it. Nevertheless when it was over he was arrested and imprisoned, and found himself in the same jail as de Valera. For both of them, and for others like them, the ideal of an Irish-speaking Ireland was to remain, no matter what side they took in the tragic divisions over the Anglo-Irish treaty of 1921. So it was

[1] *Connradh na Gaedhilge, Imtheachta na hÁrd-Fheise 1915*, pp 16–17.
[2] Translated from the Irish original, for which see *Scríbhinní Phádraig Mhic Phiarais*, p. 139.

that after 1917 there arose a national political force that was soon to put into practice the abstentionist policy that had been expounded for Ireland by George Sigerson as far back as 1868,[1] and at the same time was to show its wish for an Ireland not merely free but Gaelic as well.

With the inaugural session of the revolutionary Dáil Éireann on 21 January 1919 came the first demonstration of a commitment to Irish on the part of the organisers and members, for in it the proceedings were conducted almost completely in Irish. We have to go back to the reign of Henry VIII to find a record of a parliamentary assembly in Dublin in which Irish was used in the transaction of major business. The occasion was a meeting in June 1541 for the purpose of granting the style 'king of Ireland' to Henry, and the record says that when the bill 'was redde and declared' to the lords 'in Irisshe', 'all the hoole house most willingly and joyouslye condissended and agreid to the same'.[2]

It is one of the paradoxes of our history that these two assemblies, so different in purpose and separated by nearly 400 years during which the Irish language had declined to a point where it was threatened with extinction, should be linked by the formal use of Irish in them both. For whereas in the first instance the use of Irish was a linguistic necessity and had no political or nationalistic overtones, in the second—since Irish was not the native language of more than a few of those present—it was, in effect, a signal that Irish would henceforth be one of the 'externals' or insignia of Ireland's nationhood. It is not surprising that one of the first organisations, along with Sinn Féin, banned by the British authorities during the political and military struggle for freedom between 1919 and 1921 was the Gaelic League, for many members of Dáil Éireann and the I.R.A. were also active in the league.

That the use of Irish in the first session of the dáil was not a mere formality was shown by the subsequent establishment of a ministry for Irish with responsibility for promoting the use of the language and supporting Irish culture.[3] These stirring years saw a gesture that surely must be unique in the history of revolutionary movements in small countries. Professor Rudolf Thurneysen of Bonn, who had become the greatest authority on early Irish, had completed an extensive work on Irish literature, *Die irische Helden- und Königsage bis zum siebzehnten Jahrhundert*. Recognising the importance of this contribution to Irish studies, the ministry granted a sum of money towards the cost of publication, a fact that was recorded in an imprint when the work was published in Germany in 1921 while Dáil Éireann was still an illegal assembly under British law.

---

[1] This was done in an unsigned editorial published under the heading 'To your tents, O Israel!' in *Irishman* (29 Feb. 1868). My authority for attributing it to Sigerson is a statement made by J. O'Leary Curtin in an address to the Celtic Literary Society that was reported in Griffith's paper *United Irishman* on 3 Dec. 1904.

[2] *Cal. S. P. Ire., 1538–46*, p. 304.

[3] From the middle of 1919 Dáil Éireann employed an official Irish translator; see below, p. 430. It is noteworthy that during the peace negotiations of 1921 de Valera used Irish in letters sent to the British prime minister, Lloyd George, and supplied an English translation; see *Official correspondence relating to the peace negotiations July–September 1921* (Dublin, 1921).

The Anglo-Irish treaty of 1921 split Dáil Éireann on fundamental issues of unity and sovereignty. The debate on the treaty was a bitter one, but it is noteworthy that during it speakers on both sides emphasised their desire to see rebuilt what Griffith called 'the Gaelic civilisation broken down at the battle of Kinsale'. How this might be achieved was another matter, as Griffith's co-founder of the Irish Free State, Collins, clearly saw. Commenting on the achievements of the past and hopes for the future he wrote:

We only succeeded after we had begun to get back our Irish ways; after we had made a serious effort to speak our own language; after we had striven again to govern ourselves. We can only keep out the enemy and all other enemies by completing that task . . . The biggest task will be the restoration of the language.[1]

Collins was right. The restoration of Irish as the language of the people was a noble dream, which had immense significance before 1921. The standing accorded to Irish as the national language in the Free State constitution of 1922 reflected the earnest desires of a small number of politicians and a groundswell of goodwill on the part of a large number of people throughout the country. To transform it from being the everyday language of a small minority to become the language of the majority was a very different matter and one in which success in the schools and the continuing support of the people as a whole would be vital. The outcome lay in the future, but one thing was certain: the first government of the Irish Free State had undertaken a commitment to the language that no government in the following seven decades would formally declare abandoned.

IT has been emphasised in earlier volumes of this history that in former times scribal activity was a crucial factor in the transmission of Irish literary and historical tradition.[2] It is evident from the surviving corpus of Irish manuscripts, which numbers over 5,000 items, that while this activity continued during the second part of the nineteenth century in many parts of Ireland, both urban and rural, it did so on a much diminished scale. As in the past, many of the texts transcribed had been composed in earlier centuries, but contemporary or near-contemporary compositions are also found in the later manuscripts. It must also be said that Irish emigrants retained their interest in Irish to the extent that they brought manuscripts away with them, and this resulted in scribal activity abroad, notably in America. Alongside the decline in scribal activity in Ireland came an ever increasing activity in the areas of collection, cataloguing, study, editing, and publication of manuscript material.

Many of the mid-nineteenth-century private collectors were themselves engaged in scribal or academic work: men such as Eugene O'Curry, John O'Donovan, George Petrie, John O'Daly, William Betham, and David Comyn in Dublin, William Reeves and Robert MacAdam in Belfast, John Windle in Cork, Maurice

---

[1] Michael Collins, *The path to freedom* (Dublin, 1922; new ed., 1968), pp 100–02.
[2] Above, ii, 781–815; iii, 509–45; iv, 374–419.

Lenihan in Limerick, Nicholas Kearney in Louth and Dublin, and Peter Gallegan in Meath. The most noteworthy collector of the time outside Ireland was Sir Thomas Phillipps of Cheltenham who, with the help of Irish scholars such as Windle and Paul and Joseph Long (Ó Longain), acquired many manuscripts, including several important vellums. Despite the activity of such collectors the loss and destruction of manuscripts continued, and accordingly efforts were increased to have such manuscripts preserved in learned institutions where, in fact, interest in Irish was now growing.

At the beginning of the nineteenth century Trinity College, Dublin, was the only Irish institution to have a sizeable collection, but the change in the situation since then is reflected in the present-day location of the major collections in this country (the figures are approximate): Royal Irish Academy, 1,400; National Library of Ireland, 1,230; St Patrick's College, Maynooth, 310; University College, Cork, 250; Trinity College, Dublin, 240; University College, Dublin, 150; University College, Galway, 70; Franciscan House of Studies, Killiney, 60; St Colman's College, Fermoy, 50; Belfast Public Library, 45. Sizeable collections outside Ireland are in the British Library, 220; National Library of Scotland, 76; Manchester University Library, 70; Cambridge University Library, 56; Bodleian Library, Oxford, 40; Harvard Library, Cambridge (Mass.), 38; National Library of Wales, Aberystwyth, 35. Of these the British Library and the Bodleian Library are exceptional inasmuch as the majority of their Irish manuscripts were acquired before the middle of the nineteenth century.

With the growing interest in Irish manuscripts these began to be offered for sale, either privately or at book auctions, both in Britain and in Ireland. Thus the Stowe collection, which for the most part consisted of manuscripts that Charles O'Conor had brought with him from Belanagare in 1798 when he became librarian to the duke of Buckingham, was purchased by the earl of Ashburnham in 1849 and retained by him until 1883 when the Irish manuscripts were purchased by the British government and deposited in the Royal Irish Academy. Sir William Betham's manuscripts were sold at Sotheby's in 1854. After O'Curry's death his manuscripts, which numbered well over a hundred, were purchased for the catholic university in Dublin and eventually most of them found their way to either St Patrick's College, Maynooth, or University College, Dublin. Maynooth already had received Bishop John Murphy's collection of over a hundred manuscripts from Cork in 1848, and a further nineteen belonging to Laurence Renehan, the late president of the college, about ten years later. Robert MacAdam sold a large number of his manuscripts to William Reeves in 1889 and these were resold when Reeves died in 1892. The first sizeable acquisition by the National Library was the David Comyn collection of thirty-six manuscripts in 1907, but of course the most important addition came with the purchase of 178 volumes from the Phillipps collection in 1930. One other collection that deserves particular mention is that of Pádraig Feiritéir who emigrated from Kerry to America in 1896 and spent much of his time there collecting and copying manuscripts, which he donated to the National University of Ireland in recognition of the contribution it had made to the promotion of the Irish language by making it a required subject for matriculation.

Cataloguing of the institutional collections, such as those in Trinity College and the Royal Irish Academy, became one of the professional occupations of Irish scholars in the nineteenth century, and surviving manuscript catalogue materials include those relating to Trinity College manuscripts compiled by Edward O'Reilly and John O'Donovan and those relating to the Academy collection by O'Reilly, O'Donovan, O'Curry, Paul and Joseph Long, and others. Much of the work on the British Library manuscripts was done by Standish Hayes O'Grady between 1886 and 1892 and was completed by Robin Flower, who saw two volumes of the work published in 1926. In the meantime a catalogue of the Irish manuscripts in Trinity College had been published in 1921. Printed catalogues of the collections in the Royal Irish Academy and the National Library did not come until after that date.

The publication of Zeuss's *Grammatica Celtica* in 1853[1] had revealed the richness of the linguistic information contained in the manuscripts of Irish origin preserved in continental libraries in St Paul im Lavanttal (Carinthia), Karlsruhe, Milan, Turin, Würzburg, and elsewhere, and in the following decades early Irish became a regular subject of university teaching and research by leading European philologists. O'Curry's lectures in the catholic university in Dublin and the publication in 1861 of his *Lectures on the manuscript materials of ancient Irish history* showed the vast range and potential interest of Old and Middle Irish literature and stimulated Matthew Arnold to deliver his Oxford lectures *On the study of Celtic literature*, which were published in 1867. Ten years later a chair of Celtic was established in the University of Oxford and soon similar chairs were established in Scotland and Wales. In the meantime interest in Celtic studies had been raised to a new level by the publication in Paris in 1870 of the first volume of *Revue celtique*, a specialist periodical dealing with the Celtic languages, literature, and history. In 1897 this was joined by a German periodical, *Zeitschrift für celtische Philologie*. By that time some of the most important works of early Irish literature, as well as grammatical and linguistic studies of Old and Middle Irish, had been published. In Ireland the Royal Irish Academy was foremost in publishing Irish works, with important papers appearing in its *Transactions* and *Proceedings*, various editions of texts in its Todd lecture series, and five volumes of facsimiles of Irish manuscripts in the years 1870–96.

The efforts to promote the retention and use of Irish as a spoken language, together with growing academic interest in the language, led to research and publication in new areas, such as Early Modern Irish prose and poetry, oral literature, including folk-tales, and the scientific study of spoken Irish dialects. In 1898 the Irish Texts Society was established in London to promote the

[1] Above, p. 397.

publication of texts of various kinds, and between then and the foundation of the Irish Free State in 1922 it published over twenty volumes; the first edited by Hyde, whose versatile and productive scholarship provided further stimulus to the study of Irish with *A literary history of Ireland* (1899). In the meantime the Gaelic League had inaugurated in 1897 An tOireachtas, an annual festival that was destined to prove crucial in the development of original Irish writing.

At the beginning of the twentieth century opportunities for scientific training in Ireland in the study of Irish, and in associated subjects such as palaeography, phonetics, and philology, were not extensive, and it was this fact that led Kuno Meyer to suggest, in a lecture delivered at An tOireachtas in 1902, that a school for the higher study of Irish should be formed in Dublin with the aim of making that city what he claimed it should be: the world centre of Irish studies. So the School of Irish Learning came into being, and the first course was given by John Strachan of Manchester University in July 1903. In September of the same year Meyer gave a course on palaeography and Henry Sweet of Oxford gave a course on practical phonetics with particular reference to spoken Irish. Among those in both classes was R. I. Best, who was registrar and honorary secretary of the school and subsequently became Ireland's most illustrious palaeographer, while one of Sweet's pupils was Frank Fay who became an actor in the Abbey Theatre.[1] On his return to Oxford Sweet wrote a humorous fantasy called 'Home rule in Ireland. Before and after', which he had printed privately—with the imprint 'University Press, Clontarf. 3145'—and circulated to his friends. This little booklet contains some interesting observations on what he saw in Dublin in 1903. It is clear, for instance, that his stay in Dublin was sufficiently long for him to become aware of the suspicion with which those interested in the Irish language—even at an academic level—were liable to be regarded by Dublin Castle.

The establishment and maintenance of the School of Irish Learning was made possible through the generosity of benefactors including Lord Castletown, Lord Iveagh, Alice Stopford Green, Sarah Purser, William Delaney, S.J., Whitley Stokes, and Lady Gregory. After being only a year in existence the school established its own journal, *Ériu*, the first volume of which contained over twenty articles, including one relating to the spoken Irish of mid-Cork by Osborn Bergin.[2] Bergin had attended the 1904 summer session of the school and later that year he was awarded a scholarship, funded by Mrs Greene, to enable him to study for two years in Germany under such scholars as Heinrich Zimmer in Berlin and Rudolf Thurneysen in Bonn. On his return to Ireland in 1906 he was appointed professor in the school, and thus the scientific training in all periods of the language, from Old Irish to modern spoken Irish, became a reality. The establishment in 1908 of the national university, with chairs of Irish in all its constituent colleges, was the next step in the advancement of the higher study of

---

[1] Above, p. 362.   [2] Above, p. 409.

Irish. In the following years close cooperation between the School of Irish Learning, the Royal Irish Academy, and the Irish universities ensured that Ireland would, indeed, be a major centre for Celtic studies. The financial contribution given by Dáil Éireann in 1921 towards the cost of publication of Thurneysen's *Die irische Helden- und Königsage*[1] was an indication of goodwill and future support for Irish study and research under a native Irish government.

Although the fifty years or so between Davis's exhortations regarding the Irish language and the foundation of the Gaelic League saw a catastrophic decline in the use of Irish as a vernacular, there were factors that helped to keep alive among the diminishing number of Irish-speakers much of the richness and versatility of the language. One of these was the interest that many of them still had in their literary heritage. While relatively few of them were literate in their own language this did not prevent the average Irish-speaker from acquiring a varied repertoire of oral literature, including folk-tales, anecdotes, historical and local traditions, prayers, and poetry. The recitation of such material was one of the few sources of entertainment available to rural communities in those years, especially during the winter months. Thus the oral heritage was passed on from generation to generation, and a fair amount of it has come down to our times. For such books as *Leabhar sgeulaigheachta* (1899), *Beside the fire* (1890), *Abhráin grádh chúige Chonnacht* (1893), and *Abhráin diadha chúige Chonnacht* (1906), Hyde drew on the oral tradition still alive in Connacht, and his lead was followed in Munster by Pádraig Ó Laoghaire of south-west Cork with *Sgeuluidheacht chúige Mumhan* (1895). In the following fifty years collectors and editors were to gain an international reputation for Ireland in the area of folk literature.

Among literate members of the Irish-speaking community the clergy were the most likely to have occasion to write Irish, for they would have done so in preparing their sermons. Several examples of this genre from the nineteenth century have survived in manuscript form, one of the most extensive being a collection of sermons based on the Bible stories composed by Muiris Paodhar of Cork in 1864.[2] Very different in subject-matter is a work by a northern scholar, Aodh Mac Domhnaill, who was employed for years by Robert MacAdam of Belfast in the task of collecting Irish manuscripts, Irish music, and miscellaneous items from oral narration. Mac Domhnaill composed a number of poems, but his longest work was a prose account of natural history, which he wrote between 1849 and 1853. Like Paodhar's work this remained in manuscript form until recently.[3] A contemporary of these writers who deserves mention was Pádraig Phiarais Cúndún, a native of east Cork who emigrated to America in 1826. During his exile he kept up a correspondence with his friends at home over a period of thirty years, and his extant letters and poems provide a further example of literary

[1] Above, p. 413.
[2] Breandán Ó Madagáin (eag.), *Teagasc ar an Sean-tiomna* (Baile Átha Cliath, 1974).
[3] Colm Beckett, *Fealsúnacht Aodha Mhic Dhomhnaill* (Baile Átha Cliath, 1967).

material relatively free from any attempt to imitate the Irish of the sixteenth and seventeenth centuries.[1]

The establishment of the *Gaelic Journal* in 1882 provided a regular medium for the publication of material in Irish, and during the next fifty years the growth of the Irish revival movement was to be reflected in a proliferation of periodicals either wholly in Irish or carrying regular Irish columns, among them being *Fáinne an Lae* (1898–1900, 1918–19), *An Claidheamh Soluis* (1899–1918), *An tEurópach* (1899–1900), *Banba* (1901–6), *An Lóchrann* (1907–13, 1916–20), *An Connachtach* (1907–8), *Irisleabhar Muighe Nuadhat* (1907–   ), *Glór na Ly* (1911–12), *An Crann* (1916–21), *An Stoc* (1917–20), as well as the *New Ireland Review* (1894–1911), the *United Irishman* (1899–1906), the *Leader* (1900–   ), and *Sinn Féin* (1906–14). The same period saw a remarkable growth in the publication of books in contemporary Irish as distinct from editions of texts from earlier periods. The foremost publishers were the Gaelic League, with its subsidiary Clódhanna Teoranta, and the Irish Book Company, which published much of Peadar Ua Laoghaire's work as well as works by other writers associated with him. Irish books were also published by a number of general commercial publishers including M. H. Gill & Co., James Duffy & Co., Maunsell & Co., Educational Book Co., and Sealy, Bryer, & Walkers.

It was during those years that the spoken language came into its own as the basis for a modern Irish literature. Foremost in this development was Ua Laoghaire, whose novel *Séadna*, based on a folk-tale that he had heard as a young boy in Cork just after the famine years, began to appear seriatim in the *Gaelic Journal* in 1894 and appeared complete in book form for the first time in 1904. Ua Laoghaire was 55 when he began to write *Séadna*, but in his desire to promote the use of the living language as a medium for oral and written communication he kept up a steady stream of publications. Between 1893 and 1920, the year of his death, fifty-two books by him had been published and well over a thousand items by him had appeared in print in over forty periodicals. The range of his writings was very wide and included two novels, *Séadna* (1904) and *Niamh* (1907); several modernisations of earlier Irish tales, including *An Craos-Deamhan* (1905), *Eisirt* (1909), *An Cleasaidhe* (1913), *Bricriu* (1915), and *Guaire* (1915); an incomplete adaptation of *Don Quixote de la Mancha*; translations of Latin and Greek classical texts such as *Catilína* (1913) and *Lucián* (1924); and an autobiographical work, *Mo sgéal féin* (1915). Not surprisingly he produced a large number of religious works, including two volumes of sermons, saints' lives, a translation of Thomas à Kempis's *De imitatione Christi* entitled *Aithris ar Chríost* (1914), and translations of the four gospels (1915) and the Acts of the Apostles (1922). His most extensive religious work was his translation of the Old Testament, which he began at the age of 74 and completed within the space of two and a half years on 20 November 1916. His shorter works included a large number of essays on

[3] Risteard Ó Foghludha, *Pádraig Phiarais Cúndún* (Baile Átha Cliath, 1932).

current affairs and other topical subjects, versions of Aesop's fables, and works on grammar and vocabulary. He corresponded with many of those engaged in the Irish revival movement including MacNeill, Seosamh Laoide (J. H. Lloyd), Séamus Ó Dubhghaill, Michael O'Hickey, Osborn Bergin, and Thomas F. O'Rahilly, and many of his letters contain valuable comments on Irish linguistic usage.

Ua Laoghaire's contribution to Irish writing was recognised in a special way in 1912 when the freedom of the cities of Dublin and Cork was conferred on him. In what were memorable occasions in the fight for the recognition of Ireland's cultural identity the same honours were also conferred on Kuno Meyer of Berlin, whose zeal in promoting the study of the earlier language and in establishing the School of Irish Learning in Dublin was justly appreciated. The significance of this gesture on the part of Dublin's municipal council can be judged from the fact that in 1911 it had refused by 42 votes to 9 to present an address of welcome to George V on his visit to the city. In 1915 a majority of the members of the council, under the influence of anti-German propaganda, decided to have Meyer's name expunged from the roll of honorary burgesses; not until 1920 were amends made for this shameful act and his name restored. By that time both Meyer and Ua Laoghaire were dead.

Ua Laoghaire did not claim to have great originality as a writer. His aim was to supply abundant reading matter in good idiomatic Irish and this he did, and successive generations of learners benefited from his work. A significant comment was made by Pearse in a review of *Séadna* when it first appeared in book form:

The formative influence of *Séadna* is likely to be great. Some of our most distinctive writers have declared that it was the early chapters of *Séadna* which first taught them to write Irish. Not that they admit themselves mere imitators of Father O'Leary, but rather that *Séadna* showed them how to be themselves.

In fact Ua Laoghaire's promotion of *caint na ndaoine* (the living language) left the way open for younger writers to bring creative writing in the vernacular into new areas.

One of the areas in which modern Irish writers have been most successful is that of the short story. In the early years of the revival movement simple stories derived from folk tradition appeared in various periodicals. A new era for writers began in 1898 when in the Gaelic festival An tOireachtas four competitions for original short stories were sponsored by the *Weekly Freeman*. The winner of all four prizes of £5 was Pádraig Ó Séaghdha of south Kerry who submitted stories in idiomatic Irish, which in their form and style were on a par with short stories in other languages. His stories were published in book form in 1901, and soon two other writers had raised the Irish short story to a new level: Pádraic Ó Conaire and Pearse. Irish was not the first language of either of these writers, but they both had learned it and had achieved fluency by spending long periods in Galway Gaeltacht areas.

Ó Conaire, who was a born story-teller, learned many of the techniques of writing as well as observing various aspects of urban life during his early years as a clerk in London. He was quite young when he abandoned London and took up Irish writing as his main source of income. Indeed he was probably the only person of his generation who managed to support himself by Irish writing and some teaching. Ó Conaire, like Ó Séaghdha, won an Oireachtas prize for a short story at his first attempt in 1904, and from then on he kept up a steady flow of essays and short stories, with over 200 of these being published in the period between 1905 and the end of 1921. In those years six volumes of his short stories were published—*Nóra Mharcuis Bhig agus sgéalta eile* (1909), *An sgoláire bocht agus sgéalta eile* (1913), *An chead chloch* (1914), *Seacht mbuaidh an eirghe-amach* (1918), *An crann géagach* (1919), and *Béal an uaignis* (1921)—as well as two longer stories, *Deoraidheacht* (1910) and *Tír na niongantas* (1919). Ó Conaire's stories are uneven in quality, but the best of them are characterised by an originality and an easy style that gained for him a reputation as a writer that has endured. That some later writers succeeded in equalling or surpassing him as a story-teller is due in no small measure to the inspiration that his work gave to others.

Pearse's Irish writing began with a contribution to *An Claidheamh Soluis* in 1899, three years after he joined the Gaelic League and only one year after his first visit to the Gaeltacht of Aran. Four years later he embarked on a journalistic career as paid editor of *An Claidheamh*, and two years further on he published, under the pseudonym Colm Ó Conaire, an adventure story for boys that was well received and was described by one reviewer as a 'vigorous and idiomatic piece of modern Irish'. This was followed by other stories, most of which were intended for young readers and all of which were uncomplicated in their content and expression. They reflected his concept of life in the Gaeltacht and of the minds of people there. Two volumes of these stories are *Íosagán agus sgéalta eile* (1907) and *An mháthair agus sgéalta eile* (1916). They were republished, together with his Irish poems, some of his essays, and two plays in *Scríbhinní Phádraig Mhic Phiarais* (1919). Though his Irish writing was not extensive it was an important element in the current developments.

In view of the widespread activities of the Gaelic League it is not surprising that nearly all of those who contributed in a notable way to Irish writing in the period under review here were associated with the league's work. A good example is Mícheál Breathnach, a native of Cois Fhairrge in Galway, which he left in 1901 at the age of 20 to become secretary of the Gaelic League in London. He had already spent some years as an assistant teacher in the local school and in London he taught Irish as well as performing his secretarial and organisational duties. In 1905 he taught in the newly founded Irish college in Toormakeady, and in the following year he was appointed professor of Irish in St Jarlath's College, Tuam. Before returning to Ireland to teach he had gone to Belgium to study modern teaching methods, and he was one of the first persons to use phonetics in teaching Irish. He was a highly effective and popular teacher, but his career was interrupted by illness, which some time spent in sanatoria in Switzerland failed to cure, and he died in 1908. Breathnach had very positive views on creative Irish writing, which he published in an article in *An Connachtach*. His own writing was done in the space of seven years and, apart from a translation that he did of Charles Kickham's *Knocknagow*, it consisted mainly of essays. His best-known work is *Seilg i measg na nAlp*, a piece of good descriptive writing in which he set down observations on people he met and things he saw during his time in Switzerland. This was originally published in instalments in *An Claidheamh Soluis* but it was reprinted, along with other items, in *Sliocht de sgríbhinnibh Mhíchíl Bhreathnaigh* (1913).

Among the Irish teacher-organisers who worked for the league in the Gaeltacht and other rural areas was Pádraig Ó Siochfhradha, a native of Corca Dhuibhne in west Kerry. He was editor of the Munster periodical *An Lóchrann* and his future career was to be mainly in Irish book publishing. Like his fellow workers in the Irish movement he was aware of the needs of learners and so, as well as writing some modernisations of early tales and collecting and publishing stories, proverbs, and other material from oral narration, he wrote *An baile seo 'gainne* (1913) and *Jimín Mháire Thaidhg* (1919–20) in which he dealt with themes of rural life in an unsophisticated way but with considerable humour. Since the early years of the revival movement when Hyde adopted the pseudonym 'An Craoibhín Aoibhinn' the use of pen-names was a common practice in Irish circles, and was in fact required of entrants in Oireachtas literary competitions. Ó Siochfhradha took the name 'An Seabhac' and over the years he has probably been better known by that rather than by his real name. Séamus Ó Grianna was another writer who is well known by his pseudonym 'Máire', which he was using from about 1911 on in contributing stories and other items to periodicals. He broke new ground with *Mo dhá Róisín* (1921), a full-length novel about the Easter rising. The following years were to see him develop into one of the most productive of Irish writers.

Of the many other prose writers two more may be mentioned here—Tadhg Ó Murchadha of Cork, who was known by the pseudonym 'Seandún', and Tomás Ó Criomhthain of Kerry, both of whom produced autobiographical work. Unlike most Irish writers of his generation Ó Murchadha was a townsman whose native language was Irish, for he was born in Macroom before the famine, when the people of that town were still predominantly Irish-speaking. He trained as a tailor and then went to work in Cork where he spent the rest of his life, learned to read and write Irish, and came into contact with many of those involved in the Irish revival movement. Ó Murchadha had a fine appreciation of the flexibility of the Irish language and in his writing he sought after accuracy and polish and achieved a style that was natural and free from self-consciousness. His earliest attempt at writing was a translation of Robert Emmet's 'Speech from the dock', and he went on to translate, under the title *Toradh na Gaedhilge ar aitheasc agus ar ghréithribh na nGaedheal* (1905), William O'Brien's *The influence of the Irish language on Irish national literature and character*,[1] and then Daniel Defoe's *Robinson Crusoe* (1909). About 1912, when his sight was beginning to fail, he began to dictate an account of his life, which was transcribed by friends and admirers among whom were Diarmuid Ó Murchadha and Toirdhealbhach Mac Suibhne (Terence MacSwiney), who during the war of independence prepared a section of it dealing with the years of the fenian rising for publication in book form under the title *Sgéal 'Sheandúin'* (1920).

Tomas Ó Criomhthain was the first of the natives of the Great Blasket island off the Kerry coast to gain fame as a writer. He was born in 1856 and in the early decades of the twentieth century he came to be regarded as the leading representative of the Blasket community in matters relating to the local dialect and oral literature. Eminent scholars came from far and near to learn from him, including Carl Marstrander, professor in the School of Irish Learning and later professor of Celtic Languages at the University of Oslo, and Robin Flower, deputy keeper of manuscripts in the British Museum, as well as Osborn Bergin, T. F. O'Rahilly, and others. Among these visitors to the Blasket was Brian Ó Ceallaigh of Killarney whose encouragement led Ó Criomhthain to begin in 1919 to write a sort of diary, eventually published in 1928 under the title *Allagar na h-inise*. It was due to Ó Ceallaigh's urgings, too, that Ó Criomhthain wrote his autobiographical work *An t-oileánach*, but that was not completed until 1926.

One other development is worth recording here, for it anticipated by three decades the founding of An Club Leabhar (the Irish Book Club) in 1948. This was the establishment in 1917 of An Ridireacht Liteardha for the purpose of publishing original works in Irish on similar lines to the publication of earlier works by the Irish Texts Society, which had been operating successfully since 1898. An Ridireacht, of which Pádraic Ó Conaire was a leading advocate, sought a thousand readers to subscribe half a crown each annually in return for which they offered to supply subscribers with an original work in Irish yearly. The idea was good but two major difficulties arose: the half-crowns did not roll in and printing costs rose enormously. It took over three years to produce the first publications, *Cad ba dhóbair dó agus sgéalta eile* and *Leabhar na Pólainne* by Liam Ó Rinn, who was already well known as an essayist and in the following years was to be a prolific writer as well as being a member of the official translation staff of the Irish parliament.

Much more successful than the Ridireacht was another organisation whose aim was to encourage a greater use of Irish speech in everyday life by identifying persons who were able and willing to do so. The organisation, established early in 1916, was named An Fáinne (The Ring) and adopted a circular ring-like emblem (*fáinne*) as a badge of membership. The *fáinne* was produced in gold and silver, the gold to be worn by those who were already proficient speakers of Irish.

---

[1] Above, p. 402, n. 3.

By 1920, when the organisation had its own journal, there were 3,000 members and the use of the emblem became widespread in the following decades.

From the earliest times poetry has had a special place in Irish society—the learned poetry of the professional classes, the personal and religious poetry of the anchorites, the sub-literary poetry of the people, and so on. The nineteenth century saw the last stages of a long tradition, with scholars such as Mícheál Óg Ó Longáin (d. 1840) still occasionally using simplified forms of the old syllabic metres while for the most part using the assonantal metres that had been used only occasionally by the professional poets of the sixteenth century. There were contemporaries of Ó Longáin in Munster who lived through the famine years but whose poetry was still in the eighteenth-century mould: local poets, such as Máire Bhuidhe Ní Laoghaire (d. 1849) of Cork, and Tomás Ruadh Ó Súilleabháin (d. 1848) and Diarmaid na Bolgaighe Ó Séaghdha (d. 1850) of Kerry, whose compositions were preserved as part of the oral tradition; and the emigrant Pádraig Phiarais Cúndún (d. 1856) who brought his poetic skill with him to America. Ó Longáin and a few others were still able to compose verse with the metrical skills displayed by such poets as Eoghan Ruadh Ó Súilleabháin (d. 1784), but such expertise was rarely found among those of the next few generations whose poetry has come down to us. Worth mention here is Colum Wallace (Colm de Bhailís) of Connacht who was born in Lettermullen in Galway in 1796 and whose poetry was in circulation in his native county long before he died in 1903. He was hailed by Hyde as the last of his type—a poet of the people whose sole language was Irish.

Extant poetry from the decades between the founding of the Young Ireland movement and the death of Parnell included mediocre translations of some of Moore's *Melodies* (some of them by Archbishop John MacHale, who also composed a translation of Homer's 'Iliad'), poems occasioned by such events as the deaths of Davis and O'Connell, the failure of the potato crop in 1847, the Crimean war, and so on. And of course in those years there were in oral circulation many love poems and religious poems whose authors and dates of composition were unknown and which Hyde did so much to bring to the notice of the public in the last decades of the century. Hyde himself was publishing compositions of his own as early as 1879, but these were on the whole trivial and were often ungrammatical and devoid of metrical skill. There were others involved in the revival movement at that time whose native language was Irish and who tried their hand at verse, such as Pádraig Ó Laoghaire of Bearra in County Cork, but their efforts were generally not much better.

Four of the seven competitions in the first Oireachtas in 1897 were for verse compositions. One of these was for three short lyrics and the successful competitor was Bergin, soon to be lecturer in Celtic in Queen's College, Cork, and later an authority on Early Modern Irish bardic poetry. By 1897 he had acquired a good knowledge of west Cork Irish and these early poems were

competent in both language and metre. One of them, on the Irish language, was
composed to be sung and its refrain reflected the optimism of the time, which saw
protestants, such as Bergin and Hyde, united with catholics, such as Ua Laoghaire
and MacNeill, in a great national movement:

> Teanga ár dtíre is caoimhe ceól
> Searc ár sinsear ríoghdha romhainn,
> Ar séad glan uasal gléineach buadhach,
> Ní béarthar uainn a fuaim go deó.

(Our country's tongue of fairest music beloved by our royal ancestors of yore, our pure
noble treasure bright and victorious, never shall its sound be taken from us.)

Bergin continued to write poetry throughout most of his life, much of it
consisting of occasional verses addressed to friends and colleagues, including a
complimentary stanza for Hyde on his selection as president of Ireland in 1938.
He had a keen appreciation of music and in his love-song 'Maidean i mBéarra',
composed in 1900, we have words that fittingly grace one of our finest melodies,
the 'Londonderry air'. This, along with nineteen other poems by him, was
published in *Maidean i mBéarra agus dánta eile* (1918). Another poem in this
anthology is a national rallying song, which he entitled 'Amhrán dóchais' ('Song
of hope') and whose words he fitted to an old tune, 'Mór chluana'. Before Bergin
died in 1950 he had heard the taoiseach, John A. Costello, conclude a St Patrick's
day radio broadcast with a stanza from a poem that he had composed for St
Patrick's day 1913, and he had heard the air 'Mór chluana' mistakenly described
as 'Amhrán dóchais' when it was decided under Costello that this air would be
the basis for a musical salute to be used for the taoiseach on formal occasions.

Runner-up to Bergin in the 1897 competition was Tadhg Ó Donnchadha of
Cork, otherwise known as 'Torna'. He was thoroughly familiar with Irish prosody
and he seems to have turned out poems with great ease, for in the twenty years
or so up to 1921 he published over 300 original poems and about 400 translations,
many of them from Welsh. Some of these appeared in his *Leoithne Andeas* (1905)
and *Caitheamh aimsire* (1915).

An important factor in establishing high standards of metrical competence
among this new generation of Munster poets was the availability of good models
from earlier centuries. O'Daly's *Poets and poetry of Munster* was joined in the years
1900–16 by comprehensive editions of the poems of Séathrún Céitinn, Pádraigín
Haicéad, Dáibhidh Ó Bruadair, Aodhagán Ó Raithaille, Eoghan Ruadh Ó Súilleabháin, Piaras Mac Gearailt, and others.[1] The highly interesting syllabic poetry on
love themes was brought to the notice of the public by Thomas F. O'Rahilly in
his *Dánta grádha* (1916). Interest in poetry was such that an assembly was
convened in Cork city in 1904 for the purpose of exchanging views on it, and a
similar assembly was held in 1911. Among those present on both occasions was a
journalist and Irish enthusiast named Piaras Béaslaí who put forward quite radical

---

[1] Above, iii, 540; iv, 405.

suggestions as to how the best traditions of the language of the past might be developed in new moulds.[1] Like others of his generation he got caught up in the revolutionary movement and took part in the 1916 rising—a fact reflected in the title of an anthology of his, *Bealltaine 1916 agus dánta eile* (1920), which contains, along with poems composed in the years 1910–12, others composed while he was imprisoned in Portland in 1916, Lewes in 1917, Belfast in 1918, and Mountjoy in 1918 and 1919. Béaslaí was well able to compose in the old assonantal metres, but in line with his own ideas on poetic development he also occasionally used modernised forms of syllabic metres very effectively. Among these poems is one of great simplicity in which he recalls the feelings of himself and two companions in Kilmainham jail on 4 May 1916 when they heard the gunfire that told them of the execution of Edward Daly, Willie Pearse, and Joseph Mary Plunkett.

Willie Pearse's brother Patrick composed some poems of great feeling, including one for his mother, on the eve of his execution on 3 May. It is noteworthy that these were in English. Pearse had been composing in Irish since 1905 and had published twelve poems in his *Suantaidhe agus goltraidhe* (1914). Three additional poems were included in his *Scríbhinní*, published after his death. Among these were two marching songs for the Irish Volunteers, one of which he entitled 'An Dord Féinne' recalling the chant of the Fianna mentioned in the tale 'Bruidhean Caorthainn', which he had edited for the Gaelic League in 1908. A few of his poems are on religious themes, but the most noteworthy ones are three personal poems: 'Cad chuige dhíbh dom' chiapadh?', 'Fada liom do theacht', and 'Fornocht do chonnac thu', in which thoughts of death are very strong, especially in the last, a vision-type poem that concludes:

> Do thugas mo ghnúis
> Ar an ród so romham,
> Ar an ngníomh do–chím
> 'S ar an mbás do–gheobhad.

(I set my face towards the road before me, on the deed which I see and on the death I shall suffer).

Much of the Irish poetry of the eighteenth and nineteenth centuries was composed to be sung, and in the nineteenth century many of the song tunes were noted down by such scholars as Petrie, Joyce, and Goodman. One of the features of the Gaelic League from 1893 on was the use of social activities, such as concerts and *céilidhthe*, to attract members and retain their interest. These in turn created the need for anthologies of songs accompanied by music, and the period to 1921 saw a number of these published, including *Ceól ár sínsear* (1910), *Fuinn na smól* (1913), and *Ár gceól féinig* (1920), compiled by An tAthair Pádraig Breathnach who got many of the tunes from singers in Gaeltacht areas of Cork and Waterford, and *Amhráin Mhuighe Seóla* (1919), which contained songs from Galway and Mayo collected by Eibhlín Costello.

---

[1] Above, p. 238.

Irish was exceptional in having no drama before the revival period. However, the organisation of the Gaelic League in the form of local branches provided a good environment for dramatic activity as a form of entertainment. It is not surprising, then, that the contemporary interest in playwriting in English in Ireland led to the beginnings of theatre in Irish, nor is it surprising that Hyde was to the fore in this development. His plays, which were all short and designed to provide lighthearted entertainment, included 'Casadh an tsúgáin', which was performed in the Gaiety Theatre in Dublin in 1901, 'An tincéar agus an tsídheóg' (1902), 'An pósadh' (1903), and 'Maistín an Bhéarla' (1914). Ua Laoghaire wrote four short plays intended for staging: 'Bás Dhalláin' and 'Tadhg Saor' (1900), 'An sprid' (1902), and 'An bealach buidhe' (1906). He also wrote a more ambitious work, a dramatisation of the Ulster epic under the title 'Táin Bó Cuailgne 'n-a dhráma', which appeared in the *Cork Weekly Examiner* in 1900–01 and in book form in 1916. This was not intended for staging, but rather to convey to readers the 'Táin' story in contemporary Irish and in dialogue form, which Ua Laoghaire considered appropriate for the purpose.

Over a hundred plays were published between 1895 and 1921 and many of these were performed about the time of their first publication. Quite a number of them were translations of Anglo-Irish plays. Thus Eoghan Ó Neachtain's 'An cailín bán', published in the *Galway Pilot* in 1895, was a translation of Boucicault's 'The colleen bawn'; Mícheál Mag Ruadhrí's 'An fiaclóir', published in 1898 or 1899 and performed in Blackrock, County Dublin, in 1900, was a translation of John Cannon's 'The dentist'. A translation of Yeats's 'Cathleen Ni Houlihan' by Tomás Ó Ceallaigh was published in 1904 and was performed at the Oireachtas in Dublin in 1905. Other Anglo-Irish plays translated into Irish included works by Séamus MacManus, Pádraic Colum, Lady Gregory, Rutherford Mayne, Séamus O'Kelly, T. C. Murray, and Daniel Corkery. Among the original plays were 'Bairbre Ruadh' (1908) by Pádraic Ó Conaire, 'Íosagán' (1909) and 'An rí' (1910) by Pearse, and 'Coramac na Cuile' (1909), 'Fear na milliún púnt' (1915), and 'Cluiche cártaí' (1920) by Piaras Béaslaí.

THE role of the schools in the efforts to promote the use of Irish has been dealt with at some length, but this chapter would not be complete without some account of the steps taken to cope with the problems of teaching and learning the language. In 1894, the year following the foundation of the Gaelic League, one of its founders, Eugene O'Growney, who had himself begun to learn Irish in 1879 at the age of 16, began to publish in the *Gaelic Journal* his 'Easy lessons in Irish'. These appeared in book form in 1879–1901, and for years they served as the learner's first introduction to Irish.[1] In the course of time other grammar books—many of them much better—took their place beside them, but 'O'Growney' continued for decades to be a source of encouragement to beginners not to be afraid of making errors in

---

[1] By 1902–3 part I had reached its thirty-ninth edition and 271,000th copy. In the following year another 90,000 copies were printed.

speech and to realise the truth of the proverb *taithí a níos máistreacht* (it is practice that makes for mastery). O'Growney died in Los Angeles in 1899; the significance of his work was acknowledged when his body was brought back to Ireland in 1903 and buried with great honour in St Patrick's College, Maynooth.

Another priest who earned a place of distinction beside Peadar Ua Laoghaire and Eugene O'Growney was Patrick Dinneen (1860–1934), whose *Foclóir Gaedhilge agus Béarla*, first published in 1904 and revised for subsequent editions in 1927 and later, was the main lexicographical tool for Irish learners and writers until recent times. Dinneen was born near Rathmore in east Kerry; Irish was his native language but his special interest in it came to a head only after his ordination as a priest in 1894. His first major involvement was in the controversy about the position of Irish in secondary education in 1898. Two years later he left the Jesuits in order to devote himself full time to the Irish language. His energy and the scope of his activity as lecturer and writer were immense. His editions of earlier works include Keating's *Foras feasa ar Éirinn*, and the poems of Aodhagán Ó Rathaille, Séafradh Ua Donnchadha an Ghleanna, Eoghan Ruadh Ó Súilleabháin, and Tadhg Gaedhealach Ó Súilleabháin. His original Irish compositions include a historical novel, *Cormac Ua Conaill* (1901); some plays, the first of which was 'Creideamh agus gorta' (1901); works on local history and society such as *Cill Áirne* (1902) and *Muintear Chiarraidhe roimh an droch-shaoghal* (1905); many essays; and some poems, of which the longest is his 'Spiorad na saoirse' (1919) in which he commemorated the Easter rising. As well as writing extensively in Irish Dinneen was a very effective propagandist in English in the cause of the Irish language.

The authors mentioned in the preceding pages are only a few of those who composed many thousands of essays, stories, plays, and poems in Irish in the period to 1921. The upsurge in interest in Irish and the growth in the number of those learning it had created a demand for reading matter, which was met increasingly in the newspapers and the new periodicals. Ua Laoghaire's regular articles in the *Leader* encouraged journalists with a good knowledge of Irish, such as Béaslaí, to write in it as well as in English, and so the first decades of the twentieth century saw Irish used competently as a medium for the discussion of a variety of topics—political, economic, literary, and so on. Moreover the use of Irish in the administration of the Gaelic League in its meetings, and in its annual reports and other publications, was another factor in the development for a future role under an Irish parliament and government.

In the drive to encourage people to learn to speak and write Irish, difficulties arose because of current dialectal differences and the lack of any standard form, and considerable rivalry developed between the supporters of various dialects in the provinces of Connacht, Munster, and Ulster. Learners wishing to study in a Gaeltacht area were faced with a choice of dialect, and here the location of the various summer colleges was an important factor. An element that appeared to favour Munster Irish in the period up to 1921 was the prominence achieved by the writings of Ua Laoghaire and his associates. Connacht dialects were fairly well represented among writers, but Ulster dialects less so. The problem that dialectal variation posed for Irish in the educational system was unresolved when the Irish Free State came into being.

There were two other matters for major disagreement between scholars and writers of Irish in those years, and both had their origins in preceding centuries when the normal development of Irish as a written language closely associated with its current speech forms was inhibited under the domination of English. The first area of conflict was with regard to script and the type to be used in printing: Gaelic, which represented a continuation of the style of lettering found in most Irish manuscripts, or roman, the form used in printing English, French, and other languages. Roman type had been used in the first printed Irish book in 1567 and in some later works, including Hyde's *An sgeuluidhe Gaodhalach* (1890), but Gaelic type had been used in the first book in Irish printed in Ireland (1571) and it was Gaelic type that was favoured for publications of the learned societies in the middle of the nineteenth century and for those of the Gaelic League later on. The advantages of using roman type were argued strongly by a minority and the period to 1921 saw some indications of a shift in its favour, but Gaelic type was still that generally used by writers when the new state was founded. However, an indication of what might be the attitude of an Irish government in this matter is to be seen in the fact that in the official *Proceedings* of Dáil Éireann in the period 1919–21 roman type as well as Gaelic was used, and roman type alone was used in the publication of the *Official correspondence relating to the peace negotiations, June–September 1921*.

Type is only one of the externals of a written language. Spelling is another, and in this regard the learned societies and most writers of the mid-nineteenth century adhered to the antiquated spelling based on the sound system of thirteenth-century Irish, and this was the spelling used in the most comprehensive Irish dictionary available, O'Donovan's revised edition of O'Reilly's *Irish–English dictionary*, published in 1864. In line with the trend towards basing written Irish on the spoken language, which has been discussed above, suggestions that the spelling should be revised and simplified, to bring it more into line with spoken forms, were published in the *Gaelic Journal* and newspapers in the last decade of the nineteenth century. Among the advocates of such a change was Archbishop William Walsh of Dublin, and among its opponents was Ua Laoghaire who wrote in 1894 that 'any system of shorthand would be sure to permit what is purely Irish in the sounds . . . to slip away and be lost'.[1] Ua Laoghaire soon changed his mind and from 1900 on he was a strong supporter of moves to simplify the spelling. However, when Dinneen came to compile his dictionary he adhered to the old form of spelling although he admitted that it was 'undoubtedly cumbrous and awkward to a degree', and his lead set the fashion for most publications for years to come.[2]

[1] Peadar Ua Laoghaire to Michael Cusack (letter printed in *United Ireland*, 27 Jan. 1894).
[2] P. S. Dinneen, *Foclóir Gaeidhilge agus Béarla* (Dublin and London, 1904), p. viii.

Some of those who advocated a simplification of Irish spelling were encouraged by the spelling reform movement currently active in England, and they came together and devised a series of rules whereby the ordinary spelling could be modified and shortened by dropping consonants that were silent in speech and by using the letters *v* and *y* in addition to those normally used in writing Irish. The movement was spearheaded by Bergin, recently returned from Germany to be professor in the School of Irish Learning in Dublin, Richard O'Daly, a competent linguist and phonetician, and Seán Ó Caoimh, a journalist who had been one of the founders of the Irish College in Ballingeary, County Cork, and who changed the form of his surname to Ó Cuív in conformity with the new rules. In addition to advocating revision of the spelling they decided that roman script and type should be used, with *h* replacing the dot or mark over consonants as a mark of lenition; thus ꜰʟᴀɪᴄᴇᴀᵯᴀɪʟ was written *flahúil*. The first publication using the new system was *Irish made easy* (1907) and others soon followed, including Béaslaí's *Coramac na Cuile* (1909). In 1910 An Cumann um Letiriú Shímplí (Society for the Simplification of Irish Spelling) was set up and in November of that year Bergin delivered its inaugural lecture under the title 'Is Irish to be strangled?'. Ua Laoghaire announced his support for the society and in the following decade many of his works were issued in the new spelling. The Letiriú Shímplí was a phonemically adequate system for the transliteration of west Cork Irish for which it was mostly used, but it could, in fact, be used for dialects spoken in Connacht and elsewhere. It was an excellent aid to teachers and learners, but it was too radical to gain acceptance as a normal orthography.

From the beginning a majority of the central committee of the Gaelic League opposed the use of the revised spelling, and the unreformed spelling continued to be used in the league's publications. However, between 1910 and 1921 many writers began to adopt, though in a somewhat haphazard way, various simplifications, such as *-ú* for *-ughadh*, as in *mothú*; *-í* for *idhe* or *-eadha*, as in *filí*, or for *-idh-*, as in *oíche*; and the omission of final *dh*, as in *grá*. The use of Irish in the first dáil required that members of the secretarial staff should be proficient in that language, and in May 1919 Mícheál Ó Loingsigh, a native Irish speaker from County Cork who had taken part in the rising, was appointed as official translator. With him began the systematic development of the Irish language under official authority for its future use in all areas of government. The experience thus gained under the dáil in 1919–21 provided the basis that enabled the official translation staff of the oireachtas from 1922 on to perform its duties efficiently and to pave the way for the eventual acceptance of a reformed system of spelling for general use. This was but one of the tasks that were to devolve on state officials as a result of the constitutional designation of Irish as the 'national language' in the constitution of 1922.

APPENDIX

1 IRISH-SPEAKERS, BY COUNTIES AND PROVINCES, 1851–1911

	1851	1891	1901	1911
Province of Leinster				
Carlow	243 [0.4]	123 [0.3]	222 [0.6]	1,008 [2.8]
Dublin county	1,281 [0.9]	1,273 [0.7]	3,545 [2.2]	5,873 [3.4]
Dublin county borough	3,426 [1.3]	2,199 [0.9]	9,453 [3.3]	11,870 [3.9]
Kildare	514 [0.5]	381 [0.5]	1,198 [1.9]	1,677 [2.5]
Kilkenny county	20,830 [15.0]	3,767 [4.9]	3,568 [4.5]	3,264 [4.4]
Kilkenny	590 [3.0]	166 [1.5]		
King's County	403 [0.4]	324 [0.5]	522 [0.9]	1,933 [3.4]
Longford	1,465 [1.8]	252 [0.5]	340 [0.7]	915 [2.1]
Louth	18,762 [20.7]	2,588 [4.4]	3,204 [4.9]	3,760 [5.9]
Drogheda	599 [3.6]	88 [0.7]		
Meath	8,963 [6.4]	1,492 [1.9]	1,357 [2.0]	2,447 [3.8]
Queen's County	244 [0.2]	190 [0.3]	405 [0.7]	1,427 [2.6]
Westmeath	921 [0.8]	338 [0.5]	691 [1.1]	2,096 [3.5]
Wexford	800 [0.4]	320 [0.3]	1,300 [1.2]	2,901 [2.8]
Wicklow	135 [0.1]	176 [0.3]	631 [1.0]	1,054 [1.7]
Province of Munster				
Clare	126,996 [59.8]	46,878 [37.7]	43,486 [38.7]	36,704 [35.2]
Cork county	296,034 [52.5]	112,516 [31.0]	97,979 [29.8]	77,205 [23.8]
Cork county borough	10,381 [12.1]	7,204 [9.6]	7,737 [10.2]	6,693 [8.7]
Kerry	146,498 [61.5]	74,182 [41.4]	71,671 [43.2]	60,719 [38.0]
Limerick county	77,982 [37.4]	15,927 [13.8]	12,352 [11.4]	10,921 [10.4]
Limerick	4,204 [7.9]	1,135 [3.1]	1,708 [4.5]	2,612 [6.8]
Tipperary	62,764 [18.9]	12,312 [7.1]	9,735 [6.1]	10,020 [6.6]
Waterford county	86,823 [62.6]	36,265 [46.9]	29,460 [48.8]	21,692 [38.4]
Waterford county borough	4,103 [16.2]	1,214 [5.8]	2,140 [8.0]	2,128 [7.7]
Province of Ulster				
Antrim	3,033 [1.2]	885 [0.4]	1,012 [0.5]	2,724 [1.4]
Armagh	13,736 [7.0]	3,486 [2.4]	4,487 [3.6]	2,792 [2.3]
Belfast	295 [0.3]	917 [0.4]	3,587 [1.0]	7,595 [2.0]
Cavan	13,027 [7.5]	3,410 [3.0]	5,425 [5.6]	2,968 [3.3]
Donegal	73,258 [28.7]	62,037 [33.4]	60,677 [34.9]	59,313 [35.2]
Down	1,153 [0.4]	590 [0.3]	1,411 [0.7]	2,423 [1.2]
Fermanagh	2,704 [2.3]	561 [0.8]	1,005 [1.5]	1,563 [2.5]
Londonderry	5,406 [2.8]	2,723 [1.8]	3,476 [2.4]	4,039 [2.9]

	1851	1891	1901	1911
Monaghan	10,955 [7.7]	2,847 [3.3]	5,324 [7.1]	5,430 [7.6]
Tyrone	12,892 [5.0]	6,687 [3.9]	6,454 [4.3]	7,584 [5.3]
Province of Connacht				
Galway county	207,649 [69.7]	117,510 [59.4]	108,870 [56.5]	98,523 [54.1]
Galway	14,595 [61.4]	8,065 [47.5]		
Leitrim	15,003 [13.4]	5,622 [7.2]	4,004 [5.8]	3,923 [6.2]
Mayo	180,078 [65.6]	110,365 [50.4]	99,764 [50.1]	88,601 [46.1]
Roscommon	46,296 [26.7]	11,885 [13.0]	15,372 [15.1]	10,113 [10.8]
Sligo	49,228 [38.3]	21,336 [21.7]	17,570 [20.9]	15,927 [20.1]
Summary by provinces				
Leinster	59,176 [3.5]	13,677 [1.2]	26,436 [2.3]	40,225 [3.5]
Munster	815,785 [43.9]	307,633 [26.2]	276,268 [25.7]	228,694 [22.1]
Ulster	136,476 [6.8]	84,152 [5.2]	92,858 [5.9]	96,440 [6.1]
Connacht	512,849 [50.8]	274,783 [37.8]	245,580 [38.0]	217,087 [35.5]
all Ireland	1,524,286 [23.3]	680,245 [14.5]	641,142 [14.4]	582,446 [13.3]

The figures in square brackets are Irish-speakers as percentages of the population of the counties and provinces.

2 IRISH-SPEAKERS, BY BARONIES, 1891

	% Irish-speakers[a]	monoglots as % of Irish-speakers
County Clare		
Burren	72.6	5.7
Clonderalaw	41.3	0.9
Corcomroe	62.7	2.8
Ibrickan	52.2	1.3
Inchiquin	55.1	1.3
Moyarta	45.2	2.9
County Cork		
Bantry	44.8	3.2
Bear	51.5	7.4
Courceys	48.2	0.9
Ibane and Barryroe	53.6	1.4
Kinnatalloon	45.4	1.1
West Muskerry	54.2	4.3
County Donegal[b]		
Banagh	48.0	7.4
Boylagh	78.4	14.6
Kilmacrenan	49.9	14.5
County Galway		
Aran	88.5	30.0
Athenry	50.3	0.9
Ballymoe	56.6	2.9
Ballynahinch	74.0	13.6
Clare	74.6	6.5
Dunkellin	66.3	4.7
Galway	47.6	7.4
Killian	51.1	0.9
Kiltartan	50.7	2.4
Loughrea	40.9	0.8
Moycullen	86.3	34.3
Ross	99.3	66.0
Tiaquin	64.7	2.9
County Kerry		
Corkaguiny	71.4	14.3
Dunkerron North	64.0	5.2
Dunkerron South	59.2	5.3
Glanarought	45.8	3.7
Iveragh	69.8	9.7
County Mayo		
Burrishoole	51.2	6.4
Carra	47.2	1.9

	% Irish-speakers[a]	monoglots as % of Irish-speakers
County Mayo (contd)		
Clanmorris	43.8	1.0
Costello	43.2	0.6
Erris	75.9	14.1
Gallen	54.9	1.9
Kilmaine	70.4	5.8
Tirawley	41.6	2.3
County Waterford		
Coshmore and Coshbride	46.5	1.9
Decies within Drum	77.1	8.7
Decies without Drum	58.3	3.1
Glenahiry	47.7	3.1

[a] This table includes all baronies where more than 40 per cent of the population were Irish-speakers; monoglots are given as a percentage of the Irish-speaking population.

[b] There is a clear indication that there was a strong concentration of Irish-speakers within the barony of Raphoe throughout the nineteenth century. In 1851 there were 5,532, which represented only 10 per cent of the population, but of these 2,314 (41.8 per cent) were Irish-speaking monoglots. In the 1891 census, figures are given for Raphoe North and Raphoe South. While in Raphoe North there were only 598 Irish-speakers (3.7 per cent of the population), in Raphoe South there were 3,736 (19.7 per cent) and of these 304 (or 8.1 per cent) were monoglots. An indication of the areas of concentration of Irish-speakers is to be seen in the 1911 census figures, which show that in the barony of Raphoe South 58.0 per cent of the population of Altnapaste D.E.D. (i.e. 503 persons) were Irish-speakers, 71.4 per cent of that of Cloghan D.E.D. (i.e. 2,262 persons), 93.3 per cent of that of Graffy D.E.D. (i.e. 1,017 persons), and 68.7 per cent of that of Meencargagh D.E.D. (i.e. 313 persons).

3 DISTRICT ELECTORAL DIVISIONS, 1911

counties[a]	80% & over	50–79%	25–49%	total
Antrim	—	1	2	
Cavan	—	—	1	
Clare	2	49	43	
Cork	4	30	111	
Donegal	23	24	18	
Galway	40	87	44	
Kerry	11	44	50	
Kildare[b]	—	—	1	
Leitrim	—	—	1	
Limerick	—	—	7	
Louth	—	—	1	
Mayo	15	46	81	
Monaghan	—	—	4	
Roscommon	—	—	3	
Sligo	—	4	17	
Tipperary	—	2	1	
Tyrone	—	3	4	
Waterford	6	27	37	
total	101	317	426	884

[a] This table lists by county the number of D.E.D.s in which Irish-speakers were recorded in 1911 as numbering (a) 80 per cent or more of the population, (b) at least 50 per cent and under 80 per cent, and (c) at least 25 per cent and under 50 per cent. The total number of D.E.D.s in Ireland for 1911 was 3,751.

[b] See p. 390, n. 3.

CHAPTER XV

Visual arts and society, 1850–1900

CYRIL BARRETT AND JEANNE SHEEHY

In the second half of the nineteenth century significant changes took place in
the fortunes of the visual arts in Ireland. After the act of union, patronage of the
arts dwindled. Many of the landed aristocracy chose to migrate, drawing their
fortunes after them. Even the applied arts, silver and glass in particular, for which
the country had been renowned in the eighteenth century, ceased to flourish.
There were Irish artists, and good ones: James Arthur O'Connor, Francis Danby,
Daniel Maclise, John Henry Foley, and William Mulready. But they worked for
the most part in England, where they could get a better living, or, indeed, any
living at all.

    1851 was the year of the Great Exhibition in London. Irish crafts were
represented there and were well received.[1] The exhibition seemed to inject new
life into the arts in the British Isles and Ireland, surprisingly (given its economic
situation), was one of the quickest to respond, and rapidly applied the lessons of
the Crystal Palace. In 1852, a national exhibition was held in Cork and in 1853
an international exhibition in Dublin, both of which included the fine arts. The
exhibitions also revived a long-abandoned project for a national gallery. The
notion of a national gallery of Ireland had been very much in the air in the late
eighteenth century. Under the viceroyalty of the duke of Rutland (1784–7) it was
proposed to establish an academy of art and a national gallery to house old
masters.[2] A keeper had even been designated—Peter de Grée (d. 1789), a Dutch
painter living in Dublin. But the duke died before anything could be done, and
although the speaker John Foster took up the plan, it was dropped in favour of a
proposal by Lord Charlemont to found a museum of mechanical arts and a
repository of manufactures, which was not done either. The idea of a national
gallery then lapsed until 1853. Meanwhile an academy of arts, the Royal
Hibernian Academy, was founded by royal charter on 5 August 1823, and the
National Gallery—in London—in 1824.

    When the Dublin industrial exhibition of 1853 to be organised by the Royal
Dublin Society was mooted, William Dargan, the railway magnate, donated
£40,000 on condition that it should include a section devoted to the fine arts. To

---

[1] Above, v, 394.   [2] Above, iv, 519.

commemorate Dargan's munificence a testimonial fund was launched. The money raised was to go towards the establishment of what, in 1854, it was decided would be called the Dargan Institute. The institute would house a national collection. Meanwhile on 1 November 1853 the Irish Institution (on the model of the British Institution) was founded for the same purpose. It was to hold exhibitions of old masters, mostly from Irish collections, and acquire as many of them as possible by gift. In this way interest in the idea of a national gallery was aroused and a nucleus of a collection accumulated. The institution held six exhibitions between 1854 and 1859 (mostly in the premises of the Royal Hibernian Academy) before it was dissolved in 1863, its mission accomplished. The gallery was opened in the following year.[1]

By 1854 it was possible to set aside £5,000 out of the Dargan Testimonial Fund towards the cost of founding a gallery. In the same year an act of parliament gave formal recognition to the enterprise.[2] The act provided not only for a gallery of painting and sculpture, but also for the care of a public library (which in effect meant the housing of Marsh's library in the gallery building) and the erection of a public museum. The clause about Marsh's library was repealed in the following year and a grant of £6,000 towards the cost of building the gallery was voted.[3] A site on Leinster Lawn was donated by the Royal Dublin Society. The foundation-stone was laid by the lord lieutenant, the earl of Eglinton and Winton, on 29 January 1859. In order to preserve the symmetry of Leinster Lawn it had been stipulated that the design should conform to that of the natural history museum built on the opposite side of the lawn. The Belfast architect Charles Lanyon drew up plans, but the design used was by Captain Francis Fowke, R.E., of the department of science and art at South Kensington.

The government of the gallery was vested in seventeen governors and guardians. Of these five served *ex officio* (the president and senior vice-president of the Royal Dublin Society, the presidents of the Royal Hibernian Academy and the Royal Irish Academy, and the chairman of the board of works); two artists were to be designated by the Royal Hibernian Academy; and three were to be appointees of the lord lieutenant. The remaining seven were to be elected from among, and by, benefactors who had either donated £10 or a work valued at not less than £20, or had made an annual subscription of one guinea, provided that the number of such benefactors did not fall below a hundred; otherwise the places would be filled by nominees of the lord lieutenant. To whatever extent it is any indication of the measure of public patronage of the arts in Ireland, since 1859 these seven places have always been filled by nominees either of the lord lieutenant or of the Irish government.

---

[1] Above, v, 394; Catherine de Courcy, *The foundation of the national gallery of Ireland* (Dublin, 1985).

[2] 17 & 18 Vict., c. 99 (10 Aug. 1854).

[3] 18 & 19 Vict., c. 44 (26 June 1855). See also Muriel McCarthy, *All graduates and gentlemen: Marsh's library* (Dublin, 1980), pp 59–61.

As for the contents of the gallery, the Irish Institution had already acquired some paintings: there had been a bequest of water-colours by British and Irish artists in the will of Captain G. A. Taylor in 1855; but the most considerable contribution was made by the chairman of the board of governors, the lord chancellor, Maziere Brady, who by personal loans helped the gallery to buy thirty-nine paintings for £3,333 through his agent Robert McPherson and a Roman dealer, Aducci. It is a measure of the change in taste over 140 and 50 years respectively, that Strickland should say of this purchase: 'the only merit of many of these pictures was their size; but they helped to cover the bare walls of the newly founded gallery, and by degrees, in the subsequent years, they were weeded out.'[1] These were works by Annibale Carracci, Maratti, Lanfranco, Rosa, and Bassano, any one of which would now realise more than the present-day equivalent of what was paid for the whole collection. In 1860 George F. Mulvany, the painter and secretary of the Irish Institution, had casts from the antique made by the British Museum. These, like the paintings, helped to fill the empty spaces, and like them were eventually condemned to outer darkness, but unlike the paintings their places were not taken by other works. The government contributed £5,000 for the purchase of pictures, and private subscriptions brought in another £5,567 15s. 5d., of which £2,000 was donated by Dargan. From 1866 onwards an annual parliamentary grant of £1,000 was made available for the purchase of paintings, though it had not infrequently to be supplemented.

By 1864 105 pictures had been acquired. On 30 January of that year the gallery was formally opened by the lord lieutenant, the earl of Carlisle. One novel feature of the new gallery was that it was lit by gaslight. It was thus the first gallery in Europe that could be opened after dark. In the same year a statue of Dargan by Sir Thomas Farrell, sited in front of the gallery, was unveiled. The administrators of the testimonial funds had agreed to drop the name Dargan Institute in favour of National Gallery, if a statue, a portrait, and a commemorative plaque were erected in Dargan's honour.

Mulvany had been appointed director of the National Gallery in 1862. He continued in office until his death in 1869. It was his main achievement that he wrested the purchasing decisions out of the hands of the board of governors and into those of the director. He concentrated mainly on Italian paintings—such was the fashion of the day—but he also bought Dutch, Spanish, and German masters. In spite of Strickland's snide comment that he bought with more zeal than discretion and that the pictures were 'remarkable for their area rather than their authenticity',[2] Mulvany has to his credit the purchase of four paintings by Jordaens, two Morettos, a Parmigianino, a Murillo, a Tintoretto, a Guardi, a Coello, and a controversial Michelangelo, among many others.

Attendance at the new gallery in the first five years of its existence exceeded 100,000 a year, reaching its maximum of 128,650 in 1867—it was never to reach

---

[1] Walter G. Strickland, *A dictionary of Irish artists* (2 vols, Dublin and London, 1913), ii, 647.
[2] Strickland, *Dict. Ir. artists*, ii, 648.

anything like this figure (an average of about 350 a day) again until the late 1960s.[1] This may be partly explained by the novelty of the gallery. There was a dramatic slump in attendance in the early 1870s, reaching its lowest for the decade in 1874 (72,687); a sudden rally in 1876 (89,950); a decline, and then a steady rise to 98,147 in 1882. This was more or less maintained for a few years till it again plummetted around the mid-1880s. There were two more peaks, 1888 (87,654) and 1891 (86,633). After that there was a decline, reaching the lowest point in 1895 (64,342).

Apart from the high figures for the period 1866–71, which, as has already been stated, can be accounted for by novelty, the fluctuations in attendance at the national gallery reflect trends in other spheres. One useful guide to taste, in Dublin at least, is the attendance figures and receipts at the Royal Hibernian Academy exhibitions. In the 1850s these were low, receipts varying between £200 and £300. Towards the end of the decade there was a steady rise, reaching £400 about 1860; then a steady decline to 1866 (£151), which is reflected in the subscriptions to the art unions. There was a steady rise until 1870 and then a levelling out of academy receipts at about £430 and attendance at about 23,000. This was followed by a spectacular rise to £748 in 1879, with 35,848 (excluding season-ticket holders) attending the academy exhibition in 1880, and 98,147 attending the national gallery in 1882. From then until the end of the century there was a more or less steady decline, but, though attendance at exhibitions sank to its lowest point (7,317 in 1900), receipts at £271 in 1900 were higher than in the 1860s. The general picture shows a slump in interest in art around the mid-1860s, an abnormal rise in the late 1870s and 1880s, and a decline to something like the situation in the 1850s towards the end of the century. How these figures are to be interpreted and explained is not easy to say. The exceptional interest in the arts around 1880 requires explanation; the figures for the rest of the half-century may possibly be regarded as normal.

In his testimony before the select committee on art union laws, Michael Angelo Hayes said: 'I think all classes in Ireland have a very great taste for art; but they do not show their taste in the way it is manifested in large towns in Scotland and England.' In other words, they did not buy pictures. Hayes stated this more bluntly when he said: 'Private patronage of art is very little.' Public patronage seems to have been pretty small too. According to Hayes, on the opening day of the Royal Hibernian Academy exhibition the lord lieutenant might spend £60 or £100. He also cited the case of his brother-in-law Alderman Peter Paul McSwiney, who when lord mayor in 1864 tried to set a precedent by buying pictures, but his example was not followed. Whatever patronage was extended to art came from the middle and 'some of the higher class' rather than the 'richer' or the artisan class (these distinctions are a little unclear).[2] This was in 1866. In

---

[1] From 93,179 in 1967, attendances rose to 324,573 in 1969 and 978,000 in 1991 (figures supplied by Dr Brian Kennedy).

[2] *Report from the select committee on art union laws . . .*, pp 30, 32, H.C. 1866 (332), vii, 46, 48.

1888 it is stated in the catalogue to the Irish exhibition in South Kensington: 'The taste of the amateur or dilettante in Ireland lies more with Irish antiquities than with modern art.'[1] Lord Powerscourt, addressing the Art Union of Ireland in 1893, suggested that the artistic feeling 'which we know exists in our people' would find vent if some scheme could be devised for diverting their minds from 'the mere material interests in their small and narrow lives'.[2] A writer in the *Irish Daily Independent* in 1894 castigated Cork for neglect of its artists at the end of the century: 'artists of merit have to depart to win credit for other countries, while many, without merit or enterprise to do this, have to abandon all hope of being any more than amateurs.'[3]

In 1851 the Royal Irish Art Union (the first in Ireland, founded in 1839) and the National Art Union (founded in 1847) collapsed. Five years later a new art union, the Dublin Art Union, was founded but it too went out of existence in 1858 without making a single purchase. There had been no Royal Hibernian Academy exhibitions in 1857, for reasons to be explained later.[4] In 1858 the Art Union of Ireland was founded under the auspices of the Irish Institution. In 1860 the Shilling Art Union of Dublin was founded. All these bodies operated on the principle of collecting money by subscription; the subscriber was entitled to a chance of winning either a work of art bought with the collected funds, or a money prize that he or she was to spend on buying a work of art. Thus in the early 1860s a new stimulus was given to interest in the purchase of works of art, and this coincided with the foundation of the national gallery. As Hayes said, 'there was a great indifference to art on the part of the public until the art unions were established, but they have produced a very different feeling; in fact, the increased amount of private purchases is a proof of that.'[5]

The Irish art unions, however, had to compete with English and Scottish art unions and with lotteries for charitable purposes. This was made very clear by Hayes in his testimony to the committee on art union laws. The chief offenders were the Manchester Art Union and the Association for the Promotion of Fine Arts in Scotland. They had agents in every major city in Ireland, and the latter recruited heavily among the Dublin Scots. Although they spent some money in Ireland it never amounted to more than £300 per annum and according to Hayes averaged £160. Most of the money raised in Ireland went to support art in Great Britain, though some pictures probably found their way to Ireland. The presence of agents from these unions was one of the reasons for the formation of the Art Union of Ireland, as stated in the minutes of the first meeting in 1858. But, as Hayes pointed out, the evil that these competitors did was not so much to take away subscribers as to make the public tired of the art union idea. This was also

---

[1] *Irish exhibition in London, 1888: part I. Catalogue of pictures and sculpture . . .* ([London, 1888]), p. 6.
[2] *Irish Daily Independent*, 3 May 1893.
[3] Ibid., 30 Jan. 1894.
[4] Below, pp 443–4.
[5] *Report . . . on art union laws*, p. 32.

an effect of the charitable lotteries. But they offered an even greater threat, since the prizes often included a carriage worth £500 with a horse worth £60–70, whereas the prizes in art union draws never amounted to more than £100.[1] The decline in interest in art, which was in effect a return to customary indifference, can therefore be attributed to the causes militating against the art unions, and possibly, but to a much lesser extent, to the wearing off of the novelty of the National Gallery of Ireland. It can hardly be attributed to lack of money, since at least by the mid-1850s there was money for building and for art unions in the early years of their existence.

While on the subject of patronage it might be worth recording the following from Hayes's testimony: 'a large portion of the income of young artists has been diminished by . . . photography; and also teaching as a profession has been very much reduced in its emoluments by the schools of design.'[2] The lack of patronage had, therefore, considerable effect on Irish artists in the second half of the nineteenth century, yet more returned to or stayed in Ireland than previously. The reasons for this will be discussed later.

While on the subject of popular interest in art something must be said about the various exhibitions that took place in the second half of the nineteenth century. Mention has already been made of the Cork exhibition of 1852 and the Dublin exhibition of 1853. The Cork National Exhibition originated as a Munster exhibition, but rapidly grew in proportions. An extension (the Southern Hall) had to be added to the Cork Exchange Hall. The reasons for including fine art are interesting. To the question: 'What is the use of all this?' John Francis Maguire replies:

The occasion afforded a fitting opportunity of displaying the imitative and creative genius of our countrymen in the highest walks of art; and because the application of art to the purposes of manufacture—the blending of artistic beauty with practical utility—is becoming every day more necessary to the refined tastes of the age in which we live.[3]

This was certainly the voice of the mid-nineteenth century speaking. It is not surprising that the schools of design, which were also dedicated to these noble principles, figured prominently in this exhibition. The exhibits were confined to the works of Irish artists working at home and abroad. This seems to have been the first collective exhibition of Irish artists.

The Dublin exhibition of 1853 was on a far grander scale. It was an international exhibition, though it also called itself, modestly (and slightly inaccurately), the Irish Industrial Exhibition. The idea for the exhibition originated in Cork shortly after the opening of the Cork exhibition. Dargan offered £20,000 towards the exhibition, which was to be an enlarged version of the Royal Dublin Society

[1] Ibid., pp 30–31, 34.
[2] Ibid., p. 32. For the development of photography in this period, see Peadar Slattery, 'The uses of photography in Ireland, 1839–1900' (Ph.D. thesis, University of Dublin, 3 vols, 1992).
[3] John Francis Maguire, *The industrial movement in Ireland, as illustrated by the national exhibition of 1852* (Cork, 1853), p. 284.

triennial exhibition of manufactures. As we have seen, he made it a condition that fine art should be included. The exhibition building included, besides the society's premises in Leinster House and its court, a specially erected exhibition building of cast iron, hammered iron, and glass on the lines of the Crystal Palace, but far more elegant, erected by Sir John Benson on Leinster Lawn. One outstanding feature of the building was the quality of the light. This was especially true of the fine arts court, which, it was claimed, 'has proved to be the very best room for the suitable exhibition of paintings of all sizes, that has yet been erected'.[1]

The scale of the fine art section was quite formidable. There were 455 pieces of sculpture of, on the whole, no great merit, and 1,023 paintings of considerable value: they included works attributed to Titian, Caravaggio, the Carracci, Canaletto, Veronese, del Sarto, Domenichino, Correggio, Rubens, Rembrandt, Poussin, Claude, Watteau, Tintoretto, Lely, Kneller, Hogarth, Reynolds, Gainsborough—most of them in Irish collections (328 in all); dozens of obscure contemporary Belgian painters, and the rest a mixed bag of mainly Irish artists. The cost of transport and insurance of such a number would be prohibitive today. The attendance at the exhibition was remarkable: 589,372 paid at the door; 366,923 held season tickets. This works out at four visits *per capita* of the population of Dublin, a rate that is far in excess of the attendance of the London exhibition of 1851.

During the remainder of the nineteenth century there were six more major exhibitions of Irish art, four in Dublin, one in Cork, and one in London. In 1861 exhibitions of art and ornamental art were held in the New Hall, Kildare Street, Dublin. In 1865 a more considerable exhibition, the Dublin International Exhibition of Arts and Manufactures, was held in Earlsfort Terrace. It included 543 works of foreign schools, 292 pieces of sculpture, 159 works by old masters, 219 by the British (including the Irish) school, 137 water-colours, some engravings and architectural drawings, and 51 works by holders of the Victoria Cross (veterans of the Crimean war and Indian mutiny, presumably). The Dublin exhibition of 1872 was also held in Earlsfort Terrace. The mixture was again much as before, but among the 1,502 exhibits there were 288 photographs, and in addition there was the nucleus of a national portrait gallery containing 630 pictures.

There were only two more major exhibitions in Ireland before the end of the century and they were within a year of each other: the Exhibition of Irish Arts and Manufactures at the Rotunda, Dublin, in 1882, and the Cork Industrial Exhibition of 1883. This represents a gap of ten years, which corresponds to the falling off of attendance at the National Gallery and the Royal Hibernian Academy and the lesser peak of 1882–3. The Rotunda exhibition was mainly of Irish artists, though Watteau, Le Brun, Maratti, Vandyke, Jan Steen, and Reynolds mysteri-

---

[1] *The Irish industrial exhibition of 1853: a detailed catalogue . . .*, ed. John Sproule (Dublin and London, 1854), p. 40.

ously cropped up in their midst. The exhibition is chiefly interesting for the appearance of the Antwerp school, F. W. (as he was then known) Osborne and J. M. Kavanagh. It is also memorable for the number of Foley miniatures (twenty-three), which were offered for £5 each. The Cork exhibition, in spite of the odd Zurbarán and possible Panini (*sic*), was not up to the standard of the 1852 exhibition. Few of the artists have stood the test of time. One new name is of interest—Sarah Purser. As in gallery attendance and sales, so in exhibitions, the period 1883–1901 seems to have been a doldrum in Ireland. There were two peaks, however, one in 1888 when an exhibition of Irish art was mounted in South Kensington, and again in 1893 when an 'Irish village' was organised by Lady Aberdeen, wife of the lord lieutenant, at the Chicago World's Fair, but that was not strictly an artistic contribution—mercifully, since in the opinion of Louis Sullivan and most modern writers on art and architecture that particular event was a retrograde step in the development of art.[1]

In spite, therefore, of the founding of the National Gallery of Ireland and the popular support it received, art in Ireland was not in a very healthy state as the nineteenth century entered its third quarter—though, it must be added, no worse than it had been in the previous half-century. This is confirmed by a study of the art institutions at that time, in particular the Royal Hibernian Academy, which was passing through a crisis that was not without the element of farce. The academy had been founded in 1823, but a quarter of a century later it was in disarray. Strickland accurately and candidly summarises the history of the body when he writes:

From the time of its foundation to the present day [1912] the academy has struggled against adverse circumstances, partly from the neglect and apathy of the public and partly from the difficulty which was found in filling the ranks of the academicians with artists who could paint . . . The academy had often to elect as members of its body artists whose qualifications were of the smallest, and it is not surprising therefore that at some periods of its existence its exhibitions failed to enlist the support of the public.[2]

This last remark refers especially to the last quarter of the century. The problems with which we are concerned are of a different kind.

In 1856 the president of the academy was Martin Cregan, who had held the office since 1832; that is, for all but nine years of the academy's existence. In that year Michael Angelo Hayes was elected secretary and was determined to take the duties of his office seriously. He set about reducing the academy's debt and enforcing the rules. The latter move was resisted by the older members and things came to a head when Hayes refused to recognise George Petrie as a member for failing to exhibit at least every second year, which was a condition of membership. In December a rival faction met and elected Petrie president and Bernard Mulrenin secretary. Hayes refused to recognise the election or to hand over the

[1] Elizabeth Gilmore Holt, *From the classicists to the impressionists* (New York, 1966), pp 302–3.
[2] Strickland, *Dict. Ir. artists*, ii, 617.

keys of office, and was expelled in April 1857. In an exchange of letters in the press Hayes came out on top, but in October Petrie was duly elected by the academy as a whole. At this point the government, which had so far allowed the academy to settle its own affairs, intervened. As a result of an inquiry and a report by Norman Macleod, assistant secretary of the department of science and art at South Kensington, a new charter was drawn up, which in the event did little to improve the academy.[1] Petrie took exception to some of its provisions and resigned when it was accepted in 1859 (it came into force in 1861). Hayes was reinstated, and in 1860 was reelected secretary; so, in effect, the victory finally went to him and his party. It would hardly be an exaggeration to say that this storm in a teacup was the most momentous event in the academy's history in this period.

On the other hand, the academy's other function, the running of a school of fine art to which admission was free, was, during the late nineteenth century, not entirely unsuccessful. The reason for its rise in importance seems to have been the conversion of the Royal Dublin Society schools into a government school of design in 1849, with a consequent emphasis on the education of designers for applied rather than fine art. At the insistence of the department of science and art, women were admitted into the schools at this time. Women were admitted to the academy schools in 1893. This was partly in response to a growing demand for equality in education for women, but also, apparently, because the academy was having difficulty recruiting men. There were many notable women artists in Ireland in the late nineteenth century, among the most outstanding being Sarah Purser, Helen Mabel Trevor, Edith Somerville, Sarah Cecilia Harrison, and the water-colourists Rose Barton and Mildred Butler.[2]

SINCE the middle of the eighteenth century the Dublin Society had run a school of art, the story of which has been told in a previous volume.[3] In 1847, in its wisdom, the government decided to convert it into schools of design on the model of those in Britain. It is beyond the scope of this narrative to discuss the magnitude of the disaster that this decision brought on the teaching of art in Britain and Ireland. The ostensible purpose of the schools of design was to improve industrial design in the British dominions and make it competitive, especially against the French. With a logic comprehensible only to politicians, the method of teaching imposed on these new schools was based not on the French but on the German model. In Ireland four schools of design were set up: Dublin, Cork, Belfast, and Waterford. The first three were established on 1 May 1849 with the appointment of headmasters. Henry McManus, who had been summarily

[1] *Report upon the affairs and past management of the Royal Hibernian Academy...*, H.C. 1857–8 (294), xlvi, 477–500.

[2] See [Wanda Ryan-Smolin, Elizabeth Mayes, and Jenni Rogers (ed.)], *Irish women artists from the eighteenth century to the present day* (National Gallery of Ireland, Dublin, 1987).

[3] Above, iv, 517–19.

dismissed from the Glasgow School of Art (to the intense indignation of the students) the previous year, was appointed headmaster of the Dublin school, which was henceforth to be known as 'The Government School of Design in connection with the Royal Dublin Society'. The four society schools (figure, landscape and ornament, architecture, and modelling) continued in existence under assistant masters until 1854. The Dublin school was housed in the gallery on the west side of Leinster House. The society's practice of offering prizes was continued, and at the ninth distribution of prizes in 1851 (the first as a school of design) the aims of the newly constituted school were stated in the following terms:

Our Dublin school of design aspires to no less a task than assisting to revive the languid manufactures of Ireland, by teaching the rising generation how the beautiful may be incorporated with the useful, in order that the foreign manufacturer may be met and competed with in the home market on something like equal terms.[1]

Lord Clarendon (lord lieutenant, 1847–52), at the distribution of prizes the following year, returned to this theme when he mentioned, by way of encouraging the students, that a Parisian designer was getting £1,000 a year for supplying sketches for designs to Manchester manufacturers. Clarendon also pointed out that the ratio of awards for designs by Irish contributors at the London Exhibition of 1851 was one award to every 3.5 contributors, whereas the ratio of awards to British contributors was 1:3.25.[2] On the other hand the number of contributions was 268 as against 6,655. This would seem to argue that while Ireland lacked something in quantity of designs, the quality was reasonably high.

Among the innovations that the new school brought with it was the admission of female students, of whom there were 362 out of 1,444 in 1849. They were 'designers for worked muslin', 'painters in china', embroiderers, wood engravers, etc. Eventually the presence of these women and the increasing emphasis on applied or practical rather than fine art was to drive the more creative and artistic students to the Royal Hibernian Academy schools, so that at the end of the century they had on their books such names as William and Walter Osborne, J. M. Kavanagh, Joseph O'Reilly, Oliver Sheppard, Henry Allan, James Brenan, and H. C. Tisdall. But the new school pleased its masters and in the first government inspector's report of 1850 it was stated that 'as compared with the old drawing classes of the Royal Dublin Society, upon which the school of design has been grafted, the tuition is of a far sounder character and the productions of the pupils far more *artistic and practical* [italics added]'.[3] It will be remembered that this old drawing class produced Francis Danby, Martin Archer Shee, Richard Rothwell, Martin Cregan, Nicholas Crowley, John Henry Campbell, William Davis, John Doyle, John Faulkner, Edwin Hayes, William Howis, and Henry O'Neill, to mention only nineteenth-century painters.

[1] *Royal Dublin Society: report of the ninth public distribution of premiums* . . . (Dublin, 1851), p. 2.
[2] *Royal Dublin Society: tenth distribution. Report* . . . (Dublin, 1852), pp 20–21.
[3] Quoted in Strickland, *Dict. Ir. artists*, ii, 589.

In 1855 the staff was reduced to McManus and an assistant, Thomas Holmes. For the first time fees were charged (2s. 6d. per quarter) and evening classes were started. Finally in 1877, when the museum was taken from the Royal Dublin Society, the school of design likewise broke its connections with the society and came directly under the science and art department, South Kensington, under the title of Metropolitan School of Art.

The Cork school of design, which was opened in 1850, succeeded an earlier school founded in the 1820s as part of the Cork Institute, of which little is known. William Willes, himself a Corkman, was appointed as first headmaster. Although he died in the second year of the school's existence, he had already established the school soundly. He not only converted the Cork Institute buildings to the satisfaction of Ambrose Poynter, the government inspector, but also managed to infect the students with his own enthusiasm. He had been responsible for the first Munster art exhibition in Cork in 1815.[1] Attendance varied at first from 200 to 150, 'the males consisting chiefly of the mechanic and artisan classes, and the females of governesses, teachers, japanners, and girls engaged in embroidery and lace schools'. Maguire, from whom this quotation is taken, commenting on the satisfactory progress of the students in the first years, makes the inevitable remark: 'It [the school] has gone far towards supplying the great necessity of the day—an art-workman; without whose aid it is utterly in vain to expect lasting success for manufacturing efforts.'[2] The trades that chiefly benefited were enamelling and japanning, embroidery, and lace, and a class of 'female artisans' was being trained to supply designs 'in closer imitation of the beauty of natural forms . . . suited to the character of the material'.[3] The students in 1851 won five medals at Marlborough House in London, headquarters of the department of practical art,[4] and one is not surprised since they included James Brenan, W. L. Casey, and John J. Drummond. The presence of the casts from the antique donated by Pope Pius VII to the prince regent and given by him to Cork in 1818 is credited with some part in this success.[5]

The school received an annual grant of £200 from the Cork corporation and a further £500 from the government (raised from £200 because Poynter was so pleased with the way things had gone). But in 1854 the legality of this use of public money was questioned and the school was closed. Part of the art collection was transferred to the queen's college, opened that year. In 1855 a rate of a penny in the pound was authorised by act of parliament,[6] and the school was reopened in 1857. In 1860 James Brenan was appointed headmaster. During his thirty-odd years in office (he was appointed to Dublin in 1889), the school flourished. In 1884 a new building was erected, towards which the distiller W. H. Crawford donated £20,000. It was opened in 1885 by the prince and princess of Wales and renamed the Crawford Municipal School of Art. The building also included an art gallery, the present Crawford Municipal Art Gallery.

[1] Ibid., ii, 531.   [2] Maguire, *Industrial movement*, p. 289.   [3] Ibid.   [4] Below, p. 529.
[5] Strickland, *Dict. Ir. artists*, ii, 655; above, iv, 538.   [6] 18 & 19 Vict., c. 40 (26 June 1855).

The motives that prompted the setting up of schools of design in Britain—namely, the need to improve industrial design and hence dispense with imported designs, particularly from France—was acutely felt in Belfast with its thriving linen industry. According to Lord Dufferin, £60,000 a year was spent on linen headings from France. As early as 1836 Hugh Frazer, A.R.H.A., president of the newly formed Belfast Association of Artists, wrote: 'the leading and immediate object of the society is to obtain a building adapted for an exhibition room, and ultimately . . . forming a normal school of artistical education.'[1] A decade later, when in 1847 the notion of a school of design was first raised, 'local interest and national policy coincided'.[2] In the same year, a stationer in Belfast set up presses for printing the paper wrappers for rolls of linen. They were inferior in design to the French wrappers, but it was a beginning. The Belfast school of design, founded in 1849, was opened in April 1850. The headmaster and second master rejoiced in the auspicious names of Claude Lorraine Nursey and David Wilkie Raimbach; Nursey came, suitably, from the Leeds and Bradford schools. In all, 148 students (133 male and 15 female) were enrolled. The school got considerable voluntary support, much more than those in Dublin or Cork; in 1851 £400 was raised chiefly through the generosity of three patrons, Lord Dufferin, John Blakiston-Houston, and a Mr Hemming or Henning of Waringstown, County Down. The school was also well endowed with prizes and scholarships. Yet when in 1853 the schools of design were brought under the science and art department (the empire of Henry Cole, secretary of the department and director of the Kensington museum) and direct government grants were withdrawn (payment was henceforth by results in examinations), public subscription was not sufficient to support the Belfast school. Lord Dufferin and Nursey did what they could to save the school but it was forced to close in 1854, after only four years in existence.

Drawing classes continued in the Belfast Academical Institution, but it was not until 1870 that a new school of art was opened. This school, known as the Government School of Art, was connected with South Kensington. It remained in existence for thirty-six years. Thomas Mitchner Lindsay was appointed headmaster, and George Trobridge second master. The aims of the new school were the same as those of the schools of design, though the curriculum was broader. Lindsay seems to have been very successful: two years after its foundation, the school was rated fourth in the United Kingdom, and during the years of its existence twenty-one scholarships to the South Kensington school (the Royal College of Art) and two to Dublin were awarded to its students. Between 1890 and 1898 success in examinations trebled, so that had it remained a school of design it would have had a handsome subsidy, and in 1900 sixteen awards, including a gold medal, were won at the national competitions, held in London.

---

[1] Hugh Frazer, 'Address to the public' in *Exhibition of the Belfast Association of Artists, MDCCCXXXVI: first* (Belfast, 1836), p. 6.
[2] This phrase comes from the association's catalogue for its 1847 exhibition.

These last successes were secured under Trobridge (Lindsay had left to become headmaster of the Rugby school of art in 1880). Trobridge introduced life classes, drawing from the antique, and anatomy—in other words, fine art. This was in conformity with the general pattern of art schools: the more broadly based the more successful.

Here it might be appropriate to say a word about George Sharp. Sharp, who does not usually appear even in a footnote in most histories of art education, was in fact the one man who understood the logic of the situation: if French designers were to be counteracted then this should be done with French, not German, methods. He adopted the system of teaching employed in French government schools, that of Alexandre Dupuis, and in 1845 translated Dupuis. In 1852 he read a paper on Dupuis's method to the Royal Dublin Society, which was published as *A lecture on elementary drawing*. On the opening of the Belfast school of design, he wrote to the president of the board of trade and to Lord Dufferin, offering to put his method to the test, but was brusquely rebuffed. He exhibited his 'Methods to facilitate the teaching of drawing' in Cork in 1852.[1]

Limerick acquired a school of design in 1852. Ten years earlier, Jeremiah Hodges Mulcahy had opened a school with a view to developing dormant talent, but there is little evidence that it was awakened. The request for the school of design came from the committee of the Limerick Institution. David Wilkie Raimbach, second master in the Belfast school of design, was appointed headmaster. He was succeeded by W. L. Casey, the Cork artist, and he in turn by N. A. Brophy. In 1896 the school came under the jurisdiction of the Limerick corporation and was amalgamated with the technical school.

Limerick was lucky to have obtained a school of design, for, soon after it was established, a new kind of school, to be called a 'school of practical art', was introduced by Cole. The main difference between this and earlier schools was that the government granted £50 a year instead of £150. One of the first was opened in Waterford, a month before the Limerick school. The moving spirits in establishing the Waterford school were John A. Blake and Dean Edward Hoare of the Church of Ireland, the trustees of the Waterford Savings Bank gave premises free of rent, and J. D. Croome, R. A., was appointed headmaster. It flourished for a time, attended by male and female pupils from all walks of life, and then ceased. It was revived in 1881 and later became part of the Waterford Central Technical Institute under the department of agriculture and technical instruction.

An art school was established at Clonmel in 1854 under James A. Healy, but did not survive. In Derry an art school was opened in 1874, but in 1899 it was combined with the technical school. With the passing of the technical instruction act of 1899,[2] the policy of amalgamating art schools with technical schools, under the department of agriculture and technical instruction, was pressed ahead.

---

[1] Strickland, *Dict. Ir. artists*, ii, 327–8.
[2] 62 & 63 Vict., c. 50 (9 Aug. 1899), below, p. 530.

Before closing this section on the social aspects of art in Ireland in the late nineteenth century, mention must be made of some of the many societies and art clubs. A local drawing society was founded in Lismore, County Waterford, by six ladies, including Fanny Currey and Baroness Pauline Prochazka, in 1870. It held exhibitions in 1871 and 1872 as the Irish Amateur Drawing Society, changed its name to the Irish Fine Art Society in 1878, and eventually, in 1887, became the Water Colour Society of Ireland. It was one of the rare institutions in which women had an active role: in 1877 the committee consisted of five women and only two men; in 1892 the committee of twelve included seven women, among them the leading water-colourists Fanny Currey, Rose Barton, and Mildred Butler. In 1872 a Miss Deane and some other ladies started the Ladies' Sketching Club in Dublin, to provide a smaller exhibition than the R.H.A., where amateurs could show their work. In 1873 gentlemen were admitted, and it became the Dublin Amateur and Artists' Society. In 1888 it amalgamated with the Dublin Sketching Club, which had been set up in 1874 by a Dublin dentist, William Booth Pearsall, and included among its early members William Stokes and several other Dublin doctors, Bram Stoker, and the artists Alexander Williams and Alfred Grey. Club activities included art classes and sketching expeditions, as well as exhibitions. In 1884 the club held a loan exhibition of works by Whistler, which caused a stir in Dublin. In 1886 the Dublin Art Club was founded by a group who seceded from the sketching club, including Walter Osborne. It seems to have been the Dublin equivalent of the New English Art Club, and had links with many British naturalist painters educated in Antwerp and Paris, showing works by artists such as George Clausen, Edward Stott, and Fred Brown at its annual exhibitions. The Belfast Ramblers' Sketching Club existed from about 1879, its object being to encourage sketching from nature and original compositions. In 1891 it became the Belfast Art Society. It is an indication of the liveliness of the art world in Ireland in the late nineteenth century that so many organisations existed, and that they could encompass such a wide membership of amateurs and professionals. They seem to have had some success in their aim of educating public taste, and introducing Irish audiences to more progressive artists from abroad. It was in these smaller societies that the many talented women artists began to assert themselves, at a time when membership of the R.H.A. was closed to them.[1]

IN the year 1850 most Irish artists of any note were working in England. Sir Martin Archer Shee, the only Irishman to become president of the Royal Academy, died that year. Daniel Maclise, a Corkman, who had not severed his connections with Ireland (he exhibited at the Royal Hibernian Academy and at the Cork exhibition of 1852), was 44 and at the height of his fame. He had been elected an academician in 1840, and in 1844 received his first commission to decorate the newly built houses of parliament—he completed the giant frescoes

[1] Shirley Armstrong Duffy, 'The role of women in Irish sketching clubs in the late nineteenth century' in *Ir. women artists*, pp 12–15, and Jeanne Sheehy, *Walter Osborne* (Dublin, 1983), p. 27.

'The meeting of Wellington and Blücher' in 1861 and 'The death of Nelson' in 1865. He was on the jury of the Paris Exposition Universelle of 1855. On the death of Sir Charles Eastlake in 1865, he was offered the presidency of the Royal Academy, but declined (he was almost 60); he declined a knighthood in the following year. On his death in 1870 Charles Dickens said of him that his 'prodigious fertility of mind and wonderful wealth of intellect . . . would have made him, if he had so minded, at least as great a writer as a painter'.[1] Maclise, though an uneven and sometimes brash painter, was a good draughtsman and excelled in all forms of painting that were popular in mid-Victorian Britain: the historical subject, meticulous in detail, factually accurate (history as a scientific discipline was establishing itself), and moralistic rather than heroic; the illustration of literary incidents, particularly from Shakespeare; and genre—Maclise favoured the rumbustious, low-life scene, such as 'Snap-apple night', rather than the sentimental and everyday.

Francis Danby (1793–1861) was in his late 50s and in retirement at Exmouth, but still painting excellent pictures. His 'The evening gun' (National Gallery of Canada, Ottawa) was the sensation of the 1855 Paris exposition. Théophile Gautier said of it: 'No one has better expressed the solemn grandeur of the ocean.'[2] On his return to England in 1841, Danby had exhibited at the Royal Hibernian Academy from 1844 till 1846, and he exhibited at the Cork exhibition in 1852. But Danby belongs to the first half of the century, the period of high romanticism. The *Athenaeum*, on his death, described him as 'England's most distinguished landscape painter of the romantic school'.[3]

Another distinguished artist of Irish origin working in 1850, William Mulready (1786–1863), was already 64, yet he belongs to the mid-century more than Danby does, and at the Paris exposition, though Danby won the acclaim, Mulready was awarded the Legion of Honour. He specialised in genre and distinguished himself by his psychological insights, particularly into the behaviour of boys and dogs. He was also a superb draughtsman, particularly in his life studies. He painted the 'Bathers surprised' (National Gallery of Ireland) in 1849. His landscapes were also remarkable, and it is here that in the period under review he made his most original contribution. He may have been influenced by photography in some of his paintings—they have the photographic accuracy, redeemed with freshness and lyrical colour, beloved of the mid-century. But he was also capable of producing almost abstract landscape sketches, such as the landscape miniatures in the National Gallery of Ireland (7003–7). At the age of 68, he was capable of producing 'The young brother' (Tate Gallery) and at the age of 75, 'The toy seller' (National Gallery of Ireland). In 1860, under the new charter, he was made

[1] Strickland, *Dict. Ir. artists*, ii, 71.
[2] *The Art Journal*, new ser., ii (1856), p. 18, quoted in Eric Adams, *Francis Danby* (New Haven, Conn., and London, 1973), p. 115.
[3] *Athenaeum: journal of literature, science, and the fine arts*, no. 1739 (23 Feb. 1861), p. 264; the full obituary in no. 1740 (2 Mar. 1861), p. 294, makes Danby's Irishness clear.

an honorary member of the Royal Hibernian Academy. Ruskin's comment on him, which is meant as criticism, might be otherwise interpreted: 'Mulready . . ., while he has always produced exquisite pieces of painting, has failed in doing anything which can be of true or extensive use.'[1]

Of the other artists with established reputations in 1850, W. H. Brooke and Edward Jones were in their 70s: Martin Cregan, president of the Royal Hibernian Academy since 1832, nine years after its foundation, was in his 60s; J. P. Haverty, Samuel Lover, Henry O'Neill, William Brocas, Edward Hayes, John Doyle, Matthew Kendrick, and George Petrie were in their 50s. The artists in their prime were Richard Rothwell, Andrew Nicholl, Stephen Catterson-Smith, R. B. Beechey, J. H. Mulcahy, and G. F. Mulvany. Of this mid-century generation, the most important was Frederick William Burton, born in Corofin House, County Clare. He learned to draw from the Brocases[2] and acquired an interest in archaeology from George Petrie. After exhibiting at the Royal Hibernian Academy and the Royal Academy, in 1844 he went to Germany at the request of the king of Bavaria to copy pictures for him. He settled in Bavaria from 1851 till 1856. During this time he toured the kingdom doing water-colours (he never painted in anything else) of the Bavarian and Franconian peasantry. While in Germany he studied the old masters and he also visited the major galleries of Europe; his knowledge of art history was exceptional for his time. On his return from the Continent, he settled in London but continued to visit Ireland. In 1857 he toured the Aran Islands with Samuel Ferguson, Eugene O'Curry, and other members of the British Association. He became a founder member of the Archaeological Society of Ireland. He was appointed director of the National Gallery, London, in 1874 (the only Irishman to hold that post) and under his directorship the gallery acquired some of its most important paintings. He was knighted in 1884 and retired from the directorship in 1894. He had abandoned painting on becoming director.

Of the others working in England, Nicholas Joseph Crowley (1819–47) was a painter of enormous charm and great promise (he died while still in his 30s). He painted portraits and romantic subjects, some of which were drawn from popular plays of the time (Tyrone Power as Connor O'Gorman in 'The groves of Blarney') and others ('Lovers' farewell') look as though they might have been. William Davis (1812–73) was one of those artists who, despairing of making a living in Ireland, migrated to England. He settled in Liverpool and became known as 'Davis of Liverpool'. Until 1853, under the influence of Robert Tongue, he painted figure and still-life pictures, but later he concentrated on landscapes. He used a white priming, which gave brilliance to his colours and anticipated the techniques used by the pre-Raphaelites, by whom he was greatly admired, particularly by the two Rossettis and Ford Madox Brown. Ruskin disapproved of

---

[1] John Ruskin, *Pre-Raphaelitism* (1851) in *The works of Ruskin*, ed. E. T. Cook and Alexander Wedderburn (library edition, London, 1904), xii, 264.
[2] Above, iv, 519, 539–40.

his subject-matter (duckponds and the like) and of the flatness of his landscapes, which in fact anticipated the treatment of landscape that became accepted in the twentieth century. W. M. Rossetti went too far in the other direction, perhaps, when he said that he came nearer to the ideal landscape than anyone since Turner. Either way he is an undeservedly neglected artist.

Richard Rothwell (1800–68) is rather more typical of the Irish artist in the early and middle nineteenth century. He at first despaired of making a living by painting but persevered and at the age of 24 became a member of the Royal Hibernian Academy. In 1829 he went to London and was hailed by Sir Thomas Lawrence, for whom he worked and whose commissions he completed after his death, as the 'Irish prodigy'. Landseer is quoted as having said of him: 'An artist has come from Dublin who paints flesh as well as the old masters.'[1] And yet, in spite of his success—he had inherited Lawrence's practice—he abandoned his commissions in 1831 and left for Rome because he keenly felt his lack of knowledge of the old masters. When he returned to England in 1833 his place had been taken by others. To make matters worse, he allowed himself to be persuaded by the historical painter Benjamin Haydon to paint historical and subject pictures, some of which are of such a cloying sentimentality that, though they may have pleased the mid-century public, they were too much for the Royal Academy. He again became discouraged and returned to Dublin in 1847. He was further disturbed by the death of his eldest child and in 1852 went once more on his travels, to London, America, Rome, Warwickshire, and finally back to Rome again, where, appropriately enough, he is buried beside Keats, for in many ways Rothwell sums up the Irish artist of the first half of the nineteenth century: talented, romantic, rejected by his own people, acclaimed and rejected by others.

Of the artists who remained at home, or at least did not settle permanently abroad, Andrew Nicholl (1804–86) is perhaps the most interesting. He was a landscape painter who contributed to, or produced, various books on Irish scenery.[2] After spending ten years in London after the rejection in 1837 of his nomination for the post of master of drawing at the Royal Dublin Society schools in favour of the influential Henry Brocas, jr., he taught drawing and painting at the Colombo Academy, Ceylon. On his return he lived in Dublin, in his native Belfast, and in London. He is remarkable for his studies of flowers in landscape, whether the landscape be Ulster or Ceylon.

Of the other artists of this generation, Richard Brydges Beechey (1808–95) and Stephen Catterson-Smith, sr (1806–72), were born in England. The former, son of the painter Sir William Beechey, spent most of his life in the Royal Navy in survey ships around the Irish coast. He took up painting late in life and devoted

---

[1] Strickland, *Dict. Ir. artists*, ii, 301; *Irish art in the nineteenth century* (Cork, 1971), p. 71.
[2] Mr and Mrs S. C. Hall, *Ireland: its scenery, character, etc.* (3 vols, London, 1841–3), *passim*; Andrew Nicholl, *Five views of the Dublin and Kingstown Railway* and *Thirteen views of the Dublin and Kingstown Railway* (both Dublin, 1834); and see above, v, plates 4b, 8a, 25a.

himself mostly to marine painting. On his retirement in 1864 he settled in Monkstown, County Dublin (his wife was Irish); he was elected an honorary member of the Royal Hibernian Academy in 1868. Catterson-Smith was a Yorkshireman who settled in Ireland in 1839, rose to be president of the Royal Hibernian Academy in 1859, and died as a result of his exertions on behalf of the international exhibition in Dublin in 1872. He was chiefly a portrait painter, rarely inspired, but usually competent. He succeeded Martin Cregan[1] as the painter of fashionable portraits and was portrait painter to the lords lieutenant for thirty years.

Of the remaining artists of this generation, Jeremiah Hodges Mulcahy (d. 1889) was a landscape painter who painted at times in the eighteenth-century manner, at other times in a Turneresque style. In 1842 he opened a school of art in his native Limerick with a view to developing latent talent there,[2] but seems to have abandoned the attempt twenty years later when he settled in Dublin. George Francis Mulvany (1809–69), the first director of the National Gallery of Ireland (1862–9), was among the best of the many Mulvany painters, though his work rarely rises above mediocrity.

Those aged under 30 in 1850 do not differ appreciably in their manner of painting from their seniors by a decade, and none among them stands out as exceptional. It is interesting, however, that—with the exception of Richard Doyle (1824–83), who was born in London shortly after his parents emigrated, and never went to Ireland, though he always regarded himself as an Irishman—most of this group lived and worked in Ireland. Doyle (Dicky Doyle, as he called himself) was one of a small group of artists who were at that time fascinated by a world of fairyland. He worked for *Punch* and in 1849 produced the definitive cover (it was abandoned in the late 1950s for reasons best known to its publishers). In 1850 he resigned from *Punch* in protest against its attacks on Cardinal Wiseman and the catholic hierarchy.[3] Erskine Nicol (1825–1904) was born in Scotland but came to Ireland when he was 20, and taught in Dublin until 1850. He then returned to Scotland and recorded his impressions of his time in Ireland, the period of the famine, with a realism that was not matched by any Irish painter until Jack B. Yeats at the end of the century. Michael Angelo Hayes (1820–77) was perhaps the most outstanding of his generation. His activities as secretary of the Royal Hibernian Academy have already been recounted.[4] He specialised in military subjects (he was military painter-in-ordinary to the lord lieutenant) and was particularly successful in painting groups of people (really miniatures) against an architectural setting. He made a famous set of drawings of the Bianconi coaching establishments. His studies of cavalry led him to reject the traditional method of depicting the gallop (the 'flying-gallop'). His paper on 'The delineation of animals in rapid motion', read to the Royal Dublin Society in 1876 and later published as a pamphlet, seems, though inaccurate in detail, to have anticipated the

---

[1] Above, iv, 539. [2] Above, p. 448.
[3] For later examples of *Punch*'s stance, see above, v, plates 18*b*, 37*b*. [4] Above, pp 443–4.

photographs by Eadweard Muybridge, published after Hayes's death.[1] Almost as remarkable was his namesake, Edwin Hayes (1820–1904), who, though born in Bristol, trained as an artist in the Royal Dublin Society schools and specialised as a marine painter. Marine painting was growing in popularity throughout the nineteenth century, as Stewart Blacker's figures testify.[2] Hayes painted along the Mediterranean, as well as the Irish and British, coasts. William Osborne (1823–1901) was celebrated chiefly for his accurate and unsentimental treatment of animals, particularly dogs. He was also a reasonably good portrait painter. One of his chief titles to fame is that he was the father of Walter Osborne.

Around the middle of the century Irish painters went to the Continent, rather than solely to Britain, to study and work, rather than as mere visitors.[3] They first went to France, mainly to Paris, the forest of Fontainebleau, and Brittany. This is not surprising, since it is where the French painters went also. In the 1870s and 1880s, the Irish formed a small colony in Antwerp, though most of the Antwerp school moved on to France.

Probably the first to study in Paris was Richard Hearn, who was there in the late 1840s and studied at Couture's atelier, which Nathaniel Hone joined in 1853. Other Parisian ateliers frequented by Irish painters were those of Carolus Duran, Delécluse, Colarossi, and the Académie Julian. At first students entered the ateliers because only drawing, not painting, was taught at the École des Beaux Arts. When painting was introduced, after 1863, the habit of independent ateliers was well established, and many students attended both. Besides, it was not always easy to get into the École. Paris was becoming an increasingly important art centre, gradually outstripping Rome, Düsseldorf, Munich, and Antwerp as a centre for the study of art on the Continent. That the Irish painters went to ateliers rather than to the École may have been fortuitous, but having gone there they may have liked the informal atmosphere and international company, and spread the word at home. Among the Irish painters who studied in Paris were Frank O'Meara, George Moore, Sarah Purser, John Lavery, Edith Somerville, Roderic O'Conor, Dermod O'Brien, Paul and Grace Henry, W. J. Leech, Mary Swanzy, and May Guinness.

Hearn was also the first to follow the fashion and move on to Barbizon in the forest of Fontainebleau in 1849. Hone followed in 1857 and O'Meara in 1875. O'Meara went to Grèz-sur-Loing the same year, and was followed by Lavery in 1883 and O'Conor in 1886; both stayed some time there. The first Irish painter to go to Brittany was Hone, in 1860. He was followed by Aloysius O'Kelly and Augustus Burke in 1876 and by Walter Osborne, Joseph Malachy Kavanagh, and Nathaniel Hill, from Antwerp, in 1883. O'Conor was there from 1890 until

---

[1] *The horse in motion* (1878) was the first of several publications by Muybridge on this subject.

[2] Stewart Blacker was a founder member and honorary secretary of the Royal Irish Art Union; his testimony on the role of art unions is in *Report from the select committee on art unions; together with the minutes of evidence, appendix, and index*, pp 78–100, H.C. 1845 (612), vii, 118–40, and the accompanying tables on pp 340–51 (MS 380–91).

[3] For the continental work of eighteenth-century Irish artists, see above, iv, 521–4.

c.1904. He was a friend of Gauguin and is regarded as a member of the Pont-Aven school. Leech was there from 1903 until 1908, and many of his best-known pictures have Breton subjects. Indeed, Breton subjects were prominent in R.H.A. exhibitions in the latter part of the century and gave them a continental flavour.

There was a great incentive to study or work on the Continent after 1877, when scholarships were granted from a fund set up by the Taylor bequest.[1] Many of those who availed themselves of them went to Antwerp. The Académie Royale des Beaux Arts had a high reputation, attracting students from England, Scotland, and the U.S.A., as well as from Ireland. Founded in 1663, it was the third oldest art school in Europe; it housed many masterpieces of the baroque period, including works by Rubens; and had many excellent teachers, the most notable being Charles Verlat. The first Irish student to go to Antwerp was the sculptor Michael Hayes, who was there from 1867 until 1874. Others followed throughout the 1870s, but the major influx was in the 1880s. Osborne, Kavanagh, and Hill came in 1881; O'Conor and R. T. Moynan in 1883; Henry Allan in 1884; and Dermod O'Brien in 1887, perhaps the last. The Irish painters formed a close-knit body and evolved a distinctive style of realism, which, though not specifically Irish, singles them out among Irish painters of the time.

Nathaniel Hone (1821–1917) was a late developer. He began life as an engineer with the Midland Great Western Railway, after taking a degree at Trinity College, Dublin, and was 22 when he took up painting. In 1853 he went to Paris; what decided him to go is not clear. He studied under Yvon and Couture for two years; in 1855 he moved to Barbizon, where he was in touch with Millet, Harpignies, Manet, and Rousseau. Until 1875, when he returned to Ireland, he worked either at Barbizon, in Brittany, or on the Mediterranean coast. After his return to Ireland he settled at Malahide but travelled annually, sometimes as far as Egypt and Turkey. His means were sufficient to support him and he rarely sold his paintings—about 1,440 of them were donated by his widow to the National Gallery of Ireland. Apart from exhibiting at the Paris salons from 1867 to 1869 and once (one picture) at the Royal Academy in 1869, he rarely exhibited outside Ireland. He has thus not received the recognition he deserves. He confined himself almost entirely to landscapes. He was at his best in free and fluent sketches; of these the best are in private collections.

Hone's contemporaries included Matthew Lawless (1837–64), James Brenan (1837–1907), Augustus Burke (*c*.1838–91), Michael G. Brennan (1839–71), and John Butler Yeats (1839–1922). Both Lawless and Brennan died young. Lawless had already made a name for himself in London as an illustrator before he died at the age of 27. His works seem to have mysteriously disappeared; he is now known exclusively by 'The sick call' (National Gallery of Ireland). Brennan also worked as an illustrator in London and, like Doyle on *Punch*, resigned from *Fun* rather than caricature the pope. He suffered from consumption and sought a cure

---

[1] Above, p. 438.

in Italy, first in Rome and later on Capri, and finally he went to Algiers, as the guest of Lady Kingston, but died soon after his arrival. He is best known for his charming, romantic scenes on Capri ('Evening on a vine-covered verandah'). His namesake, James Brenan, was a solid painter, whose title to fame lies in his abilities as a teacher rather than an artist. He taught in many towns in England, was headmaster (1860–88) at the Cork School of Design (later the Crawford Municipal School of Art) (1885–9), and the Metropolitan School of Art, Dublin (1889–1904), in both of which he encouraged the applied arts. He was responsible for the fine arts section of the Cork exhibition of 1883. Burke was one of the first Irish artists to paint in Brittany, and, as Ethna Waldron suggests, may have influenced others to go there.[1] He exhibited Breton subjects at the Royal Hibernian Academy in 1876–7, when Kavanagh was a student at the Academy schools. He left Ireland after his brother Thomas Henry Burke, under-secretary for Ireland, was assassinated in the Phoenix Park in 1882.

If Burke forms a link with the next generation of Irish artists, John Butler Yeats may be said to bridge the two phases of Irish art in the nineteenth century, the mid-century and what might be described as the Irish renaissance in art, corresponding to, though only at certain points connected with, the literary renaissance. His early work is self-consciously of the earlier period. While studying in London, he came into contact with J. T. Nettleship, Edwin Ellis, and George Wilson, and set out to restore pre-Raphaelitism. His gouache 'Pippa passes' (National Gallery of Ireland) gained the approval of Dante Gabriel Rossetti when it was exhibited at the Dudley Gallery in 1871.[2] In the 1890s, however, he seems to have come under the influence of the impressionists; his pictures, mostly portraits, often take on the softness and fuzziness of pastel sketches. He was a prominent figure in the cultural life of both Dublin and London. He returned to Dublin from 1880 to 1887 and again from 1902 to 1907, when he went to the United States intending to return, but died in New York in 1922. While in London from 1887 to 1902 he and his family played an important part in the Bedford Park community, Chiswick. G. K. Chesterton, Lucien Pissarro, C. F. A. Voysey, and T. M. Rooke were also there. He painted portraits of most of the writers and scholars of the literary renaissance: Standish James O'Grady, Hyde, George Moore, Synge, Lady Gregory, George Russell (A E), and, of course, his own sons, William and Jack, forming the nucleus of a national portrait gallery. He has been eclipsed by his sons, but in his day he towered above all others with his intelligence and brilliance in conversation. His almost total lack of ambition drove Sarah Purser into paroxysms of irritation, but all her chiding and goading could not get him to change his ways.

Sarah Purser (1848–1943) was almost ten years John Butler Yeats's junior. Like him her life and work span the generations. Like Yeats she studied in Paris, at

---

[1] Ethna Waldron, 'Joseph Malachy Kavanagh' in *Capuchin Annual, 1968*, p. 318.

[2] William M. Murphy, *Prodigal father: the life of John Butler Yeats* (Ithaca, N.Y., and London, 1978), p. 74.

the Académie Julian. She took to painting as a profession after the collapse of her father's business, and went to Paris in 1878, after studying for a time at the Metropolitan School of Art, Dublin. At that time her sole aim was to become competent enough to earn a living by painting; she therefore absorbed little of what was going on outside academic circles. It was not until a decade later, when she had acquired the beginnings of a modest fortune, that she was free to travel and came under the influence of the impressionists. On her return to Ireland she began to paint portraits, and a double portrait of Eva and Constance Gore-Booth led to many lucrative commissions. These portraits were tight, detailed, naturalistic likenesses. About the turn of the century, however, when she was able to paint for herself, her style underwent an important change.

Meanwhile the pilgrimage to Brittany by way of Antwerp, Paris, or both, had begun. Of the so-called 'Antwerp school' the most important—perhaps the most important artist of this period—was Walter Osborne (1859–1903). He studied at the Royal Hibernian Academy schools, one of an increasing number of talented artists to do so,[1] before spending two years (1881–2) under Verlat at Antwerp. The next year he went to Brittany. From 1884 to 1886 he was mainly in England. Although he visited England frequently in later years, his base was Dublin. As Bodkin remarks, 'he was the one Irish artist who, with a great and growing reputation in England, elected to live and work in his own country'.[2] He took part in all the artistic activities in Dublin at that time and it was a great loss to art in Ireland when at the age of 43 he died of pneumonia contracted while cycling in the rain. His style was rapidly developing from the sort of photographic naturalism of the French realist school, in which he excelled, to a free handling of paint and a feeling for atmosphere and the play of light. He was mainly a painter of landscapes with figures, though he also did some subject studies, and in later years a great many portraits. He was an accomplished water-colourist as well as a painter in oils.

Joseph Malachy Kavanagh (1856–1918), like Osborne, studied at the Royal Hibernian Academy schools, and at the Antwerp Academy under Verlat, and painted in Brittany. He returned to Ireland in 1887 and taught at the Metropolitan School of Art, Dublin. He became keeper of the Royal Hibernian Academy in 1910 and was living in the academy premises in Abbey Street when they were gutted by fire during the 1916 rising. He escaped with some documents and the insignia, leaving behind the rest of the academy's treasures, for which he has been severely criticised. As a painter he only rarely broke from the rather limited style he had developed on the Continent, but he was sensitive to the effects of light, particularly on the surfaces of buildings. Dermod O'Brien (1865–1945), like Kavanagh, had difficulty in shaking off the restricting influences of Antwerp though in later years he occasionally managed to do so in his landscape sketches and less formal paintings. He was a skilled draughtsman but most of the

---

[1] Above, p. 445.
[2] Thomas Bodkin, *Four Irish landscape painters* (Dublin and London, 1920), p. 38.

spontaneity is lost in his finished compositions. He was a man of wide interests, which varied from music to farming and the cooperative movement. From 1910 he was president of the Royal Hibernian Academy. As with Kavanagh and O'Brien, so with Henry Allan (1865–1912); the continental influence is rarely shaken off or absorbed into something personal.

That there was nothing fatal about Antwerp is proved not only by Osborne but to an even greater extent by Roderic O'Conor (1860–1940), who was there from 1883 to 1884, after Osborne had left. O'Conor was an Irishman rather than an Irish artist. Though born in County Roscommon he was educated in England, and though he studied art in Dublin (1878–82) he never settled in Ireland, and, as far as is known, did not form part of the Irish colony at Antwerp. In 1885 he went to Paris and studied at the atelier of Carolus Duran. He exhibited at the Salon des Indépendants (1889–90) and seems to have been in touch with Van Gogh, Seurat, Signac, and Toulouse-Lautrec. In 1892 he settled at Pont-Aven in Brittany. Here he came into contact with Gauguin in 1893, on the latter's return from Tahiti, but was never greatly influenced by him. If anything, the influence went the other way: having lent Gauguin his studio, O'Conor found that Gauguin had used one of his drawings as part of a composition. At that time O'Conor was more influenced by Van Gogh. He was, moreover, a purer painter than Gauguin; there was hardly any literary element in his work. Towards the end of the century he was developing in a direction that either anticipated or at least ran parallel with that of the Fauves and the German expressionists. But O'Conor's most interesting work belongs to the twentieth century.

The last Irish artist who belongs as much to the nineteenth as to the twentieth century is John Lavery (1856–1941). Lavery was born in Belfast and grew up in such penurious circumstances that his guardians (he was an orphan) were forced to emigrate to Glasgow. He studied art in Glasgow and London, and in 1881 in Paris at the Académie Julian and the Atelier Colorossi. In 1884 he moved to the artists' colony of Grèz-sur-Loing, some years before O'Conor, and while there painted some of his best pictures, including 'The tennis party' (1886; Aberdeen Art Gallery). In 1888 he joined the Glasgow School of Art, then in its heyday, and was much influenced by Joseph Crawhall (1861–1913). He was also influenced by Whistler, whom he had met the previous year. His paintings between then and 1896, which include his studies of the Glasgow exhibition of 1888, are among his best works, showing evidence of both these influences. During these years he visited Morocco and Tangiers. In 1896 he moved to London, and in 1897 became vice-president of the International Society of Painters, Sculptors, and Engravers (founded by Whistler) and numbered Rodin among his friends. At the turn of the century Lavery was not only at the height of his powers but also one of the most promising artists working in London.

IN 1850 three major sculptors—John Hogan (1800–58), John Henry Foley (1818–74), and John Edward Carew (1784–1868)—and a number of competent sculptors—Edward Ambrose (1814–90), Richard Barter (c.1824–96), Christopher Moore (1790–1860), Patrick McDowell (1799–1870), Michael Murphy (c.1865–1938), Terence Farrell (1798–1876) and his son Thomas (1827–1900), and John Lawlor (1820–1901)—were practising, mostly in England.

Hogan had arrived back in Ireland in 1848, driven from Rome by the revolutions of that year. He arrived at a bleak time, for the effects of the famine were still being felt. His model for the memorial of Thomas Moore was passed over in favour of the vastly inferior statue by Christopher Moore that stands at the end of Westmoreland Street, Dublin. One of his few major commissions was for the O'Connell monument in the Crescent, Limerick. His tomb in Glasnevin cemetery, Dublin, with the simple inscription 'HOGAN', is a just tribute to the arrogance and simplicity of the man.

Foley, nearly twenty years Hogan's junior, was at the height of his career in 1850. In 1858 he modelled two of the finest equestrian statues of the nineteenth century, those of Lord Hardinge and Sir James Outram, both in India. He used the same model as the Hardinge statue for the horse in the Gough monument (completed by Brock and unveiled in 1880), once in the Phoenix Park, Dublin, which patriots in their wisdom sought to destroy (even though the Bolsheviks left the statue of Peter the Great in St Petersburg intact). He was commissioned by the corporation of London to supply works for the Mansion House, and replied with the delicate 'Egeria' and the slightly rhetorical 'Caractacus'. In 1870 Foley's position as the leading sculptor in England was recognised by the commission to do the figure of Prince Albert and the group 'Asia' for the Albert memorial. The latter brought about his death, for he died of pleurisy as a result of working on it in cold weather. His many other works include the statues of Goldsmith (1863) and Burke (1868) that stand outside Trinity College, Dublin. In 1866 he received the commission for the O'Connell monument now in O'Connell Street, Dublin, finished after his death by Thomas Brock and unveiled in 1882, which aroused opposition on the grounds that Brock was a 'London artist'—a charge previously made against Foley himself.[1] The statue of Grattan in College Green, Dublin, was completed by Foley just before his death and unveiled in 1876. Foley bequeathed all his casts to the Royal Dublin Society. A consignment was shipped to Dublin at the expense of the Victoria and Albert Museum; what happened to the rest is not known. He was buried in St Paul's cathedral, London. Foley's sculpture is a compromise between the neo-classical and the mid-century romantic, rhetorical, and meticulous naturalistic styles.[2]

Besides Foley, three other Irishmen worked on the Albert memorial: Samuel Lynn his assistant, Patrick MacDowell, and John Lawlor. MacDowell had exhibited at the great exhibition of 1851 in London. During the 1850s he did a number of important commissions, sculpting Turner for St Paul's cathedral (1851); Warren (1850) and Pitt (1857) for Westminster Palace; Cuvier, Leibniz,

---

[1] Strickland, *Dict. Ir. artists*, i, 359.   [2] For his 'Boy at a stream', see above, v, plate 30b.

and Linnaeus for Burlington House; and the memorial to the earl of Belfast (1855; now in Belfast city hall). He also contributed 'Leah' to the Mansion House, London, in 1870 and the group 'Europe' to the Albert memorial in 1871. Besides these commissions, MacDowell did a number of intimate works and classical subjects. He was a very pure and, one might say, innocent, neo-classical sculptor whose work had a great appeal in the mid-century. Lawlor was much more prosaic. His cast 'The bathers' won a prize at the great exhibition of 1851 and was worked in marble for Prince Albert. He contributed the group 'Engineering' and a number of plaques to the Albert memorial. He worked for a time in Ireland, when he did the quite lively 'Sarsfield' for Limerick and the almost grotesque 'Dr Delaney' for Cork. When he had a mind, he could do work of considerable delicacy.

Of the other Irish artists of the period, Ambrose, Barter, the two Farrells, and Moore all produced lively and interesting portrait busts. Ambrose did a number of charming subjects, typical of the period; Thomas Farrell, some unexciting monumental statues; and Moore one disastrous monumental statue. But compared with English, or indeed continental, sculptors of the period Irish sculptors, unlike Irish painters, were among the best—a fact that has yet to be recognised.

As Maurice Craig has pointed out,[1] Georgian classical architecture survived into the 1860s, and in some cases even into the 1870s. But as the century progressed, in Ireland as in Britain, a variety of styles made their appearance. In ecclesiastical architecture the style that predominated was revival Gothic, as opposed to the neo-classical of the earlier part of the century. Public architecture, as also institutional, varied between neo-Gothic and neo-renaissance. Private architecture added to these the neo-baronial (for the rich upper class and aristocracy) or, particularly at the end of the nineteenth and the beginning of the twentieth century, suburban neo-Tudor (for the rich middle class). Building in the late nineteenth century, however, was dominated by the larger institutions: the board of works, the poor law commissioners, the commissioners for the establishment of asylums for the lunatic poor in Ireland, the railway companies, and the churches, particularly the catholic church.

Catholic emancipation in 1829 greatly accelerated the building of catholic churches. The leading architect of the period was Patrick Byrne (1783–1864). In his early period he tended towards the neo-classical, for example St Paul's, Arran Quay, Dublin (1835–7). In the 1840s he fell temporarily under the spell of Pugin and designed churches in the neo-Gothic style for Blackrock (1842), Fairview (1859), Enniskerry (1859), and Raheny (1863–4). But by 1850 he had become ambidextrous. He had returned to his classicism. His Three Patrons church, Rathgar, Dublin (1860), and St Mary, Arklow, County Wicklow (1859–66) are examples of good work in this style.

[1] Maurice Craig, *The architecture of Ireland from the earliest times to 1880* (London and Dublin, 1982), pp 256, 289.

But the presiding genius at this period of Irish ecclesiastical architecture was Augustus Welby Northmore Pugin (1812–52), who believed that Gothic was the only possible style for a Christian society. He built St Peter's College, Wexford, in 1838–40, and in 1839–42 the church of St Michael the Archangel and the Loreto convent, Gorey, County Wexford. In the same county he built St Aidan's cathedral, Enniscorthy (1843–8), and the parish church at Tagoat, opened in 1846. He also drew up plans for St Patrick's College, Maynooth. One of the finest achievements of his career was Killarney cathedral, begun in 1842 but not finished until 1855, on account of the great famine. It was described in the *Tablet* as 'a structure which, by its arrangement and detail, fully recalls the ancient edifices of Ireland in the days of her catholic glory'. But this reflects Pugin's own views:

If the clergy and gentry of Ireland possessed one spark of real national feeling, they would revive and restore those solemn piles of buildings which formerly covered that island of saints, and which are associated with the holiest and most honourable recollections of her history. Many of these were indeed rude and simple, but, massive and solemn, they harmonised most perfectly with the wild and rocky localities in which they were erected.[1]

Pugin set great store in the honest use of materials, and the clear structural and functional purpose of the parts of a building. His Irish work is notable for its strength and vigour, a strong sense of the quality of local materials, and clarity of organisation. He would not have countenanced Patrick Byrne's use of 'Gothick' plaster vaulting and decorative arcading.

But he was not too pleased with conditions of work in Ireland. Speaking of Maynooth college, he says: 'The architect wanted one thing, the authorities another, the builder had his views, and the presiding genius, the board of works, wanted something else.' He also had harsh words for the clergy:

I regret to say that there seems little or no appreciation among the clergy. The cathedral I built in Enniscorthy has been completely ruined. The new bishop has blocked up the choir, and stuck altars under the tower; the whole building is in a most painful state of filth; the sacrarium is full of rubbish, and it could hardly have been worse treated if it had fallen into the hands of Hottentots.[2]

Most of Pugin's design for Maynooth was achieved, from 1845 onwards, except for the chapel, which was designed by J. J. McCarthy. Besides his ecclesiastical work, he worked on country houses for Lord Dunraven (Adare) and the duke of Devonshire (Lismore Castle). He was drawn to Ireland partly by his fervent catholicism (he became a convert in 1834), and partly through the Irish connections of his patron, the earl of Shrewsbury, whose wife was a daughter of William Talbot of Castle Talbot, County Wexford.[3] By his writing (for instance, in the *Dublin Review*) and his example he imposed Gothic revivalism in its moral,

[1] A. W. N. Pugin, *An apology for the revival of Christian architecture* (London, 1843), p. 23, n. 13.
[2] Benjamin Ferrey, *The recollections of A. W. N. Pugin* (London, 1861), p. 125.
[3] Denis Gwynn, *Lord Shrewsbury, Pugin, and the catholic revival* (London, 1946); Alexandra Wedgwood, *A. W. N. Pugin and the Pugin family* (London, 1985), pp 80–81.

ecclesiological, vigorous form on Irish ecclesiastical architecture from the mid-nineteenth century until the end of the century and beyond.

This is not to say that Gothic was anything more than the predominant style. As we have seen, Byrne continued with the classical. Even that determined Gothic revivalist J. J. McCarthy was induced by Cardinal Cullen to design the chapel in the Dublin seminary Holy Cross College, Clonliffe (1873), in Roman baroque. This is something that Pugin, with his passion for the architecture of the catholic medieval past, the ages of faith, would not have appreciated. The neo-classical and the baroque were associated with Rome, ancient and modern; they symbolised Roman, counter-reformation, catholicism. As the *Dublin Penny Journal* suggested,[1] this was the sort of architecture with which many, if not most, of the catholic clergy, educated on the Continent, were most familiar, and which distinguished catholic buildings from their rivals of the Church of Ireland, where Gothic had been much earlier adopted. Nevertheless, the influence of Pugin, and of the Cambridge Camden Society and the Irish Ecclesiological Society, made Gothic predominant.

Although Pugin was succeeded in Ireland by his son Edward Welby Pugin, his true heir was J. J. McCarthy (1817–82), 'the Irish Pugin' (though not Pugin's pupil), and, in Pugin's own words, 'a man raised up to do great things in Ireland'.[2] During the 1850s and 1860s he designed four cathedrals—Armagh (1854–73), Monaghan (1861–92), Thurles (1857–73), and Derry (1851–73), and about sixty churches. One of these—St Saviour's, Dominick Street, Dublin—was alleged to have been designed by Pugin, and McCarthy had to point out that, however flattered he was that it should be attributed to Pugin, he had to admit modestly that he was its author.[3] In 1875 he began the chapel at Maynooth college, which was completed in 1902 by his pupil William Hague. He was a key figure in the foundation of the Irish Ecclesiological Society in 1849. Some of the most influential of the catholic hierarchy became members; this must have appeased the ghost of Pugin, who died demented in 1852.

The main challenge to McCarthy's supremacy in the 1860s came from the firm of Pugin & Ashlin. Edward Welby Pugin (1834–75) took over his father's practice in 1852. Like his father (with whose work his is often confused) he did a number of churches, the best of which was SS Peter and Paul, Cork (1859). In 1860 he took into partnership his Irish pupil (and, later, brother-in-law) George Coppinger Ashlin (1836–1921). Together they produced a delightful little church at Monkstown, County Cork (1867–73); St Colman's cathedral, Cobh, which they won in competition in 1867; and SS Augustine and John, Thomas Street, Dublin (1860–72). They specialised in late French Gothic, with tall, slender spires and polygonal east ends. In 1870 the partnership broke up, and Ashlin's style changed in his subsequent partnership with his nephew Stephen Ashlin and Thomas

[1] Quoted in Maurice Craig, *Dublin, 1660–1860* (London, 1952), p. 294.
[2] Pugin to McCarthy, 15 Jan. 1852 (unpublished letter; copy in possession of J. I. Sheehy)
[3] Jeanne Sheehy, *J. J. McCarthy and the Gothic revival in Ireland* ([Belfast], 1977), p. 18.

Coleman. Meanwhile other Irish architects had been building in adaptations of medieval styles. For instance, William Henry Lynn (1829–1915) was not only the first Irish architect to use Lombardic detail, in the Sinclair seamen's church, Belfast (1856–7), but also the first to revive the Hiberno-Romanesque in St Patrick's, Jordanstown (1865–8).

In the second half of the century, more British architects came to work in Ireland, sometimes as winners of competitions—William Burges, for instance, whose Church of Ireland cathedral of St Fin Barre at Cork (1867–79) is a masterpiece of High French Gothic, one of the major monuments of the Gothic revival, and probably the crowning achievement of his career. Other work for the Church of Ireland included William Slater's cathedral for the diocese of Kilmore in 1857 and Christ Church, Bray, County Wicklow (consecrated 1863); and one of William Butterfield's last designs was the vigorous, polychromatic St Mark's, Dundela, Belfast (c.1875). For the catholic church, George Goldie designed St John's cathedral, Sligo (1869–75); P. C. Hardwick designed St John's cathedral, Limerick (1856–61) and St Alphonsus, Limerick (1858–62), and worked at Adare for Lord Dunraven. The Gothic revival also led to the restoration of medieval churches, notably George Edmund Street's work on Christ Church, Dublin (1871–8) and St Brigid, Kildare (1871).

In secular buildings there was a wider variety of styles. However, due to the powerful influence of Deane and Woodward, Gothic became popular in secular architecture, even in commercial or 'street' architecture. But it was secular Gothic; to be precise, Venetian Gothic; and to be still more precise, Ruskinian Venetian. As Pugin was the genius who presided over Irish ecclesiastical architecture in the nineteenth century, so Ruskin was the genius who presided over secular architecture.

Benjamin Woodward (1815–61) was steeped in Ruskin (the three volumes of *The stones of Venice* were published 1851–3). In 1845 he entered the offices of the Cork architect Sir Thomas Deane (1792–1871). He and Thomas Newenham Deane (1827–99) were taken into partnership, and the firm became Sir Thomas Deane, Son, & Woodward in 1851. In 1853 they attracted widespread attention when they won the competition for a museum, later the engineering school, for Trinity College, Dublin, described as the finest secular building the Gothic revival ever produced. Thomas Drew wrote of it in 1866: 'To this remarkable building, and this alone, we trace the inauguration of the great revolution in public taste which has since taken place.'[1]

In 1854 they won the competition for the university museum in Oxford, and attracted the attention and approval of Ruskin and the English *avant-garde*. They also designed the debating hall for the Oxford Union (1856–7). In Ireland they designed St Ann's Schools, Molesworth Street, 'the first adaptation of the Early

[1] *Ir. Builder*, viii (1866), p. 121.

English style to street architecture',[1] and the Kildare Street Club, Dublin (1858–61). They also designed the vast picture gallery for Kilkenny castle (1858–62) and much more besides.

In 1861 Woodward died of consumption, but his influence lived on, manifested in the Ruskinian use of Venetian detail, the structural polychromy (where the stones are used for their decorative qualities and not just as building materials), and the unbroken masonry surfaces, as well as the stone-carving. His partner Thomas Newenham Deane used Woodward's Ruskinian Gothic in the Meadow Buildings, Christ Church, Oxford (1862–6), and the Munster & Leinster Bank (c.1870) and Crown Life insurance office in Dame Street, Dublin (c.1871). A pupil of Woodward's, James Rogers (1838–96) adopted the style for the Caledonian insurance company, Dame Street (1860s) and the Carmichael school of medicine, North Brunswick Street (1864). It was adapted by William G. Murray for the Hibernian bank in College Green (1867). Even J. J. McCarthy, who usually favoured French or English Decorated, used it for his design for the catholic university in 1862. When John Hungerford Pollen (1820–1902) came to Dublin as professor of fine art in Newman's catholic university in 1855[2] one of his first tasks was to design the university church in St Stephen's Green. It is not unlike Woodward's work, with polychromatic brickwork, a liberal use of coloured stone, and carved decoration, and draws for inspiration on Venetian Byzantine design. Pollen worked with Woodward on the Oxford museum, and on the decoration of Kilkenny castle.

Apart from the museum building in Trinity College, the most important buildings erected in Dublin between 1850 and 1870 were the natural history museum (1857) and the national gallery (1859–64), on either side of Leinster Lawn, the one by Frederick V. Clarendon, the other by Captain Francis Fowke, employed by the department of science and art, who had rejected plans by Lanyon.[3] Leinster Lawn itself was the site of many fine, but alas ephemeral, exhibition buildings, notably those for the exhibition of 1853, designed by Sir John Benson (1812–74). One exhibition building survived. It was part of the exhibition of 1865 and later became the examination hall of the Royal University, and, in the twentieth century, the nucleus of University College, and is now the national concert hall. Other important buildings of the period were the Royal College of Physicians (1860–64) by Murray and the Mater Misericordiae hospital (1860–61) by John Bourke, both in the classical style.

As we have seen, the classical style survived in ecclesiastical architecture, for reasons already given. In spite of the influence of Deane & Woodward, it survived, in various forms, even more strongly in secular architecture. The reason

[1] *Building News*, iv (1857), p. 990. For the influence of Ruskin's views on stone-carving, see below, p. 473.

[2] Below, pp 552–3.

[3] Catherine de Courcy, *The foundation of the national gallery of Ireland* (Dublin, 1985), p. 50; above, p. 437.

for this is partly conservatism of taste; but, more importantly, it gave an appearance of stability and solidity: 'as a man is generally regarded as a gentleman because he has a good suit of clothes on his back, so too does a respectable show by a commercial establishment inspire confidence in the healthiness of its constitution.'[1]

This is nowhere more manifest than in the designs for banks and railway stations, both of which were appearing in increasing numbers in the mid-century, and, in the case of banks, well into this century. Sir Charles Lanyon used a recessed Doric portico and heavily rusticated masonry in the Northern Bank, Belfast (1852); and William G. Murray's designs for the Provincial Bank of Ireland offices in Dublin (1862) and Cork (1865) are rather Italianate, pedimented and columned. The railways, no less anxious to reassure both their passengers and shareholders, adopted either the Doric portico or colonnade—Harcourt Street by George Wilkinson (1859); Cork by Sir John Benson (1860); John Skipton Mulvany's solid 'Graeco-Egyptian' pile, Broadstone, Dublin (1850); the Italianate Kingsbridge (now Heuston) (1848).

The decade of the 1850s was a period of growing prosperity in Ireland, reflected in the urban expansion of Dublin and Belfast, and the growth of commercial buildings, warehouses, banks, and insurance offices. This growth was nowhere more manifest than in Belfast. The principal architect in Belfast and the north at this time was Sir Charles Lanyon, who became surveyor of County Antrim (including Belfast) in 1839, and built up a flourishing architectural practice. His major work in this period was the Custom House (c.1857), which, according to C. E. B. Brett, is 'Belfast's finest public building, and the peak of Lanyon's achievement'.[2] He had already to his credit the queen's college (now the Queen's University) (1849) in Oxford Collegiate Gothic, and the Northern Bank (1852), an interesting, rusticated building.

In 1854 he took into partnership the young William Henry Lynn (1829–1915). Lynn, 'scholarly, modest, reticent, unworldly' concentrated on design; Lanyon, 'good-looking, suave, extrovert, the supreme organiser' handled the business.[3] It was a partnership like that of Deane and Woodward. In his style Lynn was eclectic. As we have seen, in his ecclesiastical building he favoured the Hiberno-Romanesque and Lombardic. In his secular buildings—the Belfast Bank buildings at Newtownards (1854) and Dungannon (1855), and the Church of Ireland offices, Belfast (1867)—he favoured Ruskinian Venetian. He also designed something that was never equalled by Dublin, a warehouse of palatial proportions: Richardson Sons & Owden, Donegall Square (1869), the building to which Oscar Wilde referred when he said in 1884: 'in Belfast they had, at any rate, one beautiful

[1] *Ir. Builder*, v (1863), p. 1.
[2] C. E. B. Brett, *The buildings of Belfast, 1700–1914* (revised ed., Belfast, 1985), p. 35, and plates 25, 26, 27, and 32.
[3] Hugh Dixon, 'William Henry Lynn' in *Ir. Georgian Soc. Bull.*, xvii, nos 1–2 (Jan.–June 1974), pp 25–30.

building.'[1] Another Belfast architect of that time deserves mention: W. J. Barre (1830–67), who designed the Ulster Hall (1860) and Clanwilliam House (1864), now defaced, as well as two monuments, the Crozier memorial, Banbridge (1862), and the Albert memorial, Belfast (1865).[2]

In the 1870s and 1880s the only public buildings of any importance were town halls, erected in response to the growing power of local government. Cork was early in the field with competitions in 1851 (won by Atkins & Johnson) and again in 1881 (won by J. L. Robinson). There followed Drogheda (Barre) and Sligo (William Hague, Ruskinian Venetian), both in 1864; Dun Laoghaire (J. L. Robinson, Ruskinian Venetian) in 1879–80; Tipperary (T. G. Jackson, a mixture of 'old English' and 'Queen Anne') in 1877; and Bray, County Wicklow (T. N. Deane, half-timbered, neo-Tudor), in 1882.

The only other public building of any note was the complex on the Kildare Street side of Leinster House, the headquarters of the Royal Dublin Society, complementing the earlier work on the Leinster Lawn side.[3] In 1881 a competition was held for a science and art museum, but nothing came of it. In 1883–4 a second competition was won by T. N. Deane & Son, who produced the present national library and national museum. The design departs from the firm's Ruskinian style, perhaps out of deference to Leinster House, which the two buildings flank. It is classical, with rather heavy detail, and a domed and colonnaded rotunda in the centre of each façade. The interior decoration, especially the mosaic flooring and the carved wood and stone, follows the firm's traditions in being of very high quality. The buildings were completed in 1890.

A word must be said about Irish engineers, in particular Richard Turner (c.1798–1881) of the Hammersmith ironworks, Dublin.[4] Turner developed a light, economic structure, using beams of rolled wrought iron, capable of the wide spans needed for conservatories, exhibition buildings, and train sheds. His system was first used in the Palm House in the Royal Botanic Gardens, Kew (1845–7) and in the curvilinear greenhouses at Belfast (1839–52) and Dublin (1842–50). It was also used in the great iron and glass exhibition buildings for the Dublin exhibition of 1853, by Sir John Benson, who had been responsible for the design of the wood and glass exhibition building in Cork a year earlier. The other major iron and glass exhibition buildings were those for the Dublin exhibition of 1865, designed by Alfred Gresham Jones (c.1822–1915). The Turner system was also used in the making of passenger sheds, for instance by G. W. Hemans at Galway (1851–2) and at York Road, Belfast (1848), and in the rebuilding of Westland Row, Dublin (1875–8).

---

[1] Quoted in Brett, *Buildings of Belfast*, p. 54; and see ibid., plate 56.
[2] For the Ulster Hall and Crozier memorial, see above, v, plates 28, 30*a*.
[3] Above, p. 464.
[4] Edward J. Diestelkamp, 'The iron and glass architecture of Richard Turner' (Ph.D. thesis, University of London, 1982); for an unexecuted project by Turner, see above, v, plate 25*b*.

Besides Turner there were other Irish engineers who made important contributions to Irish building. Sir John MacNeill, who designed the great passenger shed at Kingsbridge (1845), was engineer to several Irish railway companies. His greatest contribution was the lattice girder system for bridges, which he used to span the Royal Canal for the Dublin & Drogheda railway in 1844 and for the great Boyne viaduct at Drogheda (1851–5), as well as in other parts of the British Isles. Robert Mallet (1810–81) invented the 'buckled plate', for which he took out a patent in 1852.[1] Since it combined maximum strength with minimum depth and weight, it was very useful for the flooring of bridges, notably Westminster bridge, London (1856). Bindon Blood Stoney (1828–1909), one of the first graduates from the school of engineering at Trinity College, Dublin, which opened in 1842, is renowned for his classic work, *The theory of strains in girders and similar structures* (2 vols, London, 1866–9), which marks a more rigorously scientific approach to engineering than the intuitive methods of Turner and his contemporaries. He was appointed engineer-in-chief to the port of Dublin in 1856, and his major engineering achievement was the improvement of the port.

APART from ecclesiastical and major public buildings, such as town halls, railway stations, museums, and university buildings, another group of buildings, the workhouses and lunatic asylums, came into existence. The poor law commissioners continued the vigorous building programme that they had inaugurated in 1839. Such was the volume of work that their architect George Wilkinson (1814–90), appointed in 1839 for one year, was not finally dismissed until late in 1855.[2] The building magazines of the early 1850s contain melancholy lists of new workhouses. These were, not unnaturally, loathed by the populace. Many have disappeared or been transformed out of all recognition. They were of grim appearance: rubble stone walls, with cut stone or brick dressings, and pitched roofs with dormers. What architectural embellishments there were consisted of pared-down Tudor elements with depressed arches, square hood-moulds, and diamond-paned windows. There were loud complaints that one architect, Wilkinson, an Englishman to boot, should have the monopoly of so large and lucrative a practice. Sensitive to criticisms of this kind, the board of works applied for designs for asylums for the 'lunatic poor' to 'the leading architects of the country . . ., thus avoiding any grounds of complaint as to the invidious employment of their own officers'.[3] As a result, the six district asylums built in the 1840s and 1850s were designed by different architects. The architects were reminded that they were designing hospitals, not prisons, and told to avoid the jail-like character of earlier asylum buildings. Gothic was recommended as a style with two practical

[1] Ronald C. Cox (ed.), *Engineering in Ireland, 1778–1878* (T.C.D. exhibition catalogue, [Dublin, 1978]).

[2] Michael H. Gould, *The workhouses of Ulster* ([Belfast], 1983), p. 6.

[3] *District lunatic asylums (Ireland): copy of treasury minute . . .; report of . . . commissioners*, p. 4, H.C. 1856 (9), liii, 370.

advantages: it was suited to the materials available in Ireland (as Pugin had pointed out), and it would make additions to the buildings easier. The result was some very distinguished architecture. Killarney, by Thomas Deane the elder, was built of local granite with cut limestone dressings, in an effective display of structural polychromy. According to Eve Blau, 'of all the smaller Irish asylums . . . [it] displays the greatest amount of High Victorian Gothic "realism" and explicit structural and functional expression'.[1] The other asylums were designed by William Atkins (Cork), William Deane Butler (Sligo), George Papworth (Kilkenny), William Farrell (Omagh), and J. S. Mulvany (Mullingar). Mulvany, an accomplished classicist, was not at home with Gothic, and Mullingar is built in a rather grim and dessicated Tudor.

The board of works also had charge of the building of the queen's colleges, the so-called 'Godless colleges', in Cork, Belfast, and Galway. Once again local architects were employed, and the Gothic style was used, though this does not seem to have been laid down in the conditions. The form used was Collegiate Gothic. The *Ecclesiologist* commented:

It is a curious 'fact' that all these structures have put on the garb of Christian architecture, and try to look like 'colleges', as of old the word was known; although by a curious sort of unconscious symbolism, the style in every case is the most mundane of its sort, the Third Pointed.[2]

Mundane it may be, but as the banks chose the respectability of the classical or Florentine renaissance style, so academic institutions tended to choose the respectability of the Oxford colleges as their model. Macaulay called Thomas Deane's design for Cork (1848) 'a Gothic college worthy to stand in the High Street of Oxford'.[3] Lanyon's Queen's College, Belfast, drew on details from Magdalen, though it was less obviously a translation of Oxford Gothic, but J. B. Keane's design for Galway (1849), where the gate tower is based on Tom Tower, Christ Church, is the most specific reference to Oxford.

As in ecclesiastical, so in secular architecture, Irish architects could more than hold their own against British competitors. While painters and sculptors were obliged to look abroad for a living, the country could support a respectable establishment of architects. Moreover, Irish architects, such as Woodward and Lynn, made their mark outside Ireland.

It was a period of large suburban and country house building, and Irish architects got plenty of commissions. Among the more distinguished were Lanyon, Lynn, & Lanyon, who remodelled Killyleagh Castle (1847–51) in Scottish Baronial,[4] and Glaslough, County Monaghan (*c.* 1870), in an eclectic mixture of Tudor and Italian renaissance, returning to Scottish Baronial again for

---

[1] Eve Blau, *Ruskinian Gothic* (Princeton, N. J., 1982), p. 20.
[2] *Ecclesiologist*, ix, no. 9 (Apr. 1849), pp 289–91.
[3] T. B. Macaulay, *History of England* (Everyman ed., London, 1946), ii, 344.
[4] Above, v, plate 24.

Belfast castle (1868–70). Deane & Woodward designed vigorous Ruskinian villas such as Brownsbarn, Thomastown, County Kilkenny (1858–64); Glandore, Monkstown, County Dublin (1858–9); and Clontra, Shankill, County Dublin (1858–62). Portumna Castle, County Galway (1862), in the same Venetian style but larger and more elaborate, was designed for the marquis of Clanricarde by Thomas Newenham Deane after Woodward's death. J. J. McCarthy's Cahir-moyle, County Limerick (1870–74), was influenced by Woodward's Venetian style. There was a surprising number of large, picturesque, turretted and embattled castles, such as James Franklin Fuller's Kylemore Castle, County Galway (1860); Samuel Robert's Gurteen le Poer, Kilsheelan, County Waterford (1866); and Ashford Castle, County Galway (1870s), designed by J. F. Fuller and G. C. Ashlin for Lord Ardilaun. Pugin and his designs for Adare and Lismore have been mentioned. Others worthy of mention are Fowler Jones of York with his Scottish Baronial Cloghonodfoy ('Castle Oliver'), County Limerick (c.1850); William White, an ecclesiastical architect, who designed the muscular Gothic and virtually fortified Humewood, County Wicklow (1866–70); E. W. Godwin, with another fortified pile for the earl of Limerick, with a silhouette based on the Rock of Cashel—Dromore Castle, County Limerick (1866–73); and George Devey's Killarney House (1877–80), in a mixture of Old English and Queen Anne, typical of arts and crafts architecture.

One of the most interesting stylistic developments in Irish commercial archi-tecture was the use of terracotta as a decorative and cladding material. It was first introduced when Lockwood & Mawson, a Bradford firm (terracotta was popular in the industrial north and midlands of England), won a competition for the Dublin South City Markets (1878). The assessor was Alfred Waterhouse, who had pioneered its use in the natural history museum, London, in 1873. In Ireland Albert Edward Murray, the last of that dynasty of architects, used it in the Royal City of Dublin hospital (1892) and the Working Boys Home, Lord Edward Street (1891). Murray favoured a mixture of red brick, from Ruabon in Wales, and yellowish terracotta, which led people to describe it, after a popular tobacco of the period, as 'Murray's mellow mixture'.

A feature of all functional and decorative arts towards the end of the century was a tendency to incorporate ancient Irish motifs and styles, whether genuine or bogus. In architecture this tendency found expression in the popularity of Hiberno-Romanesque. Lynn pioneered the style in 1865–8. After his partnership with Edward Welby Pugin broke up in 1870, Ashlin designed a number of buildings in this style: a domestic chapel at Mooresfort, County Tipperary (1877), St Finbar's West, Cork (1881), and All Saints, Carrick-on-Suir (1885). In 1901 he gave a presidential address to the Royal Institute of Architects of Ireland, entitled 'The possibility of the revival of the ancient arts of Ireland and their adaptation to modern circumstances'.[1] Both the Church of Ireland and the

---

[1] Quoted in *Ir. Builder*, xliv (1902), pp 1018–19.

catholic church adopted the style not only out of national sentiment but also to give support to their claim to be the true church of St Patrick. James Franklin Fuller (1835–1924) designed a Church of Ireland church at Clane, County Kildare (1883), with an interior reminiscent of Cormac's chapel, Cashel, and another at Rathdaire, Queen's County (Laois) (c.1885), with a façade based on St Cronan's, Roscrea.

Meanwhile the Gothic tradition of Pugin and McCarthy persisted. McCarthy's pupil Hague, in partnership with T. F. McNamara, designed St Eunan's cathedral, Letterkenny (1891–1901). Another of his pupils, W. H. Byrne (c.1844–1917) designed St Michael's, Enniskillen (1870–75), and St Peter's, Drogheda (1881), in partnership with John O'Neill of Belfast. On his own he designed the cathedral of Loughrea (completed 1902), soon to become the repository of some of the finest stained glass and applied art in Ireland. Later Byrne entered into partnership with his son, Ralph, and a new dynasty of architects was formed.

IRELAND produced distinguished silver, glass, and furniture in the eighteenth and early nineteenth centuries. The second half of the nineteenth century did not quite live up to these standards; on the other hand, it was outstanding for its lace and gained quite a reputation for its ceramics. The earliest reference to lacemaking in Ireland dates from the seventeenth century. But it was not until the eighteenth century that, thanks to encouragement given by the Dublin Society, the craft began to flourish modestly. At that time the sources of lace were Italy (mainly Venice), France, and Flanders. In 1816 the rector of Dunaghmoyne, County Monaghan, and Mrs Porter introduced the new method of appliqué from Italy. In 1820, to alleviate the economic distress in the locality, classes were set up to teach it. During the great famine the Shirley estate made over a house at Carrickmacross as a school and it gave its name to a truly Irish lace. This lacemaking was merely an organised cottage industry. Meanwhile, in 1829 an Englishman, Charles Walker, had established a professional lace industry in Limerick from which the special brand of Irish 'Limerick lace' emanated.

The craft, if not the art, of lacemaking spread through the country, particularly in the mid-century, thanks mainly to the convents. At the great exhibition of 1851 Irish lace was widely acclaimed. But in the next two decades quality declined. There never had been a resolution of the demands of art and craft. However, in 1883, thanks to the efforts of Alan Cole, of the department of art and science at South Kensington, and James Brenan, headmaster of the Cork school of design, lacemaking in Ireland made a spectacular recovery. Not only was it taught in art colleges, convents, and other schools, but skill and design were at last firmly mated. From 1884 prizes were given for designs, which were worked up into commissions. These were realised for such worthies as Queen Victoria and that great supporter of Irish art, Lady Aberdeen. These prize-winning designs were exhibited at the Irish lace exhibition in London in 1888. In 1907 the lord lieutenant, Lord Aberdeen, held a Lace Ball in Dublin castle. During the 1880s and 1890s a light and delicate lace was popular, but from the end of the century the heavier and more clumsy lace became fashionable. On the other hand, Irish crochet became popular in the early decades of the twentieth century.[1]

Besides lace, other textiles of quality such as Irish poplin and linen, introduced by the huguenots in the seventeenth century, continued to prosper. With the rise of nationalist feeling towards the end of the nineteenth and early twentieth century it became popular to sport Irish tweeds and jerseys. The trend towards Irish designs and fabrics accelerated in the next century.[2]

The most significant Irish contribution to ceramics came from the Belleek pottery. The factory was set up about 1856 on the shores of Lough Erne by the local landlord J. C. Bloomfield, with the assistance of the prominent Dublin merchant David McBirney and the London architect R. W. Armstrong. In its early days the firm's main production was utilitarian earthenware, but it is best known for its porcelain, manufactured from about 1863. It is characterised by the extravagant use of natural and fantastic forms—stags and dragons, a fish and a tulip—and by a creamy nacreous glaze. W. H. Gallimore, chief modeller for a Stoke-on-Trent pottery, worked there (1863–6) and devised over 500 designs, including shells, lacework, and Celtic motifs.

Glass was affected by restrictive legislation.[3] Cork glass survived into the 1840s. In spite of the lifting of the excise duty in 1845, and a triumphal appearance in the great exhibition of 1851, Waterford glass temporarily disappeared about that time. The making of high-quality glass continued in Belfast into the 1870s and in Dublin until the end of the century. In the early nineteenth century the glass that was regarded as characteristically Irish was heavy cut glass. In the 1850s Thomas and John Pugh of Dublin reintroduced the lighter engraved glass. They employed Bohemian engravers and even engraved imported glass, usually with national motifs, principally shamrocks. National motifs on glass were common in the 1780s and 1790s. Their reintroduction in the second half of the nineteenth century may be a deliberate revival prompted by nationalist feeling. On the other hand, nationalist feeling could be expressed in silver with something less symbolic than shamrocks and round towers. In 1850 the Tara brooch was discovered, and in 1868 the Ardagh chalice. Here were genuine motifs from Irish Celtic and early Christian times, animal motifs and interlacing. Admittedly they could have been copied from high crosses and manuscripts, but here they were on silver. Alas, most of the resulting silverwork was excessively ornate and lacked the delicacy of the eighteenth century.

IRISH furniture in the second half of the nineteenth century was mostly either imitation Chippendale, Hepplewhite, and Sheraton or somewhat eccentric and rather heavy, adorned with the inevitable shamrocks, round towers, wolfhounds,

---

[1] For the lacemaking industry, see above, pp 304–5.
[2] Above, pp 402–3.
[3] See Phelps Warren, *Irish glass* (2nd ed., London and Boston, Mass., 1981), pp 26, 28–9.

and harps. Nevertheless they were frequently the product of serious craftsmen— Arthur Jones, James Hicks, William Moore—the last of their kind, who won acclaim at the universal exhibitions in Dublin, Cork, and London. The most eccentric piece was surely J. Fletcher's gladiatorial table with the shield as table-top, shown at the great exhibition of 1851. Jones ran him a close second with his suite in bog yew 'illustrative of Irish history and antiquities', containing among other things a chair with arms in the forms of two wolfhounds, one at ease, the other straining forward, bearing the mottoes 'gentle when stroked' and 'fierce when provoked' respectively; and also a teapoy representing the ancient commerce of Ireland, symbolised by Hibernia, seated beneath the basalt cliffs of the Giant's Causeway, welcoming a Tyrian galley.

Bog yew and bog oak, as specifically Irish materials, became popular about the mid-century. As Jones wrote of his illustrative suite, the wood 'resembles the subject it illustrates. As the details of Irish history have been disentombed from the oblivion which conquest entails upon the records of the vanquished, the bog yew timber of ancient Ireland has been exhumed from the depths of her peat formations.'[1] Jones also exhibited at the Dublin exhibition of 1853, alongside other major furniture makers, including Patrick Beakey of Stafford Street and C. Clarke of St Stephen's Green. James Hicks of Dublin made copies of regency furniture from about 1890.

Inlaid furniture in varied coloured woods was very popular. It was known as 'Killarney work' because so much of it was made there, by, for example, Jeremiah O'Connor and J. Egan, both of Main Street, Killarney, though it was also made by Jones. Much of it was on a small scale, work-boxes and the like, suitable for the tourists who, even then, flocked to Killarney, though larger pieces, such as tables and davenports, were also made. The inlaid panels, besides depicting local beauty spots—Muckross friary or Ross castle—and the ubiquitous shamrock, frequently took the form of wreaths of ferns, for which Killarney is renowned.

By the time the arts and crafts revival had got under way at the end of the century, such work was considered hackneyed and badly designed. Reporting on the 1896 exhibition of the Arts and Crafts Society of Ireland, William Hunt felt that the workmanship in the furniture was excellent, but the designs derivative. As part of the move to develop crafts in rural areas, workshops were set up. One of these was the Bray Art Furnishing Industry, which, under the direction of Miss St John Whitty, made fittings for Christ Church, Bray, in the early years of the twentieth century.[2] The architect William A. Scott, who designed some simple seating for Loughrea cathedral, also designed sturdy, rustic-looking furniture, which was made by a local carpenter, Patrick Connolly of Gort, for W. B. Yeats's Thoor Ballylee about 1918.

---

[1] [Arthur Jones], *Description of a suite of sculptured decorative furniture, illustrative of Irish history and antiquities . . .* (Dublin, 1853), p. 3.
[2] William Garner, *Bray: architectural heritage* (An Foras Forbartha, Dublin, 1980), pp 10, 12.

THE Gothic revival, and especially the vast increase in church building, gave a great impetus to the art of stained-glass-making in the British Isles. Though a good deal of the glass was imported from the Continent, from Lobin of Tours and Mayer of Munich, for instance, over fifty small stained-glass studios proliferated in Ireland in the nineteenth century, though the great period of Irish stained glass did not begin until the early twentieth century.[1]

A notable stained-glass artist was the Dublin-born Michael O'Connor (1801–67). He was a pupil of Thomas Willement, a leading figure in the return to a medieval style in stained glass. O'Connor set up a studio in London in 1845, and was later joined by his sons Arthur and William. He designed the east window for Tuam cathedral and also for Patrick Byrne's St James's church, Dublin (1859). O'Connor & Sons also did windows for St Patrick's Church of Ireland church, Enniskerry (1862). The windows had no sooner been installed than extreme protestants smashed them.

O'Connor worked with A. W. N. Pugin in the early days of the firm, and it was Pugin who persuaded him to revive the medieval style. Pugin also had close contact with the firm of Hardman of Birmingham, a firm of ecclesiastical metalworkers whom he persuaded to expand into glass in 1845. Hardman's supplied glass for St Patrick's church, Dundalk, and Holy Trinity church, Cookstown, County Tyrone; and some fine glass in St Patrick's, Celbridge, County Kildare (1859), in which J. J. McCarthy and his wife Agnes are represented as donors.

Hardman had sufficient Irish work to set up a Dublin branch in 1853. In 1865 he resigned his Dublin business to Thomas Earley and Henry Powell. Powell had directed the Dublin branch for many years, and Earley claimed to be 'the only church decorator alive who was taught the profession by the late A. Welby Pugin'. The firm continued in existence until the late 1960s. Other Irish stained-glass firms of the nineteenth century were J. & D. Casey, F. S. Barff, and Joshua Clarke of Dublin, Watson & Co. of Youghal, and Campbell Brothers and Ward & Partners of Belfast.

The Gothic revival also increased the demand for good monumental stone-carvers. They were needed to execute the floriated ornament and figure sculpture. Particular impetus was given by Deane and Woodward, under the influence of Ruskin. Ruskin believed that the beauty of medieval work arose from the fact that the workmen were allowed a certain freedom of expression, and not forced to make mechanical copies, as in classical architecture. Woodward took up this idea and used it for his Museum Building (Trinity College, Dublin) and for the Kildare Street Club. The *Irish Builder* reported in 1861 on 'The new Kildare Street club-house':

The carving of the building has been executed upon the principles adopted in the new museums, Trinity College, and the university museums, Oxford, which is permitting the

---

[1] Nicola Gordon Bowe, David Caron, and Michael Wynne, *Gazetteer of Irish stained glass* (Blackrock, Co. Dublin, 1988), p. 15.

workmen to think for themselves and to design their own work. No drawings have been made in detail for any of the carved work in the building, a careful supervision and rough sketches, to ensure a certain character of foliage, being all that was deemed necessary.[1]

Woodward included the O'Shea brothers from Ballyhooley, County Cork, in his team. At the Oxford and Dublin museums they are said to have brought specimens of plants from which to work. They may have worked on the Kildare Street Club, but the famous billiard-playing monkeys can reliably be attributed to C. W. Harrison, who came to Dublin from Yorkshire around 1859. Harrison set up a firm of monumental masons in Great Brunswick (now Pearse) Street, which survived until the twentieth century. He did the carving on the Hibernian Bank, College Green, and the capitals in S. F. Lynn's St Andrew's church, Dublin. His firm also did the carving on the National Museum and Library; the very fine woodwork was done by J. Milligan. James Pearse, Patrick Pearse's father, came from Birmingham and served as a journeyman with Harrison until he set up with another Englishman, Edmund Sharp. The firm specialised in ecclesiastical work, especially altars.

---

[1] *Ir. Builder*, iii (1861), p. 600.

CHAPTER XVI

Visual arts and society, 1900–21

CYRIL BARRETT AND JEANNE SHEEHY

The period between the beginning of the twentieth century and 1921 saw a simultaneous increase and falling off of interest in the visual arts. The three main features of the period were the remarkable revival of Irish artistic crafts with the development of a school of stained glass; the foundation by Hugh Lane of a gallery of modern art; and the attempts to reform the art teaching establishments, the R.H.A. and the Metropolitan School of Art, Dublin. But while these events kept art before the public mind and while certain exhibitions were well attended, the indicators of sustained interest reflect a continuing apathy.

By the beginning of the twentieth century, the average attendance at exhibitions at the R.H.A. had dropped from 28,480 (1874–85) to 7,967 (1894–1905) and the receipts on commission from £124,165 (1875–84) to £38,135 (1895–1904). The reason for this, as was repeatedly pointed out in petitions to parliament and in evidence before a committee of inquiry,[1] was that the premises in Abbey Street (donated by the architect Francis Johnston in 1824), were no longer suitable. The social and intellectual centre of gravity of the city had shifted to the south side of the river. Abbey Street had become run down and no one was likely to visit it. In 1900 the architect Sir Thomas Drew was elected president and he set about with great vigour to remedy the situation.

In March 1901, Sir William Abney was instructed by the lord president of the council to report on the state of the R.H.A. to the lord lieutenant, Earl Cadogan. He recommended that, first, a new site near the National Gallery should be found; secondly, the life schools of the R.H.A. and Metropolitan School of Art should be amalgamated, but the academicians should continue to teach as visitors; thirdly, the number of academicians should be reduced to twenty (because insufficient numbers of suitable candidates were available), absentee members should be made honorary members, and an unlimited number of associates, including women, should be admitted; and fourthly, a government grant of £200 (instead of £300 to cover the cost of teaching) should be allocated. In November 1901 Drew addressed a statement approved by the academy to the lord lieutenant, requesting a new site and new galleries for the exhibition of modern and

[1] *Report by committee of inquiry into the work carried on by the Royal Hibernian Academy and the Metropolitan School of Art, Dublin . . .* [Cd 3256], H.C. 1906, xxxi, 799–922.

contemporary art near Leinster House, a new charter, the retention of the small fund realisable out of past private endowment, and the retention of the academy's autonomy. Earl Cadogan put in to the treasury a claim on behalf of the academy, which, according to Drew, was peremptorily, even discourteously, refused.

In the winter of 1902–3, at the suggestion of Hugh Lane the art dealer, recently returned to Ireland, an exhibition of 136 works by deceased English and Irish painters, from Irish collections mainly, was held at the academy. Lane organised the exhibition and financed it out of his own pocket, and it was a tremendous success: 'so charming and surprising as to attract for a few weeks to the old Hibernian Academy house in Lower Abbey Street all that is best in cultured society in Ireland'.[1]

In January 1903 Drew, in the wake of the winter exhibition, wrote a letter to the press (later published as a pamphlet) stating the academy's case. It included a comparison with the treatment of the Royal Society of Antiquaries, and veiled hints as to the source of the opposition to the R.H.A. (the empire-building of the South Kensington department of science, by then defunct).[2] In 1903 the R.H.A. put in a claim for new premises near Leinster House to the public offices sites bill committee, but was unsuccessful. That winter a retrospective of Walter Osborne and Catterson-Smith was held, and in 1905 a retrospective of G. F. Watts.

In 1905 J. J. Mooney, M.P., tabled a motion calling for a committee of inquiry into the affairs of the two teaching institutions, and in July 1905 the treasury set up a committee 'to inquire into the work carried on by the Royal Hibernian Academy and the Metropolitan School of Art in Dublin, and to report whether any—and if so, what—measures should be taken in order to enable these institutions to serve more effectually the purposes for which they are maintained'.[3] The committee took evidence in private from twenty-two witnesses between 10 October and 25 November in five sessions (four in Dublin, one in London) under the chairmanship of Lord Windsor, later earl of Plymouth. The other members of the committee were the earl of Westmeath, D. H. Madden (justice of the king's bench), George C. V. Holmes (chairman of the board of works), and J. P. Boland, M.P. The witnesses included Drew, Sir James Guthrie (president of the Royal Scottish Academy), Hugh Lane (by then a governor of the National Gallery), George Moore, William Orpen, George Russell (A E), W. B. Yeats, and Walter Armstrong. The report, published on 1 November 1906, recommended on behalf of the majority (Plymouth, Westmeath, and Holmes) that there should be only one life class, in the Metropolitan School, and that a professor of painting should be appointed in connection with it (Oliver Sheppard was already teaching

---

[1] Sir Thomas Drew, letter in *I.T.*, 19 Jan. 1903. Lane, born in Ballybrack, Co. Cork, in 1875, entered the London art trade with the help of his aunt Lady Gregory, became a successful private dealer, and built up a remarkable personal collection.

[2] Above, p. 446.

[3] *Report by committee of inquiry into . . . the Royal Hibernian Academy . . .* , p. iv (MS 802).

sculpture) under a committee of nine comprising the director of the National Gallery, two nominees of the lord lieutenant, three from the R.H.A., including the president, and three from the department of agriculture and technical instruction; that the R.H.A. premises in Abbey Street should be repaired and the gallery made suitable for exhibitions; and that a new charter should be granted, lowering the number of members to fifteen or twenty and raising the number of associates to twenty or twenty-five. Madden and Boland published a minority report in which they recommended that a new site should be found for the R.H.A. near the Metropolitan School, which might also house the collection of modern art being collected, and that the interest from the sale of the current building should be added to the annual grant of £300.

It is beyond the scope of this account to discuss the rival merits of the arguments used in the majority and minority reports. Two things, however, are clear: the majority proposals would have meant the death of the R.H.A., and the distinction between the teaching to be expected from the two institutions seems to have either escaped the majority or been wilfully ignored by them. The report produced a vigorous reaction from the academy and the art unions. On 11 February 1907 the academy presented a case to counsel (A. W. Murray, K.C., and Arthur W. Samuels, K.C.), which expressed dissatisfaction with the proposal to abolish the academy as a teaching institution, but was more concerned with refuting the suggestion that the academy came under the department of agriculture and technical instruction, and that its annual grant depended on a favourable report from an inspector of that body.

In April 1907, in *The case of the corporation of the Royal Hibernian Academy of Arts*, this was amplified to an accusation of conspiracy. The commission on art institutions is said to have

first brought to light of day disclosure of a movement obscurely hinted at since 1901, but hitherto concealed from the Irish public, viz:—that there was on foot some such movement, behind H. M. treasury, aggressively hostile to the academy, and tending to its extinction by gradual intrusion on its independence and privilege, and ultimate withdrawal of its poor subsidy.[1]

This seems to be a reference to the proposed royal college of art for Ireland. The disfavour of the treasury 'as it has been advised' was said to be due to the unwillingness on the part of the R.H.A. to come under South Kensington. The treasury was accused of drafting the terms of reference of the 1905–6 inquiry in order to favour abolishing and not strengthening the R.H.A.; the claims of the inspector were refuted in greater detail, and an appeal was made to public opinion—it was public opinion that had saved the Royal Scottish Academy.[2]

In the event neither the majority nor minority report was acted on. The government and M.P.s lost interest in the question after 1908, and so the academy

[1] *The case of the corporation of the Royal Hibernian Academy of Arts, 1907* ([Dublin, 1907]), p. 3.
[2] Ibid., pp 3–4.

continued in Abbey Street until its premises were gutted by fire during the Easter rising.[1] The annual exhibition continued to be held (at the Metropolitan School of Art and at the National College of Art until 1969, and at the National Gallery after that) and the schools continued in temporary premises until the 1940s. In 1939 the academy opened premises in Oliver St John Gogarty's former house in Ely Place.

The Dublin Science and Art Museum Act of 1877[2] brought the Dublin School of Design, the name of which was changed to the Dublin Metropolitan School of Art, under the department of science and art at South Kensington. There are conflicting reports on the teaching at the Metropolitan School between 1877 and 1900. Sir Thomas Drew, in a prize-giving speech, spoke of the older schools not having the advantage of the South Kensington system. But the general opinion of those who studied there was different. James Brenan in the prize-giving speech of 1902 said that the system consisted in working for examinations and for the national competitions. T. W. Rolleston spoke of the 'paralysing influence of South Kensington'.[3] Orpen described how he was kept to one figure for nine months in order to win a gold medal. 'They simply wanted in a particular class of work that the student should be first.' The method of teaching fine art under the South Kensington system was, he said, 'utterly bad'. W. B. Yeats stated that

The whole system of teaching at the Metropolitan School of Art was, in the opinion—I do not say of myself merely, but of all the students who had to go through with it—boring, and destructive of enthusiasm, and all kinds of individuality . . . You went through a routine . . . You were kept working at geometry; you were kept drawing eyes and noses; you were kept working from the antique.[4]

In spite, or because, of the method the school got results. Orpen won four queen's prizes (getting first in anatomy and drawing from the antique) and the Mulready prize in 1896, and a gold medal in 1897. The Metropolitan School was frequently near the top of the league table of art schools in the United Kingdom. Even Orpen had to admit that sculpture (under Oliver Sheppard), perspective, and geometry were well taught. Moreover, as Colonel Plunkett, director of the Science and Art Institution, Dublin (the body immediately responsible for the school) remarked: 'The object of this school was to turn out what are usually called designers, whose art would be decorative and applied to industry, and not to turn out painters of easel pictures.'[5] Mistaken or not as this object may have been, it partly explains the method used. The only trouble was that the school does not seem to have been too successful in its avowed aim either, as will appear later.[6]

---

[1] Above, p. 457.
[2] 40 & 41 Vict., c. ccxxiv (14 Aug. 1877).
[3] T. W. Rolleston, 'Art and industry in Ireland' in *Journal and Proceedings of the Arts and Crafts Society of Ireland*, i, no. 3 (1901), p. 231.
[4] *Report by committee of inquiry into . . . the Royal Hibernian Academy . . .*, pp 29, 60 (MS 853, 884).
[5] Ibid., p. 49 (MS 873).
[6] Below, p. 489.

In 1900 by an act of parliament the school was removed from the care of South Kensington and placed under the department of agriculture and technical instruction of Ireland, or the 'Department' as it was popularly called.[1] Under its new bosses the scope of the school was enlarged to include the teaching of the applied arts and the training of art teachers for schools. By 1905 stained glass, enamelling, metalwork, and mosaic had been introduced. These innovations were largely the work of the headmaster, James Brenan, who had introduced crafts, particularly lacemaking, when he was headmaster in Cork. He came to Dublin in 1889 and retired in 1904, handing over the job of reorganising the school to Richard Willis, who unfortunately died in 1905. In evidence before the committee of inquiry of 1906, Brenan said:

The tendency was in the direction of art for the purposes of industry. I think I foresaw that in Cork, after the exhibition of 1883 . . . though at the time many of the Cork people did not think so; and I had to endure the remarks of friends, who said—'Oh, you are destroying the character of the Cork school of art—it was the school that produced Maclise'.

It was after the Cork exhibition of 1902, he says, that craft subjects were introduced in Dublin.[2]

The school continued voluntarily to send work for examination to South Kensington, a fact that Orpen deplored: 'they were given a splendid opportunity of doing something for Irish art . . . [they] had not availed themselves of the opportunity of breaking away from that [the South Kensington] system.'[3] In spite of Brenan's gloomy forebodings that during the transitional period the students would not be as successful as before, Ethel Rhind won a king's prize for modelling from life in 1904, and Albert Power won one for sculpture in 1907. In 1908 the Metropolitan School came first in the United Kingdom in enamel, enamelled metalwork, and repoussé metalwork, and Kathleen Fox won a gold medal for design in enamel. Power won a gold medal in 1911, and Harry Clarke in that and in the two subsequent years won gold medals for stained glass. The examiners' report for 1904–5 states: 'An abundance of excellent work in every class of subject . . . Evidences of admirable direction and thorough teaching abound.' On the other hand, attendance at the Metropolitan School, which had been increasing steadily between 1899 and 1903, fell off dramatically (by eighty-six students) between 1903 and 1905. P. O'Sullivan, the art inspector for the department, attributed this partly to the rival attractions of Kevin Street technical school.[4]

As part of its task of training art teachers for schools, the Metropolitan School introduced summer courses in 1902. William Orpen conducted the first summer course. Orpen joined the staff of the school in 1906 and continued to teach for a

---

[1] 62 & 63 Vict., c. 50 (9 Aug. 1899), sect. 2 (1) (g); below, p. 530.
[2] *Report by committee of inquiry into . . . the Royal Hibernian Academy . . .*, p. 44 (MS 868).
[3] Ibid., p. 29 (MS 853).   [4] Quoted ibid., p. 38 (MS 862).

fortnight twice a term until the first world war. His influence on a whole generation of Irish artists was immense.

The school was really turning out good work, and there was a lot of promising youth—James Slater, John Keating, Miss Crilly, Miss Fox, Miss O'Kelly, and young Whelan and Touey, all with talent, and all (or mostly all) working like blacks; it was rather like a happy working family.[1]

He resigned from the R.H.A. in 1915 and abandoned a scheme for amalgamating the Metropolitan School with it. And thus he severed his connections with Ireland.

In the report of the inquiry into the Metropolitan School's affairs in 1906, it was recommended that the name be changed to 'The Royal College of Art for Ireland', in view of its wider scope in the training of teachers for the whole country. This and the other proposals affecting the school, mentioned above, were never implemented. The resources of the school were slightly augmented and its activities slightly extended.

As we have seen, a project for a gallery of modern art was for a time linked with that of a new site for the R.H.A. The idea, first publicised by Drew after the winter exhibition of 1902–3, originated with Lane: 'An academy house in the educational centre of Dublin, with the grouped art institutions for passing exhibitions of living art, and a permanent gallery of modern and living artists' works, *as advocated by him*, are the least that Dublin, among English and Irish cities, should now stand for.'[2] Lane had already in 1901, after seeing John B. Yeats's exhibition in St Stephen's Green, commissioned him to paint some portraits of prominent contemporaries.[3] This was to form the nucleus of a national portrait gallery. He also bought some (he wanted to buy all) of Nathaniel Hone's works in the exhibition, which were among the first modern works purchased by him. Hitherto his interest had been exclusively in old masters—on joining the London dealer Colnaghi in 1893, he wrote that they were 'in sympathy in preferring the old painters to the new'.[4]

Following Drew's letter a deputation of academicians called on the lord mayor to present the project. He replied, rather surprisingly, that they had the entire sympathy of the corporation, 'who had long engaged their earnest attention to the problem of forming such a gallery in Dublin'.[5] In May 1903 a special committee of the house of commons was set up under the chairmanship of Arthur Elliott 'to consider a proposal that a portion of the site allocated for the college of science

---

[1] William Orpen, *Stories of Old Ireland and myself* (London, 1924), p. 78.

[2] Quoted in Thomas Bodkin, *Hugh Lane and his pictures* ([Dublin], 1932), p. 8; and see above, p. 476.

[3] Above, p. 456.

[4] Quoted in Augusta Gregory, *Hugh Lane's life and achievement, with some account of the Dublin galleries* (London, 1921), p. 11.

[5] Bodkin, *Lane*, p. 8.

should be transferred to the Royal Hibernian Academy, who would establish thereon a gallery of modern art'. Lane and Drew gave evidence: Lane pointed out that, if a site were found, Whistler and other artists, as well as collectors, had promised to give pictures, and others to give money. The committee agreed that 'the desirability of such an institution has been clearly shown'.[1] No room was available, however, though proposals would be welcomed. Although the R.H.A. organised a retrospective exhibition of the work of Walter Osborne that winter (from which Lane bought three pictures), support for the gallery from the R.H.A. was passive, and sometimes its attitude was even hostile.

Meanwhile there had been a proposal to send an exhibition of Irish paintings to the St Louis international exhibition of 1904, and with some reluctance the department of agriculture and technical instruction entrusted it to Lane, who had a month in which to organise the exhibition and was then told that the cost of insurance was too high and that the exhibition was off. A Spanish exhibition had just been held with great success at the Guildhall, London, and Lane persuaded the curator to follow it with an Irish exhibition, with the approval of the department. The exhibition (of 465 works) opened in May 1904, and in the catalogue introduction Lane pleaded for the first time in print for a gallery of modern art for Dublin.[2] During the Guildhall exhibition Lane learned of the forthcoming sale of the Staats-Forbes collection of modern continental art, which was to be sold below the market price if destined for a public gallery. Although Lane was hitherto unacquainted with modern continental art, he seized the opportunity and persuaded the executors to allow him to exhibit in Dublin a selection (about 160 pictures) from the collection. He also persuaded the French dealer Durand Ruel to strengthen the French section with an additional forty or so pictures. To these were added 100 works that he and others were prepared to present to Dublin.

The exhibition of 'Pictures presented to the city of Dublin to form the nucleus of a gallery of modern art, also pictures lent by the executors of the late Mr Staats-Forbes and others'[3] was held in the R.H.A. in the winter of 1904–5 and in January transferred to the National Museum to make way for a paper-hangers' exhibition. Twenty-five pictures were bought: the prince of Wales bought four, the princess one, and President Roosevelt sent a cheque. On 24 March 1905 the municipal council voted £500 per annum for a gallery of modern art 'in which the valuable pictures offered to the city by Mr Lane and others might be safely housed'. In June it authorised 'the hire and maintenance of temporary premises . . . pending the erection of a permanent building in a suitable locality'. In 1907 Clonmell House (17 Harcourt Street) was acquired as a 'temporary home' for the collection. The modern gallery was in being. It was opened to the public

[1] Ibid., pp 8–9; *Report from select committee on Public Offices (Dublin) Bill* . . ., H.C. 1903 (236), viii, 541–68.

[2] *Loan collection of pictures by Irish artists* (London, 1904).

[3] This was the exhibition's title; see the published catalogue (Dublin, 1904).

on 20 January 1908. Five years later the new building was still not forthcoming. Meanwhile pressure was being brought to bear on Lane to leave his pictures to the Tate. Lane wrote to the lord mayor of Dublin pointing out that 'the next few years' had now passed. A meeting of the citizens' committee that had been formed to support Lane was called in November 1912 at the Mansion House and told that the pictures would be lost to the city if a suitable building were not found. They were then valued at something far in excess of £60,000. The collection was the admiration of the whole art world. George Bernard Shaw wrote that it was 'an instrument of culture the value of which is far beyond anything that can be expressed in figures by the city accountant'.[1] John Redmond gave his approval to efforts to find a site. In January 1913 the municipal council agreed to give £22,000 if a site plus £3,000 could be found by the citizens' committee.

A number of sites were suggested. Lane set his heart on St Stephen's Green and would have given an additional £10,000 if it were chosen, but Lord Ardilaun would not hear of it. Merrion Square was mentioned, but Edwin Lutyens—who had offered his services in return for an old master—and the citizens' committee were against it. The Turkish baths in Lincoln Place and sites in Upper Ormond Quay and Dawson Street were considered too expensive. In Lane's opinion an extension to the Mansion House would not give scope for a fine building and, having seen the plans of University College, he was opposed to Earlsfort Terrace—'nothing would induce him', wrote W. B. Yeats, 'to put a beautiful building opposite such an ugly one'.[2]

In February 1913, when every suggested site had been turned down, Lane hit on the idea of building a gallery to span the Liffey in place of the metal Wellington Bridge, which was about to be demolished. Lutyens, for whom it was 'an idea so full of imagination and possibility that it is almost impossible to resist',[3] drew a sketch for it. The city architect, C. J. McCarthy, considered that it would be a very great ornament to the city. The cost would be £45,000. It would present no legal difficulties, would be safe from fire, and would replace a bridge that had to go anyway. Yeats reported that it seemed to be conquering everybody. The only question was whether money could be raised before Lane withdrew his pictures. However, Lady Gregory was able to raise over £2,000 in America and the financial problem was solved.

The corporation set up a committee to choose a site, and it chose the river site. On 19 March 1913 the corporation approved the river site and Lutyens came over to make the designs. But meanwhile there had been mounting opposition to the whole project, led by William Martin Murphy and the *Irish Independent*. Yeats wrote: 'as the gallery was supported by Mr James Larkin . . . and important slum workers, I assume that the purpose of the opposition was not exclusively charitable.'[4] It was described as an 'aesthetic craze', for the glorification of Lane and, presumably, the benefit of his pocket. There was also opposition to

[1] Gregory, *Lane*, pp 90, 103, 104.   [2] Ibid., p. 106.   [3] Ibid., p. 110.   [4] Ibid., p. 121.

employing Lutyens, an 'English' architect, although his mother, Mary Gallway, was from an Irish catholic family. Because of the tactics used at corporation meetings the bridge site had to be abandoned in August and the city architect was instructed to make estimates for another. In September the whole project was rejected. Lane removed his pictures from the gallery, and loaned them to the National Gallery, London. On 11 October he made a will in which he bequeathed the pictures to found a collection of modern continental art in London. 'I knew he was sorry to take the French pictures away', a caretaker in the Harcourt Street gallery told Lady Gregory, 'for every other day he would have a smile for us, but on that day . . . his face was all sadness.'[1]

In February 1914, however, the trustees of the London national gallery, who had accepted the loan of Lane's pictures unconditionally, began to impose conditions. They would only hang fifteen chosen by themselves (a choice that excluded Renoir's 'Les Parapluies', Daumier's 'Don Quixote', Monet's 'Vétheuil', three Courbet landscapes, a Rousseau, and a Puvis de Chavannes) and these only on condition that they were left outright to the gallery in his will. The result was that the pictures returned to the cellars of the gallery, there to remain until 1917 when Lady Gregory, the chief executor named in the codicil to Lane's will, demanded that they be returned to Dublin. On 12 February 1914 Lane wrote to the trustees: 'I would never have dreamed of submitting my pictures for selection to members of the board.'[2]

Meanwhile his attitude towards Dublin had softened. In November 1913 he was writing to Lady Gregory and Yeats about making a new collection for Dublin. When Sir Walter Armstrong retired as director of the National Gallery of Ireland in 1914 Lane was approached by some of the governors to apply for the post. (He had been a governor since 1904.) There was some opposition to appointing a dealer, but in spite of some technical hitches Lane was elected on 24 January 1914. He severed his connection with the Johannesburg gallery that he had helped to found, and devoted all his energies to Dublin. On 3 February 1915 he wrote the famous codicil to his will, leaving to Dublin the pictures then on loan to the National Gallery, London, provided a suitable gallery was found within five years of his death. The codicil was signed (three times) and left in an envelope addressed to his sister, Mrs Shine, in his desk in the National Gallery of Ireland. But it had not been witnessed, and therefore, according to Irish and English (though not Scottish) law, was not legally valid. In May of that year he was drowned in the *Lusitania* when it was sunk by a U-boat, while returning from America and almost in sight of his birthplace.

When Lady Gregory showed the codicil to Lord Curzon, one of the trustees of the National Gallery, London, he was sympathetic and on his advice she submitted an application for the return of the pictures through solicitors in May 1915. In October 1916, when it was rumoured that a London gallery was to be

---

[1] Ibid., p. 139; cf. Bodkin, *Lane*, p. 40.   [2] Ibid., p. 226.

built to house the pictures, Lady Gregory received a letter from Lord Curzon stating that the trustees were 'waiting to be advised by their legal advisors, and in the interim it would not be right for any individual trustee to intervene'. Nevertheless it was later stated that on 9 June 1916 Sir Joseph Duveen, a trustee of the National Gallery, had given a definite promise to build a new wing to the Tate Gallery to house a collection of modern continental art 'which turned upon the possession of the Lane pictures as a nucleus'.[1] In February 1917 affidavits concerning Lane's intentions at the time of his death were sworn by his sister Mrs Shine; Ellen Duncan, curator of the Dublin municipal gallery; Lane's cousin Augustus West; and Alec Martin, a friend who saw Lane off at the boat at Liverpool before he sailed for America. During the war the matter remained in abeyance, and was resuscitated in the 1920s.

THE controversy surrounding Lane and the foundation of the municipal gallery should not eclipse the development of the national gallery, to which Lane himself made such notable contributions. Under its first director, George Mulvany, the gallery acquired a number of seventeenth-century Italian paintings. Of his successor, Henry E. Doyle, brother of Dicky Doyle and director from 1869 to 1892, Strickland says: 'Without any profound knowledge or connoisseurship he had fine judgment, an instinctive eye for a good picture, and great skill as a buyer.' His most notable contribution was to the Dutch section. He had a freer hand than his predecessor and laid the foundations of a collection of Irish artists and a national portrait gallery in 1872. By 1892, when Doyle was succeeded by Walter (later Sir Walter) Armstrong, the National Gallery had become 'one of the most interesting of the minor galleries of Europe', and the collection had grown to such an extent that an extension was necessary.[2] There was also the need to house the collection of the late Lord Milltown. In 1898 Thomas Manley Deane drew up plans for an extension, which was completed in 1903. In 1906 the Milltown collection was presented and displayed, but until 1912, when Lane persuaded the countess of Milltown to allow the collection to be merged and only the best works displayed, the rest of the gallery was rather cluttered.

Armstrong retired in 1914 and Lane succeeded him. Since his appointment as governor in 1904, Lane had tried to fill the gaps in the collection, mainly in the English, French, and Spanish schools, and mostly with gifts. His bequests and gifts included such artists as Titian, Veronese, Piazzetta, Magnasco, El Greco, Goya, Gainsborough, Hogarth, Reynolds, Stubbs, Constable, Poussin (four), Chardin, Claude, Rembrandt, Van Dyck, van Goyen, and Cuyp. What Lane might have done for the gallery had he lived we, of course, shall never know, but it is largely thanks to him that the gallery possesses one of the most balanced collections in the world; for a small country it is an art historian's paradise.

[1] Editorial, 'The Lane pictures' in *Burlington Magazine*, xliv (Jan.–June 1924), pp 263–4.
[2] Walter G. Strickland, *A dictionary of Irish artists* (2 vols, Dublin and London, 1913), ii, 648, 649.

After Lane's death in 1915 W. G. Strickland (1850–1928) acted as director. He had been registrar since 1894, and seems to have spent much of his time working on the *Dictionary of Irish artists*, which is a lasting monument to his methodical scholarship. In 1916, to Strickland's disappointment, Robert Langton Douglas (1864–1951) was appointed director. He just saw the gallery into a new era, resigning in 1923. Douglas bought soundly, though he was not a good administrator. In 1917 he had to cope with the bequest by Magdalen Hone of hundreds of paintings by her husband Nathaniel Hone. But this made no difference to the fact that, as a social institution, the National Gallery had ceased to matter. From 1900 attendance declined, and this decline continued until 1941 when an all-time low of 68,500 was recorded.

At the turn of the century Hone, Lavery, and Osborne were still at the height of their power, though Osborne was soon to die prematurely. Roderic O'Conor was going his own way in France. The first quarter of the twentieth century was a rich period for Irish art, whether home based or anchored to home. It also showed the faintest of faint indications that Irish artists might be recognised as such. The catalyst, not surprisingly, was Lane. In 1901, as a result of the powerful influence of Sarah Purser, an exhibition of the works of Hone and John Butler Yeats was held in Dublin. It implanted in Lane two ideas. First, that there must be a gallery of modern Irish art—Irish as opposed to British—which in those days was a bold intellectual step. Secondly, he commissioned Yeats to paint portraits of those most eminent in the literary, artistic, and political world in Ireland at that time. Though Yeats did not complete the task, he has left to posterity a legacy of very fine portraits of John O'Leary, John Redmond, his own sons, and many others, which form the nucleus of the national portrait gallery in Malahide Castle. It is said that his literary interests and his conversational prowess distracted him from his art. But his contribution to the Irish literary renaissance, though alas unrecorded, may have been the greater as a result.[1]

The writers Edith Somerville (1858–1949) and George Russell (A E) (1867–1935) also made a contribution, if modest, to the Irish visual arts. Somerville studied art in Paris, which she frequently visited. She was the illustrator of the books written in collaboration with her cousin Violet Martin (Martin Ross).[2] Russell had been at the Metropolitan School with W. B. Yeats. His mystical water-colours were, perhaps, an extension of his poetic vision, though had they not been by a poet of his standing they might have been dismissed as the work of a gifted amateur, which indeed they were. What is most interesting at this period of Irish cultural revival was not only the close relationship between art and literature, but the existence of this relationship within a number of gifted individuals. Someone of that generation who had also absorbed the continental influence, and who, one way or another, dominated Irish art in the first half of

[1] For details of Yeats's career, see above, p. 456; see also above, p. 480.
[2] Above, v, 514–15.

the century, was Sarah Purser. Her dominance was what might be described as political: organising exhibitions, stained-glass studios, and the Friends of the National Collections of Ireland. It was not artistic dominance, but some of her portraits (particularly spontaneous sketches) and townscapes have remarkable vitality.

Of the younger generation the most outstanding fall into two groups: those with a continental art education—Grace Henry (1868–1953) and Paul Henry (1876–1958), William John Leech (1881–1968), and Mary Swanzy (1882–1978)—and those whose artistic education was based on London—Jack B. Yeats (1871–1957) and William Orpen (1878–1931). With the exception of Paul Henry, the first group belong to a cosmopolitan movement in the art of the time, which may loosely be described as 'art for art's sake'. The subject-matter, be it a scene in Brittany, a garden, a vase of flowers, a house in the country, or even a portrait, was unimportant in itself. It was primarily a prop on which to hang a beautiful painterly composition. It carried no message and made no comment, least of all on things Irish. Mary Swanzy, whose first exhibit at the R.H.A. in 1905 was singled out for praise by the perceptive George Moore, was later to give a mystical significance to her subject-matter; but it had no direct relevance to Ireland. On the other hand, these artists regarded themselves as Irish, regularly exhibited in Ireland, and, in a small way, perhaps boosted the morale of Irish artists by exhibiting in Paris salons and winning prizes. In 1914 Leech was awarded a medal by the Société des Artistes Français at the Paris salon and Mary Swanzy exhibited at the Salon des Indépendants.

It is worth noting a curious occurrence that took place in Paris in the first half of the century, where the permanent expatriate Roderic O'Conor had established himself. For the first time an Irish artist had a direct and profound influence not only on the art of British artists but also on aesthetic theory. Before the first world war O'Conor was visited by two of the most influential British theorists of art, Roger Fry and Clive Bell. Bell at the time was an art student in Paris. After the war O'Conor had a more direct artistic influence on Duncan Grant and Matthew Smith, and the influence was acknowledged. If one reflects that these were among the most important British artists of the period, one may record a momentary reverse in influence between Britain and Ireland.

Of this group, the artist who has imprinted himself on the Irish imagination as quintessentially Irish is, of course, Paul Henry. From 1912 to 1920 he and his wife Grace lived in Achill. Assiduously and with great skill, helped no doubt by his contact with impressionism in France, he evolved a method of evoking the wild beauty and the way of life of the west of Ireland. Much of his work has been stereotyped by railway posters and cheap prints; and he tended at times to stereotype his own work. But in his best pictures he captured the reality of peasant life and the bleak beauty of the west, even if he romanticised both somewhat.

However, it was by humour rather than romanticism that the reality of Irish life was pinned down, and this by Jack B. Yeats, whose artistic career began in

London. There he worked as a cartoonist and illustrator for such magazines as *Lika Joko* (run by Harry Furniss, a fellow Irishman), *Punch*, and *Paddock Life*. As the last title suggests, he was fascinated by London low life: racing, betting, gambling, boxing, the fairground, and just loafing about. A turning-point in his artistic career was a visit to the family home in Sligo at the time of the 1798 centenary celebrations. Though he continued to work for *Punch*, from then until the 1920s low life in Ireland began to play a major part in his art, first in pen and ink, and later in oils. He edited *A Broadsheet* (1902–3) and *A Broadside* (1908–15), in both of which he portrayed life in the west: the races, the circus, boatmen dancing, fun at the fair. It was of the earth earthy. He was a man of the people, though born into the gentry. As Thomas McGreevy said, he 'filled a need that had become immediate in Ireland for the first time in three hundred years, the need of the people to feel that their own life was being expressed in art'.[1] In 1910 he settled permanently in Ireland.

Orpen was different. He had been at the Slade School, London, with Augustus John, and had outfaced him as a draughtsman. He was a consummate draughtsman. 'It was a one-man show; that man was Orpen', wrote a fellow student.[2] His 'Play scene from "Hamlet"', which won an award in 1899, was a remarkable achievement for so young a man. On graduating he became an instant success as a fashionable painter, particularly of portraits. When John B. Yeats left for America in 1908, Orpen continued the series of national portraits for Lane. At this time he taught at the Metropolitan School and set his seal on a future generation of Irish artists: Seán Keating, Leo Whelan, Patrick Touhy, Henry Lamb, and others. At the end of 1915 he enlisted in the British army, was later commissioned in the Army Service Corps, and from early 1917 was an official war artist and drew and painted some remarkable pictures of the actualities and the symbolic significance of trench warfare. He was appointed official artist at the peace conference in 1919, but his picture of a draped coffin guarded by armed and helmeted semi-nude soldiers was not accepted. In the amended version, 'To the unknown British soldier in France' (Imperial War Museum), the soldiers have been eliminated. Even then he was declining in his powers and his imagination was becoming fantastical. But it should be said that, having experienced it, he hated war, and had a profound sympathy for those who suffered and a correspondingly low opinion of politicians. Lavery shared his views on war. He too was an official war artist, and his graphic reports were every bit as harrowing as Orpen's, for being less metaphorical. Both artists were knighted in 1918, by which time they had achieved their best work.

Meanwhile Orpen's most gifted pupil, Seán Keating (1899–1977), was building up a reputation for himself. In 1915 he went for a year to London as an assistant to Orpen. That same year his 'Men of the west' was shown at the R.H.A. exhibition. The next year he was teaching at the Municipal School, and by 1919

---

[1] Thomas McGreevy, *Jack B. Yeats: an appreciation and interpretation* (Dublin, 1945), p. 19.
[2] Quoted in John Rothenstein, *Modern English painters, i: Sickert to Smith* (London, 1976), p. 215.

he was an R.H.A. His influence (and that of Orpen, both indirectly and occasionally directly, until his death in 1931) dominated Irish art in the inter-war years.

AT the turn of the century there were in Ireland two indigenous sculptors of note, John Hughes (1865–1941) and Oliver Sheppard (1865–1941), and two expatriate sculptors, Jerome Connor (1876–1943) and Andrew O'Connor (1874–1941). And there was an up-and-coming sculptor of 17 named Albert Power.

Both Hughes and Sheppard had already established themselves. During this period Hughes produced two excellent works for Loughrea cathedral, 'The man of sorrows' and 'Madonna and child'. He executed the Queen Victoria group (1903–6) that once stood outside Leinster House; the Victoria figure is now in Adelaide, Australia. He also executed the Gladstone monument (1903–19) at Hawarden and many portrait busts in Dublin. In 1905 he was a founder member of the Royal Society of British Sculptors, though along with some others he resigned in 1915. From 1903 he lived on the Continent, mostly in France, though he spent six years in Florence. His style may be described as Italianate.

Sheppard's style was more romantic. He studied in Dublin, London, and Paris. From 1903 he settled in Dublin and taught at the Metropolitan School and the R.H.A. About 1911 he executed his most famous statue, 'The death of Cú Chulainn', which now stands in the G.P.O., Dublin, to commemorate the Easter rising. His other major works are the memorials to the 1798 rising in Wexford and Enniscorthy, the bust of Mangan in St Stephen's Green, Dublin, and the die for the Tailteann games medal (1924). He too was a founder member of the Royal Society of British Sculptors. In spite of his subject-matter from the canon of Irish nationalism he exhibited eleven times between 1891 and 1928 at the Royal Academy.

Jerome Connor was born in County Kerry, but emigrated to the United States with his parents in his boyhood. He left home at 13 and worked for a time as an artisan stone-cutter. By the time he was 17 he was exhibiting sculpture. His first big commission, the Walt Whitman memorial, came in 1903. In 1912 he executed a monument to Archbishop John Carroll for Georgetown University, Washington, and began a bust of Robert Emmet for the Smithsonian Institute, a cast of which stands in St Stephen's Green, Dublin. He was a strong republican. Andrew O'Connor, though he claimed Irish nationality, was born of a Scottish father in Massachussetts. His connection with Ireland did not properly begin until the 1930s, when he took root in the country.[1]

A REMARKABLE feature of the first decades of the twentieth century was the revival of old Irish crafts and the introduction of new ones. Two factors seem to have influenced this development: first, the arts and crafts movement in England,

---

[1] O'Connor's career is described below in vol. vii.

associated with Ruskin and Morris; secondly, the growth of Irish nationalism and in particular the literary renaissance and the Gaelic revival. Of the state of Irish crafts in the late nineteenth century, T. W. Rolleston wrote:

Except in some departments of women's work, such as lace and embroidery, and there only to a very limited extent, we have practically no such thing in Ireland as the application of original artistic faculty to industry . . . There is no general diffusion of good designing, or even of decent technical ability.[1]

Lord Mayo, who was largely responsible for the formation of the Arts and Crafts Society of Ireland in 1894, was a little more benign. In attempting to solicit the support for the society from architects, he remarked: 'given good designs, the work can be properly carried out', and he instanced the glass-painting industry in Dublin.[2]

The Arts and Crafts Society of Ireland was based on the Arts and Crafts Exhibition Society, inspired by Ruskin and Morris, and founded in 1887. Its aims were to promote the artistic industries of Ireland by holding exhibitions, by providing instruction by means of lectures and the publication of a journal, and by supplying designs. During the course of its existence it held seven exhibitions (1895, 1889, 1904, 1910, 1917, 1921, and 1925). Besides holding its own meetings, its members exhibited in Glasgow in 1898, and organised the 'Historic loan collection' in the Cork exhibition of 1902 and the 'Loan collection' at the St Louis exhibition in 1904. A series of lectures was begun in 1896 in the royal university buildings. The artistic quality of the exhibitions rose progressively. Of the first exhibition in 1895, William Hunt wrote: 'your exhibitors have erred principally in treating things pictorially instead of decoratively.' But the report of the third exhibition in 1904 says that 'it testified for the first time to something like a real upspringing of artistic feeling and endeavour among Irish craftsmen and crafts-women.' R.H.A. Willis thought that though the 1904 exhibition 'savours some-what too strongly of amateurism', 'some of the work was not to be surpassed in its way'. In a foreword to the catalogue of the fifth exhibition (1917), John R. O'Connell commented: 'Since the exhibition of 1910 the general improvement in art work has been confirmed . . . This exhibition shows an appreciable advance on its predecessors . . . especially in stained-glass, embroidery, bookbinding, printing, and enamelling work.'[3]

During the last decade of the nineteenth century a large number of workshops sprang up all over the country. Most important of these were the Killarney School of Arts and Crafts, founded in 1896, which concentrated on cabinet-making,

[1] T. W. Rolleston, 'Art and industry in Ireland' in *Journal and Proceedings of the Arts and Crafts Society of Ireland*, i, no. 3 (1901), pp 230–31.

[2] Earl of Mayo, 'Inauguration of the Arts and Crafts Society of Ireland', ibid., i, no. 1 (1896), p. 10.

[3] William Hunt, 'Report on the first exhibition . . . December, 1895', ibid., i, no. 1 (1896), p. 21; report of the society's proceedings, ibid., i, no. 4 (1906), p. 253; R. H. A. Willis, 'Some impressions derived from the arts and crafts exhibition of 1904', ibid., i, no. 4 (1906), pp 261–2; *The Arts and Crafts Society of Ireland and Guild of Irish Art-Workers: catalogue of the fifth exhibition* . . . (Dublin, Belfast, Cork, 1917), pp 16, 20.

carving, and gilding, and the Fivemiletown School, County Tyrone. There were also schools in Donegal, Oughterard, Abbeyleix, Adare, Grange, and elsewhere, all of which exhibited with the Arts and Crafts Society. In 1909, the Guild of Irish Art Workers was founded. It included among its members A. E. Child; Sarah Purser; Oliver Sheppard; Albert Power; Jack, Cottie (Mary), Lily (Susan Mary), and Lolly (Elizabeth Corbet) Yeats; Ethel Mary Rhind; Michael Healy; Oswald Reeves; Harry Clarke; and Wilhelmina Geddes.

The Arts and Crafts Society of Ireland went into a decline some years after its seventh and last exhibition in 1925, both from lack of public or government support and an inability to find suitable premises for exhibitions and propaganda. By then certain old crafts had been reestablished and new ones established—roughly the list cited by John R. O'Connell above, with the addition of metalwork, carving, and *opus sectile*. But by far the most spectacular advance was in stained glass. By 1917, with the completion of the Honan hostel chapel in Cork, Irish stained-glass artists were among the foremost in the world and had surpassed anything produced since the late middle ages. Although stained-glass works had been established in Ireland by the mid-nineteenth century,[1] much of the glass in the newly built churches—their number increased towards the end of the nineteenth century—was imported. This glass, though not always as bad as is popularly believed, was often stereotyped; it was not the work of one artist and bore little of the stamp of individual imagination or feeling for the medium. On the whole it was considered trash. As Robert Elliott commented in 1903:

Though they went to Munich, they did worse in going to France, and almost as badly in going to England . . . When they went to France, as they did for the windows at Rathfarnham, they got something for their money . . . which nothing in Great Britain or Ireland can equal as downright trash. They must really be the worst windows in the world.[2]

At that time it was generally believed that art was only to be had outside Ireland, in those cradles of culture, Italy, France, Bavaria, and even England. It did not occur to clerical (or lay) patrons that these countries might have fallen from artistic grace or that the opinions of some of their fellow countrymen might enlighten them as to the artistic value of what they were buying. Nor did it occur to them, to quote a pleasantry of Elliott's, that 'it was sending money out of the country for bad glass, when just as bad could have been got at home on as reasonable terms'.[3]

This feeling, that if money should be spent on inferior work it might as well be given to Irishmen as to Germans or Frenchmen, prompted Edward Martyn, a wealthy landowner from County Galway, to turn to Irish craftsmen when it came to filling Irish churches with stained glass. In 1899 he commissioned Christopher Whall, a disciple of Morris, a student of medieval stained glass, and the best living

[1] Above, p. 473.
[2] Robert Elliott, *Art and Ireland* (reprint, Port Washington, N.Y., and London, 1970), pp 206–7.
[3] Ibid., p. 206.

stained-glass artist, to do five commemorative windows for his family at Laban, Ardrahan, County Galway. The windows were executed by Whall's assistant A. E. Child. Martyn next approached the enlightened Bishop John Healy of Clonfert, whose architecturally indifferent cathedral at Loughrea had just been completed by William Byrne, to employ Child in decorating it with stained glass. The bishop agreed and Child produced three windows in 1903: an 'Annunciation', an 'Agony in the garden', and a 'Resurrection'—not marvellous and not Irish but a cut above Munich, Birmingham, and France. At the same time Martyn persuaded T. P. Gill, secretary of the department of agriculture and technical instruction, to employ Child to teach stained-glass work in the Metropolitan School of Art. Martyn would have preferred Whall, even temporarily, but Whall could not spare the time. He generously released Child, and Ireland has no reason to complain.

Also in the year 1903 Martyn succeeded in persuading Sarah Purser to set up an open studio where Child could teach stained-glass technique. After some initial reluctance she agreed and so the studios at 24 Upper Pembroke Street, known as An Túr Gloine (the tower of glass), came into being. The earliest members of An Túr Gloine were Purser, who executed only one window (at Loughrea); Michael Healy; Child; and Beatrice Elvery (later Lady Glenavy). Catherine O'Brien joined in 1906, Wilhelmina Geddes in 1912, and Hubert V. McGoldrick in 1920. An Túr Gloine became a cooperative; the capital was repaid to Purser, and all, including Purser, became shareholders. Although they pooled the cutting and glazing (performed by Charles Williams and Thomas Kinsella), each window was individually worked on, unlike the assembly-belt method of Munich. Splendid though the Túr Gloine windows were, they were in some respects inferior to the neglected work of the Earley and Clarke studios in that they were painter's stained glass. Yet they were an immense improvement on anything that had gone before, and the war and post-war years were to disclose greater grandeurs.

In those early years the chief patronage of the newly revived craft came from two sources, Loughrea cathedral (under Bishops Healy and Thomas O'Dea, and the administrator, Fr Jeremiah O'Donovan) and St Enda's church, Spiddal, in County Galway. Between 1903 and 1912, besides work by Purser, Child, and Michael Healy, Loughrea commissioned the superb 'Risen Christ' altarpiece, the 'Virgin and child' statue by John Hughes, and Michael Shortall's baptismal font, nave capitals, and corbels. These operations, inspired by Martyn, were presided over by the architect Professor William A. Scott, who was also responsible (on Martyn's advice) for St Enda's.

But this is not the end of the story. There are in Loughrea cathedral a number of sodality banners dating from 1902 (St Ita, the first) designed by Jack and Cottie Yeats. Jack designed all the male saints except St Laurence O'Toole (designed by A E) and Cottie all the female saints except St Brigid (designed by Pamela Coleman Smith, a former columnist for Jack Yeats's *Broadsheet*). The figures were embroidered by Lily Yeats, who did them in silk, and by her girls in the Dun Emer Guild, who did the background. The Dun Emer Guild had been founded in 1903 by Evelyn Gleeson and Lily and Lolly Yeats, who had left Bedford Park, London, with their father, John Butler Yeats. They settled with him in Dundrum, Dublin, where the guild had its premises. Evelyn Gleeson was in charge of tapestry and rug-making; Lily was in charge of embroidery, and Lolly published limited editions (under the imprint of the Dun Emer Press) by Irish authors using eighteenth-century type, a hand press, and linen paper made in Saggart, County Dublin. Lolly had worked with May Morris, daughter of William Morris, while the Yeatses were at Bedford Park. All the work was done by young girls. In 1908 Evelyn Gleeson and the Yeatses split up. The Dun Emer Press became the Cuala Press. W. B. Yeats was editor from 1903 until his death in 1939. In 1940 Lolly Yeats died but the Cuala Press continued in existence until 1946 under Mrs W. B. Yeats, F. R. Higgins, and others. Gleeson retained the name 'Dun Emer', and continued to produce tapestries and rugs, as well as enamels and book bindings.

As we enter the twentieth century the work of a number of individual stained-glass artists demands attention, in particular that of Harry Clarke (1889–1931), Michael Healy (1873–1941), Wilhelmina Margaret Geddes (1888–1955), and Hubert V. McGoldrick (1897–1967). Of these four Clarke is unquestionably the most important, not only in his own right, but also in establishing a flourishing studio—sadly defunct since 1973. He studied under Child at the Metropolitan School and went to France on a scholarship in 1914. His first commission was for nine windows in the Honan chapel, University College, Cork, completed in 1917. Subsequently he made windows for Loughrea cathedral and churches in Dublin (Castleknock and Terenure) and Castlehaven, County Cork. His biggest commission and the establishment of his studio belong to a later period. Clarke was also a renowned illustrator of books. His most famous were the illustrations for the fairy-tales of Hans Andersen and Perrault, Goethe's *Faust*, Poe's *Tales of mystery and imagination*, Pope's 'The rape of the lock', and Coleridge's 'The ancient mariner', in the intricate style of Aubrey Beardsley.[1] He applied this style to his stained glass. The result is great brilliance of colour and elegance of line, but an overall impression of fantasy and unreality, even in serious subjects.

Healy in later years carried this mode of glass-making a stage further by his technique of aciding, whereby the composition is built up from tiny dots of colour rather than the traditional large areas. The chapel of Clongowes Wood contains his last work using this technique, along with an early piece in the style of Child, and for contrast some work by Evie Hone of the early 1940s. He came comparatively late to stained glass, having tried his hand as an illustrator. In 1902 he joined An Túr Gloine and studied under Child. In 1903 he was commissioned to make a window for Loughrea cathedral; in all he did eight. Subsequently he received commissions from all over Ireland, from Britain and abroad. Though his

---

[1] Nicola Gordon Bowe, *Harry Clarke: his graphic art* (Mountrath and Los Angeles, 1983), pp 149–54, and *The life and work of Harry Clarke* (Blackrock, Co. Dublin, 1989).

colour was brilliant, he was primarily a linear artist; he had, in the words of Hughes, the sculptor, a 'strong line'.

Wilhelmina Geddes showed a talent for glass-making at an early age, though she also studied painting under Orpen at the Metropolitan School. In 1912 she joined An Túr Gloine. Like Healy, her strength lay in line rather than colour. She executed many windows in Ireland and some in England.

McGoldrick joined the firm of Earley in 1913 as a stained-glass worker while attending evening classes under Child at the Metropolitan School. He joined An Túr Gloine in 1920 and continued there until 1945. Apart from designing windows for churches, he did *opus sectile*, mosaics, and posters.

DURING the last decade of the nineteenth century new building benefited from the economic boom, but with the South African war (1899–1902) there was a falling-off in demand for new buildings. The spate of ecclesiastical building that had continued since the 1860s was easing off, as the need for new churches was satisfied, but the decline in building was most noticeable in the area of domestic architecture. Fewer great houses were being built and speculative building was running ahead of demand. In 1902 the *Irish Builder* mused sadly: 'How the population of Dublin will keep on swelling so as to occupy all the new houses now being built in the suburbs is getting a sort of conundrum.'[1] In 1903 there were also thousands of unlet houses in Belfast.[2] There were conflicting verdicts about the merits of the buildings that were going up. According to J. J. Meagher, 'qualified arbitrators admit that Irish architecture and Irish architects have never reached such a high standard as they do at present'.[3] On the other hand, the northern correspondent of the *Irish Builder* said of Belfast architecture: 'In the bulk our architecture is deplorable—all Queen Anne front and Mary Anne back, as one critic has put it.' However, he had a good word for the new city hall, which was 'unsurpassed as an architectural mass' and 'utility attained with beauty'.[4]

Belfast is, in fact, a natural starting-point for an account of Irish architecture in the first years of the twentieth century, the Edwardian era. Not only does it belong to that era more fully than Dublin does, and has given it more complete architectural expression, but, more importantly, it was at the beginning of this era that Belfast reached its full stature as a city, having been granted the status of a city in 1888, when it was already overtaking Dublin city in population and far ahead in productive power. Moreover, since Gladstone's home rule bill of 1886, it had come to be regarded by protestants as no longer the second city in the country, but the capital of Irish protestantism. These two aspects of Belfast, its enormous industrial and commercial success and its role as the focal point of Irish protestantism, received eloquent expression in the architecture of the years before the first world war. As C. E. B. Brett said of the city hall, the cathedral, and the

---

[1] *Ir. Builder*, xliv (1902), p. 1495.   [2] Ibid., xlv (1903), p. 3070.
[3] J. J. Meagher, 'The Irish art renaissance' in *Ir. Builder*, xliv (1902), p. 1360.
[4] *Ir. Builder*, xlviii (1906), p. 310.

presbyterian assembly buildings, 'architecturally, they constitute the corporate expression of embattled unionism, and of an effort (perhaps largely unconscious) to convert a brash and sprawling industrial centre into a politico-religious capital city'.[1]

Of the three buildings mentioned above, the city hall is far and away the most imposing. It was built on the site of the old Linen Hall, which was demolished in 1896. In that year Alfred Brumwell Thomas of London won the competition for the new building, which was completed in 1906. If one ignores the fussiness of the corner towers, the supporters of the dome, and some of Fredrick Pomeroy's carvings, there is a dignity and gravity about its rather heavy baroque classicism. The interior is lavish in its decoration—marble, carvings, plasterwork, and stained glass, none of a high order. It is surrounded by commemorative statuary. The most symbolic of the period is Pomeroy's statue of the first marquis of Dufferin and Ava, a distinguished diplomat and a former governor-general of Canada and viceroy of India; the oddest is Thomas Brock's statue of Queen Victoria, of which the *Irish Builder* wrote: 'The majority incline to consider it [the *porte-cochère*] a mausoleum for the statue of Queen Victoria which, she not liking, stepped out of, with her pedestal, to the open ground.' King Edward VII's verdict (according to the *Belfast News Letter*) was 'Couldn't be better!' The total cost of the city hall was about £350,000, or £1 per head of the population, a staggering sum in those days.[2]

The Church of Ireland cathedral of St Anne's was lavish enough in its own way. Belfast lay within the diocese of Down, Connor, and Dromore. There were already three cathedrals—Downpatrick, Lisburn, and Dromore. Why a fourth? The reason given in a brochure published in 1896 was that it would have a good moral influence on a district 'whose present condition is by no means satisfactory'.[3] The archbishop of Canterbury was nearer the mark when, speaking in the Ulster Hall, he praised it as a gesture against disestablishment. Work was begun in 1895 and has continued ever since, though the building was consecrated in 1904. The original architects were Thomas Drew and W. H. Lynn (who left the designing to Drew) and the original design was Gothic modified in the direction of Romanesque. It was further altered by a succession of architects. In 1927, at the suggestion of Sir Edward Carson, the west front was completed as a war memorial and was, in the words of Brett, 'a remarkable anthology of architectural styles'.[4] It should be noted that, unharmonious and still incomplete, it replaces the perfectly respectable Georgian church of St Anne.

---

[1] C. E. B. Brett, *The buildings of Belfast, 1700–1914* (revised ed., Belfast, 1985), p. 65.

[2] Ibid., pp 66, 67. A comparable cost in the 1990s might be £40 million for the building (including £1,375,000 for marble work, £500,000 for carving, and £125,000 for sculpture) and £750,000 for furniture. The municipal technical institute and Royal Victoria Hospital, built in Belfast at the same period, each cost about £100,000. See also J. T. Rea, *How to estimate: being the analysis of builders' prices* (2nd ed., London, 1904).

[3] Brett, op. cit., p. 68.

[4] Ibid., pp 68, 69.

If the Church of Ireland was to have its edifice, it was reasonable to expect that the presbyterians should have one that suitably reflected their position within the community. However, they were even less fortunate in their architects and decorators. Their church house and assembly hall in Fisherwick Street were, according to the *Irish Builder*, in Tudor style, with 'sprawling senile arches that resemble nothing so much as a nonagenarian on crutches', and giving an impression that they had 'somehow been sat on so that they might squelch out and fill all the interstices of a building front commercially valuable'.[1] Brett is equally scathing on the carvings by Edgar Winter and by Purdy & Millard. These included 'a number of dragons, apparently expiring in agony, and a very sick eagle in deepest moult'.[2] If one was so inclined, one might see the hand of divine retribution in all this. The terms of the competition for the design had been drawn up by Robert Young, architect to the presbyterian church. The assessor, Sir Thomas Drew, declared them impracticable (especially within the sum allocated, £30,000), though he gave the prize to a young architect, Rupert Savage. Instead of revising the conditions, the patrons gave the contract to Young and his partner, John Mackenzie, who completed the work in 1905 at the cost of £70,000!

Belfast at the beginning of the twentieth century, however, is symbolised by its commercial buildings no less than by its public and ecclesiastical edifices. Indeed, it could be argued without much difficulty that, even architecturally, Belfast's main title to fame had lain in its commercial buildings ever since W. H. Lynn's linen warehouse and headquarters for the firm of Richardson Sons & Owden had been built in 1869.[3] The new century was greeted with the impressive Scottish Provident Institution, Donegall Square, by Young & Mackenzie (who were better at this sort of thing), which was completed in 1902, with curious carvings by Purdy & Millard. Purdy & Millard were active again the next year, doing the signs of the zodiac for the Jacobean-style Northern Bank in red brick, in the same square and by the same architects. Yet another building in Donegall Square by the same architects, built in 1900–02 in Scottish Baronial style, is the Ocean Accident Insurance building with its grotesque carvings by Winter & Thompson. Young & Mackenzie were nothing if not eclectic, and would provide anything to please the customer.

In the early years of the century there were some slight touches of the international art nouveau or *Jugendstil* style in Belfast. It appeared in, of all places, the presbyterian assembly hall and also in the Store bar, Church Lane, Belfast (1905), and Blackwood & Jury used it extensively. It had, after all, originated in Glasgow.

However unsatisfactory the Belfast public buildings may have been, the opening decades of the twentieth century in Dublin were rather thin in such buildings. In fact the only buildings of any significance were the College of Science on Merrion

---

[1] *Ir. Builder*, xlvii (1905), p. 406, quoted in Brett, op. cit., p. 70.
[2] Brett, op. cit., p. 70.   [3] Above, pp 465–6.

Street and University College, Dublin, on Earlsfort Terrace.[1] Both buildings have much in common with Belfast city hall: the gravity of the classical baroque to the point of pomposity and a certain overblown grandioseness, typical of the Edwardian era. Neither Dublin building aspires to the status of Belfast city hall; instead they partake of the restraint of earlier buildings and for that reason are probably more successful. As the *Irish Builder* said of the College of Science, it is 'in a Georgian style . . . in keeping with . . . the many other fine public buildings in Dublin erected during the latter years of the eighteenth century'.[2] These earlier buildings might have had a restraining influence on potential Edwardian exuberance, a restraint that was lacking in Belfast.

The contract for the College of Science had been given to the English architect Aston Webb (architect of the Admiralty Arch, London). As a sop to Irish feeling (the Royal Institute of the Architects of Ireland had censured the government for appointing an English architect), Thomas Manley Deane was associated with him (and knighted on its completion in 1911), yet the design was 'wholly the work of Mr Webb'.[3] In 1908, when the National University of Ireland was founded, University College, Dublin, took over the buildings that had been used by the Royal University in Earlsfort Terrace. These consisted of relics of Alfred G. Jones's exhibition buildings of 1865 (the later Winter Gardens). By 1910 W. H. Byrne had carried out some improvements, but the present classical façade was completed in limestone and granite by R. M. Butler in 1914.

The Irish Pavilion at the Glasgow Exhibition of 1901 (architect, Thomas Manley Deane) was of Irish thatch. The offices of the department of agriculture and technical instruction at the Cork exhibition of 1902 included two doorways of Celtic design based on Cormac's chapel, Cashel. But that was nothing compared with the Irish section in the St Louis exhibition of 1904 where F. G. Hicks erected, cheek by jowl, replicas of the Custom House, Cormac's chapel, the Bank of Ireland, Kate Kearney's cottage, etc. The climax of this kind of 'Irish' architecture was reached in the mock-up Irish village 'Ballymaclinton' for the Franco-British exhibition of 1908.

The period was noteworthy for certain categories of buildings: first, town halls, of which the finest were by William A. Scott (Enniskillen, 1901; Cavan, 1908; and Kells, 1914), about whom more later; secondly, technical schools and training colleges. These were mainly neo-Georgian or Queen Anne. The best of them— the Crawford municipal technical institute, Cork, by Arthur Hill (1909–12) and the technical institute, Rathmines, Dublin, by Batchelor & Hicks (1912), and Bolton Street technical college, Dublin (C. J. McCarthy, 1906–14)—have dignity, even if they are a trifle dull. The technical schools in Belfast, to quote the *Irish Builder*, preserved an 'unenviable notoriety in the matter of questionable architectural methods'. Not only was chicanery used in commissioning Samuel Stevenson without competition, but Stevenson filched the design from the war office in

---

[1] Now respectively housing government offices and the national concert hall.
[2] *Ir. Builder*, xlvi (1904), p. 281.   [3] Ibid.

London, adding 'certain architectural faults which the war office lacks'.[1] Thirdly, there were Carnegie libraries in abundance, sturdy and decent, for the most part. Fourthly, post offices, also 'somewhat Georgian in treatment' as someone described Robert Cochrane's post office in Clontarf. Fifthly, fire stations, of which C. J. McCarthy's renaissance-type brick building in Great Brunswick (now Pearse) Street, and another in Dorset Street, Dublin, are the most interesting and original.

The neo-Georgian and classical style, thought to be particularly appropriate to Dublin and some other cities and towns, was employed in public and other buildings down to the 1960s. It is a distinctive, if not a distinguished, feature of Irish architecture. It was employed to the great satisfaction of connoisseurs and public in many commercial buildings, particularly banks and insurance offices, which continued to be a seemingly inexhaustible source of employment for Irish architects. The most widely acclaimed of these buildings was the Munster & Leinster Bank (1915), Cork, by A. & H. H. Hill, described as 'one of the finest modern buildings in Ireland'.[2]

Some progressive pieces of architecture involved the use of Hennebique ferro-concrete, as used by W. Friel in Hall's warehouse, Waterford, in 1905. The theatres and cinemas of the time also deserve mention, and Murray's innovations in window fronts anticipated the modern shop window. According to Brett eight 'picture palaces' were started or completed in Belfast in the twelve months up to August 1914.[3] Most of the Dublin theatres, such as the Gaiety (C. J. Phipps, 1903) and the Queen's (Stirling, 1909), were replicas of theatres built by the same architect in England (for example, the Gaiety in the Strand, London). An exception was the Abbey by Joseph Holloway (1904), decorated with stained glass from An Túr Gloine and metalwork by the Youghal Art Metal School.

Few private houses of note were built during this period and these were on a restricted scale. C. F. A. Voysey, a disciple of Morris and a pioneer of modern architecture, built a charming house at 149 Malone Road, Belfast, in 1911. Lutyens redesigned the house on Lambay Island for Lord Revelstoke. William A. Scott even earlier (1903) designed a very simple arts and crafts house at Killyhevlin, County Fermanagh, which in feeling anticipated the modern movement. As for the rest, they were either Scottish Baronial or Tudor, half-timbered with prominent gables and leaded windows. The advance of Dublin suburbia continued, but there was now an inner ring (Ranelagh, Sandymount, and Glasnevin) and an outer (Foxrock, Bray, Greystones, Clontarf, Malahide, and Avoca—between Blackrock and Stillorgan). The change within the inner ring can be observed by travelling from St Stephen's Green to Donnybrook or from Merrion Square to Ballsbridge. As one advances into Edwardian housing, one encounters an increase in the grandiose and a loss in dignity—the houses are set back in gardens, the front door is approached by granite steps, but the fanlights

---

[1] Quoted in Brett, *Buildings of Belfast*, p. 72.   [2] *Ir. Builder*, lviii (1916), p. 10.
[3] Brett, *Buildings of Belfast*, p. 75.

and the austere proportions have gone; the fatal mistake of trying to impress by size and distance has been made. And yet, for all that, these houses are impressive. At least they are not tawdry and mean.

The most ambitious housing project of the period was Sir Robert McConnell's 'garden colony' at Cliftonville, Belfast, in 1906. The site overlooks Belfast Lough and has a view of Cave Hill on the other side. The houses were to cost between £240 and £350 and to be built in whatever style took the occupier's fancy. Besides the open spaces there were to be a bandstand, tea-house, sports ground, and gardens, but few of these amenities were built.[1]

In Dublin, Lord Iveagh contributed two important community amenities, the Iveagh market building (1906) designed by F. G. Hicks, and the Guinness play centre (1912) by McDonnell & Reid. However, as far as artisans' houses were concerned, the first decade of the twentieth century was bad. Between 1905 and 1910 no more than five houses were built each year in Dublin. Things improved generally from 1911, and until the war about 190 families were housed annually. There were also projects for housing developments outside Dublin, at Coleraine (1904) and Kilkenny (1907).

As already mentioned, the boom in church building was declining. New churches continued to be built, however, mostly in a rather dry and dull Early English Gothic style, though they often were adorned with altars and reredoses, replete with pinnacles and crochets, in the Decorated style, or some version of the Romanesque. The major firms supplying these carvings were C. W. & C. L. Harrison and Pearse (James, father of Patrick Pearse) & Sharp. Meanwhile the popularity of the Hiberno-Romanesque was increasing, encouraged by Ashlin's presidential address to the R.I.A.I. of 1901.[2] By far the most interesting work in this style was done by the outstanding architect William A. Scott. Although his style was basically Romanesque and incorporated Celtic motifs, it was distinctively his own. He had been articled to Sir Thomas Deane, had been in partnership with his father, Anthony Scott, and had worked for the London County Council. In the architects' department of the L.C.C. he could hardly have failed to come into contact with Norman Shaw and Philip Webb or with the writings of W. R. Lethaby, all forerunners of the modern movement. His work has something of the severe geometrical quality, particularly the straight vertical line, that characterises much modern architecture. His earliest essay in the Hiberno-Romanesque style was in the chapel of the Convent of Mercy, Enniskillen (1904), followed by the austere O'Growney memorial, Maynooth (1905). But it was St Enda's church at Spiddal, County Galway, in the following year that established his reputation. Elliott had already been enthusiastic about the designs in the *Irish Rosary*,[3] while the *Irish Builder* reported the claim that it represented an epoch in Irish ecclesiastical design 'by the revival of Irish romanesque architecture'.[4] This is not

---

[1] Ibid., p. 73   [2] Above, pp 469–70, 473.
[3] See Elliott, *Art and Ireland*, pp 58–9; and above, p. 491.
[4] *Ir. Builder*, xlix (1907), p. 577.

strictly true, since in the 1860s W. H. Lynn was designing what might be described as Irish Romanesque (for example, St Patrick's, Jordanstown). Scott went on to design the fine diocesan seminary, Galway (1912–13), the parish church, Edenderry (1915), with his father, and the hostel and basilica at Lough Derg (1917). He also drew up plans for a cathedral in Galway. In 1912 he was appointed to the new chair of architecture in University College, Dublin.

Among the other ecclesiastical architects active during this period mention must be made of G. C. Ashlin,[1] who designed over fifty churches, some in partnership with E. W. Pugin and later with Thomas Coleman. After 1905 he handed over his practice to his nephew Stephen, who continued the partnership with Coleman. One of their earliest designs was for the college chapel, Clongowes Wood, Naas, where concrete blocks like rock-faced ashlar were used for the first time. Another prolific designer of churches was W. H. Byrne,[2] who was joined by his son Ralph in designing the church of the Holy Name, Ranelagh, in 1914. No less prolific was R. M. Butler of Doolin, Butler, & Donnelly. During this period they had a church to their credit almost every year, including both a catholic (1902) and a presbyterian church (1909) in New Ross. Other names that frequently crop up during the period are those of George F. Beckett, who built methodist churches in Monkstown, County Dublin (1903), and Killarney (1912), and J. J. O'Callaghan (pupil of Sir Thomas Deane). By the first world war most parishes in Ireland, of whatever denomination, had a decent, if not architecturally exciting, church, and, moreover, one that corresponded to the popular notion of a church building. Had the war and the 'troubles' not intervened, church building would probably have continued, if not from necessity, at least for the sake of amelioration. As it was, it dried up completely for a decade.

---

[1] Above, pp 462–3, 469.   [2] Above, p. 470.

CHAPTER XVII

Music and society, 1850–1921

ALOYS FLEISCHMANN

BRIAN BOYDELL has shown that the slump that followed the union did not at once affect musical activity in Dublin.[1] On the contrary, there was increasing activity up to 1824, but the economic depression that hit the country in this year, coupled with the decline of Dublin as a social centre and the drift to London of the Anglo-Irish aristocracy and landed gentry, led to a corresponding decline in patronage and public interest.

Towards the middle of the century, however, the tide began to turn. In Dublin's heyday before the union, music-making had been dominated by the upper classes. As a result of increasing prosperity, the rising merchant and middle classes now began to take the lead in cultivating the arts. No less than twenty-two different music societies, chiefly choral groups, came into existence between 1841 and 1867. Among the more important of these was the Royal Choral Institute, founded in 1851 by John William Glover, the organist of St Mary's pro-cathedral, 'to establish in this country a large body of choristers composed chiefly of the working classes, capable of performing the best classical works, the performance of which is at present exclusively confined to private societies'.[2] Slater's *Directory* for 1856 lists sixty-seven music teachers, twenty-eight music shops and musical-instrument makers, three of which were also publishers, and three organ builders. Musical activity in Dublin at this time must by now have exceeded that of the pre-union period; it extended now to a far wider section of the community.

The older societies, however, consisting mainly of upper-class protestants, continued to function with undiminished vigour. The Antient Concerts Society, founded in 1844 by Joseph Robinson at the age of 18 and directed by him for twenty-nine years, produced four or five choral concerts each season. By 1843 the society had bought rooms in Great Brunswick Street (now Pearse Street), which were reconstructed as a concert hall, and known as the Antient Concert Rooms. This rapidly became the centre of Dublin's musical life. The Philharmonic Society, under various conductors, gave an average of five concerts annually, which were mainly orchestral, but like the Antient Concerts Society its programmes were of a kind such as was general all over Europe at that time, with

---

[1] Above, iv, 606–18, 628; see also above, v, 144. [2] *F.J.*, 1 Nov. 1851.

symphonies, glees, ballads, piano or cornet or flute solos, and operatic arias all interspersed. International celebrities were frequently featured. Indeed the Philharmonic Society was adversely criticised in the press for its exclusion of native talent and native music and the undue expenditure involved in engaging foreign artists, chiefly opera singers, in contrast to the support given to local artists by the Antient Concerts Society. Most of the leading Dublin musicians collaborated in each other's concerts, whether appearing as conductors, singers, or instrumentalists. But the concerts of the Philharmonic Society and the Antient Concerts Society were confined to members of these societies and their friends, evening dress was normal, and the concerts were on the whole fashionable affairs, continuing the aristocratic tradition of the previous century.

It was a time of big displays, marking the advent to Ireland of some of the prosperity that had accompanied the industrial revolution in England. In 1853, for the opening on Leinster Lawn of the Great Industrial Exhibition organised by the Royal Dublin Society,[1] Joseph Robinson conducted a choir and orchestra of a thousand performers, including five military bands and members of cathedral choirs from all over the country—the largest body yet assembled in Ireland for music on a state occasion. Such a mammoth undertaking was only possible because of the numerous societies that flourished in the city. For the Dublin International Exhibition of Fine Arts and Manufactures of 1865 Robinson again assembled a choir and orchestra of a thousand performers, with a similar programme to that of 1853, in the specially built concert hall of the Exhibition Palace in Earlsfort Terrace. This hall, with its large organ, outrivalled the Antient Concert Rooms during the following years for vocal and instrumental concerts, including promenade concerts featuring regimental bands.

Mixed programmes were still the order of the day, and it was not until 1867 that a solo recital by a single artist was given, by the pianist Charles Hallé in the exhibition hall. Major events sometimes attracted provincial support—for instance, when a festival was organised in 1869 in honour of the Swedish soprano Christine Nilsson, special trains were run for the occasion from Waterford, Limerick, Cork, and Tralee. Though the bigger concerts were expensively priced and the patronage was mainly upper-class, monthly popular concerts with programmes of good quality, chiefly chamber music, were arranged at cheaper prices, while 'Grand national concerts of Irish music' were held sufficiently often to indicate a growing interest in the native tradition—even if the main fare usually consisted of Moore's *Melodies*.

For lack of opportunities in Ireland young musicians of talent tended to emigrate at an early age, as did George Osborne and Arthur O'Leary, both to become leading figures in London; Michael Balfe and Vincent Wallace, who achieved an international reputation with their operas; and Charles Stanford, whose début as a composer was made at the age of 8 when he wrote the music

1 Above, pp 436–7, 441–2.

for a Christmas pantomime conducted by R. M. Levey at the Theatre Royal in 1860.[1] Little composition of any consequence was produced. Apart from John Smith, professor of music (1845–61) at Trinity College, Dublin, chief composer of the state music, master of the king's band of state musicians in Ireland, and composer to the Chapel Royal, Dublin, whose church music had some vogue, and the prolific Robert Prescott Stewart, who succeeded Smith in the state appointments, only three other composers were active during this period. These were the Rev. G. M. Torrance, who produced two oratorios and the opera 'William of Normandy', performed in Dublin in 1858;[2] J. W. Glover, who in 1870 wrote a much performed oratorio, 'St Patrick at Tara',[3] later given for the O'Connell and Moore centenaries, and in 1880 an opera based on Goldsmith's 'The deserted village'; and Mrs Joseph Robinson, whose cantata 'God is love' was first performed in 1868,[4] and often subsequently in Dublin and in England.

The lively cultivation of music in Dublin stemmed, at least in part, from the long established tradition of church music in the two Church of Ireland cathedrals, with their twin line of professional organists and vicars choral, who were often active music-makers in the city. Full choral services were held in both cathedrals, choral festivals were held from time to time, and organ recitals and performances of oratorio frequently given. The penal laws had hindered the development of music in catholic churches, but after 1829 the position of music in catholic churches began to improve slowly but surely after centuries of enforced neglect. Choirs began to be formed, and, owing to the lack of trained organists, foreign musicians were introduced. Haydn Corri, an Edinburgh musician of Italian extraction, was appointed to St Mary's pro-cathedral, Dublin, in 1827, and, though he was succeeded by J. W. Glover and other Irish musicians, the organists of the bigger provincial cathedral towns in the latter half of the century were often well qualified German or Belgian musicians, called in by those bishops or administrators who were interested in securing an adequate standard of music for their services. The situation had improved sufficiently to justify the formation in Dublin in 1864 of the Harmonic Society of St Cecilia, for the purpose of popularising the music of the catholic church.

In the mid-nineteenth century Belfast, with a population of about 100,000, or less than half that of Dublin, showed proportionately much less activity in music-making. The *Belfast and Province of Ulster Directory* of 1852 lists only sixteen music teachers and four music firms, two of which were piano makers, as against sixty-seven and twenty-eight respectively for Dublin. Immigrant teachers and players appeared from time to time, mainly English or German, but they tended to drift away again after a short stay. As in Dublin up to 1856, the only

---

[1] Article, 'Levey' in *Grove's dictionary of music and musicians* (5th ed., ed. Eric Blom, 10 vols, London and Basingstoke, 1954–61), v, 153–4; *F.J.*, 19 May 1863.
[2] Oratorios, *F.J.*, 17 Apr. 1855, 18 Dec. 1864; opera, *Saunders' News Letter*, 23 Mar. 1858.
[3] *F.J.*, 30 May 1870.
[4] Ibid., 22 Dec. 1868.

organised music teaching was that undertaken by the music societies, except that in Belfast the presbyterian and methodist churches were interested in promoting a knowledge of music with a view to its use in their services.

Some attempts were made in the 1850s to establish a Belfast academy of music, but by individuals rather than by groups, and none was successful. The town did, however, possess a hall specifically built for concerts by the Belfast Anacreontic Society in 1840—the Music Hall in May Street (later renamed the Victoria Memorial Hall, demolished in 1983), with a capacity of 600, thus antedating a similar achievement by the Antient Concerts Society of Dublin in 1848. Here concerts were held by various societies, chief among them the Belfast Anacreontic Society itself, founded in 1814, an orchestra composed of professional and business men, and the Belfast Classical Harmonists Society, at first a male-voice group, founded in 1851. The concerts of these societies were exclusive events, confined to members and their friends. But the Music Hall was felt to be inadequate, and the Ulster Hall Company was formed in 1859 to erect a building capable of accommodating 2,000–3,000 persons. Owing to the small size of the existing Music Hall the prices of admission had to be extravagantly high, so that persons of modest means were 'virtually excluded from every entertainment which would improve or elevate their moral and intellectual character'.[1] The Ulster Hall was opened in 1862 and still survives, a dignified, if sombre, structure, designed to house major events.[2] From 1862 to 1866 a series of organ recitals planned to interest workingmen was given in the Ulster Hall by Dr Edmund Chipp, an Englishman newly arrived in Belfast, while popular concerts were also held in the Music Hall 'with the view of affording the working classes, and the general public, an amusement of a rational and refined character'.[3] So, a little later than in Dublin, music organisations in Belfast began to open their doors to all its citizens.

Though smaller than Belfast, with a population of 82,625 in 1851, Cork's activities in the sphere of music were on a comparable scale, and the directories of the period list a score of music teachers, and seven music warehouses. The Antient Concerts Society, initiated in 1846 on the Dublin model, held two or three concerts annually in various halls with an orchestra and chorus of over a hundred, usually importing soloists from Dublin or London, and for special occasions an orchestral leader or a conductor from Dublin. Thus, when the national exhibition of 1852 was opened in Cork by the lord lieutenant, members of the Antient Concerts, Philharmonic, and Royal Choral societies of Dublin and of the Antient Concerts Society of Cork joined forces in a programme that included an 'Inauguration ode' in praise of industry, composed for the occasion and conducted by Robert Prescott Stewart. Attendance at the ordinary concerts of the Antient Concerts Society was confined to members and their friends, and though it was decided in 1851 to open unreserved seats to the general public the experiment was not repeated.

[1] *Belfast News Letter*, 12 Feb. 1859.   [2] Above, v, plate 28.
[3] *Belfast News Letter*, 19 Feb. 1864.

The Theatre Royal, George's Street, had been burned down in 1840, but the Theatre Royal in Cook Street catered for plays, variety shows, concerts, and very occasional visits from opera companies, while performances were also given in the concert room of the Imperial Clarence Hotel. January 1853 saw the reopening of the Theatre Royal in George's Street, and in 1854 the Athenaeum was erected, an imposing classical building by the Lee on the site of the present opera house, its large hall having a capacity of 2,000 seats. Two theatres and a concert hall were now in operation, resulting in a quickening of activities and of public interest in the arts. But unlike Dublin, where several choral societies endeavoured to involve the catholic population, concert activity in Cork was largely confined to protestant organisations, and catholic participation was marginal.

Of all forms of music-making, opera had the largest following. At the Theatre Royal in Dublin, opened in 1821 with a seating capacity of 3,800,[1] Italian opera seasons were usually held several times annually by visiting companies from Covent Garden and the Haymarket, and seasons of opera in English by companies such as the Pyne-Harrison company. The support accorded can be gauged from the fact that when Jenny Lind sang 'La sonnambula' at the Theatre Royal in October 1848, receipts on the first night alone totalled £1,600 (at least £80,000 in the values of 140 years later), and this directly after the great famine.[2] Enthusiasm frequently led to demonstrations, such as when Marietta Piccolomini, after a performance of 'Lucia di Lammermoor' in the Theatre Royal in 1859, was surrounded by an immense crowd on leaving the theatre, the horses were unyoked from her carriage, and hundreds of young men drew her to her hotel in triumph. But it was only big names that, as a rule, drew full houses, and the failure of many first-rate productions, just because the cast did not include a popular star, led to the opinion, often expressed, that Dublin was not a musical city in the true sense of the word.[3]

A remarkable feature was the relatively short time-lag between the production of new operas in London or on the Continent and their performance in Dublin, often after a lapse of only one or two years. The singers engaged for the Dublin opera seasons frequently toured the provinces—taking in not only Belfast and Cork, but smaller centres as well. For instance in October 1859, Jenny Lind, accompanied by the distinguished violinist Joseph Joachim, visited Cork, Killarney, Limerick, Waterford, Kilkenny, Belfast, Derry, and Ballymena. Provincial tours, however, by the opera companies that came to the Theatre Royal in Dublin or the Theatre Royal in Belfast were less frequent, and then sometimes unsuccessful. Since soloists of international status required high fees, the prices charged were often regarded as excessive and the general standard of performances severely criticised. In the provinces the earlier custom still lingered on of

[1] *The history of the Theatre Royal, Dublin* (reprinted from *Saunder's News Letter*) (Dublin, 1870), p. 147.
[2] R. M. Levey and J. O'Rorke, *Annals of the Theatre Royal* (Dublin, 1880), p. 137.
[3] Ibid., pp 59, 60, 181.

adding vocal or orchestral items, or an entire farce, after the performance of an opera, or even of presenting two operas in shortened versions on the one night. Though the larger and more sophisticated audiences of the capital were willing to accept opera on its own terms, company managers felt that provincial audiences would need extra inducements; hence the curious additions to be found on opera bills in the provinces up to the middle of the 1870s. Amateur opera was still rare, and the widespread private theatricals of the early part of the century survived only in isolated instances.

Apart from opera, military band music had the widest popular appeal. The bands of the British army in Ireland not only served military and recruiting purposes, but played a major part in the music-making of the towns. For many public occasions the participation of military bands was taken as a matter of course. In the case of concerts one or sometimes two bands shared the programme with a group of vocalists and solo instrumentalists, playing music relatively up to date for its time. At the Exhibition Palace in Dublin in 1868 Stewart conducted a 'Grand military concert' with the participation of no less than ten bands. Individual members of military bands were often used to augment orchestras when orchestral performances were given, both in Dublin and the provinces. Bands also provided the music for military and civilian balls, at which, around the middle of the century, they played quadrilles, polkas, galops, and waltzes. Up to 1856 regimental bands were paid for by the officers out of their private incomes, and the regiments vied with each other in regard to the size and quality of the bands they employed.[1] For civic or private events the officers even hired out the bands, so that these to some extent carried out the functions of the 'city music' of earlier days.[2] Most of the bandmasters engaged were civilians and foreigners. After 1856, however, the control of bands was removed from the regimental officers and taken over by the war office. Kneller Hall, Middlesex, the Royal Military School of Music, was opened in 1857, and from 1872 all British bandmasters were supposed to obtain the Kneller Hall diploma. Yet the majority of the bandmasters whose names appear in connection with military band performances in Ireland were still foreigners, chiefly Germans, up to the 1880s.

Civilian bands associated with the various trades were already in existence in the cities in the eighteenth century, for instance St James's Brass and Reed Band, the oldest surviving Dublin band, officially founded in 1800. Village bands also flourished, such as St Brigid's brass-and-reed band of Blanchardstown, still surviving, founded in 1826. Bands became associated with the crusade against heavy drinking pioneered by Father Theobald Mathew from 1838, and, as branches of his temperance society spread throughout the country, bands were to be found in almost every town from the middle of the century on.[3] In the

---

[1] Henry George Farmer, *Military music* (London, 1950), p. 30.
[2] Above, iv, 552–5.
[3] See Elizabeth Malcolm, *'Ireland sober, Ireland free': drink and temperance in nineteenth-century Ireland* (Dublin, 1986), pp 95–7.

countryside the popularity of the bands was felt by traditional musicians to be a menace to their own survival, and it is true that the temperance movement led to a decrease in piping, fiddling, and dancing, since convivial gatherings involving drinking and music-making were now increasingly frowned on, and traditional players were in lesser demand. The music played by the bands would have consisted of hymn tunes, the simpler marches, dance forms, and selections such as were played by the regimental bands—a new type of popular music for areas in which the traditional ballads, *sean-nós* (old style) singing, and Irish dance music had hitherto held undisputed sway. In the cities brass bands flourished, band contests were features of the many exhibitions held, and bands took part in political demonstrations. For instance, St James's Band headed the Dublin funeral procession for the 'Manchester martyrs' in 1867, and for a fenian amnesty demonstration in 1868. In 1887 some thirty brass, or brass and reed, bands functioned in Dublin and, towards the end of the century, over twenty fife and drum bands. The war pipes had fallen into disuse as a military instrument, and, though pipe bands were officially recognised by the war office in 1850 and the tradition of piping was carried on in Scotland for regimental purposes, it was not revived in Ireland until the close of the nineteenth century when pipes were officially introduced into Irish regiments.

While a cosmopolitan repertoire was being cultivated by an ever widening section of the community in the towns, the traditional music of the Irish countryside was suffering a sad decline. Many of the best singers, pipers, and fiddlers had been lost during the famine years, either falling victim to the famine or emigrating. A still more lethal factor was the gradual abandonment of the Irish language in the second half of the century, as the language was intimately bound up with the music of the countryside.[1] Between this and the music of the towns there had always been a chasm. On the one hand the towns concerned themselves with a cosmopolitan repertoire, Italian, German, or English, following the dictates of fashion and patterns of performances as set by London. On the other hand much of rural Ireland expressed itself in song and story in the Irish language—an oral tradition stretching back to the Gaelic world of pre-Norman times. To the townspeople, who were usually ignorant of the Irish language, the songs of rural Ireland were not only a closed book, but alien as well. To the rural Irish, the music of the towns remained identified with a foreign ascendancy and bourgeoisie that had kept them impoverished and underprivileged, and, as such, tended to excite their hostility. This language barrier and the extent of the gulf between the traditional music of the countryside and the art music of the towns largely explains the late development of formal music in Ireland.[2]

The music handed down from the singers and players of one generation to those of the next, and heard at the fireside, at the crossroads, and at fairs, constitutes one of the finest and most varied stores of folk music produced by any

[1] Above, pp 385–90.
[2] For an indication of outside influences on traditional music, see below, pp 507–8.

nation. It consists of love songs, laments, lullabies, occupational songs, humorous, drinking, and martial songs, and a wealth of dance music of somewhat later origin, but assimilated into the tradition and showing most of its peculiarities of mode and idiom. Once the words, however, of the innumerable songs heard throughout the countryside were no longer in the home language, and ceased to be understood, it was inevitable that the songs in Irish should begin to die out. Paradoxically, as they did so, interest in Irish folk-song began to grow in the cities, and an increasing number of collections began to be compiled, the most important around the middle of the century being the manuscript collections of William Forde, Henry Hudson, John Edward Pigot, and James Goodman,[1] and the first major publication after Edward Bunting—George Petrie's *Ancient music of Ireland* (1855). But the collectors, not knowing Irish, failed to note the words of the songs, so that the vast majority of the songs in manuscript or in print are literally songs without words. Moore's *Irish melodies* were at this time at the peak of their vogue, and were the means of introducing Irish folk music to the townspeople who would never have come into touch with the *sean-nós* or traditional style of singing in Irish. Moore made the songs of Ireland known to the world at large, but the general effect of the melodies is far removed from the simple, robust vigour of the originals, the words of which he displaced by graceful lyrics, tailored to the conventions of the salon of the period.

Patriotic songs were rare in the eighteenth century, other than those in which the poets chose to cloak their meanings by using symbolic names, such as 'Róisin dubh' for Ireland. But in the nineteenth century music became an ally of nationalism. The Young Ireland movement and its paper the *Nation*, published for the first time in 1842, created a demand for patriotic songs, and Thomas Davis and others wrote stirring verses in English to be sung to well known traditional tunes. Davis's original volume of poetry, *The spirit of the nation*, was republished many times, augmented by the verse of the *Nation* writers, with many of the poems set to the tunes for which they were written. Street ballads, whether narrative or political, were printed on broadsheets and sold for a penny or a halfpenny. Though the political ballads must have served to keep patriotic sentiment alive, John Mitchel's newspaper *United Ireland* complained that too much energy was being wasted in songs.[2] And in the north, Orange ballads, sturdier and less romantic than those of the south, show a vitality in defence of the Orange tradition and union with Britain as intense as the rebel songs of the nationalists. The Scots settlers would originally have brought their songs with them, and as a result of this, of the plantations, and also of the seasonal migratory labour of Irishmen to Scotland and England, many Scots and English folk tunes circulated over the centuries in Ireland, and became assimilated into the folk tradition.

[1] See Donal O'Sullivan, *Irish folk music, song and dance* (Cork, 1961), pp 14 ff.

[2] Georges-Denis Zimmermann, *Songs of Irish rebellion* (Dublin, 1967), p. 10. See also Maura Murphy, 'The ballad singer and the role of the seditious ballad in nineteenth-century Ireland: Dublin Castle's view' in *Ulster Folklife*, xxv (1979), pp 79–102.

In the second half of the century the vocal folk tradition became progressively weaker, but the instrumental continued to flourish, the chief instruments being the fiddle, the union or *uilleann* pipes, the *feadóg* or tin whistle, flute, melodeon, concertina, and accordion, with the *bodhrán* and the bones occasionally used as percussion instruments. Though song airs were also played instrumentally, it was for the dance that the instruments were mainly used—dancing at the crossroads in the summer, and in the houses during the winter. Occupational dances and mime and figure dances such as the *rinnce fada* and the hey, the sword dance, cake dance, fire dance, and potato dance, referred to in earlier sources, had virtually died out by the middle of the century, the surviving dances being the three types of jig (single, double, and hop or slip), the reel, the hornpipe, and the set dances, mainly derived from the quadrille.[1] The intricate steps of the jig and the reel were most probably invented by eighteenth- and early nineteenth-century dancing masters. The music of the jig was much influenced by the Italian style, though retaining distinctively Irish characteristics, while that of the hornpipe and reel are of English and Scottish origin respectively.

Music was associated with many old customs, some of which survived into the nineteenth century. Already about 1800 the catholic archbishop of Cashel had fulminated against the 'savage custom of howling and bawling at funerals';[2] yet the practice of hiring professional keeners to lament and sing the praises of the departed, dating from pagan times, has lasted in isolated areas to within living memory. On the feast of St Brigid a miniature effigy with a bier was carried from house to house by 'biddyboys' singing songs in honour of the saint; on Ash Wednesday holly and ivy were ceremonially burnt; bonfires were lit on St John's eve; Christmas was heralded by the blowing of horns from hilltops; 'strawboys' attended weddings; games were played at wakes, and public processions with bands and singing were held on May day and St Patrick's day. The song of the 'wrenboys' on St Stephen's day still survives, as does the practice of mumming, especially in the counties of Wexford, Dublin, and Antrim. But urbanisation and the changing pattern of country life gradually made such customs archaic, and with the nineteenth century there passed away most of the music and pageantry that had permeated Irish life in the past.

While the folk tradition declined, music began to develop as an educational subject in the schools. In 1848 J. W. Glover was appointed professor of vocal music to the Normal Training School of the national board of education. This was the first step in the official recognition of music as part of the educational system, though music had, of course, been taught sporadically. For instance, in the Christian Brothers' school in Peacock Lane, Cork, in the 1850s twenty

---

[1] The first important volume of dance music was R. M. Levey's *The dance music of Ireland: first collection* (London, 1858). For a description of the dance in Ireland see the article 'Folk music: Irish' by Donal O'Sullivan in *Grove's dictionary of music*, iii, 294–7; and Breandán Breathnach, *Folk music and dances of Ireland* (Dublin, 1971), pp 37–67.

[2] Quoted in Seán Ó Súilleabháin, *Irish wake amusements* (Cork, 1967), p. 140.

minutes was given to class singing each day, music being considered there as having a moral influence and a refining effect on the children and as 'a powerful instrument in softening their dispositions'.[1]

As regards specialised music teaching, in the eighteenth century there had been some sporadic attempts to establish a training centre in Dublin for amateur and professional musicians, but towards the middle of the nineteenth century training was exclusively in the hands of private teachers. In 1848 the Irish Academy of Music (to become the Royal Irish Academy of Music in 1872) was founded 'for the purpose of establishing a school of instrumental music in the city of Dublin, the want of which has been a great obstacle to the performance of first-class instrumental works of orchestras of the Dublin musical societies'.[2] Tuition in stringed instruments was started under the direction of R. M. Levey in the Antient Concerts Society's rooms, and in 1856 a committee was formed to reorganise the academy, the classes of which were then held at 18 St Stephen's Green, and concerts given to raise funds. From this time on the pupils of the academy played an increasing part in the musical life of the city.[3]

AFTER its thirty years of activity the Antient Concerts Society had ceased to function by 1865, but the Philharmonic Society continued to survive, giving programmes of the usual miscellaneous character while including many new as well as standard works. Sir Robert Prescott Stewart (knighted in 1872) took on the conductorship in 1874 and kept the society's orchestral concerts going for four further years in spite of declining attendances and mounting criticism. In the meantime, in 1875, Joseph Robinson had started the Dublin Musical Society with the aim of giving three choral concerts each season with a choir and orchestra of 250–350. The new society was praised for relinquishing the 'absurd idea that no one was fit to hear good music unless they are members of the society and appear at the concerts in the stuck-up attire of evening dress'.[4] For the next twenty-seven years it gave to Dublin creditable performances of all the major choral music then in vogue.

Of the many other choral societies in the city the most active was the Dublin University Choral Society. From time to time mammoth choirs consisting of members of various choral societies were still assembled for special occasions, as when Glover's 'St Patrick at Tara' was given with some 500 performers for St Patrick's day in each of the years 1873 to 1877. Dublin audiences were still incapable of accepting orchestral programmes unrelieved by vocal or solo items, as was proved by the failure of two concerts given by the Hallé Orchestra in 1878.

---

[1] *Evidence taken before her majesty's commissioners of inquiry into the state of the endowed schools in Ireland*, i, 77 [C 2336], H.C. 1857–8, xxii, pt II, p. 85.

[2] *F. J.*, 2 Jan. 1856, quoted in Michael Quane, 'The Royal Irish Academy of Music' in *Dublin Hist. Rec.*, xx (1965), p. 42.

[3] Below, p. 513.

[4] *F. J.*, 7 Apr. 1876.

In this year the Philharmonic Society came to an end after fifty-two seasons of concert giving, and was replaced in the following year by the Dublin Orchestral Union under W. H. Telford. In an effort to provide music for the masses several series of popular concerts were organised, while band promenades were initiated in the Phoenix Park in 1877, at first given by British regimental bands but later by St James's and other civilian bands. One of the most energetic workers in the field of popular music was W. A. H. Collisson, who between 1885 and 1897 organised 'Dublin popular concerts' and 'People's concerts'—concerts at cheap prices (2d., 4d., 6d.) held on Saturday evenings in the Antient Concert Rooms, the Rotunda, or from 1886 in the Leinster Hall in Hawkins Street, built on the site of the burnt-down Theatre Royal.

The Exhibition Palace built for the 1865 international exhibition was taken over by the royal university in 1883, but it continued to be used as a concert hall, while the Antient Concert Rooms, the Rotunda, and the Leinster Hall all functioned for the same purpose. In 1886 the Royal Dublin Society inaugurated a regular series of chamber music recitals given by local artists, with analytical programme notes provided by Sir Robert Stewart. From 1888, for about ten years, the unique innovation was adopted of supplying the audience with miniature scores of the music performed, in lieu of programme notes. During the years 1889–90 a series of piano recitals was introduced for the first time. These were given by Michele Esposito, a Neapolitan who had been appointed as professor of piano to the Royal Irish Academy of Music in 1882, and was to dominate musical life in Dublin for nearly half a century. The Dublin Orchestral Union was dissolved in 1891, and the city lost its two most dynamic personalities in the field of orchestral music with the death of Stewart in 1894 and of Joseph Robinson in 1898. In an attempt to provide Dublin with a permanent orchestra Esposito founded the Dublin Orchestral Society in 1899, which mustered an orchestra of over sixty players and presented an increasingly ambitious set of programmes each season. This was the start of a new era in the annals of music in the city.

In the meantime similar efforts to promote music were being made in the provincial cities. At a representative meeting of music societies held in Belfast in 1872 it was pointed out that though Belfast was increasing in wealth, importance, and population, its music societies were dying out.[1] As a result of the meeting the Belfast Musical Society was formed for the performance of large-scale choral works, and in 1874, in an effort to reconcile and absorb conflicting interests, this society united with the Classical Harmonists to form the Belfast Philharmonic Society. From then on, this society was to give an average of five concerts in the season with a choir of 200–400 and an orchestra consisting of professionals imported from Dublin, London, and British provincial cities, as well as local professionals and amateurs. But the orchestra's part in the society's performances was not considered satisfactory, and though there were three amateur orchestras

---

[1] *Belfast News Letter*, 1 Oct. 1872.

in Belfast towards the end of the century, press criticism was frequently directed at the lack of professional standards of orchestral playing. 'Monday popular concerts' begun in 1864 by the Ulster Hall Company were discontinued in 1875, but from 1887 to 1892 Collisson extended his 'Grand popular concerts' to Belfast, and under various titles such as 'Saturday night popular concerts' or 'People's concerts' these were maintained under different promoters to the end of the century.

An enterprising step was taken by the Belfast Philharmonic Society and its conductor Francis Koeller in 1891, when a competition for composers in various categories of vocal and orchestral music was announced. From nearly a hundred entries sixteen were chosen and performed at two concerts given by the society, the programmes for which included a slip on which the audiences were invited to record their choice of the best works—an early instance of the use of an audience panel in the judgement of music.

In Cork the Cork Musical Society, founded in 1869 for the cultivation of local musical talent, gave three concerts annually under Dr J. C. Marks, organist of St Fin Barre's cathedral, for the society's members and friends with an orchestra and chorus of about 150. Occasional concerts, including military band promenade concerts, were held in the Athenaeum, but decreasing support led to the closure of the latter in 1873. It reopened as the Munster Hall and housed many types of performances, including opera, until it was rebuilt in 1875 and renamed the New Theatre Royal and Opera House, a title which was shortened before long to the Opera House. In 1875 the Theatre Royal in Georges's Street was purchased by the government for the purposes of a general post office, leaving one theatre and two concert halls for the city's musical events.

In the same year W. Ringrose Atkins founded the Cork Orchestral Union, for the first time presenting programmes in Cork that were mainly orchestral. Its concerts in the Assembly Rooms were fashionable events, and in contrast with the policy of the Dublin Musical Society of 1875 evening dress was specified in the union's advertisements as late as 1882. A novel feature in the 1880 season was a concert devoted to works by Irish composers, including, apart from vocal items, the overture to Balfe's comic opera 'Le puits d'amour', Rooke's overtures 'Amilie' and 'Henrique', Field's sixth piano concerto, Jozé's 'Grand festal march', and a 'Grand fantasia on Irish airs' by Signor Bonicoli, an Italian immigrant, conducted by the composer.[1]

For the Cork industrial exhibition of 1883 a large concert hall was specially built in the corn exchange on Albert Quay, featuring a three-manual organ. No less than 181 performances took place, including choral and orchestral concerts, organ recitals, and concerts by eight regimental bands, a contest for civilian bands being won by the local Barrack Street Band. From this time on the work of protestant musicians such as J. C. Marks was supplemented by that of immigrant

[1] *Cork Constitution*, 4 Feb. 1880.

foreign organists appointed to the city's catholic churches, and a new impetus was given to church music, since they built up larger and better choirs, and performed more ambitious music according to the standards of the day—for instance, masses by Mozart, Hummel, and Gounod—sometimes, on major feastdays, using orchestral support. From March 1895 a signed weekly article on music and drama appeared in the *Cork Constitution*, the first of its kind in an Irish newspaper. Though without critical value, it served to keep Cork citizens informed about local events and contemporary artistic developments all over the world.

As organised music developed in the cities, a more discerning public was being created for the enjoyment of opera. That Dublin belonged to the international opera circuit to an increasing extent in the second half of the century is shown by the immense variety of works and composers presented by touring companies on the Dublin stage. Some 150 different operas were staged between 1850 and 1900, a high percentage of them unknown or little-known works; for this was an age when audiences were prepared to give a hearing to contemporary music, since its idiom was for the most part within their grasp. But 'Carmen' in 1878 and 'La Bohème' in 1897 were coolly received, 'Carmen' being denounced as a 'vicious and immoral work'.[1] Wagner's operas only arrived after a considerable time-lag, the first Dublin performance of 'Lohengrin' (1850) in 1875 being greeted by one critic with the remark that 'if Wagner's is the music of the future, the future is greatly to be pitied'.[2]

The Gaiety Theatre was opened in 1871, primarily to cater for light opera, which was sweeping Europe at this time. The vogue for Offenbach's operettas had begun, and from 1876 the D'Oyly Carte Company brought the Gilbert and Sullivan operettas, sometimes as often as three times in the season, to the Gaiety Theatre. Though comic opera by visiting companies and local amateur productions provided the main fare, seasons of English and of Italian opera were occasionally held at the Gaiety Theatre and also at the Queen's Theatre. In 1873 the Carl Rosa Opera Company first appeared at the Theatre Royal, returning most seasons to Dublin as well as to Belfast and Cork, and presenting a wide repertory of opera in English. When the Theatre Royal was burnt down in 1880 the Carl Rosa Opera Company appeared at the Gaiety Theatre. The reforms that this company effected, in abandoning the star system and raising the level of acting and production, were greeted as being 'amongst the notable events of the age'.[3] 'Falstaff' and 'Die meistersinger' were presented at the Gaiety Theatre in 1894 by Sir Augustus Harris's Covent Garden Company, and the Moody–Manners Company first visited the Theatre Royal in 1898, the year after its reopening.

Opera performances in the 1870s were somewhat less frequent in Belfast than in Dublin, the high prices charged for admission to Belfast's Theatre Royal (up to four and five guineas—£4.20, £5.25—for private boxes) being the subject of frequent complaint, while lack of support was attributed to poor acting and

[1] *F. J.*, 10 Sept. 1878; *I.T.*, 26, 30 Aug. 1897.   [2] *F. J.*, 11 Oct. 1875.
[3] *F. J.*, 8 Aug. 1882.

production. With the advent of the Carl Rosa and D'Oyly Carte companies the general level of performance greatly improved. Belfast had reacted rather slowly to the universal boom in operetta; but, despite occasional protests against their frivolity, the operettas of Offenbach, Planquette, and Gilbert and Sullivan, given by visiting companies, received increasing support and led to the formation of local companies such as the Belfast Amateur Operatic Society in 1892 and the Ulster Amateur Operatic Society in 1894. Thanks to this growing public, most of the operas, including Wagner's operas, presented in Dublin by touring companies were now also brought to Belfast. In 1895 the Grand Opera House was opened in Victoria Street with a seating capacity of over 2,000, and the first opera season was given there by the Belfast operatic society in 1896. But the new house was mainly used for music-hall and a variety of other purposes, and the majority of the opera seasons, two or three annually, continued to be held in the Theatre Royal.

Cork was visited regularly in the 1870s and 1880s by such companies as the Grand English Opera Company, the D'Oyly Carte Company, and groups from Covent Garden and the Haymarket. Local amateur opera developed later than in Dublin but earlier than in Belfast, one of the chief events being the production by Theo Gmür in 1890 of his own opera 'Edelweiss', which was to be revived several times within the next twenty-five years. The popularity of opera can be judged from the fact that in 1896 five different opera companies gave seasons at the Opera House.

TURNING to music in education, in 1879 music was introduced as an examination subject in the curriculum for secondary schools, though the examinations consisted merely of papers dealing with the theory of music. On the foundation of the Dublin training colleges, for catholic primary teachers in 1883 and for Church of Ireland teachers in 1884,[1] instruction in music was included and examinations in music under the national board of education were introduced in 1892. In 1900 vocal music was made compulsory in the primary schools. However, as only one inspector of musical instruction was appointed for the entire country, the amount of progress was negligible.

The Irish Academy of Music had been given a grant-in-aid of £150 annually by parliament in 1870. In the same year a house in Westland Row was purchased to accommodate the rising number of students. The title 'Royal' was bestowed in 1872 and the grant-in-aid was subsequently increased to £300. Orchestral, choral, and operatic classes were held, and numerous concerts given annually. As a result of representations made to Dublin corporation by eight amateur bands in 1888, to the effect that over a thousand young men were practising wind instruments in the city, but that the academy 'all through studiously ignored this class', the

---

[1] The catholic colleges were St Patrick's, Drumcondra, for men, and Our Lady of Mercy, Baggot Street, for women; the Church of Ireland training college has borne that name since 1884, though it originated in the Kildare Place Society formed in 1811.

corporation, in association with the academy, established a municipal school of music in the Assembly Rooms, South William Street, 'to make provision for the musical instruction of the working classes, and the organisation of amateur bands'.[1] Classes were at first confined to wind and percussion to avoid duplicating the facilities offered by the academy.

In the meantime, efforts to start a school of music were to spread to Cork, and later to Belfast. In 1877 an amending act had been passed, allowing Ireland a privilege not then enjoyed by Britain, namely, that grants could be given by municipal bodies for music.[2] Taking advantage of this, a school of music with a staff of eighteen teachers was opened on the Grand Parade in Cork in 1878, moving to larger premises on Union Quay in 1902. Similar steps were taken in Belfast in 1891 with the founding of the Belfast City School of Music by a committee consisting of the lord mayor, the president of Queen's College, and a number of prominent citizens. The school remained on a precarious footing financially, however, and ceased to function after 1907.

Professional musicians were organised for the first time in 1893, when Leinster, Ulster, and Munster sections were formed of the Incorporated Society of Musicians, founded in the north of England in 1882. The aims of the society were to provide an organisation representative of the musical profession, to raise standards of teaching, to hold examinations, and to confer a professional diploma. The society was well supported at first by Irish musicians. In 1904 the conduct of school examinations in music was entrusted to its care, but by 1912 the society had ceased to be an effective influence.

The growth of political nationalism in the latter part of the nineteenth century went hand in hand with an increased interest in Irish folklore, antiquities, literature, and music. 1873 saw the publication of R. M. Levey's second collection of *The dance music of Ireland*, and of P. W. Joyce's *Ancient music of Ireland*, and in 1888 Joyce published his *Irish music and song*, the first collection to contain words in the Irish language associated with the tunes. The generally held belief that harp playing had died out completely at the end of the previous century is disproved by the fact that in 1864 it was featured at concerts designed for the working classes in Belfast, and that in 1876 a choral festival was held there at which national melodies were sung, accompanied by a band of harps 'led by the principal professors of the instrument from London, Liverpool, Dublin, and Cork'.[3]

The formation of the Irish National Land League in 1879 gave a new impetus to the civilian band movement, especially in the south, and to the playing of patriotic airs by bands at open-air meetings. In the 1880s 'Grand concerts of Irish music' and lectures on Irish music and the Irish language became increasingly frequent both in Dublin and Belfast, music being usually associated with the

[1] Quane, 'Royal Irish Academy of Music', pp 42, 54–5; Fleischmann, *Mus. in Ire.*, pp 113–14.
[2] 40 & 41 Vict., c. 15 (28 June 1877), amending 18 & 19 Vict., c. 40 (26 June 1855).
[3] *Belfast News Letter*, 29 Mar. 1876.

commemorations of patriots such as Emmet and Davis. The Dublin Choral Union, founded by Annie W. Patterson, engaged only Irish artists 'to encourage Irish talent',[1] giving performances in the Antient Concert Rooms. On the lighter side, Percy French wrote popular songs in a racy humorous style that had a wide vogue, and collaborated with W. A. H. Collisson in the production of Irish comic operas.

After the appearance of a letter in a Dublin evening paper protesting against the neglect of Irish music by the chief representatives of musical activity in Ireland, a committee consisting of members of the Irish National Theatre Society and of the Gaelic League was formed in 1895 to found a festival for the cultivation of Irish music and its presentation to the public in a becoming manner. Annie W. Patterson, the chief initiator of the festival, was appointed one of the honorary secretaries, and the first Feis Ceoil was held in Dublin from 18 to 22 May 1897, with three concerts held in the great hall of the royal university. The competitions included one for performance on the Irish wire-strung harp, but there were no entries, and no harp music was heard in the programmes, for by this time the harp had become virtually extinct. The Feis Ceoil movement spread to Belfast where, alternating with Dublin, a Feis was held in 1898, and again in 1900 when Carl Hardebeck and Hamilton Harty were among the prize-winners.

An annual Gaelic cultural festival, An tOireachtas, similar to An Mod in Scotland and the Eisteddfod in Wales, was founded by the Gaelic League at the same time as the Feis Ceoil.[2] The first Oireachtas was held simultaneously with the first Feis, its music competitions having the same music advisers as the Feis Ceoil, namely Patterson and P. W. Joyce. In the following year, however, the music competitions of each festival were separately organised, and gradually the two were to pursue different paths, the Feis Ceoil becoming a general music festival on the lines of the English competitive festival, while the music section of An tOireachtas confined itself to the performance of traditional music and to competitions for the arranging of folk-song and for original music by Irish composers.

ESPOSITO's efforts to give Dublin orchestral music of a professional standard lasted from 1899 until 1915. With his Dublin Orchestral Society he gave an average of five concerts in the season—matinées at the Theatre Royal, evening concerts in the great hall of the royal university and later in the Gaiety Theatre. The programmes included memorable events such as the performance of Hamilton Harty's 'Irish' symphony in its first version, written for the Feis Ceoil and conducted by the composer, in 1905. The range of works extended from the classics to Wagner and to contemporary music by composers such as Strauss and Dukas. An annual grant of £50 given to the society by Dublin corporation in 1902 was discontinued in 1909, and financial crises had to be overcome periodically. In

---

[1] F. J., 12 Mar. 1892.   [2] Above, pp 417, 424.

addition to organising weekly chamber music recitals with the Chamber Music Union, Esposito in 1905 started Sunday orchestral concerts in the Antient Concert Rooms at low admission prices, fifteen concerts being given in the first season. Oratorio and choral music had been on the wane, but Vincent O'Brien's choir, mentioned below, initiated a revival in 1904, leading to the formation of the Dublin Oratorio Society in 1906. Oratorio was also presented between 1908 and 1912 by the revived Dublin Philharmonic Society under Dr Charles Marchant, organist at St Patrick's cathedral.

Popular interest centred chiefly round ballad concerts in various halls, as many as three of which were often held on the one night, consisting of a vocal quartet—soprano, alto, tenor, and bass—an instrumentalist, and a raconteur or comic singer by way of light relief. Smaller celebrity concerts took place in the round room of the Rotunda, larger ones in the Theatre Royal or the Gaiety Theatre. But the theatres were not always free, and in 1905 Jan Kubelik expressed his regret at having to perform in the Pavilion, Kingstown (Dún Laoghaire), for lack of a hall with suitable accommodation in Dublin, a sentiment much repeated both before and throughout the succeeding years, until in 1981 the National Concert Hall in Earlsfort Terrace was at last opened.

As against the continuous importation of foreign celebrities for its concerts, Ireland in turn contributed little to the international music scene. The Dublin tenor Michael Kelly had taken part as Don Curzio and Don Basilio in the first performance of Mozart's 'The marriage of Figaro' in 1786, and was in demand by various European opera houses for the next thirty years. But no singer of comparable stature emerged until John McCormack made his Covent Garden début in 1907, and his New York début in the Manhattan Opera House in 1909. Abandoning the stage, since he realised he was a poor actor, he continued his career world-wide as a recitalist, showing consummate artistry in his performances of Handel and Mozart, and also of German lieder. Unfortunately, however, he alienated the more discerning members of his audiences by including sentimental Irish ballads and trivia in the course of his programmes, though it was these, rather than his art songs, that the wider public wanted to hear.

To turn now to church music, towards the end of the nineteenth century a choir of men and boys at St Saviour's church, conducted by Vincent O'Brien, had attracted attention for its performances of music by Vittoria and Palestrina. In an article on a festival of liturgical music held at St Saviour's in 1899, Edward Martyn, patron of literature and ecclesiastical art,[1] praised the choir for singing pure liturgical music in contrast to the 'arid and uninspired'[2] compositions of the German Cecilian movement—many of which were included among the list recommended for use by the commission for ecclesiastical music of the arch-diocese of Dublin. After the resulting press controversy, Martyn in 1902 founded the Palestrina Choir at St Mary's pro-cathedral under Vincent O'Brien, who had

---

[1] Above, pp 363, 490–91. [2] *F. J.*, 26–8 Nov. 1899; *I.T.*, 11 Apr. 1900.

been appointed cathedral organist in the same year. The deed of gift stipulated that the music to be sung should be Gregorian and that of Palestrina or in the Palestrina style, no music later than the seventeenth century being permitted unless sanctioned by 'the supreme liturgical authority of the catholic church'. This was the start of an authentic tradition of catholic church music in the capital, comparable to the tradition that had flourished in Christ Church and St Patrick's cathedrals for centuries.

Dublin had its first experience of canned music when gramophone recordings of Patti, Melba, and Caruso were demonstrated at the Rotunda in 1906. In May of the following year, for the opening of the Irish international exhibition, a choir and orchestra of 500 performed under Barton McGuckin in the exhibition concert hall at Herbert Park, and gave a closing concert with 800 performers in November, the last of the capital's mammoth choral gatherings until these were revived with the Tailteann games of 1924. Enterprising orchestral programmes continued to keep Dublin in touch with contemporary music, as for instance when in 1909 Thomas Beecham and his orchestra performed Elgar's first symphony and 'Samhain', a symphonic poem by O'Brien, at the Theatre Royal. As regards popular music, in addition to open-air concerts in the Phoenix Park, national band promenades were given in 1906 and 1907 by St James's Band and the Emmet Choir at Croydon Park, Fairview, on Monday and Thursday evenings in the summer, and from 1908 to 1913 popular Saturday concerts were organised by W. F. Cope in the Sackville Hall at low rates of admission, initially 3d. and 6d., following on the tradition of the earlier popular concerts of Collisson.

To encourage orchestral playing among the younger members of the community John F. Larchet founded the Dublin Amateur Orchestral Society, which he directed from 1910 to 1912, also organising Sunday evening orchestral concerts in the summer at Bray esplanade. But the mushroom growth of cinemas in the city from 1913 on had an adverse effect on concert attendances, resulting in a drastic decrease in the number of concerts given. At first music for the films was supplied by a pianist. Then, competing with each other, the cinemas began to use instrumental combinations of up to ten players, engaging the best local soloists and even importing musicians from abroad. This development gave an impetus to string playing and teaching, since new and more lucrative openings were now available for professional players. But the drop in attendance at concerts posed a serious problem for promoters. In an effort to save the Dublin Orchestral Society, Esposito found a patron in Sir Stanley Cochrane, who in the concert hall he had built on his estate at Woodbrook, near Bray, from 1913 sponsored Sunday orchestral concerts, for which special trains were arranged from Dublin to Bray. At first the attendance was meagre, but support gradually increased, and as additional events in the August of both 1913 and 1914 the London Symphony Orchestra, conducted by Hamilton Harty, was engaged to give six concerts. Lack of consistent support, however, led to the abandonment of the whole venture by 1915.

With the outbreak of war in 1914 numerous concerts began to be given in aid of the Red Cross and various relief funds. Group activities were the first to suffer under wartime stress. On 14 February 1915 Esposito conducted the last of his Sunday orchestral concerts at the Antient Concert Rooms, and through lack of support the Dublin Orchestral Society ceased to function after 1916. The Easter rising and the imposition of martial law that followed led to the abandonment of most fixtures, but concert life was again resumed in the autumn. With the growth of the trade union movement workers became more involved in musical activities, and an orchestra started by the Dublin branch of the Amalgamated Musicians' Union inaugurated Sunday concerts in 1917. It was able to put on a vocal and orchestral concert at the Theatre Royal in October 1918, with an orchestra of over a hundred members. However, the stress of the renewed revolutionary struggle coupled with wartime unrest continued to make conditions difficult in the city.

After the war, with the growing popularity of the cinema and of music as an essential accompaniment to the silent film, it seemed to musicians that this was now the key to future developments. Even the foremost members of the profession were prepared to accept engagements at the bigger cinemas. In 1920 O'Brien conducted an orchestra of twenty-three players and the Walter McNally opera chorus of forty voices between the showing of films at the La Scala theatre (later the Capitol cinema), the first of many similar undertakings.

In spite of the political turmoil of the period, and of the curfew regulations introduced early in 1920, a new wave of concert-giving seems to have been released in Dublin. In the autumn of this year the Irish Musical League sponsored a series of eight Sunday concerts at the Abbey Theatre; the Quinlan concerts, consisting of performances by visiting celebrities, continued at the Theatre Royal; and a new orchestra, the Dublin Symphony Orchestra, conducted by O'Brien, gave a series of concerts at the La Scala Theatre, in aid of the Mater hospital, which became a feature of the city's social life.

In the meantime efforts to develop organised musical activity continued in the provinces. Belfast corporation had instituted the post of city organist in 1902. Dr William Price, the first to hold the post, gave weekly organ recitals in the Ulster Hall, and was succeeded in 1908 by John Charles Brennan, organist and director of the choir (1904–64) of the Church of Ireland cathedral of St Anne, who maintained the series of weekly recitals even during the war period, and for over fifty years played a leading part in the musical life of the city. The Belfast Philharmonic Society was taken over in 1912 by E. Godfrey Brown, who devoted much of his attention to developing the orchestral side of the repertoire, so much so that public criticism was now directed against 'too much music, and not enough singing'.[1] In 1917 he founded the Belfast Symphony Orchestra, consisting of sixty-five professional and amateur players, to supplement with orchestral concerts the mainly choral performances of the Belfast Philharmonic Society.

---

[1] *Belfast News Letter*, 8 Feb., 7 Nov. 1913.

With the outbreak of war, however, the number of concerts declined, and those given in aid of war funds tended to be of lower standard. Regimental bands were frequently featured in 'Grand patriotic' and 'Grand military' concerts. It was not until the 1919–20 season that concert activity picked up again, while the Belfast Symphony Orchestra, which had been dormant for two years, was revived to give five concerts during that season.

In Cork musical activity received a special impetus from the Cork international exhibition of 1902, for which a concert hall, with a four-manual organ (specially built by the Cork firm of T. W. Magahy at a cost of £1,200) and a seating capacity of 2,000, had been built in what is now Fitzgerald's Park, and an orchestra engaged, led by Ferruccio Grossi of Milan, violinist and conductor. Grossi and his pianist wife took up residence in Cork and developed a flourishing school of string and piano playing. The Cork Orchestral Union was revived by Grossi in 1903 but collapsed in 1910, and for the next sixteen years choral music remained as the sole medium for concerted music-making in the city. New trends made themselves felt in church music. A Palestrina choir was founded by Father Gaynor in St Vincent's church, and in St Mary's cathedral Aloys Fleischmann, sr, who was appointed organist in 1906, put the *Motu proprio* of Pope Pius X into effect by substituting boys' voices for women's, and plain chant and sixteenth-century polyphony for the florid motets and masses that had been in the repertoire up to then.

The activities of local performers increased up to the first world war, the chief recitalists being the Grossis and Tilly Fleischmann-Swertz, who was the first to give a series of solo piano recitals in the city. In 1912 Ferruccio Grossi gave a 'plebiscite recital', prospective patrons of the recital being invited to submit suggestions for the programme, which was then compiled out of those items that received most votes. Political developments were reflected in the music of the day. For instance, a 'Grand home rule concert' was given in the city hall in 1913, and after the outbreak of war 'Grand patriotic military concerts' were held. During the war of independence that followed, the city hall, with its concert hall and organ, was burned down in 1920 by auxiliary members of the R.I.C. and was not rebuilt until 1926.

The wide range of opera presented in Dublin in the latter part of the nineteenth century gradually became more restricted in the first two decades of the twentieth century. Fewer operas were given within a few years of their first production abroad, Puccini being the main exception. The main development lay in the advent of the later Wagner operas. In 1901 the Carl Rosa Company brought both 'Tristan' (1865) and 'Siegfried' (1876) to the Gaiety Theatre. In 1912 the Quinlan Opera Company presented 'The valkyrie', and in 1913 the entire 'Ring' cycle at the Theatre Royal. In contrast to the reactions to the 'Ring' in many cities abroad, both press and public were enthusiastic and bookings were unprecedented, constituting a record for Dublin. The Carl Rosa Company, which had not visited Dublin since 1911, resumed its annual visits from 1916.

Two further opera companies were founded by Irishmen about this time. One was the Joseph O'Mara Opera Company, which made its debut at the Kingstown Pavilion in 1912 and at the Gaiety Theatre in 1913, and continued to present seasons of opera in Dublin and the provincial cities until 1926. The other was the Walter McNally Opera Company, which began in 1917 and operated on a smaller scale, chiefly at the Queen's and Empire (now Olympia) Theatres. Whereas the number of opera weeks at the principal theatres in Dublin gradually diminished between 1890 and 1908, from the latter season up to 1914 it increased slightly, and after 1916, despite the war, rose to a record of seven different companies playing for twenty-three weeks in 1919. The repertoire, however, became steadily more stereotyped, with fewer new operas; and the Italian school, headed by Verdi and Puccini, became clearly ascendant.

The opera companies that visited Dublin frequently included Belfast and Cork in their tours. But the number of opera seasons remained relatively low in both cities, consisting as a rule of an annual visit by the Moody–Manners and D'Oyly Carte companies. Amateur operatic activity increased before and during the first world war, though geared almost exclusively to musical comedy.

In the field of education, a head organising inspector of music and an assistant inspector were appointed by the board of national education in 1909. The impact of these appointments, however, on some 9,000 primary and 325 secondary schools amounted to little more than a fuller recognition of the existence of music in the curriculum. The Royal Irish Academy of Music local-centre examination system had been initiated by Esposito in 1894, that of the Leinster School of Music in 1904; and with the expansion of the Dublin Municipal School of Music, which was transferred to larger premises in Chatham Row in 1908, and the foundation of the Read School of Pianoforte Playing in 1915, there were now four schools of music (two state-endowed and two private schools) operating in Dublin.

Though degrees in music had been regularly conferred by the University of Dublin in the second half of the nineteenth century, courses were not provided, and music was only introduced in the Queen's College, Belfast, in 1902, in University College, Cork, in 1906, and in University College, Dublin, in 1913. But the number of music students in all the colleges was very small, and the main function of the university music departments was to conduct examinations and to produce an occasional graduate for the few posts available for the professional musician.

As the nationalist movement gathered momentum in the first two decades of the century, the value of Irish traditional music as an incentive to the movement began to be appreciated by an ever widening circle. The foundation of the Feis Ceoil in Dublin in 1897[1] had led to an upsurge of similar festivals in other parts of the country. Numerous concerts featuring traditional singing, piping, and

---

[1] Above, p. 515.

dancing were held in Dublin under the auspices of the Gaelic League, the Feis Ceoil, and An tOireachtas, and the new interest in Irish music was even reflected on the stage. Esposito's operetta 'The post-bag' was produced at the Gaiety Theatre in 1902; O'Brien Butler's grand opera in Irish, 'Muirgheis', was given in 1903 in the Theatre Royal by the Moody–Manners company with a cast of over a hundred, and Robert O'Dwyer's opera 'Eithne' at the Gaiety Theatre with a still larger cast in 1910. Public support for these ventures, however, was scant, and least of all for 'Eithne', performed in Irish, which played to empty houses. At the Abbey Theatre a small orchestra under John F. Larchet, who was appointed director of music in 1907, performed between the acts, incidental music being provided by Larchet for many of the Abbey plays. In 1910 'The tinker and the fairy', with libretto by Douglas Hyde and music by Esposito, was given by the Dublin Amateur Operatic Society at the Gaiety Theatre. The efforts to create opera in an Irish idiom produced no durable results, since the operas were on the whole conventional and uninspired, but they represented the musical counterpart of the Irish National Theatre Society and its aims.[1]

As a parallel effort, greater attention came to be paid to the collection and transcription of Irish folk-song. In 1904 the Irish Folk Song Society was founded, to issue a journal devoted to the publication and scholarly discussion of traditional airs. Captain Francis O'Neill, chief superintendent of police in Chicago and an enthusiastic performer on the union pipes, produced two large volumes of tunes, *The music of Ireland* and *The dance music of Ireland*, published in Chicago in 1903 and 1907 respectively, drawing from earlier printed sources and from the many exponents of traditional music among Irish emigrants in the U.S.A. The foremost of the other collections to appear about this time was P. W. Joyce's *Old Irish folk music and song* (1909), based on his own and on the Forde and Pigot manuscript collections in the library of the Royal Irish Academy, and containing a representative number of peasant songs in English with their texts.

The continuing decline of traditional music in the countryside was now to some small extent offset by the introduction of this music on an organised basis into the towns. The main advance lay in the field of piping. The Cork Pipers' Club was founded in 1898, and classes formed for the study of pipes, fiddle, flageolet, and Irish dancing. The first pipers' club in Dublin was founded in 1900 with the purpose of reviving the union pipes and war pipes, for neither pipers nor pipe bands existed in the city at this time. Between 1900 and 1912 at least nine bands were formed. The club expired in 1914, but a national organisation, Píobairí na hÉireann (the Pipers' Union), had been formed in 1912 to promote the playing of the *píob mór* or war pipes, with a committee consisting of representatives from pipe bands all over the country. One of the organisation's achievements was to establish the making of war pipes as an industry in Dublin, Belfast, and Cork.

[1] Above, pp 362–3.

In northern Ireland a new type of popular music grew out of the fife and drum band, one of the oldest types of military music. The first civilian fife and drum band was formed there about 1882, but in England from the middle of the nineteenth century the keyed flute with its softer, fuller tone had begun to supersede the original fife, and towards the end of the century flute bands were founded in the north of Ireland and increased rapidly in number, for the most part connected with Orange lodges, and figuring prominently on all public occasions, whether political or social. The earliest bands played in unison, but part music was introduced for the first time at a contest in the Ulster Hall, Belfast, in 1886, and was gradually adopted. Martial airs and dance tunes, Irish as well as cosmopolitan, formed the nucleus of the repertoire, and many traditional tunes became associated with the unionist cause. The growth in the number of bands led to the foundation in 1907 of the Northern Ireland Flute Bands' Association, which in 1909 admitted brass, and brass and reed, bands to membership, and changed its title to that which it still holds today, the North of Ireland Bands' Association.

In southern Ireland arrangements of patriotic airs were increasingly played by the civilian bands, which during the struggle for independence participated in public demonstrations and at the funerals of patriots such as those of O'Donovan Rossa in Dublin in 1915, and of Thomas Ashe in 1917. At the graveside of the latter, Peadar Kearney's 'A soldier's song' (which became in 1926 the official national anthem) was for the first time played in public by St James's Band. Some of the bands were classed as 'rebel bands', and were frequently in trouble with the authorities, who prohibited bands from playing while marching. But despite the association of music with patriotism, concerts of national music, which had been on the increase up to 1916, became less frequent as the movement for independence gathered momentum. Patriotic energy was now being put into deeds rather than into songs.

CHAPTER XVIII

Pre-university education, 1870–1921

D. H. AKENSON

IN the period 1870 to 1921 Irish education below that of university level was characterised by three brief flashes of optimism against a backdrop of educational inertia and disappointment. These moments of optimism came in 1878 when the academic secondary schools were given a parliamentary grant, in 1899 when the Irish technical school system was established, and in 1900 when the national school curriculum was revised.

Because the most important innovation was in intermediate education, let us turn first to that sector. 'Intermediate schools' did not become the official designation for academic post-primary schools until 1878 but the term is adopted here for convenience in discussing the earlier period. The work of the investiga-tory commissioners of 1806–12 had led to the formation of the commissioners of education, whose task it was to oversee the endowed schools of Ireland. In actual fact, as the Rosse commission of 1881 reported, these commissioners were notable for their inactivity and for the inadequacy of their powers.[1] Throughout most of the nineteenth century the endowed intermediate schools continued unimpeded on their erratic individual courses. Even more idiosyncratic was the bewildering and ever changing cohort of private venture schools, that is, intermediate schools established for private profit and usually open to any child whose parent could muster the fees. Much more stable, but by no means uniform in academic standards, were the institutions operated by the catholic church, primarily for the education of young people with a religious vocation.

In 1871 there were in Ireland 587 'superior' schools giving academic post-primary education (including the teaching of a foreign language), with 24,170 pupils on their rolls. These totals, when compared to the 998,999 children who made at least one attendance in the national schools in the year 1870, indicate how pitifully small was the provision of intermediate education. Further, the propor-tion of catholics receiving intermediate schooling was much less than their numbers in the total population warranted. Whereas approximately 77 per cent

---

[1] *Report of the commissioners appointed by the lord lieutenant of Ireland to inquire into the endowments, funds, and actual condition of all schools endowed for the purpose of education in Ireland*, p. 229 [C 2831], H.C. 1881, xxxv, 235. There were in the late 1870s 415 endowed schools other than national schools (ibid., p. 477 (MS 483)).

of the Irish population was catholic, only about half the children in 'superior' schools in 1871 were catholics.[1]

Given the unregulated character of the intermediate schools, the general scarcity of intermediate school places, and the particular insufficiency of catholic schools, it is not surprising that the authorities of the catholic church led a drive for government assistance to intermediate schools. Initially the catholic authorities concentrated their pressures on Gladstone, who was predisposed to alleviate their grievances. However, because the wave of anti-catholicism that swept Britain after the declaration of papal infallibility in 1870 made it impossible for Gladstone to grant concessions directly to the catholics, it was left to his tory successors to placate them. Sir Michael Hicks-Beach (chief secretary, 1874–8) worked closely with Sir Patrick Keenan who, as resident commissioner of national education in Ireland, was the highest ranking and most influential Irish civil servant in matters of education. Hicks-Beach accepted Keenan's proposals for an intermediate school system, and it was Keenan's education memorandum that Hicks-Beach presented to the cabinet in late 1876. This memorandum served as the basis for a bill drawn up the next year, which, after being approved by Cardinal Cullen, who objected for a time to the inclusion of a 'conscience clause' allowing children of a minority faith to absent themselves from religious instruction of the majority, was introduced and passed in 1878.[2] Somewhat later the problem of controlling eccentric endowed schools, most of which were post-primary institutions, was solved by the Educational Endowments (Ireland) Act, 1885.[3] This act stemmed from the Kildare commission report on endowed schools of 1857–8, from the creation of an endowed schools commission in England in 1868, and from the Rosse commission report of 1881.[4] It established a permanent body that had the right to oversee educational endowments, to draft schemes of reform, and to alter conditions of endowments in the interest of educational efficiency.

The intermediate education system was simplicity itself. It was the Victorian commercial code applied to education. A seven-member unpaid board was appointed to distribute money to school managers according to the performance of their individual students at annual examinations set by the commissioners. The

[1] Although small in comparison with the number of children in national schools, the figure of 24,000 pupils on the rolls of schools giving an academic post-primary education is actually higher than that of those receiving a post-primary education in the whole Free State area in 1922. In noting this latter fact one really is pointing out the problems of statistical definition that bedevil historical work in the period. Probably the 1871 figure was inflated by the inclusion of a large number of primary schools with mostly primary pupils on the books, which nevertheless claimed to be secondary schools on the basis of their teaching a little Latin or French to some of their pupils (Department of Education, *Report of the council of education: the curriculum of the secondary school* (Dublin, 1962), p. 40).

[2] 41 & 42 Vict., c. 66 (16 Aug. 1878). For a detailed narrative of the drafting and passage of the intermediate education act see T. J. McElligott, 'Intermediate education and the work of the commissioners, 1870–1922' (M. Litt. thesis, University of Dublin, 1969), pp 21–42.

[3] 48 & 49 Vict., c. 78 (14 Aug. 1885).

[4] *Report of her majesty's commissioners appointed to inquire into the endowments, funds, and actual condition of all schools endowed for the purpose of education in Ireland* [2336], H.C. 1857–8, xxii (4 pts); and above, p. 523, n. 1.

board of intermediate education was endowed with one million pounds from the church fund and was allowed to spend annually the interest on this, which amounted to £32,500. Most of this money went to the managers of schools whose students were successful in the examinations. A smaller portion of the board's annual income was awarded in prizes and exhibitions directly to the pupils with the most outstanding examination performances. In part because their limited funds precluded the commissioners' constructing new schools, they could only work with existing institutions, and most of the schools efficient enough to earn grants were denominational. Also, it must quickly be added that by the 1870s the lesson taught by the evolution of the national system of education, namely, that nondenominationalism would not work in Ireland, had been engraved deeply on the official mind. Hicks–Beach as chief secretary had none of the apparent idealism on this point that Edward Stanley had evinced in the early 1830s. The intermediate system, therefore, was a denominational system from its inception. Indeed, it can plausibly be argued that although beneficial to all religious groups, the whole point of the intermediate education act was to assist catholic secondary schools while pretending not to, on the basis of not assisting them as such.

What were the other results of this remarkably uncomplicated system? It is clear that the system set educational standards that were sorely needed. Whereas it had been claimed at the time of the 1871 census that more than 24,000 children were receiving an intermediate-level education, only 3,954 took the first intermediate examinations set by the commissioners in 1879. The number rose above 5,500 the next year and reached a peak for the nineteenth century in 1896 when 8,711 candidates took the examinations.[1] In a parallel fashion one can contrast the 587 schools claiming to give intermediate-level instruction enumerated in 1871 and the 363 schools that actually presented students for the intermediate examinations in 1900.[2]

But laudable as was the commissioners' invocation of high academic standards, the mercenary mechanism used by them to adjudicate the distribution of grants was often harmful to individual schools. An unnecessarily high degree of rigidity and curricular conformity came to characterise many schools. Departures from the syllabus prescribed for the examinations cost the school examination fees, so school managers discouraged teachers from adapting the curriculum to the students' individual situations. At their worst the intermediate schools became cramming establishments, with every effort being bent towards satisfying the commissioners in Dublin. The commissioners unintentionally intensified the cramming mentality by allowing the subjects for which grants could be earned to increase continually.

Much to their credit the commissioners recognised many of the flaws in their system, and in 1898 they asked the lord lieutenant to constitute the intermediate

---

[1] *Curriculum of the secondary school*, p. 48.
[2] *Report of the intermediate education board for Ireland for the year 1900*, p. xi [Cd 588], H.C. 1901, xxi, 427.

board, plus any other persons he might wish to appoint, as a commission to investigate the intermediate system of education. The lord lieutenant complied with this request and appointed them as an investigatory commission, without, however, adding outsiders. Although this appointment procedure smacked of *opéra bouffe*, the actual investigation was thorough, and the commissioners made two significant suggestions. First, they suggested that inspectors be appointed to satisfy the board that the teaching staff of each school was adequate, that the sanitary conditions were acceptable, and that the school hours were reasonable. Secondly, they asked for power to loan money to school managers for purchasing equipment for the teaching of 'practical science', a precedent that one imagines could later be extended to other equipment and to the erection of school buildings.[1]

The second of these recommendations was approved by the Irish government without much difficulty, and between 1902, when the programme was inaugurated, and 1919, the last year in which advances were made, a total of £37,000 was lent to school managers to equip laboratories for teaching experimental science.[2]

On the matter of inspection, proceedings were a bit difficult but promising, none the less. To facilitate the introduction of an inspection scheme to complement the examination system, the chief secretary introduced a bill into the commons early in the session of 1900. The bill, if it had passed as originally framed, would have given the commissioners power to make any modifications they wished in their system, so long as the lord lieutenant approved; up to that time the commissioners had been bound by law to rules set out in the schedules of the 1878 act. Opposition arose, however, and the act as finally passed allowed the commissioners to change their rules only so far as necessary to implement the 1899 report, provided the lord lieutenant approved and that the rules were presented to both houses of parliament. Nevertheless, the bill gave the commissioners power to make most of the changes they desired. In particular, the power to appoint inspectors was specified in the act.[3]

Two aspects of the intermediate education act of 1900 were peculiar. First, although the act required that inspection of intermediate schools should begin, subject to the approval of the lord lieutenant and of the treasury, it did not necessarily follow that the results of the inspections would be taken into account in calculating the grant paid to each school. Whether this interconnection was to develop was to depend on inspection being proved useful in practical experiments. Accordingly, the commissioners appointed temporary inspectors, and framed a rule, in May 1902, prescribing bonuses of 10 per cent and of 20 per cent of the

[1] *Intermediate education (Ireland) commission. Final report . . .*, pp 23–4 [C 9511], H.C. 1899, xxii, 651–2.

[2] *Curriculum of the secondary school*, p. 52.

[3] 63 & 64 Vict., c. 43 (6 Aug. 1900); *Report of the intermediate education board for Ireland for the year 1903*, pp xi–xii [Cd 1670], H.C. 1903, xxi, 739–40.

school grant respectively for schools adjudged 'satisfactory' and 'highly satisfactory' by the inspectors. This rule was sanctioned by the lord lieutenant, laid before parliament, and thereby acquired force under the 1900 statute.[1]

But here the second peculiarity arose. Even though the lord lieutenant had sanctioned the new rule that introduced inspection as a factor in computing grants, the rule could not come into effect unless an adequate permanent staff of inspectors was appointed. Hence in late June 1902 the commissioners applied to the lord lieutenant and treasury for permission to appoint the permanent inspectors. After intervening correspondence, the under-secretary informed the commissioners in early December that it was thought best to let the scheme stand over until the next year for further deliberation.[2] Thus began an ugly, unseemly, six-year squabble between the intermediate education commissioners and the Irish government. The Irish government's official reasons for refusing to allow the permanent appointment of inspectors was that the commissioners were not planning to reduce the expenditure on examinations by the amount they would be expending on inspection. The commissioners replied by suggesting, politely, that the government should have thought of that when it approved the inspection rules of 1902.[3]

Impasse followed impasse until finally, in April 1908, the commissioners unanimously adopted a resolution stating that

the time has arrived when it is necessary for them to consider whether it is possible for them, in the interests of true education, to continue the administration of the funds entrusted to them for the promotion of intermediate education in Ireland in the absence of a system of inspection, the establishment of which was provided for by the legislature in the amendment act of 1900.[4]

The Irish government fenced with the commissioners for a time, but in September 1908 gave in, apparently having decided that the financial cost of the inspection scheme was less than the political embarrassment of having an entire education board resign. The appointment of six inspectors was sanctioned. A bonus school grant of 10 per cent in addition to the normal school grant was to be paid to schools rated 'satisfactory' by the inspectors and one of 20 per cent for those rated 'highly satisfactory'.[5] Some organised opposition to inspection was mounted by the catholic headmasters' association, which opposed inspectorial visits as an interference with their own prerogatives.[6] This opposition, however, was not

---

[1] *Report of the intermediate education board for Ireland for the year 1903*, loc. cit.

[2] Ibid., p. xii (MS 740).

[3] *Report of the intermediate education board for Ireland for the year 1904*, pp x–xiii [Cd 2580], H.C. 1905, xxviii, 664–6; *Report . . . for the year 1906*, pp xi–xiv [Cd 3544], H.C. 1907, xxii, 589–92; *1907*, pp ix–xii [Cd 4047], H.C. 1908, xxvii, 307–10.

[4] *Report of the intermediate education board for Ireland for the year 1908*, p. ix [Cd 4707], H.C. 1909, xx, 53.

[5] Ibid., pp ix–xii (MS 53–6); McElligott, 'Intermediate education', p. 113.

[6] 'Catholic headmasters' association. Report of general meeting, September 15, 1909' in *Irish Educational Review*, iii, no. 1 (Oct. 1909), pp 55–61; McElligott, op. cit., pp 114–15.

taken up with any great enthusiasm by the catholic bishops, so intermediate school inspection became, at last, a reality.

The catholic intermediate school managers were more effective in 1912–13 in preventing the abolition of the rule that made the basic school grant dependent solely on examinations (the inspection grant was over and above the normal grant). The commissioners, realising that such heavy dependence on the examinations was educationally unsound, suggested in their report for 1912 that school managers should be paid on a *per capita* basis, provided that the inspectors were satisfied that each school was efficient, that the teachers were qualified, and that 'a reasonable proportion' of the students passed the new school certificate examinations to be set by the commissioners. Obviously the increased emphasis on inspection would have reduced the power of individual school managers. Hence the catholic headmasters' association opposed the idea bitterly, and in the face of this opposition the government decided not to introduce a promised bill to implement the commissioners' ideas.[1]

The commissioners gained a small victory about inspection in 1913, but even this was hard won. In 1911, when they were drawing up their rules for 1913, they decided to abolish the preparatory grade of examination (taken at age 13 and under) because the tests were too severe a nervous strain on young children; instead, they proposed that the money previously granted for the education of young children on the basis of the children's examination marks should now be allocated solely on the basis of inspection. Although most of the intermediate education commissioners agreed to this course, one of their number, Lord Chief Baron Palles, wrote to the Irish government stating that the proposed new policy was illegal; under the 1878 statute that established the intermediate education system, the commissioners had the power to abolish examinations but not to compute the school grant on any other basis. The government accepted Palles's interpretation, and accordingly another intermediate education bill had to be framed. The act as finally passed involved only children aged 12 and 13; but it was a useful precedent, since for the first time it allowed the commissioners to make grants solely on the basis of school inspections.[2] Five years later, in 1918, the commissioners obtained an increase of £50,000 a year, which they distributed largely as a capitation grant according to the inspectors' reports.[3]

But these minor measures were all that was achieved. In August 1918 a viceregal committee was appointed to inquire into the intermediate system. It concluded that dependence on examinations produced a rigid, undesirable curriculum, and recommended that payment by results be abolished and a flat

[1] *Report of the intermediate education board for Ireland, for the year 1916*, pp ix–x [Cd 8630], H.C. 1917–18, xi, 633–4; *Times Ed. Supp.*, 7 Jan. 1913.
[2] 3 & 4 Geo. V, c. 29 (15 Aug. 1913); McElligott, 'Intermediate education', p. 146; *Report of the vice-regal committee on the conditions of service and remuneration of teachers in intermediate schools, and on the distribution of grants from public funds for intermediate education in Ireland*, pp 8–9 [Cmd 66], H.C. 1919, xxi, 652–3.
[3] *Curriculum of the secondary school*, p. 60.

capitation rate, subject to inspection, be substituted.[1] Nothing came of these recommendations before partition, and the governments of Northern Ireland and of the Irish Free State inherited a high-pressure, examination-bound network of intermediate schools.

JUST at the end of the Victorian era a new system of Irish education came into being: the system of technical training. Throughout the nineteenth century technical education of post-primary standard had been the orphan of the Irish educational world. In 1838 the commissioners of national education had established a model farm at Glasnevin, near Dublin, to train national school teachers in agriculture, and in 1853, when this was renamed the Albert National Agricultural Training Institution, a similar school, the Munster Institute, was founded in Cork. Most of the money for technical education, however, came from the science and art department, situated in London. This department was the product of a merger of the department of practical art, formed in 1852, and the department of science, founded in 1853.[2] The two bodies were originally under the board of trade, but when they were merged in 1856 they were transferred to the control of the committee on education of the privy council. Most of the science and art department's money was spent encouraging science classes by distributing grants calculated on the basis of examination results in scientific subjects. In 1860 there were twelve Irish schools being subsidised in part by the science and art department, and by 1868 there were seventy-six.

In the latter year the United Kingdom government decided that Ireland should have a separate science and art department of its own, but when a commission was appointed to plan for such a development it reported that Ireland did not need its own department and that its creation would be an unnecessary expense; thus, Irish technical education continued to be ruled by a committee of the British privy council. When in 1889 Ireland was included in the technical instruction act, which allowed local authorities to aid technical education through the rates and to borrow money to form technical schools, only eight Irish municipalities responded. Technical instruction continued to be carried on chiefly on an *ad hoc* basis in intermediate schools and in the higher grades of some elementary schools.[3]

Fortunately for the future of Irish education, Horace Plunkett initiated a sequence of events that eventually led to the formation of Ireland's own

---

[1] *Report of the vice-regal committee on the conditions of service and remuneration of teachers in intermediate schools and the distribution of grants from public funds for intermediate education in Ireland*, pp 32–3 (MS 676–7).

[2] See also above, pp 437, 444, 445–6.

[3] 52 & 53 Vict., c. 76 (30 Aug. 1889); Donald H. Akenson, *The Irish education experiment: the national system of education in the nineteenth century* (London and Toronto, 1970), p. 350; Graham Balfour, *The educational systems of Great Britain and Ireland* (2nd ed., Oxford 1903), pp 104–5, 111, 201–3; *Report from the commission on the science and art department in Ireland*, i, pp ii–iv, xxiv [4103], H.C. 1868–9, xxiv, 4–6; William F. Webb, 'Commercial education in Ireland' in *Stat. Soc. Ire. Jn.*, xiii, pt 94 (1914), pp 113–14.

department of agriculture and technical instruction.[1] In a letter published in a Dublin newspaper in August 1895, Plunkett proposed that a committee of all political persuasions be formed to frame legislation for the promotion of Irish agriculture and for the improvement of technical education in Ireland. This group, known as the recess committee (because its meetings were held during the parliamentary recess), issued a report in July 1896 recommending the creation of a department of agriculture and industries in Ireland. The following year the tory government introduced a bill in response to the recess committee report, but withdrew it because of the impending reorganisation of local government in Ireland. Following the creation of county and district councils in Ireland in 1898, an act was passed in 1899 that finally removed the supervision of technical instruction in Ireland from the department in London and gave it to the newly formed department of agriculture and technical instruction for Ireland.[2]

In practice, the educational activities of 'the department' (as it was called by staff) were fourfold.[3] First, it supported and controlled two Dublin central institutions, the Royal College of Science and the Dublin Metropolitan School of Art, plus two high-level agricultural schools, the Albert Institute in Glasnevin and the Munster Institute, Cork.[4] Secondly, the department carried on a good deal of what today would be called extension work; that is, it sponsored or encouraged itinerant lecturers, such as T. W. Rolleston, on agricultural or technical subjects. Thirdly, and of considerably more importance, the department made grants to intermediate schools where either practical science or drawing, or both, were taught. In so doing it was following the path of its predecessor, the London department. Obviously, in this the new Irish department was perpetuating a duality in the operation of the Irish intermediate education system. It was, in effect, claiming to control science teaching in the intermediate schools, even though the schools themselves were under the intermediate education commissioners. The commissioners, being very short of funds, chose to surrender, and from 1901 to 1915, when friction led them to reintroduce their own examinations, science and drawing in the intermediate schools were under the department of agriculture and technical instruction. Fourthly, the department granted funds to local authorities to establish and supervise local technical instruction institutes.[5]

---

[1] Above, pp 89–90, 283–7, 479–80; below, pp 588–94.

[2] 62 & 63 Vict., c. 50 (9 Aug. 1899); *A bill for establishing a department of agriculture and other industries and technical instruction in Ireland, and for other purposes connected therewith*, H.C. 1899 (180), i; *Department of agriculture and technical instruction (Ireland): report of the departmental committee of inquiry*, pp 1–6 [Cd 3572], H.C. 1907, xvii, 807–12.

[3] Above, pp 476, 479.

[4] The Glasnevin school was variously called 'Institute', 'Institution', 'College', or (in 62 & 63 Vict., c. 50) the 'Albert Agricultural and Dairy Training Department' (*Albert Agricultural College: centenary souvenir 1838–1938* [Dublin, 1938], pp 13, 15, 21, 37, 91, 93).

[5] *Report of the vice-regal committee on the conditions of service and remuneration of teachers in intermediate schools and on the distribution of grants from public funds for intermediate education in Ireland*, pp 9–10 (MS 653–4); *Second annual general report of the department of agriculture and technical instruction for Ireland, 1901–1902*, pp 18–28, 35–65 [Cd 1314], H.C. 1902, xx, 840–50, 857–87. See also above, p. 448.

Day-to-day control of the new department was exercised by a vice-president (until 1907 Plunkett held this position) and the higher civil servants; but in theory the administration was divided between a council of agriculture and a separate board of technical instruction. The council of agriculture assumed control of the Albert Institute and the Munster Institute; and the board of technical instruction took over the duties relating to technical education previously performed by the London department. The board of technical instruction was well endowed, having a basic amount of £55,000 to spend annually in the encouragement of Irish technical education above the elementary school level. This money was allocated partly to those borough councils that had founded technical schools of their own, partly to the few institutions that were previously charges on imperial funds (for example, the Royal College of Science),[1] and partly to schools that gave scientific and technical education of the sort prescribed by the board of technical instruction, usually existing intermediate schools. Unlike the board of intermediate education, the board of technical instruction made its grants to an individual school not on the basis of annual examinations but according to the number of students attending, modified by an inspector's evaluation of the school. Thus the board of technical instruction was less inhibitive of curricular innovation and of adaptation to local conditions than was the board of intermediate education.[2]

The department was remarkably successful in its educational activities. Local authorities were swift to frame technical education schemes to meet the department's specifications: in the school year 1902–3, the second full year of departmental operation, twenty-seven county schemes, twenty-four urban schemes, and six schemes for the large county boroughs were formulated.[3] As for the programmes in science and drawing, in the department's first year 152 schools carried out the required programme, involving 6,412 pupils who earned grants totalling £9,575 for their schools. By 1918–19, the number of pupils in drawing and science programmes was 16,870 and the grants distributed amounted to £33,450.[4]

Equally striking was the financial acumen of the department, which started with £55,000 a year for technical instruction. Yet in the year 1918/19 the amount available for the science and art classes and the technical schools was £114,210 from the parliamentary vote; an additional £65,867 from the board's annual endowment was spent on technical instruction, making a total of £180,077.[5] All this was in addition to the sums granted for the central agricultural institutions

[1] Below, p. 556.
[2] See 62 & 63 Vict., c. 50; *First annual general report of the department* [of agriculture and technical instruction for Ireland], *1900–1901*, pp 21–5 [Cd 838], H.C. 1902, xx, 537–41; *Regulations under section twenty-four of the Agriculture and Technical Instruction (Ireland) Act. 1899*, H.C. 1900 (132), lxviii, 3–6.
[3] *Second annual general report of the department of agriculture and technical instruction for Ireland, 1901–1902*, pp 65–8 (MS 887–90).
[4] Ibid., p. 19 (MS 841); *Department of agriculture and technical instruction for Ireland: nineteenth annual general report of the department, 1918–19*, p. 97 [Cmd 929], H.C. 1920, ix, 273.
[5] *Nineteenth annual general report of the department, 1918–19*, pp 2–3 (MS 178–9).

(the Albert and Munster institutes) and for agricultural extension work. The success of the department in obtaining large parliamentary grants is partially explained by the fact that it had been created as a result of an agitation in which nationalist M.P.s played a large, but by no means exclusive, part. Thus Irish M.P.s were inclined to press the department's case in parliament, especially as the department's highest officials took pains to establish that it was not just another 'Castle board'.[1] Also, the involvement of local government officials in the control of technical education institutions, and the requirement that local schemes should have support from local rates, fitted well with the constitutional beliefs of British politicians and treasury civil servants. This was in contrast to the systems of intermediate and national education. Although the catholic clergy were instinctively opposed to any intermeddling in education by the laity, the department's having been established with the active cooperation of the nationalist M.P.s made it impolitic for the clergy to oppose it vigorously, although they always remained suspicious of its potentially secularist character.

In the fiscal year 1914/15, a typical year, 135 separate local government bodies participated in the agricultural and technical instruction scheme and raised through local rates over £62,000 for educational purposes.[2] These activities marked the first time in the history of Irish education that local government participated in financing and controlling the schools. When the Irish Free State and Northern Ireland came into existence, one of the issues that had to be resolved by each government was whether the precedent of the technical system should be followed and the local government element in the control of education increased, or whether control of education should, as in the case of the intermediate and the national schools, remain chiefly in clerical hands.

FOR the national schools the period 1870–1921 began with the multi-volumed report of the Powis commission, a body appointed in 1868 to review the working of the system.[3] The majority of the commission appears to have been ill-disposed to the national school system. Their report was sharply critical of many of its aspects, and included 129 detailed conclusions and recommendations. These can be summarised under four major heads. In the first place the commission recommended changes in the religious rules, which would have made the national system overtly denominational. Secondly, it recommended that local rate aid be provided for each school, but this was destined never to be effected. Thirdly, it suggested the adoption of a compulsory attendance act, a measure that was not

---

[1] *Department of agriculture and technical instruction (Ireland). Report of the departmental committee of inquiry*, p. 10 [Cd 3572], H.C. 1907, xvii, 816; Horace Plunkett to T. P. Gill, 20 Oct. 1903 (N.L.I. MSS 13,478–13,526).

[2] *Agricultural and technical instruction schemes (Ireland). Local contributions (Ireland)*, pp 2–4, H.C. 1914–16 (343), liii, 8–10.

[3] *Royal commission of inquiry into primary education (Ireland)* [C 6], H.C. 1870, xxviii (5 pts). For documentation of statements of fact and interpretation concerning the primary schools in the last three decades of the nineteenth century see Akenson, *Ir. education experiment*, pp 310–75.

introduced until 1892.[1] The fourth major recommendation, in contrast to the preceding three, had a direct and almost immediate impact: that a portion of each teacher's salary be computed according to how his pupils did in standard examinations. This payment-by-results scheme was based on English precedents but was put forward by Patrick Keenan, a chief of inspection who was to become resident commissioner of national education in 1872. Under Keenan's plan each teacher was to receive a basic salary, with increments depending on the examination marks of his pupils. This was in contrast to the English practice of making the teacher's salary wholly dependent on results.

The system was adopted in 1871 and from then until the end of the century Irish primary education was subservient to the examination system. There can be no doubt that the scheme of payment by results considerably restricted the individual teacher's freedom, and thus narrowed the range of teaching in the average national school and encouraged cramming. Education journals blossomed with advertisements for review cards, sample tests, and assorted devices intended to raise the students' marks in the examinations and thus to raise the teachers' salaries.

The National School Teachers (Ireland) Act,[2] passed at the behest of the treasury in 1875, required that local poor law unions should strike an education rate to be equal to one-third of the results fees earned by the local teachers; if they did not do so, the local teachers would lose two-thirds of the results fees they had earned. This bizarre act penalised only the teachers of non-contributory poor law unions, not the officials of the unions, and was, predictably, a failure: of the 163 poor law unions in Ireland, only seventy-three were at any time contributors. Soon after the act's passage the treasury realised its mistake and pulled back slightly, granting two-thirds of the earned results fees to teachers in non-contributory unions. Subsequent changes in 1880 and 1890 undid most of the damage of the 1875 act, and in 1892 the demand for local contributions was totally withdrawn.

In the long run the policy of payment by results was most harmful because it implied that the educational process could be governed and measured in terms of money. The emergence of this attitude coincided with changes in the values that pervaded the entire United Kingdom civil service, and also coincided with an increase in the power of the treasury. Year by year the civil service was becoming more rational and more efficient, and increasingly efficiency was measured in monetary terms. Inevitably the treasury came to have great powers over all the branches of the civil service and became in many matters the final arbiter of priorities and policies. In practical terms this meant that the treasury came to make many of the Irish educational decisions that would previously have been left to the commissioners of Irish national education. On a more abstract level the evaluation of the educational process in both the primary and the intermediate

[1] 55 & 56 Vict., c. 42 (27 June 1892); below, p. 536.
[2] 38 & 39 Vict., c. 96 (13 Aug. 1875).

schools in terms of examinations, and hence in monetary terms, opened the way for the cult of efficiency, a sect whose adherents are flourishing still.

But for all its vices the results system had some virtues, the most important of which was the improvement in the regularity of attendance in the primary schools, for the teacher had a pecuniary interest in keeping attendance high in order to prepare as many children as possible for the examinations. Thus not only did the total number of children making at least one attendance during the year increase by approximately 86,000 between 1870 and 1890, a noteworthy increment in itself at a time of decreasing population, but the average daily attendance increased by 130,000.

Despite the improvement in attendance, it was clear to most informed observers that payment by results did more harm than good. By the mid-1890s Archbishop Walsh and two other leading commissioners of national education, Lord Chief Baron Palles and Professor Fitzgerald, had become convinced that a radical change in the national school curriculum was necessary because the existing one was too narrow and bookish. In March 1896 the commissioners, at the behest of Walsh, asked the lord lieutenant to appoint a commission on 'manual and practical instruction in primary schools'. Their emphasis on practical instruction was shrewd, because the Irish government was at this time considering its new scheme of technical education. The lord lieutenant responded by appointing the national commissioners as an investigatory body under viceregal warrant, with Lord Belmore, who was not a national education commissioner, as chairman.

The Belmore report of 1897–8[1] is of more than antique interest, for it not only brought an end to the scheme of payment by results, but set a curricular pattern that prevailed in the Irish Free State until the 1920s and in Northern Ireland until the 1930s. The report judged that the Irish primary school curriculum was too bookish and that it should be broadened by the introduction in the first three grades of handwork, such as clay-modelling and cardboard work, as well as drawing. Elementary science should form a part of the normal course of instruction. Cooking and needlework, though adjudged to be valuable, should not be compulsory. None of these recommendations was revolutionary, and actually the report made its most important point in a very subtle manner; it mentioned almost in passing that the recommendations on manual and practical instruction could be implemented only if payment by results was not extended to these subjects. In reality, this was a recommendation that the entire results scheme should be abandoned, because administratively it would have been nearly impossible to have some school subjects earning fees by examination results and others earning fees on a capitation basis. The report's real message, then, was that, if the curriculum was to be less bookish, annual examinations and monetary mechanisms must be abolished.

---

[1] *Commission on manual and practical instruction in primary schools . . . in Ireland. First* [etc.] *report* [C 8383–4, 8531–2, 8618–19, 8923–5], H.C. 1897, xliii; 1898, xliv.

Nearly coinciding with the impact of the Belmore report was the appointment in February 1899 of William Starkie as resident commissioner of national education, that is, as the highest full-time official in the primary education system. A catholic, Starkie had graduated from Trinity College, Dublin, and had gained a considerable reputation as a classical scholar. Energetic, talented, and outspoken, he was destined to be a thorn in the side of vested interests, including religious authorities and indolent members of his own staff. The conjunction of Starkie's appointment and the attention given to the Belmore report led to the announcement in 1900 of the revised programme. This programme was a fourfold attempt to free the Irish primary school curriculum from the shackles of the nineteenth century. In the first place the examination system of evaluating and controlling individual schools was replaced by an inspection system whereby each teacher was rated according to the quality of his teaching techniques. Secondly, in line with the Belmore suggestions, new emphasis was placed on practical subjects such as manual instruction, drawing, and physical drill. Thirdly, in the basic subjects of language and arithmetic, new techniques were introduced, especially heuristic styles of teaching in place of the old drill methods. Fourthly, each school was given considerable freedom of organisation. Teachers were allowed to arrange the school timetable to suit their students' needs, and were encouraged to intermix various subjects, for instance history and literature, when such a mixture was appropriate. Admittedly the revised programme had its weaknesses—many teachers could not adapt immediately to the sudden freedom and some inspectors preferred assessing examination papers to actually visiting schools; but this should not obscure the fact that the revised programme was a grant of emancipation to those teachers and school managers who wished to attune their school curriculum to their students' capacities and social background.[1]

Another change indicating the new curricular flexibility in primary schools was the introduction in 1904 of a bilingual programme in predominantly Irish-speaking districts.[2] In 1879 the commissioners of national education had begun to pay results fees for Irish when taught as an extra subject, and the commissioners continued these grants even after they abolished the results system. In 1901 a total of 109 schools earned grants for teaching Irish as an extra subject, but such grants were scarcely a solution to the pedagogic problems of the Irish-speaking areas, where children whose home language was Irish were being taught through the medium of English in their local schools. Accordingly, the commissioners introduced a bilingual programme in 1904, which permitted the use of both Irish and English throughout the school day in Irish-speaking and bilingual areas,

---

[1] The revised programme is described in the *Sixty-seventh report of the commissioners of national education in Ireland, year 1900, passim* [Cd 704], H.C. 1901, xxi, 561–618. A convenient precis is found in Department of Education, *Report of the council of education: . . . the function of the primary school* (Dublin, 1954), pp 58–60. For the inspectorate's problems of adapting to the new programme see *Vice-regal committee of inquiry into primary education (Ireland) 1913. Final report . . .*, pp 6–7 [Cd 7235], H.C. 1914, xxviii, 1090–91.

[2] See also above, pp 394–6, 404–5.

provided the school programme was not impeded and that the teacher had a good literary and oral knowledge of Irish. The tone of the programme made it clear that the commissioners of national education were not attempting to preserve the Irish language but were using the medium of Irish to see that the children obtained a basic primary education, by which the commissioners meant arithmetic and elementary English. The commissioners' goals rankled Irish language revivalists, but that fact is irrelevant to the main point: given their admittedly limited goals, the commissioners were making a significant attempt to adapt pedagogic methods to the background of the national school students.[1] According to the council of education report of 1954, 'by 1922 Irish was included in the curriculum of 1,900 schools, while the bilingual programme was followed in another 240'.[2] It is probable that these numbers refer to schools in the area that became the Irish Free State.

Whereas the national education commissioners, led by their resident commissioner William Starkie, were successful in renovating the primary school curriculum, they were unable to deal decisively with three issues, which were, therefore, eventually inherited by the governments of Northern Ireland and of the Irish Free State. The first was the unnecessarily low proportion of children on the school rolls who actually attended school. Admittedly the former system of payment by results had raised the regularity of attendance, but even in 1890 average daily attendance was only 59 per cent of pupils enrolled. What was needed was a compulsory attendance act similar to the English measure of 1880, requiring parents of children between the ages of 6 and 14 to send them to school for at least seventy-five days a year. An act to this effect was passed for Ireland in 1892, but its provisions covered only town-dwellers—a bad flaw in an overwhelmingly rural country.[3] Moreover, the catholic bishops were opposed to the compulsory attendance law, which they viewed as an infringement of parental rights, and in any case they were ill-disposed towards the government because it was still refusing to give grants to the Christian Brothers' schools. The most important local corporations, among them Dublin, Cork, Limerick, and Waterford, followed the bishops' lead and refused to cooperate. Thus attendance in the national schools improved only gradually, and in the years before 1920 it hovered around 70 per cent. The actual figures for the decade ranged from 68.9 per cent to 72.6 per cent.[4] Effective compulsory attendance laws such as operated in England and Scotland would have yielded 85 to 90 per cent attendance.

A second problem bedevilling the commissioners of national education was the predominance of small schools. In 1904 more than three-fifths of the schools had

[1] *Seventy-second report of the commissioners of national education in Ireland, school year 1905–6*, pp 4–22 [Cd 3154], H.C. 1906, xxix, 642–60. See also above, pp 394–6, 399.

[2] *Function of the primary school*, p. 62.

[3] 43 & 44 Vict., c. 23 (26 Aug. 1880); 55 & 56 Vict., c. 42 (27 June 1892). The 1892 act was also lenient towards absence due to the need to help in farming or fishing.

[4] Annual reports of the commissioners of national education in Ireland (1910–11 to 1920–21).

an average daily attendance of less than fifty pupils.[1] Most national schools were one-room, one-teacher schools and, nostalgic memoirs aside, were educationally deficient compared with larger schools having several teachers and more educational apparatus. The commissioners tried to raise school size by amalgamation but were thwarted by the country's shrinking rural population and by the opposition of the catholic clergy.[2] Few parish priests were willing to share control of their local school with another priest. Further, in the late nineteenth and early twentieth centuries priests were becoming increasingly sensitive to the alleged moral dangers of educating boys and girls together. The bishops were convinced that coeducational schooling was especially dangerous to girls because it was 'injurious to the delicacy of feeling, reserve, and modesty of demeanour which should characterise young girls'.[3] Thus the bishops and clergy resisted the amalgamation of boys' and girls' schools even when each school was pathetically small. The commissioners made strenuous efforts to promote amalgamation, but clearly they were outmanœuvred by the clergy: in 1904, the year before the commissioners began their amalgamation campaign, the average daily attendance per national school was fifty-six; the corresponding figure for 1919 was sixty-one, hardly a great increase.[4]

The third issue that the commissioners failed to resolve decisively was the question of what was the proper degree of civic involvement in the financial support and control of the primary schools. From its earliest years the national system had effectively excluded parents and the majority of the local citizens from a voice in the management of the national schools. Usually the local school manager was a cleric, dependent on the goodwill of his religious superior and of the national education commissioners for the maintenance of his position, but financially and operationally independent of local lay interests. The result was that, as a distinguished investigator in 1904 reported, 'except amongst the clergy, little or no local interest is manifest in the primary schools in Ireland'.[5]

Three attempts were made to correct this situation: in 1907, when Birrell introduced the Irish council bill; in 1919, when the unionists introduced a bill to permit the Belfast corporation to strike a rate for schools within its boundary; and in 1919–20 the government, with the support of the Ulster unionists, introduced bills that would have merged the national, intermediate, and technical systems

[1] *Seventy-first report of the commissioners of national education in Ireland, year 1904*, pp 13–14 [Cd 2567], H.C. 1905, xxviii, 405–6.

[2] *Minutes of the proceedings of the commissioners of national education relating to rule 127 (b) and cognate rules*, H.C. 1905 (184), lx, 371–88.

[3] 'Statements and resolutions of the Irish hierarchy at Maynooth meeting June 21' in *I.E.R.*, 4th ser., xxvii, no. 7 (July 1910), p. 92.

[4] Compare *Seventy-seventh report of the commissioners of national education in Ireland, school year 1910–11*, p. 16 [Cd 5903], H.C. 1911, xxi, 334, with *Eighty-sixth report of the commissioners of national education in Ireland, school year 1919–20*, p. 16 [Cmd 1476], H.C. 1921, xi, 462.

[5] *Report of Mr F. H. Dale, his majesty's inspector of schools, board of education, on primary education in Ireland*, p. 89 [Cd 1981], H.C. 1904, xx, 1039. Dale was considered the leading English inspector of the time.

under a ministry of education and would have established local education committees in each county and county borough to control technical education and to provide rate aid to national and intermediate as well as to technical schools.[1]

Although several *ad hoc* attempts were made at coordinating the three systems, in most matters each organisation went its own way without reference to the others. Thus there was a gap between the attainments of those who left the national schools at 14 (the normal leaving age) and the standards demanded for those entering the technical schools. On the other hand, as far as the intermediate schools were concerned, those students who stayed on at the national schools until 14 began their intermediate education at too late an age! To eliminate these problems the government in mid-1919 introduced the first of the bills referred to above, which proposed to set up a ministry of education. Although careful provisions were made to protect the existing managerial rights of the clergy in the national and intermediate schools, the catholic bishops and clergy strenuously and successfully opposed both the 1919 bill and its successor of 1920.

[1] *A bill to provide for the establishment and functions of an administrative council in Ireland and for other purposes connected therewith*, H.C. 1907 (182), ii, 481–506; *A bill to make better provision for primary education in the city of Belfast*, H.C. 1919 (24), ii, 665–84; *A bill to make further provision with respect to education in Ireland, and for other purposes connected therewith*, H.C. 1919 (214), i, 407–38; *A bill to make further provision with respect to education in Ireland, and for other purposes connected therewith*, H.C. 1920 (35), i, 563–94; and see below, pp 600–01.

CHAPTER XIX

Higher education, 1793–1908

SUSAN M. PARKES

THE development of higher education in Ireland in the nineteenth century was marked by three major movements. The first was the gradual secularisation of university education, changing it from a system that offered general education only to the clergy and gentry of a specific religious group to one that offered open access and a broad curriculum to all men and women regardless of religious affiliation. The conflict between the 'secular' and the 'religious' concept of higher education resulted in a major confrontation between the state and church authorities in Ireland that lasted for nearly fifty years. In 1845 Sir Robert Peel established three provincial 'queen's colleges' in Ireland, which were secular, funded by parliament, and linked in a common examining university, the senate of which was appointed by the government. The experiment in 'godless' education was strongly opposed, particularly by the hierarchy of the Roman Catholic church, who in 1850 founded the Catholic University of Ireland to offer higher education to the majority population within a religious context.[1] The conflict between the two concepts of higher education hampered university development, and the university question became a major political issue throughout the second half of the nineteenth century. The compromise finally reached in 1908 with the establishment of two non-denominational universities (the National University of Ireland and Queen's University, Belfast), each with its own particular religious atmosphere, was the result of many years of negotiation, frustration, and disappointment.

The second major movement of the century was the gradual broadening of the university curriculum to include modern languages, the social sciences, and the pure and applied sciences. At the beginning of the century the only existing university, the University of Dublin (Trinity College, Dublin), offered, like its ancient counterparts at Oxford and Cambridge, a general bachelor of arts degree

[1] Above, v, 397, 425–6.

I wish to acknowledge my great debt to the late T. W. Moody, Erasmus Smith's professor of modern history and oratory in the University of Dublin (1938–77), whose draft notes for this chapter were made available to me and whose major definitive work (with J. C. Beckett) *Queen's, Belfast, 1845–1949: the history of a university* (2 vols, London, 1959) provided the basis for my work. He was also my mentor and inspirer.

that consisted mostly of classics, mathematics, and logic. In the 1850s the queen's colleges, pioneers of a new style of university education, offered courses not only in modern languages and natural science but also in engineering and agriculture. The establishment of teaching professorships, the emergence of specialised subject degrees, and provision of research facilities and laboratories all contributed towards changing the function of the university in society and creating its key role in the professional life of the country. The setting up of a separate college of science, funded by parliament, in Dublin in 1867, while it indicated the reluctance of the universities to accept the importance and value of the applied sciences and technology, did not prevent the universities from becoming major educators in those fields. The establishment of the school of engineering in Trinity College in 1841 and of the chair of political economy in 1836 showed that the move towards modernisation was under way before the famine, and before the queen's colleges were established.

The third major movement was the slow but ever increasing democratisation of higher education in Ireland. The removal of religious restrictions, the increasing provision of secondary education, and the admission of women all increased the demand for higher education. In 1831 the publicly funded national school system of primary education was established, and by 1901 there were over 8,000 national schools in the country, serving a school-going population of nearly 750,000 children. In 1878 the Intermediate Education (Ireland) Act[1] provided parliamentary funds for secondary schools, and by 1901 there were nearly 500 'superior' schools with a school-going population of 35,306. However, the numbers attending universities and colleges remained small (in 1901 out of a population of four and a half million there were only 3,259, of whom only 91 were women),[2] and the major growth of higher education did not occur until the mid-twentieth century. None the less, the achievement of the nineteenth century was to establish the principle of open access to higher education and to lay the foundation of a university structure that was acceptable to the majority, had a high reputation in the country, and offered the potential for development. By 1908 the three universities of Ireland, the University of Dublin, the Queen's University, Belfast, and the National University of Ireland, had been established, and all were to flourish and expand in the twentieth century.

IRELAND at the beginning of the nineteenth century had one university, the University of Dublin, founded by Queen Elizabeth in 1592. This university had been part of the Tudor monarchy's policy of anglicisation and religious reformation, and consisted of one college. The 1592 charter referred to 'the college of the Holy and Undivided Trinity near Dublin' and incorporated it as 'the mother of a university' that would provide for the 'education, training, and instruction of youths and students in arts and faculties . . . that they may be the better assisted

---

[1] 41 & 42 Vict., c. 66 (16 Aug. 1878); above, pp 524–5.
[2] *Census Ire., 1901, general report*, pp 64, 166–7 [Cd 1190], H.C. 1902, cxxix, 82, 210–11.

in the study of the liberal arts and the cultivation of virtue and religion'.[1] Therefore from the outset Trinity College was both a university and a college, and it remained an anglican preserve and the centre of training for the clergy of the Church of Ireland. Despite later attempts to add further colleges to the University of Dublin, notably that of Gladstone's university bill of 1873, and Bryce's proposals of 1907,[2] Trinity remained the only college of the University of Dublin. Under the statutes of 1637, largely influenced by Archbishop Laud, catholics were effectively debarred from the college by the requirement of taking an oath of allegiance, the oath of supremacy, and a declaration against transubstantiation.[3] The penal legislation of the eighteenth century added the further imposition of a sacramental test that required students to receive the sacrament of holy communion according to the rites of the Church of Ireland, and this test debarred dissenters as well as catholics. The reputation and prestige of the university rose in the eighteenth century, and the development of its buildings added to its superior status. Like its medieval counterparts of Oxford and Cambridge, Trinity College was residential and nearly all the fellows were clerks in holy orders; a college statute requiring fellows to be celibate was not repealed until 1840.

The 1793 catholic relief act,[4] which gave catholics the right to vote, to hold public office, and to bear arms, also opened Trinity College to catholics and dissenters by the removal of the sacramental test and other oaths, enacting that 'it shall be lawful for papists' to take degrees 'without taking and subscribing the oaths of allegiance, supremacy, or adjuration, or making or subscribing the declaration required to be taken, made, and subscribed . . . and without receiving the sacrament of the Lord's supper according to the rites and ceremonies of the Church of Ireland'.[5] Only the provostship, fellowships, professorships, and scholarships remained confined to members of the Church of Ireland. The 1793 act allowed for the founding of further colleges within the University of Dublin provided they were non- denominational and open to all. However, two years later the government founded a separate catholic college for the education of priests. The Royal College of St Patrick, Maynooth, was established in 1795 in response to a request from the Roman Catholic hierarchy, ably led by Archbishop Troy of Dublin, for a seminary in which Irish priests could be educated safe from the revolutionary ideas of France.[6] Since the seventeenth century Irish priests had been trained in the Irish colleges in Spain, France, and Rome, but the French revolution had caused the closure of many of these. The government, equally fearful of the spread of revolutionary ideas, conceded and Maynooth was given an

---

[1] R. B. McDowell and D. A. Webb, *Trinity College, Dublin, 1592–1952* (Cambridge, 1982), p. 3.
[2] Above, p. 10; below, pp 557–8, 565–6.
[3] James Lydon, 'The silent sister: Trinity College and catholic Ireland' in C. H. Holland (ed.), *Trinity College Dublin and the idea of a university* (Dublin, 1992), p. 32.
[4] 33 Geo. III, c. 21 (9 Apr. 1793).
[5] R. B. McDowell, *Irish historical documents* (London, 1943), p. 200.
[6] John Healy, *Maynooth College; its centenary history* (Dublin, 1895), ch. IV.

initial capital sum and an annual parliamentary grant of £8,000.[1] The college was under the control of the bishops, and all the students entering had to be catholics.[2] Initially both clerical and lay students were admitted, but after 1817 Maynooth became a seminary only, enclosed and isolated on the edge of a small country town, fifteen miles west of Dublin. It became a national institution, creating the clerical leadership of the catholic church and training priests for all the dioceses in Ireland. Many of the first teaching staff came from France, and their gallican influence was to be strong in the early years. The catholic laity, however, had only Trinity College in which to avail itself of a university education, and although quite a number of middle-class catholics were to enter the college and train for professions such as law and medicine, the Church of Ireland predominance and the high cost were to deter many catholics and dissenters. If Maynooth had remained open to the laity, 'much of the controversy surrounding the question of the higher education of Roman Catholics in Ireland might have been avoided'.[3]

Meanwhile the protestant dissenters were also seeking better provision for the education of their clergy and laity. Traditionally, presbyterian clergy had been educated in the Scottish universities, particularly Glasgow and Edinburgh, but travel from Ulster was expensive and the students lacked supervision and guidance. In 1787 Thomas Orde as chief secretary had put forward a far-sighted plan for a comprehensive system of national education, which included the establishment of a second university in Ulster.[4] The plan, however, was dropped, and instead Trinity College was opened to presbyterians in 1793. However, after 1795 there was pressure again for a 'presbyterian Maynooth' but the government saw this as neither expedient nor necessary. In 1794 Richard Robinson, Baron Rokeby (archbishop of Armagh, 1765–94), bequeathed £5,000 for the setting up of a university of Armagh, provided it was established within five years of his death. Again the government was not in favour, fearing the effect of a second university on Trinity College, and so the plan failed.[5] In 1810 the Belfast Academical Institution was founded by local initiative to provide both secondary and university education in the town. It consisted of both a school and a collegiate department, which was modelled on the Scottish universities. The curriculum offered both arts and natural sciences, and courses could lead to the 'general certificate' of the institution. Secular and religious education were separate, and students of all religious persuasions were admitted. The Belfast Academical Institution was to provide an important example of the new open secular approach to education, and the presbyterians in particular gave it full support in its early years.

---

[1] Above, iv, 650–53, 688–9.
[2] 'An act for the better education of persons professing the popish or Roman Catholic religion', 35 Geo. III, c. 21 (5 June 1795).
[3] Grainne O'Flynn, 'The Dublin episcopate and the higher education of Roman Catholics, 1795–1908' (M.Ed. thesis, University of Dublin, 1973), p. 23.
[4] Above, iv, 283.
[5] Moody & Beckett, *Queen's, Belfast*, pp xxxviii–xliv.

THE idea of a secular university, one in which religious instruction was either separate or excluded, and whose main function was utilitarian rather than religious, achieved a major step forward with the founding of London University. In 1826 a group of liberals and radicals in England, frustrated by the anglican monopoly of Oxford and Cambridge, founded a university college in Gower Street, London, which was open to all and from which religious teaching was excluded. Within two years the anglicans had replied to the 'godless college of Gower Street' by founding King's College, London, in which instruction in the Christian religion would be included as an essential part of the curriculum. The University of London was incorporated in 1836 with power to grant degrees to students attending the two London colleges and other approved institutions. The influence of London University and the concept of a secular examining university were to have a profound effect in Ireland.[1]

In 1844 Sir Robert Peel began an attempt to conciliate catholic public opinion in Ireland in order to weaken the repeal movement. He first introduced two reform measures in 1844–5, the charitable bequests act and the Maynooth grant.[2] Under the first, the law governing charitable bequests was changed and a new board, consisting of both catholics and protestants, was set up to supervise charities. The bill was opposed by O'Connell and Archbishop John MacHale of Tuam, but was supported by Archbishop Crolly of Armagh and Archbishop Murray of Dublin, who agreed to serve on the board. In 1845 Peel succeeded in giving Maynooth a much needed capital sum and an increased annual grant of £26,000 from the consolidated fund. Opposition to the Maynooth grant was very strong in Britain as it was seen as direct support for Roman Catholicism, and a major split occurred in the tory party, Gladstone resigning from the cabinet.[3]

However, encouraged by the success of these two measures, Peel and the home secretary, Sir James Graham, introduced the colleges bill in May 1845.[4] The plan was to establish three queen's colleges in Belfast, Cork, and Galway, which would be secular, financed by parliamentary grant, and linked together in an examining university. Peel undoubtedly was much influenced by the model of London University, though he himself had opposed that project. There were already three colleges in Ireland affiliated to London: the Belfast Academical Institution, Carlow College, and St Kieran's, Kilkenny. Such a structure, therefore, seemed a possible solution to the problem of Irish higher education.

By 1845 the development of higher education in Ireland had become a major political issue. There was an increasing demand from the more prosperous catholic middle class, and in Belfast a bitter clash between the orthodox and

[1] Eric Ashby, *Universities, British, Indian, and African* (London, 1966), pp 24–5.
[2] 7 & 8 Vict., c. 97 (9 Aug. 1844); 8 & 9 Vict., c. 25 (30 June 1845); on the charitable bequests act see above, v, 472–6.
[3] Kerr, *Peel, priests, & politics*, pp 267–8.
[4] *Bill to enable her majesty to endow new colleges for the advancement of learning in Ireland*, H.C. 1845 (299, 400), l, 357, 365.

unitarian presbyterians had split the collegiate department of the Belfast Academical Institution and left the presbyterians once again without provision for university education. It was argued that in Scotland, with a population of only 2,000,000, there were five universities, while Ireland, with a population four times that size, had only one. There seemed to be three solutions that could be adopted. The first of these was to 'open' Trinity College, Dublin, and remove all religious tests. The difficulty with this approach was that not only would it rouse the strong opposition of protestants, both in Ireland and in England, since Trinity College was still the stronghold of the Church of Ireland and the place where its clergy were educated, but it would not please the catholics either. Only around thirty catholic students a year were entering T.C.D., as compared with 350 protestants, and it was feared, correctly or incorrectly, that catholic religious tenets were undermined by being educated at the college.

A second solution, therefore, was to separate the University of Dublin from Trinity College, and establish one or more new colleges within it. The advantage of this scheme was that it would allow the prestige and benefits of the premier university to be shared, and Trinity College could be left as a protestant college if a catholic college existed alongside it. However, Peel had seen the fierce opposition that the Maynooth grant had evoked, and he was not prepared to endow another separate catholic college. Also, since one of the purposes of the proposed higher education scheme was to wean the catholic middle classes away from support for repeal, such a college would be undesirable as it would be under clerical management. In addition the establishment of another college in Dublin would not meet the needs of the catholics in the provinces nor the demands of the northern presbyterians for a college in Ulster.[1]

A third solution was to establish a second university in Ireland that would meet the needs of both catholics and protestant dissenters, while at the same time retaining for the government some degree of control over its activities. The plan of three secular provincial colleges was therefore adopted, and was to be a sad failure. The college in Belfast was to serve mostly the presbyterians, the other two to serve the catholics in the south and west. One of the major factors in persuading Peel and Graham to choose this solution was the influence of Thomas Wyse, M.P. for Waterford city (1835–47). Wyse was an unusual and a committed advocate of educational development.[2] Born into a well-to-do catholic family in Waterford, he had been educated at Stonyhurst, the Jesuit college in Lancashire, and at Trinity College, Dublin. He became an active O'Connellite and campaigned for catholic emancipation. In 1830 he became M.P. for Tipperary; his persistent demand for a scheme of national education in Ireland earned him the nickname of 'M.P. for education'. In 1835 he chaired the select committee on

---

[1] T. W. Moody, 'The Irish university question of the nineteenth century' in *History*, xliii, no. 148 (1958), pp 90–109.

[2] See J. J. Auchmuty, *Sir Thomas Wyse, 1791–1862: the life and career of an educator and diplomat* (London, 1939).

foundation schools,[1] which presented a far-sighted and comprehensive plan for Irish educational development. There was to be an elementary school in every parish, secondary academies in each county, and four provincial colleges that would prepare students for business and professional careers as well as for the University of Dublin. The report was concerned particularly with the need for middle-class education, and it stressed that the foundation of the national school system in 1831 would lead eventually to a demand for secondary and tertiary institutions. A central board would be required to supervise the schools and colleges, and financial support should be provided by the grand juries. The provincial colleges would be modelled on the collegiate department of the Belfast Academical Institution and would be non-residential and free of all religious tests. Rev. Reuben John Bryce, principal of the Belfast Academy, had been one of the most important witnesses to the select committee, and his support for a system of provincial colleges had much influenced Wyse's plan.[2]

The publication of Wyse's report in 1838 led to the formation of a Munster college committee, which Wyse and his fellow Munsterman William Smith O'Brien, M.P. for Limerick county (1835–49), helped to organise. Eventually a petition with over a thousand signatures was presented to the queen and to parliament, requesting colleges at Cork and Limerick. Three years later, in 1841, Wyse, determined to keep the question of Irish academic education to the forefront of the political scene, wrote a letter to the chief secretary, Lord Morpeth, which was published subsequently by order of the house of commons.[3] This letter was one of several memoranda circulated by Graham to the cabinet in 1844 before the drafting of the colleges bill. It outlined the plan for provincial colleges and suggested the setting up of a university of Ireland on the lines of the University of London. Both scientific and literary courses would be offered in the colleges; religious instruction would not be excluded but taught separately 'for the several communions under the guidance of their respective pastors'.[4]

However, Wyse's 1838 plan was only one factor that influenced the drafting of the colleges bill. A memorial from the general assembly of the presbyterian church in Ireland in the autumn of 1844, requesting public money for a combined literary and theological college, reemphasised the needs of the northern community, and the desire to break up 'the solidarity of the repeal movement' and to provide a 'lay counterpart to the Maynooth bill' was paramount.[5] Under the terms of the 1845 colleges bill, the three provincial colleges were, like the Scottish universities, to be non-residential, and the teaching was to be provided by means of

[1] *Report from the select committee on foundation schools and education in Ireland*, H.C. 1837–8 (701), vii, 345–436.
[2] *Report from the select committee on education in Ireland: part I*, pp 115–17, H.C. 1836 (630), xiii, 121–3.
[3] *Copy of a letter . . . to the rt hon. lord Viscount Morpeth . . . by Thomas Wyse esq., . . . relative to the establishment and support of provincial colleges in Ireland*, H.C. 1843 (446), li, 339–46.
[4] Kerr, *Peel, priests & politics*, pp 291–6.
[5] Ibid., p. 301.

professorial lectures and examinations. There were to be three faculties (arts, law, and medicine) and all the professors were to be appointed and paid by the crown. The fees were to be low and there was to be a generous supply of scholarships. A capital grant of £100,000 was to be given for buildings and each college would receive an annual grant of £6,000 (later raised to £7,000). As the colleges were to be non-denominational, no public endowment could be used for theological teaching, though private resources could be used. The setting up of licensed boarding houses by religious bodies was also to be encouraged.[1] The decision to exclude theological teaching from public endowment was to prove a fatal flaw in the whole scheme. It was based not only on the desire to avoid denominational strife and provide a united education for catholics and protestants in Ireland, but also on the increasingly popular principle that the state should not endow any religion. The inconsistency of applying this principle to the colleges bill but not to the Maynooth grant was pointed out to Peel, but he claimed that there was a marked difference between the two measures: the parliamentary grant to Maynooth and to the Belfast Academical Institution professorships had been for professional training, whereas the colleges bill was concerned with the education of the laity.

The 1845 bill was an important pioneer venture for the government. It was the first time that there had been an attempt to establish a university financed by public funds. The experiment of the queen's colleges was to have a considerable effect on the subsequent development of universities in other parts of the British empire, principally in India and Australia. The foundations of the universities of Sydney (1850), Melbourne (1853), and Calcutta (1855) were all directly influenced by the experience gained in Ireland in the 1840s.[2]

Reaction to the bill in Ireland was mixed, but it passed through parliament and received the royal assent on 31 July 1845.[3] The repeal movement was split in two. O'Connell, borrowing the phrase used by the high-churchman Sir Robert Inglis at the opening debate when he described the bill as 'a gigantic scheme of godless education', vehemently attacked the 'godless colleges'; Davis and the Young Irelanders welcomed them as an opportunity for the united education of the young laity of Ireland.[4] The bishops also were undecided. Pleased by the outcome of the Maynooth grant earlier that year, they were anxious to avail themselves of the goodwill of the government. Under the influence of Archbishops Murray and Crolly a memorial was presented to the government requesting that more safeguards should be provided to protect the religious beliefs of catholics attending the colleges. The bishops said that they were willing to cooperate with the scheme if a fair proportion of the professors and other officeholders were catholics, if a board of trustees was appointed that included bishops, and if

[1] Moody & Beckett, *Queen's, Belfast*, pp 11–15.
[2] Ashby, *Universities*, pp 25–9.
[3] 8 & 9 Vict., c. 66 (31 July 1845).
[4] J. R. Hill, 'Nationalism and the catholic church in the 1840s: views of Dublin repealers' in *I.H.S.*, xix, no. 76 (Sept. 1975), pp 382–8; *Hansard 3*, lxxx, 378 (9 May 1845).

catholic chaplains, responsible to their bishops but paid out of public money, were appointed. On the question of lectures the bishops considered that in order to protect the beliefs of catholic students, catholic professors would be required in the crucial areas of history, logic, metaphysics, moral philosophy, geology, and anatomy.[1]

Peel and Graham, however, were unable to accede to these proposals, which they considered to be at variance with the principles of the bill. The attitude of the hierarchy hardened. A decision was made to refer the matter to Rome for its consideration and judgment. The moderates among the hierarchy, led by Archbishop Murray of Dublin and Archbishop Crolly of Armagh, wished to find a compromise that would allow catholics to make use of the new colleges; the ultras, led by Archbishop MacHale of Tuam, were determined to have the colleges totally condemned. Both parties sent missions to Rome to present their case. Pius IX had been elected pope in 1846, and he had a strong sympathy for the Irish people. Paul Cullen, rector of the Irish College in Rome, became one of the pope's chamberlains, and his conservative views much influenced papal policy towards Ireland. A papal rescript was issued in 1847 condemning the queen's colleges as 'institutions of the sort [that] would be a detriment to religion',[2] and in which the archbishops and bishops of Ireland should have no part whatever. Further rescripts followed in 1848 and 1850, and in 1850 the decrees of the synod of Thurles declared that all catholic clergy were forbidden to teach or accept office in the colleges, and that

the aforesaid colleges, because of the grave intrinsic dangers to which by the judgment of the holy see, the faith and morals of studious catholic youth are exposed in them, . . . are to be rejected and avoided by faithful catholics, who ought to prefer their faith to all temporal advantages and emoluments.[3]

This fundamental clash in the middle of the nineteenth century between the secular and religious concept of a university was to have a long-lasting effect on the history of Irish higher education. Any hope that the queen's colleges had of succeeding was greatly reduced. Their main purpose had been to provide higher education for catholics, who were now forbidden by their church to attend. On the other hand the presbyterians of Ulster found it convenient to support Queen's College, Belfast, from the outset. Disappointed as the general assembly was in not obtaining a full presbyterian theological and arts college, it none the less after much debate decided to accept the arts degree at Queen's as suitable literary training for presbyterian students, and to establish its own theological college in Belfast, which it did in 1853.[4] Therefore a sectarian divide was created by the very colleges that had been intended to unite the different creeds. Moreover, the

[1] *Catholic Directory, 1847*, pp 373-5.

[2] *First rescript on the queen's colleges from the Sacred Congregation for the Propagation of the Faith* (Rome, 1847).

[3] *Catholic Directory, 1853*, p. 148; above, v, 396-7.

[4] Robert Allen, *The Presbyterian College, Belfast, 1853-1953* (Belfast, 1954).

government's commitment to the ambitious queen's colleges scheme and the large investment that it entailed prevented its successors for many years from considering possible alternatives. The colleges, and later the queen's university, the degree-awarding body set up in 1850 to coordinate the three colleges, became in themselves vested interests and made the solution of the Irish university question a more complex issue.

Nevertheless in 1845 Peel had every hope that, despite the stern opposition, the colleges would succeed, and so plans for building went ahead. Three presidents and vice-presidents of the new colleges were appointed, and a board of colleges was formed, which met in Dublin in January 1846. The brief of the board (which had Sir Robert Kane, first president of Queen's College, Cork, as chairman) was to appoint staff, decide on courses, and recommend a structure for the proposed degree-awarding authority. In the 'memoranda of subjects'[1] presented by the government to be read at the first meeting of the board, Graham outlined his view of the purposes of the new colleges. The scheme was 'to diffuse amongst the people of Ireland, and especially the youth of the middle classes, the blessings of a full and satisfactory literary and scientific education'. It should provide the 'efficient means of instruction in those subsequent departments of study which constitute the preparation for the various practical avocations of after life'. The curriculum of the colleges should be 'in advance if possible of the systems of undergraduate education hitherto and elsewhere adopted'. Therefore the degree in arts should be broad and contain 'those branches of modern literature and science, now essential to be known by every well educated man'. In addition there should be specialised courses developed in 'those branches of practical and applied science, upon which the subsistence of the people and the wellbeing of the state' was grounded. This referred to proposed courses in both engineering and agriculture.

The B.A. degree course, which was drawn up for the colleges by 1850, was closely based on the recommendations of these memoranda. It was remarkably broad and to some extent revolutionary. The first-year arts course included both English and a modern language in addition to the traditional Greek, Latin, and mathematics, while in the second year logic, chemistry, zoology, and botany were compulsory, and Greek became an option. In the third year there were two terms of English literature and history as well as one term of physical geography and two of metaphysics, or one of jurisprudence and political economy. Such a course went far beyond that offered even by London University at that time, where there was as yet no provision for English or physical geography, chemistry, zoology, or botany.[2]

In addition to the B.A. degree, the queen's colleges also offered degrees in medicine and law (which included the three years of the arts course plus a

---

[1] Memoranda of subjects for the consideration of the board of colleges (*Report of her majesty's commissioners appointed to inquire into the progress and condition of the queen's colleges at Belfast, Cork, and Galway . . .*, appendix B, pp 315–17 [2413], H.C. 1857–8, xxi, 415–17).

[2] Ashby, *Universities*, pp 33–4.

one-year LL.B), and diplomas in engineering and agriculture. One particular innovation that pleased many was the recognition of the historic place of the Irish language by the foundation of chairs of Celtic languages in the three colleges. Each college was given a professorial teaching staff of twenty, with thirteen chairs in arts, five in medicine, and two in law. The faculty of arts was divided into a literary division and a scientific division, the former including chairs in Greek, Latin, history and English literature, modern languages, and Celtic languages; the latter including chairs in natural history, natural philosophy, mineralogy and geology, chemistry, mathematics, logic and metaphysics, civil engineering, and agriculture.

The courses, therefore, were innovative and bold in conception. What they lacked in depth they gained in breadth, and each year's course was planned in an orderly progression. Candidates who had passed the degree examination could continue to specialise for an M.A. by examination. In the years to come, queen's college graduates were to be very successful in competition with other universities in the British Isles; and in the examinations for the Indian civil service, for example, they were to win many distinctions. For instance, in 1857, two years after the open competition had been introduced, Queen's College, Belfast, obtained the top place as well as the fourth and tenth places out of the twelve offered.

The constitution of the queen's university had not been defined by the colleges act, and the opinion of the board of colleges had been sought in 1848. Some favoured a central university like London, whereas others recommended a federation of semi-independent colleges, each conducting its own examinations. The Scottish model of separate universities in each city was also a possibility. Eventually in 1850 the queen's university was established by royal charter as a centralised university to examine and award degrees to candidates who had attended a queen's college. The university was based on the London model, except that it was confined to the three colleges and was not open to other institutions. This meant that any separate catholic college that the hierarchy might set up was prevented from taking degrees. The senate of the university consisted of twenty members who, except for the presidents of the colleges, who were *ex officio* members, were appointed by the crown for life. The chancellor was also a crown appointee, and the vice-chancellor was elected annually by the senate. The office of the university was to be in Dublin castle (a decision to which some of the board of Trinity College objected) and the degree examinations were to be held there.

The three provincial colleges retained a high degree of independence, each holding its own matriculation examination and admitting its own students. In the early years many of the students did not, or could not for financial reasons, travel to Dublin to sit the university examinations, and so they left without a degree. The academic and social status of having attended one of the queen's colleges was as important as, if not more important than, obtaining the formal university degree. As the colleges were non-residential the students lived in lodgings or with friends and there were few facilities offered other than lecture halls and a library. None the less, student societies and athletic activities developed, and in 1864 a convocation of graduates was formed and granted representation on the university senate, thus contributing to its strong corporate identity.

The outstanding figure in the early years of the development of the queen's colleges was Sir Robert Kane, first president of Queen's College, Cork. Kane, born in Dublin in 1809, was representative of the new, educated, catholic middle class.[1] A graduate of Trinity College and a research chemist, he published in 1844 *The industrial resources of Ireland*, which was widely acclaimed as a pioneering and perceptive analysis of Ireland's economic potential.[2] In 1845 he became director of the new government-funded Museum of Irish Industry[3] and later that year he was offered the presidency of Queen's College, Cork. His advice and expertise were used extensively by the government, and he was chairman of the board of colleges. His career as president was chequered in that he retained his post at the museum in Dublin, which later developed into a college for the applied sciences (it became the college of science in 1867) and consequently he neglected his duties in Cork. None the less, Kane's vision of, and belief in, the value of higher education in Ireland remained undiminished, and his inaugural address in 1849 at the opening of Queen's College, Cork, illustrated how he perceived it:

We have a country abundant in capabilities, so that their enumeration has become even tiresome and commonplace. We have a people, the dormant elements of productive industry and honest wealth; and we require, in order that we may rise from the despondency into which we have allowed ourselves to fall, to utilise the resources of our country, and afford employment to our people . . . It is to afford facilities for sound industrial education among the middle and higher classes of this province that the schools of agriculture and of engineering have been established; and it will be the special object of the council of this college to conduct those schools, so that the education therein given shall be specially applicable to the practical amelioration of this country.[4]

At Belfast the first president (1845–79) was Rev. Pooley Shuldham Henry, a presbyterian minister from Armagh who, though he had no previous experience of academic life, proved a capable administrator and leader. He was ably assisted by his vice-president (1845–79), Thomas Andrews, a native of Belfast and professor of chemistry, who had studied abroad and gained an international reputation for his research. The two men formed an effective partnership for over thirty years.[5] The outstanding figure in the Belfast medical school was Alexander

[1] T. S. Wheeler, 'Sir Robert Kane, his life and work' in Royal Dublin Society, *The natural resources of Ireland* (Dublin, 1944); Deasmumhan Ó Raghallaigh, *Sir Robert Kane, first president of Queen's College, Cork: a pioneer in science, industry, and commerce* (Cork, 1942).

[2] Above, v, 144–5.

[3] Below, p. 556.

[4] Robert Kane, *Inaugural address delivered at the opening of Queen's College, Cork, 1849* (Dublin, 1849), p. 13.

[5] Moody & Beckett, *Queen's, Belfast*, pp 120–21.

Gordon, first professor of surgery (1849–86), who became an authority on the treatment of fractures, while John O'Donovan, professor of Celtic languages (1849–61), though he had no students, was eminent as a scholar of the Irish language and archaeology. At Cork William Kirby Sullivan, the chemist, who was previously at the catholic university, succeeded Kane as president in 1873 and became a leading authority on science education, while George Boole, first professor of mathematics (1849–64), was the inventor of Boolean algebra, and his published work *An investigation of the laws of thought on which are founded the mathematical theories of logic and probabilities* (1864) gained him a lasting reputation.[1] However, within ten years it became evident that the high hopes of the queen's colleges were to be unfulfilled, and many came to regard them as a costly failure. More than £375,000 had been spent on them in the first decade. In 1857 Lord Palmerston's government established a commission of inquiry into the queen's university and colleges, chaired by the marquis of Kildare, which attempted to analyse the causes of failure.[2] The average annual combined attendance at the three colleges in the first decade had been only 421, and even in the late 1870s the combined total was well below that of Trinity College, which had about 1,000–1,500. The desperate poverty and high emigration that resulted from the famine had reduced the number of potential students. The superior status of Trinity continued to attract not only all students destined for holy orders in the Church of Ireland, but also those who wished to take a degree by examination only. Even more importantly, the country lacked an organised system of secondary schooling, such as Wyse's 1838 plan had envisaged, and there was an insufficient supply of well educated recruits for the colleges. Kildare himself at the same time chaired the commission on endowed schools,[3] which recommended support for secondary schools, and the university commission reiterated this essential need.

Of the three colleges, Belfast had made the most progress, having maintained an average annual attendance of 189 during the decade. It had gained the support of the presbyterians in Ulster, who provided most of its students. The courses were regarded by the commission as being wholly satisfactory, but only the faculties of arts and medicine had grown in size. The average annual attendance in law had been only twenty, while in engineering there were only ten to fifteen in Belfast and Galway, with up to forty in Cork. Neither of these two professions yet required academic qualifications, but there was small demand for places. In agriculture the attendance had been even poorer, as most farmers could not afford to send their sons to college, so the commission recommended the abolition of the chairs of agriculture.

[1] Patrick D. Barry (ed.), *George Boole: a miscellany* (Cork, 1969).

[2] *Report of ... commissioners appointed to inquire into ... the queen's colleges*, p. 53 (MS 153). Commissions on Oxford and Cambridge had been held in 1852 and on Dublin University in 1853.

[3] *Report of her majesty's commissioners appointed to inquire into the endowments, funds, and actual condition of all schools endowed for the purpose of education in Ireland* [2336, I–IV], H.C. 1857–8, xxii, pts I–IV.

The chief factor, however, and one that the 1858 commissioners could do little about, was the continuing opposition of the catholic bishops to the queen's colleges and to the concept of a secular university. Since 1849 only 402 catholics had attended the colleges out of a total of 1,209 students (33.25 per cent), and there was little sign of any increase. The discipline and confidence of the catholic church was growing under the firm hand of Cullen, successively archbishop of Armagh (1849–52) and Dublin (1852–78), and the deaths of Archbishop Crolly of Armagh (1849) and Archbishop Murray of Dublin (1852) had ended an era of moderate leadership. The government had committed itself to a confined structure for the queen's university, and had thereby rejected the possibility of offering degrees to a catholic college affiliated to it. Nor had the position of Trinity College changed. The Dublin University commission of 1853,[1] while it had found Dublin's courses and administration more modern and efficient than those of Oxford and Cambridge, had not recommended any radical changes in the constitution of the university, and the setting up in 1854 of non-foundation scholarships for non-anglican students was the only minor concession achieved. The catholic bishops now sought to find an alternative means of providing higher education for catholic youth that would afford them learning without 'danger to faith and morals'. This led to the opening of the Catholic University of Ireland in 1854.[2]

IN the rescripts from Rome in 1847 and 1848 the Sacred Congregation for the Propagation of the Faith had urged the bishops of Ireland to unite their exertions and 'erect in Ireland a catholic academy on the model of that which the prelates of Belgium founded in the city of Louvain'.[3] The idea of a catholic university in Ireland originated as a specific countermeasure to the foundation of the queen's colleges. In 1850 at the national synod of Thurles a catholic university committee was set up consisting of eight bishops, eight priests, and eight laymen. In the synodical address signed by all the bishops it was declared that 'we have determined to make every effort in our power to establish a sound and comprehensive system of university education, that will combine all that is practically useful in the present system with all that is pure and edifying in religious doctrine'.[4] The catholic university therefore was designed as an institution for learning in which the arts and science were fully integrated with religion, and theology would hold a central place.

John Henry Newman was appointed first rector of the catholic university and came to Dublin in October 1851. As a former fellow of Oriel College, a leader of the Oxford movement, and a convert to catholicism, Newman welcomed the opportunity to create a 'catholic Oxford in Ireland', which he hoped would draw

---

[1] *Report of her majesty's commissioners appointed to inquire into the state, discipline, studies, and revenues of the University of Dublin* [1637], H.C. 1852–3, xlv.

[2] Above, v, 397.

[3] *First rescript on the queen's colleges from the College of the Sacred Congregation for the Propagation of the Faith* (Rome, 1847).

[4] *Catholic Directory, 1853*, pp 188–90.

catholic students from other parts of the English-speaking world. His philosophy and ideals of university education were set out in the famous discourses that he delivered soon after his arrival in Dublin.[1] His belief in the value of a liberal education and the importance of the education of 'gentlemen', for whom learning was an end in itself and not narrowly vocational, became an inspiration for generations of university teachers:

... what is the end of university education, and of the liberal or philosophical knowledge which I conceive it to impart [?] ... it has a very tangible, real, and sufficient end, though the end cannot be divided from that knowledge itself. Knowledge is capable of being its own end. Such is the constitution of the human mind that any kind of knowledge, if it be really such, is its own reward.[2]

However, Newman's ideas and his plans for an 'Oxford in Ireland' differed sharply from those of Archbishop Cullen and the Irish hierarchy, who regarded the catholic university as a specifically Irish institution and under episcopal control like the University of Louvain. Also Newman's philosophical ideas of the benefits of a liberal education for the independent middle classes were seen by the bishops as being unrealistic in Ireland, where the immediate needs were for professional and vocational training for the less well-off catholics.[3]

Initially support for the university was strong. The bishops appealed for funds to 'their brethren' in both England and America, but in fact most of the money was raised from catholics in Ireland, poor as they were. In 1851 £22,840 was raised in Ireland, but by 1854 only £4,000 had been raised in Britain. The lack of support from the English catholics was another disappointment for Newman and hastened his departure as rector.

The university was established in 86 St Stephen's Green, Dublin, and Newman gathered together his staff. In line with the ideals of the university, the arts and theology were given pride of place and there were to be initially four faculties: theology, law, medicine, and arts. A number of the professors appointed were English catholics whom Newman had known: T. W. Allies (modern history); Thomas Arnold (English literature), brother of Matthew Arnold and son of Thomas Arnold the headmaster (1828–42) of Rugby; Robert Ornsby (Greek and Latin literature); and John Hungerford Pollen (fine arts).[4] There were also some distinguished Irishmen, such as William Kirby Sullivan (chemistry), who later became president of Queen's College, Cork, and Eugene O'Curry (Irish history and archaeology), who was a pioneering scholar of early Irish history.

The university opened its doors in 1854; the number of students attending began at forty and rose gradually to a hundred. The medical school opened in

---

[1] J. H. Newman, *The idea of a university, defined and illustrated* (London, 1873; ed. with introduction and notes by I.T. Ker, Oxford, 1976).

[2] Ibid., pp 96–7.

[3] See V. A. McClelland, *English Roman Catholics and higher education, 1830–1903* (Oxford, 1973); Fergal McGrath, *Newman's university: idea and reality* (New York and London, 1951).

[4] Above, p. 464.

Cecilia Street in 1855, and was to be the most successful faculty in the university. In Dublin there were already four existing regulating bodies in medicine, namely the King and Queen's (later Royal) College of Physicians (1654), the Dublin University School of Physic (1711), the Royal College of Surgeons (1784), and the Apothecaries' Hall (1791).[1] While medical students at the catholic university medical school were unable to obtain degrees, they were accepted for the professional licensing examinations of the college of surgeons and the Apothecaries' Hall.[1] Thus the medical school immediately obtained the recognition of various professional bodies in the United Kingdom and had an advantage over the other faculties, for without a charter the catholic university was unable to award degrees. Professional courses in engineering, agriculture, or commerce were not offered.

In 1858 Newman resigned as rector and returned to England. His differences with Archbishop Cullen and the Irish bishops, the lack of money, the poor supply of students, and his desire to continue his work as superior of the Oratory in Birmingham, all caused him to withdraw from the venture. However, his ideals and vision remained an inspiration, and the small university college in St Stephen's Green that he helped to establish was to prove the foundation on which a university for catholics in Ireland was to be built. In 1861 Rev. Bartholomew Woodlock, who had been president of All Hallows' College, Dublin, became rector and initiated the formal laying of a foundation-stone of the catholic university buildings in Drumcondra. In reality, however, the university could not succeed as it was.

Factors militating against it were similar to those that hindered the growth of the queen's colleges—the smallness of the catholic middle class, the dearth of educational opportunities, and the lack of a system of secondary schools. However, the specific factor that hampered the catholic university was the lack of a charter and public endowment. A campaign to obtain a charter was to be carried on by Archbishop Cullen for the next twenty years, but without success. (In 1852 Laval, the catholic university in Quebec, had received a charter, and this had seemed encouraging.) The government, however, was not prepared to endow a separate catholic university in Ireland that would be in direct opposition to the newly established queen's colleges with their parliamentary grant of £30,000 a year. On the other hand, the catholic hierarchy, under the increasingly conservative and stern eye of Rome, was unable to compromise on the issue of clerical management and denominational control. The charter of the queen's university, limiting it to the queen's colleges, had been granted in September 1850, a week before the publication of the decrees of the synod of Thurles. Relations between Rome and Britain were not cordial following the 1848 revolutions and because of

---

[1] F. O. C. Meenan, 'The catholic university school of medicine, 1860–1880' in *Studies*, lxvi (1977), pp 135–6. The 'Fraternity of physicians' founded in 1654 was incorporated by charter as a college in 1667, but did not receive its present title 'Royal' till 1890; see Eoin O'Brien and Anne Crookshank with Sir Gordon Wolstenholme, *A portrait of Irish medicine* (Swords, 1984), p. 65.

the support that Britain was giving to liberal and nationalist movements in Italy. The restoration of the catholic hierarchy in England by the pope in 1850 had caused a storm of anti-catholic protest.[1] The principle of non-denominational university education had been strengthened in the 1850s by the opening of Oxford and Cambridge to dissenters and catholics and by the creation of non-foundation scholarships in Trinity College, Dublin.

An impasse was reached. None of the possible solutions seemed likely to succeed: the first, to grant a charter to an exclusively catholic university; the second, to alter the statutes of the queen's colleges and remove the objections of the catholic hierarchy to their constitution and administration; and the third, to change the charter of the queen's university to enable the catholic university to become a constituent college alongside the queen's colleges. The last solution seemed to be the most promising, and it was on this line that some efforts were made in the 1860s. In 1861 George Johnstone Stoney, secretary of the queen's university, put forward a plan to establish a new college in Dublin that would provide an arts education for students at the five medical schools in Dublin, including Cecilia Street.[2] The entire staff of Queen's College, Galway, would be transferred to Dublin. The scheme was not taken up, and Stoney then tried instead to encourage catholic students to take external degrees from the queen's university, but this move was strongly resisted by Archbishop Cullen. However, a new charter was drafted for the queen's university that extended its incorporation beyond the chancellor and senate and set up a convocation of professors and graduates.

Four years later in 1865 Palmerston's government initiated another scheme, this time to incorporate the catholic university as a catholic college but without a parliamentary grant, and to alter the queen's university charter to enable it to award degrees to all students who passed its examinations.[3] Strong opposition to this proposal came from the protestants in Ireland, particularly the presbyterians and Trinity College, who disliked the recognition of an exclusively catholic college. In 1866 Earl Russell, who had succeeded Palmerston as prime minister, issued a supplemental charter for the queen's university but did not follow it up with the necessary enabling legislation. The senate of the queen's university, augmented by six new appointees who supported Russell's proposals, accepted the charter by two votes, but the new convocation took legal proceedings and the charter became inoperative. The strength of the opposition to the supplemental charter showed the government that any further attempt to resolve the university question would have to avoid offending protestant opinion, and that support for the principle of non-denominational secular university education was increasing. On the other hand, the catholic hierarchy, while it had been closely involved in

---

[1] Above, v, 401.

[2] Moody & Beckett, *Queen's, Belfast*, p. 278.

[3] See E. R. Norman, *The catholic church and Ireland in the age of rebellion, 1859–1873* (London, 1965), pp 190–239.

the proposals of 1865–6, was still determined to gain recognition and endowment for a full catholic university, and in January 1866 in the midst of the controversy had presented two memorials to the chief secretary, Chichester Fortescue, stating their demands for denominational education at all levels and the rights of the catholic university to public endowment.[1]

In 1868 Lord Mayo, Fortescue's tory successor, attempted again to negotiate a charter for a catholic denominational university. It would have a position similar to that which Trinity College held for protestants, in that 'the governing body should consist of, and the teaching should be conducted mainly by, Roman Catholics, but that full security should be taken that no religious influence should be brought to bear on students who belonged to another faith'.[2] Mayo proposed that the chancellor, vice-chancellor, and senators should all be catholics. Of the senators, four were to be catholic bishops, six were to be laymen, and the president of Maynooth and the rectors of the colleges of the catholic university were to be *ex officio* members. Negotiations with the bishops broke down, as they considered that they could not accept less than episcopal control of the university senate, proposing that both the chancellor (who would be a bishop) and the six lay members would be elected by the senate itself and not by convocation; also that the episcopal members alone would have a veto on the first nomination of professors and lecturers and on books included in the university curriculum.[3]

The other major development of the 1860s was the establishment in 1867 of the Royal College of Science, which was outside the university sector. This college had its origins in the Museum of Irish Industry that had been founded in 1845 with as its first director Sir Robert Kane, later president of Queen's College, Cork.[4] The museum, at 51 Stephen's Green, had organised the exhibition of materials relating to Ireland's resources for agricultural, mining, and manufacturing industry. In 1853 the museum passed under the control of the department of science and art, South Kensington, and a series of public lectures and professorships were instituted. In 1867, following a five-year controversy and three parliamentary commissions as to whether the Royal Dublin Society should take over the museum and become the main provider of science education, the government decided to establish a college of science, and Kane became its first dean.[5] A three-year course of instruction in four main subjects, mining, engineer-

---

[1] *Copies of memorials addressed to the secretary of state for the home department by Roman Catholic prelates in Ireland on the subject of university and national education in Ireland*, pp 5–14, H.C. 1866 (84), lv, 247–56; above, v, 396–9, 425–6.

[2] *The Irish university education question; a statement by the annual committee of the convocation of the queen's university in Ireland* (Dublin, 1873), p. 55.

[3] Norman, *Cath. ch. & Ire.*, pp 240–80.

[4] Pat Keating, 'Sir Robert Kane and the Museum of Irish Industry' in *Proceedings of the Conference of the Educational Studies Association of Ireland, 1980*, pp 276–86 (Limerick, 1980).

[5] *Report upon the Royal Dublin Society, the Museum of Irish Industry and the system of scientific instruction in Ireland* [3180], H.C. 1863 xvii; *Report from the select committee on scientific institutions (Dublin); together with the proceedings of the committee, minutes of evidence, appendix, and index*, H.C. 1864 (495), xiii; *Report of the commission on the college of science, Dublin etc.*, H.C. 1867 (219), lv.

ing, agriculture, and manufactures, was set up, leading to a diploma of associate-ship. The college was open to women and it played a leading role in the development of science education. In 1900 it was transferred to the new department of agriculture and technical instruction, and in 1911 moved into spacious premises in Upper Merrion Street.[1]

BY the 1870s, all attempts to link the catholic university with the queen's university had failed and Gladstone decided to tackle the university problem from another angle—that of creating one single secular university for the whole country. Gladstone's reform measures in Ireland included the church act of 1869 and the land act of 1870.[2] Not only was the Church of Ireland disestablished, but the parliamentary grants to Maynooth and to the general assembly's theological college in Belfast were ended. The secularisation of universities had become widely accepted. In 1871 all religious tests were abolished at Oxford and Cambridge, and the opening of new civic universities in England, such as Manchester, Sheffield, and Leeds, emphasised the links between higher education and industry. The old ideas of a general liberal education, based on classics and mathematics, that prepared men for the church, civil service, or law, gave way to much more specialised and professional courses. The university was no longer seen as the custodian and propagator of received knowledge but rather, in the German tradition, as a centre of informed judgement and open discussion in which scholarship and research were paramount. Moreover, there had been indications that the catholic hierarchy itself was beginning to consider alternative proposals. In 1870 a formal petition had been sent by a large number of influential catholic laymen to Gladstone's government, requesting their civil and constitutional right of equality of opportunity in education. The following year the bishops, in a pastoral letter, indicated that they were prepared to consider, as a possible alternative to a charter for the catholic university, the establishment of a catholic college within an enlarged University of Dublin.

Gladstone's plan, therefore, for university education in Ireland, which he introduced in 1873,[3] was to turn the University of Dublin into a national teaching and examining university, which would incorporate not only Trinity College but also the queen's colleges and the catholic university. Queen's College, Galway, being the smallest of the three queen's colleges, was to be closed and the queen's university abolished. The finances of the university were to come from the treasury (£10,000 a year), from Trinity College (£15,000 a year), from fees (£5,000 a year), and from the church surplus fund (£23,000 a year). In order that the university itself should be totally secular it was forbidden to teach theology, modern history, or mental and moral philosophy. The colleges were to be allowed

[1] Above, p. 495.
[2] Above, v, 727–33, 746–55.
[3] *A bill for the extension of university education in Ireland*, H.C. 1873 (bill 55), vi, 329–62; see also above, p. 10.

to teach these and the university could examine in them, provided they were optional in all examinations and not eligible for prizes, scholarships, or fellowships of the university.

The 1873 university bill roused a storm of protest and pleased no one. Trinity College was enraged by the proposed loss of revenue and by the anti-liberal exclusion of specific subjects. Supporters of the queen's university were angered by the proposed closure of Queen's College, Galway, and of the queen's university itself. The catholic hierarchy, whom the bill was meant to appease, was not pleased either. The catholic college would be still unendowed and the creation of a single secular university was not what was demanded. (In fact there would have been indirect endowment of the catholic college through the university professorships, but this could not outweigh the continuing parliamentary grants to the queen's colleges). The bishops still hoped for a full catholic university, and the recognition by the Powis commission in 1870[1] of their denominational rights in the national schools had been encouraging. Also in the 1860s catholic students in England had been forbidden to attend Oxford and Cambridge, and the English bishops presently were engaged in setting up a catholic university college in London.[2]

Gladstone's university bill, therefore, based on a liberal, rational ideal, was defeated by only three votes in the house of commons, and a major attempt to found a single university that would satisfy catholics and dissenters, as well as anglicans, ended in defeat. Trinity College never forgave Gladstone, and in later years opposition to his home rule bills of 1886 and 1893 'was given a sharper edge by memories of 1873'.[3] Later that year Henry Fawcett, liberal M.P. for Brighton, introduced a bill that, enacted as the University of Dublin Tests Act, 1873, abolished all remaining religious tests in the University of Dublin and Trinity College (except in the divinity school).[4] Trinity itself had accepted the principle of this bill before the introduction of Gladstone's, and as it created a non-denominational secular university it protected the college against further attempts to separate it from the University of Dublin. In practice, however, it had little effect on the protestant nature of the college, and for the next twenty years the numbers of catholics and presbyterians attending did not increase. Moreover the catholic hierarchy now regarded Trinity College as yet another 'godless' college, and in 1875 extended the ban on the queen's colleges to Trinity. However, Fawcett's act did show increasing acceptance of the principle of secularisation, and Trinity became a place in which Irishmen of all creeds and none could mix, argue, and discuss in a free and friendly society.

Trinity College had continued to modernise and develop since the 1850s. While the ordinary B.A. degree course remained the backbone of the university

[1] *Royal commission of inquiry into primary education (Ireland)* [C 6], H.C. 1870, xxvii, pts I–IV; and above, pp 532–3.
[2] McClelland, *English Roman Catholics*, pp 269–366.
[3] McDowell & Webb, *Trinity College*, pp 252–5.
[4] 36 & 37 Vict., c. 21 (26 May 1873).

curriculum, the numbers of options in the sophister years broadened to include French and German as well as natural science. By the 1870s there were seven moderatorship honor courses—mathematics, classics, experimental science, natural science, history, political science, and modern languages—and the professional schools of law, engineering, and medicine established a high reputation, sending their graduates abroad to all parts of the British empire.

Following the introduction in 1855 of recruitment by competitive examination to the Indian civil service, the college established a chair of Sanskrit and a chair of Arabic. Later the college became a designated institution where selected candidates for the I.C.S. could reside during their probationary year and special courses of lectures were offered in Indian law, general jurisprudence, political economy, and oriental languages. A steady number of graduates won places in the I.C.S., averaging about seven per year from 1855 to 1871 (including four first places), and by 1912 a total of 180 had been recruited.[1]

There were a number of distinguished scholars at the college. The mathematician Humphrey Lloyd (provost 1867–81) was a first-class physicist who had an observatory built in the fellows' garden, and successfully encouraged scholarship and research in the college. George Salmon (regius professor of divinity 1866–88 and provost 1888–1904), was a notable mathematician and author of several treatises including *Lessons introductory to modern higher algebra*. He was also an able theologian and his strong critique of the doctrine of papal infallibility, entitled *The infallibility of the church*, was published and widely discussed in 1889. George Fitzgerald (professor of physics 1881–1901), was an outstanding and energetic scientific researcher whose work resulted in the discovery of the Fitzgerald–Lorentz contraction, which later led to the theory of relativity. John Joly (professor of geology 1897–1935) conducted experiments in photography, radioactivity, and geology, and with his successor H. H. Dixon, professor of botany, formulated the theories of the ascent of sap and of the cohesive strength of water. Edward Dowden (professor of English literature 1867–1913) was a leading Shakespeare scholar, while John Pentland Mahaffy (professor of ancient history 1869–1914 and provost 1914–19), dominated the school of classics with his work on Greek history and literature. Trinity offered a residential life to students, who attended chapel, dined on commons, and led an active social and sporting life. H. A. Hinkson in his booklet *Student life in Trinity College, Dublin* (1892) describes the pleasure of living in the college, of having a room of one's own, and of being looked after by a college 'skip':

It is a time when one stands on the very edge of life, eager for a plunge into life's pagan waters, when one has assumed the toga of one's manhood and is yet a boy at heart. Despite the responsibilities of examination and lectures, there is a delightful freedom and reckless gaiety in college life, and a camaraderie never felt in later life.[2]

[1] McDowell & Webb, *Trinity College*, p. 538; *D.U. Calendar, 1894*, pp 47–52.
[2] H.A. Hinkson, *Student life in Trinity College, Dublin* (Dublin, 1892), p. 5.

The defeat of the 1873 university bill led to Gladstone's resignation (although he resumed office within a week), and hope of finding a solution to the Irish university question faded. In the past decade the catholic bishops had had the support of both the Irish catholic M.P.s at Westminster and of Cardinal Manning in London. However, after 1873 the Irish M.P.s began to exercise a greater degree of independence of the hierarchy, and the relationship between Cullen and Manning deteriorated. After the Vatican council, Gladstone became increasingly critical of Roman Catholicism and in 1874 published his famous pamphlet *The Vatican decrees in their bearing on civil allegiance*. The catholic bishops, while they had succeeded in their prohibition on the queen's colleges, had failed to obtain either a charter or endowment for a catholic university. However, until Cullen's death in 1878, there was unlikely to be any change of policy.[1]

In 1874 Disraeli became prime minister, and Sir Michael Hicks-Beach, chief secretary, and the duke of Marlborough, lord lieutenant, were sympathetic to catholic demands in education. The problem was to find a means of channelling public money into denominational schools while still upholding the principles of secularism. A large sum of money (£1.5 million) had been put aside for educational and other purposes following the 1869 church act, and this meant that funds were readily available that could be used indirectly to support catholic education and achieve a more equitable distribution of resources. In 1878 the intermediate education act was passed, which provided grants for intermediate schools based on the principle of 'payment by results'.[2] This system of public examinations encouraged competition between schools and allowed the government to finance secondary education without interfering with the voluntary schools management structure. The principle of payment by results had been introduced into national schools in 1871, and it seemed possible that it could be applied also to university education. Early in 1879 the O'Conor Don, home rule M.P. for Roscommon county, in consultation with some of the Irish bishops, introduced a bill to establish a national examining university with affiliated colleges, which would be eligible for result fees. However, later in the year the government itself introduced a bill that proposed the setting up of a degree-awarding university in which the system of financing adopted was through state-funded university teaching fellowships, rather than through examination results. The bill was based on the idea of the supplemental charter of 1866,[3] and created a university that had the power to grant degrees to all students who matriculated and passed its examinations. Residence at specific institutions was not required except for medical degrees, and there was to be no teaching or examining in theology. The queen's university was to be abolished, as parliament could not provide for two universities.

---

[1] See Grainne O'Flynn, 'The Dublin episcopate and the higher education of Roman Catholics, 1795–1908' (M.Ed. thesis, University of Dublin, 1973), pp 154–74.
[2] Above, pp 524–5.
[3] Above, p. 555.

In 1879 the university act, which established the royal university with its teaching fellowships,[1] was accepted by the Roman Catholic hierarchy as a makeshift solution. It was the best that could be realistically obtained, and it allowed the catholic university college to offer degrees and receive indirect endowment through the fellowships. However, it fell far short of what the bishops had demanded, in that it gave neither direct endowment nor recognition to the catholic university as a teaching body in its own right. The senate of the royal university consisted of eighteen catholics and eighteen protestants, of whom thirty were appointed by the crown and the rest by convocation. Finance was provided from the church surplus fund and was to be used for university buildings (including examination rooms and a library) and for exhibitions, scholarships, and fellowships. Opposition to the scheme came from the queen's university, but the bill passed quickly through parliament in the summer of 1879 when there was little opportunity to organise protest. In fact the opposition of queen's university men to the supplemental charter in 1866 had brought about the end of their university. Henceforth students attending the queen's colleges were to receive royal university degrees.

The senate of the royal university was given the task of electing twenty-six fellows (the number could be raised to a maximum of twenty-nine) who would be paid a salary of £400 a year (unless they were already receiving payment from public funds, in which case only the difference up to £400 was to be allowed). Thirteen fellowships were allocated to the catholic university, one to Magee College, Derry, and the remainder to the queen's colleges. This gave an endowment of about £6,000 a year to the catholic university. The catholic university itself was renamed University College, Dublin, in 1882, and in 1883 was placed under the management of the Society of Jesus. There was a serious difference of opinion within the catholic hierarchy over the allocation of the catholic university fellowships. William Walsh, vice-president of Maynooth, favoured distributing the fellowships among several of the catholic colleges, in particular the French College of the Immaculate Heart of Mary (Holy Ghost Fathers), Blackrock, whereas William Delany, S.J., the new president of University College, wished to see all the fellowships placed at his college so that it could become a viable university institution. Eventually Delany was successful and Walsh resigned as a senator of the royal university. University College benefited greatly from the allocation of the fellowships, but the relations between Delany and Walsh were to remain cool, and their differences influenced the outcome of the university question.[2]

The Royal University of Ireland existed from 1879 to 1908, and although it had few admirers it served a useful purpose in providing university degrees that the catholic laity could obtain without the special permission of their bishops. The

[1] 42 & 43 Vict., c. 65 (15 Aug. 1879); and see above, p. 27.
[2] See Thomas J. Morrisey, *Towards a national university: William Delany, S.J., 1835–1924* (Dublin, 1983).

demand for higher education began to increase as the 1878 intermediate education act[1] assisted the expansion of secondary schooling. The system of competitive public examinations and exhibitions enabled young men and women to attain university entrance, and the non-residential requirement for degrees kept costs to a minimum. The common university matriculation examination set a national standard and was brought more in line with the new intermediate board examinations. It was broad and consisted of five subjects: English, Latin, mathematics, one foreign language, and experimental physics. Thus Greek became an option only. One of the major achievements of the royal university was its contribution to the higher education of women. Three women's colleges in particular (Alexandra College, Dublin; Victoria College, Belfast; and St Mary's Dominican College, Dublin) prepared students for degrees, and the number of women graduates steadily increased. By 1900 out of a total of 2,173 graduates of the royal university 501 were women, 43 of whom had continued on M.A. courses. The university also introduced innovations in its curriculum and offered not only bachelor's degrees but also master's degrees in medicine, engineering, and music.

However, the queen's colleges were unhappy with the new university. They had ceased to be the three constituent colleges of a single university and lost contact with each other. The presidents of the colleges were named, but not *ex officio*, members of the university senate, and their influence was much diminished. The numbers attending the colleges declined in the 1880s and 1890s, and while the queen's university men, rightly or wrongly, blamed the royal university, others began to criticise the colleges' waste of public money and to demand their closure. In 1884, in response to such criticisms, the lord lieutenant, Earl Spencer, appointed a commission to examine the 'well-being and efficiency of the queen's colleges'.[2] While the majority report acknowledged the generally satisfactory standard of the colleges, the minority report (signed by the chairman, Richard Carton, Q.C., and Rev. Gerald Molloy, D.D., rector of the catholic university) stated that unlike the Belfast college, the colleges at Cork and Galway did not and would not have the support of the local population unless changes in their constitution were made:

These two colleges receive two-thirds of all the endowments expended by the state on collegiate education in connection with the royal university; and yet, taken together, they have educated, during the past year, less than 9 per cent of the undergraduates in arts . . . the students will not go to these colleges because the system of education established there is inconsistent with the religious principles of the people.[3]

The injustice of spending public money on university colleges that were unacceptable on religious grounds to the majority, while denying that majority a

---

[1] Above, p. 540.
[2] *Reports of the commissioners appointed by his excellency . . . to inquire into certain matters affecting the well-being and efficiency of the queen's colleges in Ireland* [C 4313], H.C. 1884–5, xxv, 1–658.
[3] Ibid., p. 103 (MS 111).

publicly endowed university, began to be more widely recognised, and the idea that a separate university might be required for Ulster began to receive recognition once more. In 1867, at the time of the crisis over the supplemental queen's university charter, Thomas Andrews, vice-president of Queen's College, Belfast, had published a masterly pamphlet, *Studium generale*, in which he had argued for the retention of the queen's university and the creation of two independent universities, one for the north and one for the south.[1] In 1885 President Porter of Belfast once again stressed the right of Ulster to have its own university and suggested that the royal university should be replaced by a publicly endowed teaching university for catholics. However, many in Ulster rejected on principle the public endowment of a catholic university, and although in fact the royal university did provide indirect endowment for the catholic university, the idea of three denominational universities in Ireland was generally rejected.

The royal university therefore failed to satisfy the aspirations of either protestants or catholics, and as the century drew to a close the growing demand of the catholic laity for university education made the solution to the university question increasingly urgent. Pressure mounted on both the hierarchy and the government. The hierarchy was divided as to what would be the best solution. William Walsh, who became archbishop of Dublin in 1885 and a key figure in the university debate, favoured the establishment of a catholic college within the University of Dublin, which would have equal status with Trinity College; he looked back to Gladstone's 1873 bill as a lost opportunity. On the other hand William Delany favoured an extension of the royal university to include a central catholic teaching college. Under Delany's leadership University College had developed into a flourishing institution that had attracted the catholic intelligentsia and educated many of the young able men who were to lead the nationalist movement. Men such as Patrick Pearse, Eoin MacNeill, Thomas Kettle, and Francis Sheehy Skeffington, as well as James Joyce, were among its students, and the college Literary and Historical Society became a centre for political and intellectual debate. The college, though cramped and ill-equipped, proved that a catholic university college of high academic standard could be maintained, and the pioneer work of Newman's university could be fulfilled.[2]

Relationships between Walsh and Delany remained cool, and the matter was further complicated by the support among the hierarchy, chiefly from Bishop Edward O'Dwyer of Limerick, for the continuing traditional demand for a fully endowed separate catholic university. In 1889 at the meeting of the hierarchy this traditional demand was reiterated, but as the 1890s proceeded the bishops began to consider various compromises. In 1897, in answer to an invitation from A. J. Balfour, leader of the house of commons, the bishops issued a statement of their position on the university question in which they announced, contrary to what

---

[1] Thomas Andrews, *Studium generale: a chapter of contemporary history* (London, 1867).
[2] See Michael Tierney (ed.), *Struggle with fortune: a miscellany for the centenary of the Catholic University of Ireland, 1854–1954* (Dublin, 1954).

was generally believed, that they were prepared to accept a lay majority on a university governing body, and (conveniently ignoring the charter negotiations of 1868)[1] stated that 'the relative number of laymen and ecclesiastics' had never been a serious issue. The university could be open to all comers and there need be no public endowment for theology. The appointment and dismissal of professors could be entrusted to 'a well chosen board of visitors, in whose independence and judical character all parties would have confidence'.[2] The bishops' position was clarified further by an article published by Bishop O'Dwyer of Limerick in the *Nineteenth Century* in January 1898, and it became clear that the hierarchy was now prepared to accept a university that was *de facto*, if not *de jure*, catholic, in which there would be specific safeguards to protect the religious beliefs of the students. Later that year R. B. Haldane, a liberal M.P. with a keen knowledge of educational matters, came to Dublin at the request of Balfour, and met Walsh, Delany, and others.[3] He drafted a bill to establish two universities in Ireland, both non-denominational but one of which would be acceptable to catholics, the other to protestants. Balfour tested reaction to the bill through a letter to the newspapers, but after a storm of anti-catholic protest the government decided not to move. Despite opposition from the Irish protestant unionist M.P.s, however, the plan of two non-denominational universities was becoming increasingly acceptable to both the catholics and the presbyterians of Ulster.

In 1901 the government, under mounting pressure from both the hierarchy and the Irish parliamentary party, established a royal commission to examine university education in Ireland.[4] The commission, the chairman of which was Lord Robertson, a Scottish lord of appeal, was given the brief of 'inquiring into the present conditions of higher, general, and technical education available in Ireland, outside Trinity College, Dublin, and report as to what reforms, if any, are desirable in order to render that education adequate to the needs of the Irish people'. The work of the Robertson commission, which published its report in 1903, was to be a failure. Evidence was sought from the university of Louvain and from as far as Manitoba and South Australia on the provision for university education for catholics. However, eleven out of twelve commissioners expressed reservations about the proposed solutions. The exclusion of Trinity College and the University of Dublin from the brief caused Walsh to decline to give evidence because he favoured the establishment of a catholic college within the University of Dublin. On the other hand Bishop O'Dwyer of Limerick presented an eloquent and forceful case for the establishment of a separate catholic university, while Delany argued, equally forcefully, for an extended royal university. In the end the Robertson report recommended that the royal university should be reconstituted

---

[1] Above, p. 556.
[2] Statement of the Roman Catholic hierarchy, June 1897 (*Royal commission on university education in Ireland; appendix to the first report* [Cd 826], H.C. 1902, xxxi, 21).
[3] P. J. Walsh, *William J. Walsh, archbishop of Dublin* (Dublin, 1928), pp 549–53.
[4] *Royal commission on university education in Ireland: first* [etc.] *report of the commissioners* [Cd 825, 826, 899, 900, 1228, 1229], H.C. 1902, xxxi–xxxii; *final report* [Cd 1483, 1484], H.C. 1903, xxxii.

as a federal teaching and examining university, of which the queen's colleges and the catholic university college would be constituent colleges. The catholic college was to be eligible to receive state grants, and changes would be made in the constitution of the Cork college to increase local catholic influence, while the future of the Galway college was regarded as doubtful.

The decision to exclude the University of Dublin from the brief of the Robertson commission had been based on fear of strong protestant reaction, such as had occurred in 1873. However, it was clear that no solution could be found to the university question until the issue of Trinity College and the University of Dublin was examined. Walsh had published a statement of his views as a book, *The Irish university question*, in 1897, and following the Robertson commission report the chief secretary, George Wyndham, and his under-secretary, Antony MacDonnell, now consulted Walsh as to the next possible development. Wyndham, whose successful land act was passed in 1903, was anxious to solve the university question. In 1904 Lord Dunraven published in the newspapers a scheme closely based on one drafted by Wyndham and MacDonnell. Dunraven's scheme proposed, as Walsh favoured, the establishment within the University of Dublin of two new colleges: the Queen's College, Belfast, and a King's College, which would be 'well equipped financially, and should be autonomous and residential, with governing bodies selected exclusively on academical grounds'. This scheme would have given the catholics a college equal in status to Trinity College. However, O'Dwyer was strongly opposed to such a measure, and a bitter dispute took place between him and Walsh. Opposition to the scheme mounted from the protestants and it proved abortive.[1]

When the liberals took office in 1906 attention turned once again to the question of the University of Dublin and Trinity College. This time, James Bryce, the new chief secretary, set up a royal commission under the chairmanship of Sir Edward Fry, lord justice of appeal.[2] Bryce himself had chaired the commission on secondary education (1894–5) in England, and had considerable ability. However, the Fry commission was to prove no more successful than its predecessor. Its report, published in 1907, was inconclusive: five members favoured a Dunraven-style solution of an expanded royal university of Dublin; three favoured a Robertson-style solution of an expanded royal university; and one, Stephen Kelleher, the Trinity College representative on the commission, opposed both. Kelleher, a young catholic fellow of Trinity College, supported the non-denominational status of Trinity and saw no need for further colleges to be set up within the University of Dublin. Since 1895 catholic students had been permitted by their bishops to go to Oxford and Cambridge,[3] and a submission presented by 500

[1] See D. W. Miller, *Church, state and nation in Ireland, 1898–1921* (Dublin, 1973), pp 95–112; quoted passage on p. 105.
[2] *Royal commission on Trinity College, Dublin, and the University of Dublin: first* [etc.] *report of the commissioners* [Cd 3174, 3176], H.C. 1906, lvi, 601–766; [Cd 3311, 3312], H.C. 1907, xli.
[3] Above, pp 555, 557, 558.

catholic laymen to the Fry commission indicated that if such provision as a catholic chapel, a catholic theology faculty, and the duplication of the chairs of philosophy and modern history were made, Trinity College would be acceptable. Trinity had already offered some of these to the hierarchy in 1903, but they had been rejected.

The Fry commission, therefore, succeeded only in rousing the strong opposition of Trinity College; and though the college cooperated with the commission throughout, its anger was further increased when, within four days of the publication of the Fry report, Bryce announced his own scheme for university development. He proposed to introduce a bill to create a single national university, which would contain Trinity College, a new catholic college, and the queen's colleges at Belfast and Cork, while Magee College, Derry, Queen's College, Galway, and Maynooth would become 'affiliated' colleges. This revival of '1873' caused Trinity College to organise a defence committee that enlisted support from universities in Britain and presented a protest petition signed by 4,000 graduates. Provost Anthony Traill, whose 'Hands off Trinity' became the committee's battle-cry, ably led the college in the campaign, and he was supported by Queen's College, Belfast (which had no desire to be engulfed in a university dominated by Trinity), and by unionists, who objected to a 'sectarian' catholic college.[1]

Bryce resigned in 1907 to become ambassador in Washington, 'shouting', as Balfour said, ' "No surrender" ', and 'nailing his colours to somebody else's mast'.[2] His successor, Augustine Birrell, fresh from his defeat with the education bill at Westminster, took his time to reconsider the situation. He was much interested in the 1898 plan of R. B. Haldane, who was now secretary of state for war. Haldane's plan had been to create three non-denominational universities in Ireland, each with its own particular religious tradition. During the spring and summer of 1907 Birrell consulted Traill, Walsh, and Delany. Although Walsh still preferred the plan for a catholic college within the University of Dublin, he worked closely with Birrell, and his influence was to be crucial in persuading the hierarchy to accept Birrell's solution. Delany also was deeply involved in advising Birrell, whose plan ensured the future of the St Stephen's Green college.

In March 1908 the Irish universities bill was introduced in parliament.[3] It proposed to establish two new universities in Ireland, the Queen's University, Belfast, and the National University of Ireland. Both were to be non-denominational and state funded. No money was to be provided for theological teaching. The national university was to consist of three constituent colleges at Cork, Galway, and Dublin, the last being a reconstituted University College, Dublin. The Royal University of Ireland was to be abolished and its income of £20,000 a

---

[1] McDowell & Webb, *Trinity College*, pp 368–77.

[2] See *Hansard 4*, clxix, 72–3 (12 Feb. 1907), quoted in Moody & Beckett, *Queen's, Belfast*, p. 384.

[3] Papers relating to the bill, chiefly drafts of revised charters for the colleges, are in H.C. 1908, lxxxvi, 135–232.

year divided equally between the two new universities. In addition Belfast was to receive £18,000 a year, Dublin £32,000, Cork £18,000, and Galway £12,000. Capital building grants of £60,000 to Belfast and £150,000 to the national university and University College, Dublin, were to be provided also. The national university was designed as a secular university that would be acceptable to catholics by a legal protection against interference in religious beliefs, and by the *de facto* if not *de jure* presence of a large number of catholics among the staff and students, and by the opportunity for Maynooth to become a 'recognised college' under the affiliation clause of the act, which provided for the new university 'to give matriculated students of the university, who are pursuing a course of study of a university type approved by the governing body of the university in any recognised college in Ireland under teachers recognised by the governing body for the purpose, the benefit of any privileges of matriculated students of the university . . . including the right of obtaining a university degree'.[1]

The bill was widely debated but it proved acceptable to most parties. Among the bishops O'Dwyer of Limerick alone publicly denounced it because of its lack of provision for religion, the inadequate catholic representation on the senate, and the absence of control of the orthodoxy of the teaching staff. The protestant lobby and Trinity College were satisfied, as the University of Dublin was left unchanged. The *de jure* non-denominational status of the new university ensured the support of English liberal opinion, and the Irish parliamentary party had been privy to the negotiations throughout. Only the Ulster unionists bitterly opposed the bill on the grounds that it was a surrender to catholic interests, and although Belfast was to gain a university of its own, it was at the price of a separate university for catholics. The apparent impossibility of finding a university structure that would embrace both protestants and catholics, and the necessity of finding a separate solution for the north and the south, was seen, correctly, as a forerunner of the political settlement of 1920–22.

The Irish Universities Act, 1908, proved a lasting achievement, and subsequent university development was built on its foundations. Both the National University and the Queen's University were teaching universities, no religious tests were permitted for any appointment, and every professor on taking office was required to sign a declaration 'securing the respectful treatment of the religious opinions of any of his class'. Participation in higher education was encouraged by the empowering of the county councils and boroughs and the intermediate education board to provide university scholarships. Two sets of commissioners, one in Dublin and one in Belfast, were set up to oversee the establishment of the new universities. In Dublin Walsh became the first chancellor of the national university, and a catholic layman, Denis Coffey, became its first president. The Jesuits ended their stewardship of University College in 1909 and members of

---

[1] 8 Edw. VII, c. 38 (1 Aug. 1908); Grainne O'Flynn, 'Archbishop William Walsh and the Irish Universities Act, 1908' in *Proceedings of the Conference of the Educational Studies Association of Ireland* (Limerick, 1980), pp 287–96.

staff moved to appointments in the new college, among them Fr Henry Browne, professor of Greek; Fr Tom Finlay, professor of economics; Eoin MacNeill, professor of early Irish history; and Henry McWeeney, professor of mathematics. Delany, who had become unpopular at University College because of his resistance to the increasing nationalist fervour and to the admission of women, had to be satisfied with becoming a senator of the national university that he had done so much to create.[1] The site of the Royal University of Ireland buildings was used for the new University College, and the old catholic university medical school became part of the new college. Although the college received a building grant of only £110,000 and its premises were inevitably limited, the numbers attending grew each year and by 1920 had reached 1,327. The success of the college proved greater than even its inspirers had hoped.

The main controversy that dominated the national university in its first years was the question of compulsory Irish for matriculation. The influence of the Gaelic League and of the nationalist movement was very strong, and the senate of the university was faced with a difficult issue. Eoin MacNeill and Douglas Hyde of the Gaelic League were the chief advocates of compulsory Irish, and MacNeill, in his pamphlet *Irish in the national university of Ireland* (1909), declared that 'if this university does not learn to love the Irish nation, and to make itself beloved by the Irish nation, it is doomed to sterility'.[2] Delany strongly opposed the introduction of compulsory Irish, which he claimed would exclude many students and make the university less 'national'. The Gaelic League, however, gained the support of the county councils, who declared that they would not grant scholarships to the new university unless the national language was made compulsory for entry. Controversy continued within the university until finally in 1910 the senate agreed that from 1913 Irish would be an obligatory subject for matriculation. University College, Dublin, became a centre of Irish scholarship, and the national university that had been founded to fulfil the needs of catholics also played a crucial role in the creation of a separate national identity.[3]

Maynooth became a 'recognised' college of the national university, and in 1926 the Royal College of Science and the Albert Agricultural College[4] were absorbed into University College, Dublin, thus greatly extending its facilities for the applied sciences, particularly engineering. The national university had seven faculties, including Celtic studies, commerce, engineering, and architecture. A professorship of catholic theology was endowed by the catholic bishops, since the 1908 act specifically forbade the use of public money for religious teaching. The university provided professorships and statutory lectureships in the three

[1] Morrissey, *National university*, pp 244–320.
[2] Eoin MacNeill, *Irish in the national university of Ireland: a plea for Irish education* ([Dublin, 1909]), p. 3; and see above, pp 407–8.
[3] See F. X. Martin and F. J. Byrne (ed.), *The scholar revolutionary: Eoin MacNeill, 1867–1945, and the making of the new Ireland* (Shannon, 1973), pp 90–91, 149, 152, 160–61, 177.
[4] Above, p. 530.

constituent colleges, which despite their differing historical origins came to form a unified and nationally recognised institution. Its federal constitution, similar to that of the National University of Wales (1893), provided support for the two smaller provincial colleges, which the Dublin college soon outpaced.

In Belfast the queen's university also flourished. The city, which had now expanded to a population of nearly 400,000, proved fully capable of maintaining its own university. The majority of its students continued to be protestants, mostly presbyterians, but a considerable number of Roman Catholics began to attend. In 1909 the university established a chair of scholastic philosophy within the faculty of arts,[1] and a catholic dean of residence was appointed. By 1920 one-fifth of its students were catholics, and students for the priesthood from the northern dioceses regularly attended Queen's before going on to Maynooth. The acceptance of Queen's by the catholics in the north was indicative of the increasing demand for higher education and of the hierarchy's goodwill towards the new universities. Queen's became an important meeting place for young protestants and catholics in the north. Closer links with the commercial and industrial life of the city were made by the establishment of a university faculty of commerce and by cooperation with the Belfast Municipal Technical Institute, founded in 1900 by the Belfast corporation technical instruction committee as the central technical school for the city.

TRINITY College and the University of Dublin emerged unchanged by the 1908 universities act, and Trinity continued to enjoy its valued traditions and prestige. Women were admitted in 1904 and formed a small but talented intake. However, the college became increasingly isolated, and the political events of the next decade reinforced this. Relations between Trinity and the national university remained distant, particularly as the new university was faced with the formidable task of trying to establish itself and compete on such meagre resources. The existence of a university that was acceptable to catholics allowed the hierarchy to tighten its ban on Trinity College, and this was done in the years ahead. By 1920 only 20 per cent of Trinity students were catholics. However, Magee College, Derry, made an arrangement in 1909 to send its students for the sophister years to Trinity and to present themselves for a B.A. of the University of Dublin. These students, along with many other Ulstermen who preferred Trinity to Queen's, allowed the college to retain its numbers and an important north–south link even after political partition. The refusal to recognise Alexandra College as a university college for women had been a bitter disappointment to that institution, but the exclusiveness of the University of Dublin to Trinity College had been retained at a high price, and there had been no wish to break it, even in the smallest degree. The college continued to maintain its high standard of scholarship, and new buildings for science were erected, but there was a decline in student numbers,

[1] For the controversy aroused by this appointment, see Moody & Beckett, *Queen's, Belfast*, p. 408.

especially during the first world war, and in 1920 the Geikie commission recommended an annual state grant.[1]

Thus by the beginning of the twentieth century Ireland had three secular universities, each with its own peculiar religious atmosphere. All were non-denominational, offering open access to men and women of all religious persuasions or none. All offered specialised study in the natural sciences and arts, and promoted research and scholarship. The conflict between the secular and religious concept of a university had been resolved, but the Irish university system, like that of the national and intermediate schools, was to be a subtle compromise between church and state, worked out over many years of struggle. The high liberal ideals of equality in civil, religious, and educational rights were tempered by the particularly strong religious traditions in Irish society. Though the universities were secular, each retained its autonomy and was accepted as offering a suitable educational environment for students of a particular religious tradition. This was achieved only by recognising, and therefore reinforcing, the divisions within Irish society.

The creation of the queen's colleges in the 1840s was a major step forward in the modernisation of Irish higher education, for the challenge of these new state colleges was taken up not only by Trinity College, the old established university, but also by the catholic bishops. The hierarchy's efforts in the 1850s to found the Catholic University of Ireland, and their demand that adequate provision for university education for catholics should be a right, were to dominate the Irish educational and political scene for over fifty years. This resulted in the creation of three differing, yet widely respected, university institutions that were to serve Ireland well in the twentieth century.

[1] *Royal commission on the University of Dublin (Trinity College): report of the commissioners* [Cmd 1078], H.C. 1920, xiii, 1189–1220; [Cmd 1167], H.C. 1921, xi, 487–98. For the history of the grant see McDowell & Webb, *Trinity College*, pp 426–8.

CHAPTER XX

Administration and the public services, 1870–1921

R. B. MCDOWELL

THE year 1870 was a momentous one in British administrative history. At the beginning of June an order in council was made declaring that entry to the civil service was, generally speaking, to be by open competitive examination. This decision followed hard on the introduction of qualifying examinations fifteen years earlier, it being asserted in 1869 that while a standard qualifying examination had a considerable inclination to degenerate under the pressure of complaints from unsuccessful candidates, the standards of a competitive examination tended to be automatically maintained. But though it was agreed that open competition was a desirable method of selection, there was some controversy over whether there should be more than one level of competition, in fact whether there should be a single stream or two streams of entry into the service. Robert Lowe, the chancellor of the exchequer in 1870, was a strong upholder of *laissez-faire* in all spheres, and (according to him) a number of other advocates of the system were at first in favour of having one entrance examination geared approximately to a pre-university standard. But they felt that if the competition was limited to one examination at this level the public service, in its contacts with the outer world, would suffer for want of that sort of freemasonry that exists between people who have had a certain degree of education, and in the event the civil service commissioners provided for two levels of examination, the one approximating to a good university degree standard, the other planned to attract candidates with a secondary education. This entrance scheme implied that civil service clerks were to be grouped in two divisions, at first known as higher and lower, later, more tactfully, as the first and second. The first-class clerks from the outset of their careers were members of the administrative grade and were entrusted with duties demanding a considerable degree of initiative and judgement; the second-class clerks—the executive class—performed tasks of a more routine nature; and a third category was recognised, the writers or copyists, the clerical grade, whose members were often unestablished.

This tripartite division became the recognised pattern of the civil service all over the United Kingdom. In the middle 1870s second-division clerks were assigned to nine Irish departments. By 1914 second-division clerks were working in fifteen Irish departments, including the four largest. There were 500 of them employed in Ireland, and with satisfying work reasonably remunerated (in 1914 their maximum salary was £350 per annum) they formed the backbone of the civil service in Ireland. First-division men were employed in only four Irish departments in 1914: the chief secretary's office, the local government board, the national health insurance commission (a recently formed office), and the public record office (by an administrative fluke, that office being treated simply as an equivalent of the English record office, which had earlier become a first-division office). Three experienced Irish administrators, J. B. Dougherty, the under-secretary, Henry Robinson, the permanent head of the local government board, and William Starkie, the resident commissioner for national education, were all convinced in 1914 that Ireland required more first-division men with 'grasp, intelligence, knowledge of affairs that a first [-class] clerk possesses in an eminent degree'.[1] There was however another point of view expressed by T. P. Gill, the permanent head of the department of agriculture and technical instruction, who had entered the civil service after having been a newspaper editor and an M.P. Gill strongly disapproved of having a first division directly recruited by a special examination. 'These men come in', he explained, 'with the notion, from the manner in which they have been brought in, and the privileged position in which they are placed in the service from the first, that they are, so to speak, of superior clay to the men of the other divisions they find in the office.'[2] Gill visualised a civil service of two grades, the higher recruited from the lower. Men would enter the second grade at about the age of 16½, and would compete for places in the first grade at about 19, preparing themselves for the competition partly by attending evening classes and lectures, which Gill thought could be easily arranged in a city such as Dublin, well provided with educational institutions.

Gill was advocating, probably unconsciously, a scheme that had been put forward forty years earlier by a vociferous group, the Irish Civil Service Committee that had been formed at the end of the 1860s when there was widespread discontent among Irish civil servants, who were conscious that they were not as well paid as men performing similar duties in England at a time when the cost of living in Dublin had recently sharply risen. The treasury in 1869 firmly refused 'to entertain application for an increase in salary in a collective form',[3] and three years later D. R. Plunket, a young and able tory M.P., raised the question in the house. This led the treasury to appoint a commission to inquire into the condition of the civil service in Ireland. This commission decided that there had been a noticeable rise in the cost of living in Dublin and agreed in

---

[1] J. B. Dougherty, in *Royal commission on the civil service: second appendix to fourth report of the commissioners*, p. 187 [Cd 7340], H.C. 1914, xvi, 549; Robinson's view on this point appears on p. 201 (MS 563), Starkie's on pp 429–30 (MS 791–2).

[2] Ibid., p. 227 (MS 589).

[3] Quoted in McDowell, *Ir. administration*, p. 44.

recommending certain increases of salary. But the treasury representative was not prepared to accept the principle enunciated by the other two members of the committee (both Irishmen) that the levels of civil service salaries should be the same in London and Dublin. He considered that adequately qualified persons were being secured for civil service posts in Ireland, and that it was for the treasury, having taken into account the local cost of living, to fix salaries. The treasury agreed with him, offering to consider the demands of the officials in any Irish office if submitted through the departmental head. This did not satisfy the Irish civil servants and in 1873 Plunket moved a resolution in the commons in favour of equality of remuneration. It was carried in the face of strenuous opposition from the treasury bench, and from henceforth salaries tended to be on the same level on both sides of the channel.

It was shortly after this victory that the Irish Civil Service Committee had an opportunity to state its views on recruitment. In 1874 a civil service inquiry commission was appointed, and the committee submitted to it a memorandum urging that there should be a single open competitive examination for admission to the civil service, taken at about the age of 16 to 18. Successful candidates would be taken into the service as writers and termed cadets. Some years later the cadets could take 'a kind of honour examination',[1] and on the results of this, combined with reports from superior officers, a certain number would become established civil servants, those who failed having to leave the service. Discussing how candidates could prepare for the second examination, the secretary of the Irish Civil Service Committee (a third-class clerk in the board of public works) explained, apparently to the surprise of the commission, that in Dublin it was possible to take a university degree while working as a civil servant. Promotion, the committee thought, should depend on periodical reports from superiors, with a right of appeal to a standing referee or an independent tribunal.[2]

In spite of its critics, by the close of the nineteenth century the tripartite system survived and provided the conventional pattern for the civil service, but in practice it never covered all classes of civil servants. Many departments even in 1870 required officials with professional qualifications. This was especially so in Ireland towards the close of the century, when the foundation and rapid development of departments such as the land commission, the department of agriculture, and the congested districts board, created a demand for lawyers, engineers, valuators, and many types of agricultural experts and instructors. Many officials had to be selected on their professional qualifications or by limited competition. Indeed, it was even vigorously argued that one important category of official, inspectors of the local government board, could only be recruited by interview and personal knowledge, since it was essential for an inspector to possess qualities that no form of examination could assess—tact and the ability to advise elected bodies.

[1] *First report of the civil service inquiry commission; with correspondence*, p. 233 [C 1113], H.C. 1875, xxiii, 267.
[2] Ibid., pp 232–6, 329–30 (MS 266–70, 363–4).

The introduction of competitive examinations for the civil service had a considerable influence on Irish life. Early in the twentieth century it was said that even in the primary schools there was a constant looking towards civil service requirements, and the objective of the outstanding undergraduate was very often either the administrative class or the Indian civil service. There is another point perhaps worth some attention. Between 1871 and the outbreak of the first world war, government and local service had even numerically become a more significant element in the life of the community. In 1871 the census returns give about 5,800 civil servants, divided into over 4,000 officers and clerks and about 1,200 workmen and messengers. Local government and the law courts seem to have employed about 3,000. Thus the census figures would suggest that central and local government employed about 9,000 persons. The comparable figure for 1911 (when the population had fallen by about a million) was 23,000.

The institution of competitive examinations for the civil service was only one of a number of drastic reforms pushed through by Gladstone's first government, which came into office in 1868, conscious that it had a series of important and urgent tasks to perform. The condition of Ireland was one of the most pressing problems the new government had to face, and its first major measure was a remedy for Irish grievances, the disestablishment and disendowment of the Church of Ireland. This, the greatest act of nationalisation since the dissolution of the monasteries, involved a very large and complex administrative operation and the creation of a new government department, the church temporalities commission.[1]

There was already in existence a department, the ecclesiastical commissioners for Ireland, which during the past thirty-five years had effected a considerable degree of redistribution of income within the church and which by the close of the 1860s had an annual income of about £180,000 and was managing bishops' lands worth about £56,000 a year. But now the church temporalities commission was entrusted with far wider responsibilities. It had to handle an operation involving the nationalisation of property yielding an income of about £580,000 per annum and dealing with thousands of claims for compensation. The commissioners were appointed for ten years, 'a term', Gladstone declared, 'ample and sufficient for all the numerous and diversified purposes' they were expected to perform.[2] The commissioners—Lord Monck, who had been governor-general of Canada; James Lawson, a justice of the common pleas who had a keen interest in economics; and George Hamilton, the permanent secretary to the treasury—took office in the summer of 1869. All three were members of the Church of Ireland; the first two were liberals; Hamilton had been for some years a tory M.P. for the city of Dublin (1836–7) and the University of Dublin (1843–59). They were men of considerable ability, and one of their first acts was to appoint as secretary Denis Godley, an army officer who had been A.D.C. to Monck in Canada and who seems to have been a very able organiser.

---

[1] Above, v, 443, 731–3.   [2] *Hansard 3*, cxciv, 420 (1 Mar. 1869).

The commission took over the duties, staff, and headquarters in Merrion Square of the ecclesiastical commissioners. As time went on, its staff, which was organised in four departments—those of the chief clerk, the registrar, and the accountant, and the collection department—more than doubled, rising from about thirty to nearly seventy, an increase justified by the range of the commission's duties. The commissioners pointed out that though they saved labour by introducing a system of receipt and payment conducted through the Bank of Ireland, very often they had to keep their staff working beyond normal office hours.

On 1 January 1871, the day on which the church ceased to be established, its property became vested in the commissioners. The commissioners had already been busy investigating and determining the value of the interests of the clergy and lay officials (from vicars general to sextons) of the established church, and of the owners of advowsons. Over 8,000 claims were lodged, with 'the applicants being inclined to make the most of their losses', and as the commissioners, 'as guardians of public money, were bound to . . . scrutinise narrowly every charge',[1] there was a large—and in some instances lengthy—correspondence. The commission granted either annuities, which could be commuted for a capital sum, or gratuities. In addition they granted commutable annuities to over 600 presbyterian ministers and paid compensation to Maynooth for the loss of its annual grant. Since well over 90 per cent of the annuitants decided to commute, after a few years strenuous work the commission had disposed of nearly all the personal claims arising under the Irish church act. This work had both administrative and judicial aspects. The commissioners, sitting together, heard appeals against a decision by a single commissioner. Counsel appeared for the appellants and a corpus of case law, published in a textbook that rapidly ran to three editions,[2] was soon built up.

The commission was also responsible for the administration of an immense quantity of property, including the churches, burial grounds, palaces, and glebe houses of the established church. These were quickly disposed of. The churches, with those graveyards that were attached to them, were handed over to the representative body of the Church of Ireland, the other burial grounds were transferred to the poor law guardians, and the ecclesiastical residences were sold, the representative church body having the right of preemption. Finally about one hundred disused or ruinous ecclesiastical buildings 'from architectural character or antiquity worthy of preservation as national monuments' were with a capital sum handed over to the board of works; 'the task of selection was by no means an easy one'.[3] The commission also possessed other forms of property that could

[1] *Report of the commissioners of church temporalities in Ireland for the period 1869–80*, p. 4 [C 2773], H.C. 1881, xxviii, 64.

[2] W. L. Bernard, *Decisions under the Irish church act* (Dublin and London; 1st ed. 1871, 3rd ed. 1873).

[3] *Report of the commissioners of church temporalities . . . 1869–80*, p. 11 (MS 71).

not be dealt with so expeditiously: the tithe rent charge, worth about £404,000 a year, and a large acreage of land scattered throughout Ireland. The Irish church act had provided for the redemption of the tithe rent charge on what seemed easy terms, but the tithe payers, who could deduct the poor rate, which was rising, from their tithe payments, appear to have thought they might obtain even better terms in the future, and, as the commission observed, tithe redemption involved little hope of personal benefit and 'some trouble in making the application and in the subsequent correspondence';[1] with the result that after a decade only about half the tithe had been redeemed.

With about 900 estates and 10,500 tenants the commission was the largest landlord in Ireland, and in handling this complex mass of property it showed vigour and skill. As quickly as possible it converted renewable leases into easily managed perpetuities—a sensible if obvious enough step. It was, however, in managing the yearly and other short-term tenures on its estates that the commission achieved one of its most striking successes. The land purchase clauses had been inserted in the Irish church act with the aim of encouraging the creation of a peasant proprietory. These clauses obliged the commission when selling a holding to offer it first to the occupying tenant, and permitted the commission when selling a holding to the occupying tenant to give credit for up to three-fourths of the purchase price in cash, subject to interest at 4 per cent per annum, to be paid off in not more than sixty-four half-yearly instalments. The commission strove to help its tenants to avail themselves of their rights under the clauses, taking 'great pains to draw up easily intelligible forms of offer and acceptance', and trying to reduce the purchasing tenant's paperwork to the minimum.[2] As a result it was able to sell about 6,000 holdings to the occupying tenants.

In tackling novel tasks involving multitudinous detail the commissioners displayed prodigious industry, drive, and administrative inventiveness. That these virtues can be accompanied by administrative weaknesses was shown by the commission's clash with another great public department. The comptroller and auditor general had been entrusted with the duty of auditing the commission's accounts. He began by claiming that he should receive extra remuneration for doing so. The commission successfully resisted this claim and shortly afterwards the auditor general in his report commented very severely on the commission's conduct of business: there had been delays in executing mortgage deeds, and erasures and alterations of amounts in its accounts, and he also claimed that in the first three years of those accounts he had detected 1,500 to 2,000 errors and irregularities. The commissioners argued in a published report that these criticisms were either mistaken or absurdly exaggerated. They also compelled the auditor general to admit that he had no right to question 'the finality of a decision or order of the commissioners, deliberately made in their character of judges of

---

[1] Ibid., p. 13 (MS 73).   [2] Ibid., p. 15 (MS 75).

law and fact'—though he continued to insist that it was his duty to draw attention to payments that he thought should not have been made. The commission of public accounts tactfully paid tributes to both parties in the dispute, pronouncing that the commission's expenses seemed to be reasonable, and stressing the value of 'an audit so efficient' as that of the auditor general.[1]

Gladstone's other great Irish measure, the land act of 1870, though it made significant changes in the law,[2] did not alter in any way the administrative structure. But a measure that attracted practically no parliamentary attention laid, or at least greatly strengthened, the foundations for a vast amount of beneficial administrative activity. The Irish local government board act of 1872[3] was modelled on the English local government act, passed in the previous year with the aim of concentrating in one department the supervision of the laws relating to public health, local government, and the relief of the poor. The order in which the subjects are listed reflects a growing concern with public health. Irish health legislation was considered in the 1860s to have lagged seriously behind British. In 1865 the Dublin corporation, inspired by Edward Mapother, who had been appointed the first medical officer of health for the city, took vigorous steps to raise standards in Dublin, and in 1866 a public health act extended to Ireland the provisions of a number of important English sanitary measures: the public health act of 1848, the nuisances removal act of 1855, the sewage utilisation act of 1865, and the prevention of diseases acts of 1855 and 1860.[4] Just about the time the act reached the statute book, Asiatic cholera, which had been raging in England, arrived in Ireland, and in these circumstances, the poor law commissioners reported, 'it was not difficult . . . to awaken the boards of guardians to a sense of the important character of their new functions',[5] and both the guardians and the municipalities were active in bringing the act into operation.

The public health act of 1866 was completely overshadowed by the suspension of the habeas corpus act in the same year,[6] but for Ireland the act is very important as a milestone both in public health policy and in the development of local government, the duties of the municipal authorities and the boards of guardians being significantly increased. In 1874 Ireland was divided into urban and rural sanitary districts, the health authority in the former being the municipal governing body and in the latter (which corresponded to a poor law union with its urban districts subtracted) the poor law guardians.

[1] *Report of the commissioners of church temporalities in Ireland . . . to 31 December 1873*, pp 3–4, 12–30 [C 1148], H.C. 1875, xx, 39–40, 48–66; *Second report from the committee of public accounts*, pp viii–ix, H.C. 1875 (336), viii, 96–7.

[2] Above, v, 464–7, 751–4.

[3] 35 & 36 Vict., c. 69 (10 Aug. 1872).

[4] 29 & 30 Vict., c. 90 (7 Aug. 1866), pt II.

[5] *Annual report of the commissioners for administering the laws for the relief of the poor in Ireland*, p. 17 [3877], H.C. 1867, xxxiv, 414.

[6] 29 Vict., cc 1, 119 (17 Feb., 10 Aug. 1866).

The Irish local government board set up in 1872 was composed of the chief secretary who was its president, the under-secretary, a vice-president (the permanent head of the department), and two commissioners. The new department absorbed the powers both of the poor law commissioners and of the lord lieutenant in council under the public health act of 1866 and was entrusted with the duty of auditing the accounts of local authorities. Since it not only possessed advisory and supervisory functions, but in certain matters could initiate and even insist on action, it soon became a very influential force in Irish life.

In its last full session the parliament of 1868–74 passed a major English measure that indirectly but decisively affected an important sphere of Irish life, the judicature act of 1873.[1] This act fused in practice the systems of common law and equity and reshaped the judicial machinery with the aim of facilitating the distribution and dispatch of business. It was generally agreed that it was desirable to extend these changes to Ireland. Lord Cairns, the lord chancellor of Great Britain in the new tory administration, an Irishman and a Trinity College, Dublin, graduate, introduced in 1874 an Irish judicature bill closely resembling the English act. This bill reached the house of commons so late in the session that after securing a second reading it was withdrawn.

At the beginning of the next session it was decided to postpone the Irish judicature bill until the question how the court of final appeal in England should be constituted was finally settled; the Irish judges having emphasised that it was of the greatest importance to maintain uniformity in the administration of a common jurisprudence by preserving the right of a final appeal from Ireland to the same tribunal to which the right of a final appeal from the English courts should lie. In 1875 it was settled that this should be the house of lords, strengthened by the lords of appeal in ordinary, and in 1876 an Irish judicature bill had an easy passage through the lords. But when the bill reached the commons it was attacked by Butt, who argued vehemently that the task of drafting new rules of procedure under the act should not be left to the Irish judges but rather that the rules should be settled in the act. Considering Butt's 'power of obstruction'[2] the Irish solicitor general doubted if the bill would pass, and in fact it did not secure a third reading. When in the next session an Irish judicature bill was for the third time introduced, though Butt's objection was met by a schedule, it seemed as if the bill might again fail to pass as it was opposed by both Biggar and Parnell, and if their opposition was factitious they had plenty of debatable points to fasten on. Biggar, for instance, wanted compulsory retirement for judges at 70, and Parnell argued that the lord lieutenant should appoint the officials attached to the courts on the results of competitive examination—a suggestion that brought Butt to his feet in defence of judicial patronage. In the face of

---

[1] 36 & 37 Vict., c. 66 (5 Aug. 1873); above, v, 471.
[2] *Hansard 3*, ccxxx, 346 (23 June 1876).

pertinacious opposition the government persevered and the bill reached the statute book in August 1877.[1]

The act provided that the courts of chancery, queen's bench, common pleas, exchequer, probate, and matrimonial causes, and the landed estates court should be fused into one supreme court, which could administer law and equity concurrently. It was to have two permanent divisions, the high court and the court of appeal, and by 1914 the pattern was a court of appeal composed of six judges (including the lord chancellor) and a high court with twelve judges. But as four of the members of the court of appeal were also judges in the high court there were only fourteen supreme court judges in all.

The energy with which Gladstone's government interested itself in so many spheres of British and Irish life provoked a reaction, which partly, at least, accounted for the tory victory in 1874. Nevertheless the tories not only improved on their predecessors' work in local government and legal reform, but were responsible for an extension of administrative activity that led to the creation of a new department. Lord Randolph Churchill, the lively-minded and restless son of the lord lieutenant, who accompanied his father to Ireland, rapidly built up a large circle of friends in Irish academic and administrative life. At the beginning of 1878 he published a short, pungent pamphlet on the condition of Irish secondary education: 'waste, mismanagement, and general misapprehension of duties', he wrote, characterised the administration of the educational endowments intended to promote education, and far too few pupils were receiving a secondary education.[2]

In the session of 1878 the government passed an intermediate education act[3] creating an unpaid board whose function was to promote secondary education by holding examinations, granting prizes to successful candidates and paying fees, dependent on the results of the examinations, to managers of schools that complied with certain conditions. In 1878 the government also appointed a commission, the Rosse commission, to inquire into Irish educational endowments, which Lord Carlingford (formerly, as Chichester Fortescue, chief secretary 1865–6, 1868–71) declared 'had been a subject of perpetual complaint and inquiries—the inquiries always to a large extent justifying the complaints—and yet of perpetual inaction'.[4] As a result of the report of the Rosse commission in 1880 an educational endowments commission was set up in 1885, which, during its nine years of existence, effected a vast amount of legal and financial tidying up.[5]

The intermediate education board quickly built up the necessary staff and machinery for conducting its examinations, which soon became an important

[1] 40 & 41 Vict., c. 57 (14 Aug. 1877); above, v, 471–2.

[2] Lord Randolph Churchill, *Intermediate education in Ireland: a letter to Sir J. Bernard Burke* (Dublin, 1878); see Foster, *Churchill*, pp 48–50. Cf. above, pp 524–5.

[3] 41 & 42 Vict., c. 66 (16 Aug. 1878).

[4] *Hansard 3*, ccxc, 14 (4 July 1884).

[5] Above, pp 59, 524.

feature in Irish educational life. There were, of course, critics of a system that relied on examination results to direct the flow of state assistance to secondary education, and in 1898 the members of the board took the remarkable step of constituting themselves a commission of inquiry into the educational merits of their own system.[1] This inquiry emphasised the value of inspection, so that other factors, in addition to examination results, could be taken into account when fixing a school's annual grant. Following this report a new intermediate education act was passed in 1900,[2] increasing the board's membership and allowing it to substitute grants on a capitation basis for the results system. The board then had to fight hard to secure an adequate inspectorate and it carried on the struggle with a spirit that a department headed by permanent officials might not have displayed. The same sturdy independence was again shown in 1906 when the government, under house of commons pressure, pressed the board to raise the status of the Irish language. The board, in the event, yielded on the immediate issue but at the same time firmly asserted that under the 1878 act it had the duty to exercise an independent judgement on educational questions, the government, of course, having the right to dismiss the members who were in opposition to its policy—a drastic way of compelling a department to obey the instructions of the Irish executive.[3]

Disraeli's last administration ended in the throes of the great agricultural depression, which was deepened and emphasised by the disastrous results of a long period of wet weather in 1879.[4] In the August of that year, the Irish local government board asked its inspectors to report on the state of the crops in their districts. After receiving their reports the board warned the guardians to be prepared for an unusual amount of distress and informed the lord lieutenant that the potato harvest was about half an average crop, that there would be a shortage of turf, and that, with a generally poor harvest, unemployment would be widespread. The Irish government warned the treasury that 'in all probability there will be not sufficient resources in the rates to meet the whole of the expected distress', and, stressing that 'the gratuitous distribution of the necessities of life to the able-bodied population . . . would be productive of very serious evils', it suggested that landlords should be encouraged by an offer of loans on favourable terms to undertake productive works. The treasury at once agreed that a very carefully worded circular should be issued by the board of public works reminding the public of the board's lending powers.[5] This was done, but within six weeks it was obvious that the terms on which loans could be obtained were not attractive enough, and early in January 1880 the treasury agreed to the board of public works' granting loans at 1 per cent with a long period for repayment, parliamentary sanction for this being secured two months later in the Relief of Distress (Ireland) Act of 1880.[6] This act also provided for extraordinary baronial present-

[1] Above, pp 525–6.   [2] 63 & 64 Vict., c. 43 (6 Aug. 1900).
[3] McDowell, *Ir. administration*, p. 240; and see above, p. 406.   [4] Above, pp 28–37.
[5] Lords of treasury to——, 14 Nov. 1879 (P.R.O., T.14/51).   [6] 43 Vict., c. 4 (15 Mar. 1880).

ment sessions being held to sanction works and secure loans for them from the board of public works, and empowered the local government board to permit boards of guardians to grant outdoor relief to the able-bodied and to borrow for current expenses from the board of public works. The government also adopted and passed the seed supply bill, introduced by a group of Irish members, which empowered the local government board to permit or direct a board of guardians to borrow from the board of public works to buy seed potatoes or other seed to sell to small farmers.[1]

The government hoped that the problems created by distress could be met by a combination of the poor law machinery and a supply of cheap credit to encourage schemes that would provide employment. Though the management of both forms of relief was left largely to local authorities and private individuals, two government departments played an active part, the local government board and the board of public works. The former, through an augmented staff of inspectors, kept a careful watch on the situation and permitted unions to grant outdoor relief to the able-bodied and to borrow from the board of works. It pressed boards of guardians to appoint additional relieving officers and it dissolved three boards (Belmullet, Swinford, Newport, all in Mayo) that failed to strike and collect sufficient rates. The board of public works was overwhelmed with applications for loans under the terms of the relief act, and by March 1882 it had granted over 1,900 loans to landowners for improvements—drainage, levelling, and fencing. The board, of course, had to examine each application and very often arrange for the plans to be drafted by its own staff, since the applicants were incapable of preparing them. On these tasks the board employed 130 surveyors. The board also approved 2,500 baronial schemes for bridge-building and road-works—300 miles of new roads being laid out—and it made loans to railway and tramway companies and to the local authorities for sixty-eight sanitary schemes—sewerage works, water works, and, in Belfast, public baths. 'Sanitary works', the board recorded, 'have been proceeded with to a larger extent than in any former period, an impetus having been given to them by the desire on the part of local authorities to afford as much employment as possible.'[2] Finally it should be noted that one of the armed services was active in direct relief work. A squadron of small ships (including a frigate and some gunboats), under the command of the duke of Edinburgh, landed tons of food and clothing on the western islands and on parts of the coast that were difficult of access.

By April 1882 the local government board was able to report that 'all . . . temporary [relief] measures have ceased to be necessary',[3] though in a few months it was again concerned about the position in what were generally termed the distressed districts (Connacht, Donegal, Clare, Kerry, and west Cork). The board

---

[1] 43 Vict., c. 1 (1 Mar. 1880).

[2] *Forty-ninth annual report from the commissioners of public works in Ireland*, p. 9 [C 2958], H.C. 1881, xxviii, 583.

[3] *Annual report of the local government board for Ireland*, p. 4 [C 3311], H.C. 1882, xxxi, 12.

kept a careful watch on conditions in the west, appointing extra inspectors for the area, but it concluded that, though there was great poverty, poor law relief could cope with the distress. One remedy was strongly advocated by officials of the board: emigration. The arrears act of 1882[1] authorised boards of guardians to secure loans from the board of public works at very advantageous terms to assist emigration, and about twenty-five unions in the west were at first anxious to use these facilities. The lord lieutenant appointed a small commission to draw up rules regulating the selection and equipping of emigrants, and the local government board set up an emigration committee, which during the years it functioned (1883–4) helped about 25,000 emigrants.[2]

At the close of 1885 it was apparent that in the west of Galway and Mayo the potato crop was again deficient, and during the parliamentary session of 1886, while the home rule debate was in process, an Irish poor relief bill was being passed.[3] It empowered the local government board to permit boards of guardians to grant outdoor relief to the able-bodied, authorised grants totalling £20,000 to a group of unions in the west of Ireland, and provided £20,000 to be spent on public works in the same area. A commission of three (Colonel Thomas Fraser, R.E.; Christopher Redington, a public-spirited country gentleman; and Pierce Mahony, nationalist M.P. for Meath North) was appointed, and planned and executed eighty-one 'works', causeways, roads, and piers in the distressed area. At the same time the local government board authorised boards of guardians in the area to grant outdoor relief to the able-bodied, directing that, if possible, the recipients were to perform task work for eight hours a day, and that no person should be granted relief except on the express authority of the guardians. In fact the guardians, who complained that 'the work of properly investigating the cases of relief would have monopolised more time than they could spare from their own affairs',[4] were extremely lax, at least while they were confident that the government, not the ratepayers, would shoulder the burden. They seem to have simply initialled the lists of names compiled by the relieving officers, one of whom 'furnished a return of persons relieved . . . which exceeded the gross population of the district'.[5] The task work was generally badly planned and carelessly supervised.

When in 1890 the potato crop in the west was again deficient, the chief secretary, Arthur Balfour, decided that the government should keep a tight grip over relief measures. A special department was organised in the chief secretary's office to supervise relief in the west; the local government board had the responsibility of designating the areas where public works should be started and of selecting the persons to be employed on them, and at the close of 1890 Major

[1] 45 & 46 Vict., c. 47 (18 Aug. 1882).
[2] Below, pp 618–19
[3] 49 & 50 Vict., c. 17 (10 May 1886).
[4] *Poor relief (Ireland) inquiry commission: report and evidence*, p. ix [C 5043], H.C. 1887, xxxviii, 9.
[5] Ibid., p. viii (MS 8). For similar experiences during the great famine see above, v, 283–4, 301–5, 325–6.

Peacock of the Royal Engineers was put in charge of the works. Under him and some officers of his corps, seventy-four N.C.O.s and privates acted as foremen and 430 members of the R.I.C. worked as timekeepers. The workers were sometimes partly paid in seed potatoes, and seed potatoes were sent to the islands off the coast, the islanders paying part of the price in work. One scheme, much pressed on the government, was to advance money to tenants to improve their holdings. But the government considered that 'to pay a tenant in a year of distress for doing what he might have done to his own great advantage during his leisure time in past winters would be to teach him the worst of all possible lessons'.[1]

One method of coping with exceptional distress in Ireland was to intensify normal relief measures, using the machinery provided by the poor law and the legislation relating to public works. And, as has just been seen, this approach was employed when and where circumstances seemed to demand it, between 1879 and 1890. But there was widespread and strongly expressed discontent as well as distress in rural Ireland at the beginning of the 1880s, and it was believed by many that radical changes would have to be made in the whole agrarian system. The government proposed at least an immediate or short-term solution of the Irish agrarian problem,[2] the provision of machinery for establishing a 'fair' rent for every holding in Ireland, the land act of 1881 providing that if a landlord and tenant could not agree either party could appeal either to the county court or to the land commission to fix a rent, and this 'judicial' rent was to be payable for the following fifteen years. The land commission was to consist of a judicial commissioner who was to have the status of a high court judge, and two other commissioners. The first three commissioners were John O'Hagan, a Q.C. who as a young man had contributed verse to the *Nation*; Edward Falconer Litton, a Q.C. who had been elected an M.P. for County Tyrone in 1880, the first liberal to sit for that county; and J. E. Vernon, a land agent on a large scale.

The commissioners were empowered to delegate their powers to subcommissions, composed of assistant commissioners. From a decision of the subcommissions there was an appeal to the commissioners, and in certain circumstances there could be an appeal from the commissioners to the court of appeal. The land commission was also empowered to advance money to tenants wishing to buy their holdings and to purchase estates for sale to the occupying tenants. Clearly the commission was entrusted with both administrative and judicial duties, and fortunately there was in existence in 1881 an Irish government department that combined a knowledge of Irish land problems with experience in performing administrative and judicial functions: the church temporalities commission, which had been given a further lease of life by the expiring laws continuance act of 1880 for the purpose of winding up its business. The land commission was empowered to take over the duties, staff, and premises in Merrion Street of the temporalities commission, and Denis Godley, the very efficient secretary of the temporalities

---

[1] 'Relief of distress (Ireland), 1890–91'; draft report (B.L., Add. MS 49823, ff 180–236).
[2] Above, p. 47.

commission, became secretary to the land commission, and from the outset kept a firm grip on the workings of his new department. All important letters had to be submitted to him in draft, and all letters were submitted every day for his signature, 'so that the secretary has a general superintendence of everything that leaves the office'.[1]

Once the commission was constituted, the chief secretary, in consultation with the commissioners, appointed assistant commissioners, who had to be barristers, solicitors, or 'persons possessing a practical acquaintance with the value of land in Ireland'.[2] The legal assistant commissioners were almost always barristers; lay assistant commissioners had generally been land agents and farmers, either owners or tenants (and if tenants, usually large tenants), and had had, generally speaking, a good middle-class education. They were warned by the commissioners that when on circuit they should 'decline absolutely all hospitality offered to them', since it was advisable 'to avoid even the slightest shadow' of 'the suspicion which sometimes arises among the body of the people, that judicial decisions may be influenced by personal and social considerations'.[3] There was another way in which the assistant commissioners were forcibly reminded that they must observe the standards of the Victorian civil service. Godley ensured that their travelling expenses should be carefully controlled. There was 'a clerk whose special business it is to look after these things'. This clerk, Godley explained, 'is always fighting in the way that an audit office would, checking anything that he sees wrong'.[4]

The assistant commissioners were grouped in subcommissions, which were sent out on circuit. At first each subcommission consisted of a legal and two lay subcommissioners, and the practice developed that the two lay commissioners should go out and inspect holdings and then sit with their legal colleague when the subcommission was fixing rents. In 1883 it was decided that each subcommission should consist of one legal and four lay assistant commissioners, and the lay commissioners should be divided into pairs, each of which in turn would sit with the legal assistant commissioners, while the other was out inspecting. Later a subcommission was composed of a legal assistant commissioner and three or four pairs of lay assistant commissioners. The number of assistant commissioners varied. There were 85 in 1883, 21 in 1894, and 103 in 1902. In 1891 as many of the assistant commissioners as the lord lieutenant and treasury, after consultation with the commissioners, thought advisable became permanent civil servants, who were employed as valuators when not engaged in fixing fair rents.

An enormous amount of work was accomplished by the land commission in its early years. Between 1881 and 1883 the subcommissioners settled nearly 62,000 fair-rent cases and the commission disposed of nearly 3,600 appeals. By 1891 the

---

[1] *First report from the select committee of the house of lords on land law (Ireland)*, p. 4, H.C. 1882 (249) xi, 20.

[2] Ibid., p. 21 (MS 37).

[3] Ibid., p. 435 (MS 451).

[4] Ibid., p. 39 (MS 55).

land commission had fixed 157,000 rents. While it was still coming to grips with administering the land act of 1881, the commission had a large if temporary mass of new work thrust on it by the arrears act of 1882.[1] During the land war rents on many estates had fallen into arrears and in 1882 the government decided to remove this embittering issue from Irish agrarian life by a bold stroke. The arrears act provided that all arrears on holdings valued at not more than £30 a year should be cancelled, if the tenant paid the previous year's rent, the land commission paying half the antecedent arrears up to a total of not more than one year's rent. The land commission, which had to investigate applications under the act, employed a large body of local investigators, and assigned a section of its headquarters staff under its assistant secretary, W. L. Micks, later a well known congested districts board official, to handle arrears work. Within a few months 135,000 applications were dealt with.

It was while the commissioners were engaged in the threefold task of building up an organisation and dealing with the problems arising from the land act of 1881 and the arrears act, that they were subjected to severe scrutiny by a select committee of the house of lords on the land laws; this committee in 1883 issued a report that severely criticised the commission for having devised a very faulty procedure for dealing with rent cases, and for having failed to evolve and impose on its subcommissions sound principles for arriving at a fair rent. The commissioners, exasperated, took the extraordinary course of publishing a reply to the report in which they answered its charges seriatim and concluded by accusing the committee of having 'departed from the constitutional principle which protects the grounds of judicial decisions from being investigated by such a body as the committee'.[2]

If the house of lords committee of 1882–3 concluded that the land commission courts were on the whole unfair to the landlord, a house of commons committee in 1894, dominated by liberals and nationalists, reported that the commission had tended to fix rents too high. In fact, the legislature having abstained from enumerating the components of a fair rent, the land commission and its subcommissions had to solve a series of problems involving economic, legal, and even metaphysical issues. Subcommissioners understandably differed in their approach to these problems. An indignant landlord explained to the lords committee of 1882 that the first subcommissioners to sit in County Armagh were moderate in their decisions and as a result 'the tenants on one of the estates thought they did not reduce the rents low enough and they burnt the commissioners in effigy'. The subcommissioners were transferred to another county, and their successors, according to the witness, seemed to be 'under the impression that their mission is to reduce rent'—one of them, who had been an election agent for liberal candidates, having boasted at a meeting that his grandfather had carried a

---

[1] Above, pp 49, 50, 582.
[2] *Observations of the Irish land commissioners upon the fourth report from the select committee of the house of lords*, p. 19 [C 3704], H.C., 1883, lvii, 1011.

pike in '98.[1] Even the judicial commissioner, it was hinted, might not be free from bias. When Edmund Bewley, O'Hagan's successor, was giving evidence before the 1894 committee, Thomas Sexton, then nationalist M.P. for Kerry North, elicited from him that when he was practising at the bar, though he was not employed by any particular class, he had had to conduct more cases for landlords than tenants.

However, from the early 1880s it was apparent that in spite of all the hard work and the legal ingenuity that was devoted to the establishment of fair rents for holdings, this was only an interim solution of the Irish land question. Liberals and tories agreed that it was desirable to establish as quickly as possible a peasant proprietory, the tories' sense of urgency being fortified by their anxiety to secure for the landlords reasonable terms of surrender. The land purchase clauses of the act of 1881 were not a success: a tenant taking advantage of them would probably impose on himself for years a burden greater than his existing rent, and the government introduced in 1884 a bill providing better financial facilities for the purchasing tenant. It failed to pass but in 1885 Edward Gibson, Baron Ashbourne, a very able lawyer who was lord chancellor of Ireland in Salisbury's tory administration, introduced a land purchase bill, which, he pointed out, had 'this great recommendation—that it is a non-party question'. The Ashbourne act[2] provided that the whole of the purchase price should be advanced to the tenant and that the purchase branch of the commission's activities should be managed by two additional commissioners, termed the estate commissioners—'gentlemen', Ashbourne hoped, 'of energy, of capacity, of resource, and of loyal intentions'.[3] The first two estates commissioners were Stanislaus Lynch, who after having been educated at Stonyhurst and Trinity College, Dublin, had been for over ten years registrar of the landed estates court, and John MacCarthy, a Cork solicitor and historical writer who had been a nationalist M.P. for Mallow (1874–80) and a legal subcommissioner under the land act. The estates commissioners on taking office appointed examiners of title and a dozen local inspectors. In 1891 the commission was made perpetual and in 1903 it was remodelled, so that ultimately it would be composed of two judicial and three estates commissioners (one of whom would also be a land commissioner). In 1891 the lord chancellor was empowered to remove any commissioner, except a judicial commissioner, for misconduct but the removal order was not to come into operation if either house of parliament objected to it. The staff of the land commission grew from about 120 in 1885 to 560 in 1914.

The defeat of home rule in 1886 and the results of three out of the four next ensuing general elections meant that for nearly twenty years the unionists were in power. Shortly before this era of unionist rule began, Salisbury had summarised the unionists' Irish policy as twenty years of 'government that does not flinch,

---

[1] *Second report from the select committee of the house of lords on land law (Ireland)*, pp 161, 168–9, H.C. 1882 (379), xi, 715, 722–3.

[2] 48 & 49 Vict., c. 78 (14 Aug. 1885).

[3] *Hansard 3*, ccxcix, 1041, 1047 (17 July 1885); and see above, pp 59, 69.

that does not vary'.[1] But the unionists' Irish policy had another aspect: it was a tenet of the unionist creed that Irish grievances could be removed and Irish prosperity promoted under the union. The pursuance of this policy led in the administrative sphere to the reshaping of the land commission, to a remodelling of local government, and to the formation of two new departments, the congested districts board and the department of agriculture and technical instruction.

During the parliamentary sessions of 1887–8 the government was mainly concerned with maintaining law and order in Ireland, though the land act of 1887[2] strengthened the financial resources of the estates commissioners. But the debates on poor relief and the reports of the local government board for about twelve years had all tended to emphasise one feature of the Irish situation, that acute distress was largely a localised problem. There were, it was obvious, areas in the west that were either densely populated or where, even if the population was scarce and scattered, it was large in relation to the productivity of the soil. As a result very many farming families in the west of Ireland were living on holdings that even in a good year failed to provide a subsistence, the deficiency being met by the earnings of migratory labour, fishing, and kelp-burning. It was clear that, if conditions in these special areas were to be improved, state intervention on an extensive scale was called for. In 1889 an important Irish light railways act[3] provided that if the lord lieutenant declared that a light railway between certain places would contribute to the development of the fisheries or other industries of the area, then the company undertaking it could secure a grant from public funds; the board of works being entrusted with the duty of examining the engineering and economic aspects of the proposal. By 1895 thirteen lines had been completed under the act, all but one in the west. In 1891 a new department, the congested districts board, was constituted, responsible for improving economic conditions in what were termed the congested areas.[4] The term 'congested' was somewhat misleading. A congested district simply meant an area where acute poverty prevailed, defined in a ratio between the population and rateable value of poor law electoral divisions, which enabled the government to delimit as it wished the area in which the board was to function. In 1891 the congested districts, so defined, stretched from Donegal to west Cork, including about one-sixth of the area and one-ninth of the population of Ireland. The board was composed of two *ex officio* and eight paid members and from the outset considered it possessed a remarkable degree of independence, though its staff were civil servants and its accounts were audited by the comptroller and auditor general. Balfour, in a memorandum of 1892, later referred to as the board's charter of freedom, laid down that it was subordinate to the chief secretary's office, and it corresponded directly with the

---

[1] Speech at St James's Hall, London, 15 May 1886; quoted in *Annual Reg., 1886*, p. [181]; and see above, p. 86.
[2] 50 & 51 Vict., c. 33 (23 Aug. 1887).
[3] 52 & 53 Vict., c. 66 (30 Aug. 1889).
[4] Above, pp 73, 283–7.

treasury and other departments. About fifteen years after it was constituted Balfour and his brother Gerald explained to the royal commission on congestion that the board was 'hardly a government department in the full sense of the word' since it was not under a minister responsible to parliament, and that though the chief secretary was a member (and always chairman) he could only be held responsible for the actions of the board in which he concurred.[1] In practice finance proved the main limitation on the board's activities, the treasury emphatically reminding the board in 1908 that it must keep its work within the limits set by its resources.

The board was empowered to assist emigration and migration, to supply seed, and to assist the development of agriculture and industry; its function, Balfour explained, being expressed deliberately in the widest possible phraseology so that the board would not feel itself hampered in carrying out anything that might become desirable. Balfour regarded the board

as being in the nature of a machinery for giving paternal assistance to congested districts which were too poor to help themselves . . . , acting as a very wealthy and benevolent landlord might act towards an estate . . . in which he found people sunk in very great difficulties, from which they were quite incapable of extricating themselves. Evidently you would not desire to trammel the action of such a landlord by—I won't say red tape, for that is rather an offensive word, but by rules and precedents which are very proper limitations to the actions of a great government department.[2]

He added that he would view with reluctance a policy that put the whole of Ireland under such a paternal form of administration.

From the beginning the board promoted a number of schemes that would have appealed to an improving landlord. It took steps to improve the breeds of livestock and poultry. It tried to persuade farmers to spray their potatoes. It distributed seeds and planted trees. It encouraged the fisheries, setting up curing stations, providing better boats, and striving to improve market facilities. It subsidised a carpet factory and encouraged cottage industries. But soon it began the work that in time dwarfed all its other activities, the purchase of estates for resale to the tenants. This was not merely a financial operation, as the board aimed at improving estates and rearranging holdings before completing the sale. The congested districts board was thus working along the same lines as the land commission, and by the beginning of the twentieth century they were joined by a third large department, the department of agriculture and technical instruction, which began promoting the development of Irish agriculture.

In August 1895 Horace Plunkett, well known for his work for agricultural cooperation, wrote a letter to the newspapers suggesting that since it was 'good policy and good patriotism' to work for 'the material and social advancement of

---

[1] *Royal commission on congestion in Ireland: appendix to the fifth report*, pp 4, 9 [Cd 3630], H.C. 1907, xxxvi, 302, 307.
[2] Ibid., p. 1 (MS 299).

Ireland', a group of politicians drawn from all parties, together with 'practical Irishmen', should meet to discuss Irish measures that were uncontentious but which, if not thrashed out in advance by experts, 'would never ride through the crowded waterways into legislative anchorage'.[1] Plunkett in his letter mentioned two questions for discussion—an agricultural board and the improvement of technical education. A powerful committee composed of both nationalists and unionists, known as the recess committee, met and drafted a report that urged the creation of a department of agriculture and industries, with a minister responsible to parliament, aided by a consultative council, which would keep him in touch with Irish opinion.

This report was received sympathetically by the government, though there was some delay in establishing the new department since it was felt local government reform should have precedence. However, in 1899 Gerald Balfour, the chief secretary in Salisbury's third administration, carried a bill setting up a department of agriculture and technical instruction.[2] Besides being responsible for the organisation of technical and agricultural education, the new department took over from other departments the collection of agricultural statistics, the prevention of animal and plant disease, and the encouragement of fishing. It was also entrusted with the supervision of the national museum, the national library, and the botanic gardens in Dublin. To keep the department in touch with the Irish public three semi-representative advisory bodies were set up in connection with it: the agricultural council, the agricultural board, and the board of technical instruction. The council was composed of persons nominated by the county councils and the department in the ratio of two to one; the agricultural board was composed partly of persons elected by the council of agriculture, and partly of nominees of the department; the board of technical instruction was composed of persons nominated by local authorities, by the council of agriculture, by the intermediate education board, by the board of national education, and by the department. In addition to their advisory functions the two boards could veto certain forms of expenditure by the department.

By the beginning of the twentieth century there were thus three important government agencies in Ireland responsible for agricultural development—the department of agriculture and technical instruction, the land commission, and the congested districts board. Their functions tended to overlap, the last two being both engaged in land purchase, and though in 1903 the congested districts board transferred its agricultural schemes to the department, it continued to engage in activities impinging on the department's work. Plunkett, when discussing the work of the congested districts board, was quick to point out that the creation of a peasant proprietory should not proceed without regard to the optimum size of holding, a problem that of course involved an almost philosophical

[1] *I.T.*, 28 Aug. 1895; and see Trevor West, *Horace Plunkett: cooperation and politics* (Gerrards Cross, 1986), pp 44–5; and above, pp 87–91, 530–31.

[2] 62 & 63 Vict., c. 50 (9 Aug. 1899); above, pp 89–90, 282–7, 478–80, 530–32.

question—what is a subsistence? Thus it could be argued that the department of agriculture and technical instruction had a distinct interest in the problems of land purchase and resale.

Administrative tidiness definitely suggested that the congested districts board should be abolished and its functions divided between the other two departments. Sir Antony MacDonnell, an experienced and somewhat autocratic administrator who favoured the abolition of the board, managed as under-secretary (1902–8) at least to curb its independence, treating it as an ordinary department, subordinate to the chief secretary's office. But in 1909, after MacDonnell had left Ireland, the board's sphere of action was considerably enlarged and its powers in respect of land purchase increased. The government also intended to reconstruct the board on lines that would certainly have strengthened its autonomy. The land purchase bill of 1909 provided that the board was to be composed of nineteen members: three *ex officio*, two paid, five appointed, and nine representing local authorities in the congested areas. But the house of lords set to work, as Birrell put it, to 'demolish' the bill, and by the time it reached the statute book the representative element on the board had disappeared.[1]

The unionists tackled another major Irish administrative issue, local government. Local government reform, it could be argued, accorded with the unionist principle that Ireland should be encouraged to develop institutionally along English lines, and it would give Irishmen greater opportunities of managing their own affairs—within limits.[2] Certainly the pattern of Irish local government by the close of the nineteenth century urgently demanded drastic reorganisation. The counties were still governed by the grand juries and the baronial sessions. There were also the poor law unions, the urban and rural sanitary authorities, the dispensary managing committees, and the towns. There were in Ireland no fewer than 120 towns with local government. Eleven of these were governed under the provisions of the municipal government act of 1840; six under the lighting of towns act of 1828; ninety under a revised version of this act, the towns improvement act of 1854; and twelve under special acts.[3] Carrickfergus, the remaining example, was administered by a commission, appointed temporarily under the act of 1840 and made a permanent body in 1843.[4] The municipal authority in each type of town had slightly varying administrative functions and (except in the case of Carrickfergus) rating powers. The Carrickfergus commissioners were not empowered to impose a rate, but this fortunately did not matter because Carrickfergus possessed a considerable amount of municipal property.

Not only was the system confusing and unnecessarily intricate but one of the most prestigious of the local authorities, the grand jury, was not an elected body,

---

[1] 9 Edw. VII, c. 42 (3 Dec. 1909); above, pp 124, 275.

[2] Above, p. 89.

[3] 3 & 4 Vict., c. 108 (10 Aug. 1840); 9 Geo. IV, c. 82 (25 July 1828); 17 & 18 Vict., c. 103 (10 Aug. 1854).

[4] 6 & 7 Vict., c. 93 (24 Aug. 1843), sect. xxvi.

and in so far as it could be considered a virtually representative one, it represented the larger landlords, a rapidly declining class. What is surprising is that the grand juries managed to retain their administrative powers so long. Towards the close of the 1860s, witnesses before a house of commons committee on the grand jury laws urged that elected county councils should be constituted, and in the early 1880s, as might have been expected, the nationalist M.P.s launched an attack on the grand jury system of county government, T. M. Healy arguing that

the best way to train the people to habits of law and order was to enable them to govern themselves, to infuse into them a feeling of responsibility, to make them feel they were a part of the body politic, that they were within the pale of the law, and that if they were taxed they were represented.[1]

But it seems to have been accepted that the grand jury administration was economical, and the critics of the system found it hard to cite specific instances of gross maladministration—though they asserted that partiality was displayed in appointing county officers and in assessing damages in malicious injury cases. In any event, during the 1880s home rule and land legislation pushed other issues into the background.

Towards the close of the session of 1891 Balfour informed the house of commons that in the following session the government hoped to introduce an Irish local government bill based, broadly speaking, on the same principles as those on which the English and Scottish acts had been framed. And in the session of 1892 he introduced a measure reorganising Irish local government. It was to set up elective county and baronial councils to take over the administrative and fiscal duties of the grand juries and baronial sessions, and the functions of the rural sanitary authorities. Balfour was aware that this change from oligarchical to popular government would alarm conservatives, and he provided 'for a condition of Irish society, which has little or no parallel out of Ireland'[2] by incorporating in the measure a number of safeguards. The electoral districts were to be large in size and to return a number of members, and as each elector would have as many votes as there were members, minorities could secure representation. It was also provided that twenty ratepayers could petition for the removal of a council, on the grounds that it had acted illegally, corruptly, or oppressively. The petition would be tried by two high court judges, and councillors found guilty would be replaced by persons nominated by the lord lieutenant. All capital expenditure undertaken by the new authorities was to be sanctioned by a committee presided over by the high sheriff, composed of seven representatives of the county council and seven representatives of the grand jury.

The nationalists attacked the safeguards as insulting and humiliating, and at the close of the session the bill, which had only reached a second reading, was withdrawn. But after their return to office in 1895 the unionists decided again to

[1] *Hansard 3*, cclxix, 563 (12 May 1882).   [2] *Hansard 4*, i, 720 (18 Feb. 1892).

tackle the problem of Irish local government. In 1897 Balfour made a new approach to the question. He suggested that instead of enacting 'elaborate and irritating precautions'[1] they should radically alter the incidence of Irish local taxation, the treasury in the future paying half the poor rate and half the county cess. Since the poor rate was the responsibility of the landlord and the county cess that of the tenant, two very important groups in Ireland were satisfied, and the local government bill introduced in the following session had, not unexpectedly, a good reception.

The local government act of 1898[2] divided Ireland into thirty-three administrative counties (North and South Tipperary having separate status) and six county boroughs (Dublin, Belfast, Cork, Limerick, Derry, and Waterford). The governing body of the county was elected by the local government electors, that is to say the parliamentary electors, together with those persons who but for being peers or women would have been parliamentary electors. The administrative and fiscal powers of the grand jury were transferred to the county council, which became the sole authority for levying and collecting local taxation, the local authority for technical instruction, for lunatic asylums, and for the appointment of coroners, and half the joint managing committee of the county infirmary. The administrative counties were divided into urban and rural districts, to whose councils were transferred the powers of the local sanitary authorities and the duty of maintaining roads. In each poor law union the urban and district councillors elected within the union formed its board of guardians (the *ex officio* guardians being abolished) and the powers of the dispensary managing committees were transferred to the guardians. In short a two-tier system of local government, with a division of duties between the county and the district, was established over most of Ireland. The exception to this was the county boroughs, their governing bodies having the powers both of an administrative county and an urban district council.

The local government act ran to 124 clauses and was praised as a model of draftsmanship: 'the whole of Ireland', an able young barrister declared, 'topographical, municipal, rural, judicial, political, and social, seems to have been clearly and constantly before the mind's eye of the draftsman'.[3] Nevertheless before the bill could come into operation a vast amount of detail had to be filled in and innumerable points settled. The local government board tackled this great administrative task energetically. It supervised the preparation of the electoral register. It issued 119 orders altering the boundaries of poor law electoral areas to make them coincide with municipal areas, and another series of orders altering county boundaries to form satisfactory rural districts. The board also settled the electoral divisions in the counties, laid down the procedure for local elections, and appointed returning officers and deputy returning officers (the sub-sheriffs and

[1] *Hansard 4*, xlix, 1042 (21 May 1897).
[2] 61 & 62 Vict., c. 37 (12 Aug. 1898).
[3] W. J. Johnston, 'The coming changes in Irish local government' in *Stat. Soc. Ire. Jn.*, x, pt 78 (1898), p. 368.

clerks of unions), and it proudly reported that although on 6 April 1899 4,000 district elections took place in Ireland, 'there was no hitch of any kind'. The board also prescribed the forms in which the accounts of the new local bodies were to be kept—admittedly they were 'complicated', but necessarily so if statutory requirements were to be complied with. It settled the salaries to be paid to existing county officers, taking into account the increase or diminution of their duties. Finally, before the new councils met the board prepared a circular of instructions, outlining their duties as concisely as possible, which, it suggested, the newly elected members ought to 'carefully peruse'.[1]

Understandably the staff of the local government board had to be considerably increased. From a strength of about 77 in the 1890s it bounded up to 117; by 1914 it numbered about 220. And for the difficult and exceptionally busy period of 1898–1903 an additional commissioner, Richard Bagwell, was appointed. Bagwell, a diligent and impartial historian, was an uncompromising unionist and a leading country gentleman, and his appointment was probably meant in a small measure to reassure supporters of the old regime. Even with an expanding staff the department, when it was bringing the local government act into operation, was hard pushed, officials working sometimes up to midnight.

During the busy years 1899 to 1903 the board was subjected to severe parliamentary criticism by the nationalists. It was actuated, John Dillon declared, by 'the spirit of constantly desiring to dictate, interfere, and meddle'.[2] Its circulars, it was said, were marked by 'autocratic insolence' and the officials were alleged to have ridiculed and sneered at a district councillor 'because, perhaps, his grammar is not just what it ought to be'.[3] One nationalist M.P., who was a country gentleman, even compared the new system in one respect unfavourably with the old. The grand jury, he pointed out, had managed to do all the county business in eight meetings a year, but the new county council had met fifty-two times in a year. The board was strongly attacked for, generally speaking, raising salaries when fixing the remuneration of existing county officers.[4] Dillon indeed voiced the suspicion that the board was taking this course with the aim of discrediting local government by raising the rates. (Probably indeed a good deal of genuine irritation was aroused by the realisation that old grand-jury appointees were being better paid under the new local authorities than in the past). To some extent these attacks on the board reflect the hostility of Irish nationalists to Westminster legislation and the Irish executive. They also, of course, represented the almost automatic resistance that local elective bodies are likely to show to centralised, bureaucratic control. And it may be added that courts twice quashed decisions of the local government board under the act of 1898 as being based on

---

[1] *[Twenty-eighth] annual report of the local government board for Ireland*, pp i, iv, 319 [Cd 338], H.C. 1900, xxxv (no MS pagination).

[2] *Hansard 4*, lxxxiii, 1129 (24 May 1900).

[3] Ibid., 1190 (24 May 1900).

[4] Ibid., 1162, 1186 (24 May 1900).

a mistaken interpretation of the law—much to the gratification of the board's critics.

But if the magnitude of the operation is taken into account, the great revolution in Irish local government was accomplished remarkably swiftly and smoothly. And if a self-congratulatory note is clearly discernible in the board's reports, a measure of official self-satisfaction is forgivable. During the early years of the twentieth century relations between the board and the local authorities seem to have been remarkably harmonious. If in the board's attitude there was a trace of paternalism, it was also very pleased with the way in which the system was working. The board settled disputes arising between counties and districts over local taxation and the maintenance of roads. It put considerable pressure on councils to make rate collectors complete their collections on time, and when in 1912 the general body of rate collectors asked for a month's extension for the completion of their collections because, owing to an outbreak of foot-and-mouth disease, many ratepayers were having difficulty in selling stock, the board firmly refused to grant it on the grounds that it would complicate financial administration—and most of the rates were lodged on time. The board was pleased by the efforts of local authorities to improve their roads; it encouraged them to use direct labour under thorough and continuous supervision; and it approved of loans for the purchase of steamrollers—the board in the years immediately preceding the first world war strongly advocating steamrolling.

The long era of unionist government was a period of administrative change in Ireland comparable to the whig administrative revolution of the 1830s.[1] Between the resignation of Balfour's government in 1905 and the end of the war in 1918 the Irish administrative pattern altered little. The social reform legislation introduced by the liberals led to the creation in 1912 of a new department, the Irish national health commission. Under the labour exchange act of 1909,[2] labour exchanges were opened in Dublin and Belfast; and the old age pensions act of 1908[3] added, at least for a time, to the work of the heavily burdened local government board. The act provided that county councils and urban districts would appoint committees, which would determine on claims to pensions, with a right of appeal to the local government board. By March 1910 the board had received 21,000 appeals, the administration of the act being extremely difficult in Ireland where the statutory registration of births had not begun until 1864 and where it was very hard to determine the 'means' of the occupier of a small holding, especially if, as was customary, on becoming elderly he handed it over to his son. A great effort had to be made to distinguish between the bona fide transfer of a farm and a transfer made merely for the purposes of securing a pension.

It was, however, generally accepted at the beginning of the twentieth century that the administrative machinery in Ireland, 'the queerly conceived and oddly

[1] Above, v, 206–7, 245–6, 552–3.   [2] 9 Edw. VII, c. 7 (20 Sept. 1909).
[3] 8 Edw. VII, c. 40 (1 Aug. 1908); above, p. 124.

arranged departments',[1] required to be drastically reshaped. It was composed of a number of offices and commissions created to deal with specific problems, rather than a group of major departments each responsible for a large administrative area. Some of the unpaid boards displayed considerable independence when dealing with the Irish executive, which was theoretically responsible for coordinating administrative activity. The burden on the chief secretary was too heavy. James Ian Macpherson, one of the last holders of the office (1919–20), declared that when answering questions in parliament 'all that I can do is to stand up and read a carefully prepared answer, prepared by somebody else, as best I can',[2] and Birrell, with typical amiable insouciance, remarked that so far as the intermediate education board was concerned his only authority was that 'the members occasionally retire or die, and the Irish government appoints their successors'. Generally speaking, he explained, the chief secretary was 'an unfortunate mendicant', acting as the go-between 'in the endeavour to satisfy the insatiable demands of his country upon the great and wealthy British treasury'.[3]

Nationalists continually denounced the cumbersome complexities of the system and claimed that under home rule extensive economies could be effected, especially in the sphere of law and order; and the royal commission on the civil service stated in 1914 that administrative functions in Ireland should be redistributed amongst a reduced number of government departments. Lord MacDonnell (the former under-secretary), the chairman of the commission, published a scheme for grouping the Irish services under a dozen ministries, and by the summer of 1914 a major reorganisation of the Irish departments was clearly impending with the home rule bill, which would ultimately place all 'Irish services' under the control of the Irish parliament, moving towards the statute book. But before the bill received the royal assent the United Kingdom was at war and all administrative issues were overshadowed by the need to mobilise the manpower and economic resources of the community in support of the war effort.

A large number of Irish civil servants enlisted or were transferred to war work. Sixteen of the board of works staff joined the forces, and a commissioner of the board and thirteen of its staff were transferred to the ministry of munitions. Of the clerks employed by the national education board seventeen enlisted, and out of the staffs of the local government board, land commission, congested districts board, and department of agriculture, at least 375 members joined up. And by the close of 1915, thirty-three inspectors and over 500 other ranks of the R.I.C. and the D.M.P. were in the army or navy.[4]

From the beginning of the war expenditure on purposes not directly connected with the war effort was severely scrutinised. The board of works restricted its local loans, advancing money only for projects that could not be postponed without danger to public health, and it tried to keep its work on government buildings

---

[1] W. S. Churchill, *Life of Lord Randolph Churchill* (2 vols, London, 1906), ii, 77.
[2] *Hansard 5 (commons)*, cxiv, 1535 (3 Apr. 1919).   [3] Ibid., xxxviii, 443 (8 May 1912).
[4] Ibid., lxxv, 1479 (15 Nov. 1915).

down to the minimum required for maintenance. Admittedly it was discovered by the committee on accounts that in 1915 the board had extensively refurbished the viceregal stables as heated garages. But, the board explained, 'when you are dealing with a lord lieutenant you are not under quite ordinary circumstances'.[1] The local government board refused to sanction loans for roads. The land commission, owing to rising costs, found it difficult to finance land purchase and therefore was able to reduce staff. The R.I.C. was allowed to fall to 9,500 by 1915 and had barely risen above that number by the end of 1917, despite the changed political context. The national gallery lost its annual grant of £1,000 for pictures; the intermediate education board kept its expenditure on printing and stationery below the pre-war level, while pressing for increased funding on the same scale as the rest of the United Kingdom. The national education board was informed by the treasury that the board of works had been instructed not to undertake any school building, except where in default of building work the school would have to be closed, it being emphasised that in these exceptional cases treasury sanction must in each case be secured in advance; and expenditure on school buildings fell from £58,000 in 1915 to £7,170 in 1917–18. The board of national education was most unfortunate on this occasion. The viceregal commission on primary education had in January 1914 recommended better conditions of employment, including higher salaries for teachers. The board had accepted its recommendations and in July 1914 had forwarded its proposals to the Irish government, only to learn that, owing to the obvious need for economy and the restrictions on all new development, these proposals would not receive treasury sanction. However, with the cost of living rising rapidly, national school teachers (on salaries which it was agreed in 1913 were unsatisfactory) were in a perilous position; and in 1917 it was decided to introduce a new salary structure, the 'Duke scheme', on which later war bonuses were paid.

In 1915 the committee of financial experts, appointed by the treasury to investigate the possibility of retrenchment in government expenditure, decided, as Birrell put it, 'to have a battue on the Irish estimates'.[2] The committee asked three Irishmen—Sir John B. Lonsdale, unionist M.P. for mid-Armagh; Walter Kavanagh, a public-spirited country gentleman; and J.P. Boland, nationalist M.P. for south Kerry—to join them when they were surveying the Irish departments; but as the nationalist party had decided not to nominate a representative, Boland resigned. The committee received a number of statements from Irish departments outlining the economies they were making. These statements show that the departments were certainly trying to effect economies;[3] and even the treasury remembrancer, Maurice Headlam, who was expected to keep a critical eye on

[1] *Report from the committee of public accounts . . .*, p. 53, H.C. 1917–18 (123), iii, 85.

[2] Birrell to Nathan, 16 Nov. 1915 (Bodl., Nathan papers, 449).

[3] The committee found that savings had been made, but major economies would require legislation that was 'likely to prove contentious' (*Second report of the committee on retrenchment in the public expenditure* [Cd 8139], H.C. 1914–16, xxxiii, 376).

departmental expenditure, could not suggest very large savings, though he pointed out that the department of agriculture and technical instruction could be better organised (he thought it had too many watertight compartments) and he took the opportunity to deliver an attack on an area where the administrative traditions of an earlier age were still lively—the offices attached to the superior courts. He suggested the staff should be reduced by introducing a retiring age of 70 (eight or nine members were over 80) and insisted that officers should work a seven-hour day.[1]

Two departments greatly expanded their activities during the war, the local government board and the department of agriculture. At the outbreak of the war it was believed that unemployment might present a serious problem and in fact in the late summer of 1914 a number were thrown out of work by the abrupt termination of the tourist season, a sudden falling-off of orders in the building trade, uncertainty in the north over supplies of flax from Russia, and a decline in traffic at the port of Dublin owing to ships being commandeered for war purposes. The local government board responded quickly to the emergency. In August 1914 it informed the county and borough authorities that they should immediately constitute distress committees under the unemployed workmen's act of 1905[2] and representative committees composed of representatives of the local authorities, trade unions, and philanthropic agencies. The distress committees were to try to find vacancies that the unemployed might fill; the representative committees were to distribute relief from a relief fund set up for the United Kingdom. The representative committees in the first few months of the war relieved over 7,000 persons, a figure that shows that recruiting and the war industries (in which agriculture should of course be included) were soon making very heavy demands on the Irish labour market. The new labour exchanges played an important part in moving Irish labour to England and in the spring of 1915 the local government board circularised local authorities pointing out that the treasury had decided to restrict their borrowing powers within the narrowest limits, reminding them of the needs of recruiting and war manufactures and suggesting that they should economise labour as far as possible.

The local government board, however, remained concerned about employment in Dublin and female employment in the south of Ireland. It encouraged the formation of two central advisory committees for female employment, one for Ulster and one for the other three provinces. The Ulster committee soon ceased to function but the southern committee secured contracts for clothing from the war office, which afforded employment to women in a number of urban centres. The local government board also pressed the ministry of munitions to give

---

[1] Headlam ascribed the lack of further retrenchment to the government's unwillingness to oppose Redmond (Maurice Headlam, *Irish reminiscences* (London, 1947), pp 69–70, 75–6, 156–7); but it was also perceived that reduced spending in Ireland would be politically counterproductive (O'Halpin, *Decline of the union*, pp 111–12).

[2] 5 Edw. VII, c. 18 (11 Aug. 1905).

opportunities for war work to Ireland. The ministry opened five shell factories in Ireland, at Dublin (two), Cork, Galway, and Waterford. The decision to establish these factories, the permanent secretary to the ministry explained to the committee on production, was a political one rather than an economic one, to allow Ireland to participate in the general production of shells. The local government board also tried to encourage food production by sanctioning the acquisition of land for allotments and the making of loans for the purchase of seed by local authorities. Two other duties unexpectedly devolved on the board. In 1916 for about ten days after the insurrection a committee under the chairmanship of the vice-president of the board was responsible for securing foodstuffs for Dublin, and throughout the war it supervised the care of Belgian refugees in Ireland. By the end of March 1915 some 1,600 Belgian refugees had arrived, out of an eventual total of over 2,300. They were looked after by a relief committee on which the local government board was represented; the board provided the committee with a staff and arranged for the refugees to be temporarily accommodated in workhouses, as distributing centres; and 'care was taken to avoid any pauper taint, [for] the quarters of the refugees were kept distinct from those of persons on relief'.[1]

From the outset the department of agriculture appreciated the importance of Irish food supplies to the war effort. In August 1914 it convened a meeting of the council of agriculture, which approved of the department's decision to try to conserve seed and breeding stock and intensify production. During 1915 and 1916 the board campaigned hard for an increase of tillage, distributing thousands of exhortatory and advisory leaflets. At the end of 1916 the department was empowered under the defence of the realm act[2] to issue compulsory tillage regulations (at the outset these produced about 3,000 letters of inquiry from the public relating to their interpretation). The department appointed an advisory committee and threw itself into a great tillage drive. Facilities were provided for obtaining seed, and seed potatoes. Loans were made for the purchase of agricultural implements; fertilisers, sprayers, and tractors were imported. The department made great efforts to obtain tractors—by the close of 1918 the number of tractors in Ireland had risen to 640 from 70 in 1917—and, what was almost equally important, took steps to train men to drive them, starting a course for drivers at the Albert College. Eight thousand warning notices were issued to persons failing to comply with the regulations. At the beginning of 1918, acting under the terms of this act, the department appointed an agricultural wages committee with powers to fix minimum wage rates.

Two United Kingdom departments established during the war had branches in Ireland, the ministry of food and the ministry of national service. The ministry of food set up a food control committee for Ireland on 31 August 1917 and the

---

[1] *[Forty-third] annual report of the local government board for Ireland*, p. xli [Cd 8016], H.C. 1914–16, xxv, 387.
[2] 5 Geo. V, c. 8 (27 Nov. 1914).

majority of its regulations, in theory, applied to Ireland. In fact rationing, except of sugar, was little felt in a country with a large food surplus, and the ministry of food, it has been pointed out by its historian, affected Irishmen as producers rather than as consumers.[1] The national service department in Ireland was set up as the counterpart of the national service department in Great Britain, but when the latter's functions were transferred to the Irish department, with a staff of twenty-five, it continued to work apart from, and in some cases in antagonism to, the ministry of labour. It seems to have been intended that the Irish national service department should have simply been concerned with the provision of agricultural labour for the tillage scheme. But it also concerned itself with the provision of labour for aerodromes and government railways. In seventeen months it managed to find employment for 10,600 persons, but an unsympathetic committee reported that the department's correspondence was inconsiderable and its establishment top-heavy. Under the department of national service there was an Irish recruiting council with a headquarters staff in Dublin of 230, which spent a fair amount of money on printing, publicity, and motor cars. The Irish national service department seems to have been a striking example of the swollen bureaucracy that can flourish under wartime conditions. Even the chief secretary was compelled to admit that its duties might not appear to justify its separate existence—though he thought that the political influence exerted by the department had facilitated the distribution of agricultural labour. In December 1918 he issued an order ending its existence and disbanding the recruiting council by February 1919.

At the close of the war the constitutional future of Ireland was highly uncertain. The home rule act was on the statute book, but it was suspended and was likely to be amended. However, even in this unsettled period the government had to be carried on. The war years had been a time of bold experiment and development in British administrative history, and at the close of the conflict there was a widespread belief that the administrative machine must be reshaped to deal with the demands of the postwar era. In 1919 three new U.K. administrative bodies were created: the ministry of transport, the ministry of health, and the forestry commission. The ministry of transport, which was invested with all the powers possessed by any government department relating to roads, tramways, railways, canals, and harbours, took over the powers exercised by Irish departments under various acts, and a branch of the ministry was established to deal with Irish matters. The forestry commission, set up to promote the interests of forestry and the development of afforestation throughout the United Kingdom, took over the powers of the department of agriculture and technical instruction relating to forestry in Ireland.

Administrative logic may have dictated the transfer of extensive functions from Irish departments to these two new imperial departments, but the political

[1] Sir William H. Beveridge, *British food control* (London and New Haven, Conn., 1928), p. 415.

practicalities prevailed when the ministry of health was being established. In the act creating the new ministry the chief secretary was designated minister of health for Ireland 'for the purposes of promoting the health of the people in Ireland' and exercising the powers conferred by the act.[1] The Irish insurance commissioners were placed under his control, and to assist him in exercising his duties under the act an advisory council was constituted, composed of representatives of the local government board, the insurance commissioners, the registrar general, and persons having experience in public health matters. This council went briskly to work and by May 1920 had produced a long report recommending the establishment of an Irish ministry of health that would absorb the local government board, the Irish insurance commission, the registrar general's office, and the powers and duties of other departments relating to public health. The chief secretary was to remain minister for public health for Ireland and under him the department was to be headed by a vice-president (a civil servant) or by a board of coequal members (those who favoured the latter scheme arguing that the permanent head of the department would have more power than it would be desirable for any single individual to possess).

In the sessions of 1919 and 1920 the government introduced an education bill creating a department of education for Ireland. The condition of Irish education was clearly unsatisfactory.[2] The national board had been seriously concerned over the low salary levels of teachers in their schools, and though in 1920, backed by the findings of a viceregal commission, the board had managed to secure satisfactory salary scales, they were confronted with another difficulty. At the beginning of 1919 the board had received a sharp intimation from the treasury that building grants for schools were being renewed only on the understanding that they should be confined to the most urgent cases: the building resources of the country, the treasury emphasised, were bound to be severely taxed by the new housing schemes that the government had promised to encourage. The intermediate education board was facing an even more critical situation. In 1917 it had pointed out that it required a larger staff of inspectors and that secondary teachers' salaries were too low. Three years later the board in its published reports produced some statistics that dramatically illustrated the situation. Only 30 per cent of the lay secondary teachers in Ireland had salaries of over £200 per annum. The board was not surprised that many of the better teachers were emigrating and that there had even been in some schools strikes for 'a living wage'. The board in its reports hammered home that in its opinion the government was pledged to vary the grant for secondary education in Ireland in accordance with changes in the English grant—which it declared implied that Ireland should have received an additional £130,000 in 1920. It was difficult, the board declared, 'to refer to these matters in language of moderation and restraint . . . when the whole edifice

[1] 9 & 10 Geo. V, c. 21 (3 June 1919), sect. 10.   [2] Above, pp 537–8.

of secondary education in Ireland is toppling to destruction'.[1] The board had already called for the reconstruction of the entire educational system, and the government's bill at least provided the machinery for that operation. The new department of education was to absorb the powers and duties of the commissioners of national education, the commissioners of intermediate education, and the department of agriculture in relation to instruction, science, art, and the geological survey. The department was to be administered by a board consisting of the chief secretary, the vice-president of the department of agriculture and another member, referred to as 'the permanent member'. The department was to be assisted by an advisory council composed of persons interested in education and provision was made for the creation of local education authorities and the levying of an education rate. The bill was introduced late in the session of 1919 and failed to make progress in 1920 owing to the pressure of parliamentary business.

The education bill and the public health act were important steps towards simplifying and streamlining the Irish administration. But while they were being discussed conditions in Ireland were steadily making it difficult for that administration to function normally over wide areas. In January 1919 a number of Sinn Féin M.P.s from Irish constituencies met in Dublin, constituted themselves Dáil Éireann and ratified the establishment of the Irish republic. About the same time attacks on police patrols began; these rapidly multiplied and grew in scale, attempts were made to capture police barracks, military detachments were attacked, crown officials murdered. Simultaneously Dáil Éireann started to build up an administration that could compete with, or theoretically at least supplant, that of the crown in Ireland. Sinn Féin courts were set up in some areas and local authorities were asked to sever relations with the local government board.

At first the government tried to treat the situation that was developing from the beginning of 1919 as a serious outburst of lawlessness, which could be checked by the use of the machinery that had been devised during the land troubles of the 1880s. In September and October 1919 proclamations were issued under the powers conferred by the crimes act of 1887[2] declaring certain associations illegal and instituting in six counties and in Dublin a special procedure for the detention and trial of persons charged with specific offences.

During the parliamentary session of 1920 the government of Ireland act was passed,[3] setting up parliaments and administrations responsible to them in southern and northern Ireland. Each parliament was given control over certain services in its area; others were to remain imperial services. From the bill's introduction, the unionists were clearly prepared to work it in Northern Ireland, but it did not satisfy the supporters of Dáil Éireann, and the government had to contemplate carrying on the administration of Ireland until a more acceptable

---

[1] Report of the intermediate education board for Ireland for the year 1920, p. x [Cmd 1398], H.C. 1921, xi, 406.

[2] 50 & 51 Vict., c. 20 (19 July 1887).

[3] 10 & 11 Geo. V, c. 67 (23 Dec. 1920).

solution of the Irish question could be found. It was also clear from early in 1920 that over large areas in the south and west the police could scarcely perform their routine duties, and though the courts continued to function many petty sessions and county courts had to change their place of sitting owing to courthouses being burned down, and the number of cases that came before them declined sharply.

It was some time, however, before the Irish executive, or indeed many people in Ireland, realised the type of situation that was developing; at the beginning of 1919 it seemed to the authorities that it was merely a question of coping with a rise in crime and outrage, no doubt partly inspired by political motives or economic distress. In fact a combination of a determined political opposition, prepared to use legal and illegal methods, with a well directed armed force, rapidly created a state of affairs in which strong political feeling was aroused, which might manifest itself in passive resistance or violence, blended with the continuance of normal social and economic activity most of the time over most of the country. In these circumstances administrators, though dismayed at the spread of lawlessness and by the difficulties experienced in securing the public cooperation on which the normal working of the legal system depended, were slow to conclude they were fighting a civil war. This adherence to customary official ways in a time of mounting and unprecedented stresses is illustrated by the attitude of the treasury (admittedly functioning in London) to the Irish emergency measures. When it sanctioned the purchase for the chief secretary of a motor chassis on which a steel-lined body would be constructed, it laid down that there was no reason why the chassis to be acquired should be a Rolls-Royce. When asked to sanction a purchase of fifty pairs of binoculars for the use of the police, it suggested they should borrow from the admiralty, and when sanctioning a supply of 50,000 sandbags for the defence of R.I.C. barracks the treasury was glad to have an assurance that it was not proposed to allocate sandbags to barracks with small garrisons, which would not be defended in an emergency.

The government at first tried to handle the situation by applying to the seriously disturbed areas the provisions of the constabulary act of 1836[1] (which permitted an increase of the police force in a proclaimed area) and of the crimes act of 1887. This policy was probably initiated by Sir John Taylor, the assistant under-secretary, who had begun his career in the chief secretary's office in Arthur Balfour's time (1887–91) and had been private secretary to another unionist chief secretary, Walter Long (1905). Taylor, a strong conservative, fearless, aloof, an incredibly hard worker, almost incapable of delegation, was of course theoretically subordinate to the under-secretary, but Macpherson, who was appointed chief secretary in January 1919, 'ostracised' (according to the lord lieutenant)[2] the under-secretary, James MacMahon, a catholic of nationalist sympathies, with the result that there was always a missing link in the chain of responsible government.

---

[1] 6 Will. IV, c. 13 (20 May 1836).
[2] French to Bonar Law, 18 Apr. 1920 (Beaverbrook Library, London: Bonar Law papers 103/2/11).

Early in 1920, when Macpherson was replaced by Greenwood, the government of Ireland seemed to be breaking down in two respects. Attacks on the police and military were multiplying and over large areas the authority of the crown was being flouted, and at the same time, according to a hard but fair critic, the ordinary machinery in the chief secretary's office in Dublin castle, the headquarters of the Irish government, was almost non-existent.

No business that was not urgent was being attended to and business which had become urgent was disposed of, in very many cases, without proper consideration. The general state of this office on which the whole civil administration of the country should pivot was incredible.[1]

The lord lieutenant was seriously concerned and suggested an inquiry into the working of the Irish administration, and in April Sir Warren Fisher, the brilliant, at times brusque, head of the civil service, assisted by two senior officials—R. E. Harwood of the treasury and A. W. Cope of the ministry of pensions—conducted an investigation. Their reports pointed out that the Castle administration was now 'quite obsolete', the chief secretary's office having become 'merely a transmitting body' passing questions to the law adviser or the military authorities, and it was failing to advise or inform the Irish government on matters of policy.[2] In a private letter to the chancellor of the exchequer Fisher boldly stepped over the uncertain and wavering line between advising and formulating policy. The Irish 'ruling caste', he wrote after his short visit, reminded him of people in England 'mainly to be found in clubs and amongst retired warriors and dowager ladies, who spend their time denouncing the working classes'. Sinn Féin, he thought, should be recognised as a political party, in the hope that this would help to isolate the 'murder gang', and he considered that something on the lines of dominion home rule might solve the Irish problem.[3]

A number of important changes were quickly made. Taylor went on leave—permanently. Sir John Anderson, already clearly one of the outstanding civil servants of his generation, a future member of the war cabinet (1940–45), came over as joint under-secretary with the powers of a secretary of the treasury. And some other treasury officials, including Mark Sturgis, commissioner for income tax, who had been a private secretary to Asquith as prime minister, were sent over to strengthen the Irish administration, and the staff of the chief secretary's office was approximately doubled.

A few months later the restoration of order act[4] empowered the king in council to issue regulations under the defence of the realm act, providing for the trial of prisoners in certain circumstances by court martial and the suspension of grants

[1] Anderson to Greenwood, 20 July 1920 (Lloyd George papers, P.R.O., F. 19/2/14). For a very striking account of the working of the Irish administration during this time of strain, see 'The last days of Dublin Castle' in *Blackwood's Magazine*, ccxii (1922), pp 137–9; the article (by 'Periscope') is attributed to G. C. Duggan (John W. Wheeler-Bennett, *John Anderson, Viscount Waverley* (London, 1962), p. 67 n.).
[2] The reports, dated 12 May 1920, are in Lloyd George papers, P.R.O., F. 31/1/32.
[3] Fisher to chancellor of the exchequer, 15 May 1920 (Lloyd George papers, P.R.O., F. 31/1/33).
[4] 10 & 11 Geo. V, c. 31 (9 Aug. 1920).

to local authorities that failed to perform their duties, if it appeared that 'owing to the existence of a state of disorder in Ireland, the ordinary law is inadequate'. The new Irish administration continued the policy that had already begun of concentrating the police, vacating many of the smaller barracks, and trying to improve the mobility of the police by increased use of mechanised transport. It also raised a force of auxiliary police, detachments of which could be stationed in disturbed areas, and it tried to improve cooperation between the military, the police, and the civil administration.

After the government of Ireland act reached the statute book[1] the Irish executive took steps to set up administrative and judicial machinery in Northern Ireland. An assistant under-secretary was appointed for Northern Ireland with an office in Belfast, which functioned until November 1922 and to which a large number of officials were temporarily seconded from the inland revenue department to 'provide the government of Northern Ireland with the nucleus of an organisation'.[2] In June 1921 the parliament of Northern Ireland was formally opened by the king and seven government departments were constituted for the administration of the province, and from November powers were steadily being transferred to those departments. In October the high courts of justice for Northern Ireland were set up, composed of a lord chief justice—the first chief justice was Denis Henry, a catholic who had sat as unionist M.P. for Londonderry South (1916–21)—two lords justices of appeal and two puisne judges.

During this strenuous time, while the Irish administration was striving by the use of new methods and extraordinary powers to restore order, leading officials— Fisher at the treasury, Anderson, Cope—were working hard to discover a solution for the political problems that were making administration almost impossible or reducing it to a military operation for which they all had a profound distaste. Of course their powers were severely limited; the fundamental decisions on policy had to be taken by their political chiefs. Nevertheless the senior administrators concerned with Ireland worked hard in two directions: they tried to open up lines of communication with the government's opponents in Ireland so that the possibility of negotiation could be established; and they strove to impress on the ministers responsible for Ireland that the government of Ireland act, combined with the restoration of order, did not provide a basis for a satisfactory Irish policy: in short, that Southern Ireland must be offered something analogous to dominion status. On 6 December 1921 it was agreed in the Anglo–Irish treaty that this should be granted, and on 16 January 1922 the lord lieutenant, Lord FitzAlan, received the members of the provisional government appointed by Dáil Éireann and introduced them to the heads of the Irish government departments. Theoretically he was receiving his advisers.[3] The provisional government, however,

[1] 10 & 11 Geo. V, c. 67 (23 Dec. 1920).

[2] *Hansard 5 (commons)*, cxli, 433 (28 Apr. 1921)

[3] At the close of May 1922 the lord lieutenant dissolved the parliament of Southern Ireland 'on the advice of the provisional government' (*Iris Oifigiúil*, 30 May 1922).

issued a statement declaring that on 16 January they had received the surrender of Dublin Castle. Until the beginning of December 1922 the provisional government controlled the administration of Southern Ireland while the Irish Free State constitution was being drafted and approved by the dáil and the U.K. parliament. Early in March 1922 it carried through an Irish administrative revolution, creating eight ministries or departments, which took over the duties of the existing offices or departments functioning in Ireland.

At the close of January 1922 the lord lieutenant expressed the hope that the provisional government would recognise the importance of the position of the king's representative. But he was conscious that 'at present everything points to an attitude to mark a difference under the new regime from what it has been in the past'.[1] The attitude of the provisional government, Griffith explained, was to treat the lord lieutenant as a liaison officer if it was necessary to do so. FitzAlan continued as the somewhat embarrassed holder of a great historic office until the end of the year, though for much of the time he was not in Ireland. He visited Northern Ireland, where he was received with the full honours due to the king's representative, but when he went to Punchestown (County Kildare) his car was stolen by the Irregulars and he announced in advance that he and Lady FitzAlan would not attend the Dublin horse show. Finally at the beginning of December he was replaced, T. M. Healy being sworn in as governor general of the Irish Free State on 6 December 1922 and the duke of Abercorn taking office as governor of Northern Ireland on 12 December.

[1] FitzAlan to Churchill, 27 Jan. 1922 (Martin Gilbert, *Winston Churchill, iv: 1917–1922: companion, iii* (London, 1977), p. 1,737).

CHAPTER XXI

Emigration, 1871–1921

DAVID FITZPATRICK

'I THINK they all set towards the west, more or less. In my part of the country I think they have got as many relations in Boston as they have in Clare.'[1] By 1880, when the land agent Robert Vere O'Brien offered this insight into the Irishman's increasingly cosmopolitan outlook, the national 'haemorrhage' had long since become a structural element of the post-famine social order. Some 2.5 million emigrants left Ireland during the last half-century of the union. There were two periods only when hopes were aroused that the flow might be halted. In the later 1870s, a time of severe recession in North America and relative prosperity in Ireland, annual outflow reached its lowest level since the 1830s. Four decades later the combination of wartime dislocation of shipping with an economic boom at home brought about an even sharper but again temporary reduction. Otherwise, as figure 3 in volume v confirms,[2] the annual number of departures oscillated with decreasing variation about a slowly declining trend-line. The reduction of fluctuation from year to year suggests that the flickering performance of the home economy (with its sensitivity to variation in the quality and output of the harvest) played a decreasing part in the decision to stay or leave. Longer-term cycles in the volume of emigration remained important, signifying Irish responsiveness to the North American business and employment cycles. When overseas demand for employment expanded, some potential emigrants hastened their departure; when it contracted, some remained at home for a few years longer. Though others presumably delayed too long, it is likely that family pressure helped most of the group who had been 'reared for emigration' to fulfil their destiny.

Emigration had become a familiar episode in the calendar, with as many as two departures in five occurring in two months of the year (April and May). A secondary peak occurred in September and October before the hazards and discomforts of winter diminished transoceanic travel to a trickle.[3] The passenger trade had adjusted itself to shipping the emigrants from Irish rather than British

---

[1] *Minutes of evidence taken before her majesty's commissioners on agriculture* (hereafter cited as *Richmond comm. evidence*), p. 1048 [C 2778–1], H.C. 1881, xv, 1076.

[2] Above, v, 617.

[3] Monthly departures of Irish passengers from British ports, 1878–80, are tabulated in *Copy of statistical tables relating to emigration and immigration . . . in the year 1880*, p. 7, H.C. 1881 (89), xciv, 685.

ports, and by 1872 less than two-fifths of emigrants to the United States followed the precedent of their famine-driven predecessors by boarding at Liverpool. Queenstown (Cobh) was the major port of embarkation for emigrants from Munster and Connacht, while Ulster was served by Belfast and Derry, and Leinster by Dublin.[1] Emigration had become a massive, relentless, and efficiently managed national enterprise.

The rate of emigration, though below that recorded in the shadow of famine, was easily the highest in Europe throughout the later nineteenth century. Table 1 in the appendix to this chapter indicates that even in the 1890s, the decade's emigration from Irish ports amounted to a tenth of Ireland's mean population. The severity of the outflow is illustrated by the statistics of cohort depletion, the best available approximation of net outward migration for the group most at risk. About a quarter of the cohort initially aged 5-24 'disappeared' from the population before the next decennial census, and still others would have emigrated later in their lives.[2] Other estimates of net emigration suggest that in the 1870s the Irish rate tripled its nearest rivals (Norwegian, Swedish, and Scottish); while even at the height of the 'new immigration' of the 1890s, net movement from Italy was less than half as brisk as that from Ireland. No German state approached Irish rates, though provinces such as Pomerania, Posen, and East Prussia sometimes drew close.[3] Ireland's persistent preeminence was masked by its decreasing weight among European populations, which meant that the absolute volume of Irish emigration declined while that from the expanding populations of central and southern Europe increased. Ireland's share of the population of the British Isles declined from a third in 1841 to a fifth in 1871, and to a mere tenth in 1911: consequently, net emigration from Ireland between 1871 and 1911 only just exceeded that from Britain despite the much higher Irish rate *per capita*.[4] Ireland's diminished contribution to movement from the United Kingdom to North America and Australasia is reported in table 2.[5] By the early twentieth century twice as many British as Irish passengers left for the United States, while Irish emigrants comprised only a twentieth of the movement to Canada and Australasia.

The contours of Irish emigration are further defined in table 3, showing the distribution of natives of Ireland recorded in various census-takings between about 1871 and 1921. The table reveals that a substantial proportion of migrants

---

[1] Returns of the number of Irish passengers leaving each port in the British Isles between 1853 and 1872 are given in the annual *General reports of the [colonial land and] emigration commissioners*, H.C., *passim*; while returns of the number of passengers from each Irish county who left each *Irish* port between 1851 and 1875 are tabulated in the annual emigration report in *Agricultural statistics (Ireland): tables*, H.C., *passim*.

[2] Below, p. 638. Cohorts are of course depleted by mortality as well as out-migration; but for the age-group specified, decadal mortality would seldom have exceeded 6 per cent.

[3] Charlotte Erickson (ed.), *Emigration from Europe, 1815–1914: select documents* (London, 1976), p. 29.

[4] William Ashworth, *An economic history of England, 1870–1939* (London, 1960), p. 191.

[5] Below, p. 639.

(rising to a fifth by 1911) were resident in Ireland but outside their native county. Movement between counties (not to mention unrecorded migration within counties) was prompted by marriage, property transactions, and above all the search for employment. Dublin was the only city attracting substantial immigration from all counties, whereas the faster growing Belfast drew most of its immigrant work-force from north-east Ulster.[1] The distribution of the Irish overseas changed remarkably little between 1871 and 1911, the bare majority of all migratory Irish being resident in the United States. The proportion in Britain was never far from a fifth, with Australia overtaking Canada as the next most important destination. Significant Irish populations also settled in New Zealand, South Africa, and Argentina. Everywhere Irish immigrants became rapidly less conspicuous as a proportion of the local population, though this loss was counterbalanced by proliferation of the descendants of Irish settlers. Only one Australian in fifty was Irish-born in 1921, compared with one in eight half a century earlier. At the end of the period Irish natives accounted for only about 1 per cent of the population in Canada, the United States, and Britain. The impact of Irish emigration, once so important for all the major countries of settlement, was by then largely confined to the country of origin.

The great majority of Irish people who emigrated between the later 1870s and the first world war chose the United States. Table 4 shows the proportions choosing each major destination, Britain being excluded for reasons discussed in chapter XXII.[2] Despite increasingly glaring discrepancies between the major statistical series, it seems that the United States consistently attracted at least four-fifths of all Irish emigrants travelling beyond Europe. In this respect Ireland resembled Germany, which often sent more than nine-tenths of its emigrants to the United States.[3] The transatlantic flow of Irish and other European emigrants was closely linked to cyclical variation in the American economy. Thus peaks in one index of American economic growth in 1873, 1882, 1892, and 1907 were reflected in 1873, 1883, 1895, and 1907 by peaks in Irish emigration to the United States. Likewise, the economic troughs of 1878, 1885, and 1896 were echoed in the diminished emigration of 1877, 1885, and 1898.[4]

It was in periods of economic downturn in the United States that Irish emigrants were most easily diverted elsewhere, as to Britain and Australasia in the later 1870s, Britain at the turn of the century, and Canada just before the first

---

[1] Below, p. 640. For discussion of internal migration based on census birthplace returns, see David Fitzpatrick, 'Emigration, 1801–70', above, v, p. 568. Some data incorporating intra-county movement between 1901 and 1911 are presented in David Fitzpatrick, 'Irish farming families before the first world war' in *Comparative Studies in Society and History*, xxv, no. 2 (Apr. 1983), p. 366.

[2] Below, pp 641, 653–98.

[3] Robert Lee, 'Germany' in W. R. Lee (ed.), *European demography and economic growth* (London, 1979), p. 192.

[4] Richard A. Easterlin, 'Influences in European overseas emigration before World War I' in *Economic Development and Cultural Change*, ix, no. 3 (Apr. 1961), p. 347. Oddly, Ireland is excluded as 'a unique case of economic catastrophe' (p. 333). See also Brinley Thomas, *Migration and economic growth: a study of Great Britain and the Atlantic economy* (rev. ed., Cambridge, 1973), pp 103, 116.

world war. The oscillation in roughly opposite directions of the American and British economies cushioned the impact of American recession by offering Irish emigrants the prospect of employment in Britain. Some have inferred from this cyclical balance that the 'quality' and background of emigrants varied little according to destination, the latter being selected after study of the transatlantic business cycle.[1] Like all inferences based upon economic push or pull, this analysis only applies to the aberrant case of a potential emigrant possessing freedom to make an open choice. The vast majority were restricted in their choice of destination by ignorance, precedent, and links with previous emigrants: their response to American recession was generally to postpone rather than redirect their outward movement. Cultural constraints may also have dissuaded some emigrants from choosing the British colonies and dominions, just as ignorance of language ensured that South America would remain only a minor recipient of Irish immigration. High opportunity costs as well as fares impeded emigration to Australasia, while movement to Canada was restricted by the prevailing belief that 'it was a great iceberg'.[2]

Undoubtedly the most important factor in determining emigrant destinations was the location of previous emigrants. The networks of friendship, marriage, residence, and employment built up by earlier Irish settlers and their descendants exerted a powerful attraction on their Irish connections; while the chain system of migration analysed below reinforced existing patterns of settlement. After arriving overseas many emigrants continued their rambling in search of a better life, but even their rambling was often directed by information gleaned from other Irish settlers and their networks. The force of precedent in determining the patterns of Irish settlement is clearly manifest in statistics showing the Irish-born component of the migratory population of American states and British counties. Adopting the statistician's simplistic assumptions, we find that in both England and Scotland over nine-tenths of the regional clustering of Irish immigrants in 1901 may be 'explained' by the clusters recorded in 1871. A similar degree of stability applies to Irish settlement in the American states in 1870 and 1910. Despite massive turnover of population and extensive internal migration, the Irish settlers of the early twentieth century continued to gather in the regions favoured by their distant predecessors.[3] Emigrants were guided in their movements out of

---

[1] Lynn Hollen Lees and John Modell, 'The Irish countryman urbanized' in *Journal of Urban History*, iii, no. 4 (Aug. 1977), pp 20–21.

[2] *Second report from the select committee of the house of lords on land law (Ireland)*, p. 259, H.C. 1882 (379), xi, 813 (evidence of J. H. Tuke).

[3] Using census birthplace returns for each county of England (excluding home counties: n = 37) and of Scotland (Shetland and Orkney combined: n = 32), the proportion of all resident non-natives of the county born in Ireland was calculated for 1871 and 1901. The correlation for England was r = +.97, and that for Scotland was r = +.92. For each of 46 states and territories in the United States (excluding Dakota), the proportion of all foreign-born residents of the state born in Ireland was calculated for 1870 and 1910, giving the correlation r = +.88. The settlement patterns of Irish expatriates in about 1870 are analysed in David Fitzpatrick, 'Irish emigration in the later nineteenth century' in *I.H.S.*, xxii, no. 86 (Sept. 1980), pp 135–6, 140–41.

Ireland by a mental map, drawn not by some economic geographer but by the long succession of earlier Irish explorers.

Emigration, though touching every locality and every social group in Ireland, was far from uniform in its impact. Map 4 shows that the highest rates of net outward movement (as estimated by cohort depletion) were consistently recorded for the counties of the west and of the north midlands. The predominance of the Connacht region as a source of intensive migration was nothing new, having been evident from the famine period onwards.[1] After about 1880 Connacht's pre-eminence was reflected even in the defective returns of emigration from Irish ports, despite their exclusion of innumerable Connacht emigrants who travelled undetected to Britain via Dublin. The north-eastern and south-eastern counties had relatively low rates of cohort depletion, though even these usually exceeded comparable figures for net emigration from Britain. Munster, so often depicted as the hub of Irish emigration, fell far short of Connacht in rate as distinct from volume of emigration (see table 1).[2] Whichever table of emigration is analysed, it seems that regional contrasts in the rate of outward movement remained virtually unaltered between the 1870s and the outbreak of the first world war. The relative contribution of different counties thus changed little, though existing disparities were gradually accentuated.[3] Emigration rates from Connacht declined only slowly after the 1880s, the reduction being greater for Munster and Ulster, and precipitate in the case of Leinster. So emigration became increasingly a regional phenomenon, yet never to the extent of eliminating its importance even in Antrim, Kildare, or Wexford.

Emigration was consistently most intensive from counties with little employment outside agriculture (see map 8), which also tended to be heavily burdened with small farms of low valuation.[4] These statistical findings discredit the still widespread belief that lack of means, ignorance, and attachment to the Irish sod continued to block movement out of the most backward regions until the last years of the century.[5] Nor is it generally true that migration was sluggish from poorer districts within counties: even before the provision of state and private assistance for emigrants from congested areas in the 1880s, cohort

[1] Below, p. 649; and see David Fitzpatrick, 'Emigration, 1801–70', above, v, 571.

[2] Below, p. 638.

[3] For each of the thirty-two Irish counties, cohort depletion rates were calculated for 1871–81 and 1901–11, giving the correlation r = +.78. Likewise, *per capita* rates of emigration from Irish ports were calculated for 1876–85 and 1906–14, giving r = +.79. The accentuation of regional disparities is reflected in the increasing values of the coefficients of variation given in table 1.

[4] Below, p. 651. For thirty Irish counties (excluding Dublin and Antrim), three variables were calculated: (1) average of cohort depletion rates for the decades 1881–91, 1891–1901, and 1901–11; (2) the proportion of occupied males in agriculture, 1901; (3) the proportion of agricultural holdings of less than £10 valuation, 1901. The correlation between cohort depletion and agricultural occupations was r = +.80; that between cohort depletion and small holdings was r = +.67; and that between agricultural occupations and small holdings was r = +.63.

[5] G. R. C. Keep, 'The Irish migration to North America in the second half of the nineteenth century' (Ph.D. thesis, University of Dublin, 1951), p. 42.

depletion was heavier from the impoverished coastal unions of Donegal than from the county's inland region.[1] It is less clear that the group most prone to emigrate were the poorest inhabitants of the poorest localities. But in terms of neighbourhood if not personal background, the emigrants emerged disproportionately from economic contexts of rural poverty, where living standards and demand for labour fell far short of those prevailing in Britain, America, or Australasia.

Emigrant origins varied according to destination, suggesting interesting differences in the backgrounds characteristic of Irish communities overseas. Map 5 highlights these differences by ranking the counties according to the *proportions* of their emigrants choosing each major destination.[2] The association between emigration and agriculture was accentuated in the movement to the United States: thus Connacht was not merely over-represented in emigration but also overwhelmingly 'set towards the west' rather than towards Britain or Australia. The recorded origins of the Irish in Britain suggest the reverse, since the relatively prosperous and urbanised counties of the eastern and southern coastal belts sent abnormally large proportions of their emigrants to England and Scotland.[3] The predominantly protestant emigration to Canada was predictably concentrated in Ulster, the negative association between catholicism and preference for Canada being as strong as the positive association between catholicism and the proportion choosing the United States.[4] Australia had long drawn its Irish immigrants disproportionately from southern midland counties stretching from Clare to Kilkenny, with a secondary cluster in southern Ulster. There was some association between heavy emigration to Australia and rapid substitution of pasturage for tillage, reflecting the background of small-scale but market-conscious agriculture from which most Irish-Australians seem to have emerged.[5] Southern as well as Ulster protestants contributed significantly to Irish settlement in Australia. The 1911 census shows that 29 per cent of Australia's Irish-born population was non-catholic, the proportion being highest in Tasmania and lowest in South Australia. Anglicans outnumbered presbyterians and methodists together. Protestant Irish settlers were probably even more important in New Zealand and Scotland, but as in the American case no direct evidence of the religion of Irish immigrants is available. The northern origins of most Irish-Canadians were, however, demonstrated in the 1931 census, which showed that less than a quarter of the Irish-born population and a third of those claiming to be of Irish 'race' were catholics. Except in the Australian case, the regional distribution of *rates* of

---

[1] In 1871–81, cohort depletion rates for the unions of Dunfanaghy, Glenties, and Millford all exceeded that for County Donegal as a whole: see Alan Atkinson, 'The demographic effects of seasonal migration' (Trinity College, Dublin, unpublished essay, 1981). For development of this analysis see below, p. 694.

[2] Below, p. 650.

[3] For problems of interpreting statistics on the origins of the Irish in Britain, see below, pp 661–2.

[4] Fitzpatrick, 'Irish emigration', pp 138–9.

[5] Ibid., p. 133; for the Irish in Australia and New Zealand, see also below, pp 703–24.

emigration to each country changed little between 1876–85 and 1896–1905, a finding that confirms the importance of chain migration and previous settlement in shaping further movement.[1] Thus Irish emigration may usefully be envisaged as a complex network of distinct streams flowing from particular regions of origin to particular countries of settlement, even though the United States remained everywhere the majority choice.

THE Irish emigrant was not merely the product of a regional economy, but also a human being, some of whose attributes were officially recorded. Returns of sex, age, marital status, occupation, and literacy enable us to devise composite profiles of Irish emigrants, inviting comparison with the home population and with other emigrant groups. The most distinctive feature of Irish emigration was the virtually equal contribution of both sexes. Table 5 shows that the enumerators usually noticed rather more male than female departures, with the exception of the period 1893–1904 when females consistently outnumbered males according to both available sets of statistics. This finding neatly inverts Clarkson's assertion that 'women outnumbered men in Irish emigration before 1914' with the exception of the Boer war period.[2] In any case the sex differentials were minor, whereas every other major international movement except that from Sweden was dominated by men. Emigration from western counties typically contained a larger female component than that from the urbanised east, while men dominated overseas movement from the Belfast region almost as much as they did from Britain (see map 6).[3] Several factors contributed to this contrast between eastern and western counties. Since both Belfast and Dublin offered far more employment opportunities to women, much of the female labour surplus of adjoining counties was absorbed by migration to these rather than foreign cities. Women from western counties, however, often had easier access to social and employment networks in British or American cities than in Irish towns. We may also conjecture that the flood of female emigrants leaving Connacht was one symptom of demographic, social, and familial crisis in Ireland's congested regions, where demand for paid female employment had been in precipitate decline since the famine. The east–west dichotomy is reflected in the returns by sex of movement to different destinations. Passengers to the United States were more likely to be female than those choosing Canada or Australasia (which after the virtual abandonment of state assistance towards the end of the nineteenth century drew heavily on Ulster for its Irish immigrants). Between 1896 and 1907 less than two-fifths of Irish emigrants to those dominions were female.[4] The increasing prominence of women

[1] Fitzpatrick, 'Irish emigration', p. 134.
[2] Below, p. 642; and see L. A. Clarkson, 'Marriage and fertility in nineteenth-century Ireland' in R. B. Outhwaite (ed.), *Marriage and society* (New York, 1982), p. 249.
[3] Below, p. 651. Female emigrants from Connacht outnumbered males in every year between 1874 and 1914, with the exception of 1906.
[4] For the periods 1877–85, 1886–95, 1896–1905, and 1906–7, the female percentages of Irish passengers leaving British and Irish ports for the United States were 50, 51, 56, and 50; for British

in the Irish movement to the United States was encouraged by the persistent demand for domestic servants, even after the slump of 1893 had curtailed the demand for male labourers.

The even balance between male and female emigration was achieved in the absence of extensive movement in family groups. Group emigration remained far less common in Ireland than Britain, and the great majority of Irish passengers travelled alone or with companions of their own generation. Table 5 demonstrates that the proportion of emigrants ever married declined steadily during the last quarter of the nineteenth century (never exceeding one in six), before recovering slightly in the new century.[1] By contrast, married people accounted for up to a third of English emigrants between 1877 and 1907. Since young children were usually even less prominent than married emigrants, it is clear that most of those leaving Ireland were unmarried adults. Family emigration was common only from Ulster and the east, the very regions in which male emigrants tended to outnumber females (see maps 6 and 7).[2] Since these regions dominated movement to Canada and latterly Australasia, it is not surprising that married people comprised over a fifth of their intake from Ireland between 1896 and 1907. The frequency of family emigration from Ulster was often attributed to the moral and material benefits of the Ulster custom, as by a county court judge in 1872: 'by the sale of his tenant right he has the means of going and taking his family with him, whereas in the poorer parts of the country one member of the family emigrates first and then sends money to bring another, and so they bring them out by instalments.'[3] In general, though, emigration from Ireland was concentrated in the group aged 20–24, who regularly accounted for two emigrants out of five from the mid-1880s onwards. This group had reached a critical point in their life cycle: they had entered the labour market but had still to enter the marriage market. Emigration offered them the promise of employment overseas followed by marriage; whereas delay in departure threatened them with exclusion from both markets, first in Ireland but before long in the world at large.

The great majority of emigrants were returned as 'labourers' if male, and 'servants' if female, though as before these were often declarations of intention rather than fact. Though many future emigrants had whiled away their adolescence with spells of farm service or harvest labour, there is little doubt that most came from farming rather than landless backgrounds. They were themselves landless only in the sense that they were not yet landholders but dependants, who in most cases could not expect to succeed to occupancy or marry into land. When an inspector of the local government board was questioned in 1889 about the

North America, 42, 40, 37, and 36; for Australasia, 46, 46, 38, and 32. See annual *Copies of tables relating to emigration and immigration* for 1877–1907 in H.C., *passim*.

[1] Below, p. 642.
[2] Below, p. 651.
[3] *Report from the select committee of the house of lords on the Landlord and Tenant (Ireland) Act*, p. 46, H.C. 1872 (403), xi, 62 (evidence of James Hamilton, Sligo).

predominance of labourers in the emigration returns, he remarked that 'they call themselves "labourer", but we know in Ireland that they are small farmers. . . . and it is the children of those people who are emigrating [and] who are returned as labourers'.[1] The readiness to emigrate of farmers' children, even those with prospects of marriage or succession at home, was confirmed by the future novelist and canon Patrick Sheehan in 1882. He observed that the profile of emigrants leaving Queenstown (Cobh) had changed since the famine:

No longer labourers, with their wives and children, who, after many years and much labour, have put together the few pounds that will pay their passage; but the strong, intelligent artisans of our towns, and farmers' sons, who prefer the bustle and life of an American city to the monotony of country life at home; and farmers' daughters who sacrifice their dowries, and a certain prospect of marriage, for the pleasure of serving in a business house in New York, or even going into situation as housemaids in American families.

Unlike his idealised and misleading depiction of the famine exodus as a movement of families headed by labourers, Sheehan's account of the diverse background of emigrant labourers and servants in the 1880s was based on personal observation rather than hearsay.[2] Other witnesses claimed that skilled farm workers were particularly likely to leave Ireland, bearing with them the 'lost arts' of ploughing, mowing, reaping, threshing, and thatching.[3] No doubt mechanisation in farming and also in textiles generated some migration of workers with obsolescent skills; yet the occupational statistics give little hint of an Irish counterpart to the massive efflux of redundant artisans from contemporary Britain. When at the turn of the century the proportion of occupied male emigrants returned as labourers dropped from four-fifths to two-thirds, the change was caused by increasing emigration of farmers, clerks, and shop assistants rather than tradesmen. Servants continued to account for nine-tenths of occupied female emigrants up to 1910. The occupational profile of those bound for the United States diversified only gradually after 1900, whereas the emigrants choosing Canada and especially Australasia were markedly more inclined to follow professional, commercial, or skilled pursuits (see table 10).[4] Overall, those who left Ireland after 1870 were almost as likely as their predecessors to arrive overseas without skills, regular work experience, or knowledge of urban life.

Despite these drawbacks, the emigrants did their utmost to prepare themselves for life in foreign cities. They had one great advantage over their precursors of

[1] *Report from the select committee on colonisation*, p. 122, H.C. 1889 (274), x, 132 (evidence of Ruttledge-Fair). See also David Fitzpatrick, 'The disappearance of the Irish agricultural labourer, 1841–1912' in *Ir. Econ. & Soc. Hist.*, vii (1980), pp 67–9.

[2] P. A. Sheehan, 'The effect of emigration on the Irish church' in *I.E.R.*, 3rd ser., iii (1882), p. 607.

[3] *Royal commission on labour* [hereafter cited as *Devonshire comm.*]. *The agricultural labourer: Ireland. A.—Summary report by Mr W. P. O'Brien . . .*, p. 6 [C 6894–XIX], H.C. 1893–4, xxxvii, pt 1, p. 136. These observations refer to selected unions in Munster and Leinster.

[4] Below, p. 647; and see Thomas, *Migration and economic growth*, pp 383–6.

the earlier nineteenth century: literacy in English. Four-fifths of those assisted to New South Wales between 1864 and 1869 could read and write, a proportion suggesting that illiteracy was less widespread among these passengers than it was in the county populations from which they were drawn.[1] Indirect evidence confirms the prevalence of basic literacy among the emigrants at large. By applying calculations of cohort depletion to the literate cohort as against the group unable to read and write, we may ascertain the proportions of each category disappearing between census-takings. Table 6 indicates that the rapid diffusion of literacy affected emigrants as much as the home population. The proportion of emigrants able to read and write seems to have risen from three-fifths in the 1870s to well over nine-tenths by the Edwardian decade, the improvement being particularly rapid in the case of formerly 'backward' counties such as Mayo. Male emigration continued to draw disproportionately on the illiterate population; whereas, by the early twentieth century, literate women were actually over-represented in migration out of all but eight of Ireland's counties.[2] Irish emigrants were no longer seriously disadvantaged in literacy, whether compared with other emigrant groups or with the residual Irish population.

Those contemplating emigration were keenly aware that basic literacy was essential for success overseas, especially for women entering domestic service. Prospective emigrants were ceaselessly urged to better their education by influential publicists such as Margaret Anne Cusack (the Nun of Kenmare), as well as friends already overseas.[3] Children and adolescents responded by transforming the educational system into a training ground for emigration. It was reported in 1889 that specimen letters inscribed by children in national schools were 'invariably written to some friend either in the United States or Canada, or Australia, asking the person to send a ticket to take them out'.[4] Industrial classes in national schools were enthusiastically patronised by girls preparing for service in America rather than household management at home; and the same perversion was often attributed to girls and women taking the domestic economy programmes offered by the congested districts board and department of agriculture as well as the commissioners of national education.[5] National teachers adorned their drab classrooms with 'attractive pictures of doubtful veracity and descriptions

[1] Fitzpatrick, 'Irish emigration' p. 132. The annual *Reports of agent for immigration* (New South Wales, *Votes and proceedings of legislative assembly*) show that the percentage of Irish assisted immigrants who could read and write rose to 87 in 1877–80, 93 in 1881–5, and 96 in 1886–7.

[2] Below, p. 643. See David Fitzpatrick, ' "A share of the honeycomb": education, emigration and Irishwomen' in *Continuity and Change*, i, no. 2 (Aug. 1986), pp 217–34; Cormac Ó Gráda, *Ireland before and after the famine: explorations in economic history, 1800–1925* (Manchester, 1988), pp 145–6.

[3] The Nun of Kenmare, 'Education as a preparation for emigration' in *Transactions of the National Association for the Promotion of Social Science* (1881), pp 492–3; *Devonshire comm.: reports by Mr Arthur Wilson Fox . . .*, pp 64, 122 [C 6894–XXI], H.C. 1893–4, xxxvii, pt I, pp 404, 462, referring to the unions of Westport, Co. Mayo, and Skibbereen, Co. Cork.

[4] *Report from the select committee on colonisation*, p. 142, H.C. 1889 (274), x, 152 (evidence of Ruttledge-Fair).

[5] Fitzpatrick, ' "A share of the honeycomb" ', pp 226–7.

of the fertile land awaiting the young emigrant', and even obtained commissions as emigration agents (a practice forbidden after protest from the Gaelic League in 1904). In vain did the Catholic Clerical Managers' Association resolve in 1905 that 'all incentives to emigration, through the books, copybooks, or otherwise, be excluded from our national schools'.[1] Nationalist alarm was further excited by the complementary aversion to the Irish language that affected many would-be emigrants. Mark Ryan, the London fenian, recalled with shame and outrage the hostility to Irish common in the Galway of his post-famine childhood: ' "What is the use of Irish for children going to America? " the old people used to say; and many of them actually got their children punished at school for speaking Irish at home.'[2] Emigrants invariably wrote home in English, and were seldom reported as speaking Irish even among themselves. Yet emigrants came disproportionately from counties where Irish was still widely spoken; and even within those counties, the cohort depletion of Irish-speakers was almost as great as that of persons disclaiming knowledge of the language.[3] It is clear that many women, in particular, prepared for their translation overseas by courses of self-improvement combining education in English with oblivion of Irish.

Emigration resulted from innumerable distinct decisions, and should not be depicted as a monolith. The foregoing discussion has emphasised variation according to place of origin and destination. The movement out of Ulster was distinguished not only by its large protestant component and small proportion of unskilled workers, but also by its orientation towards Canada and Britain, its masculinity, and its frequent organisation in family groups. Connacht touched the opposite extremes, sending most of its emigrants to the United States as young unmarried adults without recorded occupational skills. Women predominated in Connacht emigration in virtually every year between 1874 and 1914, and showed particular eagerness to educate themselves in preparation for uprooting. Yet these diversities marked an underlying uniformity with limitless consequences for Irish development and stagnation. Emigration had become a possibility affecting the life cycle of most men and women in Ireland, regardless of their class, religion, or location. Though some groups were better placed than others to follow alternative strategies, the shadow of emigration was everywhere apparent.

---

[1] *Appendix to the eightieth report of the commissioners of national education in Ireland . . ., section I*, p. 89 [Cd 7966], H.C. 1914–16, xx, 471 (evidence of senior inspector J. S. Cussen, Castlebar circuit); *I.T.*, 12 May 1908; *Irish School Weekly*, xiv (11 May 1908), p. 454; Patrick Callan, 'Irish history in Irish national schools, 1900–1908' (M.A. thesis, N.U.I. (U.C.D.), 1975), p. 105.

[2] Mark F. Ryan, *Fenian memories* (Dublin, 1945), p. 4.

[3] In the seven counties of Galway, Mayo, Waterford, Kerry, Clare, Cork, and Donegal (where Irish was widely spoken), the cohort depletion (1881–91) of the group initially aged 10–19 was 45 per cent for those able to speak Irish, and 46 per cent for those with no Irish. For Irish-speakers elsewhere in Ireland cohort depletion was only 22 per cent, whereas for non-Irish-speakers it was 30 per cent. It is of course likely that some members of the cohort learned or forgot Irish during the decade, so reducing the accuracy of these statistics as an indicator of linguistic differentials in emigration. See above, pp 385–90, 431–5.

THE great majority of those who left Ireland between 1871 and 1921 travelled without organised assistance, being dependent for passage money and outfitting on their own resources and especially on those of their relatives. Yet their voyage was no longer a hazardous and unsupervised probe into the unknown. Most emigrants travelled by steamer rather than sailing vessel, with a resulting reduction of transit time and risk of shipwreck. Under sail, the average transatlantic crossing had taken about six weeks; but between 1867 and 1914 the length of the voyage for steam passengers was progressively reduced from over a fortnight to less than a week.[1] Fares were naturally rather higher than those available in the chaotic conditions of the 1840s on inferior vessels, when a ticket from Liverpool to New York could be found for £2 15s. or less. By 1883 all the regular shipping companies were charging four guineas for a steerage passage on the Liverpool to New York route, a quarter the price of a ticket to Australia. Discount tickets were obtainable from European ports without strict regulation of shipping, and during periods of intense competition between companies such as the so-called steamship war of 1885.[2] The higher costs of travel were mitigated by more systematic regulation of the shipping trade, consolidated under the passenger act of 1885[3] and extended to cabin passengers and traffic across the Irish Sea in 1863. Steerage conditions continued to provoke occasional howls of outrage, as in 1881 when Charlotte Grace O'Brien exposed the moral 'horrors of an emigrant ship' in a probably groundless attack on the White Star Line.[4] Regulation was further extended under the merchant shipping act of 1894, which introduced compulsory medical certification, licensing of passage brokers and runners, and detailed entitlements for cabin passengers (who accounted for nearly a third of all passengers from the United Kingdom to extra-European destinations between 1877 and 1900).[5] All these improvements could not, of course, render the ocean voyage a comfortable experience for Irish travellers ignorant and fearful of the ways of the sea. As one emigrant from Queenstown lamented in 1873: 'I was not able to bid adieu to the receding shores of dear Erin, being below by the bunks with a heavy heart and an upset stomach puking ah-awk, and so when I was passing "bara-an-valla" above I was not able to say "Erin go-bragh".'[6]

---

[1] J. D. Gould, 'European inter-continental emigration 1815–1914: patterns and causes' in *Journal of European Economic History*, viii, no. 3 (winter 1979), p. 613.

[2] *The emigrant's guide for 1883* (Pitt & Scott, London, [1883]), pp 40–41, 74; Richard Mayo Smith, *Emigration and immigration: a study in social science* (London, 1890), p. 47.

[3] 18 & 19 Vict., c. 119 (14 Aug. 1855).

[4] MacDonagh, *Pattern of govt growth*, pp 293–4, 317; Stephen Gwynn (ed.), *Charlotte Grace O'Brien: selections from her writings and correspondence, with a memoir* (Dublin, 1909), pp 55–60; *Reports with regard to the accommodation and treatment of emigrants on board Atlantic steam ships*, H.C. 1881 [C 2995], lxxxii, 93–178.

[5] 57 & 58 Vict., c. 60 (25 Aug. 1894); Stanley C. Johnson, *History of emigration from the United Kingdom to North America, 1763–1912* (London, 1913), pp 123–6.

[6] Denis Hurley (Carson, Nevada), to parents in Clonakilty, Co. Cork, 24 June 1873 (Cork Archives Institute, U 170/5).

Emigration was not entirely untouched by official encouragement and restriction. Colonial governments still offered selective subsidies to certain categories of immigrant whose labour was deemed essential, while land grants and inland transportation were sometimes offered to those venturing towards frontier regions such as Queensland and Manitoba. In 1882, for example, Irish emigrants of specified categories might apply for free passages to Queensland, the Cape of Good Hope, and Natal, and for subsidies from the governments of Quebec, New South Wales, and Tasmania, as well as Natal and Queensland. Nomination schemes were also operative in the Cape, and throughout Australasia except Victoria.[1] The stringent criteria for direct state assistance ensured that the only schemes with wide application were those requiring nomination and contributions from friends or relatives already overseas, so tending to reinforce established axes of migration rather than to extend the range of migration within the empire. Colonial assistance was further curtailed towards the turn of the century, though the foundation of the commonwealth of Australia in 1901 led to a brief revival.

The United States, far from offering inducements to emigrants, applied ever more restrictive immigration controls. Though primarily directed against the 'new immigration' rather than the influx from Britain or Ireland, the exclusion of convicts, lunatics, idiots, and destitutes in 1882 and the closer scrutiny of those brought out by friends after 1891 both tended to discourage Irish emigration. The United States did not, however, impose a quota on immigration from the British Isles until 1921, under a discriminatory scheme that scarcely affected Ireland until the end of the decade. Indeed, Irish settlers benefited from the alien scare that prompted restrictive legislation in Britain, Australia, and Canada as well as the United States, Irish immigrants being ostentatiously favoured in order to highlight the iniquities of Jewish and oriental applicants.

In the United Kingdom official assistance, though augmented during the economic crisis of the early 1880s, was never widely implemented. The treasury and hence the Irish administration showed their customary parsimony, while politicians were wary of alienating nationalist and church leaders in an era of tentative *rapprochement*. Several statutes from the period 1838–49 allowed for assistance from poor law guardians, using funds drawn either from the rates or from approved loans. These benefactions were restricted to small supplementary grants for current or prospective workhouse inmates, of whom 4,592 were helped out of Ireland during the 1870s. The number of recipients rose to 10,921 in the 1880s before subsiding to 1,057 in the 1890s and a trickle thereafter.[2] The land acts of 1881 and 1891 contained emigration clauses so dead that they were never implemented. Significant assistance was, however, smuggled into law under the

[1] *[Eleventh] annual report of the local government board for Ireland*, pp 159–63 [C 3581], H.C. 1883, xxix, 167–71.

[2] *Royal commission on congestion in Ireland* [hereafter cited as *Dudley comm.*]: *appendices to the first report*, pp 387–8 [Cd 3267], H.C. 1906, xxxii, 1017–18.

arrears of rent act of 1882 and the tramways and public companies act of 1883,[1] which together allocated £150,000 towards free grants of up to £8 *per capita*. Though the fund was not exhausted, some 24,596 emigrants received grants. In the vain hope of placating nationalist opposition, funds were also set aside for Parnell's stillborn Irish Land Purchase and Settlement Company of 1884, with its futile programme for removing pauper families to Kilcoony, County Galway, rather than to America. The parliamentary grants were mainly distributed by officials of the local government board through scheduled districts in thirty-six western unions, though in certain localities administration was left to private committees organised by philanthropists. Despite the government's intention, most of these families of assisted emigrants went to the United States rather than Canada or Australia. The scheme's impact on the agricultural structure of the congested districts was blunted by the fact that (in 1884 at least) more heads of emigrating families were labourers than landholders.[2] The government was soon happy to relinquish an expensive and controversial undertaking that it could not fully control; and despite periodic attempts to arrange Canadian colonisation schemes (as urged by the Cowper commission in 1887), no further substantial assistance was provided until 1919 when free passages were introduced to the dominions for ex-servicemen and their dependants. The congested districts board was, however, accused of clandestinely subsidising emigration by offering tenant right payments to uneconomic holders who consented to surrender their farms.[3]

Private sponsorship of emigration by entrepreneurs and landlords became less common after the 1850s, though the commercial rationales for moving selected groups from one location to another retained some exponents. Many catholic churchmen continued to believe that the creation of Irish colonies in the United States was the best strategy for propagating the faith and regulating the flock in the New World. In association with speculators who hoped to profit from the development of colonised land, a succession of bishops and lay zealots promoted Irish colonisation schemes in Minnesota, Arkansas, Nebraska, and Mississippi, the model being Bishop John Ireland's settlement programme initiated at St Paul, Minnesota.[4] The colonisation of Minnesota was further promoted by John Sweetman, a Meath landowner, and Fr Nugent in Liverpool, who organised the removal of a few families from Connemara. The craze for catholic colonisation peaked in 1879–81, before faltering as a result of the reported failure of many colonists and the financial collapse of unsound enterprises.[5] The commercial

---

[1] 45 & 46 Vict., c. 47 (18 Aug. 1882); 46 & 47 Vict., c. 43 (25 Aug. 1883); above, pp 312, 585.

[2] *[Thirteenth] annual report of the local government board for Ireland*, p. 78 [C 4400], H.C. 1884–5, xxxiv, 90.

[3] *Report of the royal commission on the Land Law (Ireland) Act, 1881*, p. 12 [C 4969], H.C. 1887, xxvi, 12; R. S. Walshaw, *Migration to and from the British Isles: problems and policies* (Liverpool, 1941 ed.), pp 34–5; *Dudley comm.: appendix to the ninth report*, pp 76–7 [Cd 3845], H.C. 1908, xli, 628–9.

[4] Above, v, 598.

[5] Sr Mary Evangela Henthorne, *The Irish Catholic Colonization Association of the United States* (Champaign, Ill., 1932), pp 106–21; James P. Shannon, *Catholic colonization on the western frontier* (London, 1957), *passim*.

motive was more overt in the case of schemes for contract labour, such as that extended to Ireland in 1882 by the Pepperell Manufacturing Co. of Biddeford, Maine. American textiles firms in search of skilled weavers and other workers appointed agents in Ireland and provided free transportation for contracted recruits, though many evidently broke their contracts on arrival in the United States. After 1885, however, the American government prohibited importation of contract labour, which was mainly drawn from Europe, as part of its programme for improving the quality of immigrants.[1]

Domestic experiments in organised emigration, always sporadic, became unusual as unorganised emigration proved its efficiency without expense to landlords, agents, or philanthropists. By 1860 most landlords had lost enthusiasm for estate reorganisation and removal of surplus population, which became more hazardous as land prices recovered and tenant solidarity intensified. Moreover depopulation weakened the belief that such a surplus existed. As Viscount de Vesci observed in 1871 of labourers in the vicinity of Abbeyleix, 'the proprietors do not now induce them to emigrate, they try to keep them on account of the scarcity of labour'.[2] The agricultural crisis of 1879–80 generated renewed interest in reorganisation, eviction, and assisted emigration. The marquis of Lansdowne offered free passage to 'a considerable number of tenants' in Kerry, but no more than four tenants accepted. In Connacht, however, 'several gentlemen' took an interest in furthering emigration: 'it is a common occurrence to be solicited to contribute towards the passage of either a man, woman, or child to America, and it is generally responded to by everybody who can do so.'[3] Yet those who tried to organise emigration of families, like Fr Nugent or Colonel King-Harman on behalf of the *New York Herald* relief fund, risked and received calumny from the nationalist press during the land war. Only two major efforts were made by philanthropists to interfere with the free flow of emigration, by James Hack Tuke (1882–4) and Vere Foster (1880–84).

Tuke, a quaker banker from York with excellent business and political connections, obtained state cooperation in an ambitious and effective scheme for removing impoverished families from coastal unions in Mayo, Galway, and Donegal. In 1880 Tuke had taken a prominent part in an abortive project for British and Irish colonisation in Manitoba and the north-west territories, supported by loans from the imperial government. The failure of this scheme, despite initial support from Sir John A. Macdonald, prime minister of Canada, persuaded Tuke to concentrate on organising emigration at the place of origin rather than destination. His fund raised nearly £70,000 in Britain and provided assistance to 9,482 emigrants, most of whom left with all or part of their immediate family and

---

[1] Charlotte Erickson, *American industry and the European immigrant 1860–1885* (Cambridge, Mass., 1957), pp 36–8, 133; Johnson, *History of emigration*, p. 144.

[2] *Report from the select committee on the law of rating (Ireland)*, p. 434, H.C. 1871 (423), x, 446.

[3] *Report of her majesty's commissioners of inquiry into the working of the Landlord and Tenant (Ireland) Act, 1870* [hereafter cited as *Bessborough comm.*], *minutes of evidence*, p. 1190 [C 2779–11], H.C. 1881, xix, 440; *Richmond comm.*, p. 666 (MS 694) (evidence of Bonar M. Deane).

settled in the United States. Even though candidates had to obtain supplementary funding from private or state sources, the cost *per capita* was unusually high at some seven guineas. In addition to ocean and rail fares averaging at least £4, provision was made for clothing, conveyance, lodging, and landing money.[1] Despite Tuke's desire to facilitate consolidation of small farms by removing entire family households, he was often frustrated by families determined to maintain their stake in land. Sometimes one household member remained on guard, while in other cases parents who had accompanied their children to America returned to a rural retirement at the first opportunity. The mechanisms of emigration were strong, supple, and resistant to tampering by even the best-intentioned social engineers.

Vere Foster, a bachelor philanthropist of limitless energy and practicality, was unique in sponsoring individual rather than family emigration. Family movement he rejected as expensive and politically imprudent, whereas individuals could be induced to leave with a modest subsidy in the knowledge that supportive kinship networks usually awaited their arrival overseas. Foster aimed to exploit existing mechanisms of emigration in order to help out those least likely to find employment in Ireland, whom he rightly identified as women. He acted on this principle to such effect that about 20,250 unmarried girls were helped out of western districts stretching from Donegal to Kerry. Each received a passage voucher for one or two pounds, with the prospect of further discounts from the shipping companies with which Foster dealt; these subventions usually capped assistance already offered by relatives overseas. Foster's obsessively meticulous records indicate that almost every catholic parish in the west of Ireland collaborated by submitting lists of candidates for assistance, one of which contained no fewer than 613 names. Applications were forwarded by 1,179 clergymen of all denominations, including 404 parish priests or administrators and 476 catholic curates. Analysis of the Clare applications confirms that virtually all catholic clergymen participated in Foster's scheme, applications being most profuse in south-west and coastal Clare rather than the less impoverished eastern and especially central parishes.[2] Delight was expressed by numerous priests at the removal of Irish girls from their 'homes of misery and wretchedness to go to a country where honest industry receives its reward', so taking 'them out of the slough of poverty and misery in which they are at present sunk'.[3] Foster's outlay of £30,000 (mostly his own money) was undoubtedly a key factor in reviving female emigration from the poorest localities. Indeed the public and private assistance of the land war period, unlike that provoked by the famine, was largely directed to those most in need of it. Many of the 60,000 recipients would have

[1] *Reports and papers relating to the proceedings of the committee of 'Mr Tuke's fund' for assisting emigration from Ireland* (private circulation, [1885]), pp 241–4.
[2] *Mr Vere Foster's Irish female emigration fund* (private circulation, Oct. 1884), in N.L.I., MS 13552.
[3] *Second report of the select committee of the house of lords on land law (Ireland)*, pp 296, 246, H.C. 1882 (379), xi, 850, 800.

found difficulty in emigrating unaided, while there is ample evidence that their remittances made possible further movement of the very poor. The general effect of assistance was to clear bottlenecks rather than to initiate a flow from western districts already deeply embroiled in emigration.

By far the most important catalyst of emigration was the 'American money' and prepaid tickets provided by those already settled overseas. Accurate statistics of individual assistance could not be compiled, since many small remittances and money orders sent to the United Kingdom had functions other than assisting Irish emigration, while much American money was sent in cash or through minor financial houses not covered by the official returns. In both respects, the quality of official data deteriorated during the later nineteenth century: returns of small transactions were no longer supplied by the port of London after 1860 or by several major Liverpool firms after 1872, and tabulation was discontinued in 1887. Thus the recorded annual flow of remittances from the United States to the United Kingdom, which as table 7 indicates reached one and a half million pounds by the 1880s, greatly understates the true amount.[1] On the other hand, the proportion of small remittances devoted to funding Irish emigration decreased. The vast expansion in the volume of money orders tells us little about long-term changes in the flow of American money after 1873, since money orders become rapidly more popular as a convenient means of sending small payments to creditors and friends as well as potential emigrants. Cyclical variation in the value of remittances and money orders is more significant, corresponding fairly closely with the American business cycle as well as with the volume of emigration from Ireland to the United States.[2] As official reports confirm, the generosity of expatriates towards their Irish connections varied (as did their other outlays) with their current earnings.[3] Table 7 gives no clear indication of the relative importance of remittances from Irish settlers outside the United States; but an experienced administrator noted in 1889 'that very large remittances come from Australia; they come in greater sums' than from America, sometimes amounting to £40.[4]

A less ambiguous though incomplete index of private assistance is provided by the returns of prepaid passages handled by Liverpool shipping houses. Even in 1872, however, many of these passage warrants were being issued to British rather than Irish emigrants. In that year only 24,837 of 168,875 passengers from Liverpool to the United States were returned as Irish-born, yet nearly 60,000

---

[1] Below, p. 644.

[2] Easterlin records American economic peaks (indicated by rate of growth of real *per capita* product) in 1873 and 1882, compared with peaks in remittances (1872 and 1883) and in money orders (1874 and 1883). Easterlin's troughs in 1878 and 1885 correspond with troughs in remittances (1875 and 1885) and money orders (1878 and 1885). See Richard A. Easterlin, 'Influences in European overseas emigration' in *Economic Development and Cultural Change*, ix, no. 3 (Apr. 1961), p. 347; see also the sources for table 7 (below, p. 644).

[3] *Twenty-third report of the postmaster general on the post office*, p. 16 [C 1863], H.C. 1877, xxvii, 216.

[4] *Report from the select committee on colonisation*, p. 126, H.C. 1889 (274), x, 136 (evidence of Ruttledge-Fair).

passage warrants worth about £5 each were handled by local shippers. Though some of these warrants were doubtless redeemed when vessels touched at Irish ports, we must infer that prepaid passages were commonplace in British as well as Irish emigration.[1] Only between 1904 and 1915 was there an official attempt to compute the proportion of all Irish emigrants to the United States whose passages were prepaid. These returns indicate that a third of all steerage passengers travelled on warrants. Not only did that proportion gradually decline, but the minority travelling as cabin passengers had risen to a tenth by 1911–15.[2] Even so, it seems likely that at least two-thirds of Irish emigrants received some form of assistance from their predecessors, though seldom to the extent of exempting them from the ancillary costs of outfit, inland transport, and landing money.

The willingness of emigrants to fund further emigration was repeatedly confirmed by clergymen, landlords, and administrators. Vere Foster stated in 1882 that 'the girls I have assisted have very frequently brought out their whole families after them'; while Tuke reported that his 10,000 beneficiaries had sent back £2,000 in 1885, rising to £8,000 by 1888 and £10,000 two years later, six years after the termination of his scheme.[3] Yet there are signs that some emigrants resented the burden, suspecting that much of their assistance was being swallowed up by household expenditure or liquor rather than provision of further emigration. Alexander Sullivan, president of the Irish National League of America, claimed in 1883 that payment of remittances was 'compulsory and of the nature of a tax'; while less illustrious Irish-Americans snarled that their Irish kinsfolk were 'cringing beggars' whose 'powers of absorption were boundless', with the result that 'the people do not like to send money to ireland it is all lost'.[4] Colonel King-Harman detected a reduction between the famine and 1882 in readiness to fund further emigration: 'nowadays the girls go out, and they generally send money home for two or three years; but they do not send it as continuously as they used to do, and they do not bring out their families in the way they used to do.'[5] Twelve years later, admittedly in the context of an American economic downturn, the registrar general observed that 'it is commonly reported that the people do not get quite so much assistance to go across as they formerly did'.[6] It would not be surprising if Irish settlers had indeed grown less willing to meet the demands of a home population that was becoming at once less impoverished and

[1] William Neilson Hancock, 'On the remittances from North America by Irish emigrants' in *Stat. Soc. Ire. Jn.*, vi (Dec. 1873), p. 281; *Thirty-third general report of the emigration commissioners* [C 768], H.C. 1873, xviii.

[2] Annual *Emigration statistics of Ireland for the years 1904 [to 1915]*, H.C., *passim*.

[3] *Second report of the select committee of the house of lords on land law (Ireland)*, p. 248, H.C. 1882 (379), xi, 802; *Report from the select committee on colonisation*, p. 203, H.C. 1890 (354), xii, 217.

[4] Kerby A. Miller, *Emigrants and exiles: Ireland and the Irish exodus* (New York, 1985), p. 510.

[5] *Second report of the select committee of the house of lords on land law (Ireland)*, pp 243–4, H.C. 1882 (379), xi, 797–8.

[6] *Minutes of evidence . . . taken before her majesty's commissioners appointed to inquire into the financial relations between Great Britain and Ireland* (hereafter cited as *Childers comm.*), p. 154 [C 7720–I], H.C. 1895, xxxvi, 152 (evidence of T. W. Grimshaw).

more reliant upon external subventions. Yet the ethnic networks serving so many expatriates provided an effective means of enforcing perceived obligations to relatives in Ireland, despite the oceans of separation. Individual generosity was demanded and reinforced by Irish emigrant communities, dependent for their perpetuation on continuance of the transatlantic drift.

Mass emigration had profound but conflicting psychological and social consequences for those at home. The ceaseless barrage of fact and rumour concerning the world outside Ireland presumably tended to soften the idiosyncrasies of Irish mentality and habit. The parish priest of Knock, County Mayo, noticed in 1907 that 'a great change is coming over the peasantry . . . They are becoming more practical and less sentimental, owing, no doubt, to their intercourse with social life in America, and to the number of emigrants who return each year from that country.'[1] Significantly, this 'great change' referred to the supposedly novel willingness of Irish countrymen and women to leave the farm, not to more efficient farming by those who remained. Indeed it is likely that emigration was more effective in retarding than promoting structural change in agriculture and rural organisation, by simultaneously raising expectations of comfort and offering the means of satisfying those expectations without radical domestic change. That means was the American money, whose arrival was urgently awaited each Christmas in uncounted rural households. The 'stream of gold' from settlers in America and elsewhere was increasingly used to maintain the home economy in addition to funding further emigration; as one witness remarked in 1907, 'the Christmas American letter is now a necessity, and the more children in America the better'.[2] Already in 1893, it was commonly said in Mayo, Roscommon, and Cork that 'we could not live without the American money'.[3] The implications were bemoaned by a Leitrim curate fourteen years later:[4]

We are living on credit, and on the returns from America. Our incomes are microscopic in their smallness. . . . Wiped out they [the farmers] would have been long ago but for American aid. Their sons and daughters practically sell themselves to slavery to keep the roofs over their parents' heads. It is they and not the land that paid the bills and paid the rent. . . . The wastrels stop at home. The unfitted survive, and the race declines.

This dubious application of Darwin was echoed by the economist Charles Oldham, who proclaimed in 1914 that 'there has been in Ireland a perpetuated survival of the unfittest, a steady debasement of the human currency—very similar

---

[1] *Dudley comm.: appendix to the ninth report*, p. 133 [Cd 3845], H.C. 1908, xli, 685 (evidence of Rev. John Fallon).

[2] *Dudley comm.: appendix to the sixth report*, p. 31 [Cd 3748], H.C. 1908, xxxix, 811 (evidence of John Quilty, Drumcliffe, Co. Sligo).

[3] *Devonshire comm.: reports by Mr Arthur Wilson Fox*, p. 16 [C 6894–xxi], H.C. 1893–4, xxxvii, pt 1, p. 356.

[4] *Dudley comm.: appendix to the sixth report*, pp 252, 255 [Cd 3748], H.C. 1908, xxxix, 1032, 1035 (evidence of Rev. Joseph Meehan, Killarga).

to Gresham's law, by which bad money continually tends to displace good money in the circulation'.[1]

The American money had a multitude of local applications. Tuke's committee reported that the sum of four or five thousand pounds sent home by his emigrants in 1882–3 was devoted to four main purposes: payment of shop debts, rent, purchase of cattle, and passage money.[2] A quarter of a century later in Mohill, County Leitrim, it was 'well known that tenant farmers borrow the money to send their oldest boy or girl to America in order that they would bring out the other members of the family, as well as send assistance home to pay the rent and keep their parents living, and shopkeepers give credit to small farmers pending the receipt of American remittances'. This witness affirmed, not without hyperbole, that the majority of local farmers derived more income from remittances than agricultural produce, and (a few minutes later) that nine-tenths of the rent paid over the last decade or so had been drawn from American money. A tenant farmer from nearby Carrigallen confirmed that most of his peers depended on remittances for their rent payments, citing the case of a family that had received over £400 from the colonies between 1868 and 1893 of which all but £100 had 'gone in rent to the landlord'. Understandably, the 'American money' was 'concealed as much as possible'.[3] In a society of debtors, it was best to keep one's creditors guessing.

Just as many emigrants resented their obligation to subsidise 'wastrels' at home, so many of the agronomists, clergymen, and other witnesses before parliamentary inquiries often deplored its mollycoddling effects. A Cavan priest lamented the vicious spiral of rural indebtedness and emigration: 'all depend for support on credit given by the local shopkeepers waiting the "American dollar"; with the further result that they become loaded with debt, and if the shopkeeper refuse there is nothing before them but the emigrant ship or the workhouse.' A shopkeeper from Roundstone, County Galway, stated to the same inquiry in 1907 that a tenth of his annual turnover of £2,000 was paid at Christmas direct from America, by emigrants settling accumulated arrears on their parents' deaths.[4] In many localities children had become the customer's chief security through their contribution to family income as seasonal workers or emigrants. As Farley McKeown of west Donegal remarks in Patrick MacGill's *Children of the dead end*, childless adults should never be sold meal on credit since 'that kind of people, who have no children to earn for them, never pay debts'.[5]

---

[1] C. H. Oldham, 'Incidence of emigration on town and country life' in *Stat. Soc. Ire. Jn.*, xiii (June 1914), p. 214.

[2] *Emigration from Ireland; being the third report of the committee of 'Mr Tuke's Fund'* (London, 1884), pp 12–13.

[3] *Dudley comm.: appendix to the sixth report*, p. 220 [Cd 3748], H.C. 1908, xxxix, 1000 (evidence of Farrell Reynolds); ibid., p. 192 (MS 972) (evidence of Thomas Smyth).

[4] *Dudley comm.: appendix to the seventh report*, p. 134 [Cd 3785], H.C. 1908, xl, 222 (evidence of Rev. Thomas McGauran); *Dudley comm.: appendix to the tenth report*, p. 39 [Cd 4007], H.C. 1908, xlii, 137 (evidence of Joseph Cloherty).

[5] Patrick MacGill, *Children of the dead end: the autobiography of a navvy* (London, 1914), p. 4.

The long-term economic consequences of emigration remain conjectural. The economist may predict the effects of a marginal reduction in emigration, but the structural repercussions of its elimination are matter for the historical sociologist. Lees and Modell belong to the succession of analysts who have maintained that emigration benefited those who remained because it 'reduced pressure on Irish resources'; whereas Brinley Thomas asserts that Ireland's 'continuous fall in the population had a paralysing effect on the inducement to invest in fixed capital and this in turn led to further emigration'.[1] Would the stoppage of emigration have generated widespread poverty and a Malthusian crisis, or would the multiplication of consumers have stimulated investment in time to avert immiseration? Clearly depopulation during and just after the famine facilitated reorganisation of the rural economy, consolidation of farms, and the substitution of livestock production for tillage. Yet O'Connor Morris's assertion in 1898 that emigration had thrown open 'millions of acres . . . to real and fruitful husbandry' became less apposite after about 1855, when the patterns of land occupancy became more static than ever before.[2] Emigration restricted the number of mouths per household without greatly reducing the number of households, so reducing pressure on resources only if replicated indefinitely. Hence, in the view of Mayo Smith and the dwindling lobby advocating family emigration from congested districts, the condition of Ireland in 1890 was 'little better now than it was forty years ago, notwithstanding the enormous emigration which has taken place of its own accord. Emigration by itself is not a remedy for the evils of overpopulation or of a low condition of the mass of the people.'[3] Many contemporaries believed that emigration, in combination with owner occupation of farms, tended to sustain rather than transform an inefficient system of agriculture, which in turn perpetuated emigration. Oldham tendentiously maintained that 'Ireland is a country with industries that are remarkable and successful, and an agriculture that is the most wasteful and ridiculous in the world. The emigration cannot be stopped unless we can develop agriculture in Ireland to provide employment for the people in the rural districts.'[4] Recent research suggests, however, that the rural economy was less static and archaic than contemporary advocates of modernisation maintained.[5] Labour productivity rose by about a quarter between 1876 and 1908, while total agricultural output rose sharply just before the first world war after declining slightly during the last quarter of the nineteenth century. Changes in land tenure did not perceptibly affect farm investment, while the diffusion of innovation was impressively rapid.[6] Even in Connacht, where holdings remained generally small and farming

[1] Lynn Hollen Lees and John Modell, 'The Irish countryman urbanized: a comparative perspective on the famine migration' in *Journal of Urban History*, iii, no. 4 (Aug. 1977), pp 39–40; Thomas, *Migration and economic growth*, p. 82.

[2] William O'Connor Morris, *Ireland 1798–1898* (London, 1898), p. 183.

[3] Richard Mayo Smith, *Emigration and immigration* (London, 1890), p. 25.

[4] Oldham, 'Incidence of emigration', p. 215.

[5] Above, pp 149–65, 260–79.

[6] Ó Gráda, *Ire. before & after famine*, pp 128–52; Michael Turner, 'Towards an agricultural prices index for Ireland, 1850–1914' in *Econ. & Soc. Rev.*, xviii, no. 2 (Jan. 1987), p. 127.

techniques relatively backward, farmers proved far more responsive to market factors after the 1870s than in the aftermath of the famine. Between 1874 and 1912 small landholders in Connacht were unusually active in substituting cattle for potatoes and cereals, when compared with farmers of similar acreage elsewhere in Ireland.[1] Ireland's agricultural economy was thus more successful and less rigid than hitherto supposed. The performance of small farms was improved by successive emigration of unproductive household members, which allowed occupiers to spend less on food production or purchase and to invest more heavily in livestock. Even so emigration, by subsidising uneconomic holdings and alleviating the pressure for consolidation as well as subdivision of farms, placed severe constraints on agricultural development. The imprint of emigration, whether positive or negative, was perceptible in every facet of economic organisation.

Many economists have argued that the benefits derived from the emigration of unproductive dependants were outweighed by the burden of their rearing costs. George O'Brien wrote in 1941 that 'every emigrant who left Europe embodied whatever investment of capital was necessary to bring him to maturity and earning capacity ... It is arguable that the under-capitalisation of Irish agriculture was partly due to the efflux of savings associated with emigration.'[2] Irish family planners were misinformed if they supposed that their expenditure in rearing children would eventually be exceeded by the insurance benefits derived from emigrant remittances. Children could only repay their rearing costs by remaining in Ireland during that phase in the life cycle when production normally exceeds consumption. If we assume that potential emigrants would have earned more than their keep had they remained in Ireland, it follows that the effect of removing low-paid workers from the home economy before the recovery of their rearing costs would be to reduce the income of those left behind while increasing *mean* income *per capita*.[3] This argument failed to satisfy the registrar general, who pointed out in 1894 that if the emigrant were 'a man who cannot get adequate means of supporting himself in this country he is a loss to the community as long as he stays there'.[4] Many believed that the stoppage of emigration would have led either to widespread pauperism at public expense, or veiled dependency within households choked by superfluous labour. Given the premise that it was desirable to bear children, the optimum strategy in Ireland was to rear most of them for

[1] This analysis is derived from returns giving land usage and livestock numbers by locality and by farm size; see Department of Industry and Commerce (Saorstat Éireann), *Agricultural statistics 1847–1926* (Dublin, 1928, 1930), pp 138–43; *Returns of agricultural produce in Ireland, in the year 1854* [2017], H.C. 1856, liii; *The agricultural statistics of Ireland, for the year 1874* [C 1380], H.C. 1876, lxxviii. The mean number of cattle on holdings of 5–15 acres, for example, rose in Connacht from 2.4 in 1854 through 2.7 in 1874 to 3.5 in 1912; whereas the figures for Ireland were 2.4, 2.9, and 3.3 respectively. Likewise the number of acres under potatoes on the Connacht holdings fell from 1.5 in 1854 through 1.4 in 1874 to 0.8 in 1912, the corresponding acreages for Ireland being 1.3, 1.2, and 0.7.
[2] George O'Brien, 'New light on Irish emigration' in *Studies*, xxx (1941), p. 26.
[3] Joel Mokyr and Cormac Ó Gráda, 'Emigration and poverty in prefamine Ireland' in *Explorations in Economic History*, xix, no. 4 (Oct. 1982), pp 360–84.
[4] *Childers comm.*, p. 145 [C 7720-1], H.C. 1895, xxxvi, 153 (evidence of T. W. Grimshaw).

emigration, since their career prospects tended to improve with distance from home. Moritz Bonn might lament in 1906 that 'the thinner the population becomes, the lonelier will Ireland be; the emptier and stiller the life of this joyous people':[1] yet his lament loses its force once we accept that Irish decisions were increasingly made in the context of the Irish world rather than the island. The emigrants amply repaid their rearing costs outside Ireland, but often within the 'moral economy' of their widely scattered families.

Granted that Ireland's economy could not have absorbed the natural increase of population in the absence of emigration, it might be argued that Irish adults were irrational not in sending their children abroad but in failing to restrict fertility. In fact the desire for children (who are seldom cost-effective) is not grounded in reason, and it is family limitation, rather than unrestricted fertility, that demands explanation in terms of self-interest. The continuing decline in Irish nuptiality after 1870 was not matched by a marked reduction in marital fertility, which remained until the first world war at levels close to those achieved by the celebrated Hutterites.[2] Ireland's failure to follow the European trend towards smaller completed family size signifies the persistence of a cultural and religious outlook glorifying procreation, in a social and economic context offering relatively weak incentives for reduction of fertility. Emigration tended to weaken those incentives still further. It is significant that the county indices of marital fertility were closely and positively correlated with those of cohort depletion. Thus Connacht was characterised by high marital fertility as well as intensive emigration. The association between fertility and emigration reflects interaction rather than mere cause and effect. Emigration reinforced a preference for large families by offering both favourable prospects for children and insurance benefits for aged parents; while high rates of fertility perpetuated underemployment in Ireland and so necessitated further emigration. The link between emigration and 'celibacy' (the proportion still unmarried at about 50) was more complex. By providing the option of employment and probably marriage overseas, emigration facilitated the evolution of a rather rigid match system for those choosing to stay at home. So long as emigration was intensive enough to drain away most of those failing to qualify for an Irish match, celibacy proportions were kept fairly low. This is manifest in the correlation between high ratios of cohort depletion and low female celibacy.[3] Yet any interruption of emigration tended to create a surplus of children who would soon become unmatchable adults, causing high or increasing celibacy proportions in regions marked by low or decreasing emigration. In this sense the secular decrease in nuptiality reflects the failure of emigration to clear the surplus. Despite that long-term failure, emigration provided essential if unreliable

---

[1] Moritz J. Bonn, *Modern Ireland and her agrarian problem* (Dublin, 1906), p. 25.
[2] Ó Gráda, *Ire. before & after famine*, pp 153–76.
[3] For thirty Irish counties (excluding Dublin and Antrim) two variables were calculated: (i) average of cohort depletion rates for the decades 1881–91, 1891–1901, and 1901–11; (ii) proportion never married of women aged 45–54 in 1911. The resultant correlation was $r = -.67$.

reinforcement for Ireland's aberrant demographic system of restrictive marriage coupled with high marital fertility.

THE persistence of heavy emigration was widely deplored by Irish observers, yet its functions as an essential prop of rural society and family structure were equally widely admitted. In 1907 a shopkeeper and small farmer in Drumcliffe, County Sligo, declared that 'as soon as their children reach the adult age, through the scarcity of employment, they join their uncles and aunts and cousins in the United States, one son remaining on the farm; and if the parents do not get him married before they die he generally sells out and goes, too. Thus the country is bleeding to death.' His report on local households showed that 13 out of 26 grown-up daughters and 15 out of 35 boys were living overseas (all in America but for 5 boys in Britain and 1 in South Africa), whereas only 9 sons and 5 daughters had found employment off the home farm in Ireland. The proportion of children living overseas was greater for small farmers whose rent ranged between £5 and £10 (56 per cent) than for those lower or higher in the social scale (32 per cent).[1] Many witnesses bemoaned the perceived tendency of the strong and healthy to depart, while the 'delicate bird in every clutch' (otherwise 'the cripples and the paralytics') stayed at home.[2] An impromptu census of 221 labourers and small farmers on the Lansdowne estate, County Kerry, revealed in 1880 that no less than 164 preferred the option of emigration to staying in Ireland.[3] Twelve years later an official in the union of Westport, County Mayo, recorded local opinions that 'it would not do for a man to stop here', that labourers would go to America 'if we get the chance', and that 'every girl who can' would make off to the United States at the age of 14.[4] The scale and popularity of emigration provoked a mixture of horror and resignation, often in the same mind. The catholic bishop of Clonfert averred in 1880 that it was 'a scandal' that 'the bone and sinew of the country is not employed in improving the land, in extending its resources, in giving railway communication, in thorough drainage, and in increasing the produce of the country'. Yet when asked if he were opposed to emigration, the bishop replied: 'I am, and I am not. I am opposed to emigration for the sake of the general welfare of the country . . . But in another sense, for the individual himself, who leaves the country and takes his youth and strength to America, it may be a blessing.'[5] Other churchmen, such as Fr Peter Sheehan at Queenstown,

---

[1] *Dudley comm.: appendix to the sixth report*, pp 29–31, 246 [Cd 3748], H.C. 1908, xxxix, 809–11, 1026 (evidence of John Quilty).

[2] Ibid., p. 153 (MS 933) (evidence of Patrick Rooney, Manorhamilton, Co. Leitrim); *Dudley comm.: first appendix to the seventh report*, p. 184 [Cd 3785], H.C. 1908, xl, 272 (evidence of Rev. P. Glynn, Kilrush, Co. Clare, who also delivered the clerical cliché that 'this dreadful haemorrhage is draining the lifeblood of Ireland away').

[3] *Richmond comm.*, p. 90 [C 2778–I], H.C. 1881, xv, 118 (evidence of Professor Thomas Baldwin).

[4] *Devonshire comm.: reports by Mr Arthur Wilson Fox*, p. 75 [C 6894–XXI], H.C. 1893–4, xxxvii, pt 1, p. 415.

[5] *Richmond comm.*, p. 500 [C 2778–I], H.C. 1881, xv, 528 (evidence of Bishop Patrick Duggan).

stressed the compensations of emigration for the church as well as the emigrant. Over the previous thirty years the church had 'lost half the merits that . . . would have been stored away in the treasury of Heaven' as well as half its funds. Yet the saving grace was that 'the exiles have prospered', becoming 'not only the apostles of a saving faith, but the only elements of the stability and strength with which these new races, proud but powerless, can be ever cemented together'.[1] Emigration, in short, hurt Ireland but helped the individual, the people, and their faith.

For many of those intent on reinvigorating Ireland, however, the nation's loss outweighed the compensating benefits. The catholic hierarchy, having denounced state-sponsored emigration at a meeting in Armagh in 1883, resolved 'that the evil can be cured in a statesmanlike manner, and with the happiest results, by promoting the migration of the surplus population of the congested districts' to vacant grasslands.[2] Seven years later, Parnell told Gerald Balfour that assisted family emigration would 'leave us none but the old men and the old women, that would be one way of dealing with the Irish question, certainly; in any case that would scarcely be a project that you could expect me to approve.' His alternative strategy for rural regeneration had shifted, however, from internal colonisation to the promotion of mining, fishing, and cottage industries.[3] So long as politicians continued to toy with projects involving state funding, nationalists could duck the embarrassing popularity of private emigration by focusing their fury on the advocates of public emigration. By the end of the century this device was obsolete. Lobbies such as the Catholic Truth Society and Anti-Emigration Society exposed 'the real evils of the exodus' from the only nation which saw 'its people leave her shores with a comparatively light heart'.[4] The *Irish Peasant* hoped that the Gaelic revival would help reverse 'the deplorable tide of emigration' by relieving the rural monotony of journalistic imagination; though Mgr O'Riordan scoffed at Sir Horace Plunkett's belief 'that they left for want of amusement at home. They left chiefly for want of work at home.'[5] Nationalist abhorrence of emigration was sharpened by its effect in depleting nationalist organisations, despite the compensating consolidation of supportive societies created by emigrants and their descendants in Britain, Australasia, and North America. The disruptive influence of emigration extended to conspiratorial as well as political organisations. In 1903 the constabulary reported that the moonlighting gangs of Miltown Malbay, County Clare, had been 'broken up and many of the members are reformed, while more are gone to America'.[6] Emigration was widely thought to promote political

---

[1] Sheehan, 'The effect of emigration on the Irish church', pp 602–5. Sheehan's enthusiasm overstrained his syntax.

[2] *Report from the select committee on colonisation*, appendix 11, p. 494, H.C. 1890 (354), xii, 508.

[3] Ibid., *minutes of evidence*, pp 344, 349, H.C. 1890 (354), xii, 358, 363.

[4] Richard J. Kelly, *The effects of emigration* (Dublin, [1904]), p. 9.

[5] Martin J. Waters, 'Peasants and emigrants' in Daniel J. Casey and Robert E. Rhodes (ed.), *Views of the Irish peasantry, 1800–1916* (Hamden, Conn., 1977), p. 171; Michael O'Riordan, *Catholicity and progress in Ireland* (London, rev. ed., 1905), p. 287.

[6] John Allingham (crime special sergeant), monthly confidential report, 2 Mar. 1903 (N.A.I., C.S.B. papers, 28288S).

stability and undermine disaffection, in Ireland if not elsewhere. This belief was as welcome to the government as it was alarming to nationalists.

Conversely, reduction of emigration menaced social and political stability by creating a surplus of young men and women without hope of advancement at home and frustrated in their expectation of finding a livelihood overseas. The first major outbreak of social unrest after the famine, the land war initiated in 1879,[1] was immediately preceded by an unprecedented reduction in net emigration and flourished in Connacht, hitherto quiescent but abnormally dependent on emigration. Though food shortage and agricultural crisis precipitated the conflict, the impact of these factors would have been far milder but for the accumulation of a surplus of dependants thwarted in their desire to depart by the American recession of the late 1870s. The heavy emigration of 1880–82 probably contributed to the subsequent reduction in the frequency of outrages. The second and more protracted interruption to emigration was to have more overt social and political consequences. As the auditor of the Trinity College Historical Society observed in 1929:

Once, and once only, during the last hundred years has the tide of emigration been stemmed—that was during the late world war. There can be little doubt that it is to the energy and vigour then accumulated that we owe our present measure of national autonomy. A five years' cessation of emigration achieved what an even greater number of centuries of violence and agitation had failed to accomplish.[2]

The chief secretary had drawn different lessons from the same assumption in July 1917, when he advised the war cabinet that the wartime stoppage of emigration had increased the disaffection as well as the number of young Irishmen.[3] This was confirmed a few months later by a journalist investigating the causes of agrarian unrest in Clare:

Emigration, the great high road to fortune for the youth of Clare, has been stopped during the war . . . There are many idle young men on scanty plots which cannot nourish a family, and side by side with the cottager's allotment there are thousand-acre farms, and even three- or four-thousand-acre estates which are only used for the feeding of cattle.[4]

The extent to which movement out of Ireland was curtailed by the war is conjectural, since no reliable enumeration of migration to Britain was undertaken. Undoubtedly the war prompted considerable short-term migration to British munitions factories, in addition to the special emigration resulting from military recruitment, overseas service, and often death or postwar settlement abroad. But munitions workers and soldiers tended to be recruited in cities and towns little affected by conventional emigration, so that the growing surplus of young adult men, and especially women, in poorer rural districts was scarcely alleviated by wartime mobility. Overseas emigration was sharply reduced in 1915 and 1916 by

[1] Above, pp 33–6.   [2] C. B. McKenna, *The depopulation of Ireland* (Dublin, 1930), p. 14.
[3] George Dangerfield, *The damnable question: a study in Anglo–Irish relations* (Boston, Mass., 1976), pp 259–60.
[4] *Manchester Guardian*, 4 Mar. 1918.

declining foreign demand for labour, becoming negligible in 1917 and 1918 because of the German submarine campaign and the commandeering of passenger vessels. After 1916 virtually all emigrants noticed by Irish police enumerators were bound for Britain, with only a few hundred risking an ocean passage. Earlier in the war the fear of conscription was said to have induced nearly 4,500 young men to leave their homes with the intention of emigrating, a figure amounting to more than half of all recorded male emigrants aged 20–39 for the period between August 1914 and November 1915. In Connacht, which provided the majority of the evaders, their number actually exceeded that of recorded emigrants.[1] The net effect of curtailing emigration and encouraging military recruitment was probably to create by 1918 a significant accumulation of would-be emigrants, male as well as female, in counties such as Mayo, Kerry, Leitrim, Galway, Donegal, and Clare. It was in these western counties that Sinn Féin won its strongest popular following in 1917–18.[2] It seems plausible, if unprovable, that thwarted emigrants contributed both personnel and passion to the great populist movements begun in 1879 and 1917; while the Ladies' Land League and Cumann na mBan were invigorated by young women for whom Ireland could offer neither jobs nor husbands.

Demobilisation of soldiers and war workers quickly followed the armistice of November 1918, yet substantial emigration did not resume until spring 1920. During those months Irish urban populations followed the precedent of the rural west by building up a labour surplus that generated heavy unemployment, especially among ex-servicemen. Returned soldiers and would-be emigrants contributed crucially to the guerrilla movement that became active in urban as well as rural areas in 1919–20. Republican organisers observed the resumption of emigration with alarm. On 25 May 1920 a Sinn Féin official at Queenstown warned Michael Collins that

some drastic steps must be taken to stop emigration . . . I believe that some of the emigration agents in the little villages and country towns are experiencing difficulty in carrying out their immoral trade openly; but they are evading the vigilance of Sinn Féin and other Irish-Ireland bodies.

The writer had already initiated a campaign 'calling on the Irish republican government to place a ban on this vicious traffic, that drains the country of its life-blood and lowers the vitality of the nation'.[3] A few days later, the minister for defence declared that

the young men of Ireland must stand fast. To leave their country at this supreme crisis would be nothing less than base desertion in the face of the enemy . . . There will be plenty

---

[1] Returns showing 'emigration of young men owing to fear of conscription' (N.A.I., C.S.O., R.P. 1915/19680).

[2] David Fitzpatrick, 'The geography of Irish nationalism, 1910–1921' in *Past & Present*, no. 78 (Feb. 1978), pp 138, 144.

[3] William Murphy to Michael Collins (N.A.I., DE 2/37).

of employment for everyone in Ireland in future. The government of the republic is at present engaged upon work which will insure this. All that is needed is a little more patience, and then a bracing-up for the final tussle.[1]

These specious assurances failed to reverse the monthly trend towards heavier emigration; a decree prohibiting emigration, issued by Dáil Éireann on 6 August 1920 to implement an earlier ministerial proclamation, also failed. It was loftily decreed that 'no citizen of the Irish republic shall be permitted to leave Ireland for the purpose of settling abroad unless with the written sanction of the government of the republic'. Applications giving 'reasons for emigrating' were to be authenticated by republican justices and court registrars, and in the case of I.R.A. personnel by their brigade commandants as well. Deputies from Cork and Sligo, more familiar with emigration than the Dublin-based leadership, proposed 'that the decree be not enforced pending the formulation of a scheme for providing employment in Ireland for intending emigrants'; but in a rare division their amendment was defeated by seven votes.[2] In early April 1921, after a month in which departures exceeded the number for any month in 1920, the dáil ministry forbade shipping and emigration agents to issue tickets or accept passage money without presentation of a permit adorned with the seal of the republic, and warned that disobedience would constitute a 'grave offence against the welfare of the state in time of war and shall be dealt with accordingly'.[3] The permit system was virtually inoperative, though by coincidence the flow of emigration slackened somewhat from June 1921 onwards. The experience of the wartime and revolutionary period offers persuasive evidence of the social and political importance of emigration. The decision to leave Ireland was essentially the outcome of economic and social factors, impervious to the rhetoric of politicians; but the organisation of politics was profoundly affected by the extent, timing, and composition of the emigrant stream.

THE shape and impact of Irish emigration were mainly determined in the immediate aftermath of famine, with only minor alterations becoming evident in the half-century after 1871. In one respect, however, the structure of migration was modified with significant consequences for Irish mentality and culture. Return movement to Ireland, once rare and spasmodic, became commonplace. Substantial reverse migration from the United States had been recorded in the 1860s; while the halving of the east-bound fare in 1874 was reported to have provoked a 'rush of steerage passengers' to Liverpool and Glasgow.[4] In 1876,

---

[1] Dáil Éireann, Department of Defence, 'Manifesto' (copy in Imperial War Museum (London), Strickland papers, P 363). See also Patrick O'Farrell, 'Emigrant attitudes and behaviour as a source for Irish history' in *Hist. Studies*, x (1976), p. 115.

[2] *Dáil Éireann proc., 1919–1921*, pp 206–7.

[3] *Round Table*, xi (1921), pp. 494–5. Monthly returns of emigrants from Irish ports for 1900–22 are in the Rialtas files (N.A.I., R2).

[4] G. R. C. Keep, 'Some Irish opinion on population and emigration, 1851–1901' in *I.E.R.*, 5th ser., lxxxiv (July–Dec. 1955), p. 384.

when emigration fell to its lowest level since the 1830s, the number of Irish passengers departing for extra-European destinations only just exceeded the number returning. Passenger traffic from the United States marginally surpassed the westward movement.[1] No systematic returns of Irish reverse migration to the British Isles were compiled until 1895. As table 8 indicates, about 44 Irish passengers returned for every 100 passengers who left between 1895 and 1913.[2] The balance of passenger movement involving the United States changed little over the period, being similar for those of Irish and British nationality. At certain periods, however, reverse movement from Canada, Australasia, and especially South Africa, approached or exceeded the outward flow. It must be emphasised that many travellers in both directions were businessmen or temporary visitors rather than permanent migrants. In 1912, when the board of trade altered its enumeration in the hope of excluding temporary migrants, the volume of recorded reverse movement to Ireland dropped sharply. Similar attempts to discriminate between permanent and temporary migrants had already been made by statisticians in the United States. Using a variety of criteria, Gould has computed 'repatriant ratios' for the Irish and other alien groups in the United States just before the first world war. According to one specification, for every alien intending to emigrate to Ireland there were sixteen Irish residents immigrating to the United States, the lowest repatriant ratio for any major country of origin.[3] Irish expatriates were far more inclined to return home as visitors than to resettle in Ireland.

Though most emigrants did not return permanently to their homeland, the 'returned Yank' as well as the Irish-born tourist had become a familiar figure in rural Ireland by the 1890s. Table 9 shows that most of them returning from the United States between 1895 and 1913 were women, whereas men were increasingly dominant in reverse movement from other countries. Table 10 provides a profile of those proposing to settle in Ireland in 1912–13.[4] The group naturally tended to be older than those emigrating in the same period: two-fifths of the passengers from North America were aged over 30, as were the majority of returned Australasians. The occupational statistics suggest that many returning migrants remained near the base of the social ladder: two-fifths of men back from

---

[1] *Copy of statistical tables relating to emigration and immigration . . . in the year 1876*, pp 12–16, H.C. 1877 (5), lxxxv, 632–6. This unique return gives immigration from each country by *port*, enabling us to estimate the number of Irish immigrants for comparison with that of emigrants (assuming that all passengers at Irish ports and a tenth of those at Liverpool were Irish). These estimates indicate that net outward migration of steerage passengers was only 838 to the United States, 122 to British North America, 686 to Australasia, and 192 elsewhere, during 1876. Net outward movement of cabin passengers to the last three destinations was 10, 59, and 106 in turn; while net interchange of cabin passengers with the United States was inward, amounting to 915 passengers.

[2] Below, p. 645.

[3] J. D. Gould, 'European inter-continental emigration: the road home: return migration from the U.S.A.' in *Journal of European Economic History*, ix, no. 1 (spring 1980), pp 55–60. Similar calculations by 'race or people' rather than birthplace produce an Irish repatriant ratio of one to six, also the lowest of Gould's series.

[4] Below, pp 646, 647.

North America were humble labourers, as were a quarter of the Irish-Australasians. A substantial minority of those from Canada and Australasia were in farming, while about half of all returning males were in trades, commerce, or the professions. Thus some but by no means all gave the appearance of having raised their social status during their residence overseas; though it is also likely that the repatriation rate was higher for emigrants of initially superior status. Among occupied women returning from the United States, servants were almost as predominant as among emigrants; whereas a fifth of women coming home from Canada and Australasia boasted commercial or professional occupations. In terms of occupation and material success, the homecomers were not easily reducible to any simple stereotype.

Local response to their arrival was correspondingly ambivalent, ranging from admiration through envy to contempt. Return, like departure, generated fierce and conflicting emotions. A Donegal man who embarked from New York at the beginning of the century remembered that 'the shouting, the roaring, and the lamentation of the people on the quays would deafen you'; whereas when he had left Derry about four years earlier there had been no quayside farewell.[1] Arrival home was often a muted occasion marked by awkwardness, alienation, and mutual wariness. Hosts and guests alike would be eager to impress each other: the Yankee would 'provide a bit of a feast' for the villagers, who in turn might have brought an outside car to the station to make his homecoming 'as "dacent" as possible'.[2] Despite dancing, drinking, and gossiping, alienation often predominated. On his first trip to Inishmaan, J. M. Synge witnessed 'the return of a native who had spent five years in New York'. He paced about 'in his neat suit, looking strangely foreign to his birthplace. . . . When the curraghs were in their places the men crowded round him to bid him welcome. He shook hands with them readily enough, but with no smile of recognition. He is said to be dying.'[3] Other reports stress the conspicuousness in 'dress, manner, and appearance' of repatriates, such as the girl who 'in her well-fitting cloth dress and jacket, looked strangely out of place in the small cottage where I found her' (near Westport, County Mayo, in 1893).[4] Some Yanks were tactful enough to discard their finery after a couple of days, like the girls whom 'George Birmingham' (Canon J. O. Hannay) observed chatting in Irish and raking the hay in their crimson flannel petticoats.[5] Yet reassimilation into Irish life was difficult even for those who had found that America 'did not suit them, and that they did not get their health there, and the working hours were too long and too different'.[6] Those who had failed abroad

[1] Michael McGowan, *The hard road to Klondike* (London, 1962), p. 139.

[2] Ibid., p. 145; P. D. Murphy, 'Village characters. II. The returned emigrant' in *Ireland's Own*, xxix (30 May 1917), p. 364.

[3] John M. Synge, *The Aran Islands and other writings*, ed. Robert Tracy (New York, 1962), pp 62–3.

[4] *Richmond comm.*, p. 1013 [C 2778–I], H.C. 1881, xv, 1041 (evidence of Charles Hare Hemphill, concerning Kerry); *Devonshire comm.: reports by Mr Arthur Wilson Fox*, p. 57 [C 6894–XXI], H.C. 1893–4, xxxvii, pt 1, p. 397.

[5] George A. Birmingham, *The lighter side of Irish life* (Edinburgh, new ed., 1924), pp 213–14.

[6] *Report of the royal commission on the Land Law (Ireland) Act, 1881*, p. 42 [C 4969], H.C. 1887, xxvi, 74 (evidence of A. Newton Brady, Connemara).

tended to be despised at home while those who had succeeded were greeted with resentment. As Birmingham wrote:[1]

We do not, as a rule, much like them either as settlers or visitors. If they come home for good and all, they put up the price of land, bidding up small holdings which happen to be for sale to quite ridiculous prices. Then they build houses which are out of keeping with our humble dwellings. Their ways of life are a continual reproach to our easy-going habits ... If they come as visitors their conversation annoys us.

Irish networks of kinship and friendship, so efficient in overcoming physical separation, came under severe strain when that separation was unexpectedly terminated.

The successful returned emigrant was often stereotyped as either a woman in search of a husband or a man in search of property. In north Longford it was the custom for returning women to devote their ample fortunes to rescuing debt-burdened farmers, so earning the epithet 'redeemer'.[2] In 1907 the Dudley commission was told that numerous girls returned from America to Knock, County Mayo, with fortunes of one or two hundred pounds, so being 'sure to get husbands'. In Carna, County Galway, girls brought back dowries of between £50 and £300; while the range reported in Roscommon was £50–200.[3] Occasionally men returned in search of Irish wives, as in the case of a reformed alcoholic who returned in the 1860s from the Victorian diggings 'to the Old Land with the reward of his labour, and seriously talked about "picking up some young woman" to shed the radiance of her smiles within his cottage home of ease'.[4] The prominence of Yanks in purchasing tenant right, often at inflated prices, is confirmed by testimony from counties as disparate as Wexford and Donegal (1880), Cork and Galway (1897), and Leitrim (1907). In Dungloe, County Donegal, a small farmer and shopkeeper claimed that 'the American money raised the price of land. Many who paid large prices for farms on their return with their savings from America have, since the bad times, had to go back to the States.'[5] A similar case was reported in Carna (Connemara), where a Boston man bought for £28 four adjacent holdings whose tenants had been evicted:[6]

The man returned from America, when his relative bought the places, and he expended about £40 or £45 on it, and made a very superior country house. When he had all that

---

[1] Birmingham, op. cit., p. 211.

[2] Marjolein 't Hart, 'Irish return migration in the nineteenth century' in *Tijdschrift voor Economische en Sociale Geografie*, lxxvi, no. 3 (1985), p. 225.

[3] *Dudley comm.: appendix to ninth report*, p. 133 [Cd 3845], H.C. 1908, xli, 685; *appendix to tenth report*, p. 50 [Cd 4007], H.C. 1908, xlii, 148; *appendix to fifth report*, p. 167 [Cd 3630], H.C. 1907, xxxvi, 465 (evidence of Rev. John Fallon, Rev. Michael McHugh, and John Fitzgibbon respectively). See also Arnold Schrier, *Ireland and the American emigration, 1850–1900* (Minneapolis, 1958), pp 130–31.

[4] *Emigration! Where shall I go? By an Australian colonist* (London, 1869), p. 13.

[5] *Bessborough comm.: appendix D*, p. 1546 [C 2779–III], H.C. 1881, xix, 796 (evidence of Daniel O'Donnell).

[6] *Royal commission of inquiry into the procedure and practice and the methods of valuation . . .: minutes of evidence*, p. 889 [C 8859], H.C. 1898, xxxv, 941 (evidence of James Berry).

done the land was incapable of improvement, and he failed on the spot and sold it, with his house, for £30, and went off to America.

In Mallow, County Cork, two Americans returned in the mid-1880s with capital raised from diamond-mining and sheep-farming, and 'at once picked up' any farms that had since come on to the market.[1] Local hostility was aroused not only by the alleged inflation of land prices, but also by the readiness of returned emigrants to 'grab' evicted farms and by their agricultural incompetence. An organiser of the United Irish League in Mohill, County Leitrim, asserted that the only farmers able to buy land were returned or returning Americans: 'I never saw one of them fit for a spit in agriculture. They have exhausted their energies in America earning this money.'[2]

Those who returned as settlers or tourists, though often greeted with reserve and suspicion, helped bridge the cultural gap between Ireland and the urban world. Their speech, clothing, and manners inevitably infected the home population, producing a droll blend of Ireland, Britain, and America. The evident possibility of return encouraged emigrants to leave Ireland with less fuss than before. Even in 1871, Wexford people were matter-of-fact about going to America: 'in fact, they speak of it now as they spoke formerly of going from one county into another.'[3] The American wake and wail were still reported, but as Robert Lynd remarked of emigrant girls boarding trains in Connemara, 'sometimes, the lamenting girl seems to lose her grief as suddenly as she found it, and as she arrives at various railway stations she leans out of the window to see if there are any friendly faces about which will be wakened into interest by her momentary tragedy'.[4] In 1882 Tuke described the departure of his second shipload of assisted emigrants from Clifden, County Galway: 'I did not hear a single "wail" as we left the ship; but before we steamed out a multitude of hand-shakings and blessings were showered upon me, and three cheers rang across the bay.'[5] As Mgr O'Riordan observed in 1905,[6]

the 'American wake' has ceased to be what it once was. The wailing which was once witnessed at the parting of old friends and the separating of families is heard no more. Most of our present emigrants are leaving friends at home only to join others beyond the sea. Children learn from their childhood that their destiny is America; and as they grow up, the thought is set before them as a thing to hope for.

Pity, once lavished upon Ireland's 'exiles', now greeted those who had failed to escape.

[1] Ibid., p. 660 (MS 712) (evidence of Thomas Barry).
[2] Dudley comm.: appendix to sixth report, p. 221 [Cd 3748], H.C. 1908, xxxix, 1001 (evidence of Farrell Reynolds).
[3] Report from the select committee on law of rating (Ireland) . . ., minutes of evidence, p. 328, H.C. 1871 (423), x, 340 (evidence of Michael FitzHenry Sweetman).
[4] Robert Lynd, Home life in Ireland (London, 1909), p. 121.
[5] J. H. Tuke, 'With the emigrants' in Nineteenth Century, xii (July 1882), p. 152.
[6] O'Riordan, Catholicity and progress, p. 292.

APPENDIX

1 RATES OF OUT-MIGRATION FROM IRELAND, 1871–1911

	cohort depletion				emigration from Irish ports			
	1871–81	1881–91	1891–1901	1901–11	1871–80	1881–90	1891–1900	1901–10
Leinster	18.67	21.66	14.95	12.41	8.51	11.24	4.30	3.67
Munster	27.22	33.79	27.74	24.56	13.30	20.09	15.82	10.64
Ulster	26.19	27.50	19.73	19.79	13.69	13.00	5.43	6.70
Connacht	33.17	40.28	36.11	34.97	10.39	20.93	17.29	13.54
Ireland	25.82	29.98	23.35	21.46	11.79	15.60	9.46	7.82
coefficient of variation	11.9	15.9	17.1	29.1	22.3	26.8	55.6	43.9

Sources: *Census Ire., 1871–1911*; *Agricultural statistics, Ire., 1871–5*; *Emigration statistics of Ireland, 1876–1910*: in H. C. papers. See also Vaughan & Fitzpatrick, *Ir. hist. statistics*, pp 261–5, 269–353.

Cohort depletion is the percentage depletion over an intercensal decade of the cohort initially aged 5–24 years. Rates of emigration from Irish ports give the number of 'permanent' emigrants (natives of Ireland) for each decade enumerated by the constabulary, multiplied by 100, and divided by the mean census population for the decade. The coefficient of variation gives the standard deviation of percentages for 30 counties (excluding Dublin and Antrim) multiplied by 100, and divided by the mean percentage for those counties.

2 NATIONALITY OF EMIGRANTS FROM UNITED KINGDOM PORTS BY DESTINATION, 1853–1910

	Irish emigrants as % of U.K. emigrants to certain destinations			
years	total[a]	United States of America	British North America	Australasia
1853–60	56.1	71.4	52.4	25.2
1861–70	52.1	61.0	30.8	31.0
1871–80	33.3	41.3	14.5	20.4
1881–90	28.7	36.6	14.7	14.9
1891–1900	26.4	37.3	5.7	9.0
1901–10[b]	17.1	33.3	4.5	5.1

[a] Totals include passengers contracted to land at other extra-European destinations.
[b] For 1908–10 only, 'U.K.' emigrants include a few 'British subjects' of colonial nationality (amounting to 0.8% of all 'U.K.' emigrants for 1901–10).

Sources: *Tables relating to emigration, 1901–10*: in H.C. papers, *passim*. Statistics refer to passengers of 'English'. 'Scotch', and 'Irish' nationality who were returned as leaving U.K. ports for extra-European destinations (excluding 'foreigners' and passengers of unspecified nationality).

3 DISTRIBUTION OF IRISH-BORN OUTSIDE THEIR NATIVE COUNTIES, 1871–1921

year	Ireland	Britain	U.S.A.	Canada	Australia	total (5 cols)	native county
			(thousands)				
1871	489.2	774.3	1,855.8	223.2	213.8	3,556.3	4,817.6
1881	479.8	781.1	1,854.6	185.5	214.8	3,515.8	4,582.5
1891	459.3	653.1	1,871.5	149.2	229.2	3,362.3	4,122.1
1901	483.9	631.6	1,615.5	101.6	185.8	3,018.4	3,843.0
1911	500.0	550.0	1,352.3	92.9	141.3	2,636.5	3,733.2
1921	600.0[a]	523.8	1,037.2	93.3	106.3	2,360.6[a]	3,800.0[a]
% of migratory Irish-born in each region							
1871	13.8	21.8	52.2	6.3	6.0	100	
1881	13.6	22.2	52.8	5.3	6.1	100	
1891	13.7	19.4	55.7	4.4	6.8	100	
1901	16.0	20.9	53.5	3.4	6.2	100	
1911	19.0	20.9	51.3	3.5	5.4	100	
1921	25.4[a]	22.2	43.9	4.0	4.5	100[a]	
% of local population in each region							
1871	9.0	3.0	4.8	6.0	12.9	4.7	
1881	9.3	2.6	3.7	4.3	9.5	3.8	
1891	9.8	2.0	3.0	3.1	7.2	3.1	
1901	10.9	1.7	2.1	1.9	4.9	2.4	
1911	11.4	1.3	1.5	1.3	3.2	1.8	
1921	13.4[a]	1.2	1.0	1.1	2.0	1.4[a]	

Statistics are derived from national census returns for dates proximate to the stated years (preceding year for U.S.A.).

[a] These Irish figures (1921) are partly based upon the registrar-general's estimate for that year, and are especially imprecise. Precise criteria of enumeration varied between countries. The Isle of Man and the Channel Islands are excluded from British statistics. Irish settlers in other regions such as New Zealand, South Africa, and South America are ignored.

4 DESTINATIONS OUTSIDE EUROPE OF IRISH EMIGRANTS, 1876–1914

destination	number (thousands)				percentage			
	1876–85	1886–95	1896–1905	1906–14	1876–85	1886–95	1896–1905	1906–14
emigrants from Irish ports								
U.S.A.	453.3	522.3	318.9	200.1	83.50	92.56	94.17	80.63
British North America	34.0	16.5	9.6	38.5	6.26	2.93	2.84	15.53
Australasia	53.9	22.6	6.7	7.6	9.94	4.01	1.97	3.05
other	1.6	2.9	3.5	2.0	0.30	0.51	1.02	0.79
total outside Europe	542.9	564.3	338.6	248.2	100	100	100	100
Irish emigrants from U.K. ports								
U.S.A.	474.0	541.4	382.5	309.8	80.90	90.90	87.62	80.02
British North America	40.0	19.6	16.2	49.2	6.83	3.28	3.71	12.72
Australasia	66.1	26.1	10.2	15.5	11.27	4.38	2.35	3.99
other	5.8	8.6	27.6	12.6	0.99	1.44	6.33	3.27
total outside Europe	585.9	595.6	436.5	387.1	100	100	100	100

For definitions and sources, see note to table 5.

Statistics of Irish emigrants from U.K. ports for the first decade exclude 1876, for which breakdowns by destination and nativity are unavailable. Statistics of emigrants from Irish ports exclude those bound for Britain (approximately 226,700 between 1876 and 1914), France (300) and other parts of Europe (200). The 'other' destinations recorded were Africa (5,700) and South America (3,300). Inconsistencies in totals are attributable to rounding.

5 EMIGRATION OF NATIVES OF IRELAND BY QUINQUENNIA, 1871–1914

groups	1871–5	1876–80	1881–5	1886–90	1891–5	1896–1900	1901–5	1906–10	1911–14
emigrants from Irish ports (each group is shown as a percentage of the total)									
male: total	56.21	52.96	51.01	51.61	47.34	45.34	47.45	52.56	53.16
under 15 years	7.06	4.93	8.36	5.47	4.17	3.67	4.52	4.50	3.83
20–24 years	18.21	16.32	18.01	21.59	19.91	18.65	20.03	22.03	23.67
ever married			7.42[a]	5.81	4.63	4.17	4.58	4.57	4.65
female: total	43.79	47.04	48.99	48.39	52.66	54.66	52.55	47.44	46.84
under 15 years	6.89	4.60	8.01	5.24	4.11	3.68	4.49	4.32	3.74
20–24 years	15.23	15.37	16.16	18.66	21.94	25.78	21.28	18.16	18.51
ever married			9.57[a]	7.97	7.16	6.55	6.86	5.71	5.27
number (thousands)	364.1	259.8	414.2	356.5	243.0	190.3	187.2	158.9	111.2
Irish emigrants from U.K. ports (each group is shown as a percentage of the total)									
male: total		51.64[b]	51.02	51.05	47.30	45.09	46.95	50.14	50.19
under 12 years		6.36[b]	7.41	5.34	4.00	3.17	3.75	4.11	4.12
ever married		5.81[b]	5.10	3.86	3.43	3.42	4.37	4.95[b]	
female: total		48.36[b]	48.98	48.95	52.70	54.91	53.05	49.86	49.81
under 12 years		6.21[b]	7.27	5.26	4.12	3.34	3.78	3.93[b]	3.99
ever married		7.39[b]	7.47	6.11	5.80	5.48	6.86	7.62[b]	
number (thousands)	329.5	213.2	398.7	335.8	259.8	201.1	235.4	250.0	137.1

Sources: *Agricultural statistics of Ireland, 1871–5*; *Emigration statistics of Ireland, 1876–1914*; *Tables relating to emigration, 1877–1914*: in H.C. papers.

Statistics by age-group and conjugal status refer to the percentage of all emigrants for whom relevant data were returned. The upper part of the table concerns 'permanent' emigrants (natives of Ireland) enumerated at Irish ports: the war year of 1915 is omitted from statistics for the final quinquennium. The lower part of the table refers to passengers from U.K. ports (recorded as natives of Ireland) bound for destinations outside Europe. For the latter part of the final period only (Apr. 1912 to Dec. 1913), statistics refer to the more restricted class of 'emigrants' last resident for a full year in Ireland, and intending to spend at least a year outside Europe. These statistics are not available for 1914.

[a] Data available only for the years 1883–5.
[b] Data unavailable for part of the quinquennium. For 1876–80, details of sex, age, and conjugal status were not available for 1876. For 1906–10, details of conjugal status were published only for the first two years.

6 COHORT DEPLETION AND LITERACY FOR IRELAND AND MAYO, 1871–1911

	Ireland				Mayo			
	1871–81	1881–91	1891–1901	1901–11	1871–81	1881–91	1891–1901	1901–11
depletion as % of cohorts								
literates								
males	33	40	34	31	38	49	47	44
females	33	39	32	30	43	52	49	48
illiterates								
males	48	56	46	37	51	63	52	45
females	38	48	33	29	40	59	41	44
% of total depletion								
literates								
males	61	71	83	92	44	57	78	90
females	62	75	89	95	43	56	84	93

Sources: *Census Ire., 1871–1911: reports*, in H.C. papers. For full references to census reports and population figures, see Vaughan & Fitzpatrick, *Ir. hist. statistics*, pp 355–7.

Cohort depletion is the percentage depletion over an intercensal decade of the cohort initially aged 15–24 years, calculated separately for each sex and for the cohorts able to read and write, and illiterate (including those able to read but not write), respectively. The depletion statistics slightly overstate the out-migration of persons initially unable to read and write, since some people aged over 15 presumably became literate thereafter.

7 VOLUME OF SMALL REMITTANCES TO THE UNITED KINGDOM, 1871–1915

	remittances		money orders			
	U.S.A.	Australia[a]	U.S.A.	Australia	New Zealand	British North America
		annual average (£'000)				
1871–5	603	—[b]	177[c]	112[c]	50[c]	100[c]
1876–80	832	51	163	139	73	48
1881–5	1,502	74	474	230	77	109
1886–90	1,514[d]	68[d]	819	273	54	135
1891–5	—	—	839	196	46	110
1896–1900	—	—	755	134	66	120
1901–5	—	—	1,166	132	97	251
1906–10	—	—	2,198	153	141	866
1911–15	—	—	2,161	466	195	1,947

[a] Data for 'Australia and other places', relying in part on returns from colonial agents-general.
[b] Where no figure is shown, returns are not available.
[c] Average for years 1873–5 (first available returns distinguishing countries).
[d] Average for years 1886 and 1887 (last returns).

Sources: *Tables relating to emigration, 1871–87*; *Reports of the postmaster general on the post office, 1873–5, 1875–6, . . . 1915–16*: in H.C. papers, *passim*.

Returns of remittances from 'North America' (including a negligible quantity from British North America) were based on imperfect returns from 'banks and mercantile houses connected with America', excluding at least one major Liverpool house and those at the port of London. Statistics exclude money passed through private hands, such as money orders, and no account is taken of remittances sent out of the U.K. Returns of money order transactions in the U.K. show the *excess* of foreign orders cashed in the U.K. over foreign-bound orders paid for in the U.K. (excluding official and military orders). Remittance statistics refer to calendar year, whereas money order returns refer to the calendar year for 1873–5 and the year beginning April thereafter (no statistics having been published for the first quarter of 1876).

8 'IRISH' IMMIGRATION AS PERCENTAGE OF EMIGRATION BY DESTINATION, 1895–1913[a]

years	total	U.S.A.	British North America	Australasia	British South Africa	other
1895	0.48	0.46	0.81	0.91	0.93	1.28
1896–1900	0.48	0.47	0.67	0.55	0.46	0.87
1901–5	0.47	0.47	0.32	0.48	0.65	1.25
1906–10	0.44	0.43	0.25	0.53	1.59	1.26
1911–13[b]	0.29	0.28	0.18	0.22	1.07	1.05
total	0.44	0.43	0.28	0.43	0.83	1.14

[a] Statistics refer to passengers of 'Irish' nationality who were returned as travelling between U.K. ports and extra-European countries.

[b] From Apr. 1912 onwards, statistics refer to British subjects intending to change their permanent residence from (or to) Ireland, and travelling beyond Europe.

Sources: *Tables relating to emigration, 1895–1913*: in H.C. papers, *passim*.

9 FEMALE PERCENTAGE OF IRISH MIGRATION BY DESTINATION, 1895–1913[a]

years	emigration		immigration	
	U.S.A.	other	U.S.A.	other
1895	57	39	53	39
1896–1900	57	37	55	36
1901–5	55	35	57	33
1906–10	52	38	57	34
1911–13[b]	53	40	55	37
1895–1913	55	38	56	35

[a] Statistics refer to passengers of 'Irish' nationality who were returned as travelling between U.K. ports and extra-European countries.

[b] From Apr. 1912 onwards statistics refer to British subjects intending to change their permanent residence from (or to) Ireland, and travelling beyond Europe.

Sources: *Tables relating to emigration, 1895–1913*: in H.C. papers, *passim*.

10 'PERMANENT' MIGRATION BETWEEN IRELAND AND EXTRA-EUROPEAN COUNTRIES, 1912–13

groups	total		U.S.A.		British North America		Australasia	
	to	from	to	from	to	from	to	from
groups as percentage of all migrants								
female	51	49	54	56	42	32	40	36
aged under 18	15	13	12	11	21	11	19	11
aged 18–29	69	46	74	50	58	48	56	35
aged over 30	16	41	14	39	21	41	26	54
number (thousands)	82.1	11.2	60.4	6.7	15.1	1.9	4.7	1.1
groups as percentage of all occupied male migrants								
labourers	44	34	48	42	45	37	14	23
in agriculture	33	14	34	9	24	19	54	25
in trades	11	28	10	27	14	28	15	26
commercial, professional	11	24	8	22	17	15	16	25
groups as percentage of all occupied female migrants								
in service	85	81	87	84	80	66	73	69
in trades	10	8	10	7	12	15	13	12
commercial, professional	5	11	3	8	8	20	14	19

Sources: *Copy of tables relating to emigration and immigration, 1913 and 1914*: in H.C. papers, 1913 (183), lv, 865–932; 1914 (295), lxix, 941–1000.

Statistics refer to British subjects enumerated at ports in the United Kingdom, Apr. 1912 to Dec. 1913, who proposed to change their country of 'permanent residence' (duration twelve months or more) to or from an extra-European country, and from or to Ireland. Totals include migration involving British South Africa and other countries. Adults of unspecified age have been distributed in proportion to those of specified age for each country and sex separately. Occupational data exclude migrants of 'miscellaneous' or unspecified occupation, and those of age specified as 17 or less.

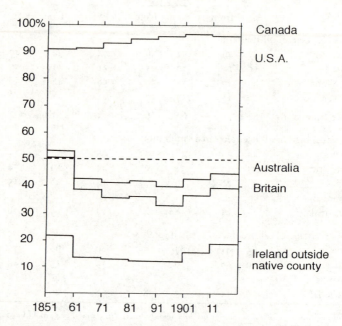

Figure 6 MIGRATORY IRISH-BORN POPULATION, 1851–1911; PERCENTAGE
DISTRIBUTION BY PLACE OF RESIDENCE, DISTINGUISHING FOUR COUN-
TRIES AND IRISH RESIDENTS LIVING OUTSIDE THEIR NATIVE COUNTY,
by David Fitzpatrick

Source: *Saorstat Éireann, census of population 1926*, i (Dublin, 1928), and national censuses.

Statistics are drawn from birthplace returns for each region, using the census most proximate to the
first year of each decade. Australian figures for 1851–71 involve estimation. Statistics exclude outlying
islands (Britain), outlying territories in British North America, and minor countries of Irish settlement
such as New Zealand, South Africa, and Argentina.

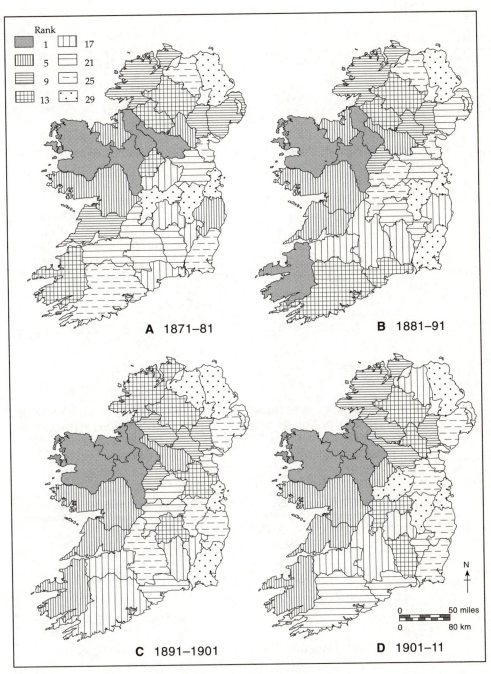

Rank
1 17
5 21
9 25
13 29

A 1871–81

B 1881–91

C 1891–1901

D 1901–11

N

0   50 miles
0   80 km

Map 4 COHORT DEPLETION, 1871–1911, by David Fitzpatrick

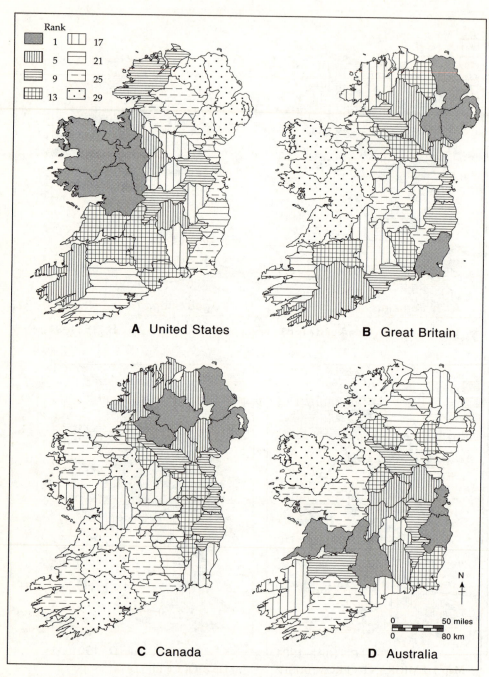

Map 5 EMIGRANT DESTINATIONS, 1876–1914, by David Fitzpatrick

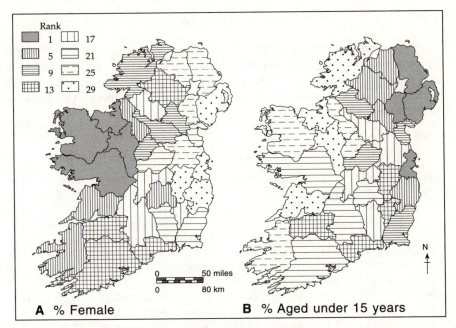

A % Female   **B** % Aged under 15 years

Map 6 EMIGRANTS FROM IRISH PORTS, 1876–1914, by David Fitzpatrick

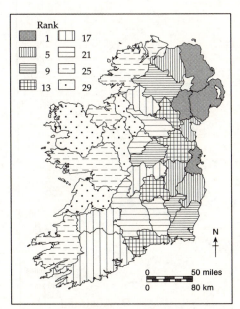

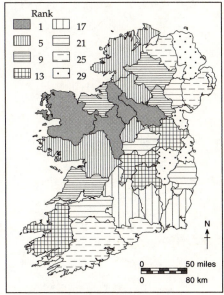

Map 7 EMIGRANTS FROM IRISH
PORTS, 1883–1914: PERCENTAGE
EVER MARRIED, by David Fitzpatrick

Map 8 OCCUPIED MALES IN
AGRICULTURE, 1911, by David
Fitzpatrick

NOTE ON MAPS 4–8

In these maps the counties of Ireland are shaded according to rank order, in eight groups, each including four counties ranked 1–4, 5–8, 9–12, 13–16, 17–20, 21–4, 25–8, 29–32. The following table shows for each map the highest value in each group and also the lowest value among the thirty-two counties. All figures are percentages.

map	rank								
	1	5	9	13	17	21	25	29	32
4a	35.68	32.09	31.46	29.60	28.59	27.16	25.53	22.80	1.01
4b	41.36	39.39	37.30	32.82	31.53	30.98	28.47	27.01	6.34
4c	38.20	34.55	32.75	28.95	26.79	25.52	24.62	21.61	−4.82
4d	37.63	33.26	30.74	24.80	22.48	21.43	20.75	16.30	1.60
5a	94.30	90.03	86.33	83.42	81.41	77.39	70.42	59.73	41.27
5b	35.16	18.19	12.52	9.42	7.79	4.25	3.97	2.34	1.53
5c	17.90	11.14	7.83	4.25	3.08	2.71	1.89	1.55	1.06
5d	10.47	7.06	5.84	5.02	3.43	2.99	2.56	2.13	0.75
6a	58.58	52.06	51.11	49.07	48.67	48.14	46.73	42.96	41.71
6b	23.52	13.98	12.01	10.61	9.79	9.61	9.05	8.03	7.28
7	23.19	17.39	14.78	13.25	12.60	11.51	9.99	8.90	8.52
8	87.10	80.77	77.69	73.03	67.63	63.38	55.06	46.59	7.72

CHAPTER XXII

The Irish in Britain, 1871–1921

DAVID FITZPATRICK

THE Irish who came to Britain during the half-century before 1871 were mainly reluctant immigrants. Even more so than those who settled in America or Australasia, they were a restless, transient people. Many stayed in Britain just long enough to earn sufficient to ward off destitution at home, or else to pay for their passage to the New World. For those who lingered, transience within Britain was encouraged by the virtual exclusion of Irish immigrants from secure employment and housing. The restricted range of demand for immigrant labour, aggravated by native distaste for the newcomers with their 'wild Milesian features',[1] ensured that Irishmen were concentrated in the most menial, casual, and impermanent sectors of manual employment. Female immigrants, unlike their counterparts in the colonies or America, found in many towns that even domestic service was largely reserved to natives of the host country. The warped occupational distribution of the immigrants was reflected in their housing and patterns of settlement. Though Irish ghettos developed virtually nowhere in Britain, the settlers were clustered in the most congested and decaying districts of most British towns, among which they moved with startling rapidity from one insalubrious lodging to another. The relative deprivation of the immigrants was manifest in the statistics of pauperism and criminality, which revealed Irish over-representation in virtually all categories.

Alienation from British culture, the obverse of enforced exclusion from British institutions and paths of upward mobility, was not cushioned by the creation of an immigrant community with an autonomous subculture. Despite energetic efforts by Roman Catholic priests and nationalist politicians, the Irish in mid-century Britain were notably lax in their observance of both religious and political rites. Their culture remained that of Ireland, and their modest political involvement was largely directed towards sustaining organisations within Ireland rather than serving the interests of expatriates. Immigrant alienation, though most pronounced for catholics, also applied to the substantial minority of protestant Irish settlers. The continued obsession with Irish grievances was manifest in the reiterated collisions between 'orange' and 'green', particularly in

---

[1] Thomas Carlyle, *Chartism* (2nd ed., London, 1840), p. 28.

Scotland and northern England where Ulster settlers were most prominent. Thus the settlers of 1871 constituted neither an integrated element of British society nor a self-sustaining community: their process of adaptation had scarcely begun.

The subsequent half-century did not witness the complete transformation of the Irish in Britain into either an expatriate community or a fully accepted ingredient of British society. Yet the acuteness of immigrant estrangement was abated, not least because the Irish-born minority became less obvious and therefore less resented. In England the Irish population exceeded 600,000 only in 1861, steadily diminishing thereafter to about one-third of a million in 1921. In Scotland the decline was delayed for several decades, the number of Irish-born just exceeding 200,000 at most censuses between 1851 and 1901. But in both kingdoms Irish prominence declined sharply as the non-Irish population increased. Table 1 in the appendix to this chapter indicates that the Irish component of England's population dropped from one-fortieth to one-hundredth between 1871 and 1921,[1] meanwhile halving from a peak of one-sixteenth in the Scottish case. The Irish also became less important as a component of the total migratory population of Britain, and by the end of the century their notoriety as undesirable guests was probably exceeded by that of the Jewish immigrant aliens from Russia and eastern Europe.[2]

The slow shrinkage of the Irish-born population did not signify any stoppage of immigration, for substantial movement was required to compensate for heavy losses from overseas emigration and mortality. Enumerators at Irish ports counted about 131,000 'permanent emigrants' to England between 1876 and 1910, together with 90,000 to Scotland. The true number was far greater, partly because the two elderly enumerators at the port of Dublin made no attempt to count emigrants taking ferries to Britain. Indeed the age-distribution of Irish natives in various parts of England in 1911 suggests that the *net* immigration from Ireland since 1876 probably amounted to about 300,000, far more than double the recorded total for *gross* immigration.[3] Thus bureaucrats, like so many

---

[1] Below, p. 690.

[2] In references to statistics, 'England' includes Wales, but 'Britain' excludes the Isle of Man and the Channel Islands.

[3] 'Reverse survivorship ratios' were used to estimate the number of emigrants required to account for the Irish-born population of England (1911), as follows: (a) the Irish-born population of each sex was assigned to eight age-groups using the recorded age-distribution for London, Birmingham, Bradford, Liverpool, Manchester, Middlesbrough, and Glamorganshire; (b) generational life tables were used to estimate the probability of death between age 20 and age recorded in 1911, assuming that all settlers left Ireland when aged 20 and were thereafter subject to the prevailing English risk of death for their sex; (c) net immigration between 1876 and 1911 was taken to be the sum of all those surviving to 1911 who had reached 20 years after 1876, adjusted as above for likely mortality between arrival in England and 1911. Estimated immigration amounted to 302,000. See R. A. M. Case and others, *Serial abridged life tables: England and Wales, 1841–1960* (London, 1963); Cormac Ó Gráda, 'A note on nineteenth-century Irish emigration statistics' in *Population Studies*, xxix, no. 1 (1975), pp 143–9, where a somewhat similar technique is applied to immigration to Britain between 1851 and 1911.

contemporaries and historians, understated the importance of Britain as a destination for the migratory Irish. In fact, the British element in Irish migration scarcely diminished over the period. Of all the Irish-born living outside their home counties, roughly one-fifth were living in Britain at every census year between 1871 and 1911, compared with one-half in the United States.[1] The enumerators' returns, indicating that Britain was the destination for less than one-twelfth of emigrants, are clearly misleading. Emigration to Britain declined between 1871 and 1921, but its decline was almost matched by that of Irish emigration as a whole.

The declining pace of immigration had important consequences for the profile of Britain's Irish-born population. As with most movements out of Ireland, that to Britain was dominated by young unmarried adults rather than family groups, so that the proportion of youngsters was always small. Decreasing migration aggravated this problem by causing a general ageing of the immigrant population. Census returns for Scotland show that the proportion of Irish-born residents under 20 years dropped steadily from one-seventh in 1871 to one-tenth in 1911. Selective returns for England also indicate a reduction in the proportion of juvenile settlers over that period. Moreover the age distribution of adult Irish settlers in 1911 was strongly biased towards older age-groups. Compared with the total adult population, they were almost twice as likely to have passed beyond normal working age. Since many Irish households contained English-born children it is likely that the Irish 'dependency ratio' was abnormally burdensome, though no census returns were compiled for those of Irish stock.[2]

This effect was usually mitigated by the preponderance of male immigrants, who were more likely to participate in the labour force. In Scotland, as in the case of most Ulster migrations, there was invariably a marked male majority, though in England females had the bare majority in both 1871 and 1921. The prominence of women among Irish settlers was least at the turn of the century, reflecting the fact that American demand for unskilled male labour had declined before that for female servants. In 1911 nearly two-thirds of England's Connacht natives were male, whereas three-fifths of Connacht's emigration to all destinations over the two preceding decades had been female. Thus to some extent the Irish in Britain were the residue of those drawn towards more enticing countries, united only in their disappointment at having missed the transatlantic boat. By comparison with their mid-century predecessors, who were most likely to be young adults and also female, the vitality of Irish settlers as producers and reproducers had diminished by the early twentieth century. They were outnumbered, almost certainly, by the more shadowy and less aberrant population of the second generation.

The increasingly decrepit expatriate population remained heavily concentrated in a few counties, though even in these the Irish were far less conspicuous than

---

[1] Table 3, above, p. 640.
[2] For the seven districts named above, p. 654, n. 3, the proportion of adult Irish-born settlers aged 65 or more was 16.7 per cent, compared with 8.7 per cent for the English adult population (1911).

in the mid-nineteenth century. By 1901 the Irish proportion of the migratory population (those born outside their county of residence) exceeded one-fifth in only two counties, Lanark and Renfrew. In Ayr, Dumbarton, Wigtown, and Linlithgow, together with Lancashire and Cumberland in England, they exceeded one-tenth. Variation between counties in the Irish component of migratory residents was as marked in 1921 as it had been fifty years earlier, in Scotland at least. The county distribution of Irish settlers in Britain, which had been largely determined before the famine, changed remarkably little over the period up to 1921.[1] Even so, the gradual process of diffusion of Irish settlers through the urban networks of northern England and southern Scotland continued. Table 2 indicates that the relative importance of the three major English cities was much reduced between 1871 and 1901, though Glasgow's contribution increased until it accounted for more than one-tenth of Britain's Irish population.[2] After 1871 two-thirds of the settlers lived outside London, Liverpool, Manchester, and Glasgow, though of these the vast majority lived in towns. In 1911 just under half of Lancashire's Irish population lived outside Liverpool and Manchester (including Salford), while almost one-quarter was dispersed among the county's other fourteen boroughs. Likewise in Scotland in 1921 nearly half of the Irish outside Glasgow lived in the twenty-two burghs with over 20,000 inhabitants. The younger immigrants' choice of town depended on current employment opportunities, so that in towns with a contracting demand for unskilled labour the Irish population tended to be older and more settled. In 1911 almost two-thirds of the Glamorganshire Irish were active adults aged between 20 and 45, compared with half in London, over two-fifths in Manchester, Liverpool, Birmingham, and Middlesbrough (that mid-Victorian phenomenon of industrial expansion), and only one-third in the decaying textiles centre of Bradford. Women predominated in many towns of long-standing Irish settlement, especially London, but in certain localities such as Middlesbrough and Glamorganshire they were vastly outnumbered by men responding to local demand (in these cases for metalworkers and miners respectively). Britain's Irish population remained predominantly urban and responsive to localised fluctuations in industrial demand for immigrant labour.

Even the most blinkered observer could no longer claim that the Irish were confined to ghettos and 'Irishtowns' within major cities. Engels, who had so eloquently depicted the horrors of Manchester's 'Little Ireland' and its denizens in 1844, admitted in the 1892 edition of the same work that ' "Little Ireland" had disappeared' in company with many other slums, as a result of the extension of sanitation and drainage, which under Chadwick's direction had transformed the

---

[1] Analysis of the ratio of Irish-born inhabitants to those born outside the county of residence gives coefficients of variation (C.V.) for Scotland (32 counties) of 1.09 (1871), 1.13 (1901), and 1.13 (1921); and for England (37 counties excluding the home counties and Wales) of 1.11 (1871), and 0.98 (1901). The correlation coefficients (r) for the distributions of 1871 and 1901 are + 0.92 for Scotland and + 0.97 for England, while that for the Scottish distributions of 1901 and 1921 is + 0.98.

[2] Below, p. 691.

appearance, smell, and ethnic character of urban England. The Liverpool Irish of 1871 were still slightly more segregated in their patterns of residence than other immigrant groups, yet their distribution was not very different from that of native Liverpudlians.[1] In London the Irish population had long been diffused throughout the metropolis, with Irish settlers participating in the general drift from central to suburban districts. In 1881 the Irish were still over-represented in the centre, but thirty years later the reverse was the case. As Booth's survey had demonstrated, the familiar Irish enclaves were rapidly disappearing. One pocket of the East End was still 'an Irish colony, called locally the "Fenian barracks" ', whose inhabitants were reputedly not human but 'wild beasts'; yet neighbouring districts no longer had more than a sprinkling of Irish residents. In the former 'Irish colony of the Mile End Old Town', Booth found that 'the Irish there are giving place to the Jews'. Many Irish had been forced out of Clerkenwell by a boom in non-residential construction: whereas non-Irish protestants had been accommodated locally in new model dwellings, 'the evicted Irish seem to be gathering together further west in Kensal Town and Notting Hill'. The 'poor Irish' had largely left their familiar haunts in Soho and Westminster, while south of the river the demolition of slum courts in West Southwark was forcing them eastwards.

Demolition and eviction did not always entail subsequent improvement in Irish living conditions. The Sultan Street district of south London, rebuilt only a quarter-century before Booth's survey, had become 'a collection of streets where beastly men and women live bestially', a repulsive haunt of the second-generation 'Cockney Irish'.[2] As Engels maintained, the eradication of ancient pockets of urban overcrowding and poverty was often counterbalanced by the creation of new pockets of suburban poverty. The uprooting of established Irish settlements tended to disrupt the already fragile communal networks of Irish settlers in British towns. This process was lamented by a writer in a catholic journal in the case of Glasgow in 1913. Forty years earlier, so he alleged, they had 'lived in distinct quarters—with few exceptions—mostly on the south side of the river Clyde'; but now they were 'diffused in batches all over the city. There is practically no meeting centre, no district in which a majority of Ireland's natives hold possession'. Once, the 'old-fashioned Irish landlady' had provided immigrants with 'a resting place and a certain amount of security amongst their own class';

---

[1] Friedrich Engels, 'The condition of the working class in England' in Karl Marx and Friedrich Engels, *On Britain* (Moscow, 1953), pp 20–21, 94–6; Colin G. Pooley, 'The residential segregation of migrant communities in mid-Victorian Liverpool' in *Transactions of the Institute of British Geographers*, ii, no. 3 (1977), pp 369–72.

[2] Charles Booth, *Life and labour of the people in London*, 3rd ser. (7 vols, London, 1902), i, 17; ii, 41, 141, 187; iii, 84–5; iv, 13; vi, 19. Analysis of the Irish-born proportion of the population in various divisions of London gives C.V. = 0.55 (1881) and 0.54 (1911), while the proportion of Irish settlers resident in the 'central district' fell from 42.1 per cent (1881) to 18.3 per cent (1911). This district accounted for 35.2 per cent of London's population (1881) and 18.5 per cent (1911). See Booth, *Life & labour*, 1st ser. (1902), iii, 118–19, 150–66; Lynn Hollen Lees, *Exiles of Erin* (Manchester, 1979), p. 61; *Census of England and Wales, 1911: report* [Cd 8491], H.C. 1917–18, xxxv, 483.

whereas by 1913 the newcomers had to live dangerously among protestants and Scots.[1] Geographical dispersion inhibited the growth of an Irish community without always improving immigrant conditions of life.

Stark evidence of continued deprivation among Irish immigrants was provided by the returns of pauperism. The famine settlers had been notorious for their unmatched degree of dependence on parochial relief, and the spectre of immigrant pauperism continued to trouble British ratepayers long after the mass of victims had died, emigrated, or otherwise become independent of relief. Applicants for English relief who could not prove their continuous residence in the chargeable union for a period of one year were still subject to removal across the Irish Sea, though the practice had almost fallen into disuse by 1881–2 when only 248 paupers were removed from England to Ireland.[2] In Scotland both the legislation and the practice were more severe. Relief applicants without a parish settlement (acquired after five years' residence) were subject to removal until 1898, when the qualifying period was reduced to three years with a discretionary clause operative after a year's residence. Between 1875 and 1910 just over 7,000 paupers and their dependants were removed from Scotland to Ireland, this being equivalent to one-eighth of the recorded immigration during the period. Yet by comparison with the deportations of 1847 or 1848, when over 10,000 Irish removals were executed, this constituted a mere trickle. The resident Irish population of Scotland remained over-represented among recipients of relief, but the number of Irish recipients, including Scottish-born dependants, seldom exceeded 10,000 between 1890 and 1919. No relative reduction in immigrant pauperism occurred during the half-century under review, and evidence for Pollokshaws (1870) indicates that Irish protestants as well as catholics were prominent among recipients. The persistent excess of Irish paupers was largely attributable to an ageing population of Irish workhouse inmates, of whom there were nearly 2,000 in Scotland (1894). One-fifth of all inmates were Irish natives or their dependants, compared with one-tenth of those who received outdoor relief and only one-fifteenth of the lunatic poor.[3] Irish pauperism in Britain no longer signified the vulnerability of an entire immigrant population, but rather the failure of an unfortunate substratum to grasp the modest livelihood that Britain offered its newcomers.

The poorest class of expatriate Irish not actually dependent on relief was that of migratory labourers, a significant component of the British farm labour force up to the first world war. As usual, detailed enumeration began only when the flow was slackening and therefore countable. Official statistics for 1880–1915, abstracted in table 3,[4] show a reduction in the number of migratory workers

---

[1] Engels, 'Condition of working class in England', pp 20–21; P. Dougan, 'Irish life in Glasgow' in *Catholic Bulletin*, iii (1913), p. 730.

[2] Michael E. Rose, 'Settlement, removal, and the new poor law' in Derek Frazer, (ed.), *The new poor law in the nineteenth century* (London, 1976), pp 25–44.

[3] *Reports of the board of supervision for the relief of the poor in Scotland*, H.C. papers, *passim*; James Edmund Handley, *The Irish in modern Scotland* (Cork, 1947), pp 255–60; *Returns showing the number of paupers*, H.C. 1895 (54), lxxxv.

[4] Below, pp 692–3.

known to the Royal Irish Constabulary from 20,000 to 8,000, interrupted by a brief surge at the turn of the century. Conflicting returns from railway and shipping companies, though confirming this trend over time, suggest that the actual annual movement from Ireland to Britain was about twice as great. The magnitude of regular annual migration was evidently larger in the 1870s, the subsequent decrease being usually ascribed to the gradual substitution of machinery for labour in British farming. An inquiry of 1883 suggests that this applied most of all to the western counties of northern England and southern Scotland. The general decrease in Irish migration to eastern counties stretching from Yorkshire to Edinburgh was seldom attributed to mechanisation, and may represent failure of labour supply rather than demand as longer-distance migrants drifted into urban industry. Men mostly journeyed by rail from north-western Ireland to Dublin before proceeding to Britain, leaving the cheaper but longer sea voyage to women, who often admitted 'that they dread the voyage owing to seasickness, and that it is as trying as the whole season's work'.[1] Many migrants left Ireland immediately after major cattle fairs, before the proceeds could be squandered in the shebeen, a few receiving subsidies from rent-hungry landlords. Even the United Irish League occasionally subsidised migration; but by June 1921 their nationalist successors had come to regard seasonal migration as a menace comparable with emigration, causing Michael Collins to recommend the provision of £2,500 to 'keep the bulk of the necessary officers and men' of the I.R.A. at home in Donegal.[2]

Donegal, together with the five counties of Connacht and Armagh, provided virtually all the regular migratory labour from pre-war Ireland. In 1880 these seven counties contained four-fifths of all the migratory labourers counted by the constabulary, a proportion that reached 97 per cent before the end of the century. Mayo's contribution ranged between half and three-fifths during the three decades after 1886, while the proportion of migrants from Donegal doubled to one-fifth. The recovery of migration from Donegal was reflected in the proportion of migrants making for Scotland, which attracted few workers from other counties. Seasonal migration, to a far greater extent than in pre-famine times, was a highly localised movement between certain coastal districts in north-western Ireland and a shrinking belt of agricultural Britain. It was composed of men rather than women, and farmers' sons rather than landholders, who when they did migrate were usually very small farmers. Thus, in a few districts, it provided an alternative to permanent emigration for the surplus population of young

[1] William Neilson Hancock, 'On the equal importance . . .' in *Stat. Soc. Ire. Jn.*, viii, pt 56 (1880), pp 52–3; *Report . . . as to the diminution in the number of migratory labourers from Ireland*, H.C. 1884 (218), lxii; Cormac Ó Gráda, 'Seasonal migration and post-famine adjustment in the west of Ireland' in *Studia Hib.*, xiii (1973), p. 66; *Devonshire comm.: reports by Mr Arthur Wilson Fox*, p. 60 [C 6894–XXI], H.C. 1893–4, xxxvii, pt 1, p. 400.
[2] *Devonshire comm.: reports by Fox*, pp 78–9 (MS 418–19); Collins to de Valera, 29 June 1921, (N.A.I., DE 2/446); and see above, pp 623–3.

unmarried adult males. For many of these it was in fact the prelude to a less easily reversible departure. It provided both a taste for life elsewhere and the means for indulging that taste. Indeed seasonal and permanent migration were often complementary rather than alternative experiences, seasonal movement being a normal adolescent episode whereas emigration occurred slightly later in the male life cycle, when the transfer of farm occupancy between generations was being accomplished. The counties of heavy seasonal migration all had high emigration rates, and this relationship applied also to smaller districts within Donegal and Mayo. Here seasonal migration propped up a curious demographic system whereby frequent marriage and rapid natural increase were counteracted by heavy net emigration (see table 4).[1] Yet the practice of annual migration to Britain survived the curtailment of permanent emigration after the 1880s, so that in Mayo (1901) the number of harvesters almost equalled the entire recorded male emigration over the subsequent decade. Though diminishing, seasonal migration remained as a relic of the transience and impermanence that had once typified the Irish experience in Britain.

The familiar farming operations of reaping, potato-lifting, or turnip-singling no longer exhausted the employment sought by migratory workers. By 1870 Kerry labourers had virtually abandoned their annual migration to British farms, but a few went to the mines of Wales and Cornwall with 'no fixed intention of returning within any definite period to their own country' (a change similar to that noted in Waterford, Antrim, and Newry). Kerry women took up regular migration 'to the iron furnaces in South Wales and such places . . . though it is not a very nice occupation for women, yet the women do the work in spring after the potatoes are planted'.[2] When non-agricultural workers were first enumerated in 1901, one-seventh of male and nearly one-quarter of female migrants were seeking employment off the farm. In descending order, their favoured occupations were in mining, factory work, public works, railways, and navvying. Those in farming performed a narrowing range of tasks in a shrinking region, which by now excluded the once popular destinations of southern Cambridgeshire, the Oxford district, and the home counties.

The practice of importing gangs under the direction of a gaffer persisted, at least in the case of female potato-lifters: one Achill girl aged 18 in 1893 had already spent four seasons in Scotland, the last in the company of her father (the gaffer), twenty-seven girls, and three boys.[3] Many migrated regularly to particular

---

[1] Below, p. 694.

[2] *Reports from poor law inspectors as to the existing relations between landlord and tenant*, pp 25, 75, 127, 112, 113 [C 31], H.C. 1870, xiv, 61, 111, 163, 148, 149; *Dudley comm.: appendix to eighth report*, p. 21 [Cd 3839], H.C. 1908, xli, 95.

[3] *Report and tables relating to Irish migratory agricultural and other labourers*, pp 44–5 [Cd 850], H.C. 1902, cxvi, pt II, pp 130–31; *Devonshire comm.: reports by Fox*, p. 84 (MS 424). The percentages seeking off-farm employment in 1901 were 7.3 (among migrants bound for England), 28.3 (Scotland), and 55.3 (other parts of Ireland). Analysis of 'favoured occupations' refers to those bound for Britain, thus excluding many migrants seeking work in fishing and domestic service within Ireland.

employers, but others prowled about northern England and southern Scotland to barter their services at the numerous hiring fairs or pursue contacts with farmers known to provide 'paddy houses'. They played the labour market with skill, so that in 1898 Irish labourers were observed in three-fifths of Britain's higher-wage counties but in only one-eighth of the lower-wage counties.[1] Variations in method of payment (usually by piece), duration of employment, and specific occupation make it difficult to estimate the typical net return of a season's employment. Mayo's 10,000 or so migratory workers sent home postal orders amounting to more than £100,000 annually between 1876 and 1880 in advance of their return home; while a group of 425 mainly female migrants from Achill to Scotland in 1901 earned £5,240, exclusive of payments in kind.[2] Individual earnings ranged between about £4 and £20, averaging perhaps £12. This represented a substantial portion of a small farmer's family earnings: an inspection of congested districts in the 1890s indicated that over one-third of a typical family's annual earnings in the Rosses of Donegal was derived from annual migrations to the 'Laggan' or to Scotland.[3] The total return from seasonal work may well have amounted to one-third of the remittances received from overseas emigrants, which often served similar functions in the home economy by facilitating payment of shop debts or rent.

The non-seasonal Irish population of Britain emerged from a more variegated home background. In the mid-nineteenth century a great proportion of Irish settlers in Yorkshire, and doubtless other northern English counties, had come from Connacht; whereas Ulster had dominated settlement in Scotland. By 1911, when Irish counties of origin were first distinguished in the English census, Connacht accounted for only one-sixth of England's springtime Irish population (seasonal workers normally arrived shortly after the census). The census indicated that Mayo, Sligo, and Roscommon were still relatively important sources of movement to Britain, but many of the predominantly male Connacht settlers were probably former seasonal workers who had lingered on out of season. The counties most inclined to generate settlers in England were (in descending order) Kildare, Mayo, Louth, Dublin, Cork, Waterford, Wexford, and Sligo, which suggests fairly intensive movement from southern and eastern coastal counties. The statistics of permanent emigration to Britain between 1876 and 1910 give a very different distribution of origins, with relatively heavy movement from

---

[1] *Report by Mr Wilson Fox on the wages and earnings of agricultural labourers in the United Kingdom* [Cd 346], H.C. 1900, lxxxii. Seventy-seven districts of Britain were ranked according to the average weekly wage of ordinary agricultural labourers, and assigned to four groups of nineteen or twenty districts each in descending rank order. The numbers of districts in each group with 'some' or 'many' Irish migratory workers were 13 (highest wages), 10 (high wages), 4 (low wages), and 1 (lowest wages). See also E. H. Hunt, *Regional wage variations in Britain, 1850–1914* (Oxford, 1973), chs 1, 8.

[2] *Thom's Official Directory* (Dublin, 1883), p. 637; *Royal commission on the poor laws and relief of distress: appendix XIX.B: report by Mr Cyril Jackson*, p. 26 [28] [Cd 4890], H.C. 1909, xliv, 889.

[3] Anne O'Dowd, ' "Sweeten that to your liking"—Irish seasonal workers in fact and fiction' in *Folk Life*, xx (1981–2), p. 76; W. G. S. Adams estimated that the savings of migratory labourers in 1905, whether remitted or carried home, exceeded £275,000 (*Report and tables relating to Irish migratory agricultural labourers*, p. 20 [Cd 2865], H.C. 1906, cxxxiii, 1058).

north-east Ulster and little movement from Connacht. Most emigrants from Connacht and Leinster evidently escaped enumeration by taking the Dublin ferries: indeed the police enumerators seem to have missed about one-seventh of emigrants leaving Munster, compared with two-fifths from Ulster, four-fifths from Leinster, and nearly nine-tenths from Connacht. One should beware of drawing inferences from the official emigration returns, despite the apparent coincidence of intensive movement to Britain and relatively great urbanisation at home, which might suggest circulation of town workers within the urban networks of the British Isles.[1]

The returns of emigration to Scotland are somewhat less misleading, since fewer emigrants slipped through Dublin. They indicate heavy contributions from all Ulster counties with only a trickle from elsewhere, with the exceptions of Leitrim, Sligo, and Louth. The six counties now in Northern Ireland regularly provided three-quarters of recorded emigrants bound for Scotland, though the Scottish census reports for 1921 and 1931 suggest a much smaller northern majority. Northern emigrants clustered together, so that they outnumbered southern settlers in only ten British counties, mainly in south-western Scotland. The highest proportions were recorded in Wigtown (four-fifths), Ayr and Renfrew (two-thirds), and Cumberland in north-western England (three-fifths).[2] These statistics illustrate the persistence of the historic link between north-eastern Ireland and north-western Britain, though even Ulster's emigrants usually preferred overseas destinations. Antrim, which sent half its recorded emigrants to Britain during the decade 1876–85, is the solitary exception. For northerners and southerners alike, settlement in Britain remained a minority preference.

The Irish settlers of pre-1914 Britain, like their famine-driven predecessors, were mainly confined to menial occupations requiring negligible skill. Studies of York and several Lancashire towns between 1851 and 1871 reveal no general reduction in the propensity of Irish workers to belong to lowly occupations such as general labouring.[3] The inaccessibility until recent years of English census enumerators' forms for subsequent years has inhibited detailed statistical study of ethnic social status and mobility, though the great urban surveys of the turn of the century make incidental reference to persistent Irish deprivation. In York the Irish population had declined since the disappearance of chicory cultivation: 'of those who remain, many find work as general labourers, while some of the women

[1] *Emigration statistics of Ireland, 1876–1910*, H.C. papers, *passim*; estimate of net movement from each province to England, 1876–1911, using sources and procedures given above, p. 654, n. 3. There is no general correlation between the county distributions of these two estimates of immigration. See also Vaughan & Fitzpatrick, *Ir. hist. statistics*, pp 344–53.

[2] Statistics are drawn from the first available census returns distinguishing northern from southern Irish residents of British counties (1921: England; 1931: Scotland); Irish settlers without known county of origin are ignored.

[3] Frances Finnegan, *Poverty and prejudice: the Irish immigrants in York* (Cork, 1982), pp 99, 103, 105; W. J. Lowe, 'The Irish in Lancashire, 1846–71: a social history' (Ph.D. thesis, University of Dublin, 1975), pp 600–06. York data include occupations of children and spouses of immigrants; Lancashire statistics relate only to Irish-born occupied household heads.

pick up a more or less precarious livelihood by working in the fields outside the city, often tramping out for miles in the early morning to their work.' In London also, familiar sources of employment had vanished: the brawny Irish presence at the West India dock allegedly dissipated when sugar ceased to be imported in hogsheads. Irish casual dockers were still conspicuous in East London in 1888, when the future Beatrice Webb observed that

Paddy enjoys more than his proportional share of dock work with its privileges and its miseries. He is to be found especially among the irregular hands, disliking as a rule the 'six to six business' for six days of the week. The cockney-born Irishman, as distinguished from the immigrant, is not favourably looked upon by the majority of employers.

The Irish comprised one-eighth of casual workers at various dockland warehouses but only four of the 276 regular staff.[1] The only survey of immigrant occupations published for the English census, a rather slapdash analysis of 1,000 adult males of Irish birth in Liverpool in 1891, confirms their low status: nearly half were dock labourers, over five times the proportion for the entire local work-force. The Irish were also over-represented among coal porters and heavers, sailors, and general labourers, though few general porters and carters, or artisans and shopkeepers, were immigrants.[2] No studies are available of Irishwomen's occupations after 1871, though their access to domestic service (already restricted by discrimination as well as geography) probably diminished with the contraction of that sector during the period under review.[3] In England, Paddy (and doubtless Biddy) remained proletarian.

In Scotland, so it has been claimed, Irish upward mobility was more manifest. A Glasgow observer reported in 1913 that 'what were called "low jobs" in the city are not now exclusively left to the Irish', many of whom were now employed at good wages as insurance agents, railway clerks, telegraph workers, and bartenders. One protestant publican had even advertised in search of a young man 'for spirit trade; Irish R.C. preferred; also *without experience*'.[4] This assessment may be tested using the comprehensive occupational analysis of the Irish in Scotland published for the 1911 census, the results of which are abstracted in table 5.[5] This confirms that Irishmen were fully represented among Glasgow's insurance agents and bartenders, and also that Irish immigrants very seldom preponderated in the

[1] B. Seebohm Rowntree, *Poverty: a study of town life* (London, 1901), p. 10; Booth, *Life & labour*, 1st ser., iv, 22; iii, 90–95. Data on birthplace of casuals are limited to East London warehouses, whereas data for regulars cover the East and West India docks and town warehouses.

[2] *Census Eng., general report*, p. 62 [C 7222], H.C. 1893–4, cvi, 696. Comparisons with the occupations of the Liverpool male population are imprecise, since categories differ somewhat from those used in the regular occupational tables.

[3] Theresa McBride, *The domestic revolution* (London, 1976), pp 112–13; Mark Ebery and Brian Preston, *Domestic service in late Victorian and Edwardian England* (Reading, 1976). As Ebery and Preston show at pp 36–8, the ratio of female indoor domestics to families was high in the London region, low in areas of heavy Irish settlement such as south Wales and northern England, and lowest of all in the towns of Lancashire.

[4] Dougan, 'Irish life in Glasgow', pp 730–31.

[5] Below, p. 695.

most menial occupations of any Scottish region. In the case of occupations selected for table 5 there were only four cases of Irish local majorities (among builders' labourers in Dumbarton, Lanark, and Renfrew, and dockworkers in Dumbarton). Nowhere did Irishwomen constitute even one-quarter of any sector work-force, partly because the relatively small number of female immigrants were abnormally prone to have 'no gainful occupation' whatever.

Though few menial occupations were Irish-dominated, most Irish workers were confined to menial occupations. Using the regional data for 1911, we may compare the occupational distributions of immigrants and their neighbours, so eliminating distortion caused by Irish concentration in industrial towns. The resultant weighted index of Irish over-representation indicates that the seeming paucity of Irish farm workers was a function of location rather than occupational choice within regions, while the prominence of Irish workers in iron, steel, and shipbuilding cannot be explained away by their residential choices. Irishmen were at least three times as likely as the general population to be found in building and construction, dock labour, chemical manufacture, municipal service, and general labour. Almost all of their preferred occupations, except shoemaking and hawking, involved manual labour; whereas strikingly few Irishmen were occupied as shopkeepers, clerks, or even (outside Glasgow) as waiters. Irishwomen were also clustered in unattractive pursuits such as hawking, farm labour, and charring, though unlike their menfolk they were also prominent in the lower grades of service and professional work as teachers, nurses, waitresses, and domestics. The Irish in Scotland were beginning to penetrate more desirable sectors of society, yet in 1911 they were still disadvantaged by comparison with their hosts.

The social convulsion occasioned by the first world war inevitably disturbed Irish patterns of settlement and occupation in Britain. Military service, always most attractive to the urban lumpenproletariat, had long been a popular source of employment for Irishmen in Britain as distinct from their rural brothers at home. Army returns of medical inspection show that the proportion of Irish-born recruits inspected outside Ireland dropped from over two-fifths (1860–63) to perhaps one-eighth (1911–13), suggesting that the ageing immigrant population was no longer remarkable as a source of recruitment. Second-generation settlers continued to flock into the army, which probably contained as many Roman Catholics born in Britain as in Ireland at the outbreak of war.[1] In Ireland itself wartime recruiting lagged markedly behind British rates, and conscription was never enforced in the face of furious popular and ecclesiastical opposition. But Britain's Irish and catholic populations, concentrated in the least essential sectors of the wartime economy, showed no disinclination to joining the forces. In Newcastle upon Tyne, 5,500 men were recruited for four battalions of Tyneside

---

[1] Army Medical Department, *Annual reports, 1859–1913*, H.C. papers, *passim* (relevant statistics available only for stated years); H. J. Hanham, 'Religion and nationality in the mid-Victorian army' in M. R. D. Foot (ed.), *War and society* (London, 1973), pp 176–81. All statistics exclude officers and those outside the regular army. See also above, pp 162, 189–90, 334.

Irish within two months of the war office's grudging sanction of a scheme proposed and funded by local businessmen and home rulers. As with most 'Irish' units the officers were drawn from all over the British empire, almost half being born neither in Ireland, Northumberland, nor Durham; but the brigade staff sported shamrock badges and most of the other ranks were presumably of Irish extraction.[1] By February 1915, T. P. O'Connor was urging John Redmond to assert publicly that 'we had already raised 115,000 Irishmen in Great Britain': the criteria and evidence for this remarkable claim are obscure. O'Connor's United Irish League of Great Britain urged Irish cooperation with the Derby enlistment scheme in 1915, and neither nationalist nor catholic opposition to British conscription was attempted. Despite noisy protests from Francis Meynell's tiny Guild of the Pope's Peace, the English hierarchy under Cardinal Bourne and the laymen comprising the Catholic Union of Great Britain were at pains to dissociate the catholic church in England from the agitation in Ireland. Only a handful of conscientious objectors cited the catholic faith as justification.[2] Throughout the war, Irish immigrant military participation was remarkable only for its normality.

Immigrants were prominent in manning the munitions factories and controlled establishments, which at the beginning of 1916 employed over a million men. The shortage of civilian manpower in Britain further promoted Irish migration to undertake government work, though some munitions operatives soon returned. As the west Cork constabulary reported in March 1916: 'Many of them were earning £2 a week, but they state that the work was too hard. These men as a class all belong to the ne'er-do-well community.'[3] Irish labour was obtained by the ministry of munitions not only through the employment exchanges, but also through direct recruiting by officials, agents, and contractors. After interdepartmental discussion these irregular methods were banned in February 1918, yet demand for Irish labour via the exchanges remained strong enough to provoke a ministry of labour complaint that Irish restriction of travel permits was inhibiting the supply of labour. The Irish inundation predictably generated anger among Scottish workers, who reportedly regarded the proposed

extension of conscription to Ireland almost [sic] as equitable. Indeed, the introduction of Irish labour . . . which has been possible because of the military conditions in Ireland, has always been resented, and it has been stated that any measure terminating such immigration should be welcomed by organised labour.[4]

[1] Felix Lavery (compiler), *Irish heroes in the war* (London, 1917). Birthplaces of 145 officers in four of the five battalions were extracted from lists on pp 159–63, 181–5, 202–5, and 224–31. Of these 8 were born in Ulster, 13 elsewhere in Ireland, 54 in the regimental area (Northumberland and Durham), 47 elsewhere in England, 15 in Scotland, and 6 overseas (2 cases unknown).

[2] O'Connor to Redmond, 27 Feb. 1915 (Redmond papers, N.L.I. MS 15215); Ian S. Wood, 'John Wheatley, the Irish, and the labour movement in Scotland' in *Innes Review*, xxxi, no. 2 (1980), p. 84; Alan Wilkinson, *The Church of England and the first world war* (London, 1978), p. 315; John Rae, *Conscience and politics* (London, 1970), pp 80, 250–51. See also above, pp 189–90, 234–6; below, pp 716–19.

[3] County inspector, R.I.C., monthly confidential report (P.R.O., C.O. 904/99).

[4] W. G. Greene to munitions council, 18 Feb. 1918 (P.R.O.: MUN 5/57, HR 320/31); R.I.C. circular (9 May 1918) and associated files, HO 45/10957: 54b; report for week ending 27 Apr. 1918,

The armistice was quickly followed by the closure of munitions factories, demobilisation, and renewed unemployment, whereupon the immigrant work-force reverted to something very like its pre-war complexion. As the 1921 Scottish census revealed, the occupational clustering of Irish immigrants just after the war differed little from that recorded a decade before.[1] For Irish immigrant men, as for British women, wartime indispensability proved to be a revolution that was all too easily reversible.

If Irish indispensability was temporary, British hostility towards the immigrants was enduring. By the end of the century, however, sectarian and ethnic animosities were more often expressed through political struggles on school boards or local councils rather than in rioting or window-smashing. A macabre case arose in 1897 in Dumbarton when catholics applied to the Bonhill parish council to buy a thousand lairs 'to be used exclusively for catholic burial', a proposal that alarmed future denizens of the adjoining ornamental sector of the cemetery. The *Glasgow Observer* detected 'a fear that those who can afford grandeur after death might not wish to lie so close to the poor despised Irishman. At all events, rampant bigotry was shown, and the demand would in all probability have been refused had not the catholics offered to buy the choice ground as well.'[2] Their successful attempt to buy up some corner of a foreign cemetery serves as a fit, if ambiguous, symbol of immigrant upward mobility in Scotland. In England, violent conflict also became less common after the early 1870s, when the frenzy engendered by fenianism and militant evangelicalism had dissipated. Irish outrages such as the Phoenix Park murders in 1882 could still provoke anti-Irish outrages in Britain, including the attack on Brighouse catholic chapel in Yorkshire, and the expulsion of Irish ironworkers from Tredegar in Monmouthshire.[3]

Few English towns, however, experienced conflict comparable with that in Liverpool, where raw enmities within the working class continued to be fostered by heavy unemployment and immigration. In 1906 Liverpool catholics stoned the congregation of George Wise, a pastor and local councillor, whose supporters thereupon assaulted two protestant missionaries who had injudiciously donned

---

MUN 2/15. In Mar. 1918 (just before introduction of permits), the average daily passenger traffic in *each* direction (reportedly) between Britain and Ireland was 2,840, of which 70 per cent comprised military or naval personnel (report by Burgess, CO 904/169/4).

[1] Occupational categories used in 1921 are not precisely comparable with those for 1911 (see table 5, below, pp 695–6). The index of over-representation for Irish male workers ranged from 419 (utilities), 332 (chemicals), 313 (vehicles and ships), and 246 (building), to 39 (paper), 37 (agriculture), 29 (instruments), 22 (private clerical work), and 3 (fishing). The index for women ranged from 142 (personal service), 140 (agriculture), and 133 (non-clerical professions), to 61 (paper), and 35 (private clerical work).

[2] *Glasgow Observer*, 26 Mar. 1898.

[3] John Denvir, *The Irish in Britain* (London, 1894), pp 296–313; Jon Parry, 'The Tredegar anti-Irish riots of 1882' in *Llafur*, iii, no. 4 (1983), pp 20–23. The chief constable of Monmouthshire reported that 'every Irishman who showed himself out of his house was stoned, and his house, in many cases, gutted, his furniture being thrown out and destroyed'.

shamrocks for St Patrick's day. Sectarian rage was further excited by the eucharistic congress of 1908: forty-seven schools had to be closed for a week after the children and mothers of St Anthony's catholic school had exchanged blows with their protestant counterparts at St Polycarp's, and defence associations were formed in the interests of each denomination. As a contemporary observed:

religious rioting is a favourite summer amusement among the submerged tenth in Liverpool. A so-called band, playing party tunes, will readily collect a Saturday or Sunday crowd of followers, who chant taunting airs, and regard stone-throwing and window-smashing as exhilarating pastimes. Of course, no self-respecting Irishman, catholic or protestant, associates with this ignorant rabble; but, as orange and green colours are used, Ireland gets the blame for this rowdyism.[1]

Elsewhere the passions and loyalties that had once given rise to 'party fights' were largely subsumed, as in Ireland, into politics and games. When London's Gaelic Athletic Association arranged a tournament in 1897, it announced that 'together with the usual running, jumping, weight-throwing, hurling, and football competitions the programme will also include an international tug-of-war (Irish Gaels versus Scottish Gaels)'.[2] Ethnic violence was increasingly directed against Jewish, Chinese, or black targets, with Irish settlers offering enthusiastic support to their British neighbours: thus in Cardiff (1919) one-third of those arrested for attacking black seamen (mainly resident in quarters once identified as Irishtowns) had Irish names.[3] As in the American case, native hostility to the Irish immigrant was mitigated by shared revulsion against a later generation of newcomers.

The gradual blunting of ethnic conflict could not, however, obscure the persistent social alienation of the Irish in Britain. Irish settlers and their descendants continued to commit a startlingly high proportion of crime: even in 1911, Irish-born accounted for one-tenth of all offenders committed to Lancashire prisons and over one-third of Scottish offenders. As table 6 indicates,[4] Irish settlers were five times more likely to go to prison than the population of England as a whole, and nearly ten times more likely than that of Scotland. Between 1861 and 1911 no reduction was discernible in the relative criminality of the immigrants, which remained even more excessive for women than men. The Irish excess was too great and too uniform to be wholly attributable to factors such as police hostility or class composition. Less is known about the criminality of British-born descendants of Irish parents, though some instructive statistics were gathered showing the declared religious adherence of offenders. In Scotland the catholic proportion rose from one-fifth in 1852 to one-third in 1872 and 1906, with somewhat higher figures recorded for Glasgow. The importance of the

---

[1] P. J. Waller, *Democracy and sectarianism* (Liverpool, 1981), pp 230, 517; A. Shallice, 'Orange and green and militancy' in *North West Labour History Society Bulletin*, vi (1979–80), pp 24–8; *The Liverpool Irishman* (Liverpool, c.1907; copy in N.L.I.), p. 6.

[2] Notice in Dillon papers, T.C.D. MS 6735/140a.

[3] Neil Evans, 'The South Wales race riots of 1919' in *Llafur*, iii, no. 1 (1980), p. 23.

[4] Below, p. 697.

protestant Irish contribution to crime as well as immigration was reflected in the Scottish returns for 1906, which revealed more Irish-born than catholic criminals. Over half of Lancashire's prisoners were catholic in 1872, compared with two-thirds in Liverpool and one-quarter in England as a whole; these remarkable proportions had fallen only slightly by 1906. By ignoring the minorities of non-Irish catholics and non-catholic Irish in England, we may obtain rough estimates of the relative criminality of catholic descendants of Irish immigrants. No precise statistics of England's catholic population are available, but a comparison of the proportion of English marriages conducted by catholic priests with the proportion of the population born in Ireland gives ratios of 1.6 (1861), 1.6 (1871), 3.1 (1901), and 4.2 (1911). Since the ratio of catholic to Irish-born offenders rose from 1.3 (1864) through 1.8 (1872) to 3.2 (1906), it would appear that catholics born outside Ireland were almost as likely as Irish immigrants to commit offences.[1] The Irish in pre-war Britain did much to merit their popular reputation for lawlessness, combined with artlessness in evading punishment.

Contrary, however, to stereotype, Irish settlers in Liverpool and Manchester at least were over-represented in virtually all categories of crime. Between 1871 and 1891 the Irish share of crime varied little according to category, being as great in the case of larceny as in that of assaults on policemen. No longer were Irish offenders particularly inclined to commit assault or breach of the peace, appear drunk and disorderly, or cause malicious and wilful damage. In short, the criminal profile of the late Victorian immigrants was almost indistinguishable from that of their British counterparts, and Irish criminality could no longer be laughed off as the outcome of Celtic exuberance and inebriety.[2] Even more worrying to many observers were the patterns of crime evident among the children of Irish settlers. Mayhew and Binny reported as early as 1862 that

the habitual criminals of London are said to be, in nine cases out of ten, 'Irish cockneys', that is, persons born of Irish parents in the metropolis; and this is doubtlessly owing to the extreme poverty of the parents on their coming over to this country, and the consequent neglect experienced by the class in their youth, as well as the natural quickness of the Hibernian race for good or evil.

Unlike the immigrants, Irish cockney criminals were most prominent among professional thieves and perpetrators of brutal violence. On their tour of Holloway prison the investigators

saw a clever little boy, of fourteen years of age, with engaging countenance, and soft Irish tongue. Though young in years he was an old offender, and an adroit pickpocket . . . He stated that his parents came from Manchester, and his father was a bricklayer, and addicted to intoxicating drink; that he himself lived by thieving, and chiefly frequented London Bridge and Whitechapel.

---

[1] Returns of prisoners in H.C. 1852–3 (908), lxxxi; 1864 (150), xlix; 1873 (156), liv; 1906 (138), xcix. For data on the birthplace of prisoners, see note to table 6, below, p. 697.
[2] Lowe, 'Irish in Lancashire', pp 222 ff.

While in conversation with the prison governor he 'often arched his eyebrows and protruded his tongue in an artful manner, and appeared to be proud of what he had done'.[1] The contrast between alcoholic father and delinquent son, rejoicing in his criminal professionalism, provides a grotesque example of intergenerational upward mobility.

Neither aggregate statistics nor contemporary stereotypes enable us to unravel the interacting influences of nationality, religion, occupation, and environment on Irish criminality. Mayhew and Binny posited a composite of racial and environmental factors in their explanation of Irish cockney crime, while other observers often insinuated that immigrant criminality was a consequence of the moral turpitude endemic among catholics. In refuting this thesis, one priest with pastoral experience in England argued that the expatriate criminals, unlike the majority of Irish people whether at home or in Britain, were not 'virtuous catholics' but persons living 'in a state of mortal sin'. The Englishman had 'natural habits' that gave him 'power and protection in certain temptations, and which Irish immigrants do not possess at all, and seldom acquire'. Ill-educated and unprepared for urban life, the immigrants were abnormally vulnerable to temptation in the squalid and socially disorganised industrial city.[2] A crude test of these conflicting explanatory models may be conducted using the returns of admission to Barlinnie prison in 1882–3, which allow tabulation of prisoners according to their religion, birthplace, occupation, and category of offence (see table 7).[3] Barlinnie was the newly opened receptacle in Glasgow for medium-term male offenders from all parts of Scotland, and its inmates roughly typify the Scottish criminal population, excluding both the most dangerous convicts and the casual drunks who were rounded up each Saturday night for drying out in police cells and local jails.

Just under one-fifth of the Barlinnie prisoners were Irish-born: of these one-quarter were protestant, and three-quarters from Ulster. For every catholic prisoner born in Ireland there were two catholics born elsewhere, mostly no doubt of Irish extraction. Religion influenced the occupational distribution of prisoners more than birthplace, and unskilled or semi-skilled employment accounted for two-thirds of catholics but only two-fifths of protestants. Catholics of both Irish and Scottish birth were over-represented in general labour, mining, building, and also dealing. Thus (at least within the criminal population) protestant immigrants differed little in legitimate occupation from their Scottish hosts, whereas catholics of both the first and later generations were of lower status. By contrast, the patterns of offences most favoured by Barlinnie prisoners seem to have been determined more by birthplace than by religion or occupation. As table 7

---

[1] Henry Mayhew and John Binny, *The criminal prisons of London* (London, 1862), pp 165, 386, 402, 549–50; cf. J. M. Feheney, 'Delinquency among Irish catholic children in Victorian London' in *I.H.S.*, xxiii, no. 92 (Nov. 1983), pp 319–29.

[2] Rev. J. S. Flanagan, P.P. (Adare) to William Monsell, 26 Nov. 1864 (Monsell Papers, N.L.I. MS 20683).

[3] Below, p. 698.

indicates, the lowest stratum of workers (general labourers) were more likely than others to breach the peace, less likely otherwise to commit assaults, and equally inclined to thieve. Yet the differences between offenders of various occupations were minor compared with those between immigrants and offenders born outside Ireland. Irish-born prisoners of both religious persuasions were unusually prone to commit assaults and breaches of the peace rather than to thieve or rob. Even so, they contributed to almost all categories of offence, and were not averse to perpetrating crimes of fraud, assaults on their wives, or lewd practices against pre-pubescent girls. Like their criminal counterparts in Ireland (though not, as we have seen, in Lancashire), the immigrants were disposed to commit offences against the person and the peace rather than property. The descendants of catholic immigrants conformed more closely to Scottish patterns of working-class aliena-tion by specialising in the illicit acquisition of property. The criminal disposition was affected less by matters of faith than by the problem of uprooting and readjustment.

The social status of Britain's Irish population improved only gradually over the half-century after 1871, and the familiar signs of deprivation (poor housing, menial employment, and criminality) persisted. Continuing native hostility, however attenuated, reinforced the immigrant's sense of grievance. As the nationalist politician John O'Connor Power, M.P. for Mayo, wrote in 1880,

it has been said that the 'era of reconciliation' has set in, but the Irish in England are marked with the effects of the same policy that pursued their fathers at home. They have had to go through all the work of life with the ban upon them of being Irish . . . Social recognition is slow to wait upon those who cannot forget that they are Irish.

The interaction of British hostility and Irish pride ensured, so Power asserted, that the Irish showed not 'the slightest tendency to amalgamation with those around them'.[1] Irish clannishness and cultural distinctiveness were often noted by British observers, though such impressions are always biased in favour of distinctiveness since those setting aside their ethnicity become socially invisible. In his investigation of York (1901), Rowntree found that two of the town's three disreputable drinking clubs were

largely frequented by Irish labourers. Entrance to them is jealously guarded, and exact information regarding the number of members or conditions of membership cannot be given . . . Drunken men have been seen through the windows of one of these clubs lying on the wooden forms, but the members are careful not to allow any one to leave the club until he is sober enough to escape the risk of a summons for being drunk in the streets.

Ethnic eating habits also attracted notice: in pre-1914 Salford Irish families 'were ridiculed for their Sunday habit of boiling cabbage, pork ribs, and "murphies" all in one iron pan, then letting the mess serve for every meal far into the following

---

[1] J[ohn] O'Connor Power, 'The Irish in England' in *Fortnightly Review*, xxvii, no. 159 (1880), pp 418, 420.

week'.[1] These accounts illustrate the cultural consequences of immigration rather than cultural transference: Salford's Irish would seldom have smelt either pork or cabbage before emigration, while the secretive insobriety of York contrasted sadly with the shameless bibulousness of a Connacht town on market-day. Far from forming a cohesive community, the immigrants were divided among those who tried to replant their Irish culture in Britain, those who created a hybrid immigrant culture, and those who did their best to 'forget that they were Irish'.

For most immigrants, Roman Catholicism was pervasive in the culture of their Irish upbringing. Their restricted participation in the rites and institutions of the church in Britain therefore suggests that cultural transference was incomplete. In 1864 the Rev. J. S. Flanagan had observed that 'vast numbers of the Irish immigrants and their descendants are living in habitual neglect of every religious duty, i.e. they never come to mass, and never make their Easter confession and communion . . . I am inclined to think they are the majority'.[2] Neglect of duties remained commonplace throughout the nineteenth century, though the catholic church avoided the rapid decline in participation experienced by some of its major rivals. In the Liverpool diocese the number of Easter communicants increased by half between 1866 and 1885, yet the majority of nominal catholics still ignored their obligation. A census of religious attendance in Liverpool borough in 1881 revealed virtually no increase since the official census of 1851. Less than two-fifths of catholics attended any Sunday service, twice the Anglican proportion but well below that for nonconformists. Attendance at catholic services in Sheffield (1881), Glasgow (1881), Greenock (1881), Aberdeen (1891), York (1901), and London (1902–3) somewhat exceeded the attendance returned in 1851, but in each case the increment fell short of the increase in total town population. At least in London, where nearly two-thirds of catholic attenders were women, 'lapsing' was evidently more common among men.[3] Adolescent boys were deemed particularly vulnerable: as Booth remarked in his survey of London, 'the best hope is to catch the young men again a few years later when they marry'.

Booth's clerical informants reported that intermarriage with protestants was rare, but a less sanguine assessment was offered by a prominent catholic nationalist:

There are few places where the Irish are more intermixed and intermarried into the general population than in Birmingham. London is the nearest approach to it. This is in striking

---

[1] Rowntree, *Poverty*, pp 326–7; Robert Roberts, *The classic slum* (Manchester, 1971), p. 84.

[2] See above, p. 669, n. 2. Flanagan had been chaplain of the Birmingham workhouse.

[3] Lowe, 'Irish in Lancashire', ch. 7; R. B. Walker, 'Religious changes in Liverpool in the nineteenth century' in *Jn. Ecc. Hist.*, xix, no. 2 (1968), pp 203, 211; E. R. Wickham, *Church and people in an industrial city* (London, 1969), pp 109, 148, 279; Robert Howie, *The churches and the churchless in Scotland* (Glasgow, 1893), pp xxi, 97–100; Rowntree, *Poverty*, pp 346–7; Hugh McLeod, *Class and religion in the late Victorian city* (London, 1974), pp 308–14; *Census G.B. 1851. Religious worship. England and Wales. Report and tables* [C 1690], H.C. 1852–3, lxxxix; *Religious worship and education. Scotland. Report and tables* [C 1764], H.C. 1854, lix. Scottish figures refer to attendance at the most populous service, English to total Sunday attendance. For data concerning Britain's catholic population and problems of interpretation, see Robert Currie and others, *Churches and churchgoers* (Oxford, 1977).

contrast to Liverpool, Manchester, and other north-country towns, where they are more homogeneous, and but rarely marry outside their own creed and nationality.[1]

There is no reason to suppose that intermarriage became more common after the 1850s: in England the catholic proportion of all marriages remained remarkably constant at about one-twentieth up to 1914, while in Scotland the proportion stayed close to one-tenth. In accordance with both catholic doctrine and Irish practice, immigrant families were evidently large: for every catholic marriage conducted in Britain between 1911 and 1914 there were about 4.6 baptisms.[2] High fertility within marriage was also encouraged by Irish concentration in occupational groups prone to the procreation of large families, as demonstrated by the Scottish fertility census for 1911.[3] In general, the returns of Easter obligation, church attendance, marriages, and baptisms indicate that, in a period of rapid secularisation, the catholic church in Britain elicited stable but by no means general participation from its nominal membership.

Even stability was hard won, the outcome of heavy involvement of manpower and capital in the struggle to stem secularism. Under the influence of Henry Edward Manning and Herbert Alfred Vaughan, the church showed greater readiness than ever before to cater for its Irish majority of adherents as well as its more accepted native minority: Manning reflected in 1887 that he had spent his 'life in working for the Irish occupation of England'.[4] Between 1885 and 1905 the number of catholic churches in Britain increased by over one-quarter and the number of clergy by half, a considerable proportion of whom were Irishmen.[5] Under Vaughan's direction in Salford and later Westminster, the church endeavoured to mobilise the educated laity in order to recover the lapsed souls of the usually Irish poor. Booth remarked on the 'extraordinary degree of adaptability' in social work manifested by London's priests (unlike their protestant counterparts); and bodies such as the Catholic Truth Society (founded in 1884) and the

---

[1] Booth, *Life & labour*, 3rd ser., vii, 244–5; Denvir, *Irish in Britain*, p. 415.

[2] Currie, *Churches & churchgoers*, *passim*. Church returns record 309,000 catholic baptisms between 1911 and 1914 (including perhaps 4,000 adult conversions in Scotland only), while the registrars general reported 67,000 catholic marriages. Over the same period the ratio of all registered births to all registered marriages in Britain was only 3 : 1. The catholic proportions of all marriages occurring in each of eleven registration divisions changed little in relative terms between 1851 and 1919, despite the overall increase from 4.5 per cent to 6.7 per cent ($r = +0.93$).

[3] *Census Scotland: report*, *III*, pp 288–90 [Cd 7163], H.C. 1914, xliv, 734–6, gives the number of children ever born to men of various occupations who had married women aged 22–6 years at least fifteen years before the census. For the twenty-four groups of occupied males analysed in table 5, the mean number of children (weighted according to the distribution of Irish-born workers among these groups) was 6.2, compared with the Scottish mean of 5.8. In fourteen of the sixteen groups in which the Irish were over-represented (unweighted index), family size exceeded the Scottish mean, whereas it fell short of the Scottish mean in seven of the eight groups with disproportionately few Irish workers.

[4] Denis Gwynn, 'The Irish immigration' in George Andrew Beck (ed.), *The English catholics, 1850–1950* (London, 1950), p. 265.

[5] *The Catholic Directory 1885*, p. 344; *1905*, p. 444. About one-third of catholic clergy in five dioceses (1881 and 1900) had Irish names, according to E. D. Steele, 'The Irish presence in the north of England, 1850–1914' in *Northern History*, xii (1976), p. 239.

Catholic Social Union (1892) augmented the work of guilds and sodalities in diversifying the cultural impact of catholicism. Of even greater importance was the rapidly extending network of catholic voluntary schools, whose financial security and standard of education were gradually enhanced by the provision of public money. Whereas most catholic children in Glasgow, for example, had no contact with any school whatever in the 1860s, the great majority of eligible children were enrolled in church-run schools by the early twentieth century.[1] Catholic adult education was provided by newspapers purporting to provide catholic glosses on current events: Charles Diamond, who emigrated from Maghera to Newcastle upon Tyne in the late 1870s, constructed a newspaper empire, centred on the *Glasgow Observer*, which comprised thirty-seven publications at the time of his death in 1934.[2] Through these means the church exercised an increasingly subtle and variegated influence on the mentality of a good many of its ostensible members. Yet, as a Franciscan publicist reflected in 1902, 'so long as a few catholics are scattered amongst a large population of non-catholics, nothing will prevent a large leakage, especially in these busy industrial days'.[3]

Always conscious of its vulnerability as a minority instrument, the church as a body did not reinforce the political element of Irish community in Britain. In some countries of Irish settlement such as Australia, the clergy fostered or, where necessary, invented Irish nationalism in the belief that the catholic transplant would wither unless set in a rich mulch of Irish sentiment.[4] Nationalism, with its elusive objective and populist appeal, was an excellent foil for socialism: indeed it has been suggested that the Dundee clergy 'fostered the politics of nationalism as a distraction from the politics of class'.[5] On St Patrick's day, of course, the church could not hope to prevent outpourings of Irish sentiment in and about its parish churches, schools, and halls. But in Britain its strategy was largely negative: three days' abstinence from drink was regularly imposed in order to avoid intoxication and riot, while church-directed festivals, concerts, and reunions were arranged in order to discourage political celebrations. By the turn of the century church manipulation of the Patrician ritual had rendered a once volatile occasion bland and even amusing, a folk festival conducted by beaming priests before an indulgent British audience. When the newly established Irish population of Kensal New Town (recently evicted from Clerkenwell) formed a mile-long procession with banners, they were met not with jeers but 'the delight of the inhabitants at large'.[6] So long as Irishness signified nothing more sinister than

---

[1] Booth, *Life & labour*, 3rd ser., vii, 252; J. H. Treble, 'The development of Roman Catholic education' in David McRoberts (ed.), *Modern Scottish catholicism, 1878–1978* (Glasgow, 1979), pp 111–39.

[2] Owen Dudley Edwards, 'The catholic press in Scotland' in McRoberts, *Modern Scottish catholicism*, pp 156–82.

[3] K. S. Inglis, *Churches and the working classes in Victorian England* (London, 1963), p. 129.

[4] Below, pp 709–22.

[5] W. M. Walker, 'Irish immigrants in Scotland' in *Hist. Jn.*, xv (1972), p. 663.

[6] Booth, *Life & labour*, 3rd ser., iii (1902), 142.

saints and shamrocks, it could be treated with benevolence by British catholics, protestants, and unbelievers alike.

Yet the deliberate identification of British catholicism with Irish culture remained abhorrent to many native churchmen, who not only feared inundation by a more bigoted and less orderly backwater of the faith, but also deplored the demand for Irish self-government. The English hierarchy held that the latter was a political matter beyond the competence of the church, and intermittently came into conflict with nationalist leaders by instructing laymen to test electoral candidates on the education question rather than on home rule. The demand for public funding of voluntary schools touched the church's institutional interest, and could therefore be raised in the pulpit or in ostensibly apolitical bodies such as the Catholic Young Men's Society. In 1885, when Parnell urged immigrants 'to vote against all liberals and radicals',[1] the church stimulated widespread rejection of his advice in constituencies where tory candidates displayed secularist tendencies.

Subsequently the liberal party posed the major menace to school funding, so tending to alienate the catholic church in Britain from the Irish parliamentary party during its effective alliance with Gladstonian liberalism after 1886. In 1904 Archbishop Bourne of Westminster icily declined to provide catholic schools as meeting places for the United Irish League, on the grounds that the church should stand 'outside and above all sectional political combinations . . . especially in countries where political differences are wide and profound'. He dismissed the insinuation of the league's secretary, J. F. X. O'Brien, that 'a policy of political divorce between priest and people' might augment still further 'the numbers of Irish who have fallen away from the faith in this country—numbers which if they could be enumerated would, I fear, run into millions'.[2] After the election of January 1910, at which the Catholic Federation ineffectively solicited Irish support for tory candidates in key constituencies, the liberal government shelved its secularism and the church avoided further collision with the league. The Scottish hierarchy had also tried to placate nationalists by reversing its singular ruling of 1899 that the sacraments be withheld from members of the Ancient Order of Hibernians, a stridently catholic society, which by 1910 dominated the home rule movement.[3] But the church's enduring distaste for mainstream nationalism resurfaced after 1916 when the republic became the focus of Irish populist agitation. Whereas most Irish bishops gave at least tacit support to Sinn Féin in order to avert the 'political divorce' of which O'Brien had warned, their British counterparts greeted the revolutionary movement with loyal disgust. Though Bourne eventually admitted that official reprisals were no less repugnant

[1] Above, p. 61.

[2] C. H. D. Howard, 'The Parnell manifesto of 21 November 1885' in *E.H.R.*, lxii, no. 242 (1947), pp 42–51; correspondence of Nov. 1904 in J. F. X. O'Brien papers, N.L.I. MS 13454.

[3] Neal Blewett, *The peers, the parties and the people* (London, 1972), pp 349–53; Handley, *Irish in modern Scotland*, p. 283.

to catholics than the outrages of 'fenianism' (as he termed republicanism in February 1921), he sought above all to avoid alienation of the church from British non-catholic opinion: 'I am an archbishop in England and in London . . . In Ireland, it is Ireland that counts. In England it is not only Ireland but also England and the whole empire.'[1]

Despite church equivocation and sporadic hostility, nationalist organisers struggled hard to involve immigrants in the concerns of Ireland and her politics. After the fenian alarms of the 1860s the character of that involvement was transformed. Through its front organisations the Irish Republican Brotherhood continued to perform social and recreational functions for many Irish settlers in Britain, but as a conspiracy it became ridiculous. Few immigrants joined the brotherhood itself: according to its own return in 1884 there were one-third as many members in Britain as in Ireland, with 6,000 in north-eastern England, 2,500 in the south-east, and 3,000 in Scotland. The centres of many circles were 1867 men who had fled to Britain, and often (as in Glasgow and London) they remained so for the rest of the century. Some circles were of startlingly small radius, as in the case of Tyne dock (South Shields) where 'Bill Heron and his 5 sons comprised the circle'. Others were evanescent, fading quickly on the departure of roving organisers or the migration of members. One organiser recollected that 'as a result of the migratory work of the Irish in Scotland it was very difficult to keep the circles together. A circle might almost disappear in a few months.' Circles maintained their vitality, if at all, by acquiring and shipping arms to Ireland where they would never be used, by plotting the empire's overthrow over dinner table or bar, and above all by ritual celebration of past battles. In Scotland the brotherhood's year was focused on three 'special celebrations': 4 March (Emmet commemoration), 18 September ('smashing of the van in Manchester'), and 23 November (execution of the 'Manchester martyrs'), each of which was marked by a lecture from some Irish celebrity such as Maud Gonne, O'Donovan Rossa, or Constance Markievicz.[2] But the fenians of Britain seem to have played little part in the bombing and dynamiting campaigns of 1881–7 carried out by Rossa's 'Skirmishers' and the Clan na Gael. Those responsible for attacks on barracks, public buildings, bridges, and tube stations in Britain were almost invariably American-Irish visitors, and their strategy was opposed by the brotherhood's supreme council for Ireland and Britain. In Glasgow a few 'ribbonmen' were trained for service by Rossa, while in the north of England the brotherhood's executive directed in 1883 'that travellers who may visit them with proper credentials are to be received'.[3] Yet, in contrast with the fenian movement of the 1860s, the outrages of the 1880s were generally attributed by the courts,

---

[1] D. G. Boyce, *Englishmen and Irish troubles* (London, 1972), pp 78–9.

[2] 'Secret societies in Ireland and America', memorandum of 26 Mar. 1889, in B.L., Balfour papers 13/9; Patrick McCormick papers, N.L.I. MS 15337.

[3] K. R. M. Short, *The dynamite war* (Dublin, 1979), pp 259–60, 159–60, 147; Mark F. Ryan, *Fenian memories* (Dublin, 1945), pp 107, 130–36, 178.

the government, and the public to a handful of American specialists rather than to the immigrant population. Physical force was no longer a popular strategy for Irish nationalists in Britain, either in reality or in the imagination of their neighbours.

The brotherhood's political significance derived from its unrivalled expertise in providing patriotic entertainment during the years of awaiting revolution. By creating or infiltrating an impressive network of political and cultural organisations, it succeeded in implanting a sentimental trace of the fenian vision in a wide range of immigrants. The reiterated campaigns for amnesty for Irish republican prisoners generated well publicised public meetings and extensive immigrant participation, often with the blessing of moderate nationalists such as Butt. Even the *Tablet*, the loyal organ of the English hierarchy, remarked with approval on the 'singularly temperate' speeches delivered to the amnesty meeting of 25,000 at Hyde Park in 1874, an assembly of 'for the most part respectable artisans and their families, for there were many women and children'.[1] As shown below, individual fenians, sometimes no doubt under official direction, were prominent in organising the Irish electorate in Britain under Butt, Parnell, and Redmond.[2] Numerous literary and discussion groups were formed, according to one fenian organiser, with the intention of 'attracting and educating young Irishmen who would make desirable recruits for the fenian organisation'. In *fin-de-siècle* London, as Dr Mark Ryan attested, 'the active agents in all the political bodies were practically the same, and the primary object of many of them was to strengthen the fenian movement'. Fenian headquarters at 55 Chancery Lane accommodated the Young Ireland Society (founded in 1882), the Parnellite Leadership Committee (1891), the Parnellite Irish National League of Great Britain (1891), the Amnesty Association (1892), the Gaelic League (1896), the Gaelic Athletic Association (1895), the O'Donovan Rossa Reception Committee, the John Daly Reception Committee, the '98 Centenary Association, the Irish National Club (1899), Cumann na nGaedheal (1903), and Sinn Féin (1905), all but one of whose committees included Mark Ryan.[3]

The organisational ubiquity of a gaggle of fenian doctors and journalists does not imply that the young revivalists of Celtic or Gaelic culture themselves became conspirators. London Irish poets such as Yeats fed on the illicit glamour emanating from John O'Leary, but employed it to manufacture poems rather than bombs. Romantic Ireland had particular appeal for better educated expatriates and their children, providing an attractive image of the Irish past that was not (as in Ireland) seen to be painfully at odds with the drab materialism of the Irish present. Language classes and bracing lectures on Irish history now supplemented the singing of lachrymose Irish airs round the piano in the parlour of the respectable immigrant household. By 1902 there were 1,500 members of the Gaelic League in London alone, with up to fifty Irish classes weekly in fourteen

---

[1] *Tablet*, 21 Mar. 1874, p. 354. [2] Below, p. 677. [3] Ryan, *Fenian memories*, pp 171–2.

schools. Moist-eyed 'exiles' heard Irish-language sermons on St Patrick's day at the dockland catholic church, relished 'an atmosphere of the country fireside gatherings' of their childhoods at league meetings, and organised language summer schools in Irish holiday resorts.[1] The Gaelic revival served a further function for immigrants by encouraging a belief in the community of Celtic peoples, which might provide immigrants in bleak Britain with allies among the Welsh, the Scots, and the Manx. Though Irish settlers in Britain had little contact with Britain's 'Celtic fringe', which was of course restricted to remote rural districts virtually devoid of immigrants, feelings of abstract solidarity flourished in the absence of chilling first-hand acquaintance. The mystique of race helped ameliorate the immigrants' sense of alienation from their country of settlement as well as separation from their country of birth.

A more prosaic and practical version of Irish nationalism was promulgated by the network of clubs and committees supporting the Irish parliamentary party in British towns. Their leadership and membership overlapped with both fenian and revivalist organisations. The first executive of the Home Rule Confederation of Great Britain (1873) included four ex-fenians, of whom John Denvir and John Barry had both belonged to a 'sort of inner circle of the I.R.B.'. But apart from the secretary of the Land League of Great Britain, who was suspected of involvement in the Phoenix Park murders, few of the party's organisers seem to have remained active as revolutionaries or conspirators.[2] Involvement in constitutional nationalism was not a cover for men impatiently awaiting revolution, but an acknowledgement that revolution was no longer practicable. The eminent practicality of the home rule movement in Britain tended to alienate sentimental Gaels, despite intermittent attempts by politicians to promote Irish-Ireland. These attempts generated more rivalry than concord. As senior organiser in Britain, J. F. X. O'Brien (leader of the Bottlehill rising in 1867 and inveterate wearer of 'Irish materials almost exclusively') tried 'without avail' to interest anti-Parnellite branches in Irish manufactures, and later urged the United Irish League 'to form Gaelic classes . . . especially as the Gaelic League is rather unfriendly to us, as a rule'. In 1902, when 1,500 people attended a sports meeting at Birkenhead organised by the Gaelic Athletic Association with the assistance of the Gaelic League, the Liverpool United Irish League staged a rival and more popular tournament at Greenwich Park.[3] Fruitless efforts were occasionally made to coordinate all strands of patriotic enthusiasm in a single campaign. In 1898 several centennial coordinating committees vied for authority over an increasingly restive network of Irish societies, only 1,000 of whose members had joined any Scottish centenary club by June 1898, while 1,600 had joined in northern

---

[1] Liam P. Ó Riain, 'Twenty years of the London Gaelic League' (Art O'Brien papers, N.L.I. MS 8346); and see above, pp 403–24.

[2] John Denvir, *The life story of an old rebel* (Dublin, 1910), p. 175; Ryan, *Fenian memories*, pp 132–3.

[3] J. F. X. O'Brien to Alfred Webb, 7 Nov. 1900 (J. F. X. O'Brien papers, N.L.I. MS 13456); home office, crime special branch précis, 7 Aug. 1902 (N.A.I., Carton 3).

England.[1] Incorrigible dreamers and conspirators tended to drift away from the home rule movement, with its ever contracting tunnel vision; but it was the hard-headed manipulators and vote-fixers who elicited most support from the immigrant population.

The home rule movement took organisational shape in Britain even earlier than in Ireland, where it remained for some years nothing but a form of words adopted by a few hundred protestant gentlemen.[2] In December 1871 the Glasgow Home Government branch was formed by John Ferguson, an independent-minded publisher whose Belfast presbyterian background doubtless added fire to his reiterated battles with home rule orthodoxy over the next four decades. In Liverpool a home rule committee was set up by John Denvir, a jack of all movements who had worked for Fr James Nugent as well as the I.R.B., and Alfred Crilly, an admirer of the Sullivanite strand of moral-force nationalism. As Denvir rather complacently recalled: 'Whatever was the national organisation in Ireland for the time being we two—Alfred Crilly and myself—always did our best to have its counterpart in Liverpool . . . our people there invariably looked to us to take the initiative in every national movement.' Twenty such associations formed the Home Rule Confederation of Great Britain in January 1873, which was addressed at its first convention by Isaac Butt despite his justified dread of manipulation by old schemers such as Denvir. Butt, like Parnell seven years later, used the British confederation as a launching-pad prior to rallying organised support for his leadership within Ireland. The title of the British organisation with its constituent branches was several times altered over the next quarter-century, but its character and functions changed little.[3] In 1884 Parnell abolished the local general councils that had allowed all too audible a voice to dissident nationalists; thereafter, the British organisation was tightly and overtly controlled by members of parliament despite recurrent efforts by Ferguson and other immigrant activists to restore branch representation on the executive. In Britain as in Ireland the reunification of the movement after 1900 brought some decentralisation;[4] but the Irish parliamentary party retained effective control over the United Irish League by nominating half the members of its executive. All British home rule organisations were virtually limited to men (apart from ladies' and juvenile auxiliaries), excluded officials of British political parties, and eschewed sectarian discussion. In practice protestants were sometimes unwelcome: thus the Irvine branch of the Irish National League, ironically named after Robert Emmet, restricted its band membership to catholics. The political focus was explicitly Irish rather than British: 'the self-government of Ireland is the supreme purpose of the organisation, and to that purpose all others must remain subordinate'; though 'one of the

---

[1] Ibid., June 1898 (N.A.I., Carton 2).

[2] Above, pp 3–25.

[3] Denvir, *Life story of an old rebel*, pp 150, 175; Handley, *Irish in modern Scotland*, pp 269–80; Bernard O'Connell, 'Irish nationalism in Liverpool, 1873–1923' in *Éire-Ireland*, x, no. 1 (1975), pp 24–37.

[4] Above, pp 92–9.

objects . . . shall be the protection of the general interests of the Irish population of Great Britain'.[1] The major political organisation enrolling Irish immigrants sought to reinforce their preoccupation with the Irish past rather than the British present.

Most immigrants avoided all Irish organisations, but far more joined home rule clubs than conspiratorial or revivalist societies. Just before the split the Irish National League of Great Britain reached its peak membership of 41,000 in 630 branches, a threefold increase over the five years since 1885. Since the Irish-born population of adult males in Britain exceeded 300,000, it is clear that the great majority of eligible immigrants (and indeed of Irish electors) remained outside the league.[2] The Parnellites received little organised support in Britain during the 1890s, though London's fenians under the ubiquitous Dr Mark Ryan formed innumerable committees in Chancery Lane. The executive of 1890 had consisted of eight Parnellite and ten anti-Parnellite M.P.s, and each group subsequently claimed the allegiance of the league's branches. But political squabbling led to local apathy and disorganisation, with many branches lapsing and others declining to forward subscriptions to any executive. A meeting at Christmas 1890 to establish a new anti-Parnellite branch in Southwark attracted twelve participants, of whom ten failed to join, while only four came to the next meeting.[3] The paid-up membership of the larger league had fallen below 15,000 by 1898, and even its ebullient president T. P. O'Connor could not deny 'the influence of apathy produced by faction and dissension'. Reports in the *Glasgow Observer* indicate vigorous activity by social organisations such as the Irish National Foresters or the Glasgow Hibernian Swimming Club, but little enthusiasm for politics. The Thomas Davis branch in Glasgow organised a competition to attract new members, with the enticement of 'a third-class return ticket to Dublin as a second prize'.[4] Party reunification in 1900 was soon followed by reinvigoration of the British movement under the United Irish League, though the divisions between local bosses such as Austin Harford and T. P. O'Connor in Liverpool, or Ferguson and Diamond in Glasgow, took several years to paper over. By 1908 the league's strength was almost 25,000, with 74 subscribing branches in Scotland and 216 in England. Ferguson's troublesome Home Government branch remained easily the largest in Britain. Apart from Glasgow (with 2,600 members), the towns with most leaguers were Leeds (1,800), London (1,500), Manchester and Salford (1,200), Liverpool (800), Bradford (700), and Newcastle upon Tyne (400).[5]

---

[1] Ian Wood, 'Irish immigrants and Scottish radicalism, 1880–1906' in Ian MacDougall (ed.), *Essays in Scottish labour history* (Edinburgh, 1978), pp 71–4; O'Connell, 'Irish nationalism in Liverpool', p. 29; United Irish League of Great Britain, *Annual report* [1908], pp 56–8 (copy in N.L.I.).

[2] O'Brien, *Parnell and his party* (Oxford, 1957), pp 274–5.

[3] Ryan, *Fenian memories*, pp 151–4; Denvir, *Life story of an old rebel*, pp 377–8; report by Denvir to executive committee, I.N.L. of G.B., 31 Dec. 1890 (J. F. X. O'Brien papers, N.L.I. MS 13467).

[4] Irish National League of Great Britain, *Annual convention* [report] (London, 1898), p. 3 (copy in Dillon papers, T.C.D. MS 6762/361); *Glasgow Observer*, 1 Jan. 1898, 22 Jan. 1898.

[5] U.I.L. of G.B. (1908), pp 6–16. Membership is calculated from receipts on account of membership cards, branches being required to forward 1s. per member.

The size and achievement of the home rule movement in Britain betokened rather low political vitality by comparison with other Irish emigrant populations. Michael Davitt estimated that British organisations had subscribed only £20,000 to the national movement during the quarter-century from the formation of the Land League, equivalent to one-twenty-fifth of American or one-third of Australasian contributions.[1] British revenue certainly exceeded this sum, but the net contribution to party funds may well have been still lower. At its peak between 1886 and 1890, the Irish National League's income of £15,000 was outweighed by the party's expenditure of £5,500 on British electoral expenses and £13,000 on British propaganda through the Irish Press agency. During the 1890s the anti-Parnellite League had 'the greatest difficulty' in paying its way, and had to sell office furniture and borrow from the party to pay rent and salaries. Gross annual income from branches fell below £2,000, returning after reunification to a plateau at about £4,000 of which less than half found its way into the parliamentary fund.[2] The modest circulation of nationalist newspapers in Britain provides further evidence of immigrant indifference towards organised nationalism. Even 'in its best days' William O'Brien's *United Ireland* sold only 8,000 copies in London and just 226 to the substantial Irish population of Newport and Wales; while at the turn of the century, the London circulation of its successor the *Irish People* was 2,500 copies.[3] The appeal of organised nationalism was strongest among electors and hence weakest in the lumpenproletariat. As the labour organiser Harry McShane recalled, 'the membership of the United Irish League in Glasgow was mostly middle-class Irishmen: publicans, grocers, iron merchants, and suchlike—men who were making their way.'[4] In Liverpool the league's relatively small membership was but one symptom of immigrant social disorganisation. According to a pamphlet published in 1907, 'it is calculated that 90 per cent of the Liverpool Irishmen are at present not connected with any Irish society in the city. There is no social bond of brotherhood uniting the people.' Irish Liverpudlians were urged indiscriminately to join the Gaelic Athletic Association, Gaelic League, Irish Literary Society, and Irish National Foresters, form an Irish cooperative society and Sinn Féin club, and develop the suburban network of the United Irish League so that 'guidance would be given to the Irish voters at election times'.[5] Britain's immigrant population, apart from an ageing core of enthusiasts still bedded in Irish political culture, gave at best half-hearted support to the nationalist cause.

[1] Below, pp 711–13.
[2] Davitt, *Fall of feudalism*, p. 713; O'Brien, *Parnell and his party*, pp 274–5; J. F. X. O'Brien to Dillon, 9 Dec. 1896 (Dillon papers, T.C.D. MS 6735/135); miscellaneous I.N.L. accounts in Dillon papers, T.C.D. MSS 6762, 6735; annual reports of I.N.L. of G.B., and U.I.L. of G.B. Davitt's estimate of the British contribution, though not based on financial accounts, was evidently informed by advice from J. F. X. O'Brien: see copy of Davitt to O'Brien, 2 Jan. 1904 (J. F. X. O'Brien papers, N.L.I. MS 13420).
[3] Thomas O'Dwyer to J. F. X. O'Brien, 11 Jan. 1900 (J. F. X. O'Brien papers, N.L.I. MS 13432).
[4] Harry McShane and Joan Smith, *Harry McShane: no mean fighter* (London, 1978), p. 11.
[5] *The Liverpool Irishman* [1907], pp 6–8.

The *raison d'être* of all home rule organisations in Britain was electoral. Branches were required to take 'an active part in all parliamentary elections, and in other elections in those districts where such elections are contested on political principles', voting only for 'supporters of Gladstone's Irish policy'.[1] The party's alliance with liberalism after 1886 was thus extended to electoral choices in Britain, though some discretion was exercised by the executive as Rosebery, Campbell-Bannerman, and Asquith (in his first years of office) wriggled away from the Gladstonian commitment. Reiterated efforts by convention delegates to modify the Irish test for candidates or apply other criteria were blocked; and under the direction of T. P. O'Connor, a member of the National Liberal Club, home rule managers closely coordinated their electoral tactics with their liberal counterparts. Liberal officials could not, however, take office in the league, and league members were forbidden to accept liberal money without branch permission. The constituency strategy of league branches was analogous to that of the Irish parliamentary party at Westminster: not to win majorities, but to hold the balance between the major British parties. Despite heavy Irish settlement in the Glasgow region, it was the Scotland division of Liverpool that elected Britain's only home ruler M.P. (T. P. O'Connor, who held the seat for forty-four years after his election in 1885). In 1908, O'Connor defended the league's expensive but failed attempt to return Alderman O'Hanlon for Jarrow by claiming that he was 'not despairful of the time coming when we will be able to return Irishmen for some seats in Great Britain'. Meanwhile, 'the Irish vote in England may be the deciding factor in given circumstances with regard to the fate of the government or party', provided that the minority acted 'as one man'.[2]

Yet even without bickering between branches and conflict with the Catholic Federation, Irish electoral influence would have been disproportionately small. Despite the franchise extension of 1885, the severe residence and valuation requirements for householders discriminated against Irishmen, who were unusually mobile and inclined to reside in inferior accommodation on short-term lettings. Moreover, we should not glibly assume that all qualified electors born in Ireland or of an Irish parent could under any circumstances have been induced to vote as one man: as in the United States and Australia, the 'Irish vote' in Britain was in part a bogey invented by political opponents in order to exploit anti-Irish sentiment.[3] Historical psephology is hindered by the shared tendency of nationalist organisers and their rivals to magnify the unity and power of the Irish electorate. This applies particularly to the 1885 election, the last at which the Irish parliamentary party was free to instruct its British followers to vote against liberal candidates.[4] Disappointed liberals as well as cock-a-hoop Parnellites

---

[1] This rule applied to both the I.N.L. and the U.I.L. of G.B., though qualifying clauses were occasionally amended. For a decade up to 1898, the league was bound to support Gladstonian candidates 'adopted by the liberal leaders and by the authorised liberal association' unless the executive approved 'Irish candidates'. See annual reports, *passim*.

[2] U.I.L. of G.B. (1908), pp 18–20.

[3] Below, pp 712–13.

[4] Above, pp 61, 674.

attributed at least twenty-five tory gains to Parnell's tactical reversal, a claim rendered implausible by the evident disunity within both the liberal party and the nationalist movement. In Glasgow, where Ferguson opposed Parnell's manœuvre, all seven liberal candidates were successful; while in several English constituencies the catholic church effectively undermined party strategy.[1] Thereafter the fragility of the nationalist vote as an independent force was concealed by the liberal alliance, though the incessant squabbling over league support for particular anti-tory candidates reflected deep divisions within the immigrant population as well as power play among league managers. O'Connor and his team were often less severe in their interpretation of Gladstonian policy than were their party leaders. Thus in September 1900 O'Connor urged Redmond to 'discourage their pressing liberal candidates too closely on the question of home rule', drawing the sharp response that the league 'should only support when home rule declaration unequivocal'. The British organisers were keenly aware that their branches could neither avoid entanglement with competing liberal factions, nor afford alienation of likely winners. Even the style of nationalism required modification in the drab British context, as indicated by a complaint to J. F. X. O'Brien from a Manchester official in 1887. The writer was a colourful example of fenian turned fixer, a man who had helped carry the baggage of his 'old commanding officer' to Bottlehill in 1867. But he knew that Irish theatricality was not easily exportable, warning that 'a large number of Englishmen connected with the Home Rule Union have been alienated from us' by the profligacy of league organisers and especially by the braggadocio of William O'Brien, who was 'daily lounging about town *à la* Oscar Wilde, or coquetting at big local meetings'.[2] In parliamentary elections the league became little more than a pressure group within liberalism, pragmatic in its tactics and humdrum in its tone.

It was the rise of labour as a political factor that placed the unity of the Irish vote and the liberal alliance under greatest strain. As J. F. X. O'Brien wrote to Dillon in December 1891, 'the desire of the labour party for parliamentary representation is showing as a rock ahead in many places . . . the liberals have no policy in this matter—and *laissez faire* is landing them *and us* in difficulty in several places'.[3] The source of difficulty was the rapid extension of trade unionism

---

[1] Alan O'Day, *The English face of Irish nationalism* (Dublin, 1977), pp 110–12; C. H. D. Howard, 'The Parnell manifesto of 21 November 1885' in *E.H.R.*, lxii, no. 242 (1947), pp 42–51; John McCaffrey, 'The Irish vote in Glasgow in the later nineteenth century' in *Innes Review*, xxi, no. 1 (1970), pp 30–36; P. F. Clarke, *Lancashire and the new liberalism* (Cambridge, 1971), pp 37–8, 427–31. In the Lancashire region, as Clarke's analysis of newspaper reports indicates, the Irish vote was concentrated in constituencies with low proportions of registered electors. Only 4 of the 16 constituencies where the Irish (or catholic) factor was worthy of enumeration had proportions above the median for the 66 constituencies in the region. This analysis, though referring to 1910, concerns elections held under the 1885 franchise.

[2] O'Connor to Redmond, 26 Sept. 1900, and Redmond's notes for reply, 28 Sept. (Redmond papers, N.L.I. MS 15215); J. W. O'Hea to J. F. X. O'Brien, 15 Sept. 1887 (J. F. X. O'Brien papers, N.L.I. MS 13432.).

[3] O'Brien to Dillon, 23 Dec. 1891 (Dillon papers, T.C.D. MS 6735/70).

among unskilled and semi-skilled workers, which disproportionately affected the once disorganised Irish work-force. Irish immigrants or their sons, such as Will Thorn, Ben Tillett, and Jim Sexton, became prominent organisers of gas and dock workers in the 1880s and 1890s; while the heavy involvement of Irish stevedores in the London dock strike of 1889 encouraged Cardinal Manning to make his celebrated intervention to settle the dispute. The Irish stereotype was hastily modified from strike-breaker to strike-maker, and in 1898 the Irish National League attributed its loss of income to the heavy involvement of its members in the great engineering dispute.[1] Trade unionists and their supporters among Irish settlers often pressed league branches to support labour representatives at elections, even where they were repudiated by liberal managers. Labour candidacies tended to promote conflict within and between local branches, between branches and executive, and between the British executive and the party leadership. Party leaders apart from Davitt normally backed the liberal managers, as in the case of Keir Hardie's candidature for Mid Lanark in 1888. Even Davitt and his Scottish ally Ferguson temporarily closed ranks against Hardie in 1892, when he urged working-class support for tories against liberals. O'Connor's executive, answerable to both the party and their working-class membership, generally combined rhetorical approval of labour's cause with dutiful condemnation of particular labour candidacies. From 1906 onwards the league was committed to giving preference to labour candidates who had passed the Irish test and who were expected to win seats, a proviso that at first excluded virtually all labour nominees.[2] But the skilful wordplay of nationalist leaders could not conceal the enduring divisions among Irish voters in the localities. The *Glasgow Observer*, though itself prominent in support of Irish catholic labour organisers such as John Wheatley in his early years, bitterly denounced those league officials for whom 'trade unionism is more than home rule'. Its antagonist, the Home Government branch, was described as 'a very narrow circle of Glasgow publicans and Glasgow I.L.P. men who happen to be Irish in nationality, and anxious to use the Irish movement to further their own purposes'.[3] The promotion of Irish working-class interests by prosperous publicans was not merely a droll exportation of Irish ambiguities, but above all a symbol of the changing political alignments of industrial Britain.

The failure of Irish settlers to create an autonomous community in politics was most evident in local government. Despite the democratisation of the 1890s, the usual municipal manifestation of large Irish minorities was the entrenchment of

[1] I.N.L. of G.B. (1898), p. 3.

[2] T. W. Moody, 'Michael Davitt and the British labour movement' in *R. Hist. Soc. Trans*, 5th ser., iii (1953), pp 53–76; Clarke, *Lancashire and the new liberalism*, p. 253.

[3] *Glasgow Observer*, 8 Jan. 1898; Ian S. Wood, 'John Wheatley, the Irish, and the labour movement in Scotland' in *Innes Review*, xxxi, no. 2 (1980), pp 71–85. Wheatley, who had emigrated as a child from Waterford to Greenock, became an active leaguer and Forester and a reporter on the *Observer*. His subsequent involvement in the Catholic Socialist Society and I.L.P. made him a favourite target for clerical and *Observer* abuse by 1914.

large anti-Irish majorities on local councils. Irish settlers were slow to achieve representation. The first Irishman to sit as a nationalist on an English town council is said to have been Bernard McAnulty in Newcastle upon Tyne, formerly a precursor, repealer, confederate, and tenant leaguer, but elected as a home ruler between 1874 and 1882. In 1875 another home ruler was elected in Liverpool, so challenging the middle-class Catholic Club's claim to represent the Irish interest within the city council's seemingly permanent liberal minority (1844–92). By 1877 the club had dropped its opposition to home rule, and (despite recurrent challenges from more aggressive nationalists) an effective local alliance between liberals and respectable home rulers was soon secured. Most of Liverpool's nationalist councillors in 1898 were locally born rather than sons of Ireland, and their political culture was that of urban Lancashire. As Diamond's *Catholic Herald* rhetorically enquired, 'beyond making city councillors for the liberal party and jerrymandering seats in safe Irish wards for the favoured few, what has the Irish National League of Liverpool ever done?'[1] Harford and the Liverpool United Irish League skilfully rode the working-class wave from liberalism towards labour, and the local organisation not only outlasted the league's terminal convention (1918) but even increased its municipal representation from fourteen to twenty-three over the next quinquennium. The nationalist organisation had survived intact by sleight of hand, Irish voters having abandoned the Irish priorities of the league's constitution and regrouped as one strand in the tangled web of proletarian rivalries. Yet the retention of the old party label was counterproductive, enabling Salvidge's Workingmen's Conservative Association (which excluded catholics until 1935) to exploit 'Orange' prejudice in order to reinforce tory control over the city.[2] In most other towns the process of political integration was signified by the disappearance rather than the transmutation of explicitly Irish organisations. By the time of the first world war, the cause of Ireland was becoming ineffectual as a rallying-cry for the catholic working class of urban Britain.

The residual power of Irish agitation to levy active support from Britain's immigrant population was tested by the revolutionary events of 1916–21. The British vestiges of the I.R.B. made little contribution to the Easter rising, though under Seán MacDermott's instructions the Scottish executive sent a few men to Belfast who spent Easter searching for a rising. Thereafter the brotherhood exerted itself to supply arms to Ireland, including those seized in eight raids on Clydeside munitions works. Apart from window-smashing in London and warehouse-burning in Liverpool, little diversionary action was attempted in Britain. When a detective was killed during a Scottish assault on a van carrying

---

[1] T. P. MacDermott, 'Irish workers on Tyneside' in Norman McCord (ed.), *Essays in Tyneside labour history* (Newcastle, 1977), pp 166–8; Bernard O'Connell, 'Irish nationalism in Liverpool' in *Éire-Ireland*, x, no. 1 (1975), pp 26–7; P. J. Waller, *Democracy and sectarianism* (Liverpool, 1981), pp 186, 180.

[2] O'Connell, 'Irish nationalism in Liverpool', pp 32–4; A. Shallice, 'Orange and green and militancy' in *North West Labour History Society Bulletin*, vi (1979–80), pp 17–18.

an Irish prisoner, it was condemned by the Irish Volunteer leadership.[1] Though a few 'wild men' such as Brugha proposed extending armed struggle across the Irish Sea, the British policy of Sinn Féin and Dáil Éireann was to win public support by propaganda against unjust and oppressive government, rather than to alienate support through murder and arson.[2] Propaganda was conducted along three channels: by supplying British and foreign journalists and public figures with the republican version of current events as in the *Irish Bulletin*; by encouraging the formation of sympathetic pressure groups by influential non-Irish men and women; and by establishing networks of republican clubs among the Irish in Britain. The first two campaigns, directed towards British rather than immigrant opinion, were fairly effective in promoting opposition to coercion and pressing Lloyd George into negotiating truce and treaty in 1921. The Peace with Ireland Council was formed in October 1920 by a medley of old and new radicals of all parties, as a 'purely English movement', which would be 'therefore more effective' than a mere tool of Sinn Féin.[3] In March 1921 de Valera asked Art O'Brien, the republic's main organiser in Britain, 'to get a relief committee formed of the English who were opposed to their government's present policy in Ireland . . . not for the cash it might raise, but because a relief campaign would give the best cue for an attack by them upon their own government'. This committee was presumably linked to the Irish White Cross, a classic front organisation whose original trustees included Arthur Griffith and Michael Collins as well as Archbishop Walsh of Dublin.[4]

The third strategy of republican propagandists was to demonstrate that in Britain, as in Ireland, home rulers had been converted *en masse* to self-determination. New networks of Irish societies were created using well tried organisational techniques to enrol old activists under new banners. Though Sinn Féin itself formed branches in many British towns, the largest British network was the Irish Self-Determination League of Great Britain, formed in about October 1919. Ostensibly to avoid suppression, the league refrained from committing itself to the republic, instead promising to 'support their compatriots in Ireland, and use every means in their power to secure the application of the principle of self-determination for Ireland'. But the deletion at the first delegate conference of the proposed 'recognition of the Irish republic' and of Dáil Éireann probably owed as much to the sensibilities of old home rulers as those of the police.[5] P. J. Kelly, the league's president, was a close associate of Liverpool's United Irish

---

[1] McCormick papers, N.L.I. MS 15337; John Archer Jackson, *The Irish in Britain* (London, 1963), p. 124; Handley, *Irish in modern Scotland*, pp 297–300. Handley alleges that 'almost every town' in Scotland had Volunteer companies, and that the number of Sinn Féin clubs was increased from twenty to eighty on the visit in 1918 of the organiser Seán O'Sheehan.

[2] Above, p. 249.

[3] Boyce, *Englishmen and Irish troubles*, pp 65–6.

[4] De Valera to O'Brien, 19 Mar. 1921, quoted in Boyce, *Englishmen and Irish troubles*, p. 83; *The story of the Irish White Cross, 1920–1947* (Dublin, 1948), pp 6–7. Its president was Cardinal Logue.

[5] I.S.D.L. of G.B., *1st annual delegate conference . . . agenda* (London, 1920), and *Constitution and rules* (n.p., n.d.; both in N.L.I.).

League leader Austin Harford. Like their predecessors, its organisers went 'tramping about in the rain every day interviewing priests and others to try and get order out of chaos', forming local committees, selling newspapers at church doors, and fixing public meetings. In Ashton-in-Makerfield (Lancashire), the league was at first compelled by 'strong opposition' to hold its meetings in 'outlying districts', but subsequently acknowledged 'the generosity of the committee of the U.I.L.' in making its rooms available.[1]

Despite its indebtedness to the home rule organisation, the Irish Self-Determination League was far more restrictive in its objects, membership, and political tactics. Members were required to be of 'Irish birth or descent resident in Great Britain', and to avoid participation 'in English politics, either local government or parliamentary', without specific authority from Sinn Féin in Dublin. These restrictions brought reiterated but ineffectual protests from branches hoping to broaden membership to include spouses, English catholics, or sympathisers, and to involve themselves in local politics either independently or in the labour interest. The executive kept a tight rein on branch activity, and was itself dominated by Art O'Brien, who was also the key official of Sinn Féin and the Gaelic League in England. As in Ireland, the remodelling of nationalism was accompanied by superficial reinvigoration of the Irish-Ireland movement after its pre-war decline. By 1920 the London Gaelic League had over a thousand paid-up members, half its strength in 1903; while a few hurling, football, and camogie teams were assembled in February 1921. In April 1922 the Irish Self-Determination League claimed

the largest membership of any Irish organisation in the history of the Irish in Britain . . . Apart from our political objective during the period under review [1919–22], hundreds of branches of the Gaelic League have been formed, several Irish musical societies established, numerous literary and debating societies have been called into being and are in full swing, and clubs for Irish games and pastimes are now preparing for the Irish Race Olympic.[2]

These claims were exaggerated. In a more sober moment and a private context, the league's secretary had complained that 'although the Irish population of Great Britain is about 1,500,000, the total membership of the league is at present only 26,000'; and membership never reached the level claimed by the Irish National League in 1890. Indeed paid-up membership for the year of greatest activity (1921–2) only just exceeded 20,000, with no branches at all in Scotland and far fewer in Liverpool than in London, Manchester, or Tyneside.[3] The league's

---

[1] Seán McGrath to Art O'Brien, 28 Oct. 1919, report from Newcastle (Art O'Brien papers, N.L.I. MS 8433); *Irish Exile*, i, no. 4 (June 1921).
[2] I.S.D.L. of G.B., *Constitution and rules*; *Agenda* (1920); *2nd annual delegate conference . . . agenda* (London, 1921); *Irish Exile*, i, no. 4 (June 1921); report of 3rd annual delegate conference (Art O'Brien papers, N.L.I. MS 8433). The agendas of the first two conferences included ten branch resolutions seeking relaxation of membership restrictions and eight calling for permission to participate in English politics.
[3] Boyce, *Englishmen and Irish troubles*, p. 83; various returns in Art O'Brien papers (N.L.I. MS 8433).

organ, the *Irish Exile*, was selling obout 10,000 copies in late 1921, and the political and relief funds forwarded to Ireland by the I.S.D.L. amounted to only £37,000, of which one-quarter was committed to the Irish national loan. In addition £1,000 was sent direct from Wales, £600 from Sheffield, and £12,000 from Liverpool. Thus immigrant funding of the independence movement, though nominally at least exceeding Davitt's estimate of £20,000 for the nationalist movement between 1879 and 1904, was trifling by comparison with American contributions. The White Cross raised only £13,000 in Britain, scarcely one-hundredth of the amount sent by the associated American Committee for Relief in Ireland.[1] The I.S.D.L.'s inability to unite immigrant nationalists was underlined by the separate operations of the Council of Irish Societies (Liverpool and district), which organised its fund-raising through church collections, made 'confidential reports to priests of parishes', appointed a priest as auditor, and contributed money to Diamond's *Catholic Herald* while that organ was engaged in 'venomous attacks' on the I.S.D.L.[2] Nationalist disunity in Britain became all the more obvious after the dáil's approval of the treaty terms. Despite thinly veiled anti-treaty propaganda in Art O'Brien's *Irish Exile*, the league's conference of April 1922 voted by two to one to avoid explicit commitment to the republic pending an Irish election. The league soon disintegrated in a cloud of mutual recrimination and snide suggestions of embezzlement, leaving all factions disheartened by 'mass apathy' in Britain.[3] Irish nationality would never again be the focus of political activity for Britain's Irish population, for whom the partial reversion to Ireland-orientated agitation between 1919 and 1921 was but a feeble flash in the pan.

The half-century after 1871 did not witness the creation in Britain of an Irish community. Despite their persistently low social status, Irish settlers adopted patterns of residence, religious practice, political participation, and criminality that do not suggest a segregated population locked together in defensive ethnicity. Integration into British working-class life, a process encouraged by the multiplication of persons of Irish descent rather than birth, did not entail proletarian solidarity but merely the reorientation of factional conflict. Irish and British workers found some common ground in their shared fear and dislike of the Jewish

---

[1] Report of 3rd conference, loc. cit.; Council of Irish Societies (Liverpool and district), *Prisoners' dependents [sic] and Irish distress fund: confidential report* (31 Mar. 1922), and associated memoranda (Cusack papers, N.L.I. MS 10972); *White Cross*, p. 12. Statistics of funds raised by the I.S.D.L. and other bodies include sums remitted to the White Cross (not always distinguished).

[2] Council of Irish Societies, *Prisoners' dependents . . . report*; report of 3rd conference, loc. cit. Diamond, despite his antipathy to the I.S.D.L., had given belated support through his newspapers to Sinn Féin and had been imprisoned for justifying the attempt to murder French in 1919 (Owen Dudley Edwards, 'The catholic press in Scotland' in David McRoberts (ed.), *Modern Scottish catholicism, 1878–1978* (Glasgow, 1979), pp 156–82; Handley, *Irish in modern Scotland*, pp 296–7).

[3] *Irish Exile*, new ser., no. 3 (Jan. 1922), no. 6 (Apr. 1922); George O'Brien (Liverpool) to Eamon Donnelly (anti-treaty Sinn Féin), 11 May 1922 (N.A.I., 1094/5/13).

[4] 5 Edw. VII, c. 13 (11 Aug. 1905), effective from 1 Jan. 1906.

immigration between 1870 and 1907, when intake was restricted under the aliens act.[4] As a midwife recollected of London's East End:

it used to be a street occupied by poor English and Irish people. In the afternoons you would see the steps inside cleaned, and the women with their clean white aprons sat in summer times inside the doors, perhaps at needlework, with their little children about them. Now it is a seething mass of refuse and filth. . . . They are such an unpleasant, indecent people.

Cartoonists sharpened their focus from forehead and chin to nose, and the 'poor Irish people' enjoyed a shove up the ladder of civilisation.[1] Yet Irish settlers and their British neighbours retained their mutual awareness of each other's racial inferiority. Indeed this was the heyday of that bogus sociology that explained social and political behaviour in terms of racial inheritance. The Scottish census of 1871 warned that the 'invasion of Irish is likely to produce far more serious effects on the population of Scotland than even the invasions of the warlike hordes of Saxons, Danes, or Norsemen', spreading immorality as well as ignorance among innocent Scots.[2] Conversely, the *Freeman's Journal* lamented in November 1890 that 'it is living in England that has contaminated Mr Parnell and were he living at home in Ireland he would never have fallen in with the O'Sheas'. Three decades later, the *Irish Exile* exclaimed:

Where does the common mind exist between the Irish and English peoples? In the first place the Irish people are Gaelic and the English Anglo-Saxon—the Irish are catholic and the English protestant. . . . The fact that most of the Irish people speak better English than most of the English people does not prove community of mind, but difference in intelligence.[3]

Yet racist banter no longer expressed the grim group hatreds that had formerly alienated the Irish in Britain from their competitors. Republican propagandists might play at racial superiority, but their more serious design was to cultivate influential Englishmen whose sympathies were capable of crossing both racial and religious barriers. Integration, however fractious, in the British working class, however alienated from its masters, was the most rational strategy for Britain's shrinking Irish minority. As early as 1880 the former fenian O'Connor Power had written:

For weal or woe the great mass of the Irish who have settled in England are destined to remain in the land of their adoption. They have children born to them on English soil, all

---

[1] John A. Garrard, *The English and immigration, 1880–1910* (London, 1971), p. 51; cf. Lloyd P. Gartner, *The Jewish immigrant in England, 1870–1914* (London, 1973).
[2] *Census Scotland, 1871: report, vol. 1*, p. xix [C 592], H.C. 1872, lxviii, p. 19; cf. Handley, *Irish in modern Scotland*, p. 240. The Irish census commissioners refuted these insinuations with spirit, and won the qualified support of *The Times* (9 Dec. 1875).
[3] O'Brien, *Parnell and his party*, p. 287; *Irish Exile*, i, no. 3 (May 1921).

their worldly interests are centred in England, and their prospects in life are practically bounded by the English shore.[1]

For Power this posed a threat to Irish identity; but for T. P. O'Connor a third of a century later, partial integration into the 'British environment' had made the Irishman in Britain 'broader in his outlook' than his fellows at home. He now occupied 'a curious middle place between the nationality to which he belongs and the race among which he lives'.[2]

[1] J[ohn] O'Connor Power, 'The Irish in England' in *Fortnightly Review*, xxvii, no. 159 (1880), p. 418.
[2] Felix Lavery (compiler), *Irish heroes in the war* (London, 1917), pp 31–2.

APPENDIX

1 IRISH-BORN POPULATION OF GREAT BRITAIN, 1871–1921

year	number	as % of population	% female	% under 20
England and Wales				
1871	566,540	2.49	50.01	11.97
1881	562,374	2.17	48.35	n.a.
1891	458,315	1.58	48.81	n.a.
1901	426,565	1.31	47.26	n.a.
1911	375,325	1.04	48.88	n.a.
1921	364,747	0.96	51.01	n.a.
Scotland				
1871	207,770	6.18	47.79	14.43
1881	218,745	5.86	46.40	13.73
1891	194,807	4.84	45.71	11.99
1901	205,064	4.59	41.95	11.51
1911	174,715	3.67	42.77	10.11
1921	159,020	3.26	43.66	10.78

Sources: *Census of England and Wales*, and *Census of Scotland*, 1871–1921, reports: in H.C. papers.

2 IRISH-BORN POPULATION OF BRITISH TOWNS, 1871–1921

year	London	Liverpool	Manchester[a]	Glasgow	elsewhere	Britain
as % of local population						
1871	2.80	15.56	8.59	14.32	2.32	2.97
1881	2.12	12.85	7.45	13.12	2.15	2.63
1891	1.58	9.12	4.59	10.04	1.64	1.98
1901	1.33	6.67	3.69	8.88	1.42	1.71
1911	1.14	4.64	2.64	6.73	1.14	1.35
1921	1.16	3.90	2.36	6.35[b]	0.99[b]	1.22
as % of total Irish-born population in Britain						
1871	11.77	9.91	5.59	8.82	63.90	100
1881	10.34	9.09	4.94	8.59	67.05	100
1891	10.18	7.23	4.94	10.12	67.53	100
1901	9.53	7.23	4.46	10.70	68.07	100
1911	9.58	6.30	4.54	9.60	70.17	100
1921	9.97	5.97	4.34	12.54[b]	67.18[b]	100
index of over-representation[c]						
1871	94	524	289	482	78	100
1881	81	489	283	499	82	100
1891	80	461	232	508	83	100
1901	78	391	216	520	83	100
1911	85	344	196	500	84	100
1921	95	318	193	518[b]	81[b]	100

Sources: As for table 1.

[a] Including Salford.

[b] Glasgow boundaries extended 1921.

[c] The index of over-representation shows the Irish-born percentage of each district's population divided by the Irish-born percentage of the entire population of Britain.

3 IRISH SEASONAL MIGRATION, 1880-1915

	1880	1881-5	1886-90	1891-5	1896-1900	1901-5	1906-10	1911-15	1880-1915
thousands per annum									
from									
Mayo	10.2	7.9	7.4	8.5	9.5	9.3	7.3	4.9	7.9
Donegal	2.4	1.5	1.1	1.5	2.5	2.3	1.8	1.7	1.8
5 counties[a]	5.8	4.8	3.3	4.1	5.1	4.7	3.1	1.5	3.8
other	4.5	1.8	0.7	0.4	0.5	1.3	0.6	0.3	0.9
to									
England	17.0	12.7	10.5	12.0	13.7	12.8	9.5	5.7	11.2
Scotland	3.8	2.4	1.5	2.1	3.6	3.7	2.4	2.1	2.6
other Ireland	2.1	1.1	0.6	0.4	0.4	1.1	0.8	0.4	0.7
total *estimate* (A)	22.9	16.1	12.5	14.5	17.7	17.7	12.7	8.3	14.5
estimate (B)	*22.9*	*16.1*	*12.5*	*14.5*	*17.7*	*14.5*	*10.3*	*6.8*	*13.5*
estimate (C)	*42.3*	*36.6*	*31.8*	*33.8*	*36.8*	*35.7*	*30.6*	*n.a.[b]*	*34.4[b]*
percentage of total estimate (A)									
from									
Mayo	44.5	49.2	59.4	58.8	53.9	52.7	57.3	58.6	54.7
Donegal	10.6	9.4	8.8	10.1	14.2	13.3	14.0	20.9	12.4
5 counties[a]	25.3	29.9	26.6	28.1	28.9	26.6	24.0	17.5	26.6
other	19.5	11.4	5.3	3.0	3.0	7.4	4.7	3.1	6.7
to									
England	74.2	78.6	83.4	83.1	77.8	72.7	74.6	69.0	77.2
Scotland	16.5	14.8	11.9	14.3	20.1	21.1	18.9	25.8	17.8
other Ireland	9.4	6.6	4.7	2.6	2.1	6.2	6.5	5.2	5.0

Sources: *Reports and tables relating to Irish migratory agricultural labourers* for 1880 to 1915 (variant titles): in H.C. papers. From 1901 onwards the returns included a few female and non-agricultural workers, and some women were included also in returns for 1880–84. Three sets of annual average *total* estimates of seasonal migration are given:

(A) labourers enumerated by the police each June, including those intending to leave later in the year.
(B) as above, excluding females and excluding the estimated number of male migratory labourers not engaged in agriculture (based upon the proportion so recorded for 1901).
(C) from returns by railway companies of 'harvesters' tickets' to Britain via Dublin, together with the number of 'temporary emigrants' enumerated up to the end of Aug. at all ports except Dublin.

  a The 'five counties' of major migration (apart from Mayo and Donegal) were Galway, Roscommon, Sligo, Leitrim, and Armagh.
  b Estimate (C) is obtainable only up to 1911, after which harvesters' tickets were discontinued. It overstates the true number of migratory workers since those making multiple journeys were double-counted, and since numerous 'jobbers', drovers, and temporary visitors left Irish ports and used the concessionary fares.

4 DEMOGRAPHY OF MAYO AND DONEGAL,
c. 1881–91

| | period | variable seasonal migration | | | |
| | | Mayo | | Donegal | |
		high	low	high	low
cohort depletion[a]					
male	1881–91	44.7	38.5	35.9	34.3
female	1881–91	41.4	40.0	34.6	31.8
natural increase[b]	1881–91	11.0	9.4	9.3	5.6
celibacy[c]					
male	1901	11.3	13.7	20.5	29.7
female	1901	9.1	12.1	20.5	28.7
SMAM[d]					
male cohort	1861–1911	31.0	31.2	31.0	32.1
female cohort	1861–1911	26.8	26.0	26.1	28.8

Sources: *Census Ire., 1881–1911*; *Agricultural statistics, Ireland; report and tables relating to migratory agricultural labourers* [C 5221], H.C. 1887, lxxxix. Demographic variables were calculated for two sections of the counties of Mayo and Donegal, divided according to the rate of seasonal migration in 1886 as a percentage of the population in 1881, in each poor law union (or portion) lying within those counties. In Mayo, the four unions with seasonal migration exceeding 2 per cent were categorised as having 'high' seasonal migration, whereas in Donegal the borderline was 1 per cent. The four unions with 'high' seasonal migration in Mayo were Swineford (5.5 per cent), a portion of Castlereagh (4.8 per cent), Claremorris (4.0 per cent), and Castlebar (3.3 per cent). In Donegal, the three unions with 'high' seasonal migration were Dunfanaghy (1.8 per cent), Glenties (1.6 per cent), and Millford (1.1 per cent). The residual population of each county was categorised as having 'low' seasonal migration.

[a] Percentage depletion over decade of the cohort initially aged 5–24.
[b] Excess of registered births over registered deaths during decade, as a percentage of mean population.
[c] Number never married as percentage of cohort aged 45–54.
[d] SMAM = singulate mean age at marriage, in years, for cohort born in about 1861 and remaining in union, derived from proportions never married at successive age-groups between 1881 and 1911.

5 IRISH-BORN WORKERS AS PERCENTAGES OF CERTAIN OCCUPATIONS, SCOTLAND (1911)

occupation	(1) percentage	(2) index	(3) weighted index
males			
building	32.0	531	487
drainage	18.4	305	363
docks	21.8	361	329
chemicals	27.9	463	325
general labour	17.6	292	318
gasworks	21.9	363	286
navvying	15.5	257	286
iron and steel	24.4	404	193
railway labour	10.3	171	180
farm labour	2.8	46	175
shoemaking	8.5	141	159
engine driving	9.8	163	147
hawking	9.3	154	139
iron founding	10.4	173	133
shipbuilding	14.6	242	129
mining	7.4	123	104
insurance	6.1	102	94
publicans	6.5	108	90
carters, carmen	4.6	76	73
waiters	4.5	74	63
tailors	3.2	53	58
police, etc.	4.2	69	57
grocers	2.7	45	46
clerks	1.4	23	18
total	6.0	100	100
females			
hawking	8.9	340	310
farm labour	2.8	108	249
charwomen	5.5	213	202
waitresses	5.5	210	180
hemp and jute	3.4	129	131
teaching	3.2	121	124
domestic service	2.4	92	116
nursing	3.5	135	111
dressmaking	2.2	84	77
cotton	3.6	138	70
clerks	1.0	38	30
total	2.6	100	100

Source: *Report on the twelfth decennial census of Scotland*, ii [Cd 6896], H.C. 1913, lxxx, 45–740; iii [Cd 7613], H.C. 1914, xliv, 393–736.

Occupational descriptions are imprecise, referring sometimes to sector and sometimes to function. For each occupation three figures are given, showing (1) Irish natives as a percentage of all workers of the same sex thus occupied in Scotland; (2) an index of over-representation dividing (1) by the Irish-born percentage of the entire Scottish male (or female) work-force; (3) a weighted index derived from the index values obtained for each of the ten districts with substantial Irish-born work-forces, weighted according to the proportions of all Irish male (or female) workers counted in each of those ten districts (the cities of Glasgow, Edinburgh, and Dundee; the counties of Edinburgh and Lanark excluding the cities of Edinburgh and Glasgow respectively; and the counties of Ayr, Dumbarton, Fife, Renfrew, and Stirling). These districts accounted for 92.3 per cent of the Irish male work-force in Scotland and 91.9 per cent of the Irish female work-force. The selected occupations accounted for 63.8 per cent of the Irish male work-force, and 54.0 per cent of the Irish female work-force.

6 IRISH-BORN OFFENDERS IN BRITAIN, 1861–1911

	as % of all offenders						index of over-representation					
	1861	1871	1881	1891	1901	1911	1861	1871	1881	1891	1901	1911
arrests												
Manchester	30	22	17	13			1.9	2.3	2.3	2.8		
Liverpool	37	34	24	16			2.0	2.2	1.9	2.1		
Preston	26	28	27	26			3.1	5.2	6.1	8.4		
Bradford	19	24	15	5			3.3	4.2	3.5	2.0		
committals to prisons												
Middlesex	16	12	8	5	5	4	4.2	4.2	3.6	3.1	3.9	3.1
Lancashire	31	28	24	15	12	10	3.5	4.0	3.9	3.7	3.7	4.2
England and Wales	15	14	12	8	7	5	4.9	5.7	5.7	5.3	5.6	5.2
Scotland					42	36					9.1	9.7

Sources: Lowe, 'Irish in Lancashire', pp 222 *et seq.*, figures read off graphs (for Manchester, Liverpool, Preston); C. Richardson, 'The Irish in Victorian Bradford' in *The Bradford Antiquary*, xlv (1971), p. 311 (for Bradford); *Judicial statistics. England and Wales, 1861–1911* (H.C.P.) (for Middlesex, Lancashire, England & Wales); *Report on the judicial statistics of Scotland, 1901, 1911* (H.C.P.) (for Scotland).

Arrests refer to all natives of Ireland placed in custody on apprehension by the police. Committals refer to Irish natives committed during year stated to local prisons only, excluding convict, military, and debtor prisoners (in England and Wales); and (in Scotland) to those committed to all prisons and police cells, excluding 'civil' prisoners. Statistics for Bradford refer to 1860, 1870, 1880, and 1890, while the earliest figure for Liverpool refers to 1863. The index of over-representation gives the Irish percentage of offenders divided by the Irish proportion of the local population at the nearest census.

7 MALE PRISONERS ADMITTED TO BARLINNIE PRISON, GLASGOW, 1882–3

offence	number Irish		number non-Irish			percentage Irish		percentage non-Irish		
	R.C.	other	R.C.	other	total	R.C.	other	R.C.	other	total
all occupations breach of										
peace	12	2	19	24	57	19	9	15	10	12
assault	33	11	40	81	165	52	48	31	33	36
theft	19	10	71	142	242	30	43	55	57	52
total	64	23	130	247	464					
general labourers breach of										
peace	7	—	11	10	28	26	—	21	18	20
assault	11	2	20	9	42	41	50	38	16	30
theft	9	2	22	36	69	33	50	42	65	50
total	27	4	53	55	139					
other occupations breach of										
peace	5	2	8	14	29	14	11	10	7	9
assault	22	9	20	72	123	59	47	26	38	38
theft	10	8	49	106	173	27	42	64	55	53
total	37	19	77	192	325					

Source: Glasgow (Barlinnie) prison, *Register of criminal prisoners, 1882–5*, Scottish Record Office, Edinburgh, HH.21.70/1.

The table classifies convicted criminal prisoners by birthplace (Irish or other), religion (Roman Catholic or other), occupation (general labourer or other), and broad category of offence. Breaches of the peace include breaches of crimes act, and riotous and disorderly behaviour; assaults include culpable homicide, attacks upon women, and assaults with intent to rob; thefts include resets of theft, housebreaking, robbery, and unlawful possession, excluding cases coupled with assault or breach of the peace. Prisoners analysed are those admitted between 15 Aug. 1882 and 13 Mar. 1883, excluding seventy-two convicted of offences not falling within the three stated categories.

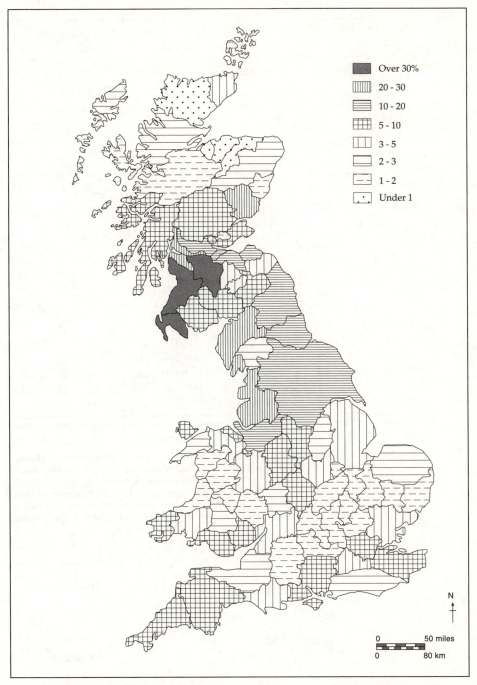

Map 9 BRITISH COUNTIES, 1871: IRISH-BORN AS PROPORTION OF
POPULATION BORN OUTSIDE COUNTY OF RESIDENCE,
by David Fitzpatrick

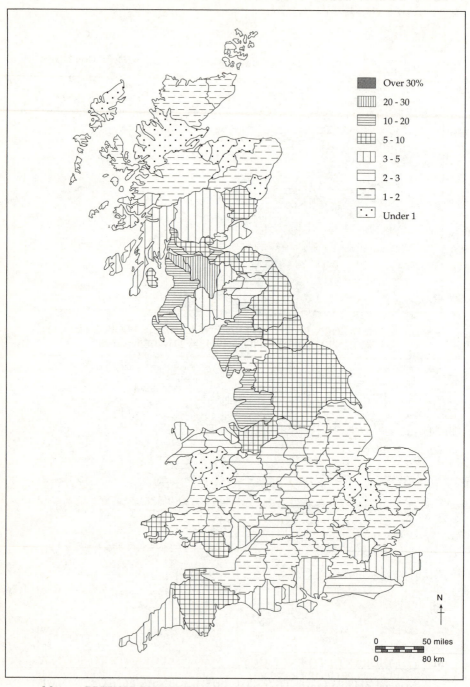

Map 10 BRITISH COUNTIES, 1901: IRISH-BORN AS PROPORTION OF
POPULATION BORN OUTSIDE COUNTY OF RESIDENCE,
by David Fitzpatrick

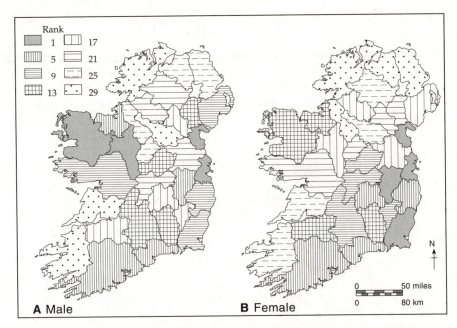

Map 11 IRISH-BORN RESIDENTS IN ENGLAND AS PROPORTION OF
COUNTY POPULATION, 1911, by David Fitzpatrick

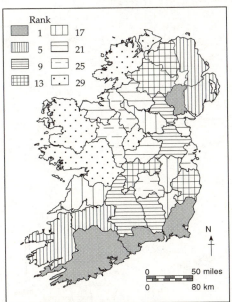

Map 12 EMIGRANTS TO ENGLAND,
1876–1914, AS PROPORTION OF
COUNTY POPULATION, 1911,
by David Fitzpatrick

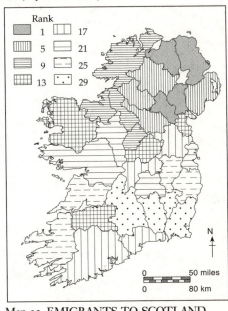

Map 13 EMIGRANTS TO SCOTLAND,
1876–1914, AS PROPORTION OF
COUNTY POPULATION, 1911,
by David Fitzpatrick

NOTE ON MAPS 11–13

In these maps the counties of Ireland are shaded according to rank order, in eight groups, each including four counties ranked 1–4, 5–8, 9–12, 13–16, 17–20, 21–4, 25–8, 29–32. The following table shows for each map the highest value in each group and also the lowest value among the thirty-two counties. All figures are percentages.

map	rank								
	1	5	9	13	17	21	25	29	32
11a	17.73	11.42	9.44	7.78	7.22	6.34	5.65	4.91	2.36
11b	17.53	11.49	10.67	9.38	7.83	6.26	5.35	4.37	2.19
12	11.29	3.73	2.89	2.39	1.66	1.40	1.24	0.94	0.41
13	7.87	4.38	2.25	0.84	0.46	0.36	0.26	0.16	0.13

CHAPTER XXIII

The Irish in Australia and New Zealand, 1870–1990

PATRICK O'FARRELL

By the 1870s, the number of Irish-born living in Australia had begun to decline: the influx of Irish immigrants into Queensland in the 1880s and 1890s was not sufficient to offset diminishing numbers elsewhere.[1] As MacDonagh has indicated, 'it follows that generalisations about an ethnic group based solely upon birthplace returns become progressively more circumscribed and tenuous, as time proceeds'.[2] That is, as home rule becomes the dominant national cause in Ireland, the Irish element in Australia becomes increasingly composed of persons of Australian birth who identify, to a greater or less degree, with the country of their extraction. Determining the size and Irishness of this element is a complex task, particularly as the various colonies present differing experiences.

The usual means of tracing the Irish group is to take advantage of the strong correlation between Irishness and catholicism. In 1911, Queensland was, marginally, the most catholic of the colonies (23 per cent), South Australia the least (13 per cent); Victoria (21 per cent) was less catholic than New South Wales (23 per cent).[3] Yet Victoria was the most Irish of the colonies; nowhere was the impress of the Irish element 'more deep and clear, nowhere was its part in the cultural interchanges more vigorous'.[4] Whereas in Victoria the Irish element was assertive

---

[1] The Irish-born in Queensland increased rapidly from 28,295 in 1881 to 40,157 in 1886 and 43,036 in 1891, but by 1901 dropped to 37,636 (M. E. R. MacGinley, 'A study of Irish migration to and settlement in Queensland, 1885–1912' (M.A. thesis, University of Queensland, 1972), pp 47–53). In Victoria, the number of Irish-born fell from 100,468 in 1871 to 85,307 in 1891 (Oliver MacDonagh, 'The Irish in Victoria, 1851–91: a demographic essay' in *Hist. Studies*, viii (1971), pp 90–92). A similar decline occurred in New South Wales.

[2] MacDonagh, op. cit., p. 69.

[3] The case of the Irish in South Australia, and the questions it raises in regard to received generalisations about the Australian Irish, have been raised speculatively by Eric Richards in an article available in two forms: 'Irish life and progress in colonial South Australia' in *I.H.S.*, xxvii, no. 107 (May 1991), pp 216–36; and a longer version, 'The importance of being Irish in colonial South Australia' in John O'Brien and Pauric Travers (ed.), *The Irish emigrant experience in Australia* (Dublin, 1991), pp 62–102. This book also includes MacGinley, 'The Irish in Queensland: an overview' (pp 102–9). The general survey by Chris McConville, *Croppies, Celts and catholics: the Irish in Australia* (Melbourne, 1987), has a strongly Victorian orientation and content.

[4] MacDonagh, op. cit., p. 70.

and socially abrasive, in Queensland it was hardly less pervasive, but much milder, more accepting of its environment. These differences between colonies reflect a complex interaction between important local factors: the number and proportion of Irish catholics in the community, the stage of development when they arrived in the colony or became important in it (later in New South Wales, at the beginning in Victoria), their character and class composition, the temperaments and policies of their clerical leaders, and the effect of particular local circumstances and events. Not only were the Irish who came to Australia and New Zealand throughout the nineteenth century not homogeneous, but the colonial circumstances in which they found themselves were diverse, as were their responses. Nevertheless, their hibernicity and predominant catholicism were sufficiently intense and distinctive to make generalisation possible, though this raises the elusive question of the relative importance of national origin and religion in determining the cohesion and behaviour of the Irish element.

J. F. Hogan's *The Irish in Australia*, published in 1888, uses the terms 'Irish' and 'Irish-Australian' interchangeably.[*] Both can indicate either Irish or Australian birth. To Hogan, his subject-matter is persons of dual allegiance, who identify themselves with both Ireland and Australia, making some kind of personal balance between the demands of the two identities and blending them when possible. However, despite Hogan's assumptions and the title of his book, those with a predominantly Irish identity were very few. The very much larger group whose origins were Irish, and whose culture and loyalties were partly or sometimes Irish, were decisively Australian.

Explanation is best made through contrast with the Irish in the U.S.A. In Australia the Irish, like the rest of the population, tended—despite some areas of concentration—to be widely dispersed geographically, and relatively thinly spread on a vast continent. The mobility of a pioneering society, and adequate economic opportunity, minimised personal and group frustrations and allowed upward economic and social movement to a degree not possible in the more settled and resistant American communities, especially those of New York and other urban magnets that attracted the Irish. An equivalent to the Irish-American ghetto proletariat did not develop in Australia, nor did a political machine of the Irish-American kind.[1] In the 1880s nearly half of Victoria's Irish lived outside metropolitan Melbourne, with similar wide distributions in other colonies.[2] The

---

[*]EDITOR'S NOTE: The hyphenated form 'Irish-Australian' appears in this chapter, conforming with usage elsewhere in the *New history*. Professor O'Farrell recommends 'Irish Australian' as less historically misleading, for the reasons explained in his *Vanished kingdoms: the Irish in Australia and New Zealand; a personal excursion* (Sydney, 1990), p. xxii.

[1] This is not to deny that some inner-city slum areas did develop a particularly Irish character. For the case of Collingwood in Melbourne, see Niall Brennan, *John Wren, gambler: his life and times* (Melbourne, 1971); and for Richmond in Melbourne, see Janet McCalman, *Struggletown: public and private life in Richmond, 1900–1965* (Melbourne, 1984). For Surry Hills in Sydney, see Ruth Park's novel *The harp in the south* (Sydney, 1948; reprint, Victoria, 1975).

[2] G. M. Tobin, 'The sea-divided Gael: a study of the Irish home rule movement in Victoria and New South Wales, 1880–1916' (M.A. thesis, Australian National University, 1969), p. 23; for

self-image of the Irish-Australians was that of independent and reasonably prosperous small farming. An Irish immigrant could reach the status of farmer by way of wage labouring or the gold diggings, or through other employment, and in this he did not differ radically from his English or Scots counterparts. Landholding was encouraged by the catholic church. The Australian bishops' 1885 pastoral enjoined catholics to 'strive to secure for themselves a just share of the public lands, otherwise their children must necessarily be shearers or farm labourers, wandering from shed to shed, and from harvest to harvest'.[1] Such exhortations pointed, of course, to the considerable section of Irish catholics who were spendthrift migratory labourers, and ignored those whose ambitions were not related to landholding: many Irish succeeded in commerce, particularly the liquor trade, and in other pursuits that required little capital, the gambling spirit, and some luck: contracting, property speculation, middle-manning of all kinds. Whatever the avenue, the openness of the colonial economy and society quickly won the allegiance of the Irish. The Irish farming ideal was to a very significant extent realised, even, as in some areas of Victoria, to the extent of reproducing the potato cultivation and village society of Munster.[2] But Irish potatoes in Victoria commanded the lucrative Melbourne city market. If few of these Irish farmers became wealthy—generally they lacked capital to develop their land—most of them made a reasonable and contented living.

The half of the Irish immigrants that remained in the cities was significantly over-represented in unskilled occupations and at the bottom of the socio-economic scale. They tended to seek employment with government agencies—the railways were particularly popular—as offering greater security and more protection from prejudice than private employers. A salient characteristic of Irish female immigrants was their employment, before marriage, in domestic service.[3] The overwhelming dominance of Irish girls in domestic service had a detrimental effect on the image of the Irish in the community generally: servant girls by definition were lazy, insolent, slatternly, and unsatisfactory in

Queensland, see M. E. R. MacGinley, 'A study of Irish migration to and settlement in Queensland, 1860–1885' (M.A. qualifying thesis, University of Queensland, 1970), pp 109–11. The suburban detail, down to street distribution, is a feature of the work of Chris McConville, 'Emigrant Irish and suburban catholic: faith and nation in Melbourne and Sydney, 1851–1933' (Ph.D. thesis, University of Melbourne, 1984). For a Victorian application, see McConville's 'The Victorian Irish emigrants and families, 1851–1891' in Pat Grimshaw and others, *Families in colonial Australia* (Sydney, 1985), pp 1–8.

[1] Quoted in Patrick and Deirdre O'Farrell, *Documents in Australian catholic history, 1788–1968* (2 vols, London, 1969), ii, 19. The Queensland bishop Robert Dunne, who was responsible for the wording of this pastoral, made these concerns a virtual obsession from the 1860s to the 1880s. Neil J. Byrne has developed a thesis study of Dunne (M.A. qualifying thesis, University of Queensland, 1981) into a full-scale biography: *Robert Dunne, archbishop of Brisbane* (Brisbane, 1991).

[2] Tobin, op. cit., pp 23–30.

[3] In 1857 more than a third of catholic marriages in New South Wales were celebrated in St Mary's cathedral. Of 316 brides in that year, 259 were Irish-born and 237 of these (over 90 per cent) had been in domestic service (marriage registers, St Mary's cathedral archives, Sydney).

the estimation of their employers, and these defects became associated with Irishness.[1]

The fact that the Irish element tended to be grouped heavily at the bottom of the socio-economic scale, especially in the cities, meant that it related itself very naturally to the trade union movement as it emerged in the 1870s and 1880s, and to labour political parties as they were formed in the 1890s. So the Irish came to exercise a very powerful influence on Australian politics and society through the labour movement. However, this influence was never distinctively Irish or catholic. The Irish element within the labour movement was of Irish descent rather than birth, and it was concerned with its Australian socio-economic position, not with Irish issues. Moreover, the labour movement, with secularist roots and non-sectarian intentions, was strongly resistant to catholic pressures and demands. The labour movement became the avenue for the economic aspirations, and for the political and organising abilities, of those of Irish descent, but these were firmly anchored to Australian circumstances.[2]

The basic reason for the failure of any distinctive, militant Irish leadership to emerge in nineteenth-century Australia seems very simple. The Irish as a whole did not want it. They could identify happily enough with an Australia that was sufficiently open to allow Irish migrants to assimilate into it with success from

[1] Beverley Kingston, *My wife, my daughter, and poor Mary Anne: women and work in Australia* (Melbourne, 1975), pp 16–23. A very different picture of Irish girls as domestic servants is given by J. F. Hogan, *The Irish in Australia* (Melbourne, 1888), pp 26–7. Irish women immigrants have been a neglected research topic, although a section with that title (for the nineteenth century) appears in the substantial entry on the Irish in James Jupp (ed.), *The Australian people: an encyclopedia of the nation, its people, and their origins* (Sydney, 1988), pp 553–95; and there are a few specific articles, e.g. Sharon Morgan, 'Irishwomen in Port Phillip and Victoria, 1840–60' in Oliver MacDonagh and W. F. Mandle (ed.), *Irish-Australian studies: papers delivered at the fifth Irish-Australian conference* (Canberra, 1989), pp 231–49; Malcolm Campbell's paper 'Irish women in nineteenth-century Australia: a more hidden Ireland', presented to the sixth Irish-Australian conference at Melbourne 1990 (awaiting publication), is more a study of the neglect than a major attempt to remedy it. There is considerable relevant material on the twentieth-century Irish heritage in Sally Kennedy, *Faith and feminism: catholic women's struggles for self-expression* (Sydney, 1985), including a chapter 'Challenging the Irish-catholic model'. However, the most substantial historical literature on Irish women in Australia is to be found in the histories of female religious congregations. Most such congregations have published histories. Both typical and professionally executed are M. E. R. MacGinley, *Roads to Sion: Presentation Sisters in Australia, 1866–1980* (Clayford, Queensland, 1983), and M. S. McGrath, *These women? Women religious in the history of Australia: Sisters of Mercy, Parramatta 1888–1988* (Sydney, 1989). For a review of catholic women, concentrating on images and opinions, see Patrick and Deirdre O'Farrell, 'The status of women: some opinions in Australian catholic history *c.*1860–*c.*1960' in *Bulletin of Christian Affairs*, special, no. 2 (Nov. 1975), pp 3–42.

[2] The linkage between Irish catholics and the Australian labour movement is frequently discussed in general Australian histories. The work most central to the theme is Celia Hamilton, 'Irish catholics of New South Wales and the labour party, 1890–1910' in *Historical Studies*, viii, no. 31 (Nov. 1958), pp 254–67, and 'Catholic interests and the labour party: organised catholic action in Victoria and New South Wales, 1910–1916', ibid., ix, no. 33 (Nov. 1959), pp 62–73. The linkage is also discussed in Patrick O'Farrell's three books *The catholic church and community: an Australian history* (revised ed., Sydney, 1992), *The Irish in Australia* (Sydney, 1987), and *Vanished kingdoms*. See also Frank Farrell, 'J. H. Scullin, the Irish question, and the Australian labour party' in Colm Kiernan (ed.), *Australia and Ireland 1788–1988: bicentenary essays* (Dublin, 1986), pp 156–69.

about 1810. To offset what resistance to them existed in Australian society, and what dissatisfactions they experienced, were considerations of necessity. Distance was too great for much hope of return or for any feeling of real involvement in Ireland's affairs. The U.S.A., in contrast, was not only much closer to Ireland, but a republic that owed its existence to successful rebellion against Britain. Its atmosphere was very different from Australia and New Zealand: contented parts of the British empire, reliant on the empire for defence, status, self-image, and cultural orientation. In this loyalist colonial world Irishmen lived as a mostly dispersed minority, and to a very large extent they accepted its dominant ethos and attitudes.[1] A more affluent body of Irish immigrants came to Australia.[2] Certainly the fact that the famine migration was overwhelmingly to North America seems to have spared Australia that particularly bitter injection of anti-British venom.

The pressures existing in overwhelmingly British colonies, remote from Ireland, offering real opportunities for a good life, induced substantial conformity among the Irish-Australians. This was encouraged by most catholic clerics, but especially by Cardinal Patrick Francis Moran, who was translated from Ossory to Sydney in 1884, and dominated the catholic church in Australia until his death in 1911.[3] The cardinal's policy was one of encouraging a close Irish-Australian identification with Australian life and with imperial enterprises. The reverse policy was demonstrated by the episcopate of Bishop Patrick Moran, another Irish cleric, in Otago, New Zealand, from 1871 to 1895: he succeeded in leading his Irish catholic flock into a position of antagonism and conflict with the community on Irish and catholic issues, in contrast with the better relations that prevailed in other New Zealand dioceses.[4] In Australia, particularly between 1916 and 1923, Archibishop Daniel Mannix of Melbourne had a similar polarising function. Mannix had come to Melbourne in 1911 from the presidency of St Patrick's College, Maynooth, and remained a controversial figure until his death in 1963.[5]

---

[1] It is notable that the Australian republican movement of the 1890s had little Irish-Australian support. The same applies to the reappearance of this movement in 1991.

[2] The most detailed investigative work on this point has been done by David Fitzpatrick; see his *Irish emigration, 1801–1921* (Dublin, 1984); 'Irish emigration in the later nineteenth century' in *I.H.S.*, xxii, no. 86 (Sept. 1980), pp 126–43; ' "Over the foaming billows": the organisation of Irish emigration to Australia' in Eric Richards (ed.), *Poor Australian immigrants in the nineteenth century* (Canberra, 1991), pp 133–52; and above, v, 562–615. See also, for a more literary and impressionistic but confirmatory view, MacDonagh, op. cit., p. 76; Brennan, op. cit., p. ix; and O'Farrell, *Ir. in Australia*, pp 54–114. For a view of immigrant mentality see Patrick O'Farrell, 'Landscapes of the Irish immigrant mind' in John Hardy (ed.), *Stories of Australian migration* (Sydney, 1988), pp 33–46.

[3] A biography of Cardinal Moran is being written by A. E. Cahill of Sydney University; his entry on Moran in the *Australian Dictionary of Biography* is the best brief overview of the cardinal's career. The chapter in O'Farrell, *Catholic church*, is more critical.

[4] Richard P. Davis, *Irish issues in New Zealand politics, 1868–1922* (Dunedin, 1974); Hugh M. Laracy, 'The life and context of Bishop Patrick Moran' (M.A. thesis, Victoria University of Wellington, 1964); Hugh M. Laracy, 'Bishop Moran: Irish politics and catholicism in New Zealand' in *Jn. Relig. Hist.*, vi, no. 1 (June 1970), pp 62–76.

[5] The controversy remains. The most substantial recent biographies are Michael Gilchrist, *Daniel Mannix, priest and patriot* (Blackburn, Victoria, 1982), and B. A. Santamaria, *Daniel Mannix: a*

However numerous and large the exceptions, the general rule was that the Irish in Australia and New Zealand thought their adopted society essentially a good one. Their most serious criticisms, of intolerance or inequality or injustice, were in the context of a recognition of the substantial freedom and opportunities the colonies provided. Certainly there were tensions and conflicts between the Irish and the rest of the community, but the generalisation that the Irish as a group were 'agin the government' is false. On the contrary, the Irish in Australia and New Zealand accepted, indeed took pride in, belonging to Australia and the empire. In accepting the freedom of the city of Dublin in 1888, Cardinal Moran declared:

And while the Australians are thus one in heart and hand with their brothers in the dear mother country, we are not the less loyal to the empire of which we are proud to form part. In our sympathy with your struggles in the cause of liberty, we are impelled not by hatred of England, but by love of Ireland. The freedom which we enjoy is the mainstay of the empire's strength; and we desire that Ireland should, to the fullest extent enjoy the same freedom, without which the empire cannot stand.[1]

Obviously, such attitudes were in warm accord with the home rule movement in Ireland, producing a comfortable harmony, which existed from the 1880s until the 1916 rebellion destroyed it.

Moran, and leading Irish-Australians generally, saw the empire as the protective context for the freedom of diverse elements. The dominant groups in Australian society took a much narrower, monolithic view of empire, equating it with all that was most conservatively English. The Irish in Australia generally were happy to be included in colonial societies constructed on the British model, but they wanted inclusion as themselves, not as imitation Anglo-Saxons. A colonial society determined to be English did not readily admit members on such conditions, and the insistence that the Irish abandon any element of divergent identity led to conflict. This conflict between colonial society and its Irish elements was intensified by stress on, and exaggeration of, Irish divergencies and deficiencies. Colonial society took its image of the Irish not from those who were 'respectable' and constantly preferred imperial and Australian loyalties, but from those Irish who were criminal, drunken, insane, or violent; to this it added animosity derived from sectarian divisions, and resentment of the separateness of catholics, as expressed in the catholic education system and prohibition of mixed marriages. The response of the leaders of Irish-Australia was to construct a counter-image.

biography (Melbourne, 1984). In 1985 Professor James Griffin disputed Mannix's capacities and intellectual stature in an address published as 'Daniel Mannix and the cult of personality' in Oliver MacDonagh and W. F. Mandle (ed.), *Ireland and Irish-Australia: studies in cultural and political history* (London, 1986), pp 95–118; and again in Griffin's entry on Mannix in the *Australian Dictionary of Biography*. This provoked vigorous defence, commentary, and exchanges in various journals, mainly *Quadrant*, continuing into 1991. For a critique of the Mannix literature see R. M. Sweetman, 'Daniel Mannix and his biographers' in *Australian Studies*, no. 1 (June 1988), pp 61–71.

[1] Quoted in O'Farrell, *Documents*, ii, 100–01.

Cardinal Moran told the second Australasian catholic congress of 1904 that 'the sons and daughters of Ireland are, beyond all question, the most enlightened, the most progressive, and the most virtuous people of Christendom at the present day'.[1] This flattering stereotype was also applied to descendants. Monsignor M. J. O'Reilly explained to the 1911 New South Wales catholic educational conference: 'It was true that their children were not Irish—they were Australians—but everything that was best and noblest in Australia was Irish.'[2] Celebration of the enlightenment, progressiveness, and virtue of the Irish in Australia became the standard reply to allegations of their ignorance, degradation, and disloyalty.

Were the Irish of the 1890s 'a breed apart, firebranded like travelling stock in a strange country'?[3] As a rule, they were not: the identification of most Irish with their Australian environment is made evident in many ways, not least in their organisations. Before the 1880s the few Irish organisations that were set up were nearly all ephemeral, often non-denominational, mainly social in aims, or associated with some short-term Irish charitable purpose—such as famine relief—or with local religious projects such as church-building. Societies with an Irish political orientation, such as the Repeal Association set up in Sydney in 1842, were rare, tiny, and very short lived. The largest flourishing Irish society in Australia was the Hibernian Australasian Catholic Benefit Society, originating in Victoria in 1871 and spreading rapidly throughout Australia and New Zealand in the 1880s. Despite its relatively large membership (24,710 in Australia and New Zealand in 1905),[4] the H.A.C.B.S. remained an insurance organisation, whose Irish character was largely that of sentiment. It did have an Irish nationalist function in that it acted on an organisational structure through which such persons as home rule emissaries might be welcomed, but it seldom took any initiative in nationalist matters and what it did take was in the nature of mild sympathetic resolutions and counsels of moderation. The absence of any political motivation was also evident in the Melbourne Celtic Club, the next oldest surviving Irish organisation: it was formed in 1887 for purely social purposes, as was the Queensland Irish Association, founded in 1898.[5] The larger Australian

---

[1] P. F. Moran, *The priests and people of Ireland in the nineteenth century* (Melbourne, 1904), p. 3. The classic Australasian refutation of charges that the Irish were leaders in violence and crime was that of Rev. H. W. Cleary, editor of the New Zealand catholic *Tablet*, in *An impeached nation, being a study of Irish outrages* (Dunedin, N.Z., 1909). This confined itself to Irish reference; a range of recent research confirms that the colonial Irish were substantially in excess of their population proportion in prisons and mental institutions; see also above, pp 667–70.

[2] Quoted in O'Farrell, *Documents*, ii, 121.

[3] Herbert M. Moran, *Viewless winds* (London, 1939), p. 10.

[4] *Hibernian Australasian Catholic Benefit Society: report of proceedings in connection with the third biennial meeting . . . Adelaide . . . 26th and 27th April 1905* (Sydney, 1905), p. 10. For a history see Patrick H. O'Connor, *The Hibernian Society of New South Wales, 1880–1980: a centenary history* (Sydney, 1980), and Mary Smith, 'The Hibernian Australasian Catholic Benefit Society of New South Wales: a study of social organisation within the Irish working class during 1870–1900' (B.A. thesis, University of New South Wales, 1980).

[5] There is a recent history of the Celtic Club: D. J. O'Hearn, *Erin go bragh—Advance Australia fair: a hundred years of growing, 1887–1987* (Melbourne, 1990).

Irish societies were cautious and respectable; the smaller ones, before 1915, were seldom militant and never survived long.

One reason for this—and further evidence of the extent to which the Irish assimilated—was the general failure of Irish-Australians to retain their cultural traditions, other than by way of sentimental ornament. The distinctive folk culture and the Irish language seem to have vanished almost instantly on arrival in Australia.[1] Attempts from the 1890s to import the Gaelic revival into Australia met with very little response. What vestiges of genuine Irish culture were maintained depended on the enthusiasm of a very few, most notably the Australian-born Melbourne medical practitioner Dr Nicholas O'Donnell, who was Australia's foremost (indeed almost only) Gaelic scholar in the early 1900s,[2] and Morgan P. Jageurs, a Melbourne stonemason of German-Irish ancestry. Jageurs also illustrates another characteristic of the Irish-Australian. He was a foundation member of almost every Irish organisation founded in Melbourne from the 1880s—the Irish Pipers Club, the Irish Land League, the Irish National League, the Celtic Club, and the United Irish League. Several of these organisations were dependent on his personal energy. What Irish activity there was in Australia depended in very large degree on the enthusiasm and activity of a few people. None of these were radicals and very few had any social prominence. The result was that they had negligible influence, even among Irish-Australians. The multiplicity of Irish-Australian organisations disguises a remarkable degree of common membership, particularly among the officeholders. The mass of the Irish-Australians would not join such organisations.

The strongest continuing focus for Irish-Australian activity remained St Patrick's day. The centre of the celebrations in the 1880s was a procession through city streets, maintained in Melbourne until the 1970s, but discontinued in Sydney in the mid-1890s. The procession had a strong tendency to disperse into hotels, which is one reason why Cardinal Moran disapproved of it, and why in 1896 he took control of the celebrations. He substituted a major sports meeting intended as a mass demonstration of catholicity, and diverted the proceeds from the home rule cause to catholic charities. The associated banquet was transformed from what amounted to a home rule meeting into a formal catholic occasion of an elevated kind, attended by political and social leaders assembled with regard to

---

[1] This does not deny the existence of distinctive habits of character and behaviour, or of a residuum of sentiment and balladry, associated with the Irish in Australia. A collection of these popular evidences has been made by Bill Wannan, *The wearing of the green: the lore, literature, legend, and balladry of the Irish in Australia* (Melbourne, 1965). The matter of sociolinguistic interaction between the Irish and both aborigines and English in Australia has been opened up in a historical context by Jakelin Troy, ' "Der mary this is Fine cuntry is there is in the wourld": Irish-English and Irish in late eighteenth-century and nineteenth-century Australia' in O'Brien & Travers, *Ir. emigrant experience*, pp 148–80. Contemporary Irish interaction with aborigines is dealt with from personal experience by Clare Dunne, *People under the skin* (Sydney, 1988). The idea of a 'hidden Ireland' in Australia is explored in 'Kings deposed?' ch. 1 of O'Farrell, *Vanished kingdoms*.

[2] O'Donnell was a friend of Douglas Hyde, central figure of the Gaelic revival (above, pp 400–14); see Douglas Hyde, *Legends of saints and sinners* (London, N.D.), p. 40.

distinction, not religion or Irish connection.[1] But by 1914 Sydney's celebrations were teetering on the verge of collapse: only 4,685 of Sydney's 185,000 catholics attended the 'monster' sports meeting. As for the Melbourne Irish, as late as March 1916 the St Patrick's day procession halted outside the federal parliament house while 'God save the king' was played. The tone and content of the celebrations indicated a loyalty to Australia and the empire, and a sentimental recalling of Ireland's past glories, rather than any wish to claim active involvement in Ireland's more recent history or continuing problems.

The same may be said of the Irish-Australian attitude to the home rule movement. From 1880 to 1891 there was a widespread upsurge of interest in Irish affairs, but it was the threat of famine, not Irish politics, that first captured attention. Significantly it was the catholic church that provided both the initial stimulus and practical organisation that raised £95,000 for Irish relief in 1880—though the appeal attracted considerable support from the general community. Similar practical sympathy had been expressed from Australia in earlier periods of Irish distress. On this occasion interest was sustained among the ordinary Irish-Australians by the dramatic struggle of the Irish peasants for land, not only because so many Irish-Australians had come from that very peasant class and were now farmers in Australia, but because the land war was being fought most bitterly in those localities (mainly in Clare and Tipperary) from which they had themselves come.[2] The land war had, for them, a reality that the elevated and remote home rule movement previously lacked.

However, a deep interest did not necessarily lead to any immediate commitment. The course of events in Ireland was obscured and confused by passing through the pro-British Australian press, and by the month's delay in receiving news direct from Ireland. The land war and the activities of Parnell, moreover, had connotations of violence and anarchy that revealed divisions among Irish-Australians. When, late in 1881, the movement to collect money for a Parnell Defence Fund developed into a campaign to establish branches of the land league, the moving spirits were 'men and women of the labouring classes' not 'leading Irishmen'.[3] This division—which was to be again evident later—probably reflects more than class position: it was also a matter of different generations of migration, of the degree of assimilation in Australia, and the immediacy of direct experience of Irish conditions.

The 1883 tour of Australia and New Zealand by John and William Redmond, representing the Irish parliamentary party and national league, won over many of the colonial Irish, but it also deepened their divisions. Arriving in the midst of allegations that the Irish parliamentary party was implicated in the Phoenix Park

---

[1] For these developments see Malcolm C. Campbell, 'St Patrick's day in Sydney in the 1890s: an exploration of the influences upon, and dimensions of, the celebration' (B.A. thesis, University of New South Wales, 1984).

[2] Above, pp 612, 639–41, 645–7.

[3] O'Farrell, *Irish in Australia*, p. 222.

murders, John Redmond recollected: 'I received a chilling reception. All the respectable people who had promised support kept away. The priests would not help me. . . . The Irish working men stood by me, and in fact saved the situation.'[1] Moreover the Redmond visit aroused the active hostility of anti-Irish elements in the general community, and of Irish protestants who opposed home rule: public allegations of extremism and sedition abounded.[2] Many Irish-Australians, particularly those most prominent and successful, were unhappy about the tour, for it forced them to commit themselves. If they attended the Redmond meetings they risked odium in the general community; if they stayed away they courted charges of cowardice and national betrayal. Redmond urged that a convention be held to consolidate and unify all Irish organisations in Australia and New Zealand. It was held in Melbourne in November 1883 to the enthusiasm of those who attended, but in a public atmosphere typified by the remark of the *Sydney Morning Herald*: 'an Irish convention in Australia is a mischievous anomaly however considered. Irish-Australian it cannot be, because an Irish-Australian is a creature of whom we cannot possibly conceive. He is or he is not one of us . . .'[3] A few leaders of Irish-Australian organisations wished to assert their distinctive identity, and to express sharp criticism of English rule in Ireland, but most Irish-Australians wished to avoid both issues. However, they were prepared to be generous with their money. To subscribe to the nationalist cause salved Irish-Australian consciences, testified to group allegiance, and satisfied sentiment and pride, all without too deep an involvement.

The enthusiasm and the organisations generated by the Redmond visit rapidly disappeared. It was Gladstone who revived Ireland's cause in Australia; his commitment to home rule in 1886 made it generally respectable, so great was his colonial reputation. But, with Gladstone now on their side, Australian home rulers could not resist the temptation to rejoice and to gloat over the discomfiture of their former opponents. Pro-union Irish protestants felt at first betrayed, then determined to campaign against the colonial home rule assistance movement. In the realm of general colonial opinion, the press and politicians abandoned their hostility to home rule, but opposition did not disappear. Instead it narrowed and became concentrated among the Orange sympathisers in the colonies, who were determined, outspoken, and vigorously formidable in their enmity. Sectarian issues, always latent, were now stridently brought forward, and remained inextricably involved with Irish affairs in Australasia for the next forty years. Home rule became a catholic cause, and opposition to it an anti-catholic one. Indeed the issue tended to be sustained not so much for itself as for what it symbolised: to catholics, justice and community recognition; to anti-catholics,

[1] Denis Gwynn, *The life of John Redmond* (London, 1932), pp 52–3.
[2] For the Redmond visit to Victoria, and the home rule cause in the 1880s, see Geoffrey Serle, *The rush to be rich: a history of the colony of Victoria 1883–1889* (Melbourne, 1971), pp 237–44. See also D. L. Evans, 'Reaction to home rule and the visit of John and William Redmond in 1883, as reflected in some of the contemporary colonial press' (B.A. thesis, University of New South Wales, 1980).
[3] *Sydney Morning Herald*, 7 Nov. 1886.

catholic sedition and tyranny. In Australia, home rule's connotations became sectarian more than national or political, an identification that applied thereafter to every Irish cause.

The arrival in Australia in March 1889 of John Dillon, John Deasy, and Sir Thomas Esmonde proved once again that direct contact with Irish politicians was the only means whereby anything like widespread Irish-Australian support could be mustered for Irish causes. The object of the tour was to collect funds desperately needed to sustain the plan of campaign, and it was a tremendous success.

At no other point . . . did developments in the colonial extension of the home rule movement have as close a bearing on the tactical situation in Ireland itself. The £30,000 which Dillon took back with him from that tour was of critical importance in rescuing the plan of campaign from collapse . . .[1]

However, the colonial Irish were not conscious of filling any such decisive role, nor were they aware of the differing policies and personalities within the Irish nationalist movement, of which they had a simple impression of undisturbed unity. During Dillon's visit they were much more concerned with the reaction of colonial society. The fact that this was much more tolerant than it had been towards the Redmonds gave them much greater satisfaction than assisting the cause of Ireland.

This self-concerned orientation was glaringly revealed by the reactions of the colonial Irish to the fall of Parnell in 1890–91. The intense bitterness and sense of betrayal that welled up against Parnell among colonial home rulers was prompted by the damage he was felt to have done to them personally: that is, humiliated and degraded them publicly in the eyes of a critical colonial society to whose opinions they were so sensitive. It was an indignity they did not wish to court again, and the subsequent factional disputes in Irish politics disillusioned the colonial Irish to the point of disgust. Michael Davitt was welcomed in 1895 because he, of all Irish politicians, had retained most Australian respect, as untainted by factionalism.[2] But apathy, tinged with revulsion for any involvement in Irish politics, prevailed.

From the mid-1890s Irish nationalism came more and more under clerical control, particularly that of Cardinal Moran. Moran wished to prove 'that they who love Ireland most are at the same time the best citizens of Australia'.[3] He saw support for the general principle of home rule, and avoidance of too deep an involvement in the particularities of Irish politics, as forwarding that end, which was to harmonise Irish catholicity with its Australian setting. Moran's ideal had

---

[1] Tobin, 'Sea-divided Gael', pp 199–200; this is confirmed by Lyons, *Dillon*, p. 106.
[2] Davitt's account of his tour is given in his *Life and progress in Australasia* (London, 1898). The tour and Davitt's role in the politics and perceptions of the Australian Irish (he was a columnist on Irish affairs for the Melbourne Irish catholic *Advocate*) are the subjects of two as yet unpublished articles by Dr Noel McLachlan of the University of Melbourne.
[3] *Freeman's Journal* (Sydney), 14 Mar. 1896.

already taken some practical form in the distinctive subculture to be immortalised in Fr P. J. Hartigan's *Around the boree log*, a depiction in verse of Hartigan's childhood in the 1880s and 1890s in southern New South Wales. Hartigan's world was that of sturdy and pious Irish peasant catholicity thriving in the Australian bush:

> Where the settlers battle gamely, beaten down to rise again,
> And the brave bush wives the toil and silence share,
> Where the nation is a-building, in the hands of splendid men,
> There's a little Irish mother always there.[1]

Here was the aspiration and, in part, the reality of the mingling of Ireland and Australia in creative harmony.

However, there were those in Australia who denied that such harmony was possible, mainly because Irish causes were associated with catholicism.[2] Over twenty years of militant anti-catholicism opened with the formation in June 1901 of the Australian Protestant Defence Association. Its manifesto claimed that home rule meant Rome rule, and its leader was the dynamic demagogue Rev. Dill Macky, an Irish presbyterian minister who had been brought up in Derry, where he had been a member of the Apprentice Boys. The standard unionist arguments against home rule were soon made vigorously clear to an Australian public that was sensitive to all questions of imperial loyalty, if not catholic subversion.

In New Zealand developments similar to those in Australia, together with similar regional variations, had been occurring since the 1870s. There, however, due to the different character of the settlements, the issues, conflicts, and regional differences were somewhat more muted. The colonisation of New Zealand had been accomplished without Irish convicts, with a smaller proportion of Irish immigrants (reaching a peak of only 6.5 per cent (46,037) in 1896), and with a catholic clergy substantially French and English in composition. The outcome was a greater Irish catholic conformity to a New Zealand environment that was more English and Scots than the Australian environment, but also more tolerantly so.[3]

---

[1] 'John O'Brien' (P. J. Hartigan), *Around the boree log* (Sydney, 1921), p. 7. Hartigan's biography, which includes treatment both of his verse and of his substantial historical writings, has been written by Frank Mecham: '*John O'Brien' and the boree log* (Sydney, 1981).

[2] This was the dominant image and impression, but it ignored the significant (up to 20 per cent) element of Irish in Australia who were Anglo-Irish or Ulster protestant. For detailed documentation from Ulster protestant sources, see Patrick O'Farrell, *Letters from Irish Australia, 1825–1929* (Sydney, 1984), where the major emphasis is on correspondence from the 1880s and later. A study of the Anglo-Irish in Australia, by Dr Gordon Forth of Deakin University, is in progress. Dr Forth has already published a monograph study of one Anglo-Irish family, *The winters on the Wannon* (Warrnambool, 1991), and has compiled and edited *A biographical register and annotated bibliography of Anglo-Irish colonists in Australia* (Warrnambool, 1991). The history of the Orange Lodge movement in Australia has been largely neglected, but see Andrew Gill, ' "To the glorious, pious, and immortal memory of the great and good King William": the 12th July in Western Australia, 1887–1930' in Lenore Layman and Tom Stannage, *Celebrations in Western Australian history: Studies in Western Australian History*, x (Apr. 1989), pp 75–83; Tas Vertigan, *The Orange order in Victoria* (Melbourne, 1979).

[3] The subtle complexities of the New Zealand Irish situation cannot be pursued within this space. Davis, *Irish issues*, gives a useful account of major political issues, but appears to generalise from the

Cardinal Moran, whether through tactics or preference, had attempted to avert the danger that the home rule cause might become negatively identified with the Irish-Australian cause; he saw both of them as most appropriately pursued at the highest possible political and social levels, and by the most prominent and prestigious personalities in Irish catholic society. In taking over control of the home rule cause and its fund-raising activities, Moran ignored the old home rule organisations, run by manual workers and the lower middle class. In 1905 a campaign was mounted to get the commonwealth parliament, formed in 1901, to pass a resolution in favour of home rule. The motion passed easily, but had no practical effects other than conferring a sense of community acceptance on those, like Moran, who sponsored it. The visits of the last of the home rule delegations (Joseph Devlin and J. T. Donovan in 1906, and William Redmond,[1] Richard Hazleton, and J. T. Donovan in 1911–12) were financially successful, but the prevailing mood was not excitement, simply the certainty that home rule must come. The placing of home rule on the statute book in September 1914 seemed, from the distance of the colonies, a total resolution of all Ireland's problems. There were monster meetings of celebration, that in Sydney being attended by the New South Wales prime minister W. A. Holman. Even in the previous year Irish-Australian organisations were making arrangements to send representatives to the anticipated opening of an Irish parliament in Dublin. Soon Ireland, like Australia, would be free, within the British empire.

WHEN news of the 1916 rising reached Australia, the only organisation to welcome it was the newly formed Irish National Association. This had been set up in Sydney in July 1915 at the initiative of Albert Thomas Dryer, a young Australian of Irish and German descent, who, although he had never visited Ireland, had experienced an intellectual and emotional conversion to the cause of uncompromising Irish nationalism. The I.N.A. broke radically with Irish-

extreme case of Bishop Moran's Otago to indicate a degree and kind of conflict not warranted by wider analysis. The history of Irish catholicism in New Zealand is not well served by Eileen Duggan, 'New Zealand' in Corish, *Ir. catholicism*, vi, fasc. 7. In 1991 a new, popular history of New Zealand catholicism was commissioned. The only substantial general treatment of the Irish in New Zealand is D. H. Akenson, *Half the world from home: perspectives on the Irish in New Zealand, 1860–1950* (Wellington, 1990); Professor Akenson makes clear that this is not a full history but 'an initial probe' dealing with some central aspects—which it does to great stimulatory effect. The Ulster genealogical review *Familia* devoted its 1989 issue (ii, no. 5) to essays on New Zealand, and its 1985 issue (ii, no. 1) included a survey article by Michael Bellam, who is engaged on a history of the Irish in New Zealand. O'Farrell, *Vanished kingdoms*, is substantially devoted to a case-study of the author's Irish parents and their families, who emigrated to New Zealand from 1906. D. H. Akenson has published a small number of New Zealand Irish letters in 'Reading the texts of rural immigrants: letters from the Irish in Australia, New Zealand, and North America' in D. H. Akenson (ed.), *Canadian papers in rural history*, vii (Gananoque, Ontario, 1990), pp 307–406. David McGill has written a history of a pro-fenian incident in Hokitika in 1868, *The lion and the wolfhound: the Irish rebellion on the New Zealand goldfields* (Wellington, 1990), whose subtitle sensationalises, for popular consumption, a minor protest, but one regarded with hysterical seriousness by authority at the time.

[1] For an account of his private visit in 1905 see William Redmond, *Through the new commonwealth* (Dublin, 1906).

Australian tradition. It wanted an Irish republic, not home rule. It was associated with neither the catholic church nor the Australian labour movement. It was militant and its membership was mostly working-class and Irish-born. Above all, its orientation was towards Irish affairs, to the exclusion of Australia. Not surprisingly, it was unpopular with the church authorities and the existing Irish organisations, and its membership was tiny, being 211 in January 1916. At that time there were over 22,000 Irish-born living in Sydney and its suburbs, and around 150,000 of Irish descent. But the I.N.A. had radical contacts in Ireland and America, and the rising gave its ideals and orientation a firm basis in Irish events, which continued to sustain its existence.[1]

Nevertheless, the I.N.A. remained an oddity in the Irish-Australian scene. Among prominent Irish-Australian organisations and personalities, the rising provoked reactions ranging from emotional denunciations, and fervent declarations of loyalty to the empire, to saddened regret and repudiation. This sprang from feelings much more basic than loyalty to home rule. The home rule solution to the question of Ireland's political status suited Irish-Australians perfectly—Ireland, like Australia, would be free within the empire. The Irish-Australians could thus reconcile, without difficulty, their old and their new loyalties: they could be loyal to Ireland, Australia, and the empire, all at once, in a piece, without any conflict or tension. The rising altered this radically by making loyalty to Ireland and loyalty to the empire mutually exclusive. Irishmen, aided by Germany, had taken up arms against Britain, which was fighting Germany with Australian aid. The howl of anguished repudiation that arose, from Irish organisations throughout Australia, testified to their dismay that Irish affairs should cast doubts on their Australian loyalties and jeopardise their reputation, comfort, and security in Australia.

Hostility to the rising's leaders was immediate, but when the initial shocked fury had passed, this began to be seen as willingness to accept the discreditable proposition that Irishmen alone were to blame for what had happened. The same impulses that had led to initial denunciation of the rising—pride, aspirations to community acceptance, a sense of what was right and honourable—made an anti-Irish interpretation of the rising unacceptable. Soon most Irish-Australians moved on to blame British provocation. In this they had the leadership of Archbishop Mannix. Indeed, without Mannix it seems likely that the issues of Irish rebellion and independence would have received small attention in Australia. Most Irish-Australians would have preferred to avoid them, but Mannix made this impossible, for he said what many thought but for reasons of peace or comfort did not say, and the attacks he attracted forced them to take his side. This fostered an extremism in regard to Irish matters quite abnormal in Australia.

---

[1] See Patrick O'Farrell, 'Dreaming of a distant revolution: A. T. Dryer and the Irish National Association of Australia' in *Journal of the Royal Australian Historical Society*, lxix, pt 3 (Dec. 1983), pp 145–60.

The execution of the rising's leaders engendered a widespread surge of bitter resentment among Irish-Australians. This sprang less from sympathy with the rebels than from alarm about the implications for Irish-Australians. The executions, followed by repression, martial law, and mass deportations, seemed to brand the Irish—wherever they were—as traitors and criminals, and to arraign them all, by association, as potentially disloyal. Archbishop James Duhig of Brisbane[1] was most concerned about the damage British policy would do to what he regarded as a major element in the process of Irish integration into Australian life—enlistment in the armed forces. Irish-Australian opinion deserted the Irish parliamentary party very rapidly, but this desertion was much more a bitter disillusionment with its policies and their outcome than conversion to separatism. Home rulers felt cheated and betrayed, but this did not produce enthusiasm for the rising: they had no wish to be associated with violence. Undoubtedly, the dominant wish was to opt out of the local embarrassments that flowed from the Irish question. But this was complicated by genuine indignation at British policy, and by the urge to respond to the increasing questioning of the loyalty of Irish catholics in Australia.

The progress of events in Ireland, and the rapid polarisation of opinion on the issue in Australia, made a noncommittal or conservative Irish stance less and less tenable. Conservatives, such as Archbishop Michael Kelly of Sydney,[2] would have liked to forget the rising, but loyalists and super-patriots would not allow them to. What had happened in Ireland was seized on by protestant extremists—many of them Irish protestants committed to unionism—as proving the most fantastic assertions of catholic international conspiracy, disloyalty, and sedition. These attacks evoked a defence in the form of justification of what had occurred in Ireland—and, of course, swiftly added to such exchanges a sectarian element that soon dwarfed all other considerations.[3]

Tighe Ryan, editor of the Sydney *Catholic Press*,[4] produced a solution to the problem of the apparent conflict between loyalty to the empire and support for Ireland's freedom. He argued that the true concept of empire was a democratic

---

[1] T. P. Boland, *James Duhig* (Brisbane, 1986), is an excellent biography which sets Duhig in the Queensland Irish scene from his arrival as a boy in 1885 to his death as archbishop and K.B.E. in 1965.

[2] For Archbishop Kelly's attitudes, see Patrick O'Farrell, 'Archbishop Kelly and the Irish question' in *Journal of the Australian Catholic Historical Society*, iv, pt 3 (1974), pp 1–19.

[3] For the development of this sectarian dimension from the Irish crisis, see J. C. Gleeson, 'The enemies within: a study of sectarianism in Victoria, 1917' (B.A. thesis, University of Melbourne, 1970), pp 24 ff; Michael McKernan, *Australian churches at war: attitudes and activities of the major churches, 1914–1918* (Sydney and Canberra, 1980); Michael Hogan, *The sectarian strand: religion in Australian history* (Victoria, 1987), ch. 7, 'Sectarian consolidation', pp 170–205.

[4] This had been founded in 1895 by clerics as a more religious rival to the long established (1850), and more militantly Irish, Sydney *Freeman's Journal*. A similar duality existed in Melbourne with the *Advocate* (1860) and the *Tribune*. Appreciating the influence of their own press in forming and controlling Irish opinion, in all Australian states from the 1890s clerics and bishops were moving towards take-overs or new foundations in the field of Irish catholic journalism. The only substantial work on any aspect of this important topic is Noel McLachlan, 'Irish organs and reversible nationalism: the *Irish-Australian* and Irish Australia, 1894–5' in MacDonagh & Mandle, *Irish-Australian studies*, pp 185–216; this has appendices listing journalists of Irish birth or descent.

one, held by a mass of ordinary people, enshrined in dominion status, and in conflict with 'the brutal antiquated tory spirit'.[1] The numerous demands from organisations and public meetings all over Australia, for an end to martial law in Ireland and for immediate home rule, were invariably made on the grounds that this would best serve the empire and the war effort. This reflected genuine concern both for Ireland and the empire, but also more personal considerations. If the empire had no room for a free Ireland, with its own particular local identity, would it have room for Irish identity within Australia? Archbishop Mannix, openly in favour of rebel Ireland, had no doubts about what his loyalties would be if such problems arose: 'if he could not be loyal to the commonwealth and to the empire without forgetting his own people in Dublin and Ireland, then he was no longer loyal to the commonwealth; no longer loyal to the empire. The hypothesis was, of course, absurd.'[2] His critics, however, did not think it absurd at all: they regarded him and all other Irish catholics with him as no longer loyal.[3] However, Mannix's supporters denied such disloyalty. They were not choosing Ireland and rejecting Australia and the empire, but demanding that the Irish problem be accepted and resolved within the empire.

These divisions and demands came to a head during the conscription referenda campaigns of 1916 and 1917. The contemporaneous public prominence of Irish affairs and Ireland's champion Archbishop Mannix, the most prominent opponent of conscription, created the impression, then and after, that Ireland was a decisive factor in the defeat of conscription.[4] The historical realities suggest that this is a massive exaggeration, and that the rejection of conscription was the expression of many things, but mostly an Australia-wide inward-turned reaction of a selfish materialist kind.[5] The evidence, moreover, suggests that Irish-Australians opposed conscription not because of events in Ireland but because of local grievances, resentments, and animosities that existed in Australia long before 1916. They were moved by a deep conviction (though one certainly reinforced by what had happened in Ireland) that the dominant forces in Australian society sought to exclude or demean catholics, and conscription seemed the programme of the ascendancy party in microcosm.[6] As Mannix told an anti-conscription

---

[1] *Catholic Press*, 17 Aug. 1916.

[2] Quoted in O'Farrell, *Catholic church*, p. 220.

[3] These critics included some Australian catholics. 'To me it seems nothing short of criminal for any priest to use the influence that has come [to] him through his spiritual office to sway the minds of ignorant people in a crisis . . . to avenge his own wrongs or the wrongs of his country by playing the traitor' (Geoffrey Hughes to Sir Thomas and Lady Hughes, 14 Jan. 1917; Hughes papers, Mitchell library).

[4] The standard statement of this argument is Alan D. Gilbert, 'The conscription referenda, 1916–17: the impact of the Irish crisis' in *Historical Studies*, xiv, no. 53 (Oct. 1969), pp 54–72. See also D. J. Murphy, 'Religion, race, and conscription in World War I' in *Australian Journal of Politics and History*, xx, no. 2 (Aug. 1974), pp 155–63; R. P. Davis, 'Tasmania and the Irish revolution, 1916–22' in *Papers and Proceedings, Tasmanian Historical Research Association*, xxii, no. 2 (June 1974), pp 69–88.

[5] The best analysis is T. A. Metherell, 'The conscription referenda, October 1916 and December 1917: an inward-turned nation at war' (Ph.D. thesis, University of Sydney, 1971).

[6] For this argument, see O'Farrell, *Catholic church*, pp 225–9.

meeting late in 1917, 'Sinn Féin has nothing to do with us at the present'.[1] The mass of Irish-Australians were concerned with Australian affairs, not Irish ones, and their identification with, and concern for, the sufferings of Ireland continued only so long as these seemed to symbolise their own.

This conclusion is supported by the remarkably weak response in Australia and New Zealand to directly republican causes. The I.N.A. reached its peak of membership in 1919—about 1,500. Many members regarded it as a social club. In June 1918 seven members were interned in Sydney as being members of the Irish Republican Brotherhood.[2] This small group of militants had some contacts with the American I.R.B., and—although the authorities did not discover this—had set up a tiny camp in the Blue Mountains to train men to fight in Ireland. The military detention of seven active champions of Ireland's independence was an obvious and ready-made cause for the expression of a massive Irish-Australian declaration of support for their ideas and ideals. No such declaration was made. The tiny I.R.B. group and its alleged seditious activities were irrelevant to the real and great concerns that agitated Irish catholics in Australia: these were catholic and Australian concerns. At bottom there was consensus that the I.R.B. detainees were cranks whose activities were completely out of place.

A similar reaction can be discerned in relation to the case of Hugh Mahon, labour member for Kalgoorlie, in November 1920. Mahon had been gaoled in Kilmainham for his land league activities in the 1880s. During a protest demonstration in Melbourne occasioned by the hunger-strike of Terence Mac-Swiney, lord mayor of Cork, Mahon savagely attacked British policy in Ireland. As a consequence he was expelled from the federal parliament as 'by reason of seditious and disloyal utterances . . . guilty of conduct unfitting him to remain a member of this house'.[3] There were protests, but none was large, and they soon ceased; another potential cause, around which Irish-Australians might have rallied had they been vitally interested, was soon forgotten.

Although the Irish-Australian response to the British government's prevention in August 1920 of Archbishop Mannix's visit to Ireland[4] was much more

[1] *Catholic Press*, 6 Nov. 1917.
[2] The case is considered in Patrick O'Farrell, 'The Irish Republican Brotherhood in Australia: the 1918 internments' in Oliver Macdonagh, W. F. Mandle, and Pauric Travers (ed.), *Irish culture and nationalism 1750–1950* (London, 1983), pp 182–93.
[3] See H. J. Gibbney, 'Hugh McMahon: a political biography' (M.A. thesis, Australian National University, 1969); R. G. Dryen, 'The significance of the expulsion of Hugh McMahon, M.H.R., from federal parliament, 12 November 1920' (B.A. thesis, University of New South Wales, 1967).
[4] The incident is described by Thomas E. Hachey in 'The quarantine of Archbishop Mannix: a British preventive policy during the Anglo-Irish troubles' in *Ir. Univ. Rev.*, i (1970), pp 111–30. Several Irish-born bishops, from Australian sees, played some part in the Anglo–Irish negotiations of 1920–21, notably Archbishop Patrick Clune of Perth, but also Archbishops William Barry of Hobart, Michael Kelly of Sydney, and Mannix of Melbourne. See John T. McMahon, *'The cream of their race': Irish truce negotiations, December 1920–January 1921* (Ennis, [1972?]); J. T. McMahon, *College, campus, cloister* (Nedlands, 1969); David W. Miller, *Church, state, and nation in Ireland 1898–1921* (Dublin, 1973), pp 473–6; O'Farrell, 'Archbishop Kelly', pp 9–11. However, the fullest and most recent account of Mannix's contacts with Irish politics is Dermot Keogh, 'Mannix, de Valera, and Irish nationalism'

vigorous, it still had little purely pro-Irish content. There were large protest meetings, but they aroused religious rather than nationalist sensibilities. In November 1919 the Australian hierarchy had acted to assert its determination to remain the arbiter of Irish sentiment in Australia, as well as to demonstrate the respectability of the Irish cause. An Irish Race Convention was summoned in Melbourne by Archbishop Mannix at the request of the hierarchy and the Irish societies in Australia. Essentially it was a clerical device to maintain control of an Irish catholic sentiment that had become markedly more interested in, and sympathetic towards, Irish independence. Its theme was support for self-determination, and it allowed Irish catholics to demonstrate their solidarity behind their hero, Archbishop Mannix.[1] The self-determination movement led to the establishment of the Irish Self-Determination League of Australasia in February 1921; it fitted the traditional pattern of offering an outlet for moral and financial support for Ireland.

The relative success of the moderate league, and the unwillingness of the Irish-Australians to be provoked by incidents that might have been regarded as persecution of their nation, testify again to their reluctance to go beyond that point where active sympathy with Irish causes would involve them in direct conflict with other Australians. Moreover, the years of Anglo–Irish war (1919–21) made it clear that very few Irish-Australians wanted any association with the struggle for Irish independence if it involved killing, maiming, and destruction in war against Britain. Ireland had become a considerable embarrassment to its Australian sons and daughters, a painful situation that they ardently wished would end. To the vast majority of Irish-Australians, the Anglo-Irish treaty of 6 December 1921, creating the Irish Free State, was an end to the unfortunate business, and an honourable liberation for them from an intolerable involvement.

BRIEFLY, and in a more subdued fashion, the same Irish-catholic-centred animosities dominated the New Zealand scene. Australian and Irish acrimonies were imported into New Zealand via the Protestant Political Association, formed in July 1917 by Orangemen, and via the Maoriland Irish Societies, established throughout 1917. The most spectacular subsequent incident was that of the prosecution for sedition—and acquittal—of Bishop James Liston of Auckland, following his criticism of British policy in Ireland at a St Patrick's day gathering in 1922.[2] This, however, was untypical of the New Zealand reaction, and

---

in *Australasian Catholic Record*, lxv, no. 2 (Apr. 1988), pp 159–73; no. 3 (July 1988), pp 343–57. A shorter version of this paper, under the same title, is in O'Brien & Travers, *Ir. emigrant experience*, pp 196–225.

[1] O'Farrell, 'Archibishop Kelly', p. 9.

[2] See Davis, *Irish issues*, pp 196–8; P. J. O'Farrell, *Harry Holland: militant socialist* (Canberra, 1964), pp 91–3; H. S. Moores, 'The rise of the Protestant Political Association: sectarianism in New Zealand during World War 1' (M.A. thesis, University of Auckland, 1966). The fullest treatment at present available is R. M. Sweetman, 'New Zealand catholicism and the Irish issue, 1914–1922' in W. J. Shiels and Diana Woods (ed.), *The churches, Ireland and the Irish* (Oxford, 1989), pp 375–84. It is to be hoped

something of an anachronism. In Australia and New Zealand active enthusiasm for Irish independence had died before the Anglo–Irish treaty, a distant casualty of the Anglo–Irish war, and an immediate victim of local sectarian battles. Irish-Australasian catholics would not sanction or accept Irish violence, and they were tired of the constant sectarian warfare, and denials of their loyalty, that involvement in Irish affairs had brought in its train.

What was dead was buried, in disgust, during the Irish civil war. As Irishman killed Irishman in Ireland, they also killed what little remained of Irish-Australian interest in Ireland's cause—whatever that was, for few understood what was at issue. Only Archbishop Mannix remained a committed republican of de Valera's stamp; his erstwhile supporters fell from him like autumn leaves. Irish republican envoys were deported from Australia in June 1923. In 1923 Bishop Michael O'Farrell of Bathurst reported to Ireland: 'No one wants to speak of the Irish question out here.'[1] 'I am completely disillusioned', wrote Archbishop William Barry from Tasmania in 1927; 'this is not the Ireland of my youth and dreams.'[2] Identification with Ireland's causes had been, for many, the pursuit of ideals, a search for lost youth, a quest for the realisation of their dream worlds. All this was shattered and destroyed by Irish realities.[3] Among Irish catholics in Australia, Ireland had been the epitome of all that was noble and holy; it had betrayed their trust. And not only did they turn from Irish politics, there was also a reaction against the most potent Irish influence within Australia, the Irish clergy of the catholic church. From 1919 pressure intensified within the priesthood itself to end the domination of the Australian church by Irish clerics.[4] With Archbishop Gilroy's succession to Sydney in March 1940, Australianism had effectively arrived: the long episcopates of Archbishop Mannix and Archbishop James Duhig of Brisbane, ending with their deaths in the 1960s, were the protraction of an Irish phase that had ended long before, though aspects of its powerful heritage linger to the present day.[5]

By the 1930s the Australian catholic community was paying little heed to its Irish derivation, other than by way of pious acknowledgement.[6] In 1946, a Melbourne priest reported: 'I asked a young friend of mine what he thought

that Dr Sweetman's recently completed Cambridge Ph.D. on New Zealand catholicism in this period will soon be published.

[1] Michael O'Farrell to Fr O'Donnell, 27 Mar. 1923 (All Hallows College archives, Dublin). For a study of some Australian reactions, see Susan Grinsell, 'The Sydney press and Irish affairs, 1920–24' (B.A. thesis, University of New South Wales, 1972).

[2] William Barry to Fr O'Donnell, 5 Aug. 1927 (All Hallows College archives, Dublin).

[3] Not entirely; some few colonial individuals maintained their belief in an ideal Ireland. See O'Farrell, *Vanished kingdoms*, ch. 8, 'Dreams of Irelands', pp 199–239.

[4] See O'Farrell, *Documents*, ii, 191–209; K. T. Livingston, 'Terence Maguire and the Manly Union, 1914–1924' in *Australasian Catholic Record*, xlviii, no. 3 (July 1971), pp 237–54. Livingston's book *The emergence of an Australian catholic priesthood, 1835–1915* (Sydney, 1977), deals with the pre-history of these developments.

[5] The effects of this Irish legacy are the central concern of O'Farrell, *Vanished kingdoms*.

[6] For some aspects of the 1930s, see Louise Meyer, 'The image of Ireland in New South Wales' (B.A. thesis, University of New South Wales, 1974).

should be done about Irish history and sentiment in Australia. "Forget about them", he replied at once with a smile."[1] But not until the late 1960s did the descendants of the Irish in Australia become sufficiently free of the authoritarian and traditionally sacred seriousness of their heritage to poke fun at it. This exercise was first performed, with considerable comic skill, by the novelist Thomas Keneally in *Three cheers for the Paraclete*, published in 1968, in which traditional Irish catholic culture received satiric treatment. The attempt to slough off Irish-Australia, or at least to appraise it critically, became part of the great Australian identity quest characteristic of the 1950s and 1960s. It was given sharp point by the disintegration, from 1954, of the half-century-old identification of Irish catholics with the Australian labour party. This profound convulsion marked the end of any significant political unity among catholics. While it may be possible to interpret some of what happened then in terms of Irish habits of mind, descended through Irish and Australian history,[2] the issues that split the labour movement and catholics at that time were in no way Irish, but Australian and catholic. At this most recent point of crisis, Ireland was entirely irrelevant to Australian catholicism.[3]

After 1920 an interest in Irish affairs became confined to those of Irish birth, mainly recent immigrants, and not many of those: interest among those of Irish descent virtually disappeared. Just how slight was that interest was not conclusively demonstrated until 1948, when Eamon de Valera and Frank Aiken toured Australia and New Zealand. They received enthusiastic welcomes, but the enthusiasm was one of sentiment, and completely ephemeral. De Valera was preaching the message of anti-partition, and he left Albert Dryer with the task of organising an Australian League for an Undivided Ireland. The outcome was little better than a fiasco. Despite Dryer's prodigious efforts, he aroused almost no interest or support. After the ignominious collapse of his anti-partition campaign, it could be conclusively said that the cult of Ireland by a substantial section of the Australian population had quite expired; to some it was a minor embarrassment, to most it was an utter irrelevance. Irish-Australia was at an end.[4]

What remained were the Irish-born. Postwar assisted immigration took this to a new peak of 47,673 in 1954. Most of these were young labourers, among whom were sufficient militants to establish small Sinn Féin organisations in the early 1950s. Their significance in the general community was negligible, though they

---

[1] Melbourne *Advocate*, 13 Mar. 1946.

[2] This is the argument of Niall Brennan, *The politics of catholics* (Melbourne, 1972), pp 13–17.

[3] The two best accounts make this clear by omission: Robert Murray, *The split* (Melbourne, 1970), and Paul Ormonde, *The movement* (Melbourne, 1972). Again, not quite entirely. That events in 1956 echo impulses and attitudes evident among Irish clerics in the Parnell period is an argument suggested in O'Farrell, *Vanished kingdoms*, pp 276–9.

[4] See Patrick O'Farrell, 'Irish-Australia at an end: the Australian League for an Undivided Ireland, 1948–54' in *Papers and proceedings, Tasmanian Historical Research Association*, xxi, no. 4 (Dec. 1974), pp 142–60.

were an irritant to the membership of some older Irish organisations, such as the
I.N.A., which they attempted to take over. The older organisations were social,
and wanted nothing to do with the Irish Republican Army. The reemergence
from 1968 of violence in Northern Ireland did little to alter this, though it
attracted intense interest, roused some old emotions, and drew sympathy in a
financial form, eventually leading to the formation of an Australian Aid for Ireland
organisation.[1] By this time a new factor had entered the situation—the permanent
establishment in 1964 of an Irish embassy in Canberra, following negotiations that
went back to 1946.[2] Those negotiations had stemmed from the postwar interest
of both small powers in seeking wider international recognition, and in particular
from the ambitions of the Australian foreign minister, H. V. Evatt, and the
pro-Irish enthusiasm of the minister for immigration, Arthur Calwell. However,
moves towards a full ambassadorial exchange ground to a long halt over questions
of style and titles, Australian governments refusing to accept recognition of
'Ireland', as implying acceptance of the republic's claims to the north. While the
impasse continued, Ireland sent T. J. Kiernan in what amounted to an ambassadorial role to Australia, while Australia responded with lesser levels of diplomatic
representation—and for a long period none—in Dublin. Eventually the problem
was resolved by some verbal ingenuity that allowed both countries their own
interpretations of the meaning of the formal documents, and full ambassadors
were exchanged. This not only formalised the relations between the two countries
at a governmental level, but gave the relationship a continuous and serious
content, and—with a succession of innovative ambassadors at both ends—formed
a structure and focus for closer ties and productive cultural initiatives. Diplomatic
relations provided the framework within which both Australia and Ireland
developed their awareness of the connections between them and took practical
steps to further their knowledge of each other, which had grown dim since the
1920s. Links were made between universities; sports teams were exchanged;[3] and
artists, theatre companies, poets, as well as parliamentarians and businessmen

---

[1] Little research has been done on the Australian response to the Northern Ireland situation. For
reminiscence see Vincent Buckley's two books *Cutting green hay: friendships, movements, and cultural
conflicts in Australia's great decades* (Victoria, 1983) and *Memory Ireland* (Victoria, 1985). See also, for
some aspects of the Australian press reaction, Jane Noble, 'Some aspects of the Australian perception
of the conflict in Northern Ireland, 1968–85, using selected public sources' (B.A. thesis, University of
New South Wales, 1990). On the social geography of the Sydney Irish from the 1950s to the 1980s,
see Séamus Grimes, 'Postwar Irish immigrants in Australia: the Sydney experience' in Séamus Grimes
and Gearóid Ó Tuathaigh (ed.), *The Irish-Australian connection* (Galway, 1989), pp 137–59.
[2] For the history of this evolution and this background of politicking, see Patrick O'Farrell,
'Irish-Australian diplomatic relations' in *Quadrant*, xxiv, no. 151 (Mar. 1980), pp 11–20.
[3] Another area of historical neglect has been that of Irish sporting activity in Australia: although
research compilations exist with regard to Irish games, nothing substantial has as yet been published.
However, controversy has long raged over the question whether Irish influence was important in the
origins of 'Australian rules' football, the major form of football in Victoria. Despite substantial
scholarly research suggesting the contrary, Irish enthusiasts remain unconvinced and claim credit for
inventing the game.

visited each other's countries.[1] These visits, multiplying and diversifying in the 1980s, were set in a context of a major increase in Irish emigration, both permanent and temporary, to Australia. Whereas in 1984–5 the Australian embassy in Dublin issued 5,270 visas, in 1987–8 it issued 14,390. In the same period the number of Irish clubs, organisations, and sporting groups virtually doubled to close on a hundred for the whole of Australia.

These were the new Irish, the arrivals of the 1960s to the 1990s, most choosing to have no deep encounter with Australia.

Rather they were sojourners, visitors, casuals, hived-off and happy inhabitants of their own particular division of multi-culture . . . content to be permanently Irish while resident in Australia. These new arrivals, airborne, with money, and a ticket home in their heads if not their pockets, educated, with a republic of their own, self-confident in their identity and proud of their culture . . ., were far distant in character, outlook, mission, from those Irish whose Ireland predated 1916, 1921.[2]

For Australia and New Zealand the age of the great ocean saga had ended, the Irish dimension of that experience especially sad and proud: the distance so great, the homeland so beloved, the lifelines so tangled. It had ended happily in working holidays, cash in hand, sunny days, friends in the pub, home a phone call away. Australia discovered? Or was it Australia, once formed in the sweat of their progenitors, now lost, merely a warm parking space off the edge of the real earth?[3]

---

[1] Irish participation in Australian politics and poetry, as well as literature and art, is well documented historically. Less well known is the contribution of the Anglo-Irish, in particular to Australian academic and intellectual life. See F. B. Smith, 'Stalwarts of the garrison: some Irish academics in Australia' in O'Brien & Travers, *Ir. emigrant experience*, pp 120–47. The same paper is also available in *Australian Cultural History*, vi (1987), pp 74–93. See also T. A. Boylan and T. P. Foley, 'Tempering the rawness: W. E. Hearn, Irish political economist, and intellectual life in Australia' in Grimes & Ó Tuathaigh, *Irish-Australian connection*, pp 91–119.

[2] O'Farrell, *Vanished kingdoms*, pp xxv–xxvi.

[3] The history of the Irish in Australia from 1788 is examined in greater detail in Patrick O'Farrell, *The Irish in Australia* (Sydney, 1987). The revised 1992 edition contains an additional chapter on 'The new Irish', bringing the coverage into the 1990s.

CHAPTER XXIV

The remaking of Irish-America, 1845–80

DAVID NOEL DOYLE

BETWEEN 1845 and 1880 Irish-America was dramatically remade, then matured, and by 1921 was beginning to decline. The commonplace perception that it had always been an urban, industrial, and catholic community (quite inaccurate as to its character before 1820, and only partially true before 1845) well describes it for a full century after that date. The decisive years of change were between 1845 and 1880; the following forty years saw a maturing of the patterns then established. Before 1845, diverse experiences in both the United States and in British North America had made for scattered, varied, and disunited communities: Irish protestants and catholics had mingled as farmers, traders, and artisans in varying proportions across a vast continent. Smallish numbers and protestant preeminence had not only accelerated Americanisation (or Canadianisation) in terms of both acculturation and outright absorption, but also eased the direct contributions of the immigrants to still fluid host cultures.

Four major changes altered all this after 1845. First, the famine multiplied massively the numbers going to North America: 'more people left Ireland in just eleven years than during the preceding two and one-half centuries', or 1.8 million between 1846 and 1855.[1] Declining demand for agricultural labour in Ireland, and the fall of Irish wages compared with those in America, inclined millions more to follow the great outflow between 1855 and 1921. Secondly, as many as nine-tenths of these famine and post-famine emigrants to the U.S.A. were catholics, which, together with the vast numbers and a major new effort by churchmen in Ireland and North America to secure fuller levels of churchgoing than before, not merely cut the protestant element in Irish-America, but (except in Canada) inclined the body of Irish protestant migrants to dissociate themselves from their fellow countrymen. In the United States this trend was accelerated by a more sharply anti-Irish nativism,[2] which was now more strictly anti-catholic, so that Irish

---

[1] Kerby Miller, *Emigrants and exiles* (Oxford and New York, 1985), p. 291; see above, p. 640, table 3.

[2] Nativism: an American political movement emphasising 'nationality, protestant piety, temperance, craft-exclusiveness, and anti-Irishism' (above, v, 719).

protestants were now no longer subjected to it, unlike those who had come to colonial America. Thirdly, the triumph of Irish nationalist ideology, if in varying forms, among the Irish at home in this period, created an ethos of distinctiveness and techniques of group advancement that took renewed root, for other reasons, in the overseas communities. Fourthly, this expanded migration was given new form and concentration by America's rapid industrialisation from the early 1840s and its focus in certain regions.

It is striking that in British North America, where the transition from a mixed protestant and catholic migration was less marked, where industrialisation was very limited, and where the hegemony of British traditions persisted (marginalising Irish nationalism), 'Irish-Canada' remained well into the 1880s what Irish-America had ceased to be after Andrew Jackson (president 1829–37): largely rural and agricultural, largely led by protestants, and largely scattered. (The very inclusion of the Irish harp as a minor element in the flag of the dominion of Canada in 1867 appropriately reflected this.) By contrast, by the 1860s a new Irish-America, which was urban, industrial, and catholic, had become intensely aware of itself, especially of its notable share in the armies and casualties of the civil war (only now passing from cliché to documentation).[1] Indeed, these new Irish-Americans were overwhelmingly more urban than were native Americans or Irish-Americans of colonial antecedents. They were found at all social levels of the burgeoning commercial as well as factory cities, which they humanised by networks of connections based on common local and regional origins in the old country. If churchmen instigated parish creation, they found myriads of natural cooperators amongst these newcomers.

The full period 1845–1921 thus has a natural unity. Continuous arrivals from Ireland counteracted dispersal and assimilation; those going to the U.S.A. greatly outnumbered those going to any other destination.[2] Thus the main story after 1845 plainly relates to the United States, where communities grew by continuous infusions from home, as well as by industrial concentration and the intergenerational loyalty between Irish-born and their American offspring. The Roman Catholic church there became the most distinctively 'Irish' institution outside Ireland. Such cohesion underpinned the role of the American Irish in funding and encouraging the Irish independence movement, especially in the 1880s and from 1910 to 1922, and in securing transatlantic attention for its objectives. This solidarity influenced the ethnic and religious simplifications surrounding the 'Irish question' in the British Isles and also matters of minority rights and power in the United States. Whether either Irish independence, or the full form of religious pluralism attained by metropolitan America by 1910, would have been attained,

[1] David Power Conyngham, *The Irish Brigade and its campaigns*, ed. L. F. Kohl (New York, 1994); W. J. K. Beaudot and L. J. Herdegen (ed.), *An Irishman in the Iron Brigade: the civil war memoirs of James F. Sullivan* (New York, 1994); L. F. Kohl and M. C. Richard (ed.), *Irish green and union blue: the civil war letters of Peter Welsh* (New York, 1993).
[2] Above, p. 641, table 4.

without such self-conscious organisation around the symbols of national identity and catholic belief, remains matter for doubt.

In America the Irish pioneered a distinctive new society: fluid, democratic, innovative, yet locally catholic and competently industrial. They interacted as before with Anglo-Americans for most public and economic purposes, and aligned after the 1850s with German catholics for religious and cultural ones. From 1880, they drew many other Europeans to themselves, providing both examples and leadership for the enclaves from which Italians and Poles, then many others, would gather the fruits of a modern mass society.

Some scholars have written as though the famine exodus and its continuation to 1914 gave Irish-America its distinctive characteristics.[1] Others have sought to emphasise the continuing consequences after 1845 of previous protestant and mixed migrations, by reason both of their offspring, and of continuing lesser protestant flows from Ireland.[2] Protestant migrants did modify the remaking of Irish-America, and some indeed continued to identify with it despite the great change in its composition and traditions: the nationalists John Mitchel and George Pepper are prominent examples. These matters are shown best by contrast with Canada: scholars agree that the famine migration did not make for a distinctive Irish-Canada.[3] Canada was a different case, even apart from its chronology, whereby in much of the country the Irish preserved an older pattern after the famine, in an imperial framework, in which the protestant Irish enjoyed both numerical supremacy and a preferential position. But what was the typical Irish-Canadian experience? Was it the religiously mixed (yet segregated) pre-famine rural settlements, or the post-famine industrial and labouring parishes of cities such as Hamilton, Kingston, Toronto, or even Montreal? Particularly in Ontario (and later in the western provinces) the catholic Irish were discreetly and quietly subordinate to an Anglo-Canadian supremacy, of which Irish protestants were favoured clients. The history of all the Irish in Canada was indeed an 'untold

[1] This is true even of works giving attention to pre-famine elements: Carl Wittke, *The Irish in America* (Baton Rouge, La., 1956), p. 23 and *passim*; Miller, *Emigrants & exiles*, pp 293–344, 492–555; Nicholas Nolan, 'The Irish emigration: a study in demography' (Ph.D. thesis, N.U.I. (U.C.D.), 1935), pp 135, 284–96; Oliver MacDonagh, 'The Irish famine emigration to the United States' in *Perspectives in American History*, x (1976), pp 430–46; Donald H. Akenson, *Being had: historians, evidence, and the Irish in North America* (Port Credit, Ont., 1985), pp 46–9.
[2] David N. Doyle, 'Afterward' in David N. Doyle and Owen Dudley Edwards, *America and Ireland, 1776–1976* (Westport, Conn., and London, 1980), pp 324–5; Ronald A. Wells, 'Aspects of northern Ireland migration to America: definitions and directions' in *Ethnic Forum*, iv, no. 1 (1984), pp 49–63; Christopher McGimpsey, 'Internal ethnic friction: Orange and Green in nineteenth-century New York, 1868–1872' in *Immigrants and Minorities*, i (1982), pp 39–59; Akenson, *Being had*, pp 60–74; Miller, *Emigrants & exiles*, pp 348, 350, 352–3, 371, 378, 380.
[3] Akenson, *Being had*, pp 77–102, quantifies more generally known facts; see Robert O'Driscoll and Lorna Reynolds, *Untold story: the Irish in Canada* (2 vols, Toronto, 1988), i, 30, 171–98, 203–11, 215–29; 253–8, 263–94, 309–35. Apart from urban factory districts, only New Brunswick possibly owed the body of its Irish population and traditions to the years of the famine and after (ibid., pp 231–2), but cf. Donald McKay, *Flight from famine: the coming of the Irish to Canada* (Toronto, 1990), pp 150–63; despite his title, McKay also stresses the pre-famine theme, even for New Brunswick.

story', until a descendant, Brian Mulroney, became the dominion's prime minister in 1984. Their traditions were better remembered in isolated catholic Irish 'holylands' than among catholic scholars or among the Anglo-Canadian protestants of largely Irish descent. To present the nineteenth-century Ontario, therefore, as an ideal interplay of Irish identities and autonomies is wide of the mark. While Thomas D'Arcy McGee fled from New York in 1857, disenchanted with the poverty, urban captivity, and political manipulation of his countrymen there during the height of nativism, seeking a 'pastoral utopia' in Canada's 'tidy church-centred Irish catholic farm communities', yet notably he was invited in as leader by the Irish of French, not English, Canada.[1] In 1873 a French churchman in New York reversed McGee's basic contrast: in Canada, 'Irishmen are not at liberty to show the same feeling for their native country, and prove equally useful to her [as here] . . . they seem almost paralysed in their actions as Irish people.'[2]

Although experience after 1845 varied greatly in the U.S.A., the trend of change was clear. The urban and labouring Irish population, newly populous, more wholly catholic, salved its trauma and poverty and maintained its self-esteem and cohesion by constructing a peculiar subculture around the familiarities of the neighbourhood, the saloon, and the parish. Within these, Irishmen met, talked, and organised for the protection of their livelihood, the improvement of their social position, and the maintenance of their religious faith. The formal sides of these concerns saw the creation of trade unions and fraternal clubs, the support of the urban organisations ('machines') of the national Democratic party, and the multiplication of catholic churches, schools, and hospitals. Within these, in turn, Irish-American support for Irish independence grew inevitably from past experience, from present marginality, from the lessons of American republicanism, and from the respectability of the cult of nationalism, following in the wake of the war against Mexico and the civil war.

Yet most of the originating cultural and institutional pattern of Irish-America had emerged before 1845, if only skeletally and only in the Atlantic port cities. It would have grown anyway without the famine, as the U.S. economy boomed between 1849 and 1857. On conservative estimates of an annual increase of 0.5 per cent in the population of Ireland during the period 1846–60, and assuming a stable flow of emigration westwards at average pre-famine rates, roughly one million would have settled compared with the actual two million who apparently did so. Then the Irish experience of Atlantic migration would have been closer to Scandinavian and rural British patterns, if more numerous, and the whole experience would be less melodramatised by historians. Such counter-factual possibilities also show that not all famine emigrants were refugees from the

[1] Quoted in Thomas N. Brown, 'The Irish layman' in Corish, *Ir. catholicism*, vi, fasc. 2, pp 71–2.
[2] A. J. Thébaud, *The Irish race in the past and the present* (New York, 1873), p. 465; the author, born in Nantes in 1807, had been rector of Fordham College and served Irish-Americans in three states and in Canada.

tragedy. Many would have left home in any case: up to a quarter of the 1846–50 flow, and perhaps half of that for 1851–60, would have emigrated. In short, the trends of demography and emigration, coupled with available foundations laid in America by 1845, would have themselves assured the remaking of Irish-America, if on a less imposing scale and with a less dramatic transition.

The decades 1861–80 are more straightforward. The United Kingdom commissioners of emigration reported 1,140,394 Irish bound for the United States, whose officials in turn reported 872,649 arrivals.[1] Since such discrepancies had previously been reversed (with better arrival than departure data), probably this under-reporting in America was due partly to civil war disruptions and the desire of incoming young Irishmen to avoid the draft. It was also due to a century-long pattern in which Irish departees reported their ultimate planned destination, but stopped off to work at intermediate points (usually in English and Scottish cities) on hearing of recession in America, this time in 1865–6 and throughout the 1870s. Nevertheless, annual rates of direct emigration to the U.S. settled at levels around or slightly above those reached just before the famine—in the 1870s they were at 8.5 per thousand of population, the rate of 1842.

The effects of the famine bulge thus had already thinned out. The post-famine pull of relatives, and the diffusion of the custom of maintaining a viable farm by sending off most of its offspring to such kin-pools, were somewhat reduced by the diminished domestic population on which they operated.[2] The full period 1845–80, nevertheless, bears the clear impress of the famine itself. Most Irish-born in America in the thirty years after 1850 would have clear memories associated with the famine. From 1880 to 1921, however, two new generations set the tone there, one born in the United States, the other the product of later Victorian Ireland, both without such direct recollection. The fusion of constitutional nationalism and agrarian radicalism with fenianism in the 'new departure' of 1878 reflects a compromise between leaders moulded in the first era with the more pragmatic attitudes of these two rising generations. Although the famine cannot be willed away, its effects were thus not unlimited.

Yet the effects of the famine were very important. It tested the narrow and conventional limits of government intervention in Britain, Ireland, and British North America, as well as the United States; it accelerated the tide of romantic humanitarianism intolerant of widespread suffering; it instigated reforms, which in the United States were chiefly municipal, from wide-ranging health and welfare reforms, to accelerated provision of schools and prisons. Emigrant numbers were greatly boosted, although abnormal death rates pursued the emigrants from Ireland, and shadowed their children and successors right into the 1920s. Already between 1840 and 1845 past ease of assimilation had been disrupted by the press

---

[1] Cormac Ó Gráda, 'A note on nineteenth-century Irish emigration statistics' in *Population Studies*, xxix (1975), table 1, p. 144.

[2] J. A. Dunlevy and H. A. Gemery, 'British-Irish settlement patterns in the U.S.: the role of family and friends' in *Scottish Journal of Political Economy*, xxiv (1977), pp 257–63.

of incoming crowds. Between 1847 and 1854 the influx varied from three to six times the rate of the early 1840s; each year over 100,000 people were squeezed into or through America's still smallish ports. Probably a minimum of 200,000 died within three years of arrival, although deaths on the incoming vessels have been much exaggerated. The destitution of many newcomers and the anxiety of all, as they crowded available accommodation and employment, so darkened public views of the Irish that their real character and their recent (and then subsequent) progress were obscured. Political nativism was reborn, prejudicial stereotypes replaced friendliness, and hard treatment resulted, quite apart from hard labour.

The suffering of such large numbers also quickened charity: in many cities the first major catholic hospitals, orphanages, and welfare funds were set up. The tide of the poor overwhelmed the young church and other voluntary agencies; public provision by municipalities had to be greatly expanded. There were extraordinary efforts too, by men prominent in both Irish and non-Irish communities, to send aid direct to the starving in Ireland—from cities as distinct as New Orleans and Boston, and by men as varied as post-frontier politicians and Philadelphia gentlemen merchants. Choctaws in Indian territory, the blacks of the North Liberties and Kensington (the Irish districts of greater Philadelphia), Shakers in Ohio, Jews in New York, military cadets at West Point, even the future Know-Nothing candidate Millard Fillmore, gave money. In both the house of representatives and senate, however, the bills providing federal aid failed. (In any case President Polk believed that they were unconstitutional and planned to veto them.) Irish-Americans naturally raised most money: $623,193 in New York city, Boston, Philadelphia, and Baltimore in the first two months of 1847 alone, against $143,540 raised by the general relief committees of the same four cities from November 1846 to early 1848. All this expressed the old conjoint pattern of leadership in pre-famine Irish communities in America, with deference both to general city and state leaderships and to their own leading merchants and lawyers; it also was a final flourish of immigrant protestant Irish solidarity with the old country, characteristic of Irish-America since the American revolution. It seems that donor fatigue came more quickly to non-Irish Americans, however, than to the Irish, alerted by letter and church networks to continuing hardship well beyond 1847. Misery on one side, charity on the other, diminished the usual factionalism of Irish civic life in America, and briefly replaced the recent tensions with its hosts. Yet now more emotionally 'Irish', the communities were even less amenable to rapid Americanisation than in the changing 1830s, even had native-stock Americans continued generally sympathetic. The great outpouring of compassion and aid by the latter for Ireland itself did not survive the wretched horde-like influx from Ireland. Boston in 1847 demanded a bond of $1,000 from each sick passenger, which deflected many of the poor to New Brunswick and the St Lawrence, in addition to those already bound for the British North American ports.

Although the organised nativists and their animus, numbers, and political presence revived as the most wretched scenes receded, yet no one, not even the nativists, ever sought even partial exclusion of the Irish as such, nor sought to deny (as distinct from delay) their ultimate citizenship. Open ports and borders were perhaps America's greatest generosity of the time, and in turn the famine immigration greatly reinforced the humanitarian argument for an open immigration policy, with America as a haven for Europe's oppressed and miserable, which then ironically survived as long as mass immigration included substantial Irish and other north European components. The tendency of Irish-American scholars to emphasise the role of anti-Irish and anti-catholic strains in U.S. culture, in catalysing the emergence of the conscious, defensive, and institutionalised Irish-America after 1850, tends to neglect this broader receptivity, even friendliness, and the role it played in allowing in the crowds whose numbers and dispositions were themselves sufficient cause to construct a subculture.

The famine trauma itself gave emigrants the need for an outlook in which continuing ill-fortune, whether providential or imposed, was a national fate to be nobly endured.[1] Famine, followed by a rough passage and migratory insecurity, was accompanied for many by culture shock, disease, poverty, hardship, and unemployment. American coldness, if not obloquy, hurt most. Finally the armies of the civil war beckoned many with deadly finality. Thus the contexts nurturing a new fatalism were surely more extreme than those experienced in the hardened lives of pre-famine Irish country people.

Irish writers visiting America from 1850 to 1875 could only see the hard and meagre lives of their fellow countrymen, and could not perceive the dynamics of America's exciting polity and economy. The emphasis of Victorian popular culture on the pain felt by those who left an empty nest proved as much goad as catharsis to their feelings: Stephen Foster (himself of Ulster-American descent) wrote from 1851 to 1863, and Thomas Moore remained the favourite lyric writer of all Americans. Thus even the migrants' change of country and often language did not save them from an emotionalised view of past associations.

The coming of a Young Irish élite of refugees after the rising of 1848 reinforced much of this. Disabused, romantic, assertive, and articulate, their highly charged sensibilities mixed with the chiaroscuro attitudes of their lowly fellow countrymen to incline both together away from any common-sense judgement that the worst was over by the mid-1850s. Both the journalism of the former and the ordinary letters of the latter confirm their common noble pessimism. Irish-Americans in the generation after 1850 were thus veined with a sadness that obscured their gifts, veiled their religious faith, and either shadowed or distanced their American-born children.

Ironically the famine emigrants could hardly have come at a better time. By the treaty of Guadalupe Hidalgo (1848), the United States had newly added title to, or reconfirmed, possession of lands now one-third of its continental territory—

---

[1] Miller, *Emigrants & exiles*, pp 299 ff.

over one million square miles. The country's rail network grew tenfold from 3,000 to 30,000 miles between 1840 and 1860, chiefly after 1850, multiplying construction jobs and quickening development of the north-eastern industrial core, and its integration with the midwest's spreading wheat and maize fields. Although most factory workers up to the 1830s had been native Americans, not immigrants, by the 1850s most of them preferred life in trade, on farms, or as white-collar workers, leaving expanding industrial work to foreigners. Indeed, 3 million American-born left the Atlantic states for the interior by 1860, whereas very few then migrated the other way to compete with the incoming Irish. Manufacturing plants increased from 123,000 in 1849–50 to 140,000 in 1860, but their employment increased by a huge 50 per cent as the scale of the larger, nationally oriented ones grew rapidly, although most remained small, averaging less than ten workers each. The *per capita* annual income in the north-eastern states was $181 in 1860, which exceeded that of every other country except Australia, and indeed that of every other American region, except Texas and Louisiana.

Politics also broadly suited the Irish. The Democrats, who courted them, held federal power from 1845 to 1849, and from 1853 to 1861. The Mexican war, slavery, sectionalism, and competitive expansion distracted attention from the Irish, even when their arrival was agitated by the Know-Nothings as a counter-issue. In short, had they entered a confined, united, and economically stagnant land, the brief flurries of nativism might well have proved more general, hostile, and enduring. Instead they came to a booming country, divided and distracted by vast questions linked to its growth. Rarely can almost 2 million newcomers anywhere have escaped becoming a matter of real and continuing obsession; yet in North America between 1845 and 1860 the Irish did so. Few enough of them realised all this at the time, and those that did, such as Thomas D'Arcy McGee, resented still the accompanying injustices. Most lived far from such broad perspectives, each in his or her own harassed, anxious place.

WHO actually came, during the famine, in its aftermath, and thereafter?[1] A balanced view cannot rest on the images and self-images that sprang from the immediacy of disaster. The answers are vital to assessing the history of Irish-Americans. How can one explain their rapid diffusion and adaption, if they were the 'wretched refuse of storm-tossed shores', the uprooted of Oscar Handlin's portrait,[2] or the Gaelic and post-Gaelic prisoners of a collectivism incapable of

---

[1] The first real effort to raise this was by MacDonagh, in 'Irish famine emigration', pp 357–91, 418–30; while mapping the outflow, he still generalises it and assumes that departures meant equally proportionate arrivals, as was implied earlier in his 'Irish overseas emigration during the famine' in R. Dudley Edwards and T. Desmond Williams (ed.), *The great famine* (Dublin, 1956), pp 320–26, 376, 380–81.

[2] Oscar Handlin, *Boston's immigrants* (Cambridge, Mass., 1941; rev. ed., 1959); most monographs on the nineteenth-century urban Irish followed this thesis before *c*.1970, notably Stephan Thernstrom, *Poverty and progress: social mobility in a nineteenth-century city* (Cambridge, Mass., and Oxford, 1964). This too was a study of an 1850s Massachusetts community, which must be balanced nationally; see below, pp 740–46.

enterprise and individualism, who became the victims of an immature industrialism, as in Kerby Miller's portrait?[1] It is not surprising that Oliver MacDonagh accepted their initial immiseration and proletarianisation in America.[2] The Handlin or Miller pictures logically entail a sequence whereby they were at first the passive playthings of masterful forces they but gradually and dimly understood. Their proletarianisation was thus but the corollary of their ignorance, and the counterpart to the stewardship of the American-born élites who moulded the country, and forcefully remade the very circumstances and texture of Irish life within it. Such ideas tend to fuse with the view that on both sides of the Atlantic the Irish were also victims of a thoughtless fecundity.[3] The other side of the picture has received less emphasis: that the Irish were a versatile people availing themselves of fresh opportunity and diminishing prejudice to build an intelligent subcommunity open to all the ways of American life, and contributing considerably to its dynamism.[4] Neither a close study of the emigrants' backgrounds nor of their actual lives in America supports the pessimistic view of their fortunes, unless one concentrates on the misery of two groups: emigrants from Ireland's congested west coast, and tenement-dwelling, unskilled Irish newcomers in New England.

The characteristics of the migrants depended on where they came from. If the whole famine outflow came from places where previous migration was rare, then indeed Irish-America was remade even in its origins, especially if those coming after 1850 were relatives of the famine emigrants, and then the later mid-Victorian migration consisted of siblings, nieces, and nephews of these predecessors. The traditional view that Irish-America from 1850 to 1921 was the product of the famine would in that respect hold up. Yet study of depopulation and emigration rates by county, together with analysis of birth cohort depletion, support the broad conclusion that the famine brought firstly a new intensity of emigration from the 'old' zones of south Ulster, north Connacht, and the midlands, from which emigration was long established,[5] and only then, in its aftermath, a shift in zones of relative intensity into the west and south-west. Initially, heavy transatlantic outmigration came from areas suffering high excess mortality and general destitution—if relatives outside Ireland could assist escape or even simply attract

[1] Miller, *Emigrants & exiles*, pp 296–9, 303–4, 315–19, 325–8; Kerby Miller, Bruce Boling, and David Doyle, 'Emigrants and exiles: Irish cultures and Irish emigration to North America, 1790–1922' in *I.H.S.*, xxii, no. 86 (Sept. 1980), pp 97–125.

[2] MacDonagh, 'Irish famine emigration', pp 360–64, 434–40.

[3] Thus MacDonagh: 'Two conclusions . . . The first is the importance of emigration in cutting the Gordian knot of overpopulation . . . [The famine exodus] may be looked upon as a population movement unnaturally postponed' (Edwards & Williams, *Great famine*, pp 328, 331); and Handlin: 'Fecundity was the only contribution of the Irish toward a solution of the community's social problems' (*Boston's immigrants*, p. 117).

[4] Notable are Dennis Clark, *The Irish in Philadelphia* (Philadelphia, 1973); his *Hibernia America* (Westport, Conn., 1986) and his 'The Irish in the American economy: the industrial period' in P. J. Drudy (ed.), *The Irish in America: emigration, assimilation, impact* (Cambridge, 1985), pp 234–42; as earlier Wittke, *Irish in America*, pp 23–113, 193–240.

[5] Above, pp 610–12.

it. South Ulster, north Connacht, and the north midlands (Fermanagh, Monaghan, and Cavan; Sligo, Roscommon, Leitrim; Longford and Westmeath) all rank in the top half of county emigration rates before 1841, and all were in the upper half of county mortality rates during 1846–50. The first seven of these eight counties, plus contiguous Mayo, accounted for the top eight county emigration rates for the years 1846–51, with Westmeath also in the top half. Yet rates, as opposed to numbers, are deceptive: this region provided less than one-third of all emigrants between 1846 and 1855.[1] The real and distinguishing crowds now came from Munster (and nearby Galway).

For a new pattern that pointed to the future now intruded, although not without its own precedents. If a few anomalous counties at first suffered high famine mortality without commensurate recorded emigration, notably Cork and Clare in the south-west, and Galway and Mayo in the west, there is evidence that they too had sent away large numbers (if not proportions) of their people in the past and sent even more in 1846–50.[2] Thus they too were equipped with their own bridges out of disaster. Thereafter they indeed provided the most numerous flows abroad. Well over half a million people left County Cork from 1846 to 1921, and over a quarter of a million left from each of Counties Mayo and Galway.[3] Of older emigration zones, only County Antrim, the Scots-Irish heartland, kept pace in sheer numbers, with over 300,000 migrants in the same years. In this vital sense, maps of total county outflow are more useful than those of emigration rates now generally used.[4] In sum, there was a massive overlap between past emigration habits and famine consequences. The poorest might not have been able to escape

[1] S. H. Cousens, 'The regional variation in emigration from Ireland between 1821 and 1841' in *Transactions and Papers of the Institute of British Geographers*, xxxvii (Dec. 1965), fig. 4, p. 22; Cousens, 'The regional pattern of emigration during the great Irish famine, 1846–51' ibid., xxviii (1960), fig. 1, p. 121; David Fitzpatrick, map 14, above, v, 620; Joel Mokyr, *Why Ireland starved* (London, 1982), p. 267. Roscommon apart, the discrepancies between Cousens and Fitzpatrick are less on this than the latter claims (above, v, 571), and the general pattern has been confirmed by Mokyr (unpublished data, reported by Donnelly, above, v, 354–5).

[2] The largest numbers of newcomers seeking knowledge of 'missing friends' and relatives in the *Boston Pilot*, 1831–50, were (in rank order) from Cork, Tipperary, Limerick, Mayo, and Galway; see Ruth-Ann Harris and Donald M. Jacobs (ed.), *The search for missing friends: Irish immigrant advertisements placed in the Boston Pilot* (Boston, 1989), map A, p. xxxvi.

[3] Standard figures are Cork, 575,000; Antrim, 325,000; Mayo, 258,000; Galway, 252,000; Kerry, 226,000; Tipperary, 224,000 (see MacDonagh, 'Irish famine emigration', pp 419–20, added to Miller, *Emigrants & exiles*, pp 570–71). But it must be stressed that 'cohort depletion', constabulary reports, and ships' manifests all suggest that Galway and Mayo figures were much higher again for the years 1851–71, with the other counties somewhat higher. The headlong rush of 1846–51 would indicate this should be even more true of these years (for which we lack all these controls). See above, v, 608; Cormac Ó Gráda, 'Some aspects of nineteenth-century Irish emigration' in L. M. Cullen and T. C. Smout (ed.), *Comparative aspects of Scottish and Irish economic and social history* (Edinburgh, 1977), pp 68–71. The discrepancies are too great to be reconciled, but at the maximum suggest total Galway and Mayo outflow could be increased up to one-third, that from Cork and Kerry up to one-fifth. Such numbers are consistent with the internal American evidence.

[4] Contrast the maps of totals below, ix, 69, with those of rates above, v, 620, and in Cousens, 'Regional variation . . . between 1821 and 1841', pp 19, 20, 22, and 'Regional pattern . . . 1846–51', p. 121.

immediately, but, through kin and neighbours, they too knew the way out and, as destitution and sickness receded, they took it.

The provinces of Munster and Connacht, from the famine (and until the 1930s), sent disproportionately more of their inhabitants to the United States than did Leinster or Ulster. America's appeal to Munster people, especially to those from Cork, was strong. So too was it to those Connacht people who could afford to get there. Some of Connacht's lost 'cohort depletion' of the 1840s and 1850s (those born by 1841 or 1851 and unaccounted for in the migration or mortality statistics of 1851 and 1861) undoubtedly broke from the main flow to Britain to arrive in industrial Pennsylvania or on the construction sites of mid-Victorian Canada. Connacht's representatives in New York's Irish middle class seem an anomaly, and originated in a pre-famine select flow from its better towns and families, notably from Sligo.

Thus, while the period 1846–55 increased Munster and Connacht elements within Irish-America, it diminished the shares of Leinster and Ulster, the politically important, commercially more advanced, and culturally more diverse provinces. Distribution throughout the U.S.A. seems to have been proportionate to these flows. Munster emigrants were everywhere boosted to preponderance by the famine, even if they took longer to establish social and business leadership. It is thus not by chance that the chief contemporary investigators of Irish-America between 1850 and 1880 were Munstermen, usually from Cork, notably the nationalist politicians J. F. Maguire and William Smith O'Brien, the priests Michael Buckley and Hugh Quigley, and the journalist Jeremiah O'Donovan (who should not be confused with Jeremiah O'Donovan Rossa). Probably 30 per cent of all America's Irish immigrants in 1846–55 were from Munster.

Ulster was displaced, therefore, almost everywhere, by Munster as the most characteristic source of the Irish-born in North America. The exceptions are themselves revealing. New York city's mid-century middle-class Irish were heavily of Ulster background, and equally protestant and catholic, while Pennsylvania remained partly an Ulster stronghold, even if now presbyterian farmers were less prominent than catholic miners and mill workers.[1] Migration from Ulster, from 1846 to 1855, was less than its population warranted by total Irish patterns. But Cavan, Monaghan, and Fermanagh did have high rates, as did the glens of Antrim. Large numbers emigrated from Tyrone, Donegal, and south Down, so that together the 'outer Ulster' zones sent away from 330,000 to 350,000. It was

---

[1] Cormac Ó Gráda, 'Across the briny ocean: some thoughts on pre-famine emigration to America' in T. M. Devine and David Dickson (ed.), *Ireland and Scotland, 1600–1850* (Edinburgh, 1983), table 7, p. 127; Victor A. Walsh, 'Across the "Big wather"; the Irish-catholic community of mid-nineteenth century Pittsburgh' in *Western Pennsylvania Historical Magazine*, lxvi (1983), table 1, p. 4; Harris and Jacobs, *Search for missing friends*, table 3, p. xx; Ruth-Ann Harris, ' "On the whole I'd rather be lost in Philadelphia": a profile of Irish migrants in Philadelphia, 1831–1851' (unpublished paper, 1988); Marion Casey, 'A quantitative analysis of New York city's Irish and Irish-American middle-class community in the middle of the nineteenth century' (unpublished seminar paper, New York U., 1988), figs 1 and 3, table 3, pp 15, 17, 29.

in these areas that the famine struck most severely in Ulster.[1] One can safely assume that American indications of Ulster arrivals are of these people. Yet whether from northern or southern Ireland, in its regional composition the remade Irish-America was recruited from its own pre-famine foundations, if with a tilt in the originating axis within Ulster to its more catholic zones, and along the axis towards inland Munster.[2]

All this helped set the catholic character of Irish-America for the next three generations, which strengthened the drift to a more homogenous Irish-America, under way since the mid-1820s. Even excluding special calculations for Ulster, provincial figures show that 1.6 million or 85 per cent of emigrants leaving Ireland in these years were Roman Catholic; and given the special migration patterns of the protestants, this implies that nine out of ten migrants to the United States were likewise catholic.[3] This produced a series of self-reinforcing tendencies among Irish-Americans, in the outlook of native Americans, and (not least) in the growing preference for Canada among protestant emigrants. Irish-America now thought of itself as catholic in essence; native Americans, to a greater or lesser degree, agreed with them; and the descendants of the earlier presbyterian emigrants now distinctive abandoned their usual past identification of themselves as Irish for the distinctive and relatively novel (if not inaccurate) identification 'Scotch-Irish'. Indeed there was unconscious irony in the fact that most Irish-Americans, grasping the right to a dual national identity and culture as an immigrant people, denied that right to the presbyterians of Ulster, aspects of whose culture were strongly retained and transmitted in the United States.

The nature of the migration's epicentre, its axis stretching from mid-Tyrone and Monaghan south to east Cork and Kilkenny, together with Connacht's outflow coming heavily into the pattern, meant that its Irish-speaking component was very considerable, although not a majority one. Some half a million people, perhaps 550,000, from Munster and Connacht, or two-thirds their outflow from 1846 to 1855, were then Irish-speaking. Barony analysis of depopulation in Ulster and north Leinster, as in Kilkenny, shows higher incidence in residually

---

[1] See P. Mac Doinleibhe, 'Glimpses of the famine in Fermanagh' in *Clogher Rec.*, iv (1962), pp 187–9; Brian Ó Mórdha (ed.), 'The great famine in Monaghan: a coroner's account' in *Clogher Rec.*, iv (1960–61), pp 29–41, 175–86; Mullagh Historical Committee, *Portrait of a parish: Mullagh, Co. Cavan* (Cavan, 1988), pp 52–61; Peadar Livingstone, *The Fermanagh story* (Enniskillen, 1969), pp 196–203; Wallace Clark, *Rathlin: its story* (2nd ed., Limavady, 1988), pp 139–40; Ambrose Macaulay, *Patrick Dorrian: bishop of Down and Connor, 1865–85* (Dublin, 1987), pp 59–72; James Grant, 'The famine in Ulster' (Ph.D. thesis, Q.U.B., 1986).

[2] This balances Fitzpatrick's assertion, 'The catastrophe of the famine thus generated an immediate and lasting transformation in the regional patterns of outward migration' (above, v, 571).

[3] Evidence from Detroit (1853) and Pittsburgh (1850) confirms this, the more convincingly since the early sample dates cover more mixed pre-famine immigration, and since the one was on the border with the new Ulster settlements of Ontario, the other was the effective capital of largely Ulster-American west Pennsylvania (J. E. Vinyard, *The Irish on the urban frontier: Detroit, 1850–1880* (New York, 1976), pp 98–9; Walsh, ' "Big wather" ', p. 2 and n. 7).

Irish-speaking areas than in English-speaking ones in the same years.[1] From 1856 to 1880 at least a half-million or more Irish-speakers left for America.[2] Most were bilingual, and over time the importance of their speaking Irish diminished, yet at mid-century both priests and politicians knew the value of Irish, and protestant missionaries believed five-eighths of the Irish in New York city to be Irish-speakers.[3] From the 1870s the Irish language revival movement took its initial force, and much of its finance, from America. (All this is not to confound the mid-Victorian migration with that of the later nineteenth century: unlike those after 1880, even Irish-speakers came more from Ireland's interior than from its western seaboard.)

This brings us back to the geographical, economic, and social background of the migrants. The east Munster and south Leinster region was well served by banks and trade networks, by roads and carriage services, and by schools. Population densities were hardly overwhelming, approximating those of northern France; land values were high.[4] Thackeray fond the bookishness of its plain people unusual; Mgr Michael Buckley believed Cork people bought six of ten of all the books bought in Ireland, a fond if revealing judgement. The region had anticipated Pius IX's 'devotional revolution': the pre-famine religious commitments of the area had long been properly institutionalised and catechised, despite residual folkloric survivals. This was more so of smallholders' families, which produced youthful emigration, than of labourers, too immiserated to go.[5] Most of the people were also strongly nationalist in politics, largely in the moderate framework advanced by Daniel O'Connell before 1845, but many also in the informal and sometimes violent conspiracies of men with more pressing grievances. Indeed, geographically, this was the most politicised region of the country until the late 1870s.[6] As emigrants, they were far from the hopeless, uprooted

---

[1] For Ulster, collate *Census Ire., 1851*, H.C. 1852–3, xcii, 36, 61, 99, 150, 185, 224, 251, 285, 326, with ibid., *general report*, H.C. 1856, xxxi, pp xiv, 390, 404, 434, 448, 464, 475, 488, 500, 514. For Leinster, collate *Census Ire., 1851*, H.C. 1852–3, xci, 117, 185, 226, with ibid., *general report*, H.C. 1856, xxxi, 82, 117, 134; and T. Jones Hughes, 'East Leinster in the mid-nineteenth century' in *Ir. Geography*, iii, no. 5 (1958), pp 235–6, 239–40.

[2] Miller, *Emigrants & exiles*, p. 579, table 9.

[3] John T. Ridge, 'The hidden Gaeltacht in old New York' in *New York Irish History*, vi (1991–2), p. 15.

[4] Cf. 'Densité de la population rurale, 1845' in René Rémond, *Atlas historique de la France contemporaine, 1800–1965* (Paris, 1966), p. 36, with the regional population maps in T. W. Freeman, *Pre-famine Ireland* (Manchester, 1957), pp 168, 177, 184, 212, 220, 226; W. J. Smyth, in Patrick O'Flanagan and C. G. Buttimer, *Cork: history and society* (Dublin, 1993), pp 657, 682–96.

[5] Patrick J. Corish, *The catholic community in the seventeenth and eighteenth centuries* (Dublin, 1981), pp 101–9; Kevin Whelan, 'The catholic church in County Tipperary, 1700–1900' in William Nolan and Thomas McGrath (ed.), *Tipperary: history and society* (Dublin, 1985), pp 215, 230–54.

[6] Nolan & McGrath, *Tipperary*, pp 241, 255; end-maps in Angus MacIntyre, *The Liberator: Daniel O'Connell and the Irish party, 1830–1847* (London, 1965); K. T. Hoppen, 'Landlords, society, and electoral politics...' in C. H. E. Philpin (ed.), *Nationalism and popular protest in Ireland* (Cambridge, 1987), pp 287–90; see further the articles by M. J. Bric, M. R. Beames, and L. P. Curtis, jr, in the same volume, with a dissenting essay by Tom Garvin, which locates Ribbonism in the least formally politicised outer Ulster regions: the balance of agrarian outrage incidents does not support him.

lemmings of the implicit imagery of Handlin or Freeman. They were not already without some prior knowledge of, and leverage on, the arts and skills of mid-Victorian modernity, before going to America, British North America, or Britain: this indeed explains why they moved so easily between the four countries. While their capacities were real, however, they did fall short of a measured grasp of the innovations, structures, and power in those countries. This helps explain the heroic superficiality, the courageous error, of the fenianism of so many of them after 1858; those who did better understand these things, by preparation or by observation, usually had the wit to stand back from such adventurism.

There were indeed the truly uprooted and bewildered. These came from the south-western mountains and peninsulas, from parts of Clare and the more congested regions of Connacht. In the Atlantic seaboard areas, holdings were tiny, often still strips in common fields, English was little used, books and newspapers were little known, potato dependence almost absolute, population densities (in the habitable pockets) extraordinary, and real knowledge of the wider world—while not absent—mostly scraps gleaned from harvesting stays in Britain. Political consciousness was either dependent or inchoate.[1]

Outer Ulster was also distinctive. Population densities were very high, 300–350 per square mile in 1845, and normal holdings similar to Munster's, from five to twenty-five acres. But the canny marketing of skills, labour, and produce had partly withstood the decline of its chief base in domestic textiles, leaving a still monetised if precarious economy. Unlike Munster, outer Ulster had few proper towns; indeed, contrary to stereotype, only 9 per cent of the province's people lived in centres of 2,500 or more, most in the factory and mill towns of north-eastern, inner Ulster.[2] The anomaly in outer Ulster of a literate, market-oriented rural economy, without significant urbanisation, was unique in Ireland, although not unknown in parts of western Pennsylvania, to which many had gone since the 1790s, and to which many continued to go from the 1830s to the early 1860s. If the newer migrants were now largely catholic, they were sometimes more superstitious and less well catechised than those from Munster and Leinster, although by the later 1850s a striking improvement was clear across the province.[3] Yet they had the advantage of knowing both plain and poorer protestants; unlike those from Munster, they did not normally associate protestants with an oppressive and inherited social order. It is striking that such Ulster catholics, in marked contrast with our own times, were rarely found among the national-

---

[1] Hoppen, 'Landlords, society, and electoral politics . . .'; T. W. Freeman, *Pre-famine Ireland* (Manchester, 1957), pp 235–50, 264–8; Patrick Hickey, 'Famine, mortality, and emigration: a profile of six parishes . . .' in O'Flanagan & Buttimer, *Cork*, pp 873–917.
[2] W. H. Crawford, 'The evolution of the Ulster town, 1750–1850' in Peter Roebuck (ed.), *Plantation to partition* (Belfast, 1981), pp 140–56.
[3] S. J. Connolly, 'Catholicism in Ulster, 1800–1850' in Roebuck, *Plantation to partition*, pp 157–66; Oliver P. Rafferty, *Catholicism in Ulster, 1603–1983* (Dublin, 1994), pp 98–111, 145–55; Macaulay, *Patrick Dorrian*; Edward McCarron, *Life in Donegal, 1850–1900* (Cork, 1981), pp 15–22, 52, 87–90.

ist ideologues of Irish-America between 1850 and 1900. The exceptions, such as John Mitchel, John McClenahan, and William Carroll, were presbyterian townsmen.

Many small farmers fled all three of these distinctive regions, and more yet of their sons and daughters. They had much in common, despite what has just been said. Though few had capital and many were inured to hardship and privation, most had experience of money and markets, many of town life, almost all of labour and produce transactions, some of the law and the courts. Few came from the lowest, landless strata; few, by Irish rural standards, had been destitute. The tendency of most young immigrants to be described (or to describe themselves) from the late 1840s onwards as labourers and servants, before departure, confounds the crucial distinction of the Irish countryside between those who were actually so as their parents had been also, and smallholders' offspring so denoted by reason of recent work with their own or others' families.[1] Most had a rudimentary education and were literate, adaptable, and (if Irish-speaking) bilingual.[2] Almost all, as noted, were catholic, if they varied as to the seriousness of it. The men were politically inclined, if not politically skilled. Despite cliché, most were young and vigorous; few were heads of families. Convinced that Ireland had now failed them, they were determined on survival and improvement: 'in certain respects well fitted for the life he was to enter', the emigrant was 'from the moment of landing a special category of American, not a special category of Irish'.[3] Such was true even of Irish-speakers. Men such as Brooklyn real-estate dealer Michael Logan (founder of *An Gaodhail*) and William Hughes of Detroit (later editor of the *Michigan Catholic*) made wholly English-speaking careers, no less than did the nationalist leaders Michael Doheny and John O'Mahony. Only in isolated pockets, such as the Schuylkill mining valleys, was Irish commonly used; and only in very remote ones, such as Beaver Island in Lake Michigan, or the Mirimichi basin in New Brunswick, was it commonly transmitted to the next generation.[4] All this confirms a broader Americanisation among both Irish- and English-speakers. 'There are very few Irish people who do not pick up the

[1] Thus throughout the period 1837–1900 such categories rose from 65 per cent (1837) to 87 per cent (1855) to 91 per cent (1900) of all U.S. migrants (P. J. Blessing, table 22.3, in Drudy, *Irish in America*, p. 20), although labourers fell from 56 per cent of Ireland's agricultural workers (1841) to 38 per cent (1881) to 23 per cent (1926), with sons and relatives taking over much of the work (Samuel Clark in P. J. Drudy (ed.), *Ireland: land, people and politics* (Cambridge, 1982), table 2.1, p. 22, and Damian Hannan, ibid., table 7.1, p. 145).

[2] This was then noted (as novel) in the annual report of the American Protestant Society, 1849: 'many of the children and youth who now arrive from Ireland can read' (quoted in Ridge, 'Hidden Gaeltacht in old New York', p. 17); see data in John Logan, 'Sufficient to their needs: literacy and elementary schooling in the nineteenth century' in Mary Daly and David Dickson, *The origins of popular literacy in Ireland* (Dublin, 1990), fig. 1, p. 116.

[3] MacDonagh, 'Irish famine emigration', p. 430.

[4] See the articles by Proinsias Mac Aonghusa, Breandán Ó Buachalla, Liam Ó Dochartaigh, Breandán Ó Conaire, and Tomás de Bhaldraithe in Stiofán Ó hAnnracháin (ed.), *Go Meiriceá Siar: na Gaeil agus Meiriceá* (Dublin, 1979); Dennis Clark, *The Irish relations* (Rutherford, N.J., 1982), p. 222; Ridge, 'Hidden Gaeltacht in old New York', pp 13–17.

American accent, and the American form of speech', granted that those who 'studiously conceal that they are Irish . . . are units in thousands'.[1]

Such change was oddly accelerated by the very provincialism of residual Irish identities. 'The northerns look down on the southerns, and both dislike the Connachtfolk. The "far downs" i.e., the northerns, are despised by the "Corkeys", while the latter are odious to the former in a similar degree.'[2] For most, the evening balm of memory was thus of natal locality, not nationality, and scarcely threatened a workaday Americanism. Hence the vast provincial outflows from Ireland did not immediately constitute a common and vigorous Irish subculture in America to qualify the impact of the new society and polity. Instead Irish-America had to be actually made, partly by men with clear ideas of its possible potential forms, and partly more indirectly by the interplay of shared Irish traditions and the impact of America. Leaders were most effective when shaping the latter: churchmen in moulding inchoate belief against the shock of the new country's impersonal secularity and aggressive evangelicalism, politicians and nationalists in turning community bonds and customs into instruments for group pride and urban improvement. So competing provincial biases did but limited damage, though they remained obstacles to a more unified Irish-America. Irish provincialism thus oddly speeded acculturation and even assimilation. But the character of the emigrant was evident less in how the past constrained him than in what he did in America.

THE rapid urbanisation of the Irish says most about their adaptability.[3] Certainly by 1850 they had already concentrated in the industrialising northern states touching the Atlantic: here 748,000 of 962,000 of them lived—78 per cent, as against 40 per cent of all Americans. We lack evidence as to when this began, but so marked a pattern so close to 1847 suggests that it was no overnight product of the famine. By 1880, 1.2 million of 1.8 million Irish-born lived in the same states, or 67 per cent.[4] William V. Shannon, following Carl Wittke's views of 1939, and those of many others, put it crisply: 'The Irish were a rural people in Ireland and became a city people in the United States.' By contrast, D. H. Akenson bluntly replies: 'In 1870 even the Irish immigrants (much less the second or third

---

[1] Michael Buckley, *Diary of a tour in America in 1870 and 1871* (Dublin, 1889), pp 52, 151. Cf. the comments of a visiting English hatter, and of a leading Yankee intellectual convert to catholicism, both often thought anti-Irish: 'Irishmen or the sons of Irishmen are often more American than the natives' (J. D. Burn, *Three years among the working classes in the United States* (London, 1865)); 'The Irish people, the laity, are far less unAmerican than their clergy' (Orestes Brownson to Isaac Hecker, undated [1 June 1855], in J. F. Gower and R. M. Lelinert (ed.), *The Brownson–Hecker correspondence* (Notre Dame, Ind., 1979), p. 183).

[2] Buckley, *Diary of a tour*, p. 152 (Boston, 25 Sept. 1870).

[3] This is the realistic master-theme of the five books (*Irish in Philadelphia; Irish relations; Hibernia America; Erin's heirs* (Lexington, Ky., 1991); and *The Irish in Pennsylvania* (University Park, Pa., 1991)) and thirty papers of Dennis Clark.

[4] Harris and Jacobs, *Search for missing friends*, table 6, p. xxiv; Patrick J. Blessing, *The Irish in America: a guide to the literature and the manuscript collections* (Washington, D.C., 1992), pp 290–91. I have followed Harris, not Blessing, Winsberg, or the U.S. census bureau, by including Delaware, Maryland, and Washington, D.C., in this region, as it was for both Irish and Scots-Irish before them.

generation) were not a city people.' All three scholars are referring to this main migration.[1] Yet new research confirms the pattern of urbanisation to be indeed fundamental, and even remarkable. For not only were the incoming Irish now urbanised almost *en bloc* in the United States (and considerably so in British America), they became among the most urbanised people in the world, notably more so than the Americans as a whole, and more so than almost all peoples in Europe, except in Britain and the Low Countries. They remained thus for half a century, until other major ethnic groups, and populations elsewhere, began to catch up.[2] While most notable in America's industrialised 'core' area, as has long been argued,[3] the precise patterns were more distinctive than those of the core itself. Well over four-fifths of the specialised regional literature on the Irish in the United States deals with the Irish in towns and cities. It includes most of the earlier scientific literature on Irish-America, pioneered not by Irish-Americans seeking modernist credentials, but rather by America's founder scholars of urban history, such as Arthur Schlesinger, sr, Marcus Hansen, and Oscar Handlin.

In short, from the 1840s, building on precedents,[4] Irish-Americans became the people of the country's urban future, rather than of its then present of farms, commerce, and villages, much less of its almost wholly rural past. That the descendants of the previous migrants, for whom we lack data, may indeed have largely replicated native American (rather than newly immigrating Irish) patterns, and stayed or migrated within the countryside, probably hastened the division between the 'old' and the newer Irish-America, and further distanced the 'Scotch-Irish' from others.

By 1870, just nine out of ten Irish-born, or 1.68 million out of 1.85 million, lived in the eighteen states of the nation's developed northern core.[5] This ran 500 miles from Portland in southern Maine to Baltimore in Maryland, and thence a

[1] W. V. Shannon, *The American Irish* (rev. ed., New York, 1966), p. 27; Carl Wittke, *We who built America* ([1939], rev. ed., Cleveland, 1964), p. 145; Wittke, *Irish in America*, pp 23–31; Akenson, *Being had*, pp 37–107; D. H. Akenson, *Small differences: Irish catholics and Irish protestants, 1815–1922* (Kingston and Montreal, 1988), p. 107. Earlier versions by Akenson follow his own Canadian studies by refusing to distinguish Scots-Irish migrants, and other early nineteenth-century protestant Irish settlers, from the post-1845 exodus, so that one may more charitably regard his assertion 'there is no positive evidence available . . . for the existence of the fundamental "fact" of the history of the Irish as an ethnic group in America—that they were a city people' (D. H. Akenson, 'Data: what is known about the Irish in North America?' in Oliver MacDonagh and W. F. Mandle (ed.), *Ireland and Irish-Australia* (London and Sydney, 1986), p. 10).
[2] David N. Doyle, 'The Irish as urban pioneers in the United States, 1850–1870' in *Journal of American Ethnic History*, x (1990), pp 36–59.
[3] David Ward, *Cities and immigrants* (New York, 1971), pp 59–81; R. K. Vedder and L. E. Gallaway, 'The geographical distribution of British and Irish emigrants to the United States after 1800' in *Scottish Journal of Political Economy*, xix (1972), pp 19–35; Vedder and Gallaway with V. Shukla, 'The distribution of the immigrant population in the United States: an economic analysis' in *Explorations in Economic History*, ii (1974), pp 213–26.
[4] Of earlier scholars alert to this urban reality, one did realise the pattern was well begun before the famine: George Potter, *To the golden door: the story of the Irish in Ireland and America* (Boston and Toronto, 1960), pp 170–75, dealing with 1820–40.
[5] What follows summarises Doyle, 'The Irish as urban pioneers'.

thousand miles westwards to southern Minnesota, and south to central Missouri at St Louis. This vast area, roughly rhomboid in shape, was only one-fifth of the whole country, and as yet its industrial zones were confined to the east coast and the river valleys there, apart from a few outliers such as Pittsburgh and Cincinnati. But the region contained over three-quarters of the country's urban population, about two-thirds of all its people, and the great bulk of its manufacturing capacity. Elsewhere there were considerable numbers of Irish in only two states: 54,000 in California and 17,000 in Louisiana. Whereas the American-born were well distributed throughout these twenty states in the core plus California and Louisiana, 70 per cent (1.3 million) of the Irish lived in less than one-seventh of the twenty states' component counties (in but 146 out of 1,090 counties). These 146 counties were all urban and industrial, or occasionally mining, counties (or both).

The roots of such urban patterns go back to the later eighteenth century, but its reality owed most to the convergence of post-1840 mass migration with America's industrialisation. Yet urban precedents in Ireland, the newer models of livelihood in Britain, and a distaste for wide-open spaces and their lack of community were contributory factors. The pattern in the core states was already established by 1850, pioneered by pre-famine arrivals, as was settlement in Louisiana. California, the sole post-famine addition to the pattern, owed its position to the coincidence of annexation, gold rush, and famine migration. From 1850 to 1870 concentration, as a proportion of all Irish in the U.S.A., neither markedly increased nor diminished in the major industrial states of the core zone (New York, Pennsylvania, Massachusetts, and Ohio). It did increase, however, in New Jersey and Illinois, as these were absorbed into the manufacturing areas of the zone by the New York Central railroad and its auxiliaries, a grid complete by 1860. Indeed, later nineteenth-century change was only towards even further concentration within the zone, rather than dispersal away from it. After 1870, and especially after 1880, relative Irish densities in lower New England, in New York, New Jersey, and Pennsylvania, began to rise again, for reasons similar to those of the 1840s: a renewed Irish outflow seeking former neighbours and kinfolk in cities enjoying further rounds of industrial growth, now based not only on steam, water power, iron, and coal, but also on steel, oil, and chemicals. Even with the larger plants this new industrialism brought, most factories remained small. But the preference of male newcomers for mobile, often outdoor work, from the 1870s onward found men disproportionately taking railroad and construction jobs, and leaving much factory work to immigrant single women, a major change since the 1840s. Despite this, the years 1845–70 plainly laid out the pattern of the urban and industrial settlements of the Irish, a geography as distinct as that of the Scotch-Irish settlers a century before them, and for many of the same reasons: expanding and available livelihoods, kinship networks, familiarity of terrain, and the chance to re-create church and community. Both waves of Irish settled the available, unclosed America of their own times, and occasionally overlapped:

James Crockett settled the still empty land of mid-Pennsylvania as a pioneer presbyterian farmer in 1810, and was still alive when catholic miners filled the region's new anthracite mining hamlets after 1845.

The urban-industrial counties of the core states contained grids of small cities, factory towns, and mill villages (called 'villes' in Connecticut), and sometimes a large city, or mining centre, or a railway junction. Such varied counties were not unknown to migrants who had lived in the Lagan valley, or remigrants who had worked in the Scots lowlands, northern England, or south Wales. Settlements, like workplaces, were small-scale. They were rarely far from each other before 1870. The Irish preferred counties geared to their own sense of distance, as they did towns of a certain intimacy. Finding these things, they dug in, even as America's industrialism distended geographically. This helps explain the irony that their concentration increased even as urban America spread. Industrial south New England was no larger than Munster and Leinster combined; New York city was only 88 miles from Philadelphia and 218 from Boston. By contrast, western distances chilled the newcomers: New York was 830 miles from Chicago and 1,300 from Omaha. The chief eastern factory districts were thus accessible to each other, even on foot for poorer job-seekers.

This too explains why, within a broad continuity in the counties of the developed core region, there appear three changing stages of relative Irish settlement patterns as between their cities. First, an initial overconcentration in the largest cities, usually ports, to 1850. Secondly, a gradual dispersal from these through all the cities of the main eighteen-state core region and elsewhere, between 1850 and 1860. Thirdly, after 1860, a slow abandonment of most interior and southern cities (except Chicago, Cleveland, Pittsburgh, and St Louis), a renewed identification with the country's leading fifteen cities, notably those of the Atlantic north-east, and a distinct web of lesser Irish centres in which their share of the inhabitants dwarfed these smaller cities' importance. These too were in the intimate, industrial north-east, notably Lowell, Worcester, and Cambridge. Despite a doubling of the number of American cities between 1870 and 1900, these latter trends held constant thereafter to the end of the century.[1]

Originally forced to become continent-wide pioneers by the famine crisis and the labour gluts created by it, chasing unskilled and semi-skilled livelihoods wherever they offered (like the Mexican *braceros* of more recent times), eventually, given a choice, migrants sought locales that were congenial, familiar, and receptive: the heavily Irish working-class and catholic subcultures of the north-eastern factory cities, or alternatively the cosmopolitan great cities, such as New York, Chicago, and San Francisco, each too large to permit imposition of a single cultural standard. Elsewhere, throughout the south and midwest, two major changes began to make the Irish uncomfortable in the local cities. First, even by

---

[1] U.S. *Seventh census* [De Bow] (1850), p. 399; *Eighth census* [Kennedy] (1860), xxxi–xxxii; *Ninth census* (1870), i, 386–91; *Eleventh census* (1890), pt 1, cxl; *Twelfth census* (1900), i, 430–43, 796–800, 874–7.

1860, both regions had ceased on balance to draw native-born Americans from the east coast states. Secondly, after 1870 these regions migrated their own children either further west, or to the new cities (e.g. Tulsa, Rockford, Birmingham) or established ones (e.g. Milwaukee, Cincinnati, Atlanta), booming in their own zones. Both areas were now more local in tone.[1]

Thus the obvious thesis that the Irish avoided contracting opportunity cannot be sustained. Economically the more open midwestern region was growing. Indeed, while the relationship in the south between low wages for labouring and slow population growth and low in-migration does help account for virtual Irish abandonment of the zone by 1870, the midwest experienced high labouring wages, much foreign in-migration, and high population growth rates, and yet a dramatic fall-off in Irish new arrivals between 1850 and 1869. The comparison with New England and the Atlantic coast cannot explain it (except in so far as the labouring and other opportunities were there innumerable, though not markedly better paid).[2] For in the midwest there was no simple pattern of either increasing or declining opportunity, either for Irish newcomers or for long-term Irish residents. In Jacksonville, Illinois, the Irish were at the bottom of the social and occupational heap in 1880 as in 1850, whereas in Ripon, Wisconsin, they had markedly improved their situation. Midwestern pay levels and costs together were neither markedly better nor worse by the 1870s than in the east for incoming labourers and other workers granted initially favourable differences in the 1850s. True, for the highest levels of factory operatives, such as machinists, pay became somewhat higher in the east, as the market share of larger enterprises based there increased, but such positions were infrequently held by the Irish. On the railroads, which drew so many Irish, the real differentials of pay were between the various midwestern trunk systems in the mid-1870s, if differentials between labourers and skilled workers were sometimes less in the east. Perhaps a housing shortage directed the young Irish away from the midwest as they reached the stage of family formation. Above all, however, the real differences were in longer-term prospects for those who stayed around. The very 'openness' of the midwest (and the mountain and Pacific states) itself posed a barrier against latecomers; in societies of so many recent 'winners' the unsuccessful were more usually deemed to deserve their fate than in the more settled eastern states, as it was 'the general temper of western society . . . to make its poorer members feel not only unfortunate but infamous'.[3] It did not make it easier for Irish 'losers', 'on the other side of the tracks', that many of their Irish contemporaries, having migrated perhaps

[1] Lawrence Gelfand, 'The problem of the eastward movement in America, 1850–1930' in Ciaran Brady (ed.), *The American city* (Dublin, 1988), pp 39–44.

[2] Stanley Lebergott, *Manpower in American economic growth: the American record since 1800* (New York, 1964), figures at pp 79–82, 86.

[3] *Valedictory of the Hon. Thos Selby* . . . (San Francisco, 1871), p. 14, quoted in R. A. Burchell, *The San Francisco Irish, 1848–1880* (Manchester, 1979), p. 71; U.S. Dept of the Treasury, Bureau of Statistics [Edward Young, compiler], *Labor in Europe and the United States* (Philadelphia, 1875), pp 739–47, 751, 753, 758–9, 785–8, 796–9, 804, 806.

only a few years before them, were prosperously ensconced in good neighbour-hoods nearby.

By contrast, in the south wages and conditions were fairly consistent, and lower than elsewhere. If provisions were as cheap as in the midwest, tenement rents were very high (after the civil war they were three times New England rates). Battered by yellow fever and malaria, despised even by free blacks, enclaves of Irish labourers diminished, lacking social mobility, or even secure niches, in the south's hierarchic, semi-tropical isolation. The exceptions networked the great railroads (once built)—a grid of opportunity, high wages, and promotion, unusually immune to southern patterns. Other Irish improved incrementally in the industrialising cities of the post-reconstruction south, especially if they brought acquired industrial skills.

Thus cultural and regional factors, the 'personality' of individual cities, and even the attitudes of the Irish already there, played vital parts in redirecting Irish migration, doing so even from the south. Increasingly, the humbler Irish chose small factory cities, where low incomes and limited chances to rise were redeemed by Irish dominance and where working daughters (sons being more apt to roam) could supplement limited family budgets. Some more ambitious immigrants now chose those great cities mixed and fluid enough to allow blue-collar entry and white-collar upward mobility, even power, and (if desired) anonymity and secularity; others found in them a counterpointing familiarity and parish catholi-cism to humanise the excitement of the large.

Catholicism of itself did not draw: western cities in the 1850s had consistently more catholic church provision relative to their populations than most eastern ones,[1] often funded by quite up-market 'old' families who also had made an earlier start in the provision of catholic secondary education. The new Irish clannishly preferred investment in their own social infrastructure: schools, churches, hospi-tals, orphanages, clubs. Orestes Brownson was not entirely the catholic nativist that Irish editors held him when he noted: 'The mass of our catholics think only of enjoying their religion for themselves.'[2]

If the famine scattered the Irish as urban pioneers everywhere in the United States, and created their urban precedents in Canada, by the 1870s they were becoming less adventurous, and settling for the predictable. They now more rarely went to non-eastern cities dominated by native protestant,[3] or even German-American, populations, even those with a founding catholic American

[1] Vinyard, *Irish on the urban frontier*, pp 333, 346.
[2] Brownson to Isaac Hecker, 29 Sept. 1857 (Gower & Lelinert, *Brownson–Hecker corr.*, p. 201); the problems of declining priest–people ratios in Ireland until 1847, and of servicing the diaspora thereafter, partly account for this frame of mind (Edmund M. Hogan, *The Irish missionary movement . . . 1830–1980* (Dublin, 1990), pp 13–24, 62–8).
[3] 'Though the native stock were in a numerical minority, they had most firmly set their imprint on the form of San Francisco, and settled . . . what the major lines of development would be' (Burchell, *San Francisco Irish*, p. 180). Classic studies by Richard Wade on the urban frontier, Bayrd Still on Milwaukee, Bessie L. Pierce on Chicago, and Melvin Holli on Detroit show the same of those cities with demographically 'foreign stock' majorities.

element. Yet far from being demoralised 'pioneers of the urban ghetto', many Irish early desired a secure social footing in prospering but open cities in which they were ghettoised neither by prejudice nor by their own parochial fears, but rather were able both to see themselves and their children improve their own livelihood and circumstances, and yet offer nephews and nieces from Ireland abundant, if more modest, beginnings. Only very rarely did they cling to a relatively declining city, though Albany offered one example. After 1880, there were major differences between the limited social mobility open to the Irish in New England factory towns, the greater chances open to them in New York and Pennsylvania (especially in both the cities with populations of over a million, and in towns in their interiors), and the relative equality of opportunity offered more widely in the midwest, so that their growing preference after 1860 against direct midwestern settlement might appear a mistaken gamble. Possibly the greater availability of skilled jobs in the east, as it grew and diversified so rapidly, meant that labourers and semi-skilled Irishmen, for whom there were midwestern openings, sensed that the next rungs—if only for their sons—were eastwards. Possibly that very availability absorbed the more venturesome anyway. But, even more interestingly, it seems that the supplements to 'family economy', which made the difference between poverty and comfort in Irish working families, were less available in the west. San Francisco in 1852 had only one job for an Irish girl or woman for every twenty-five jobs for Irish men, and even in 1880 but one to four. New York city had about two women's jobs for every three men's among the Irish in 1855.[1] The midwest was generally closer to the western than the eastern pattern: domestics in the midwest were usually native-born, German, or Scandinavian, and in the south, of course, black. By contrast, the heavy concentration of Irish in Rhode Island was due to the existence of large numbers of mill jobs, not merely for young women, but—unlike elsewhere in the north—even for children into the 1880s.[2] In short, it was not job opportunities so much as 'family' survival patterns, born of necessity, that were involved. There are still unanswered questions about the Irish urban pattern of the mid-century and its long-term results, since adult job availability alone was not seemingly crucial after the 1850s. Certainly by 1870 their urban networks of 1900 were strikingly set already.[3]

AMERICA's cities were for many a sequence of temporary resting places; for others, death camps that soon turned escape into a graveyard; for others, a transfer

---

[1] Burchell, *San Francisco Irish*, pp 54–5; Michael R. Haines and Claudia Goldin in Theodore Hershberg (ed.), *Philadelphia: work, space, family, and group experience in the nineteenth century. Essays toward an interdisciplinary history of the city* (New York and Oxford, 1981), ch. 7, pp 256–79, and ch. 8, pp 280–96; and Robert Ernst, *Immigrant life in New York city, 1825–1863* (Syracuse, 1994), pp 65–9, 214–17, recalculated.

[2] In 1851, Welcome Sayles noted that many of these children, 'chained to the wheel by poor or exacting parents', had had their only schooling in Ireland (Peter J. Coleman, *The transformation of Rhode Island, 1790–1860* (Providence, R.I., 1963), pp 234–5, 238–41).

[3] Below, pp 756–7.

from threadbare rural destitution to grinding tenement poverty, with the added burden of unremitting labour unknown in peasant society. Early death rates were appalling, if variable. While the great difference between rates in Philadelphia and those in lower Manhattan and in Broad Street and Fort Hill in Boston confirms the destructiveness of the worst slums, yet the persistence of high levels of mortality, after the severest poverty in America receded, raises questions, as do the lower levels among poor German catholics in the Manhattan slums. Among Irish men, high rates were plainly related to hard physical labour, which lowered life expectancy well into the medically more competent early twentieth century. To the typhus, typhoid, and dysentery that spread through all the Irish settlements after 1845 but receded after 1849, were added a major cholera outbreak in the latter year, and, above all, the beginnings of mass endemic tuberculosis, which thereafter dogged the urban Irish beyond the 1920s. If slums made for the highest density of typhus, typhoid, and cholera deaths—partly sparing Philadelphia with its better housing for workers—dysentery was most common where (as in Boston or Lowell) civic sanitation was primitive. Tuberculosis, by contrast, followed the Irish disproportionately, almost regardless of their dwellings, just as it hit fewer immigrants from continental European cities, no matter how overcrowded their tenements. This was plainly a matter of previous exposure and the gradual genetic immunity acquired by continentals, in contrast with those from rural Ireland, where the disease had been rare or unknown. It multiplied in the moist, warm air of textile mills (falling off during lockouts and unemployment) and in apartments warmed by steam heat.

In the early and mid-1850s, death rates of the Irish-born in Boston were 142 per cent of those of the native-born; but they were only 60 per cent of native death rates in New York city, and 58 per cent in Philadelphia. Thus Irish rates differed markedly by city: in 1855, Boston lost 37.7 per thousand of Irish birth, New York 21.1, and Philadelphia 12.2. Different circumstances of livelihood, housing, and sanitation were involved. Further, the Boston community was all but an overnight, famine-rooted one; those of the other cities were much older, so that in them the Irish made a high contribution to 'native' deaths due to the high mortality of their offspring. This confuses direct contrast, as do the low death rates of established 'old' Irish families.[1] The Irish were not unresponsive to the lessons taught. There was a persistent migration from the pest centres of the east coast upstate or inland. Most dramatically, an early diffusion throughout the cities of the south was rapidly scaled down, with few newcomers after the

---

[1] Clark, *Irish in Philadelphia*, pp 48–9, 200 n. 49; D. B. Cole, *Immigrant city: Lawrence, Massachusetts, 1845–1921* (Chapel Hill, N.C., 1963), p. 29; Handlin, *Boston's immigrants*, pp 114–17; Jay P. Dolan, *The immigrant church: New York's Irish and German catholics, 1815–1865* (Baltimore, 1975), pp 33–40; Ernst, *Immigrant life in New York city*, pp 50–54; Brian C. Mitchell, *The Paddy camps: the Irish of Lowell, 1821–61* (Champaign, Ill., 1988), pp 106–8, and table 4, p. 158. These death rates are the more startling when one notes that the age pyramid of the Irish-born disproportionately excluded those (under 15 and over 55) most subject to mortality (Deirdre Mageean, 'Nineteenth-century emigration' in Drudy, *Irish in America*, fig. 3.1, p. 52).

mid-1850s. There pandemic yellow fever and malaria added to the usual hazards, with extraordinary death rates from 1845 to 1860, peaking with a rate of about 200 per 1,000 in New Orleans in the epidemic year of 1853.[1]

High Irish death rates persisted in eastern cities, and indeed improvements after the 1850s were sometimes very slow: New York state in 1910 had a rate for Irish-born males of 25.9 compared with 13.8 for those of U.S. birth, and 12.9 for Italians (who had generally poorer living conditions). Even the American-born Irish reflected this. As late as 1920, the offspring of Irish mothers had mortality rates between one-third and one-half higher than those of native parentage in Chicago, as in Pennsylvania and New York state. A more balanced sample from various areas still showed a median differential of 42 per cent. The children of the Irish suffered less in the 1920s than in the 1850s, but still unequally so: their infant mortality rate was 90.7 per 1,000 births compared with 75.8 for the infants of American-born mothers (though better than the 112.9 for those of Austrian-born mothers). The contrast of their higher adult mortality with those of poorer 'new immigrants' from eastern and southern Europe (except in the matter of infant mortality), cannot be explained by housing, livelihood, or sanitation, and raises still unanswered questions. Little wonder a leading Irish medical man in New York city correctly noted in 1918: 'The Irish in America have by far the poorest resistance to diseases in general than [*sic*] all the immigrants from Europe', concluding America was a graveyard by contrast with home. Indeed, Irish life expectancy had for half a century been higher in Ireland's countryside than in America's cities (for men, but less so for women). Plainly, if mere economics do not explain the settlement patterns of the Irish in America, likewise the traditional measure, that holds life expectancy to be the arbiter and mirror of living standards, cannot explain (as the same doctor conceded) why nothing could hold the young from America.[2]

The key to their movement was the density of both life and prospects in the American city, which they learned before most native Americans. The United States was predominantly rural even in 1914, with its growing trend towards

---

[1] Earl F. Niehaus, *The Irish in New Orleans, 1800–1860* (Baton Rouge, La., 1965; New York, 1976), pp 31–3, though his conclusion (that the Irish stayed put, and did not respond by out-migration and curbing in-migration) is in error: see above, pp 743, 745.

[2] Austin O'Malley, M.D., Ph.D., LL.D., 'Irish vital statistics in America' in *Studies*, vii (1918), pp 623–32; L. I. Dublin and G. W. Baker, 'Mortality of race stocks in Pennsylvania and New York' in *Journal of the American Statistical Association*, xvii (1920), pp 13–44; James J. Walsh, M.D., commentary thereon in *Studies*, x (1920), pp 628–32; Robert E. Kennedy, *The Irish: emigration, marriage and fertility* (Berkeley, Calif., 1973), pp 45–65; U.S. Bureau of the Census, Dept of Commerce, *Immigrants and their children, 1920* (Washington, D.C., 1927), pp 198–9, 202–7; none of these figures is directly comparable to those of the 1850s because of standardisation adopted to counteract the different age-pyramids of immigrants and native-born populations. It is striking that O'Malley attributed the causes to degeneracy caused by change of climate (in *Studies*, v (1916), p. 530) when so many of the conditions he saw, studied, and treated were stress-related, from cardio-vascular deaths to mental disorders, or rooted in cultural poverty, as with high infant mortality; journalists better understood the pressures on the Irish, e.g. John Spargo, *The bitter cry of the children* [1906], ed. W. Trattner (Chicago, 1968), pp 25–7.

urbanisation largely populated from Irish and other European countries; not dissimilar portions of the Irish at home lived in towns until that time.[1] And the earlier disproportionate urbanisation of the Irish in the United States, together with continuing migration from Ireland, meant that the head start of the Irish element in the make-up of urban America was not lost throughout the nineteenth century. Indeed by 1900 the offspring of Irish-born parents added between 100 per cent and 200 per cent to the Irish-born populations of most American cities. Total Irish elements in many of them (especially in the north-east) were thus not dissimilar to those between 1850 and 1870, despite the coming of millions of 'new immigrants' from continental Europe. This dynamism of the Irish—in terms of livelihood, family formation, reproduction, and continuing in-migration—meant that, whether larger or smaller, American cities remained magnets of familiarity to newcomers. In Ireland, while towns represented impressive proportions of town-dwelling by the continental European standards of the time, they were after 1850 the residua of a people in decline, with the number of towns of between 2,500 and 100,000 inhabitants actually falling from 104 in 1841 to 87 in 1901. By contrast, America's towns and cities were the engines of a people in rapid growth. In 1840 there were but 129 places of those sizes (2,500 to 100,000), where in 1900 there were 2,654; in 1840, but three larger cities (of over 100,000), in 1900 another 61 (where Ireland still had but two large ones: Dublin and Belfast, the latter having surpassed Cork). The old commonplace that the cities of the Irish were in America acquires new meaning. In the case of County Cork, preeminent source of emigrants, it was indeed as though the very habit of urbanism itself underwent Atlantic migration.[2]

Frequent participation in Ireland in town rituals and exchanges, at irregular fairs and more regular markets, habituated country folk to urban patterns (in Ireland fairs and markets were frequently in inverse proportion to formal urbanisation, so that even those from the Atlantic west and outer Ulster thereby compensated for lack of formal experience of towns). Thus a people used to some urban living and excitement made the American city partly in their own image in its formative era, and then held on to it by demography, migration, and politics until the first world war. Moreover the style and type of city in these years suited their jumbled, face-to-face custom of market and town relations. This crowded city—in which businesses, tenements, workshops, and small factories, stalls, shops, and carts all crowded brick-lined streets, in common neighbourhoods—

---

[1] Percentage of population in cities over 2,500:

	1840/41	1870/71	1900/01	1920/26
Ireland	13	21	32	35
U.S.A.	10.7	25	40	51

Data computed from Vaughan & Fitzpatrick, *Ir. hist. statistics*, pp 28–48; *U.S. historical statistics to 1970*, ser. A 57–72.

[2] Patrick O'Flanagan, in O'Flanagan & Buttimer, *Cork*, pp 410–67.

only later began to alter its character by segregating its districts both functionally and socially. One of these old, mixed, part-Irish streets (Polk Street, in San Francisco) has been remembered as 'still little changed . . . still lit with gas, still bustling with a big-city-neighbourhood community life—modest, shoddy, and now so out of date'.[1]

Livelihood was neither life nor community, but was indispensable to both. The Irish then, and their historians since, are divided as to whether the American city offered more, or less, than the Irish countryside in decline. D. W. Cahill, linguist, scientist, and priest, who came to America in 1859, conceded the new country's 'exceptional poverty, its local distresses, its grinding destitutions', but held on balance that steady employment, high wages, and the chance of savings all made for the estimable 'position, condition, and social life of the labouring classes in America'. At home, Irish labourers rarely acquired farms or shops, or escaped the condition 'of the half-starved slave of daily trade', so that the young and unmarried Irish were better off coming to the States. Others agreed, though Thomas Mooney saw that labouring was for those with no other skill, and to be abandoned quickly, except that the early marriage of new immigrants kept them 'in the nasty labour which is alone open to friendless strangers' until they could put their daughters in service to improve their position. But Michael Kennedy, an immigrant for ten years, replied to Cahill from Troy (a heavily Irish iron and textiles town) that the Irish were 'the hardest worked, the worst paid, the most abused, the oftenest insulted, and the least respected (by Americans) of any other [*sic*] people in this country'.[2]

Kerby Miller gives the modern version of this:

Nearly all studies of the Irish in mid-century North America exhibit a deadening and depressing sameness. Irish emigrants were disproportionately concentrated in the lowest-paid, least-skilled, and most dangerous and insecure employment, with the highest rates of transience, residential density and segregation, inadequate housing and sanitation, commitals to prisons and charity institutions, and excess mortality. Upward occupational mobility was unusually slight.[3]

Such deadening sameness, punctuated only by misfortune and unemployment, would not have continued to draw millions from Ireland after 1855. True, the great body of male immigrants were increasingly drawn from among labourers at home (if one includes small farmers' sons calling themselves such);[4] and many would initially serve as general labourers after emigration. Had previous experience made many think favourably of labouring? Did American experience of it give grounds for hope? In Ireland seasonal agricultural labour, paying as little as

[1] Kenneth Rexroth, 'Afterword' in Frank Norris, *McTeague: a story of San Francisco* (New York, 1964), p. 343; Sam Bass Warner, jr, *The urban wilderness* (New York, 1972), pp 81–4.

[2] Cahill in *Boston Pilot*, 28 Jan. 1860; Kennedy in *Tipperary Advocate*, 21 July 1860; Thomas Mooney, *Nine years in America* (Dublin, 1850), pp 37–41.

[3] Miller, *Emigrants & exiles*, p. 315.

[4] Rising from 39 per cent in 1831 to 85 per cent in 1867 (above, v, tables 4 and 5, pp 611, 612, and pp 575–7). See also p. 739, n. 1.

4*d*. daily in Munster in 1845, or temporary public works labour during the famine, could be much improved if one got a job amongst the 30,000–40,000 railroad labourers of the country's brief railroad boom of 1847; a remarkable 18*d*. daily was normal, and status was commensurate, quite unlike that of contemporary 'railway navvies' in Britain. In America, labouring proved for some a lottery and for others a life sentence, sometimes mitigated by some job security and by family earnings. Comparison of the labouring communities from 1850 shows that they did not engross the majority of Irish working people anywhere; that the numbers and proportions so engaged differed widely; that there were great varieties of working condition among labourers; that their living conditions and housing also differed greatly; and that their chance to alter their condition, while low and uncertain, was not foreclosed.[1] Moreover, in the 1850s higher proportions of the Irish workforce were labourers in western, southern, and midwestern towns than in the east coast cities, though oddly labourers' wages were then higher in the east. Roughly between one-fifth and two-fifths of male immigrants were labourers in eastern cities between 1850 and 1870; inland and westwards, up to one-half of them were (although their numbers were much smaller).[2] The sheer visibility of gangs of Irish labourers in construction, railroad-making, freightage, iron-making, and much else probably deflected attention from the majority of the Irish in blue-collar jobs. In 1855 New York city had 19,000 Irish labourers and porters in a city workforce of over 200,000 (of whom 85,000 were Irish-born). In 1850 Philadelphia had 8,000 in a male workforce of 100,000 (of whom 27,000 were Irish-born), and Boston had 7,000 in a workforce of 44,000 (of whom 15,000 were Irish-born). To the west, Buffalo had 600 labourers among 2,700 Irish heads-of-family.[3]

Such numbers should surely alter stereotypes. Extraordinary differences of condition separated $2.75-a-day rail-layers from 80c.-a-day labourers; or the well paid in San Francisco in the 1850s from those scrabbling for subsistence in

[1] See Ernst, *Immigrant life in New York city*, pp 61–72; Thernstrom, *Poverty & progress*, pp 15–32; Mark Wyman, *Immigrants in the valley: Irish, Germans, and Americans in the upper Mississippi country, 1830–1860* (Chicago, 1983), pp 75–105; Clark, *Hibernia America*, pp 23–33; Wittke, *Irish in America*, pp 37–9.

[2] Given, or recalculated from data (East) in Handlin, *Boston's immigrants*, tables XIII and XV, pp 251, 253; Ernst, *Immigrant life in New York city*, table 27, pp 214–17; Clark, *Irish in Philadelphia*, p. 74, and table 1, p. 75; Theodore Hershberg and others, 'Occupation and ethnicity in five nineteenth-century cities: a collaborative inquiry' in *Historical Methods Newsletter*, vii (1974), pp 174–216, graph 5; (West, Midwest) Walsh, 'Across the "Big wather" ', p. 10; Vinyard, *Irish on the urban frontier*, pp 150, 390–91; Bessie Louise Pierce, *History of Chicago, ii: 1848–1871* (Chicago, 1940), p. 499; R. D. Weber, 'Socioeconomic change in Racine, 1850–1880' in *Journal of the West*, xiii (1974), pp 105–6; Burchell, *San Francisco Irish*, pp 54–5; P. J. Blessing, 'West among strangers: Irish migration to California, 1850–1880' (Ph.D. thesis, U.C.L.A., 1977), table 6.7, p. 289; Vinyard, *Irish on the urban frontier*, table A.48, p. 420; Lebergott, *Manpower . . . since 1800*, table A-25, p. 541.

[3] Handlin, *Boston's immigrants*; Ernst, *Immigrant life in New York city*; B. Laurie, T. Hershberg, and G. Alter, 'Immigrants and industry: the Philadelphia experience, 1850–1880' in Hershberg, *Philadelphia*, pp 107, 110; L. A. Glasco, *Ethnicity and social structure: Irish, Germans and native-born of Buffalo, N.Y., 1850–1860* (New York, 1980), pp 94–7. As the N.Y. 1855 state census was conducted in summer, when male heads of family were often unlisted (being out of town as railroad, farm, or other labourers), the Buffalo and N.Y. city figures are under-enumerations.

Hartford or Providence during construction downturns in 1857 or 1877; or both from the migratory labourers who travelled seasonally to the American south in winter and worked in northern camps in summer; above all, great differences separated those in semi-permanent employment from those fleeing from job to job. Once turned family men, Irish labourers sometimes accumulated property (houses and furniture) faster than other immigrants, and much faster than their analogues among native Americans. Boarding houses, trackside shanties, and casual work were, at best, traded for security of place and task.[1] If among native Americans labouring was increasingly linked to low-living social marginals and outcasts, the Irish saw it otherwise—as a youthful probation for more varied work or a more stable situation. Thomas Mooney in 1850 pointed out that common labour fetched 80c. or 3s. 4d. daily (four times the then Irish rate); that provisions were only a third of their Irish cost, although clothing, house rent, and fuel were closer to costs at home, 'and [there was] a certainty of employment and the facility of acquiring houses and lands, and education for your children, a hundred to one greater' than in Ireland. Twenty-five years later, Mgr Buckley reluctantly reached the same conclusions, a view then carefully supported by the touring representative of British and Irish agricultural labour, Peter O'Leary, in 1877.[2] While cruel exploitation was real enough, much of the labourers' hyperbole and aggression as to exploitation, disease, casual dismissal, and charges against their wages had to do with the failure of expected savings and of improving chances; but labouring in America still offered a real hope of improvement, denied at home. Indeed, wage data suggest this was more so for immigrant labourers than for artisans.[3] Yet they

[1] Hershberg and others, 'Occupation and ethnicity', tables 9, 10, and 11; Thernstrom, *Poverty & progress*, table 7, p. 119; Glasco, *Ethnicity and social structure*, pp 132–40; Clark, *Irish in Philadelphia*, pp 54–60; Burchell, *San Francisco Irish*, pp 61–6; Clark, *Hibernia America*, p. 28.

[2] Mooney, *Nine years in America*, pp 21–2; William Smith O'Brien, *Lectures on America* (Dublin, 1860), p. 15; Buckley, *Diary of a tour*, pp 144, 241; Peter O'Leary, *Travel and experiences in Canada, the Red River territory and the United States* (London, 1877), pp 1, 6, 178–9, 220.

[3] Labourers' daily wages, Ireland and the U.S., 1850–70 (U.S. cents)

1850 Ireland	farm, without board	12.5 <
	Dublin, builder's labourers	32–52
1850 U.S.A.	North Atlantic and midwest: farm, with board	46
	general labour, national average	87
	N.Y.city, Erie Canal, Michigan: general labour	88 < 91
1870 Ireland	farm labour, with board	17 < 61
	farm labour, without board	24 < 97
	urban and construction labour	48 < 62
1870 U.S.A.	North Atlantic & midwest: farm, with board	95 < 145
	farm, without board	136 < 196
	general labour	106 < 168
	Pa., N.Y., and Mass.: railroads, iron mills	140 < 156

Sources: Fergus D'Arcy, 'Wages of labourers in the Dublin building industry' in *Saothar*, xiv (1989), pp 23, 24, 26; Lebergott, *Manpower . . . since 1800*, p. 299, table A-25, p. 541; U.S. Bureau of Statistics [Edward Young], *Labor in Europe and America* (Philadelphia, 1875), pp 359–61, 739, 741, 743, 750, 758–9, 765, 785–6; Burchell, *San Francisco Irish*, table 13, p. 67; *Historical statistics of the United States . . . to 1970*, pp 163–5. For comparison with artisan differentials, see below, p. 753, n. 4.

too suffered the not unusual tendency of the Irishman eventually to reverse the normal pattern of self-betterment, and to lose both better paid employment and better housing as age weakened his resistance to the effects of a lifetime's overwork.

Most Irish immigrants did not work as labourers.[1] In 1852, the New York *Irish American* ventured that 'one-half (at least) of the mechanics' of the city were Irish.[2] The editor was somewhat exaggerating, but was close enough for his pride to be pardonable. In 1855 the city had around 27,000 Irish-born skilled and semi-skilled artisans, roughly 42 per cent of all city workers in such categories, and around 51 per cent of their own male workforce. Joined to a lesser middle-class and white-collar group of around 7,500 (from grocers, publicans, and hoteliers to officials, clerks, and policemen),[3] these artisans (and their providers of food, beer, and order) constituted the backbone of New York Irish society: modest, industrious, self-conscious, perhaps patriarchal, family men already or by intention. As yet, however, the real bourgeoisie of propertied merchants, lawyers, and manufacturers, if growing, was small, and distant from their fellows. The pressure on them was to try to dissociate from their fellow countrymen, as Buckley recognised by 1871. For to non-Irish members of higher society, distinctions between Irish labourers, artisans, and indeed the Irish generally did not matter: they were all 'poor, ignorant, helpless, and degraded'.

By Irish standards, nevertheless, money was to be made. How much, relative to living costs, was problematic. Irish craftsmen seemed to arrive with inflated expectations.[4]

---

[1] The widespread artificial linkage of 'domestic service' with 'general labouring' as a single occupational category, in tables both of outflowing emigrants and of the mid-century and later Irish American workforce, distorts this by consistently showing majorities of the Irish in the lowest bracket. But before *c.*1880 there was a familial migration, with daughters, in service before marriage, supplementing incomes either at home or in America (Tom Mooney warned labourers they must so put their girls in service to avoid poverty); from 1880 onwards, this pattern overlapped with an increasing differentiation of male and female experiences of America.

[2] Ernst, *Immigrant life in New York city*, p. 73.

[3] Recalculated from ibid., pp 214–17, and Sean Wilentz, *Chants democratic* (New York, 1984), pp 405–6.

[4] Daily craft wages in Ireland and America, 1850 and 1870 ($)

year	carpenters	masons	bricklayers	printers	machinists	tailors
1850 Ireland	1.20	1.04	1.20	1.25 <	< 1.08	.60 <
1850 U.S.A	1.50	1.50		1.40	1.30 <	1.60
1870/73 Ireland	1.32	1.32	1.32	1.75 <	1.80	1.22
1870 U.S.A.	2.88	3.00	3.16	3.30	2.67 <	2.48
1860 U.S.A.	1.52	1.78		1.64	1.64	

Sources: Fergus D'Arcy, 'Wages of skilled workers in the Dublin building industry, 1667–1918' in *Saothar*, xv (1990), pp 25–31; Maura Cronin, 'Work and workers . . . 1800–1900' in O'Flanagan & Buttimer, *Cork*, 730–31; Ernst, *Immigrant life*, pp 77–78; Wilentz, *Chants democratic*, pp 404, 405; Laurie and others, 'Immigrants and industry' in Hershberg (ed.), *Philadelphia*, pp 104–5; Burchell, *Irish in San Francisco*, p. 67; Young, *Labor in Europe and America*, pp 360–61, 745–8, 761–2, 795; *Historical statistics of the United States to 1970*, pp 163, 165. I have chosen maximum rates available in eastern U.S. cities, as in Ireland, but as a corrective the *c.*1860 figures give Lebergott's calculations of real wages for the period from 1860 (effectively to 1880); apart from civil war and post-war fluctuations, he held these years to be ones of no real rise (*Manpower . . . since 1800*, pp 154, 298–301).

Their own sources spoke most commonly of higher wage levels, and were less forthcoming on living costs.[1] Where they could, Irish artisans in New York dominated higher-paying skills, especially in construction, on its masonry, bricklaying, and stonecutting sides. It was their good fortune that New York was now (belatedly) following Philadelphia and Baltimore away from wooden building. The Irish were also the leading suppliers of the city's blacksmiths, plumbers, coopers, glassworkers, and brass- and coppersmiths, as of its dressmakers.[2] They were not ousted from preeminence in these in half a century, fastening their hold as unions grew.[3] They were replaced as the chief source of tailors by Germans by 1855. Men not worried about mere survival sought security and sufficiency through craft routes familiar at home, and through job-networking and protection. Income was much improved, not so much due to higher wage rates (of themselves almost cancelled by higher living costs) but rather because craft work was in chronic short supply in Irish towns and usually abundant in New York.[4]

In cities other than New York half the younger Irish were artisans, construction and transport workers, and machine operatives, though smaller proportions of middle-aged men were such. By contrast, few young arrivals had white-collar positions, but over 10 per cent of the immigrants over thirty years old had. Including New York city, Irish male household heads enjoyed a firmer economic footing and thus some more social information and leadership than one expects: overall, from one-third to three-fifths of Irish-born males were skilled or white-collar employees in five leading cities at mid-century.[5] Such gains were not sustained. The well known simplification in the occupational profile of later Irish arrivals was not the only reason. The years from 1850 to 1880 were ones in which the convergence of further mechanisation and workplace organisation with mass immigration meant there was no effective gain in real wages, with immigrants in the 1850s constituting 91 per cent of the labour force increase. Almost half these were Irish,[6] a heavy inflow that may explain why subsequently the proportions of Irish males in manufacturing trades fell significantly between 1850 and 1880, as in Philadelphia.[7]

[1] E.g. Francis Wyse, *America* (London, 1846), iii, 10–26; Mooney, *Nine years in America*, pp 37, 84–93, 133–54.

[2] Wilentz, *Chants democratic*, table 15, p. 406.

[3] David Doyle, 'The Irish and American labour, 1880–1920' in *Saothar*, i (1975), p. 43.

[4] Greagoir Ó Dughaill (ed.), 'Return of the tradesmen of the town of Galway, their rates of wages . . . 15 Dec. 1845' in *Saothar*, i (1975), pp 66–7; cf. E. Almquist, 'Pre-famine Ireland and the theory of European proto-industrialisation: evidence from the 1841 census' in *Jn. Econ. Hist.*, xxxix (1979), pp 699–718.

[5] Ernst, *Immigrant life*, pp 214–17; Dale B. Light in Drudy, *Irish in America*, table 6.2, p. 118; Handlin, *Boston's immigrants*, pp 250–51; Vinyard, *Irish on the urban frontier*, pp 62, 68; Glasco, *Ethnicity and social structure*, p. 97; Burchell, *San Francisco Irish*, p. 54. Recalculations are based on the classifications given by Vinyard, p. 363.

[6] Lebergott, *Manpower . . . since 1800*, pp 62–3.

[7] Hershberg and others, 'Occupation and ethnicity', graph 5; Laurie, Hershberg, and Alter, in Hershberg, *Philadelphia*, p. 107; Clark, *Irish in Philadelphia*, pp 76–87.

The speed with which the refugees from famine sought to establish homes and families is remarkable, as is their dependence on the models of their immediate pre-famine predecessors. Such patterns have been best studied in communities away from the eastern seaboard, but migration inland was not necessary to begin them. In large coastal cities the flight from tenements required the coming of streetcars, street railways, and large-scale Irish-controlled savings and loan societies to begin the process; in inland cities, cheap frame houses were available just off downtown itself from the start. Already from the 1850s to the 1870s the fringes of eastern cities saw similar developments, such as to midtown Manhattan, to the Flatbush area of Brooklyn, to Roxbury and Charlestown in Boston, and to outer Kensington, outer Moyamensing, and West Philadelphia in the latter city.[1] By 1855 Buffalo at the western end of New York's Erie canal was funnelling the grain of the midwest eastwards, and outranked Odessa as the world's leading grain port. A wave of largely married Irish worked their way slowly up the Hudson river and along the Erie in 1849–53 to offload the grain from lake boats and in to canal barges. Not an Irishman survived there from the canal-building days of the 1820s. Quickly the Irish entrenched themselves in Buffalo. Living there an average seven years, they were one-fifth of the city's 15,400 households. They clustered largely along the canal itself, four-fifths of them with an immediate Irish neighbour. They left the main downtown wards to the city's German catholics, the largest group there. The youngest Irish, in their twenties, were least likely to be labourers: the consequence both of spreading literacy and the use of English in Ireland or (if brought over as children) of American upbringing; the older, often pre-famine immigrants, were more likely to be labourers. A quarter of working household heads had skilled or semi-skilled jobs, proportions varying only slightly by length of residence. By the time they were aged 35–50, most immigrants had established family homes, usually by renting, but commonly acquiring a cheap wooden house if the male could keep a semi-skilled or skilled job in the town more than seven years. This was more usual than job improvement. To sustain this, the Irish in Buffalo had a 'niche' based on a system whereby each ethnic group 'either dominated or was severely underrepresented in an occupation', a system unaffected by length of residence, and in place by 1855. Similar patterns characterised other western cities, if some had a larger Irish middle class.[2]

Home life made it all not just tolerable, but acceptable: 'the Irish in general chose family life if they could.'[3] The Irish at home responded to the pre-famine and post-famine livelihood crises by increasingly delaying, then even avoiding,

---

[1] Handlin, *Boston's immigrants*, pp 94–100; Clark, *Irish in Philadelphia*, pp 50, 52, 55–60; Alan Burstein and Stephanie Greenberg in Hershberg, *Philadelphia*, pp 183–6, 194–9; and pp 214–23; John T. Ridge, *The Flatbush Irish* (Brooklyn, 1983), pp 6 ff.

[2] Glasco, *Ethnicity and social structure*, pp 15–21, 31–4, 42–3, 52–5, 60–61, 71, 80–139; Vinyard, *Irish on the urban frontier*, pp 49–79, 87–8, 94–101, 193, 365–79; Kathleen N. Conzen, *Immigrant Milwaukee, 1836–1860* (Cambridge, Mass., 1976), pp 63–153; Burchell, *San Francisco Irish*, pp 47–72.

[3] Burchell, *San Francisco Irish*, p. 46.

family formation. Thus the young chose late marriage, emigration, or celibacy to protect a single stem-family succession, linked to a viable farm or small shop or craft. Abundant if straitened livelihoods in America allowed general family formation. As in the far west of Ireland, the commitment to young and fertile marriage persisted in the diaspora to the end of the nineteenth century (until migrants from a sadder and more calculating Ireland began to arrive from about 1890). All this gave a very different tone to Irish life in the United States as against Ireland between 1845 and 1921, and helps to explain the compelling attraction of America to the young.[1] The course of life of most Irish immigrants was built towards and around marriage and child-bearing, not away from it as increasingly was the case at home. This began as the famine receded. In Buffalo by 1855 as many as 85 per cent of women would expect to marry, given established patterns (and even more of the men who stayed around or returned). Nine out of ten married Irish-born spouses; in other cities, the pattern was almost the same. Effective fertility rates were twice those of native New England-born women (as they were also for the German catholic majority there). But Irish families in Buffalo in 1850 were no larger than native, averaging 2.1 children (as in San Francisco), suggesting even then very high infant mortality as well as younger, incomplete families. There was a general adaption of pre-famine Irish rural patterns to American circumstances: general, early, and fertile marriage, the family as an economic unit, the desire to keep the young at home until they were twenty where possible, coupled with the readiness to send them off early if necessary, and finally the search for money support and perhaps even a licit fertility control in the migratory work habits of established poorer fathers. Even the adjustments made to cut the growth rate were carried to America: some delay on marriage age, and a celibacy rate of between 10 and 15 per cent, especially among labourers, who had fewer children than skilled or white-collar workers.[2] On the other hand, losses to infant mortality were perhaps greater than those of rural Ireland before the famine (which were high); this must have given poignancy to American experience, and sharpened the drive to better one's living standards. By 1875–80 these losses seem indeed to have been partly reduced.

All this suggests the Irish after 1845 were hardly 'pioneers of the ghetto' in its modern sense of communities of the chronically unemployed, the familially broken, and the socially disorganised. Given the sixty-hour, six-day weeks then so common, the Irish were in a sense overemployed, while often appallingly housed. Thus arose the problems of their own Americanising children, many of

---

[1] Kerby Miller, David Doyle, and Patricia Kelleher, ' "For love and for liberty": Irishwomen, emigration, and domesticity in Ireland and America, 1815–1920' in Patrick O'Sullivan (ed.), *The Irish world wide*, vol. iv, *Irish women and Irish migration* (Leicester and London, 1995), pp 41–65.

[2] Generally for this paragraph Blessing, 'West among strangers', pp 201, 284, 351–8; Conzen, *Immigrant Milwaukee*, pp 46–52; Glasco, *Ethnicity and social structure*, pp 141–225; Vinyard, *Irish on the urban frontier*, pp 106–13, 184–8, 192, 380–88, 409–19; Burchell, *San Francisco Irish*, pp 78–87; Lynn H. Lees and John Modell, 'The Irish countryman urbanized: a comparative perspective on the famine migration' in Hershberg, *Philadelphia*, pp 352–5; Mokyr, *Why Ire. starved*, pp 32–7, 71–4.

whom were in turn orphaned or 'half-orphaned' (as was then said) by the high adult death rates. A great deal of their response to their poverty, overwork, and threatened disorganisation was rooted in the harsh but important adaptions of rural Ireland, whose lessons were all intensified by the great famine, and were a preparation for the relative indifference of native American property-owners and employers throughout most of this period.[1]

The social conservatism of catholic bishops in America from 1845 to 1880 partly reflected their reading of the hopelessness of foreign and religious minorities' attempting to change the country's social order, and mirrored the greater conservatism of the dominant protestant churches. Yet these bishops were ready to see Irish immigrants and religious adapt to local conditions the patterns both of self-help and of reliance on political intervention, learnt first at home. Only where the 'trade unionism' of the poor was secretive, oath-bound, illegal, and disposed to violence did bishops and middle-class Irish opinion (as in Ireland) condemn it, although generally the church was quicker to distinguish between the necessity of such things and their less acceptable expressions in alien urban America than it was in Ireland. As in Ireland, one gets the impression of the various fragments, 'the scattered debris' indeed of a people, groping their way to survival, then to mutuality, amid their own 'churning motion' in the new cities.[2] The surprise is how much was achieved, and even attempted, before even 1865, and how much more thereafter. Both ingenuity and cooperation made real contributions to alleviating the community's social problems.[3]

Irish experience of course had negative features. Neither in Ireland nor in the United States did it encourage dependence on government. As the organ of the Boston Irish put it in 1852, 'It is a crime in Massachusetts to be poor. People are sentenced to our public institutions because they are destitute.'[4] This drove the

---

[1] For poverty in Irish America see Dolan, *Immigrant church*, pp 32–7, 123–5; Dennis Clark, 'Ramcat and Rittenhouse Square' in *Irish relations*, pp 158–69; Ernst, *Immigrant life in New York city*, pp 39–40, 48–60; Handlin, *Boston's immigrants*, pp 88-123; Neihaus, *Irish in New Orleans*, pp 59–70, 135–46; Thernstrom, *Poverty & progress*, pp 20–32, 42–56; Carole Groneman, 'The bloody ould Sixth: a social analysis . . .' (Ph.D. thesis, U. of Rochester, 1973). For poverty in Ireland, see Mokyr, *Why Ire. starved*, pp 6–29, 278–94; Timothy P. O'Neill, 'The state, poverty, and distress in Ireland, 1815–1845' (Ph.D. thesis, N.U.I. (U.C.D.), 1971).

[2] Clark, *Erin's heirs*, pp 50–51, 54; James Roohan, *American catholics and the social question, 1865–1900* (New York, 1976), pp 40–71; Henry F. May, *The protestant churches and industrial America* (New York, 1967) pp 3–72; John R. Bodo, *The protestant clergy and public issues, 1812–1848* (Princeton, 1954; repr., 1980), *passim*; R. F. Hueston, *The catholic press and nativism, 1840–1860* (New York, 1976), pp 140–46, 185, 229, 249–74; H. J. Browne, *The catholic church and the Knights of Labor* (New York, 1976); Fergus McDonald, *The catholic church and the secret societies in the United States* (New York, 1946). Quoted phrases are from Dolan, *Immigrant church*, pp 33, 42.

[3] Aaron Abell, *American catholicism and social action: a search for social justice, 1865–1950* (Notre Dame, Ind., 1963; repr., Westport, Conn., 1980), pp 1–53; Florence D. Cohalan, *A popular history of the archdiocese of New York* (Estero, Fla., 1983), pp 78–9, 90–94; James F. Connelly, *The history of the archdiocese of Philadelphia* (Philadelphia, 1976); Dolan, *Immigrant church*, pp 121–40; Charles Shanabruch, *Chicago's catholics: an evolution of an American identity* (Notre Dame, Ind., 1981) pp 7, 22; Handlin, *Boston's immigrants*, pp 117, 161–3, 168–9.

[4] *Boston Pilot*, 3 Jan. 1852, quoted in Hueston, *Catholic press and nativism*, p. 143.

Irish into close-meshed reliance on their networks, on the catholic church and its own institutions, but especially on their own families. Overworked and thus overburdened, such families bore much; and there was less margin for that helping of others that had carried so many in Ireland through the shortfall season each year when crops had been good. However, apart from meeting the non-competing needs of others' pressing wants and of hospitality and work-sharing among friends, often the Irish 'lower classes are unduly harsh and unfeeling towards each other in pecuniary matters' (as Daniel O'Connell admitted in 1825), and had been even more demonstrably so in matters of land.[1] This too carried over to hamper their urban cooperation, if also to prepare them for the harsh winds of Yankee individualism, short-term labour contracts, and the primacy of debt obligation. Their lately functioning 'family economy' had been as close to monetary imperatives as to any supposed 'moral economy of the poor'; for the Irish, sentiment and survival had been inextricable in families, and it proved true also in the United States throughout the nineteenth century.

IN 1845 there were 1.1 million catholics in the United States. By 1860 this had tripled to 3.1 million; in 1880 there were 6.3 million. Less than 4 per cent of Americans in 1840, they were over 12 per cent by 1880. Irish immigration accounted for roughly half the increase between 1845 and 1860; the surviving offspring of Irish parents for maybe one-third of the balance. The increase was made more visible as it mirrored the north-eastern distribution of the immigrants, and coincided with the growth of cities thrust to preeminence by the north's victory in the civil war and continuing industrialisation. The early diocesan structure had reflected the dual southern and northern bases of independent America, with Baltimore as the effective leading see. But the populous new dioceses set up after 1840 reflected first the coming of the Irish and then that of the Germans. In about half of them the bishops were Irish-American or Irish for the rest of the century, often beyond that. Contrary to ethnic protest and rivalry after 1880, the Irish-born were consistently under-represented at hierarchic levels, in so far as their numbers empowered church expansion, and indeed even the American-born Irish were never over-represented before the 1890–1940 period. Apart from New York, created an archiepiscopal see in 1850 (and anticipated or balanced by the creation of those of Oregon City, St Louis, New Orleans, and Cincinnati), the other leading American cities and Irish-American centres, Philadelphia, Boston, and Chicago, waited a further quarter-century to achieve

---

[1] Timothy P. O'Neill, 'Poverty in Ireland' in *Folklife*, xi (1974), pp 22–37; 'Clare and Irish poverty' in *Studia Hib.*, xiv (1974), pp 7–27; O'Connell, quoted in Mokyr, *Why Ire. starved*, p. 220; David Fitzpatrick, 'Class, family, and rural unrest in nineteenth-century Ireland' in P. J. Drudy (ed.), *Irish Studies II: Ireland: land, politics, and people* (Cambridge, 1982), pp 37–75; but this contrast of mutual aid and mutual harshness must be qualified by the comment of John Stanley in 1845: 'Irish farmers, from want of capital, could not . . . carry out production, with a high rate of wages . . . Again money wages does [*sic*] not enter into the calculation of Irish farmers, commonly operating' (cited in O Gráda, *Ire. before & after famine*, pp 59–60).

similar rank, along with such minor cities at that time as Santa Fé and Milwaukee. The Vatican was plainly moved neither by Irish demography nor by Irish politicking, but rather by an urge towards a balanced vision of America's prospects analogous to that of Henry Clay and Daniel Webster in secular matters, a vision it shared with most leading U.S. prelates, Irish or not.[1]

The Irish were usually portrayed as the core of the history of nineteenth-century American catholicism by scholars working from the 1880s to the early 1960s. To be sure, they made a judicious distinction between U.S.-born, or long Americanised, bishops and clergy, and those more recently come from Ireland or enfolded by their fellow countrymen in the U.S.A. From the scholarship of John Gilmary Shea to that of the students of Mgr Peter Guilday and R. J. Purcell, the Americanised Irish were given credit for the skill with which they adapted the Irish catholic inheritance to distinct American civic and religious circumstances— and the more narrowly Irish leadership was faulted for provoking reaction and hostility. Yet in both views the Irish contribution was seen as primary. Since the 1950s the role has been subject to an increasing change of emphasis, as the church has sought more distinctively American antecedents, and as ethnically diverse contemporary catholics began to emphasise their forerunners' presence in the mosaic of the previous century. Then, too, a liberal (at times even modernist) establishment in the universities founded by the church has sought to distance itself from the Irish and their traditions: supposedly illiberal, authoritarian, provincial, and Roman among clergy, and tribal, ill-informed, unintellectual, familial, pragmatic, and devotionalist among ordinary emigrants. The counter-view, once common, is still encountered among some clergy of Roman, German, or Polish training or background in the United States: that Irish catholics were lax, undisciplined, and too secular, too uncritical of the dangers posed by America to the faith, and corrupt in their lay political leaderships. Indications that the mid-century Irish were less rigorously catholic than their successors have been exaggerated in these contexts, although modern scholarship has reversed the more negative findings on these matters.[2] As early as 1855 the *New York Times*, then

---

[1] In sequence (with those of Irish episcopal succession italicised) *Pittsburgh, Chicago, Hartford (Conn.), Little Rock (Ark.)*, and Milwaukee all in 1843; *Albany, Buffalo*, Cleveland, and Galveston in 1847; *Wheeling, St Paul*, and Savannah in 1850; *Brooklyn, Erie*, Newark, Burlington (Vt.), *Portland (Maine)*, Quincy (Ill.), Covington, and San Francisco in 1853; Fort Wayne (Ind.), and Sault St.-Marie (Wis.) in 1857; Wilmington (Del.), *Scranton, Harrisburg, Rochester*, Columbus, Green Bay, and LaCrosse (both Wis.), *St Joseph (Mo.)*, Grass Valley (now *Sacramento*), all in 1868; *Springfield (Mass.)* in 1870; Ogdensburg (N.Y.) and Providence, both in 1872; and Peoria, 1875, Leavenworth (Kan.), 1877, and Allegheny (Pa.) in 1876. Data from Theodore Roemer, *The catholic church in the United States* (St Louis, 1950), maps and appendices, pp 202, 318 ff, 384 ff, 401–14, and J. B. Code, *Dictionary of the American hierarchy* (New York, 1940). Additionally in these years Portland (Ore.), Walla-Walla, and Nesqually were created as missionary dioceses in the far north-west, and Santa Fé, San Antonio, and St Augustine in once Spanish or Mexican lands.

[2] D. W. Miller, 'Irish catholicism and the great famine' in *Journal of Social History*, ix (1975), pp 81–98; Sean Connolly, *Religion and society in nineteenth-century Ireland* (Dundalk, 1985), pp 7–17, 41–60, which does not cite P. J. Corish, *The catholic community in the seventeenth and eighteenth centuries* (Dublin, 1981), pp 82–115; see also Corish, *The Irish catholic experience*, pp 166–215.

four years old and acceptable to the better-off Irish, could yet brand attempts to update, deepen, and discipline catholic practice in Ireland as a plot to make its clergy 'more Roman and less Irish' and ensure 'catholic Ireland would become a mere province or spiritual appendage of the Vatican'.[1] Such artificial antitheses have dogged the understanding of nineteenth-century Irish catholicism in America, as at home, amongst both its friends and its critics.

At least 2 million Irish-born and German-born catholics in 1870 made up 45 per cent of the country's 4.5 million catholics, as they did 35 per cent of its 5.6 million foreign-born overall. There were probably more. With their children, and adult offspring, they dominated the church. Even allowing that one-fifth of the Irish-born were not affiliated to parishes, whether as protestants, or by reason of choice or of unattached youth, the Irish-born component was at least twice that of the German (which had in fact considerably higher rates of non-affiliation).[2] Yet more interesting is the evidence of very different patterns of church identification, so often compounded by historians. Contrast of seating availability with Irish- and German-born adherents in 1870 for leading industrial counties suggests that the Irish provided best for themselves where the catholic community was overwhelmingly their own (as in Scranton or Albany) and when additionally stimulated by a vigorous native protestantism (as in New England cities). They were less fully active in the great cosmopolitan cities, where secularity, and a variety of rival cultures, met the disorientation and youthfulness of newcomers: notably in New York city and its satellites or Philadelphia; but also in poorer new industrial ones, especially where, as in Pittsburgh, many of them came from less well catechised roots. Where German or 'old American' catholics were preponderant, Irish minorities seem to have been sometimes encouraged (especially if more settled) but also sometimes put off. Oddly, there are no direct correlations between these patterns and the relative preponderance (or not) of an Irish-American clergy.[3] In short, the old story of majority Irish religiosity has been so oft told that such diversities have gone unexamined, as of course has the protestantism of a signal minority, both of mid-century migrants and of converts from catholicism, who were few.[4]

Irish visitors appreciated even by the 1860s the pressures towards a certain secularisation operating in the United States; Irish churchmen were surprised at the levels of conviction and piety found equally in New York and County Cork. Plainly, while the ordinary (if not the more heroic) activities of churchmen were

[1] 'The Roman Propaganda in Ireland' in *New York Times*, 24 Oct. 1855; Emmet Larkin, 'The devotional revolution in Ireland, 1850–75' in *A. H. R.*, lxxvii (1972), pp 623–52.

[2] Jay P. Dolan, *The American catholic experience: a history from colonial times to the present* (Notre Dame, Ind., 1992), p. 207.

[3] See further David N. Doyle, 'The Irish in Australia and the United States: some comparisons, 1800–1939' in *Ir. Econ. & Soc. Hist.*, xvi (1989), pp 86–92 and citations; M. Doorley, 'The Irish and the catholic church in New Orleans, 1835–1918' (M.A. thesis, U. of New Orleans, 1987), tables 3 to 17, pp 66–77.

[4] R. A. Wells, *Ulster migrants to America: letters from three families* (New York, 1991); *Fifth annual report of the American Protestant Society* (New York, 1848), p. 3.

self-explanatory, the general commitment of the immigrants requires more perceptive study. As Oscar Handlin noted, the famine migrants, turned harassed operatives and servants, found vital explanation and solace in Christian mysteries. But this went further. Since a minority found in America the promise (if not always the reality) of a more this-wordly individualism, of an escape from the material deprivation, social obligations, and guilty anxieties of rural Irish society—and most emigrants were youthful in years and in their reading of such things—what drew the majority back to rebuilding their childhood convictions afresh, unsurrounded by censorious elders and the associations of the past? Was it the transplanting of the most carriageable and adaptable institution of their culture, as a refuge to the uprooted, a source of familiarity, an enclave of mutual trust, a point of reference drawing all the vague yearnings for the lost point of origin? Was it a reaction to the force of native prejudice, driving the Irish in on themselves, causing them to assert their worth in an incontestable framework, that of their souls' worth against the obloquy of Americans?

Yet American experiences nurtured shocks of recognition that gave life to the stale catechetical clichés of Irish childhoods. Neither evangelicals, nor Know-Nothings, nor many Republicans believed that, given free schooling, free access to scripture, and the experience of a free society, the Irish would grow away from priestly tutelage. America gave the Irish access to an extraordinarily diverse book of life, uncoded by the rigid socio-religious polarities of home. One must assume that the lessons they learnt were neither preconditioned, nor those always intended by their hosts. Yet why find such wisdom almost exclusively in its catholic reinforcement? It became shared and socialised in the dense life of the Irish parish, as Jay Dolan convincingly demonstrated, even as it was given deeper import by familiar liturgy and sacrament.[1] Yet it would be false to see it as solely a collective expression of the Irish against the world. Work needs to be done on the interactive nature of Irish-American catholicism from the start. It is striking that the Irish were deeply impressed by the catholicism of those not of their own nationality, especially when it was so often placed in their service. Examples include in New York the Cuban Felix Varela, the Haitian Pierre Toussaint, the Frenchman Alphonse Thébaud; in Philadelphia, the Czech bishop John Neumann; in Boston or in Ohio the Frenchmen Jean de Cheverus or Jean Baptiste Lamy; even in remote Natchez, Bishops John Chanche and James Van de Velde, who both died serving the Irish, and everywhere numerous German clerics. It meant more in an age when such example was guaranteed by word of mouth in small 'walking cities'. Indeed, most of the orders of nuns either founded in, or transplanted to, America in these years, and drawing so many thousands of young Irish women, had continental European (or American) founders. The impact of native American catholics and converts was equally strong and reinforcing: only

[1] Dolan, *American catholic experience*, pp 165–8, 195–8; and his *Immigrant church*, pp 13–14, 21–2, 45–67, 121–58.

a handful (such as Orestes Brownson and Isaac Hecker) seem to have disliked the Irish, and even their shared animus disguised lifelong contact with Irish acquaintances, publishers, penitents, associates, and confessors. While indeed the Irish seem to have preferred the parish to be mostly their own, as at home, the church as a whole came to them in a new form: as a witness of truth transcending their own pronounced provincialisms, reassuring them that their final convictions were no local idiom, but a language of universal import, equal to the bewildering and exciting enormity of the American world. Before 1880, the Irish were as much debtors as creditors of the church in America, and in this era seem to have accepted rather than resented this.

A continuous and unpredictable nightmare may destroy faith; but, among the Irish, successive traumas were set off against a continuing and youthful search for a promising normality. Their convictions and community carried them towards goals that many attained, with the promise of eternal redress where the balance often seemed set to subvert their modest efforts. 'I feel a sort of anticipated consolation in reflecting that the religion which gave us comfort in our early days . . . enabled us to endure the stroke of affliction and endeared us to each other', wrote one. For the American-born Irish, reflection on their parents' very limitations could shape their key role as mediators between generations in the lay church. As John Gilmary Shea recalled of his father, an anti-episcopal activist: 'In my case we were negative poles and almost spontaneously I took the opposite. As soon as I saw those who went to their duties cling to the bishop it gave him a halo in my boyish fancy.' For many, no such reaction to large dissent, but parental neglect, drunkenness, or disorder may have had a similar engrafting effect. And then there was the long-standing effect of native American good example, protestant and catholic: 'A greater latitude and indifference on the score of religion is allowed to prevail amongst emigrants lately arrived . . . than amongst the Americans themselves. It is admitted by many Irish clergymen . . . that they [are] before our country people in their religious practice, particularly the catholics.'[1] Yet these experiences were neither confining nor prescriptive. On the contrary, by contrast with German catholicism, Irish immigrants enjoyed a comprehensive latitude in their secular pursuits: their clubs, benefit societies, saloons, militia companies, trade union activities, political alignments, and even the schooling of most of their children before the 1880s, had no formal church connection (though the informal press of numbers in Irish localities gave them a catholic tone). Church societies drew only minorities of the devout. The deinstitutionalisation of catholicism, by contrast with that of Germany, was in Ireland the consequence of a long history of proscription and marginalisation.

---

[1] Thomas Brady to Bishop John McCloskey, 1 Jan. 1861 (Mary C. Taylor, *History of the foundation of catholicism in northern New York* (Yonkers, 1976), p. 187); J. Gilmary Shea to James F. Edwards, 16 Aug. 1890 (Richard Shaw, *John Dubois: founding father* (Yonkers, 1976), p. x; Patrick O'Kelly, *Advice and guide to emigrants going to the United States of America* (Dublin, 1834), p. 19. O'Kelly had spent five years in America.

Time would show it was not an ideal model for industrial America, and attempts to change it were well under way by the 1870s. But such informality gave the young incoming Irish a space in which to work out their own relations to America, while attaching themselves to a parish for essential religious continuity.

BIBLIOGRAPHY

HELEN F. MULVEY AND CHARLES BENSON

INTRODUCTION

THE introductions to the bibliographies of all previously published volumes of the *New history* have been, in effect, brief essays on the range of published sources for the history of their periods. For the history of the period 1800–1921 the single most important fact is the enormous mass and variety of potential source material. As has been observed in the introduction to the present volume, the period is perhaps the most thoroughly and variously documented available to historians of Ireland;[1] and although this refers specifically to the half-century 1870–1921 the observation holds good for the whole period of the union. The development and expansion of British administration in Ireland, the importance of Irish affairs in the politics of the United Kingdom, and the development of Irish political, economic, and cultural life, culminating in the setting up of an independent state, have combined to produce great bodies of primary and secondary source material on all subjects and of all shades of opinion, providing the foundation for a rapidly increasing number of scholarly studies. The extent of this latter body of work was charted in 1966–71 in three articles by Helen Mulvey.[2] In the quarter-century that has followed, not only has the sheer bulk of published work continued to grow, but wider areas of subject-matter have been explored—economic and social, constitutional and administrative, technical and medical, arts and communications, biographical studies and reference material. The large body of work published on Northern Ireland since 1969 belongs mainly, of course, to the period covered by volume VII of the *New history*, but is often relevant to the period 1800–1921. It is clear from any instalment of the serial bibliographies listed below that more has been published on this period than on any other in Irish history, and that this continues to be the case despite the growth of studies in other periods.

This *embarras de richesses* has determined not only the content but the organisation of the following bibliography. Under the standard bibliographical plan of the *New history*, other volumes have included sections on manuscript sources, records, and contemporary writings, and the original plan for this volume included also newspapers, maps, drawings, and photographs. In practice, the demands on space of this extended treatment would have been inordinate; as a result a large compilation by Charles Benson of records, contemporary writings, and other source material has had to be dropped. We have therefore compiled an extended section of 'bibliographies and guides' (sections IA and IB), providing fuller assistance towards further reading in all types of source material; and followed solely by the four normal categories of secondary works. It can only be regretted that this leaves no place for such basic source material as the papers of the chief secretary's office, or for such achievements of modern scholarship as Maurice O'Connell's monumental eight-volume edition (1972–80) of the correspondence of Daniel O'Connell, the work of M. R. D. Foot

---

[1] Above, p. xxxvii.
[2] See below, pp 860–61.

and H. C. G. Matthew on the Gladstone diaries, or the continuing series of ordnance survey memoirs edited by Angélique Day and Patrick McWilliams (1990–).

Among secondary works, owing to constraints of space, there has also been an *embarras du choix*. As a general rule, we have not included works written or published before 1921 or after 1991, although some important works, more recently published, have been added. Where an author has followed an article with a book covering the same subject, the latter has been entered but not the former. We have included some sources cited in the footnotes of this volume and its predecessor, but not all; in particular, the footnotes of David Doyle's chapter[3] list many further sources on the Irish in America. Where a composite work, considered as a whole, merits entry, we have not entered its constituent articles separately, although exceptions have been made for articles deserving special attention.

We are grateful to the editors and contributors of this and other volumes of the *New history*, and to other scholars in several fields, including the members of the Military History Society of Ireland, for their advice and suggestions; to Helen Aitner of the library of Connecticut College, for assisting Helen Mulvey with interlibrary loans; and to Janet McKee of the library of University College, Dublin, for checking references to periodicals.

[3] Above, pp 725–63.

CONTENTS

I BIBLIOGRAPHIES AND GUIDES

A BIBLIOGRAPHIES

Adams, J. N., and Davies, M. J. *A bibliography of nineteenth-century legal literature.* 2 vols. Newcastle upon Tyne, 1992–3.
  Covers A–Q for period 1801–70.
Bibliography of works on Irish history published in the U.S.S.R. In *Saothar,* ii (1976), pp 62–3.
Black, R. D. C. *A catalogue of pamphlets on economic subjects published between 1750 and 1900 . . . in Irish libraries.* Belfast, 1969.
Block, Andrew. *The English novel, 1740–1850.* New ed., London, 1961.
Bourke, F. S. The rebellion of 1803: an essay in bibliography. In *Bibliog. Soc. Ire. Jn.,* v, no. 1 (1933), pp 3–16.
Brady, Anna. *Women in Ireland: an annotated bibliography.* New York and London, 1988. (Bibliographies in Women's Studies, 6.)
British Library. *The British Library general catalogue of printed books to 1975.* 366 vols. London, 1979–88. CD-ROM, London, 1989. *1976–82,* 50 vols, London, 1983; *1982–5,* 26 vols, London, 1986; *1985–7,* 22 vols, London, 1988.
—— *Catalogue of printed maps, charts, and plans.* 15 vols. London, 1967. Ten-year supplement (1965–74), London, 1977.
—— *Bibliography of biography, 1988* [etc.]. London, 1989– .
  Annual.
British union-catalogue of periodicals. 4 vols. London, 1955–8.
Brown, L. M., and Christie, I. R. *Bibliography of British history 1789–1851.* Oxford, 1977.
Brown, Stephen J. *Ireland in fiction.* Dublin, 1915; 2nd ed., Dublin, 1919. Reprint with introduction by Desmond Clarke, Shannon, 1969.
—— and Clarke, Desmond. *Ireland in fiction,* vol. 2. Cork, 1985.
Brye, D. L. (ed.). *European immigration and ethnicity in the United States and Canada: a historical bibliography.* Santa Barbara, Calif., and Oxford, 1983.
Cambridge University Library. *A catalogue of the Bradshaw collection of Irish books.* 3 vols. Cambridge, 1916.
Carty, James. *Bibliography of Irish history, 1870–1911.* Dublin, 1940.
—— *Bibliography of Irish history, 1912–1921.* Dublin, 1936.
Collins, Timothy. *Floreat Hibernia: a bio-bibliography of Robert Lloyd Praeger, 1865–1953.* Dublin, 1985.
Cullen, Sara. *Books and authors of County Cavan.* Cavan, 1965.
De Hae, Risteárd. *Clár litridheacht na Nua-Ghaeilge 1850–1936.* 3 vols. Dublin, 1938–40.
Denson, Alan. *Printed writings by George W. Russell (A E): a bibliography.* London, 1961.
Doughan, David, and Souchez, Denise. *Feminist periodicals, 1855–1984: an annotated critical bibliography of British, Irish, commonwealth, and international titles.* Brighton, 1987.
Doyle, David N. The regional bibliography of Irish America, 1800–1930: a review and addendum. In *I.H.S.,* xxiii, no. 91 (May 1983), pp 254–83.

Eager, A. R. *A guide to Irish bibliographical material: a bibliography of Irish bibliographies and sources of information.* 2nd ed., revised and enlarged, Westport, Conn., and London, 1980.

Edwards, John. *The Irish language: an annotated bibliography of socio-linguistic publications, 1772–1982.* New York and London, 1983.

Elmes, R. M. *National Library of Ireland. Catalogue of engraved Irish portraits, mainly in the Joly collection, and of original drawings.* Dublin, 1938.

—— *National Library of Ireland. Catalogue of Irish topographical prints and original drawings.* Dublin, 1943. New ed., revised by Michael Hewson, Dublin, 1975.

Flynn, Mary E. Ten-year retrospective bibliography of Irish labour history, 1963–1972. In *Saothar*, xiv (1989), pp 143–57.

—— A retrospective bibliography of Irish labour history, 1960–1972. In *Saothar*, xvi (1991), pp 144–58.

  See below O'Connell, Deirdre.

Fordham, Henry. The roadbooks and itineraries of Ireland, 1647 to 1850: a catalogue. In *Bibliog. Soc. Ire. Jn.*, ii, no. 4 (1923), pp 63–76.

French books on Irish subjects, 1801–1900. In *I.B.L.*, xvi, no. 2 (Mar.–Apr. 1928), pp 42–3; no. 3 (May–June 1928), pp 59–61.

Gilbert, V. F. Current bibliography of immigrants and minorities: monographs, periodical articles, and theses, 1981. Minority groups, Irish. In *Immigrants and Minorities*, iii (1984), p. 203.

Gilcher, E. *A bibliography of George Moore.* DeKalb, Ill., 1970.

—— *Supplement to a bibliography of George Moore.* Westport, Conn., and Gerrards Cross, 1989.

Glandon, Virginia. Index of Irish newspapers, 1900–1922. In *Éire-Ireland*, xi, no. 4 (winter 1976), pp 84–121; xii, no. 1 (spring 1977), pp 86–115.

Gmelch, George, and Gmelch, S. B. Ireland's travelling people: a comprehensive bibliography. In *Journal of the Gypsy Lore Society*, i, no. 3 (1977), pp 159–69.

Hanham, H. J. *Bibliography of British history 1851–1914.* Oxford, 1976.

Harmon, Maurice. *Select bibliography for the study of Anglo-Irish literature and its backgrounds.* Dublin, 1977.

Hartigan, Maureen (compiler), and Hickman, Mary J. (ed.). *The history of the Irish in Britain: a bibliography.* London, 1986. (Irish in Britain History Centre.)

Hayes, R. J. (ed.). *Sources for the history of Irish civilisation: articles in Irish periodicals.* 9 vols. Boston, 1970.

Hayley, Barbara. *A bibliography of the writings of William Carleton.* Gerrards Cross, 1985.

—— A detailed bibliography of editions of William Carleton's *Traits and stories of the Irish peasantry* published in Dublin and London during the author's lifetime. In *Long Room*, no. 32 (1987), pp 28–55; no. 33 (1988), pp 20–40.

Herries Davies, Gordon L. *The history of Irish science: a select bibliography.* 2nd ed., Dublin, 1985.

Houghton, Walter (ed.). *The Wellesley index to Victorian periodicals, 1824–1900.* 5 vols. Toronto and London, 1966–89.

  Vol. IV includes *Dublin University Magazine.*

Joannon, Pierre. Liste des ouvrages consacrés à l'histoire, la politique, les institutions de l'Irlande. In *Études Irlandaises*, no. 3 (1974), pp 57–73; no. 4 (1975), pp 189–211; i (1976), pp 231–44; ii (1977), pp 237–47; iii (1978), pp 87–99; iv (1979), pp 339–48; v

(1980), pp 261–8; vi (1981), pp 211–20. Continued as 'Bibliographie selective: histoire, politique, institutions Irlandaises' in vii (1982), pp 233–9; viii (1983), pp 331–9; ix (1984), pp 323–30; x (1985), pp 283–96; xi (1986), pp 217–27; xii, no. 2 (Dec. 1987), pp 235–47; xiii, no. 2 (Dec. 1988), pp 191–206; xiv, no. 2 (Dec. 1989), pp 221–8; xv, no. 2 (Dec. 1990), pp 215–28; xvi, no. 2 (Dec. 1991), pp 209–24; xvii, no. 2 (Dec. 1992), pp 211–26. In progress.

Kavanagh, Mary. *A bibliography of the County Galway*. Galway, 1965.

Kavanagh, Michael V. *A contribution towards a bibliography of the history of County Kildare in printed books*. Kildare, 1976.

Keaney, Marian. *Westmeath authors*. Mullingar, 1969.

Kinane, Vincent. Trinity Closet Press, 1973–1994: a chronology and a bibliography. In *Long Room*, no. 39 (1994), pp 60–63.

MacLysaght, Edward. *Bibliography of Irish family history*. 2nd ed., Blackrock, 1982.

McParland, Edward. A bibliography of Irish architectural history. In *I.H.S.*, xxvi, no. 102 (Nov. 1988), pp 161–212.

McTernan, John C. *Historic Sligo: a bibliographical introduction* . . . Sligo, 1965.

——*Here's to their memory: profiles of distinguished Sligonians of bygone days*. Dublin, 1977. Bibliography, pp 411–21.

Maher, Helen. *Galway authors*. Galway, 1976.

——*Roscommon authors*. Roscommon, 1978.

Martin, G. H., and MacIntyre, Sylvia. *A bibliography of British and Irish municipal history*. Leicester, 1972.

Maxwell, L. F., and Maxwell, W. H. *A legal bibliography of the British commonwealth of nations, iv: Irish law to 1956*. London, 1957.

Murray, James; Ford, Alan; McGuire, J. I.; Connolly, S. J.; O'Ferrall, Fergus; and Milne, Kenneth. The Church of Ireland: a critical bibliography, 1536–1992. In *I.H.S.*, xxviii, no. 112 (Nov. 1993), pp 345–84.

Pts v (1800–70) and vi (1870–1992), pp 369–84.

The national union catalogue: pre-1956 imprints. 754 vols. Chicago and London, 1968–81.

Nelson, E. Charles. Three centuries in Irish botanical gardens: an epitome and a bibliography. In *Long Room*, no. 34 (1989), pp 14–28.

Nevin, Donal. Bibliography of writings about James Larkin. In *Saothar*, iv (1978), pp 57–61.

Nineteenth-century short title catalogue. Newcastle upon Tyne, 1984– . 1st ser., phase I (1801–15). 6 vols. 1984–6. 2nd ser., phase I (1816–70). 1986– .

North, J. S. *The Waterloo directory of Irish newspapers and periodicals, 1800–1900*. Waterloo, Ont., 1986.

O'Connell, Deirdre. A bibliography of Irish labour history . . . [from 1973]. In *Saothar*, v (1979), pp 97–108; vi (1980), pp 124–32; vii (1981), pp 128–32; viii (1982), pp 107–14; ix (1983), pp 139–44; x (1984), pp 123–30; xi (1986), pp 124–34; xii (1987), pp 107–27; xiii (1988), pp 131–46; xiv (1989), pp 129–57; xv (1990), pp 113–23; xvi (1991), pp 136–43; xvii (1992), pp 122–36. In progress.

See above Flynn, Mary E.

O'Hanrahan, Brenda. *Donegal authors: a bibliography*. Blackrock, 1982.

O'Hegarty, P. S. *A bibliography of books written by Standish O'Grady*. Dublin, 1930.

——*A bibliography of books written by P. H. Pearse*. Dublin, 1931.

——*A bibliography of books written by Thomas MacDonagh and Joseph Mary Plunkett*. Dublin, 1931.

O'Hegarty, P. S. *A bibliography of books by Seumas O'Kelly*. Dublin, 1934.

—— *A bibliography of books by The O'Rahilly, Tom Clarke, Micheál Ó hAnnracháin and Countess de Markievicz*. Dublin, 1936.

—— *A bibliography of Dr Douglas Hyde*. Dublin, 1939.

O'Higgins, Paul. *A bibliography of periodical literature relating to Irish law*. Belfast, 1966. *First supplement*, Belfast, 1973. *Second supplement*, Belfast, 1983.

—— *A bibliography of Irish trials and other legal proceedings*. Abingdon, 1986.

Ó Macháin, Pádraig. *Catalogue of Irish manuscripts in the National Library of Ireland*. Fasc. xi (MSS G 501–G 599). Dublin, 1990.

O'Neill, Patrick. German literature and the *Dublin University Magazine*, 1833–50: a check list and commentary. In *Long Room*, no. 14–15 (autumn 1976/spring–summer 1977), pp 20–31.

Ó Suilleabháin, Seán. *Longford authors*. Mullingar, 1978.

O'Toole, James. *Newsplan: report of the Newsplan project in Ireland*. London and Dublin, 1992.

    Contains a union list of holdings of Irish newspapers.

Peddie, R. A. *Subject index of books published up to and including 1880*. London, 1933; 2nd ser., London, 1935; 3rd ser., London, 1939; new ser., London, 1948.

Prendeville, P. L. A select bibliography of Irish economic history. Part three: the nineteenth century. In *Econ. Hist. Rev.*, 1st ser., iv, no. 1 (Oct. 1932), pp 81–90.

Rafroidi, Patrick. Bibliographie. In *Études Irlandaises*, no. 1 (1972), pp 23–5.

—— *Irish literature in English: the romantic period (1789–1850)*. Atlantic Highlands, N.J., 1980. First published as *L'Irlande et le romantisme*. Paris, 1972.

    Vol. I, parts 1–3; vol. II, part 4, bibliography (list of and commentary on principal Irish periodicals, pp 379–92).

—— Alluin-Popot, Raymonde; Deboulonne, Marie-Jocelyne; Escarbelt, Bernard; Neville, Grace; and Rafroidi, Anne. The year's work in Anglo-Irish literature. In *Études Irlandaises*, no. 3 (1974), pp 41–55; no. 4 (1975), pp 157–88; i (1976), pp 205–30; ii (1977), pp 209–36; iii (1978), pp 59–86; iv (1979), pp 311–38; v (1980), pp 241–60. Continued as 'The year's work in Irish-English literature' in vi (1981), pp 195–210; vii (1982), pp 211–31; viii (1983), pp 297–329; ix (1984), pp 299–321; x (1985), pp 265–81; xi (1986), pp 195–215. Continued as 'Irish literature in English: the year's work' in xii, no. 2 (Dec. 1987), pp 211–33; xiii, no. 2 (Dec. 1988), pp 161–89; xiv, no. 2 (Dec. 1989), pp 197–220; xv, no. 2 (Dec. 1990), pp 181–214; xvi, no. 2 (Dec. 1991), pp 173–207; xvii, no. 2 (Dec. 1992), pp 175–209. In progress.

Schneider, Jürgen, and Sotscheck, Ralf. '*Irland*': eine Bibliographie selbständiger deutschsprachiger Publikationen: *16. Jahrhundert bis 1989*. Darmstadt, 1990.

Select bibliography of writings on Irish economic and social history, published in 1973 [etc.]. By Marie Boran, S. A. Caskey, S. J. Connolly, Richard English, T. P. Geary, Raymond Gillespie, S. R. Greenlees, Carla Keating, Triona Kennedy, Graeme Kirkham, Desmond McCabe, D. P. McCracken, Eamonn McKee, Martin Maguire, Stella Morrison, Niall Ó Ciosáin, Vivienne Pollock, Margaret Whelan, [etc.]. In *Ir. Econ. & Soc. Hist.*, i (1974), pp 67–70; ii (1975), pp 66–71; iii (1976), pp 83–7; iv (1977), pp 79–83; v (1978), pp 78–83; vi (1979), pp 74–80; vii (1980), pp 99–105; viii (1981), pp 113–24; ix (1982), pp 80–93; x (1983), pp 100–14; xi (1984), pp 129–41; xii (1985), pp 125–38; xiii (1986), pp 124–41; xiv (1987), pp 87–104; xv (1988), pp 107–23; xvi (1989), pp 102–15; xvii (1990), pp 101–16; xviii (1991), pp 62–80; xix (1992), pp 88–109. In progress.

Sharkey, B. R. A bibliography of printed material relating to County Antrim. [F.L.A. thesis. Belfast, 1972.]

Slade, Bertha Coolidge. *Maria Edgeworth, 1767–1849: a bibliographical tribute.* London, 1937.

Trinity College, Dublin. *Catalogus librorum impressorum.* 9 vols. Dublin, 1864–87. Reprinted in microfiche, Dublin, 1988.

Wade, Allan. *A bibliography of the writings of W. B. Yeats.* 3rd ed., revised by Russell K. Alspach, London, 1968.

Watson, George. *The new Cambridge bibliography of English literature.* 5 vols. Cambridge, 1969–77.

    Vol. III, 1800–1900; vol. IV, 1900–50.

White, Stephen. Soviet writings on Irish history, 1917–80: a bibliography. In *I.H.S.*, xxiii, no. 90 (Nov. 1982), pp 174–86.

Willging, Eugene, and Hatzfeld, Herta. *Catholic serials of the nineteenth century.* 15 vols. Washington, D.C., 1959–68.

Wolff, Robert Lee. *Nineteenth-century fiction: a bibliographical catalogue based on the collection formed by Robert Lee Wolff.* 5 vols. New York and London, 1981–6.

B GUIDES

Adams, J. R. R. *Northern Ireland newspapers; checklist and locations.* Belfast Library Association, 1980.

Bishop, A. W., and Ferguson, Kenneth. *Index to The Irish Sword, volumes I to XVIII, 1949–1992; compiled for volumes I to X by A. W. Bishop; continued to the end of volume XVIII and prepared for publication by Kenneth Ferguson.* [Dublin], 1992.

Blessing, Patrick J. *The Irish in America: a guide to the literature and the manuscript collections.* Washington, D.C., 1992.

Burchell, R. A. The historiography of the American Irish. In *Immigrants and minorities*, i, no. 3 (Nov. 1982), pp 281–305.

Calkin, Homer. The United States government and the Irish: a bibliographical study of research materials in the U.S. national archives. In *I.H.S.*, ix, no. 33 (Mar. 1954), pp 28–52.

Canning, Joseph. Nineteenth-century British parliamentary papers as a source for local history. In *Ulster Local Studies*, xi, no. 1 (1989), pp 5–9.

Cullen, L. M. Irish Manuscripts Commission survey of business records. In *Ir. Econ. & Soc. Hist.*, x (1983), pp 81–91.

Donnelly, Brian. Irish Manuscripts Commission survey of business records: archives report. In *Ir. Econ. & Soc. Hist.*, xvi (1989), pp 95–7.

—— Records of the Royal College of Physicians. In *Irish Archives*, i (1989), pp 31–4.

—— and Warke, Oonagh (ed.). Maritime history sources issue. *Irish Archives*, ii, no. 1 (summer 1992).

    Seven articles covering sources in Ireland, with bibliography of published works.

Études Irlandaises: a bilingual journal of Irish history, civilisation, and literature. Index [1972–92]. Sainghin-en-Mélantois, [1993].

Feldman, David. 'There was an Englishman, an Irishman, and a Jew . . .': immigrants and minorities in Britain [review article]. In *Hist. Jn.*, xxvi, no. 1 (1983), pp 185–99.

Finneran, Richard J. (ed.). *Anglo-Irish literature: a review of research.* New York, 1976. Supplement, 1983. (Modern Language Association of America.)

Flatman, Richard. A visit to the National Archives (head office). In *Irish Family History*, vi (1990), pp 91–100.

Hamell, P. J. *Index to the Irish Ecclesiastical Record (1864–1917): documents, articles, correspondence and reviews*. Dublin, 1963; 2nd ed. (1864–1963), Dublin, 1965.

Hannigan, Ken. Trade union records in Ireland. In *Archivum*, xxvii (1980), pp 73–9.

Harmon, Maurice. Anglo-Irish literature: a survey of general works. In *Études Irlandaises*, xvi, no. 2 (Dec. 1991), pp 19–26; xvii, no. 1 (June 1992), pp 157–67.

Hayes, R. J. (ed.). *Manuscript sources for the history of Irish civilisation*. 11 vols. Boston, 1966.

Hayley, Barbara, and McKay, Enda (ed.). *Three hundred years of Irish periodicals*. Dublin and Gigginstown, Co. Westmeath, 1987.

Helferty, Seamus, and Refaussé, Raymond (ed.). *Directory of Irish archives*. Dublin, 1988; 2nd ed., 1993.

Holzapfel, Rudolf P. *A survey of Irish literary periodicals from 1900 to the present day*. Dublin, 1964.

Inglis, K. S. Catholic historiography in Australia. In *Historical Studies*, viii (1958), pp 233–53.

Irish Historical Studies: supplement 1. Dublin, 1968.
    Includes index (by Esther Semple) for vols i–xv (1938–67).

Keaney, Marian. *Westmeath local studies: a guide to sources*. Mullingar, 1982.

Lester, Dee Gee. *Irish research: a guide to collections in North America, Ireland, and Great Britain*. Westport, Conn., 1987.

Library Associations of Ireland. *Directory of libraries in Ireland*. 2nd ed., Dublin and Belfast, 1988.

Lindsay, Deirdre, and Fitzpatrick, David. *Records of the Irish famine: a guide to local archives, 1840–1855*. Dublin, 1993.

Lohan, Rena. *Guide to the archives of the office of public works*. Dublin, 1994.

Lunn, Kenneth. The Irish in Britain: some recent work. In *Saothar*, viii (1982), pp 116–17.

Mac Giolla Choille, Breandán. Fenian documents in the state paper office. In *I.H.S.*, xvi, no. 63 (Mar. 1969), pp 258–84.

McTernan, John. *Sligo: sources of local history. A catalogue of the local history collection with an introduction and guide to sources*. Sligo, 1988.

MacWhite, Eoin. Guide to Russian writings on Irish history, 1917–63. In *Melbourne Slavonic Studies*, no. 3 (1969), pp 40–96.

Maltby, Arthur, and Maltby, Jean. *Ireland in the nineteenth century: a breviate of official publications*. Oxford and New York, 1979.

Marman, Ed (compiler and ed.). *Eire-Ireland, the comprehensive index, 1966–1988*. Index issue, vols i–xxiii (1992).

Metress, Séamus P. *The Irish-American experience: a guide to the literature*. Washington, D.C., 1981.

—— and Annable, Kathleen R. *The Irish in the Great Lakes region: a bibliographic survey*. Toledo, Ohio, 1990.

Neville, Grace. Westward bound: emigration to North America in the Irish Folklore Commission archives. In *Études Irlandaises*, xvii, no. 1 (June 1992), pp 195–207.

O'Connell, Declan. The Irish in Australia: some recent work. In *Saothar*, viii (1982), p. 115.

Ó Duilearga, Séamus. An untapped source of Irish history. In *Studies*, xxv (1936), pp 399–412.
　　Archives of the Irish Folklore Commission.
Ó Gráda, Cormac. *Irish agricultural history, recent research*. Dublin, 1989.
　　Bibliography, pp 1–8.
Osborough, W. N. Recent writing on modern Irish legal history. In *Zeitschrift für neuere Rechtsgeschichte*, viii (1986), pp 180–94.
O'Sullivan, S. The work of the Irish Folklore Commission. In *Oral History*, ii, no. 2 (1974).
Palmer, Samuel. *Index to The Times, 1790–1905*. CD-ROM, Cambridge, 1995.
Prochaska, Alice. *Irish history from 1700: a guide to sources in the Public Record Office*. London, 1986.
Refaussé, Raymond. Church of Ireland records. In *Irish Family History*, vi (1990), pp 101–11.
Ryan, James G. *Irish records: sources for family local history*. Salt Lake City, 1988.
Studies: an Irish quarterly review. General index of volumes i–l (1912–61). Roscrea, 1967.
Wallace, Janet. The central archives of the British Museum. In *Archives*, xix, no. 84 (Oct. 1990), pp 213–23.
Ward, John M. The historiography of the British commonwealth. In *Historical Studies*, xii, no. 48 (Apr. 1967), pp 556–70.
Weaver, J. W., and Lester, Dee Gee. *Immigrants from Great Britain and Ireland: a guide to archival and manuscript sources in North America*. Westport, Conn., 1986.
Wilentz, Robert S. Industrialising America and the Irish: towards the new departure. [Review essay.] In *Labor History*, xx, no. 4 (fall 1979), pp 579–95.
Woods, C. J. A guide to Irish biographical dictionaries. In *Maynooth Review*, vi, no. 1 (May, 1980), pp 16–34.
Writings on Irish history, 1936– . Dublin, 1938– . In progress.
　　Published annually in *I.H.S.* to 1979; lists for 1979–83 published in microfiche by Irish Committee of Historical Sciences; lists from 1984 published as annual booklets by I.C.H.S. in association with *I.H.S.* and (from 1986) with A New History of Ireland.
Yurdan, Marilyn. *Irish family history*. London, 1990. (Batsford Local History Series.)
　　Guide to archives and research procedures.

II SECONDARY WORKS

A GENERAL HISTORY

Bardon, Jonathan. *A history of Ulster*. Belfast, 1992.
Beckett, J. C. *The making of modern Ireland, 1603–1923*. London and New York, 1966; paperback ed., London and Boston, 1981.
—— *Confrontations: studies in Irish history*. London, 1972.
　　Contains essays on period 1800–1921.
—— *A short history of Ireland*. 6th ed., London, 1979.
Boyce, D. G. *Nineteenth-century Ireland: the search for stability*. Dublin, 1990. (New Gill History of Ireland, 5.)
Brady, Ciaran; O'Dowd, Mary; and Walker, B. M. (ed.). *Ulster: an illustrated history*. London, 1989.

Collins, M. E. *Ireland, 1800–1970*. London, 1976. 1st ed. published as *Ireland Three: union to the present day* (Dublin, 1972).

Cullen, L. M. *The emergence of modern Ireland, 1600–1900*. London, 1981.

Edwards, R. D. *A new history of Ireland*. Dublin, 1972.

Foster, R. F. *Modern Ireland, 1600–1972*. London, 1988; paperback ed., 1989.

Hoppen, K. Theodore. *Ireland since 1800: conflict and conformity*. London and New York, 1989.

Inglis, Brian. *The story of Ireland*. London, 1956.

Kearney, Hugh. *The British Isles: a history of four nations*. Cambridge, 1989.

Kee, Robert. *The green flag: a history of Irish nationalism*. London, 1972.

Lee, J. J. *Ireland, 1912–1985: politics and society*. Cambridge, 1989.

—— *The modernisation of Irish society*. Dublin, 1973. New impression, 1989. (Gill History of Ireland, 10.)

Lyons, F. S. L. *Ireland since the famine*. London, 1971; paperback ed., 1973.

McCaffrey, L. J. *The Irish question, 1800–1922*. Lexington, Ky., 1968.

McCartney, Donal. *The dawning of democracy in Ireland, 1800–1870*. Dublin, 1987. (Helicon History of Ireland, 9.)

MacDonagh, Oliver. *Ireland: the union and its aftermath*. Englewood Cliffs, N.J., 1968; rev. ed., London, 1977.

Mansergh, P. N. S. *The Irish question, 1840–1921*. 3rd ed., London, 1975. First ed. published as *Ireland in the age of reform and revolution* (London, 1940).

Moody, T. W. *The Ulster question, 1603–1973*. Dublin and Cork, 1974; 3rd ed., 1978.

—— and Martin, F. X. (ed.). *The course of Irish history*. Cork, 1967; 2nd ed., 1984. Further revised and enlarged ed., ed. F. X. Martin, Cork, 1994.

—— and Beckett, J. C. (ed.). *Ulster since 1800: a political and economic history*. London, 1954.

—— and —— *Ulster since 1800: a social survey*. London, 1957.

Murphy, J. A. *Ireland in the twentieth century*. Dublin, 1975; new impression, 1989.

Norman, E. R. *A history of modern Ireland*. London, 1971.

O'Farrell, P. J. *England and Ireland since 1800*. London, 1975.

O'Hegarty, P. S. *A history of Ireland under the union, 1801–1922*. London, 1952.

Ó Tuathaigh, Gearóid. *Ireland before the famine, 1798–1848*. Dublin, 1971; new impression, 1989.

Ranelagh, J. O. *A short history of Ireland*. Cambridge, 1983.

Stewart, A. T. Q. *The narrow ground: aspects of Ulster, 1609–1969*. London, 1977.

Strauss, E. *Irish nationalism and British democracy*. New York and London, 1951.

Travers, Pauric. *Settlements and divisions: Ireland, 1870–1922*. Dublin, 1988. (Helicon History of Ireland, 10.)

Vaughan, W. E. (ed.). *A new history of Ireland, V: Ireland under the union, 1801–1870*. Oxford, 1989.

B SPECIAL FIELDS AND TOPICS

1 POLITICAL HISTORY

Allen, Kieran. *The politics of James Connolly*. London, 1990.

Alter, Peter. *Die irische national Bewegung zwischen Parlament und Revolution: der konstitutionelle Nationalismus in Ireland, 1880–1918*. Munich and Vienna, 1971.

—— Symbols of Irish nationalism. In *Studia Hib.*, xiv (1974), pp 104–23.

Arnstein, Walter L. Parnell and the Bradlaugh case. In *I.H.S.*, xiii, no. 51 (Mar. 1963), pp 212–35.

Bartlett, Thomas. The origin and progress of the catholic question in Ireland, 1690–1800. In T. P. Power and Kevin Whelan (ed.), *Endurance and emergence: catholics in Ireland in the eighteenth century* (Dublin, 1990), pp 1–20.

—— The rise and fall of the protestant nation, 1690–1800. In *Éire-Ireland*, xxvi, no. 2 (summer 1991), pp 7–18.

—— *The fall and rise of the Irish nation: the catholic question, 1690–1830.* Dublin, 1992.

Beames, M. R. *Peasants and power: the Whiteboy movements and their control in pre-famine Ireland.* Brighton and New York, 1983.

Bedarida, François. *Irlande: la participation des classes populaires au mouvement national (1800–1921).* Paris, 1971.

Best, G. F. A. The protestant constitution and its supporters, 1800–1829. In *R. Hist. Soc. Trans.*, 5th ser., viii (1958), pp 105–27.

Bew, Paul. The problems of Irish unionism. In *Economy and Society*, vi, no. 1 (Feb. 1977), pp 89–109.

—— *Conflict and conciliation in Ireland, 1890–1910; Parnellites and radical agrarians.* Oxford, 1987.

—— Sinn Féin, agrarian radicalism, and the war of independence, 1919–21. In D. G. Boyce (ed.), *The revolution in Ireland, 1879–1923* (Basingstoke, 1988), pp 217–35, 265–7.

—— James Connolly (1868–1916) and Irish socialism. In Ciaran Brady (ed.), *Worsted in the game: losers in Irish history* (Dublin, 1989), pp 159–68.

—— The real importance of Sir Roger Casement. In *History Ireland*, ii, no. 2 (summer 1994), pp 42–5.

Biggs-Davison, John, and Chowdharay-Best, George. *The cross of Saint Patrick: the catholic unionist tradition in Ireland.* Bourne End, Kensal, 1984.

Blewett, Neal. *The peers, the parties, and the people: the general election of 1910.* London, 1972.

Bolton, G. C. *The passing of the Irish act of union: a study in parliamentary politics.* London, 1966.

Bowman, John. *De Valera and the Ulster question 1917–73.* Oxford, 1982.

Boyce, D. G. *Englishmen and Irish troubles; British public opinion and the making of English policy, 1918–22.* Cambridge, Mass., and London, 1972.

—— 'One last burial': culture, counter-revolution, and revolution in Ireland, 1886–1916. In D. G. Boyce (ed.), *The revolution in Ireland, 1879–1923* (Basingstoke, 1988), pp 115–36.

—— (ed.). *The Irish question in British politics, 1868–1986.* Basingstoke and London, 1988; New York, 1988.

Boyle, J. W. The Belfast Protestant Association and the Independent Orange Order, 1901–10. In *I.H.S.*, xiii, no. 50 (Sept. 1962), pp 117–52.

Brown, T. N. Nationalism and the Irish peasant, 1800–1846. In *Rev. Pol.*, xv, no. 4 (Oct. 1953), pp 403–45.

Brynn, Edward. *Crown and Castle: British rule in Ireland, 1800–1830.* Dublin, 1978.

Buckland, P. J. *Irish unionism: one – the Anglo-Irish and the new Ireland, 1885–1922.* Dublin and London, 1972.

—— *Irish unionism: two – Ulster unionism and the origins of Northern Ireland, 1886–1922.* Dublin, 1973.

Buckland, P. J. (ed.). *Irish unionism, 1885–1923: a documentary history*. Belfast, 1973.

—— The unity of Ulster unionism, 1886–1939. In *History*, lx (1975), pp 211–23.

—— *The Northern Ireland question, 1886–1986*. London, 1987. (Historical Association: New Appreciations in History, 3.)

—— The southern Irish unionists, the Irish question, and British politics. In Alan O'Day (ed.), *Reactions to Irish nationalism* (Dublin, 1987), pp 365–92.

—— Irish unionism and the new Ireland. In D. G. Boyce (ed.), *The revolution in Ireland, 1879–1923* (Basingstoke, 1988), pp 71–90.

Buckley, Mary. John Mitchel: Ulster and Irish nationality, 1842–48. In *Studies*, lxv (spring 1976), pp 30–44.

Budge, Ian, and O'Leary, Cornelius. *Belfast: approach to crisis: a study of Belfast politics, 1613–1970*. London, 1973.

Bull, Philip. The United Irish League and the reunion of the Irish parliamentary party, 1898–1900. In *I.H.S.*, xxvi, no. 101 (May, 1988), pp 51–78.

—— Land and politics, 1879–1903. In D. G. Boyce (ed.), *The revolution in Ireland, 1879–1923* (Basingstoke, 1988), pp 23–46.

—— The significance of the nationalist response to the Irish land act of 1903. In *I.H.S.*, xxviii, no. 111 (May 1993), pp 283–305.

Cahill, Gilbert. Irish catholicism and English toryism. In *Rev. Pol.*, xix, no. 1 (Jan. 1957), pp 62–76.

—— Some nineteenth-century roots of the Ulster problem, 1829–48. In *Ir. Univ. Rev.*, i, no. 2 (spring 1971), pp 215–37.

Cahill, Liam. *Forgotten revolution: Limerick soviet, 1919. A threat to British power in Ireland*. Dublin, 1990.

Callanan, Frank. *The Parnell split, 1890–91*. Cork, 1992.

Carroll, F. M. The American commission on Irish independence and the Paris peace conference of 1919. In *Irish Studies in International Affairs*, ii, no. 1 (1985), pp 103–18.

Clark, G. S. Kitson. 'The romantic element', 1830–50. In J. H. Plumb (ed.), *Studies in social history: a tribute to G. M. Trevelyan* (London and New York, 1955), pp 211–39.
    Discusses Young Ireland.

Clark, Samuel. The political mobilisation of Irish farmers. In Alan O'Day (ed.), *Reactions to Irish nationalism* (London, 1987), pp 61–77.

Clarke, Randall. The relations between O'Connell and the Young Irelanders. In *I.H.S.*, iii, no. 9 (Mar. 1942), pp 18–30.

Clarkson, J. D. *Labour and nationalism in Ireland*. New York, 1925; repr., New York, 1970.

Comerford, R. V. France, fenianism and Irish nationalist strategy. In *Études Irlandaises*, no. 7 (Dec. 1982), pp 115–25.

—— Anglo-French tension and the origins of fenianism. In Lyons & Hawkins, *Ire. under the union* (1980), pp 149–71.

—— *The fenians in context; Irish politics and society, 1848–1882*. Dublin and Atlantic Highlands, N.J., 1985. (Topics in Modern Irish History, 3.)

Condon, Mary D. The Irish church and the reform ministries. In *Jn. Brit. Studies*, iii (1964), pp 120–42.

Connell, Paul. The rise and fall of the repeal movement in County Meath, 1840–1845. In *Ríocht na Midhe*, vii, no. 2 (1982–3), pp 90–113.

—— Repeal and the Roman Catholic clergy in County Meath, 1840–45. In *Ríocht na Midhe*, vii, no. 3 (1984), pp 44–60.

Cooke, A. B., and Vincent, J. R. *The governing passion; cabinet government and party politics in Britain, 1885–6*. Brighton, 1974.

Corfe, Tom. *The Phoenix Park murders: conflict, compromise, and tragedy in Ireland, 1879–1882*. London, 1968.

Costello, F. J. Lloyd George and Ireland, 1919–21: an uncertain policy. In *Canadian Journal of Irish Studies*, xiv, no. 1 (July, 1988), pp 5–16.

—— The Irish representatives to the London Anglo–Irish conference in 1921: violators of their authority or victims of contradictory instructions? In *Éire-Ireland*, xxiv, no. 2 (summer 1989), pp 52–78.

—— The role of propaganda in the Anglo–Irish war, 1919–1921. In *Canadian Journal of Irish Studies*, xiv, no. 2 (Jan. 1989), pp 5–24.

Cullen, L. M. The cultural basis of modern Irish nationalism. In Rosalind Mitchison (ed.), *The roots of nationalism: studies in northern Europe* (Edinburgh, 1980), pp 91–106.

Curran, J. M. *The birth of the Irish Free State, 1921–23*. University, Ala., 1980.

Curtis, L. P., jr. *Coercion and conciliation in Ireland, 1880–1892: a study in conservative unionism*. Princeton, N.J., 1963.

—— Moral and physical force: the language of violence in Irish nationalism. In *Jn. Brit. Studies*, xxvii, no. 1 (Jan. 1988), pp 150–89.

D'Alton, Ian. *Protestant society and politics in Cork, 1812–44*. Cork, 1980.

D'Angelo, Giovanni. *Italy and Ireland in the nineteenth century: contacts and misunderstandings between two national movements*. Athlone, 1975.

Dangerfield, George. *The damnable question: a study in Anglo–Irish relations*. London, 1977.

D'Arcy, F. A. The artisans of Dublin and Daniel O'Connell, 1830–47: an unquiet liaison. In *I.H.S.*, xvii, no. 66 (Sept. 1970), pp 221–43.

—— Charles Bradlaugh and the Irish question: a study in the nature and limits of British radicalism, 1853–91. In Cosgrove & McCartney, *Studies in Ir. hist.* (1979), pp 228–56.

Davies, John. Wales, Ireland, and Lloyd-George. In *Planet: the Welsh Internationalist* (Feb.–Mar. 1988), pp 20–28.

Davis, Peter. The liberal unionist party and the Irish policy of Lord Salisbury's government, 1886–1892. In *Hist. Jn.*, xviii, no. 1 (1975), pp 85–104.

Davis, Richard. *Arthur Griffith and non-violent Sinn Féin*. Dublin, 1974.

—— Ulster protestants and the Sinn Féin press, 1914–22. In *Éire-Ireland*, xv, no. 4 (winter 1980), pp 60–85.

—— *The Young Ireland movement*. Dublin, 1987.

De Cogan, Donard. Ireland, telecommunications, and international politics, 1866–1922. In *History Ireland*, i, no. 2 (summer 1993), pp 34–8.

Dewar, M. W.; Brown, John; and Long, S. E. *Orangeism: a new historical appreciation*. Belfast, 1967; 2nd ed., Belfast, 1969.

Donnelly, James S., jr. The land question in nationalist politics. In T. E. Hachey and L. J. McCaffrey, *Perspectives in Irish nationalism* (Lexington, Ky., 1989), pp 79–98.

Drake, Michael. The mid-Victorian voter. In *Journal of Interdisciplinary History*, i, no. 3 (spring 1971), pp 473–90.

Dutton, David. Unionist politics and the aftermath of the general election of 1906: a reassessment. In *Hist. Jn.*, xxii, no. 4 (1979), pp 861–76.

Dyas, Éamon. *Federalism, Northern Ireland, and the 1920 government of Ireland act*. Belfast, 1988.

Edwards, Owen Dudley. *The sins of our fathers: roots of conflict in Northern Ireland*. Dublin, 1970.

—— Evans, Gwynfor; Rhys, Ioan; and Mac Diarmid, Hugh. *Celtic nationalism*. London, 1968.

Edwards, R. Dudley. The contribution of Young Ireland to the Irish national idea. In Séamus Pender (ed.), *Féilscríbhinn Torna: essays and studies presented to Tadg Ua Donnchadha* (Cork, 1947), pp 115–33.

Fair, J. D. The Anglo–Irish treaty of 1921: unionist aspects of the peace. In *Jn. Brit. Studies*, xii, no. 1 (Nov. 1972), pp 132–49.

—— *British interparty conferences: a study of the procedure of conciliation in British politics, 1867–1921*. Oxford, 1980.

—— From liberal to conservative: the flight of the liberal unionists after 1886. In *Victorian Studies*, xxix, no. 2 (winter 1986), pp 291–314.

Fanning, Ronan. The unionist party and Ireland, 1906–10. In *I.H.S.*, xv, no. 58 (Sept. 1966), pp 147–71.

—— The Irish policy of Asquith's government and the cabinet crisis of 1910. In Cosgrove & McCartney, *Studies in Ir. hist.* (1979), pp 279–303.

—— Britain, Ireland, and the end of the union. In British Academy and Royal Irish Academy, *Ireland after the union* (Oxford, 1989), pp 105–20.

Feingold, W. L. *The transformation of local government in Ireland, 1872–1886*. Boston, 1984.

Fergusson, James. *The Curragh incident*. London, 1963.

Fitzpatrick, David. *Politics and Irish life, 1913–21: provincial experience of war and revolution*. Dublin, 1977.

—— The geography of Irish nationalism, 1910–21. In *Past & Present*, no. 80 (1978), pp 113–44.

Foster, R. F. Parnell and his people: the ascendancy and home rule. In *Canadian Journal of Irish Studies*, vi, no. 1 (June 1980), pp 105–34.

—— To the northern counties station: Lord Randolph Churchill and the prelude to the Orange card. In Lyons & Hawkins, *Ire. under the union* (1980), pp 237–87.

—— Together and apart: Anglo-Irish agreements, 1886–1986. In *History Today*, xxxvi (May 1986), pp 6–9.

—— Anglo-Irish literature, Gaelic nationalism, and Irish politics in the 1890s. In British Academy and Royal Irish Academy (ed.), *Ireland after the union* (Oxford, 1989), pp 61–82.

Ford, Trowbridge. Dicey's crusade against Parnell. In *Studia Hib.*, xix (1979), pp 118–46.

Fox, R. M. *The history of the Irish Citizen Army*. Dublin, 1942.

Fraser, Peter. The liberal-unionist alliance: Chamberlain, Hartington, and the conservatives, 1886–1904. In *E.H.R.*, lxxvii, no. 302 (Jan. 1962), pp 53–78.

—— Unionism and tariff reform: the crisis of 1906. In *Hist. Jn.*, v, no. 2 (1962), pp 149–66.

—— The unionist débâcle of 1911 and Balfour's retirement. In *Jn. Mod. Hist.*, xxxv (Dec. 1963), pp 354–65.

Gailey, Andrew. *Ireland and the death of kindness; the experience of constructive unionism, 1890–1905*. Cork, 1987. (Studies in Irish History, new ser., vol. 2.)

—— Failure and the making of the new Ireland. In D. G. Boyce (ed.), *The revolution in Ireland, 1879–1923* (Basingstoke, 1988), pp 47–70.

Gallagher, Michael. Socialism and the nationalist tradition in Ireland, 1798–1918. In *Éire-Ireland*, xii, no. 2 (summer 1977), pp 63–102.

Garvin, Tom. *The evolution of Irish nationalist politics*. Dublin, 1981.

—— Defenders, Ribbonmen and others: underground political networks in pre-famine Ireland. In *Past & Present*, no. 96 (Aug. 1982), pp 133–55.

—— The anatomy of a nationalist revolution: Ireland, 1858–1928. In *Comparative Studies in Society and History*, xxviii (1986), pp 468–501.

—— Priests and patriots: Irish separatism and fear of the modern, 1890–1914. In *I.H.S.*, xxv, no. 97 (May 1986), pp 67–81.

—— *Nationalist revolutionaries in Ireland, 1858–1928*. Oxford, 1987.

—— The politics of language and literature in pre-independence Ireland. In *Ir. Political Studies*, ii (1987), pp 49–64.

—— Great hatred, little room: social background and political sentiment among revolutionary activists in Ireland, 1890–1922. In D. G. Boyce (ed.), *The revolution in Ireland, 1879–1923* (Basingstoke, 1988), pp 91–114.

Gash, Norman. *Politics in the age of Peel: a study in the technique of parliamentary representation, 1830–1850*. London, 1953; 2nd ed., with new introduction, London, 1977.

—— *Reaction and reconstruction in English politics, 1832–52*. Oxford, 1965. (Ford lectures, 1964.)

Geary, L. M. *The plan of campaign, 1886–1891*. Cork, 1986.

—— John Mandeville and the Irish crimes act of 1887. In *I.H.S.*, xxv, no. 100 (Nov. 1987), pp 358–75.

Gibbon, Peter. *The origins of Ulster unionism: the formation of popular protestant politics and ideology in nineteenth century Ireland*. Manchester, 1975.

Glaser, J. F. Parnell's fall and the nonconformist conscience. In *I.H.S.*, xii, no. 46 (Oct. 1960), pp 119–38.

Glandon, Virginia. John Dillon's reflections on Irish and general politics, 1919–21. In *Éire-Ireland*, ix, no. 3 (autumn 1974), pp 21–43.

Goldring, Maurice. *Faith of our fathers: the formation of Irish nationalist ideology, 1890–1920*. Dublin, 1982.

Goodlad, G. D. The liberal party and Gladstone's land purchase bill of 1886. In *Hist. Jn.*, xxxii, no. 3 (1989), pp 627–41.

Graham, A. H. The Lichfield house compact, 1835. In *I.H.S.*, xii, no. 47 (Mar. 1961), pp 209–25.

Gray, John. *City in revolt: James Larkin and the Belfast dock strike of 1907*. Belfast, 1985.

Gray, Trevor. *Nationalist and unionist: Ireland before the treaty*. Glasgow, 1989.

Greaves, T. Desmond. *Liam Mellows and the Irish revolution*. London, 1971; 1987.

Gutze, David W. Rosebery and Ireland: a reappraisal. In Alan O'Day (ed.), *Reactions to Irish nationalism* (London, 1987), pp 285–95.

Gwynn, Denis. *O'Connell, Davis, and the colleges bill*. Cork, 1948.

—— *Young Ireland and 1848*. Cork and Oxford, 1949.

Hachey, T. E. *Britain and Irish separatism from the fenians to the Free State, 1867–1922*. Chicago, 1977; Washington, D.C., 1985.

Hamer, D. A. The Irish question and liberal politics. In Alan O'Day (ed.), *Reactions to Irish nationalism* (London, 1987), pp 237–58.

Hancock, W. K. *Survey of British commonwealth affairs: problems of nationality, 1918–36*. Vol. I. London and New York, 1937.

   Two chapters on Ireland.

Hanham, H. J. Mid-century Scottish nationalism. In Robert Robson (ed.), *Ideas and institutions of Victorian Britain* (London and New York, 1967), pp 143–79.

Harbinson, J. F. *The Ulster unionist party, 1882–1973: its development and organisation.* Belfast, 1973.

Harrison, Henry. *Parnell. Joseph Chamberlain, and 'The Times'.* Dublin, 1953.

Hartley, Stephen. *The Irish question as a problem in British foreign policy, 1914–18.* Dublin and New York, 1986.

Hawkings, F. M. A. Defence and the role of Erskine Childers in the treaty negotiations of 1921. In *I.H.S.*, xxii, no. 87 (Mar. 1981), pp 251–70.

Hechter, Michael. *Internal colonialism: the celtic fringe in British national development, 1536–1966.* Berkeley, Calif., and London, 1975.

Hepburn, A. C. The Ancient Order of Hibernians in Irish politics, 1905–14. In *Cithara*, x (1971), pp 5–18.

—— The Irish council bill and the fall of Sir Antony MacDonnell, 1906–7. In *I.H.S.*, xvii, no. 68 (Sept. 1971), pp 470–98.

—— *The conflict of nationality in modern Ireland.* New York and London, 1980.

Heyck, T. W. *The dimensions of British radicalism: the case of Ireland, 1874–95.* Urbana, Ill., and London, 1974.

Hill, Jacqueline. Nationalism and the catholic church in the 1840s: views of Dublin repealers. In *I.H.S.*, xix, no. 76 (Sept. 1975), pp 371–95.

—— The intelligentsia and Irish nationalism in the 1840s. In *Studia Hib.*, xx (1980), pp 73–109.

—— The protestant response to repeal: the case of the Dublin working class. In Lyons & Hawkins, *Ire. under the union* (1980), pp 35–68.

—— The politics of privilege: Dublin corporation and the catholic question, 1792–1823. In *Maynooth Review*, vii (Dec. 1982), pp 17–36.

—— National festivals, the state, and 'protestant ascendancy' in Ireland, 1790–1829. In *I.H.S.*, xxiv, no. 93 (May 1984), pp 30–51.

—— The meaning and significance of protestant ascendancy, 1787–1840. In British Academy and Royal Irish Academy, *Ireland after the union* (Oxford, 1989), pp 1–22.

Hinde, Wendy. *Catholic emancipation: a shake to men's minds.* Oxford and Cambridge, Mass., 1992.

Holt, Edgar. *Protest in arms: the Irish troubles, 1916–23.* London, 1960.

Hoppen, K. T. *Elections, politics, and society in Ireland, 1832–1885.* Oxford, 1984.

Howard, C. H. D. Joseph Chamberlain, Parnell, and the Irish 'central board' scheme, 1884–5. In *I.H.S.*, viii, no. 32 (Sept. 1953), pp 324–61.

Hunseler, Wolfgang. *Das deutsche Kaiserreich und die Irische Frage, 1900–14.* Frankfurt-on-Main, 1978.

—— Die Irische Bürgerkriegsgefahr im Kalkul der deutschen Grossbrittanienpolitik in der Julikrise 1914. In *Militärgeschichtliche Mitteilungen*, xxxii (1982), pp 35–44.

Hurst, Michael. Ireland and the ballot act of 1872. In *Hist. Jn.*, viii, no. 3 (1965), pp 326–52.

—— *Joseph Chamberlain and liberal reunion: the Round Table conference of 1887.* Newton Abbot, 1970.

Hutchinson, John. *The dynamics of cultural nationalism: the Gaelic revival and the creation of the Irish nation-state.* London, 1987.

Jackson, Alvin. *The Ulster party: Irish unionists in the house of commons, 1884–1911.* Oxford, 1989.

—— The failure of unionism in Dublin, 1900. In *I.H.S.*, xxvi, no. 104 (Nov. 1989), pp 377–95.

—— The social and political roots of Irish partition. In *Revue française de civilisation brittanique*, v (1989), pp 13–28.

—— Unionist politics and protestant society in Edwardian Ireland. In *Hist. Jn.*, xxxiii, no. 4 (1990), pp 839–66.

—— Larne gun-running, 1914. In *History Ireland*, i, no. 1 (spring 1993), pp 35–8.

Jalland, Patricia. A liberal chief secretary and the Irish question: Augustine Birrell, 1907–1914. In *Hist. Jn.*, xix, no. 2 (1976), pp 421–51.

—— *The liberals and Ireland: the Ulster question in British politics to 1914*. Brighton and New York, 1980.

—— Irish home-rule finance: a neglected dimension of the Irish question, 1910–14. In *I.H.S.*, xxiii, no. 91 (May 1983), pp 233–53.

Jenkins, Brian. *Fenianism and Anglo-American relations during reconstruction*. Ithaca, N.Y., and London, 1969.

—— *Era of emancipation: British government of Ireland, 1812–1830*. Kingston and Montreal, Canada, 1988.

Jenkins, T. A. *Gladstone, whiggery, and the liberal party, 1874–1886*. Oxford, 1988.

Joannon, Pierre. L'Irlande et la France en 1848. In *Études Irlandaises*, xii, no. 2 (Dec. 1987), pp 133–54.

Jordan, Donald. John O'Connor Power, Charles Stewart Parnell and the centralisation of popular politics in Ireland. In *I.H.S.*, xxv, no. 97 (May 1986), pp 46–66.

—— *Land and popular politics in Ireland: County Mayo from the plantation to the land war*. Cambridge, 1994.

Jupp, P. J. *British and Irish elections, 1784–1831*. Newton Abbot, 1973.

—— Irish parliamentary elections and the influence of the catholic vote, 1801–20. In *Hist. Jn.*, x, no. 2 (1967), pp 183–96.

Kemp, Betty. The general election of 1841. In *History*, xxxvii (June 1952), pp 146–57.

Kennedy, B. A. Sharman Crawford's federal scheme for Ireland. In H. A. Cronne, T. W. Moody, and D. B. Quinn (ed.), *Essays in British and Irish history* (London, 1949), pp 235–54.

Kline, Benjamin. Churchill and Collins, 1919–22: admirers or adversaries? In *History Ireland*, i, no. 3 (autumn 1993), pp 38–44.

Kluge, H. D. *Irland in der deutschen Geschichtswissenschaft, Politik und Propaganda vor 1914 und im ersten Weltkrieg*. Frankfurt-on-Main, 1985.

Knowlton, Stephen R. *Popular politics and the Irish catholic church: the rise and fall of the independent Irish party, 1850–59*. New York, 1991.

Koss, Stephen. *The rise and fall of the political press in Britain*. London, 1981; 2nd ed., 1990.

Kriegel, A. D. The Irish policy of Lord Grey's government. In *E.H.R.*, lxxxvi, no. 338 (Jan. 1971), pp 22–45.

Laffan, Michael. The unification of Sinn Féin in 1917. In *I.H.S.*, xvii, no. 67 (Mar. 1971), pp 353–79.

—— *The partition of Ireland, 1911–1925*. Dundalk, 1983. (Dublin Historical Association, student paperbacks, 2nd ser., I.)

Lawlor, Sheila. *Britain and Ireland, 1914–23*. Dublin and Totowa, N.J., 1983.

Lee, J. J. Irish nationalism and socialism: Rumpf reconsidered. In *Saothar*, vi (1980), pp 59–64.

Loughlin, James. *Gladstone, home rule, and the Ulster question, 1882–1893*. Dublin and Atlantic Highlands, N.J., 1986.

    Contains extensive bibliography.

—— T. W. Russell, the tenant-farmer interest, and progressive unionism in Ulster, 1886–1900. In *Éire-Ireland*, xxv, no. 1 (spring 1990), pp 44–63.

Lowe, W. J. The Chartists and the Irish confederates: Lancashire, 1848. In *I.H.S.*, xxiv, no. 94 (Nov. 1984), pp 172–96.

Lubenow, W. C. *Parliamentary politics and the home rule crisis: the British house of commons in 1886*. Oxford, 1988.

Lyne, D. C., and Toner, P. M. Fenianism in Canada, 1874–84. In *Studia Hib.*, xii (1972), pp 27–76.

Lyne, Gerald J. Daniel O'Connell, intimidation, and the Kerry election of 1835. In *Kerry Arch. Soc. Jn.*, iv (1971), pp 74–97.

Lyons, F. S. L. *The Irish parliamentary party, 1890–1910*. London, 1951; repr., 1975.

—— The machinery of the Irish parliamentary party in the general election of 1895. In *I.H.S.*, viii, no. 30 (Sept. 1952), pp 115–39.

—— *The fall of Parnell, 1890–91*. London, 1960.

—— *Culture and anarchy in Ireland, 1890–1939*. Oxford, 1979.

Mac an Ghallóglaigh, Domhnall. The land league in Leitrim, 1879–83. In *Breifne*, vi, no. 22 (1983–4), pp 155–87.

McCaffrey, L. J. Home rule and the general election of 1874 in Ireland. In *I.H.S.*, ix, no. 34 (Sept. 1954), pp 190–212.

—— *Irish federalism in the 1870s: a study in conservative nationalism*. Philadelphia, 1962. (American Philosophical Society, Transactions, lii, pt 6.)

—— *Daniel O'Connell and the repeal year*. Lexington, Ky., 1966.

McCartney, Donal. The church and fenianism. In *University Rev.*, iv, no. 3 (winter 1967), pp 203–15.

—— De Valera's mission to the United States, 1919–20. In Cosgrove & McCartney, *Studies in Ir. hist.* (1979), pp 304–23.

McCracken, Donal P. *The Irish pro-Boers, 1877–1902*. Johannesburg, 1989.

McCready, H. W. Home rule and the liberal party, 1899–1906. In *I.H.S.*, xiii, no. 52 (Sept. 1963), pp 316–48.

MacDermot, Brian (ed.). *The catholic question in Ireland and England, 1798–1822: the papers of Denis Scully*. Dublin, 1988.

MacDonagh, Oliver. The contribution of O'Connell. In Brian Farrell (ed.), *The Irish parliamentary tradition* (Dublin and New York, 1973), pp 160–69.

—— Ambiguity in nationalism: the case of Ireland. In *Historical Studies*, xix, no. 76 (Apr. 1981), pp 337–52.

McDougall, D. J. Lord John Russell and the Canadian crisis, 1837–41. In *Canadian Historical Review*, xxii (1941), pp 369–88.

    Refers to Russell's Irish policy.

McDowell, R. B. *Public opinion and government policy in Ireland, 1801–46*. London, 1952; 2nd ed., Westport, Conn., 1975.

McEwen, J. M. The coupon election of 1918 and unionist members of parliament. In *Jn. Mod. Hist.*, xxxiv, no. 3 (Sept. 1962), pp 294–306.

—— The liberal party and the Irish question during the first world war. In *Jn. Brit. Studies*, xii, no. 1 (Nov. 1972), pp 109–31.

Machin, G. I. T. The catholic emancipation crisis of 1825. In *E.H.R.*, lxxviii, no. 308 (July 1963), pp 458–82.

—— *The catholic question in English politics, 1820–30.* Oxford, 1964.

MacIntyre, Angus. *The Liberator: Daniel O'Connell and the Irish party, 1830–47.* London, 1965.

McKillen, Beth. Irish feminism and national separatism, 1914–23. In *Éire-Ireland*, xvii, no. 3 (fall 1982), pp 52–67; no. 4 (winter 1982), pp 72–90.

MacLysaght, Edward. *East Clare, 1916–21.* Ennis, 1954.

McMinn, Richard. Presbyterianism and politics in Ulster, 1871–1906. In *Studia Hib.*, xxi (1981), pp 127–46.

—— Liberalism in north Antrim, 1900–14. In *I.H.S.*, xxiii, no. 89 (May 1982), pp 17–29.

—— The myth of 'Route' liberalism in County Antrim, 1869–1900. In *Éire-Ireland*, xvii, no. 1 (spring 1982), pp 137–49.

Mandle, W. F. *The Gaelic Athletic Association and Irish nationalist politics, 1884–1924.* London and Dublin, 1987.

Mansergh, Nicholas. *The unresolved question: the Anglo-Irish settlement and its undoing, 1912–72.* New Haven, Conn., and London, 1991.

Martin, F. X. Eoin MacNeill on the 1916 rising. In *I.H.S.*, xii, no. 47 (Mar. 1961), pp 226–71. (Select Documents, XX.)

—— Easter 1916: an inside report on Ulster. In *Clogher Rec.*, xii, no. 2 (1986), pp 192–208.

Metscher, Priscilla. *Republicanism and socialism in Ireland: a study in the relationship of politics and ideology from the United Irishmen to James Connolly.* Frankfurt-on-Main, Berne, and New York, 1986.

Miller, D. W. *Church, state and nation in Ireland, 1898–1921.* Dublin, 1973.

—— *Queen's rebels: Ulster loyalists in historical perspective.* Dublin, 1978.

Mitchell, Arthur. William O'Brien, 1881–1968, and the Irish labour movement. In *Studies*, lx (autumn–winter 1971), pp 311–31.

—— *Labour in Irish politics, 1890–1930: the Irish labour movement in an age of revolution.* Dublin, 1974.

Moody, T. W. The 'new departure' in Irish politics, 1878–9. In H. A. Cronne, T. W. Moody, and D. B. Quinn, *Essays in British and Irish history* (London, 1949), pp 303–33.

—— Michael Davitt and the British labour movement, 1882–1906. In *R. Hist. Soc. Trans.*, 5th ser., iii (1953), pp 53–76.

—— The Irish home-rule movement and the British liberal party. In *Topic*, xiii (1967), pp 44–59.

—— The *Times* versus Parnell and Co., 1887–90. In *Hist. Studies*, vi (1968), pp 147–82.

—— Anna Parnell and the Land League. In *Hermathena*, cxvii (summer 1974), pp 5–17.

Morgan, Austen. *Labour and partition: the Belfast working class, 1905–23.* London and Concord, Mass., 1991.

Morgan, Kenneth. Lloyd George and the Irish. In British Academy and Royal Irish Academy, *Ireland after the union* (Oxford, 1989), pp 83–104.

Munck, Ronald. At the very doorstep: Irish labour and the national question. In *Éire-Ireland*, xviii, no. 2 (summer 1983), pp 36–51.

Munsell, F. D. Charles Edward Trevelyan and Peelite Irish famine policy, 1845–6. In *Societas*, i (1971), pp 299–315.

Murphy, Brian. *Patrick Pearse and the lost republican ideal.* Dublin, 1991.

—— The first Dáil Éireann. In *History Ireland*, ii, no. 1 (spring 1994), pp 41–7.

Murphy, Cliona. *The women's suffrage movement and Irish society in the early twentieth century.* New York and Philadelphia, 1989.

Murphy, Detlef. *Die Entwicklung der politischen Parteien in Irland: Nationalismus, Katholizismus . . . als Determinenten der irischen Politik von 1823 bis 1977.* Oplanden, 1982. (Sozialwissenschaftliche Studien, 19.)

Murphy, Maura. Municipal reform and the repeal movement in Cork, 1833–44. In *Cork Hist. Soc. Jn.*, lxxxi, nos 233–4 (Jan.–Dec. 1976), pp 1–18.

——The ballad singer and the role of the seditious ballad in nineteenth-century Ireland: Dublin Castle's view. In *Ulster Folklife*, xxv (1979), pp 79–102.

——Fenianism, Parnellism, and the Cork trades, 1860–1900. In *Saothar*, v (May 1979), pp 27–38.

Murphy, Richard. Faction in the conservative party and the home rule crisis, 1912–14. In *History*, lxxi, no. 232 (June 1986), pp 222–34.

——Walter Long and the making of the government of Ireland act, 1919–20. In *I.H.S.*, xxv, no. 97 (May 1986), pp 82–96.

Murray, A. C. Agrarian violence and nationalism in nineteenth-century Ireland: the myth of Ribbonism. In *Ir. Econ. & Soc. Hist.*, xiii (1986), pp 56–73.

——Nationality and local politics in late nineteenth-century Ireland: the case of County Westmeath. In *I.H.S.*, xxv, no. 98 (Nov. 1986), pp 144–58.

Newsinger, John. John Mitchel and Irish nationalism. In *Literature and History*, vi (1980), pp 182–200.

——Canon and martial law: William O'Brien, catholicism, and Irish nationalism. In *Éire-Ireland*, xvi, no. 2 (summer 1981), pp 59–70.

——Old chartists, fenians, and new socialists. In *Éire-Ireland*, xvii, no. 2 (summer 1982), pp 19–45.

Ní Chinnéide, Síle. The Gaelic contribution to Irish nationalism. In *University Rev.*, ii, no. 9 (1960), pp 67–76.

Nowlan, K. B. *The politics of repeal: a study in the relations between Great Britain and Ireland, 1841–50.* London and Toronto, 1965.

O'Brien, Conor Cruise. *Parnell and his party, 1880–1890.* Oxford, 1957. Corrected impression, 1964.

——Revolution and the shaping of modern Ireland. In Robert O'Driscoll (ed.), *The Celtic consciousness* (Portlaoise, 1982), pp 427–35.

O'Brien, J. V. *William O'Brien and the course of Irish politics, 1881–1918.* Berkeley, Calif., and London, 1976.

Ó Broin, Leon. *Dublin Castle and the 1916 rising: the story of Sir Matthew Nathan.* Dublin, 1966; 2nd rev. ed., London, 1971.

Irish version published as *Na Sasanaigh agus éirí amach na Cásca: scéal Nathan* (Dublin, 1967).

——*The chief secretary: Augustine Birrell in Ireland.* Hamden, Conn., and London, 1970.

——*Fenian fever: an Anglo-American dilemma.* London and New York, 1971.

——*The prime informer: a suppressed scandal.* London, 1971.

——*Revolutionary underground: the story of the Irish Revolutionary Brotherhood, 1858–1924.* Dublin, 1976.

——The Phoenix conspiracy. In *Ir. Sword*, xiv, no. 54 (summer 1980), pp 25–46; no. 55 (winter 1980), pp 157–71.

—— *Protestant nationalists in revolutionary Ireland: the Stopford connection.* Dublin and Totowa, N.J., 1985.

—— *W. E. Wylie and the Irish revolution, 1916–21.* Dublin, 1989.

O'Day, Alan. *The English face of Irish nationalism: Parnellite involvement in British politics.* Dublin, 1977; 2nd ed., Aldershot, 1994.

—— *Parnell and the first home rule episode, 1884–87.* Dublin, 1986.

O'Ferrall, Fergus. *Catholic emancipation: Daniel O'Connell and the birth of Irish democracy, 1820–30.* Dublin, 1985.

—— Daniel O'Connell and Henry Cooke: the conflict of civil and religious liberty in modern Ireland. In *Irish Review*, i (1986), pp 20–27.

—— *Liberty and catholic politics, 1790–1990.* Belfast, 1990.

O'Higgins, Rachel. The Irish influence in the Chartist movement. In *Past & Present*, no. 20 (Nov. 1961), pp 83–96.

—— Irish trade unions and politics, 1830–50. In *Hist. Jn.*, iv, no. 2 (1961), pp 208–17.

O'Leary, Cornelius. *The elimination of corrupt practices in British elections, 1868–1911.* Oxford, 1962.

—— *Celtic nationalism.* Belfast, 1982. (Q.U.B.; New Lecture Series, no. 132.)

O'Mahony, Seán. *Frongoch: university of revolution.* Dublin, 1987.

O'Neill, Máire. The Dublin Women's Suffrage Association and its successors. In *Dublin Hist. Rec.*, xxxviii, no. 4 (Sept. 1985), pp 126–40.

Ó Tuathaigh, Gearóid. Gaelic Ireland, popular politics, and Daniel O'Connell. In *Galway Arch. Soc. Jn.*, xxxiv (1974–5), pp 21–34.

—— Nineteenth-century Irish politics: the case for normalcy. In *Anglo-Irish Studies*, i (1975), pp 71–81.

Owens, Gary. Hedge schools of politics: O'Connell's monster meetings. In *History Ireland*, ii, no. 1 (spring 1994), pp 35–41.

Owens, Rosemary (and Women in Community Publishing). *Did your granny have a hammer? a history of the Irish suffrage movement, 1867–1922.* Dublin, 1985.

Pakenham, Frank. *Peace by ordeal.* London, 1935; new ed., 1962.

Palmer, Norman D. *The Irish Land League crisis.* New Haven, Conn., 1940; repr., New York, 1978.

Patterson, Henry. *Class conflict and sectarianism: the protestant working class and the Belfast labour movement, 1868–1920.* Belfast, 1980.

—— Ireland: a new phase in the conflict between nationalism and unionism. In *Science and Society*, liii, no. 2 (summer 1989), pp 192–218.

Petler, D. N. Ireland and France in 1848. In *I.H.S.*, xxiv, no. 96 (Nov. 1985), pp 493–505.

Phillips, W. A. *The revolution in Ireland, 1906–23.* London, 1926.

Phoenix, Eamon. *Northern nationalism: nationalist politics, partition, and the catholic minority in Northern Ireland, 1890–1940.* Belfast, 1994.

Pomfret, J. E. *The struggle for land in Ireland, 1880–1923.* Princeton, N.J., 1930.

Prill, Felician. *Ireland, Britain, and Germany, 1871–1914: problems of nationalism and religion in nineteenth-century Europe.* Dublin, 1975.

Quinault, R. E. Lord Randolph Churchill and home rule. In *I.H.S.*, xxi, no. 84 (Sept. 1979), pp 377–403.

Quinlivan, Patrick, and Rose, Paul. *The fenians in England, 1865–1972: a sense of insecurity.* London and New York, 1982.

Ramsden, John. *The age of Balfour and Baldwin.* London, 1978.

Rempe, Paul. Sir Horace Plunkett and Irish politics, 1890–1914. In *Éire-Ireland*, xiii, no. 3 (fall 1978), pp 6–20.

Reynolds, J. A. *The catholic emancipation crisis in Ireland, 1823–9*. New Haven, Conn., 1954.

Riach, Douglas. Daniel O'Connell and American anti-slavery. In *I.H.S.*, xx, no. 77 (Mar. 1976), pp 3–25.

Robbins, Keith. Core and periphery in modern British history. In *Brit. Acad. Proc.*, lxx (1984), pp 275–97.

Rodner, W. S. Leaguers, covenanters, moderates: British support for Ulster, 1913–14. In *Éire-Ireland*, xvii, no. 3 (fall 1982), pp 68–85.

Rose, Paul. *The Manchester martyrs: the story of a fenian tragedy*. London, 1970.

Rumpf, Erhard, and Hepburn, A. C. *Nationalism and socialism in twentieth-century Ireland*. Liverpool, 1977.

Ryan, A. P. *Mutiny at the Curragh*. London, 1956.

Ryan, Desmond. *The rising: the complete story of Easter week*. Dublin, 1949; 3rd ed., 1957.

Ryan, Mark. *Fenian memories*. Dublin, 1945.

Savage, D. C. The origins of the Ulster unionist party, 1885–6. In *I.H.S.*, xii, no. 47 (Mar. 1961), pp 185–208.

—— The Irish unionists: 1867–1886. In *Éire-Ireland*, ii, no. 3 (autumn 1967), pp 86–101.

Savage, D. W. The attempted home rule settlement of 1916. In *Éire-Ireland*, ii, no. 3 (autumn 1967), pp 132–45.

Schneider, F. D. British labour and Ireland, 1918–21: the retreat to Houndsditch. In *Rev. Pol.*, xl, no. 3 (July 1978), pp 368–91.

Senior, Hereward. *Orangeism in Ireland and Britain, 1795–1836*. London and Toronto, 1966.

—— *The fenians and Canada*. Toronto, 1978.

Shannon, Richard. Gladstone and home rule, 1886. In British Academy and Royal Irish Academy, *Ireland after the union* (Oxford, 1989), pp 45–60.

Sheehy-Skeffington, A. D., and Owens, Rosemary. *Votes for women: Irish women's struggle for the vote*. Dublin, 1975.

Steele, E. D. Ireland and the empire in the 1860s: imperial precedents for Gladstone's first Irish land act. In *Hist. Jn.*, xi, no. 1 (1968), pp 64–83.

—— *Irish land and British politics: tenant right and nationality, 1865–1870*. London, 1974.

—— Cardinal Cullen and Irish nationality. In *I.H.S.*, xix, no. 75 (Mar. 1975), pp 239–60.

—— Gladstone, Irish violence, and conciliation. In Cosgrove & McCartney, *Studies in Ir. hist.* (1979), pp 257–78.

Stewart, A. T. Q. *The Ulster crisis: resistance to home rule, 1912–1914*. London, 1967; paperback ed., 1969. Repr., Aldershot, 1993.

Stubbs, John D. The unionists and Ireland, 1914–1918. In *Hist. Jn.*, xxxiii, no. 4 (1990), pp 867–93.

Sturgis, J. L. *John Bright and the empire*. London, 1969.
    Three chapters on Ireland.

Taylor, Rex. *Assassination: the death of Sir Henry Wilson and the tragedy of Ireland*. London, 1961.

Thirle, P. F. *Chamberlain, Irland, und das Weltreich, 1880–1895*. Frankfurt-on-Main, 1977.

Thompson, Frank. Attitudes to reform: political parties in Ulster and the Irish land bill of 1881. In *I.H.S.*, xxiv, no. 95 (May 1985), pp 327–40.

Thornley, David. *Isaac Butt and home rule*. London, 1964.

Townshend, Charles. The Irish railway strike of 1920: industrial action and civil resistance in the struggle for independence. In *I.H.S.*, xxi, no. 83 (Mar. 1979), pp 265–82.

—— *Political violence in Ireland: government and resistance since 1848*. Oxford, 1983.

Travers, Pauric. The financial relations question, 1800–1914. In F. B. Smith (ed.), *Ireland, England, and Australia* (Cork and Canberra, 1990), pp 43–69.

Vincent, J. R. *Pollbooks: how Victorians voted*. Cambridge, 1967.

—— Gladstone and Ireland. In *Brit. Acad. Proc.*, lxiii (1977), pp 193–238.

Walker, B. M. The Irish electorate, 1868–1915. In *I.H.S.*, xviii, no. 71 (Mar. 1973), pp 359–406.

—— Party organisation in Ulster, 1865–92: registration agents and their activities. In Peter Roebuck (ed.), *Plantation to partition* (Belfast, 1981), pp 191–209.

—— *Ulster politics: the formative years, 1868–86*. Belfast, 1989.

—— Ulster society and politics, 1801–1921. In Ciaran Brady, Mary O'Dowd, and B. M. Walker (ed.), *Ulster: an illustrated history* (London, 1989), pp 158–81.

Ward, A. J. *Ireland and Anglo-American relations, 1899–1921*. Toronto and London, 1969.

—— Lloyd George and the 1918 conscription crisis. In *Hist. Jn.*, xvii, no. 1 (1974), pp 107–29.

—— *The Easter rising: revolution and Irish nationalism*. Arlington Heights, Ill., 1980.

Ward, Margaret. *Unmanageable revolutionaries: women and Irish nationalism*. Dingle, 1983.

Warwick-Haller, Sally. *William O'Brien and the Irish land war*. Dublin, 1990.

Whyte, J. H. *The independent Irish party, 1850–9*. Oxford, 1958.

—— Daniel O'Connell and the repeal party. In *I.H.S.*, xi, no. 44 (Sept. 1959), pp 297–316.

—— The influence of the catholic clergy on elections in nineteenth-century Ireland. In *E.H.R.*, lxv (1961), pp 239–59.

—— *The Tenant League and Irish politics in the eighteen-fifties*. Dundalk, 1963, 1972. (Dublin Historical Association; Irish History Series.)

—— Landlord influence at elections in Ireland, 1760–1885. In *E.H.R.*, lxxx, no. 317 (Oct. 1965), pp 740–60.

Woods, C. J. The general election of 1892: the catholic clergy and the defeat of the Parnellites. In Lyons & Hawkins, *Ire. under the union* (1980), pp 289–319.

van der Wusten, H. H. *Iers verzet tegen de staatkundige eenheit der Britse Eilanden 1800–1921: een politick-geografische studie van integratie en desintegratie processen*. Amsterdam, 1977.

—— The United Kingdom and its Irish contenders, 1800–1922. In *Netherlands Journal of Sociology*, xvi, no. 2 (Oct. 1980), pp 171–84.

Younger, Calton. *A state of disunion: Arthur Griffith, Michael Collins, James Craig, and Eamon de Valera*. London, 1972.

2 CONSTITUTIONAL, ADMINISTRATIVE, AND LEGAL HISTORY

Best, G. F. A. The constitutional revolution, 1828–32. In *Theology*, lxii (1959), pp 226–34.

Blewett, Neal. The franchise in the United Kingdom, 1885–1918. In *Past & Present*, no. 32 (Dec. 1965), pp 27–56.

Blythe, E. P. The D.M.P. [Dublin Metropolitan Police]. In *Dublin Hist. Rec.*, xx, no. 3–4 (June–Sept. 1965), pp 116–26.

Boyce, D. G. Dicey, Kilbrandon, and devolution. In *Political Quarterly*, xlvi (1975), pp 280–92.

Boyce, D. G., and Hazelhurst, Cameron. The unknown chief secretary: H. E. Duke and Ireland, 1916–18. In *I.H.S.*, xx, no. 79 (Mar. 1977), pp 286–311.

Brady, J. C. English law and Irish land in the nineteenth century. In *N. I. Legal Quart.*, xxiii, no. 1 (spring 1972), pp 24–47.

—— *Religion and the law of charities in Ireland.* Belfast, 1976.

Brennan, Gerard. The Irish and law in Australia. In *Ir. Jurist*, xxi (1986), pp 95–106.

  Also in Oliver MacDonagh and W. F. Mandle, *Ireland and Irish Australia* (London, 1986), pp 18–32.

Brett, C. E. B. *Long shadows cast before: nine lives in Ulster, 1625–1977.* Edinburgh and London, 1978.

  Account of family of attorneys in Ulster.

Brewer, J. D. *The Royal Irish Constabulary: an oral history.* Belfast, 1990. (Institute of Irish Studies.)

Broeker, Galen. *Rural disorder and police reform in Ireland, 1812–36.* London and Toronto, 1970.

Casey, James. Republican courts in Ireland, 1919–22. In *Ir. Jurist*, v (1970), pp 321–42.

—— The genesis of the dáil courts. In *Ir. Jurist*, ix (1974), pp 326–38.

Casey, J. P. *The office of the attorney general of Ireland.* Dublin, 1980.

  Ch. 2 on characteristics before 1922.

Cochrane, Nigel. Public reaction to the introduction of a new police force, Dublin, 1838–45. In *Éire-Ireland*, xxii, no. 1 (spring 1987), pp 72–85.

Cohen, Emmeline. *The growth of the British civil service, 1780–1939.* London, 1941.

Conway, T. G. The approach to an Irish poor law, 1828–33. In *Éire-Ireland*, vi, no. 1 (spring 1971), pp 65–81.

Costello, F. J. The republican courts and the decline of British rule in Ireland, 1919–1921. In *Éire-Ireland*, xxv, no. 2 (summer 1990), pp 36–55.

Costello, Kevin. A constitutional antiquity?—the Habeas Corpus (Ireland) Act 1782 revisited. In *Ir. Jurist*, xxiii (1988), pp 240–54.

Crossman, Virginia. Emergency legislation and agrarian disorder in Ireland, 1821–41. In *I.H.S.*, xxvii, no. 108 (Nov. 1991), pp 309–23.

—— *Local government in nineteenth-century Ireland.* Belfast, 1994.

Curran, C. P. Figures in the hall [of the Four Courts]. In *Record of the centenary of the charter of the Incorporated Law Society of Ireland, 1852–1952* (Dublin, 1953), pp 75–82.

Davitt, Cahir. The civil jurisdiction of the courts of justice of the Irish Republic, 1920–22. In *Ir. Jurist*, iii (1968), pp 112–30.

Dawson, N. M. Illicit distillation and the revenue police in Ireland in the eighteenth and nineteenth centuries. In *Ir. Jurist*, xii (1977), pp 282–94.

De Blagd, E. P. 'Tim Kelly, guilty or not guilty?' Phoenix Park murders, 1882. In *Dublin Hist. Rec.*, xxv, no. 1 (Dec. 1971), pp 12–24.

Delany, V. T. H. Lord Justice Christian and law reporting: a sidelight on Irish legal history. In *N.I. Legal Quart.*, xii, no. 1 (Nov. 1956), pp 46–52.

—— Irish and Scottish land resettlement legislation. In *International and Comparative Legal Quarterly*, viii, pt 2 (Apr. 1959), pp 299–319.

—— The history of legal education in Ireland. In *Journal of Legal Education*, xii (1960), pp 396–406.

—— *Law relating to charities in Ireland.* Dublin, 1962.

Donaldson, A. G. *Some comparative aspects of Irish law.* Durham, N.C., and London, 1957; rev. ed., London, 1967.

Fair, J. D. The king, the constitution and Ulster: inter-party negotiations of 1913 and 1914. In *Éire-Ireland*, vi, no. 1 (spring 1971), pp 35–52.

Farrell, Brian. *The founding of Dáil Éireann: parliament and nation-building*. Dublin, 1971.

Flanagan, Kieran. The chief secretary's office, 1853–1914: a bureaucratic enigma. In *I.H.S.*, xxiv, no. 94 (Nov. 1984), pp 197–225.

Geary, L. M. John Mandeville and the Irish crimes act of 1887. In *I.H.S.*, xxv, no. 100 (Nov. 1987), pp 358–74.

Girvin, Stephen D. Three Irish-born judges at the Cape, 1861–96. In *Ir. Jurist*, xxiv (1989), pp 99–112.

Griffin, Brian. Religion and opportunity in the Irish police forces, 1836–1914. In R. V. Comerford, Mary Cullen, J. R. Hill, and Colm Lennon (ed.), *Religion, conflict, and coexistence in Ireland* (Dublin, 1990), pp 219–34.

Griffith, Margaret. The Irish record commission, 1810–30. In *I.H.S.*, vii, no. 25 (Mar. 1950), pp 17–38.

Griffiths, A. R. G. The Irish board of works in the famine years. In *Hist. Jn.*, xiii, no. 4 (1970), pp 634–52.

Harrison, R. S. *Irish insurance, historical perspectives* [1650–1939]. Cork, 1992.

Hart, Jennifer. Sir Charles Trevelyan at the treasury. In *E.H.R.*, lxxv, no. 294 (Jan. 1960), pp 92–110.

Hawkins, Richard. Gladstone, Forster, and the release of Parnell, 1882–8. In *I.H.S.*, xvi, no. 64 (Sept. 1969), pp 417–45.

——Liberals, land, and coercion in the summer of 1880: the influence of the Carraroe ejectments. In *Galway Arch. Soc. Jn.*, xxxiv (1974–5), pp 40–57.

——The 'Irish model' and the empire: a case for reassessment. In D. M. Anderson and David Killingray (ed.), *Policing the empire: government, authority, and control, 1830–1940* (Manchester and New York, 1991), pp 18–32.

Healy, Maurice. *The old Munster circuit*. London, 1948.

Heaney, Henry. Ireland's penitentiary, 1820–31: an experiment that failed. In *Studia Hib.*, xiv (1974), pp 28–39.

Hinde, R. S. E. Sir Walter Crofton and the reform of the Irish convict system, 1854–61. In *Ir. Jurist*, xii, pt 1 (1977), pp 115–47; pt 2, pp 295–338.

Hogan, Daire. *The legal profession in Ireland, 1789–1922*. Dublin, 1986.

——and Osborough, W. N. (ed.). *Brehons, serjeants, and attorneys: studies in the history of the Irish legal profession*. Blackrock, 1990.

Hughes, J. L. J. The Dublin court of conscience. In *Dublin Hist. Rec.*, xv, no. 2 (Apr. 1959), pp 42–9.

Jalland, Patricia. United Kingdom devolution, 1910–14: political panacea or tactical diversion? In *E.H.R.*, xciv, no. 373 (Oct. 1979), pp 757–85.

Johnson, D. S. The trials of Sam Gray: Monaghan politics and 19th-century Irish criminal procedure. In *Ir. Jurist*, xx (1985), pp 109–34.

Kendle, John. *Ireland and the federal solution: the debate over the United Kingdom constitution, 1870–1921*. Kingston and Montreal, 1989.

Kennedy, Denis. The Irish whigs, administrative reform, and responsible government, 1782–1880. In *Éire-Ireland*, viii, no. 4 (winter 1973), pp 55–69.

Kenny, Colum. The exclusion of catholics from the legal profession in Ireland, 1537–1829. In *I.H.S.*, xxv, no. 100 (Nov. 1987), pp 337–57.

Kenny, Colum. Paradox or pragmatist? 'Honest Tristram Kennedy' (1805–85): lawyer, educationalist, land-agent and member of parliament. In *R.I.A. Proc.*, xvii, sect. C (1993), pp 1–35.

—— Counsellor Duhigg—antiquarian and activist. In *Ir. Jurist*, xxi (1986), pp 300–25.

Kiernan, T. J. *History of the financial administration of Ireland to 1817.* London, 1930.

Kotsonouris, Mary. Revolutionary justice: the Dáil Éireann courts. In *History Ireland*, ii, no. 3 (autumn 1994), pp 32–6.

Large, David. The house of lords and Ireland in the age of Peel, 1832–50. In *I.H.S.*, ix, no. 36 (Sept. 1955), pp 367–99.

Larkin, J. F. Aspects of the career of John Blake Powell, 1861–1923. In *Ir. Jurist*, xx (1985), pp 403–24.

Leitch, W. A. The four burglars and the carving knife [the affair of Mr Purcell of Co. Cork, 1811]. In *N.I. Legal Quart.*, xviii, no. 3 (Sept. 1967), pp 322–9.

Lowe, W. J., and Malcolm, E. L. The domestication of the Royal Irish Constabulary, 1836–1922. In *Ir. Econ. & Soc. Hist.*, xix (1992), pp 27–48.

Lubenow, W. C. *The politics of government growth: early Victorian attitudes towards state intervention.* Newton Abbot and Hamden, Conn., 1971.

McAree, Noel. *Murderous justice: a study in depth of the infamous Connemara murders.* Limerick, 1990.

   The Maamtrasna murders of Aug. 1882.

McBride, L. W. *The greening of Dublin Castle: the transformation of bureaucratic and judicial personnel in Ireland, 1892–1922.* Washington, D.C., 1991.

McCabe, Desmond. Magistrates, peasants and the petty sessions courts: Mayo, 1823–50. In *Cathair na Mart*, v, no. 1 (1985), pp 45–53.

—— 'The part that laws or kings can cause or cure': crown prosecution and jury trial at Longford assizes, 1830–45. In Raymond Gillespie and Gerard Moran (ed.), *Longford: essays in county history* (Dublin, 1991), pp 153–72.

McColgan, John. *British policy and the Irish administration, 1920–22.* London, 1983.

MacDonagh, Oliver. *A pattern of government growth: the passenger acts and their enforcement, 1800–1860.* London, 1961.

—— The last bill of pains and penalties: the case of Daniel O'Sullivan, 1869. In *I.H.S.*, xix, no. 74 (Sept. 1974), pp 136–55.

—— *Early Victorian government, 1830–1870.* New York, 1977.

—— *The inspector-general: Sir Jeremiah Fitzpatrick and the politics of social reform, 1783–1802.* London, 1981.

McDowell, R. B. *The Irish administration, 1801–1914.* London, 1964; Westport, Conn., 1976.

—— *The Irish convention, 1917–18.* London and Toronto, 1970.

McEldowney, John. The case of 'The queen v. McKenna' (1869) and jury packing in Ireland. In *Ir. Jurist*, xii (1977), pp 339–53.

—— Lord O'Hagan (1812–1885): a study of his life and period as lord chancellor of Ireland (1868–1874). In *Ir. Jurist*, xiv (1979), pp 360–77.

—— William Neilson Hancock (1820–1888). In *Ir. Jurist*, xx (1985), pp 378–402.

—— Legal aspects of the Irish secret service fund, 1793–1833. In *I.H.S.*, xxv, no. 98 (Nov. 1986), pp 129–37.

—— and O'Higgins, Paul (ed.). *The common law tradition: essays in Irish legal history.* Dublin, 1990.

McGowan, James. Nineteenth-century developments in Irish prison administration. In *Administration*, xxvi, no. 4 (1978), pp 496–508.

Maley, William. The Crosshill railway murder. In *History Ireland*, i, no. 1 (spring 1993), pp 24–7.

Mansergh, Nicholas. The government of Ireland act, 1920, its origins and purposes: the working of the 'official mind'. In *Hist. Studies*, ix (1974), pp 19–48.

Marnane, E. J. *Cork county council, 1899–1985*. Cork, 1987.

Micks, W. L. *An account of the constitution, administration, and dissolution of the congested districts board from 1898 to 1923*. Dublin, 1925.

Middleton, C. R. Irish representative peerage elections and the conservative party, 1832–1841. In *American Philosophical Society, Proceedings*, cxxix, no. 1 (1985), pp 90–111.

Monaghan, H. J. Administration of the land acts. In *Public administration in Ireland* (1944), pp 125–42.

Newark, F. H. *Notes on Irish legal history*. Belfast, 1960. Reprint, with revisions, from *N.I. Legal Quart.*, vii, no. 2 (May 1947), pp 121–39. See also next item, pp 203–28.

—— *Elegantia juris: selected writings of F. H. Newark*. Ed. F. J. McIvor. Belfast, 1973.

Nowlan, K. B. The meaning of repeal in Irish history. In *Hist. Studies*, iv (1963), pp 1–17.

Ó Ceallaigh, Tadhg. Peel and police reform in Ireland, 1814–18. In *Studia Hib.*, vi (1966), pp 25–48.

Ó Duill, Greagoir. Founding the office: archival reform in the nineteenth century. In *Administration*, xxv (1977), pp 561–80.

—— Sir John Gilbert and archival reform. In *Dublin Hist. Rec.*, xxx, no. 4 (Sept. 1977), pp 136–42.

O'Halpin, Eunan. H. E. Duke and the Irish administration, 1916–18. In *I.H.S.*, xxii, no. 88 (Sept. 1981), pp 362–76. (Historical Revision XX.)

—— Sir Warren Fisher and the coalition, 1919–1922. In *Hist. Jn.*, xxiv, no. 4 (Dec. 1981), pp 907–27.

—— *The decline of the union: British government in Ireland, 1892–1920*. Dublin and Syracuse, N.Y., 1987.

O'Higgins, Paul. Blasphemy in Irish law. In *Modern Law Review*, xxiii (1960), pp 151–66.

—— English law and the Irish question. In *Ir. Jurist*, i (1966), pp 59–65.

O'Loan, John. Nineteenth century administrators: William Thomas Mulvany. In *Administration*, viii, no. 4 (winter 1960), pp 315–32.

    Shorter version of prize-winning essay.

Osborough, W. N. Law in Ireland, 1916–26. In *N.I. Legal Quart.*, xxiii, no. 1 (spring 1972), pp 48–81.

—— *Borstal in Ireland, 1906–74*. Dublin, 1975.

—— In search of Irish legal history: a map for explorers. In *Long Room*, no. 35 (1990), pp 28–38.

—— Puzzles from Irish law reporting history. In P. B. H. Birks (ed.), *The life of the law* (London and Rio Grande, 1993), pp 89–111.

—— (ed.). A treatise on impressing. [By] Alexander Hamilton [1804]. In *Ir. Jurist*, viii (1973), pp 117–42.

Ó Tuathaigh, M. A. G. *Thomas Drummond and the government of Ireland, 1835–41*. Dublin, 1978. (O'Donnell Lectures.)

Palmer, Stanley. *Police and protest in England and Ireland, 1780–1850*. Cambridge, 1988.

Plunkett, E. A. Attornies and solicitors in Ireland. In *Record of the centenary of the charter of the Incorporated Law Society of Ireland, 1852–1952* (Dublin, 1953), pp 38–74.

Power, T. P. 'The Black Book of King's Inns': an introduction with an abstract of contents. In *Ir. Jurist*, xx (1985), pp 135–212.

Robinson, Howard. *The British post office*. Princeton, N.J., 1948.
 Ch. 14, the Irish mail.

Robinson, H. W. *A history of accountants in Ireland*. Dublin, 1983.

Ryan, John. William Thomas Mulvany. In *Studies*, xii (Sept. 1923), pp 378–90.

Shannon, Catherine. The Ulster liberal unionists and local government reform, 1885–98. In *I.H.S.*, xviii, no. 71 (Mar. 1973), pp 407–23.

Sheills, Derek. The resident magistrates in Ireland, 1860–1922. In *International Association for the History of Crime and Criminal Justice Bulletin*, xv (Feb. 1992), pp 39–53.

Sheridan, L. A. Irish private law and the English lawyer. In *International and Comparative Legal Quarterly*, 4th ser., i, pt 2 (Apr. 1952), pp 196–212.

Shipkey, Robert. Problems of Irish patronage during the chief secretaryship of Robert Peel, 1812–18. In *Hist. Jn.*, x, no. 1 (1967), pp 41–56.

Smith, B. A. The Irish general prisons board, 1877–1885: efficient deterrence or bureaucratic ineptitude? In *Ir. Jurist*, xv (1980), pp 122–36.

—— The Irish prison system, 1885–1914: land war to world war. In *Ir. Jurist*, xvi (1981), pp 316–49.

Townshend, Charles. Martial law: legal and administrative problems of civil emergency in Britain and the empire, 1800–1940. In *Hist. Jn.*, xxv, no. 1 (1982), pp 167–95.

Tulloch, Hugh. A. V. Dicey and the Irish question, 1870–1922. In *Ir. Jurist*, xv (1980), pp 137–65.

Turner, John. *Lloyd George's secretariat*. Cambridge, 1980. Ch. 7, Ireland.

Waldron, Jarlath. *Maamtrasna: the murders and the mystery*. Dublin, 1992.

Weston, Corinne. The liberal leadership and the lords' veto, 1907–10. In *Hist. Jn.*, xi, no. 3 (1968), pp 508–37.

Wylie, J. C. W. *Irish land law*. London, 1975; 2nd ed., 1986.

3 ECCLESIASTICAL HISTORY

Ahern, John. The plenary synod of Thurles. In *I.E.R.*, lxxv (May 1951), pp 385–403; lxxviii (July 1952), pp 1–20.

Akenson, D. H. *The Church of Ireland: ecclesiastical reform and revolution, 1800–1885*. New Haven, Conn., and London, 1971.

Allen, Robert. *The Presbyterian College, Belfast, 1853–1953*. Belfast, 1954.

Bane, Liam. John McHale and John MacEvilly: conflict in the nineteenth-century catholic hierarchy. In *Archiv. Hib.*, xxxix (1984), pp 45–52.

Barkley, J. M. *Short history of the presbyterian church in Ireland*. Belfast, 1959.

Barry, P. C. The holy see and the Irish national schools. In *I.E.R.*, xcii (Aug. 1959), pp 90–105.

—— The legislation of the synod of Thurles, 1850. In *Ir. Theol. Quart.*, xxvi (1959), pp 131–66.

Bell, P. M. H. *Disestablishment in Ireland and Wales*. London, 1969.

Best, G. F. A. Popular protestantism in Victorian Britain. In Robert Robson (ed.), *Ideas and institutions of Victorian Britain* (London, 1967), pp 115–42.

Bolster, Sr M. Angela. *Mercy in Cork, 1837–87*. Cork, 1987.

Bowen, Desmond. *Paul, Cardinal Cullen, and the shaping of modern Irish catholicism*. Dublin, 1983.

Brady, John. Ireland and the ecclesiastical titles bill. In *I.E.R.*, xcix (1963), pp 338–49.

Broderick, J. F. *The holy see and the Irish movement for the repeal of the union with England, 1829–47*. Rome, 1951.

Brooke, Peter. *Ulster presbyterianism: the historical perspective, 1610–1970*. Dublin, 1987.

Brose, Olive. *Church and parliament: the reshaping of the Church of England, 1828–60*. Oxford, 1959.

Brown, Lindsay T. The presbyterians of Co. Monaghan (part I). In *Clogher Rec.*, xiii, no. 3 (1990), pp 7–54.

Brynn, Edward. *The Church of Ireland in the age of catholic emancipation*. New York and London, 1982.

Butler, T. C. *John's Lane: history of the Augustinian friars in Dublin, 1280–1980*. Dublin, 1983.

Cahill, Gilbert. The Protestant Association and the anti-Maynooth agitation of 1845. In *Cath. Hist. Rev.*, xliii, no. 3 (Oct. 1957), pp 273–308.

Cannon, Seán. *Irish episcopal meetings, 1788–1882: a juridico-historical study*. Rome, 1979.

Carey, Patrick. Voluntaryism: an Irish catholic tradition. In *Church History*, xlviii, no. 1 (Mar. 1979), pp 49–62.

Coldrey, B. M. *Faith and fatherland: the Christian Brothers and the development of Irish nationalism, 1838–1921*. Dublin, 1988.

Comerford, R. V.; Cullen, Mary; Hill, J. R.; and Lennon, Colm (ed.). *Religion, conflict, and coexistence in Ireland: essays presented to Monsignor Patrick J. Corish*. Dublin, 1990.

Connolly, S. J. *Priests and people in pre-famine Ireland, 1780–1845*. Dublin, 1982.

——*Religion and society in nineteenth-century Ireland*. Dublin, 1985. (Studies in Irish Economic and Social History, 3.)

Corish, P. J. The Catholic Truth Society of Ireland: the first fifty years, 1899–1949. In Catholic Truth Society of Ireland (ed.), *First fifty years, 1899–1949* (Dublin, 1949), pp 11–26.

——Cardinal Cullen and Archbishop MacHale. In *I.E.R.*, xci (June 1959), pp 393–408.

——Cardinal Cullen and the National Association of Ireland. In *Reportorium Novum*, iii, no. 1 (1961–2), pp 13–61.

——Catholic Ireland, 1864. In *I.E.R.*, cii (Oct. 1964), pp 196–205.

——Political problems, 1860–1878. In Corish, *Ir. catholicism*, v, fasc. 3 (1967).

——The church since emancipation: catholic education. In Corish, *Ir. catholicism*, v, fasc. 6 (1971).

——Gallicanism at Maynooth: Archbishop Cullen and the royal visitation of 1853. In Cosgrove & McCartney, *Studies in Ir. hist.* (1979), pp 176–89.

——*The Irish catholic experience: a historical survey*. Dublin, 1985.

Cunningham, T. P. Church reorganisation. In Corish, *Ir. catholicism*, v, fasc. 7 (1970).

De Brún, Pádraig. The Irish Society's bible teachers, 1818–27. In *Éigse*, xx (1984), pp 34–92; xxi (1986), pp 72–149; xxii (1987), pp 54–106; xxiv (1990), pp 71–120.

Deems, L. E. The story of the Harcourt Street Baptist Church, Dublin. In *Ir. Baptist Hist. Soc. Jn.*, xiv (1981–2), pp 23–34.

Ellis, J. T. *Cardinal Consalvi and Anglo-papal relations, 1814–24*. Washington, D.C., 1942.

Fahey, Tony. Nuns in the catholic church in Ireland in the nineteenth century. In Mary Cullen (ed.), *Girls don't do honours* (Dublin, 1987), pp 7–30.

Ford, Alan; McGuire, James; and Milne, Kenneth. *As by law established: the Church of Ireland since the reformation*. Dublin, 1995.

Gilley, Sheridan. Protestant London, no-popery, and the Irish poor, 1830–60. In *Recusant History*, x, no. 4 (Jan. 1970), pp 210–30; xi, no. 1 (Jan. 1971), pp 21–46.

—— The Roman Catholic mission to the Irish in London. In *Recusant History*, x, no. 3 (Oct. 1969), pp 123–45.

—— The Roman Catholic Church and the nineteenth-century Irish diaspora. In *Jn. Ecc. Hist.*, xxxv (1984), pp 188–207.

—— The catholic church and revolution. In D. G. Boyce (ed.), *The revolution in Ireland, 1879–1923* (Basingstoke, 1988), pp 157–72.

Grogan, Geraldine. *The noblest agitator: Daniel O'Connell and the German catholic movement, 1830–50*. Dublin, 1991.

Grubb, Isabel. *Quakers in Ireland, 1654–1900*. London, 1927.

Haire, J. L. M. (ed.). *Challenge and conflict: essays in Irish presbyterian history and doctrine*. Belfast, 1981.

Hempton, D. N. The methodist crusade in Ireland, 1795–1845. In *I.H.S.*, xxii, no. 85 (Mar. 1980), pp 33–48.

—— Methodism in Irish society, 1770–1830. In *R. Hist. Soc. Trans.*, 5th ser., xxxvi (1986), pp 117–42.

Hempton, David, and Hill, Myrtle. *Evangelical protestantism in Ulster society, 1740–1890*. London and New York, 1992.

Hepburn, A. C. Catholics in the north of Ireland, 1850–1921: the urbanisation of a minority. In A. C. Hepburn (ed.), *Minorities in history* (London, 1978), pp 84–101.

Hexter, J. H. The protestant revival and the catholic question in England, 1778–1829. In *Jn. Mod. Hist.*, viii (1936), pp 297–318.

Hill, Myrtle. Popular protestantism in Ulster in the post-rebellion period, c.1790–1810. In W. J. Shiels and Diana Wood, *The churches: Ireland and the Irish* (Oxford, 1989), pp 191–202.

Hogan, E. M. *The Irish missionary movement: a historical survey, 1830–1980*. Dublin, 1990; Washington, D.C., 1991.

Holmes, R. F. *Our Irish presbyterian heritage*. Belfast, 1985.

Hurley, Michael (ed.). *Irish anglicanism, 1869–1969: essays presented to the Church of Ireland, on the occasion of the centenary of its disestablishment, by a group of methodist, presbyterian, quaker, and Roman Catholic scholars*. Dublin, 1970.

Hynes, Eugene. Nineteenth-century Irish catholicism, farmers' ideology and national religion: explorations in cultural explanation. In R. O'Toole (ed.), *Sociological studies in Roman Catholic religion: historical and contemporary perspectives* (New York, 1989).

Jeffery, Frederick. *Irish methodism: an historical account of its traditions, theology, and influence*. Belfast, 1964.

Jenkins, Hilary. The Irish dimension of the British Kulturkampf: vaticanism and civil allegiance, 1870–5. In *Jn. Ecc. Hist.*, xxx, no. 3 (July 1979), pp 355–77.

Johnston, T. J.; Robinson, J. L.; and Jackson, R. W. *A history of the Church of Ireland*. Dublin, 1953.

Keenan, D. J. *The catholic church in nineteenth-century Ireland: a sociological study*. Dublin and Totowa, N.J., 1983.

Kennedy, T. P. Church building. In Corish, *Ir. catholicism*, v, fasc. 8 (1970).

Kerr, D. A. *Peel, priests, and politics: Sir Robert Peel's administration and the Roman Catholic church in Ireland, 1841–46*. Oxford, 1982.

—— Under the union flag: the catholic church in Ireland, 1800–1870. In British Academy and Royal Irish Academy, *Ireland after the union* (Oxford, 1989), pp 23–44.

—— 'A nation of beggars'? Priests, people, and politics in Famine Ireland, 1846–52. Oxford, 1994.

Larkin, Emmet. Church and state in Ireland in the nineteenth century. In *Church History*, xxxi, no. 3 (Sept. 1962), pp 294–306.

—— The quarrel among the Roman Catholic hierarchy over the national system of education in Ireland, 1838–41. In R. B. Browne, W. J. Roscelli, and Richard Loftus (ed.), *The Celtic cross: studies in Irish culture and literature* (Purdue, Ind., 1964), pp 121–44.

—— Socialism and catholicism in Ireland. In *Church History*, xxxiii, no. 4 (Dec. 1964), pp 462–83.

—— Economic growth, capital investment, and the Roman Catholic church in nineteenth-century Ireland. In *A.H.R.*, lxxii, no. 3 (Apr. 1967), pp 852–84.

—— The devotional revolution in Ireland, 1850–75. In *A.H.R.*, lxxvii, no. 3 (June 1972), pp 625–52.

—— *The Roman Catholic church and the creation of the modern Irish state, 1878–86*. Philadelphia, 1975.

—— *The Roman Catholic church and the Plan of Campaign in Ireland, 1886–8*. Cork, 1978.

—— *The Roman Catholic church in Ireland and the fall of Parnell, 1888–1891*. Chapel Hill, N.C., 1979.

—— *The making of the Roman Catholic church in Ireland, 1850–60*. Chapel Hill, N.C., 1980.

—— *The historical dimension of Irish catholicism*. Washington, D.C., 1984.

—— Socialism and catholicism in Ireland. In *Studies*, lxxiv, no. 293 (spring 1985), pp 66–92.

—— *The consolidation of the Roman Catholic church in Ireland, 1860–1870*. Chapel Hill, N.C., and Dublin, 1987.

—— The problem of Irish clerical avarice in the nineteenth century. In *Éire-Ireland*, xxiv, no. 3 (1989), pp 33–41.

—— *The Roman Catholic church and the home rule movement in Ireland, 1870–1874*. Chapel Hill, N.C., 1990.

Leighton, C. D. A. Gallicanism and the veto controversy: church, state, and catholic community in early nineteenth-century Ireland. In R. V. Comerford, Mary Cullen, J. R. Hill, and Colm Lennon (ed.), *Religion, conflict, and coexistence in Ireland* (Dublin, 1990), pp 135–58.

Loughridge, Adam. *The covenanters in Ireland: a history of the reformed Presbyterian Church of Ireland*. Belfast, 1984.

Lowe, W. J. The Lancashire Irish and the catholic church, 1846–71: the social dimension. In *I.H.S.*, xx, no. 78 (Sept. 1976), pp 129–55.

Lysaght, Moira. Daniel Murray, archbishop of Dublin, 1823–52. In *Dublin Hist. Rec.*, xxvii, no. 3 (June 1974), pp 101–8.

Macauley, Ambrose. William Crolly, archbishop of Armagh, 1835–49. In *Seanchas Ardmhacha*, xiv, no. 1 (1990), pp 1–19.

MacDonagh, Oliver. The politicization of the Irish catholic bishops, 1800–1850. In *Hist. Jn.*, xviii, no. 1 (1975), pp 37–53.

McDowell, R. B. *The Church of Ireland, 1869–1969*. London, 1975. (Studies in Irish History, 2nd ser.)

McGlade, Joseph. The missions: Africa and the Orient. In Corish, *Ir. catholicism*, vi, fasc. 8 (1967).

McGrath, Fergal. The university question. In Corish, *Ir. catholicism*, v, fasc. 6 (1971).

Machin, G. I. T. Lord John Russell and the prelude to the ecclesiastical titles bill, 1846–51. In *Jn. Ecc. Hist.*, xxv, no. 3 (July 1974), pp 277–95.

—— *Politics and the churches in Great Britain, 1832–1868*. Oxford, 1977.

—— *Politics and the churches in Great Britain, 1869–1921*. Oxford, 1987.

MacMahon, J. A. The catholic clergy and the social question in Ireland, 1891–1916. In *Studies*, lxx (1981), pp 263–88.

MacNamee, Brian. The 'second reformation' in Ireland. In *Ir. Theol. Quart.*, xxxiii (1966), pp 39–64.

——J.K.L.'s letter on the union of the churches. In *Ir. Theol. Quart.*, xxxvi, no. 1 (Jan. 1969), pp 46–69.

Macourt, M. P. A. The religious inquiry in the Irish census of 1861. In *I.H.S.*, xxi, no. 82 (Sept. 1978), pp 168–87.

MacRedmond, Louis. *To the greater glory: a history of the Irish Jesuits*. Dublin, 1991.

Mac Suibhne, Peadar. Ireland at the Vatican council. In *I.E.R.*, xciii (Apr.–May 1960), pp 209–22, 295–307.

Miller, D. W. Irish catholicism and the great famine. In *Journal of Social History*, ix, no. 1 (1975), pp 81–98.

—— Presbyterianism and 'modernisation' in Ulster. In *Past & Present*, no. 80 (1978), pp 66–90.

Milne, Kenneth. *The Church of Ireland: a history*. Dublin, 1966.

Mooney, Gary. British diplomatic relations with the Holy See, 1793–1830. In *Recusant History*, xiv (1978), pp 193–210.

Murphy, Ignatius. Some attitudes to religious freedom and ecumenism in pre-emancipation Ireland. In *I.E.R.*, cv (Feb. 1966), pp 93–104.

—— Primary education. In Corish, *Ir. catholicism*, v, fasc. 6 (1971).

Murphy, J. A. The support of the catholic clergy in Ireland, 1750–1850. In *Hist. Studies*, v (1965), pp 103–21.

—— Priests and people in modern Irish history. In *Christus Rex*, xxiii, no. 4 (Oct. 1969), pp 235–59.

Murphy, J. H. The role of Vincentian parish missions in the 'Irish counter-reformation' of the mid-nineteenth century. In *I.H.S.*, xxiv, no. 94 (Nov. 1984), pp 152–71.

Murphy, Maura. Repeal, popular politics, and the catholic clergy of Cork, 1840–50. In *Cork Hist. Soc. Jn.*, lxxxii (1977), pp 39–48.

Newsinger, John. Revolution and catholicism in Ireland, 1848–1923. In *European Studies Review*, ix, no. 4 (1979), pp 457–80.

Norman, E. R. *The catholic church and Ireland in the age of rebellion, 1859–73*. London and Ithaca, N.Y., 1965.

—— *The catholic church and Irish politics in the 1860s*. Dundalk, 1965. (Dublin Historical Association.)

—— The Maynooth question of 1845. In *I.H.S.*, xv, no. 60 (Sept. 1967), pp 407–37.

Nowlan, K. B. The catholic clergy and Irish politics in the eighteen thirties and forties. In *Hist. Studies*, ix (1974), pp 119–35.

Ó Ceallaigh, Tadg. Disestablishment and church education. In *Studia Hib.*, x (1970), pp 36–69.

O'Connell, M. R. Daniel O'Connell and religious freedom. In *Thought*, l (1975), pp 176–87.

O'Donoghue, Patrick. Causes of the opposition to tithes, 1830–8. In *Studia Hib.*, v (1965), pp 7–28.

—— Opposition to tithe payments in 1830–31. In *Studia Hib.*, vi (1966), pp 69–98.

—— Opposition to tithe payments in 1832–33. In *Studia Hib.*, xii (1972), pp 77–108.

Ó Fiaich, Tomás. The catholic clergy and the independence movement. In *Capuchin Annual*, xxxvii (1970), pp 480–502.

O'Neill, Timothy P. The catholic church and the relief of the poor, 1815–45. In *Archiv. Hib.*, xxxi (1973), pp 132–45.

O'Shea, James. *Priest, politics, and society in post-famine Ireland: a study of County Tipperary, 1850–1891.* Atlantic Highlands, N.J., and Dublin, 1983.

Ó Suilleabháin, S. V. Secondary education. In Corish, *Ir. catholicism*, v, fasc. 6 (1971).

Phillips, W. A. (ed.). *History of the Church of Ireland from the earliest times to the present day.* 3 vols. Oxford, 1933–4.

Pickering, W. S. F. The 1851 religious census: a useless experiment? In *British Journal of Sociology*, xviii (1967), pp 382–407.

Porter, Norman. Irish baptists and Orangeism. In *Ir. Baptist Hist. Soc. Jn.*, xviii (1985–6), pp 4–17.

Presbyterian Church in Ireland General Assembly. *A history of congregations in the Presbyterian Church in Ireland, 1610–1982.* Belfast, 1982.

Purcell, Mary. *The story of the Vincentians: a record of the achievements in Ireland and Britain of the priests and lay-brothers of the Congregation of the Mission, founded by St Vincent de Paul.* Dublin, 1973.

Quigley, E. J. The year of grace. In *I.E.R.*, lix (May 1942), pp 453–60.
The Ulster revival of 1859.

Roberts, Patricia. *The life and ministry of Edward Cooney.* Enniskillen, 1990.

Roche, K. F. The relations of the catholic church and the state in England and Ireland, 1800–1852. In *Hist. Studies*, iii (1961), pp 9–24.

Sharpe, John. *Reapers of the harvest: the Redemptorists in Great Britain and Ireland, 1843–1898.* Dublin, 1989.

Shearman, Hugh. *How the Church of Ireland was disestablished.* Dublin, 1970.

Shiels, W. J., and Wood, Diana (ed.). *The churches: Ireland and the Irish.* Oxford, 1989. (Studies in Church History, 25.)

Shillman, Bernard. *A short history of the Jews in Ireland.* Dublin, 1945.

Stewart, David. *The seceders in Ireland, with annals of their congregations.* Belfast, 1950.

Taggart, Norman. *The Irish in world methodism, 1760–1960.* London, 1986.

Thompson, Joshua. Irish baptists and the 1859 revival. In *Ir. Baptist Hist. Soc. Jn.*, xvii (1984–5), pp 4–10.

Turner, Michael. The French connection with Maynooth College, 1795–1855. In *Studies*, lxx (1981), pp 77–87.

Turpin, John. John Hogan and the catholic religious revival. In *Maynooth Review*, v, no. 1 (May 1979), pp 64–70.

Vale, Mary. The origins of the Catholic University of Ireland, 1845–1854. In *I.E.R.*, lxxxii (1954), pp 1–16, 152–64, 226–41.

Walsh, T. J. *Nano Nagle and the Presentation Sisters.* Dublin, 1959.

Whyte, J. H. The influence of the catholic clergy on elections in nineteenth-century Ireland. In *E.H.R.*, lxxv, no. 295 (Apr. 1960), pp 239–59.

Whyte, J. H. Newman in Dublin: fresh light from the archives of Propaganda. In *Dublin Review*, no. 483 (spring 1960), pp 31–9.

—— The appointment of catholic bishops in nineteenth-century Ireland. In *Cath. Hist. Rev.*, xlviii, no. 1 (Apr. 1962), pp 12–32.

—— Fresh light on Archbishop Cullen and the tenant league. In *I.E.R.*, xcix (Mar. 1963), pp 170–76.

—— Political problems, 1850–60. In Corish, *Ir. catholicism*, fasc. v (1967).

Woods, C. J. Ireland and Anglo-papal relations, 1880–85. In *I.H.S.*, xviii, no. 69 (Mar. 1972), pp 29–60.

—— The politics of Cardinal McCabe, archbishop of Dublin, 1879–85. In *Dublin Hist. Rec.*, xxvi, no. 3 (June 1973), pp 101–10.

4 MILITARY HISTORY

Allendorfer, F. W. The Western Irish Brigade: 23rd Illinois Infantry Regiment. In *Ir. Sword*, ii, no. 7 (winter 1955), pp 177–83.

—— An Irish regiment in Brazil, 1826–1828. In *Ir. Sword*, iii, no. 10 (summer 1957), pp 28–31.

Babington, A. *The devil to pay: the mutiny of the Connaught Rangers, India, July 1920.* London, 1991.

Barry, Tom. *Guerrilla days in Ireland.* Dublin, 1949; Cork, 1955. New ed., with introduction by M. J. Costello, Dublin, 1981.

—— *The reality of the Anglo-Irish war, 1920–21, in West Cork: refutations, corrections, and comments on Liam Deasy's 'Towards Ireland free'.* Dublin, 1974.

Bateman, R. J. Captain Timothy Deasy, fenian. In *Ir. Sword*, viii, no. 31 (winter 1967), pp 130–37.

Beckett, I. F. W., and Jeffery, Keith. The Royal Navy and the Curragh incident. In *Historical Research*, lxii, no. 147 (Feb. 1989), pp 54–69.

Beesley, Patrick. *Room 40: British naval intelligence, 1914–18.* London, 1982. Paperback ed., Oxford, 1984.

Belchem, John. Republican spirit and military science: the 'Irish brigade' and Irish-American nationalism in 1848. In *I.H.S.*, xxix, no. 113 (May 1994), pp 44–64.

Bell, J. Bowyer. *The secret army: the I.R.A., 1916–79.* Revised ed., Dublin, 1989.

—— The Thompson sub-machine-gun in Ireland, 1921. In *Ir. Sword*, viii, no. 31 (winter 1967), pp 98–108.

Bennett, Richard. *The Black and Tans.* London, 1959.

Berkeley, G. F. H. *The Irish battalion in the papal army of 1860.* Dublin, 1929.

Bowden, Tom. The Irish underground and the war of independence, 1919–21. In G. R. Mosse (ed.), *Police forces in history* (London, 1975), pp 57–78.

—— *The breakdown of public security: the case of Ireland, 1916–21, and Palestine, 1936–39.* London, 1977. (Sage Studies in 20th-century History.)

Brennan, Michael. *The war in Clare 1911–1921: personal memoirs of the Irish war of independence.* Dublin, 1980.

Bruce, W. M. L. *The thunder maker: General Thomas Meagher.* Milwaukee, 1959.

Bryan, Dan. Thomas Davis as a military influence. In *An Cosantoir*, v (1945), pp 551–8.

Callan, Patrick. Recruiting for the British army in Ireland during the first world war. In *Ir. Sword*, xvii, no. 66 (summer 1987), pp 42–56.

Carles, P. Le corps irlandais au service de la France sous le consulat et l'empire. In *Revue historique des armes*, ii (1976).

Caulfield, Max. *The Easter rebellion*. London, 1964.

Clark, Brian. Napoleon's Irish legion, 1803–15: the historical record. In *Ir. Sword*, xii, no. 48 (summer 1976), pp 165–72.

Conran, Phil. Military and naval aviation in Ireland, 1913 to 1922. In *An Cosantóir*, xxxii (Sept. 1972), pp 158–62.

Crawford, Fred. *Guns for Ulster*. Belfast, 1947.

Crean, C. P. The Irish battalion at the defence of Spoleto, 1860. In *Ir. Sword*, iv, no. 14 (summer 1959), pp 52–60; no. 15 (winter 1959), pp 99–104.

Cronin, Seán. 'The country did not turn out': the Young Ireland rising of 1848. In *Éire-Ireland*, xi, no. 2 (1976), pp 3–17.

Crossman, Virginia. Irish barracks in the 1820s and 1830s: a political perspective. In *Ir. Sword*, xvii, no. 68 (1989), pp 210–13.

—— Preserving the peace in Ireland: the role of military forces, 1815–45. In *Ir. Sword*, xvii, no. 69 (1990), pp 261–72.

Cryan Pancani, M. J. New light on the background to the Irish participation in the papal army of 1860. In *Ir. Sword*, xvi, no. 64 (summer 1986), pp 155–64.

Cunliffe, Marcus. *The Royal Irish Fusiliers, 1793–1968*. 2nd ed., Oxford, 1970.

Denman, Terry. The 10th Irish Division, 1914–15: a study in military and political interaction. In *Ir. Sword*, xvii, no. 66 (summer 1987), pp 16–25.

—— The catholic Irish soldier in the first world war: the 'racial environment'. In *I.H.S.*, xxvii, no. 108 (Nov. 1991), pp 352–65.

—— *Ireland's unknown soldiers: the 16th (Irish) Division in the great war*. Dublin, 1992.

Dooley, Thomas P. Politics, bands, and marketing: army recruitment in Waterford city, 1914–15. In *Ir. Sword*, xviii, no. 72 (winter 1991), pp 205–19.

Dublin's fighting story. Tralee, 1949.

Duffy, C. J. The Irish in the imperial service: some observations. In *Ir. Sword*, v, no. 19 (winter 1961), pp 69–74.

Duggan, G. C. The fenians in Canada: a British officer's impressions. In *Ir. Sword*, viii, no. 31 (winter 1967), pp 88–91.

Duggan, J. P. German arms and the 1916 rising. In *An Cosantóir*, xxx (Mar. 1970), pp 97–104.

Edmunds, G. J. *The Irish rebellion: the 26th Sherwood Foresters' part in the defeat of the rebels in 1916: their early training*. London, 1965.

Ellis, Peter Berresford-. The battle of Ridgeway, 2 June 1866. In *Ir. Sword*, xvi, no. 65 (winter 1986), pp 245–67.

—— and King, Joseph A. Fenian casualties and prisoners: fenian invasion of British North America, June 1866. In *Ir. Sword*, xvii, no. 73 (summer 1992), pp 271–85.

Elting, J. R. *Swords around the throne: Napoleon's Grande Armée*. London, 1988.
 Ch. 18, 'Régiments étrangers'.

Enoch, V. J. *The Martello towers of Ireland*. Dublin, 1975.

Fergusson, James. *The Curragh incident*. London, 1964.

Forde, Frank. The New South Wales Irish Rifle Regiment. In *Ir. Sword*, viii, no. 33 (winter 1968), pp 306–8.

—— The Sixty-Ninth Regiment of New York. In *Ir. Sword*, xvii, no. 68 (1989), pp 145–58.

Fox, R. M. *The history of the Irish Citizen Army*. Dublin, 1943.

Gallagher, Edward. The Irish brigade at Fredericksburg: the story of a glorious failure. In *An Cosantóir*, ii (1942), pp 337–44.

Gallagher, John G. Conflict and tragedy in Napoleon's Irish legion: the Corbet/Sweeny affair. In *Ir. Sword*, xvi, no. 64 (summer 1986), pp 145–54.

Garland, J. L. Irish soldiers of the American confederacy. In *Ir. Sword*, i, no. 3 (1951–2), pp 174–80.

—— The formation of Meagher's Irish brigade. In *Ir. Sword*, iii, no. 12 (summer 1958), pp 162–5.

—— Michael Corcoran and the formation of his Irish legion. In *Ir. Sword*, xvii, no. 66 (summer 1987), pp 26–40.

Gavin, Joseph, and O'Sullivan, Harold. *Dundalk: a military history*. Dundalk, 1987.

Gibbon, Monk. *Inglorious soldier*. London, 1968.
    Officer in British army during 1916 rising.

Goodspeed, D. J. *The conspirators: a study of the coup d'état*. London, 1962.
    Ireland and Europe, 1903–44.

Greenhous, Brereton. An Irish gunner on the upper Mississippi, 1814. In *Ir. Sword*, x, no. 41 (winter 1972), pp 245–54.

Griffin, W. D. Irish generals and Spanish politics under Fernando VII. In *Ir. Sword*, x, no. 38 (summer 1971), pp 179–87.

Haire, David N. In aid of the civil power, 1868–90. In Lyons & Hawkins, *Ire. under the union* (1980), pp 115–47.

Hally, P. J. The Easter 1916 rising in Dublin: the military aspects. In *Ir. Sword*, vii, no. 29 (winter 1966), pp 311–26; viii, no. 30 (summer 1967), pp 48–57.

Hanham, H. J. Religion and nationality in the mid-Victorian army. In M. R. D. Foot (ed.), *War and society: historical essays in honour and memory of J. R. Western, 1928–71* (London, 1973), pp 159–81.

Harris, Henry. *The Irish regiments in the first world war*. Foreword by G. A. Hayes-McCoy. Cork, 1968.

Harris, R. G. *The Irish regiments: a pictorial history, 1683–1987*. Tunbridge Wells, 1989.

[Hayes, Karl E.; Conran, Phil; Kearns, A. P.; and Smyth, Damian.] *A history of the Royal Air Force and United States Naval Air Service in Ireland, 1913–1923*. Killiney, 1988.

Hayes-McCoy, G. A. The raising of the Connaught Rangers, 1793. In *Galway Arch. Soc. Jn.*, xxi, no. 3–4 (1945), pp 133–9.

—— The defence of Ireland a century ago. In *An Cosantóir*, viii (1948), pp 486–91, 540–47, 607–11.

—— The Irish company in the Franco-Prussian war, 1870–1. In *Ir. Sword*, i, no. 4 (1952–3), pp 275–83.

—— *Irish battles: a military history of Ireland*. London, 1969. Paperback ed., 1990.

—— *Captain Myles Walter Keogh, United States Army, 1840–1876*. Dublin, n.d.

Healy, F. J. A famous Franco-Irish soldier: General William Corbet. In *Journal of the Ivernian Society*, iii (1910–11), pp 239–44; iv (1911–12), pp 39–55.

Heffernan, J. B. Ireland's contribution to the navies of the American civil war. In *Ir. Sword*, iii, no. 11 (winter 1957), pp 81–7.

Heuston, John. *Headquarters battalion, Easter week 1916*. Dublin, 1966.

Holmes, R. *The little field marshal: Sir John French*. London, 1981.

Hume, Geraldine, and Malcomson, Anthony. *Robert Emmet: the insurrection of 1803*. Belfast, 1976.

Ireland, John de Courcy. Irish soldiers and seamen in Latin America. In *Ir. Sword*, i, no. 4 (1952–3), pp 296–302.

—— Admiral Brown at Martin Garcia and Montevideo. In *Ir. Sword*, iii, no. 10 (summer 1957), pp 20–24.

—— Irish naval links with the Adriatic. In *Ir. Sword*, vi, no. 23 (winter 1963), pp 76–80.

—— Thomas Charles Wright: soldier of Bolivar; founder of the Ecuadorian navy. In *Ir. Sword*, vi, no. 25 (winter 1964), pp 271–5.

—— *The sea and the Easter rising*. Dublin, 1966.

—— Fenianism and naval affairs. In *Ir. Sword*, viii, no. 30 (summer 1967), pp 10–22.

—— The confederate states at sea in the American civil war: the Irish contribution. In *Ir. Sword*, xiv, no. 54 (summer 1980), pp 73–94.

—— John Philip Holland: pioneer in submarine navigation. In *N. Munster Antiq. Jn.*, x (1967), pp 206–12.

Jeffery, Keith. *The British army and the crisis of empire, 1918–22*. Manchester, 1984.

Johnson, T. *Orange, green, and khaki: the story of the Irish regiments in the great war, 1914–1918*. Dublin, 1992.

Jones, P. *The Irish Brigade*. New York, 1969.

Karsten, Peter. Irish soldiers in the British army, 1792–1922: suborned or subordinate? In *Journal of Social History*, xvii, no. 1 (fall 1983), pp 31–64.

Kerry's fighting story, 1916–1921. Tralee, 1949.

Kilfeather, T. P. *The Connaught Rangers*. Tralee, 1969.

Krueger, C. *Saint Patrick's battalion*. New York, 1960.

Lambert, Eric. General O'Leary and South America. In *Ir. Sword*, xi, no. 43 (winter 1973), pp 57–74.

—— Irish soldiers in South America, 1818–1830. In *Ir. Sword*, xvi, no. 62 (summer 1984), pp 22–35.

Lambrick, H. T. *Sir Charles Napier and Sind*. Oxford, 1952.

Lemass, Seán. I remember 1916. In *Studies*, lv (spring 1966), pp 7–9.

McAnally, Henry. *The Irish militia, 1793–1816: a social and military history*. Dublin, 1949.

McCarthy, J. M. (ed.). *Limerick's fighting story, 1916–1921*. Tralee, 1949.

McCarthy, P. J. The R.A.F. and Ireland, 1920–22. In *Ir. Sword*, xvii, no. 68 (1989), pp 174–88.

MacCauley, J. A. The Dublin Fusiliers. In *Ir. Sword*, vi, no. 25 (winter 1964), pp 257–70; x, no. 38 (summer 1971), pp 54–67.

McCormack, R. B. The San Patricio deserters in the Mexican war, 1847. In *Ir. Sword*, iii, no. 13 (winter 1958), pp 246–55.

McCracken, Eileen. Alfred Aylward: a fenian in South Africa. In *Ir. Sword*, xii, no. 49 (winter 1976), pp 261–9.

McCullagh, Gilbert. The South African Irish Regiment. In *Ir. Sword*, xv, no. 60 (summer 1983), pp 145–8.

McGrath, Walter. The fenian rising in Cork. In *Ir. Sword*, viii, no. 33 (winter 1968), pp 245–54.

Maguire, W. A. Major General Ross and the burning of Washington. In *Ir. Sword*, xiv, no. 55 (winter 1980), pp 117–28.

Maher, Jim. *The flying column: West Kilkenny, 1916–21*. Dublin, 1987.

Melvin, Patrick. Colonel Maurice Griffin Dennis, 1805–63. In *Ir. Sword*, xiii, no. 50 (summer 1977), pp 45–59.
  Irishman in the British army in India and Africa.

Miller, Robert Lyal. *Shamrock and sword: the Saint Patrick's Battalion in the U.S.–Mexican war*. Norman, Okla., 1989.

Morris, R. K. John P. Holland and the fenians. In *Galway Arch. Soc. Jn.*, xxxi, no. 1 & 2 (1964–5), pp 25–38.

Muenger, Elizabeth. *The British military dilemma in Ireland: occupation politics, 1886–1914*. Lawrence, Kan., and Dublin, 1991.

Mulcahy, Risteárd. The development of the Irish Volunteers: 1916–22. In *An Cosantóir*, xl, no. 2 (Feb. 1980), pp 35–40; no. 3 (Mar. 1980), pp 67–71; no. 4 (Apr. 1980), pp 99–102.

Mullen, T. J. The Irish brigades in the union army, 1861–5. In *Ir. Sword*, ix, no. 37 (winter 1970), pp 39–56.

Murphy, J. J. W. Three Irish cavalry regiments at Balaclava. In *Ir. Sword*, iv, no. 16 (summer 1960), pp 182–90.

——Kipling and the Irish soldier in India. In *Ir. Sword*, ix, no. 37 (winter 1970), pp 318–29.

Newsinger, John. 'I bring not peace but a sword': the religious motif in the Irish war of independence. In *Journal of Contemporary History*, xiii, no. 3 (1978), pp 609–28.

Ó Cathaoir, Breandán. American fenianism and Canada, 1865–71. In *Ir. Sword*, viii, no. 31 (winter 1967), pp 77–87.

——Terence Bellew McManus: fenian precursor. In *Ir. Sword*, xvi, no. 63 (winter 1984), pp 105–9.

O'Donnell, P. D. Dublin's military barracks: three centuries. In *An Cosantóir*, xli, no. 3 (Mar. 1981), pp 73–7; no. 7 (Apr. 1981) pp 102–7.

O'Donoghue, Florence. *No other law: the story of Liam Lynch and the Irish Republican Army, 1916–23*. Dublin, 1954.

——Plans for the 1916 rising. In *University Rev.*, iii, no. 1 (1962), pp 3–21.

——Guerrilla warfare in Ireland. In *An Cosantóir*, xxiii (1963).

——Easter week, 1916. In G. A. Hayes-McCoy (ed.), *The Irish at war* (Cork, 1964), pp 83–95.

——The failure of the German arms landing at Easter, 1916. In *Cork Hist. Soc. Jn.*, lxxi, no. 213–14 (Jan.–Dec. 1966), pp 49–61.

O'Farrell, Padraic. *The Seán Mac Eoin story*. Dublin, 1981.

O'Flaherty, P. *The history of the Sixty-ninth Regiment in the Irish brigade, 1861 to 1865*. New York, 1986.

O'Neill, Eoghan. The battle of Dublin, 1916. In *An Cosantóir*, xxvi, no. 5 (May 1966), pp 211–22.

O'Neill, Thomas P. Fintan Lalor and the 1849 movement. In *An Cosantóir*, x, no. 4 (Apr. 1950), pp 173–9.

Orr, Philip. *Road to the Somme: men of the Ulster division tell their story*. Belfast, 1987.

Pakenham, Valerie. Sir Edward Pakenham and the battle of New Orleans. In *Ir. Sword*, ix, no. 34 (summer 1969), pp 32–7.

Palmer, S. H. Major-general Sir Charles James Napier: Irishman, chartist, and commander of the northern district in England in 1839–41. In *Ir. Sword*, xv, no. 59 (winter 1982), pp 89–100.

Pollock, Sam. *Mutiny for the cause: the story of the revolt of Ireland's 'Devil's own' in British India.* London, 1970.
 Connaught Rangers.
Quinn, Anthony. Flanders Fields and Irish recollections. In *Capuchin Annual*, xliv (1977), pp 342–50.
Razzell, P. E. Social origins of officers in the Indian and British home army, 1758–1962. In *British Journal of Sociology*, xiv (1963), pp 248–68.
Robbins, Frank. *Under the starry plough: recollections of the Irish citizen army.* Dublin, 1977.
Ruda, Richard. The Irish Transvaal brigades. In *Ir. Sword*, xi, no. 45 (winter 1974), pp 201–11.
Ryan, A. P. *Mutiny at the Curragh.* London, 1956.
Ryan, Desmond. *Sean Treacy and the third Tipperary brigade.* Tralee, 1945.
—— *The rising.* Dublin, 1949.
Ryan, F. W. A projected invasion of Ireland in 1811. In *Ir. Sword*, i, no. 2 (1950–51), pp 136–41.
Semple, A. J. The fenian infiltration of the British army. In *Journal of the Society for Army Historical Research*, lii, no. 211 (1974), pp 133–60.
Short, K. R. M. *The dynamite war: Irish-American bombers in Victorian Britain.* Dublin and Atlantic Highlands, N.J., 1979.
Staunton, Martin. Kilrush, Co. Clare, and the Royal Munster Fusiliers: the experience of an Irish town in the first world war. In *Ir. Sword*, xvi, no. 65 (winter 1986), pp 268–76.
Sutcliffe, Sheila. *Martello towers.* Newton Abbott, 1972.
 Ch. 8, Ireland.
Toner, P. M. The military organisation of the 'Canadian' fenians, 1866–1870. In *Ir. Sword*, x, no. 38 (summer 1971), pp 26–37.
—— The 'green ghost': Canada's fenians and the raids. In *Éire-Ireland*, xvi, no. 2 (summer 1981), pp 27–47.
Townshend, Charles. *The British campaign in Ireland, 1919–1921: the development of political and military policies.* Oxford, 1975.
—— The Irish Republican Army and the development of guerrilla warfare, 1916–21. In *E.H.R.*, xciv, no. 371 (Apr. 1979), pp 318–45.
—— *Britain's civil wars: counter-insurgency in the twentieth century.* London, 1986.
—— Military force and civil authority in the United Kingdom, 1914–1921. In *Jn. Brit. Studies*, xxviii, no. 1 (Jan. 1989), pp 262–92.
Verney, Peter. *The Micks: the story of the Irish Guards.* London, 1970.
Waller, Hardress. Robert Waller: a Kabul hostage of 1842. In *Ir. Sword*, xviii, no. 73 (summer 1992), pp 248–54.
Wells, Roger. *Insurrection: the British experience.* Gloucester, 1985.
Willoughby, Roger. *A military history of the University of Dublin.* Limerick, 1989.

5(a) HISTORICAL GEOGRAPHY

Aalen, F. H. A. Some historical aspects of landscape and rural life in Omeath, Co. Louth. In *Ir. Geography*, iv, no. 4 (1962), pp 256–78.
—— Enclosures in eastern Ireland: report of a symposium, Dublin, 23 Sept. 1964. In *Ir. Geography*, v, no. 2 (1965), pp 29–39.
—— *Man and the landscape in Ireland.* London, 1978.

Andrews, J. H. Notes on the historical geography of the Irish iron industry. In *Ir. Geography*, iii, no. 3 (1956), pp 139–49.

—— Road planning in Ireland before the railway age. In *Ir. Geography*, v, no. 1 (1964), pp 17–41.

—— Simms, Anngret; Clarke, H. B.; and Gillespie, Raymond (ed.). *Irish Historic Towns Atlas*. Dublin, 1986– . (R.I.A.) In progress. *I: Kildare*. By J. H. Andrews (1986). *II: Carrickfergus*. By Philip Robinson (1986). *III: Bandon*. By Patrick O'Flanagan (1988). *IV: Kells*. By Anngret Simms with Katherine Simms (1990). *V: Mullingar*. By J. H. Andrews with K. M. Davies (1992). *VI: Athlone*. By Harman Murtagh (1994). I–IV ed. J. H. Andrews and Anngret Simms; V–VI ed. J. H. Andrews, Anngret Simms, and H. B. Clarke.

Buchanan, R. A., and Walker, B. M. (ed.). *Province, city, and people: Belfast and its region*. Antrim, 1987.

Butlin, R. A. (ed.). *The development of the Irish town*. London and Totowa, N.J., 1977.

Camblin, Gilbert. *The town in Ulster: an account of the origin and building of the towns of the province and the development of their rural setting*. Belfast, 1951.

Cawley, M. E. Aspects of continuity and change in nineteenth-century rural settlement patterns: findings from County Roscommon. In *Studia Hib.*, xxii–xxiii (1982–3), pp 106–27.

Currie, E. A. Land tenures, enclosures, and field patterns in Co. Derry in the eighteenth and nineteenth centuries. In *Ir. Geography*, ix (1976), pp 50–62.

Duffy, P. J. Carleton, Kavanagh and the south Ulster landscape, *c.*1800–1950. In *Ir. Geography*, xviii (1985), pp 25–37.

Evans, E. E. *Mourne country*. Dundalk, 1951; 2nd ed., 1967.

—— *Irish folk ways*. London, 1957. Paperback ed., 1967.

—— *The personality of Ireland: habit, heritage, and history*. Cambridge, 1973; rev. ed., Belfast, 1981.

—— and Jones, Emrys. The growth of Belfast. In *Town Planning Review*, xxvi (1955–6), pp 92–111.

Freeman, T. W. Historical geography and the Irish historian. In *I.H.S.*, v, no. 18 (Sept. 1946), pp 139–46.

—— *Pre-famine Ireland: a study in historical geography*. Manchester, 1957.

—— *Ireland: its physical, historical, social, and economic geography*. London, 1950; 4th ed., 1969; reprint, with revisions, 1972.

Graham, B. J., and Pomfret, L. J. *An historical geography of Ireland*. London, 1993.

Green, E. R. R. *Industrial archaeology of County Down*. Belfast, 1963.

Harkness, David, and O'Dowd, Mary (ed.). *The town in Ireland*. Belfast, 1981. (*Hist. Studies*, xiii.)

Horner, A. A. Carton, Co. Kildare: a case study in the making of an Irish demesne. In *Ir. Georgian Soc. Bull.*, xviii, no. 2–3 (1975), pp 45–104.

—— Planning the Irish transport network: parallels in nineteenth- and twentieth-century proposals. In *Ir. Geography*, x (1977), pp 44–57.

—— The scope and limitations of the landlord contribution to changing the Irish landscape, 1700–1850. In Viggo Hansen (ed.), *Collected papers presented at the permanent European conference for the study of the rural landscape*. Copenhagen, 1981.

Hughes, T. Jones. East Leinster in the mid-nineteenth century. In *Ir. Geography*, iii, no. 5 (1958), pp 227–41.

—— Landlordism in the Mullet of Mayo. In *Ir. Geography*, iv, no. 1 (1959), pp 16–34.

—— The origin and growth of towns in Ireland. In *University Rev.*, ii, no. 7 (1960), pp 8–15.

—— Administrative divisions and the development of settlement in nineteenth-century Ireland. In *University Rev.*, iii, no. 6 (1964), pp 8–15.

—— Society and settlement in nineteenth-century Ireland. In *Ir. Geography*, v, no. 2 (1965), pp 79–96.

—— Village and town in mid-nineteenth-century Ireland. In *Ir. Geography*, xiv (1981), pp 99–106.

—— Historical geography of Ireland from *circa* 1700. In *Ir. Geography*, golden jubilee issue (1984), pp 149–66.

—— Continuity and change in rural County Wexford in the nineteenth century. In Kevin Whelan and William Nolan, *Wexford: history and society* (Dublin, 1987), pp 342–72.

Hutchinson, W. R. *Tyrone precinct: a history of the plantation settlement of Dungannon and Mountjoy to modern times*. Belfast, 1951.

Johnson, J. H. The population of Londonderry during the great Irish famine. In *Econ. Hist. Rev.*, 2nd ser., x (1957–8), pp 273–85.

Jones, E. A. *A social geography of Belfast*. London, 1960.

McCutcheon, W. A. The Lagan navigation. In *Ir. Geography*, iv, no. 4 (1962), pp 244–55.

—— *The industrial archaeology of Northern Ireland*. Belfast, 1980. (H.M.S.O.)

Mitchell, Frank. *The Shell guide to reading the Irish landscape*. Dublin, 1986.
   Revised and redesigned ed. of *The Irish landscape* (1976).

—— The influence of man on vegetation in Ireland. In *Journal of Life Sciences*, iii, pt 1 (1982), pp 7–14.

Nolan, William (ed.). *The shaping of Ireland; the geographical perspective*. Dublin, 1986. (Thomas Davis Lectures.)

O'Connor, P. J. *Exploring Limerick's past: an historical geography of urban development in county and city*. Newcastle West, 1987.

Orme, A. R. Youghal, County Cork: growth, decay, resurgence. In *Ir. Geography*, v, no. 3 (1966), pp 121–49.

O'Sullivan, Peter (ed.). *Newcastle Lyons: a parish of the Pale*. Dublin, 1986.

Royle, Stephen. The historical legacy in modern Ireland. In R. W. G. Carter and A. J. Parker, *Ireland: a contemporary geographical perspective* (London, 1989), pp 113–44.

Smyth, W. J. Continuity and change in the territorial organisation of Irish rural communities. In *Maynooth Review*, i, no. 1 (June 1975), pp 51–78; no. 2 (Nov. 1975), pp 52–101.

—— Estate records and the making of the Irish landscape: an example from County Tipperary. In *Ir. Geography*, ix (1976), pp 29–49.

—— and Whelan, Kevin (ed.). *Common ground: essays on the historical geography of Ireland presented to T. Jones Hughes*. Cork, 1988.

Stephens, Nicholas, and Glasscock, R. E. (ed.). *Irish geographical studies in honour of E. Estyn Evans*. Belfast, 1970.

Thomas, Colin (ed.). *Rural landscapes and communities: essays presented to Desmond McCourt*. Dublin, 1986.

Whelan, Kevin. The catholic parish, the catholic chapel, and village development in Ireland. In *Ir. Geography*, xvi (1983), pp 1–15.

—— Town and village in Ireland: a socio-cultural perspective. In *Irish Review* (1988), pp 34–43.

5(b) HISTORY OF GEOGRAPHY

Andrews, J. H. *History in the ordnance map: an introduction for Irish readers.* Dublin, 1974.

—— *A paper landscape: the ordnance survey in nineteenth-century Ireland.* Oxford, 1975.

—— Ireland in maps. In *Ir. Geography*, golden jubilee issue (1984), pp 280–92.

—— *Plantation acres: an historical study of the Irish land surveyor and his maps.* Belfast, 1985. (Ulster Historical Foundation.)

Bannon, M. J. The making of Irish geography, III: Patrick Geddes and the emergence of modern town planning in Dublin. In *Ir. Geography*, xi (1978), pp 141–8.

Boyne, Patricia. Letters from the County Down: John O'Donovan's first field work for the ordnance survey. In *Studies*, lxxiii (summer 1984), pp 106–16.

Haughton, J. P. The Atlas of Ireland. In *Ir. Geography*, xii (1979), pp 1–9.

Herries Davies, G. L. Dr Anthony Farrington and the Geographical Society of Ireland. In *Ir. Geography*, iv, no. 5 (1963), pp 311–20.

—— Thomas Walter Freeman and the geography of Ireland: a tribute. In *Ir. Geography*, vi, no. 5 (1973), pp 521–8.

—— The making of Irish geography, II: Grenville Arthur James Cole (1859–1924). In *Ir. Geography*, x (1977), pp 90–94.

—— The Geographical Society of Ireland. In *Ir. Geography*, golden jubilee issue (1984), pp 1–23.

Lockhart, Douglas. The land surveyor in northern Ireland before the coming of the ordnance survey *circa* 1840. In *Ir. Geography*, xi (1978), pp 102–9.

Madden, P. G. The ordnance survey of Ireland. In *Ir. Sword*, v, no. 20 (summer 1962), pp 155–63.

Seymour, W. A. (ed.), *A history of the ordnance survoy*, Folkestone, 1980.

Smyth, W. J. Social geography of rural Ireland: inventory and prospect. In *Ir. Geography*, golden jubilee issue (1984), pp 204–36.

6 ECONOMIC AND SOCIAL HISTORY

Aalen, F. H. A. The rehousing of Irish rural labourers under the Labourers (Ireland) Acts, 1883–1919. In *Journal of Historical Geography*, xii, no. 3 (July 1986), pp 287–306.

—— The working-class housing movement and the emergence of planning in Dublin, 1850–1914. In M. J. Bannon (ed.), *A hundred years of Irish planning* (Dublin, 1986), pp 131–88.

—— *The Iveagh Trust: the first hundred years, 1890–1990.* Dublin, 1990.

—— Ireland. In C. Pooley (ed.), *The comparative study of housing strategies in Europe, 1880–1930* (Leicester, 1992), pp 132–65.

—— Constructive unionism and the shaping of modern Ireland, *c.*1880–1920. In *Rural History*, iv, no. 2 (1993), pp 137–65.

Akenson, D. H. *Small differences: Irish catholics and Irish protestants, 1815–1922: an international perspective.* Kingston and Montreal, 1988.

Allen, R. G., and Ó Gráda, Cormac. On the road again with Arthur Young: English, Irish, and French agriculture during the industrial revolution. In *Jn. Econ. Hist.*, xlviii, no. 1 (Mar. 1988), pp 93–116.

Almquist, E. L. Pre-famine Ireland and the theory of European proto-industrialization: evidence from the 1841 census. In *Jn. Econ. Hist.*, xxxix, no. 3 (Sept. 1979), pp 699–718.

Anderson, E. B. *Sailing ships of Ireland.* Dublin, 1951.

Arensberg, C. M. *The Irish countryman: an anthropological study*. New York, 1937; reprint, 1959.

—— and Kimball, S. T. *Family and community in Ireland*. 2nd ed., Cambridge, Mass., 1968.

Armstrong, D. L. Social and economic conditions in the Belfast linen industry, 1850–1900. In *I.H.S.*, vii, no. 28 (Sept. 1951), pp 235–69.

—— *An economic history of agriculture in Northern Ireland, 1850–1900*. Oxford, 1989.

Baker, Michael C. *Irish railways since 1916*. London, 1972.

Baker, Sybil. *Edwardian Belfast: a social profile*. Belfast, 1982.

Bannon, M. J. (ed.). *A hundred years of Irish planning, 1: the emergence of Irish planning, 1880–1920*. Dublin, 1986.

Barrington, Thomas. A review of Irish agricultural prices. In *Stat. Soc. Ire. Jn.*, xv (1926–7), pp 249–80.

Barrow, G. L. *The emergence of the Irish banking system, 1820–45*. Dublin, 1975.

Barrow, Lennox. The use of money in mid-nineteenth-century Ireland. In *Studies*, lix (spring 1970), pp 81–8.

Bartlett, Thomas. A people made rather for copies than for originals: the Anglo-Irish, 1760–1800. In *International History Review*, xii (1990), pp 11–25.

Beames, M. R. *Peasants and power: the Whiteboy movements and their control in pre-famine Ireland*. Brighton and New York, 1983.

Bell, Jonathan. Hiring fairs in Ulster. In *Ulster Folklife*, xxv (1979), pp 67–78.

—— and Watson, Mervyn. *Irish farming: implements and techniques, 1750–1900*. Edinburgh, 1986.

Bergman, M. The potato blight in the Netherlands and its social consequences, 1845–47. In *International Review of Social History*, xii (1967), pp 390–431.

Bew, Paul. *Land and the national question in Ireland, 1858–82*. Dublin, 1979.

Bielenberg, Andy. *Cork's industrial revolution, 1780–1880: development or decline?*. Cork, 1991.

Black, R. D. Collison. The progress of industrialization, 1850–1920. In T. W. Moody and J. C. Beckett (ed.), *Ulster since 1800: a political and economic survey* (London, 1954), pp 50–59.

—— Economic policy in Ireland and India in the time of J. S. Mill. In *Econ. Hist. Rev.*, 2nd ser., xxi, no. 2 (1968), pp 321–36.

—— The Irish dissenters and nineteenth-century political economy. In *Hermathena*, cxxxv (winter 1983), pp 120–37.

Bolger, Patrick. *The Irish cooperative movement: its history and development*. Dublin, 1977.

—— (ed.). *And see her beauty shining there: the story of the Irish Countrywomen*. Dublin, 1986.

Bonn, Moritz. The psychological aspect of land reform in Ireland. In *Economic Journal*, xix (1909), pp 374–94.

Bourke, Joanna. *Husbandry to housewifery: women, economic change, and housework in Ireland, 1890–1914*. Oxford, 1993.

Bourke, P. M. A. *'The visitation of God'?: the potato and the great Irish famine*. Ed. Jacqueline Hill and Cormac Ó Gráda. Dublin, 1993.
     Compilation of earlier articles on the famine and Irish agriculture.

Boyd, Andrew. *The rise of the Irish trade unions, 1729–1970*. Tralee, 1972; 2nd ed., 1985.

Boyle, J. W. *The Irish labour movement in the nineteenth century*. Washington, D.C., 1988.

Boyle, Phelim, and Ó Gráda, Cormac. Fertility trends, excess mortality, and the great Irish famine. In *Demography*, xxiii, no. 4 (Nov., 1986), pp 543–62.

Bradley, D. G. *Farm labourers: Irish struggle, 1900–1976*. Belfast, 1988.

Brahimi, Michèle. Nuptialité et fécondité des mariages en Irlande. In *Population*, xxxiii, no. 3 (mai–juin 1978), pp 663–703.

Breen, Richard. Farm servanthood in Ireland, 1900–1940. In *Econ. Hist. Rev.*, xxxvi, no. 1 (Feb. 1983), pp 87–102.

——Population trends in late nineteenth- and early twentieth-century Ireland: a local study. In *Econ. & Soc. Rev.*, xv, no. 2 (Jan. 1984), pp 95–108.

Brodie, Malcolm. *One hundred years of Irish football*. Belfast, 1980.

Brooke, David. *The railway navvy: 'that despicable race of men'*. Newton Abbot, 1983.

Brown, K. D. Larkin and the strikes of 1913: their place in British history. In *Saothar*, ix (1983), pp 89–99.

Buckley, A. D. On the club: friendly societies in Ireland. In *Ir. Econ. & Soc. Hist.*, xiv (1987), pp 39–58.

Buckley, K. The fixing of rents by agreement in Co. Galway, 1881–5. In *I.H.S.*, vii, no. 27 (Mar. 1951), pp 149–79.

Burke, Helen. *The people and the poor law in 19th-century Ireland*. Dublin, 1987.

Burn, W. L. Free trade in land: an aspect of the Irish question. In *R. Hist. Soc. Trans.*, 4th ser., xxxi (1949), pp 61–74.

Burtchael, Jack. 19th-century society in County Waterford. In *Decies* (1985–6), xxx, 25–34; xxxi, 35–42; xxxii, 48–57; xxxiii, 15–20.

Butlin, N. G. A new plea for the separation of Ireland. In *Jn. Econ. Hist.*, xxviii (1968), pp 274–91.

Byrne, Liam. *History of aviation in Ireland*. Belfast, 1980.

Capie, Forrest, and Perren, Richard. The British market for meat, 1850–1914. In *Agricultural History*, liv (1980), pp 502–15.

Carney, F. J. Pre-famine Irish population: the evidence from the Trinity College estates. In *Ir. Econ. & Soc. Hist.*, ii (1975), pp 35–45.

Carr, Alan. *The Belfast labour movement, 1885–1893*. Belfast, 1974.

Carter, J. W. H. *The land war and its leaders in Queen's County, 1879–82*. Portlaoise, 1994.

Casserley, H. C. *Outline of Irish railway history*. Newton Abbot, 1974.

Christianson, G. E. Secret societies and agrarian violence in Ireland, 1790–1840. In *Agricultural History*, xlvi (1972), pp 369–84.

——Landlords and land tenure in Ireland, 1790–1830. In *Éire-Ireland*, ix, no. 1 (1974), pp 25–58.

Clark, Samuel. *Social origins of the Irish land war*. Princeton, N.J., 1979.

——Landlord domination in nineteenth-century Ireland. In *Unesco Yearbook on Peace and Conflict Studies* (1986), pp 7–29.

Clarke, Desmond. The contribution of the Royal Dublin Society to science and technology in Ireland. In *Administration*, xv (1967), pp 25–34.

Clarke, Wallace. *Linen on the green: an Irish mill village, 1730–1982*. Belfast, 1982; 2nd ed., 1983.

Clarkson, L. A. Irish population revisited, 1687–1821. In Goldstrom & Clarkson, *Ir. population* (1981), pp 13–36.

——Population change and urbanisation, 1821–1911. In Liam Kennedy and Philip Ollerenshaw (ed.), *Economic history of Ulster* (Manchester, 1985), 137–57.

—— Conclusion: famine and Irish history. In E. M. Crawford, (ed.), *Famine: the Irish experience* (Edinburgh, 1989), pp 220–36.

—— and Crawford, E. M. Dietary directions: a topographical survey of Irish diet, 1836. In Rosalind Mitchison and Peter Roebuck (ed.), *Economy and society in Scotland and Ireland, 1500–1939* (Edinburgh, 1988), pp 171–92.

Clear, Catriona. *Nuns in nineteenth-century Ireland*. Dublin and Washington, D.C., 1987.

—— The limits of female autonomy: nuns in nineteenth-century Ireland. In Maria Luddy and Cliona Murphy (ed.), *Women surviving: studies in Irish women's history in the nineteenth and twentieth centuries* (Swords, 1989), pp 15–50.

Coakley, Davis, and Coakley, Mary. *Wit and wine: literary and artistic Cork in the early nineteenth century*. Dun Laoghaire, 1985.

Coe, W. E. *The engineering industry of the north of Ireland*. Newton Abbot, 1969.

Cohen, Marilyn. Peasant differentiation and proto-industrialisation in the Ulster country-side: Tullylisk, 1825–1960. In *Journal of Peasant Studies*, xvii, no. 3 (1990), pp 413–32.

Cohn, R. L. The determinants of individual immigrant mortality on sailing ships, 1836–1853. In *Explorations in Economic History*, xxiv, no. 4 (Oct. 1987), pp 371–91.

Coleman, J. C. The craft of coopering. In *Cork Hist. Soc. Jn.*, xlix (1944), pp 79–89.

Collins, Brenda. Proto-industrialisation and pre-famine emigration. In *Social History*, vii, no. 2 (May 1982), pp 127–46.

Collins, E. J. T. Migrant labour in British agriculture in the nineteenth century. In *Econ. Hist. Rev.*, xxix, no. 1 (1976), pp 38–59.

Connell, K. H. *The population of Ireland, 1750–1845*. Oxford, 1950.

—— Essays in bibliography and criticism: the history of the potato. In *Econ. Hist. Rev.*, iii, no. 3 (1951), pp 388–95.

—— The potato in Ireland. In *Past & Present*, no. 23 (Nov. 1962), pp 57–71.

—— *Irish peasant society: four historical essays*. Oxford, 1968.

Connell, Peter. Famine and the local economy: Co. Meath 1845–1855. In *Riocht na Midhe*, vii, no. 4 (1985–6), pp 114–25.

Connolly, S. J. *Religion and society in nineteenth-century Ireland*. Dundalk, 1985. (Dublin Historical Association: Studies in Irish Economic and Social History, no. 3.)

Conroy, J. C. *A history of railways in Ireland*. London, 1928.

Conway, T. G. The approach to an Irish poor law, 1828–33. In *Éire-Ireland*, vi, no. 1 (spring 1971), pp 65–81.

Court, Artelia. *Puck of the Droms: the lives and literature of the Irish tinkers*. Berkeley, Calif., 1985.

Cousens, S. H. The regional pattern of emigration during the great famine, 1846–51. In *Transactions and Papers of the Institute of British Geographers*, xxviii (1960), pp 119–34.

—— Emigration and demographic change in Ireland, 1851–1861. In *Econ. Hist. Rev.*, xiv, no. 2 (1961), pp 275–88.

—— The regional variations in mortality during the great Irish famine. In *R.I.A. Proc.*, lxiii, sect. C (1963), pp 127–49.

—— The regional variations in population changes in Ireland, 1861–1881. In *Econ. Hist. Rev.*, xvii, no. 2 (1964), pp 301–21.

—— The regional variations in emigration from Ireland between 1821 and 1841. In *Transactions and papers of the Institute of British Geographers*, xxxvii (Dec. 1965), pp 15–30.

—— Population trends in Ireland at the beginning of the twentieth century. In *Ir. Geography*, v (1968), pp 387–401.

Craig, E. T. *An Irish commune: the experiment at Ralahine, County Clare, 1831–33; with essays by James Connolly (1910) and Cormac Ó Gráda (1974)*. Dublin, 1983. (Irish Cooperative Studies, 4.)

Crawford, E. M., Indian meal and pellagra in nineteenth-century Ireland. In Goldstrom & Clarkson, *Ir. population* (1981), pp 113–33.

—— (ed.). *Famine: the Irish experience, 900–1900: subsistence crises and famines in Ireland*. Edinburgh, 1989.

—— William Wilde's table of Irish famines, 900–1850. In E. M. Crawford (ed.), *Famine: the Irish experience* (Edinburgh, 1989), pp 1–30.

—— Diet and the labouring classes in the nineteenth century. In *Saothar*, xv (1990), pp 87–95.

Crawford, W. H. *Domestic industry in Ireland: the experience of the linen industry*. Dublin, 1972.

—— Landlord-tenant relations in Ulster, 1609–1820. In *Ir. Econ. & Soc. Hist.*, ii (1975), pp 5–21.

—— The evolution of Ulster towns, 1750–1850. In Peter Roebuck (ed.), *Plantation to partition* (Belfast, 1981), pp 140–56.

—— The evolution of the linen trade in Ulster before industrialisation. In *Ir. Econ. & Soc. Hist.*, xv (1988), pp 32–53.

—— The significance of landed estates in Ulster, 1600–1820. In *Ir. Econ. & Soc. Hist.*, xvii (1990), pp 44–61.

Crotty, Raymond. *Irish agricultural production: its volume and structure*. Cork, 1966.

—— Modernisation and land reform: real or cosmetic: the Irish case. In *Journal of Peasant Studies*, xi, no. 1 (1983), pp 101–16.

—— *Ireland in crisis: a study in capitalist colonial underdevelopment*. Dingle, Co. Kerry, 1986.

Cuddy, M., and Curtin, C. Commercialisation in west of Ireland agriculture in the 1890s. In *Econ. & Soc. Rev.*, xiv (1983), pp 173–84.

Cullen, L. M. Problems in the interpretation and revision of eighteenth-century Irish economic history. In *R. Hist. Soc. Trans.*, 5th ser., xvii (1967), pp 1–22.

—— Irish history without the potato. In *Past & Present*, no. 40 (July 1968), pp 72–83.

—— *Life in Ireland*. London, 1968.

—— *The formation of the Irish economy*. Cork, 1969.

—— *Six generations: life and work in Ireland from 1790*. Cork, 1970.

—— *Merchants, ships and trade, 1660–1830*. Dublin, 1971.

—— *An economic history of Ireland since 1660*. London, 1972.

—— Population growth and diet, 1600–1850. In Goldstrom & Clarkson, *Ir. population* (1981), pp 89–112.

—— Landlords, bankers, and merchants: the early Irish banking world, 1700–1820. In *Hermathena*, cxxxv (winter 1983), pp 25–44.

—— *Princes and pirates: the Dublin chamber of commerce*. Dublin, 1983.

—— and Butel, Paul (ed.). *Négoce et industrie en France et en Irlande aux XVIIIᵉ et XIXᵉ siècles*. Paris, 1980.

—— and Furet, François (ed.). *Ireland and France, 17th–20th centuries: towards a comparative study of rural history*. Paris, 1980.

—— and Smout, T. C. (ed.). *Comparative aspects of Scottish and Irish economic and social history, 1600–1900*. Edinburgh, 1977.

Currie, J. R. L. *The Northern Counties Railway.* 2 vols. Newton Abbot, 1973–4.
    Vol. I, 1845–1903; vol. II, 1903–72.
Curtis, L. P., jr. The Anglo-Irish predicament. In *Twentieth-century Studies,* iv (Nov. 1970), pp 37–63.
—— Incumbered wealth: landed indebtedness in post-famine Ireland. In *A.H.R.,* lxxxv, no. 2 (Apr. 1980), pp 332–68.
Daly, M. E. Women in the Irish workforce from pre-industrial to modern times. In *Saothar,* vii (1981), pp 74–82.
—— *A social and economic history of Ireland since 1800.* Dublin, 1981.
—— Social structure of the Dublin working class, 1871–1911. In *I.H.S.,* xxiii, no. 90 (Nov. 1982), pp 121–33.
—— *Dublin: the deposed capital: a social and economic history, 1860–1914.* Cork, 1984.
—— An alien institution: attitudes toward the city in nineteenth- and twentieth-century Irish society. In *Études Irlandaises,* x (Dec. 1985), pp 181–94.
—— *The famine in Ireland.* Dundalk, 1986.
—— Housing conditions and the genesis of housing reform in Dublin, 1880–1920. In M. J. Bannon (ed.), *A hundred years of Irish planning* (Dublin, 1986), pp 77–130.
—— A tale of two cities: 1860–1920. In Art Cosgrove (ed.), *Dublin through the ages* (Dublin, 1988), pp 113–32.
Daly, Miriam. Women in Ulster. In Eiléan Ní Chuilleanáin (ed.), *Irish women, image and achievement: women in Irish culture from earliest times* (Dublin, 1985), pp 51–60.
Daly, Seán. *Cork, a city in crisis: a history of labour conflict and social misery, 1870–72.* Cork, 1978.
Danaher, Kevin. *The year in Ireland.* Cork, 1972.
—— *The hearth and stool and all: Irish rural households.* Cork and Dublin, 1986.
D'Arcy, Fergus. An age of distress and reform: 1800–1860. In Art Cosgrove (ed.), *Dublin through the ages* (Dublin, 1988), pp 93–112.
—— Irish trade unions before Congress. In *History Ireland,* ii, no. 2 (summer 1994), pp 25–30.
Davies, A. C. The first Irish industrial exhibition: Cork, 1852. In *Ir. Econ. & Soc. Hist.,* ii (1975), pp 46–59.
—— Roofing Belfast and Dublin, 1896–8: American penetration of the Irish market for Welsh slate. In *Ir. Econ. & Soc. Hist.,* iv (1977), pp 26–35.
—— Ireland's Crystal Palace, 1853. In Goldstrom & Clarkson, *Ir. population* (1981), pp 249–70.
Day, Angélique. 'Habits of the people': traditional life in Ireland, 1830–40, as recorded in the ordnance survey memoirs. In *Ulster Folklife,* xxx (1984), pp 22–36.
De Burca, Marcus. *The G. A. A.: a history.* Dublin, 1980.
Delany, Ruth. *The Grand Canal of Ireland.* Newton Abbot, 1973.
—— *Ireland's inland waterways.* Belfast, 1986.
—— *The shoemaker's canal.* Dublin, 1992.
Delany, V. T. H., and Delany, D. R. *The canals of the south of Ireland.* Newton Abbot, 1966.
Devine, T. M., and Dickson, David (ed.). *Ireland and Scotland, 1600–1850: parallels and contrasts in economic and social development.* Edinburgh, 1983.
Dewey, Clive. Celtic agrarian legislation and the Celtic revival: historicist implications of Gladstone's Irish and Scottish land acts, 1870–86. In *Past & Present,* no. 64 (Aug. 1974), pp 30–70.

Dickson, David. Aspects of the rise and decline of the Irish cotton industry. In L. M. Cullen and T. C. Smout, *Comparative aspects of Scottish and Irish economic history* (Edinburgh, 1977), pp 100–15.

——In search of the old Irish poor law. In Rosalind Mitchison and Peter Roebuck, *Economy and society in Scotland and Ireland* (Edinburgh, 1988), pp 149–59.

Donnelly, J. S., jr. *Landlord and tenant in nineteenth-century Ireland*. Dublin, 1973. (Insights into Irish History.)

——*The land and the people of nineteenth-century Cork*. London and Boston, 1975.

——The Irish agricultural depression of 1859–64. In *Ir. Econ & Soc. Hist.*, iii (1976), pp 33–54.

——Factions in pre-famine Ireland. In Audrey Eyler and Robert Garratt (ed.), *The uses of the past: essays on Irish culture* (Newark, Del., 1988), pp 113–30.

——The Terry Alt movement, 1829–31. In *History Ireland*, ii, no. 4 (winter 1994), pp 30–35.

Doyle, Oliver, and Hirsch, Stephen. *Railways in Ireland, 1834–1984*. Dublin, 1983.

Drake, Michael. Marriage and population growth in Ireland, 1750–1845. In *Econ. Hist. Rev.*, xvi, no. 2 (1963), pp 301–13.

Duffy, P. J. Irish landholding structures and population in the mid-nineteenth century. In *Maynooth Review*, iii, no. 2 (Dec. 1977), pp 3–27.

Dunleavy, J. C., and Dunleavy, G. W. The hidden Ireland of Irish landlords: manuscript evidence of oral tradition. In *Anglo-Irish Studies*, iv (1979), pp 47–58.

Dunlevy, Mairead. *Dress in Ireland*. London, 1989.

Dwyer, D. L., and Symons, L. J. The development and location of the textile industries in the Irish Republic. In *Ir. Geography*, iv, no. 6 (1963), pp 415–31.

Ehrlich, Cyril. Sir Horace Plunkett and agricultural reform. In Goldstrom & Clarkson, *Ir. population* (1981), pp 271–85.

Ellis, Peter Berresford. *A history of the Irish working class*. London, 1972.

Farrell, Michael. *The poor law and the workhouse in Belfast, 1838–1848*. Belfast, 1978.

Fetter, Frank. *The Irish pound, 1797–1826*. London, 1955.

Fitzpatrick, David. The disappearance of the Irish agricultural labourer, 1841–1912. In *Ir. Econ. & Soc. Hist.*, vii (1980), pp 66–92.

——Irish farming families before the first world war. In *Comparative Studies in Society and History*, xxv (1983), pp 339–74.

——*Irish emigration, 1801–1921*. Dundalk, 1984. (Studies in Irish Economic and Social History, I.)

——A share of the honeycomb: education, emigration, and Irishwomen. In *Continuity and Change*, i, no. 3 (Sept. 1986), pp 217–34.

——Divorce and separation in modern Irish history. In *Past & Present*, no. 114 (Feb. 1987), pp 173–96.

——The modernization of the Irish female. In Patrick O'Flanagan, Paul Ferguson, and Kevin Whelan (ed.), *Rural Ireland: modernisation and change* (Cork, 1987), pp 162–80.

Flanagan, Patrick. *Transport in Ireland, 1880–1910*. Dublin, 1969.

Flood, D. T. The decay of Georgian Dublin. In *Dublin Hist. Rec.*, xxvii, no. 3 (June 1974), pp 78–100.

Flynn, Gabriel. Bishop Thomas Nulty and the Irish land question. In *Riocht na Midhe*, vii, no. 3 (1984), pp 14–28; no. 4 (1985–6), pp 93–110.

Freeman, T. W. The congested districts of the west of Ireland. In *Geographical Review*, xxxiii, no. 1 (Jan. 1943), pp 1–15.

Froggatt, Peter. The census in Ireland of 1813–14. In *I.H.S.*, xiv, no. 55 (Mar. 1965), pp 227–35.

—— The demographic work of Sir William Wilde. In *Ir. Jn. Med. Sc.*, 6th ser., no. 473 (1965), pp 213–30.

—— Sir William Wilde and the 1831 census of Ireland. In *Medical History*, ix (1965), pp 302–27.

Gailey, Alan. The Scots element in north Irish popular culture. In *Ethnologia Europaea*, viii, no. 1 (1975), pp 2–22.

—— *Ulster folkways: an introduction*. Belfast, 1978.

—— Introduction and spread of the horse-powered threshing machine to Ulster farmers in the nineteenth century: some aspects. In *Ulster Folklife*, xxx (1984), pp 37–54.

Geary, Frank. The Belfast cotton industry revisited. In *I.H.S.*, xxvi, no. 103 (May 1989), pp 250–67.

—— and Johnson, W. Shipbuilding in Belfast, 1861–1986. In *Ir. Econ. & Soc. Hist.*, xvi (1989), pp 42–64.

Geoghegan, Vincent. Ralahine: an Irish Owenite community. In *International Review of Social History*, xxxvi, no. 3 (1991), pp 377–411.

Gibbon, Peter. Arensberg and Kimball revisited. In *Economy and Society*, ii (1973), pp 479–98.

—— Colonialism and the great starvation in Ireland, 1845–9. In *Race*, xvii, no. 2 (1975), pp 131–40.

—— and Curtin, Chris. Irish farm families: facts and fantasies. In *Comparative Studies in Society and History*, xxv (1983), pp 375–80.

—— and Higgins, M. D. Patronage, tradition, and modernisation: the case of the Irish 'gombeenman'. In *Econ. & Soc. Rev.*, vi, no. 1 (1974), pp 27–44.

Gill, Conrad. *The rise of the Irish linen industry*. Oxford, 1925; repr., 1964.

Gilligan, H. A. *History of the port of Dublin*. Dublin, 1988.

Gmelch, George, and Gmelch, S. B. The emergence of an ethnic group: the Irish tinkers. In *Anthropological Quarterly*, xlix, no. 4 (1976), pp 225–38.

Goldstrom, J. M. Irish agriculture and the great famine. In Goldstrom & Clarkson, *Ir. population* (1981), pp 153–71.

—— and Clarkson, L. A. (ed.). *Irish population, economy, and society: essays in honour of the late K. H. Connell*. Oxford, 1981.

Grant, James. The great famine and the poor law in Ulster: the rate-in-aid issue of 1849. In *I.H.S.*, xxvii, no. 105 (May 1990), pp 30–47.

Gray, John. *City in revolt: James Larkin and the Belfast dock strike of 1907*. Belfast, 1985.

Greaves, C. D. *The Irish Transport and General Workers Union: the formative years, 1909–23*. Dublin, 1982.

Green, E. R. R. *The Lagan valley, 1800–1850: a local history of the industrial revolution*. London, 1949.

Gribbon, H. D. *The history of water power in Ulster*. Newton Abbot, 1969.

Gribbon, Sybil. The social origins of Ulster unionism. In *Ir. Econ. & Soc. Hist.*, iv (1977), pp 66–72.

—— *Edwardian Belfast: a social profile*. Belfast, 1982. (Explorations in Irish History.)

Griffin, Brian. Social aspects of fenianism in Connacht and Leinster, 1858–1870. In *Éire-Ireland*, xxi, no. 1 (spring 1986), pp 16–39.

Griffin, Padraig. *The politics of Irish athletics, 1850–1900*. Ballinamore, Co. Leitrim, 1990.

Guttmann, J. M. The economics of tenant right in 19th-century Irish agriculture. In *Economic Inquiry*, xviii (1980), pp 408–24.

Hall, F. G. *The Bank of Ireland, 1783–1946*. Dublin and Oxford, 1949.
    Architectural chapter by C. P. Curran (pp 412–71); biographical notes by Joseph
        Hone (pp 473–513).

Harris, Ruth-Ann. Seasonal migration between Ireland and England prior to the famine. In *Canadian Papers in Rural History*, vii (1990), pp 363–86.

Harrison, J. F. C. *The second coming: popular millenarianism, 1780–1850*. London and New Brunswick, N.J., 1979.

Harvey, Brian. Changing fortunes on the Aran Islands in the 1890s. In *I.H.S.*, xxvii, no. 107 (May 1991), pp 237–49.

Hatton, Helen. Friends' famine relief in Ireland, 1846–9. In *Quaker History*, lxxvi (1987), pp 18–32.

Hearn, Mona. *Below stairs: domestic service remembered in Dublin and beyond, 1880–1922*. Dublin, 1993.

Heelan, Louis J., and Henry, E. W. Capital in Irish industry: statistical aspects; financial and related aspects. In *Stat. Soc. Ire. Jn.*, xxi, pt 1 (1962–3), pp 135–90.

Hepburn, A. C. Work, class, and religion in Belfast, 1871–1911. In *Ir. Econ. & Soc. Hist.*, x (1983), pp 33–50.

—— and Collins, B. Industrial society: the structure of Belfast, 1901. In Peter Roebuck (ed.), *Plantation to partition* (Belfast, 1981), pp 210–28.

Herring, I. J. Ulster roads on the eve of the railway age, c.1800–1840. In *I.H.S.*, ii, no. 6 (Sept. 1940), pp 160–88.

Holohan, Patrick. Daniel O'Connell and the Dublin trades: a collision, 1837–8. In *Saothar*, i (1975), pp 1–17.

Hooker, E. R. *Readjustments of agricultural tenure in Ireland*. Chapel Hill, N.C., 1938.

Horn, P. L. R. The National Agricultural Labourers' Union in Ireland, 1873–9. In *I.H.S.*, xvii, no. 67 (Mar. 1971), pp 340–52.

Hughes, T. Jones. The estate system of landholding in nineteenth-century Ireland. In William Nolan (ed.), *The shaping of Ireland: the geographical perspective* (Dublin, 1986), pp 137–50.

Hurst, J. W. Disturbed Tipperary, 1831–60. In *Éire-Ireland*, ix, no. 3 (autumn 1974), pp 44–59.

Huttman, J. P. The impact of land reform on agricultural production in Ireland. In *Agricultural History*, xlvi (1972), pp 353–68.

Hyman, Louis. *The Jews of Ireland from earliest times to the year 1910*. Shannon, 1972.

Hynes, Eugene. The great hunger and Irish catholicism. In *Societas: a review of social history*, viii (1978), pp 137–56.

Ireland, John de Courcy. *Ireland's sea fisheries: a history*. Dublin, 1981.

—— *Ireland and the Irish in maritime history*. Dun Laoghaire, 1986.

Jackson, Pauline. Women in nineteenth-century Irish migration. In *International Migration Review*, xviii, no. 4 (winter 1984), pp 1004–20.

Jacobson, D. S. The political economy of industrial locations: the Ford motor company at Cork, 1912–26. In *Ir. Econ. & Soc. Hist.*, iv (1977), pp 36–55.

James, N. O. G. *A forestry centenary: the history of the Royal Forestry Society of England, Wales, and Northern Ireland.* Oxford, 1982.

Jeffers, Brendan. Westport: an early Irish example of town planning. In *Cathair na Mart*, ix, no. 1 (1989), pp 48–59.

Jenkins, R. P. Witches and fairies: supernatural aggression and deviance among the Irish peasantry. In *Ulster Folklife*, xxiii (1977), pp 33–56.

Johnson, J. H. The population of Londonderry during the great Irish famine. In *Econ. Hist. Rev.*, 2nd ser., x (1957), pp 273–85.

—— Marriage and fertility in nineteenth-century Londonderry. In *Stat. Soc. Ire. Jn.*, xx, pt I (1958), pp 99–117.

—— Agriculture in Co. Derry at the beginning of the nineteenth century. In *Studia Hib.*, iv (1964), pp 95–103.

—— Harvest migration from nineteenth-century Ireland. In *Transactions of the Institute of British Geographers*, xli (June 1967), pp 97–112.

—— The distribution of Irish emigration in the decade before the great famine. In *Ir. Geography*, xxi (1988), pp 78–87.

Johnston, Joseph. *Irish agriculture in transition.* Dublin, 1951.

Jones, E. L., and Mingay, G. E. (ed.). *Land, labour, and population in the industrial revolution.* London, 1967.

Jones, Mary. *These obstreperous lassies: a history of the Irish Women Workers Union.* Dublin, 1988.

Jordan, Donald. *Land and popular politics in Ireland: County Mayo from the plantation to the land war.* Cambridge, 1994.

Kearney, H. F. Father Mathew: apostle of modernisation, In Cosgrove & McCartney, *Studies in Ir. hist.* (1979), pp 164–75.

Kemmy, James. The Limerick soviet. In *Saothar*, ii (1976), pp 45–52.

Kenneally, J. J. Sexism, the church, Irish women. In *Éire-Ireland*, xxi, no. 3 (fall 1986), pp 3–16.

Kennedy, Líam. A sceptical view on the reincarnation of the Irish gombeen man. In *Econ. & Soc. Rev.*, viii, no. 3 (1972), pp 213–22.

—— Adoption of a group innovation in Irish agriculture, 1890–1914: an exercise in applied history. In *Oxford Agrarian Studies*, vi (1977), pp 57–70.

—— The early response of the Irish catholic clergy to the cooperative movement. In *I.H.S.*, xxi, no. 81 (Mar. 1978), pp 55–74.

—— Retail markets in rural Ireland at the end of the nineteenth century. In *Ir. Econ. & Soc. Hist.*, v (1978), pp 46–63.

—— The Roman Catholic church and economic growth in nineteenth-century Ireland. In *Econ. & Soc. Rev.*, x, no. 1 (1978), pp 45–60.

—— Traders in the Irish rural economy, 1880–1914. In *Econ. Hist. Rev.*, xxxii, no. 2 (May 1979), pp 201–10.

—— Regional specialisation, railway development, and Irish agriculture in the nineteenth century. In Goldstrom & Clarkson, *Ir. population* (1981), pp 173–93.

—— Studies in Irish econometric history. In *I.H.S.*, xxiii, no. 91 (May 1983), pp 193–213.

—— Social change in Northern Ireland. In *Studies*, lxxiv, no. 295 (autumn 1985), pp 242–51.

—— and Ollerenshaw, Phillip. *Economic history of Ulster, 1820–1939.* Manchester, 1985.

Kennedy, R. E. *The Irish: emigration, marriage, and fertility.* Berkeley, Calif., and London, 1973.

Keogh, Dermot. *The rise of the Irish working class*. Belfast, 1982.

Kerr, Barbara. Irish seasonal migration to Great Britain, 1800–1830. In *I.H.S.*, iii, no. 12 (Sept. 1943), pp 365–80.

Kerrigan, Colm. The social impact of the Irish temperance movement, 1839–45. In *Ir. Econ. & Soc. Hist.*, xiv (1987), pp 20–38.

Kinealy, Christine. The poor law during the great famine: an administration in crisis. In E. M. Crawford (ed.), *Famine: the Irish experience* (Edinburgh, 1989), pp 157–75.

Kirby, R. G., and Musson, A. E. *The voice of the people: John Doherty, 1798–1854: trade unionist, radical, and factory reformer*. Manchester, 1975.

Kirkpatrick, R. W. Origins and development of the land war in mid-Ulster, 1879–85. In Lyons & Hawkins, *Ire. under the union* (1980), pp 201–35.

Knott, J. W. Land, kinship and identity: the cultural roots of agrarian agitation in eighteenth- and nineteenth-century Ireland. In *Journal of Peasant Studies*, xii, no. 1 (1984), pp 93–109.

Lane, P. G. An attempt at commercial farming in Ireland after the famine. In *Studies*, lxi, no. 24 (spring 1972), pp 54–66.

——The encumbered estates court, Ireland: 1848–9. In *Econ. & Soc. Rev.*, iii, no. 3 (1972), pp 413–53.

——The general impact of the encumbered estates act of 1849 on Counties Galway and Mayo. In *Galway Arch. Soc. Jn.*, xxxiii (1972–3), pp 44–74.

——The management of estates by financial corporations in Ireland after the famine. In *Studia Hib.*, xiv (1974), pp 67–89.

——The impact of the encumbered estates court upon the landlords of Galway and Mayo. In *Galway Arch. Soc. Jn.*, xxxviii (1981–2), pp 45–58.

——Purchase of land in Counties Galway and Mayo in the encumbered estates court, 1849–1858. In *Galway Arch. Soc. Jn.*, xliii (1991), pp 95–127.

Langer, W. L. Europe's initial population explosion. In *A.H.R.*, lxix, no. 1 (Oct. 1963), pp 1–17.

Large, David. The wealth of the greater Irish landowners, 1750–1815. In *I.H.S.*, xv, no. 57 (Mar. 1966), pp 21–47.

Larsen, S. V., and Snoddy, Oliver. 1916—a workingman's revolution? An analysis of those who made the 1916 revolution in Ireland. In *Social Studies*, ii, no. 4 (Aug. 1973), pp 377–98.

Leckey, J. J. The railway servants' strike in Co. Cork, 1898. In *Saothar*, ii (1976), pp 39–45.

Lee, J. J. Marriage and population growth in Ireland, 1750–1845. In *Econ. Hist. Rev.*, xvi, no. 2 (1963), pp 301–13.

——Money and beer in Ireland, 1790–1875. In *Econ. Hist. Rev.*, xix, no. 1 (1966), pp 183–90.

——The construction costs of Irish railways, 1830–1853. In *Business History*, ix (1967), pp 95–109.

——Marriage and population in pre-famine Ireland. In *Econ. Hist. Rev.*, xxi, no. 2 (1968), pp 283–95.

——The provision of capital for early Irish railways, 1830–1853. In *I.H.S.*, xvi, no. 61 (Mar. 1968), pp 33–63.

——Irish agriculture. [Review article.] In *Agricultural History Review*, xvii (1969), pp 64–76.

——The dual economy in Ireland, 1800–1850. In *Hist. Studies*, viii (1971), pp 191–201.

—— On the accuracy of the pre-famine Irish censuses. In Goldstrom & Clarkson, *Ir. population* (1981), pp 37–56.

Lees, Lynn Hollen. Mid-Victorian migration and the Irish family economy. In *Victorian Studies*, xx, no. 1 (autumn 1976), pp 25–43.

Leighton, C. D. A. *The Irish manufacture movement, 1840–43.* Maynooth, 1987. (Maynooth Historical Series, 5.)

Leister, Ingeborg. *Das werden der Agrarlandschaft in der Grafschaft Tipperary (Irland).* Marburg, 1963.

Lewis, C. A. *Hunting in Ireland: an historical and geographical analysis.* London, 1975.

Lockington, J. W. The Rev. Dr John Edgar and the temperance movement of the nineteenth century. In *Bulletin of the Presbyterian Historical Society of Ireland*, no. 12 (1983), pp 1–15.

Lowe, W. J. Landlord and tenant on the estate of Trinity College, Dublin, 1851–1903. In *Hermathena*, cxx (summer 1976), pp 5–24.

Luddy, Maria. Women and charitable organisations in nineteenth-century Ireland. In *Women's Studies International Forum*, xliv (1989), pp 301–5.

—— Irish women and the contagious diseases acts. In *History Ireland*, i, no. 1 (spring 1993), pp 32–5.

—— and Murphy, Cliona (ed.). *Women surviving: studies in Irish women's history in the nineteenth and twentieth centuries.* Swords, Co. Dublin, 1990.

Lynch, Patrick, and Vaizey, John. *Guinness's brewery in the Irish economy, 1759–1876.* Cambridge, 1960.

Lyne, G. J. John Townsend Trench's reports on the Lansdowne estates in Kerry, 1863–73. In *Kerry Arch. Soc. Jn.*, no. 19 (1986), pp 5–64.

Lyons, F. S. L. (ed.). *Bank of Ireland, 1783–1983: bicentenary essays.* Dublin, 1983.

McCarthy, Charles. *Trade unions in Ireland, 1894–1960.* Dublin, 1977.

McCarthy, J. C. History of pig breeding in Ireland. In *Dept. Agric. Jn.*, lxiii (1966), pp 55–60.

McCarthy, R. B. *The Trinity College estates, 1800–1923: corporate management in an age of reform.* [Dundalk], 1992.

McCaughan, Michael. *Steel ships and iron men: shipbuilding in Belfast, 1894–1912.* Belfast, 1989.

—— and Appleby, John (ed.). *The Irish Sea: aspects of maritime history.* Belfast, 1989.

McCourt, Desmond. Infield and outfield in Ireland. In *Econ. Hist. Rev.*, 2nd ser., vii, no. 3 (1955), pp 369–76.

—— The decline of rundale, 1750–1850. In Peter Roebuck (ed.), *Plantation to partition* (Belfast, 1981), pp 119–39.

McCourt, Eileen. The management of the Farnham estates during the nineteenth century. In *Breifne*, iv, no. 16 (1975), pp 531–60.

McCracken, D. P. The management of a mid-Victorian Irish iron-ore mine: Glenravel, County Armagh, 1866–87. In *Ir. Econ. & Soc. Hist.*, xi (1984), pp 60–72.

—— and McCracken, Eileen. A register of trees, Co. Cork, 1790–1860. In *Cork Hist. Soc. Jn.*, lxxxi, nos 233–4 (1976), pp 39–60.

McCracken, Eileen. *The Irish woods since Tudor times: distribution and exploitation.* Newton Abbot, 1971.

—— Tree-planting by tenants in Meath, 1800–1850. In *Ríocht na Midhe*, viii, no. 2 (1988–9), pp 3–20.

McCutcheon, Alan. *Wheel and spindle: aspects of Irish industrial history*. Belfast, 1977.

McCutcheon, W. A. *The canals of the north of Ireland*. London, 1965.

—— Industrial archaeology: a case study in Northern Ireland. In *World Archaeology*, xv, no. 2 (Oct. 1983), pp 161–72.

McDowell, R. B. (ed.). *Social life in Ireland, 1800–1845*. Dublin, 1957; repr., 1963.

McFeely, Mary Drake. *Lady inspectors: the campaign for a better workplace, 1893–1921*. Oxford, 1988.

    Three chapters on work of women factory inspectors in Ireland.

McGowan, Pádraig. *Money and banking in Ireland: origins, development, and future*. Dublin, 1990.

McGuire, E. B. *Irish whiskey: a history of distilling, the spirit trade, and excise controls in Ireland*. Dublin and New York, 1973.

McHugh, John. The Belfast labour dispute and riots of 1907. In *International Review of Social History*, xxii (1977), 1–20.

McKenna, E. E. Marriage and fertility in post-famine Ireland: a multivariate analysis. In *American Journal of Sociology*, lxxx, no. 3 (Nov. 1974), pp 688–705.

—— Age, region, and marriage in post-famine Ireland: an empirical examination. In *Econ. Hist. Rev.*, 2nd ser., xxxi, no. 2 (1978), pp 238–56.

Mac Lochlainn, Alf. Social life in County Clare, 1800–1850. In *Ir. Univ. Rev.*, ii, no. 1 (1972), pp 55–78.

McNeill, D. B. *Irish passenger steamship services, I: North of Ireland*. Newton Abbot, 1969.

Mac Philip, Seamus. Profile of a landlord in folk tradition and in contemporary accounts: the third earl of Leitrim. In *Ulster Folklife*, xxxiv (1988), pp 26–40.

Maguire, W. A. *The Downshire estates in Ireland, 1801–1845*. Oxford, 1972.

—— Lord Donegall and the sale of Belfast: a case history from the encumbered estates court. In *Econ. Hist. Rev.*, xxix, no. 4 (1976), pp 570–84.

—— The 1822 settlement of the Donegall estates. In *Ir. Econ. & Soc. Hist.*, iii (1976), pp 17–32.

—— *Living like a lord: the second marquis of Donegall, 1769–1844*. Belfast, 1984.

Malcolm, Elizabeth. *Ireland sober, Ireland free: drink and temperance in nineteenth-century Ireland*. Dublin and Syracuse, N.Y., 1986.

—— Asylums and other 'total institutions' in Ireland: recent studies. In *Éire-Ireland*, xxii, no. 3 (fall 1987), pp 151–60.

Malins, Edward. *Irish gardens and demesnes from 1830*. London, 1980.

Martin, J. H. The social geography of mid-nineteenth-century Dublin city. In W. J. Smyth and Kevin Whelan (ed.), *Common ground* (Cork, 1988), pp 173–88.

Maxwell, Constantia. *Dublin under the Georges*. London, 1936; 2nd ed., 1956.

—— *Country and town in Ireland under the Georges*. London, 1940; 2nd ed., Dundalk, 1949.

Meenan, F. O. C. The Georgian squares of Dublin and the professions. In *Studies*, lviii (winter, 1969), pp 405–14.

Meenan, James, and Webb, D. A. (ed.). *A view of Ireland: twelve essays on different aspects of Irish life and the Irish countryside*. Dublin, 1957. (British Association for the Advancement of Science.)

Messenger, Betty. *Picking up the linen threads: a study in industrial folklore*. Austin, Tex., 1978.

Micks, W. L. *An account of the Congested Districts Board for Ireland from 1891 to 1923*. Dublin, 1925.

Middlemass, Tom. *Irish standard gauge railways*. Newton Abbot, 1981.

Miller, D. W. (ed.). *Peep o' Day Boys and Defenders*. Belfast, 1990.

Mitchison, Rosalind, and Roebuck, Peter (ed.). *Economy and society in Scotland and Ireland, 1500–1939*. Edinburgh, 1988.

Mogey, J. M. *Rural life in Northern Ireland: five regional studies*. London, 1947.

Mokyr, Joel. *Why Ireland starved: a quantitative and analytical history of the Irish economy, 1800–1850*. London, 1983. Paperback ed., with corrections, 1985.

—— and Ó Gráda, Cormac. Poor and getting poorer? Living standards in Ireland before the famine. In *Econ. Hist. Rev.*, xli, no. 2 (1988), pp 209–35.

Molumby, Patrick D. Lighting Dublin. In *Capuchin Annual*, xl (1973), pp 75–85.

Monaghan, J. J. The rise and fall of the Belfast cotton industry. In *I.H.S.*, iii, no. 9 (Mar. 1942), pp 1–17.

Mooney, Desmond. The origins of agrarian violence in Meath, 1790–1828. In *Ríocht na Midhe*, viii, no. 1 (1987), pp 45–67.

—— A society in crisis: agrarian violence in Meath, 1828–1835. In *Ríocht na Midhe*, viii, no. 2 (1988–9), pp 102–28.

Moore, Gerry. Socio-economic aspects of anti-semitism in Ireland, 1880–1905. In *Econ. & Soc. Rev.*, xii, no. 3 (Apr. 1981), pp 187–201.

Moore, John. *Motor makers in Ireland*. Belfast, 1982.

Morgan, Austen. *Labour and partition: the Belfast working class, 1905–1923*. London, 1991.

Morgan, D. H. *Harvesters and harvesting, 1800–1900: a study of the rural proletariat*. London, 1982.

Morgan, Valerie, and Macafee, W. Irish population in the pre-famine period: evidence from County Antrim. In *Econ. Hist. Rev.*, xxxvii (1984), pp 182–96.

Moss, Michael, and Hume, John R. *Shipbuilders to the world: 125 years of Harland and Wolff, Belfast 1861–1986*. Belfast and Wolfeboro, 1986.

Mulligan, Fergus. *One hundred and fifty years of Irish railways*. Belfast, 1983.

Munck, Ronald. Class and religion in Belfast: a historical perspective. In *Journal of Contemporary History*, xx, no. 2 (1985), pp 241–59.

—— Class conflict and sectarianism in Belfast: from its origins to the 1930s. In *Contemporary Crises*, ix (1985), pp 149–67.

Munn, C. W. The emergence of central banking in Ireland: the Bank of Ireland, 1814–50. In *Ir. Econ. & Soc. Hist.*, x (1983), pp 19–32.

Murphy, A. E. (ed.). *Economists and the Irish economy from the eighteenth century to the present day*. Dublin, 1984.

Murphy, Cliona. *The women's suffrage movement and Irish society in the early twentieth century*. New York, 1989.

Murphy, Maura. The working classes of nineteenth-century Cork. In *Cork Hist. Soc. Jn.*, lxxxv (1980), pp 26–51.

Murray, A. C. Agrarian violence and nationalism in nineteenth-century Ireland: the myth of Ribbonism. In *Ir. Econ. & Soc. Hist.*, xiii (1986), pp 56–73.

Murray, K. A. *The Great Northern Railway*. Dublin, 1944.

—— William Dargan. In *Ir. Railway Rec. Soc. Jn.*, ii (1950–51), pp 94–102.

—— *Ireland's first railway*. Dublin, 1981.

Neeson, Eoin. *A history of Irish forestry*. Dublin, 1991.

Nelson, E. C., and Brady, Aidan (ed.). *Irish gardening and horticulture*. Dublin, 1979. (Royal Horticultural Society of Ireland.)

Newsinger, John. James Connolly and the Easter rising. In *Science and Society*, xlvii, no. 2 (summer 1983), pp 152–77.

—— 'A lamp to guide your feet': Jim Larkin, the *Irish Worker*, and the Dublin working class. In *European History Quarterly*, xx, no. 1 (Jan. 1990), pp 63–99.

Nicholas, Stephen, and Shergold, P. S. Human capital and the pre-famine Irish emigration to England. In *Explorations in Economic History*, xxiv, no. 2 (Apr. 1987), pp 158–77.

—— and—— Irish intercounty mobility before 1840. In *Ir. Econ. & Soc. Hist.*, xvii (1990), pp 22–43.

Nolan, William. New fields and farms: migration policies of state land agencies, 1891–1980. In W. J. Smyth and Kevin Whelan (ed.), *Common ground* (Cork, 1988), pp 296–319.

O'Brien, Gerard. The establishment of poor law unions in Ireland, 1838–43. In *I.H.S.*, xxiii, no. 90 (Nov. 1982), pp 97–120.

—— The new poor law in pre-famine Ireland: a case history. In *Ir. Econ. & Soc. Hist.*, xii (1985), pp 33–49.

—— Workhouse management in pre-famine Ireland. In *R.I.A. Proc.*, lxxxvi, sect. C (1986), pp 113–34.

O'Brien, J. B. *The catholic middle classes in pre-famine Cork*. Dublin, 1979. (O'Donnell Lecture.)

—— Merchants in Cork before the famine. In Paul Butel and L. M. Cullen (ed.), *Cities and merchants* (Dublin, 1986), pp 221–32.

O'Brien, J. V. *'Dear dirty Dublin': a city in distress, 1899–1916*. London, 1982.

Ó Ceallaigh, Séamus. *Story of the G.A.A.* Limerick, 1977.

O'Connor, Emmet. *Syndicalism in Ireland 1917–1923*. Cork, 1988.

—— *A labour history of Waterford*. Waterford, 1989.

—— *A labour history of Ireland, 1824–1960*. Dublin, 1992.

Ó Danachair, Caoimhín. The death of a tradition. In *Studies*, lxiii (autumn 1974), pp 219–30.

—— (ed.). *Folk and farm: essays in honour of A. T. Lucas*. Dublin, 1976.

O'Donnell, P. D. *The Irish faction fighters of the nineteenth century*. Dublin and Tralee, 1975.

O'Donovan, John. *The economic history of livestock in Ireland*. Cork, 1940.

O'Dowd, Anne. *The Irish migrant farm worker, 1830–1920*. Dublin, 1990.

O'Flanagan, Patrick; Ferguson, Paul; and Whelan, Kevin (ed.). *Rural Ireland: modernisation and change, 1600–1900*. Cork, 1987.

Ó Gallchobhair, Proinnsias. *The history of landlordism in Donegal*. Ballyshannon, 1962.

Ó Gráda, Cormac. A note on nineteenth-century Irish emigration statistics. In *Population Studies*, xxix (Mar. 1973), pp 143–9.

—— Seasonal migration and post-famine adjustment in the west of Ireland. In *Studia Hib.*, xiii (1973), pp 48–76.

—— Agricultural head-rents, pre-famine and post-famine. In *Econ. & Soc. Rev.*, v, no. 3 (1974), pp 385–92.

—— The Owenite community at Ralahine, Co. Clare, 1831–3: a reassessment. In *Ir. Econ. & Soc. Hist.*, i (1974), pp 36–48.

—— The investment behaviour of Irish landlords, 1830–75: some preliminary findings. In *Agricultural History Review*, xxiii, pt 2 (1975), pp 139–55.

—— Supply responsiveness in Irish agriculture during the nineteenth century. In *Econ. Hist. Rev.*, 2nd ser., xxviii, no. 2 (1975), pp 312–17.

—— The beginnings of the Irish creamery system, 1880–1914. In *Econ. Hist. Rev.*, 2nd ser., xxx, no. 2 (1977), pp 284–305.

—— The population of Ireland, 1700–1900: a survey. In *Annales de Demographie Historique 1979*, pp 281–99.

—— Primogeniture and ultimogeniture in rural Ireland. In *Journal of Interdisciplinary History*, x, no. 3 (winter 1980), pp 491–7.

—— Malthus and the pre-famine economy. In *Hermathena*, cxxxv (winter 1983), pp 75–95.

—— *Catholic families weren't always bigger: religion, wealth, and fertility in rural Ulster before 1911.* Dublin, 1984.

—— Irish agricultural output before and after the famine. In *Journal of European Economic History*, xiii, no. 1 (spring 1984), pp 149–65.

—— Did Ulster catholics always have large families? In *Ir. Econ. & Soc. Hist.*, xii (1985), pp 79–88.

—— *Éire roimh an nGorta: an saol eacnamaioch.* Dublin, 1986. (Monograif Staire agus Cultur.)

—— *Ireland before and after the famine: explorations in economic history, 1800–1925.* Manchester, 1988.

—— *The great Irish famine.* Basingstoke, 1989. (Economic History Society.)

—— The 'lumper' potato and the famine. In *History Ireland*, i, no. 1 (spring 1993), pp 22–4.

—— *Ireland: a new economic history, 1780–1939.* Oxford, 1994.

Ollerenshaw, Philip. *Banking in nineteenth-century Ireland: the Belfast banks, 1825–1914.* Manchester, 1987.

O'Loan, John. Origin and development of arterial drainage in Ireland and the pioneers. In *Dept. Agric. Jn.*, lix (1962), pp 46–73.

O'Mahony, Colman. Shipbuilding and repairing in nineteenth- century Cork. In *Cork Hist. Soc. Jn.*, xciv (1989), pp 74–87.

O'Malley, Eoin. The decline of Irish industry in the nineteenth century. In *Econ. & Soc. Rev.*, xiii, no. 1 (Oct. 1981), pp 21–42.

O'Neill, James. A look at Captain Rock: agrarian rebellion in Ireland, 1815–1845. In *Eire-Ireland*, xvii, no. 3 (fall 1982), pp 17–34.

O'Neill, Kevin. *Family and farm in pre-famine Ireland: the parish of Killashandra.* Madison, Wis., 1984.

O'Neill, Thomas P. The Society of Friends and the great famine. In *Studies*, xxxiv (1950), pp 203–13.

—— From famine to near-famine, 1845–1879. In *Studia Hib.*, i (1961), pp 161–71.

O'Neill, Timothy P. The catholic church and relief of the poor, 1815–1845. In *Archiv. Hib.*, xxxi (1973), pp 132–45.

—— Fever and public health in pre-famine Ireland. In *R.S.A.I. Jn.*, ciii (1973), pp 1–34.

—— *Life and tradition in rural Ireland.* London, 1977.

—— The food crisis of the 1890s. In E. M. Crawford, (ed.), *Famine: the Irish experience* (Edinburgh, 1989), pp 176–97.

Orridge, Andrew. *The Irish Land League: the social origins of an agrarian movement.* Birmingham, 1980.

—— Who supported the land war? an aggregate-data analysis of Irish agrarian discontent, 1879–1882. In *Econ. & Soc. Rev.*, xii, no. 3 (1981), pp 203–33.

Osborne, J. W. William Cobbett and Ireland. In *Studies*, lxx (1981), pp 187–95.

Ó Suilleabháinn, Seán. *Irish folk custom and belief.* Dublin, 1967.

O'Sullivan, C. J. *The gasmakers: historical perspectives on the gas industry.* Dublin, 1987.

Owens, Rosemary Cullen. *Smashing times: a history of the Irish women's suffrage movement, 1889–1922.* Dublin, 1984.

Patterson, Henry. *Class conflict and sectarianism: the protestant working class and the Belfast labour movement, 1868–1920.* Belfast, 1980.

—— Independent orangeism and class conflict in Edwardian Belfast: a reinterpretation. In *R.I.A. Proc.*, lxxx, sect. C (1980), pp 1–27.

Phelan, M. M. Fr Thomas O'Shea and the Callan Tenant Protection Society. In *Old Kilkenny Rev.*, new ser., ii, no. 2 (1980), pp 49–58.

Powell, F. The Irish poor law controversy. In *Social Policy and Administration*, xv, no. 3 (autumn 1981), pp 286–303.

Proudfoot, Lindsay. The management of a great estate: patronage, income and expenditure on the duke of Devonshire's Irish property, *c.*1816 to 1891. In *Ir. Econ. & Soc. Hist.*, xiii (1986), pp 32–55.

Rhodes, R. M. *Women and the family in post-famine Ireland.* Hamden, Conn., 1991.

Robins, Joseph. *The lost children: a study of charity children in Ireland, 1700–1900.* Dublin, 1980.

Robinson, Olive. The London companies as progressive landlords in nineteenth-century Ireland. In *Econ. Hist. Rev.*, 2nd ser., xv, no. 1 (1962), pp 103–18.

—— The London companies and tenant right in nineteenth-century Ireland. In *Agricultural History Review*, xviii (1970), pp 54–63.

Roebuck, Peter. The Donegall family and the development of Belfast, 1600–1850. In Paul Butel and L. M. Cullen (ed.), *Cities and merchants* (Dublin, 1986), pp 125–38.

—— Rent movement, proprietorial incomes, and agricultural development, 1730–1830. In Peter Roebuck (ed.), *Plantation to partition* (Belfast, 1981), pp 82–101.

Royle, S. A. The economy and society of the Aran Islands, County Galway, in the early nineteenth century. In *Ir. Geography*, xvi (1983), pp 36–54.

—— Irish famine relief in the early nineteenth century: the 1822 famine on the Aran Islands. In *Ir. Econ. & Soc. Hist.*, xi (1984), pp 44–59.

Salaman, R. N. *The influence of the potato on the course of Irish history.* Dublin, 1944.

—— *The history and social influence of the potato.* Cambridge, 1949. Revised impression, ed. T. G. Hawkes, 1985.

Shearman, Hugh. State-aided land purchase under the disestablishment act of 1869. In *I.H.S.*, iv, no. 13 (Mar. 1944), pp 58–80.

Shepherd, W. E. *The Dublin and South-Eastern Railway.* Newton Abbot, 1974.

Shields, Lisa, and Fitzgerald, Denis. The night of the 'big wind' in Ireland, 6–7 January 1839. In *Ir. Geography*, xxii (1989), pp 31–43.

Simpson, Noel. *The Belfast Bank, 1827–1970: 150 years of banking in Ireland.* Belfast, 1975.

Sinclair, R. C. *Across the Irish sea: Belfast–Liverpool shipping since 1819.* London, 1990.

Smyth, Hazel. *The B. & I. line: a history of the British and Irish Steampacket Company.* Dublin, 1984.

Smyth, W. J. Landholding changes, kinship networks and class transformation in rural Ireland: a case-study from County Tipperary. In *Ir. Geography*, xvi (1983), pp 16–35.

—— Flax cultivation in Ireland: the development and demise of a regional staple. In W. J. Smyth and Kevin Whelan (ed.), *Common ground* (Cork, 1988), pp 236–52.

Socolofsky, H. E. *Landlord William Scully.* Lawrence, Kan., 1980.

Solar, P. M. The agricultural trade statistics in the Irish railway commissioners' report. In *Ir. Econ. & Soc. Hist.*, vi (1979), pp 24–40.

—— Why Ireland starved: a critical review of the econometric results. In *Ir. Econ. & Soc. Hist.*, xi (1984), pp 107–15.

—— The reconstruction of Irish external trade statistics for the nineteenth century. In *Ir. Econ. & Soc. Hist.*, xii (1985), pp 63–78.

—— A Belgian view of the Ulster linen industry in the 1840s. In *Ulster Folklife*, xxxiv (1988), pp 16–25.

—— The great famine was no ordinary subsistence crisis. In E. M. Crawford (ed.), *Famine: the Irish experience* (Edinburgh, 1989), pp 112–33.

—— The Irish butter trade in the nineteenth century: new estimates and their implications. In *Studia Hib.*, xxv (1989–90), pp 134–61.

—— The Irish linen trade, 1820–52. In *Textile History*, xxi (1991), pp 57–85.

Solow, B. L. *The land question and the Irish economy, 1870–1903.* Cambridge, Mass., 1971.

—— A new look at the Irish land question. In *Econ. & Soc. Rev.*, xii, no. 4 (July 1981), pp 301–14.

Strain, R. W. M. *Belfast and its charitable society: a story of urban social development.* London, New York, and Toronto, 1961.

Staehle, H. Statistical notes on the economic history of Irish agriculture, 1847–1913. In *Stat. Soc. Ire. Jn.*, xviii (1950–51), pp 444–71.

Stevenson, Jane. The beginnings of literacy in Ireland. In *R.I.A. Proc.*, lxxxix, sect. C (1989), pp 127–65.

Taylor, L. J. The priest and the agent: social drama and class consciousness in the west of Ireland. In *Comparative Studies in Society and History*, xxvii (1985), pp 696–712.

TeBrake, Janet, K. Irish peasant women in revolt: the land league years. In *I.H.S.*, xxviii, no. 109 (May 1992), pp 63–80.

T'Hart, Marjolein. Irish return migration in the nineteenth century. In *Tijdschrift voor Economische en Sociale Geografie*, lxxvi, no. 3 (1985), pp 223–31.

Thompson, Francis. The landed classes, the Orange order, and the anti-Land League campaign in Ulster, 1880–81. In *Éire-Ireland*, xxii, no. 1 (spring 1987), pp 102–21.

Thuente, M. H. Violence in pre-famine Ireland: the testimony of Irish folklore and fiction. In *Ir. Univ. Rev.*, xv, no. 2 (autumn 1985), pp 129–47.

Turner, Michael. Livestock in the agrarian economy of Counties Down and Antrim from 1803 to the famine. In *Ir. Econ. & Soc. Hist.*, xi (1984), pp 19–43.

—— Towards an agricultural prices index for Ireland, 1850–1914. In *Econ. & Soc. Rev.*, xviii, no. 2 (Jan. 1987), pp 123–36.

—— Output and productivity in Irish agriculture from the famine to the great war. In *Ir. Econ. & Soc. Hist.*, xvii (1990), pp 62–78.

Vaizey, John. *The brewing industry, 1886–1951.* London, 1960.

Vaughan, W. E. Agricultural output, rents and wages in Ireland 1850–80. In L. M. Cullen and François Furet (ed.), *Ireland and France* (Paris, 1980), pp 85–97.

—— Richard Griffith and the tenement valuation. In G. L. Herries Davies and R. C. Mollan (ed.), *Richard Griffith, 1784–1878* (Dublin, 1980), pp 103–22.

—— Farmer, grazier, and gentleman: Edward Delany of Woodtown, 1851–99. In *Ir. Econ. & Soc. Hist.*, ix (1982), pp 53–72.

—— *Sin, sheep and Scotsmen: John George Adair and the Derryveagh evictions, 1861.* Belfast, 1983.

Vaughan, W. E. *Landlords and tenants in Ireland, 1848–1904.* Dublin, 1984. (Studies in Irish Economic and Social History, 2.)

—— Potatoes and agricultural output. In *Ir. Econ. & Soc. Hist.*, xvii (1990), pp 79–92.

—— *Landlords and tenants in mid-Victorian Ireland.* Oxford, 1994.

Verrière, Jacques. *La population de l'Irlande.* Paris, 1979.

Walsh, B. M. Marriage rates and population pressure: Ireland, 1871 and 1911. In *Econ. Hist. Rev.*, xxiii, no. 1 (1970), pp 148–62.

Webb, J. J. *The guilds of Dublin.* Dublin, 1929.

Weir, R. B. In and out of Ireland: the Distillers Company Ltd and the Irish whiskey trade, 1900–39. In *Ir. Econ. & Soc. Hist.*, vii (1980), pp 45–65.

Westropp, M. S. D. *Irish glass: an account of glassmaking in Ireland from the XVIth century to the present day.* London, 1920; 2nd ed., London, 1978.

Whelan, Kevin. The geography of hurling. In *History Ireland*, i, no. 1 (spring 1993), pp 27–31.

Williamson, J. G. The impact of the Irish on British labor markets during the industrial revolution. In *Jn. Econ. Hist.*, xlvi, no. 3 (Sept. 1986), pp 693–720.

Wilson, Thomas. The great landowners of Meath, 1879. In *Ríocht na Midhe*, vii, no. 1 (1980–81), pp 99–110.

Winstanley, M. J. *Ireland and the land question, 1800–1922.* London, 1984.

Woodham-Smith, Cecil. *The great hunger: Ireland, 1845–1849.* London and New York, 1962.

Woods, Christopher. American travellers in Ireland before and during the great famine: a case of culture-shock. In Wolfgang Zach and Heinz Kosok (ed.), *Literary interrelations* (Tübingen, 1987), iii, 77–84.

7 HISTORY OF ENGLISH LANGUAGE AND LITERATURE

Atkinson, Colin, and Atkinson, Jo. Sydney Owenson, Lady Morgan: Irish patriot and first professional woman writer. In *Éire-Ireland*, xv, no. 2 (summer 1980), pp 60–90.

Bareham, Tony (ed.). *Charles Lever: new evaluations.* Gerrards Cross and Lanham, Md., 1991.

Begnal, Michael. *Sheridan Le Fanu.* Lewisburg, Pa., 1971.

Bliss, A. J. The language of Synge. In Maurice Harmon (ed.), *J. M. Synge centenary papers, 1971* (Dublin, 1972), pp 35–62.

Boue, André. *William Carleton, 1794–1869: romancier Irlandais.* Paris, 1973.

Boyd, Ernest. *Ireland's literary renaissance.* 2nd ed., New York, 1922; repr., Dublin, 1968.

Brogan, Howard. Thomas Moore, Irish satirist and keeper of the English conscience. In *Philological Quarterly*, xxiv (1945), pp 255–76.

Bromwich, Rachel. *Matthew Arnold and Celtic literature: a retrospect, 1865–1965.* Oxford, 1965.

Brown, M. J. *George Moore: a reconsideration.* Seattle, 1955.

—— *The politics of Irish literature: from Thomas Davis to W. B. Yeats.* London, 1972.

Browne, Nelson. *Sheridan Le Fanu.* London, 1951.

Bushrui, Suheil Badi, and Benstock, Bernard (ed.). *James Joyce: an international perspective.* Gerrards Cross and Totowa, N.J., 1982.

Cahalan, J. M. *Great hatred, little room: the Irish historical novel.* Syracuse, 1983.

Carpenter, Andrew (ed.). *My uncle John: Edward Stephens's life of J. M. Synge.* London, 1974.

Carpentier, Godeleine. Kickham's panorama of rural Ireland, 1840–70. In *Tipperary Historical Journal* (1990), pp 63–74.

Chestnutt, Margaret. *Studies in the short stories of William Carleton*. Gothenburg, Sweden, 1976.

Chuto, Jacques. Mangan, Petrie, O'Donovan, and a few others: the poet and the scholars. In *Ir. Univ. Rev.*, vi, no. 2 (autumn 1976), pp 169–87.

Colgan, Maurice. After Rackrent: ascendancy nationalism in Maria Edgeworth's later Irish novels. In Heinz Kosok (ed.), *Studies in Anglo-Irish literature* (Bonn, 1982), pp 37–42.

Corkery, Daniel. *Synge and Anglo-Irish literature*. Cork, 1931.

Costello, Peter. *The heart grown brutal: the Irish revolution in literature from Parnell to the death of Yeats, 1891–1939*. Dublin and Totowa, N.J., 1977.

Cronin, John. *The Anglo-Irish novel*. 2 vols. Belfast, 1980, 1990.
> Vol. I, the nineteenth century; vol. II, 1900–40.

Deane, Séamus. The literary myths of the revival: a case for their abandonment. In Joseph Ronsley (ed.), *Myth and reality in Irish literature* (Waterloo, Ont., 1977), pp 317–29.

——*A short history of Irish literature*. London and Notre Dame, Ind., 1986.

Diskin, Patrick. The poetry of James Clarence Mangan. In *University Rev.*, ii, no. 1 (1960), pp 21–30.

Dowden, W. S. 'Let Erin remember': a reexamination of the journal of Thomas Moore. In *Rice University Studies*, lxi (1975), pp 39–50.

Dunne, Tom. *Maria Edgeworth and the colonial mind*. Cork, 1984. (O'Donnell Lecture.)

——Haunted by history: Irish romantic writing, 1800–1850. In Roy Porter and Mikulas Teich (ed.), *Romanticism in national context* (Cambridge, 1988), pp 68–91.

Ellmann, Richard. *Yeats, the man and the masks*. New York, 1948. Paperback ed., 1958.

Esslinger, P. M. The Irish alienation of Sean O'Casey. In *Éire-Ireland*, i, no. 1 (spring 1966), pp 18–25.

Fallis, Richard. *The Irish renaissance: an introduction to Anglo-Irish literature*. Syracuse, N.Y., 1977; Dublin, 1978.

Faulkner, Peter. *Yeats and the Irish eighteenth century*. Dublin, 1965. (Yeats Centenary Papers, v.)

Flanagan, Thomas. *The Irish novelists, 1800–1850*. New York, 1959.

Foster, J. W. *Forces and themes in Ulster fiction*. Dublin and London, 1974.

——*Fictions of the Irish literary revival, a changeling art*. Syracuse, N.Y., and Dublin, 1987.

——The revival of saga and heroic romance during the Irish renaissance. In Heinz Kosok (ed.), *Studies in Anglo-Irish literature* (Bonn, 1982), pp 126–36.

Foster, Roy. Protestant magic: W. B. Yeats and the spell of Irish history. In *Brit. Acad. Proc.*, lxxv (1989), pp 243–66.

Greene, D. H., and Stephens, E. M. *J. M. Synge, 1871–1909*. New York, 1959.

Gwynn, Denis. *Edward Martyn and the Irish revival*. London, 1930.

Hall, W. E. *Shadowy heroes: Irish literature of the 1890s*. Syracuse, N. Y., 1980.

Harmon, Maurice. Aspects of the peasantry in Anglo-Irish literature from 1800 to 1916. In *Studia Hib.*, xv (1975), pp 105–27.

Haslam, Richard. Lady Morgan's novels from 1806 to 1833: cultural aesthetics and national identity. In *Éire-Ireland*, xxii, no. 4 (1987), pp 11–25.

Hayes-McCoy, G. A. Sir Walter Scott and Ireland. In *Hist. Studies*, x (1976), pp 91–108.

Hayley, Barbara. *Carleton's 'Traits and stories' and the nineteenth-century Anglo-Irish tradition*. Gerrards Cross and Totowa, N.J., 1983.

Hickey, Kieran. *Faithful departed: the Dublin of James Joyce's Ulysses.* Dublin, 1982.

Hone, J. M. *The life of George Moore.* New York, 1936.

—— *W. B. Yeats, 1865–1939.* New York, 1943.

Howarth, Herbert. *The Irish writers: literature and nationalism, 1890–1940.* New York, 1959.

Hurst, Michael. *Maria Edgeworth and the public scene: intellect, fine feelings, and landlordism in the age of reform.* London and Coral Gables, Fla., 1969.

Hyde, Douglas. *A literary history of Ireland from earliest times to the present day.* London, 1899. New ed. with introduction by Brian Ó Cuív, London and New York, 1967.

Jeffares, A. N. *W. B. Yeats: man and poet.* New Haven, Conn., 1949.

—— *Anglo-Irish literature.* Dublin, 1982.

—— (ed.) *Yeats the European.* Savage, Md., 1989. (Princess Grace Irish Library Series, no. 3.)

Johnston, Conor. Parsons, priests, and politics: Anthony Trollope's Irish clergy. In *Éire-Ireland*, xxv, no. 1 (1990), pp 80–97.

Jordan, H. H. *Bolt upright: the life of Thomas Moore.* 2 vols. Salzburg, 1975. (Salzburg Studies in English Literature.)

Kain, Richard. *Dublin in the age of William Butler Yeats and James Joyce.* Norman, Okla., 1962. (Centers of Civilisation, 7.)

Kelly, J. S. The fall of Parnell and the rise of Irish literature: an investigation. In *Anglo-Irish Studies*, ii (1976), pp 1–23.

Kenny, Desmond. The ballads of *The Nation*: a study in a popular concept. In *Cahiers du Centre d'Études Irlandaises*, iii (1978), pp 31–45.

Kiberd, Declan. *Synge and the Irish language.* London, 1979.

—— The perils of nostalgia: a critique of the revival. In Peter Connolly (ed.), *Literature and the changing Ireland* (Gerrards Cross, 1982), pp 1–24.

Kilroy, James. *James Clarence Mangan.* Lewisburg, Pa., 1970.

Kinsella, Thomas, and Yeats, W. B. *Davis, Mangan, Ferguson? tradition and the Irish writer: writings by W. B. Yeats and by Thomas Kinsella.* Dublin, 1970.

Knapp, J. E. History against myth: Lady Gregory and cultural discourse. In *Éire-Ireland*, xxii, no. 3 (fall 1987), pp 30–42.

Komesu, Okifumi, and Sekine, Masaru (ed.). *Irish writers and politics.* New York, 1990.

Kosok, Heinz (ed.). *Studies in Anglo-Irish literature.* Bonn, 1982.

Kuch, Peter. *Yeats and A. E.* London, 1985.

Lloyd, D. C. *Nationalism and minor literature: James Clarence Mangan and the emergence of Irish cultural nationalism.* Berkeley, Calif., 1987.

Loftus, R. J. *Nationalism in modern Anglo-Irish poetry.* Madison, Wis., 1964.

Lucy, Seán (ed.). *Irish poets in English.* Cork and Dublin, 1973. (Thomas Davis Lectures.)

Lyons, F. S. L. The twilight of the Big House. In *Ariel: review of international English literature*, i, no. 3 (July 1970), pp 110–22.

McCormack, W. J. *Sheridan Le Fanu and Victorian Ireland.* Oxford, 1980.

—— *Ascendancy and tradition in Anglo-Irish literary history from 1789 to 1929.* Oxford, 1985.

MacDonagh, Oliver. *The nineteenth-century novel and Irish social history: some aspects.* Dublin, 1971. (O'Donnell Lectures.)

McHugh, Roger. William Carleton. In *Studies*, xxvi, no. 101 (1937), pp 47–62.

—— and Harmon, Maurice. *Anglo-Irish literature.* Dublin, 1980.

—— and —— *Short history of Anglo-Irish literature from its origins to the present day.* Dublin, 1982.

MacWhite, Eoin. Thomas Moore and Poland. In *R.I.A. Proc.*, lxxii (1972), pp 49–62.

Malins, Edward. *Yeats and the Easter rising.* Dublin, 1965. (Yeats Centenary Papers, i.)

Manganiello, Dominic. *Joyce's politics.* London, 1980.

Mannin, Ethel. *Two studies in integrity: Gerard Griffin and the Rev. Francis Mahony ('Father Prout').* London and New York, 1964.

Marcus, P. L. *Standish O'Grady.* Lewisburg, Pa., 1970.

—— *Yeats and the beginning of the Irish renaissance.* Ithaca, N.Y., and London, 1970.

Mercier, Vivian. *The Irish comic tradition.* London, 1962.

O'Brien, Conor Cruise. Passion and cunning: an essay on the politics of W. B. Yeats. In A. N. Jeffares and K. G. W. Cross (ed.), *In excited reverie* (New York, 1965), pp 207–78.

O'Connor, Frank [Michael O'Donovan]. *A short history of Irish literature: a backward look.* New York, 1967.

O'Driscoll, Robert. *An ascendancy of the heart: Ferguson and the beginnings of modern Irish literature in English.* Dublin, 1976.

Ó Muirithe, Diarmaid (ed.). *The English language in Ireland.* Dublin and Cork, 1977; repr., 1978.

O'Neill, Patrick. *Ireland and Germany: a study in literary relations.* New York, Berne, Frankfurt-on-Main, 1985. (Canadian Studies in German Language and Literature.)

Partridge, A. C. *Language and society in Anglo-Irish literature.* Totowa, N.J., 1984.

Power, P. C. *The story of Anglo-Irish poetry, 1800–1922.* Cork, 1967.

—— *A literary history of Ireland.* Cork, 1969.

Quin, E. G. The collectors of Irish dialect material. In Diarmaid Ó Muirithe (ed.), *The English language in Ireland* (Dublin and Cork, 1977), pp 115–26.

Rafroidi, Patrick. The uses of the Irish myth in the nineteenth century. In *Studies*, lxii (autumn/winter 1973), pp 251–61.

Robinson, Hilary. *Somerville and Ross: a critical appreciation.* Dublin and New York, 1980.

Sheeran, P. F. Colonists and colonized: some aspects of Anglo-Irish literature from Swift to Joyce. In *The Yearbook of English Studies*, xiii (1983), pp 97–115.

Sloan, Barry. *The pioneers of Anglo-Irish fiction, 1800–1850.* Totowa, N.J., 1986.

Stevenson, Lionel. *The wild Irish girl: the life of Sydney Owenson, Lady Morgan, 1776–1859.* London, 1936; repr., 1969.

—— *Dr Quicksilver: the life of Charles Lever.* London, 1939; repr., New York, 1969.

Tessier, Thérèse. *La poésie lyrique de Thomas Moore (1779–1852).* Paris, 1976.

—— *The bard of Erin: a study of Thomas Moore's Irish melodies, 1808–1834.* Dover, N. H., 1981. (Salzburg Studies.)

Thompson, W. I. *The imagination of an insurrection.* New York, 1967.

Tomelty, Joseph. Patrick MacGill. In *Ir. Bookman*, i, no. 12 (1947), pp 25–32.

Torchiana, Donald. *W. B. Yeats and Georgian Ireland.* Evanston, Ill., 1966.

Vance, Norman. Celts, Carthaginians and constitutions: Anglo–Irish literary relations, 1780–1820. In *I.H.S.*, xxii, no. 87 (Mar. 1981), pp 216–38.

—— *Irish literature: a social history. Tradition, identity, and difference.* Oxford, 1990.

Warner, Alan. *William Allingham.* Lewisburg, Pa., 1975.

—— *A guide to Anglo-Irish literature.* Dublin, 1981.

Watson, G. J. *Irish identity and the Irish literary revival: Synge, Yeats, Joyce, and O'Casey.* London and New York, 1979.

Weekes, Anne Owens. *Irish women writers: an uncharted tradition*. Lexington, Ky., 1991.

Whitaker, T. R. *Swan and shadow: Yeats's dialogue with history*. Chapel Hill, N. C., 1964.

Wilson, F. A. C. *W. B. Yeats and tradition*. London, 1958.

Zach, Wolfgang, and Kosok, Heinz (ed.). *Literary interrelations: Ireland, England and the world*. 3 vols. Tübingen, 1987.

8 HISTORY OF IRISH LANGUAGE AND LITERATURE

Adams, G. B. Language in Ulster, 1820–1850. In *Ulster Folklife*, xix (1973), pp 50–55.

—— The 1851 language census in the north of Ireland. In *Ulster Folklife*, xx (1974), pp 65–70.

—— Language census problems, 1851–1911. In *Ulster Folklife*, xxi (1975), pp 68–72.

Blaney, Roger. *Presbyterians and the Irish language*. Belfast, 1991.

Caird, Donald. A view of the revival of the Irish language. In *Éire-Ireland*, xxv, no. 2 (1990), pp 96–108.

Comerford, R. V. Nation, nationalism, and the Irish language. In T. S. Hachey and L. J. McCaffrey (ed.), *Perspectives on Irish nationalism* (Lexington, Ky., 1989), pp 20–41.

Corkery, Daniel. *The hidden Ireland*. Dublin, 1925; repr., 1980.

—— *The fortunes of the Irish language*. Dublin, 1954.

Cullen, L. M. The hidden Ireland: reassessment of a concept. In *Studia Hib.*, ix (1969), pp 7–47.

—— Patrons, teachers, and literacy in Irish, 1700–1850. In Mary Daly and David Dickson (ed.), *Origins of popular literacy in Ireland* (Dublin, 1990), pp 15–44.

Daly, D. P. *The young Douglas Hyde: the dawn of the Irish revolution and renaissance*. Dublin, 1974.

De Blacam, Aodh. *Gaelic literature surveyed: with an additional chapter by Eóghan Ó Hanluain*. Dublin, 1973.

    1st ed., Dublin, 1929.

De Blaghd, Earnán. *The state and the language*. Dublin, 1947; 2nd ed., 1951.

—— *Trasna na Buinne*. Dublin, 1957.

De Brún, Pádraig. Scriptural instruction in Irish: a controversy of 1830–31. In *Folia Gadelica: essays presented by former students to R. A. Breathnach* (Cork, 1983), pp 134–59.

De Fréine, Seán. *The great silence*. Dublin, 1965.

De hÓir, Éamonn. *Sean Ó Donnabháin agus Eóghan Ó Comhraí*. Dublin, 1962.

Doyle, J. J. *David Comyn, 1854–1907: a pioneer of the Irish language movement*. Cork, 1926.

Duffy, Seán. Antiquarianism and Gaelic revival in Co. Louth in the pre-famine era. In *Louth Arch. Soc. Jn.*, xxi, no. 4 (1988), pp 343–68.

Durkacz, V. E. *The decline of the Celtic languages: a study of linguistic and cultural conflict in Scotland, Wales, and Ireland from the reformation to the twentieth century*. Edinburgh, 1983.

Fagan, Patrick. The decline of the Irish language in Westmeath. In *Ríocht na Midhe*, vii, no. 3 (1984), pp 94–101.

FitzGerald, Garret. Estimates for baronies of minimum level of Irish-speaking among successive decennial cohorts: 1771–81 to 1861–71. In *R.I.A. Proc.*, lxxxiv, sect. C (1984), pp 117–55.

—— The decline of the Irish language. In Mary Daly and David Dickson (ed.), *Origins of popular literacy in Ireland* (Dublin, 1990), pp 59–72.

Fitzsimons, J. The official presbyterian Irish-language policy in the eighteenth and nineteenth centuries. In *I.E.R.*, lxxii (Sept. 1949), pp 255–64.

French, R. B. D. J. O. Hannay and the Gaelic League. In *Hermathena*, cii (1966), pp 26–52.

Gleeson, D. F. Peter O'Connell: scholar and scribe, 1755–1826. In *Studies*, xxxiii (Sept. 1944), pp 342–8.

Greene, David. Fifty years of writing in Irish. In *Studies*, lv (spring 1966), pp 51–9.

—— Robert Atkinson and Irish studies. In *Hermathena*, cii (spring 1966), pp 6–15.

Hindley, Reg. *The death of the Irish language: a qualified obituary*. London and New York, 1990.

Hyde, Douglas. *Mise agus an Connradh*. Dublin, 1937.

—— *Mo thúras go h-Americe*. Dublin, 1937.

Joyce, Mannix. The Joyce brothers of Glenosheen. In *Capuchin Annual*, xxxvi (1969), pp 257–87.

  Patrick Weston Joyce and Robert Dwyer Joyce.

Kiberd, Declan. *Synge and the Irish language*. London, 1979.

MacCarthy, B. G. Jeremiah J. Callanan. In *Studies*, xxxv (1946), pp 215–29, 387–99.

  Pt I, his life; pt II, his poetry.

Matonis, A. T. E., and Melia, Daniel F. (ed.). *Celtic language, Celtic culture: a festschrift for Eric P. Hamp*. Van Nuys, Calif., 1990.

Murphy, Brian. Father Peter Yorke's 'Turning of the tide' (1899): the strictly cultural nationalism of the early Gaelic League. In *Éire-Ireland*, xxiii, no. 1 (spring 1988), pp 35–44.

Ní Shéaghdha, Nessa. Collectors of Irish manuscripts: motives and methods. In *Celtica*, xvii (1985), pp 1–28.

Nic Eóin, Máirin. *An litríocht reigiunach*. Dublin, 1982.

  Historical survey of literature in the Gaeltacht.

Ó Broin, Leon. The Gaelic League and the chair of Irish at Maynooth. In *Studies*, lii (winter 1963), pp 348–62.

Ó Buachalla, Breandán. *I mBéal Feirste cois cuain*. Dublin, 1968.

  Belfast as centre of Irish language revival.

—— A speech in Irish on repeal. In *Studia Hib.*, x (1970), pp 84–94.

—— Ó Corcora agus an 'Hidden Ireland'. In *Scríobh*, iv (1979), pp 109–37.

Ó Buachalla, Séamas. Educational policy and the role of the Irish language from 1831 to 1981. In *European Journal of Education*, xix, no. 1 (1984), pp 75–92.

Ó Ceallaigh, Seán. *Eoghan Ó Grainnaigh: beath aisneis*. Dublin, 1968.

Ó Conluain, Proinsias. The last native Irish speaker of Tyrone. In *Dúiche Néill*, iv (1989), pp 101–18.

Ó Cuív, Brian. *Irish dialects and Irish speaking districts*. Dublin, 1951.

—— (ed.), *A view of the Irish language*. Dublin, 1969.

Ó Fiaich, Tomás. Irish poetry and the clergy. In *Leachtaí Cholm Coille*, iv (1975), pp 30–56.

Ó hAilin, Tomás. The Irish Society agus Tadg Ó Coinnialláin. In *Studia Hib.*, viii (1968), pp 60–78.

Ó hÓgáin, Dáithí. *The hero in Irish folk history*. Dublin, 1985.

O'Leary, Denis. The first professor of Irish in Q.C.C.: Owen Connellan. In *Cork Univ. Rec.*, no. 9 (1947), pp 37–44.

O'Leary, Philip. 'Children of the same mother': Gaelic relations with other Celtic revival movements, 1882–1916. In *Proceedings of the Harvard Celtic Colloquium*, vi (1986), pp 101–30.

Ó Luing, Seán. Douglas Hyde and the Gaelic League. In *Studies*, lxii (summer 1973), pp 123–38.

—— William Maunsell Hennessy, Celtic scholar, 1829–89. In *Kerry Arch. Soc. Jn.*, xix (1986), pp 80–120.

Ó Murchadha, Tadhg. Micheál Óg Ó Longáin (1766–1837). In Séamus Pender (ed.), *Féilscríbhinn Torna: essays and studies presented to Tadg Ua Donnchadha* (Cork, 1947), pp 11–17.

O'Neill, Séamus. The hidden Ulster: Gaelic pioneers of the north. In *Studies*, lv (spring 1966), pp 60–66.

Ó Raifeartaigh, Tarlach. An Bord Naisiúnta agus an Ghaeilge, 1831–70. In *Studies*, lxxii (1949), pp 481–94.

O'Rourke, Brian. *Pale rainbow: an dubh ina bhán. A selection of Gaelic folk songs with prose translations and verse equivalents.* Blackrock, 1989.

Ó Sé, Liam. The Irish language revival: Achilles heel. In *Éire-Ireland*, i, no. 1 (spring 1966), pp 26–49.

Ó Sé, Seán. Pádraig Feiritéar (1856–1924): a shaol agus a shaothar. In *Kerry Arch. Soc. Jn.*, iii (1970), pp 116–30.
    Land League and Gaelic activist.

Ó Snodaigh, Pádraig. *Hidden Ulster.* Dublin, 1973.

Ó Súilleabháin, Donncha. *Connradh na Gaeilge in Londain, 1894–1917.* Dublin, 1989.

O'Sullivan, Donal. Thaddeus Connellan and his books of Irish poetry. In *Éigse*, iii (1941–2), pp 278–304.

—— The Bunting collection. In *Ir. Folk Song Soc. Jn.*, v (1967), containing original vols xxii–xxiii (1927) devoted to the Bunting collection.

Ó Tuama, Seán. Donal Ó Corcora agus filiocht na Gaeilge. In *Studia Hib.*, v (1965), pp 29–41.

—— (ed.). *The Gaelic League idea.* Cork, 1973. (Thomas Davis Lectures.)

—— Donal Ó Corcora. In *Scríobh*, iv (1979), pp 94–108.

Piatt, D. S. *Mhaireadar san ardchathair.* Dublin, 1957.

Power, Victor. Eugene O'Growney, Arizona, the Catholic University of America, and the Irish language revival. In *Éire-Ireland*, xxii, no. 2 (summer 1987), pp 131–52.

Ryan, Desmond. *The sword of light: from the Four Masters to Douglas Hyde.* London, 1939.

Tierney, Michael. What did the Gaelic League accomplish? 1893–1963. In *Studies*, lii (winter 1963), pp 337–47.

Tuinleigh, Críostóir. Sémas Ó hArgadáin, 1782–1855. In *Galvia*, iii (1956), pp 47–61.
    James Hardiman.

Wall, Maureen. The decline of the Irish language. In Brian Ó Cuív (ed.), *A view of the Irish language* (Dublin, 1969), pp 81–90.

Wall, Thomas. Teige MacMahon and Peter O'Connell, seanchaí and scholar in Co. Clare. In *Béaloideas*, xxx (1962), pp 89–104.

Waters, Martin. Peasants and emigrants: considerations of the Gaelic League as a social movement. In D. J. Casey and Robert Rhodes (ed.), *Views of the Irish peasantry, 1900–1916* (Hamden, Conn., 1977), pp 160–77.

Welch, Robert. *A history of verse translation from the Irish, 1789–1897*. Gerrards Cross and Savage, Md., 1988. (Barnes & Noble Irish Literary Studies, 24.)

Withers, C. W. J. *Gaelic in Scotland, 1698–1981: the geographical history of a language*. Edinburgh, 1984.

9 HISTORY OF EDUCATION

Akenson, D. H. *The Irish education experiment: the national system of education in the nineteenth century*. London and Toronto, 1970.

Allen, Robert. *The Presbyterian College, Belfast, 1853–1953*. Belfast, 1954.

Angelsea, Martyn. *The Royal Ulster Academy of Arts: a centennial history*. Belfast, 1981.

Atkinson, Norman. *Irish education: a history of educational institutions*. Dublin, 1969.

Auchmuty, J. J. *Irish education: a historical survey*. Dublin, 1937.

Bailey, K. C. *A history of Trinity College, Dublin, 1892–1945*. Dublin, 1947.

Barnes, Jane. *Irish industrial schools, 1868–1908: origins and development*. Blackrock, 1989.

Birch, Peter. *St Kieran's College, Kilkenny*. Dublin, 1951.

Boyne, Patricia. The cardinal and the professor. In *Studies*, lxxix (1990), pp 360–67.

Brady, John. The lay college, Maynooth. In *I.E.R.*, lxi (1943), pp 385–8.

Branigan, C. G. Quaker education in 18th- and 19th-century Ireland. In *Ir. Educational Studies*, iv, no. 1 (1984), pp 54–72.

——Ballitore school and its unique curriculum, 1726–1836. In *Ir. Educational Studies*, v, no. 2 (1985), pp 302–14.

Breathnach, Eileen. Women and higher education in Ireland (1879–1914). In *Crane Bag*, iv, no. 1 (1980), pp 47–54.

——Charting new waters: women's experience in higher education, 1879–1908. In Mary Cullen (ed.), *Girls don't do honours* (Dublin, 1987), pp 55–78.

Brenan, Martin. *Schools of Kildare and Leighlin, 1775–1835*. Dublin, 1935.

Burke, Andrew. Trinity College and the religious problem in Irish education. In James Kelly and Uaitear Mac Gearailt, *Dublin and Dubliners* (Dublin, 1990), pp 95–126.

Burton, E. F. Richard Lovell Edgeworth's education bill of 1799: a missing chapter in the history of Irish education. In *Irish Journal of Education*, xiii, no. 1 (1979), pp 24–33.

Byrne, Kieran. Mechanics' institutes in Ireland, 1825–50. In *Proceedings of the Educational Studies Association of Ireland Conference* (Dublin, 1979), pp 32–47.

——The department of agriculture and technical instruction: administrative structure and educational policy. In *Ir. Educational Studies*, ii (1982), pp 233–52.

——The provision of technical education in the city of Cork. In *Ir. Educational Studies*, v, no. 2 (1985), pp 243–60.

Cashman, John. The 1906 education bill: catholic peers and Irish nationalists. In *Recusant History*, xviii (1987), pp 422–39.

Clune, Michael. Technical instruction in Ireland, 1900. In *Oideas*, xxv (1982), pp 14–25.

Coldrey, Barry. *Faith and fatherland: the Christian Brothers and the development of Irish nationalism, 1828–1921*. Dublin, 1988.

Cole, R. Lee. *Wesley College, Dublin: an historical summary*. Dublin, 1963.

Condon, Kevin. *The missionary college of All Hallows, 1842–1891*. Dublin, 1986.

Coolahan, John. Three eras of English reading in Irish national schools. In *Studies in Reading* (1977), pp 12–26.

——*Irish education: its history and structure*. Dublin, 1981.

Coolahan, John. The daring first decade of the board of national education, 1831–41. In *Irish Journal of Education*, xvii, no. 1 (1983), pp 35–54.

—— The fortunes of education as a subject of study and of research in Ireland. In *Ir. Educational Studies*, iv, no. 1 (1984), pp 1–34.

Corcoran, Timothy. *Education systems in Ireland from the close of the middle ages*. Dublin, 1928.

—— *The Clongowes Record, 1814–1932*. Dublin, 1932.

Corish, P. J. *Maynooth College, 1795–1895*. Dublin, 1995.

Costello, Peter. *Clongowes Wood: a history of Clongowes Wood College, 1814–1989*. Dublin, 1989.

Curtis, Bruce. Capitalist development and educational reform: comparative material from England, Ireland, and Upper Canada to 1850. In *Theory and Society*, xiii (1984), pp 41–68.

Cullen, Mary (ed.). *Girls don't do honours: Irishwomen in education in the nineteenth and twentieth centuries*. Dublin, 1987.

Daly, Mary. The development of the national schools system, 1831–40. In Cosgrove & McCartney, *Studies in Ir. hist.* (1979), pp 150–63.

—— and Dickson, David (ed.). *The origins of popular literacy in Ireland: language change and educational development, 1700–1920*. Dublin, 1990.

Dowling, Maurice. A history of the Irish Baptist College. In *Ir. Baptist Hist. Soc. Jn.*, xiii (1980–81), pp 29–41.

Dowling, P. J. *The hedge schools of Ireland*. London, 1935.

—— *A history of Irish education: a study in conflicting loyalties*. Cork, 1971.

Durcan, T. J. *History of Irish education with special reference to manual instruction*. Bala, Wales, 1972.

Edwards, R. D. The beginnings of the Irish intermediate education system. In *Catholic University Centenary Book, 1867–1967* (Dublin, 1967), pp 47–58.

Fathers of the Society of Jesus. *A page of Irish history: story of University College, Dublin, 1883–1909*. Dublin, 1930.

Flanagan, Kieran. The shaping of Irish anglican secondary schools, 1854–1878. In *History of Education*, xiii, no. 1 (1984), pp 27–43.

Foley, T. P. 'A nest of scholars': biographical material on some early professors at Queen's College, Galway. In *Galway Arch. Soc. Jn.*, xlii (1989–90), pp 72–86.

Goldstrom, J. M. Richard Whately and political economy in school books, 1833–1880. In *I.H.S.*, xv, no. 58 (Sept. 1966), pp 131–46.

—— *The social content of education, 1808–1870: a study of the working-class reader in England and Ireland*. Dublin, 1972.

Griffin, Seán. The Glasnevin experiment, 1847–1877: a case study of official and religious involvement in an industrial model school. In *Ir. Educational Studies*, viii (1989), pp 37–55.

Hayes, Charles. The educational ideas of Paul, Cardinal Cullen. In *Proceedings of the Educational Studies Association of Ireland Conference* (Dublin, 1979), pp 1–10.

—— Cullen, Newman, and the Irish university. In *Recusant History*, xv (1980), pp 201–12.

Hegarty, W. J. The Irish hierarchy and the queen's colleges (1845–50). In *Cork University Record*, no. 5 (1945), pp 35–50.

Hoban, James. The survival of the hedge schools: a local study. In *Ir. Educational Studies*, iii, no. 2 (1983), pp 21–36.

Holland, C. H. (ed.). *Trinity College Dublin and the idea of a university*. Dublin, 1991.

Holmes, R. F. G. *Magee, 1865–1965*. Belfast, 1965.

Hyland, Áine. The treasury and Irish education, 1850–1922: the myth and the reality. In *Ir. Educational Studies*, iii, no. 2 (1983), pp 57–82.

—— The process of curriculum change in the Irish national school system, 1868 to 1986. In *Ir. Educational Studies*, vi, no. 2 (1986–7), pp 17–38.

—— The multi-denominational experience in the national school system in Ireland. In *Ir. Educational Studies*, viii (1989), pp 89–114.

Jamieson, John. *The history of the Royal Belfast Academical Institute*. Belfast, 1959.

Keating, Patrick. Sir Robert Kane and the museum of Irish industry. In *Proceedings of the Educational Studies Association of Ireland Conference* (Dublin, 1979), pp 276–86.

Kelleher, D. V. *James Dominick Burke: a pioneer of Irish education*. Blackrock, 1988.

Kelly, Noel. Music in Irish primary education, 1831–1922. In *Proceedings of the Educational Studies Association of Ireland Conference* (Dublin, 1979), pp 48–56.

Kennedy, David. The Ulster academies and the teaching of science, 1785–1835. In *I.E.R.*, 5th ser., lxiii (Jan. 1944), pp 25–38.

Kinzer, Bruce. John Stuart Mill and the Irish university question. In *Victorian Studies*, xxxi, no. 1 (autumn 1987), pp 59–77.

Logan, John. How many pupils went to school in the nineteenth century? In *Ir. Educational Studies*, viii (1989), pp 23–36.

McCaffrey, Patricia. The Wyndham university scheme, 1903–4. In *I.E.R.*, 5th ser., cx, no. 6 (Dec. 1968), pp 329–49.

McCann, Peadar. Charity schooling in Cork city in the late eighteenth and early nineteenth centuries. In *Cork Hist. Soc. Jn.*, lxxxvi, no. 243 (1981), pp 30–37, 109–15; lxxxvii, no. 245 (1982), pp 51–7, 133–41.

McCartney, Donal. Lecky and the Irish university question. In *I.E.R.*, 5th ser., cviii (Aug. 1967), pp 102–12.

McDowell, R. B. and Webb, D. A. *Trinity College, Dublin, 1592–1952: an academic history*. Cambridge, 1982.

McElligott, T. J. *Secondary education in Ireland, 1870–1921*. Dublin, 1981.

McGrath, Fergal. *Newman's university: idea and reality*. Dublin, 1951.

Mac Shamhráin, A. S. Ideological conflict and historical interpretation: the problem of history in Irish primary education, c.1900–1930. In *Ir. Educational Studies*, x (1991), pp 229–43.

Marshall, Ronald. *Methodist College, Belfast*. Belfast, 1968.

Maxwell, C. A. *A history of Trinity College, Dublin, 1591–1892*. Dublin, 1946.

Meenan, James (ed.). *Centenary history of the Literary and Historical Society of University College, Dublin, 1855–1955*. Tralee, [1956].

Metscher, Priscilla. Padraic Pearse and the Irish cultural revolution: the significance of Pearse as an Irish educationalist. In Kosok, *Studies in Anglo-Ir. literature* (1982), pp 137–47.

Milne, Kenneth. The Irish charter schools: the grand design in principle and practice. In *Ir. Educational Studies*, iv (1984), pp 35–54.

Moody, T. W. The Irish university question of the nineteenth century. In *History*, xliii (1958), pp 90–109.

—— and Beckett, J. C. *Queen's, Belfast, 1845–1949: the history of a university*. 2 vols. London, 1959.

Ó Buachalla, Séamus (ed.). *Education policy in twentieth-century Ireland*. Dublin, 1988.

Ó Canáinn, Séamus. The educational inquiry, 1824–26, in its social and political context. In *Ir. Educational Studies*, iii, no. 2 (1983), pp 1–20.

Ó Ceallaigh, Tadgh. Disestablishment and church education. In *Studia Hib.*, x (1970), pp 36–69.

O'Connell, Philip. *Schools and scholars of Breifne*. Dublin, 1942.

O'Connell, T. J. *History of the Irish National Teachers' Organisation, 1868–1968*. Dublin, 1968.

O'Connor, A. V. Influences affecting girls' secondary education in Ireland, 1860–1910. In *Archiv. Hib.*, xli (1986), pp 83–98.

—— The revolution in girls' secondary education in Ireland, 1860–1910. In Mary Cullen (ed.), *Girls don't do honours* (Dublin, 1987), pp 31–54.

—— and Parkes, S. M. *Gladly learn and gladly teach: Alexandra College and school, 1866–1966*. Dublin, 1984.

O'Donoghue, T. A. Educational innovation in the Kerry Gaeltacht: 1904–22. In *Kerry Arch. Soc. Jn.*, xix (1986), pp 121–35.

—— Bilingual education in Ireland in the late nineteenth and early twentieth centuries. In *History of Education*, xvii (1988), pp 209–21.

O'Donovan, P. F. Archbishop Walsh and the commission on manual and practical instruction. In *Ir. Educational Studies*, vi, no. 2 (1986–7), pp 76–87.

O'Driscoll, Finbarr. St Dominic's: the rise and fall of a training college. In *Ir. Educational Studies*, iv, no. 1 (1984), pp 98–114.

—— Equal rights for women in higher education: a forgotten aspect of the Royal University. In *Ir. Educational Studies*, vi, no. 2 (1986–7), pp 39–55.

O'Farrell, Pádraic. *'Tell me, Sean O'Farrell': the story of an Irish schoolmaster*. Cork and Dublin, 1986.

Ó hEideáin, Eustas. *National school inspection in Ireland: the beginnings*. Dublin, 1967.

Ó Raifeartaigh, T. O. Mixed education and the synod of Ulster, 1831–40. In *I.H.S.*, ix, no. 35 (Mar. 1955), pp 281–99.

O'Sullivan, Denis (ed.). *Social commitment and adult education: essays in honour of Alfred O'Rahilly, an Irish educator*. Cork, 1989.

Parkes, S. M. *Irish education in the British parliamentary papers in the nineteenth century and after, 1801–1920*. Cork, 1978.

—— *Kildare Place: the history of the Church of Ireland Training College, 1811–1969*. Dublin, 1984.

—— George Fletcher and technical education in Ireland, 1900–1927. In *Ir. Educational Studies*, ix, no. 1 (1990), pp 13–29.

Purser, Olive. *Women in Dublin University, 1904–1954*. Dublin, 1954.

Roberts, Ruaidhri. *The story of the People's College*. Dublin, 1986.

Stanford, W. B. *Ireland and the classical tradition*. Dublin and Totowa, N.J., 1976.

Tierney, Michael. *Education in a free Ireland*. Dublin, 1919.

—— (ed.). *Struggle with fortune: a miscellany for the centenary of the Catholic University of Ireland, 1854–1954*. Dublin, 1954.

Tynan, Michael. *Catholic instruction in Ireland, 1720–1850*. Dublin, 1985.

Vale, Mary. The origins of the Catholic University of Ireland, 1845–1854. In *I.E.R.*, 5th ser., lxxxii (1954), pp 1–16, 152–64, 226–41.

Walker, Brian, and McCreary, Alf. (R. H. Buchanan, consulting editor.) *Degrees of excellence: the story of Queen's, Belfast, 1845–1995*. Belfast, 1994.

Wall, P. J. The catholic hierarchy and education, 1898–1908. In *Oideas*, xxiv (1981), pp 18–30.

Walsh, Lorcan. Images of women in nineteenth-century schoolbooks. In *Ir. Educational Studies*, iv, no. 1 (1984), pp 73–87.

Whiteside, Lesley. *A history of the King's Hospital.* Dublin, 1975.

Wilkinson, R. The educational endowments act, 1885, as part of nineteenth-century educational reform. In *Ir. Educational Studies*, iii (1983), pp 98–119.

10 HISTORY OF IDEAS

Beringause, A. F. The presentness of the past in Ireland. In *Jn. Hist. Ideas*, xvi, no. 2 (Apr. 1955), pp 240–46.

Black, R. D. C. *Economic thought and the Irish question, 1817–70.* Cambridge, 1960.

Boyce, D. G. *Nationalism in Ireland.* Baltimore, 1982.
> Rev. ed., 1991; new concluding chapter on revisionism.

Boylan, T. A., and Foley, T. P. John Elliott Cairnes, John Stuart Mill and Ireland: some problems for political economy. In *Hermathena*, cxxxv (winter 1983), pp 96–119.

—— and —— *Political economy and colonial Ireland; the propagation and ideological functions of economic discourse in the nineteenth century.* London, 1991.

Brooks, G. P. The use of psychological concepts in the writings of an Irish psychiatrist in the nineteenth century. In *Irish Journal of Psychology*, ii, no. 2 (1973), pp 102–12.

Bryson, M. E. 'Our one philosophical critic': John Eglinton. In *Éire-Ireland*, x, no. 2 (summer 1975), pp 81–8.

Callan, Patrick. Aspects of the transmission of history in Ireland during the latter half of the nineteenth century. In *Ir. Educational Studies*, vi, no. 2 (1986–7), pp 56–75.

Clarke, Desmond. *Church and state: essays in political philosophy.* Cork, 1985.

Conniff, James. Edmund Burke's reflections on the coming revolution in Ireland. In *Jn. Hist. Ideas*, xlvii, no. 1 (Jan.–Mar. 1986), pp 37–59.

Curtis, L. P., jr. *Anglo-Saxons and Celts: a study of anti-Irish prejudice in Victorian England.* Bridgeport, Conn., 1968.

—— *Apes and angels: the Irishman in Victorian caricature.* Washington, D.C., and Newton Abbot, 1971.

Dangerfield, George. James Joyce, James Connolly, and Irish nationalism. In *Ir. Univ. Rev.*, xvi, no. 1 (spring 1986), pp 5–21.

Deane, Seamus. *The French revolution and enlightenment in England, 1789–1832.* Cambridge, Mass., 1988.

Dunleavy, John. Faith and fatherland: the conflict between Catholic Action and Irish nationalism before the first world war. In *Irish Studies in Britain*, xiv (1989), pp 14–16.

Dunne, Tom. La trahison des clercs: British intellectuals and the first home rule crisis. In *I.H.S.*, xxiii, no. 90 (Nov. 1982), pp 134–73.

Edwards, Owen Dudley. Ireland. In Owen Dudley Edwards, Gwynfor Evans, Ioan Rhys, and Hugh Mac Diarmid, *Celtic nationalism* (London, 1968), pp 1–209.

Ensor, R. C. K. Some political and economic interactions in later Victorian England. In *R. Hist. Soc. Trans.*, 4th ser., xxxi (1949), pp 17–28.

Farrell, Seán. Patrick Pearse and the European revolt against reason. In *Jn. Hist. Ideas*, l, no. 4 (Oct.–Dec. 1989), pp 625–43.

Ford, T. H. Dicey's conversion to unionism. In *I.H.S.*, xviii, no. 72 (Sept. 1973), pp 552–82.

Freyer, Grattan. *W. B. Yeats and the anti-democratic tradition*. Dublin, 1982.

Glandon, V. E. Arthur Griffith and the ideal Irish state. In *Studies*, lxxiii (spring 1984), pp 26–36.

Harvie, C. T. Ideology and home rule: James Bryce, A. V. Dicey, and Ireland, 1880–87. In *E.H.R.*, xci, no. 359 (Apr. 1976), pp 298–314.

——Ireland and the intellectuals, 1848–1922. In *New Edinburgh Review*, xxxviii–xxxix (summer–autumn 1977), pp 35–42.

Hazelkorn, Ellen. Reconsidering Marx and Engels on Ireland. In *Saothar*, ix (1983), pp 79–87.

——The social and political views of Louie Bennett, 1870–1956. In *Saothar*, xiii (1988), pp 32–44.

——Why is there no socialism in Ireland? Theoretical problems of Irish Marxism. In *Science and Society*, liii, no. 2 (summer 1989), pp 136–64.

Hoppen, K. Theodore. Ireland, Britain, and Europe: twentieth-century nationalism and its spoils. In *Hist. Jn.*, xxxiv (1991), pp 505–18.

Kabdebo, Thomas. *The Hungarian-Irish parallel and Arthur Griffith's use of historical sources*. Maynooth, 1988.

Kearney, Richard (ed.), *The Irish mind: exploring intellectual traditions*. Dublin and Atlantic Highlands, N.J., 1985.

Koot, G. M. T. Cliffe Leslie, Irish social reform, and the origins of the English historical school of economics. In *History of Political Economy*, vii, no. 3 (1975), pp 312–36.

Lebow, R. N. *White Britain and black Ireland: the influence of stereotypes on colonial policy*. Philadelphia, 1976.

Lyons, F. S. L. *Culture and anarchy in Ireland, 1890–1939*. Oxford, 1979.

McCartney, Donal. *Democracy and its nineteenth-century Irish critics*. Dublin, 1979. (O'Donnell Lecture.)

MacDonagh, Oliver. Ambiguity in nationalism: the case of Ireland. In *Historical Studies*, xix, no. 76 (April 1981), pp 337–52.

McDonnell, M. A. Malthus and George on the Irish question: the single tax, empiricism, and other positions shared by the 19th-century economists. In *American Journal of Economics and Sociology*, xxxvi (1977), pp 401–16.

McKillen, Beth. Irish feminism and national separation, 1914–23. In *Éire-Ireland*, xviii, no. 3 (1981), pp 52–67; xviii, no. 4 (1981), pp 72–90.

Mercier, Vivian. Victorian evangelicalism and the Anglo-Irish literary revival. In Peter Connolly (ed.), *Literature and the changing Ireland* (Gerrards Cross, 1982), pp 59–101.

Murphy, Brian. The canon of Irish cultural history: some questions. In *Studies*, lxxvii, no. 305 (spring 1988), pp 68–83.

——J. J. O'Kelly, the *Catholic Bulletin*, and contemporary Irish cultural historians. In *Archiv. Hib.*, xliv (1989), pp 71–88.

O'Brien, Conor Cruise. *Writers and politics*. London, 1965.

Ó Danachair, Caoimhín. The progress of Irish ethnology, 1783–1982. In *Ulster Folklife*, xxix (1983), pp 3–17.

O'Farrell, Patrick. Millennialism, messianism, and utopianism in Irish history. In *Anglo-Irish Studies*, ii (1976), pp 45–68.

O'Halloran, Clare. Irish re-creation of the Gaelic past: the challenge of MacPherson's Ossian. In *Past & Present*, no. 124 (Aug. 1989), pp 69–95.

O'Neill, Thomas P. The economic and political ideas of James Fintan Lalor. In *I.E.R.*, lxxiv, no. 1 (spring 1950), pp 398–409.

Princess Grace Irish Library (ed.). *Irishness in a changing society*. Gerrards Cross, 1988.

Roach, John. Liberalism and the Victorian intelligentsia. In *Camb. Hist. Jn.*, xiii (1957), pp 71–88.

Sack, J. J. The memory of Burke and the memory of Pitt: English conservatism confronts its past, 1806–1829. In *Hist. Jn.*, xxx, no. 3 (1987), pp 623–40.

Steele, E. D. J. S. Mill and the Irish question. In *Hist. Jn.*, xiii (1970), pp 216–36, 419–50.

Townshend, Charles. The making of modern Irish public culture. In *Jn. Mod. Hist.*, lxi, no. 3 (Sept. 1989), pp 535–54.

Williams, Martin. Ancient mythology and revolutionary ideology in Ireland, 1878–1916. In *Hist. Jn.*, xxvi, no. 2 (1983), pp 307–28.

Zastoupil, Lynn. Moral government: J. S. Mill on Ireland. In *Hist. Jn.*, xxvi, no. 3 (1983), pp 707–17.

11 LEARNED SOCIETIES

Black, R. D. C. *The Statistical and Social Inquiry Society of Ireland: centenary volume 1847–1947 with a history of the society*. Dublin, 1947.

Deane, Arthur (ed.). *The Belfast Natural History and Philosophical Society, centenary volume, 1821–1921*. Belfast, 1924.

Herries Davies, G. L. The Geological Society of Dublin and the Royal Geological Society of Ireland, 1831–1890. In *Hermathena*, c (summer 1965), pp 66–76.

Kelham, B. B. The Royal College of Science for Ireland, 1867–1926. In *Studies*, lvi (autumn 1967), pp 297–309.

Killen, John. *A history of the Linenhall Library, 1788–1988*. Belfast, 1990.

MacSweeney, M., and Reilly, J. The Cork Cuvierian Society. In *Cork Hist. Soc. Jn.*, lxiii, no. 197 (1958), pp 9–14.

Meenan, James, and Clarke, Desmond. *R.D.S.: the Royal Dublin Society, 1731–1981*. Dublin, 1981.

Ó Raifeartaigh, Tarlach (ed.). *The Royal Irish Academy: a bicentennial history, 1785–1985*. Dublin, 1985.

Pettit, S. F. The Royal Cork Institution: a reflection of the cultural life of a city. In *Cork Hist. Soc. Jn.*, lxxxi, nos 233 and 234 (Jan.–Dec. 1976), pp 70–90.

Stewart, A. T. Q. *Belfast Royal Academy: the first century, 1785–1885*. Belfast, 1985.

White, Terence de Vere. *The story of the Royal Dublin Society*. Tralee, 1955.

12 MEDICAL, SCIENTIFIC, AND TECHNICAL HISTORY

Barr, A. A short account of tuberculosis in Ireland, 1850–1900. In *Ir. Jn. Med. Sc.*, 6th ser., no. 362 (Feb. 1956), pp 58–67.

Barrington, Ruth. *Health, medicine, and politics in Ireland, 1900–1970*. Dublin, 1987.

Bennett, J. A. *Church, state, and astronomy in Ireland: 200 years of Armagh observatory*. Armagh Observatory, in association with the Institute of Irish Studies, Q. U. B., 1990.

Bourke, P. M. A. The scientific investigation of the potato blight in 1845–6. In *I.H.S.*, xiii, no. 49 (Mar. 1962), pp 26–32. (Historical Revision XIV.)

Browne, O'Donel T. D. *The Rotunda Hospital, 1745–1945*. Edinburgh, 1947.

Clarke, Desmond. An outline of the history of science in Ireland. In *Studies*, lxii (autumn–winter 1973), pp 287–302.

Coakley, Davis. *The Irish school of medicine: outstanding practitioners of the nineteenth century.* Dublin, 1988.

Connolly, S. J. The 'blessed turf': cholera and popular panic in Ireland, June 1832. In *I.H.S.*, xxiii, no. 91 (May 1983), pp 214–32.

Cox, Ronald (compiler). *Engineering Ireland, 1778–1878: the catalogue of an exhibition in Trinity College, Dublin, 1978.* Dublin, 1978.

——(ed.). *Robert Mallet, 1810–1881: papers presented at a centenary seminar, 1981.* Dublin, 1982.

Craig, D. H. *Belfast and its infirmary: the growth of a hospital from 1838 to 1948.* Belfast, 1985.

Crowe, Morgan. The origin and development of public health services in Ireland. In *Ir. Jn. Med. Sc.*, 6th ser., no. 265 (Jan. 1948), pp 1–19.

Deeney, James. The development of the Irish tuberculosis services. In *Supplement*, pp 29–33, to *Ir. Jn. Med. Sc.*, cliv (May 1985).

Dixon, F. E. Dunsink observatory and its astronomers, In *Dublin Hist. Rec.*, xi, no. 2 (Mar.–May 1950), pp 33–50.

——Richard Kirwan: the Dublin philosopher. In *Dublin Hist. Rec.*, xxiv, no. 3 (June 1971), pp 53–64.

Donaldson, Peggy. *Yes, matron: a history of nurses and nursing at the Royal Victoria Hospital, Belfast.* Belfast, 1989.

Doolin, William. *Wayfarers in medicine.* London, 1947.

——Dublin surgery 100 years ago. In *Ir. Jn. Med. Sc.*, 6th ser., no. 279 (Mar. 1949), pp 97–111.

——Newman and his medical school: the fateful first lustrum, 1855–60. In *Studies*, xlii (June 1953), pp 151–68.

—— *Dublin surgeon-anatomists and other essays. A centenary tribute. Ed.* J. B. Lyons. Dublin, 1987.

Fallon, Martin. *Abraham Colles, 1773–1843: surgeon of Ireland.* London, 1972.

Farrington, Anthony, and others. Robert Lloyd Praeger, 1865–1953. In *Irish Naturalist's Journal*, xi, no. 6 (1954), pp 141–76.

Feeney, J. K. *The Coombe lying-in hospital.* Dublin, 1983.

Finnane, Mark. *Insanity and the insane in post-famine Ireland.* London and Totowa, N.J., 1981.

Fleetwood, J. F. Dublin's private medical schools. In *Ir. Jn. Med. Sc.*, 6th ser., no. 265 (Jan. 1948), pp 20–31.

——An Irish field ambulance in the Franco–Prussian war. In *Ir. Sword*, vi, no. 24 (1963–4), pp 137–48.

—— *The history of medicine in Ireland.* Dublin, 1951; 2nd ed., 1983.

Froggatt, Peter. Sir William Wilde, 1815–1876. In *R.I.A. Proc.*, lxxvii, sect. C, no. 10 (1977), pp 261–78.

——Dr James MacDonnell, M. D. (1763–1845). In *The Glynns*, ix (1981), pp 16–31.

——The response of the medical profession to the great famine. In E. M. Crawford (ed.), *Famine: the Irish experience* (Edinburgh, 1989), pp 134–56.

Herries Davies, G. L. The earth sciences in Irish serial publications, 1787–1977. In *Journal of Earth Sciences: Royal Dublin Society*, i, no. 1 (1978), pp 1–23.

—— *Sheets of many colours: the mapping of Ireland's rocks, 1750–1890.* Dublin, 1983. (Royal Dublin Society: Historical Studies in Irish Science and Technology, no. 4.)

—— Irish thought in science. In Richard Kearney (ed.), *The Irish mind* (Dublin, 1985), pp 294–310.

—— Sir Robert Stawell Ball, 1840–1913. In *Hermathena*, cxxxviii (summer 1985), pp 41–56. Astronomer royal of Ireland and professor of astronomy, T.C.D.

Hughes, N.J. *Irish engineering, 1760–1960*. Dublin, 1982. (Institution of Engineers of Ireland.)

Jarrell, R. A. The Department of Science and Art and control of Irish science, 1853–1905. In *I.H.S.*, xxiii, no. 92 (Nov. 1983), pp 330–47.

Johnston, Roy. Science and technology in Irish national culture. In *Crane Bag*, vii (1983), pp 58–63.

Jones, Greta. Eugenics in Ireland: the Belfast Eugenics Society, 1911–15. In *I.H.S.*, xxviii, no. 109 (May 1992), pp 81–95.

Kirkpatrick, T. P. C. *The history of Dr Steevens' hospital, Dublin, 1720–1920*. Dublin, 1924.

—— The Dublin medical journals. In *Ir. Jn. Med. Sc.*, 6th ser., no. 78 (June 1932), pp 243–60.

—— Mercer's Hospital: its foundation and early days. In *Ir. Jn. Med. Sc.*, 7th ser., no. 109 (Jan. 1935), pp 7–15.

Logan, Patrick. *Making the cure: a look at Irish folk medicine*. Dublin, 1972.

Lyons, J. B. *The citizen surgeon: a biography of Sir Victor Horsley, 1857–1916*. Dublin, 1966.

—— *James Joyce and medicine*. Dublin, 1973.

—— Sir William Wilde, 1815–1876. In *Journal of the Irish Colleges of Physicians and Surgeons*, v, no. 4 (Apr. 1976), pp 147–52.

—— *Scholar and sceptic: the career of James Henry, 1798–1876*. Dún Laoghaire, 1985.

—— *The quality of Mercers': the story of Mercers' Hospital, 1734–1991*. Dublin, 1991.

—— *What did I die of? The deaths of Parnell, Wilde, Synge, and other literary pathologies*. Dublin, 1991.

McConnell, A. J. The Dublin mathematical school in the first half of the nineteenth century. In *R.I.A. Proc.*, i, sect. A, no. 6 (1945), pp 75–88.

McKenna, S. M. P. Astronomy in Ireland from 1780. In *Vistas in Astronomy*, ix (1968), pp 283–96.

McLaughlin, P. J. Richard Kirwan, 1733–1812. In *Studies*, xxviii, no. 111 (Sept. 1939), pp 461–74; xxviii, no. 112 (Dec. 1939), pp 593–605; xxix, no. 113 (Mar. 1940), pp 71–83; xxix, no. 114 (June 1940), pp 281–300.

—— The Irish inventor of the dynamo. In *Studies*, xxxvii (June 1948), pp 179–88.

—— Some Irish contemporaries of Faraday and Henry. In *R.I.A. Proc.*, lxiv, sect. A, no. 2 (1964), pp 17–35.

—— *Nicholas Callan: priest-scientist, 1799–1864*. Dublin and London, 1965.

Malcolm, Elizabeth. *Swift's hospital: a history of St Patrick's hospital, Dublin, 1746–1989*. Dublin, 1989.

Mason, T. H. Dublin opticians and instrument makers. In *Dublin Hist. Rec.*, vi, no. 4 (Sept.–Nov. 1944), pp 133–49.

Meenan, F. O. C. The Georgian squares of Dublin and their doctors. In *Ir. Jn. Med. Sc.*, 6th ser., no. 484 (Apr. 1966), pp 149–54.

—— The Victorian doctors of Dublin: a social and political portrait. In *Ir. Jn. Med. Sc.*, 7th ser., i, no. 7 (July 1968), pp 311–20.

—— *Cecilia Street: the Catholic University School of Medicine, 1855–1931*. Dublin, 1987.

Mitchell, David. *'A peculiar place': the Adelaide Hospital, Dublin: its times, places, and personalities, 1839–1989*. Tallaght, 1989.

Moore, Patrick. *Armagh observatory: a history, 1790–1967.* Armagh, 1967.

—— *The astronomy of Birr castle.* London, 1971.

O'Brien, E. T. (ed.). *Essays in honour of J. D. H. Widdess.* Dublin, 1978.

—— (ed.). *The charitable infirmary, Jervis Street, 1718–1987: a farewell tribute.* Monkstown, 1987.

O'Connell, T. C. J. Something old and something new (19th century surgery). In *Ir. Jn. Med. Sc.,* 6th ser., no. 414 (1960), pp 249–61.

O'Keefe, P. J. *The development of Ireland's road network.* Dublin, 1973. (Institution of Engineers of Ireland.)

O'Malley, Kevin, and O'Brien, Eoin (ed.). *The bicentenary of the Royal College of Surgeons in Ireland, 1784–1984.* Dublin, 1987.

O'Neill, Thomas P. The scientific investigation of the failure of the potato crop in Ireland, 1845–6. In *I.H.S.,* v, no. 18 (Sept. 1946), pp 123–38.

—— Fever and public health in pre-famine Ireland. In *R.S.A.I. Jn.,* ciii (1973), pp 1–34.

O'Rahilly, Ronan. *A history of the Cork Medical School, 1849–1949.* Cork and Oxford, 1949.

Powell, Malachy. The Royal Academy of Medicine in Ireland: the first hundred years. In *Ir. Jn. Med. Sc.,* cli (Jan. 1983), pp 3–11.

Praeger, R. L. *Some Irish naturalists: a biographical note-book.* Dundalk, 1949.

Reilly, J., and MacSweeney, D. T. William Higgins: a pioneer of the atomic theory. In *Scientific Proceedings of the Royal Dublin Society,* new ser., xix, no. 15 (1929), pp 139–57.

—— and O'Flynn, N. Richard Kirwan, an Irish chemist of the eighteenth century. In *Isis,* xiii (2), no. 41 (1930), pp 298–319.

Robins, Joseph. *Fools and mad: a history of the insane in Ireland.* Dublin, 1986.

Simington, R. C., and Farrington, Anthony. A forgotten pioneer: Patrick Ganly, geologist, surveyor, and civil engineer (1809–1899). In *Dept. Agric. Jn.,* xl (1949), pp 36–50.

Somerville-Large, L. B. Dublin's eye hospitals in the nineteenth century. In *Dublin Hist. Rec.,* xx, no. 1 (Dec. 1964), pp 19–28.

Stendall, J. A. S. *Robert Bell, geologist: a biographical sketch.* Belfast, 1938.

Strain, R. U. M. The foundations of Belfast medicine. In *Ulster Medical Journal,* xl, no. 1 (1971), pp 17–42.

Webb, D. A. William Henry Harvey, 1811–66, and the tradition of systematic botany. In *Hermathena,* ciii (autumn 1966), pp 32–45.

Wheeler, T. S. Life and work of William K. Sullivan. In *Studies,* xxxiv, no. 133 (Mar. 1945), pp 21–36.

—— Newman and science. In *Studies,* xlii (summer, 1953), pp 179–96.

—— and Partington, J. R. *The life and work of William Higgins, chemist (1763–1825).* Oxford, 1960.

—— and others. *The natural resources of Ireland: a series of discourses delivered before the Royal Dublin Society in commemoration of the centenary of the publication by the society of Sir Robert Kane's 'The industrial resources of Ireland'.* Dublin, 1944.

Widdess, J. D. H. The beginnings of medical microscopy in Ireland. In *Ir. Jn. Med. Sc.,* 6th ser., no. 274 (Oct. 1948), pp 668–78.

—— *A Dublin school of medicine and surgery: an account of the schools of surgery, Royal College of Surgeons, Dublin, 1789–1948.* Edinburgh, 1949.

—— Robert McDonnell—a pioneer of blood transfusion: with a survey of transfusion in Ireland, 1832–1922. In *Ir. Jn. Med. Sc.,* 6th ser., no. 313 (1952), pp 11–20.

—— *A history of the Royal College of Physicians of Ireland, 1654–1963.* Edinburgh, 1963.

—— (ed.). *The Charitable Infirmary, Jervis Street, Dublin, 1718–1968.* Dublin, 1968.

—— *The Richmond, Whitworth and Hardwicke hospitals, St Lawrence's, Dublin, 1772–1972.* Dublin, 1972.

—— *The Royal College of Surgeons in Ireland and its medical schools, 1784–1984.* 3rd ed., Dublin, 1984.

Wilkins, Noel. *Ponds, passes and parcs: aquaculture in Victorian Ireland.* Dublin, 1989.

Wilson, D. J. Napoleon's doctors on St Helena: the Irish five. In *Ir. Jn. Med. Sc.*, cxl, no. 1 (Jan. 1971), pp 30–44.

13 LOCAL AND FAMILY HISTORY

ANTRIM. *Sentry Hill: an Ulster farm and family.* By Brian M. Walker. Dundonald, 1981.

ARAN. *Inis Beag, isle of Ireland.* By John C. Messenger. New York, 1969.

—— Economy and society of the Aran Islands, County Galway, in the early 19th century. By Stephen A. Royle. In *Ir. Geography*, xvi (1983), pp 36–54.

ARDAGH. *History of the diocese of Ardagh.* By James J. McNamee. Dublin, 1954.

AYLWARD. The family of Aylward. By Julian C. Walton. In *Ir. Geneal.*, iv (1968–73), pp 157–66, 252–66, 397–416, 584–97; v (1974–9), pp 51–71, 216–33, 506–21.

BALLINASLOE. *The parish of Ballinasloe: its history from the earliest times to the present.* By Patrick Egan. Dublin and London, 1960.

BALLYMONEY. *Ballymoney. Sources for local history.* Belfast, 1975. (P.R.O.N.I.)

BELFAST. *Belfast: an illustrated history.* By Jonathan Bardon. Belfast, 1982.

—— *Belfast: the origin and growth of an industrial city.* Ed. J. C. Beckett and R. E. Glasscock. London, 1967.

—— *Belfast: the making of the city, 1800–1914.* By J. C. Beckett and others. Preface by E. Estyn Evans; foreword by R. E. Glasscock. Belfast, 1983; repr. 1988.

BRENNAN. *A history of the O'Brennans of Iclough, Co. Kilkenny.* By T. A. Brennan. New York, 1975.

BUTLER. The Butlers of Co. Clare. By Sir Henry William Butler Blackall. In *N. Munster Antiq. Jn.*, vi (1949–52), pp 108–29; vii, no. 1 (1953), pp 153–67; no. 2 (1955), pp 19–45. Reprinted as booklet, n.p. [1955].

CASTLE CALDWELL. *A history of Castle Caldwell and its families.* By J. B. Couningham. Enniskillen, 1980.

CASTLECOMER. *Castlecomer connections: exploring history, geography, and social evolution in north Kilkenny environs.* By Tom Lyng. Castlecomer, 1984.

CAVAN. *Diocese of Kilmore.* By P. O'Connell. Dublin, 1938.

Christiansen, Reider. Regional survey and local history. In *Béaloideas*, xvi (1948), pp 126–40.

CLOGHER. *Diocese of Clogher: parochial records.* By James E. McKenna. 2 vols. Enniskillen, 1920.

CLONEGAL (CO. CARLOW). *Clonegal parish.* By P. Mac Suibhne. Carlow, 1975.

COLE. *The Cole family of West Carbery.* By R. Cole. Belfast, 1943.

COLERAINE. *Coleraine in Georgian times.* By T. H. Mullin. Belfast, 1977.

CORK. *The city of Cork, 1700–1900.* By Seán Pettit. Cork, 1977.

—— *Steps and steeples: Cork at the turn of the century.* By Colm Lincoln. Dublin, 1980. (Urban Heritage Series, 1.)

CORK. *Cork: history and society. Interdisciplinary essays on the history of an Irish county.* Ed. Patrick O'Flanagan and Cornelius G. Buttimer; editorial adviser Gerard O'Brien. Dublin, 1993. (Irish County History Series.)

DERRY. *Derry, Donegal, and modern Ulster.* By Desmond Murphy. Derry, 1981.

DEVEREUX. The Devereux family of Co. Wexford. In *Kilmore Parish Journal*, xv (1985–6), pp 14–18.

DILLON. The noble line of the Dillons, Irish swordsmen of France. By Renagh Holohan. In *Études Irlandaises*, xiv, no. 2 (1989), pp 135–42.

DONAGHMORE (CO. TYRONE). *Domhnach Mor (Donaghmore): an outline of parish history.* By Éamon Ó Doibhlin. Omagh, 1969.

DONEGAL. *Donegal's changing traditions: an ethnographic study.* By Eugenia Shanklen. New York and London, 1984.

DOWN. *A history of Dundonald, County Down.* By Peter Carr. Dundonald, 1987.

DUBLIN. *Victorian Dublin.* Ed. Tom Kennedy. Dublin, 1980.

—— *Dublin and Dubliners: essays on the history and literature of Dublin city.* Ed. James Kelly and Uaitear Mac Gearailt. Dublin, 1990.

—— *Dublin city and county: from prehistory to present. Studies in honour of J. H. Andrews.* Ed. F. H. A. Aalen and Kevin Whelan. Dublin, 1992. (Irish County History Series.)

DUNGARVAN. *A maritime and general history of Dungarvan, 1670–1978.* By J. M. Young. Dungarvan, 1978.

DUNKERRIN (CO. TIPPERARY). *Dunkerrin: a parish in Ely O'Carroll . . .* By Séamus Ó Riain. Dunkerrin History Committee, 1988.

ENNISKILLEN. *The history of Enniskillen: with references to some manors in County Fermanagh and other local subjects.* By W. C. Trimble. 3 vols. Enniskillen, 1919–21.

EYRE. *Signpost to Eyrecourt: portrait of the Eyre family.* By M. Fahy. Bath, 1975.

FASSADININ. *Fassadinin: land, settlement, and society in south-east Ireland, 1600–1850.* By William Nolan. Dublin, 1979.

FERMANAGH. *The Fermanagh story: a documented history of the County Fermanagh.* By Peadar Livingstone. Enniskillen, 1969; 2nd printing, 1974.

—— *Passing the time in Ballymenone: culture and history of an Ulster community.* By Henry Glassie. Philadelphia and Dublin, 1982.

FERMOY. *Fermoy, 1791–1840: a local history.* By Niall Brunicardi. [Fermoy], 1976. Companion to the author's *Fermoy to 1790: a local history* (1975).

GALWAY. *Old Galway.* By M. O'Sullivan. Cambridge, 1942.

—— *Galway, town and gown, 1484–1984.* Ed. Diarmuid Ó Cearbhaill. Dublin, 1985.

GALWEY. The Galweys of Munster. By Sir Henry William Butler Blackall. In *Cork Hist. Soc. Jn.*, lxxi (1966), pp 138–58; lxxii (1967), pp 20–51, 122–34; lxxiii (1968), pp 161–74.

Glassie, Henry. *Irish folk history: folk tales from the north.* Philadelphia and Dublin, 1982.

GOLA (CO. DONEGAL). *The life and last days of an island community.* By F. H. A. Aalen and Hugh Brody. Cork, 1969.

Harrison, R. S. (ed.). *Beara and Bantry Bay: a history of Rossmacowen.* Bantry, 1990.

ISLANDMAGEE (CO. ANTRIM). *Between two revolutions: Islandmagee, County Antrim, 1798–1920.* By D. H. Akenson. Don Mills, Ont., 1979.

JEPHSON. *An Anglo-Irish miscellany.* By M. D. Jephson. Dublin, 1964.

—— Mallow castle and the Jephson family. By J. Copps. In *Mallow Field Club Jn.*, iii (1985), pp 42–54.

JOLY. The Joly family: Jasper Robert Joly and the National Library. By Patrick Henchy. In *Ir. Univ. Rev.*, vii, no. 2 (autumn 1977), pp 184–98.

KERRY. *Discovering Kerry: its history, heritage, and topography.* By T. J. Barrington. Monkstown, Co. Dublin, 1976.

KILKENNY. *Kilkenny: an urban history, 1391–1843.* By W. G. Neely. Belfast, 1989.

—— *Kilkenny: history and society. Interdisciplinary essays on the history of an Irish county.* Ed. William Nolan and Kevin Whelan. Dublin, 1990. (Irish County History Series.)

—— *Kilkenny: its architecture and history.* By K. M. Lanigan and Gerald Tyler. Belfast, 1986.

KILLALOE. *The diocese of Killaloe, 1800–1850.* By Ignatius Murphy. Dublin, 1992.

KILLORGLIN. *History of Killorglin.* By Kieran Foley. Killorglin, 1988.

KILMORE. *The diocese of Kilmore: its history and antiquities.* By Philip O'Connell. Dublin, 1937.

KING. *The Kings, earls of Kingston.* By R. King-Harman. Cambridge, 1957.

LAOIS. *The landscape of Slieve Bloom: a study of its natural and human heritage.* By John Feehan. Dublin, 1979.

—— *Laois: an environmental history.* By John Feehan. Stradbally, 1983.

LEITRIM. *History of Leitrim.* By T. M. O'Flynn. Dublin, 1937.

LIMAVADY. *Limavady and the Roe valley.* By T. H. Mullen. Limavady, 1983.

LIMERICK. *The diocese of Limerick from 1691 to the present time.* By J. Begley. 3 vols. Dublin, 1938.

—— *The story of Limerick.* By Robert Wyse Jackson. Dublin and Cork, 1973.

—— *Exploring aspects of Limerick's past.* By Patrick J. O'Connor. Newcastle West, 1987.

—— The maturation of town and village life in County Limerick, 1700–1900. By P. J. O'Connor. In W. J. Smyth and Kevin Whelan, *Common ground* (Cork, 1988), pp 149–72.

—— *History of Limerick.* By James Dowd. Ed. Ciaran O'Carroll. Dublin, 1990.

LISTOWEL. *Listowel and its vicinity.* By J. A. Gaughan. Tralee, 1973.

LONDONDERRY. *The Londonderrys: a family portrait.* By H. Montgomery Hyde. London, 1979.

LONGFORD. *Longford: essays in county history.* Ed. Raymond Gillespie and Gerard Moran. Dublin, 1991.

MACDONALD. *The MacDonalds of Mayo.* By G. A. Hayes-McCoy. In *Galway Arch. Soc. Jn.*, xvii (1936), pp 65–82.

MAYO. *The living landscape: Kilgalligan, Erris, County Mayo.* By Séamus Ó Catháin and Patrick O'Flanagan. Dublin, 1975.

—— *A various county: essays in Mayo history, 1500–1900.* Ed. Raymond Gillespie and Gerard Moran. Westport, Co. Mayo, 1987.

—— ISLANDS. Settlement, population and economy of the Mayo islands. By Stephen Royle. In *Cathair na Mart*, ix (1989), pp 120–33.

—— The natural history of our western islands. By Tony Whilde. In *Cathair na Mart*, ix (1989), pp 79–90.

MEAGHER. Migration and upward mobility. The Meagher family in Ireland and Newfoundland. By John Mannion. In *Ir. Econ. & Soc. Hist.*, xv (1988), pp 54–70.

MEATH. *A short history of the diocese of Meath, 1867–1937.* By T. Brady. Navan, 1937.

MOATE. *Moate, County Westmeath: a history of the town and district.* By Liam Cox. Athlone, 1981.

MONAGHAN. *The Monaghan story.* By Peadar Livingstone. Enniskillen, 1980.

MURROE AND BOHER. *Murroe and Boher: the history of an Irish country parish*. By Mark Tierney. Dublin, 1966.

NAGLE. The Nagles of Garnavilla. By B. M. O'Connell. In *Ir. Geneal.*, iii (July 1956), pp 17–24.

NAVAN. *Changing forces shaping a nineteenth century Irish town: a case study of Navan*. By Peter Connell. Maynooth, 1978.

NEWCASTLE LYONS. *Newcastle Lyons: a parish of the Pale*. By Peter O'Sullivan. Dublin, 1986.

NEWRY. *Frontier town: an illustrated history of Newry*. By Tony Canavan. Belfast, 1989.

Nolan, William. *Tracing the past: sources for local studies in the Republic of Ireland*. Dublin, 1982.

OFFALY. *Sources for Offaly history*. By Michael Byrne. Tullamore, 1977.

O'Neill, Thomas P. *Sources of local history*. Dublin, 1958.

OSSORY. *The history and antiquities of the diocese of Ossory*. By William Corrigan. 4 vols. Dublin, 1905. Facsimile reprint with foreword by James Carey, introduction and bibliography by John Bradley, Kilkenny, 1981.

PETTY-FITZMAURICE. *Glanerought and the Petty-Fitzmaurices*. By N. W. E. Fitzmaurice, marquis of Lansdowne. London, 1937.

POOLE. *The Pooles of Mayfield, and other Irish families*. By Rosemary ffolliott. Dublin, 1958.

RAPHOE. *A history of the diocese of Raphoe*. By Edward Maguire. 2 vols. Dublin, 1920.

RIVERS. Bartholomew Rivers of Waterford, banker, and his kindred. By Hubert Gallwey. In *Decies*, no. 12 (Sept. 1979), pp 53–61.

Rogers, Alan. *Approaches to local history*. London and New York, 1972; 2nd ed., 1977. First ed. published as *This was their world*.

ROSCREA. *Roscrea and district: monuments and antiquities*. By George Cunningham. Roscrea, 1976.

SALTEE ISLANDS. *Saltees: islands of birds and legends*. By R. Roche. Dublin, 1977; new ed., 1987.

SHACKLETON. The Shackletons and Ballitore. By A. Tracey. In *Carloviana*, i, no. 4 (Nov. 1951), pp 161–6.

SLIGO. *History of Sligo, county and town, from the earliest ages . . .* By W. G. Wood-Martin. 3 vols. Dublin, 1882–92.

SOMERVILLE. *Records of the Somerville family of Castlehaven and Drishane from 1174 to 1940*. By E. and B. Somerville. Cork, 1940.

THOMASTOWN. *In the valley of the Nore: a social history of Thomastown, County Kilkenny, 1840–1893*. By P. H. Gulliver and Marilyn Silverman. Dublin, 1986.

THURLES. *Thurles: the cathedral town. Essays in honour of Archbishop Thomas Morris*. Ed. William Corbett and William Nolan. Dublin, 1989.

TIPPERARY. *Romantic Slievenamon in history, folklore, and song: a Tipperary anthology*. By James Maher. Mullinahone, Co. Tipperary, 1957.

—— *Land and violence: a history of west Tipperary from 1660*. By Denis G. Marnane. Tipperary, 1985.

—— *Tipperary: history and society. Interdisciplinary essays on the history of an Irish county*. Ed. William Nolan and Thomas McGrath. Dublin, 1985. (Irish County History Series.)

—— *History of south Tipperary*. By Patrick Power. Cork and Dublin, 1989.

TIPPERARY–KILKENNY. *Gleann an Óir: ar thóir na staire agus na litríochta in Oirthear Mumhan agus i nDeisceart Laighean*. By Eoghan Ó Néill. Dublin, 1988.

TORY ISLAND (CO. DONEGAL). *The Tory Islanders: a people of the Celtic fringe.* By R. Fox. Cambridge, 1978.

TYRONE. *Tyrone folk quest.* By Michael J. Murphy. Belfast, 1973.

VALENTIA ISLAND. *Man and environment in Valentia Island.* By Frank Mitchell. Dublin, 1969. (R.I.A.)

—— *Valentia: portrait of an island.* By Daphne D. C. Pochin Mould. Dublin, 1978.

WALL. *The Wall family in Ireland.* By H. D. Gallwey. Naas, 1970.

WATERFORD. *Waterford & Lismore: a compendious history of the united dioceses.* By Patrick Power. Dublin, 1937.

—— *A history of Waterford city and county.* By Patrick Power. Cork, 1990.

—— *Waterford: history and society. Interdisciplinary essays on the history of an Irish county.* Ed. William Nolan and Thomas P. Power; associate editor Des Cowman. Dublin, 1992. (Irish County History Series.)

WESTMEATH. *South Westmeath: farm and folk.* By Jeremiah Sheehan. Dublin, 1978.

WEXFORD (Hooke peninsula). *The promontory of Hooke.* By Billy Colfer. Wexford, 1978.

—— *Carrig-on-Bannow.* By T. C. Butler. Bannow, 1981.

—— *The families of Co. Wexford.* By Hilary Murphy. Dublin, 1986.

—— (Newbawn). *A history of Newbawn.* Ed. K. Whelan. Newbawn, 1986.

—— (Davidstown). *Davidstown-Courtnacuddy, some of its history.* By P. Hennessy. Davidstown, 1987.

—— *Wexford: history and society. Interdisciplinary essays on the history of an Irish county.* Ed. Kevin Whelan and William Nolan. Dublin, 1987. (Irish County History Series.)

WICKLOW. *Wicklow: history and society. Interdisciplinary essays on the history of an Irish county.* Ed. Ken Hannigan and William Nolan. Dublin, 1994. (Irish County History Series.)

14 HISTORY OF THE IRISH ABROAD

Adams, W. F. *Ireland and Irish emigration to the new world from 1815 to the famine.* New Haven, Conn., 1932; repr., 1967.

Akenson, D. H. *The United States and Ireland.* Cambridge, Mass., 1973.

—— An agnostic view of the historiography of the Irish Americans. In *Labour,* xiv (1984), pp 123–59.

—— *The Irish in Ontario.* Montreal, 1984.

—— *Being had: historians, evidence, and the Irish in North America.* Port Credit, Ont., 1985.

—— *Half the world from home: perspectives on the Irish in New Zealand, 1860–1950.* Wellington, N.Z., 1990.

Alter, Peter. *'Niedrigste Klasse der Bevölkerung': die Iren in Viktorianischen England.* Vameland der Handarbeit, 1981.

Amos, Keith. *The fenians in Australia, 1865–1880.* Kensington, N.S.W., 1988.

Belchem, John. English working-class radicalism and the Irish, 1815–1850. In *Éire-Ireland,* xix, no. 4 (winter 1984), pp 78–93.

Billington, R. A. *The protestant crusade, 1800–1860.* New York, 1938.

Birmingham, Stephen. *Real lace: America's Irish rich.* London, 1974.

Bolger, S. G. *The Irish character in American fiction, 1830–1860.* New York, 1976.

Brady, L. W. *T. P. O'Connor and the Liverpool Irish.* London and New Jersey, 1983. (Royal Historical Society: Studies in History, 39.)

Broehl, Wayne G., jr. *The Molly Maguires.* Cambridge, Mass., 1965.

Brown, T. N. *Irish-American nationalism, 1870–1890*. Philadelphia, 1966.
—— The United States of America: the Irish layman. In Corish, *Ir. catholicism*, vi, (1970).
Buckley, J. P. *The New York Irish: their view of American foreign policy, 1914–21*. New York, 1976.
Burchell, R. A. *The San Francisco Irish, 1848–1880*. Manchester and New York, 1979; Berkeley, Calif., 1980.
Carroll, F. M. *American opinion and the Irish question, 1910–23*. Dublin, 1978.
—— De Valera and the Americans: the early years, 1916–1923. In *Canadian Journal of Irish Studies*, viii, no. 1 (June 1982), pp 36–54.
Clark, Dennis (ed.). *The Irish in Philadelphia*. Philadelphia, 1973.
—— *The Irish relations*. Rutherford, N.J., 1982.
—— *Hibernia America: the Irish and regional cultures*. Westport, Conn., 1986.
—— *Erin's heirs*. Lexington, Ky., 1991.
—— *The Irish in Pennsylvania*. University Park, Pa., 1991.
Cleary, P. S. *Australia's debt to Irish nation builders*. Sydney, 1933.
Coleman, Terry. *The railway navvies*. London, 1965.
Costello, Con. *Botany Bay: the story of the convicts transported from Ireland to Australia, 1791–1853*. Cork, 1987.
Coughlan, Neil. The coming of the Irish to Victoria. In *Historical Studies*, xii, no. 45 (Oct. 1965), pp 68–86.
Cross, R. D. *The emergence of liberal catholicism in America*. Cambridge, Mass., 1958.
Cuddy, J. E. *Irish America and national isolationism, 1914–20*. New York, 1976.
Curti, Merle, and Burr, Kendall. The immigrant and the American image in Europe, 1860–1914. In *Mississippi Valley Historical Review*, xxxvii (1950–51), pp 203–30.
D'Arcy, Fergus. The Irish in nineteenth-century Britain: reflections on their role and experience. In *Irish History Workshop*, i (1981), pp 3–12.
D'Arcy, William. *The fenian movement in the United States: 1858–1886*. Washington, D.C., 1947.
Davis, Graham. *The Irish in Britain, 1815–1914*. Dublin, 1991.
Davis, R. P. *Irish issues in New Zealand politics, 1868–1922*. Dunedin, N.Z., 1974.
Devine, T. M. (ed.). *Irish immigrants and Scottish society in the nineteenth and twentieth centuries*. Edinburgh, 1991.
Dickason, G. B. *Irish settlers to the Cape: a history of the Clanwilliam 1820 settlers from Cork harbour*. Cape Town, 1973.
Diner, H. R. *Erin's daughters in America: Irish immigrant women in the nineteenth century*. Baltimore and London, 1983.
Dolan, J. P. *The immigrant church: New York's Irish and German catholics, 1815–1865*. Baltimore and London, 1976.
Doyle, D. N. The Irish and American labour, 1880–1920. In *Saothar*, i (1975), pp 42–58.
—— *Irish-Americans: native rights and national empires: the structures, divisions, and attitudes of the catholic minority in the decade of expansion, 1890–1901*. New York, 1976.
—— *Ireland, Irishmen, and revolutionary America, 1760–1820*. Cork, 1981.
—— The Irish in Australia and the United States: some comparisons, 1800–1939. In *Ir. Econ. & Soc. Hist.*, xvi (1989), pp 73–94.
—— The Irish in Chicago. In *I.H.S.*, xxvi, no. 103 (May 1989), pp 293–303.
—— and Edwards, O. D. (ed.). *America and Ireland, 1776–1976: the American identity and the Irish countryside*. Westport, Conn., and London, 1980.

Durey, Michael. The survival of an Irish culture in Britain, 1800–1845. In *Historical Studies*, xx, no. 78 (Apr. 1982), pp 14–35.

Egan, P. K. *The influence of the Irish on the catholic church in America*. Dublin, 1968. (O'Donnell Lecture.)

Elliott, Bruce. *Irish migrants in the Canadas: a new approach*. Kingston, Montreal, and Belfast, 1988.

Ellis, Eilish. State-aided emigration schemes from crown estates in Ireland *c*.1850. In *Anal. Hib.*, no. 22 (1960), pp 329–407.

Erickson, Charlotte. Emigration from the British Isles to the U.S.A. in 1831. In *Population Studies*, xxxv, no. 2 (1981), pp 175–98.

Ernst, Robert. *Immigrant life in New York city, 1825–1863*. New York, 1949.

Feheney, J. M. Delinquency among Irish catholic children in Victorian London. In *I.H.S.*, xxiii, no. 92 (Nov. 1983), pp 319–29.

Finnegan, Frances. *Poverty and prejudice: a study of Irish immigrants in York, 1840–1875*. Cork, 1982.

Firedeng, Steven. *Class and ethnicity: Irish catholics in England, 1880–1939*. Buckingham, 1993.

Fitzpatrick, David. Irish emigration in the later nineteenth century. In *I.H.S.*, xxii, no. 86 (Sept. 1980), pp 126–43.

—— *Irish emigration, 1801–1921*. Dundalk, 1984. (Studies in Irish Economic and Social History, I.)

—— 'That beloved country, that no place else resembles': connotations of Irishness in Irish-Australasian letters, 1841–1915. In *I.H.S.*, xxvii, no. 108 (Nov. 1991), pp 324–51.

Foley, Billy. The Irish in Argentina. In *Irish Family History*, vi (1990), pp 5–14.

Foner, Eric. Class, ethnicity, and radicalism in the gilded age: the Land League and Irish America. In *Marxist Perspectives*, i (1978), pp 6–55.

Funchion, M. F. *Chicago's Irish nationalists, 1881–90*. New York, 1976. (Arno Press series: Irish-Americans.)

—— Irish-America: an essay on the literature since 1970. In *Immigration History Newsletter*, xvii (1985), pp 1–8.

Gilbert, A. D. The conscription referenda, 1916–17: the impact of the Irish crisis [on Australia]. In *Historical Studies*, xiv, no. 53 (Oct. 1969), pp 54–72.

Gilley, Sheridan. Papists, protestants, and the Irish in London, 1835–70. In *Studies in Church History*, viii (1972), pp 259–66.

—— English attitudes to the Irish in England, 1780–1900. In Colin Holmes (ed.), *Immigrants and minorities in British society* (London, 1978), pp 81–110.

—— The Roman Catholic church and the nineteenth-century Irish diaspora. In *Jn. Ecc. Hist.*, xxxv, no. 2 (Apr. 1984), pp 188–207.

Glazer, Nathan, and Moynihan, Daniel. *Beyond the melting pot: the negroes, Puerto-Ricans, Jews, Italians, and Irish of New York city*. Cambridge, Mass., 1964; rev. ed., 1970.

Greeley, Andrew. *The Irish-Americans: the rise to money and power*. New York, 1980.

Green, J. J. American catholics and the Irish land league, 1879–1882. In *Cath. Hist. Rev.*, xxxv, no. 4 (Apr. 1949), pp 19–42.

Griffin, W. D. *A portrait of the Irish in America*. New York, 1981.

Groneman, C. Working-class immigrant women in mid-nineteenth-century New York: the Irish women's experience. In *Journal of Urban History*, iv, no. 3 (1978), pp 255–74.

Gutman, H. G. *Work, culture, and industrialising society*. New York, 1976.

Handley, J. E. *The Irish in Scotland, 1798–1845*. Cork, 1943.

—— *The Irish in modern Scotland*. Cork, 1947.

Handlin, Oscar. *Boston's immigrants, 1790–1880: a study in acculturation*. Rev. ed., Cambridge, Mass., 1959.

Hansen, Marcus Lee. *The Atlantic migration, 1607–1860*. Cambridge, Mass., 1940.

Harris, Ruth-Ann. The failure of republicanism among Irish migrants to Britain, 1800–1840. In *Éire-Ireland*, xxi, no. 4 (winter 1986), pp 122–36.

Henderson, T. M. *Tammany Hall and the new immigrants: the progressive years*. New York, 1976.

Heuston, R. F. *The catholic press and nativism, 1840–60*. New York, 1976.

Hickey, John. *Urban catholics: urban catholicism in England and Wales from 1829 to the present day*. London, 1967.

Higham, John. *Strangers in the land, 1860–1925*. New York, 1963.

Holmes, Colin (ed.). *Immigrants and minorities in British society*. London, 1978.

Hornby-Smith, M. P., and Dale, Angela. The assimilation of Irish immigrants in England. In *British Journal of Sociology*, xxxix, no. 4 (1988), pp 519–44.

Houston, C. J. *The sash Canada wore: a historical geography of the Orange order in Canada*. Toronto, 1980.

—— and Smyth, W. J. The Irish abroad: better questions through a better source, the Canadian census. In *Ir. Geography*, xiii (1980), pp 1–19.

—— and—— *Irish emigration and Canadian settlement: patterns, links, and letters*. Toronto and Belfast, 1990.

Inglis, K. S. *The Australian colonists: an exploration of social history, 1788–1870*. Melbourne, 1974.

Jackson, J. A. *The Irish in Britain*. London and Cleveland, Ohio, 1963.

Jackson, Pauline. Women in nineteenth-century Irish migration. In *International Migration Review*, xviii, no. 4 (1984), pp 1004–20.

Johnson, H. J. M. *British emigration policy, 1815–1830*. Oxford, 1972.

Johnson, J. H. Harvest migration from nineteenth-century Ireland. In *Transactions and Papers of the Institute of British Geographers*, xli, no. 41 (June 1967), pp 97–112.

—— The context of migration: the example of Ireland in the nineteenth century. In *Transactions of the Institute of British Geographers*, new ser., xv (1990), pp 259–76.

Jones, M. A. *American immigration*. Chicago and London, 1980.

—— The Scotch-Irish. In Stephan Thernstrom, Oscar Handlin, and Ann Orlov (ed.), *Harvard encyclopaedia of American ethnic groups* (Cambridge, Mass., and London, 1980), pp 896–908.

Joyce, W. L. *Editors and ethnicity: a history of the Irish-American press, 1848–83*. New York, 1976.

Keep, G. R. C. Official opinion on Irish emigration in the later nineteenth century. In *I.E.R.*, lxxxi (June 1954), pp 412–21.

—— Some Irish opinion on population and emigration, 1851–1901. In *I.E.R.*, lxxxiv (Dec. 1955), pp 377–86.

Kiernan, Colm (ed.). *Ireland and Australia*. Dublin and Cork, 1984. (Thomas Davis Lectures.)

—— *Daniel Mannix and Ireland*. Victoria, 1985.

—— (ed.). *Australia and Ireland, 1788–1988: bicentenary essays*. Dublin, 1986.

Kiernan, T. J. *Transportation from Ireland to Sydney, 1791–1816*. Canberra, 1954.

Knobel, D. T. A vocabulary of ethnic perception: content analysis of the American stage Irishman, 1820–1860. In *Journal of American Studies*, xv, no. 1 (1981), pp 45–72.

Korol, Juan Carlos, and Sabato, Hilda. *Como fue la immigración irlandesa en Argentina.* Buenos Aires, 1981.

Lawton, R. Irish immigration to England and Wales in the mid-nineteenth century. In *Ir. Geography*, iv, no. 1 (1959), pp 35–54.

Lees, Lynn Hollen. *Exiles of Erin: Irish migrants in Victorian London.* Manchester, 1979.

Levine, E. M. *The Irish and Irish politicians.* Notre Dame, Ind., 1966.

Lewis, C. R. The Irish in Cardiff in the mid-nineteenth century. In *Cambria*, vii (1980), pp 13–41.

Lowe, W. J. *The Irish in mid-Victorian Lancashire: the shaping of a working-class community.* New York and Berne, 1989. (Irish Studies, 1.)

McCaffrey, L. J. *The Irish diaspora in America.* Bloomington, Ind., 1976; 2nd ed., Washington, D.C., 1984.

—— Skerrett, E.; Funchion, M. F.; and Fanning, C. *The Irish in Chicago.* Urbana, Ill., and Chicago, 1987.

McCracken, Donal. The Irish in nineteenth-century South Africa. In *Irish Heritage Links*, iii, nos 8–9 (1990), pp 15–21.

McCracken, J. L. *New light at the Cape of Good Hope: William Porter, the father of Cape liberalism.* Belfast, 1993.

MacDonagh, Oliver. The Irish catholic clergy and emigration during the great famine. In *I.H.S.*, v, no. 20 (Sept. 1947), pp 287–302.

—— The Irish in Victoria, 1851–91: a demographic essay. In *Hist. Studies*, viii (1971), pp 67–92.

—— The Irish famine emigration to the United States. In *Perspectives in American History*, x (1976), pp 357–446.

McGrath, Walter. The fenians in Australia. In *Cork Hist. Soc. Jn.*, xcii (1988), pp 45–54.

MacKay, Donald. *Flight from famine: the coming of the Irish to Canada.* Toronto, 1990.

MacKenzie, H. A. *The Irish in Cape Breton.* Antigonish, Nova Scotia, 1979.

McManamin, F. G. *The American years of John Boyle O'Reilly, 1870–1890.* New York, 1976.

McWhinney, Grady. *Cracker culture: Celtic ways in the old south.* Prologue by Forrest McDonald. Tuscaloosa, Ala., 1988.

Madgwick, R. B. *Immigration into eastern Australia, 1788–1851.* London, 1937; repr., Sydney, 1969.

Maguire, J. F. *The Irish in America.* London, 1868; repr., New York, 1969.

Mannion, John. *Irish settlements in eastern Canada.* Toronto, 1974.

—— (ed.). *The peopling of Newfoundland.* St Johns, 1977.

Marshall, P. D. A founding minority: Scotch-Irish contributions to the growth of the American republic. In J. W. Blake (ed.), *The Ulster-American connection* ([Coleraine], 1981), pp 26–32.

Meagher, Timothy. *From Paddy to Studs: Irish-American communities in the turn of the century era, 1880–1920.* London, 1986.

Merwick, Donna. *Boston priests, 1848–1910: a study of social and intellectual change.* Cambridge, Mass., 1976.

Messenger, J. C. The most distinctively Irish settlement in the New World. In *Ethnicity*, ii (1975), pp 281–303.

Miller, K. A. *Emigrants and exiles: Ireland and the Irish exodus to North America*. New York, 1985.

—— Bolling, Bruce, and Doyle, D. N. Emigrants and exiles: Irish cultures and Irish emigration to North America, 1790–1822. In *I.H.S.*, xxii, no. 86 (Sept. 1980), pp 97–125.

Miller, R. M., and Wakelyn, J. L. (ed.). *Catholics in the old South*. Macon, Ga., 1983.

Morton, Grenfell. Ulster emigrants to Australia, 1850–1890. In *Ulster Folklife*, xviii (1972), pp 111–20.

Neal, Frank. *Sectarian violence: the Liverpool experience, 1819–1914, an aspect of Anglo–Irish history*. Manchester, 1988.

Nicholas, Stephen, and Shergold, P. S. Human capital and the pre-famine Irish emigration to England. In *Explorations in Economic History*, xxiv, no. 2 (Apr. 1987), pp 158–77.

Niehaus, E. F. *The Irish in New Orleans*. Baton Rouge, La., 1965.

Nolan, Janet. *Ourselves alone: women's emigration from Ireland, 1885–1920*. Lexington, Ky., 1989.

O'Brien, E. M. *The foundation of Australia*. 2nd ed., Sydney, 1950.

O'Brien, John, and Travers, Pauric (ed.). *The Irish emigrant experience in Australia*. Swords, 1991.

O'Brien, M. J. R. Cork women for Australia: assisted emigration, 1830–1840. In *Cork Hist. Soc. Jn.*, xciii, no. 252 (1988), pp 21–9.

O'Carroll, Íde. *Models for movers: Irish women's emigration to America*. Dublin, 1990.

O'Connor, Kevin. *The Irish in Britain*. London, 1972.

O'Driscoll, Robert, and Reynolds, Lorna (ed.). *The untold story: the Irish in Canada*. 2 vols. Toronto, 1988.

O'Farrell, Patrick. Emigrant attitudes and behaviour as a source for Irish history. In *Hist. Studies*, x (1976), pp 109–31.

—— Dreaming of a distant revolution: A. T. Dryer and the Irish National Association, Sydney, 1915–16. In *Journal of the Royal Australian Historical Society*, lxix, pt 3 (Dec. 1983), pp 145–60.

—— The Irish Republican Brotherhood in Australia: the 1918 internments. In Oliver MacDonagh, W. F. Mandle, and Pauric Travers (ed.), *Irish culture and nationalism, 1750–1950* (London and Canberra, 1983), pp 182–93.

—— *The catholic church and community: an Australian history*. Rev. ed., Sydney, 1992.

—— *The Irish in Australia*. Sydney, 1987; rev. ed., 1992.

—— *Vanished kingdoms: the Irish in Australia and New Zealand: a personal excursion*. Sydney, 1990.

Ó Gráda, Cormac. A note on nineteenth-century Irish emigration statistics. In *Population studies*, xxix, no. 1 (1975), pp 143–9.

O'Grady, J. P. *Irish-Americans and Anglo–American relations, 1880–1888*. New York, 1976.

Osofsky, Gilbert. Abolitionists, Irish immigrants, and the dilemmas of romantic nationalism. In *A.H.R.*, lxxx, no. 4 (Oct. 1975), pp 889–912.

Ó Tuathaigh, M. A. G. The Irish in nineteenth-century Britain: problems of integration. In *R. Hist. Soc. Trans.*, 5th ser., xxxi (1981), pp 149–73.

Quinn, E. G. Of myths and men: an analysis of Molly Maguireism in nineteenth-century Pennsylvania. In *Éire-Ireland*, xxiii, no. 4 (winter 1988), pp 52–61.

Ready, W. B. The Irish and South America. In *Éire-Ireland*, i, no. 1 (Mar. 1966), pp 50–63.

Richards, Eric. Irish life and progress in colonial South Australia. In *I.H.S.*, xxvii, no. 107 (May 1991), pp 216–36.

——(ed.). *Poor Australian immigrants in the nineteenth century*. Canberra, 1991.

Robinson, Portia. *The women of Botany Bay: a reinterpretation of the role of women in the origins of Australian society*. Sydney, 1988.

Robson, L. J. *The convict settlers of Australia: an enquiry into the origin and character of convicts transported to New South Wales and Van Diemen's Land, 1787–1852*. Melbourne, 1965.

Rodechko, J. P. *Patrick Ford and his search for America: a case study of Irish-American journalism, 1876–1913*. New York, 1976.

Rudé, George. *Protest and punishment: the story of the social and political protesters transported to Australia, 1788–1868*. Oxford, 1978.

Schrier, Arnold. *Ireland and the American emigration, 1850–1900*. Minneapolis and London, 1958.

Senior, Hereward. *The fenians and Canada*. Toronto, 1978.

Sewell, M. J. Rebels or revolutionaries? Irish-American nationalism and American diplomacy, 1865–1885. In *Hist. Jn.*, xxix, no. 3 (1986), pp 723–33.

Shannon, J. P. *Catholic colonisation on the western frontier*. New Haven, Conn., and London, 1957.

Shannon, W. V. *The American Irish*. New York, 1963; rev. ed., 1966.

Shaw, A. G. L. *Convicts and colonies: a study of penal transportation from Great Britain and Ireland to Australia and other parts of the British empire*. London, 1966.

Steele, E. D. The Irish presence in the north of England, 1850–1914. In *Northern History*, xii (1976), pp 220–41.

Sutton, T. L. *Catholic society in New South Wales, 1788–1860*. Sydney, 1974.

Swift, Roger, and Gilley, Sheridan (ed.). *The Irish in the Victorian city*. London, 1985.

Swords, Liam. *The green cockade: the Irish in the French revolution, 1789–1815*. Dublin, 1989.

Taylor, Philip. *The distant magnet*. London, 1971.

Thernstrom, Stephan. *The other Bostonians, 1880–1970*. Cambridge, Mass., 1973.

Treble, J. H. O'Connor, O'Connell, and the attitudes of Irish immigrants towards chartism in the north of England, 1838–48. In J. Butt and J. F. Clarke (ed.), *The Victorians and social protest: a symposium* (Newton Abbot, 1973), pp 33–70, 220–28.

Vedder, R. K., and Gallaway, L. E. The geographical distribution of British and Irish emigrants to the United States after 1800. In *Scottish Journal of Political Economy*, xix (Feb. 1972), pp 19–35.

Vinyard, J. E. *The Irish on the urban frontier: Detroit, 1850–1880*. New York, 1976.

Waldersee, James. *Catholic society in New South Wales, 1788–1860*. Sydney, 1974.

Walker, William. Irish immigrants in Scotland: their priests, politics, and parochial life. In *Hist. Jn.*, xv, no. 4 (1972), pp 649–68.

Walsh, J. P. *The Irish: America's political class*. New York, 1976.

Werly, John. The Irish in Manchester, 1832–49. In *I.H.S.*, xviii, no. 71 (1973), pp 345–58.

Williamson, J. G. The impact of the Irish on British labour markets during the industrial revolution. In *Jn. Econ. Hist.*, xlvi, no. 3 (1986), pp 693–720.

15 HISTORY OF ARCHITECTURE, PAINTING, AND DECORATIVE ARTS

Anglesea, Martyn. David Wilson, 1873–1935. In *Irish Arts Review Yearbook* (1990–91), pp 57–70.

Arnold, Bruce. *A concise history of Irish art.* London, 1968.

—— *Orpen: mirror to an age.* London, 1981.

—— *Mainie Jellett and the modern movement in Ireland.* New Haven, Conn., and London, 1991.

Barrett, Cyril. Irish art in the nineteenth century. In *Connoisseur*, clxxviii, no. 718 (1971), pp 230–37.

—— Irish nationalism and art. In *Studies*, lxiv (winter 1975), pp 393–409.

Barry, Michael. *Across deep waters: bridges of Ireland.* Dublin, 1985.

Bence-Jones, Mark. William Tinsley: Victorian or Georgian? In *Ir. Georgian Soc. Bull.*, iii, no. 2 (1960), pp 13–20.

—— A city of vanished waterways. [Cork I] In *Country Life*, cxlii, no. 3674 (3 Aug. 1967), pp 250–53.

—— Two pairs of architect brothers. [Cork II] In *Country Life*, cxlii, no. 3675 (10 Aug. 1967), pp 306–9.

—— Ireland's great exhibition. In *Country Life*, cliii, no. 3951 (15 Mar. 1973), pp 666–8. Discusses John Benson's exhibition building of 1853 in Dublin.

—— *Burke's guide to country houses, 1: Ireland.* London, 1978.

Benington, Jonathan. *Roderic O'Conor.* Dublin, 1992.

Betjeman, John. Francis Johnston, Irish architect. In Myfanwy Evans (ed.), *The pavilion* (London, 1946), pp 20–38.

Black, Eileen. James Green Wilson. In *Irish Arts Review Yearbook* (1990–91), pp 99–102.

Blau, E. M. *Ruskinian gothic: the architecture of Deane and Woodward, 1845–1861.* Princeton, N.J., 1982.

Bodkin, Thomas. James Barry. In *Studies*, xi (1922), pp 83–96.

—— *Hugh Lane and his pictures.* Dublin, 1956.

Bowe, Nicola Gordon. *Harry Clarke: his graphic art.* Mountrath and Los Angeles, 1983.

—— The life and work of Harry Clarke. Blackrock, 1989.

—— The Irish arts and crafts movement, 1886–1925. In *Irish Arts Review Yearbook* (1990–91), pp 172–85.

—— Caron, David, and Wynne, Michael. *Gazetteer of Irish stained glass.* Blackrock, 1988.

Breathnach, Kathleen. The last of the Dublin silk weavers. In *Irish Arts Review Yearbook* (1990–91), pp 134–43.

Brett, C. E. B. *Courthouses and market houses of the province of Ulster.* Belfast, 1973.

—— *Roger Mulholland, architect of Belfast, 1740–1818.* Belfast, 1976.

—— *Buildings of Belfast, 1700–1914.* London, 1967; rev. ed., Belfast, 1985.

Campbell, Julian. *The Irish impressionists: Irish artists in France and Belgium, 1850–1914.* Dublin, 1984.

—— *Nathaniel Hone the younger.* Dublin, 1991.

Casey, Christine, and Rowan, Alistair. *North Leinster: the counties of Longford, Louth, Meath, and Westmeath.* London, 1993. (The Buildings of Ireland.)

Clarke, John ('Benmore'). *Memorials of John Hogan.* Glenarm, Co. Antrim, 1927.

Craig, Maurice. *Dublin 1660–1860.* London and Dublin, 1952.

—— *Classic Irish houses of the middle size.* London, 1976; New York, 1977.

—— *The architecture of Ireland from the earliest times to 1880.* Dublin, 1989.

Crookshank, Anne. *Irish art from 1600 to the present day*. Dublin, 1979. (Dept. of Foreign Affairs: Aspects of Ireland, 4.)

—— *Irish sculpture from 1600 to the present day*. Dublin, 1984.

—— and the knight of Glin. *The painters of Ireland, c.1600–1920*. London, 1978.

—— and—— *The watercolours of Ireland: works on paper in pencil, pastel, and paint, c.1600–1914*. London, 1994.

Curl, J. S. *The Londonderry plantation, 1609–1914. The history, architecture, and planning of the estates of the city of London and its livery companies in Ulster*. Chichester, 1986.

Curran, C. P. Benjamin Woodward, Ruskin, and the O'Sheas. In *Studies*, xxix, no. 114 (June 1940), pp 255–68.

—— Michael Healy: stained glass worker, 1873–1941. In *Studies*, xxxi (1942), pp 65–82.

—— *Newman House and University Church*. Dublin, 1953.

—— Evie Hone: stained glass worker, 1894–1955. In *Studies*, xliv (summer 1955), pp 129–42.

—— The architecture of the Bank of Ireland, pt I: the parliament house, 1728–1800. In *Ir. Georgian Soc. Bull.*, xx, nos 1 and 2 (Jan.–June 1977), pp 3–36.

—— The architecture of the Bank of Ireland, pt II: the building of the bank, 1800–1946. In *Ir. Georgian Soc. Bull.*, xx, nos 3 and 4 (July–Dec. 1977), pp 40–70.

Danaher, Kevin. *Ireland's vernacular architecture*. Cork, 1975.

De Breffny, Brian, and ffolliott, Rosemary. *The houses of Ireland: domestic architecture from the medieval castle to the Edwardian villa*. London, 1975.

—— and Mott, George. *The churches and abbeys of Ireland*. London, 1976.

De Courcy, Catherine. *The foundation of the National Gallery of Ireland*. Dublin, 1985.

Denson, Alan. *An Irish artist: W. J. Leech, R. H. A. (1881–1968)*. 2 vols. Kendal, 1968–9.

—— *John Hughes, sculptor, 1865–1941*. Kendal, 1969.

Diestelkamp, Edward. Richard Turner and the Palm House at Kew Gardens. In *Transactions of the Newcomen Society*, liv (1982–3), pp 1–26.

Dixon, Hugh. *An introduction to Ulster architecture*. Belfast, 1975. (Ulster Architectural Heritage Society.)

—— Honouring Thomas Jackson, 1807–1890. In *Belfast Natur. Hist. Soc. Proc.*, 2nd ser., ix (1978), pp 23–31.

Eiffe, June. Lyons, Co. Kildare. In *Ir. Georgian Soc. Bull.*, xxvii (1984), pp 1–37.

Evans, David, and Patton, Marcus. *The diamond as big as a square: an introduction to the towns and buildings of Ulster*. Belfast, 1981. (Ulster Architectural Heritage Society.)

Fenlon, Jane; Figgis, Nicola; and Marshall, Catherine (ed.). *New perspectives: studies in art history in honour of Anne Crookshank*. Blackrock, 1987.

Forbes, J. D. *Victorian architect: the life and work of William Tinsley*. Bloomington, Ind., 1953.

Francis, Peter. Franz Tieze (1842–1932) and the reinvention of history on glass. In *Burlington Magazine*, cxxxvi, no. 1094 (May 1994), pp 291–302.

See also letters, ibid., no. 1098 (Sept. 1994), pp 621–2.

Gailey, Alan. *Rural houses of the north of Ireland*. Edinburgh, 1984.

Galloway, Peter. *The cathedrals of Ireland*. Belfast, 1992.

Garner, William. *Bray: architectural heritage*. Dublin, 1980.

Gilmartin, John. Peter Turnerelli, sculptor, 1774–1839. In *Ir. Georgian Soc. Bull.*, x, no. 4 (Oct.–Dec. 1967), pp 1–19.

Graby, John (ed.). *150 years of architecture in Ireland: R.I.A.I. 1839–1989*. Dublin, 1989.

Gregory, Augusta. *Hugh Lane's life and achievements*. London, 1921.

Guinness, Desmond. *The Irish house*. Dublin, 1975.

—— *Georgian Dublin*. London, 1979.

—— and Ryan, William. *Irish houses and castles*. London, 1971.

Harbison, Peter; Potterton, Homan; and Sheehy, Jeanne. *Irish art and architecture from prehistory to the present*. London, 1978.
    Extensive bibliography.

Heleniak, K. M. *William Mulready*. New Haven, Conn., and London, 1980. (Studies in British Art.)

Hussey, M. O. A century of Dublin portrait painters, 1750–1850. In *Dublin Hist. Rec.*, xvii, no. 4 (1963), pp 101–21.

—— Nathaniel and all the Hones. In *Dublin Hist. Rec.*, xxiii, no. 2/3 (Dec. 1969), pp 72–85.

Hutchinson, John. *James Arthur O'Connor*. Dublin, 1985.

Jeffery, Keith. Irish artists and the first world war. In *History Ireland*, i, no. 2 (summer 1993), pp 42–6.

Johnston, Roy. *Roderic O'Conor*. London, 1985.

Jones, Barbara. *Follies and grottoes*. London, 1974.

Kennedy, Brian P., and Gillespie, Raymond (ed.). *Ireland: art into history*. Dublin, 1994.

Larmour, Paul. *The arts and crafts movement in Ireland*. Belfast, 1992.

Lavery, John. *The life of a painter*. London, 1940.

Longfield, Ada. Old wallpapers in Ireland. In *Ir. Georgian Soc. Bull.*, x, no. 1 (Jan.–Mar. 1967), pp 1–25.

Lyons, Mary Cecelia. *Illustrated incumbered estates: Ireland, 1850–1905*. Whitegate, Co. Clare, 1993.

McConkey, Kenneth. *A free spirit: Irish art, 1860–1960*. London, 1990.

McCullough, Niall, and Mulvin, Valerie. *A lost tradition: the nature of architecture in Ireland*. Dublin, 1987.

McParland, Edward. Francis Johnston, architect, 1760–1829. In *Ir. Georgian Soc. Bull.*, xii, nos 3 and 4 (July–Dec. 1969), pp 61–139.

—— The wide streets commissioners: their importance for Dublin architecture in the late 18th–early 19th century. In *Ir. Georgian Soc. Bull.*, xv, no. 1 (Jan.–Mar. 1972), pp 1–32.

—— Sir Richard Morrison's country houses, I: the smaller villas. In *Country Life*, cliii (24 May 1973), pp 1462–6.

—— Building in the grand manner: Sir Richard Morrison's country houses, II. In *Country Life*, cliii (31 May 1973), pp 1538–41.

—— *The buildings of Trinity College, Dublin*. London, 1978. Reprinted from *Country Life*, clix (1976), pp 1166–9, 1242–5, 1310–13.

—— *James Gandon, Vitruvius Hibernicus*. London, 1985. Photographs by David Davison.

Malins, Edward, and Bowe, Patrick. *Irish gardens and demesnes from 1830*. London, 1980.

Moore, D. F. The Royal Hibernian Academy. In *Dublin Hist. Rec.*, xxi, no. 1 (Mar.–May 1966), pp 28–37.

National Gallery of Ireland [Ryan-Smolin, Wanda; Mayes, Elizabeth; and Rogers, Jenni (ed.)]. *Irish women artists*. Dublin, 1987.

O'Connor, Ciaran, and O'Regan, John (ed.). *Public works: the architecture of the office of public works, 1831–1987*. Dublin, 1987.

Includes Frederick O'Dwyer on board of public works, 1831–1923.

O'Doherty, Brian. Paul Henry, the early years. In *University Rev.*, ii, no. 7 (1960), pp 25–32.

O'Dwyer, Frederick. *Lost Dublin.* Dublin, 1981.
Chapter on unexecuted works, 'Unbuilt Dublin'.

—— and Williams, Jeremy. Benjamin Woodward. In Tom Kennedy (ed.), *Victorian Dublin* (Dublin, 1980), pp 38–63.

O'Grady, J. M. Sarah Purser, 1848–1943. In *Capuchin Annual*, xliv (1977), pp 89–104.

Pointon, Marcia. *Mulready.* London, 1986.

Popplewell, S. P. Domestic decorative painting in Ireland, 1720 to 1820. In *Studies*, lxviii (spring–summer 1979), pp 46–65.

Potterton, Homan. *The O'Connell monument.* Ballycotton, Co. Cork, 1973.

—— *Andrew O'Connor.* Ballycotton, Co. Cork, 1974.

—— *Irish church monuments, 1570–1880.* Belfast, 1975.

Pressly, W. L. *The life and art of James Barry (1741–1806).* New Haven, Conn., and London, 1981.

Pyle, Hilary. *Estella Solomons: portraits of patriots.* Dublin, 1966.

Purcell, Mary. *Dublin's pro-cathedral.* Dublin, 1975.

Raftery, Patrick. The last of the traditionalists: Patrick Byrne, 1783–1864. In *Ir. Georgian Soc. Bull.*, vii, nos 2–4 (Apr.–Dec. 1964), pp 48–67.

Richardson, D. S. *Gothic revival architecture in Ireland.* 2 vols. New York and London, 1983.

Rothery, Sean. Parnell monument: Ireland and American beaux arts. In *Irish Arts Review*, iv, no. 1 (spring 1987), pp 55–7.
Discusses collaboration between Augustus St Gaudens and Henry Bacon on the design.

Rowan, Alistair, *North-west Ulster: the counties of Londonderry, Donegal, Fermanagh, and Tyrone.* Harmondsworth, 1979. (The Buildings of Ireland.)

Rowan, Ann M. (ed.). *The architecture of Richard Morrison (1767–1849), and William Vitruvius Morrison (1794–1838).* Dublin, 1989.

Rynne, Etienne. The revival of Irish art in the nineteenth and early twentieth century. In *Topic*, no. 24 (1972), pp 29–36.

Shaffrey, Patrick, and Shaffrey, Maura. *Buildings of Irish towns: treasures of everyday architecture.* Dublin, 1983; London and Springfield, Ill., 1984.

—— and —— *Irish countryside buildings: everyday architecture in the rural landscape.* [Companion volume to *Buildings of Irish towns*.] Dublin, 1985.

Sheehy, Jeanne. *Kingsbridge Station.* Ballycotton, Co. Cork, 1973.

—— *Walter Osborne.* Ballycotton, Co. Cork, 1974.

—— Railway architecture: its heyday. In *Ir. Railways Rec. Soc. Jn.*, xii, no. 68 (Oct. 1975), pp 125–38.

—— *J. J. McCarthy and the Gothic revival in Ireland.* Belfast, 1977. (Ulster Architectural Heritage Society.)

—— *The rediscovery of Ireland's past: the Celtic revival, 1830–1930.* London, 1980.
Photographs by George Mott.

Snoddy, Oliver. Augustus Saint Gaudens. In *Capuchin Annual*, xxxviii (1971), pp 197–208.

Stratton-Ryan, Mary. Augustus Nicholas Burke, R.H.A., 1838–1891. In *Irish Arts Review Yearbook* (1990–91), pp 103–10.

Turpin, John. Daniel Maclise and his place in Victorian art. In *Anglo-Irish Studies*, i (1975), pp 51–69.

—— Exhibitions of art and industries in Victorian Ireland, pt I: the Irish arts and industries exhibition movement, 1834–1864; pt II, Dublin exhibitions of art and industries, 1865–1885. In *Dublin Hist. Rec.*, xxxv, no. 1 (Dec. 1981), pp 2–13; no 2 (Mar. 1982), pp 42–51.

—— Ireland's progress: the Dublin exhibition of 1907. In *Éire-Ireland*, xvii, no. 1 (spring 1982), pp 31–8.

—— *John Hogan, Irish neo-classical sculptor in Rome, 1800–1858*. Blackrock, 1982.

—— The Royal Dublin Society and its School of Art, 1849–1877. In *Dublin Hist. Rec.*, xxxvi, no. 1 (Dec. 1982), pp 2–20.

—— The South Kensington system and the Dublin Metropolitan School of Art, 1877–1900. In *Dublin Hist. Rec.*, xxxvi, no. 2 (Mar. 1983), pp 42–64.

—— The Dublin Society and the beginnings of sculptural education in Ireland, 1750–1850. In *Éire-Ireland* xxiv, no. 1 (spring 1989), pp 40–58.

—— Irish history painting. In *Irish Arts Review Yearbook* (1989–90), pp 233–47.

Wedgwood, Alexandra. *The Pugin family*. Farnborough, 1977. (Catalogue of the Drawings: Collection of the Royal Institute of British Architects.)

—— *A. W. N. Pugin and the Pugin family*. London, 1985.

Wheeler, H. A., and Craig, M. J. *The Dublin city churches of the Church of Ireland*. Dublin, 1948.

White, James, and Wynne, Michael. *Irish stained glass*. Dublin, 1977.

Williams, Jeremy. *A companion guide to architecture in Ireland, 1837–1921*. With a foreword by Mark Girouard. Blackrock, 1994.

Wilson, J. C. *Conor, 1881–1968: the life and work of an Ulster artist, with a critical appreciation by John Hewitt*. Belfast, 1981.

16 HISTORY OF MUSIC AND THEATRE

Boydell, Brian (ed.). *Four centuries of music in Ireland: essays based on a series of programmes broadcast to mark the 50th anniversary of the B.B.C. in Northern Ireland*. London, 1980.

Breathnach, Brendan. *Folk music and dances of Ireland*. Dublin, 1971.

—— Francis O'Neill: collector of Irish music. In *Dal gCais*, iii (1977), pp 111–19.

Bruford, Alan. *The complete Irish street ballads*. 2 vols. London, 1984.

Butler, Hubert. The Kilkenny theatre, 1801–1819. In *Butler Soc. Jn.*, ii (1981), pp 32–44.

Calder, Grace J. *George Petrie and the 'Ancient music of Ireland'*. Dublin, 1968.

Coxhead, Elizabeth. *J. M. Synge and Lady Gregory*. London, 1962.

De Valera, Terry. Philip Cogan (1750–1833), pianist and composer. In *Dublin Hist. Rec.*, xxxix, no. 1 (1985), pp 2–12.

Diskin, Patrick. Moore's Irish melodies. In *University Rev.*, ii, no. 8 (1960), pp 34–40.

Downer, A. S. *The eminent tragedian William Charles Macready*. Cambridge, Mass., 1966.

Duggan, G. C. *The stage Irishman: a history of the Irish play and stage characters from the earliest times*. Dublin, 1937.

Ellis-Fermor, Una. *The Irish dramatic movement*. London, 1939; 2nd ed., 1954; paperback ed., 1967.

Faoilain, Turlough. *'Blood on the harp': Irish rebel history in ballad*. Troy, N.Y., 1983.

Fay, Gerard. *The Abbey theatre: cradle of genius*. London, 1958.

Fitzsimon, Christopher. *The Irish theatre*. New York, 1983.

Flannery, J. W. *W. B. Yeats and the idea of a theatre: the early Abbey Theatre in theory and practice*. New Haven, Conn., and London, 1976.
—— *Miss Annie F. Horniman and the Abbey Theatre*. Dublin, 1970; repr., 1976. (Irish Theatre Series, 3.)
Fleischmann, Aloys (ed.). *Music in Ireland: a symposium*. Cork, 1952.
Gailey, Alan. *Irish folk drama*. Cork, 1969.
Gillen, Gerard, and White, Harry (ed.). *Musicology in Ireland*. Dublin, 1990.
Greaves, C. D. *The Easter rising in song and ballad*. London, 1980.
Gregory, Augusta. *Our Irish theatre*. London and New York, 1913; Gerrards Cross, 1972.
    Reprint with introduction by Daniel J. Murphy, New York, 1965.
Grindle, Harry. *Irish cathedral music: a history of music at the cathedrals of the Church of Ireland*. Belfast, 1989.
Healy, J. N. (ed.). *Irish ballads and songs of the sea*. Cork, 1967.
—— *The Mercier book of old Irish street ballads*. 3 vols. Cork, 1967.
Hogan, I. M. *Anglo-Irish music, 1780–1830*. Cork, 1966.
Hogan, R. G. *After the Irish renaissance: a critical history of Irish drama since 'The plough and the stars'*. Minneapolis, 1967.
—— *Dion Boucicault*. New York, 1969.
—— and others. *The modern Irish drama: a documentary history. I The Irish literary theatre, 1899–1901; II Laying the foundations, 1902–1904; III The Abbey Theatre: the years of Synge, 1905–9; IV The rise of the realists, 1910–15; V The art of the amateur, 1916–1920*. Dublin and Atlantic Highlands, N.J., 1975–9; Portlaoise and Atlantic Highlands, 1984. (Irish Theatre Series, 6–8, 10, 12.)
    Co-authors: I–III, James Kilroy; IV, Richard Burnham and Daniel P. Poteet; V, Richard Burnham.
Hunt, Hugh. *The Abbey: Ireland's national theatre, 1904–78*. Dublin, 1979.
Jordan, H. H. Thomas Moore: artistry in the song lyric. In *Studies in English literature*, ii (1962), pp 403–40.
Kavanagh, Peter. *The story of the Abbey Theatre*. New York, 1950.
Kelly, Máire. John Field. In *Studies*, xxxiii (Dec. 1944), pp 516–26.
Kilroy, James. *The 'Playboy' riots*. Dublin, 1971.
King, M. C. *The drama of J. M. Synge*. Syracuse, N.Y., 1985.
Krause, David. *Sean O'Casey: the man and his work*. Rev. and enlarged ed., New York, 1975.
—— *Sean O'Casey and his world*. London and New York, 1976.
McClelland, Aiken. The Irish harp society. In *Ulster Folklife*, xxi (1975), pp 15–24.
Mac Líammóir, Micheál. *Theatre in Ireland*. Dublin, 1964.
Macnamara, Brinsley. *Abbey plays, 1899–1948, including the productions of the Irish literary theatre*. Dublin, 1949.
Malone, A. E. *The Irish drama*. London, 1929; repr., New York, 1965.
Maxwell, D. E. S. *A critical history of modern Irish drama, 1891–1980*. Cambridge and New York, 1984.
Meeks, L. H. *Sheridan Knowles and the theatre of his time*. Bloomington, Ind., 1933.
Nelson, J. M. From Rory and Paddy to Boucicault's Myles, Shaun, and Conn: the Irishman on the London stage, 1830–60. In *Éire-Ireland*, xiii, no. 3 (fall 1978), pp 79–105.
Ní Chinnéide, Veronica. The sources of Moore's melodies. In *R.S.A.I. Jn.*, lxxxviii (1958), pp 109–34.

O'Driscoll, Robert (ed.). *Theatre and nationalism in twentieth century Ireland*. London, 1971.
—— and Reynolds, Lorna (ed.). *Yeats and the theatre*. London, 1975.
Ó Madagáin, Breandán. Functions of Irish song in the nineteenth century. In *Béaloideas*, liii (1985), pp 130–216.
O'Sullivan, Donal (ed.). *Irish folk music, song, and dance*. Dublin, 1952; rev. repr., 1961, 1969.
—— *Songs of the Irish: an anthology of Irish music and poetry with English verse translations*. Dublin, 1959.
    Biographical and historical notes.
Quane, Michael. The Royal Irish Academy of Music. In *Dublin Hist. Rec.*, xx, no. 2 (Mar. 1965), pp 42–56.
Robinson, Lennox. *Ireland's Abbey Theatre: a history, 1899–1951*. London, 1951.
Saddlemyer, Ann. *In defence of Lady Gregory, playwright*. Dublin, 1966.
Setterquist, Jan. *Ibsen and the beginnings of Anglo-Irish drama: I John Millington Synge; II Edward Martyn*. New York, 1974. (Uppsala Irish Studies.)
Skelton, Robin. *J. M. Synge and his world*. New York, 1971.
—— and Saddlemyer, Ann (ed.). *The world of William Butler Yeats: essays in perspective on the occasion of the W. B. Yeats centenary festival . . .* Dublin, 1965.
Stevenson, P. J. The Antient Concert Rooms. In *Dublin Hist. Rec.*, v, no. 1 (Sept.–Nov. 1942), pp 1–14.
Tessier, Thérèse. *The bard of Erin: a study of Thomas Moore's Irish melodies, 1808–1834*. Dover, N. H., 1981. (Salzburg Studies.)
Thornton, Weldon. *J. M. Synge and the western mind*. New York, 1979.
Watt, S. M. Boucicault and Whitbread: the Dublin stage at the end of the nineteenth century. In *Éire-Ireland*, xviii, no. 3 (fall 1983), pp 23–53.
White, Harry. Music and the perception of music in Ireland. In *Studies*, lxxix, no. 313 (spring 1990), pp 38–44.
Wright, R. L. *Irish emigrant ballads and songs*. Bowling Green, Ohio, 1975.
Zimmermann, Georges-Denis. *Songs of Irish rebellion: political street ballads and rebel songs, 1780–1900*. Dublin, 1967. First published as *Irish political street ballads and rebel songs*. Geneva, 1966.

17 HISTORIOGRAPHY

Archer, J. R. Necessary ambiguity: nationalism and myth in Ireland. In *Éire-Ireland*, xix, no. 2 (summer 1984), pp 23–37.
Beckett, J. C. *The study of Irish history*. Belfast, 1963.
    See also Beckett, *Confrontations*, pp 11–25.
—— Ireland under the union. In J. C. Beckett, *Confrontations: studies in Irish history* (London, 1972), pp 142–51.
    Originally published in *Topic*, xiii (1967), pp 34–44.
Boyce, D. G. Brahmins and carnivores: the Irish historian in Great Britain. In *I.H.S.*, xxv, no. 99 (May 1987), pp 225–35.
Bradshaw, Brendan. Nationalism and historical scholarship in modern Ireland. In *I.H.S.*, xxvi, no. 104 (Nov. 1989), pp 329–51.
Brady, Ciaran (ed.). *Ideology and the historians*. Dublin, 1991. (*Hist. Studies*, xvii.)
Canny, N. P. Fusion and faction in modern Ireland: a review article. In *Comparative Studies in Society and History*, xxvi, no. 2 (1984), pp 352–65.

Clarke, Aidan. Robert Dudley Edwards (1909–1988). In *I.H.S.*, xxvi, no. 102 (Nov. 1988), pp 121–7.

Corish, P. J. Irish ecclesiastical history since 1500. In Lee, *Ir. histor. 1970–79*, pp 154–72.

Cosgrove, R. A. The relevance of Irish history: the Gladstone–Dicey debate about home rule, 1886–7. In *Éire-Ireland*, xiii, no. 4 (winter 1978), pp 6–21.

Cullen, L. M. The reinterpretation of Irish economic history. In *Topic*, xiii (1967), pp 68–77.

Curtis, L. P., jr. Editorial introduction to W. E. H. Lecky, *A history of Ireland in the eighteenth century* (new abridged ed., Chicago and London, 1972).

—— On class and class conflict in the land war. [Review article.] In *Ir. Econ. & Soc. Hist.*, viii (1981), pp 86–94.

—— Ireland since 1500. In Richard Schlatter (ed.), *Recent views on British history* (New Brunswick, 1984), pp 401–49.

Donnelly, James S., jr. The great famine: its interpreters, old and new. In *History Ireland*, i, no. 3 (autumn 1993), pp 27–33.

Dunne, Tom. Haunted by history: Irish romantic writing, 1800–1850. In Roy Porter and Mikulas Teich (ed.), *Romanticism in national context* (Cambridge, 1988), pp 68–91.

Edwards, R. D. The fall of Parnell, 1890–91: seventy years after. In *Studia Hib.*, i (1961), pp 199–210.

   Essay on F. S. L. Lyons, *The fall of Parnell* (1960).

—— An agenda for Irish history, 1978–2018. In *I.H.S.*, xxi, no. 81 (Mar. 1978), pp 3–19.

Ellis, Stephen G. Historiographical debate: representations of the past in Ireland: whose past and whose present? In *I.H.S.*, xxvii, no. 108 (Nov. 1991), pp 289–308.

Finnegan, Francis. Maurice Lenihan, historian of Limerick. In *Studies*, xxxv (1946), pp 407–14; xxxvi (1947), pp 97–104, 358–65; xxxvii (1948), pp 91–6.

Fitzpatrick, David. Recent writing on Irish nationalism. In *Hermathena*, cxxxii (summer 1982), pp 47–52.

—— Unrest in rural Ireland: review essay. In *Ir. Econ. & Soc. Hist.*, xii (1985), pp 98–105.

—— Was Ireland special? Recent writing on the Irish economy and society in the nineteenth century. In *Hist. Jn.*, xxxiii, no. 1 (1990), pp 169–76.

—— Women, gender and the writing of Irish history. In *I.H.S.*, xxvii, no. 107 (May 1991), pp 267–73.

Foster, John. Completing the first task: Irish labour in the nineteenth century. [Review article.] In *Saothar*, xv (1990), pp 65–9.

Foster, R. F. History and the Irish question. In *R. Hist. Soc. Trans.*, 5th ser., xxxiii (1983), pp 169–92.

—— *Francis Stewart Leland Lyons, 1923–1983*. London, 1986.

—— 'We are all revisionists now'. In *Irish Review*, i (1986), pp 1–5.

Hayes-McCoy, G. A. Twenty-five years of Irish military history. In *Ir. Sword*, xii (1975–6), pp 90–97.

Hill, Jacqueline. Popery and protestantism, civil and religious liberty: the disputed lessons of Irish history, 1690–1812. In *Past & Present*, no. 118 (Feb. 1988), pp 96–129.

Hughes, E. W. Remembering Patrick O'Leary, 1856–1931. In *Old Kilkenny Rev.*, new ser., ii (1983), pp 475–93.

Inglis, K. S. Catholic historiography in Australia. In *Historical Studies*, viii, no. 31 (Nov. 1958), pp 233–53.

Kelleher, J. V. Matthew Arnold and the Celtic revival. In H. Levin (ed.), *Perspectives of criticism* (Cambridge, Mass., 1950), pp 197–221.

Kinzer, B. L. J. S. Mill and Irish land: a reassessment. In *Hist. Jn.*, xxvii, no. 1 (1984), pp 111–27.

Laffan, Michael. Insular attitudes: the revisionists and their critics. In Máirín Ní Dhonnchadha and Theo Dorgan (ed.), *Revising the rising* (Derry, 1991), pp 106–21.

Lebow, R. N. *John Stuart Mill on Ireland*. Philadelphia, 1979.

Lee, J. J. Some aspects of modern Irish historiography. In Ernst Schulin (ed.), *Gedenkschrift Martin Guhring: studien zur Europäischen geschichte* (Wiesbaden, 1968), pp 431–43.

—— Irish economic history since 1500. In Lee, *Ir. histor., 1970–79*, pp 173–224.

—— (ed.). *Irish historiography, 1970–79*. Cork, 1981.

Lyons, F. S. L. The dilemma of the Irish contemporary historian. In *Hermathena*, cxv (summer 1973), pp 45–56.

—— *The burden of our history*. Belfast, 1979. (W. B. Rankin Memorial Lecture.)

McCartney, Donal. The writing of history in Ireland, 1800–30. In *I.H.S.*, x, no. 40 (Sept. 1957), pp 347–62.

—— Lecky's *Leaders of public opinion in Ireland*. In *I.H.S.*, xiv, no. 54 (Sept. 1964), pp 119–41.

—— James Anthony Froude and Ireland: a historiographical controversy of the nineteenth century. In *Hist. Studies*, viii (1971), pp 171–90.

—— The political use of history in the work of Arthur Griffith. In *Journal of Contemporary History*, viii, no. 1 (1973), pp 3–19.

—— *Democracy and its nineteenth-century Irish critics*. Dublin, 1979. (O'Donnell Lecture.)

—— *W. E. H. Lecky, historian and politician, 1838–1903*. Dublin, 1994.

MacDonagh, Oliver. *States of mind: a study of Anglo-Irish conflict, 1780–1980*. London, 1985.

MacGrath, Kevin. Writers in the *Nation*, 1842–5. In *I.H.S.*, vi, no. 23 (Mar. 1949), pp 189–223.

Martin, F. X. The Thomas Davis lectures, 1953–67. In *I.H.S.*, xv, no. 59 (Mar. 1967), pp 276–302.

—— 1916: myth, fact, and mystery. In *Studia Hib.*, vii (1967), pp 7–126.

—— The 1916 rising: a coup d'état or a 'bloody protest'? In *Studia Hib.*, viii (1968), pp 106–37.

Miller, David. Irish catholicism and the historian. In *Ir. Econ. & Soc. Hist.*, xiii (1986), pp 113–16.

Mokyr, Joel. Malthusian models and Irish history. In *Jn. Econ. Hist.*, xl, no. 1 (Mar. 1980), pp 159–66.

—— Three centuries of population change. [Review article.] In *Economic Development and Cultural Change*, xxxii, no. 1 (Oct. 1983), pp 183–92.

—— and Ó Gráda, Cormac. New developments in Irish population history, 1700–1850. In *Econ. Hist. Rev.*, xxxvii, no. 4 (Nov. 1984), pp 473–88.

Moody, T. W. The writings of Edmund Curtis. In *I.H.S.*, iii, no. 12 (Sept. 1943), pp 393–400.

—— Edmund Curtis, 1881–1943. In *Hermathena*, lxiii (May 1944), pp 69–78.

—— (ed.). *Irish historiography, 1936–70*. Dublin, 1971.

—— Irish history and Irish mythology. In *Hermathena*, cxxiv (summer 1978), pp 7–24.

Mulvey, H. F. The historian Lecky: opponent of Irish home rule. In *Victorian Studies*, i, no. 4 (June 1958), pp 337–51.

—— Modern Irish history since 1940: a bibliographical survey (1600–1922). In E. C. Furber (ed.), *Changing views in British history* (Cambridge, Mass., 1966), pp 345–78.

—— Nineteenth-century Ireland, 1801–1914. Twentieth-century Ireland, 1914–1970. In Moody, *Ir. histor.*, *1936–70*, pp 71–136.

    For an earlier version see *I.H.S.*, xvii, no. 65 (Mar. 1970), pp 1–31; no. 66 (Sept. 1970), pp 151–84.

—— Theodore William Moody: an appreciation. In *I.H.S.*, xxiv, no. 94 (Nov. 1984), pp 121–30.

Murtagh, Harman. The historical writings of G. A. Hayes-McCoy. In *Ir. Sword*, xii (1975–6), pp 83–9.

Nowlan, Kevin. Writings in connection with the Thomas Davis and Young Ireland centenary, 1945. In *I.H.S.*, v, no. 19 (Mar. 1947), pp 265–72.

Ó Broin, Leon. R. R. Madden: doctor, historian, and public servant. In *Ir. Jn. Med. Sc.*, 6th ser., no. 391 (1958), pp 315–26.

O'Callaghan, Margaret. Irish history, 1780–1980. [Review article.] In *Hist. Jn.* xxix, no. 2 (1986), pp 481–98.

O'Farrell, Patrick. Whose reality? The Irish famine in history and literature. In *Historical Studies*, xx, no. 78 (Apr. 1982), pp 1–13.

Ó Gráda, Cormac. *'For Irishmen to forget?': recent research on the great Irish famine*. Dublin, 1988.

Ó Tuathaigh, M. A. G. Ireland, 1800–1921. In Lee, *Ir. histor.*, *1970–79*, pp 85–131.

Palmer, N. D. Sir Robert Peel's 'Select Irish library'. In *I.H.S.*, vi, no. 22 (Sept. 1948), pp 101–13.

Phelan, M. M. Rev. James Graves (1816–1886). In *Old Kilkenny Rev.*, 2nd ser., iii, no. 3 (1986), pp 267–76.

    Founder of Kilkenny Archaeological Society.

Phillips, Walter. Australian catholic historiography: some recent issues. In *Historical Studies*, xiv, no. 56 (Apr. 1971), pp 600–11.

Reaney, B. Historians and nineteenth-century Irish working-class history. In *Ruskin History Workshop*, xiii (1979), pp 10–19.

Schlatter, Richard (ed.). *Recent views on British history: essays on historical writing since 1966*. New Brunswick, N.J., 1984. (Conference on British Studies.)

    Chapter on Ireland by L. P. Curtis, jr.

Shaw, Francis. The canon of Irish history: a challenge. In *Studies*, lxi (summer 1972), pp 113–53.

Silke, J. J. The Roman Catholic church in Ireland, 1800–1922: a survey of recent historiography. In *Studia Hib.*, xv (1975), pp 61–104.

Swift, Roger. The outcast Irish in the British Victorian city: problems and perspectives. In *I.H.S.*, xxv, no. 99 (May 1987), pp 264–76.

Tierney, Mark. Eugene O'Curry and the Irish tradition. In *Studies*, li (winter 1962), pp 449–62.

Townshend, Charles. Modernisation and nationalism: perspectives in recent Irish history. In *History*, lxvi, no. 217 (June 1981), pp 233–43.

Varley, Tony. The primacy of the political? State, class, and the dynamics of change in Ireland. [Review essay.] In *Saothar*, xv (1990), pp 70–75.

Walsh, Katherine. The opening of the Vatican archives (1880–81) and Irish historical research. In *Archiv. Hib.*, xxxvi (1981), pp 34–43.

Whyte, J. H. Whitehall, Belfast, and Dublin: new light on the treaty and the border. In *Studies*, lx (autumn–winter 1971), pp 233–42.

Williams, Martin. Ancient mythology and revolutionary ideology in Ireland, 1878–1916.
    In *Hist. Jn.*, xxvi, no. 2 (1983), pp 307–28.
Wyatt, Anne. Froude, Lecky, and 'the humblest Irishman'. In *I.H.S.*, xix, no. 75 (Mar.
    1975), pp 261–85.

18 HISTORY OF PRINTING AND PUBLISHING

Adams, J. R. R. *The printed word and the common man: popular culture in Ulster, 1700–1900.*
    Belfast, 1987.
Aspinall, Arthur. *Politics and the press, 1780–1850.* London, 1949.
Benson, Charles. Printers and booksellers in Dublin, 1800–1850. In Robin Myers and
    Michael Harris (ed.), *Spreading the word: the distribution networks of print, 1550–1850*
    (Detroit, 1990), pp 47–59.
Bowen, B. P. Dublin humorous periodicals of the 19th century. In *Dublin Hist. Rec.*, xiii,
    no. 1 (Mar.–May 1952), pp 2–11.
Brown, Lucy. The treatment of the news in mid-Victorian newspapers. In *R. Hist. Soc.*
    Trans., 5th ser., xxvii (1977), pp 23–39.
Callan, Patrick. D. P. Moran, founder editor of *The Leader*. In *Capuchin Annual*, xliv
    (1977), pp 274–87.
Campbell, A. A. *Belfast newspapers past and present.* Belfast, 1921.
Clifford, Brendan (ed.). *Reprints from the Cork Free Press.* Belfast and Cork, 1984.
Cullen, L. M. *Eason and son: a history.* Dublin, 1989.
Davis, Richard. Ulster protestants and the Sinn Féin press, 1914–22. In *Éire-Ireland*, xv,
    no. 4 (winter 1980), pp 60–85.
Dickson, David. Historical journals in Ireland: the last hundred years. In Barbara Hayley
    and Enda McKay (ed.), *Three hundred years of Irish periodicals* (Dublin and Gigginstown,
    1987), pp 87–103.
Earls, Maurice. The Dublin penny press, 1830–50. In *Long Room*, no. 32 (1987), pp 7–26.
Edwards, O. D., and Storey, P. J. The Irish press in Victorian Britain. In Roger Swift and
    Sheridan Gilley (ed.), *The Irish in the Victorian city* (London, 1985), pp 158–78.
Epstein, J. A. Feargus O'Connor and the *Northern Star*. In *International Review of Social*
    History, xxi (1976), pp 51–97.
Glandon, Virginia. *Arthur Griffith and the advanced nationalist press, Ireland, 1900–1922.*
    New York, 1985. (American University Studies, 9th ser.: History, 2.)
Gray, Peter. *Punch* and the great famine. In *History Ireland*, i, no. 2 (summer 1993), pp 26–34.
Hall, Wayne. The first year of the *Dublin University Magazine*. In *Éire-Ireland*, xxii, no. 4
    (winter 1987), pp 26–35.
Hammond, J. W. The *Dublin Gazette*, 1705–1922. In *Dublin Hist. Rec.*, xiii, nos 3 and 4
    (1953), pp 108–17.
Hayley, Barbara. Irish periodicals from the union to the *Nation*. In *Anglo-Irish Studies*, ii
    (1976), pp 83–108.
——'A reading and thinking nation': periodicals as the voice of nineteenth-century
    Ireland. In Barbara Hayley and Enda McKay (ed.), *Three hundred years of Irish periodicals*
    (Dublin and Gigginstown, 1987), pp 29–48.
——and McKay, Enda (ed.). *Three hundred years of Irish periodicals.* Dublin and
    Gigginstown, Co. Westmeath, 1987.
Herbert, Robert. *Limerick printers and printing. Part one of the local collection in the city of*
    Limerick public library. Limerick, 1942.

Inglis, Brian. *The freedom of the press in Ireland, 1784–1841*. London, 1954.

—— The press. In R. B. McDowell (ed.), *Social life in Ireland, 1800–45* (Dublin, 1957), pp 98–111.

Irish Independent. *Golden jubilee edition: the story of fifty years, 1905–55*. Dublin, 1955.

Kain, R. M. Irish periodical literature, an untilled field. In *Éire-Ireland*, vii, no. 3 (fall 1972), pp 93–9.

Kennedy, Brian. Seventy-five years of *Studies*. In *Studies*, lxxv, no. 300 (winter 1986), pp 361–73.

Kinane, Vincent. *A history of the Dublin University Press, 1734–1976*. Dublin, 1994.

Loh, Gerhard. *Irland in der Berichterstaltung deutscher Tageszeitungen, 1914–18*. 2 vols. Frankfurt, 1987.

McCabe, Bryan. *From Linenhall to Loopbridge: the story of McCaw, Stevenson, & Orr Ltd, printers, 1876–1990*. Antrim, 1990.

McClelland, Aiken. The Ulster press in the eighteenth and nineteenth centuries. In *Ulster Folklife*, xx (1974), pp 89–99.

McDowell, R. B. The Irish government and the provincial press. In *Hermathena*, liii (May 1939), pp 138–47.

McKay, Enda. A century of Irish trade journals, 1860–1960. In Barbara Hayley and Enda McKay (ed.), *Three hundred years of Irish periodicals* (Dublin and Gigginstown, 1987), pp 103–22.

MacLaughlin, P. J. Dr Russell and the *Dublin Review*. In *Studies*, xli (June 1952), pp 175–88.

Millar, Liam. The Dun Emer Press. In *The Irish Book*, ii (1963), pp 43–52.

Murphy, Sean. Women and *The Nation*. In *History Ireland*, i, no. 3 (autumn 1993), pp 34–8.

Ó Casaide, Séamus. Clonmel printing, 1826–1900. In *I.B.L.*, xxv, nos 4–6 (July–Dec. 1937), pp 90–98.

O'Neill, Thomas P. Notes on Irish radical journals. In *An Leabharlann*, xii, no. 4 (Dec. 1954), pp 139–44.

Ó Suilleabháin, Pádraig. Catholic books printed in Ireland, 1740–1820, containing lists of subscribers. In *Collect. Hib.*, vi (1964), pp 231–3.

Sadleir, Michael. *The Dublin University Magazine: its history, contents, and bibliography*. Dublin, 1938.

Stockwell, La Tourette. The Dublin pirates and the English laws of copyright, 1710–1801. In *Dublin Mag.*, xii, no. 4 (Oct.–Dec. 1937), pp 30–40.

Sullivan, D. J. Standish James O'Grady's *All Ireland Review*. In *Studia Hib.*, ix (1969), pp 125–36.

Wall, Thomas. *The Irish Ecclesiastical Record* and Maynooth. In *I.E.R.*, lxvi (Nov. 1945), pp 322–30.

—— *The sign of Doctor Hay's head: being some account of the hazards and fortunes of catholic printers and publishers in Dublin from the later penal times to the present day*. Dublin, 1958.

—— Catholic periodicals of the past [1834–56]. In *I.E.R.*, ci (Apr., May, June 1964), pp 234–44, 289–303, 375–88; cii (July, Aug., Sept., Oct. 1964), pp 17–27, 86–100, 129–47, 206–24.

Wheeler, W. G. The spread of provincial printing in Ireland up to 1850. In *Irish Booklore*, iv (1978), pp 7–19.

Williams, H. H. *Book clubs and printing societies of Great Britain and Ireland.* London, 1929; Ann Arbor, Mich., 1971.

Wilson, K. M. Sir John French's resignation over the Curragh affair: the role of the editor of the *Morning Post.* In *E.H.R.,* xcix, no. 393 (Oct. 1984), pp 807–12.

19 BIOGRAPHY

ALEXANDER. *Primate Alexander, archbishop of Armagh, a memoir.* Ed. Eleanor Alexander. London, 1913.

ANDERSON. *John Anderson, entrepreneur.* By Niall Brunicardi. Fermoy, 1987.

ARMOUR. *Armour of Ballymoney.* By W. S. Armour. London, 1934.

ASHE. *I die in a good cause; a study of Thomas Ashe, idealist and revolutionary.* By Seán Ó Luing. Tralee, 1970.

ASQUITH. *Life of Herbert Henry Asquith, Lord Oxford and Asquith.* By J. A. Spender and Cyril Asquith. 2 vols. London, 1932.

——*Asquith.* By Stephen Koss. London and New York, 1976; repr., 1985.

BALFOUR. *Arthur J. Balfour and Ireland, 1874–1922.* By Catherine B. Shannon. Washington, D.C., 1989.

BARRY. *Kevin Barry and his time.* By Donal O'Donovan. Sandycove, Co. Dublin, 1989.

BENNETT. *Louie Bennett: her life and times.* By R. M. Fox. Dublin, 1957.

BERNARD. *Archbishop Bernard: professor, prelate, and provost.* By R. B. Murray. London, 1931.

BIANCONI. *Bianconi, king of the Irish roads.* By M. A. C. O'Connell and S. J. Watson. Dublin, 1962.

BIRRELL. *Things past redress.* By Augustine Birrell. London, 1937.

——*The chief secretary: Augustine Birrell in Ireland.* By Leon Ó Broin. London, 1969.

BLAKE. *Edward Blake, Irish nationalist.* By Margaret Banks. Toronto and Oxford, 1957.

BONAR LAW. *The unknown prime minister. The life and times of Andrew Bonar Law, 1858–1923.* By Robert Blake. London, 1955.

BREEN. *The Dan Breen story.* By Joseph G. Ambrose. Dublin, 1981.

BRENNAN. *Allegiance.* By Robert Brennan. Dublin, 1950.

BRUGHA. *Cathal Brugha.* By Seán Ua Ceallaigh. Dublin, 1942.

——*Cathal Brugha: a shaol is a thréithe.* By Tomás Ó Dochartaigh. Dublin, 1969.

BURKE. *Brother James Dominic Burke: a pioneer of Irish education.* By Daniel V. Kelleher. Dublin, 1988.

BUSHE. *An incorruptible Irishman: being an account of Chief Justice Charles Kendal Bushe and of his wife Nancy Crampton and their times, 1767–1843.* By E. Œ. Somerville and Martin Ross. London, 1932.

BUTT. *The road of excess.* By Terence de Vere White. Dublin, 1946.

——*Isaac Butt and home rule.* By David Thornley. London, 1964.

CARSON. *The life of Lord Carson.* 3 vols. London, 1932–6.

Vol. 1 by Edward Marjoribanks; vols II–III by Ian Colvin.

——*Sir Edward Carson.* By Alvin Jackson. Dundalk, 1993.

CASEMENT. *Roger Casement.* By Brian Inglis. London, 1973.

——*The lives of Roger Casement.* By B. L. Reid. London, 1976.

CHILDERS. *Erskine Childers.* By [Arthur Frederic] Basil Williams. London, 1926.

——*The zeal of the convert: the life of Erskine Childers.* By Burke Wilkinson. Washington, D.C., 1976.

—— *The riddle of Erskine Childers.* By Andrew Boyd. London, 1977.

CHURCHILL, LORD RANDOLPH. *Lord Randolph Churchill: a political life.* By R. F. Foster. Oxford, 1981.

CHURCHILL, WINSTON. *Churchill and Ireland.* By Mary Bromage. Notre Dame, Ind., 1964.

CLARKE. *Tom Clarke and the Irish freedom movement.* By Louis Leroux. Dublin, 1936.

CLARKE. *Revolutionary woman: Kathleen Clarke, 1878–1972, an autobiography.* Ed. Helen Litton. Dublin, 1991.

COLLINS. *Michael Collins and the making of a new Ireland.* By Piaras Beaslai. 2 vols. Dublin, 1926.

—— *Michael Collins.* By Rex Taylor. London, 1958.

—— *Michael Collins: the lost leader.* By Margery Forester. London, 1971; reissue, 1989.

—— *Michael Collins: a biography.* By T. P. Coogan. London, 1990.

Colum, Mary Maguire. *Life and the dream.* London, 1947; rev. ed., Dublin, 1966.

CONNOLLY. *The mind of an activist: James Connolly.* By Owen Dudley Edwards. Dublin, 1971.

—— *James Connolly: a biography.* By Samuel Levenson. London, 1973.

—— *Young Connolly.* By Seán Cronin. Dublin, 1978.

—— *James Connolly: a political biography.* By Austen Morgan. Manchester, 1988.

COOKE. *Henry Cooke.* By Finlay Holmes. Belfast, 1981.

CORRIGAN. *Conscience and conflict: a biography of Sir Dominic Corrigan, 1802–1880.* By Eoin O'Brien. Dublin, 1983.

CRAIGAVON (CRAIG). *Craigavon: Ulsterman.* By St John Ervine. London, 1949.

—— *James Craig.* By Patrick Buckland. Dublin, 1980.

CROKE. *Croke of Cashel: the life of Archbishop Thomas William Croke, 1823–1902.* By Mark Tierney. Dublin, 1976.

CULLEN. *Paul Cullen and his contemporaries: with their letters from 1820 to 1902.* By Peadar Mac Suibhne. 6 vols. Naas, 1961–77.

—— *Paul Cardinal Cullen and the shaping of modern Irish catholicism.* By Desmond Bowen. Dublin and Waterloo, Ont., 1983.

CUSACK. *Margaret Anna Cusack: one woman's campaign for women's rights: a biography.* By Irene Eagar. 2nd ed., Dublin, 1979; preface by Margaret MacCurtain.
First published as *The nun of Kenmare* (Cork, 1970).

CUSACK. *Michael Cusack and the G.A.A.* By Marcus de Burca. Dublin, 1989.

DAVIS. *Thomas Davis: the memoirs of an Irish patriot, 1840–1846.* By Sir Charles Gavan Duffy. London, 1890.

—— *Thomas Davis, 1814–45.* By T. W. Moody. Dublin, 1945.

—— Thomas Davis and the Irish nation. By T. W. Moody. In *Hermathena*, cii (1966), pp 5–31.

DAVITT. *Davitt and Irish revolution, 1846–82.* By T. W. Moody. Oxford, 1981.

DENVIR. *The life story of an old rebel.* By John Denvir. Dublin, 1910; new ed., 1914. Reprint with introduction by Leon Ó Broin, Shannon, 1972.

DELANEY. *Towards a national university: William Delaney, S. J., 1835–1924.* By Thomas Morrissey. Dublin, 1983.

DESPARD. *An unhusbanded life: Charlotte Despard, suffragette, socialist, and Sinn Feiner.* By Andro Linklater. London, 1980.

—— *Charlotte Despard: a biography.* By Margaret Mulvihill. London, 1989.

DE VALERA. *De Valera*. By Tomás Ó Neill and Pádraig Ó Fiannachta. 2 vols. Blackrock, 1968, 1970.
    In Irish; for comparison with the English version (next entry), see J. H. Whyte in *I. H. S.*, xvii, no. 68 (Sept. 1971), pp 593–5.
—— *Eamon de Valera*. By the earl of Longford and Thomas P. O'Neill. London, 1970.
—— *De Valera and the Ulster question, 1917–73*. By John Bowman. Oxford, 1982.
—— *Éamon de Valera*. By Owen Dudley Edwards. Washington, D.C., 1987.
DEVOY. *Recollections of an Irish rebel*. By John Devoy. London, 1929.
—— *John Devoy*. By Seán Ó Luing. Dublin, 1961.
DILLON, JOHN BLAKE. *John Blake Dillon: Young Irelander*. By Brendán Ó Cathaoir. Dublin, 1990.
DILLON, JOHN. *John Dillon: a biography*. By F. S. L. Lyons. London, 1968.
DOHENY. Michael Doheny: Young Irelander and fenian. By Patrick O'Flaherty. In *Ir. Sword*, xvi (1987–8), pp 81–9.
DORRIAN. *Patrick Dorrian, bishop of Down and Connor, 1865–1885*. By Ambrose Macaulay. Blackrock, 1987.
DUFFY, CHARLES GAVAN. Sir Charles Gavan Duffy: Young Irelander and imperial statesman. By Helen F. Mulvey. In *Canadian Historical Review*, xxxiii (1952), pp 369–86.
—— *Charles Gavan Duffy and the repeal movement*. By K. B. Nowlan. Dublin, 1963. (O'Donnell Lecture.)
—— *Charles Gavan Duffy*. By Leon Ó Broin. Dublin, 1967.
—— *My life in two hemispheres*. By Charles Gavan Duffy. 2 vols. New York, 1898. Reprint with introduction by J. H. Whyte, Shannon, 1969.
—— *The three lives of Gavan Duffy*. By Cyril Pearl. Kensington, N. S. W., 1979.
DUFFY, GEORGE GAVAN. *George Gavan Duffy, 1881–1951: a legal biography*. By G. M. Goulding. Dublin, 1982.
EDGEWORTH. *Maria Edgeworth: a literary biography*. By Marilyn Butler. Oxford, 1972.
—— *Maria Edgeworth and the public scene*. By Michael Hurst. London, 1969.
EMMETT. *The unfortunate Mr Robert Emmet*. By Leon Ó Broin. Dublin and London, 1958.
FERGUSON. *Sir Samuel Ferguson: a centenary tribute*. *Ed.* Terence Brown and Barbara Hayley. Dublin, 1988.
FITZGERALD. *Memoirs, 1913–16*. By Desmond Fitzgerald. London, 1968.
FOSTER. *Vere Foster, 1819–1900: an Irish benefactor*. By Mary McNeill. Newton Abbot, 1971.
FRENCH. *Life of Field-marshal Sir John French*. By Gerald French. London, 1931.
FROUDE. *James Anthony Froude: a biography*. By Waldo H. Dunn. 2 vols. Oxford, 1961, 1963. Vol. I, 1818–50; vol. II, 1857–94.
GLADSTONE. *Gladstone and the Irish nation*. By J. L. Hammond. London, 1938; 2nd ed., with new introduction by M. R. D. Foot, Hamden, Conn., 1964.
—— Gladstone and Ireland. By E. D. Steele. In *I. H. S.*, xvii, no. 65 (Mar. 1970), pp 58–88.
—— *Gladstone and Ireland*. By John Vincent. London, 1978.
    (*Proceedings of the British Academy*, lxiii (London, 1977), pp 193–238.)
GOGARTY. *Oliver St John Gogarty: the man of many talents: a biography*. By J. B. Lyons. Dublin, 1980.
GONNE. *Maud Gonne: lucky eyes and a high heart*. By Nancy Cardozo. London, 1978.

—— *Maud Gonne: Ireland's Joan of Arc*. By Margaret Ward. London, 1990. Retitled *Maud Gonne: a life*, 1993.

GOUGH. *Johnnie Gough, V.C.* By Ian F. W. Beckett. London, 1989.

GREEN. *Alice Stopford Green: a passionate historian*. By R. B. McDowell. Dublin, 1967.

GREGORY, LADY. *Lady Gregory: a literary portrait*. By Elizabeth Coxhead. London, 1961.

—— *Seventy years, 1852–1922: being the autobiography of Lady Gregory*. Ed. Colin Smythe. New York, 1974.

—— *Lady Gregory: the woman behind the Irish renaissance*. By Mary Lou Kohfeldt. New York, 1985.

—— *Lady Gregory fifty years after*. Ed. Ann Saddlemyer and Colin Smythe. Gerrards Cross and Totowa, N.J., 1987.

GREGORY, SIR WILLIAM. *Sir William Gregory of Coole*. By Brian Jenkins. Gerrards Cross, 1986.

GRIFFITH, ARTHUR. *Art Ó Griofa*. By Seán Ó Luing. Dublin, 1953.

—— *Arthur Griffith*. By Padraic Colum. Dublin, 1959.

—— *Arthur Griffith*. By Richard Davis. Dublin, 1976. (Dublin Historical Association.)

—— *Arthur Griffith*. By Calton Younger. Dublin, 1981.

GRIFFITH, RICHARD. Sir Richard Griffith—the man and his work. By Mary Olive Hussey. In *Dublin Hist. Rec.*, xx, no. 2 (Mar. 1965), pp 57–75.

—— *Richard Griffith, 1784–1878*. Ed. G. L. Herries Davies and R. C. Mollan. Dublin, 1980.

HAMILTON. *Sir William Rowan Hamilton*. By Thomas L. Hankins. Baltimore and London, 1980.

—— *William Rowan Hamilton: portrait of a prodigy*. By Seán O'Donnell. Dublin, 1984. (Profiles of genius: I.)

HARCOURT. *The life of Sir William Harcourt*. By A. G. Gardiner. 2 vols. London, 1923.

HART. *Hart of Lisburn, Northern Ireland: the story of Sir Robert Hart*. By Stanley Bell. Lisburn, 1985.

HOGAN, DAVID. *The four glorious years*. By David Hogan. Dublin, 1953.

HOGAN, JOHN. *John Hogan: Irish neo-classical sculptor in Rome, 1800–1858: a biography and catalogue raisonné*. By John Turpin. Dublin, 1982.

HOLLAND. *John P. Holland, 1841–1914: inventor of the modern submarine*. By Richard K. Morris. Annapolis, 1966.

HYDE. *The young Douglas Hyde: the dawn of the Irish revolution and renaissance*. By Dominic Daly. Dublin and Totowa, N.J., 1974.

—— *Dubhglas de h-Íde, 1860–1949: a ceannrodaí cultúrtha, 1860–1910*. By Risteárd Ó Glaisne. Dublin, 1990.

—— *Douglas Hyde: a maker of modern Ireland*. By Janet Egleson Dunleavy and Gareth Dunleavy. Berkeley, Calif., 1991.

JOHNSON. Thomas Johnson, 1872–1963, a pioneer labour leader. By Arthur Mitchell. In *Studies*, lviii (winter 1969), pp 396–404.

—— *Thomas Johnson, 1872–1963*. By J. A. Gaughan. Dublin, 1980.

JOYCE. *James Joyce remembered*. By C. P. Curran. London and New York, 1968.

—— *James Joyce*. By Richard Ellman. New York, 1959; rev. ed., 1982.

KANE. *Sir Robert Kane, first president of Queen's College, Cork: a pioneer in science, industry and commerce*. By Deasmumhan Ó Raghallaigh. Cork, 1942.

—— Sir Robert Kane: an apostle of Irish industries. By J. J. Kerr. In *Dublin Hist. Rec.*, v, no. 4 (June–Aug. 1943), pp 137–46.

KANE. Sir Robert Kane: life and work. By T. S. Wheeler. In *Studies*, xxxiii (1944), pp 158–68, 316–30.

—— Sir Robert Kane: first president of Q. C. C. By T. S. Wheeler. In *Cork University Record*, no. 3 (1945), pp 29–38.

—— Sir Robert Kane's soil survey of Ireland: the record of a failure. By R. C. Simington and T. S. Wheeler. In *Studies*, xxxiv, no. 136 (Dec. 1945), pp 539–51.

KETTLE, THOMAS. *The enigma of Tom Kettle: Irish patriot, essayist, poet, British soldier*. By J. B. Lyons. Dublin, 1983.

—— Tom Kettle (1880–1916). By J. B. Lyons. In *Dublin Hist. Rec.*, xliii, no. 2 (1990), pp 85–98.

KICKHAM. *Charles J. Kickham, 1828–82: a study in Irish nationalism and literature*. By R. V. Comerford. Dublin, 1979.

LALOR. *James Fintan Lalor: patriot and political essayist*. Ed. L. Fogarty. Dublin, 1918; rev. ed., Dublin, 1947.

—— *Fiontan Ó Leathlobhair*. By Tomás P. Ó Néill. Dublin, 1962.

—— *James Fintan Lalor: radical*. By David N. Buckley. Cork, 1990.

LARKIN. *James Larkin: Irish labour leader, 1876–1967*. By Emmet Larkin. London, 1965; repr. 1977.

LAVELLE. *A radical priest in Mayo. Fr Patrick Lavelle: the rise and fall of an Irish nationalist, 1825–86*. By Gerard Moran. Blackrock, 1994.

LONG. *Walter Long, Ireland and the union, 1905–1920*. By John Kendle. Dún Laoghaire, 1992.

LONGFIELD. *Mountifort Longfield: Ireland's first professor of political economy*. By L. S. Moss. Ottawa, Ill., 1976.

MCAULEY. *Catherine McAuley: the first Sister of Mercy*. By R. Burke Savage. Dublin, 1955.

MCCRACKEN. *The life and times of Mary Ann McCracken, 1770–1866*. By Mary McNeill. Dublin, 1960.

—— Mary Anne McCracken: a critical Ulsterwoman within the context of her time. By Priscilla Metscher. In *Études Irlandaises*, xiv, no. 2 (1989), pp 143–58.

MacCURTAIN. *Tomás MacCurtain, soldier and patriot*. By Florence O'Donoghue. Tralee, 1971.

MacDERMOTT. *Seán Mac Diarmada, 1883–1916*. By C. J. Travers. In *Breifne*, iii, no. 9 (1966), pp 1–46.

MacDONAGH. *Thomas MacDonagh: the man, the patriot, the writer*. By Edd W. and Aileen W. Parks. Athens, Ga., 1967.

—— *Thomas MacDonagh: a critical biography*. By Johann Norstedt. Charlottesville, Va., 1980.

MCGEE. *Thomas D'Arcy McGee: the prophet of Canadian nationality*. By D. C. Harvey. Winnipeg, 1923.

—— D'Arcy McGee and the fenians. By R. B. Burns. In *University Rev.*, iv (1967), pp 260–73.

MACHALE. *John MacHale, archbishop of Tuam*. By Nuala Costello. Dublin, 1939. (Noted Irish Lives.)

MacMANUS. *Terence Bellew MacManus, 1811(?)–1861: a short biography*. By T. G. McAllister. Maynooth, 1972. (Maynooth Historical Series, no. 2.)

MacNEILL. *The scholar revolutionary: Eoin MacNeill, 1867–1945, and the making of a new Ireland*. Ed. F. X. Martin and F. J. Byrne. Shannon, 1973.

—— Eoin MacNeill: a reappraisal. By Nicholas Mansergh. In *Studies*, lxiii (1974), pp 133–40.

—— *Eoin MacNeill: scholar and man of action.* By Michael Tierney. *Ed.* F. X. Martin. Oxford, 1980.

MacSWINEY. *Terence MacSwiney.* By M. Chevasse. Dublin, 1961.

MAHAFFY. *Mahaffy: a biography of an Anglo-Irishman.* By W. B. Stanford and R. B. McDowell. London, 1971.

MANGAN. *The life and writings of James Clarence Mangan.* By D. J. O'Donoghue. Edinburgh and Dublin, 1897.

MANNING. *Cardinal Manning: his public life and influence, 1865–1892.* By V. A. McClelland. London, 1962.

—— *Cardinal Manning: a biography.* By Robert Gray. London, 1985.

MANNIX. *Daniel Mannix, priest and patriot.* By Michael Gilchrist. Blackburn, Victoria, 1982.

MARKIEVICZ. *Constance de Markievicz in the cause of Ireland.* By Jacqueline Van Voris. Amherst, N. H., 1967.

—— *Prison letters of Countess Markievicz.* New introduction by Amanda Sebestiyen. London, 1987. 1st ed., 1934.

—— *Constance Markievicz, an independent life.* By Anne Haverty. London, 1988.

—— *Terrible beauty: a life of Constance Markievicz, 1868–1927.* By Diana Norman. London, 1987; Dublin, 1988.

MARTIN. *Humanity Dick Martin, M.P., 1754–1834, 'king of Connemara'.* By Shevawn Lynam. London, 1975; paperback ed., Dublin, 1989.

MATHEW. *Father Mathew.* By J. F. Maguire. London, 1863.

—— *Father Theobald Mathew, apostle of temperance.* By Patrick Rogers. Dublin, 1943.

—— *Father Theobald Mathew, apostle of temperance.* By Moira Lysaght. Dublin, 1983.

—— *Father Mathew and the Irish temperance movement, 1838–1849.* By Colm Kerrigan. Cork, 1992.

MAXWELL. *General Sir John Maxwell.* By Sir George Arthur. London, 1932.

MEAGHER. *Thomas Francis Meagher: an Irish revolutionary in America.* By Robert G. Athearn. Boulder, Colo., 1949.

—— *Thomas Francis Meagher.* By Denis Gwynn. Dublin, 1962. (O'Donnell Lecture.)

MELLOWS. *Liam Mellows and the Irish revolution.* By C. D. Greaves. London, 1971.

MEYER. *Kuno Meyer, 1858–1919; a biography.* By Seán Ó Luing. Dublin, 1991.

MIDLETON. *Records and reactions, 1856–1939.* By William St John Brodrick, earl of Midleton. London, 1939.

MITCHEL. *A life of John Mitchel.* By William Dillon. 2 vols. London, 1888.

—— *Irish Mitchel: a biography.* By Séamus MacCall. London, 1938.

—— John Mitchel's wilderness years in Tennessee. By Dee Gee Lester. In *Éire-Ireland*, xxv, no. 2 (1990), pp 7–13.

MOORE, GEORGE AUGUSTUS. *The life of George Moore.* By Joseph Hone. London, 1936.

MOORE, THOMAS. *The harp that once: a chronicle of the life of Thomas Moore.* By Howard Mumford Jones. New York, 1937.

—— *The minstrel boy: a portrait of Tom Moore.* By L. A. G. Strong. London, 1937.

—— *Thomas Moore, the Irish poet.* By Terence de Vere White. London, 1977.

MORGAN. *The wild Irish girl: the life of Sydney Owenson, Lady Morgan, 1776–1859.* By Lionel Stevenson. London, 1936; repr. 1969.

—— *Lady Morgan.* By Mary Campbell. London, 1988.

MORPETH. *Morpeth: a Victorian public career.* By Diana Davids Olien. Washington, D.C., 1983.

G. W. F. Howard, chief secretary (as Viscount Morpeth) 1835–41; lord lieutenant (as earl of Carlisle) 1855–8, 1859–64.

MULALLY. *A valiant Dublin woman: the story of George's Hill, 1766–1960.* By R. B. Savage. Dublin, 1940.

MULVANY. *W. F. Mulvany: an Irish pioneer in the Ruhr, Great Britain, and industrial Europe, 1750–1870.* By W. O. Henderson. Liverpool, 1954.

MURRAY. Daniel Murray, archbishop of Dublin, 1823–1852. By Moira Lysaght. In *Dublin Hist. Rec.,* xxvii, no. 3 (June 1974), pp 101–8.

—— Archbishop Murray of Dublin and the great famine in Mayo. By David Sheehy. In *Cathair na Mart,* xi (1991), pp 118–28.

NAGLE. *Nano Nagle and the Presentation Sisters.* By J. J. Walsh. Dublin, 1959.

NATHAN. *Sir Matthew Nathan: British governor and civil servant.* By Anthony Haydon. St Lucia, Queensland, 1976.

NEWMAN. *Newman: light in winter.* By Meriol Trevor. London, 1962.

——*John Henry Newman.* By C. S. Dessain. London, 1966.

——*John Henry Newman: a biography.* By Ian Ker. Oxford, 1988.

——Newman: the man and his legacy. By Finula Kennedy. In *Studies,* lxxix (1990), pp 343–52.

——*Newman and his age.* By Sheridan Gilley. Darton, 1990.

NUGENT. *Father Nugent of Liverpool.* By John Bennet. Liverpool, 1949.

O´BRIEN, GEORGE. *George O'Brien: a biographical memoir.* By James Meenan. Dublin, 1980.

O´BRIEN, WILLIAM (1852–1928). *The life of William O'Brien, the Irish nationalist: a biographical study of Irish nationalism, constitutional and revolutionary.* By Michael MacDonagh. London, 1928.

—— *William O'Brien and the Irish land war.* By Sally Warwick-Haller. Dublin, 1990.

O´BRIEN, WILLIAM (1881–1968). *Forth the banners go; reminiscences of William O'Brien, as told to Edward MacLysaght.* Dublin, 1969.

O´BRIEN, WILLIAM SMITH. William Smith O'Brien. By Denis Gwynn. In *Studies,* xxxv (Dec. 1946), pp 448–58; xxxvii (Mar. 1948), pp 7–17, 149–60.

—— *William Smith O'Brien and his revolutionary companions in penal exile.* By Blanche Touhill. St Louis, Mo., 1981.

—— *William Smith O'Brien: Ireland—1848—Tasmania.* By R. P. Davis. Dublin, 1989.

O´CONNELL. *King of the beggars.* By Sean O'Faolain. London, 1938.

——*Daniel O'Connell: nine centenary essays.* Ed. Michael Tierney. Dublin, 1949.

——Daniel O'Connell: income, expenditure, and despair. By Maurice R. O'Connell. In *I.H.S.,* xvii, no. 66 (Sept. 1970), pp 200–20.

——*Daniel O'Connell: nationalism without violence.* By Raymond Moley. New York, 1974; paperback ed., 1975.

——*Daniel O'Connell and his world.* By R. Dudley Edwards. London, 1975.

——*Daniel O'Connell.* By Fergus O'Ferrall. Dublin, 1981.

—— *The hereditary bondsman: Daniel O'Connell, 1775–1829.* By Oliver MacDonagh. London and New York, 1988.

—— *The emancipist: Daniel O'Connell, 1830–47.* By Oliver MacDonagh. London and New York, 1989.

——*Daniel O'Connell studies.* By Maurice O'Connell. Blackrock, 1989.

—— *The world of Daniel O'Connell.* Ed. Donal McCartney. Cork, 1980.

—— *Daniel O'Connell: portrait of a radical.* Ed. K. B. Nowlan and M. R. O'Connell. Belfast, 1984. (Thomas Davis Lectures.)

—— *The great Dan: a biography of Daniel O'Connell.* By Charles Chenevix Trench. London, 1984.

o´connor, feargus. *Feargus O'Connor: Irishman and chartist.* By Donald Read and Eric Glasgow. London, 1961.

—— *The lion of freedom: Feargus O'Connor and the chartist movement.* By James Epstein. London, 1982.

o´connor, t. p. *T. P. O'Connor.* By Hamilton Fyfe. London, 1934.

o´donnell. *A political odyssey: Thomas O'Donnell, M.P. for West Belfast, 1900–1918.* By J. A. Gaughan. Dublin, 1983.

o´donovan. *John O'Donovan (1806–61): a biography.* By Patricia Boyne. Kilkenny, 1987. (Studies in Irish Art and Archaeology.)

o´higgins. *Kevin O'Higgins.* By Terence de Vere White. London, 1948.

o´leary. *John O'Leary: a study in Irish separatism.* By Marcus Bourke. Tralee, 1967.

o´rahilly. *Alfred O'Rahilly.* By J. A. Gaughan. Dublin, 1986.

—— *Winding the clock: O'Rahilly and the 1916 rising.* By Aodogan O'Rahilly. Dublin, 1991.

palles. *Christopher Palles, lord chief baron of her majesty's court of exchequer in Ireland, 1874–1916.* By V. T. H. Delany. Dublin, 1960.

parnell, charles stewart. *Life of Charles Stewart Parnell.* 2 vols. By R. Barry O'Brien. London, 1898.

—— *Parnell vindicated: the lifting of the veil.* By Henry Harrison. London, 1931.

—— *Parnell: beath aisnéis.* By Leon Ó Broin. Dublin, 1937.

—— *Parnell's vindication.* By Henry Harrison. In *I. H. S.*, v, no. 19 (Mar. 1947), pp 231–43. (Historical Revision, viii.)

—— *Parnell and his party, 1880–90.* By Conor Cruise O'Brien. Oxford, 1957; 2nd impression, 1964.

—— *Parnell.* By F. S. L. Lyons. Dundalk, 1963. (Dublin Historical Association.)

—— *Charles Stewart Parnell: the man and his family.* By R. F. Foster. Hassocks, 1976.

—— *Charles Stewart Parnell.* By F. S. L. Lyons. London, 1977; paperback ed., 1978.

—— Towards a psychoanalytic interpretation of Charles Stewart Parnell. By Joseph M. Woods. In *Bulletin of the Menninger Clinic*, xlii, no. 6 (1978), pp 463–92.

—— *C. S. Parnell.* By Paul Bew. Dublin, 1980.

—— *Parnell in perspective.* Ed. D. G. Boyce and Alan O'Day. London, 1991.

—— *Parnell: the politics of power.* Ed. Donal McCartney. Dublin, 1991.

parnell, mrs charles stewart. *The uncrowned queen of Ireland: the life of Kitty O'Shea.* By Joyce Marlow. New York, 1975.

—— *Kitty O'Shea: a life of Katherine Parnell.* By M. R. Callaghan. London, 1989.

parnell. *Fanny and Anna Parnell: Ireland's patriot sisters.* By Jane M. Cote. London, 1991.

—— The Parnell sisters. By Marie Hughes. In *Dublin Hist. Rec.*, xx, no. 11 (Mar. 1966), pp 17–27.

pearse. *Patrick Pearse: the triumph of failure.* By Ruth Dudley Edwards. London, 1974.

peel. *Mr Secretary Peel: the life of Sir Robert Peel to 1830.* By Norman Gash. London, 1961.

—— *Sir Robert Peel: the life of Sir Robert Peel after 1830.* By Norman Gash. London, 1972.

PETRIE. *George Petrie, 1789–1866.* By Myles Dillon. In *Studies,* lvi (1967), pp 266–76.

—— *George Petrie and the ancient music of Ireland.* By Grace J. Calder. Dublin, 1968.

PLUNKETT, COUNT GEORGE. *An Pluincéadach.* By Labhrás Breathnach. Dublin, 1971.

PLUNKETT, HORACE. *Horace Plunkett: an Anglo-American Irishman.* By Margaret Digby. Oxford, 1949.

—— *Horace Plunkett, cooperation and politics: an Irish biography.* By Trevor West. Gerrards Cross and Washington, D.C., 1986.

QUINN. *The man from New York: John Quinn and his friends.* By B. L. Reid. New York, 1968.

REDMOND. *Life of John Redmond.* By Denis Gwynn. London, 1932.

RICE. *Edmund Rice, founder and first superior general of the brothers of the Christian schools in Ireland.* By J. D. Fitzpatrick. Dublin, 1945.

—— *Edmund Rice: the man and his times.* By Desmond Rushe. Dublin, 1981.

ROBINSON. *Memories: wise and otherwise.* By Sir Henry Augustus Robinson. London, 1923.

—— *Further memories of Irish life.* By Sir Henry Augustus Robinson. London, 1924.

ROLLESTON, T. W. *Portrait of an Irishman: a biographical sketch.* By C. H. Rolleston. London, 1939.

RUSSELL, CHARLES WILLIAM. *Dr Russell of Maynooth.* By Ambrose Macaulay. London, 1983.

RUSSELL, GEORGE. *That myriad-minded man: a biography of George William Russell, A E, 1867–1935.* By Henry Summerfield. London and Totowa, N.J., 1976.

RYAN, DESMOND. *Remembering Sion.* By Desmond Ryan. London, 1934.

RYAN, MARK. *Fenian memories.* By Mark Ryan. Dublin, 1945.

SAUNDERSON. *Colonel Edward Saunderson: land and loyalty in Victorian Ireland.* By Alvin Jackson. Oxford, 1995.

SHEEHY SKEFFINGTON, FRANCIS. *With wooden sword: a portrait of Francis Sheehy Skeffington, militant and pacifist.* By Leah Levenson. Boston and Dublin, 1983.

SHEEHY SKEFFINGTON, HANNA. *Hanna Sheehy Skeffington: Irish feminist.* By Leah Levenson and Jerry H. Natterstad. Syracuse, N.Y., 1986.

SHEEHY SKEFFINGTON, OWEN. *Skeff: a life of Owen Sheehy Skeffington, 1909–1970.* By Andrée Sheehy Skeffington. Dublin, 1991.

SOMERVILLE, EDITH, AND ROSS, MARTIN. *Somerville and Ross: a biography.* By Maurice Collis. London, 1968.

—— *The Irish cousins: the books and background of Somerville and Ross.* By Violet Powell. London, 1970.

STACK. *Austin Stack: portrait of a separatist.* By J. A. Gaughan. Dublin, 1977.

STARKEY-O'SULLIVAN. *Séamus O'Sullivan: a critical biography.* By Jane Russell. London and Toronto, 1987.

STEPHENS. *The fenian chief: a biography of James Stephens.* By Desmond Ryan. *Ed.* Patrick Lynch and Owen Dudley Edwards. Dublin and Sydney, 1967.

SULLIVAN. *Recollections of troubled times in Irish politics.* By T. D. Sullivan. Dublin, 1905.

TRENCH. *The man of ten talents: a portrait of Richard Chenevix Trench, 1807–86, philologist, poet, theologian, and bishop.* By John Bromley. London, 1959.

TYNDALL. *Life and work of John Tyndall.* By A. S. Eve and C. H. Creasy. London, 1945.

—*John Tyndall: essays on a natural philosopher*. *Ed.* W. H. Brock, N. D. McMillan, and R. C. Mollan. Dublin, 1981. (Royal Dublin Society.)

WALSH. *William J. Walsh, archbishop of Dublin*. By Patrick Walsh. Dublin, 1928.

WHATELY. *A protestant in purgatory: Richard Whately, archbishop of Dublin*. By D. H. Akenson. Hamden, Conn., 1981.

WILDE, OSCAR. *Oscar Wilde*. By Richard Ellmann. London, 1987.

WILDE, SIR WILLIAM. *Victorian doctor: being the life of Sir William Wilde*. By T. G. Wilson. New York, 1946.

—— *The Wildes of Merrion Square: the family of Oscar Wilde*. By Patrick Byrne. London and New York, 1953.

—— *The parents of Oscar Wilde: Sir William and Lady Wilde*. By Terence de Vere White. London, 1967.

WILDE, LADY. *Speranza: a biography of Lady Wilde*. By Horace Wyndham. London and New York, 1951.

WILSON. *Field-marshal Sir Henry Wilson*. By C. E. Callwell. London, 1927.

—— *Brass hat: a biography of Sir Henry Wilson*. By Basil Collier. London, 1961.

—— *The lost dictator: a biography of Field-marshal Sir Henry Wilson, Bart, G.C.B.* By Bernard Ash. London, 1968.

WINDLE. *Sir Bertram Windle: a memoir*. By Monica Taylor. London, 1932.

—— Sir Bertram Windle, 1858–1929: a centenary tribute. By Denis Gwynn. In *University Rev.*, ii, no. 3 (1958), pp 48–58.

WYSE. *Sir Thomas Wyse, 1791–1862: the life and career of an educator and diplomat*. By J. J. Auchmuty. London, 1939.

YEATS, JACK. *Jack B. Yeats: a biography*. By Hilary Pyle. London, 1970.

—— *The charmed life*. By Jack B. Yeats. London, 1974.

YEATS, JOHN BUTLER. *Prodigal father: the life of John Butler Yeats, 1832–1922*. By W. M. Murphy. Ithaca, N.Y., and London, 1978.

YEATS, W. B. *W. B. Yeats: a new biography*. By A. Norman Jeffares. London, 1989.
   3rd (rev.) ed.; 1st and 2nd eds (1949, 1962) published under title *W. B. Yeats: man and poet*.

C BIOGRAPHICAL AND OTHER WORKS OF REFERENCE

Andrews, J. H. *Irish maps*. Dublin, 1978.

The Annual Register, or a view of the history, politicks and literature for the year 1758 [etc.]. London, [1759]– .

Atlas of Ireland, prepared under the direction of the Irish National Committee for Geography. Dublin, 1979. (Royal Irish Academy.)

Australian encyclopaedia. Sydney, 1958.

Baillie, L., and Sieveking, P. *British biographical archive*. London, 1984.
   Booklet and microfiche: a one-alphabet cumulation of 324 of the most important English-language biographical reference works published between 1601 and 1929.

Ball, F. E. *The judges in Ireland, 1121–1921*. 2 vols. London, 1926; New York, 1927.

Bank, D., and Esposito, A. *British biographical index*. London, 1990.

Bence-Jones, Mark. *A guide to Irish country houses*. London, 1988.

Boylan, Henry. *A dictionary of Irish biography*. Dublin and New York, 1978; 2nd ed., Dublin, 1985.

Breathnach, Diarmuid, and Ní Mhurchú, Máire. *1882–1982 Beathaisnéis.* 3 vols. Dublin, 1986–92.

Burke, J. B. *The landed gentry of Ireland.* London, 1858; with revisions, 1899, 1904, 1912, 1958.

——*Dormant, abeyant, extinct, and forfeited peerages of the British empire.* London, 1883.

Burtchaell, G. D. and Sadleir, T. U. (ed.). *Alumni Dublinenses: a register of the students, graduates, fellows, and provosts of Trinity College in the University of Dublin* [*1593–1846*]. London, 1924. New ed. (*1593–1860*), Dublin, 1935.

Cleeve, Brian. *Dictionary of Irish writers.* 3 vols. Cork, 1967–71. Rev. ed., Gigginstown, 1985.

C[okayne], G. E. (ed.). *The complete baronetage.* 6 vols. Exeter, 1900–9.

——*The complete peerage of England, Scotland, Ireland, Great Britain, and the United Kingdom. Ed.* Vicary Gibbs and others. 13 vols. London, 1910–59.

The concise dictionary of national biography: from earliest times to 1985. 3 vols. Oxford and New York, 1992.

Cordasco, Francesco. *Dictionary of American immigration history.* Metuchen, N.J., 1990.

Coxhead, Elizabeth. *Daughters of Erin: five women of the Irish renaissance.* London, 1965.

Crone, J. S. *A concise dictionary of Irish biography.* Dublin, 1928; 2nd ed., [1937].

De Breffny, Brian (ed.). *Ireland: a cultural encyclopaedia.* London, 1983.

The dictionary of National Biography. Ed. Leslie Stephen and Sidney Lee. 66 vols. London, 1885–1901. Reprint, with corrections, 22 vols, London, 1908–9.

Dictionary of American Biography. Ed. Allen Johnson and Dumas Malone. 20 vols. New York and London, 1928–37.

Doherty, J. E., and Hickey, D. J. *A chronology of Irish history since 1500.* Dublin, 1990.

Eden, Peter (ed.). *Dictionary of land surveyors and local cartographers of Great Britain and Ireland, 1550–1850.* 2 pts and supp. Folkestone, 1975–9.

Edwards, Ruth Dudley. *An atlas of Irish history.* London, 1973. 2nd ed., London, 1981.

Encyclopaedia of Ireland. Ed. Victor Meally and others. Dublin, 1968.

Farrar, Henry. *Irish marriages: being an index of the marriages in Walker's Hibernian Magazine, 1771 to 1812.* 2nd ed., Baltimore, 1972.

Foley, Timothy P. A nest of scholars: biographical material on some early professors at Queen's College, Galway. In *Galway Arch. Soc. Jn.,* xlii (1989–90), pp 72–86.

Forth, Gordon (ed.). *A biographical register and annotated bibliography of Anglo-Irish colonists in Australia.* Warrnamborrl, 1991.

Fox, R. M. *Rebel Irishwomen.* Cork, 1935.

Haigh, Christopher (ed.). *The Cambridge historical encyclopaedia of Great Britain and Ireland.* Cambridge, 1985.

Harbison, Peter. *Guide to the national monuments of Ireland.* Dublin, 1970.

——Potterton, Homan, and Sheehy, Jeanne. *Irish art and architecture from pre-history to the present.* London, 1978.

Harris, Ruth-Ann, and Jacobs, D. M. (ed.). *The search for missing friends; Irish immigrant advertisements placed in the Boston Pilot.* Vol. 1: 1831–1850. Boston, 1989.

Hickey, D. J., and Doherty, J. E. (ed.). *A dictionary of Irish history since 1800.* Dublin, 1980.

——and ——*A chronology of Irish history since 1500.* Savage, Md., 1990.

Hogan, Robert (ed.). *Dictionary of Irish literature.* Dublin, 1980.

Holmes, Michael. *The country house described: an index to the country houses of Great Britain and Ireland.* Winchester, 1986.

Hughes, James L. *Patentee officers in Ireland, 1173–1826*. Dublin, 1960.

Kavanagh, Peter. *The Irish theatre: being a history of the drama in Ireland from the earliest period up to the present day*. Tralee, 1946.

Lewis, Samuel. *A topographical dictionary of Ireland*. 2 vols and atlas. London, 1837. Reissue, Port Washington, N.Y., 1970.

Lyons, J. B. *Brief lives of Irish doctors*. Dublin, 1978.

MacLysaght, Edward. *Irish families: their names, arms, and origins*. Dublin, 1957.

—— *More Irish families*. Galway and Dublin, 1960.

—— *Guide to Irish families*. Dublin, 1964.

—— *Supplement to Irish families*. Dublin, 1969.

Massingberd, H. M. (ed.). *Burke's Irish family records*. London, 1976.

Meehan, P. F. *The members of parliament for Laois and Offaly, 1801–1918*. Portlaoise, 1983.

Mitchell, Frank, and others. *The book of the Irish countryside*. Belfast, 1987.

Mollan, Charles; Davis, William; and Finucane, Brendan. *Some people and places in Irish science and technology*. Dublin, 1985.

—— —— and—— *More people and places in Irish science and technology*. Dublin, 1990.

O'Connell, Niall (ed.). *The forests of Ireland: history, distribution and silviculture*. Dublin, 1984.

O'Connor, Ulick. *All the Olympians: a biographical portrait of the Irish literary renaissance*. New York, 1984.

O'Day, Alan (ed.). *Reactions to Irish nationalism*. Dublin, 1987. Compilation of articles from periodicals.

O'Donoghue, D. J. *The poets of Ireland*. Dublin, 1912.

O'Flanagan, J. R. *Lives of the lord chancellors and keepers of the great seal of Ireland from the earliest times to the reign of Queen Victoria*. 2 vols. London, 1870.

Praeger, R. L. *Some Irish naturalists*. Dundalk, 1949.

Reece, B. N. (ed.). *Letters from Erin: convict lives in Ireland and Australia*. London, 1991.

Room, Adrian. *A concise dictionary of modern place-names in Great Britain and Ireland*. Oxford, 1983.

Royal Historical Society. *Handbook of British chronology*. 3rd ed., London, 1986.

Share, Bernard. *Irish lives*. Dublin, 1971.

Shaw, Henry. *The Dublin pictorial guide and directory of 1850*. Belfast, 1988.

Stockwell, La Tourette. *Dublin theatres and theatre customs, 1637–1820*. Kingsport, Tenn., 1938; repr., New York, 1968.

Strickland, W. G. A. *A dictionary of Irish artists*. 2 vols. Dublin, 1913; repr., Blackrock, 1989.

Thom's Irish almanac and official directory for the year 1844 [etc.]. Dublin, 1844 [etc.].

Vaughan, W. E., and Fitzpatrick, A. J. *Irish historical statistics: population, 1821–1971*. Dublin, 1978. (A New History of Ireland: ancillary publications II.)

Walker, B. M. *Parliamentary election results in Ireland, 1801–1922*. Dublin, 1978. (A New History of Ireland: ancillary publications IV.)

—— *Parliamentary election results in Ireland, 1918–92*. Dublin and Belfast, 1992. (A New History of Ireland: ancillary publications V.)

Wallace, Martin. *100 Irish lives*. Totowa, N.J., 1983.

Webb, D. A. *Of one company: biographical studies of famous Trinity men*. Dublin, 1951.

Widdess, J. D. H. *An index to the biographical notices, papers on the history of medicine, etc., in the Irish Journal of Medical Science from Sept. 1916 to Dec. 1954*. Dublin, 1955.

D COMPOSITE WORKS

Alexander, Yonah, and O'Day, Alan (ed.). *Terrorism in Ireland*. London and New York, 1984.

Almquist, Bo; Mac Aodha, Breandán; and Mac Eóin, Gearóid (ed.). *Hereditas: essays and studies presented to Professor Séamus Ó Duilearga*. Dublin, 1975.
   Foreword on historical background, by Michael Tierney.

Bartlett, Thomas, and others (ed.). *Irish studies: a general introduction*. Dublin and Totowa, N.J., 1988.

Bastable, J. D. (ed.). *Newman and Gladstone: centennial essays*. Dublin, 1978.

Boal, F. W., and Douglas, J. N., with assistance of Orr, J. A. E. *Integration and division: geographical perspectives on the Northern Ireland problem*. London, 1982.

Bossy, John, and Jupp, Peter (ed.). *Essays presented to Michael Roberts, sometime professor of modern history in the Queen's University of Belfast*. Belfast, 1976.

Boyle, J. W. (ed.). *Leaders and workers*. Cork, 1965.

British Academy and Royal Irish Academy (ed.). *Ireland after the union*. Oxford, 1989.

Browne, R. B.; Roscelli, William; and Loftus, Richard (ed.). *The Celtic cross: studies in Irish culture and literature*. Purdue, Ind., 1964. (Purdue University Studies.)

Byrne, C. J., and Harry, Margaret (ed.). *Talamh an Eisc: Canadian and Irish essays*. Halifax, Nova Scotia, 1986.

Carpenter, Andrew (ed.). *Place, personality, and the Irish writer*. Gerrards Cross, 1977.

Casey, D. J., and Rhodes, Robert (ed.). *Views of the Irish peasantry, 1900–1916*. Hamden, Conn., 1977.

Clark, Samuel, and Donnelly, J. S., jr (ed.). *Irish peasants: violence and political unrest, 1780–1914*. Madison, Wis., and Manchester, 1983; paperback ed., Dublin, 1983.

Corish, P. J. (ed.). *Radicals, rebels, and establishments*. Belfast, 1985. (*Hist. Studies*, xv.)

Cosgrove, Art (ed.). *Marriage in Ireland*. Dublin, 1985.

—— and McCartney, Donal (ed.). *Studies in Irish history presented to R. Dudley Edwards*. Dublin, 1979.

—— and McGuire, J. I. *Parliament and community*. Belfast, 1983. (*Hist. Studies*, xiv.)

Cronne, H. A.; Moody, T. W.; and Quinn, D. B. (ed.). *Essays in British and Irish history in honour of James Eadie Todd*. London, 1949.

Crozier, Maurice (ed.). *Cultural traditions in Northern Ireland*. Belfast, 1989. (Institute of Irish Studies.)

Curtin, Chris; Jackson, Pauline; and O'Connor, Barbara (ed.). *Gender in Irish society*. Galway, 1987.

—— Kelly, Mary, and O'Dowd, Liam (ed.). *Culture and ideology in Ireland*. Galway, 1984.

De Breffny, Brian (ed.). *The Irish world: the history and cultural achievements of the Irish people*. London, 1977.

De Paor, Liam (ed.). *Milestones in Irish history*. Cork and Dublin, 1986.

Dickson, David (ed.), *The gorgeous mask: Dublin, 1700–1850*. Dublin, 1987. (Trinity History Workshop.)

Drudy, P. J. (ed.) *Irish Studies I; Irish Studies II: Ireland: land, politics, and people; Irish Studies III: Ireland and the European Community; Irish Studies IV: the Irish in America: emigration, assimilation and impact; Irish Studies V: Ireland and Britain since 1922*. Cambridge, 1980–86.

Dunne, Tom (ed.). *The writer as witness: literature as historical evidence.* Cork, 1987. (*Hist. Studies*, xvi.)

Edwards, O. D, and Pyle, Fergus (ed.). *1916: the Easter rising.* London, 1968.

Edwards, R. D. (ed.). *Ireland and the Italian Risorgimento: 1848–70.* Dublin, 1960.

—— and Williams, T. D. (ed.). *The great famine: studies in Irish history, 1845–1852.* Dublin, 1956; New York, 1957.

   Reprint, with introduction by E. R. R. Green, New York, 1976. Reissue, with an introduction by Cormac Ó Gráda (new bibliography), Dublin, 1994.

Eyler, Audrey, and Garratt, Robert (ed.). *The uses of the past: essays on Irish culture.* Newark, Del., 1988.

Farrell, Brian (ed.). *The Irish parliamentary tradition.* Dublin and New York, 1973.

—— (ed.). *Communications and community in Ireland.* Dublin, 1984.

Fitzpatrick, David (ed.). *Revolution in Ireland 1917–23.* Dublin, 1990. (Trinity History Workshop.)

Gailey, Alan (ed.). *The use of tradition: essays presented to G. B. Thompson.* Cultra, Co. Down, 1988.

—— and Ó hÓgáin, Dáithí (ed.). *Gold under the furze: studies in folk tradition presented to Caoimhín Ó Danachair.* Dublin, 1982.

Gallagher, S. F. (ed.). *Women in Irish legend, life and literature.* Gerrards Cross, 1983. (Irish Literary Studies, 14.)

Genet, Jacqueline (ed.). *The big house in Ireland.* Lanham, Md., 1991.

Gillespie, Raymond, and O'Sullivan, Harold (ed.). *The borderlands: essays on the history of the Ulster–Leinster border.* Belfast, 1989.

Green, E. R. R. (ed.). *Essays in Scotch-Irish history.* London and Belfast, 1969.

Grimes, Séamus, and Ó Tuathaigh, M. A. G. (ed.). *The Irish-Australian connection: An Caidréamh Gael-Australach.* Galway, 1989.

Hachey, T. E., and McCaffrey, L. J. (ed.). *Perspectives on Irish nationalism.* Lexington, Ky., 1989.

Hayley, Barbara, and Murray, Christopher (ed.). *Ireland and France, a bountiful friendship: essays in honour of Patrick Rafroidi.* Lanham, Md., 1992.

Hepburn, A. C. (ed.). *Minorities in history.* London, 1978. (Hist. Studies, xii.)

—— (ed.). *The conflict of nationality in modern Ireland.* New York, 1980.

Jeffares, A. N., and Cross, K. G. W. (ed.). *In excited reverie: a centenary tribute to William Butler Yeats, 1865–1939.* New York, 1965.

—— (ed.). *Yeats, Sligo, and Ireland: essays to mark the 21st Yeats International Summer School.* Gerrards Cross and Totowa, N.J., 1980. (Irish Literary Studies, 6.)

Keating, Carla (ed.). *Plunkett and cooperatives: past, present, and future.* Cork, 1983. (U.C.C., Bank of Ireland Centre for Cooperative Studies.)

Kennelly, Brendan (ed.). *Ireland, past and present.* Dublin, 1987.

   Contains two essays by Liam de Paor (18th and 19th century), and Thomas Brown (20th century).

Lackner, B. K., and Philp, K. R. (ed.). *Essays on modern European revolutionary history.* Austin, Tex., 1977. (Walter Prescott Webb memorial lectures.)

Lyons, F. S. L., and Hawkins, R. A. J. (ed.). *Ireland under the union: varieties of tension. Essays in honour of T. W. Moody.* Oxford, 1980.

MacCurtain, Margaret, and Ó Corráin, Donncha (ed.). *Women in Irish society: the historical dimension.* Dublin, 1978.

MacDonagh, Oliver, and Mandle, W. F. (ed.). *Ireland and Irish Australia: studies in cultural and political history*. London, 1986.

—— and —— (ed.). *Irish-Australian studies: papers delivered at the fifth Irish-Australian conference*. Canberra. 1989.

———— and Travers, Pauric (ed.). *Irish culture and nationalism, 1750–1950*. London and Canberra, 1983.

McHugh, Roger (ed.). *Dublin, 1916*. London, 1966.

Martin, Augustine (ed.). *The genius of Irish prose*. Cork and Dublin, 1984. (Thomas Davis Lecture.)

Martin, F. X. (ed.). *The Irish volunteers, 1913–15*. Dublin, 1963.

—— (ed.). *The Howth gun-running, 1914*. Dublin, 1964.

—— (ed.). *1916 and University College, Dublin*. Dublin, 1966.

—— (ed.). *Leaders and men of the Easter rising: Dublin, 1916*. London and Ithaca, N.Y., 1967.

Mingay, G. E. (ed.). *The Victorian countryside*. 2 vols. London, 1981.

Mommsen, W. J., and Hirschfeld, Gerard (ed.). *Social protest, violence, and terror in nineteenth- and twentieth-century Europe*. London, 1982.

Moody, T. W. (ed.). *The fenian movement*. Dublin and Cork, 1978.

—— (ed.). *Nationality and the pursuit of national independence*. Belfast, 1978. (*Hist. Studies*, xi.)

Morgan, Austen, and Purdie, Bob (ed.). *Ireland: divided nation, divided class*. London, 1980.

Murtagh, Harman (ed.). *Irish midland studies: essays in commemoration of N.W. English*. Athlone, 1980.

Ní Chuilleanáin, Eiléan (ed.). *Irish women, image and achievement: women in Irish culture from earliest times*. Dublin, 1985.

Ní Dhonnchadha, Máirín, and Dorgan, Theo (ed.). *Revising the rising*. Derry, 1991.

Nowlan, K. B. (ed.). *The making of 1916: studies in the history of the rising*. Dublin, 1969.

O'Brien, Conor Cruise (ed.). *The shaping of modern Ireland*. London, 1960; repr. 1970.

O'Day, Alan (ed.). *Reactions to Irish nationalism*. London, 1987.

O'Driscoll, Robert (ed.). *The Celtic consciousness*. New York, 1982.

Orel, Harold (ed.). *Irish history and culture: aspects of a people's heritage*. Lawrence, Kan., 1980.

Ó Tuathaigh, M. A. G. (ed.). *Community, culture, and conflict*. Galway, 1986.

Philpin, C. H. E. (ed.). *Nationalism and popular protest in Ireland*. Cambridge, 1987.

Princess Grace Irish Library (ed.). *Irishness in a changing society*. Gerrards Cross, 1988.

Reid, Richard, and Johnston, Keith (ed.). *The Irish Australians: essays for Irish and Australian family historians*. Sydney and Belfast, 1984.

Roebuck, Peter (ed.). *Plantation to partition: essays in Ulster history in honour of J. L. McCracken*. Belfast, 1981.

Rynne, Etienne (ed.). *North Munster studies: essays in commemoration of Monsignor Michael Moloney*. Limerick, 1967.

Siegmund-Shulte, Dorothea (ed.). *Irland: Gesellschaft und Kultur*, vi. Halle Wittenburg, 1989.

Skelton, Robin, and Saddlemyer, Ann (ed.). *The world of W. B. Yeats: essays in perspective on the occasion of the W. B. Yeats centenary festival held at the University of Victoria*. Dublin, 1965.

Smith, F. B. (ed.). *Ireland, England, and Australia: essays in honour of Oliver MacDonagh*. Cork and Canberra, 1990.

Topic, a journal of the liberal arts, no. 13. Washington, D.C., and Jefferson College, Pa., 1967.

    Issue devoted to Irish subjects; various authors.

Townshend, Charles (ed.). *Consensus in Ireland: approaches and recessions.* Oxford, 1988.

Williams, T. D. (ed.). *The Irish struggle, 1916–26.* London, 1966.

—— (ed.). *Secret societies in Ireland.* Dublin and New York, 1973.

INDEX

All persons of rank are indexed primarily under the family name, cross references being given from the title.

The following abbreviations are used:

abp	archbishop	L.L.	lord lieutenant
bp	bishop	n.	note
C.S.	chief secretary	P.	protestant
L.C.	lord chancellor	R.C.	Roman Catholic

Abbey Theatre, 123, 173, 357, 365–8, 377, 378, 417, 518; established, 107–8; 'Playboy' riots, 111, 119–21, 359, 366, 372–3; Yeats plays, 358–9; ensemble playing, 362–3; building, 497; music, 521

Abbeyleix, Queen's County, 28, 490, 620

Abercorn, duke of, *see* Hamilton, James Albert Edward

Aberdeen, 671

Aberdeen, earl and countess of, *see* Gordon, Ishbel, and Gordon, John Campbell Hamilton

Abney, Sir William, 475

abstention policy, 240, 413

Académie Royale des Beaux Arts, 455

Achill, Co. Mayo, 289, 393, 660

act of union, 436

Adare, Co. Limerick, 461, 463, 490

administration, 168–9, 379, 571–605; costs of, 335, 353; effects of, 353–4; censorship, 373; and Irish language, 417; *see also* Dublin Castle, local government

Aducci, art dealer, 438

A E, *see* Russell, George

Agar-Robartes, Thomas Charles Reginald, M.P., 132

agrarian disturbances, 3, 27, 158, 160–61, 631; crime rates, 45; rent strikes, 69, (1918), 234; *see also* Irish National Land League; land war; United Irish League; plates 8, 57

agricultural board, 589

agricultural council, 589

agricultural wages committee, 598

agriculture, li, 148–9, 583; distress, 36–8, 51; prices, 80, 272–3, 314–18; cooperative movement, 87–91; cattle industry, 100, 160; cattle drives, 161; pasturage, 164–5; report on pig-breeding, 184; post-famine, 263–6; livestock, 264, 272–4, 279–81, 282; housing, 276–7; improvements, 278–83; investment in, 324–5; rural society, 341–2; swine fever, 343; first world war, 343–6; effects of emigration, 626–7; *see also* agrarian disturbances

—, labourers, 151–3, 165–6, 174, 263, 276, 277–8; housing, 55, 59, 99; support for national league, 55; wages, 318–19, 320

agriculture and technical instruction, department of, 99, 290, 304, 481, 491, 572, 573, 595, 597, 601; established, 90–91, 271, 529–30, 588–9; report on pig-breeding, 184; activities of, 282–3, 531–2; congested districts transferred to, 285; art schools transferred to, 448, 477, 479; college of science transferred to, 556; first world war, 597, 598–9

Aiken, Frank, 722

Akenson, Donald Harman, 740–41

Albert College, 283, 529, 530, 531, 532, 568, 598

Albert memorial, (Belfast) 466, (London) 459–60

Alexandra College, Dublin, 562, 569

Alfred Ernest Albert, duke of Edinburgh, 581

aliens act (1907), 687

All-for-Ireland League, 126, 127, 235

All Hallows' College, Dublin, 554

All-Ireland committee, 89

All Ireland Review, 361

All Saints church, Carrick-on-Suir, Co. Tipperary, 469

Allan, Henry, 445, 455, 458

Allies, Thomas William, 553

Allingham, William, 360

Amalgamated Musicians' Union, 518

Ambrose, Edward, 459, 460

America, *see* United States of America

American civil war, 265, 267, 293, 298, 728, 729, 731

American Committee for Relief in Ireland, 687

American Land League, 65

Amery, Lord, 228n

Amnesty Association, 1–2, 7, 676

amnesty campaign, 27–8

Ancient Order of Hibernians, 115, 126, 154, 674

Anderson, Sir John, joint under-secretary (1920–22), 603, 604

—, Robert Andrew, 88, 164

Andrews, Thomas, 550, 563

—, William, 291

1. Earthenware chamber-pot with portrait of W. E. Gladstone, *c.*1870

2. 'The ancient oratory of St Clement, at Rome', 1872

3. 'Dublin obsequies of Lord Mayo: landing the coffin at the Custom House Quay', 1872

5. 'The O'Connell centenary celebration in Dublin', 1875

RETURNING FROM AN ORANGE DEMONSTRATION

AN ORANGE DECORATION—THE PURSUIT OF KING JAMES BY KING WILLIAM

AN ORANGE SERMON

4. 'The twelfth of July in the north of Ireland', 1875

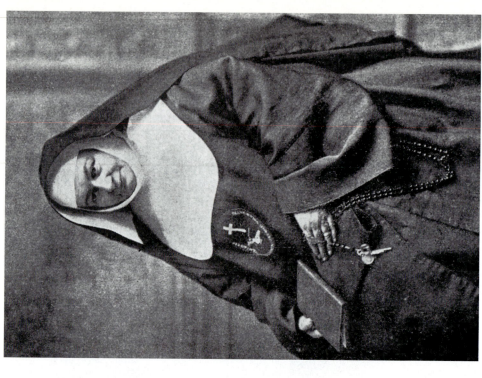

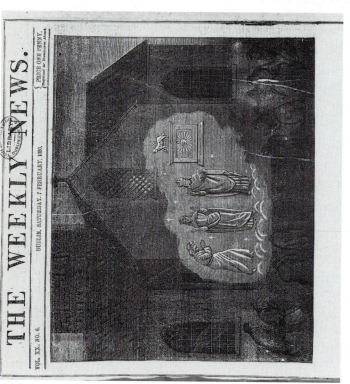

THE WEEKLY NEWS.

VOL. XX. NO. 6.

DUBLIN, SATURDAY, 7 FEBRUARY, 1880.

PRICE ONE PENNY,
(Registered for Transmission Abroad.

6. The apparition at Knock, 21 Aug. 1879, represented six months later

7. Margaret Anne Cusack, the 'Nun of Kenmare', 1889

8. 'Waiting for the landlord!', by Charles Keene, 1878: 'Sure, Tirince, I hope the ould gintleman hasn't mit wid an accidint!!!'

9. 'The right pig by the ear', by Linley Sambourne, 1883: an Orange peer is removed
from the magistracy

10. Rev. James Healy of Bray, Co. Wicklow

11. Cartoon by Percy French, 1890

PARNELL AND YOUNG IRELAND

12. 'Parnell and Young Ireland', by Harry Furniss, Sept. 1891

13. 'A dramatic incident at Mr Parnell's funeral', by W. S. Stacey, Oct. 1891: the packing case of the coffin being broken up for mementoes

14. The dining room, Carton House, Maynooth, Co. Kildare, c.1890

15. Grand Lodge room, Freemasons' Hall, Dublin

16. Mr MacSimius: 'Well, Oi don't profess to be a particularly cultivated man meself; but at laste me progenitors were all educated in the hoigher branches!', by Bernard Partridge, 1897

17. 'Last of the vi-kings and first of the tea-kings', by Leonard Raven-Hill, 1903;
Sir Thomas Lipton, millionaire grocer, philanthropist, and yachtsman

18 (a) Edward VII inspecting an R.I.C. guard of honour, 1907

(b) Royal party at the viceregal lodge, Dublin, July 1911

19. Rev. James Cullen (centre), founder of the Pioneer Total Abstinence League of the Sacred Heart

20. 'Irish Tichbornites reading the verdict' by W. H. Hill Marshall

21. 'The marriage of Princess Aoife of Leinster with Richard de Clare,
earl of Pembroke (Strongbow)' by Daniel Maclise (detail)

22. 'The Aran fisherman's drowned child' by F. W. Burton

23. 'The banks of the river Seine, near Paris' by Nathaniel Hone the younger

24. 'Towards the night and winter' by Frank O'Meara

25. 'The Four Courts, Dublin' by Walter Osborne

26. 'The fish market' by Walter Osborne

27. 'The fine art academy, Antwerp' by Dermod O'Brien

28. 'Field of corn, Pont Aven' by Roderic O'Conor

29. 'In the west of Ireland' by Paul Henry

31. 'John O'Leary' by John B. Yeats

30. 'The rogue' by Jack B. Yeats

32. 'Roger Casement' by Sarah
Purser

33. The buildings of the
Dublin industrial exhibition,
1853, Sir John Benson architect

GREAT INDUSTRIAL EXHIBITION,
DUBLIN 1853.

Sir J. Benson, Architect

34. St Finn Barre's cathedral, Cork,
William Burges architect

35. St Patrick's church, Jordanstown,
Co. Antrim, under construction,
W. H. Lynn architect

36. St Patrick's College, Maynooth, Co. Kildare; design drawings by
A. W. N. Pugin, 1846

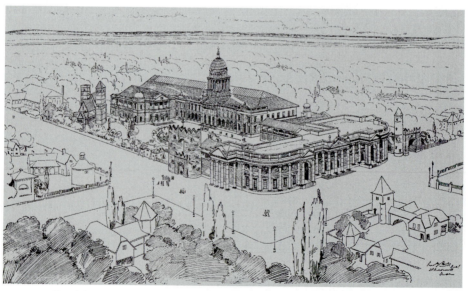

37. 'Louisiana Purchase Exposition, St Louis, 1904. Bird's eye view of special Irish
section', by F. G. Hicks

38. St Colman's cathedral, Cobh, E. W. Pugin and G. C. Ashlin architects

39. First design for art gallery over Liffey between Aston Quay and Bachelors Walk, Dublin, by Edwin Lutyens

KILLYHEVLIN C? FERMANAGH FOR W. E. HURST ESQ.   ERECTED 1903   W. A. SCOTT A.R.I.B.A. M.S.A. 72 HOLYBANK ROAD DRUMCONDRA DUBLIN

40. House at Killyhevlin, Co. Fermanagh, W. A. Scott architect, 1903

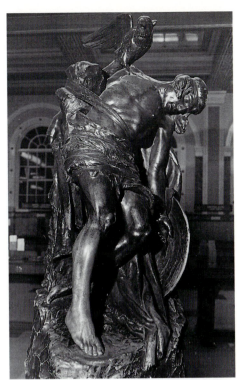

41. William Dargan, bronze statue by Thomas Farrell

42. (*above right*) 'The death of Cú Chulainn', bronze statue by Oliver Sheppard

43. 'Erin unveiling her first pot'; Belleek china, *c*.1863

44. (*above left*) Drinking goblet with Williamite
inscription, *c*.1850, from Bohemia

45. (*above*) Drinking goblet with Williamite
inscription, *c*.1860, from Novy Svet glassworks,
northern Bohemia

46. Glass jug engraved with Irish patriotic
emblems, *c*.1880, by Franz Tieze

48. James J. (Gentleman Jim) Corbett, world heavyweight boxing champion, 1892–7, born in San Francisco of parents from Co. Mayo

DRACULA

BY

BRAM STOKER

WESTMINSTER
ARCHIBALD CONSTABLE AND COMPANY
2 WHITEHALL GARDENS
1897

47. Title page of first edition of *Dracula*

49. The political caricaturist's art: Lord Salisbury (above), Arthur Balfour (left), and the model (above left), by Harry Furniss, 1905

50. G. W. Russell (A E), 1901

51. Standish O'Grady, 1894

52. W. B. Yeats, 1894

53. Douglas Hyde and A. P. Graves, 1894

54. Dr and Mrs Colohan of
Blackrock, Co. Dublin, in the
first petrol-engined car in
Ireland, *c.* 1898

55. James (Jimmy) Tyrrell of Ballyfoyle, Co. Kilkenny, as (a) Irish countryman (standing, left) and
(b) British colonial official (centre), c. 1900

56. 'A negligible quantity', by Bernard Patridge, 1906: Redmond no longer holds the balance at Westminster

57. 'Desperate remedies', by Linley Sambourne, 1907: Birrell's 'softly, softly' approach to cattle-driving

58. '"We want to remain with you": Edward Carson 1914: an Orange man'
by Cecil Cutler

59. '"A" Company, 2nd Royal Inniskilling Fusiliers' (1911); the battalion went into action on the extreme left of the British line, 26 Aug. 1914

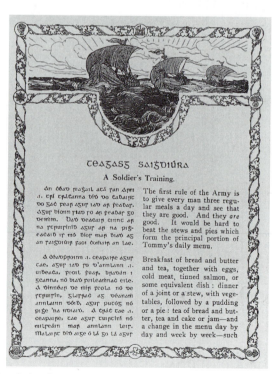

τeαzαsz sαιzσιúrα
A Soldier's Training.

Aη óбaσ riazaιl açá ιαη Άτη .ι. τρί τριlcαηηα bíσ σο ταбαιτ σο zαó ιεατ αzυτ ιασ αη ιεαбατ. αzυτ bιοηη ιιασ τo αη ιεαбατ zo σειήη. σασ σεαcαιτ cιηητ ατ ηα ιτιιητ αzυτ αη ηα τιzεασαι ιτ ήо бιοτ ήατ bιασ αz αη ταιzσιúιτ ιαοι σοήαιη αη τaε.

The first rule of the Army is to give every man three regular meals a day and see that they are good. And they *are* good. It would be hard to beat the stews and pies which form the principal portion of Tommy's daily menu.

Á óбaσττοιηη .ι. cεαραιτε αzυτ ταε, αzυτ ιασ τo σ'αηηιαηη .ι. υιбεαсα, τεοιl ιυατ, bτασáη ι zcαηηα, ηó bιασ ιειlεαήηαс ειlε. Á σιηηéατ σε ήιτ τεοιa ηó σε τειυιτιη, zιιτσασ αz σéαηαή αηηιαηη σóιb, αzυτ ιιτóz ηó ιτ z 'ηα ησιαισ. Á сτáτ ταε .ι. cεαραιτε, ταε αzυτ τιιτcιηι ηó ήιτεáηη ήατ αηηιαηη τειτ. Μαlιιτ bíσ αιzε ó lá zo lá αzυτ

Breakfast of bread and butter and tea, together with eggs, cold meat, tinned salmon, or some equivalent dish : dinner of a joint or a stew, with vegetables, followed by a pudding or a pie : tea of bread and butter, tea and cake or jam—and a change in the menu day by day and week by week—such

60. *Ireland's cause* [1915]; parallel texts in Irish and English

61. 'Major-general Sir Oliver Nugent', by William Conor

62. Two Irish chaplains of the third battle of Ypres: (a) Rev. William Doyle;
(b) Rev. G. A. Studdert Kennedy, 'Woodbine Willie'

63. 'H.M.S. *Vindictive*' by K. D. Shoesmith; Belfast-built aircraft-carrier

64. Memorial at Thiepval to 36th (Ulster) Division, J. A. Bowden and A. L. Abbott architects

65. Missionaries about to leave for Africa; Cork, 1920